Operations Management

A Supply Chain Approach

D1346826

INTERNATIONAL THOMSON BUSINESS PRESS

I(T)P An International Thomson Publishing Company

London Bonn Boston Johannesburg Madrid Melbourne Mexico City New York Paris
Singapore Tokyo Toronto Albany, NY Belmont, CA Cincinnati, OH Detroit, MI

Operations Management: A Supply Chain Approach

Copyright © 1999 International Thomson Publishing

IⓉ**P**® A division of International Thomson Publishing Inc.
The ITP logo is a trademark under licence

British Library Cataloguing-in-Publication Data
A catalogue record for this book is available from the British Library

---

First published 1999 by International Thomson Business Press

Typeset by Saxon Graphics
Printed in Spain by Mateu Cromo

ISBN 1-86152-415-3

International Thomson Business Press
Berkshire House
168–173 High Holborn
London WC1V 7AA
UK

http://www.itbp.com

Contents

Acknowledgements

I would like to thank the following persons who directly, or indirectly, knowingly or unknowingly helped in the preparation of the text either by reviewing certain sections, providing useful information, organising plant visits, or giving critical advice.

- **ARNOULD**, Francis; French Government
- **FILLON**, David; Renault Véhicles Industriels, Bourg en Bresse, France
- **HAAG**, Alain; Renault Véhicles Industriels, Vennisieux, France
- **LAVIALLE**, Thierry; Dickson PTL, Lyon, France
- **MONTIER**, Alain; Panzini, Lyon, France
- **RAMMELOO**, Charles; Pittance Constructors (Retired), Dardilly, France
- **RANKIN**, Dan; Pasadena, California, USA

Students from E.M. Lyon:
Diane-Audrey CHANUT ● Anne CHEVILLARD ● Christelle CUIOC ● Laure GAILLARD ● Sidney GRÜNBERGY ● Régis LAFFONT ● Jocelyn NGUYEN ● Bertrand POISONNET ● Nathalie PUPIN ● Dominique SALAÜN ● Benoit STOS ● Christophe SURGEY ● Anne-Caroline ULRICH ● Christian WILD.

This book is dedicated to my family for their patience ...

Christine, Delphine, and Guillaume

———————————

... and to the following who guided me during my education and career:

- John Cooper (for his implicit trust)
- Betty Preston (for her patience and determination)
- Frank Manning (for his direction and encouragement)
- Ken Peet (for always being prepared to listen)
- Hugh Baird (for his enthusiasm and support)

Derek L. Waller, November 1998.

About this textbook

Overview

This textbook, *Operations Management: A supply chain approach* is designed to be a complete, practical, and integrated document covering the operations management environment and the associated supply chain in both manufacturing and services. The material is international but has a strong European emphasis. It contains 26 detailed chapters, divided into the following four principal sections preceded by an opening Chapter 1 presenting the field of operations management.

Chapter 1	Positioning Operations Management
Part I.	STRATEGIC DECISIONS AND OPERATIONS
Part II.	DESIGN IN OPERATIONS MANAGEMENT
Part III.	PLANNING, ORGANISING, AND CONTROL
Part IV.	FURTHER ANALYSIS

Part I covers the strategic elements of the organisation and some of the drivers of the operations and supply chain including corporate strategy, site selection, quality management, and the ecological environment. Part II underscores the organisation as a system and the interrelation of product design, design of the process and operations network, and the human resources in the system design. Part III gives the core elements of operations management and the supply chain including forecasting, layout, inventory management, capacity planning, material requirements planning, scheduling, lean production and just-in-time, purchasing, managing the supply chain, project management, and reliability and maintenance. Finally, Part IV contains further analytical approaches to further improve the operations and supply chain system including decision making and risk, statistical quality control, waiting lines or queuing, financial analysis, and auditing operations. The linkage of these elements is illustrated on the attached flow sheet.

Illustrations

There are over 450 illustrations, diagrams (some in cartoon-form), charts, tables and graphs are included in the text. Their purpose is to synthesise and give a thumbnail overview of a particular subject, to aid in the retention of the material, and also to remove some of the *dryness* of the subject of Operations and Supply Chain Management. Transparency masters of all of these, plus many more based on the text (some 500) are available to instructors as hard copies.

Articles

There are nearly 30 complete articles from leading international business publications including the Wall Street Journal Europe, The Economist, Business Week and The Sunday Times, to illustrate the practical application of the material.

Worked Examples and Microsoft Excel

In the chapters which cover quantitative elements are worked examples with detailed solutions based on the Microsoft Excel software.

References and Bibliography

At the end of each chapter is a listing of the references cited in the text plus other selected bibliographic readings giving a total of some 1,160. Some of the references are from well known business publications again to illustrate the pragmatic nature of this text.

Review and Discussion Questions

There are a total of 180 review and discussion questions presented at the end of each chapter which can be used in classroom sessions to stimulate understanding of chapter material. Many of these are of a broad nature to further illustrate the *real world application*. Suggested responses to these questions will be available to instructors in a separate publication.

Exercises

After many of the chapters are numerous quantitative exercises. Solutions to these exercises will be available to instructors in a separate publication and/or on diskette based on the Microsoft Excel program.

Cases

At the end of many chapters are real world cases. Again, suggested responses to these will be available to instructors in a separate publication.

Glossary

At the end of the text there is a glossary containing over 700 defined terms related to operations management and the supply chain.

Currency Units

Although this text has a European emphasis, the principal currency units employed for illustrative examples and cases is $US as it is felt at the present time this will still be the dominant international currency. There is uncertainty on the role of the European currency unit, the dominance of the British Pound on international markets, and the stability of Asian currencies.

OPERATIONS MANAGEMENT: A Supply Chain Approach

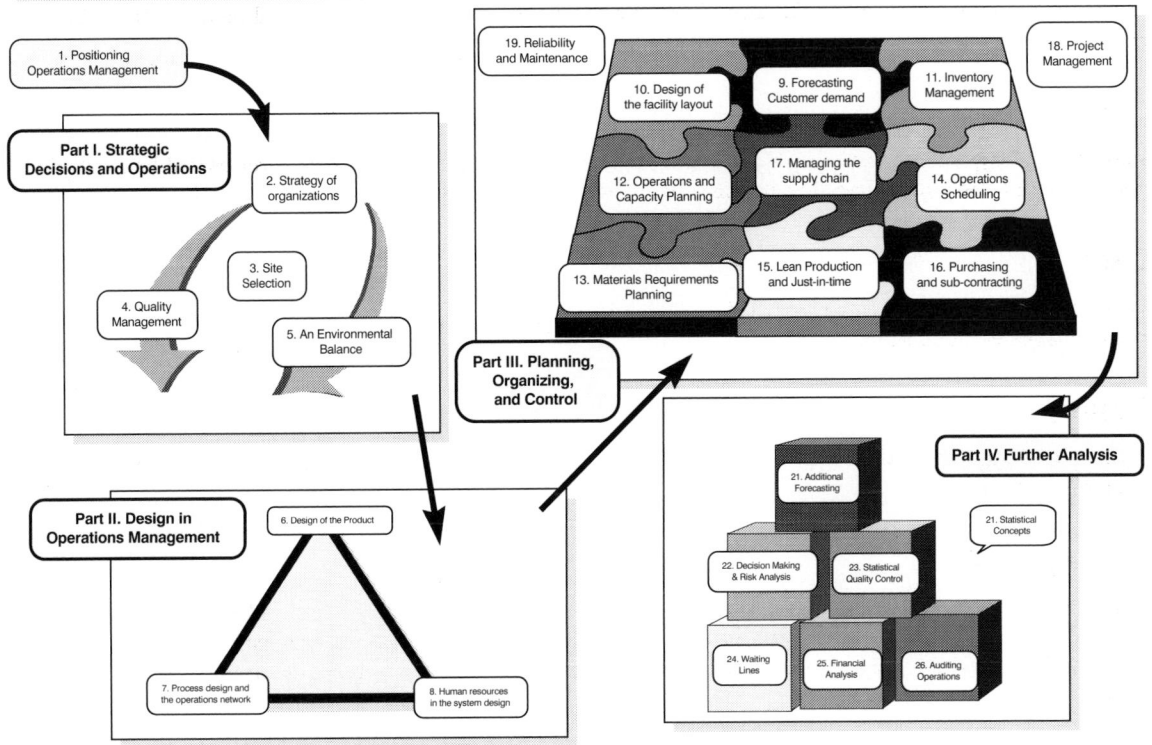

1 | Positioning operations management

Objectives and overview

The purpose of this chapter is to position operations management and to enumerate its role and function in the global business environment in both services and manufacturing. The chapter first discusses the scope of operations, its link with the supply chain and the importance of the client. It distinguishes between manufacturing and service industries, as well as describing the part played by non-profit organizations. The international element of operations is detailed for a broad spectrum of organizations, as well as the changing employment pattern in the operations environment today. A simple model of operations is presented and the elements of added value, productivity and resource utilization are discussed. The overlap between various operations management activities and other business functions is given particular emphasis. A systems approach to operations management is presented. Finally, the last section deals with technological evolution, detailing how it has impacted the operations environment.

DEFINING OPERATIONS MANAGEMENT

Scope of operations management

One is constantly confronted with the operations environment. The daily repetitive activity, through waking, showering, dressing, feeding the dog, reading the newspaper, having breakfast, dropping the children off at school and catching the train to work, represents several interrelated operations. Many people try to 'manage' these activities by optimizing, or minimizing the time necessary so that they can sleep in as late as possible and still arrive at work on time! The beds we sleep in, the water for washing, the clothes we wear, the breakfast we eat, the veterinary service for the dog, the news we hear on the radio, the newspaper that is delivered, the school the children attend, the train schedule for the commuter, are all products originating from the operations management environment.

Operations management is the effective planning, organizing and control of all the resources and activities necessary to provide the market with tangible goods and services. Operations activities are vast and apply to manufacturing industries, and service firms, in the private sector, as well as to non-profit organizations and even government.

Linkage operations and the supply chain

Operations management is not an isolated function, just covering the activities that transform raw materials into finished products. It is an integral part of a complex supply chain, involving the delivery of inputs from suppliers to the transformation area, movement of materials within the transformation zone and distribution of finished products to the client. In addition to material flow, there is an information supply chain with a reverse sense, communicating product needs, specifications and timing. The link operations and the supply chain are critical when one considers that today business firms are international, having perhaps up to 80 per cent of their work performed by subcontractors, many overseas. Operations and the supply chain have to be considered as an integrated system, since merely producing a product or service has no meaning to the customer unless it is delivered in a timely manner.

The supply chain is perhaps most easily conceptualized in manufacturing, since there is physical flow of goods. However, a supply chain is very much present in the service sector; in order to be successful, airlines, financial institutions, consulting companies, distribution firms, retail outlets, etc. rely on timely information flow through a sophisticated communications network.

Serving the client

The ultimate driving force behind the operations manager is the client. He or she is expecting to have a product delivered at the right time, at an acceptable quality, at a reasonable price and courteously. Even in a non-profit organization or in government, although there is no commercial gain, there is a client. The client should be considered as king!

MANUFACTURING AND SERVICE FIRMS

Classification

Traditionally, market-driven businesses that survive on the basis of generated profits are broadly classified into two groups, manufacturing and services.

Manufacturing industries

The principal role of the manufacturing firm is to turn physical raw materials into tangible products. A tangible product is one that can be physically touched, described by dimensional terms, such as weight, length, height, volume, etc., valued in monetary terms and visualized.

Service industries

A service industry also provides a 'product' but one that is often intangible and cannot be described in the same dimensional terms as manufactured goods.

Major industries, according to the two classifications, are illustrated in Figure 1.1.[1]

The economic triad

The manufacturing and service sector can also be differentiated according to its economic triad.

The primary sector

The primary sector, which is almost pure manufacturing, covers extraction of minerals, such as oil, coal, gold and silver, and agricultural activities, such as wheat farming, cattle rearing and fruit growing.

The secondary sector

The secondary sector involves the transformation of primary resources into manufactured products, such as steel into automobiles, gold into jewellery, crude oil into petrol, wheat into bread and cattle into hamburgers.

The tertiary sector

The tertiary sector covers services and administration activities found in government, schools, social services, etc. Tertiary activities are treated in more detail in the next section, as not-for profit organizations.

Classification anomalies

The separation into manufacturing and services is clearly not black and white. Some service firms violate the *intangible product* rule. The following are illustrations:

- Engineering and construction firms build bridges, oil refineries, and commercial complexes. These can be touched and visualized.
- Food service firms, or restaurants, provide meals or 'inventory' which can be touched.
- Retail stores are involved in the sale of products, that is, the movement of finished goods inventory.

Thus, businesses can also be considered as a continuum, where one moves from pure services, such as insurance, to steel production, which is almost pure manufacturing as illustrated in Figure 1.2.

Services in manufacturing

A further anomaly in the classification is that within all manufacturing industries there are service elements:

- an after-sales service for repair or replacement of faulty products;
- legal services for employee rights, problems with suppliers and customers, interpreting government regulations;
- purchasing services, such as providing assistance to suppliers to improve the quality of products supplied;
- services providing internal company training that is deemed necessary to ensure effective performance of the manufacturing organization;
- the human resource department, a service that hires new employees, follows promotion, administers salaries and terminates people's employment;
- the company restaurant, a service to employees.

Client contact

In the service industry, there is generally more client contact in all phases of the operating environment than there is in manufacturing. Personnel in medical services, restaurants and hotels have client contact on a daily

Figure 1.1 Service and manufacturing industries.

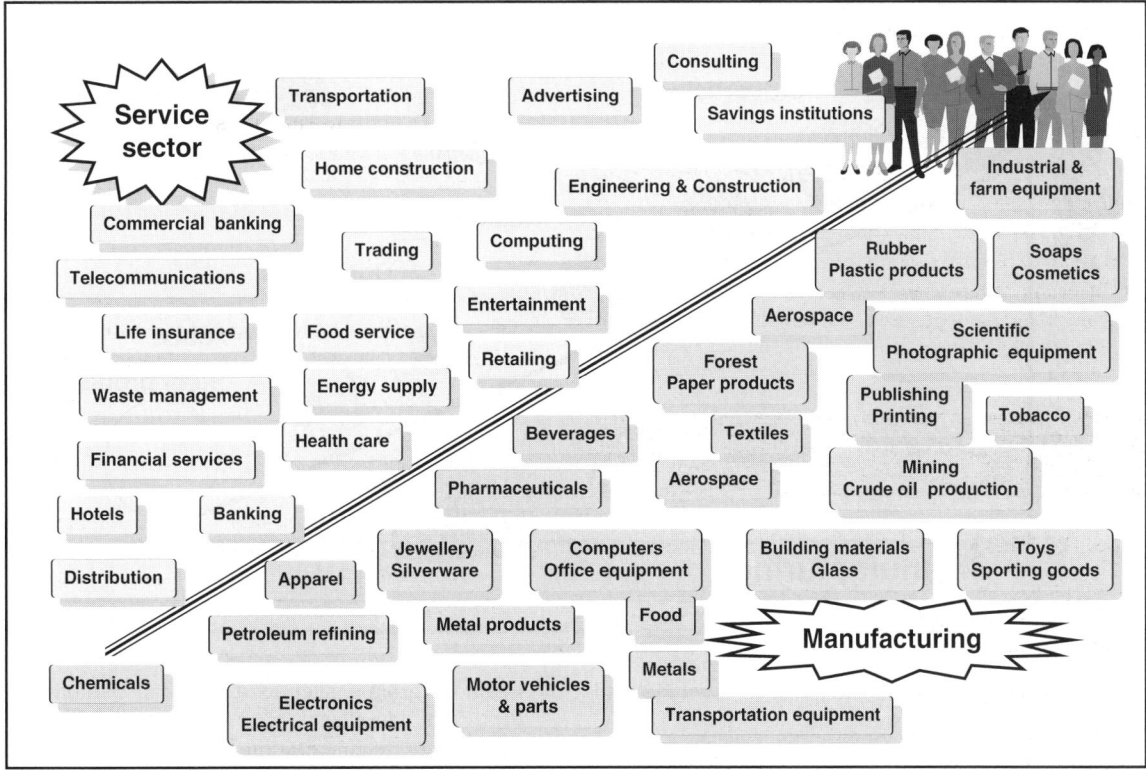

basis. This is not the case in the production of automobiles, the brewing industry, or a light bulb manufacturer, for example, where the client only makes an appearance on delivery of the finished product. This client differentiation characteristic often gives a secondary classification in operations, where those persons in services are more people oriented than to those in manufacturing, where there is usually a higher proportion of technicians and engineers.

NOT-FOR-PROFIT SERVICE ORGANIZATIONS

In addition to market-driven operations, the economy also includes numerous not-for-profit (or non-profit) service organizations. Here the driving force is a desire to do good, rather than to serve any commercial interest. However, although non-profit organizations are not constrained by the profit motive, they are nevertheless operations that need to be managed so that they use resources effectively and serve the end users of their services at a reasonable cost.

Not-for-profit organizations can be broadly classified into two groups. The first group would include those that are directly, or indirectly, managed by national and local governments and usually funded by tax receipts. The second group includes those organizations allowed a non-profit status by government because they serve the public at large, to educate, inform, provide health care, support cultural events, provide social services, etc., which is something private industry is unable to provide. Funding for these groups may come from donations, foundations, revenue generating activities within the organization or partial government funding. Although these organizations may make a 'net income', all of this income is ploughed back into the organization to benefit the users of the service.

Examples of organizations in these two categories are given below. The distinction is not always clear cut, because, for example, some non-profit organizations may have their operations influenced by governments, particularly if they receive some government funding. Universities would be an example. On the other side, some government agencies may be quite independent of government control. The United Nations, although

Figure 1.2 Content of the service function in business.

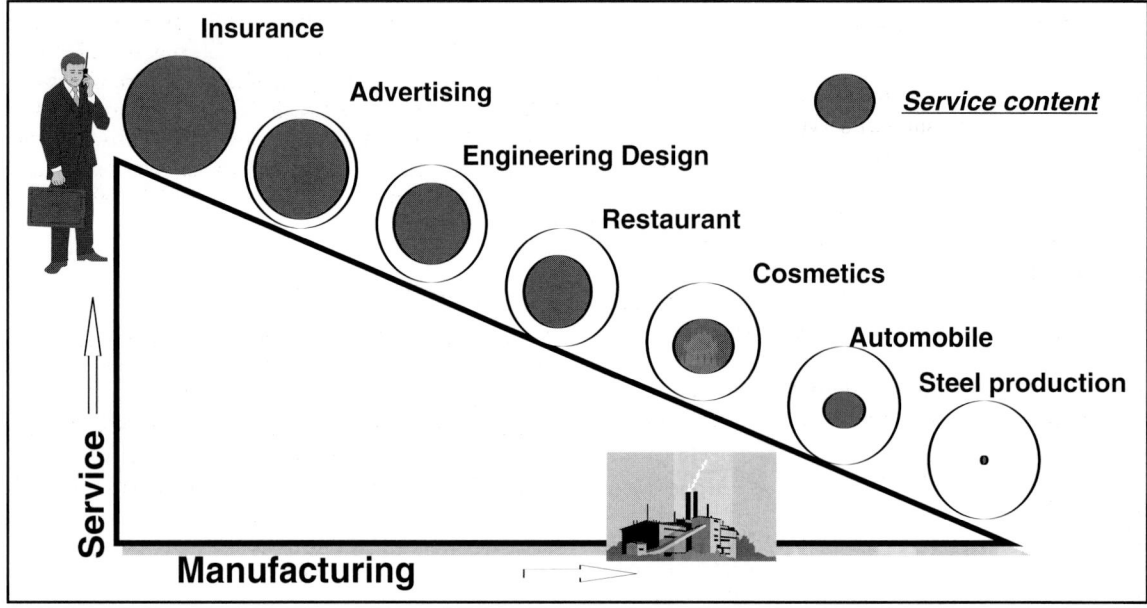

entirely funded by governments, makes very independent decisions.

Government or quasi-government organizations

- National, state and local governments themselves
- Military services – army, air force and navy
- Agencies within governments, such as those regulating transportation, trade, environmental, industrial and transportation safety policies
- Health services and hospitals (in the USA, some are 'for profit' organizations)
- North Atlantic Treaty Organization (NATO)
- Groups that provide personal safety, such as the police, the US Federal Bureau of Investigation (FBI), or the International Criminal Police Organization (Interpol)
- United Nations Organization
- Schools (some are private and, though they have similar curriculum, are non-profit)
- World Health Organization (WHO)
- Postal services
- Rail and bus services in some countries

Organizations with non-profit status

- Humanitarian organizations, such as the Salvation Army and the Red Cross

- Religious groups, such as the Roman Catholic and Protestant churches
- Universities (depending on the country, these may be controlled by the government)
- Boy and Girl Scout organizations
- Museums and cultural centres
- The British Council
- Sports events, such as the Olympic movement

OPERATIONS ARE INTERNATIONAL

Increasingly, the operations environment is international. Some reasons include the following:

- There has been a reduction in trade barriers, brought about by the creation of such entities as the European Union (EU) with its current 15 members, or the North Atlantic Free Trade Association (NAFTA) between the USA, Canada, and Mexico.
- Foreign labour is often less expensive than domestic labour in countries such as Japan, Germany, the UK, France, Italy and Canada.
- Domestic markets are saturated, so that new markets are being developed away from the home country.
- The international transport of goods, services and people has become easier and cheaper. As an illustration, the cost of ocean freight has fallen by some 60 per cent in the 60 years since 1930 and air transportation cost has fallen by some 80 per cent.[2]

The manufacturing firm

A manufacturing firm may have, for example, the following:

- headquarters in New York, USA, which provides top management and support services;
- manufacturing facilities in Argentina, Ukraine and Singapore;
- product distribution centres in Central USA, Columbia, Norway and Western Australia;
- purchasing activities in China and the Philippines;
- clients throughout South America, California, Europe, Eastern and Western Europe.

This is conceptualized in Figure 1.3. As an example, the British/French joint-venture GEC/Alsthom has 120 factories in 40 countries.[3]

The real-world international extent of manufacturing firms is illustrated below by excerpts from the activities of Exxon,[4] an oil company based in Irving, Texas, USA (Box 1.1); Boeing,[5] an aircraft manufacturer based in Seattle, Washington, USA (Box 1.2), and Siemens,[6] a consumer and industrial equipment manufacturer with its headquarters in Munich, Germany (Box 1.3).

Service firms

Major service firms survive simply by being international, with offices, activities and communication networks worldwide, Examples of activities are illustrated below by excerpt summaries from British Airways,[7] London, UK, in air transportation (Box 1.4), Accor[8] the hotel chain based in Paris, France (Box 1.5), and Crédit Suisse,[9] in banking, based in Zurich, Switzerland (Box 1.6).

Non-profit organizations

The strength of many non-profit organizations is worldwide coverage. Consider, for example, the Roman Catholic Church, the World Health Organization, NATO, the Salvation Army and the Red Cross. Box 1.7 describes the international scope of Euronews, a non-profit television news channel and a competitor to BBC World News.

Products are international

As well as the actual operations of a firm, many of the manufactured products have international input, even

Figure 1.3 Operations are international.

Box 1.1 Exxon

Exxon drilled another oil discovery in the Norwegian North Sea. Called Tau, the well is near the Elli discovery, a significant oil find drilled in 1994. Overall, Exxon participated in eight discoveries in the North Sea in 1995. Elsewhere in Europe, Exxon continued to have success in the Netherlands with five gas finds. In Germany, BEB, in which Exxon has a 50 per cent interest, discovered two gas fields onshore, both of which are expected to begin producing in 1996.

An Exxon-operated consortium signed a production-sharing agreement for Sakhalin I off Sakhalin Island, Russia. The area contains estimated recoverable resources of 2.5 billion barrels of oil and 15 trillion cubic feet of gas. Additional seismic and drilling activity can begin once the Russian government develops the necessary legislative and regulatory framework. Exxon joined with another US company on an exploration block covering three million acres in Kazakstan, in which Exxon has a 50 per cent interest and will conduct seismic operations in 1996. In Azerbaijin Exxon began negotiating agreements on exploration blocks in the Caspian Sea.

In Africa, Exxon participated in drilling six wells in Angola, including a new discovery. Exxon began drilling in Nigeria in late 1995. In Chad it worked on the development of three large oil discoveries containing resources of nearly one billion barrels of oil. Early in 1995, an Exxon-operated consortium signed an agreement for piping oil from Chad to a marine terminal on the Atlantic coast of Cameroon. In Niger, it obtained operation management approval and increased ownership to 80 per cent in more than nine million acres containing discovered oil and gas resources.

Exxon added 29 blocks in the high-potential deep water in the Gulf of Mexico, which resulted in a year-end 1995 inventory of 153 federal leases. On its own, and in conjunction with Petronas Carigali, the operating arm of Malaysia's National Oil Company, Exxon conducted seismic surveys and completed four discoveries on several concessions in offshore Malaysia. It acquired a 100 per cent interest in a large exploration block in Papua New Guinea near its two existing concessions, where drilling confirmed a large gas discovery in 1993. In 1995 it completed new agreements in the East China Sea, the Qaidam Basin and the Songliao Basin near Daqing Field, China's largest producer. In the USA Exxon is the nation's largest producer and proved reserves holder.

From Exxon Corporation Annual Report (1995)

Box 1.2 The Boeing Company

Boeing has long set the industry standard for customer service. It maintains field representatives in 60 countries, supporting nearly 600 airlines. It opened a new avionics service centre in Singapore during 1995 to provide more support for customer airlines in Asia, and it maintains seven spare parts distribution centres in Atlanta, Los Angeles, and Seattle, USA; Beijing, China; Brussels, Belgium; London, UK; and Singapore. It is the only aeroplane manufacturer that offers next-day shipment of routine spares, and can ship parts within two hours when an aircraft is grounded for urgent repairs. Because Boeing stocks parts around the world and provides such prompt shipment to airlines, it can reduce other companies' costs of holding their own parts inventory.

Boeing is making sweeping improvements in the way it delivers technical information to airline customers around the world. It is the first aeroplane manufacturer to offer customers direct on-line access to a central database that provides engineering drawings and parts lists needed for aircraft maintenance and repair. In mid-1996 it will begin offering online delivery of service bulletins and maintenance and repair documentation. The switch from paper to digital formats will allow the company to provide more data more efficiently and to help customers reduce the cost of their Boeing fleets.

In 1996, Boeing and China will celebrate 25 years of cooperation. Since the first sale of 707s to China in 1972, the Boeing presence in China has grown dramatically. Today there are more than 240 Boeing jetliners operating in China – the fastest growing air travel market in the world. In addition to meeting the demand for commercial aircraft, Boeing is helping China train more pilots and improve safety and air traffic control. China is also becoming an important Boeing supplier, providing parts and assemblies for the 737, 757 and 747. Between now and the year 2015, Boeing projects that China will require about $100 billion worth of new commercial jet aircraft.

From Boeing Corporation Annual Report (1995)

Box 1.3 Siemens

Siemens, with headquarters in Munich, Germany, is a leading manufacturer of high-technology industrial and consumer equipment. Its products include: gas turbines, control systems and transmission equipment for power generation; automatic and robotics equipment for industrial use, such as automatic letter sorting machines and bottling machine systems; telecommunications equipment including telephones, networks, Internet applications and server systems; transportation equipment such as the tramways used in Lisbon, Portugal and Vienna, Austria; X-ray and echography testing equipment used in the medical field; semiconductors for the television and computer industry; and lighting and household equipment in collaboration with Bosch, also of Germany.

Siemens has worldwide manufacturing facilities in the United States, Canada, Venezuela, Columbia, Argentina, Brazil, South Africa, India, China, Australia, Russia, Turkey and almost every country in Europe. In addition to the manufacturing sites, it has sales offices in just about every country of the world. In 1995–96 it employed 379 000 people and had revenues of DM 94,180 million, of which 39 per cent was from Germany, 27 per cent from the rest of Europe, 17 per cent from North and South America, 11 per cent from Asia/Pacific and 6 per cent from Africa and the former Soviet Union.

From Siemens Corporation Annual Report (1996)

Box 1.4 British Airways

In air transportation, British Airways is one of the world leaders for business and holiday travel. In 1996–1997 it had revenues of £8359 million, carried 38.2 million passengers and 0.72 million tons of cargo worldwide. Its principal operations are based out of London's Heathrow and Gatwick airports in the south of England. At Manchester International Airport it has a substantial operation to serve customers in the north west of England. The operation of flying aeroplanes encompasses numerous other operating activities, including route planning, aircraft maintenance, restaurant services, booking, charter holiday travel, refuelling logistics, weather operations, cleaning, inventory management of parts and the human resources element in dealing with passengers.

In addition to operating in its own right, British Airways' global activities are aided by multinational alliances and franchises. With Qantas of Australia it has significant operations in the Asia/Pacific region. In North America it works with Canadian Airlines and has a proposed alliance with American Airlines in the United States. Its operations in Europe include a majority stake in Air Liberté and TAT European Airlines of France, while in Germany its alliance partner is Deutsche BA and it also has franchises with Sun-Air of Denmark and British Mediterranean Airways. In South Africa it has a franchise network with Comair. British Airways' global operations, including its alliances, covers all the five continents to 474 scheduled destinations in 103 countries.

From British Airways Report and Accounts 1996–97

Box 1.5 Accor

In the hotel and restaurant service area, Accor of France ranks among one of the world's leaders. In 1995 it had operations in 126 countries, employed 120 000 people and had revenues of FF 91 billion. About 31 per cent of its business was in France, 47 per cent in the rest of Europe, 11 per cent in North America, 10 per cent in Latin America, and 1 per cent in other countries.

Accor operates 2378 hotels with 268 256 rooms in 68 countries, including names such as Sofitel, Novotel, Mercure, Ibis, Formula 1, and Motel 6. In the restaurant service to industry, its operations include the management of Ticket

Restaurants or Luncheon Vouchers throughout Europe, company restaurants under the Compass Group name including 1129 restaurants in Brazil and Italy. It operates the Carlson Wagonlit travel agency serving business travel with 4100 offices in 125 countries. It has 678 roadside and motorway restaurants including L'Arche, Courte Paille and Le Notre. It operates the Wagon Lit railway sleeping cars with 4.5 million clients per year and also the Europcar car rental agency with an average car volume of 60 000 vehicles.

From Accor, Evry France, *Direction de la communication*, July 1996

Box 1.6 Crédit Suisse

Crédit Suisse, based in Zurich, Switzerland, is one of the world's leading financial service groups with operating activities on every continent and in all the world's major financial centres. In 1996 it had a net operating income of SF 12.9 billion, had a staff of 34 821 and 470 offices.

The Crédit Suisse Group is made up of four business units. The first is Crédit Suisse, which provides banking services to corporate and individual clients in Switzerland with 240 locations. It has subsidiary arrangements in leasing, car leasing and real-estate leasing, as well as insurance with Winterthur, Switzerland's largest insurer. The second business unit is Crédit Suisse Private Banking, which provides services in portfolio management and financial advice for private clients worldwide. It has 50

operating units in Switzerland, and 40 international operating units. The third business unit is Crédit Suisse First Boston with two locations in Switzerland and 50 internationally. This unit offers integrated services in corporate and investment banking, with a presence in all of the worlds principal financial centres. The last business unit is Crédit Suisse Asset Management, which focuses on institutional investors and includes Credis, the investment fund company serving Switzerland and Europe. In August 1997 Crédit Suisse announced a $9.5 billion merger with the insurer Winterhur. This merger will create one of the world's ten biggest financial service companies with combined assets of $465 billion[10].

From Crédit Suisse Group Annual Report 1996/97

though they are assembled and sold in one country. As an illustration, Table 1.1 gives the different countries that supply some of the component parts for the Ford Escort automobile, assembled and marketed principally in Britain.[11]

Foreign sales and country size

Another characteristic of the international component of companies is that many of them generate a large portion of their revenues outside their home country.

As an illustration, of the world's 20 biggest multinational firms in 1993 Nestlé, the food manufacturer, generated 98 per cent of its revenues outside Switzerland. Philips, the electronics firm of The Netherlands was next with about 88 per cent. Asea Brown Boveri, industrial equipment, also of Switzerland, was close behind. Japanese companies also obtain large portions of their revenue outside their home country. On the other hand, US companies, although they have many big multinational firms, possess a much bigger domestic market than

---

Box 1.7 Euronews

Euronews was created on 1 January 1993 with the support of the European Union and in partnership with 19 public television channels, including RTBF of Belgium, RAI of Italy, RTVE of Spain, SSR-SRG of Switzerland and France's Channels 2 and 3. The primary operating objective of Euronews is to provide news coverage for European and Mediterranean basin viewers.

News programmes are available on an almost 24-hour basis, either by satellite, cable or regular television channels, in many languages including English, French, German, Italian and Spanish. This language diversity gives Euronews an advantage over its major competitors, BBC World News and CNN International. In addition to direct news coverage, throughout the week there are related magazine programmes covering European-oriented events, such as politics, economics, sports, health, fashion, travelling, leisure and analysis of daily events.[12]

Euronews has an office in Paris, but the operating centre is at Ecully, some 8 km west of Lyon, France. Here there are 80 journalists of all nationalities, assisted by 80 technicians and 60 administrative personnel. News programmes are compiled by multilanguage teams of eight journalists, each directed by a project leader. News bulletins, from which programmes are developed, are received continuously by an international computer network from such world sources as Reuters, APTV and WTN. The operation is very flexible and programme format can be modified at the last minute, according to the direction of the editorial chief, to handle news breaking items. (At the time of the author's visit two bomb attacks in Israel had just occurred.)

As of March 1997, the operation of Euronews was received in over 87.7 million homes in some 42 countries. This included all of the European Union countries plus Switzerland and Norway, 12 countries in the former Eastern Europe and 13 in the Mediterranean Basin (Greece, Turkey, Lebanon, Israel, Jordan, Saudi Arabia, Syria, Morocco, Algeria, Tunisia, Egypt, Cyprus and Malta).[13]

European or Japanese firms, and generally, with the exception of Exxon, generate much less of their revenues overseas. This comparison is illustrated in Figure 1.4.[14]

In Appendix I there are tabulations giving further examples of major international manufacturing and service firms.

EMPLOYMENT IN OPERATIONS

Manufacturing

Historically, in Europe and the USA manufacturing industries have employed a large proportion of the workforce, as people moved from farming into the heavy industries. In the late 1800s the heavy industries were principally iron and steel for locomotives and railroad construction. Then, in the early 1900s, the automobile was born from manufacturing firms like General Motors and Ford of the USA, Daimler of Germany and Panhard and Levassor of France. Labour demand in manufacturing increased in the hundred years up to 1920. Then, except for the period 1940–1950, when manufacturing output increased as a result of the war effort and the subsequent reconstruction, the proportion of persons in manufacturing has declined. This profile is illustrated for the USA in Figure 1.5.[15]

Europe

Europe has also shed manufacturing jobs as is illustrated in Figure 1.6.[16] In the period since 1970, Britain's share has reduced some 50 per cent, France 20 per cent and Germany some 17 per cent.

Manufacturing output

It must be pointed out that, as illustrated in Figure 1.7,[17] that, even though the absolute level of manufacturing employment has been flat and is now declining, manufacturing output has continued to increase, principally because of the replacement of labour by technology. (Technological innovations are reviewed in the section 'Technology' in this chapter.)

Table 1.1   Countries supplying parts for the Ford Escort

Country of supply	Components supplied
Denmark	Cooling and air conditioning belts
The Netherlands	Tyres, paint, control systems
Switzerland	Carpeting, speedometer
Norway	Straps for exhaust system, tyres
Germany	Pistons, cylinder bolts, steering column
Austria	Tyres, radiator, heating lines
Japan	Starter, alternator, bearings
USA	Catalytic converter, wheel bolts, windows
Belgium	Inner tubes, seat cushions, brakes and linings
Sweden	Tubular columns, cylinder bolts, stamped sections
Italy	Engine block, carburettor, lights, de-icing system
Spain	Radiator and heater leads, air filters, batteries, rear mirrors
France	Master cylinder, brakes, gear-box casing, waterproof joints
Canada	Windows, radio
UK	Oil pumps, heating system, direction indicators, petrol tank, steering wheel

Figure 1.4 The larger multinationals – foreign sales as a percentage of total sales (1993).

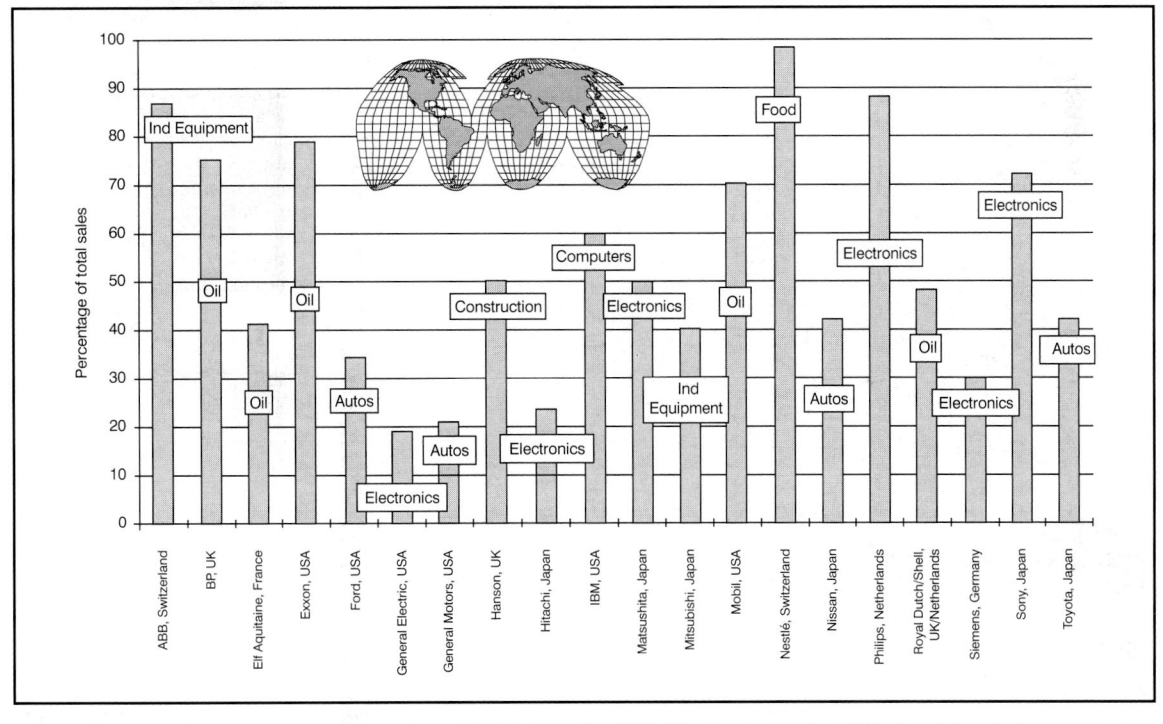

Service industries

Service industries, notably the travel industry, medical care – partly as a result of the ageing population – and financial services, have absorbed large portions of the labour force with detriment to manufacturing. This is illustrated in Figure 1.8.[18] In Britain, for example, in the period 1970–1993 the proportion of persons in services has grown from about 52 to 75 per cent. In Germany, the change is less pronounced climbing from about 52 to 60 per cent.

Figure 1.5 Manufacturing employment in the USA (source: US Bureau of Labor Statistics – *The Economist* 5 March 1994)

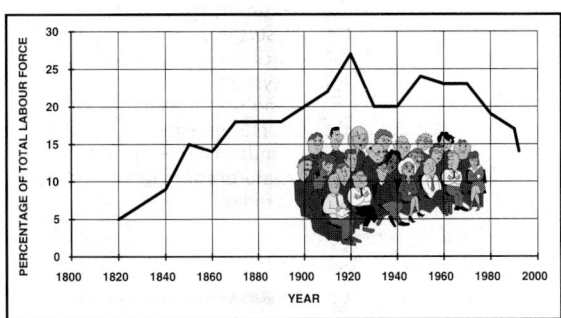

Developing regions

Developing regions, notably the Far East, Latin American countries and former Eastern European countries, have increased their manufacturing output. This is either because European and North American countries have moved some of their production operations to these low-labour-cost countries. Alternatively, the countries themselves have established their own manufacturing operations and have developed alternatives to US and European products, as illustrated by the article in Box 1.8 concerning the manufacture of computers and associated components.[19]

Accounting changes

Although manufacturing employment is decreasing, structural changes in companies have also modified the method of accounting for labour levels. For example, a large manufacturing company in the USA had a significant printing centre for copying, printing and binding of documents, brochures and books. The company realized that the cost of this service was very high compared to purchasing the service from outside. It decided to close this department, which in formal

Figure 1.6   Change in manufacturing employment in Europe.

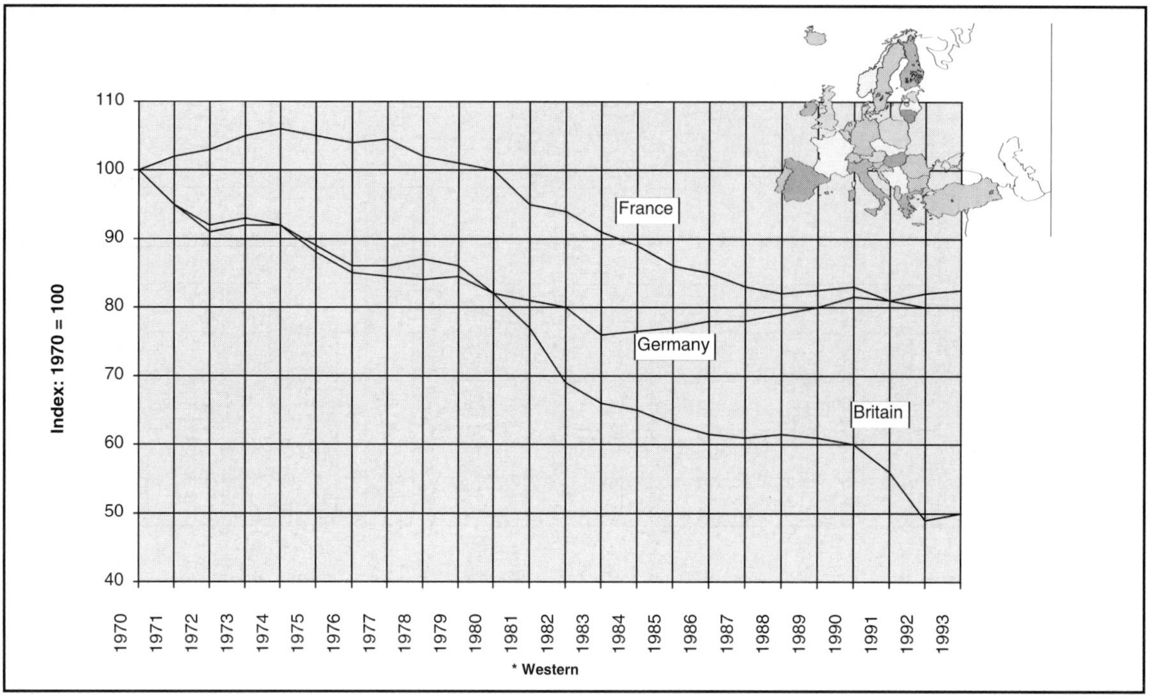

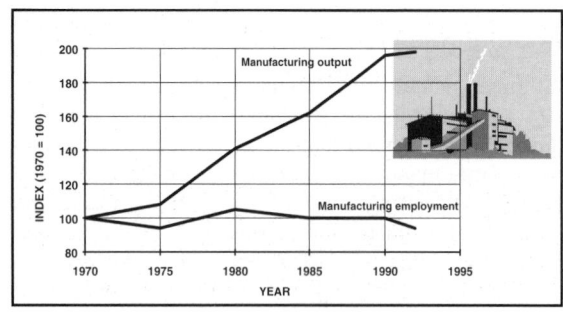

*Graph showing Index: 1970 = 100 on y-axis (40 to 110) and years 1970 to 1993 on x-axis, with lines labelled France, Germany, and Britain. * Western*

terms reduced the level of people involved in manufacturing. However, the persons who formerly worked in the printing department purchased all the associated printing equipment and set up their own company. Then they were contracted by their former employer to continue performing all the printing services. Thus, in accounting employment, originally the printing staff were in manufacturing; then they were in a service industry. However, the work they were performing was the same!

Figure 1.7   Change in manufacturing in the USA (source: US Bureau of Labor Statistics – *The Economist* 5 March 1994).

Graph: INDEX (1970 = 100) on y-axis (80 to 200), YEAR on x-axis (1970 to 1995), showing Manufacturing output and Manufacturing employment.

MODEL OF OPERATIONS

The operations model is a supply chain

A simple model for any operation is a supply chain comprising three basic blocks, inputs, transformation and outputs, which when integrated provide the network of product flow to clients. Then, in the opposite sense, is an information flow network providing all the necessary details of the products demanded. Such a model is illustrated in Figure 1.9 for nine industry types, four in manufacturing (food, automobiles, chemicals and textiles) and five in services (insurance, health care, distribution, engineering and construction and the entertainment industry). In general:

- ■ 'Inputs' is where the raw materials are received by the operating firm. These may originate locally, nationally or internationally.
- ■ 'Transformation' is where the state of the received raw materials is modified according to desired requirements. The transformation may be in a multitude of steps and occur at different locations.
- ■ 'Outputs' is where the desired product is finished and distributed to customers. The customers may be local, national or international.

Figure 1.8 Employment changes in services and manufacturing.

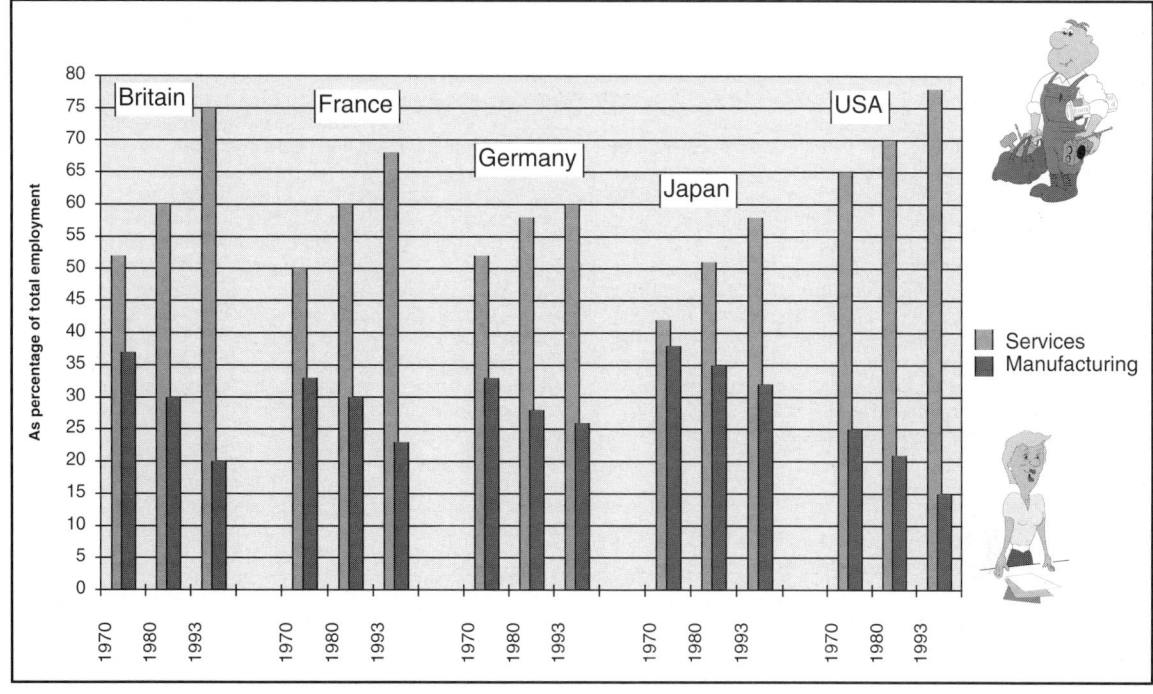

Box 1.8 Up the Ladder. U.S. multinationals take 'brain work' to plants overseas. Job competition and pressure on wages begin to reach America's labor elite. Malaysia model offers lesson. By G. Pascal Zachary, Staff Reporter

PENANG, Malaysia – Yoon Chong Leong runs a team of Hewlett-Packard Co. engineers here and at a Boise, Idaho, plant halfway around the globe. His far-flung people are building a new production line for Penang, and Mr. Leong, after years of taking cues from his American superiors, relishes his leadership role.

When H-P opened shop here in 1974, "people expected [Malaysians] to remain an unequal partner," he says. "Now Americans work for me."

American multinationals such as H-P came to Malaysia mainly for low wages. But in the process they have bred a fast-growing class of cosmopolitan professionals like Mr. Leong and legions of skilled factory hands who have the kind of high-skilled jobs Americans covet.

White Collar Competition

The Malaysian scenario has already played out in more advanced Asian countries such as Taiwan, and is just starting in less-developed nations such as China and Indonesia. It means that some of America's and Europe's most skilled workers are increasingly likely to face the same punishing

competition and wage pressures from abroad already felt by blue-collar workers.

"There are some, new high-tech jobs, but they are not reserved for you in the First World," Edith Holleman, counsel for the House Committee on Science, Space and Technology, told a meeting of U.S. engineers this month. "As international corporations move their facilities to cheaper locations, jobs in fields such as product design, process engineering and software development are moving with them."

Of course, the creation of one professional or skilled job in Malaysia doesn't necessarily subtract one in the U.S. A robust world economy can help all around. Still, its benefits will be spread unevenly because of an extraordinary shift in investment by industrialized nations.

This shift is sending billions of dollars of capital to countries like Malaysia from the U.S. and Japan, fueling the growth of high-paying jobs overseas. American companies doubled their annual foreign investment over the past four years to a record $50 billion in 1993, according to the United Nations' World Investment Report.

Smart and Flexible

In Malaysia alone, multinationals have invested more than $20 billion in manufacturing over the past six years, accelerating the transformation of its industrial workers into the kind of smart, flexible force extolled by U.S. Labor Secretary Robert Reich. In the 1970s, Malaysia's manual laborers earned a dollar a day. Now they earn $8 a day plus ample over time – the result of 8.6% average annual economic growth in Malaysia since 1988. Many senior managers and engineers earn $30,000 or more a year. The unemployment rate is less than 3%, and wages for many jobs are rising at 10% a year.

"The trend is definitely towards a higher-skilled, higher-paid Malaysian workforce," says Paul Lubeck, a professor at the University of California at Santa Cruz who has studied Malaysia's growth. "Professionals are not yet on the leading edge, but they are moving up the skill hierarchy and fast becoming specialists in a global economy."

If all countries could benefit from multinational investment as efficiently as Malaysia, elite workers in the U.S., Japan and Europe would face a graver threat. But so far, it is mostly Asian countries – and not all of them – that have taken full advantage of foreign investment. By becoming a haven for multinationals, "Malaysia offers lessons to many poorer countries, especially those in the African environment," says Saha Dhevan Meyanathan, a World Bank economist.

Always Vulnerable

Even so, Malaysia hasn't reached full industrialization, and it is vulnerable as multinationals constantly look for sources of cheaper labor – raising the specter that some could abandon Malaysia for a place where people toil for less.

Malaysians concede that their economy is heavily dependent on outsiders. "We still need foreign investment. We can't live without it," says Nafaruddin Arshad, a senior fellow at the Malaysian Institute of Economic Research, an independent body.

Despite labor's rising cost here, multinationals show no signs of disaffection and indeed are deepening their ties to Malaysia. They are sticking around for clear, self-interested reasons: Suppliers and important Asian markets are nearby; many workers speak English, a holdover from British colonialism; unions are toothless; the government rewards foreign investors with tax breaks; and the country is peaceful. Even as companies such as chip-maker Advanced Micro Devices Inc. shift manual labor to lower-wage countries, higher-skilled jobs are retained here, spawning a prosperous class of local technicians, designers, managers and even some entrepreneurs.

These Malaysian professionals are setting their sights high. "We are perfectly positioned" to help multinaticnals "penetrate low-wage areas elsewhere in Asia, and especially China," says P.Y. Lai, president of Motorola's Greater China division and a Penang native.

Intel Corp. typifies the new Malaysia. Its Penang factory makes three times as many chips as it did 10 years ago – with the same number of workers, 2,000. One in every six employees is now an engineer, compared with only one in 40 in 1980. Locals run every part of the plant, including operating an ultrasensitive tool that can pinpoint a single bad circuit on Intel's three million-circuit Pentium chip. Coveted design jobs, once the sole province of the Santa Clara, California, company's U.S. offices, have come to Malaysia too. Intel recently asked 100 engineers in Penang to design future chips, brain work formerly done by Americans in Arizona.

The story is similar at Hewlett-Packard, whose Penang factory each day makes a million light-emitting diodes, which are used for illuminating signs, cars and electronic displays. Since opening in 1972, the plant has grown steadily more automated and autonomous. It no longer relies on U.S. pilot lines or engineering support to solve production snafus. Little work is done by hand. Output is shipped directly to many customers. Plant engineers build their own test and machining gear and even dabble in product design.

"When we first started, we basically executed instructions given us by the U.S.," says Tan Bian Ee, the plant's managing director. "Today we are a full-fledged business partner."

And one that is testing the bounds of independence. Ng Chee Mang, a Malaysian-trained scientist, is the emblem of the H-P plant's fitful transformation. Last year, Mr. Ng, the son of an auto mechanic, discovered how to improve the light-emitting diodes greatly by altering the makeup of the clear epoxy that encases them. The epoxy now withstands thousands of hours of sunlight – instead of hundreds – without turning yellow.

Mr. Ng's breakthrough won him celebrity at the plant, stock options and bonuses. Thirtysomething and single, he lives a life similar to many American professionals: He works long hours, dresses casually and relaxes by jogging and scuba diving. H-P pampers him with glitzy computers and the time to pursue his own ideas. Even so, "my constant worry is how to keep him motivated," says Ban Ee Keong, his boss. In a show of deference, Mr. Ban calls Mr. Ng "Doctor" and encourages him to speak with and visit researchers in the U.S. Mr. Ban has tried but failed to convince H-P that Mr. Ng should be put in charge of the company's world-wide epoxy research, which would mean that American scientists would report to the Malaysian researcher.

Mr. Ng's situation illustrates the tug-of-war between multinationals and their Malaysian proxies. Locals often push for more authority. Three years ago, Motorola Inc. refused to let its Penang plant, which makes mobile phones, design new software for cellular conference calls. The company gave its approval only after the Malaysians agreed to do the task in addition to their existing jobs. After the code was written, the plant won approval to hire a permanent software team. "People here are very persistent," says S.K. Ko, the plant's chief. "We never give up."

Malaysian workers consistently rank among the highest in the world on quality benchmarks, with U.S. executives marveling at their discipline and group orientation. At Ms. Ko's plant, when workers were first asked a decade ago to suggest improvements, they responded with one tip each in the first year. Today, they average 20 a year; about two-thirds of the suggestions yield beneficial changes in operations.

New engineering graduates receive multiple job offers. Rather than wait for recognition at the company they join, they often "talk in the canteen about how they can get more money," says Hooi Tan, a manager at Seagate Technology's plant here.

Even experienced factory workers are sought after, with job-hopping commonplace. To keep favored workers, multinationals have devised elaborate training programs, some more generous than those in the U.S. and Europe. "They have made a virtue out of of necessity," says Mr. Meyanathan, the World Bank economist.

Motorola pays for the college educations of promising Malaysian high-school students and, in return, gets first crack at hiring them. Manual workers also are trained. Advanced Micro is sending dozens of laborers to school full-time to learn new skills. The employee gets a raise, and the company gets a skilled worker.

Labor is in such short supply that some companies move people here from the Philippines or Indonesia, then house them near factories. Seagate, while relying on imported workers, also has hired hundreds of young Malaysians from *kampongs*, or peasant villages. Many have never seen machines or felt air conditioning.

Umika, one newcomer, spent her first few days at work confused and shivering in the chill air. But within a month she had mastered[???] scope, aligning a piece of metal with a grid, then tightening a screw. Another recent arrival, Asman, feared his machine at first, but now calls it "my friend."

The multinationals, once feared, are now considered friends too. When the first wave quietly opened small factories in the early 1970s on a converted rice paddy near Penang's airport, the locals were dubious. "We felt the multinationals would stay a short while and then go, so we called them 'fly by nights,'" says A. Balasakaran, who then ran a small TV and radio repair shop.

In those early years, the plants mainly needed people to assemble chips and other tiny electronic devices. Most workers were women, sometimes derided as "*minah keran*," or electric women. Mr. Balasakaran eventually closed his repair shop and joined Advanced Micro as a technician. His wife, Kam, fretted then: "What if they just close and go home? Then you have nothing."

Twenty years later, Advanced Micro is still here. Mr. Balasakaran, though still a technician, has gained broader duties and higher pay. He and his wife own an apartment, and their oldest daughter, Ireeny, is in college in the Malaysian capital, Kuala Lumpur. During visits home, she programs on her father's personal computer.

"I have a bunch of friends who are nuts about computers," she says. "We're hoping to be pioneers."

Malaysia could use them. For all their accomplishments, professionals here are innately cautious. "You give them a set of rules and tell them to follow them all the time, and it's done," says Seagate's Mr. Tan. "Things work in Malaysia because people do what they're told."

This tradition of regimentation is one trait that Americans, running hard to justify wages that are at least double those paid Malaysians, can perhaps be thankful for. Though Malaysia's government is encouraging creativity and risk-taking in its people, it might take decades for this new ethic to flourish. Says Mr. Tan, who is 30: "I can't see in my lifetime a Malaysian team coming up with the Pentium chip."

Wall Street Journal Europe, 30 September 1994
Reprinted by permission of *Wall Street Journal, Europe*,
© 1994 Dow Jones & Company, Inc.
All Rights Reserved Worldwide.

Figure 1.9   Operations model.

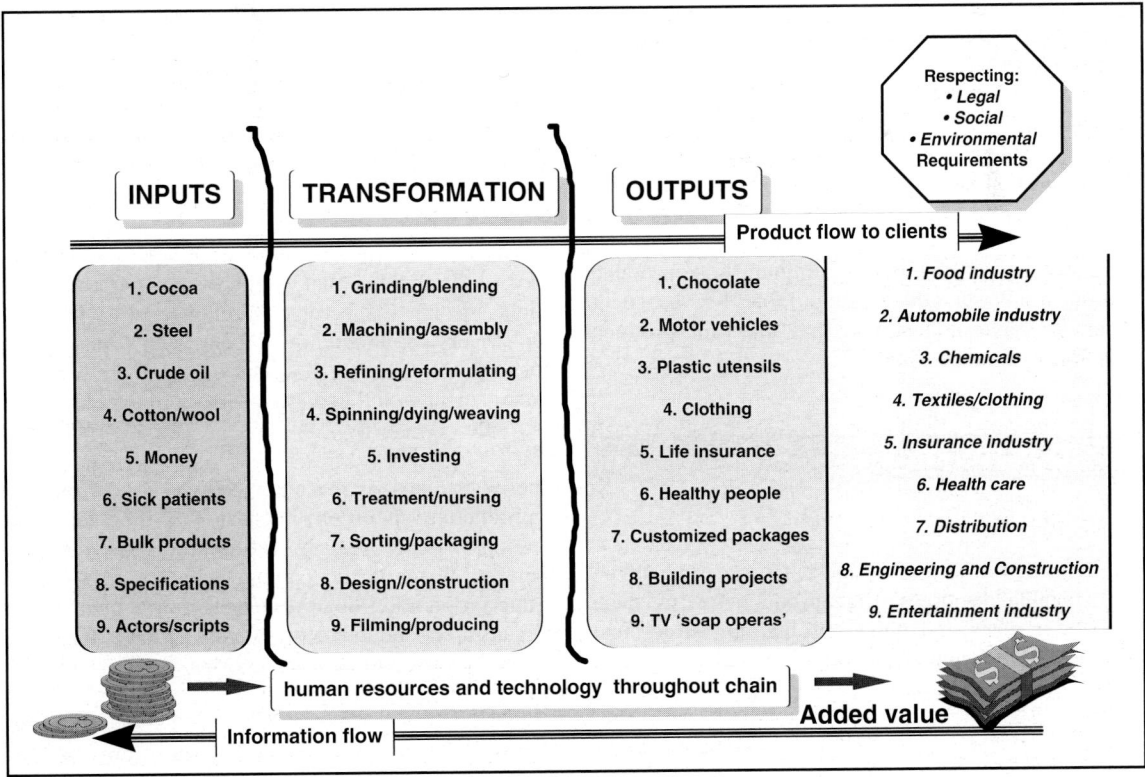

No matter the type of operation, the chain functions basically by a combination of human resources and technology that respects current legal, social and environmental regulations.

Model economics

In any operation, as presented in the model, the economic value of the output is greater than the economic value of the input:

$$\frac{\text{output value}}{\text{input value}} > 1$$

From a marketing point of view, the margin obtained from the output product is greater than the margin that would be obtained from the input product. In the model examples shown:

- A slab of chocolate has a higher value than the input raw cocoa beans.
- An automobile has a higher added value than raw steel.
- A healthy patient has a higher value than one who is sick when entering a hospital.
- A life insurance policy has a greater value than non-invested cash.
- A six-pack of beer has a higher added value in a retail store than six cans of beer coming off the filling line in a brewery.

Product added value

Different products have different added values and companies that have multiple business units may have a marketing strategy to retain the production of those products that have the highest added value (which translates into profit) and discontinue those products that have a lower added value. Table 1.2, based on Japanese studies, illustrates that different products have different 'added value'.[20]

PRODUCTIVITY

Resources

The objective in any operation is to use productively the available resources. High productivity translates into lower costs and higher profits. Resources may include the following elements.

Surface area

This could be the raw land surface available for building construction, the storage area for warehousing,

Table 1.2 The added value of various products

Product	Value added ($US/kg)
Satellite	10 000
Jet fighter	1 250
Supercomputer	850
Aeroplane engine	450
Jumbo jet	175
Video camera	140
Mainframe computer	80
Semiconductor	50
Submarine	20
Colour television	8
Numerical-controlled machine tool	5
Luxury automobile	5
Standard automobile	2
Cargo ship	0.5

floor available for manufacturing or surface area available for offices in a service operation.

Materials

Materials would include all the tangible items used in production, such as steel, plastic, wood, packaging material, liquids, etc.

Direct labour

The direct labour is the amount of labour, measured in time units, that can be directly associated with the product, such as the numbers of machine operators, welders, wiring personnel, packaging people, etc.

Indirect labour

The indirect labour is the amount of labour, also measured in time units, that supports an operation. This might include inspectors, warehouse personnel and supervisory people. Indirect labour, such as inspection, does not add value to an operation and therefore good management would keep this activity to a minimum.

Energy and water

Energy includes oil, gas and electricity used directly in a production operation, but also that used for space heating, cooling or, say, refrigeration for the food industry. Water is the cooling water used, say, in a refinery operation or in a nuclear power plant or the actual water used in the production process, for example in the food and paper industries.

Financial resources

Financial resources in the broad sense are the cash needed to finance land purchase, building construction, new machines, salaries, purchasing of raw materials, maintenance expenditures, travel costs, etc.

Measurement of productivity

Productivity is a measure of how resources are used. Globally it is given by the ratio of the value of the inputs used to achieve the desired outputs. Or, simply:

$$\text{productivity} = \frac{\text{output}}{\text{input}}$$

Productivity in an operation increases if an amount of output has increased without any increase in the corresponding amount of input. Productivity improvements are often a bargaining element in union contracts. An increase in productivity is a way in which a firm can afford to raise wages while still remaining competitive in an increasingly global economy.

The productivity ratio is somewhat analogous to the value-added ratio, but it is not the same. As an illustration, from the basic raw materials, an automobile built in Japan may have the same added value as one built in the UK. However, the productivity of arriving at the finished product may be different in the two countries. Alternatively, the perceived added value to a hotel customer may be the same with two companies, but the productivity of providing the service may be quite different.

Specific productivity measurements depend on the industry being considered. Some examples of ratios used to measure productivity in certain industries are described in the following sections.

Manufacturing

Productivity here might be expressed in units produced per employee or hours needed per product. As an illustration, in a study by J. D. Powers, the productivity of automobile construction for three continents in 1989 in terms of hours/car was as follows:[21]

- Japan: 16.8;
- USA: 25.1;
- Europe: 36.2.

Service firms

The ratio employed here depends on the type of firm. The following are some illustrations:

- airline industry: passenger mile/aeroplanes in service;
- engineering: design hours per project;
- hotel industry: no of hotel rooms filled per period;
- railways: passengers per network mile;
- television: viewers per programme;

- education: students per professor;
- fast food restaurant: time to make a hamburger.

Some firms use revenues as the numerator in the productivity ratios. For example, revenues per passenger mile in the travel industry, or revenues per unit in manufacturing. However, this is not really a good measure for analysing the productivity since revenues can be increased by increasing price with no changes in the inputs.

Productivity improvements

What is often of interest is not the absolute value of the productivity, but the change in the value over time. Thus, one has a basis of comparison to see if improvements are being made.

Manufacturing versus services

Figure 1.10 illustrates how productivity since 1958 has changed in the USA in the two industrial sectors.[22] Before the 1970s productivity in services and manufacturing advanced at roughly equal rates and then after this period the two rates diverged. Part of the explanation appears to be that, as the result of the explosion of the service sector, a large proportion of young and inexperienced workers were employed. Furthermore, service firms did not invest as much in capital equipment and technology as did the manufacturing firms. The manufacturing profile underscores the increase in manufacturing output, although a decline in employment, as discussed in this chapter in the section *Employment in Operations*.

Productivity changes on a country basis

Figure 1.11 illustrates how productivity has changed for various countries in the two periods 1979–1985 and 1985–1993.[23] Britain's manufacturing productivity

Figure 1.10   Productivity in manufacturing and services in the USA.

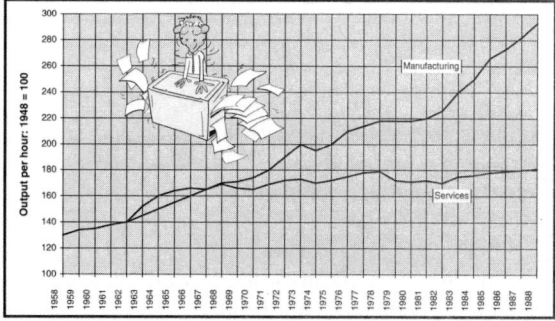

Figure 1.11   Manufacturing productivity for various countries (output/hour: average percentage yearly increase).

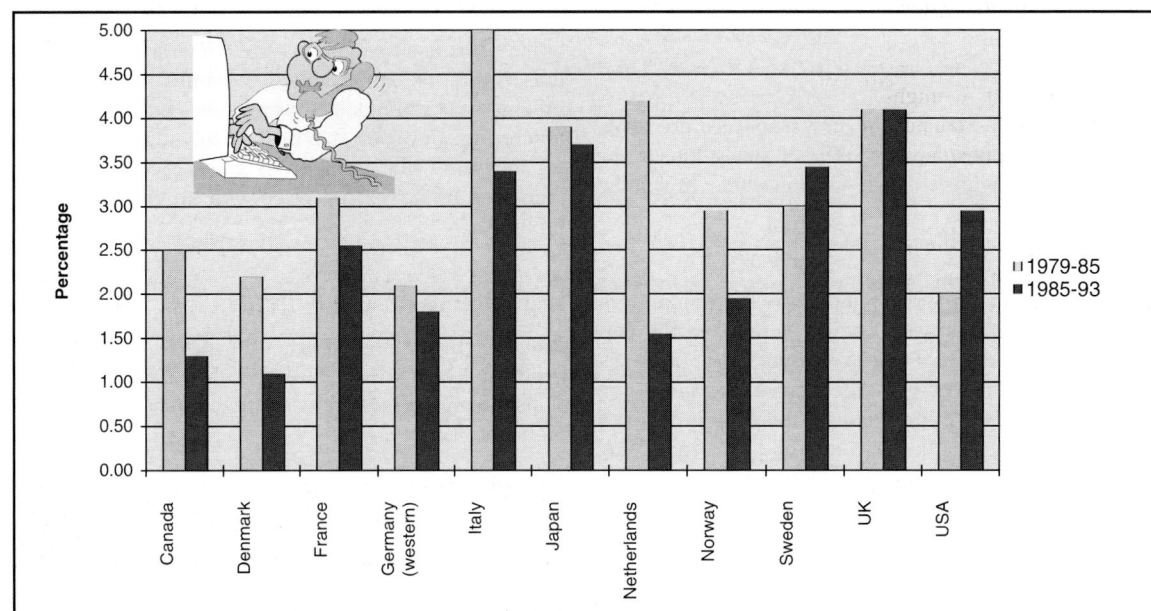

grew by an average 4.1 per cent. In the second period it outpaced all the countries in the survey – note that Margaret Thatcher was in power during part of this period. Denmark was the worst performer with an average yearly increase of about only 1.1 per cent in the 1985–1993 period.

MANAGEMENT ACTIVITIES IN OPERATIONS

Interface with other functions

Operations management involves not only direct operating activities but, because of the supply chain in business, also a significant interface with other functional areas. Some of these are described in the following sections.

Sales

The interface here involves working with marketing personnel to respond to sales forecasts and specific customer requirements and to translate and develop these into operating requirements.

Financial

Here, the interface means working with financial and accounting personnel on product costs, budgets, inventory levels, labour costs and purchase decisions for raw materials, sub-contractor components and capital equipment.

Operational

Some of the operational activities would include:

- working with top management and financial persons to plan capacity requirements over the long range;
- deciding what production capacity will be needed over the short range to satisfy client needs;
- deciding what raw materials, parts and sub-assemblies should be purchased or produced, at what time period, and in what quantity;
- optimizing the levels of inventory to keep investment at a minimum;
- implementing just-in-time production and other approaches in order to achieve 'lean manufacturing'.

Environmental

This would include working with research and development personnel on what strategy the organization should adopt in order to minimize downstream pollution. This includes considering the product design, the product life cycle, minimizing the use of toxic materials, recycling methods and packaging materials.

Human resources

This would involve determining how to use effectively the personnel assigned to an operation, the level of communicating and motivation in a continually changing environment. It might also involve staff selection and training of personnel who will work in the production and operations departments.

Layout

This would involve determining the optimum layout of machines, equipment, storage areas or office space. With new evolving technologies and new products, design layouts are often changed.

Location

This would involve working with top management when new production facilities are to be added to decide where they should be located.

Maintenance

This would involve organization of the operation so that routine maintenance reduces the number of unplanned shutdowns and emergency situations.

Productivity

This would include analysing the effective use of the resources and determining how productivity can be maintained or improved.

Purchasing

This is working with suppliers so that quality, price and delivery times are respected.

Scheduling

This involves deciding on the optimum method to schedule operations such as organizing machines, equipment and personnel to avoid bottlenecks.

Distribution

This involves working with warehouses and distribution centres in order to manage properly the finished goods inventory that is ultimately supplied to the final client.

Project management

When projects arrive in the operation, then this activity involves how these should be effectively managed, budgeted and controlled.

Quality assurance

This is continually looking at quality in the operation to see how it can be improved.

Information systems

This is working with computer personnel to update information systems on a continuous basis, so as to have an efficient supply chain.

Organization charts

All businesses have organization charts that define the relationships between functional departments in the organization. Three organization charts are illustrated for two service firms (Figures 1.12 and 1.13) and a manufacturing company (Figure 1.14). These charts indicate where some of the operations management activities that have been presented fit into to the overall business organization.

SYSTEMS APPROACH TO OPERATIONS

Any organization, be it manufacturing, services or non-profit, can be considered as a system, an approach developed by Jay Forrester.[24] A system is a grouping, perhaps complex, of interdependent components, variables, activities or subsystems. The objective of the system design is that the final output, performance or appearance is optimized or maximized. The following are illustrations (Figure 1.15):

- *The human body*: In the system that is the human body, the arms, legs, head, feet, fingers, etc. would be the subsystems. The optimum human would be intelligent, athletic and good looking.
- *The automobile*: In the system that is the automobile, the engine, transmission, differential, wheels and brakes are components or subsystems. The optimum automobile would be top-performing, reliable, comfortable and attractive.
- *The business firm*: The business firm is a system and Marketing, Operations and Finance are the principal subsystems. High profits, large market share, low costs and high employee moral would be indicators of an optimum firm.

System performance

Most systems are considered open systems in that they are in continuous interaction with the external environment, which imposes on them certain constraints. As a result, a condition of suboptimal performance probably exists.

Figure 1.12 Organization chart for a food distribution centre.

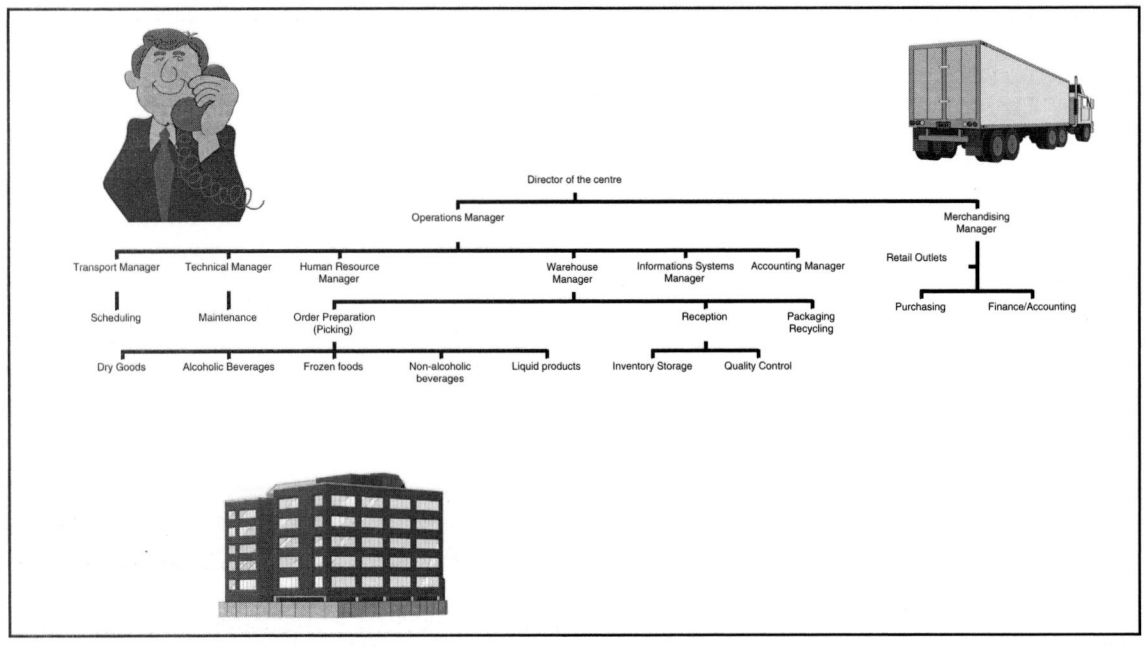

Figure 1.13 Organization of Scandinavian Airlines (SAS), 1997 (Source: SAS Annual Report).

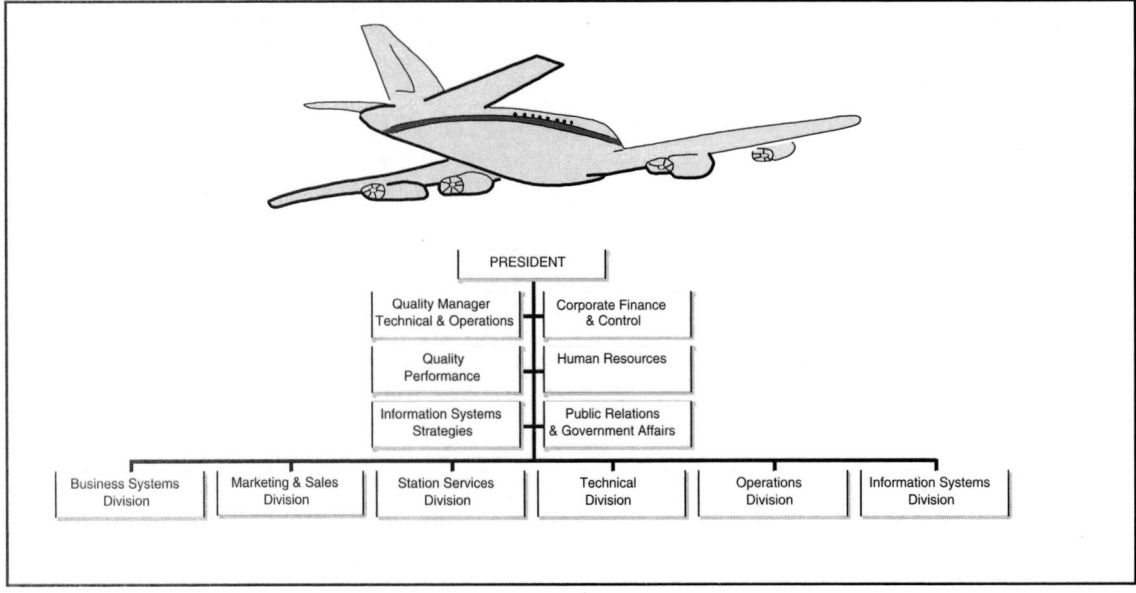

Figure 1.14   Organization chart for a small pharmaceutical manufacturer.

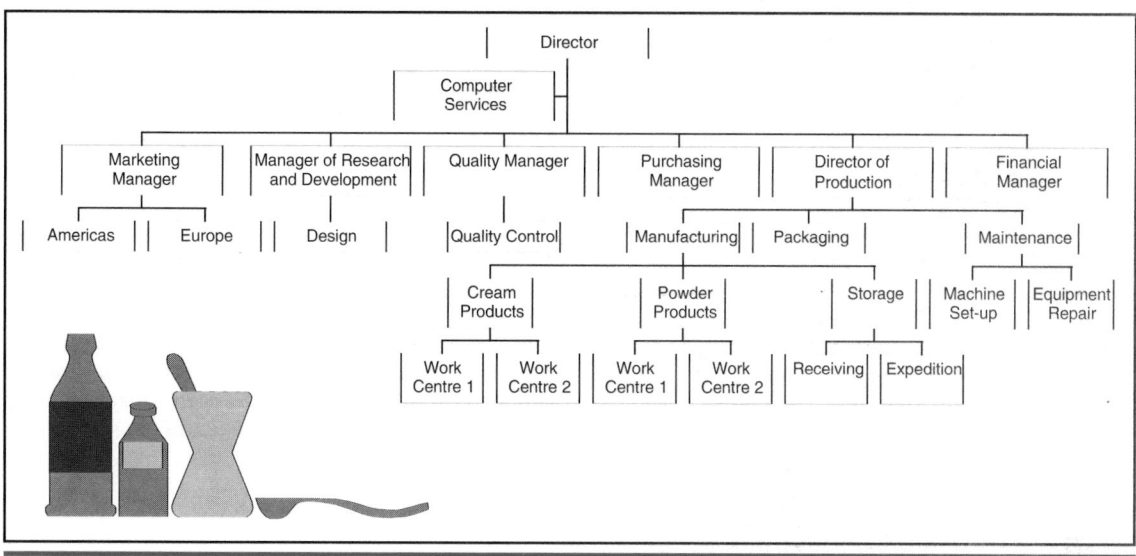

Figure 1.15   A system ... with subsystems.

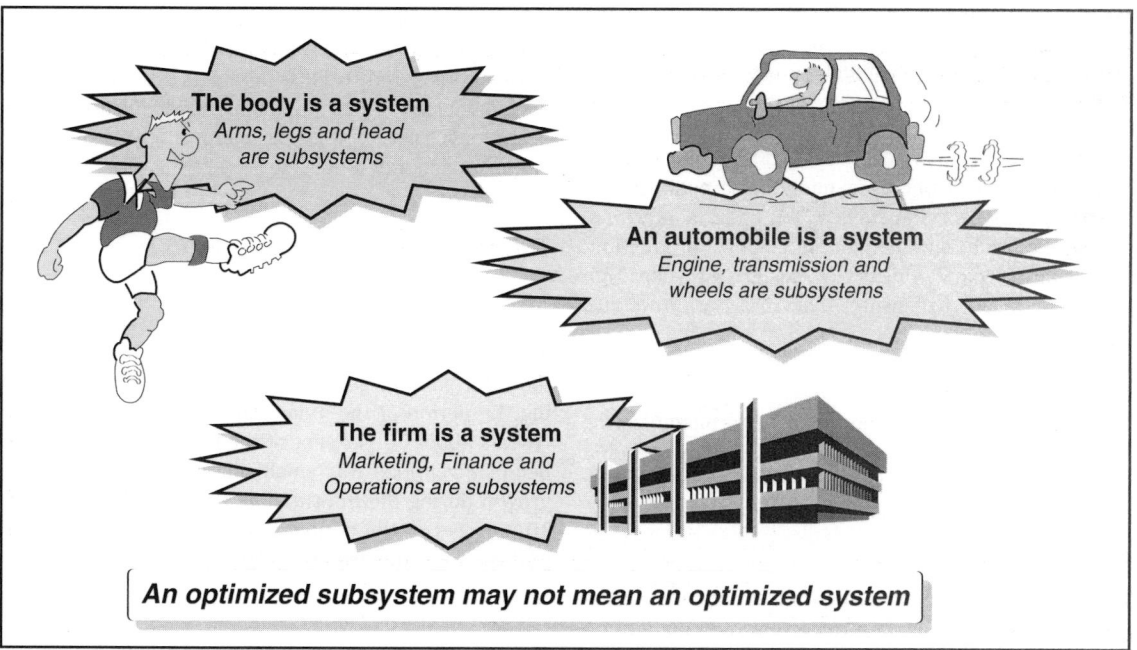

Suboptimal performance

Suboptimal is the condition when optimization of one component, or subsystem, results in less than optimal performance of the overall system, and vice-versa. For the three illustrations given above:

■ Attention to the body's physical performance to give optimum performance (an athlete), may leave insufficient time to educate the mind. Thus, the human being may not be considered '*optimum*'.

■ An optimum-designed engine may be high performing, but the end product, the automobile, may be very noisy and polluting. Incorporating the legally imposed environmental controls reduces the performance of the automobile.

■ In business, optimization of one department's (subsystem's) activity may not be optimum for the entire firm.

System performance of an organization

In the real world, optimum system performance may imply suboptimal performance of the subsystem, since it is not possible to satisfy all requirements of the subsystem. As an illustration, some of the principal objectives of the three major subsystems, Operations, Marketing and Finance, might be described as in the following sections.

Operations

The objectives of Operations might be to minimize the operating costs of the facility, minimize shutdowns, reduce the product range, maintain a level production, standardize product or service designs or keep high inventory levels to ensure that material flows are always met.

Marketing

The objectives of Marketing might be to maximize the number of units sold, maximize market share, develop custom-designed products or services, develop new products or have very short client delivery times.

Finance

The objectives of Finance might be to maximize company profits, minimize any risky ventures, maintain a liquid cash position, maintain low inventory levels or keep borrowing low.

Because of the conflicting objectives of each of these subsystems, there is potential for suboptimality to occur between the three functions:

■ Production prefers to minimize costs by standardized designs, whereas Marketing wants to have more custom designs to satisfy the clients.

■ Finance wants to keep investments in inventory low, while Production wants to keep inventory high as a security measure to minimize the risk of shutdown.

■ Marketing wants to expand the sales territory, but Finance is hesitant because of the capital investment requirement.

Thus, in practice, Marketing, Production and Finance need to work as a team to ensure that products or services conform to customer requirements, are ready on time and are at an acceptable price and that the necessary investment is available for their development and commercialization. The goals of each subsystem must be properly tuned so that the output of the system (the firm) attains the desired objectives. This situation is summarized in Figure 1.16.

TECHNOLOGY

Technological developments, probably more than anything else, have had the biggest impact on the operations management environment. The industrial revolution is considered to have heralded the technological movement and, since then, growth, in terms of new inventions, has followed an increasingly exponential curve, as illustrated in Figure 1.17.[25]

The evolution of technology

Technological evolution may be broken down into four time frames, as illustrated in Figure 1.17, the Industrial Revolution, the Electric Age, the Electronic Age and the Information Age. It is significant to note that during the period of the industrial revolution, which represents about 56 per cent of the time period, the number of inventions was small relative to the explosive growth during the Information Age, which is less than 10 per cent of the period. Summaries of the activities in these four time frames follow.

The industrial revolution

The industrial revolution (1733–1878) is considered to have started when, in 1733, John Kay of Britain invented the flying shuttle for weaving textiles. Other notable inventions in this period included the development of the steam engine by James Watt in 1765 and the cotton gin by Eli Whitney in 1793, which enabled an

Figure 1.16   Interaction of major business functions in operations.

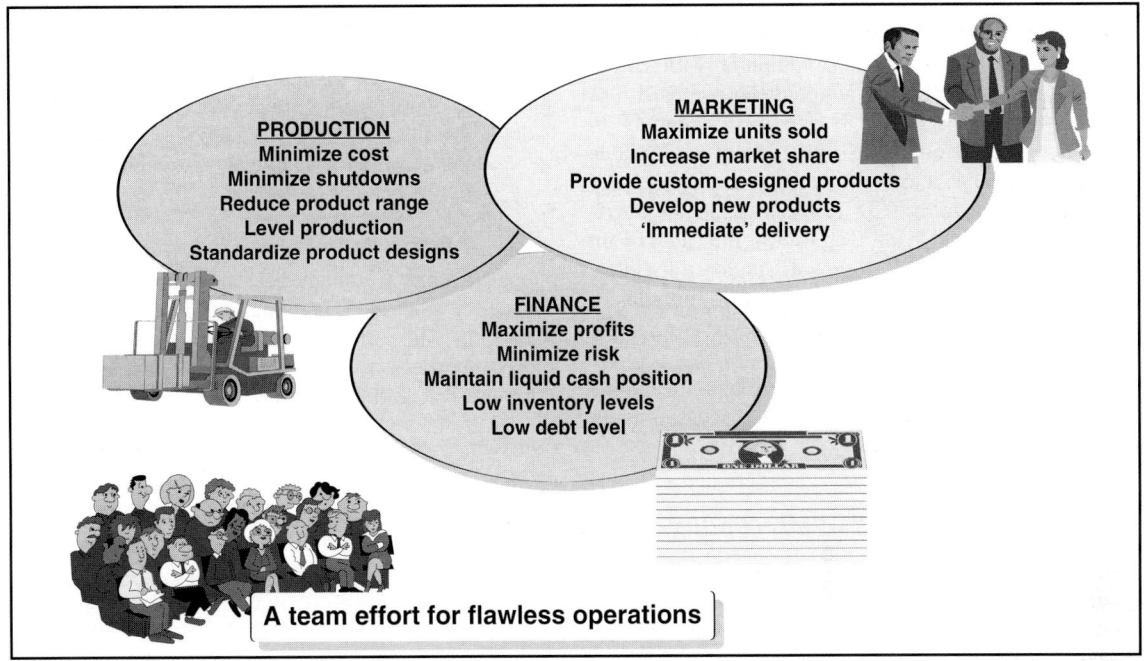

The PRODUCTION
Minimize cost
Minimize shutdowns
Reduce product range
Level production
Standardize product designs

MARKETING
Maximize units sold
Increase market share
Provide custom-designed products
Develop new products
'Immediate' delivery

FINANCE
Maximize profits
Minimize risk
Maintain liquid cash position
Low inventory levels
Low debt level

A team effort for flawless operations

increase in the rate at which seeds could be combed from cotton. In 1837 Samuel Morse patented the telegraph and in 1876 Alexander Graham Bell did the same for the telephone.

The electric age

The Electric Age (1879–1946) began with the invention of the electric light bulb by Thomas Edison and Joseph

Figure 1.17   Technological evolution.

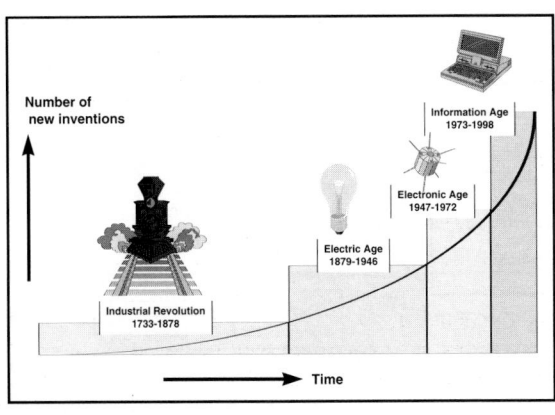

Number of
new inventions

Information Age
1973-1998

Electronic Age
1947-1972

Electric Age
1879-1946

Industrial Revolution
1733-1878

Time

Swan. This period saw the development of the first successful petrol-driven automobile by Karl Benz in 1885 and Marconi's invention of wireless telegraphy in 1895. At the turn of the century, in 1903, Orville and Wilbur Wright made the first extended aeroplane flight. Computers came on the scene when, in 1930, Vannevar Bush, invented the first analogue computer.

The electronic age

The period of the Electronic Age (1947–1972) included the development of the transistor at the Bell Laboratories (now Lucent Technologies) in 1947. In 1956 FORTRAN became the first computer programming language. Other inventions included the launching of the Telstar 1 commercial communications satellite in 1962 and, in the same year, the introduction of the compact cassette by Philips of The Netherlands. The first computers to use integrated circuits were invented by the Burroughs Corporation in 1968 and the production of the first home video cassette recorders (VCR) was in 1972.

The information age

The information age (1973–1998+) is the explosion of information technology and includes such inventions as the ability to put 10 000 units on a one square centimetre computer chip in 1973, the transmittal in six minutes of the first international fax in 1974. In 1977 Apple brought out the first personal computer with colour graphics and in 1981, IBM adopted the standard disk operating system (DOS) for its personal computers. In 1983 Motorola introduced the first cellular telephone and in 1984 Philips and Sony brought out the compact disc read only memory (CD-ROM). In 1990 the development of the World Wide Web on the Internet began. And, in 1995 and 1998, Microsoft, under Bill Gates, introduced Windows 95 and Windows 98, upgrades of the operating system used for most personal computers.

A comprehensive list of some of the major inventions and discoveries during the periods discussed is in Appendix II.[26]

Operations and the twentieth century

In the twentieth century, some global technological developments that have played a major role in operations are illustrated in Figure 1.18. Some of the impact that these technology changes have had on the operations environment are considered in the following sections.

Production processes

Automatic welding machines increase the speed and accuracy of joining metal sheeting. Robots for painting improve the uniformity and the quality of finishing on automobile body work. And bottling and canning of fruits, vegetables and meat is faster, of better quality and less prone to bacteriological contamination.

Service operations

Money can be withdrawn from the bank by using a simple plastic card. Compact discs store a wealth of information for insurance, banking and other applications. Bar codes, and the associated electronic scanners, speed the process through a store checkout and money can be transferred internationally in seconds.

Communication

Electronic mail allows worldwide communication at any hour of the day. Stock prices are available almost instantaneously. With portable phones one can telephone from anywhere to anywhere.

Transportation times

In the 1950s it took three weeks to travel from Europe to Australia by boat, but now with Jumbo jets it takes a matter of hours. Motorways and improved technology

Figure 1.18   Key technological developments in the twentieth century.

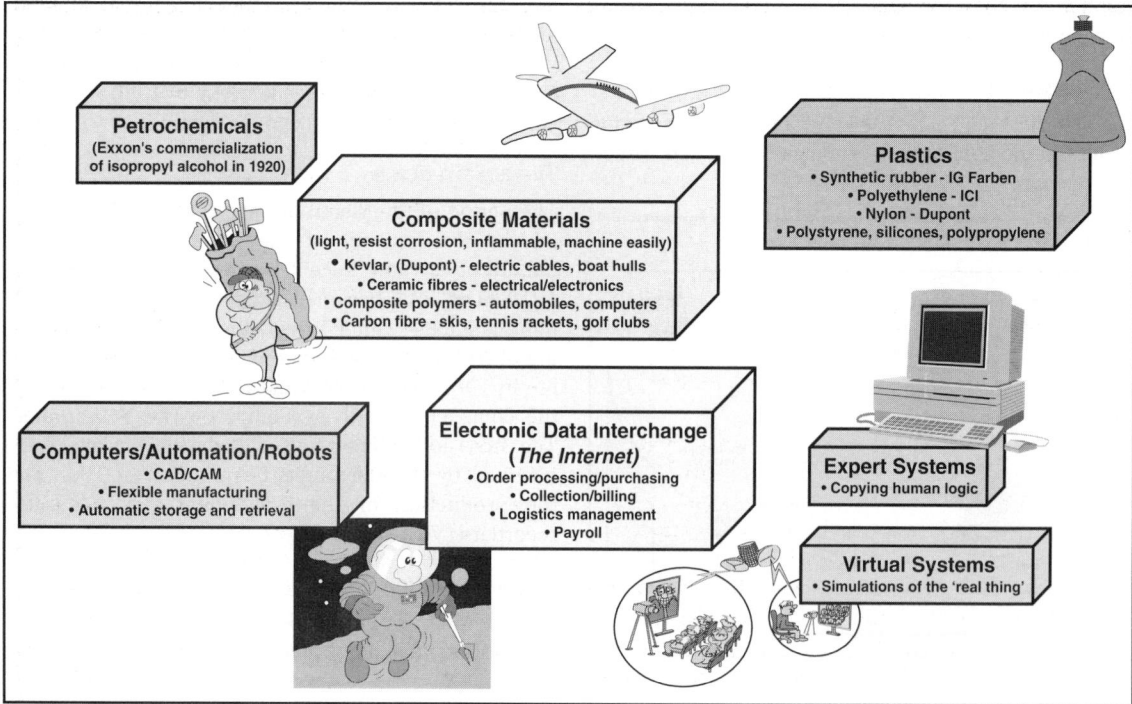

of road construction make delivery of food and other products much quicker. The Bullet trains in France, Japan and Germany have reduced intercity travel time to a matter of hours.

The variety of products available

The number of drugs on the market for asthma, heart disease and ulcers has multiplied. Clothing, in a variety of colours, styles and size, can be obtained in natural or synthetic materials and the models, engine sizes, and colours of automobiles have come a long way since Henry Ford's Model T.

Job conditions

Automatic cutting and drilling machines have reduced the backbreaking work in mines. Thanks to automatic washing machines and dryers, gone is the scrubbing of clothes and turning them through the mangle, and computers have simplified and increased the speed of the reservations process in the travel industry.

Product and process quality

Paint colours on wallpaper, on carpeting and in photography are more uniform, and the colour can be repeated. The quality of results for medical treatment such as electrocardiographs, X-rays and DNA tests is much improved, while computer programs have improved the quality (accuracy) of financial analyses. Finally, transportation, in terms of the miles travelled, is safer.

Product delivery time

Automation allows automobiles to be produced within days. Chemical feeds allow chickens, geese and turkeys to be bred at a faster rate (although views differ on whether this is a good thing). Microwave ovens allow aeroplanes rapidly to serve meals that approach restaurant quality.

Product prices

Production methods for the computer have put the price of computers in the range of most consumers. New construction materials have brought down the cost of homes. The real cost of many drugs and medical treatments has come down, making them available to a broader spectrum of patients.

Reduced labour needs

The need for labour on the assembly line has dropped. Tellers are not needed in the banking industry. Operators are not needed in the telephone industry. And on certain metro lines, such as in Lyon, France, there are no drivers.

SUMMARY OF KEY ELEMENTS

- Operations management is the planning, organizing and control of all the resources and activities to provide goods and services. It applies equally to manufacturing and services in the private and public sectors and even in government.
- The driving force in operations management is the 'king' client who requires products at the right time, at an acceptable quality, at a reasonable price and courteously.
- A manufacturing firm turns physical raw materials into tangible products. These products can be seen and touched, described in dimensional terms, such as weight, length, height and volume, and have monetary value.
- Services provide a 'product', often intangible, which cannot be described in dimensional terms. Compared to manufacturing, there is more client contact in services and so operations personnel are often more people-oriented.
- As well as market-driven firms, there are non-profit service organizations. Here the driving force is a desire to do good, rather than to serve commercial interests. Although not constrained by the profit motive, they are nevertheless operations that need to be managed effectively, so that they can serve end client users at a reasonable cost.
- The employment level in manufacturing in developed nations continues to decline because of technology replacing labour, relocation to cheaper labour regions and the explosive growth of service industries.
- Operations are increasingly international because of reduction in trade barriers, less expensive foreign labour, expanding markets in emerging economies, coupled to saturated domestic markets, and cheaper and easier international transportation.
- An operations model is a supply-chain network of three blocks, inputs, transformation and outputs of end products, which is coupled to an information flow with the reverse sense. The economic value of the outputs is greater than that of the inputs.
- The objective of operations is to use available resources productively, as this translates into lower costs and higher profits. Resources include surface area, materials, direct and indirect labour,

energy and water, and finances. Globally productivity is given by the ratio of output to input.

■ Operations involve activities related to sales, finance, the environment, human resources, facility layout, site selection, maintenance, productivity improvements, purchasing, scheduling, distribution, project management, quality assurance and information systems.

■ The firm, or organization, can be considered as a system, of which operations, sales and finance are the three subsystems. Optimizing the firm may lead to suboptimization of the operations management function.

■ Technological developments, probably more than anything, have had the biggest impact on the operations management environment, including the development of new products, process design and the reduced requirement for labour.

REVIEW AND DISCUSSION QUESTIONS

1 **Linking supply chain and operations.** The supply chain refers to the purchasing, transformation and delivery of finished goods to the client. All along the supply chain are 'clients'. The client is king (or 'queen')! What is meant by this axiom in the supply chain? In your day-to-day living in dealing with businesses, the university, stores, etc. are you treated as 'king'. Discuss, in particular, where you think improvements are warranted.

2 **Distinction, services and manufacturing.** The distinction is often made between manufacturing and services. What is the usefulness of such a distinction? Is it meaningful? What purpose does it serve? Illustrate your discussion with real companies or industries.

3 **Medical care.** Medical health coverage in France and Britain are principally not-for-profit service-type organizations. People are getting older and so are increasing the demands on the system. Pharmaceutical products are expensive and research and development are high. The medical systems in both these countries are heavily in debt. How would you think that the operation of the health system can be improved, by reducing costs, but not severely reducing the quality of service to the client?

4 **International firms.** On the international scene, the text makes reference to Exxon (oil industry), Boeing (aircraft manufacture), Siemens (industrial and consumer goods), British Airways (transportation), Accor (Hotels), Crédit Suisse (Banking) and Euronews (non-profit communications). Discuss, in global terms, the supply chain and operations of these types of international industries from the points of view of personnel, materials, cost and operations.

5 **Employment.** Manufacturing-sector employment has dropped dramatically in favour of the service sector. Do you believe this trend will continue? What impact will this have on developed countries and in developing (emerging) countries? Discuss these trend in relationship to the high unemployment levels in France and Germany. Why is unemployment level lower in Great Britain than in Germany and France?

6 **Organization chart.** Not using those already presented, find an organization chart for the following:
(a) a manufacturing company;
(b) a service company.

Identify the firms and identify the systems approach in that organization and the types of interaction that will occur with the departments illustrated.

7 **Modelling.** Develop a simple flow scheme, or model of operations, for the following, indicating which is the main value-added step in the operation:
(a) local grocery store;
(b) university or business school;
(c) dentist's or doctor's office;
(d) Post Office;
(e) a large department store.

8 **Productivity.** Discuss how productivity would be measured in the following:
(a) a plumbing service company that makes house calls;
(b) a retail store;
(c) a travel agent;
(d) a milk-bottling company.

9 **Managing technology.** People often talk about 'Managing Technology' in business, because technology is considered a resource. Discuss what you believe are the important elements to be considered in managing technology, taking into consideration the rapid changes in techniques and methods in operations.

10 **Technology in the firm.** Consider the following operations:
(a) the house where you live;
(b) a university or business school;
(c) a medical centre;
(d) a library;
(e) stores that you use.
Where do you think technology would improve the efficiency, decrease the cost and reduce the time in these operations? What would be the downside of adding your proposed technical innovations.

11 **Technical change.** Many people resent technical change. A classic illustration is the Luddites who during the Industrial Revolution smashed the cropping frames as they felt their jobs in the textile industry were being threatened. Unions often cite technological changes as a reason for reductions in the work force. People are 'afraid to use computers'. Do you believe people's fears are justified? Do you believe that the introduction of new technology is always a good thing? How do you think managers should cope with these changes in relation to their staff?

12 **United Parcel Services and Volvo Automobiles.** United Parcel Services (UPS), based in the USA, is a service company providing express delivery of letters, pack-

ages and equipment to customers worldwide. Volvo, based in Sweden, is a manufacturer of automobiles. One is a service company, the other is manufacturing.

(a) What are the similarities between the operating aspects of these two firms?

(b) What are the differences between the operating aspects of these two firms?

(c) What are the challenges facing these two firms in the 21st century?

In your analysis consider, at least (but you are not limited to), strategies, technology, organization, human resources, international challenges, customers, quality and facility layout.

CASE STUDY: PANGAS

Situation[27]

Pangas, in Liverpool, England was created in 1976 and is now owned by the current president. Its business is the servicing, maintenance and installation of electric and gas heating appliances. Its principal clients are individual homes, small businesses (printing shops, stores, car repair stores, etc.) and blocks of flats owned by the community. In 1995 its revenues amounted to £1.5 million.

Pangas currently has 37 employees, of which 14 are administrative and 23 are technicians, who perform the maintenance and installation work. The service area covers all of Liverpool and some of the surrounding areas. At present the company has 18 500 maintenance/contracts, of which one third are for homes and flats and two thirds are for small businesses. These contracts have been negotiated at a fixed price and usually have a duration of three to five years.

The revenues of Pangas are growing at about 2 to 3 per cent per year, although there is considerable pressure on the price of the service as a result of competitive pressure. The cost of the work for Pangas is as follows:

- 60 per cent salaries;
- 15 per cent pieces purchased for the repair work;
- 9 per cent telephone, communication, vehicle maintenance, insurance, computer service charges and rent for office space;
- 3 per cent for taxes;
- 1 per cent depreciation;
- 1 per cent gasoline for service vehicles

Operational activity

There are several types of service activities for Pangas. The maintenance contracts are serviced two to three times per year. The planning for this activity is entered into the computer system, from which the administrators generate a print-out each day and enter it into the planning for the service technicians. Installation of new equipment, which constitutes about 5 per cent of the revenues, is usually planned about two to three weeks in advance. For this type of work, the appliances are purchased by the client and the technician's responsibility is the installation. However, there are often situations where the technicians have to buy additional parts because of special considerations. The other activity is emergency service work such as the breakdown of appliances, poor operation, etc., which is difficult to plan and often involves the secretaries rescheduling the routing of the technicians. In total, the technicians make about 35 000 visits per year. Not all of these are productive because clients are not at home, keys for the house/flat cannot be located or the technician does not have the correct parts in his van.

When a client has a problem he/she telephones Pangas and a telephonist takes down the required information and enters it directly into the computer system. With the client on the line, she directly proposes a date and time for the service work. For this purpose, she has a planning programme for each technician according to the geographic zone and the type of work. She would plan about four visits for the morning and five for the afternoon. This information would be confirmed to the client by mail sent two to three weeks in advance of the service date. The telephonists do not have the full details regarding the competence of each technician and the scheduling, so sometimes modifications have to be made. When the job has been performed, the technician fills out the form containing the necessary details of the job, has it signed by the client and gives this to accounting. Accounting bills the customer accordingly and asks for payment within 60 days if the work falls outside the terms of the contract. This may be when parts are not included or when the work is beyond the scope of the contract.

Required

1 Present how you believe this service firm would operate from reception of a client call, through to performing the work, to billing the customer. What do you think are some of the problems likely to be encountered (typical of many service organizations where house or small business visits are made)?

2 Develop an appropriate organization chart for the Pangas company.

3 How should the productivity of the company be measured? Based on your ideas, how might the productivity be improved?

CASE STUDY: STENA LINE

Situation

Stena Line is the world's largest company for international ferry traffic. The Group's route network consists of 15 well-positioned ferry routes in north-western Europe. These cover the business areas of the Kattegatt (Sweden–Denmark–Germany–Poland), the Skagerack (Norway–Denmark–Sweden)), the English Channel (Britain–France–Belgium–Holland) and the Irish Sea (Ireland–England–Scotland).

In 1995, nearly 15 million passengers, 2.7 million private cars and 930 000 trucks, trailers, containers and railway carriages were transported on the Group's ferries. The fleet consists of 35 ferries, most of which are large multipurpose ferries for passengers, cars and trucks, but some of which are straightforward freight ferries for wheelborne freight traffic. Two of the Group's routes are operated by high-speed catamarans, which can carry both passengers and private cars.

The Stena Line Group owns four harbours in the UK (Harwich, Fishguard, Holyhead and Stranraer). In Denmark, it runs three hotels (two in Frederikshavn and one in Grena) as an integrated part of the ferry operations.

The Group's income is generated by the Travel, Onboard and Freight/Ports Divisions. In 1995, the Travel Division, which covers all ticket revenue from passengers, private cars and caravans, as well as hotel and travel-agency sales, accounted for 36 per cent of the operating income. Onboard, comprising sales in restaurants, duty free shops, etc., accounted for 38 per cent of income. Freight/ports, which covers marine transportation and forwarding services, together with the business from other shipping companies who use the Group's harbours, accounted for the other 26 per cent of the operating income.[28]

Required

Discuss broadly what you believe are the operating activities and challenges for this international service firm. Include in your discussion how you believe its operating plans differ from its strategic plan. In general terms, how do the operations of this type of firm differ from those of a manufacturing firm? Consider using the Internet for more information.

NOTES AND REFERENCES

1. *Fortune* (1995) 15 May.
2. Institute for International Economics (1991) 'Transportation and communication costs,' *The Economist* 20 July.
3. Mahler, Robert, Directeur Général, GEC Alsthom T&D (1997) G7 Management Conference, Lyon Graduate School of Business, 16 May.
4. *Exxon Corporation* (1995) *Annual Report 1995*.
5. *Boeing Corporation* (1995) *Annual Report 1995*.
6. Siemens *Rapport Annuel* 1996, Siemens AG, Wittelsbacherplatz 2, Munich, Germany. (French version of the original Annual Report published in German.)
7. British Airways (1997) *Reports and Accounts 1996–97*.
8. Accor (1996) *Direction de la communication*, Accor, Evry, France, July.
9. Crédit Suisse Group (1997) *Annual Report 1996/97*, Zurich, Switzerland.
10. Shotgun Wedding? Crédit Suisse Plans $9.5 billion merger with Winterthur (1997) *Wall Street Journal Europe* 12 August.
11. 'Les Firmes Multinationales', *Mémo, Larousse*, Encyclopédie, 1990: 600
12. Visit on 30 July 97 with Mr Tombaccini and Euronews company brochure.
13. Euronews Distribution (1997) 31 March.
14. *The Economist* (1996) 23 March.
15. US Bureau of Labour Statistics (1994) *The Economist* 5 March.
16. OECD National Statistics (1994) *The Economist*, 19 March.
17. US Bureau of Labour Statistics (1994) *The Economist* 5 March.
18. OECD National Statistics (1994) *The Economist*, 19 March.
19. Zachary, G. Pascal (1994) Up the Ladder. US Multinationals Take Brain Work to Plants overseas: Job competition and pressure on wages begin to reach America's Labour Elite, *Wall Street Journal Europe* 30 September.
20. *The Economist* (1989) 2 December.
21. Powers, J. D. (1992), Survey: The Car Industry, *The Economist* 17 October: 10.
22. Council of Economic Advisors (1989) *Wall Street Journal Europe* 1 June.
23. *The Economist* (1994) 15 October.
24. Forrester, Jay (1964) *Industrial Dynamics*, Cambridge, MA: MIT Press.
25. Based on Roach, S.S. 'Computers can do a great job – Yours', *Time*, 13 November 1995.
26. *Mémo Larousse Encyclopédie* (1990) Libraire Larousse and others
27. Based on a study by Dominique Salaün and others, CESMA, Groupe ESC Lyon, 1996–1997.
28. Stena Line AB (1995) *Annual Report 1995*.

FURTHER READING

Many of the references here include general textbooks on production and operations management. These reference books contain useful information related to many of the functional areas discussed in this textbook.

Amrine, H. T., Ritchey, J. A., Moodie, C. L. (1987) *Manufacturing Organisation and Management*, Englewood Cliffs, NJ: Prentice Hall.

Banker, R. D. and Khosla, I. S. (1995) 'Economics of operations management: A research perspective', *Journal of Operations Management* 12(3,4): 423–35.

Broadberry, S. N. (1997) 'The long run growth and productivity performance of the United Kingdom', *Scottish Journal of Political Economy* 44(4): 403–24.

Buffa, E. S. and Sarin, R. K. (1987) *Modern Production/Operations Management*, New York: Wiley.

Burton, F., Yamin, M. and Young, S. (1996) *International Business and Europe in Transition*, Basingstoke: Macmillan.

Cartwright, R. Collins, M. Green, G. and Candy, A. (1993) *Managing Operations*, Oxford: Blackwell Business.

Chase, R. B. and Aquilano, N. J. (1989) *Production and Operations Management, A Life Cycle Approach*, Homewood, IL: Irwin.

Dilworth, J. (1993) *Production and Operations Management*, New York, London: McGraw-Hill.

Emery, F. E. (1969) *Systems Thinking: Selected Readings*, Harmondsworth, UK: Penguin.

European Commission (1989) *Employment in Europe – 1989*, Luxembourg: EUR-OP.

European Commission (1996) *Services of General Interest in Europe*, Luxembourg: EUR-OP.

Freeman, C., Sharp, M. and Walker, W. (1991) *Technology and the Future of Europe: Global Competition and the Environment in the 1990s*, London: Pinter.

Gaither, N. (1994) *Production and Operations Management*, Fort Worth, TX, London: Dryden Press.

Haeckel, S. H. (1993) 'Managing by wire', *Harvard Business Review*, October, 71(5): 122–32.

Harrison, M. (1996) *Principles of Operations Management*, London: Pitman.

Heap, J. P. (1992) *Productivity Management: A Fresh Approach,* New York: Cassell.

Heizer, J. and Render, B. (1996) *Production and Operations Management,* Upper Saddle River, NJ: Prentice Hall.

Ingrassia, P. and White, J. B. (1994) *Comeback: The Fall and Rise of the American Automobile Industry,* New York, London: Simon and Schuster.

Johnston, R. (1994) 'Operations: From factory to service management', *International Journal of Service Industry Management* 5(1): 49–63.

Krajlewski, L. J. and Ritzman, L. P. (1993) *Operations Management Strategy and Analysis*, Harlow: Addison-Wesley.

Marshall, J. N. (1988) *Services and Uneven Development,* Oxford: Oxford University Press.

Meredith, J. R. (1992) *The Management of Operations,* New York, Chichester: Wiley.

Muhlemann, A. P., Oakland, J. S. and Lockyer, K. G. (1993) *Production and Operations Management,* London: Pitman.

Nahmias, S. (1997) *Production and Operations Analysis,* Homewood, IL: Irwin.

Naylor, J. (1996) *Operations Management,* London: Pitman.

Noori, H., Laurier, W. and Radford, R. (1995) *Production and Operations Management: Total Quality and Responsiveness,* New York: McGraw-Hill.

Prokopenko, J. (1992) *Productivity Management,* Geneva: International Labour Office.

Roman, D. D. and Puett, J. F. (1983) *International Business and Technological Innovation,* New York, Oxford: North Holland.

Russell, R. S. and Taylor, B. W. III (1995) *Production and Operations Management,* Englewood CLiffs, NJ: Prentice Hall.

Sawaya, W. J. (1993) 'Improving company performance through operations management training for production workers', *Production and Inventory Management Journal,* 2nd quarter, 34(2): 18–22.

Schmenner, R. W. (1990) *Productions/Operations Management: Concepts and Situations,* New York: Macmillan; London: Collier Macmillan.

Schonberger, R. J. and Knod, E. M. (1988) *Operations Management: Serving the Customer,* Homewood, IL: Business Publications Inc.

Schroeder, R. (1993) *Operations Management: Decision Making in the Operations Function,* New York, London: McGraw-Hill.

Sheu, C. and Wacker, J. (1994) 'A planning and control framework for non-profit humanitarian organisations', *International Journal of Operations and Production Management* 14(4) 64–78.

Skinner, W. (1985) *Manufacturing: The Formidable Competitive Weapon,* Wiley.

Slack, N., Chambers, S., Harrison, A., Johnston, R. and Harland, C. (1998) *Operations Management,* London: Pitman.

Starr, M. K. (1989) *Managing Production and Operations,* Englewood Cliffs, NJ: Prentice Hall.

Stevenson, W. (1995) *Production/Operations Management,* Homewood, IL: Irwin.

Tassey, G. (1992) *Technology Infrastructure and Competitive Position,* Norwell, MA: Kluwer Academic.

Toni, A. D., Filippini, R. and Forza, C. (1992) 'Manufacturing strategy in global markets: an operations management model', *International Journal of Operations and Production Management* 12(4): 7–18.

Victor, B. and Boynton, A. C. (1993) 'Making mass customisation work', *Harvard Business Review* 71(5): 108–119.

Weiss, H. J. and Gershon, M. E. (1989) *Production and Operations Management,* Boston, MA: Allyn and Bacon.

Wilson, B. (1990) *Systems: Concepts Methodologies and Applications,* New York, Chichester: Wiley.

Wilson, J. M. (1995) 'An historical perspective on operations management', *Production and Inventory Management Journal* 36(3): 61–66.

Womack, J. P., Jones, D. T. and Roos, D. (1990) *The Machine that Changed the World,* New York, Oxford: Rawson Associates/Maxwell Macmillan International.

Zachary, W. B. and Richman, E. (1993) 'Building an operations management foundation that will last: TQM, JIT, and CIM', *Industrial Engineering,* August, 25(8): 39–43.

Part I.
Strategic decisions and operations

An organization, either services or manufacturing, is driven by top management's strategy and it is this that sets in motion operations and the associated supply-chain linkage. The four chapters in this part of the book describe some of the organization's global strategic elements. Chapter 2 gives an overview of corporate strategy and its market orientation. Chapter 3 discusses the strategy of where to locate the firm, with factors such as cost, labour and other resources taken into account. The subsequent two chapters, 4 and 5, concern quality management and maintaining an environmental balance. Without a certain quality level, a company will have difficulty retaining clients. And, without maintaining an environmental balance, a firm will lose its credibility. In either case, if these elements are not part of the organization's strategy, its long-term survival will be in doubt.

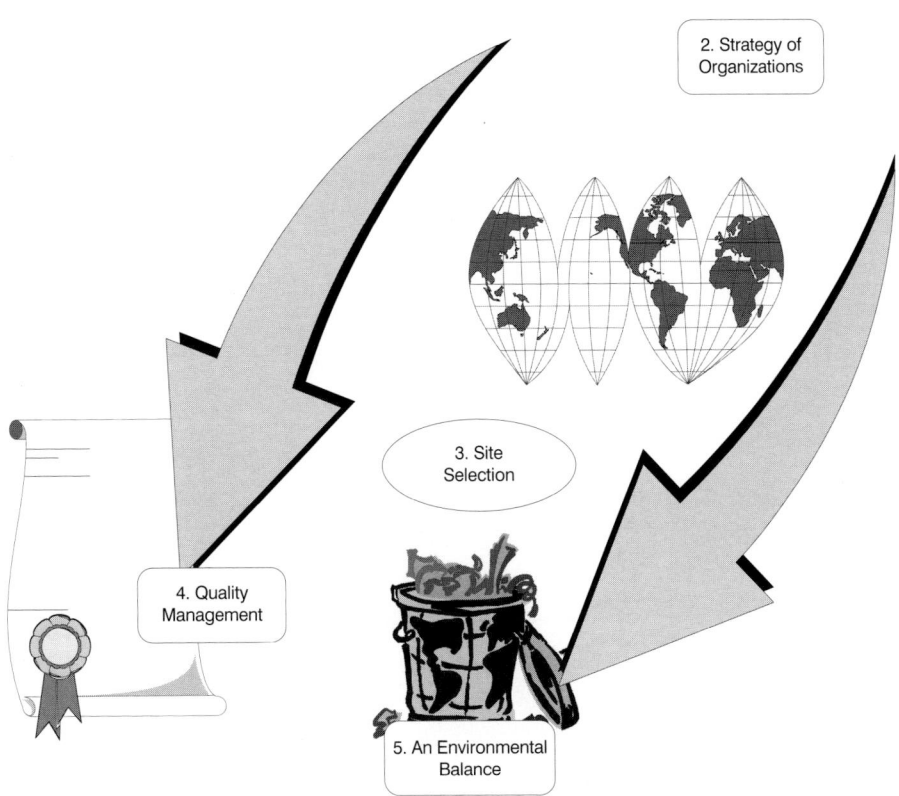

2. Strategy of Organizations

3. Site Selection

4. Quality Management

5. An Environmental Balance

2 | Strategy of organizations

Objectives and overview

The objective of this chapter is to review the strategy of organizations with emphasis on the interrelationship between corporate strategy and operations management. The first section discusses global strategies of both market-driven and non-profit organizations. The next section is concerned with the various elements of a strategic plan including the time frame, mission statements, using a SWOT analysis and developing action plans. There is a section on overlap strategy and operations with a pro-forma financial statement for a firm used as an illustration, in which the marketing and financial activities are compared with operations. Finally, the chapter summarizes the real-world corporate objectives of three international firms.

GLOBAL STRATEGIC OBJECTIVES

Every manufacturing, service firm or non-profit organization must have a long-term objective. Globally the objectives would encompass: Where do we want to be? Who do we want to be? What do we want to do? The strategy then includes the measures to take in order to arrive at the organization's stated objectives. Senior managers in the organization would have the ultimate responsibilities for these measures. Then, once these are established, they would be the drivers for setting the strategies or objectives for the operations and supply-chain functions.

Objectives, and strategy, have their roots in war time. The objectives of a nation are of course to win the war and the strategy is how the country will mobilize its resources to achieve this objective.

Market-driven organizations

As discussed in Chapter 1, *Positioning Operations Management*, the firm is an open system, which interacts continually with the external environment. The external environment is constantly in a state of flux demographically, politically, economically and socially. Markets and consumer needs change; laws are modified; and technology is constantly being updated and improved. It is in this competitive environment that the firm operates and as such it has basically three options:

- ignore the environment;
- adapt enough to survive;
- grow by exploiting opportunities.

Ignore the environment

In the long run, if the firm maintains its *status quo*, this will lead to disaster. The failure of many firms is as a result of complacency and ignoring the changing business environment. Eventually these firms are consumed by the changing events.

Adapt enough to survive

Some conservative firms adhere to the familiar path because of the fear of taking risks. Firms is this category eventually find their market share dwindling and they are eventually swallowed.

Grow by exploiting opportunities

In order to grow, the firm must innovate and change. It must seize opportunities, but at the same time avoid dangers that are constantly being created by the ever-changing environment. Every business enterprise makes decisions that ultimately decide its future. Choices are made that influence long-term outcomes and those made on accurate business environmental forecasts will lead to growth and profitability.

Profit

In the long run, the global objective of a business firm must be to make a profit. With this profit:

- Shareholders will receive dividends and may invest further in the business.
- Salaries can be increased or employees may receive bonuses that can have an indirect effect of motivating their work effort.
- Funds are available for capital expansion, which will lead to higher employment. Capital expansion will mean increasing business in the surrounding community to support the increased number of employees.

If the company does not continue to make a profit in the long run, it will fail.

Non-profit organizations

Non-profit organizations are also open systems in that they interact with the surrounding environment. However, their objectives are usually not constrained by the push to generate profits or to battle competitors. Their existence is to provide to the public at large the service established according to their charter, such as education, humanitarian aid, postal delivery, transportation services, etc. The objectives are overseen by a board of directors, who will establish a strategy for the operational personnel.

Regina E. Herzlinger, at Harvard University, in a study of hundreds of non-profit organizations over the last 25 years, has developed the following four interrelated criteria to aid the board of directors achieve these objectives.[1]

Consistency with financial resources

The organizational goals should be consistent with the organization's financial resources. In broad terms, this means that if a large proportion of society is not benefiting from the service, then it should be reduced or curtailed. This philosophy was behind the actions of the British Government's Dr Beeching who announced in March 1964 the closure of many rail services in the then nationalized British Railways. The principal argument was, that although a public service, the operating cost of some lines was inconsistent with the number of users.[2]

Equitable services for all generations

This guideline is that objectives of today should not jeopardize the services offered in the future, and vice-versa. As an illustration, when a charity saves an excessively large proportion of its resources to help future users, it denies benefits to present users. Conversely, when it consumes virtually all its assets to serve present users, it denies the benefits of the organization's services to future users.

Sources and uses of funds should be matched

Non-profit organizations have expenses that are fixed in the sense that they are exceedingly difficult to reverse. The remuneration of, say, a tenured professor at a university, a noted conductor at a symphony orchestra or the head of a public hospital represent fixed expenses. These fixed expenses should be funded by sources that can be readily controlled, and should yield a steady stream of income. For example, the income from endowment capital invested in a relatively risk-free portfolio should be used to match fixed expenses. It would be inappropriate to match the salaries of a professor with research grants, because, if these dried up, teaching capacity at universities would have to be decreased.

Sustainability of the organization

If the first three criteria are satisfied, then normally the *status quo* of the organization can be sustained if it is maintained on an inflation-adjusted constant value. Preparation of a strategic plan, together with an associated pro-forma financial statement (discussed later), would demonstrate that continuation of present policies will enable the organization to survive in its present form. An illustration of this is the government-managed social securities programmes of many major industrialized countries (USA, Britain, France, Germany and Japan), which are technically 'bankrupt'. In this case, the changing demographic environment is showing that the organization is unable to meet the first three criteria:

- Goals are not consistent with the financial resources.
- It will be impossible to have equitable services for all generations.
- It is difficult to match sources and uses of funds.

As such, many countries' social security programmes are not sustainable in their present form.

Note that, unlike the market-driven organization, the *status quo* of the non-profit organization is the major element in its sustainability. The Catholic Church, the Red Cross and the Elementary School have barely changed. However, compare this to the British coal industry, British shipbuilding or Smith Corona Typewriters, where all three have been unable to adapt to the changing environment.

THE STRATEGIC PLAN

A strategic plan is the detail of how an organization proposes to arrive at its desired objectives. Elements of the strategic plan depend on the particular organization, but they would generally include such items as the time frame and the mission of the firm, or in the case of a non-profit organization, a charter. The strategic plan would attempt to analyse the current and future external environment and particularly those elements that would have a strong impact on the organization. Furthermore, the plan would include a rigorous analysis of the organization's strength's and weaknesses, both internal and external.

Strategic plans for business firms are ultimately developed by top management personnel, such as the president or the vice-presidents of marketing, finance, operations and human resources and they usually have to be approved by the board of directors. For non-profit firms it is often the board of directors who develop the plans. However, in all cases, strategic plans are built up from input provided by operating personnel.

Time frame

A strategic plan is generally long-term. The time frame is nominally about five years, but in reality depends upon the organization. For non-profit organizations, such as universities, hospitals and the military, five years may be reasonable. However, for companies that are involved in activities that are strongly influenced by technological changes, such as IBM (computers), AT&T (telecommunications) and Microsoft (software development), the strategic plans may be less than five years because the technology field changes so rapidly. Aircraft firms (Boeing and Airbus), nuclear power plant constructors and oil companies have strategic plans that go beyond five years, because of the enormous time needed for activities like development, design and product commercialization. Consider the following article for an oil company.

Mobil oil

Box 2.1 refers to the development of an oil field off Newfoundland, Canada and illustrates the lengthy strategy process in oil companies.[3]

Dates for key events are summarized below. The time frame is almost 40 years and still the plan's objectives have not been reached!

Box 2.1 Old Gusher. Four decades later, oil field off Canada is ready to produce. Politics, money and nature put vast deposit on ice; now it may last 50 years. 'Shot in the Arm for U.S' By Allanna Sullivan, Staff Reporter

GREAT MOSQUITO COVE, Newfoundland – Just as the ice-filled seas near here hid the secrets of the Titanic for decades, so too has the stormy North Atlantic concealed vast reserves of oil deep beneath its seabed.

But now, almost 40 years after the effort to tap those reserves began, the ocean is about to release its loot. The Hibernia field, one of the largest oil discoveries in North America in decades, should deliver its first oil by year end. At least 20 more fields may follow, offering well over one billion barrels of high-quality crude and promising that a steady flow of oil will be just a quick tanker-run away from the energy-thirsty Eastern Seaboard of the U.S.

At a time when most of America's oil comes from politically risky nations, the security of a nearby oil reserve largely owned by U.S. companies and in a friendly country is hard to overestimate. "It's a big shot in the arm for U.S. supply," says David Oake, a former official in Newfoundland's industry ministry.

Three Enemies

That Hibernia will finally happen is a triumph over the industry's three biggest enemies: nature, politics and economics. Fluctuating oil prices, a partner's financial woes and lengthy squabbles between Canada's federal and Newfoundland's regional governments repeatedly threatened to halt the project.

Even now, nature could still interfere. So dangerous is the territory that operators will track icebergs by plane, helicopter and ship. The oil rig's serrated platform, the only

one of its kind in the world, is designed to take the impact of an iceberg on one of its 16 giant teeth. In addition, the platform will be equipped with radar to detect ice. Once the field is up and running, a fleet of huge tugs will lasso errant icebergs with heavy cables and drag them away.

But the $4.2 billion effort, which has an estimated 50-year lifespan, is well worth the risk to project leader Mobil Corp. and its partners. Hibernia's two reservoirs alone hold a minimum of 615 million barrels of oil, and likely more, says Paul Hoenmans, Mobil executive vice president, and reserves of this magnitude are rare indeed.

Most of the world's new high-profile discoveries are in distant lands where rebels, dictators or terrain make development a slow process. Hibernia and related fields, as well as a natural-gas find nearby, will boost the Fairfax, Virginia, oil company's production, ultimately increasing Mobil's North American oil and natural-gas output by 30%. "The east coast of Canada is a major growth area for us," says Jerry Anderson, chief executive of Mobil Canada.

Though the Hibernia field, about 310 kilometers southeast of St. John's, and the surrounding area bear an uncanny geographic resemblance to the giant North Sea complex, oil companies ignored it for years because of its location in "iceberg alley." Don Axford, a retired Mobil executive, says he first considered the region might hold promise during a routine 1959 executive meeting, when he took a good look at Sable Island's location on a wall map, south of Hibernia's location. "I got to wondering why that speck of an island was sitting out there in the ocean all by itself," he says.

Island High

Fixated on the island, off Nova Scotia in the Grand Banks fishing shoals, Mr. Axford, then Mobil's chief research geologist in Canada, began to wonder, "Could it be a high?" – a geological term for a rocky dome-shaped formation that sometimes holds oil.

He and his team of geologists spent months researching the prospect, but managers twice turned away his theory. Finally, though, he was given permission to buy up permits covering one million acres (400,000 hectares) beneath the glacial waters off eastern Canada – the first exploration permits granted to a major oil company there. "Just in case," he was told by Arthur Dutmar, then president of Mobil's Canadian unit.

Mr. Axford didn't get a chance to drill for eight years, and then he chose to try Sable itself. Loading a rig onto a World War II landing craft, he ran it up onto the beach and had it dragged to the middle of the island. When he and his crew drilled straight down, they hit gas – but it wasn't a big enough strike to be commercial. Still, "the well showed us the resource was there," Mr. Axford says, his voice still showing elation after all these years.

Soon, drilling had moved offshore and oil companies, following Mobil, were scooping up permits and sinking holes all over the Grand Banks, where fishing for years was the main occupation. With new seismic data showing evidence of oil on the ocean bottom, Mobil picked up a second sweep of permits in 1965 for just several cents an acre, including the terrain that became Hibernia. (In contrast, Amoco Corp. in 1995 spent $65.7 million for a small exploration lease near Hibernia.)

Despite the treacherous conditions, Mobil in 1973 drilled Adolphus No. 1, the first well in the Hibernia formation. Again it struck oil, but again it was far too little to be commercial. With better projects elsewhere, such as Alaska's Prudhoe Bay, geologists' attention turned away.

Scrapping Governments

In the meantime, the federal and provincial governments in Canada started scrapping over who owned the offshore mineral rights. Newfoundland claimed them, but the federal government argued the province ceded those rights in joining Canada in 1949. Oil companies, in a defensive posture, began requesting permits from both governments. In some cases, the same acreage was leased to two companies. The governments "were fighting over the spoils before there were any," says Newfoundland's premier, Brian Tobin.

The Supreme Court of Canada decided in favor of the federal government. By then, Mobil had taken on partners, including Chevron Corp., which drilled the well that discovered commercial oil on the Hilbernia prospect in 1979, the same year as the second Arab oil embargo.

Oilmen, first ecstatic over a colossal strike in friendly waters during such a politically sensitive period, became disenchanted when the governments continued bickering. The issue finally was resolved after Brian Mulroney became prime minister in the 1984. John Crosbie, a savvy politician from Newfoundland, was one of the prime minister's most trusted cabinet members, and he urgently lobbied Mr. Mulroney to distribute the bulk of Hibernia's wealth to the province. Mr. Mulroney was familiar with the poverty and hardships of Newfoundland's natives and he soon moved to negotiate a 1985 accord that ultimately granted all royalty rights to the Newfoundland government. "The people of the province didn't want anymore bloody handouts from the

federal government," Mr. Mulroney explains today, "And without Hibernia, there was no future for them."

Tough Negotiator

In addition, Mr. Mulroney's government took a tough negotiating stance with the oil companies, successfully insisting that Newfoundland get a piece of some of the construction business.

Meanwhile, the project had a run-in with tragedy. In 1982, the Ocean Ranger, a semisubmersible drilling rig balanced on two giant pontoons, went down in a winter storm while exploring the Hibernia prospect, killing all 84 people on board. The loss helped persuade operators to build an extraordinarily heavy platform that can withstand nature's volleys, rather than the more typical floating rig.

Later, oil prices became a worrisome issue. By 1988, Mobil was eager to delay the project because the day's prices didn't justify it. After a series of meetings between the company and government officials failed to reach a resolution, Arne Nielsen, chief executive of Mobil's Canadian unit at the time, says he told Canadian government officials at a tension-filled meeting in Montreal that Mobil and its partners were quitting plans to develop the field.

With Newfoundland desperately in need of the economic boost, Mr. Nielsen says Marcel Masse, Canada's energy minister at the time, told him: "The project must go ahead. What do you need to proceed?"

On behalf of the consortium of companies that wanted to tap Hibernia, Mr. Nielsen demanded that the Canadian government put up a whopping $700 million up front and guarantee loans for about one-third of the $4.2 billion capital costs. "I personally thought it was the end of Hibernia," Mr. Neilsen recalls. "But, by Jove, they accepted the terms."

With all parties finally in step with each other, design and construction plans got under way. But then, another crisis hit. In January 1992, Gulf Canada Resources Ltd., which had a 24% stake in the project, said it was pulling out. "It was like someone shot me," says Rex Gibbons, Newfoundland's natural-resources minister.

Gulf, owned then by the financially strapped Reichmann family of Canada, couldn't keep up the payments, leaving Mobil, Chevron and Petro-Canada without a major partner. The pullout sparked fresh public criticism about the project's viability and work stopped for a year as the remaining partners scoured the world for a replacement. Every company with the financial muscle to take on the stake, including Royal Dutch/Shell Group and Exxon Corp., said no.

It finally looked like the end of Hibernia. Though construction had already begun, "we believed the project was in serious jeopardy," said Martin Sheppard, deputy minister of Newfoundland's Energy Department.

That is, until independent Murphy Oil Corp. of El Dorado, Arkansas, still 25% owned by founder Charles Murphy and family, offered to pick up 6.5%, paying for the purchase with loans backed by the Canadian government, according to Murphy Chief Executive Claiborne P. Deming. That inspired Mobil and Chevron to pick up another 5% each. And the Canadian government, already up to its neck in loans and subsidies; took on an 8.5% interest.

That oil will begin flowing soon was clear in late February when two giant barges, balancing the top of the oil platform destined for Hibernia, moved around the snow-crusted bluff near Come-By-Chance, a small town in southeast Newfoundland. The platform was headed toward a partially submerged pillar so big that workmen poured concrete nonstop for more than 50 days to construct it.

Six-Hour Trip

The 1.5-kilometer journey, which left the mammoth topsides hovering over the almost-submerged pillar, took six hours. Once in place, water, used as ballast, was pumped out of the column, allowing the concrete pillar to quietly rise up underneath the platform and lift it high into the air. Now finally together, the structure stands 60 stories – taller than the United Nations building in New York.

In May, it will be floated out to the Hibernia location with great ceremony, and by August the platform will be anchored to the ocean floor. The next chapter is up to geologist David Slater, who with colleagues will decide where to direct the drill bits after they pierce the seabed, headed nearly five kilometers down. On a recent Saturday, Mr. Slater paced the narrow hallway outside his small office in a nondescript building in downtown St. John's, Newfoundland's capital, studying the squiggles of three-dimensional seismic renderings of existing exploration wells and reservoir geology.

Tens of millions of years ago, drifting continents crunched together and pulled apart at least twice to create oceans where Hibernia and the other oil fields now lie. The geology left by this turmoil is very complex and hard to decipher, but Mr. Slater believes he is ready to take on the challenge. He nods his head as he stares at the scattering of papers thumbtacked to the walls and says softly, "The wells are speaking to me."

Wall Street Journal Europe, 2 April 1997
Reprinted by permission of *Wall Street Journal Europe*,
© Dow Jones & Company, Inc.
All Rights Reserved Worldwide.

- 1959: Permits of one million acres (400 000 hectares) were purchased by Mobil.
- 1965: A second batch of permits was bought by Mobil.
- 1973: Mobil drilled the first well in the Hibernia formation.
- 1979: Together with Chevron Oil, Mobil discovered commercial oil.
- 1982: The drilling rig, *Ocean Ranger*, collapsed, killing all 84 people aboard.
- 1985: All royalty rights to the oil were granted to the Newfoundland government.
- 1988: Mobil considered delaying the project as oil prices did not justify the project.
- 1992: Gulf Canada Resources, a major partner, pulled out of the venture.
- 1997: A drilling platform is almost in place ready to start commercializing the oil.

Mission statement

A mission statement globally defines the business and the objectives of an organization. It is the start point of the strategic plan. As illustrations, the mission statements of some organizations might be as in the following:

- *Railways*: In the business of providing transportation services for people and goods at prices that are competitive with other transportation means.
- *Business school*: To be one of the top ten international business schools in Europe, providing programmes at the undergraduate, masters, executive and doctorate level.
- *Engineering and construction*: To provide top-quality services in the process, energy and food industries, both domestically and internationally.
- *Hotel*: In the business of providing accommodation and restaurant services to private and business clients in the European market.
- *Volkswagen (in 1937)*: To manufacture and sell an automobile that is affordable by everyone.

SWOT analysis

A SWOT analysis is a strategic planning tool that attempts to match the internal strengths and weaknesses of the organization with external opportunities and threats. (SWOT is an acronym for Strengths, Weaknesses, Opportunities and Threats.) The objective of the analysis is that if an organization carefully reviews such strengths, weaknesses, opportunities and threats, then an appropriate strategy for meeting objectives can be developed. Several general considerations for an organization are illustrated in Figure 2.1.[4]

Strengths

As a concrete example in a SWOT analysis, the following gives strengths of an engineering and construction service company, while the next section gives the weaknesses.

- Ability, and the reputation, to perform quality and innovative engineering in the petroleum refining, chemical process, pharmaceutical and food industries.
- A documented record of completing projects within budget and on schedule.
- Record of trouble free start-ups and excellent first-year level of plant operation.
- Ability to offer a broad range of services in the oil and gas production area both on and off shore.
- Growing capability in the international arena.

Figure 2.1   Considerations for a SWOT analysis.

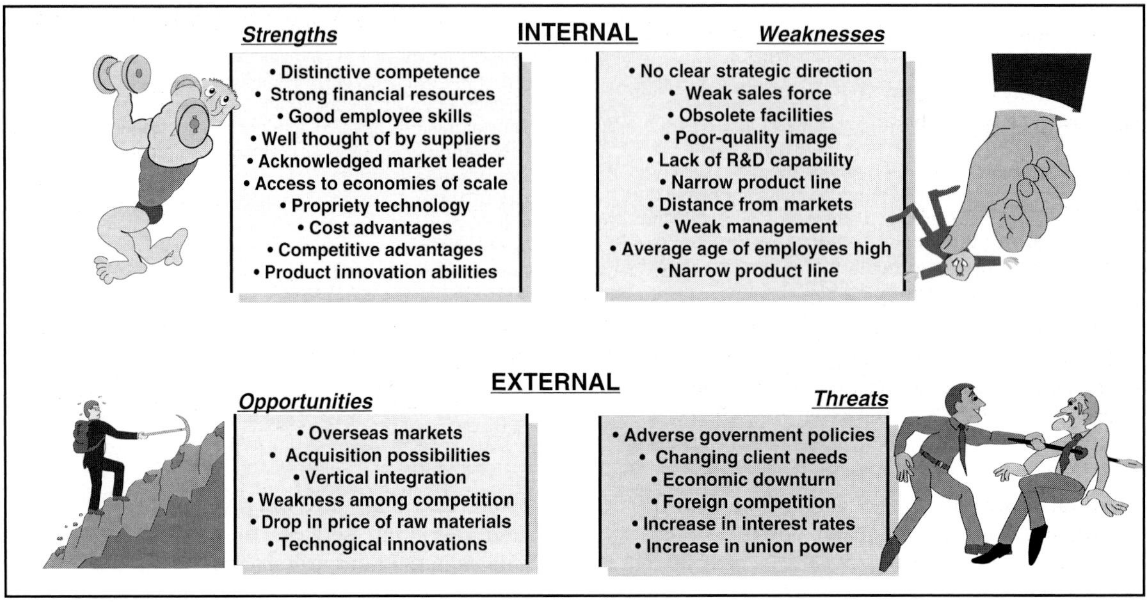

Strengths   **INTERNAL**   *Weaknesses*

- Distinctive competence
- Strong financial resources
- Good employee skills
- Well thought of by suppliers
- Acknowledged market leader
- Access to economies of scale
- Propriety technology
- Cost advantages
- Competitive advantages
- Product innovation abilities

- No clear strategic direction
- Weak sales force
- Obsolete facilities
- Poor-quality image
- Lack of R&D capability
- Narrow product line
- Distance from markets
- Weak management
- Average age of employees high
- Narrow product line

EXTERNAL

Opportunities   *Threats*

- Overseas markets
- Acquisition possibilities
- Vertical integration
- Weakness among competition
- Drop in price of raw materials
- Technogical innovations

- Adverse government policies
- Changing client needs
- Economic downturn
- Foreign competition
- Increase in interest rates
- Increase in union power

Weakness

The weaknesses are:

- Perception of a lack of flexibility in dealing with clients during contract negotiations and the execution phase of the project.
- Lack of engineering design offices in strategic areas such as Asia, Europe and the US Gulf Coast.
- Lack of cold-climate (Alaska, Siberia, etc.) and harsh-environment (Middle East, and Central America) facilities and experience.
- Tendency to develop our own design systems and tools rather than investigating more efficient, and less expensive, systems designed by others.

Opportunities

Examples of opportunities in different environments include:

- *Demographic changes:* For airlines, an increase in disposable income and more free time as a result of early retirement is significantly increasing the demand from vacation travellers. In the pharmaceutical industry there is an increasing demand for products as a result of the ageing population.
- *New geographic markets*: New markets are opening in China, the Eastern European countries with the fall of the Berlin Wall, South Africa now liberated from apartheid and Central and South America,

which have become more politically stable with democratic governments.

- *New products*: Government regulations on exhaust emissions are pushing the development of electric cars by such companies as Renault, General Motors and Mercedes. New drugs are being developed by pharmaceutical companies to combat AIDS.
- *Government deregulation*: Government deregulation is opening up new markets and permitting strategic alliances in, say, the airline industry (British Airways, Lufthansa, and US airlines) or in telecommunications (BT, France Telecom and Deutches Telecom).

Threats

Examples of threats in different environments include:

- *Government regulation*: Stricter regulations from governments for drug approval are making the introduction of new products a slow process for the pharmaceutical industry. Furthermore, pressure to reduce medical costs, particularly in Europe, the USA and Japan, is cutting into profit margins.
- *Market saturation*: For automobile firms, market saturation, the low level of vehicle replacement, and route saturation, pushing people into public transportation, is cutting into sales of new vehicles.

Action plans to achieve objectives

Some of the long-range plans to meet the objectives of the strategic plan might include some of the following actions. Many of these are discussed in further detail in later sections of this book.

New facilities

Constructing, or opening, new facilities is one sure way of increasing market exposure. Examples would include BMW of Germany building a new automobile facility in the USA, BT of the UK opening telecommunication facilities in Europe, Formula I of France building hotels elsewhere in Europe and McDonald's rapid expansion of fast food restaurants; McDonald's hamburger chains are now present in over 100 countries.

Expansion

As an alternative to the construction of a new facility, an existing one might be expanded. Oil refineries are often expanded, as are automobile manufacturing facilities, storage warehouses for distribution companies and even supermarkets and other retail stores.

Acquisitions

Companies may resort to acquiring other companies as a route to market. Ford of the US acquired Jaguar of the UK in 1989. Rhône Poulenc of France acquired Fisons of the UK in 1995. In the USA, Burlington Northern Railways swallowed Santa FE Pacific and Wells Fargo bought First Interstate Bank in 1995–96. In France, as the government will not allow construction of new hypermarkets, take-overs are occurring in the retail business. Auchan acquired Dock de France in 1996 and in September 1997 Promodes made a hostile bid for Casino.[5]

New technology

With the rapid pace of technological growth, firms have to update their facilities or products. This may include the installation of a new computer network for operations planning, telecommunication companies financing the launching of new communication satellites, automating an existing operating facility or developing biotechnology methods for new pharmaceutical products.

Quantitative components of the strategic plan

In developing the strategic plan, it is necessary to quantify the objectives in the plan. Then, at the end of the plan period, one would be able to compare actual results with planned objectives.

Business firms

Market-driven organizations might have quantitative statements such as:

- 'To increase market share by 15 per cent in five years, so that we are a market leader.'
- 'To increase profits by 10 per cent per year over the next five years.'
- 'To have 5 per cent of our business in China by 2000.'

Non-profit organizations

Non-profit organizations might be able to quantify actions by such statements as:

- 'To have a 95 per cent literacy rate in a certain country within five years.'
- 'To completely eradicate a disease in five years.'
- 'To increase an intake of students by 25 per cent over the next five years.'

Pro-forma financial statements

Pro-forma financial statements are estimated income and balance sheet statements, which are often prepared for each year during the planning period. They are developed by making estimates or forecasts of revenues and costs and, as such, quantify in detail the expected outcomes from the defined strategic plan.

SYNERGY STRATEGY AND OPERATIONS

As mentioned, organizations develop global strategies and then plan, design, organize and manage the operation in order to meet the strategic objectives. As such, strategies and operations are closely interwoven:

- For a desired strategy to be realized, all the operating plans need to be in place.
- For operations to be successful, there has to be a well-defined strategy.

A strategy is very often long term, is often unique and is definable, although some organizations may have short-term strategies in, say, manufacturing, distribution or sales in order to meet some well-defined objective. In contrast to these strategic elements are operations that have a time frame of usually less than one year and are continuous and repetitive. Figure 2.2 illustrates the elements in the interface strategy/operations. The top part of the loop shows those that are principally strategic in nature. The bottom part of the loop includes those that are principally operating in nature. However, the separation is not always clearly black and white:

- Quality management is a long-term activity, but requires day-to-day attention.
- Environmental management is a long-term strategy, but needs a day-to-day involvement.
- Facility layout is shown as operational because the design can be changed in the short term. However, changing the design is expensive and some firms may put the layout in a long-range plan.
- Project management is a daily activity, but projects themselves can be long term.

The strategic importance of operations

In the previous chapter, a systems approach to the organization was presented, highlighting that Operations, Marketing and Finance were the principal subsystems of the business firm. In this system, the strategic importance of Operations is illustrated with reference to the pro-forma income statement of Hershey, a US food company manufacturing food products including chocolate items (its principal products), sweets and pasta. Table 2.1 presents the actual 1996 income statement[6] and the pro-forma statements based on three hypothetical assumptions concerning three

possible strategies in each of the subsystems. These are described in the following sections.

Marketing

The strategy for the firm is that sales are to be increased by 50 per cent above those obtained in 1996. In arriving at a new net income, cost of goods sold is assumed to increase by 50 per cent, as are selling, marketing and administrative expenses. All other costs and expenses and the tax rate remain the same. As illustrated in the pro-forma statement, this strategy would give an increase in net income of 59 per cent.

Finance

The strategy for the firm is that the interest expense is to be reduced by 80 per cent below that incurred in 1996. All other costs and expenses and the tax rate remain the same. As illustrated in the pro-forma statement, this strategy would give an increase in net income of 8 per cent.

Operations

The strategy for the firm is that operating costs are to be reduced by 25 per cent below those incurred in 1996. In arriving at a new net income, sales are assumed to be unchanged and other expenses and the

Figure 2.2   Synergy of the strategic and operating environments.

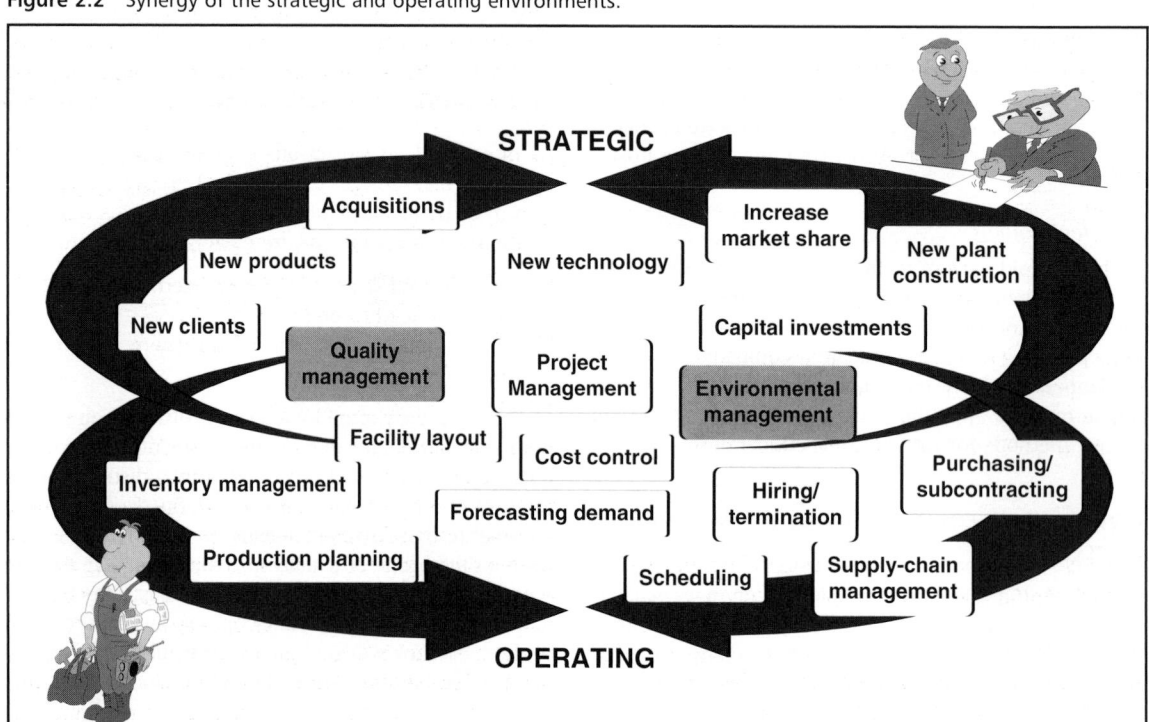

Table 2.1 Hershey Foods: Strategic importance of operations ($000s). For the sales option, selling, marketing and administrative expense are increased by same proportion

	Actual 1996 income statement	Strategic options for various hypothesis		
		Increase sales by 50%	Reduce interest expense by 80%	Reduce operating costs by 25%
Sales	3 989 308	5 983 962	3 989 308	3 989 308
Cost of goods sold	2 302 089	3 453 134	2 302 089	1 726 567
Gross margin	1 687 219	2 530 829	1,687 219	2 262 741
Selling, marketing, administration	1 124 087	1 686 131	1 124 087	1 124 087
Total cost & expenses	3 426 176	5 139 264	3 426 176	2 850 654
Loan on disposal of businesses	–35 352	–35 352	–35 352	–35 352
Income before taxes and interest	527 780	809 346	527 780	1 103 302
Interest expense	48 043	48 043	9 609	48 043
Income before taxes	479 737	761 303	518 171	1 055 259
Tax provision	206 551	327 779	223 099	454 342
Net income	273 186	433 524	295 072	600 917
Tax rate on provision (per cent)	43.06	43.06	43.06	43.06
Net income/sales (per cent)	6.85	7.24	7.40	15.06
Increase in net income		160 338	21 886	327 731
Increase in net income (per cent)		58.69	8.01	119.97

tax rate remain the same. As illustrated in the proforma statement, this strategy would give an increase in net income of 120 per cent.

Although there can be arguments about the exact changes to the financial data, the direction is clear. The key entity in a company's strategy is its operations.

Responsibilities of the firm

Whether a firm is considering its strategies, or its operations, it has responsibilities to three principle parties as illustrated in Figure 2.3.

Employees

Poor employee relations as a result of the type of work, poor conditions in the production centre, low salaries and the like can reduce productivity. At the worst, a strike can stop production as Box 2.2 illustrates.[7]

Customers

Dissatisfied customers can reduce both net income and market share as they turn to the competitors.

Shareholders

These are the owners of the business. Owners who are not happy with the firm can sell their portion of ownership, which will push down the price of the stock.

Dissatisfied shareholders can influence the management of the firm.

These principal parties are an integrated force. If the responsibilities are lacking to any one, the firm's activities will suffer. British Airways is a strong proponent of the use of this triangle to illustrate who are the stakeholders in their company though they put the customers at the apex of the triangle because, for British Airways, they are the most important. British Airways says the customer is the product and if not treated correctly, they are perishable.[8] This type of triangle does not have the same importance to non-profit organizations, though there might be some similarities if one considers the government as a shareholder.

Challenges for the firm

Business firms have competitors and this 'jungle-type' environment represents a challenge to the firm. No matter the product, or service, the major challenges revolve around Quality, Delivery and Cost and can be represented by three axes, as illustrated in Figure 2.4. A company that continually offers Quality products will enhance its business. In this respect, Marks and Spencer of the UK is a good example. Delivery, the thrust of the supply chain, is meeting the planned time to market, or the due date promised to the client. The Cost is either the producer's cost, or the price a con-

Figure 2.3 Responsibilities of the firm.

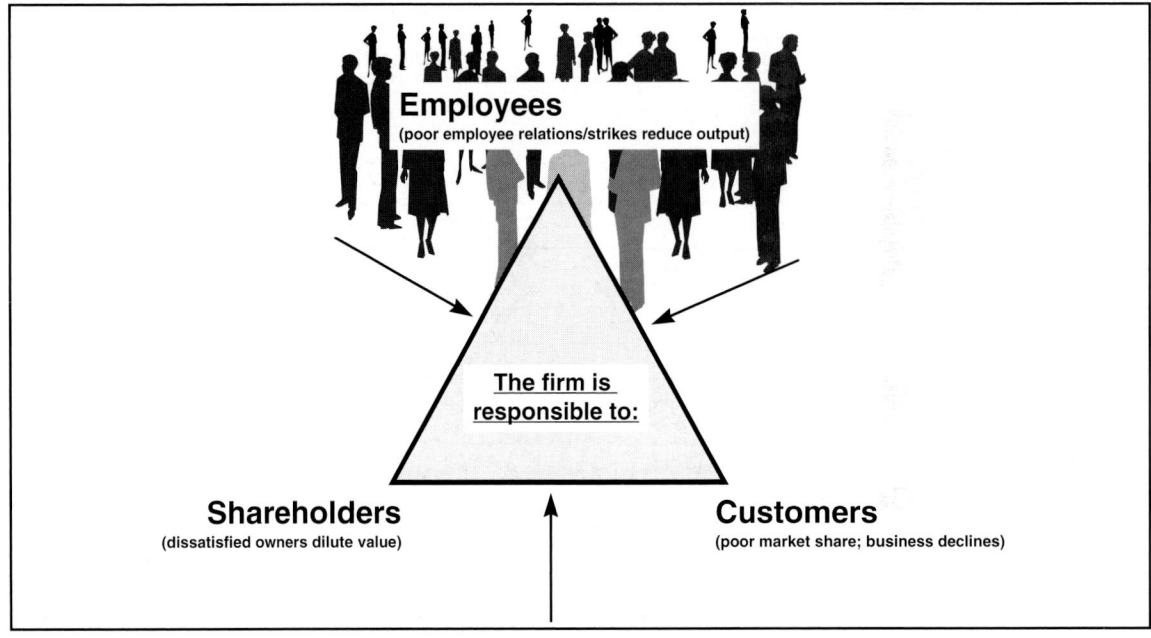

Box 2.2 GM, Chrysler face strikes as local unrest remains. By Nichole M. Christian and Gabriella Stern, Staff Reporters.

DETROIT – With a strike at a passenger-car plant in its third week, **General Motors** Corp. faced a strike deadline late Tuesday at a Pontiac, Michigan, assembly plant that builds full-size pickup trucks.

A walkout by 5,400 United Auto Workers members at the Pontiac East plant would halt production of GM's bread-and-butter pickups, potentially biting into the No. 1 auto maker's profits and hampering GM in the increasingly competitive pickup market.

Meanwhile, GM is grappling with a strike at its Oklahoma City car assembly plant, which began April 5, and is recovering from a March strike at its Fort Wayne, Indiana, pickup-truck assembly plant. At the same time, **Chrysler** Corp. is contending with a two-week-old strike at an engine plant that has crippled much of its light-truck production.

What's going on in Detroit? All this labor unrest suggests that even though the Big Three U.S. auto makers signed new three-year national labor pacts last fall, serious disagreements with the UAW about staffing levels and the farming out of parts work remain unresolved at the local level. (**Ford Motor** Co. has been free of local strikes so far this year because it is relatively more productive than its domestic rivals and thus is putting less pressure on the UAW.)

UAW officials at the international and local levels acknowledge that GM and Chrysler need to improve factory efficiency in order to remain competitive. However, they are resisting what they view as excessively low staffing levels in some plants. They also cite efforts by the companies to skirt previous local agreements.

National contracts generally set broad guidelines for wages, benefits, training and grievances, but they leave room for local unions to hammer out day-to-day plant operating details which are ultimately spelled out in individual factory contracts. As a result, some powerful locals can end up unraveling some of the auto makers' gains in the national contract.

Indeed, the new three-year contract left an extraordinary amount of wiggle room for local management and union leaders to craft distinct deals. GM, for instance, is still trying to negotiate new plant-level contracts with some 30 UAW locals around the country. It has reached agreements with the other 75 locals.

Chrysler is close to completing its local negotiations; the engine plant in Detroit is the last one. The two-week strike by 1,800 workers has crippled the No. 3 U.S. auto maker's ability to produce most of its highly profitable sport-utility vehicles and pickups. Because the engine plant feeds 16 of Chrysler's truck plants, a total of 23,000 assembly and parts workers have been idled in the U.S., Canada and Mexico.

Analyst Jack Kirnan of Salomon Brothers says the strike already has had a 20-cents-a-share impact on second-quarter earnings and is costing the company $12 million a day in profit. The main issue is the UAW's charge that Chrysler wants to shift at least 300 jobs to an outside supplier. Chrysler pledges no jobs will be lost.

UAW officials at GM's Pontiac East plant contend that the auto maker is violating a 1995 local agreement that included promises to hire permanent assembly workers and slow the pace of work being farmed out to non-UAW suppliers.

Under that agreement, which ended a six-day strike at the plant in the spring of 1995, GM has hired about 80 people and assigned them all to nonassembly jobs in the plant, according to officials with Local 594.

Wall Street Journal Europe, 23 April 1997
Reprinted by permission of *Wall Street Journal Europe*,
© 1997 Dow Jones & Company, Inc.
All Rights Reserved Worldwide.

Figure 2.4 Challenges for the firm.

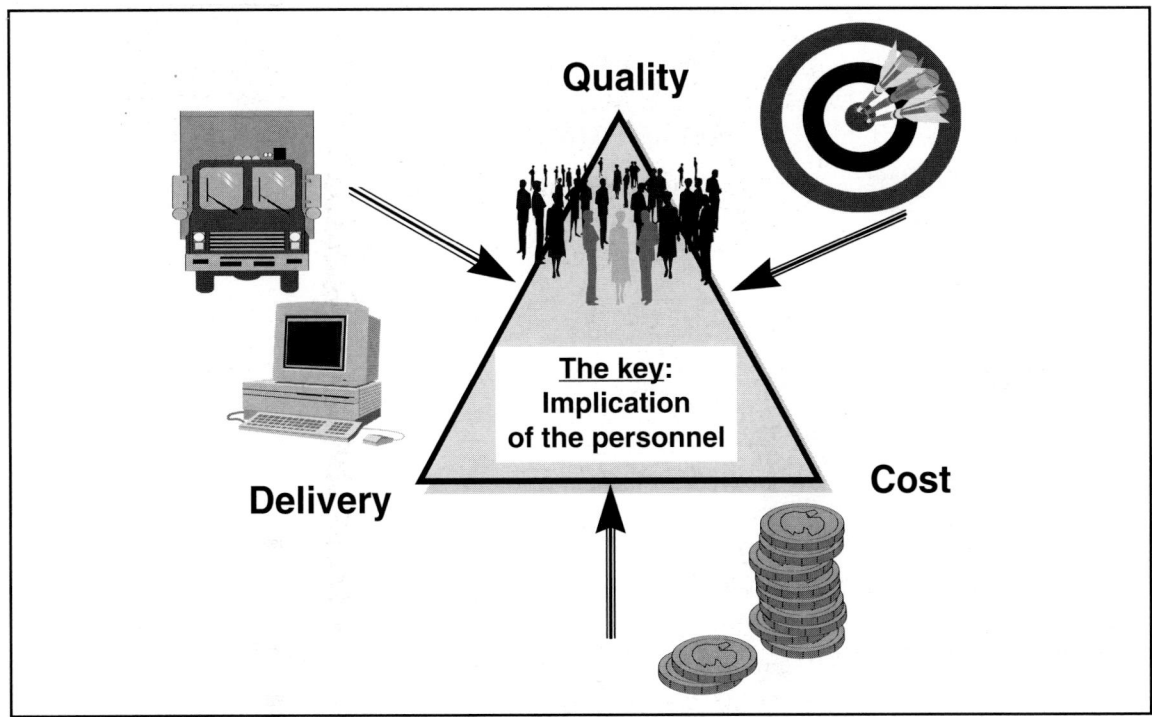

sumer has to pay 'his or her cost'. These three are explicitly, or implicitly, part of the strategy, but they are also operational in that they are of daily concern.

REAL-WORLD CORPORATE STRATEGIC OBJECTIVES

The following illustrates the real-world corporate objectives of some major corporations. They all stress the importance of the customer in the strategy.

Hewlett Packard

As illustrated in Figure 2.5, this company, based in California, USA, has seven corporate objectives as elaborated below.[9] The objective brings stress on the importance of profit, though profit integrated with other essential elements of a successful organization.

Profit

To achieve sufficient profit to finance our company growth and to provide the resources we need to achieve our other corporate objectives.

Customers

To provide products and services of the highest quality, and the greatest possible value to our customers, thereby gaining and holding their respect and loyalty.

Fields of interest

To participate in those fields of interest that build upon our technology and customer base, that offer opportunities for continuing growth, and that enable us to make a needed and profitable contribution.

Growth

To let our growth be limited only by our profits and our ability to develop and produce innovative products that satisfy real customer needs.

Our people

- To help Hewlett Packard people share in the company's success, which they make possible.
- To provide employment security based on their performance.
- To ensure them a safe and pleasant work environment.
- To recognize their individual achievements.

Figure 2.5 Corporate objectives (Hewlett Packard).

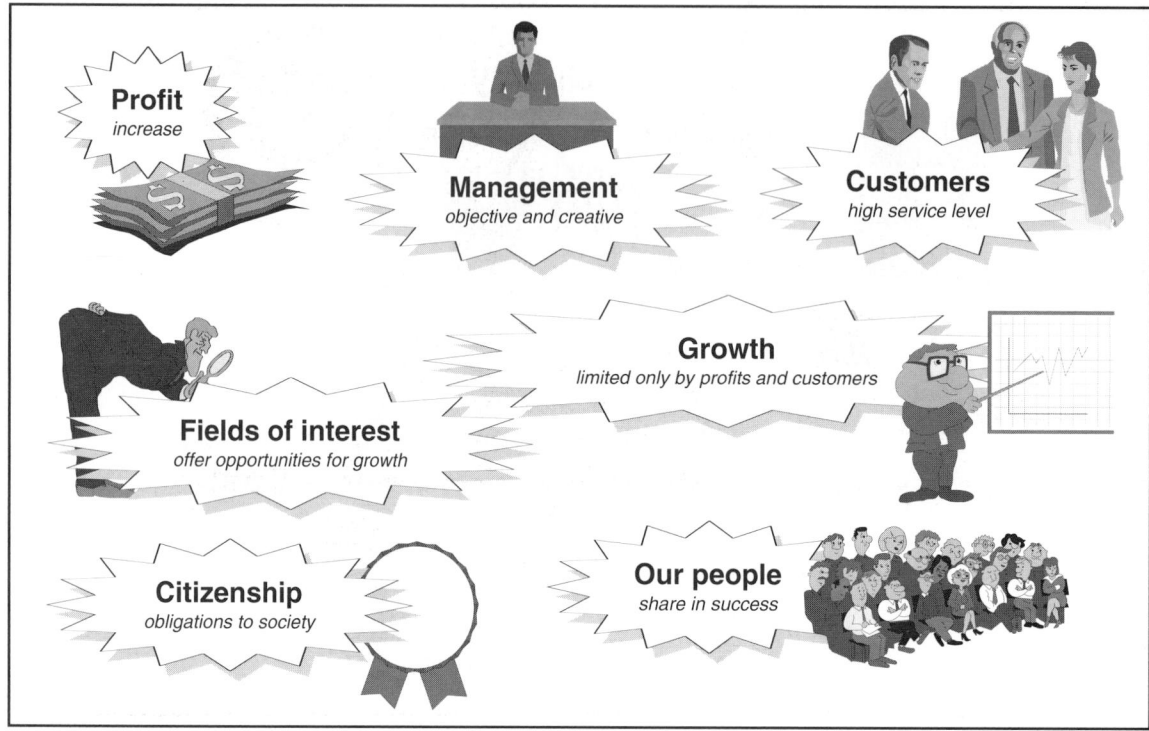

■ To help them gain a sense of satisfaction and accomplishment from their work.

Management

To foster initiative and creativity by allowing the individual great freedom of action in attaining well-defined objectives.

Citizenship

To honour our obligations to society by being an economic, intellectual and social asset to each nation and each community in which we operate.

British Airways

This UK-based airline has four strategic objectives for its company, as illustrated in Figure 2.6.[10] They are elaborated below.

Inspired people

This is considered the dominant objective of the firm and relates to the company employees who need to be continually motivated and able to learn, and who benefit from the corporate success.

Customer choice

British Airways clients have a choice in the service offered by the airline.

Truly global

The company recognizes that it has to have presence internationally and this is one of its reasons for a proposed alliance with American Airlines.

Strong profitability

No firm can succeed without a strong balance sheet. Here, the cost is king!! For the year ending 31 March 1996 British Airways' profit rose 9.4 per cent to $1.05 billion.[11]

To succeed in its strategy the company has a four-pronged approach:[12]

■ Develop a marketing plan with universal appeal.
■ Help employees understand the company's global vision.
■ Benchmark off mistakes that others may have made in the past.
■ Select the right partners for joint ventures overseas.

Figure 2.6   Objectives of British Airways.

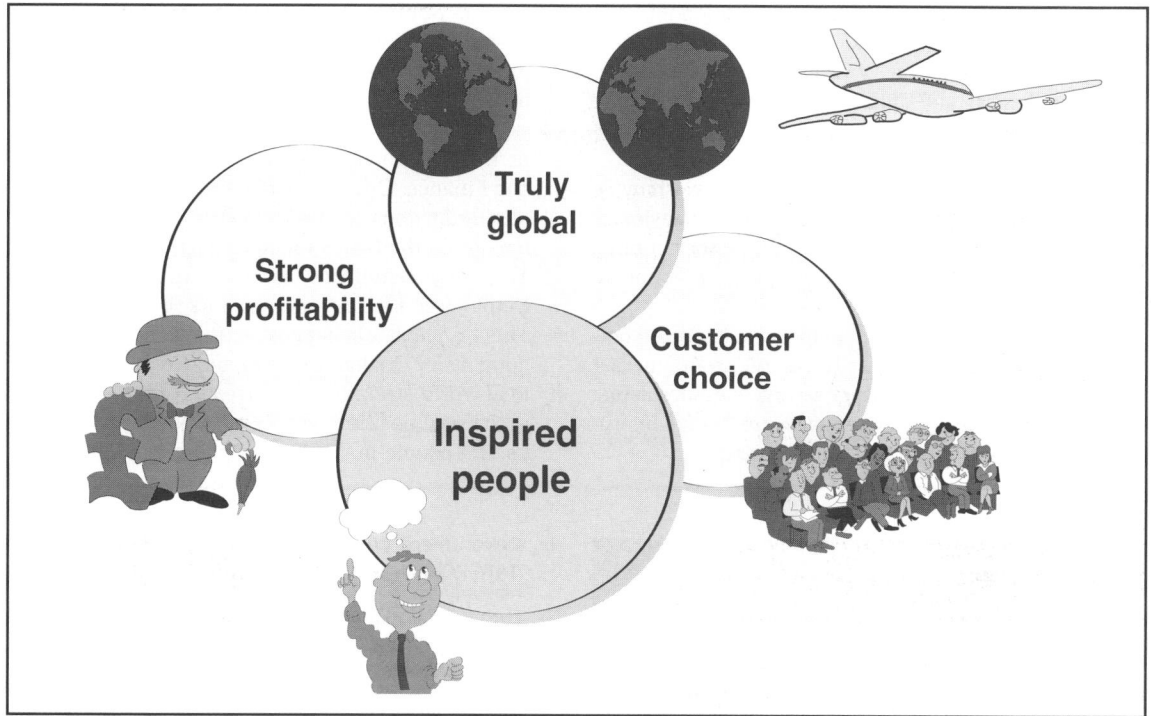

IBM

Back in the late 1980s IBM was regarded as a national disaster. It was famous for blanketing big corporations with legions of pin-striped marketing and field-engineering troops. It had become distant, arrogant and unresponsive. Now, with Louis V. Gerstner Jr as the Chairman and Chief Executive Officer, IBM is once again one of the most profitable computer makers. Gerstner's strategy is customer relationships; talking to customers, learning their needs and figuring out how to satisfy them. Gerstner says:[13]

■ You start the day with customers.
■ You start thinking about a company around its customers.
■ You organize around customers.

With IBM's customer-oriented strategy, Richard C Watts, general manager of Hewlett Packard's computer system group says that IBM is now much harder to fight than it used to be.

SUMMARY OF KEY ELEMENTS

■ The global strategic objective of the firm is to grow by exploiting opportunities. If firms ignore the external environment, or adapt only enough to survive, they will eventually fail or be swallowed.

■ The global strategic objectives of a non-profit organization are essentially sustainability and maintaining the *status quo*. Its operation must be consistent with financial resources, its sources and use of funds should be matched; and it should provide equitable services for all generations.

■ The time frame of a strategic plan is nominally five years, but may vary according to the industry. New, high-technology firms may have a shorter time frame, whereas established firms with high capital projects may have a much longer time frame.

- A mission statement, or charter, describes in general terms the activity of the organization and it is the start point, or the root, of the strategic plan.
- A SWOT analysis (Strengths, Weaknesses, Opportunities and Threats) is a strategic planning tool to help an organization match its internal characteristics with the external environment.
- Action plans to achieve strategic objectives may be the construction of new facilities, the expansion of existing facilities, the acquisition of other companies, the creation of new markets or the application of new technology.
- A strategic plan needs to quantify its expected outcome, which may be in terms of profit, market share, geographic territory or unit measurements. Pro-forma financial statements are useful instruments for quantifying a strategic plan.

- A firm's strategy and operations are closely interwoven. Neither exists without the other. For a desired strategy to be realized, all the operating plans need to be properly defined. For operations to be successful, there has to be a well-defined strategy.
- In the integrated system, Operations, Marketing and Finance, Operations plays a dominant role and cost reductions in this area can have the biggest impact on the firm's financial performance.
- The responsibilities of the firm are to its Employees, its Customers and its Shareholders.
- The principal challenges to the firm are in the domains of Quality, Delivery and Cost.
- Real-world strategic objectives have the customer in the pole position. This is often followed by profits, the people in the firm and continued growth.

REVIEW AND DISCUSSION QUESTIONS

1 **Proactive or reactive.** What firms do you believe today are pursuing a proactive strategy and which a reactive strategy? Explain your reasoning. Do their financial results support your conclusions?
2 **Mission statements.** What do you believe would be the mission statement of:
 (a) A medical centre?
 (b) A hypermarket/supermarket firm like Tesco or Sainsbury in the UK or Carrefour, Leclerc in France?
 (c) A law firm?
 (d) An armaments factory?
 (e) A cigarette company?
3 **New business opportunities.** Where do you believe are the new business opportunities today according to:
 (a) Geographical location?
 (b) New products?

4 **Government policies and strategies.** How do government policies affect the strategies of firms? Justify your reasoning and, where possible, give real illustrations.
5 **Firm's responsibilities.** The text indicates that a firm has a responsibility to its employees, clients and owners. Some companies say that their responsibilities are solely to their owners, since it is the owners who provide the financing and who take the risk for the firm. On the other hand, employees are remunerated with salaries, so that the company's responsibilities are abrogated. Very often, when a company announces layoffs, the market value, as indicated by the stock price, rises (Renault, AT&T, IBM). Similarly, useful products are provided to the client and this nullifies any further responsibility. What is your opinion?
6 **SWOT analysis.** You are studying at university or business school for a career. Develop a SWOT analysis for yourself. What do you perceive to be your strengths and weaknesses? What are the opportunities and threats posed to you, taking into consideration your career objectives?

CASE STUDY: GROUP MICHELIN

Situation

The Group Michelin, famous for developing the radial tyre almost 50 years ago during the Second World War, is the French tyre maker based in Clermont-Ferrand, France. A headlong US expansion in the 1970s and 1980s gave Michelin a string of 13 North American manufacturing sites with headquarters based in South Carolina, including the 1990 acquisition of Uniroyal Goodrich Tire Co. in a debt-financed acquisition. This activity transformed Michelin from a medium-sized European tyre maker into the world's leading producers after Bridgestone, Japan as illustrated in Figure 2.7. Today, Michelin has production facilities in many countries and sales and service outlets covering over 170 countries. Where there are no production facilities (Australia for example), Michelin has a significant import operation.

By 1991, debt from expansion put the company into deep financial trouble. Costs were getting out of control. The company was getting complaints from valued customers and distributors such as Sears Roebuck & Co., Michelin's biggest US distributor. Sears Roebuck's complaint was too slow deliveries, so that they then started buying more tyres from Goodyear, one of Michelin's competitors. By the end of 1993 Michelin's debt was more than double equity.

François Michelin, the head of the company has put his son, Edouard Michelin, in control and started to make cutbacks in all sites including the US and European manufacturing operations in Belgium, Britain, Germany, Italy, Netherlands, Spain and its home base in France.

Some of Michelin's problems grew from the need to keep quality uniform during the expansion. French systems, that were transferred to US plants, were simply not understood by US employees. Eager for discipline, the company sometimes hired former military people in the US. To protect what it considered superior technology and process methods, it guarded secrets even from employees. Many decisions were centralized, which made it difficult to control costs. Big customers had trouble getting Michelin's highly structured manufacturing plants to respond to unexpected orders.

On 21 February 1997 Michelin announced redundancies of 1445 jobs in France which brings the total decline in the tyre-maker's workforce since 1990 to 25 000 or almost one job in five. Some 700 of those who lose their jobs will be given part-time work, or work at other Michelin factories. However, this will not save the reputation of the firm that once took pride in looking after its workers from cradle to grave. After seven difficult years, Michelin understands that it must turn itself from a smug and lumbering national champion into a general multinational firm.

Tyres are made up of over 200 components and worldwide about 700 000 tires are produced per day. There are about 10 000 references to finished products. In addition to tyres, the company also makes some of the wheels and, of course, publishes the famous Michelin Guides, although these two segments only constitute about 2 per cent of the business. Michelin has large research facilities, and road circuits for testing tyres in France and the USA. A new technology process, C3M, is a machine for making tyres that will also reduce both labour and inventory levels, two areas in which Michelin currently outspends its competitors. Michelin is very vertically integrated, making everything including the synthetic rubber, the steel bands in the tyres and even the machines which are used to assemble the tyres. It also owns some of the rubber plantation plants in Brazil and Nigeria. For tyres that are used in heavy service about half the rubber is natural.

Michelin serves every market segment, including agricultural machinery, two-wheeled vehicles, aeroplanes, heavy earth-moving equipment, trucks, cars, buses and all tourist vehicles. Tyre sales enter into two markets, first-mounted and replacements. First-mounted are on new vehicles and this constitutes about one third of the business. For this, the market clients are the automobile constructors (Renault, Ford, GM, Groupe PSA, etc.) Replacements, approximately two-thirds of the business, are sold through distributors, such as Carrefour, Intermarché and LeClerc in France as well as specialized auto stores. After-sales service is very important in tyre sales. This includes advice on technical information, communication, stock levels for future sale, and billing.[14]

Required

1 In 1997, what would be an appropriate Mission Statement for the Michelin Group?
2 Based on the information given, what should be some of the major strategic elements for the company?
3 Analyse the internal and external strengths and weakness of the firm.
4 What are some of the operating characteristics for Michelin that must support its strategy?

Figure 2.7 The world tyre market (percentage of world sales, 1995).

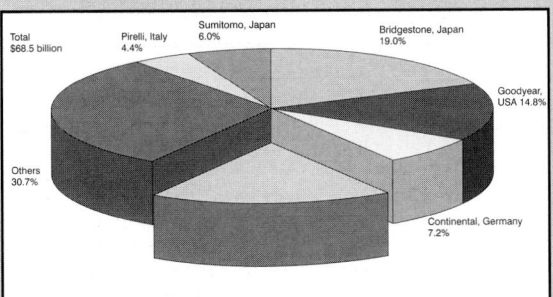

CASE STUDY: BRITISH PETROLEUM (BP)

Situation

Lima is a town in western Ohio, USA, some 100 km from the Canadian border. It was in that region, in 1885, that Benjamin C Faurot discovered oil and the following year, John D Rockefeller purchased 151 acres of navy bean fields for $200 to build the Solar oil refinery at Lima. In 1931, Standard Oil of Ohio (Sohio) bought the Lima refinery from Solar. In 1948 they carried out a $30 million refinery expansion and then the following year, Sohio, jointly with Sun Oil, started work on a 1600 km long pipeline from Texas to Ohio through Mid-Valley Pipeline Co., a jointly owned affiliate. These construction projects made Lima an important oil centre.

In 1967 Sohio spent another $75 million to expand the refinery and, in the following two years, British Petroleum agreed with Sohio to trade part of its interest in the Alaska Prudhoe Bay oil field for minority stock ownership in the Lima refinery. As production increased from Prudhoe Bay, BP's percentage ownership in the refinery increased. In 1987, purchase of the remaining Sohio stock for $7.6 billion made BP the sole owner of the Lima refinery.[15]

In January 1996, BP announced plans to rationalize its international refining system and this included closing its Lima refinery, even though productivity had risen by 30 per cent. In addition, it planned to close another facility at Lavera in Southern France and the Pernis section of the Nerefco refinery complex at Rotterdam, The Netherlands. BP's rationale was that there was over-capacity in its refineries and the profit margins at these sites were low. BP said that it would only operate refineries that are among the top 25 per cent in efficiency and profitability in their respec-

tive regions. At that time the Lima facility, with a capacity of 160 000 barrels/day, employed 455 people, Lavera, with a capacity of 200 000 bbls/day, employed 620 and the Nerefco complex of some 420 000 bbls/day employed 875 people. BP said that it hoped to minimize layoffs, but would make no guarantee. In November 1996 BP announced that only three bids had been received for the sale of the Lima facility, all of which were unacceptable. Thus, the refinery would be closed within two years and probably turned into a terminal. BP's stock price began climbing on the news of the closures.[16]

The impact on the small community of 48 000 at Lima will be enormous. The city not only relies on the refinery for jobs, but it covers 260 hectares of real estate which generates $26 million annually in fees to utilities plus $11 million to local businesses. The concern is that the land will just become a wasteland. However, the response from BP's Vice-President, David Atton was, 'BP realizes that the decision made here has severe ramifications. On the other hand, it has an international and national reputation to defend. BP's first responsibility is to our shareholders.'

More than ever communities are suffering as large multinational firms cease their operations in efforts to cut costs and respond to the demands of shareholders. In Papendrecht, the Netherlands, 1200 people were made redundant when Daimler Benz of Germany stopped funding the NV Fokker aeroplane company in 1996. Similarly, in early 1997, the residents of Vilvoorde, Belgium learnt of a similar fate when 3100 workers and as many as 1000 suppliers were told they would be axed when Renault decided to close its automobile facility.[17]

Required

1 Review this strategic decision to close down an operation and its impact.

(a) What are your opinions? Do you agree with management's decision?

(b) What is its impact?

(c) Do you believe that there are any alternatives?

(d) Do you think that international companies should have long-term obligations to local communities where they establish operations?

Give as much detail and justification as you feel is necessary.

NOTES AND REFERENCES

1. Herzlinger, Regina E. (1994) Effective oversight: A guide for non-profit directors, *Harvard Business Review* July–August: 52–60.
2. 'The reshaping of British Railways' (1964) *A British Railways Board Report,* Chairman Dr Beeching.
3. Sullivan, A. (1997) 'Old Gusher: Four decades later, oil field off Canada is ready to produce. Politics, money and nature put vast deposit on ice. Now it may last 50 years. Shot in the arm for the US', *Wall Street Journal Europe* 2 April.
4. Based on Certo, Samuel C. (1989) *Principles of Modern Management,* 4th edition, Boston: Allyn and Bacon: 144.
5. 'Food Fight: Promodes shakes up France in hostile bid for Casino, Rallye', (1997) *Wall Street Journal Europe,* 2 September.
6. *Hershey Corp,* Hershey, Pennsylvania, *1996 Annual Report,* Pennsylvania.
7. Christian, N. M. and Stern, G. (1997) 'GM, Chrysler face strikes as local unrest remains', *Wall Street Journal Europe* 23 April.
8. George Cooper, European Director of British Airways (1997) Presentation at the G7 Management Conference, Lyon Graduate School of Business 16 May (with permission).
9. *The HP way* (1994) Hewlett Packard, Company Brochure (with permission).
10. George Cooper, European Director of British Airways.
11. *Wall Street Journal Europe* (1997) 20 May.
12. 'Flying High, Going Global' (1997) *Fortune.* 7 July: 87–89.
13. 'How IBM became a growth company again: It's raking in new business, its stock is roaring, and it's regaining the respect of Corporate America. What's Gerstner's secret?' (1996) *Business Week,* 9 December: 36.
14. Adapted from 'Debt-laden Michelin sets off down road to transformation: French tire maker removes strict systems, reduces secrecy in bid to modernise', *Wall Street Journal Europe,* 7 September 1994 and *The Economist* 1 March 1997.
15. The Lima News Home page, http://www.limanews.com/bp/bphist.html, April 1996.
16. BP Homepage, http://www.bp.com/press/pr2.html, April 1996.
17. *Wall Street Journal Europe* (1996) 25 March.

FURTHER READING

Argyris, C. (1985) *Strategy, Change and Defensive Routines,* London: Pitman.
Baranson, J. (1978) *Technology and the Multinationals: Corporate strategies in a changing world economy,* Lexington, MA: Lexington Books.
Butler, T. W., Leong, G. K. and Everett, L. N. (1996) 'The operations management role in hospital strategic planning', *Journal of Operations Management* 14(2): 137–56.
Craig, S. C. and Douglas, S. P. (1996) 'Responding to the challenges of global markets: Change complexity, competition and conscience', *Columbia Journal of World Business* 31(4): 6–18.
Flynn, J. E. and Flynn, B. B. (1996) 'Achieving simultaneous cost and differentiation competitive advantages through continuous improvement: World class manufacturing as a competitive strategy', *Journal of Managerial Issues* 8(3): 360–379.
Harrison, M. (1996) *Operations Management Strategy,* London: Pitman.
Hill, T. (1993) *Manufacturing Strategy: The Strategic Management of the Manufacturing Function,* Basingstoke, Macmillan.
Hofer, C. W. and Schendel, D. (1980) *Strategy Formulation: Analytical Concepts,* St Paul, MN: West.
Kono, T. (1984) *Strategy and Structure of Japanese Enterprises,* London: Macmillan.
Leavy, B. and Wilson, D. (1994) *Strategy and Leadership,* London: Routledge.
Markides, C. (1993) 'Corporate Refocusing', *Business Strategy Review* 4(1): 1–15.
Menda, R. and Dilts, D. (1997) 'The manufacturing strategy formulation process: Linking multifunctional viewpoints', *Journal of Operations Management* 15(4): 223–42.
Montgomery, C. A. and Porter, M. E. (1991) *Strategy: Seeking and Securing Competitive Advantage,* Cambridge, MA: Harvard Business School.
Russell, K. (1997) 'Strategic manufacturing for competitive advantage: transforming operations from shop floor to strategy', *Technology Analysis and Strategic Management* 9(2): 238–39.
Sefertzi, E. (1996) 'Flexibility and alternative corporate strategies', *Industrial Relations–Quebec* 51(1): 97–116.
Snyder, A. V. and Ebeling, W. H. Jr (1992) 'Targeting a company's real core competencies', *Journal of Business Strategy* 13(6): 26–32.
Tulip, S. (1997) 'Building the future', *Supply Management* 2(7): 28–30.
Uyterhoeven, H. E. R., Ackerman, R. W. and Rosenblum, J. W. (1977) *Strategy and Organisation: Text and Cases in General Management,* Homewood, IL: Irwin.
Winter, D. and Zoia, D. (1997) 'Ford's component strategy taking shape', *Ward's Auto World* 33(7): 73–74.
'A rescue at sea in South Korea: How do you turn a bankrupt Korean shipyard into an international showcase? A management brief at how Daewoo performed this trick through a mixture of technical inventiveness and corporate paternalism' (1994) *The Economist* 26 November.
'Crunch at Chrysler' (1994) Management Brief, *The Economist* 12 November.

3] Site selection

Objectives and overview

The purpose of this chapter is to underscore the importance of site selection in a firm's operation and to enumerate some of the many factors that need to be taken into consideration
before a site-selection decision is made. The chapter begins by reviewing the strategic
nature of site selection and its relations with the operations management environment, and
gives a mention of historical corporate towns. The chapter then goes on to emphasize the
importance of markets, labour costs and other human-resource-related issues. There are
sections which discuss inherent local conditions, the infrastructure of a region, construction
factors for new facilities, considerations that directly impact cash flow, financial aid offered
by governments and the proximity of resources. The last section of the chapter presents in
detail four quantitative methods for site selection, including weighting, break-even, probability and centre-of-gravity methods. Although site-selection elements are discussed individually, there are close interrelationships between some, if not all, of the factors.

DEFINING SITE SELECTION

Site selection, or facility location, for either manufacturing or service organizations, is deciding on a location for constructing, expanding or acquiring a physical entity of a firm in order to reach new markets,
increase production capacity and/or serve clients better. As illustrated in Figure 3.1, the physical entity
may be a warehouse for raw materials, a manufacturing centre, a distribution centre for finished products
or a retail outlet. These would all represent physical
plant in a material supply chain. Alternatively, the new
facility may be an office block with communication
equipment, an airport, a hospital, a school, hotel, etc.
to serve an expanding market better. In the supply
chain, the location of the operating facility is a critical factor in timely delivery of tangible products or
services.

The nature of the facility

A chosen site for a new facility may be grass roots, that
is to say virgin land on which a completely new installation will be built, or, the location may contain an existing facility that needs to be modified to serve the needs
of the firm. Site selection may be relatively easy for a
small regional company or very complex for large multinationals, where many factors come into play. A selected site may be domestic, in the country where the par-

ent company is based, or it may be international, located hundreds of miles away from the parent office in a
foreign country. The following sections illustrate this.

Domestic site

- General Motors, based in Detroit, Michigan, selects
  to build the new Saturn automobile facility in Spring
  Hill, Tennessee, 56 km south of Nashville, USA.
- Valéo, a manufacturer of automobile parts, based in
  Paris, France, constructs a facility for assembling
  starter motors in L'Isle d'Abeau near Lyon.
- British Petroleum, based in London, UK, expands its
  ethylene capacity at its facility in Grangemouth,
  Scotland from 270 000 to 600 000 tonnes per year
  in 1992.
- Sainsbury's, a food company in the UK, decides to
  build a new store in Watford, north of London, in
  the 1990s.

International site

- Nissan of Japan locate an automobile facility in
  Smyrna, Tennessee, USA in 1981.
- Daimler-Benz of Germany decides to build a factory
  in Tuscaloosa, Alabama, USA in September 1993.
- ABB/CEE a subsidiary of Switzerland's Asea Brown
  Boveri builds a power plant in Indonesia in 1989.
- Marks and Spencer, the British retail store, opens a
  store in Lyon, France in the 1980s.
- Mckinsey Consulting of the USA opens up a new
  consulting office in Osaka, Japan in the late 1980s.

Figure 3.1 Site selection.

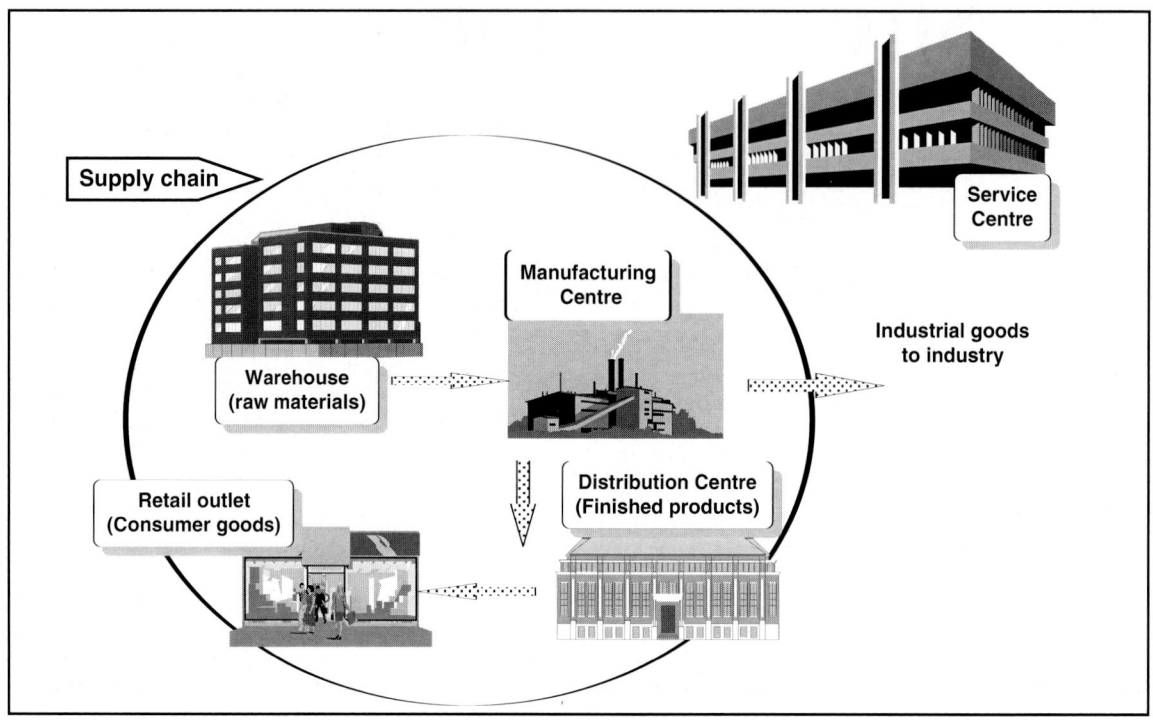

McDonald's of the USA opens a new fast food restaurant in Beijing, China in the 1990s.

The ultimate decision on site selection is often based on the cost of operating the new facility, or on the level of revenues expected to be generated. Site selection for a manufacturing facility is more complex than for an office facility, retail outlet or distribution centre as there is a bigger capital investment, a higher content of labour requirements and, thus, a greater downside risk. Deciding on a location for a new facility may take many months because of the many variables to be taken into consideration.

Strategy and operations

Site selection is a strategic, long-term decision made at top management level. However, it is part of the operations management environment because:

- Operations management personnel are solicited for their opinions concerning site selection.
- Operations management will be responsible for running the new facility once construction is finished.
- The choice of a site can mean the success or failure of an operation and the efficiency of the supply chain. Operations managers would need to respond to such considerations as.
  - Are costs controllable?
  - Is the labour force adaptable?
  - Are energy sources reliable?
  - Is there stability in the region?
  - Are suppliers nearby and dependable?
  - Is there a reliable transportation system?

Markets

The ultimate objective of a business firm is to sell the product or service. Thus, the proximity and reliability of the final market is a key concern. That is, what is the expected risk? Even though potential markets exist, companies need to be able to evaluate the expected market growth, competition from local firms and the expectation of new competitors moving into the area. For service companies, such as financial institutions, restaurants, hotels, retail outlets, consulting firms and the like, the site selected has to be very close to the client. For manufacturing firms this may not be so critical because physical products can be shipped from one location to another. Certainly, many manufacturing firms locate in low-cost production areas and then export their products to other regions.

Asia

Many companies are locating in emerging economies in Asia, particularly China, not necessarily just because labour is cheaper but also because that region is a target market. The criterion is that these areas represent a very large untapped market relative to developed economies, which have a relatively stagnant market. Table 3.1 illustrates the potential size of the Asian market relative to other regions. Of the Asian population, China has about 1.2 billion people, or 22 per cent of the world population.[1]

Automobile companies (General Motors, Toyota and Group PSA), telecommunications firms (AT&T and British Telecom), construction companies (Bechtel, Fluor and Bouygues) and nuclear plant designers and constructors (Electricité de France and Framatome) are some examples of companies with facilities in China.

The strategic role of foreign factories

Kasra Ferdows, in the *Harvard Business Review*, has developed a classification of foreign factories. He has described how the strategic role of foreign factories can be divided into six types.[2]

■ *Offshore factory*. This is established to produce specific items, at a low cost, which are then later exported. At this site, there is little development or engineering.

■ *Source factory*. This also produces at low cost, but operations managers have greater control over procurement, production planning, process planning and design decisions.

■ *Server factory*. This is set-up to supply national or regional markets. It provides, for the parent firm, a way to overcome tariffs, reduce taxes, minimize logistics costs and/or exposure to fluctuating foreign exchange rates.

■ *Contributor factory*. This also serves national or regional markets, like the server factory, but it goes further, in that its responsibilities extend to product design, process engineering and supplier selection.

■ *Outpost factory*. The primary role of this type of factory is to collect information for strategic purposes for the parent firm. As such, it is located in areas where there are competitors, research laboratories and customers. Of course, to justify its existence, the outpost factory is also a producer, but this is often a secondary strategic role.

■ *Lead factory*. This creates new process, products and technologies for the entire company. Operations managers in these facilities have a key role in the choice of suppliers and the type of development work.

Factors in site selection

There are numerous factors to be considered in site selection – staffing, local conditions, construction feasibility, financial factors, proximity of subcontractors and suppliers, availability of energy and raw materials, etc. Within these are subconsiderations, which makes the whole selection process complex. These are all discussed later in this chapter. However, site selection may sometimes be made on a whim, or a personal preference of the owners or top management personnel, as illustrated in Figure 3.2.

CORPORATE TOWNS

Historical

From the turn of the century, up to the early 1950s, when companies were very paternalistic, site selection of facilities was often governed by offering employees a host of benefits in addition to employment. This phenomena gave birth to company towns, where the firm was in many respects able to 'control the life of the employees', even when they were not in the work centre. Some examples are given below:[3]

■ Corning, a technology firm (Corning Glass), was established in a small town naming it Corning, in the Appalachians, in upstate New York. Half of the 12 000 inhabitants work for Corning and many of the rest work for subsidiaries or their dependants.

■ IBM has its headquarters in Endicott, also in New York state. Here there are several manufacturing

Table 3.1 World population

	Millions	Percentage of total
Asia	3 245	59
Africa	660	12
Europe	550	10
Former Soviet Union	330	6
Latin America	440	8
North America	275	5
Total	5 500	100

Figure 3.2   Not all site selections are based on economics.

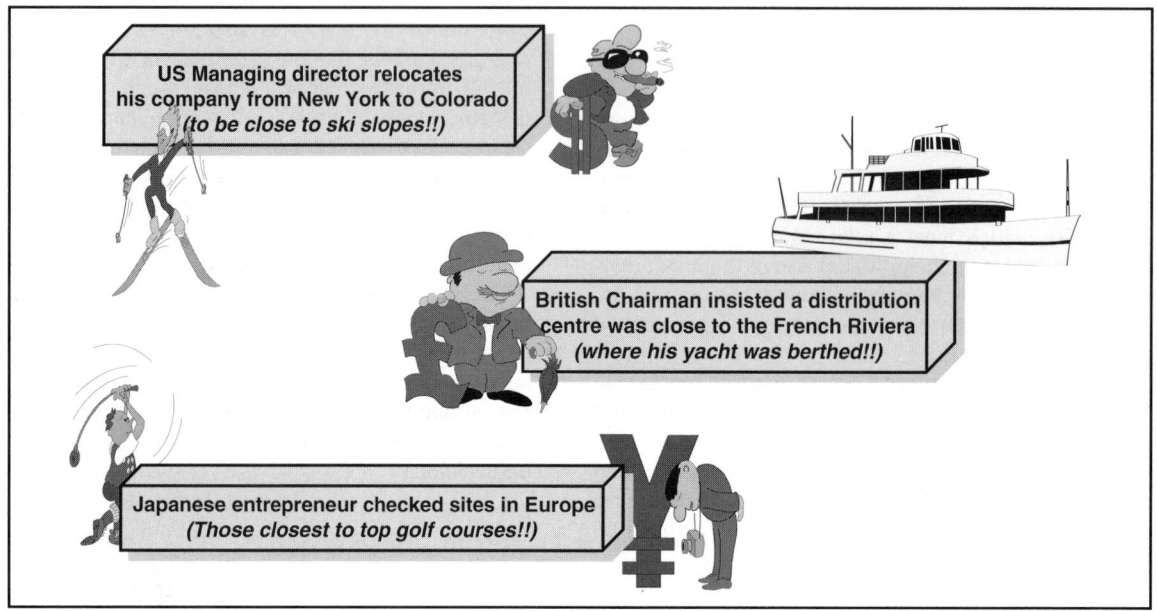

plants, the IBM golf course and a street, Watson Boulevard, named after Thomas Watson, a former chairman.

- Boeing aircraft company has its headquarters in Seattle, Washington, USA. The firm once so dominated this city that Senator Henry Jackson was once known as the senator from Boeing. (Microsoft now also has its headquarters in Seattle, Washington.)

- Hitachi, the engine maker, is at a site 160 km north of Tokyo called Hitachi city.

- Ford Motor's River Rouge plant outside Detroit was once one of the world's biggest company towns. There the company smelted its own steel, as well as building automobiles.

- Cadbury (now Cadbury-Schweppes) was relocated by its founder, George Cadbury, from the grime of Birmingham to Bourneville on the outskirts to escape from the 'unwholesomeness of city life'. Bourneville cocoa was once one of its main products.

- Lever Brothers, founded by William Lever, the soap baron, selected a model site outside Liverpool, called Port Sunlight, to give a more rural lifestyle to the employees.

- Rowntree, started by Joseph Rowntree, built New Earswick in England as his company town. This was a traditional-looking village that one of his architects said 'gave life just that order, that crystalline structure it had in feudal times'.

- Krupp steel company chose a company site in Margaretenhohe, near Essen, Germany.

- Pullman, the railroad car builder started by George Pullman, built a beautiful town for its employees on the outskirts of Chicago in the 'belief that a rational and aesthetic order would elevate the character of his workers'.

- Broken Hill Proprietary Co., the Australian Mining company, established Newman in a desolate part of Western Australia as its company town.

- Philips Petroleum chose Bartelesville, Oklahoma, USA as its company town because of the crude oil in this region. Bartelesville has since fallen on hard times.

- Phelps Dodge, a copper producing company, selected Tyrone, in a remote corner of New Mexico, USA, as the site of its company town.

Company towns are just about non-existent today as industries have merged, reorganization has taken place, other firms have moved into the area and employees have become much less dependent on a single employer.

STAFFING

Staffing for a firm includes the hiring of all the types of personnel needed to run a facility, including direct and indirect operating personnel and management. Some of the factors in staffing are discussed below.

Labour costs

The cost of direct wages is probably one of the most important criteria in site selection. It helps to explain why many international companies, based in the USA, Europe and Japan, have built facilities away from their own country. Labour costs enter directly into the cost of manufactured products or the cost of providing a service. The higher the labour costs, the higher is the product, or service, cost. Labour costs include not only the basic salary, or wages, but all social and other charges (the burden) paid to the employee or paid by the employer to the government in the form of taxes for the employee in question.

Social charges

Social charges cover medical insurance, social security payments, paid vacations, retirement benefits, unemployment benefits and, in some cases, paid educational programs. These charges are mandated by the law of the country. Figure 3.3 illustrates labour costs for major industrialized countries, breaking them down in terms of wages and the social charges or benefits.[4] The impact of the social charge can reverse the impact of the other. For example, wages paid in Denmark are higher than in Germany, but when German social charges are added, Germany has the highest total cost.

Social laws

Social laws, which directly impact social charges, concern labour flexibility and include such areas as the basic work week, overtime permitted, weekend working, hiring and termination laws. This is also a strong factor on deciding where a company should locate. In the European Union, Britain opted out of the Social Chapter of the Maastricht Treaty in 1992, allowing it more flexibility in its employment practices. The objectives of the European Union Social Chapter include:

> ... the promotion of employment, improved living and working conditions, proper social protection, dialogue between management and labour, the development of human resources with a view to lasting employment and the combating of social exclusion ...

The fact that Britain at present does not comply with the Social Chapter is one of the reasons why companies 'relocate' to Britain as Box 3.1 illustrates.[5] (The new government of Tony Blair, who became prime minister in 1997, made a commitment that Britain will sign the Social Chapter.) Another impediment to France and Italy is the consideration that they may adopt a 35 hour working week.

Figure 3.3 Labour costs in manufacturing (1993).

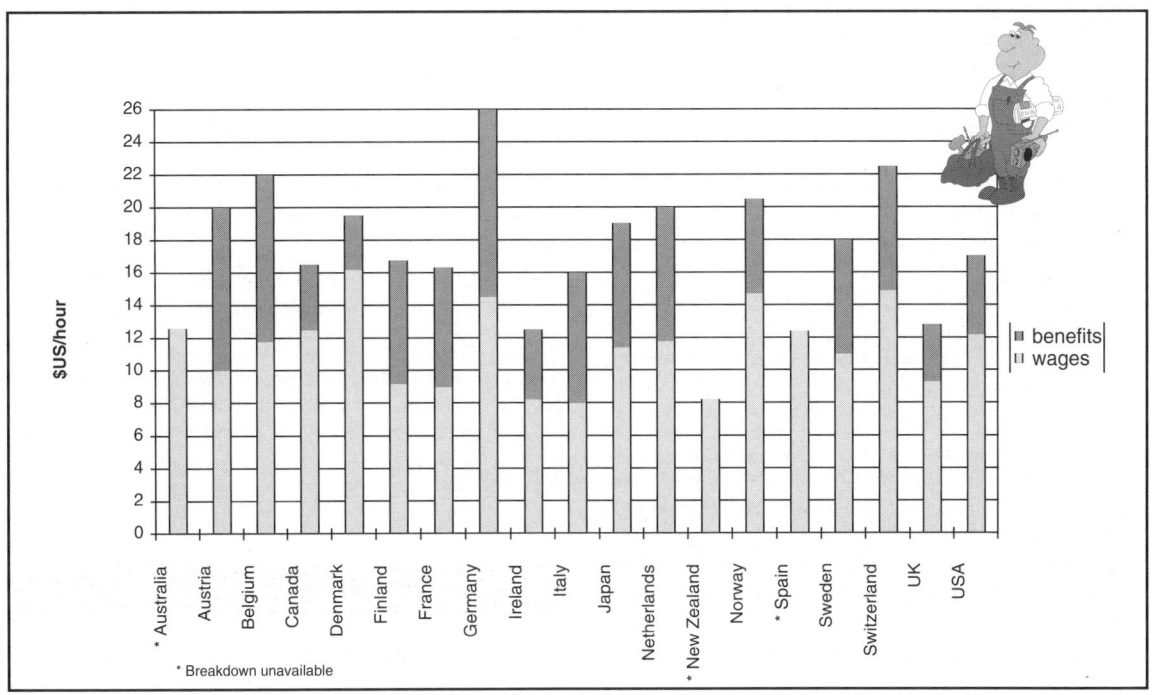

Box 3.1 Fugitive from the German disease

Labour is committed to the Social Chapter. **Claire Oldfield** meets a businessman who knows just how damaging it can be.

The stated objectives of the Social Chapter are: "... the promotion of employment, improved living and working conditions, proper social protection, dialogue between management and labour, the development of human resources with a view to lasting employment and the combating of social exclusion."

LAST AUTUMN, Technic Group in Burton-on-Trent increased its output of retread tyres from 45,000 to 65,000 a week and said sales had climbed to £30m. The firm epitomised the best of British entrepreneurial activity. But to achieve this, Peter Webber, chief executive, had to relocate an entire plant from Germany to England to escape the crippling burden placed on the firm by the European Union's Social Chapter.

The move was not made because the company is anti-European. In the nine years since Technic was founded, it has forged strong links on the Continent. Exports now contribute 80% of its business. Webber says: "We had set it up as a European business and saw Europe as our natural market-place. Germany was our largest customer base."

Two years ago, one of Technic's largest German competitors decided its retread arm was no longer commercially viable and negotiated with Webber to take it over. The German firm then employed 380 workers and produced 12,000 tyres a week.

When Webber and his team moved in, they encountered staggering waste, the result of German working practices reinforced by the Social Chapter of the Maastricht Treaty signed by EU members in 1992.

John Major secured a British opt-out from the Social Chapter, but Tony Blair has committed a Labour government to signing it.

Many experts fear that such a move could open the floodgates to a torrent of regulations that would land Britain with German-style inflexibility and costs, and cripple smaller firms.

Webber says: "The social costs in Germany are about 50% of the wage bill compared with 16% in Britain. Workers are restricted by the number of hours they can work, they are highly unionised and do not work weekends or after 6pm. Part-time workers have the same benefits as full-time staff. Holiday arrangements are very generous. There are even laws governing moving products around on Sundays."

All this resulted in an expensive, inefficient workforce, low production and the expense of shutting down machines overnight and at weekends. The Burton-on-Trent factories, meanwhile, worked 24 hours a day, seven days a week for most of the year.

The only way to fight what Webber saw as a ludicrous series of regulations was to move the entire production to Burton-on-Trent, where extra machinery was installed. Soon, production rose by 20,000 tyres a week.

When it was signed, the Social Chapter was heralded as a boon to workers, strengthening their rights and social protection. But however worthy the objectives, in practice it can be damaging, especially for small firms. Andrew Godfrey at Grant Thornton, the accountant, says: "The Social Chapter is a good thing in essence, but is pricing Europe out of the world market. Having all the social benefits in the world is not very helpful if you don't have a job."

At present the Social Chapter allows common rules to be introduced by a qualified voting majority and for agreements reached at EU level between employer and trade union federations to be made legally binding in all the 14 member states that adopted the regulations, also by a qualified majority. Working conditions and sex equality at work are among areas to be covered by the legislation.

So far, two directives have been enacted by member states under the chapter: the European works-council directive, which sets out requirements for all firms operating in more than one of the 14 signatory states, and above a specific size, to inform and consult their employees at European level; and the parental-leave directive, which entitles men as well as women to three months' unpaid leave after the birth of a child.

Many large British companies have introduced works councils, despite our opt-out, because they think it better to initiate them than have them imposed later.

On paternity leave, Stephen Davies at the Institute of Directors (IoD) says: "It is not such an enormous imposition on big companies, but for a small business to have a key worker out for three months could be enormously disruptive."

In a recent survey of members, the IoD found that most feared the Social Chapter measures. At the time of its survey the IoD said it was especially concerned about the impact of legislation on small firms, not just directly but in the imposition of additional bureaucratic burdens.

Davies is also concerned about the proposals on combating sexual discrimination, now under discussion.

He says: "Shifting the burden of proof in sex discrimination cases and allowing indirect discrimination would be very hard for small firms to deal with, especially in the case of unreasonable claims. The small-business owner cannot afford to take the time off. People tend to say that the damaging aspects of the Social Chapter are vastly hyped. But that is thinking of it in terms of large business. For small firms, they are not."

If Britain were to give up its opt-out of the Social Chapter, firms would automatically be subject to its legislation, which could not be overruled by the British government.

Small-firm lobby groups oppose any move towards opting in. Stan Mendham at the Forum of Private Business says: "If it isn't broke, why mend it? In the past four years, Britain has created more jobs than the rest of Europe put together, so why change our winning formula in return for signing the Social Chapter, which, although not critically damaging at the time, would irrevocably lock us into laws that could be inflicted on British firms without the opportunity of a veto?"

Last week Tony Blair attempted to calm fears about the Social Chapter. He called small firms the bedrock of a successful enterprise community and claimed: "The Social Chapter would have no adverse effect on small companies, or indeed large ones."

Clearly many of those who actually run small firms or advise them disagree.

The Sunday Times 16 February 1997,
© Times Newspapers Limited, 1997.

The basic salary can somewhat be controlled by the company, but obligatory social charges usually cannot. When social charges are higher, paid vacations longer and the working week shorter, then labour costs are higher. For equal labour skills, it is often these factors that determine whether a company should set up a facility overseas where the labour costs are lower.

Availability of competent labour

In site selection, there must be a good pool of labour that can be appropriately trained for the type of work. Choosing a region where there is a high level of unemployment is an indicator of labour availability. IBM and Compaq Computer of the USA located in a region close to Glasgow, Scotland. One reason they chose this area was that, because of the demise of the coal and steel industries, there was a significant labour pool. In Spain, in the 1980s, over 18 per cent of the labour force was engaged in agriculture and this provided a labour pool for prospective employers. Figure 3.4 illustrates the unemployment levels for 17 countries both in total and for young adults (under 25).[6] Most countries shown have youth unemployment levels higher than the total, except countries with apprentice systems, such as Austria, Germany and Switzerland. Here youth unemployment levels are close to those of the total.

Minimum-wage laws exacerbate high unemployment levels, particularly among young adults.

Productivity

A large labour pool also has to be associated with the productivity of this labour. As discussed in Chapter 1, *Positioning Operations Management*, absolute productivity is measured as the output divided by the input of resources. Countries in south-east Asia, such as South Korea and Hong Kong, have a reputation for the high productivity of their labour force, which, coupled to the low labour cost, gives a reason for companies to locate to these regions. Currently, poor labour productivity in some Eastern European countries, as a result of years working under centralized planning, puts these regions at a disadvantage.

Measuring productivity with labour cost

When a site is selected either for productivity levels or labour cost, the two elements have to be considered together. Assume that the information in Table 3.2 was known for two sites. If one selected purely on the basis of labour cost, Site A would be selected. If one selected purely on the basis of productivity measured by output, Site B would be selected. However, if the unit cost is calculated by dividing labour cost by productivity,

Figure 3.4 Unemployment as a percentage of the labour force (September–October 1994).

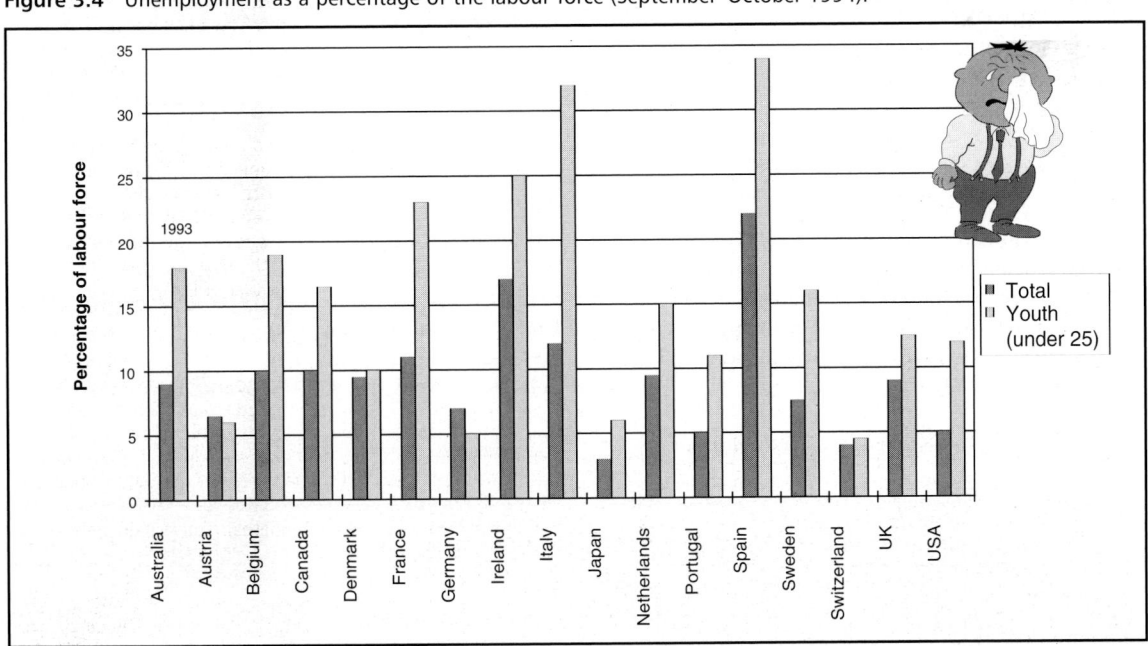

Table 3.2 Labour cost and productivity

Variable element	Site A	Site B
Labour cost, £/hour	16.00	20.00
Productivity, units/hour	100.00	125.00
Cost per unit, £/unit	0.16	0.16

there would be a trade-off between the two sites. There is a break-even situation at £0.16 per unit.

Trade unions

Strong trade-union power in a country is a strong deterrent against a firm locating in that region. Many trade unions in industrial countries, concerned about unemployment, are rigid, unwilling to modernize and unable to accept new technology or to adopt labour enhancements to improve a firm's productivity. Tony Blair, the UK prime minister, underscored these facts about union rigidity in a speech to the Trade Union Congress (TUC) in Brighton on 9 September 1997. Box 3.2 gives part of a report of the speech.[7]

Union membership

Overall, union membership in industrialized countries is declining, as illustrated in Figure 3.5,[8] for 17 OECD countries in 1980 and 1990. Only Finland and Sweden are exceptions. Trade-union power suffered the biggest decline in Spain, where membership fell from 25 per cent to 11 per cent during the decade. Union membership was lowest in France, where in 1990 only 10 per cent of French workers belonged to a union. By contrast, 83 per cent of Swedish workers belonged to a union in 1990. On average, trade-union membership in OECD countries fell by 6.4 per cent in the period 1980–1990. Some reasons for union decline are that:

- Service industries, which are usually non-unionized, are replacing manufacturing firms, which historically have been the bedrock of unions.
- Women, who make up a fast growing part of the labour force, are not eager to join unions that are almost exclusively run by men!

- Self-employed individuals, or small businesses, a fast-growing sector of the economy, in most cases do not belong to unions. These groups have to be *flexible* and *competitive* to survive and thus are not attracted by rhetoric that continually casts scorn on those two words.
- Young people are also thinly unionized. Seemingly they are reticent to join the ranks of predominantly middle-aged union members.

Industrial action

Related to the union membership as a factor in site selection is the country's history of industrial action, or strikes, which is illustrated in the Figure 3.6.[9] Generally, strikes have diminished in most countries since 1984. In the 22 countries shown on the chart, only Austria, Holland, Greece and Turkey had more days lost by strikes in the period 1989–1993 than in the period 1984–1988. However, Austria and Holland were two countries least affected by strikes in the ten-year period analysed. Greece tops the list for the most strike action with on average 4.5 working days lost per employee in the period 1989–1993. This is up from about three days in the previous five-year period. This Greek labour unrest, coupled with government instability, are the underlying reasons for tyre makers Goodyear and Pirelli pulling out of the country, together with clothing company Levi Strauss.[10]

Education level

Technology is becoming more and more sophisticated in the operation of companies. Thus, a significant criterion in site selection is the education level of the available work force, how much training would be required and what are the training facilities available. As an illustration, in the USA, North Carolina is an attractive state in these respects. It has 58 community colleges, a high-calibre research park plus three universities, North Carolina State University, Duke University and the University of North Carolina. These factors, in the five years between 1987 and 1992, have helped to make the state of North Carolina the first

---

Box 3.2 Union rigidity

Unions had no influence over a Labour Government, and they risked being left behind unless they came to terms with the challenges of a more competitive world. They must shed old-fashioned attitudes, modernise their political structure, and accept new responsibilities. Labour and unions must not repeat the past mistakes of heavy-handed state intervention, nationalisation, and industrial conflict. Unions should adopt the modern way and build a true

enterprise economy facing up to the reality that industry must be adaptable, flexible, and open to change in a global economy. Today services are more valuable than manufacturing. The British economy employs more people in design, than in the car industry, and sells abroad more rock music, than steel.

From 'No return to industrial warfare: Join the real world, Blair tells unions' *The Times* 10 September 1997, © Times Newspapers Limited, 1997.

Figure 3.5 Union membership 1980 and 1990.

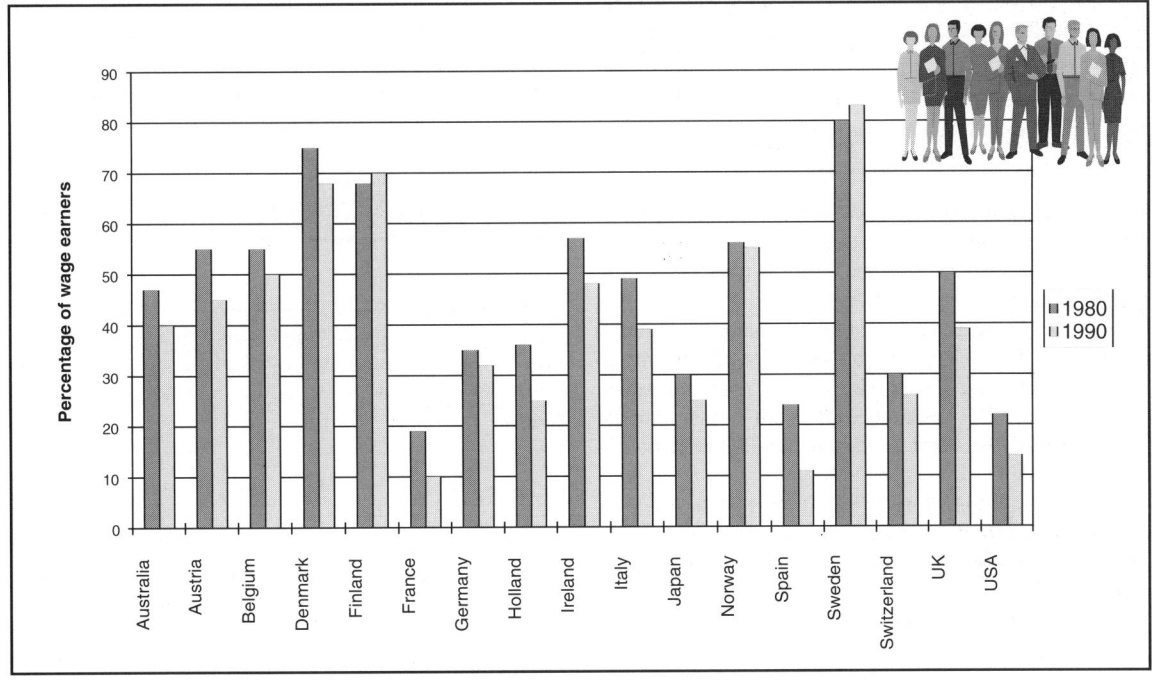

Figure 3.6 Industrial action between 1984 and 1993.

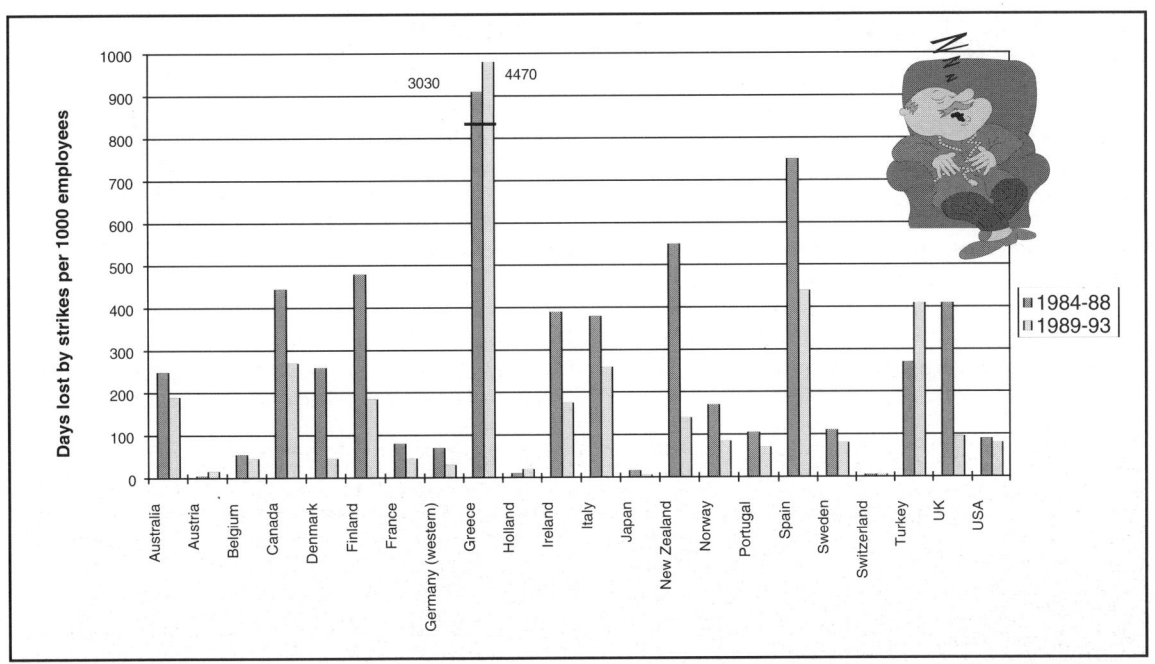

choice in the USA for locating manufacturing facilities. In worker training schemes since 1963 some 250 000 people have been trained for some 3000 firms, many of them international.[11]

Ability of local labour to handle sophisticated plant technology

Continuous-flow facilities, such as oil refineries and chemical and food processing plants, often have complex process-control systems that require a certain sophistication in the operating labour. Problems can arise if the labour pool cannot be adequately trained in order that the facility can be operated according to specification design, including safety considerations. This was one of the factors cited as the reason for the Union Carbide accident at Bhopal, India, described in Box 3.3.[12]

Sometimes, when it is critical to select a site in a location when the labour lacks the required sophistication, the complexity of the plant is reduced to adapt to the level of the local labour. Such was the case of an ethylene plant designed by a US constructor for the Middle East in the late 1970s. A less efficient conversion process was installed because it was less complicated to manage.[13]

Labour mix

The labour mix concerns regulations governing the percentage of local labour that must be used in either the construction of a new facility, or its subsequent operation. Some countries specify minimum levels of local labour to ensure that their own people benefit from the economic advantages of the new facility. If this is the case, it puts a limit on the amount of expatriate labour that can be employed. Regulations such as these can cause problems for the country concerned if the local labour does not have the required educational capacity to perform the work. In the Bhopal situation described above, it was pressure from the Indian Government in 1982 which required that the plant be turned over to Indian personnel, as opposed to Union Carbide expatriate personnel who had previously operated the plant.

INHERENT LOCAL CONDITIONS

Inherent local conditions include factors such as climate, culture and language, which are important not only to the personnel employed by the company but to their associated families. Some considerations are as follows.

Climate

Regions where there are many days of sunshine and good weather present attractive locations for facilities. People prefer to live in these regions and consequently it is easier to recruit personnel if a company is located in the 'sun belt'. In the USA this explains the rapid growth of California, Florida and Texas to the detriment of the harsher climate of the north-east. In Europe, Sophia-Antipolis, a science park created in 1969 on 2300 hectares on the French Mediterranean coast has proved to be a magnet for many industrial companies. It has attracted nearly 1000 different firms, including IBM, Cordis, a US medical company, Tepar, an oil company joint venture including Texaco, and Elf Aquitaine. Even though it is an expensive area to live in, with high rents and rigid planning controls, there is a waiting list for new occupants. Similarly, the agreeable climate is one of the reasons why Spain, Malta and Greece are attractive.[14] However, as previously discussed, Greece loses its attraction because of its poor labour relations.

Box 3.3 Union Carbide and Bhopal

Union Carbide of the USA built a pesticide facility in India in 1969 because one was needed as a result of the increased production of wheat, rice and corn. The pesticide plant used the highly toxic methyl isocyanate (MIC) as a raw material and initially this was imported. To eliminate the need for imports, a methyl isocyanate plant was constructed at Bhopal, India by Humphreys & Glasgow of the UK between 1975 and 1980. In 1982 the facility was turned over to Indian personnel.

On 3 December 1984 a worker cleaned out a pipe in the MIC storage system without installing a slip blind (used to prevent back-flow of fluid). This violated maintenance procedures. As a result, water entered the MIC storage tank, causing an exothermic reaction. The temperature and pressure of the tank increased rapidly. Refrigeration units used to cool tanks were inoperable as they had been shut down five months earlier as an economy measure. The gas pressure increased to such a level that the safety release valve opened, releasing MIC gas into the atmosphere. A safety scrubber used to neutralize MIC gas could not be used because that was down for maintenance. Similarly, the flare tower designed to burn off gases was also down for repairs. Emergency transfer tanks for the MIC could not be used as they were full.

In two hours 45 tons of methyl isocyanate gas leaked into the atmosphere. The result was an official death toll of 2347 and extensive injuries due to blindness and respiratory ailments.

As well as the benefits to employees, a warmer climate translates into lower operating energy costs. Also, the cost of construction materials may be lower in warmer regions as insulation requirements are not as rigorous and foundation depth can be less if there is no danger of deep freezing. In addition, a new facility can be built more quickly in warmer climates because almost 12 months of the year are available for construction. In the northern climates the 'window' may be reduced by four months or more because of bad weather. In Alaska, USA it is even worse and construction project planning is complicated because the 'window' for construction is only about five months. This was one of the constraints presented to C.F. Braun, a Southern California construction company, building an ammonia facility on the Kenai Peninsular in the 1970s.[15]

Climate was an important factor for the location of the Port Aventura Theme Park south west of Barcelona, Spain by the consortium of Anheuser-Busch (USA) and Tussauds Group (UK) in 1995.[16] Eurodisney on the other hand, with a similar product, chose the Paris region of France, even though Spain was originally a consideration. The Paris region, with its relative proximity to the population of Northern Europe and good transportation links for Disney Corporation, overrode the negative impact of the northern French climate.

Culture

In the rapid expansion periods after World War II, companies, particularly from the USA, employed large numbers of expatriate personnel in their overseas facilities. Expatriates are nationals of the country where the head office is located, who are sent overseas on a time-limited contract. They are usually paid a premium on their salary according to the 'difficulty' of the location. Saudi Arabia would be considered more difficult than England, for example. Using expatriates is very costly, not only because of the salary premium, but because housing and transportation have to be provided for the employees and, if they are married, their families. In addition, using expatriates is not always successful because either the employee, or his or her spouse and family cannot adapt and this puts a stress on the employee. Box 3.4 gives three actual situations concerning cultural adaptation.[17]

As a result of the high cost, finding the right individuals and the requirement of foreign governments to use local people, the use of expatriate personnel has declined.

Box 3.4 Cultural adaption problems

Engineer

In the late 1960s a single expatriate chemical engineer from England was sent on a two-year operating assignment in a Middle East oil refinery. He was housed in a sparsely furnished villa on a company-owned housing complex. Other residents included roughly 100 Moslems, and five expatriate families, including the British General Manager. He put in long hours at the refinery, including working Saturday morning and doing several stints on the night shift. He was highly regarded by the local engineers and the local Refinery Manager. Social life for a single person was extremely dull. The only café in the village seemed to be exclusively for men to drink tea, chat, and play cards. The engineer met an American woman, a teacher from a nearby US military base. After a period, they lived together. Some local families on the complex strongly disapproved of this 'Western behaviour' and registered a complaint to the Expatriate General Manager. The General Manager called the engineer into his office and told him he had to stop living with the girl, as this type of behaviour was not acceptable to the host country. If not, he would have to leave the country. The engineer's response was 'You can tell me what to do during work hours, but the evening time is mine'. The engineer's assignment was terminated shortly afterwards!

Operations manager

In the early 1970s a US-based company was constructing a petrochemical facility on the Gulf of Izmit, Turkey. One US expatriate operations manager from Texas was not adapting to the assignment and began drinking. He was very critical of the culture of the Turkish people. One evening, at an important banquet where there were many senior personnel from the parent company present, he became very drunk. At one point, he stubbed his cigarette out in the mayonnaise sauce. He was removed from his assignment the following day!

Marketing manager

In the late 1980s a large French food and retail group purchased a similar operation in Southern California, USA. To understand the French operation better, a marketing manager from the Southern California store was brought to France. He came with his wife and two children, ostensibly for a two-year period. The company paid his travel, provided furnished accommodation in a comfortable villa in an agreeable part of France, paid expenses associated with the children's schooling and provided two automobiles. Adapting was not easy because of the language and culture of middle-France compared to those of Southern California. The wife had great difficulty in adapting to the life style, felt that the quality of medical services was poor and was critical of the education her children were receiving in French schools. She made many trips back to the US, leaving her husband behind. The whole family left the assignment before a year had expired!

Ethics

Western companies whose ethical principles do not always match those of other countries have difficulties in adapting to the 'different ethical cultures' that are found in some Asian, Middle Eastern and African countries. The US government's regulations on ethics can be a road block on American companies doing business in these regions. (See Chapter 16, *Purchasing and Subcontracting*, regarding ethics) In Europe, Italy puts itself at a disadvantage for possible investors because of its Mafia dealings and the French island of Corsica has similar problems.

Language

Although English is the language of business, in continental Europe it is a necessity to speak several languages for an international company to be successful. One reason why the UK is attractive to US companies is the common language. The UK is also attractive to Japanese companies for this reason, because English is the second language for the Japanese. Many companies are now looking to establish facilities in the former communist Eastern Europe. One of their handicaps is to attract qualified personnel who speak German, Russian or other appropriate languages. On the other side of the Atlantic, the province of Quebec in Canada attracts French companies because of the common language.

INFRASTRUCTURE

Infrastructure in the broadest sense includes physical facilities put in place by the region, laws enacted by the government and the business environment that has evolved, or perhaps declined, through the years as a result of that country's management.

Family services

'Family services' covers housing, schools, universities, shops, medical services, etc. and is an element in attracting personnel. Schooling often presents a problem to expatriate families with children at the lycée or high-school level. For those in the Middle East or Africa, it often means leaving their children in boarding schools in their own country.

Communication

Communication covers telephone, fax lines, computer network facilities and video conferencing, all of which imply the need for cable and satellite connections.

Often, locating a facility in a developing region presents a problem with communication links. In France in the early 1960s, telephone communication was very difficult compared to other developed countries and this made firms non-competitive. President Valéry Giscard d'Estaing was instrumental in forging ahead rapidly with new telephone links in the 1970s, now making France a leader in telecommunications. According to a survey by Plant Location International in 1993, of 300 international companies questioned, the availability and quality of telephone, fax and data lines was the most important criterion in the selection of facility location, as illustrated in the survey data in Table 3.3.[18]

Environmental regulations

Environmental regulations cover local, regional and national rules for air, water, land and noise pollution. Locating a facility in an area where the environmental laws are strict can be costly. In Germany, where environmental regulations are some of the toughest in the world, this factor is often quoted as a reason why German companies look to install facilities away from their own turf. In California, USA, an environmental impact statement has to be prepared before a company can construct. This document has to address all the possible effects that construction and operation will have on the environment. Preparation of such a report can be lengthy, entailing a delay longer than normal for plant construction. For this reason, companies are shying away from California, preferring sites in neighbouring Arizona and New Mexico. Changing environmental laws can impact an existing operating facility. Again in Southern California, there are many oil refineries that were constructed before strong environmental regulations were put in place. Now, with the tighter regulations mandated by the Southern California Air Resources Board, companies have been

Table 3.3 Plant location survey

Priority	Average score out of 10
Availability and quality of telephone, fax and data lines	8.48
A stable political situation	7.91
Reasonable level of labour costs	7.68
Reliability of power supply	7.54
Market proximity	7.23
Healthy economic situation	7.15
A stable social climate	7.15
Availability of skilled workers	7.04

obliged to install expensive pollution abatement equipment, or simply close down.

Legal framework

Litigation laws vary enormously from country to country. The USA has probably the most severe liability laws. Damage claims for infringement, such as faulty products, faulty operation, environmental spills and the like, can run into the millions of dollars. In addition, in the USA, companies are required to have in place affirmative action programmes, the objective of which is to stress the hiring and promotion of minority and disadvantaged individuals. These groups are based on race, sex and physical disability. Affirmative action programmes arose out of the US Government's 1964 and 1972 Equal Employment Opportunity Commissions (EEOC). In Southern California in the 1980s, a French travel company ran into problems with the law because it promoted a man to a position above a woman who was better trained and had more seniority with the company. Both were French citizens. Affirmative action laws in the USA are in many instances now being reconsidered.[19]

Transportation

This covers the transportation facilities and networks for raw materials, finished goods and personnel. A good rail service and road network are important for the delivery of raw materials and then for dispatching finished goods. Transportation costs can add significantly to the cost of finished products, for example a facility in Asia supplying European markets. For some facilities where export is a major priority, or where raw materials are imported, locating close to a port may be an important criteria. If the transportation network is unreliable, the company may have to envisage constructing suitable storage facilities to act as an inventory buffer for the raw materials and finished goods. A site close to a major airport may be critical for companies where there is considerable movement of site personnel. Europe, recognizing the importance of a good transport network for business, including the travel industry, is investing millions of dollars in the road and rail infrastructure.[20] Specifically, in the late 1980s and early 1990s, Spain considerably improved its road and rail network and this has been a positive factor in attracting foreign investment to the country. Conversely, the degradation of a transportation network, such frequent road bottlenecks, is sometimes a reason for companies to relocate. Such has been the case for companies in New York and Los Angeles, USA, and for companies in England, which have moved their offices from Central London to the Docklands further east.

Rental costs

For service firms office rental cost plays an important consideration in site selection, since, of course, it increases the cost of the service (and hence the price to the consumer). Some companies, which desire to locate to a particular country establish an office, not in the capital city where rental rates are very high, but in adjacent towns, where costs are lower. Among the industrialized countries, Tokyo continues to be the most expensive location for offices and, in Europe, Paris and London are among the highest as illustrated in Figure 3.7.[21]

Living costs

Living costs cover all the expenses for employees to live in the area. Regions of high living cost may make it difficult to recruit the appropriate personnel because prospective employees find it prohibitive to relocate. Alternatively, if the company is responsible for paying the living cost, then this is an added burden on the corporation. Figure 3.8 illustrates the wide variation in living costs of various principal cities in 25 different countries relative to New York, USA, which is given an index of 100.[22] Again, as for rental rates, Tokyo is the most expensive location, with living costs over twice as high as New York. In Europe, Zurich is some 25 per cent more expensive than New York and Paris is not far behind. Eastern Europe, as represented by Prague in the Czech Republic and Warsaw in Poland, are low-cost regions, which the data show as half as expensive as New York.

Country stability

Some regions present a high risk to companies for site selection because of the fragility of the government, the threat of civil strife or locals plainly distrustful of foreign companies. A qualitative analysis of the risk of various countries is illustrated in Figure 3.9.[23] This is a measure of the credit risk rating of 26 countries in emerging markets, based on economic and political factors. Of the countries considered, Iraq is the riskiest with a maximum rating of 100. Other countries with high risk are Russia, Venezuela, Nigeria, Mexico and Brazil. Singapore is the least risky of the countries considered, even after the collapse of the UK Baring's Bank.

Dupont, USA has experienced difficulties in this respect in trying to build a US $190 million chemicals

Figure 3.7 Office rents for prime business areas (June 1997).

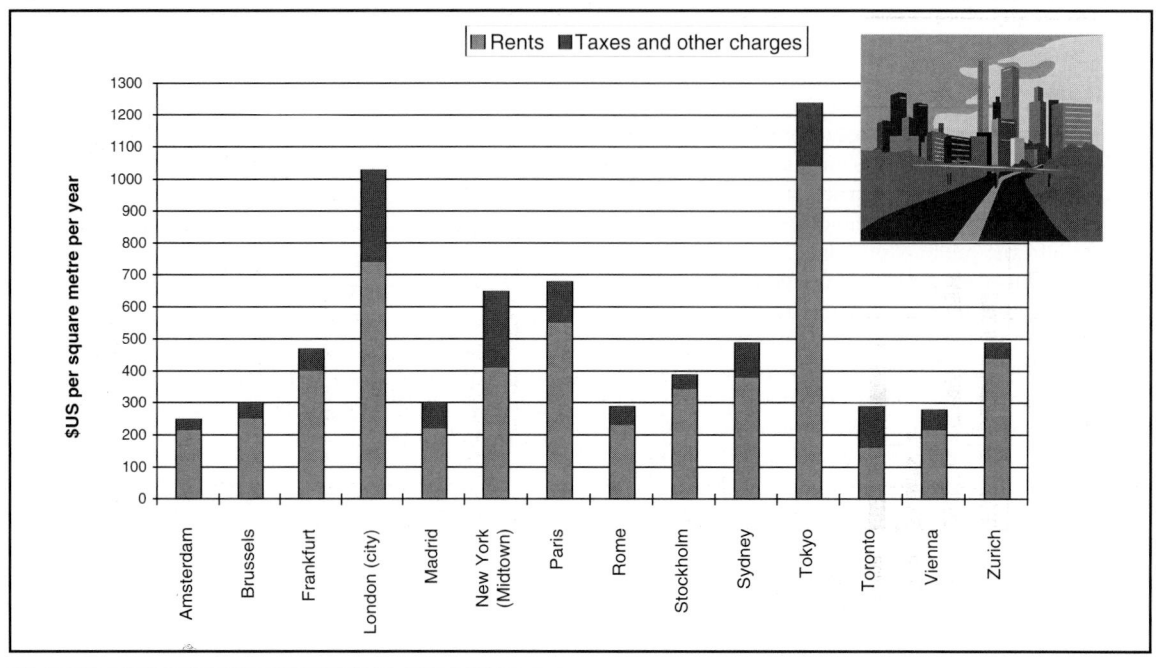

Figure 3.8 Cost of living internationally (Spring 1994).

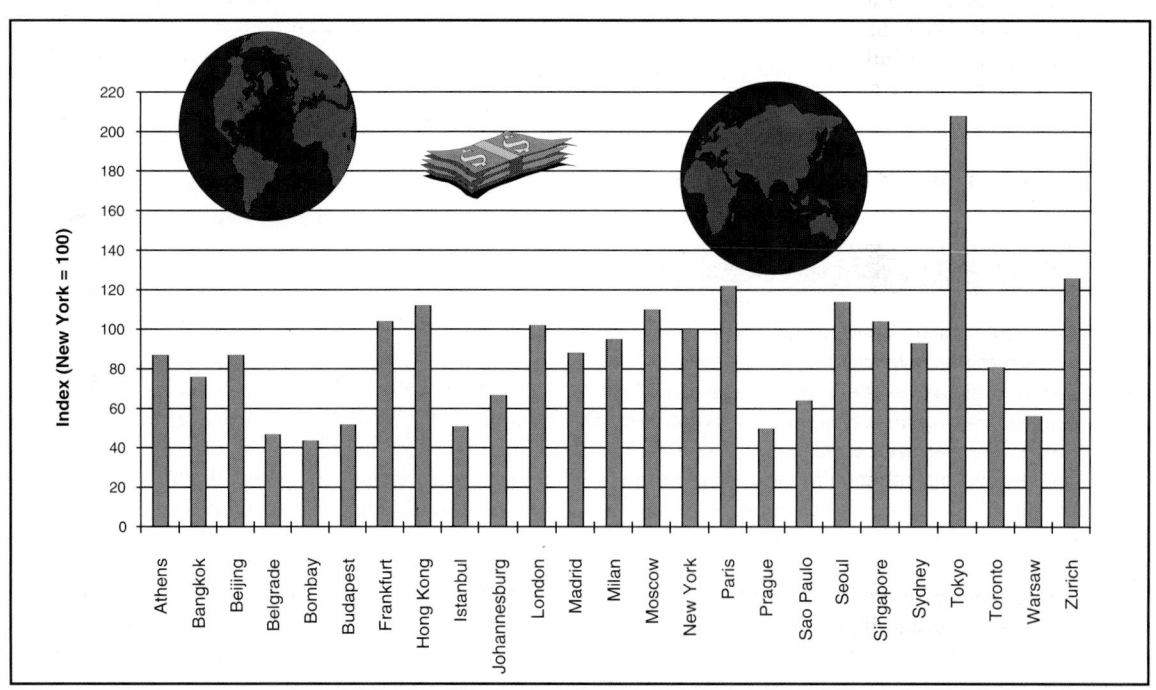

Figure 3.9 Country risk (fourth quarter 1994).

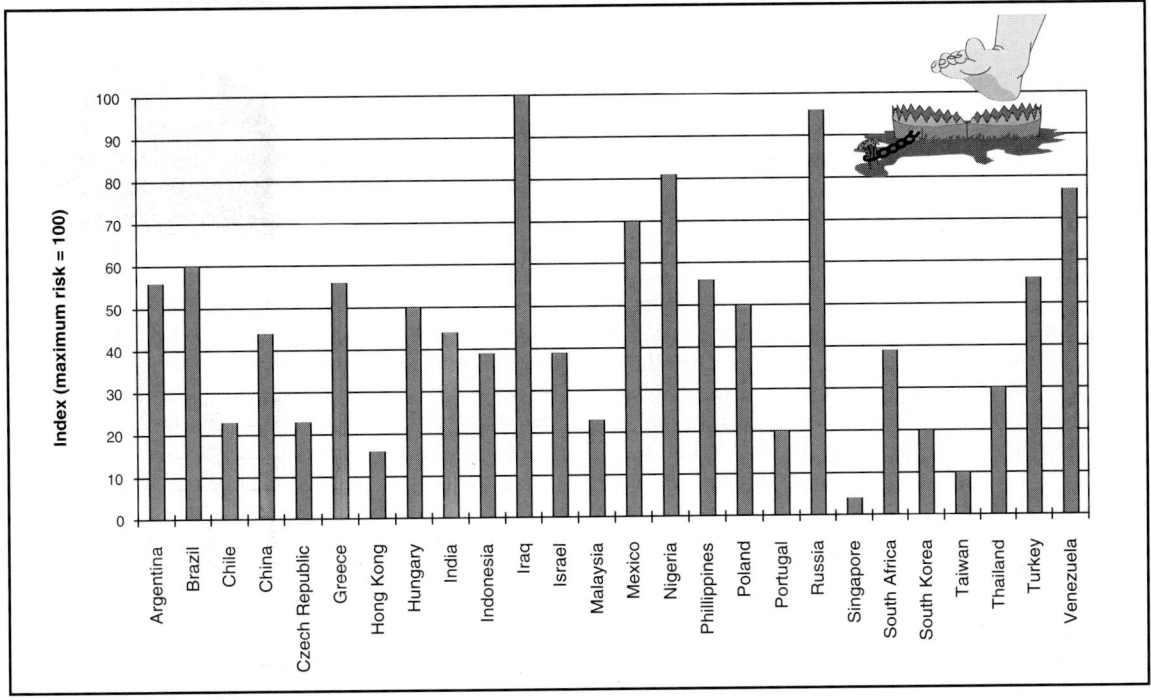

facility in the Southern State of Goa, India. The project was proposed in 1987, but the company has run into constant problems, including local distrust from residents concerning safety and environmental damage.[24] (Memories of the Bhopal disaster still linger.) In January 1995 police killed a local protester and the outcome of the project is uncertain.

CONSTRUCTION

Before a plant can be operational, it has to be built. Since construction costs are usually depreciated over a certain period of the plant's operating time, high construction costs can reduce the profitability of the facility. Some of the elements have been mentioned in the previous section, but others are highlighted here.

Land cost

The cost of land, including taxes by local or national governments, is often high where land is scarce. Europe is high relative to many other regions. In the USA, land cost in Southern California is high relative to

the Mid-West. However, tax incentives on the part of regional or national governments may make the ultimate land cost cheaper, as was the case for Disney Corp., which received tax incentives on the land at Marne La Vallée, France when it constructed the Euro Disney entertainment facility in the 1980s.

Construction labour

This covers the pool of construction labour available (as opposed to operating labour). In developing regions finding the appropriate crews may be difficult, meaning that labour has to be imported for the duration of the construction. In addition, there may be local regulations requiring a certain proportion of local labour in the construction crews.

Land preparation

'Land preparation' covers the work necessary to prepare land for construction of the facility. Industrial parks, created by regional districts for the purpose of attracting companies, require little land preparation and often all the utility hook ups are in place as well.

This may not be the case in many developing regions, such as the Philippines, Brazil or the Middle East.

Expansion possibilities

After a company has built a new facility, there may be need for expansion. Thus, in selecting a site location, consideration needs to be given to whether expansion possibilities exist. Hewlett Packard, which has a facility in Grenoble, France, has expanded considerably its operation in that country. However, on the original site there was not room for expansion and the company had to purchase land in l'Isle d'Abeau, near Lyon, some 120 km from the plant at Grenoble. As a result, the company was obliged to put in place a daily delivery service between the two sites. Lorries deliver and collect components and finished products daily, which adds to the logistics and inventory planning.

Zoning regulations

These cover laws regarding construction in a particular area. In most countries, an area has to be designated as an industrial zone before a plant can be constructed.

Environmental regulations

These may be included in the zoning regulations and would cover the type of plant being constructed. The environmental regulations would cover both the construction phase and the operation phase as discussed in the section entitled *Local conditions*.

Materials availability

Construction materials such as cement, fibre board, wood and construction steel may not be available locally and have to be imported, adding to costs.

FACTORS THAT IMPACT CASH FLOWS

Most of the factors reviewed earlier enter into the financial equation of site selection. Other financial considerations that directly impact a firm's cash flow are discussed below.

Fluctuating exchange rates

Currency stability is important in selecting a site for an operating company. Relative to the currency of the country of the parent company, wide variations can sharply impact the revenues realized, the cost of raw materials, operating costs and investment amounts needed. Figures 3.10 and 3.11 illustrate how currencies have fluctuated for specific time periods.[25,26]

In developed countries the German Mark, the Swiss Franc and the Dutch Guilder have increased in strength over 20 per cent relative to the US dollar during the period March 1994 to March 1995. The impact during this period on revenues to a US company, say, with a facility in Germany is that revenues accrued to the US parent in US dollars have increased by some 20 per cent or in the reverse situation, revenues accrued to a German firm will have decreased by a similar amount. For emerging regions, such as the case of a US company with a facility in Brazil operating during the period December 1993 to December 1994, revenues accrued to the US parent with a Brazilian facility will have dropped some 90 per cent. Within Europe, the introduction of a common European currency will eliminate exchange-rate problems for participating countries.

The changes in operating cost and raw material cost depend on the currency in which the costs are denominated. Crude oil, which is the basic raw material for oil refineries and chemical plants and also the energy source for facilities, is denominated in US dollars. Thus, when the dollar becomes stronger (it takes more foreign currency units to purchase a dollar), then the cost of oil increases, which increases the cost of raw materials and energy with the effect of depressing net income.

A strong currency, although an indicator of the stability of a country, can also be a deterrent for investment in new facilities. The strength of the German Mark is one reason why German companies, such as Mercedes-Benz, Hoechst and Deutsche Telekom have opted to invest in facilities in the USA rather than locally. Similarly, in Switzerland, where the currency is strong, companies are looking to invest more in the USA, where there is a comparatively weak dollar but a stable economy. The down side is that, when the operating revenues from these companies are translated into German Marks or Swiss Francs, the returns may not look attractive.

Repatriation of funds

'Repatriation of Funds' concerns the ability of the parent company to repatriate the funds to the country where the headquarters are located. Some countries, particularly emerging economies, have strict exchange controls, so that transfer is not easy.

Taxes on operations

Countries levy taxes on companies that do business in their territory. Taxes paid will diminish the net return

Figure 3.10 Currency exchange against the $US (developed countries).

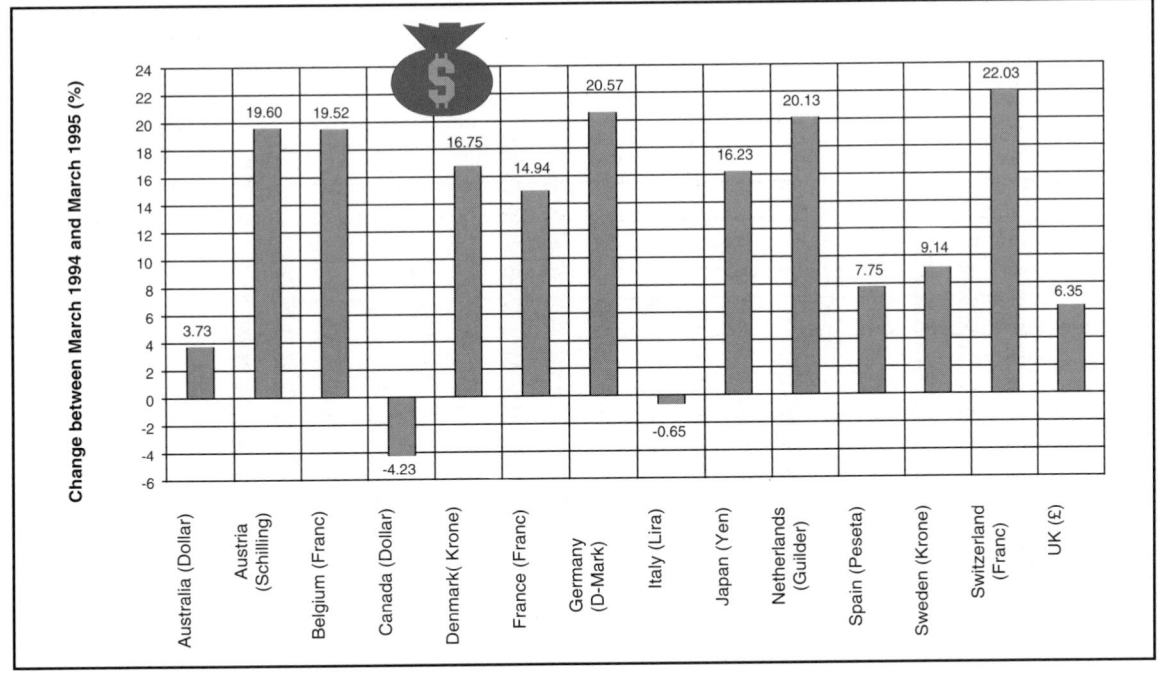

Figure 3.11 Currency exchange against $US (emerging economies).

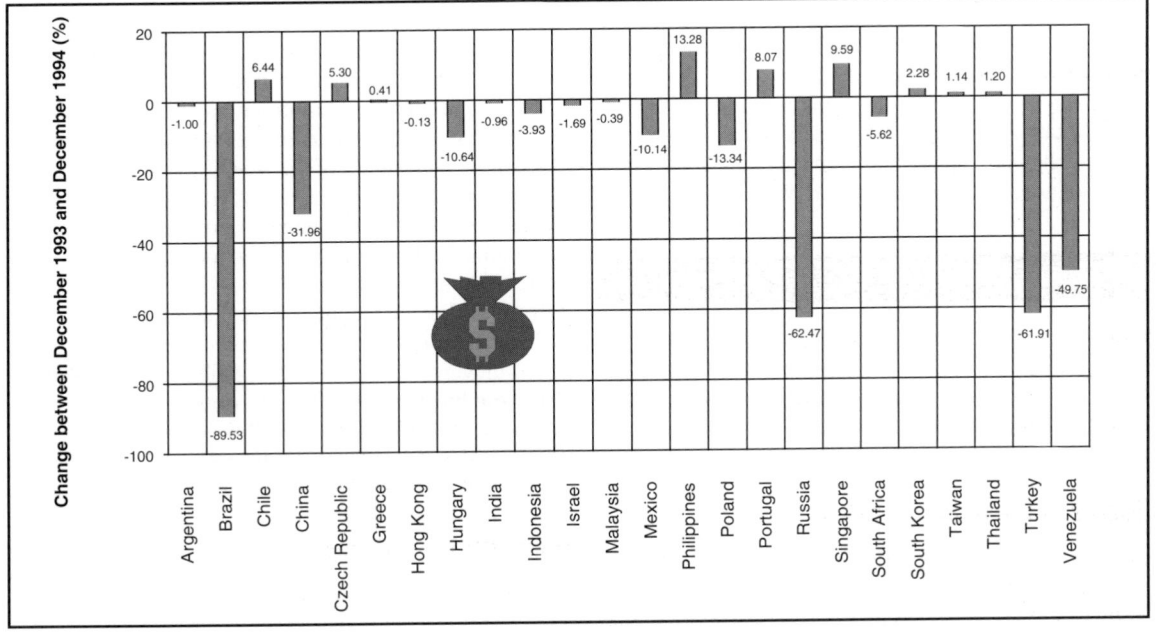

Figure 3.12 Corporate income tax (top rate, July 1994).

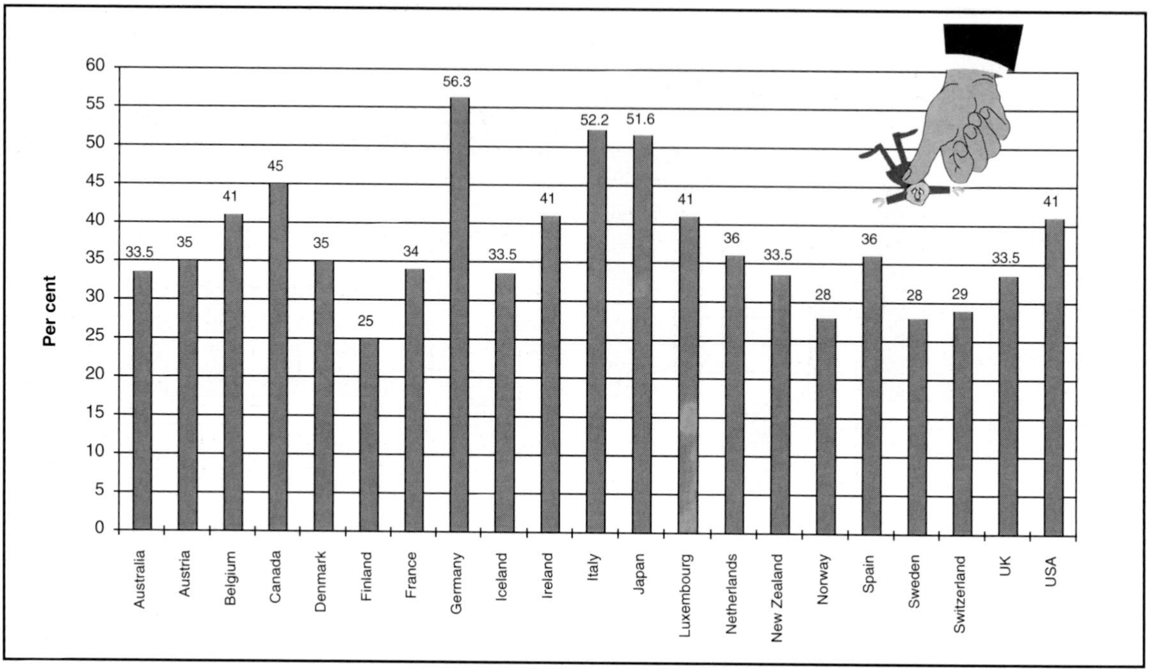

to the corporation. Figure 3.12 illustrates the taxes on company profits, including national, local, municipal, and others in the OECD countries.[27] The average is 37.3 per cent with Germany topping the list at 56.3 per cent, followed by Italy at 52.2 per cent and Japan at 51.6 per cent. Finland, Sweden and Norway exhibit the lowest rates with 25, 28 and 28 per cent respectively. However, this is compensated by the higher social security and other benefit costs born by the company.

In California, USA, there is a long-running unitary taxation situation concerning the ability of the State to tax not only the operation of a foreign company in the State, but also income generated by worldwide operations.

FINANCIAL AID

Financial aid from regional, local or national governments can be a vital factor in the selection of a site. The financial aid might include direct cash grants or tax incentives on the land, operation or products produced. The following sections illustrate the point.[28]

USA

In April 1993 Mercedes-Benz of Germany announced that it planned to build a US $300 million plant somewhere in the USA to produce a new four-wheel drive sports utility vehicle. It began the site selection process by establishing a team advised by Fluor-Daniels, the Los Angeles based engineering and construction company. This team first established an initial list of 150 sites based in 30 states, using criteria such as transport costs, quality of the work-force and financial proposals from government agencies. The list was subsequently reduced to 64 sites in 21 states by considering the distance to nearby residential areas and the distance to existing automotive operations as further evaluation criteria. Then, in-depth studies covering infrastructure, education, availability of the work-force and productivity narrowed the selection to 20 sites in 11 states. When factors covering distance to suppliers, training programmes and quality of life were added, this left just six sites in six states – Tennessee, Nebraska, South Carolina, North Carolina, Georgia and Alabama.

A further detailed analysis then covered the proximity of universities and colleges, other companies in the area, the business climate, a re-evaluation of the work force, and operating and investment costs. This reduced the short list to three sites in three southern states – North Carolina, South Carolina and Alabama. These three all presented the attraction of a relatively low-cost but skilled and abundant work-force, anti-union sentiments, affordable housing, attractive life style and good transport links with Europe. In addition, they all had governments willing to throw money at companies ready to locate in their state. The governments of the three states under consideration all offered attractive financial incentives. A site at Tuscaloosa, Alabama was finally selected. The state's financial package amounted to incentives totalling an up-front sum of $253 million, including $17.4 million to purchase and develop the plant site for Mercedes, $42.6 million for building construction, $30 million for a training centre, $60 million to train Mercedes workers and $77 million to develop the related infrastructure, such as roads and water lines. In addition, the package qualified Mercedes-Benz for tax breaks related to its profits and head count, which were estimated at $9.2 million per year for up to 25 years – an additional amount of some $230 million.

Another state in the USA that has been successful in attracting industry is Utah. In addition to financial aid, the Utah Mormon culture offers a disciplined labour force.[29]

United Kingdom

In Europe, the UK has been successful in attracting foreign firms. Financial aid, as well as the language and cheap labour relative to the rest of Europe, is an incentive as illustrated in the article in Box 3.5. As the

article mentions, the relocating company, LG Group of South Korea, is expected to benefit from subsidies running into hundreds of millions of dollars.[30]

PROXIMITY OF RESOURCES

Raw materials

For some facilities, particularly process-flow plants, proximity of raw materials and energy are critical factors in site selection. Processing facilities, such as coal power stations, are often located close to coal mines because it is cheaper to process the coal *in situ* rather than to ship the coal by rail to a power plant some distance away. Also, for environmental reasons, often the only feasible way to produce electricity is to burn the coal in a remote region and then to transmit to power by high tension cable to the user area, for example the power stations in the remote Four Corners area of New Mexico, USA, which transmit their power to Los Angeles.

Oil refineries, which produce gasoline, kerosene and diesel from crude oil, are sometimes located close to the oil fields and then the finished products are shipped to the customers. Similarly, metal-processing

---

Box 3.5 Shock therapy. Britain sends message on EU jobs by winning $2.6 billion investment. LG will build plants in Wales, reflecting firms' interest in labor-market reforms. The U.K. is "very, very stable". By Nicholas Bray, Staff Reporter

LONDON – No pain, no gain.

That's the message Britain is sending its European Union partners as it savors its latest foreign investment plum: A gigantic $2.6 billion project by South Korea's LG Group to build two electronics factories in Wales.

After years of recession and social upheaval, Britain is at last reaping the fruits of some of the most sweeping changes in social and work legislation in any Western European country since World War II. Experts say it has become the most attractive country for a foreign firm wanting to set up a manufacturing presence in the EU.

Ending months of speculation about possible sites for the project, LG announced Wednesday that it would invest a total of £1.7 billion ($2.6 billion) to build a semiconductor factory and a television plant in a 100-hectare industrial park near Newport in southern Wales. When completed in the year 2002, the two plants will employ 6,100 people in the biggest industrial project ever launched in Western Europe by a non-European company.

Top Foreign Investment

The project is also the biggest-ever foreign investment in Britain, dwarfing a £1.1 billion project announced last year by Germany's Siemens AG for a microchip factory in northern England.

British Prime Minister John Major was jubilant at winning the deal against competition from France and Ireland. "Britain ... has again attracted the pick of the inward investment decisions," Mr. Major said in a statement. "It reinforces Britain's progress in becoming the unrivaled enterprise center of Europe."

With only months to go before U.K. general elections due at the latest by May, Mr. Major's remarks inevitably smacked of campaign rhetoric. But his message can hardly be ignored – either by his political opponents or by his EU partners, which are mired in a jobs crisis brought on partly by the high cost of employing people on the Continent.

Since 1993, more than 1,300 foreign direct investment projects have been announced in Britain, creating 120,000 jobs and safeguarding nearly 300,000 others, according to British government officials. In the 12 months ended April 30, Britain took 38% of all foreign direct investment into the EU, including 40% of all Japanese investment into the union. Behind those figures, economists say, lies a story of accelerating social change.

Differences With Continentals

"The differences between Britain and, say, Germany are enormous in terms of the opportunities available to companies," says Simon Briscoe, an economist at Nikko Europe. "It will take many years for other countries to be as attractive as Britain for inward investment."

LG's choice of Wales over alternative sites backs up that assertion. As part of a deal with the British government and local authorities, LG is expected to benefit from subsidies running into hundreds of millions of dollars. But U.K.

officials insist that these weren't the deciding issue, as LG could have obtained similar incentives elsewhere.

Instead, they argue, LG chose Wales because of a combination of factors – ranging from Britain's low labor costs, low tax rates and flexible labor conditions to the local availability of a skilled workforce. Newport is on the western end of Britain's M4 motorway from London, which in recent years has become a focus for thousands of high-tech firms along what is known as the M4 corridor.

The deal also offers LG a chance to tap the expertise of London University's Imperial College. The industrial park where the factories are to be built is a joint venture between the college and local Welsh authorities, and Imperial College officials expect to play a key role in training staff and providing research facilities for LG.

Export Base for EU

"This sort of exercise will require a lot of staff education and a graduate work force," says David Thomas, Imperial College's pro-rector in charge of research coordination and business development. "We can attract people and train people and do advanced research for them."

LG executives in Britain say the Newport initiative is part of a strategy to increase LG's world-wide sales fivefold to $360 billion by 2005. The Korean company plans to use Britain as a manufacturing base for everything from components to finished goods, for distribution throughout Western Europe and for export to the U.S. Thanks to Britain's EU membership, foreign manufacturers who set up shop here enjoy tariff-free access to the main Continental European markets.

Under the two-part project, LG Semicon Inc. is investing $1.9 billion to build a semiconductor plant. Due to open in 1999, it will produce 30,000 20-centimeter chips a month, for use in home appliances to control information and communications systems. Another LG unit, LG Electronics Inc., is to spend $690 million on building an electronics plant. Starting from the end of next year, a $350 million first phase will produce two million computer monitors and three million wide-screen color television tubes a year. In addition to direct employment of 6,100, the project is expected to create jobs for as many as 10,000 people in supplier and support industries.

For Wales, badly hit in recent years by closures in the coal-mining industry, a sharp reduction in jobs in steel manufacturing and a decline in employment in the British military, the project comes as a big boost. "It's the most significant boost for us this century," Labour Party politician Paul Flynn enthused. "It will provide well-paid, secure jobs for our young people well into the next century."

In the past few years, Wales has made a big push to lure high-tech industries. The region now hosts subsidiaries belonging to 50 Japanese companies and is home to 23% of all consumer electronics jobs in the U.K.

Uncomfortable Truth

Behind the rhetoric and investment figures, however, some uncomfortable truths are also becoming increasingly evident. Many of the reasons why foreign companies prefer Britain to Continental Europe relate to the tax cuts, privatization selloffs, antiunion legislation and other measures introduced by the Conservative Party over the past 17 years, in the teeth of bitter opposition from the Labour Party. If Labour wins

Britain's next general elections, as opinion polls suggest is likely, it will have to decide whether to stick with these changes or play to its supporters on the far left by withdrawing them.

"The most important reason why Britain is so successful with inward investment is the reforms to the labor market that have been taking place since 1980," says Nikko's Mr. Briscoe. These include such measures as the removal of restrictions on the number of hours that young people between the ages of 16 and 19 can work; the abolition of a minimum wage for people under 21; reductions in maternity, unfair dismissal and redundancy rights; access for women to factory jobs from which they had been excluded; and measures to promote more part-time jobs. Though such measures might seem "socially unattractive," Mr. Briscoe says, they have had a strong impact on the economy.

A decade ago, there were five million people working part time in Britain; today there are six million. Numbers of self-employed people have risen by more than 20%. Some are people who lost full-time jobs through corporate downsizing or closures. Others are young people coming onto the labor market who either prefer part-time work or self-employment – or haven't been able to find full-time jobs. "For companies this adds up to much greater flexibility in the labor market," Mr. Briscoe says.

Why is Britain so attractive to foreign companies? "Low production costs," echoes Yasunori Taga, who plans manufacturing strategy for Japan's Hitachi group in Europe. In Wales, according to local politicians, as many as 42,000 people work for wages of less than £2.50 an hour, including 12,000 who are paid less than £1.50. And social-security charges are only a fraction of what's levied in countries like Germany, France and Spain.

'Low Production Costs'

In macroeconomic terms, the benefits for Britain of low wages and flexible labor laws are beginning to show through, not only in increased investment from abroad but also in a strengthening pound, lower interest rates and a vibrant stock market. Britain's go-it-alone stance on European monetary issues has also helped. While other European countries are jacking up taxes in a bid to meet the Maastricht Treaty's requirements on government debt and deficit, Britain is talking about cutting taxes. While other countries' unemployment rates are rising or stagnating, Britain's jobless rate is falling.

It's too early yet to say Britain's economic problems have been solved. But while the debate over future regulation and tax levels will dominate Britain's coming electoral campaign, industrial investors are likely to keep flocking in from Korea, Japan and other parts of the world to take advantage of other British attractions: the English language, a stable society and a temperate climate.

"Most Korean people speak English, not French," says Han Soo Park, marketing manager for the Korean Trade Association in Britain. "If I go to France, imagine: It would be terrible. In Italy, the weather is better, but there's too much bribery. In the U.K., nothing changes. It's very, very stable, politically and economically. We know what to expect."

Wall Street Journal Europe, 11 July 1996.
Reprinted by permission of *Wall Street Journal Europe*,
© 1996 Dow Jones & Company, Inc.
All Rights Reserved Worldwide.

plants, such as copper, iron ore and aluminium smelters, are most often located close to the mine because it is less expensive to ship the refined product rather than the raw material.

Process and utility water

Oil refineries and metal-processing plants use a large quantity of utility water for cooling and/or in the process itself. Thus, these types of plants need to be located close to a reliable water supply, such as inland lakes or rivers, or to the sea.

For food-processing plants, particularly the brewing and soft drinks industry, the water supply is an integral part of the product and so the quality of the water is very important. Coors Beer of the USA has facilities in Colorado because the quality of the mountain water is considered critical to the finished product. Other brewing facilities (e.g. Heineken, the Netherlands) have water purification plants on their site that upgrade the water before it is used in the process. Companies that sell bottled water (Evian, Contrex, Badoit, etc.) of course have their processing facilities at the water source.

Reliability of power supplies

Reliability of power supplies is important. In some emerging economies, such as Africa, electrical supplies are not always reliable. In this case, if a site in these areas is selected, then backup power facilities need to be constructed close to the facility. (See Chapter 19, *Reliability and Maintenance*.)

Suppliers or subcontractors

Companies may depend heavily on suppliers and subcontractors in their operation. In this case, a consideration in site selection is that proposed suppliers of products or services are readily available, so that in the supply chain there is no risk of production being interrupted. Reliability in delivery of goods is particularly important if a just-in-time production criterion is used at the company (see Chapter 15, *Lean Production and Just-in-Time*). Furthermore, it may be a requirement that the quality of subcontracted work is certified by codes such as the European ISO-9000. (See Chapter 4, *Quality Management*).

QUANTITATIVE APPROACHES TO SITE SELECTION

If parameters and variables related to site selection can be estimated with some certainty, the following four

quantitative methods might be used as a basis for selection:

- weighting the site criteria;
- break-even analysis;
- probability analysis
- centre-of-gravity method.

These approaches are useful in that they quantitatively determine the 'best' location. However, they are not foolproof as the input data used may change and thus alter the results. The four methods are explained in the following sections, each with a worked example.

Weighting the selection criteria

This method applies weighting factors to the criteria for site selection. The site that has the highest overall value would be the preferred location. This method is similar to the weighting criteria used in supplier selection presented in Chapter 16, *Purchasing and Subcontracting*.

Procedure

- Select the site criteria that are considered the most important for the site. These might be, for example, cost, labour availability, transport, etc.
- Assign a weighting factor F to all the site criteria according to their importance in the selection. The total weighting will be equal to unity.
- Apply a numerical score S (out of 100, for example) for all the site criteria for each possible location being considered.
- Multiply the weighting factor by the numerical score, $F \times S$ for each site and for each criterion.
- Sum the total $F \times S$.
- The value $\Sigma (F \times S)$ that is the maximum indicates the preferred site.

The worked example for *Steel King* illustrates this method.

Break-even analysis

Break-even analysis is a common evaluation method when costs can be determined with some certainty. The technique is also illustrated in Chapter 16, *Purchasing and Subcontracting*.

Procedure

- Determine the fixed and variable costs for each site.
- If a site has a variable cost higher than another site, but a lower fixed cost, then there will be a break-even point. There will be no break-even point if both the fixed costs and variable costs are higher than the corresponding costs at another location.

- Determine the production level expected from each site.
- The preferred site will be that which has the lowest total cost.

The worked example for *Ramona Co.* illustrates this method.

Uncertainty and risk

Uncertainty and risk uses the decision methods described in Chapter 22, *Decision Making and Risk Analysis*.

Uncertainty

Uncertainty is when it is difficult to assign probabilities to a situation. In this case, the criteria of Maximax, Maximin, Equally likely and Minimax regret may be used, depending on the approach of the decision maker.

Probabilities

If probabilities can be assigned, then the expected outcome of a particular site selection may be determined by weighting according to the various probabilities.

These two approaches are illustrated in the worked example for *Pike Company*.

Centre of gravity

The centre-of-gravity method is a technique that may be used to establish, for example, the location of a primary central distribution centre that supplies secondary distribution centres. The method takes into account the volume of goods shipped from the central to the secondary sites and also the distance between sites. The assumption of the method is that unit shipping costs are the same regardless of location. The object of this technique is to find the *centre of gravity* for the network or to optimize the location of the site as far as shipping movements are concerned.

Procedure

- Position the network on a grid identified by X and Y coordinates. The units of the coordinates are not important, but they must be created such that the grid is to scale with the network.
- The coordinates of the centre of gravity are then calculated from the following relationships:

$$X_c = \frac{\Sigma X_i Q_i}{\Sigma Q_i} \text{ and } Y_c = \frac{\Sigma Y_i Q_i}{\Sigma Q_i}$$

where:
X_c and Y_c are the coordinates for the centre of gravity;
X_i and Y_i are the coordinates for supply centre i;
Q_i is the quantity delivered from the central site to secondary centre i.

This method is illustrated by the worked example for *Prismode Co.*

WORKED EXAMPLE: STEEL KING

Situation

Steel King, a company with corporate offices based in London, manufactures high-quality office furniture. Production capacity at the existing production centres is now saturated and the company has decided to construct a new production facility somewhere in Europe to satisfy its expanding market.

After a study of the possible locations, the following were the five leading contenders:

1. Bari, Italy
2. Lille, France
3. Munich, Germany
4. Valence, Spain
5. Watford, England

Steel King's department of Strategic Planning proposed to use six comprehensive criteria for analysing the various sites:

- *Productivity.* This was based on data provided by an external consultant and covered such elements as union regulations, quality of work, turnover, absenteeism and work ethic.

- *Construction cost.* This covered the turnkey cost of constructing the facility, including land cost, construction time and cost incentives provided by the region.
- *Labour cost.* Included in the wage rates were all the social charges and the costs of hiring and termination.
- *Proximity to clients.* This was based on the existing clients and on an estimation of new clients. Transportation costs were an important consideration in this factor.
- *Proximity to suppliers.* Steel King ran its production operation on a just-in-time basis and so distance, as related to on-time delivery, was an important criteria in this factor. There were about 25 key suppliers, who furnished the steel, wheels, tubing, locks, plastic components and the like.
- *Weather/quality of living.* An agreeable environment, including weather and surroundings for the work force, was a consideration in the evaluation, albeit not a major one.

Table 3.4 gives:

- the various weighting factors, for a total of 10;
- the numerical score assigned to each site.

The score was out of a maximum of 100. The higher the score, the more favourable was the site. For example, labour costs at Bari were lower than at Munich and hence the weighting factor for Bari was higher. However, productivity at Munich was considered higher than at Bari, so the weighting factor for Munich was higher.

Table 3.4 Weighting factors and scores for each site

Site criteria	Weighting factor F	Bari S	Lille S	Munich S	Valence S	Watford S
Productivity	2.75	25	65	90	60	75
Construction cost	1.35	60	50	30	70	40
Labour cost	2.50	70	30	25	35	50
Proximity to clients	1.25	40	75	85	60	55
Proximity to suppliers	1.15	30	65	55	35	45
Weather/quality of living	1.00	85	25	25	90	35
Total	10.00					

Required

1 Based on the data provided (Case 1), determine the preferred location for the construction of a new production facility for Steel King.
2 If the labour cost value for Munich was re-evaluated to 30 and the construction cost for Watford re-evaluated to 50 (Case 2), would this change the decision based on the information given?
3 What can you say about the sensitivity of using this approach for site selection?

Solution

1 The weighting factor F is multiplied by the score S for each location and the total $\Sigma (F \times S)$ is determined. The values are given in the last line of Table 3.5. Based on the information given, Valence would be the preferred location.

If the labour cost value for Munich was re-evaluated to 30, and the construction cost for Watford re-evaluated to 50, would this change the decision based on the information given? See Table 3.6 for Case 2. In fact Watford, Munich, and Valence are very close, so the decision would be different.

Table 3.5 Steel King: Case 1 (the higher the site factor, the more positive for the location)

Site criteria	Weighting factor	1 Bari	2 Lille	3 Munich	4 Valence	5 Watford
Productivity	2.75	25	65	90	60	75
Construction cost	1.35	60	50	30	70	40
Labour cost	2.50	70	30	25	35	50
Proximity to clients	1.25	40	75	85	60	55
Proximity to suppliers	1.15	30	65	55	35	45
Weather/quality of living	1.00	85	25	25	90	35
Total	10.00	494.25	514.75	545.00	**552.25**	540.75
Maximum score	**552.25**					
Preferred location	**Valence**					

Table 3.6 Steel King: Case 2

Site criteria	Weighting factor	1 Bari	2 Lille	3 Munich	4 Valence	5 Watford
Productivity	2.75	25	65	90	60	75
Construction cost	1.35	60	50	30	70	50
Labour cost	2.50	70	30	30	35	50
Proximity to clients	1.25	40	75	85	60	55
Proximity to suppliers	1.15	30	65	55	35	45
Weather/quality of living	1.00	85	25	25	90	35
Total	10.00	494.25	514.75	**557.50**	552.25	554.25
Maximum score	**557.50**					
Preferred location	**Munich**					

2 This approach for selection is very sensitive to the weighting and the scores given for each location.

WORKED EXAMPLE: RAMONA COMPANY

Situation

The Ramona Company, based in Hull, England, manufactures a line of heating units, which it sells domestically; it also has a large export market. The success of its models is based on a patent-protected exchanger and fin unit built into the units coupled to the thermostat control. The company is looking to expand its production capacity. It has selected three possible sites:

- Dijon, France;
- Sitges, Spain;
- Hull, England.

In analysing the sites, the company estimated the costs as shown in Table 3.7.

Table 3.7 Costs for the possible sites for Ramona Co.

	Dijon, France	Sitges, Spain	Hull, UK
Fixed costs, £/year			
Salaries, management/staff	3 400 000	2 700 000	3 200 000
Depreciation	750 000	600 000	400 000
Insurance	250 000	225 000	210 000
Energy costs	310 000	275 000	290 000
Taxes	100 000	90 000	80 000
Total	4 810 000	3 890 000	4 180 000
Variable costs, £/unit			
Raw materials	21.50	25.90	24.75
Labour	12.50	11.30	11.10
Packing	1.30	2.05	1.50
Transportation	0.30	1.10	0.95
Total	35.60	40.35	38.30

Required

1 What are the break-even levels in terms of number of units produced between the three sites?
2 Based on the cost information what would seem to be the preferred location if the production level was:
   (a) at 100 000 units per year?
   (b) at 200 000 units per year?
   (c) at 300 000 units per year?
   (d) at 400 000 units per year?
   Assume that there is no appreciable difference in the cost information for the various production levels.
3 Illustrate the cost information according to production levels on a line graph.

Solution

1 Break-even point is:

   Total costs = Fixed Costs + Variable cost × Production level.

The total fixed costs and the variable costs for the three sites are as given in Table 3.7.

■ If Dijon and Sitges are compared, the fixed costs are higher for Dijon than for Sitges, but the reverse is true for the variable costs. Thus, a break-even situation occurs between these two sites when for some production quantity Q the total costs are equal.
■ If Hull and Sitges are compared, the fixed costs are higher for Hull than for Sitges, but the reverse is true for the variable costs. Thus, a break-even situation occurs between these two sites when for some production quantity Q the total costs are equal.
■ If Dijon and Hull are compared, the fixed costs are higher for Dijon than for Hull, but the reverse is true for the variable costs. Thus, a break-even situation occurs between these two sites when for some production quantity Q the total costs are equal.

The total costs for the Dijon site, using the subscript d for Dijon, can be represented by the relationship:

$$TC_d = FC_d + Q_d \times VC_d.$$

Similarly, total costs for the Sitges site, using the subscript s for Sitges, can be represented by the relationship:

$$TC_s = FC_s + Q_s \times VC_s.$$

The break-even point is when the total costs are equal for the two sites at some production level Q or:

$$FC_d + Q \times VC_d = FC_s + Q \times VC_s.$$

Reorganizing the equation gives:

$$Q = \frac{(FC_d - FC_s)}{(VC_s - VC_d)}.$$

Similar relationships hold between Hull and Sitges and between Dijon and Hull. Table 3.8 gives the values of the production units at the break-even point, and the total costs for each of the twin sites. These are obtained using the last equation for Q to determine the break-even units and then substituting this value into the corresponding total cost equation (TC). The equal break-even units are in bold type.

Table 3.8

Units produced to break even	Total costs (£) Dijon, France	Sitges Spain	Hull, UK
141 463	9 846 098	**9 598 049**	**9 598 049**
193 684	**11 705 158**	**11 705 158**	11 598 105
233 333	**13 116 667**	13 305 000	**13 116 667**

2 Production levels:

Table 3.9 below gives the Total costs (Fixed + Variable) for the four production levels (minimum in bold).

Table 3.9 The Total costs (Fixed + Variable) for the four production levels (minimum in bold)

Production (units)	Dijon, France (£)	Sitges, Spain (£)	Hull, England (£)
100 000	8 370 000	**7 925 000**	8 010 000
200 000	11 930 000	11 960 000	**11 840 000**
300 000	**15 490 000**	15 995 000	15 670 000
400 000	**19 050 000**	20 030 000	19 500 000

Thus at a production level of:

■ 100 000 units, the site at Sitges has the lowest total costs.
■ 200 000 units, the site at Hull has the lowest total costs.
■ 300 000 units, the site at Dijon has the lowest total costs.
■ 400 000 units the site at Dijon has the lowest total costs.

3 Graphical information:
   Figure 3.13 shows a line graph for the production level and the corresponding total costs with the various break-even levels. This figure is developed from Table 3.10.

Table 3.10 Total costs versus units produced for the three sites

Units produced	Total costs (£) Dijon France	Total costs (£) Sitges Spain	Total costs (£) Hull England
0	4 810 000	3 890 000	4 180 000
20 000	5 522 000	4 697 000	4 946 000
40 000	6 234 000	5 504 000	5 712 000
60 000	6 946 000	6 311 000	6 478 000
80 000	7 658 000	7 118 000	7 244 000
100 000	8 370 000	7 925 000	8 010 000
120 000	9 082 000	8 732 000	8 776 000
140 000	9 794 000	9 539 000	9 542 000
160 000	10 506 000	10 346 000	10 308 000
180 000	11 218 000	11 153 000	11 074 000
200 000	11 930 000	11 960 000	11 840 000
220 000	12 642 000	12 767 000	12 606 000
240 000	13 354 000	13 574 000	13 372 000

Figure 3.13 Ramona – break-even analysis.

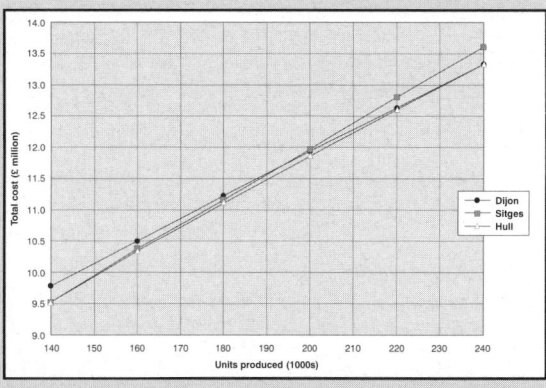

WORKED EXAMPLE: PIKE COMPANY

Situation

The Pike Company, based in Germany, manufactures and distributes jogging shoes principally for the European market. As a result of an expected increase in demand for its product, the company is considering four possibilities for capacity expansion:

■ a new facility in Mexico in a joint venture operation with a local company;
■ a new facility in Hong Kong, which will be 100 per cent owned by Pike;
■ a new, relatively small facility in southern Europe;
■ limited expansion of an existing facility in Poland.

An estimation of the profit over five years from each facility, in German Marks, is given in Table 3.11 according to various market changes. The numbers take into account all construction costs, transportation, risks associated with currency changes, and financial assistance from government, and regional authorities.

Required

1 Based on the data provided, what would be the preferred site:
  (a) If management is optimistic in its approach?
  (b) If management is pessimistic in its approach?
  (c) If management takes a middle-of-the-road approach.
  (d) Using the concept of minimax regret.

2 Assume that the probability of the market changes were estimated as follows:

Market change over five years	50 per cent increase	25 per cent increase	Flat	10 per cent decline
Probability of occurrence	30 per cent	45 per cent	20 per cent	5 per cent

Using expected values, what decision would be made for site selection?

3 After further analysis and consultation, the probabilities of the market changes were revised. The new data were as follows:

Market change over five years	50 per cent increase	25 per cent increase	Flat	10 per cent decline
Probability of occurrence	50 per cent	40 per cent	5 per cent	5 per cent

Using expected values, would the decision for site selection be modified?

Table 3.11 Estimates of the profits from each facility in German marks

Market change over five years	50 per cent increase	25 per cent increase	Flat	10 per cent decline
Mexico/joint venture	22 250 000	19 250 000	–625 000	–11 250 000
Hong Kong	26 290 000	15 500 000	–1 479 000	–18 925 000
Southern Europe	6 273 500	5 250 000	–1 790 000	–12 920 000
Expand existing	7 400 000	5 500 000	–50 000	–100 000

Solution

1   The results are given in Table 3.12.

(a) If management is optimistic in its approach then this implies using a maximax approach, or selecting the alternative that has the maximum estimated return. In this case, management will select the Hong Kong site, which has an estimated profit of DM 26 290 000 based on a 50 per cent market increase in five years.

(b) If management is pessimistic in its approach, then this implies using a maximin approach, or selecting the alternative that has the best estimated return of the worst possible outcomes. In this case, management will select to expand the existing facility because DM –100 000 for the expansion is the best of all the worst possible outcomes.

(c) If management takes a middle-of-the-road approach, then a way to arrive at a decision is to take the simple average of the outcomes of all of the possible profit numbers and to select that choice which has the highest average. The average values are given in the last column of Table 3.12. On this basis, the preferred

site would be in Mexico under a joint venture, with an average of all of the possible outcomes of DM 7 406 250.

(d) In the minimax regret, the maximum regret is determined for each column. This value is the difference between the maximum outcome in that column and the possible outcome for each cell. The maximum for each possible decision is determined. The minimum of this maximum is then chosen. In this case it is the Mexico joint venture.

2   The results are given in Table 3.13(a). The expected value is obtained by multiplying the probability of the market change by the estimated outcome and then obtaining the sum. This information is given in the last column of the table.

Based on this method, the preferred site is in Mexico as a joint venture, which has an expected (weighted average value) of DM 14 650 000.

3   The results are given in Table 3.13(b). Based on this method, the preferred site is in Hong Kong, which has an expected (weighted average value) of DM 13 619 950.

Table 3.12   Pike Co. – uncertainty

Market change	50 per cent increase	25 per cent increase	Flat	10 per cent decline	Maximum
Maximax (optimistic approach)					Maximum
Mexico/joint venture	22 250 000	19 250 000	–625 000	–11 250 000	22 250 000
Hong Kong	26 290 000	15 500 000	–1 479 000	–18 925 000	**26 290 000**
Europe	6 273 500	5 250 000	–1 790 000	–12 920 000	6 273 500
Expand existing	7 400 000	5 500 000	–50 000	–100 000	7 400 000
Maximum of maximum	26 290 000				
Choose: Hong Kong					
Maximin (pessimistic approach)					Minimum
Mexico/joint venture	22 250 000	19 250 000	–625 000	–11 250 000	–11 250 000
Hong Kong	26 290 000	15 500 000	–1 479 000	–18 925 000	–18 925 000
Europe	6 273 500	5 250 000	–1 790 000	–12 920 000	–12 920 000
Expand existing	7 400 000	5 500 000	–50 000	–100 000	**–100 000**
Maximum of minimum	–100 000				
Choose: Expand existing					
Equally likely (middle of the road)					Average
Mexico/joint venture	22 250 000	19 250 000	–625 000	–11 250 000	**7 406 250**
Hong Kong	26 290 000	15 500 000	–1 479 000	–18 925 000	5 346 500
Europe	6 273 500	5 250 000	–1 790 000	–12 920 000	–796 625
Expand existing	7 400 000	5 500 000	–50 000	–100 000	3 187 500
Maximum of average	7 406 250				
Choose: Mexico/joint venture					
Minimax regret matrix (Result = maximum regret)					Maximum regret
Mexico/joint venture	4 040 000	0	575 000	11 150 000	11 150 000
Hong Kong	0	3 750 000	1 429 000	18 825 000	18 825 000
Europe	20 016 500	14 000 000	1 740 000	12 820 000	20 016 500
Expand existing	18 890	13 750 000	0	0	18 890 000
Minimum of max regret	11 150 000				
Choose: Mexico/joint venture					

Table 3.13(a) Pike Co. – Risk – Probability situations

Probability Market change	30 per cent 50 per cent increase	45 per cent 25 per cent increase	20 per cent Flat	5 per cent 10 per cent decline	100 per cent Weighted average
Mexico/joint venture	22 250 000	19 250 000	–625 000	–11 250 000	14 650 000
Hong Kong	26 290 000	15 500 000	–1 479 000	–18 925 000	13 619 950
Europe	6 273 500	5 250 000	–1 790 000	–12 920 000	3 240 550
Expand existing	7 400 000	5 500 000	–50 000	–100 000	4 680 000
Maximum of EV	14 650 000				

Choose: Mexico/joint venture

Table 3.13(b) Pike Co. – Risk – Probability situations

Probability Market change	50 per cent 50 per cent increase	40 per cent 25 per cent increase	5 per cent Flat	5 per cent 10 per cent decline	100 per cent Weighted average
Mexico/joint venture	22 250 000	19 250 000	–625 000	–11 250 000	18 231 250
Hong Kong	26 290 000	15 500 000	–1 479 000	–18 925 000	18 324 800
Europe	6 273 500	5 250 000	–1 790 000	–12 920 000	4 501 250
Expand existing	7 400 000	5 500 000	–50 000	–100 000	5 892 500
Maximum of EV	18 324 800				

Choose: Hong Kong

WORKED EXAMPLE: PRISMODE COMPANY

Situation

The Prismode Company is a large European retail outlet in France, which is negotiating a merger with another major retailer in Spain. If the merger is completed, the new organization will provide a large distribution/sales network throughout Europe.

One of the decisions to be made in the new organization is where to locate the primary distribution centre to serve already-established secondary distribution centres, which are located in Rennes, France; Oporto, Portugal; Valencia, Spain; Naples, Italy; Frankfurt, Germany; Athens, Greece; Göteborg, Sweden, Bergen, Norway, and Birmingham, England. Initial studies have indicated that the average monthly delivery of consumer goods from the primary distribution centre to the secondary centres will be as shown in Table 3.14.

Table 3.14 Average monthly delivery of consumer goods the secondary centres

Secondary distribution centre	Units/month (000s)
Rennes	5 536
Oporto	5 784
Valencia	4 055
Naples	3 521
Frankfurt	2 420
Athens	5 130
Göteborg	1 431
Bergen	2 272
Birmingham	5 595

Required

1 Using the centre-of-gravity method, determine in the vicinity of which major city the central distribution centre would best be located. Assume that unit transportation costs between the central and all secondary sites is the same.

2 In the merger proposal there is some uncertainty about the acquisition of the outlets in Frankfurt, Göteborg and Birmingham. If these sites were not included in the merger proposal, and the unit deliveries at the other sites remained the same, near what major city would the centre-of-gravity method now suggest locating the primary centre?

Solution

■ The network is first located on a grid with X and Y coordinates. This is given in Figure 3.15.

■ From the map/grid, the corresponding X and Y coordinates are established for each secondary distribution site. These are given in Table 3.15 (columns 2 and 3).

■ The product (coordinate × number of units delivered) is then calculated for each site (Table 3.16, columns 5 and 6).

■ The centre-of-gravity coordinates are then determined from the relationship

$$\frac{\Sigma \text{ coordinate} \times \text{quantity}}{\Sigma \text{ quantity.}}$$

1 The x coordinate is 6.00 and the y coordinate is 3.80. This puts the centre of gravity near Lyon, France.

2   The x coordinate is 6.02 and the y coordinate is 2.86. This puts the centre of gravity near Marseille, France.

As with all quantitative data, the final result is sensitive to the input data. A change in the numbers of units delivered could change the final result.

Figure 3.14   Prismode – site selection.

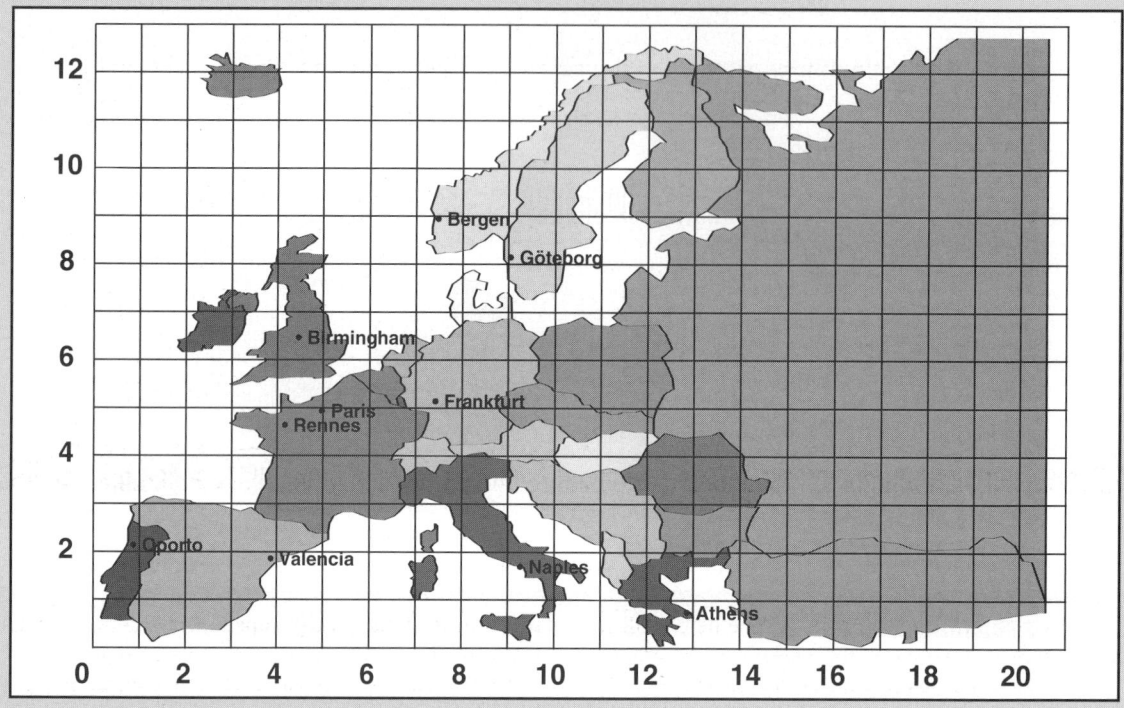

Table 3.15(a)   Centre-of-gravity method for Prismode

Question 1 (All secondary sites)

1	2 x coordinate	3 y coordinate	4 Units/month (000s)	5 $x \times$ units (Col 2) $\times$ (Col 4)	6 y $\times$ units (Col 3) $\times$ (Col 4)
Rennes	4.2	4.8	5 536	23 253	26 574
Oporto	0.9	2.1	5 784	5 206	12 147
Valencia	3.5	1.4	4 055	14 193	5 677
Naples	9.2	1.8	3 521	32 396	6 338
Frankfurt	7.5	5.2	2 420	18 147	12 582
Athens	12.9	0.8	5 130	66 174	4 104
Göteborg	9.0	8.1	1 431	12 879	11 591
Bergen	7.5	9.0	2 272	17 041	20 449
Birmingham	4.5	6.5	5 595	25 175	36 365
Total			35 744	214 464	135 827
Centre of gravity:					
Lyon, France	6.0	3.80			

Table 3.15(b)

Question 2 (Birmingham, Frankfurt and Göteborg not included)

1	2 x coordinate	3 y coordinate	4 Units/month (000s)	5 x × units (Col 2) × (Col 4)	6 y × units (Col 3) × (Col 4)
Rennes	4.2	4.8	5 536	23 253	26 574
Oporto	0.9	2.1	5 784	5 206	12 147
Valencia	3.5	1.4	4 055	14 193	5 677
Naples	9.2	1.8	3 521	32 396	6 338
Frankfurt	7.5	5.2	0	0	0
Athens	12.9	0.8	5 130	66 174	4 104
Göteborg	9.0	8.1	0	0	0
Bergen	7.5	9.0	2 272	17 041	20 449
Birmingham	4.5	6.5	0	0	0
Total			26 299	158 262	75 289

Centre of gravity:
Marseille, France 6.02 2.86

SUMMARY OF KEY ELEMENTS

- Site selection is a market-driven strategic decision with considerable operations management involvement. Operations management personnel may have input to the site selection or they may ultimately be involved in operating the new facility,

- Foreign factories may be classified according to six strategic roles relating to the parent firm. This classification may be as offshore factory, source factory, server factory, contributor factory, outpost factory or lead factory.

- Historically, at the beginning of the twentieth century, company paternalism led to the selection of sites that grew into corporate towns. However, the impact of corporate towns today has been minimized as a result of mergers, acquisitions and employee mobility.

- Labour costs, including social charges and labour flexibility, form a key element in site selection. Areas with high unemployment, as a result of the loss of traditional industries such as coal mining and steel production, may provide a pool of competent labour.

- The productivity of labour, as an element in site selection, must be considered in conjunction with labour costs. The rigidity of unions often weakens productivity.

- Regions with good training facilities present a magnet in the countries in which they are located, because it is important that local labour has the competence to handle the sophisticated technology used by firms.

- Cultural differences, including language, often make it difficult for expatriates to adapt to the new environment. Furthermore, emerging economies are demanding higher proportions of local labour in the operation of a firm which selects a site in their country. This often means a reduction in the use of expatriate labour.

- A warm climate, a developed infrastructure, political stability, reasonable living costs, balanced environmental regulations, and a manageable legal framework are all positive considerations in site selection.

- In constructing a new facility on a virgin site, land costs, construction labour, the amount of land preparation, expansion possibilities, zoning and environmental regulations, and material availability are important considerations.

- Fluctuating exchange rates, ease of repatriating funds and taxes on operations have an impact on a firm's cash flows at foreign sites.

- All other factors being equal, the financial aid offered by local or national governments can swing the balance in site selection.

- Country instability, because of economic fragility or political instability, is a strong negative factor in site selection.

- As well as labour costs, for manufacturing firms the proximity of raw materials, process and utility water, the reliability of power supplies and the closeness and reliability of suppliers are other important considerations in site selection.

- Quantitative methods for evaluating the location of a site include weighting the evaluation criteria, a financial break-even analysis, probability analysis of the various returns, and the centre of gravity method to balance transportation.

REVIEW AND DISCUSSION QUESTIONS

1 **Emerging Economies.** The following are emerging economies:
(a) India;
(b) China;
(c) Mexico;
(d) Korea.
   What are the reasons why a corporation might establish a business in these regions? What are some of the risks that might be encountered?
2 **Raw materials.** How important is it today to locate a facility close to raw materials? Illustrate your arguments with actual industries.
3 **Euro Currency.** Discuss the advantages and disadvantages that adopting a common currency would have over site selection in the European community.
4 **Social Charter of the European Union.** Tony Blair, the UK Labour prime minister, has said that he will adopt the Social Chapter of the European Union. What impact will this have on selecting a site in Britain?
5 **Local authorities.** Local authorities often make financial inducements to attract businesses, conferences (G7 to Denver, USA in 1997), or major sporting events (The

Winter Olympic Games to Albertville, France in 1992). These inducements are paid out of local taxes. Not all residents approve of these decisions, particularly when the cost far exceeds revenues. What do you believe is correct? Discuss the pros and cons of these site selection decisions.
6 **Quantitative methods.** How might one use the quantitative approaches to site selection in conjunction with the qualitative approaches, as reviewed in this chapter?
7 **Weighting method.** What are the limitations of the weighting method for site selection?
8 **Break-even analysis.** In using the break-even analysis, of which of the two costs, fixed or variable would one have the most confidence in the analysis? What is the danger of using this method in inflationary periods?
9 **Uncertainty.** In conditions of uncertainty one makes estimates of future outcomes. How are 'future outcomes' developed? How sensitive are these estimates to external situations? As a decision maker, would you tend to be optimistic or pessimistic in deciding the outcome of site selection using the relevant criteria? Justify your response.
10 **Centre of gravity.** Discuss the advantages, and disadvantages, of using the centre of gravity method for site selection. What are some of the costs that are not considered with this method?

EXERCISE PROBLEM: COMPUTERS

Situation

A computer company based in the USA is considering four possibilities in new facilities for increasing its production capacity:

■ USA (100 per cent owned facility);
■ China (joint venture);
■ India (expansion of an existing facility);
■ Ireland (small new facility).

An estimate of the returns over five years from each facility, in US dollars, is given in Table 3.16 according to various market changes. The numbers take into account all construction costs, transportation, risks associated with currency changes and financial assistance from government and regional authorities.

Table 3.16 An estimate of the returns (US dollars)

Market change	50 per cent increase	25 per cent increase	Flat	5 per cent decline
USA (100 per cent owned)	40 500 000	27 250 000	–2 000 000	–18 500 000
China (joint venture)	29 500 000	13 500 000	–1 500 000	–8 000 000
India (expansion)	15 500 000	10 000 000	–1 000 000	–4 500 000
Ireland (new)	10 000 000	6 500 000	0	–1 000 000

Required

1 Based on the data provided, what would be the preferred site:
(a) If management is optimistic in its approach?
(b) If management is pessimistic in its approach?
(c) If management takes a middle-of-the-road approach?
(d) Using the concept of minimax regret?
2 Assume that the probability of the market changes were estimated as follows:

Probability	40 per cent	30 per cent	25 per cent	5 per cent
Market change	50 per cent increase	25 per cent increase	Flat	5 per cent decline

Using expected values, what decision would be made for site selection?
3 If the probability of a 25 per cent increase in the market and that of a flat market remained unchanged, to what level would the 50 per cent increase in market have to decrease (at the expense of an increase in the case of a 5 per cent decline) in order that the decision in Question 2 should be changed? Do you believe this situation would be realistic?

EXERCISE PROBLEM: JJ DAUNAY

Situation

The JJ Daunay Company, a British-based firm that manufactures various types of beauty products in ointment form, is investigating new sites for the construction of a new facility in Europe. Four possible locations are being considered:

- Bergen, Norway;
- Graz, Austria;
- Bristol, England;
- Helsinki, Finland.

An estimate of average costs on an annual basis for the four sites is given in Table 3.17.

Table 3.17 An estimate of average costs (£) on an annual basis for the four sites

	Bergen, Norway	Graz, Austria	Bristol, England	Helsinki, Finland
Salaries	3 100 000	3 020 000	2 900 200	3 100 000
Depreciation	250 000	350 000	450 000	350 000
Insurance	125 000	175 000	250 000	220 000
Energy costs	29 000	31 000	35 000	29 000
Taxes on facilities	26 000	31 000	46 000	37 000
Variable costs				
Raw material cost/unit	7.50	8.25	8.50	7.95
Labour cost/unit	12.85	10.85	9.75	10.00
Packing cost/unit	1.30	1.05	1.50	1.50
Distribution cost/unit	0.25	0.85	0.65	0.75

Required

1 What are the break-even levels in terms of number of units produced for each of the four sites?
2 Based on the cost information, what would seem to be the preferred location if the production level was:
 (a) 50 000 units per year?
 (b) 100 000 units per year?
 (c) 200 000 units per year?
 (d) 300 000 units per year?

Assume that there is no appreciable difference in the cost information for the various production levels.

3 Illustrate on a line graph the cost information according to production levels.

EXERCISE PROBLEM: DISTRIBUTION CENTRE

Situation

A company is considering establishing a new distribution platform in northern Europe to serve its retail outlets in the Benelux countries, France and Germany. Table 3.18 shows the distribution outlets and an estimate of the number of journeys per day from the distribution centre to the retail outlet.

Table 3.18 The distribution outlets and an estimate of the number of journeys per day from the distribution centre to the retail outlet

Retail outlet	Round trips per day
Paris, France	12
Rotterdam, Netherlands	12
Charleroi, Belgium	9
Nancy, France	8
Groningen, Netherlands	15
Köln, Germany	8
Strasbourg, France	14

Required

1 Using the centre-of-gravity method, determine in the vicinity of which major city the distribution centre would best be located. Assume that unit transportation costs between all sites are the same.

EXERCISE PROBLEM: TEXTILES

Situation

A European-based company is considering developing a new textile facility principally for producing ladies and children's clothing. There are five possible international locations in the following countries: China; Mexico; France; India; England.

Part of the decision-making process is based on weighting various criteria for the five sites. This information is given in Table 3.19.

Table 3.19 The weighting of the various criteria for the five sites

Site criterion	Weighting factor	1 China	2 Mexico	3 France	4 India	5 England
Productivity	3.00	70	70	80	65	85
Construction cost	2.00	55	60	25	60	35
Labour cost	3.00	90	80	45	75	55
Proximity to clients	1.50	50	50	100	60	90
Proximity to suppliers	0.50	50	45	60	55	30

The table gives:

■ the various weighting factors, with a total of 10;
■ the numerical value assigned to each site. This numerical value is out of a maximum of 100. The higher the score, the more favourable is the site.

Required

1   Based on the data provided, determine the preferred location for the facility.
2   Illustrate with a graph the sensitivity of the weighted score for France according to the numerical value of the labour cost for numerical values of the labour cost from 45 to 100 in increments of 5. Assume that the weighted score for all the other sites remains constant at the values calculated in Question 1. What would have to be the numerical values of the labour cost for France in order that it 'breaks even', that is the weighted score is the same as for the other sites?

CASE STUDY: HOLGER COMPANY

Situation

In the late 1800s, Franz Holger and his brother Roland started a small company making small machine tools in the Cologne area of Germany. Originally these tools were destined for the coal mining industry in the Ruhr area. The company grew at a rapid pace and ventured into the larger machines that operated the mine-shaft elevators and the small trains used underground in the mine tunnels. In the 1930s the Holger Company employed almost 1000 people, including engineers, a large number of operating personnel and sales agents. When the car industry began its accelerating growth, Holger started supplying machine components for Volkswagen and Mercedes. Holger had no debt. During this period it was privately owned and financed all its investment from internal operations.

As war in Europe started looming, Holger was forced to start providing machine tools and components for the military. This included tanks and aircraft components. The allies, familiar with Holger's war effort, targeted the manufacturing facility and in 1944 the factory was heavily bombed. The result was that in 1945 Holger Company was almost non-existent and the allies were of a mind to liquidate the firm. However, after discussions, the Holger Company (now in the hands of three of the sons of the founders) was allowed to continue, with the infusion of 30 per cent of the capital from a British group.

In the 1950s through to the late 1970s the Holger Company grew at an impressive pace. The company was well known for the quality of its products, prices were very competitive and it provided excellent after-sales service. It remained in its core business of machine tools and automated machines, but also provided specialized components for the automobile industry. Whereas originally the firm's market had been Germany, now it had a broad territory in the European Union and a growing market in Eastern Europe. However, its manufacturing facilities remained in the Cologne region of Germany.

In 1981 Holger received a large order from Hyundai in South Korea, which also required an infusion of capital into the company. This order, and subsequent work, gave a market distribution, according to revenues, of 20 per cent in South Korea and other Asian countries, 70 per cent in Europe and 10 per cent in North America. Capital ownership of Holger was now 60 per cent German, 30 per cent British and 10 per cent South Korean.

In the late 1980s profit margins for Holger started to decline. Business was getting very competitive and the company was having difficulties controlling its manufacturing costs. In 1996 the board of Holger, composed of personnel from the three countries, discussed a major strategic decision to move the manufacturing operations out of Germany. Discussions were acrimonious and difficult. Two serious possibilities were being considered. One was in northern England, at a new site close to Newcastle-upon-Tyne. Newcastle had been dependent on coal mining and shipbuilding, but both of these industries had declined. The other site selection was at Inchon, a coastal town in South Korea, not far from the capital, Seoul. If the company moved to England, it was felt that about 90 key members of the company and their families would be asked to relocate. This would include design personnel, key operators and management people in the commercial and manufacturing area. If South Korea was selected, it was believed that only about 50 of Holger's people would relocate. Whichever site was selected, redundancies in Germany would include some 850 people, including work-centre operators, maintenance people and secretarial staff.

Required

1   Discuss what might have been some of the reasons for the high costs of the manufacturing operation in Germany?
2   What would be the impact, in Germany, of the company relocating its facility out of Germany?
3   What are the advantages to the firm in relocating to England? What do you believe could have been some of the inducements offered?
4   What are some of the disadvantages in relocating the operation to England?
5   What do you believe are some of the advantages in relocating to South Korea?
6   What are the disadvantages in relocating to South Korea.

Consider in your response the global impact of the operation, including sales, products, personnel and costs.

CASE STUDY: HOOVER CORPORATION

Situation

Hoover Corporation is a division of the US Maytag Co. In January 1993, it made a logic business decision to shut down its vacuum-cleaner manufacturing line in Longvic near Dijon, France and to relocate the work to Cambuslang near Glasgow, Scotland. This relocation would result in the redundancy of 600 workers in Dijon. Hoover justified its decision by recognizing that, in global markets, the company needs to take whatever action is necessary to remain competitive.

In France, reaction to the Hoover news was swift. Employees in Dijon immediately went on strike. There were talks of a nationwide boycott of Hoover products. 'This is the end of the world for us. There are no jobs within hundreds of kilometres', said Jean Verglasier, one striker.[31] French politicians, who faced parliamentary elections in less than two months, were not surprisingly furious. Dominique Strauus-Kahn, Minister for Industry and Foreign Trade, fumed that British workers had been so cowed by 12 years of Thatcherist policies that they would accept anything. Socialist Prime Minister, Pierre Bérégovoy, claimed that Britain was stealing jobs from the rest of Europe. Roland Dumas, France's Foreign Minister, called the decision 'a serious incident', which was strong language for the diplomatic Mr Dumas.[32]

France vowed to take the issue to Brussels in the hope that sympathetic European Community (EC) officials might block the move. In the end, the EC admitted that it could do nothing to help the French workers and Hoover was acting within Community rules. Nonetheless, European Commission President, Jacques Delors, suggested that Britain was guilty of the moral offence of 'job poaching'.

At the time, unemployment in both countries stood above 10 per cent and in France the numbers were fast approaching three million. It was a reminder that in hard economic times nations, to say nothing of workers and unions, put their own well-defined interests such as jobs before the less understood needs of the European Community. Nowhere was that more true than in Glasgow, where the unemployment rate was nearly 20 per cent. The city had been hard hit by the decline of heavy industry, especially in the south-eastern part of the city near the Hoover facility.

The Hoover announcement was particularly tough as it came close on the heels of a decision by US Rockwell Graphic Systems to move part of its activity from the region of Nante, to Preston in England.[33] In addition, there was a pending decision by Grundig, a German television maker to move 890 jobs from Creutzwald in north-eastern France to Vienna in Austria.

Required

1 What do you believe might have been some of the factors in this relocation decision?
2 Do you agree that Hoover is justified in moving jobs from one European country to another? Do you agree with the idea that it is job poaching?
3 The text states, 'that, in global markets, the company needs to take whatever action is necessary to remain competitive'. In production, where manufacturing and assembly are concerned, how does site location impact the competitiveness of the product?

NOTES AND REFERENCES

1. United Nations (1994) *The Economist* 12 March.
2. Ferdows, Kasra (1997) 'Making the most of foreign factories', *Harvard Business Review* March–April: 73–88.
3. 'Company Towns. The strange death of corporationville: The company town was invented by the industrial revolution. Will it be killed off by the information age?' (1995) *The Economist* 23 December–5 January 1996: 77–80.
4. Swedish Employer's Confederation (1994) *The Economist* 27 August.
5. 'Fugitive from the German Disease' (1997) *The Sunday Times* 16 February.
6. *The Economist* (1994) 3 December.
7. 'No return to industrial warfare: Join the real world, Blair tells unions' (1997) *The Times* 10 September.
8. OECD (1994) *The Economist* 23 July.
9. UK Dept of Employment (1995) (Adapted from *The Economist*, 21 January.
10. 'Island Getaway. Greek Labour Unrest, red tape drive out foreign companies' (1996) *Wall Street Journal Europe* 14 October.
11. 'Locating in North America' (1993) *Financial Times* 28 October.
12. Steiner, G. A. and Steiner, J. F. (1988) 'The Union Carbide Corporation and Bhopal: A case study of Management Responsibility', *Business Government and Society, A Managerial Perspective*, Random House, New York: 303.
13. Project worked on by the author.
14. 'Business Locations in Europe: The driving force behind much of the business location activity across Europe arises from the need to consolidate manufacturing, distribu-

tion, and management functions, and to adjust to a wider European market of 400 million people' (1993) *Financial Times* 11 October.
15. Author's experience.
16. 'With one eye on Disneyland: A theme park may lift all Catalonia' (1995) *Business Week* 27 March: 5.
17. Personal situations encountered by the author.
18. Plant Location International (1993) *Financial Times* 11 October.
19. 'The battle of Piscataway' (1997) *The Economist* 30 August: 35.
20. 'All aboard the supertrains' (1989) *Newsweek* 31 July.
21. Richard Ellis (1997) *The Economist* 30 August.
22. *The Economist* (1994) 25 June.
23. *The Economist* (1995) 4 March.
24. 'Bad chemistry for Dupont: A scuttled plant is a new setback for multinationals in India' (1995) *Business Week* 27 March: 20.
25. *The Economist* (1995) 18 March.
26. *The Economist* (1994) 10 December.
27. KPMG (1994) *The Economist* 30 July.
28. *Financial Times* (1993) 11 October.
29. 'Utah's own Lehi wins high-tech plant: Micron joins slew of firms in Mormon country' (1995) *Wall Street Journal Europe* 14 March.
30. Bray, N. (1996) 'Shock Therapy: Britain sends message on EU jobs by winning $2.6 billion investment. LG will build plants in Wales, reflecting firms' interest in labour-market reforms. The U.K is very very stable', *Wall Street Journal Europe* 11 July.
31. *Newsweek* (1993) 15 February.
32. *The Economist* (1993) 6 February: 67.
33. *Le Nouvelle Economiste* (1993) 5 February: 12.

FURTHER READING

Andel, T. (1997) 'Ready to go global', *Transportation & Distribution* June: 34–44.

Bartmess, A. and Cerny, K. (1993) 'Building competitive advantage though a global network of capabilities', *California Management Review* 35(2): 78–103.

Busillo, T. (1997), 'Laura Ashley debuts the Dallas Home Store', *Home Textiles Today* 19(3): 4, 15.

Chaudray, S. S., Choi, I.-C. and Smith, D. K. (1995) 'Facility Location with and without constraints through the p-median problem', *International Journal of Operations and Production Management* 15(10): 75–81.

Chen, Y. (1997) 'Why Acer shunned Russia', *Corporate Location* July/Aug: 72.

Colvin, R. (1997) 'Regions vie for new investment', *Modern Plastics* 74(8): 64.

Costanzo, C. S. (1997) 'Think before you build', *Cellular Business* 14(10): 34–38.

Davies, J. (1997) 'Getting what you pay for', *International Business* 10(3): 20–23.

Davis, T. (1997) 'Technical skills are important when locating your call centre', *Telemarketing & Call Center Solutions* May: 22, 140.

Farkas, D. (1997) 'The site is right, isn't it?', *Restaurant Hospitality* 81(10): 55–62.

Khami, J. (1997) 'Restaurant site selection', *Commercial Investment Real Estate Journal* 16(3): 20–23.

Kroehe, J. Jr. (1995) 'Relocation reconsidered', *Across the Board* 32(2): 40–46.

Mars, L. (1997) 'Euro Headquarters goes to historic site', *Corporate Location* September/October: 160.

Mervosh, E. M. (1997) 'An HQ here, an HQ there . . .', *Industry Week* 246(19): 90–95.

Milmo, S. (1997) 'BASF investment to focus on its integrated site strategy', *Chemical Market Reporter* 252(8): 7.

Murdoch, A. (1997) 'Who pays wins', *Management Today* April: 60–68.

Raiszadeh, F. M. E., Helms, M. M. and Varner, M. C. (1995) 'Critical Issues to consider when developing business operations in Eastern bloc countries', *European Business Review* 95(6): 12–20.

Randhawa, S. U. and West, T. M. (1995) 'An integrated approach to facility location problems', *Computers and Industrial Engineering* 29(1–4): 261–65.

Ristelhueber, R. (1997) 'India: Asia's new chip hub', *Electronic Business Today* 23(4): 29–30.

Sanders, C. (1997) 'The China syndrome', *Corporate Location* May/June: 56.

Selwitz, R. (1997) 'Sofitel builds in New York', *Hotel and Motel Management* 7 April: 3,64.

Slofstra, M. (1997) 'Dutch-based services firm chooses Canada to flagship its North American Operations', *Computing Canada* 23(19) 8.

Thisse, J.-F. and Wildasin, D. E. (1995) 'Optimal transportation policy with strategic locational choice', *Regional Science and Urban Economics* 25(4): 395–410.

4 Quality management

Objectives and overview

Quality is a key strategic concern, which impacts net income and costs. The objective of this chapter is to give a give an in-depth analysis of the quality challenge and to highlight the fact that quality is not an isolated issue, but impacts the supply chain, operations and strategic activities of the entire organization. The chapter reviews quality concerns and the importance of the customer. It explains the accepted definition of quality and some of the subrequirements. It explains total quality management (TQM) and what it requires, and reviews the philosophy of some leading experts in quality management. The chapter then goes on to detail the cost elements of quality and to summarize quality control concepts. Some accepted quality-related practices to improve the firm are highlighted. The chapter then describes the International Standards Organization (ISO) 9000 quality certification and reviews quality award programmes from the European Foundation for Quality Management, as well as the Cranfield UK Best Factory Award and the US Malcolm Baldrige Quality Award. Finally, the chapter concludes by explaining the link between quality and ethics.

QUALITY CONCERNS

One issue which is, or should be, a key concern to all organizations is the quality of the goods, process or services offered. To the consumer, or client, quality-related incidents occur all the time. The car will not start in the morning. The train is late. The packaging is torn. The receptionist was rude. At the least, quality problems can be irritating. At the worst, they can be tragic, as for example the DC-10 aeroplane accident in Chicago in 1979, which killed all the passengers and crew. The problem was in part due to a bad mounting assembly on one of the engines. (See also Chapter 19, *Reliability and Maintenance*).

Quality issues for specific industries

Some quality-related concerns in specific industries would include the following.

- *Travel.* Are customers treated courteously? Is the accommodation comfortable? Does the publicity conform to actuality? Is the transportation punctual?
- *Distribution.* Is the product delivered on time? Are the delivery agents courteous? Does the product arrive in good order? Is the product installed correctly?
- *Automobiles.* Does the vehicle perform as expected? Do the accessories work properly? Is it safe

during operation? Does it conform to environmental regulations?
- *Education.* Are courses well structured? Is the professor competent? Is the material up-to-date? Is the teaching interactive?
- *Food.* Do products have an agreeable taste? Is processing under hygienic conditions? Do products have the correct ingredients? Do products have a reasonable shelf life?
- *Fertilizers.* Is the chemical composition correct? Is the packaging durable? Do particle sizes meet specifications? Are use instructions clearly indicated?
- *Medical services.* Is the patient treated with understanding? Are visitors treated courteously? Is the prescribed treatment appropriate? Is the environment pleasing for recovery?

Quality is a strategic issue

Quality-related problems occur daily and, initially, one might put them at the operational level. However, the cause of quality is very deep rooted and ultimately can be traced to incorrect design and poor organization; in particular it is related to people. Employees and managers who lack motivation become sloppy in their work and this translates into errors in production or a poor attitude in dealing with customers. Thus, quality involves long-term planning and organization and, as such, is a strategic issue.

Quality and the supply chain

Quality issues have a strong impact on the material supply chain. Even though flow is efficient and timely throughout the chain, poor quality at any point will impede the success of the organization. This issue is discussed more fully in this chapter in the section on *Total Quality Management*.

Customers drive quality

Customers judge quality. If a tangible product has a reputation for quality, customers will purchase. All else being equal, the company will benefit. German machine tools have a reputation for good quality and, as a consequence, enjoy a reasonably healthy market share. In the 1970s, the then independent Jaguar Motor Company of the UK had a poor reputation for quality and this impacted their sales. The joke went: 'If you want a Jaguar automobile, buy two. One to have as a spare while the other is in the garage for repairs!' (Jaguar is now owned by Ford, USA[1]). Service industries use quality aspects as a strong marketing tool. British Airways, partly as a result of a reputation for good service, enjoyed a strong growth period in the 1980s and now in the 1990s is one of the most successful airlines. Harvard University of the USA enjoys a reputation for quality programmes, and producing quality graduates. It has minimal problems in recruitment or obtaining industrial financing. Supermarkets, Tesco and Sainsbury's in the UK, Carrefour and Auchon in France for example, continually compete on the quality of their fresh foods.

Net income and quality

Producing superior quality products, or providing a quality service, is vital to the continued growth and success of a firm because:

- It gives a positive company image.
- It improves competitive ability both nationally and internationally.
- It increases market share, which translates into improved profits.
- Overall, it reduces costs, which also translates into improved profits.
- It reduces, or eliminates, product liability problems, avoiding unnecessary costs.
- It creates an atmosphere for high employee morale, which improves productivity.

In summary, as illustrated in Figure 4.1, quality has a direct impact on the bottom line.

DEFINITION OF QUALITY

If one asks someone what they mean by quality, the response is certain to be different because people's appreciation or requirements of a product, or service, vary:

- For some, the Volvo Estate is considered a reliable and robust vehicle and this translates into a quality product. For others, the car is not stylish and there is no quality message in the product.
- At a retail store a simple 'No' from a sales agent may seem curt and disrespectful to some customers and thus be translated into poor quality service. However, others may consider this response sufficient and not attach any importance to it.
- Some products are marked 'hand craft leather', 'hand painted,' or 'hand sewn'. Some people consider that the manual-labour input signifies good quality. Others may consider that hand-fabricated items are of a lower quality than those made by machine because humans make errors and machines are more consistent in their operation.
- Students' evaluation of the quality of a university course can vary enormously. A professor who is rigid and has a well-structured course may be considered excellent by some. Others may feel that the course lacks flexibility and the professor lacks warmth, so for them the quality is poor.

International Standards Organization

The International Standards Organization, ISO (presented in more detail in the section *International Standards Organization and ISO-9000*) defines quality as *'the totality of features and characteristics of a product, process, or service that bear on its ability to satisfy stated or implied needs'*.[2] In this definition there are:

- *Stated needs*, which imply a contractual obligation for quality and would be specified in a written document such as the labelling on packaging. For example, 'the fertilizer contains 10 per cent by weight of phosphorus, 5 per cent potassium, and 15 per cent nitrogen'.
- *Implied needs* are the expectations of the customer and these needs are probably not in writing. For example, one expects courteous service, food that is fresh, mail delivered on time and lecture courses that are relevant and well presented.
- *Evolution.* Needs in the quality definition may change with time. This is particularly so with chang-

Figure 4.1 Quality increases net income.

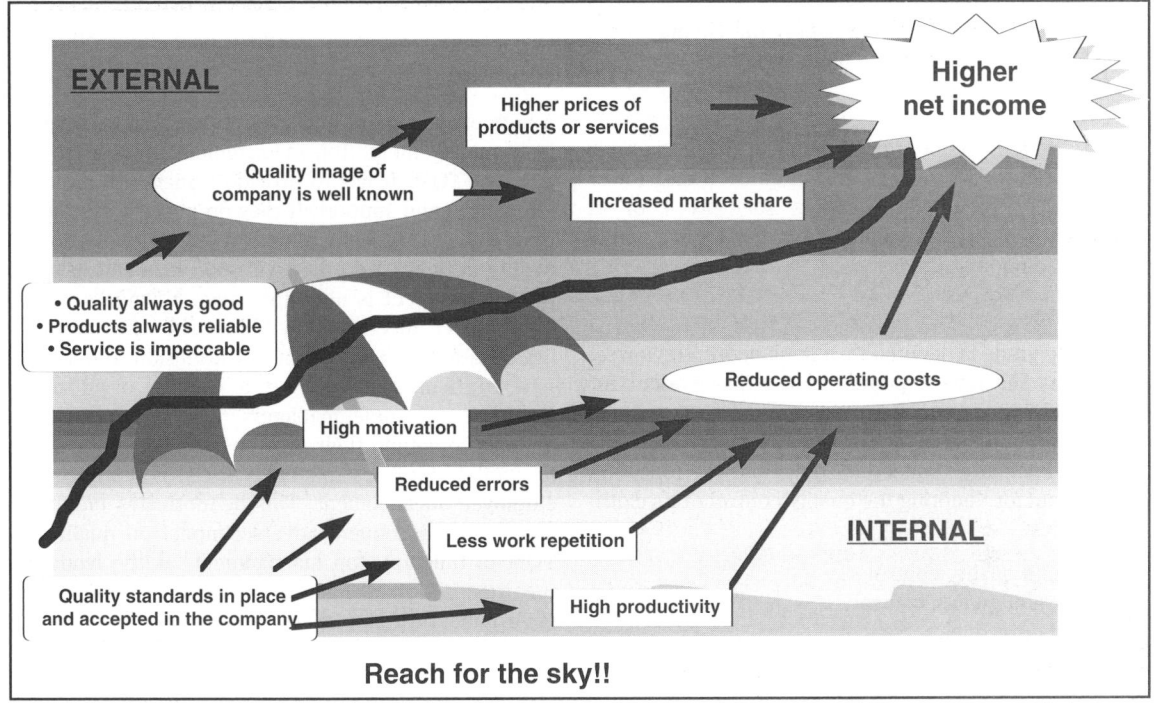

ing technology and so product designs and specifications have to be updated to satisfy the customer. For example, automobile designs and safety features have evolved enormously over the years and the range of services offered by a financial institution is now more than just simple checking services.

Specification

A specification, or standard in some countries, is the document that describes in detail the requirements which the product, process or service, has to meet. The specification includes drawings, patterns, tables of dimensions and other relevant information. The document should also indicate the means and criteria whereby conformity to the specification can be checked. Sometimes a specification may be more precisely identified such as one of the following: design specification; purchase specification; testing specification; manufacturing specification; quality system specification; or an operating specification.

Grade

For many similar products there may be different levels of quality, usually referred to as grades. A grade is

an indicator of category, or rank, applied to products, processes or services that are intended for the same functional use, but for an otherwise different set of needs. Examples are: a Porsche automobile and a Ford; a Hilton Hotel and a Formula 1 Hotel; stainless steel and carbon steel; business-class and first-class air travel; Visa 'Gold Card' and 'Regular Card'; full service or a fast-food restaurant.

The grade may reflect a planned difference in requirements; if it is not planned, then there is a recognized difference. The difference is often evidenced by the ratio of the cost to the functional use, which would be higher for the better grades. The concept is elaborated on further in the following.

Travel

If the question is just getting to a destination, then flying first or second class makes no difference. A similar logic applies if one drives from Rome to Milan in a Porsche or a Ford. In both examples, the cost/function relationship of the first mode is higher.

Adequacy of quality

A high-grade article can be of inadequate quality for satisfying customer needs, and vice-versa. For example, a luxurious hotel that does not offer a porter, well-dressed waiters and room service would not satisfy some very wealthy customers. A Formula 1 hotel offering these services would not satisfy the clients either, because the needs of these clients are different.

Numerical notation

Where grade is denoted numerically, it is common for the highest grade to have the number 1 and lower grades to have higher numbers such as 4 or 5. However, in a student examination, the lowest points denote the poorest grade.

Point score

When the grade is denoted by a point score, the lowest grade has the fewest points. In the star system for hotels, the highest number represents the best grade – a five-star hotel compared to a two-star hotel. The clothing company, Pimkie, in France has the following star system for denoting the quality control of its clothing articles:

*   Rapid quality control
**   Careful quality control
***   Superior quality control
****   Guaranteed high-quality control.

Its articles are priced accordingly. One-star items are less expensive than four-star items.

National origin

At one time quality in products or services could be identified by their country of origin:

- Germany for machine tools, and automobiles;
- France for wine, cuisine and perfume;
- USA for televisions and other consumer products;
- Switzerland for watches and banking services;
- Sweden for industrial engines and paper.

However, with the internationalization of many businesses, changes in cost structure and the dominance of Japan in many industrial and consumer goods, this identification is no longer dominant. Furthermore, as the article in Box 4.1 illustrates the former communist eastern European countries are now also moving into the picture.[3]

TOTAL QUALITY MANAGEMENT

Total Quality Management (TQM) or Total Quality Control (TQC) is where attention to quality pervades the whole operation, and not just one particular sector.

The driving wheel of TQM lies in the word *Management* and, more precisely, Top Management.

Top management

A high proportion of quality problems can be traced to poor management. Top management must be the initiator of TQM. It has to provide leadership, direction, motivation and support. If they do not, the system will breakdown. If assembly-line workers are conscious of quality in their work, they will soon lose enthusiasm if top management is not supportive. Managers who do not respect meeting schedules, who are sloppy in organization or who do not pay attention to detail will have difficulty in running a quality organization. Furthermore, some managers, who are 'afraid' and anxious to defend their own position, create a barrier to collaboration, communication, creativity and employee advancement. This de-motivates employees and has a consequent adverse impact on quality. For TQM to function, top management, as the leaders of the organization, needs to provide an appropriate work environment for employees as illustrated in Figure 4.2.

Quality-related training

A key element in TQM is that quality-related training must be available for everyone in the company. This goes from the work centre to the board room, including line personnel, staff and clerical people and must also include suppliers. Furthermore, customers need to made aware of a company's quality programme. Training should be a continuous and integrated process, such as every month. A once-only training program is soon forgotten and does not give evidence of a company's commitment to quality. Renault Automobiles, France, which introduced TQM in about 1988, continues to send employees on refresher quality-related training courses. This training (*formation*) consumes one tenth of the training budget and is equivalent to a large 5 per cent of the total wage bill.[4]

A manufacturing quality supply chain

Quality is also a supply-chain operation as illustrated in Figure 4.3. For a tangible product, quality starts at conception and continues as the product moves from design through production, packaging and transportation to retail outlet, purchase and use by the final customer. A break in any link of the chain impacts the whole firm. Some key considerations are discussed in the following sections.

Box 4.1 New competitor. East Europe's industry is raising its quality and taking on West. Swift change in work habits yields exportable goods while costs remain low. A halt to drinking on the job. By Dana Milbank, Staff Reporter.

KECSKEMET, Hungary – Most businesses this side of the Berlin Wall spent the past few decades specializing in the production of one thing: junk.

But now, more and more companies in Central and Eastern Europe, no longer content to make shoddy autos and second-rate textiles, are rapidly raising the quality of their products to Western standards. Their success suggests that these countries – especially Poland, Hungary and the Czech Republic – are rejoining the West more quickly than many people expected.

Their gains could serve as a warning to Western producers. Industry in Central and Eastern Europe, prodded by Western investors and competition from Western imports, is combining its old advantage of cheap labor with newly upgraded merchandise to pose a more serious export threat. The Czech Republic, for example, has increased exports to the West to 70% of total exports from 31% in 1989.

"There have been very dramatic improvements in quality of products," says Charles Harman, a CS First Boston specialist in the region.

A Changed Scene

The far-reaching change is obvious at Petofi Printing & Packaging Co., a maker of cardboard boxes, wrappers and other containers here in Kecskemet. Only a few years ago, Petofi's employees drank beer at work. Flies buzzing in open windows got stuck in the paint and pressed into the paperboard. Containers were delivered in wrong colors and sizes. But customers didn't dare complain. Instead, they bribed the state company with chocolates and liquor to take their orders.

But after being privatized in 1990, Petofi began overhauling itself, leapfrogging Western companies with state-of-the-art machinery. It whipped its work force into shape with a combination of inducements and threats. Now, most of its products are exported, and its customers include multinationals such as Unilever NV of the Netherlands and General Electric Co. and Philip Morris Cos. of the U.S. Some are shifting orders from Western suppliers.

Petofi's quality "compares very favorably," says Gerry Flanagan, a purchaser for Pepsi Co Inc., which buys Petofi wrappers for some snack-food products. "They have filled the gap between competitive quality and best cost."

Industrial Heritage

Vladimir Lich, who heads A.T. Kearney Inc.'s management-consultancy office in Prague, says the region's companies could become tougher competitors than Latin America or the Far East because of their heritage of industrial strength. "They have the tradition and they have the know-how," he says. "They may have obsolete equipment and bad habits, but in cases where they have good management, they can compete almost immediately."

Goldsun Ltd., a Hungarian frozen-vegetables company, took 12 hours to process fresh corn in 1991, and only 30% of its produce was export-grade. Now, Goldsun processes corn in four hours, and 96% of it passes muster. Goldsun is exporting 60% of its production.

In Hungary, some 40 companies have received "ISO-9000" certification, by meeting a series of quality standards from the International Standards Organization. Another that expects to get ISO certification soon is the Budafok packaging plant in the Budafok industrial area of Budapest. The state company, now being sold to Tenneco Inc.'s Packaging Corp. of America, has poured $9 million into new machinery.

Time-Consuming Process

But ISO certification doesn't guarantee Western quality. And as Ferenc Fonyodi, Budafok's operations director, notes, "Improving quality is not an overnight process." Although Budafok's products generally meet Western grades, the company must cull 20% to 25% of them because they fail its own quality inspection. That is better than before, when even damaged goods were shipped, but it shows that something is still awry in Budafok's production. The company hasn't landed any major Western orders.

Among many Hungarian-owned businesses, in fact, progress toward quality remains uneven. At Videoton Holding Co., a military supplier that slid into bankruptcy in 1991 after the Soviet Union collapsed, quality is a major theme of the new management. But of the 36 Videoton companies, many in consumer electronics, only 12 have begun quality-assurance programs.

Most of those 12 have done so because of Western joint-venture partners. At Videoton's huge complex in Szekesfehervar, a facility making VCR components for Philips NV looks like any in the West: clean and bright with charts on the wall showing statistical process controls and a banner on the wall that says Quality. But nearby, at a hot and dirty plant that makes oil-pump parts for cars, customers still send back 15% of goods shipped.

"The systematic approach is missing" at Hungarian companies, says Istvan Szabo, a former Videoton worker who now is quality manager for an American company. "It's a matter of culture – generations have to change."

However, the generations are changing quickly in this part of the world. Some Hungarian businesses see high-end exports as their best opportunity. They can't count on underpricing foreign competitors with low labor costs; wages are higher than in the Far East and are rapidly nearing Western European levels.

"If you want to export, you have to produce top quality," says Eszter Papai, export manager for Kandelaber Ltd., near Budapest. Using that philosophy, tiny Kandelaber doubled its experts last year, to one-third of total output. And the exports aren't cheap stuff: Kandelaber sells light fixtures, made from solid brass and cast iron by craftsmen, for $600 to $2,000.

For others, the quality drive isn't about exports but about defending their own turf. With imports flooding in from Western Europe, Japan and the U.S., local companies realize that they have to improve quality if they are to keep even the Hungarian market.

That's what Peter Zwack concluded when he bought back the old family liquor business, Zwack Unicum Co. Though the business was partially protected by quotas, Mr. Zwack knew that Western rivals would soon be producing here.

He had reason to worry. Zwack, nationalized in 1948 when he was a teenager, had been ruined by 40 years of communism. The company's star brand, a bitter called Unicum, had deteriorated. When ingredients such as rhubarb and ginseng weren't available, they were simply left out. The state stopped aging the liquor and resorted to cheap packaging.

Regaining an Image

Mr. Zwack resolved to regain the mystique of the 200-year-old company. "What we want to do is bring back the Austro-Hungarian image, the cradle of culture," he says. "We had a great quality image. What we have to regain is that image."

Aided by investments from Underberg AG of Switzerland and Grand Metropolitan PLC of Britain, the renewed Zwack installed new equipment for $4 million, imported top-quality herbs, eliminated variations in Unicum's ingredients and ordered new packaging. It improved delivery and numbered each bottle of Unicum to be able to trace quality problems. New sales, marketing and customer-service departments trumpet its quality theme.

The company, again profitable, has increased exports of Unicum, apricot brandy and plum brandy to 5% of sales – and seems to be heading for 20% by the end of 1990s. Moreover, Mr. Zwack promises to close his other plant, in Italy, and move production here when Hungary joins the European Union, a development expected within a few years. "We feel we're going to be very successful in the West," says Mr. Zwack, sitting in his father's old office.

Success in the West requires new attitudes as well as new equipment. At Petofi, the printing plant, the equipment was the easy part. The communist era machines at its Kecskemet plant were decades behind Western standards. Instead of box-cutting machines, Petofi "had a bench and 50 burly women with rubber mallets pounding waste paper off the edges all day long," says Stephen Frater, a Hungarian-American investor who orchestrated Petofi's privatization. The products' quality and color depended on which paints and materials were available; if red paint was running low, orange would do. Not surprisingly, only 7% of Petofi's production was exported, and that went east.

Equipment-Buying Splurge

Financed by the World Bank, the European Bank for Reconstruction and Development and various investors such as Cofinec Group (a group backed by Carlo de Benedetti, the Italian industrialist), Petofi pumped $35 million into new equipment between 1990 and 1993 and called in Western consultants. It now has 40 new machines, including computer-controlled laser equipment to make prototypes, offset printers, computerized color analyzers to mix the Wrigley green or Marlboro red, ultraviolet varnishing, and cameras to check for printing imperfections.

Petofi also set up a quality-assurance lab to check raw materials and to sack suppliers who were sending poor goods because they thought a Hungarian company wouldn't care.

But more important and more difficult has been changing the people who run the new machinery. In the old days, managers opened the schnapps in the morning, and, Mr. Frater recalls, "by 11 o'clock everyone was in the bag." Petofi allocated products to customers. "They would give us a sample box, and we'd make something close to that," says Tibor Szabados, the production chief. "It didn't matter. They couldn't complain. There were people lining up at the door for more and more."

The sales staff didn't make calls; it set up visiting hours when customers could plead their case. Workers had high absentee rates, and managers told them not to waste material even if that meant shipping junk. "We got paid no matter what," says Bela Szel, who now heads the local union.

The Work Ethic

No longer. Cofinec, which owns half of Petofi, demanded an end to drinking on the job and overhauled Petofi's top management. The new managers offered workers huge incentives to improve: a 40% pay raise (wages now average $600 a month), year-end bonuses and better working conditions. It also brought customers onto the shop floor and took workers to trade shows to teach them the importance of quality.

In case workers don't get the message Petofi reminds them. If customers reject a shipment, Petofi traces the mistake to the workers responsible and docks their wages. If a worker opens a beer on the job, he loses a third of his monthly wage. If the offense is serious, the worker is fired – a serious deterrent in a community with double-digit unemployment. Only a few workers have actually been disciplined.

Petofi offered early-retirement packages to its older workers, who have had more trouble kicking old habits. Now, the average age at the plant is 36, and the young staff is changing quickly. "Nothing like this has ever happened in our lives," says Miklos Toth, a 31-year-old printer. Mr. Toth, who no longer takes a full lunch period, misses the long coffee breaks and on-the-job beers. But with a $1,000-a-month salary, he figures, he has more money to buy beer after work.

Petofi still can slip. Shortly after winning a big order from Henkel KGa of Germany for detergent boxes with a rebate promotion, Petofi discovered that one of its workers was stealing the empty boxes and sending in the rebate coupons. Although the worker was fired Petofi regained Henkel's trust only with heavy persuasion. Occasionally, Petofi has trouble with wrong colors, late deliveries and slow pricing and payment systems.

Company More Competitive

But Petofi is steadily becoming more competitive with Western rivals. It has won awards from the World Packaging Organization and received its ISO-9000 certification last year. Aided by tax breaks and low labor costs, it has gross profit margins of about 30%, one-third higher than most of its competitors. It can undercut Western rivals' prices by 10% to 15%, taking away customers and driving down prices in the industry. Its output is growing 30% annually in a flat European market.

Development and design

Quality should be considered from the point at which a product is conceived and designed. It is difficult to rectify a poorly conceived product when it is at the production stage. The performance of the product, reliability, durability and the way the product is offered will all be elements of quality to the final customer. Design engineers should work closely with operating personnel to ensure that the designed product can be properly manufactured in order to give the desired quality.

Purchased materials

Raw materials and purchased component parts must be according to specification. If they are not, they will impact the quality of the final product. Suppliers must be aware of a company's quality requirements. An important criterion in the selection of a supplier is the quality of the production process employed and the products. (See Chapter 16 *Purchasing and Subcontracting*)

Manufacturing

Every employee in the work centres must be conscious of quality production. At an upstream work position the operator must pass to the downstream work position a product of specified quality. If a defect is detected, the worker should have the responsibility to stop the production line until the cause of the defect has been detected. (See Chapter 15, *Lean Production and Just-in-Time*).

Finished product to consumer

TQM must also include the packaging, shipping and, if necessary, the installation of the product. A poorly packaged product will degrade the perceived image of the product itself. There will be a similar effect if the product, such as a water heater, electric stove or

Figure 4.2 Quality and management: the requirements.

Figure 4.3 Quality chain in manufacturing.

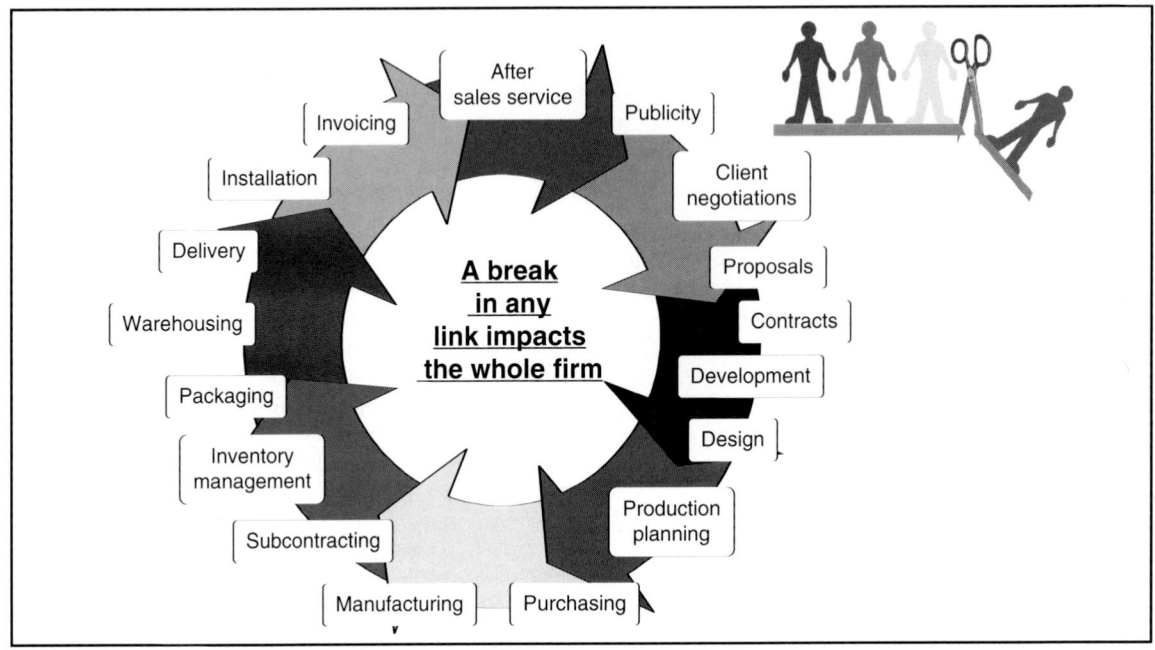

copier machine, is badly installed. Thus, even if the product was originally of specification quality, poor packaging, damage in shipping or incorrect installation may be equated by the customer with poor product quality. Thus, the often-subcontracted service functions of shipping, distribution and installation should also be committed to perfect quality.

Invoicing

Sloppy accounting can be translated by a customer to a poor-quality organization. In one incident, a customer ordered 1000 cases of beer, but he was invoiced for 2000! Not intentionally, but as a result of poor communication with the organization.

The service quality chain

In a service industry the chain analogy also exists, although the 'chain' is often shorter and the difference is that company personnel are dealing much more closely with the client than in the case of manufacturing. As such, quality in services includes how courteous company agents are with customers. Are they honest, responsive and patient, etc? Do they always have a smile? Illustrations of the chain-like reaction might include the following:

■ Accounting errors in a banking operation can destroy the confidence of the client in a particular bank.

■ Products delivered damaged will impact the image of a delivery firm.
■ Poor food on an airline flight, perhaps subcontracted, can discredit the airline company.
■ Unresponsive assistants in a retail store can tarnish the image of that retail firm.

Communication

Poor communication between parties concerned in an operation can result in perceived poor quality. In Figure 4.4 the final product delivered was not what the client had in mind and the perception is, therefore, of poor quality, even though the product itself was actually of good quality. The illustrated *perceived nonquality* is the difference been the quality level expected and what was delivered. At each step in the communication, the quality *degrades*. In Taguchi Methods (discussed in a later section) this is analogous to the quality loss function.

Necessity for total quality management

TQM activities, and procedures, need to be in place because:

■ TQM adds value to the services offered to the client.
■ All personnel are implicated, which improves motivation and commitment.

Figure 4.4 Quality level is reduced in the chain (communication).

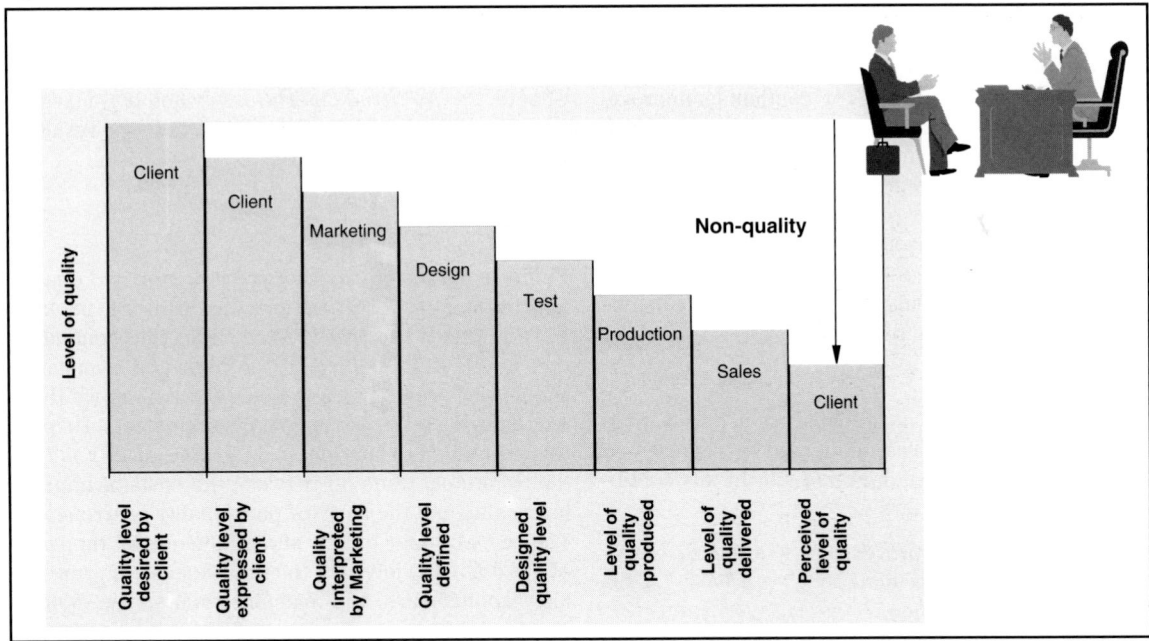

- TQM provides assurance that performance and processes are well understood.
- TQM is economic in the long term to both the company and its clients.

HJ Heinz, the food firm, introduced a TQM programme in the late 1980s and they believed they could reduce costs by over $250 million over three years by eliminating waste and rework.[5]

LEADING PROPONENTS OF QUALITY MANAGEMENT

There are many proponents who have developed concepts and ideas in quality management, most insisting that management accept responsibility for building good quality systems. Notable individuals include Deming, Juran, Crosby and Feigenbaum of the USA and Taguchi and Ishikawa of Japan. The philosophies of the US gurus are presented here. Taguchi and his quality methods are discussed later in this chapter and Ishikawa is discussed in Chapter 26, *Auditing Operations*.

Deming

Dr W. Edwards Deming, who died in 1994 and was by training a statistician, was a professor at New York University, as well as being a consultant to industry. After the Second World War he was invited to Japan at the request of the Japanese government to help improve the quality of Japanese products. He worked extensively with Japanese industries and was so successful that the government established the annual Deming prize for innovation in quality management. Deming is well known for establishing the following 14 criteria for quality improvement.[6]

Fourteen criteria for quality improvement

1 Create consistency of purpose toward product quality.
2 Refuse to allow commonly accepted levels of delay for mistakes, defective material and defective workmanship.
3 Build quality into the product; stop depending on inspections to catch problems.
4 Build long-term relationships with suppliers based on performance instead of awarding business on the basis of price.
5 Implement programmes for continuous improvements of costs, quality, service and productivity.
6 Start training to make full use of all employees.
7 Focus supervision on helping people to do a better job. Provide the tools and techniques for people to have pride of workmanship.
8 Eliminate fear and encourage two-way communication.

9 Break down barriers between departments and encourage problem solving through teamwork.

10 Eliminate the use of numerical goals, slogans and posters for the work force.

11 Use statistical methods for continuing improvement of quality and productivity and eliminate all standards prescribing numerical quotas.

12 Remove barriers to pride of workmanship.

13 Institute a vigorous programme of education and training to keep people abreast of new developments in materials, methods and technologies.

14 Clearly define management's permanent commitment to quality and productivity.

Wheel of quality

Deming's idea was that quality improvement is a cyclical and continuous process and could be represented by a wheel, as illustrated in Figure 4.5. In this continuum there were four stages.[7]

1 Plan for quality improvements – organize everything that needs to be done.

2 Put the plan into action.

3 Check the plan and verify that improvements are being obtained by measuring changes that are occurring.

4 Improve and correct the plan if necessary. Then repeat the cycle.

Juran

Joseph M. Juran was another pioneer, in the 1970s and 1980s, in helping the Japanese to improve product quality. Like Deming, he believed strongly in top-management commitment, support and involvement in quality and also in teamwork to continually strive to raise quality standards. He also focused on the customer in an effort to define quality as fitness for use and not necessarily according to written specifications. Juran popularized the 80/20 rule of Pareto (see Chapter 26, *Auditing Operations*) when he suggested that 80 per cent of a firm's problems are the result of only 20 per cent of the causes.

Crosby

Philip B. Crosby, another contributor to quality improvement in organizations, published a book in 1979 entitled, *Quality is Free*.[8] Here, he contended that any level of defects is too high and companies should put programmes in place that will move them continuously towards the goal of zero defects. He postulated that the main idea behind free quality is that the traditional trade-off between the costs of improving quality and the costs of poor quality is erroneous. The costs of poor quality should include all the costs of not doing the job right the first time: scrap, rework, lost labour-hours and machine hours, the hidden costs of customer ill will, lost sales and warranty costs. He strongly believed that the cost of poor quality is so understated that unlimited amounts can be profitably spent on improving quality. Quality-related costs are developed in more detail in the following section.

Feigenbaum

Armand V. Feigenbaum published a book in 1983 entitled *Total Quality Control*, in which he emphasized that the responsibility for quality has to rest with the persons who perform the associated work – secretaries, sales persons, machinists, suppliers, etc.[9] This is referred to as quality at the source and is discussed later in Chapter 15, *Lean Production and Just-in-Time*.

Feigenbaum, with his brother, created a consultancy business and worked extensively with US firms on quality issues. In their work the Feigenbaums estimated that the quality failure costs (cost of non-quality) average 10 per cent of gross sales in world-class US companies, but a high 25 per cent in most other major US companies. To illustrate, as a result of work by the Feigenbaums, Union Pacific (US railroads) has eliminated more than $700 million per year in quality-related costs since 1988 by upgrading scheduling, maintenance and customer service. Similarly, Tenneco (Energy) has increased operating yield by $250 million annually by improving quality.[10]

Figure 4.5 Quality improvement: a continuous circular process (Deming).

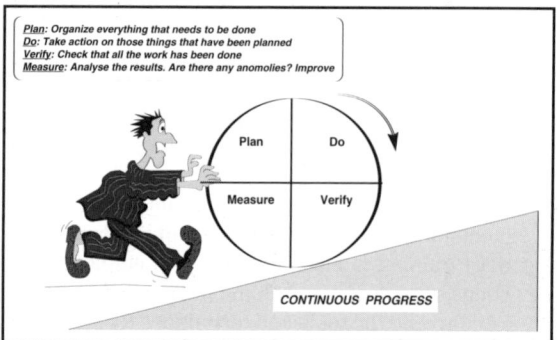

Plan: Organize everything that needs to be done
Do: Take action on those things that have been planned
Verify: Check that all the work has been done
Measure: Analyse the results. Are there any anomalies? Improve

Plan
Do
Measure
Verify

CONTINUOUS PROGRESS

COSTS OF QUALITY AND NON-QUALITY

The costs associated with quality, total quality costs, referred to by Crosby and the Feigenbaums, as discussed in the previous section, may be represented by an equation, as illustrated in Figure 4.6. This shows that total quality costs are the sum of four elements, external and internal costs and evaluation and prevention costs. These are dealt with in more detail below and are summarized in Figure 4.7.

External Faults

In an external fault, which is the cost of non-quality, a product has left the factory and is subsequently found to be defective. Either the fault is detected at the distribution level, the client determines the fault or a government determines that the product is faulty. Box 4.2 is an illustration.[11]

Costs resulting from external failure would include:

- time for an employee to deal with problem;
- replacing the defective item;
- use of a repair service to put the product back in order;
- transport cost to return product to the factory;
- loss of profit (client refuses to accept a replacement);
- deterioration of company image;
- potential loss of future clients;
- product, or process, liability suits.

A contributor to external failures is the rush to meet client demand so that products are produced rapidly and quality is put on the back burner. This has been one of the problems with the electronic lock systems now commonly used in hotels. In the USA, in only a few years, electronic locks have been installed in a third of the nation's 3.2 million hotel rooms and poor quality is evidenced by guests unable to get into their rooms or worse, unable to get out! The precise failure rate is not known, but Chicago-based EMG Associates Inc., which sells and services electronic locks, said that in 1995 it sold about 5 000 electronic locks, and repaired about 5 500.[12]

Product, or process, liability is one of the severest quality-related repercussions to a producer arising

Figure 4.6 Relationship concerning the cost of quality.

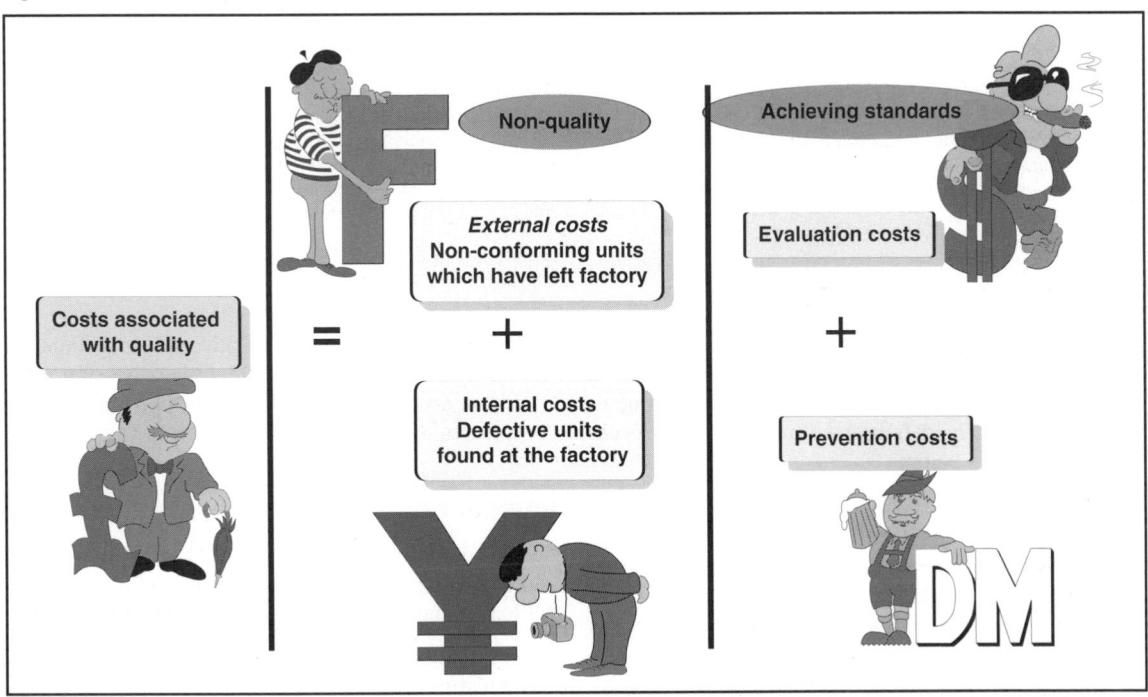

Figure 4.7 Cost associated with quality.

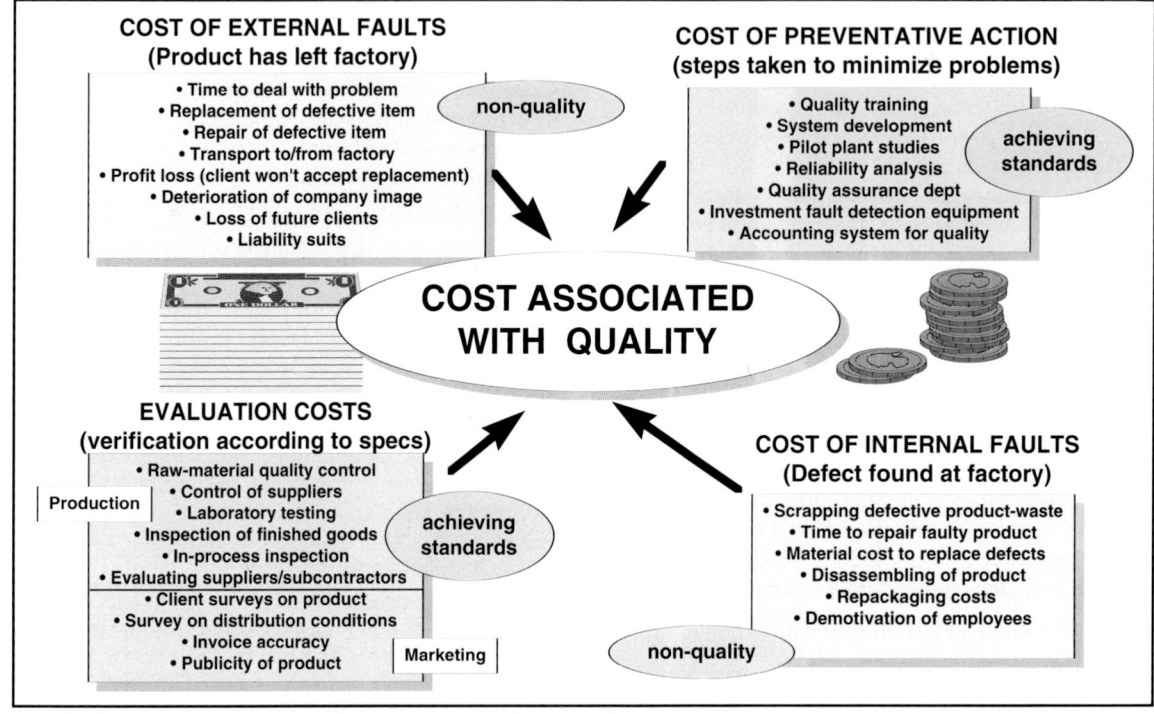

COST OF EXTERNAL FAULTS
(Product has left factory)
- Time to deal with problem
- Replacement of defective item
- Repair of defective item
- Transport to/from factory
- Profit loss (client won't accept replacement)
- Deterioration of company image
- Loss of future clients
- Liability suits

non-quality

COST OF PREVENTATIVE ACTION
(steps taken to minimize problems)
- Quality training
- System development
- Pilot plant studies
- Reliability analysis
- Quality assurance dept
- Investment fault detection equipment
- Accounting system for quality

achieving standards

COST ASSOCIATED WITH QUALITY

EVALUATION COSTS
(verification according to specs)
- Raw-material quality control
- Control of suppliers
- Laboratory testing
- Inspection of finished goods
- In-process inspection
- Evaluating suppliers/subcontractors
- Client surveys on product
- Survey on distribution conditions
- Invoice accuracy
- Publicity of product

Production

achieving standards

Marketing

COST OF INTERNAL FAULTS
(Defect found at factory)
- Scrapping defective product-waste
- Time to repair faulty product
- Material cost to replace defects
- Disassembling of product
- Repackaging costs
- Demotivation of employees

non-quality

Box 4.2 Vehicle Recalls

Automobile makers recalled a whopping 11 million vehicles in the US in 1993 to fix a range of defects. This was the most since 1977, when 12.9 million vehicles were recalled. Included in the recalls were the Honda Accord and Prelude, Ford Taurus, Chevy Pickup, Volkswagen, Hyundai, Audi and Jaguar. As a percentage of vehicles sold, Honda Motor topped the list of the six largest automobile makers, recalling 966 572 Accords and Preludes, or 134 per cent of the 716 546 cars it sold last year. The recall came after Honda had already recalled 900 000 vehicles in 1992 for the same problem, petrol leaks in older cars that can cause fires. Hyundai sold 108 796 vehicles in 1993 but recalled 515 000 of its 1986 through 1989 Excels the manual transmissions of which would sometimes jam, causing the vehicle to stop suddenly. The industry's recall total of 11 million vehicles last year was up sharply from 10.1 million in 1992, and 9.7 million in 1991.

From *Wall Street Journal Europe* 24 February 1994

---

from external faults. The limits of liability vary from country to country according to national legislation. In the USA, liability settlements are very much higher than in Europe. The definitions of product and process liability are given below.

Product and process liability

■ The risk that a producer, or others, may have to bear the responsibility for the personal injury, or harm, resulting from the use of a product or process that they have supplied.

■ The legal retribution that may have to be made by those responsible for supplying a product or process that causes personal injury, or harm.

■ The onus on a producer, or others, for the financial loss or other harm suffered by the users of a product or process that they were responsible for putting into circulation.

Internal Faults

An internal fault is also part of the cost of non-quality and this is where the defect is found before the product leaves the factory. The costs may include:

■ scrapping the defective product so that there would be material waste;

■ reprocessing time for employees to repair the faulty product;

- material cost to replace the defective product;
- disassembling the product;
- repackaging costs;
- management/employee irritation, which could lead to reduced productivity.

Preventive Measures

As preventive measures, a firm develops methods to eliminate, or minimize, quality problems and so these become costs to achieve quality. They may include:

- quality-related employee training programmes;
- systems development for quality improvement;
- pilot plant to use for quality programmes;
- a Quality Assurance Department.

Detection and/or evaluation

Detection and/or evaluation would include activities associated with verifying that a product is according to specification quality and so again these aspects represent costs to obtain quality. They might be divided into costs at the production stage and costs at the marketing stage.

Production

Costs at the production stage would include:

- sampling of raw materials for conformity;
- inspection of in-process products;
- inspection of finished goods;
- laboratory testing for conformity;
- client surveys for opinion on the quality of manufactured products;
- evaluating suppliers, licensees or subcontractors for quality conformance.

Marketing

Costs at the marketing stage would include:

- client surveys for opinion on the quality of final products;
- survey of distribution chain, including transportation systems;
- accuracy of invoicing documents;
- presentation and display of final products.

Percentage cost of quality

If the above four elements are considered as parts of the cost of quality, then a mathematical relationship, as a percentage, is:

$$\text{Cost of quality} = \frac{C_e + C_i + C_d + C_p}{C_B + C_e + C_i + C_d + C_p} \times 100$$

Where:
C_e is the cost of external faults;
C_i is the cost of internal faults;
C_d is the cost of detection;
C_p is the cost of prevention;
C_B is the measured base production cost (no costs for quality).

In practice, it is difficult to separate all the costs, but even making an estimation would give a manufacturer or service operator some idea as to how much is involved. As an illustration, the following section summarizes the costs associated with quality for a food packing and distribution firm in France.[13]

Food distribution firm

This company has two principal activities. One is the reception of bulk dry foods, including rice, beans, herbs, etc. and then packaging them on automatic filling machines into one and five kilogram sacks for delivery to supermarkets. The second activity is the mixing, processing, bottle filling and packaging of soft drinks, such as cola, orange, lemon, etc. also for supermarket clients.

The company recognized that it had a quality problem and its first step in 1995 to tackle the situation was to determine the total cost of all the quality-related activities in the firm. To do this, it determined the time spent on quality problems for each department and multiplied this by the average salary to come up with a cost. Prevention and detection costs were based on the time spent on all the associated laboratory work and control studies carried out in the packing area. The costs of non-quality were the time spent on activities such as:

- quality control of raw materials;
- maintenance because of unplanned machine shutdowns;
- taking back poor quality products from clients;
- time lost in reception or production because bags would break.

Figure 4.8 summarizes the results. On a percentage basis these were:

- internal costs 71.1 per cent;
- external costs 0.2 per cent;
- detection 12.8 per cent;
- prevention 15.9 per cent.

The total was equivalent to 8.2 per cent of revenues, or FF 211 000 per employee.

Figure 4.8 Cost of non-quality/quality for a food packing and distribution firm.

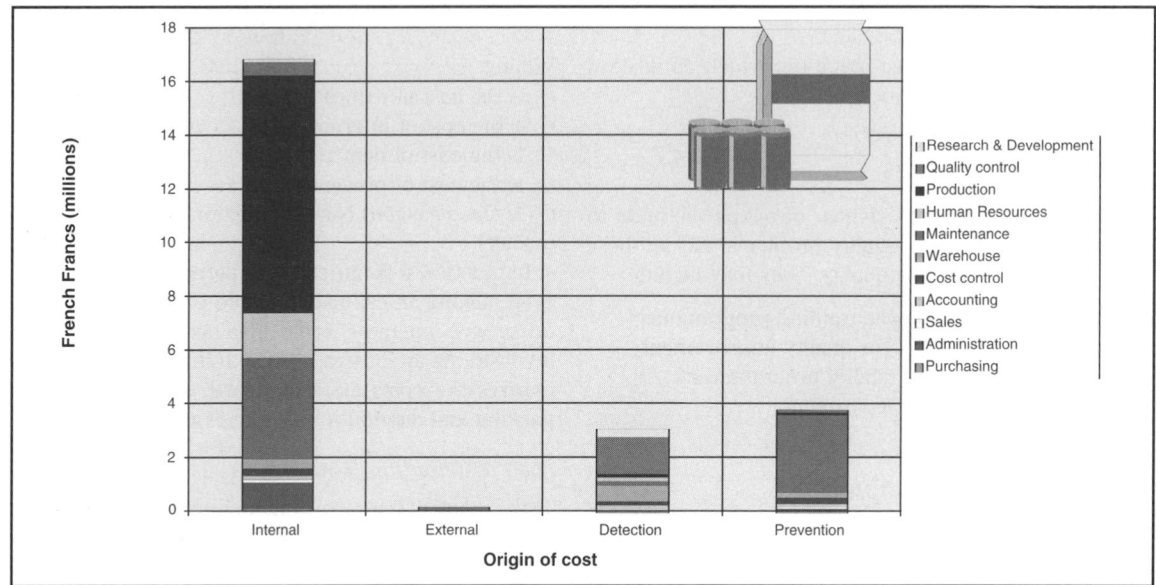

Costs are long term

Changing levels of quality does not happen overnight. Improved results from training programmes, design modifications or installing fault-detection equipment take time but in the long run, the benefits are positive. A graph showing the direction of the changes, is given in Figure 4.9. The explanations are:

■ *No quality programme*. With no quality management programme in place, then additional manufacturing or service related costs would be incurred arising from external and internal faults. This is represented by the upper curve labelled 'Costs with no quality programme'.

■ *With a quality programme*. With a quality programme in place, then, over time, both external and internal costs would decline as illustrated by the curve, 'Costs with quality programme'. On the contrary, detection and prevention costs would generally increase, although they would probably even off as personnel were effective in managing the detection and prevention systems. The net result is that additional costs would be less than with no such quality programme, as illustrated by the vertical difference between the two curves.

Costs and level of quality design

Quality has a cost and the more one improves a product through quality enhancements, the higher are produc-

tion related costs. These higher production costs are passed along to the consumer. However, there is a limit to how much a customer is willing to pay for a certain product – 'You get what you pay for.' It makes no sense to 'gold plate' an article if it is priced out of the market.

The type of relationship that exists between the product price and the production cost is shown in Figure 4.10. The shape of the curve will differ according to the product, quality improvements and the like. However, the relationship will be similar. The cost of improving the quality design will increase in an exponential form. The price a customer would be willing to pay will level out as the additional quality enhancements add no marked increase in value in the eyes of the customer. Some illustrations are:

■ *Books*. A hardback book is more attractive and durable, and to many represents better quality than

Figure 4.9 Long-term quality programmes reduce cost.

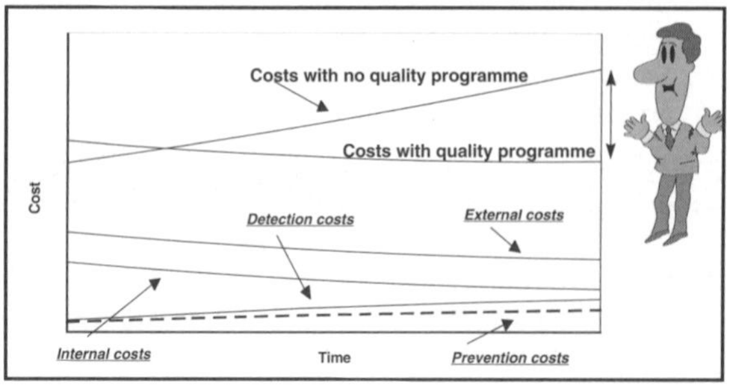

Figure 4.10 Limit to quality design.

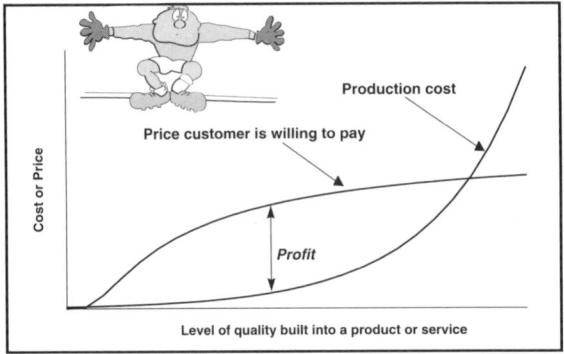

the same text as a softback. Very often a publisher will price a hardback version higher than a soft. Customers, particularly students, may not necessarily be willing to pay for such hardback editions when a softback will suffice. After all, it is the text inside which is important.

■ *Automobiles.* An automobile can be fitted with leather upholstery, a teak-wood dashboard, stainless-steel wheel mouldings and the like. However, this would price it out of the market for many people, who see a car as a basic utility vehicle. Only for clients who will pay the high price, such as for a Jaguar, are these fittings acceptable.

■ *Jewellery.* With new techniques, it is hard for most people to see the difference between costume and fine jewellery. For many customers, the price and appearance of costume jewellery is sufficient as fine jewellery may be outside their budget.

■ *Furniture.* Similarly with furniture, new manufacturing techniques make possible a wide range of furniture constructed from compressed wood chips or plywood. Finishing the product with oak, walnut or teak laminations gives it the same appearance as if it were made from solid wood.

■ *Matches.* Matches are produced at low quality levels and low production costs per unit. People do not care as long as they light.

■ *Nails and screws.* Customers will not pay the price for precision stainless steel nails or screws when simple carbon-steel products do the same job.

QUALITY CONTROL

Quality control covers the operational techniques and activities used to satisfy quality requirements including monitoring a process and eliminating the causes of unsatisfactory performance at all stages of the quality chain. The quality control programme depends very much on the industry, but an organization might have in place a quality control programme for Manufacturing, Purchasing, Customer Relations, Transportation, Warehousing, etc. Quality control will almost certainly include statistical quality control, which comprises the analytical techniques for verifying conformity for a process or for a product. These are dealt with in detail in Chapter 23, *Statistical Quality Control*. The purpose of this section is to highlight some of the terms and qualitative aspects related to quality control.

Defective product

A defective product can mean a broad range of problems. If for example the product is a television, it might be defective because it plainly does not work, the reception is poor, because it makes a strange noise or, say, because the screen has a scratch. The strict definition of a defective product is one where there is non-fulfilment of intended usage requirements. This means that there is a departure or absence of one or more quality characteristics from intended usage requirements.

Reliability or durability

Durability, or reliability, in quality control is to verify that products function, without failing for a reasonable period of time, under prescribed or stated conditions. (Reliability is discussed further in Chapter 19, *Reliability and Maintenance*). For example:

■ grocery bags that do not collapse when full of food items;
■ zippers on clothing that are reliable for the duration of the life of the garment;
■ filler caps on bottles that do not leak.

Reproducibility

Reproducibility in quality control is the ability to produce products that are reproducible in quality and in their characteristics. For example, reproducibility according to colour might be applied to textiles, paint colours, photographic reprints, food dressing, wall paper and carpets.

Quality control departments

Historically, and even now in some firms, manufacturing, engineering and construction companies had quality control departments. Those in Quality Control were staff, as opposed to line, personnel whose responsibility was to establish quality specifications and monitor, measure and report on the quality of products or designs produced by the corresponding department or work centre.

In production, the principal responsibility was to maintain throughput, keep unit costs low and produce at an acceptable quality level. In many instances, the main criteria for judging production were quotas and costs. Thus, as a result, quality took a back seat and this put Production and Quality Control departments in conflict. Quality Control policed Production to ensure that quality was according to standards. Production tried to meet their quantity quotas, but the surveillance by Quality Control created stress in the organization. Quality Control was not a line function, and had no responsibility to shut down an operation or to enforce design changes.

To manage an organization so that quality takes precedence, people must work as a team. Sales, design engineers, production, suppliers, maintenance and the like have to take the responsibility for the quality of their work. Their 'customer', be it end user of the product, the next work station, an industrial client or a contractor, has to be provided with a product that meets the quality expectations or specifications, that is, quality at the source as espoused by Feigenbaum. To achieve quality at the source, the following should be the rule, and not the exception:

- *Responsibility.* Complete quality responsibility is assigned to the person performing the work, that is, quality becomes a line, rather than a staff, function.
- *Self-inspection.* The production function is enlarged, so that workers inspect their own work. If workers are properly informed and trained, this makes the activity more motivating. In this case, the number of staff people formerly involved in quality control can be reduced and surplus personnel reassigned to the value-added production operation.
- *Remove the policeman.* The Quality Control department, rather than being a policeman, is responsible for establishing the quality specifications, for training personnel in quality control and providing whatever assistance is needed in quality matters. (Very often today, Quality Control Departments are referred to as Quality Assurance Departments.)

Inspection in quality control

Ideally, no inspection is needed if quality work is performed a hundred per cent of the time. Unfortunately, this is not the case and so inspection, preferably at a minimum level, is performed in certain circumstances. The term 'inspection' covers all activities such as measuring, examining, testing or gauging one or more characteristics of a product, process or service by sampling and then comparing these results with designated requirements. (See also Chapter 23, *Statistical Quality Control*). Some tools for quality control inspection of products would include:

- surface finishing gauges to test surface finish;
- weigh scales;
- callipers to measure diameter;
- chemical analysis;
- electronic meters;
- a viscosity meter for measuring the 'pouring' characteristics of lubricating oils.

Extent of inspection

The extent of inspection depends on the type of products produced. Where the product has a high value, every product coming off the production line is subject to some level of final inspection. This is the case for automobiles, computers and electrical switch gear for instance. In many cases, because of economics, not all final manufactured products are 100 per cent inspected. This is the case for standard products coming off an assembly line, such as canned beer, screws or books. Where destructive testing is required, such as would be the case for ammunition, fire extinguishers and concrete, 100 per cent testing would destroy all the output! In all these cases, samples are selected at random, tested and, on the basis of statistical analysis, decisions are made whether to accept or reject the entire lot (Chapter 23, *Statistical Quality Control*).

In sampling there is a risk. Some faulty items would be analysed before they reach the customer, but other faulty items would escape inspection and end up with the customer. However, as there is a cost associated with inspection, there is an optimum level, or a balance between the amount of inspection employed and the 'cost' associated with defective products reaching the market place, as illustrated in Figure 4.11. The larger the proportion of final products inspected, the greater is the cost. However, in this case the risk of defective units being passed onto the customer is lower, and so the cost of non-quality is lower. On the opposite side, with little inspection, there is a lower inspection cost, but a greater chance of defective items being passed along to the customer. The graphical illustration is similar to inventory movements in balancing purchasing costs and holding costs presented in Chapter 11, *Inventory Management*.

When and where to inspect

When it is uneconomic to inspect all products, the following are some general guidelines when to inspect in an operation:

Figure 4.11 Balance between inspection and cost.

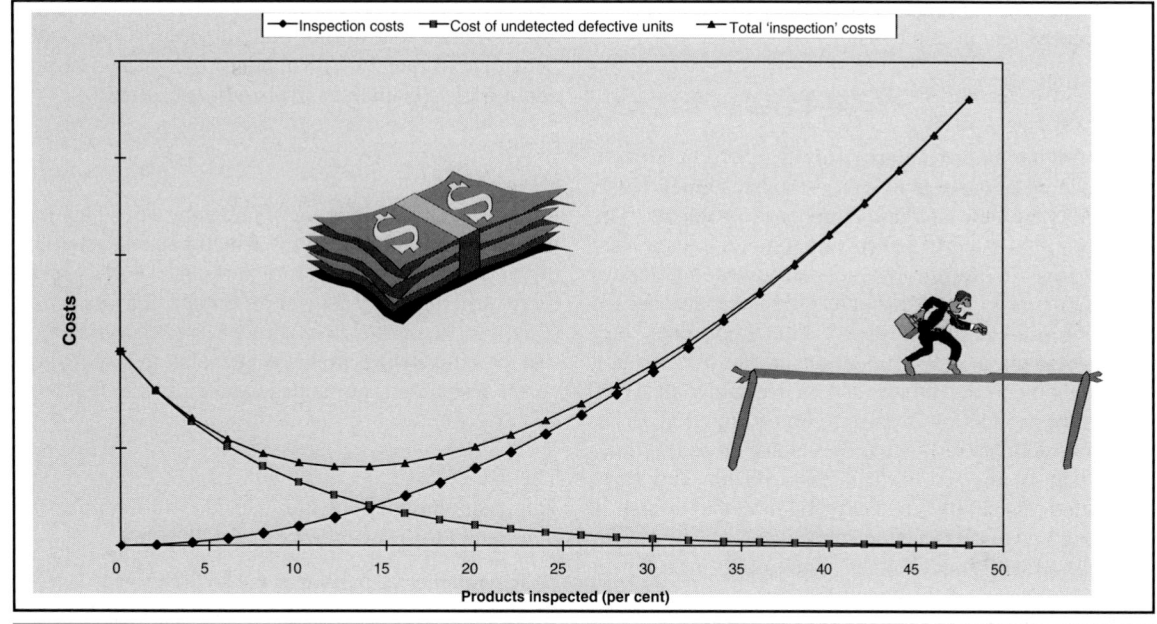

- Raw materials and purchased parts, inspect at a supplier's facility. This will help to avoid reception of non-conforming products.
- Inspect on receipt of supplier's products if inspection at the supplier's location is not possible. (Starting with faulty raw materials will be a bad start in the quality chain.)
- Inspect after a new team has been working on an operation.
- Inspect at licensee's facility to verify processing conditions (brewery for example).
- Inspect at a franchise facility to verify quality standards (McDonald's for example).
- Inspect after operations that are complex and are known to produce faulty items (intricate soldering or assembly).
- Inspect before costly operations. Do not waste costly labour or machine time on items that are already defective. In a book printing/binding operation, to print a large quantity of books that have not been well proofed is very costly.
- Inspect before an irreversible process, e.g. in manufacturing some plastics. Polyethylene is made from ethylene and, if the ethylene feed is not according to specification, then the final product will be off specification.
- Inspect before operations that cover up defects. Painting, plating, soldering, and assembling can often hide defects.

- Inspect before assembly operations that cannot be undone.
- On automatic machines, inspect first and last on the production runs, but fewer in between.
- Inspect finished products if it is economic to do so. Customer satisfaction is important, the firm's image is at stake and the firm is liable for faulty products. Repairing or replacing defective products in the field is more expensive than at the factory. If this occurs, the seller is probably responsible for shipping costs and a client may hold up final payments pending delivery of non-defective goods.
- Inspect distributors or transport operators to verify their handling practices.

Traceability

Traceability in quality control is the ability to trace the history, application or location of an item or activity by means of recorded identification. The identification may be a date stamp, a lot number or, very often, a bar code. Traceability is a requirement of the ISO certification discussed later.

QUALITY-RELATED PRACTICES

Companies can improve upon the quality of their products, services, processes or organization by adopting certain practices. The following sections give illustrations and many of them, as indicated, are described in detail elsewhere in this book.

Continuous improvement, Kaizen

A continuous improvement process (CIP), or Kaizen, means continuously trying to establish higher levels of quality by, say, isolating sources of problems. The ultimate goal is zero defects, the objective espoused by Crosby. In Kaizen the concept is 'don't always strive for new breakthrough products, but try to improve on existing designs'. This logic was very much evident in the production of the Volkswagen Beetle, which was introduced in Germany in 1937 and, until production in Europe was stopped in 1978, over 22 million VW Beetles were sold, more than any other car in the world. The basic design and style remained essentially unchanged for close to half a century, but quality-related improvements were continually added. Today, in the automobile industry in Germany, the article in Box 4.3 illustrates the concept of Kaizen at Opel (a division of General Motors) and Robert Bosch an automotive supplier.[14]

Phantom customer in services

Phantom customers are used, for example, in automobile dealerships, banks, retail stores and restaurants to monitor the quality of its operations. At any unspecified time a *customer*, who is in reality a company employee, visits the site requesting a service. When the service is completed, this *customer* evaluates the service outlet on quality of work, price, time and the way the customer was treated.

Taguchi methods

Taguchi methods, named after Genichi Taguchi, are methods aimed at quality improvement in both product and process design. They are based on making designs robust by building in tolerances for manufacturing variables known to be unavoidable. Taguchi's philosophy is that missing the quality target in a consistent manner can be better than hitting it a few times with the rest being scattered all over the board.[15] The three basic concepts in the Taguchi Methods are presented in Chapter 6, *Design of the Product*.

Activity based costing

Conventional cost management does not put a cost on reworking, delays, inventory storage or bottlenecks. Activity based costing (ABC) is a technique that measures costs at each step of the supply chain, or the production process, in a way that uncovers inefficiencies and activities that do not add value and often lead to poor overall quality. The concept is reviewed in more detail in the Chapter 15, *Financial Analysis*.

Keep designs simple

Keep designs simple is the philosophy of reducing the number of parts in a product which helps to minimizes the probability of error. More parts in a product means there are more areas where things can go wrong. (Chapter 19, *Reliability and Maintenance* analyses this logic further). Simple designs also reduce material costs, assembly time, and inventory costs. Below are two illustrations.

General Motors

The rear bumper of the Seville automobile was redesigned with the following results.[16]

- The number of parts was cut by half to 63.
- The assembly time was reduced by 57 per cent to less than eight minutes.
- The estimated annual labour saving was $462 000.

IBM

IBM's Laser Printer has fewer parts, and fewer screws, than the comparable Hewlett-Packard LaserJet III.[17]

Just-in-time

Just-in-time (JIT) production (covered in detail in Chapter 15, *Lean Production and Just-in-Time*) is a management practice where the exact quantities of a product are produced, or delivered, just when needed. Delay times, and inventory levels, are kept to an absolute minimum since the philosophy is that unnecessary inventories, or delays, mean an inefficient use of resources. Thus, practising JIT enforces adherence to product quality.

Benchmarking

Benchmarking, in global terms, is the comparison of one firm's business practices with others. From a quality point of view, however, it is the comparison of product quality between firms. For example, in a 1994 benchmarking study, by J D Power and associates, of new-car defect rates in the first 90 days of ownership, Toyota scored 70 per 100 vehicles to Chrysler's 125.[18] Benchmarking is described in detail in Chapter 16, *Auditing Operations*.

Box 4.3 On the line. Automotive suppliers in Germany take aim at years of inefficiency. Facing likely shakeout, plants try Japanese techniques to boost competitiveness. Catching up in common sense. By Brandon Mitchener, Staff Reporter

EDENKOBEN, Germany – These are tough times for the 3,000 German companies that make auto parts.

One in three is losing money. One in two plans to shift some production outside Germany, according to a government survey. And the German Automotive Industry Association estimates that 75,000 German supplier jobs – one in every five – will be lost in the next five years.

But a visit to the Edenkoben plant of Walker Gillet Europe GmbH shows that, despite all the industry's problems, German auto suppliers can survive – if they cut away many years' accumulation of corporate fat and inefficiency.

The plant, located 120 kilometers south-west of Frankfurt, makes automotive exhaust systems. Using Japanese *kaizen* management methods – which seek to boost efficiency through continual improvement – the factory reduced reject rates more than 5% and cut inventories to one-two days from four-five days. Output rose 15% last year, and helped Walker Gillet – part of the automotive unit of U.S. conglomerate Tenneco Inc. – return to profitability after losing money the previous two years.

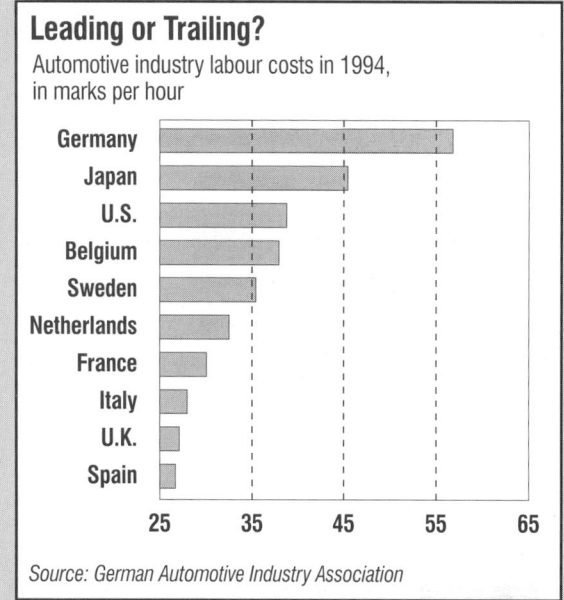

Leading or Trailing?

Automotive industry labour costs in 1994, in marks per hour

Germany
Japan
U.S.
Belgium
Sweden
Netherlands
France
Italy
U.K.
Spain

25   35   45   55   65

Source: German Automotive Industry Association

Closing a Gap

"It wouldn't have been possible under the old system," says Klaus Bellgardt, a Walker Gillet manager, shaking his head at the waste that used to exist in the plant.

German industry faces myriad problems: oppressively high wage levels, combined with generous hours and holidays; hefty tax and social-security levies; restrictive environmental regulations; and slow approval processes. IKB Deutsche Industriebank AG, which has many customers among small and medium-size German suppliers, warned in a recent report that the situation for suppliers is getting "riskier."

Indeed, experts warn that those who can afford to get out of the automotive-supplies business might be wise to do so, because there's little doubt that the sector faces a shakeout likely to claim many victims. Analysts also note that the kaizen continual-improvement system may only help some German manufacturers start to close a broad gap between them and their chief industrial rivals. After all, Walker Gillet and other automotive companies are only now seizing on a system embraced in the U.S. some 10 years ago and in Japan much earlier.

In addition, kaizen-style improvements are often no more than a starting point for German companies such as Daimler-Benz AG and Hoechst AG, which can only become more competitive by divesting themselves of peripheral, often unprofitable businesses and concentrating on what they do best.

Nonetheless, as the Edenkoben plant shows, there is a lot of entrenched inefficiency that German companies can root out to improve their health, even at times when demand is slack and manufacturing conditions unfavorable. And catching up through kaizen is better than slipping further behind.

"There's so much waste in most companies that if you look at it as reserves, they're rich," says Peter Willats, a co-founder and managing partner of the Kaizen Institute. The Zurich-based consultancy sells European manufacturers on the idea of using kaizen, a term popularized by Japanese

management guru Masaaki Imai in a 1986 book of the same name.

While German technology is generally considered state of the art, manufacturing methods often lag standards in Japan and even the U.S.

The waste message hasn't been lost on many big German companies, which have had to make dramatic gains in efficiency to offset the rise in the value of the mark and other competitive disadvantages. Between 1992 and 1994, the productivity of German industry jumped almost 20% as a result of this corporate drive, according to the Organization for Economic Cooperation and Development. In many cases, the higher productivity has come about as a result of layoffs that have pushed German unemployment to postwar highs. But as Walker Gillet and many other companies are finding, there are other ways of becoming more efficient.

German auto makers have been in the vanguard of companies adapting Japanese-style lean-management and lean-production techniques, and profits in the industry are on the rise. A spokesman for Volkswagen AG says the company has conducted 14,000 kaizen-style workshops in its factories over the past three years.

But auto makers' suppliers, most of which are barely sputtering along, have only begun to change. The Kaizen Institute's first customers in Germany were Adam Opel AG, a unit of General Motors Corp., and Robert Bosch GmbH, one of the country's biggest suppliers. Now, the institute is increasingly advising companies lower down on the automotive food chain.

Employing Common Sense

While traditional consulting often aims to bring about dramatic cost savings immediately, the kaizen method, according to Mr. Willats, employs common sense to identify and eliminate waste through continual improvement.

In a huge company like VW, where factories are still going through their first brush with kaizen-style workshops, it often takes years to determine whether the improvement

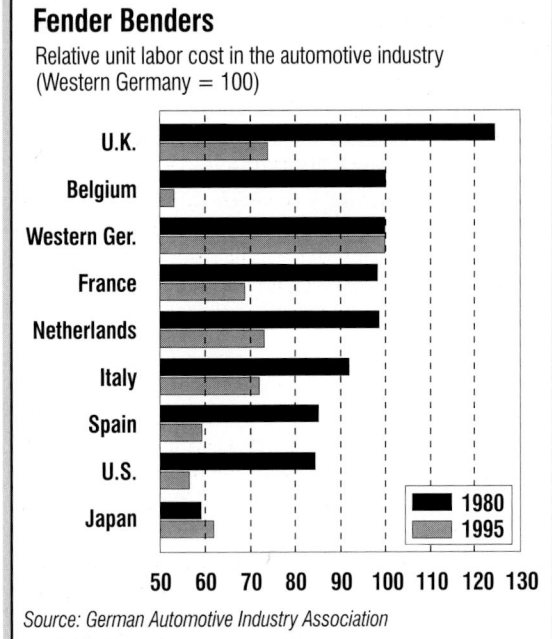

Fender Benders

Relative unit labor cost in the automotive industry
(Western Germany = 100)

Legend:
- 1980
- 1995

Countries: U.K., Belgium, Western Ger., France, Netherlands, Italy, Spain, U.S., Japan

X-axis: 50 60 70 80 90 100 110 120 130

Source: German Automotive Industry Association

process has become "continual." "Successive improvements naturally get smaller, but by the time we're through with the first pass, it'll be time to start over at the beginning," says Peter Schlelein, a VW spokesman.

When the kaizen warriors descended on Edenkoben in August 1994, the common-sense problems were fairly obvious. At one large horseshoe-shaped station where two pieces of a muffler housing were welded together, there could be as much as two to three days' worth of unfinished work accumulating along the line between the start and end of the process. Now, that's down to one day. Instead of being moved around by forklift in bulk, parts are placed in small bins and pushed around by hand.

At another station, Walker Gillet was able to free up 20% more space, reduce the distance parts had to travel between manufacturing steps by 42% and increase output by 40% – and all in one week. "The traditional German approach would have been to buy a singing and dancing Rolls Royce of new machinery," says Mr. Bellgardt, a managementboard member in charge of original-equipment operations. "We just moved things around."

Throughout the plant, black floors that hid oil leaks were replaced with colorful, easy-to-clean flooring; tools were color-coded to match the section where they were used and mostly put within arm's reach instead of in a central spot; and right angles were eliminated to simplify movements.

Reaping the Benefits

As quickly as the changes were made, the benefits became apparent.

The setup time to change dies at one seaming station was cut to 12 hours from 80 hours. Preventive maintenance reduced the need for repairs and downtime. And while competitors were giving discounts that eroded their margins – Walker Gillet's customers demanded rebates ranging from 20% to 24% last year alone – "we were able to hold our

ground" and salvage a small profit, says Mr. Bellgardt, despite flat sales at 300 million marks ($201.9 million).

Both GM and VW gave Walker Gillet awards for its improvements. Porsche AG plans to dump its current supplier for complete exhaust systems and make Walker Gillet its sole source as of June.

Walker Gillet has been so successful at cutting its own costs that one of its own workers, a veteran of 40 years of "old system" manufacturing, is now conducting kaizen workshops at Walker Gillet suppliers.

"We've recognized that this is the only way to be more competitive than we have been," Mr. Bellgardt says.

Strong Mark Strikes Again

To be sure, the kaizen method can't work miracles in a country hampered by one of the world's strongest currencies. Despite all the improvements, the Edenkoben plant lost 40 million marks in business to sister plants in Britain and Spain. Like many automotive suppliers caught up in a wave of mergers and acquisitions world-wide, Walker Gillet has to contend not only with other competitors in Germany, but also with its own eight factories elsewhere in Europe.

Moreover, some analysts warn that kaizen-based changes could prove to be only stop-gap measures. "These programs have been a very important aspect of the improved productivity of German industry, but for most German companies they are a defensive, catch-up operation to minimize the widening competitive gap," says Edmund Chew, an analyst at Auto Business Ltd., in a recent report for UBS Phillips & Drew.

Strategic Partnerships

Many analysts and industry experts say companies also must standardize their products to improve economies of scale, reduce their work force at every opportunity and seek strong partners.

Robert Fieten, a professor of process management in Duesseldorf, Germany, told a recent meeting of supplier-company executives that one of their best chances of surviving lies in entering strategic partnerships with competitors, particularly for research and development and purchasing. Many foreign companies still find German suppliers attractive potential partners or acquisitions for both their proprietary technology and their access to German auto makers.

But Mr. Fieten said many outfits should consider finding another line of work before their balance sheets are completely ruined. That's especially true for smaller companies without the resources to become single-source suppliers for increasingly internationally minded customers, he argued. "One strategy many suppliers have to consider is getting out of the automotive business altogether," he said.

Mr. Willats at the Kaizen Institute agrees: "Any supplier who can get out of the business is trying to do so." But for the bigger companies like Walker Gillet that have too many fixed assets to sell, the only way out is to soldier on, and there "kaizen" can help, he believes.

"There's so much waste that suppliers have a chance to improve faster than their customers," Mr. Willats says.

Wall Street Journal Europe, 6 February 1996
Reprinted by permission of *Wall Street Journal Europe*,
© 1996 Dow Jones & Company, Inc.
All Rights Reserved Worldwide.

Re-engineering

Re-engineering, or Business Process Re-engineering (BPR), is an idea that had its roots in the USA in the late 1980s and has been taking hold in Europe. It means a complete revaluation and shake-up of a firm with the ultimate objective of increasing its performance, to be more flexible, more reactive and closer in touch with the needs of the client. With this increase in performance is included (it is hoped) improved quality of products and services. Re-engineering is further reviewed in Chapter 7, *Process Design and the Operations Network*.

Downsizing and quality

Re-engineering, or restructuring, has been practised by many companies since the late 1980s. The practice has in many cases been synonymous with downsizing, or employee redundancy, as illustrated in Table 4.1 for five major US companies.[9]

As a result of this type of layoffs, re-engineering, which is supposed to make a company more reactive and more quality conscious, is sometimes having the reverse effect. This situation is underscored in Box 4.4 which discusses the practices of Deming to illustrate the point.[20]

Poka Yoke

The concept of Poka Yoke is a fail-safe approach with the objective of increasing the reliability, and thus the quality, of a product, process or service. The concept, which is discussed in detail in Chapter 19, *Reliability and Maintenance*, means incorporating into the system fail-safe devices, perhaps mechanical or electrical, to prevent inadvertent mistakes by the user or the operator.

INTERNATIONAL STANDARDS ORGANIZATION AND ISO-9000

International Standards Organization

The International Standards Organization (ISO), is an international, non-governmental organization, whose principal goal is to decrease trade barriers by promoting worldwide product standardization, such as in manufacturing practices, paper sizes and film speeds. The ISO was founded in 1947, with headquarters in Geneva Switzerland. There are 119 countries in the organization, including the USA represented by the American Standards Institute (ANSI), UK by the British Standards Institute (BSI), France by the Association Française de Normalisation (AFNOR), Germany by Deutsches Institut für Normung (DIN) and Ireland by National Standards Authority of Ireland (NSAI).

Europe and ISO Quality Standardization

The ISO-9000 series is a series of quality standards, launched in 1987 by the International Standards Organization and aimed at assuring quality consistency in the business of both manufacturing and service organizations.

ISO-9000 is based on the British Standard BS 5750, which was put in place in 1979. BS 5750 itself was modelled on Britain's military procurement standards to ensure the quality of UK-manufactured defence equipment and it also proved a useful marketing tool.[21] BS 5750 was initially introduced into the rest of Europe as EN 29000, from which was developed the ISO standards. European firms have adopted the ISO series as a measure of the quality standards of an operation, design or process, although adoption of the norms is completely voluntary.[22] As of the first half of 1993, it was estimated that over 34 000 European companies were registered in compliance with the ISO-9000 standards, compared to over 1 000 companies in the United States.[23] In France, the ISO norms were adopted for the first time in 1989.

Basic requirements for certification

The basic requirements for ISO-9000 certification are:

- *Documentation*. Write down everything that has to be done, that is, rigorously develop the required documentation of procedures for carrying out any activity in the operation.

Table 4.1 Lay offs in five major US companies

Company	Activity	Layoffs	Since	Net earnings (millions)
IBM	Computers	63 000	July 1993	-$4 965 (1992)
Sears	Retailing	50 000	January 1993	-$3 932 (1992)
AT&T	Telecommunications	40 000	January 1996	$270 (1995 estimate)
Boeing	Aircraft	28 000	February 1993	$552 (1992)
Digital Equipment	Computers	20 000	May 1994	-$251 (1993)

Box 4.4 The straining of quality. American companies are discovering what happens when total quality meets total chaos

HAS life lost a little of its quality for American firms? W. Edwards Deming, the American who set off the total-quality revolution, is dead. Joseph Juran, the co-founder of the quality movement, gave his farewell lecture tour last year. The American Quality Foundation has been disbanded. And, tellingly, applications for the Baldrige award, America's prestigious prize for quality, have slumped. In 1994 only 71 firms vied for a Baldrige, a fall of a third in three years.

Optimists believe that waning interest in the Baldrige award is evidence of American firms' new-found self-confidence in the quality of their quality—after all, why bother to take part if you know you're the tops? Indeed, a recent study by Boston University, Tokyo's Waseda University and INSEAD, a European business school, concluded that American companies had caught up with and overtaken their Japanese competitors in terms of quality.

Perhaps. But the Baldrige's decline is more a reflection of corporate America's increasing tussle with total-quality management (TQM). Even the 1980s' most ardent adherents of quality are finding that TQM does not readily blend with wave after wave of restructuring, downsizing and re-engineering. And the challenge of developing products and bringing them to market ever more swiftly—especially in industries where prices are tumbling, such as computers—adds to the strain on TQM. So far, America is bearing the brunt of this quality chaos. But Japan and Western Europe, increasingly obsessed with fads such as re-engineering, could soon be in its throes.

In their hearts, American managers want to believe that TQM amounts to a viable way of cutting costs. They would dearly love to emulate Richard Buetow, director of quality at Motorola. He reckons that, thanks to fanatical devotion to quality, the chips-to-cellphones maker has saved a staggering $6.5 billion in manufacturing costs since 1987 (the year before it won a Baldrige). But, outside Motorola, most managers still believe that cutting jobs cuts costs faster. According to Challenger, Gray & Christmas, a Chicago consultancy, 2.6m American workers have been sacked since early 1990.

The snag is that downsizing undermines a cornerstone of TQM: employee motivation. To achieve perfect quality, said Deming, companies must "drive out fear, so that everyone may work effectively." Yet downsizing fosters fear, as Xerox, the world's biggest photocopier maker (and a Baldrige winner in 1989), has discovered. Hector Motroni, head of quality at Xerox, says the firm has been through "11 years of wrenching change" since it adopted TQM in 1983. And although Mr Motroni credits total quality with reinvigorating the firm, he concedes that job cuts and the loss of management layers—Xerox is in the process of cutting its workforce by another 12%, to 85,000—has damaged motivation and made it harder to sell the TQM message.

To overcome this, the firm encourages individual workers (instead of, say, departments) to focus on the needs of customers. All employees are given responsibility for quality. This, hopes Mr Motroni, will give workers a goal; it should also help bypass broken lines of communication. Dick LeVitt, director of corporate quality at Hewlett-Packard, agrees that such "empowerment" is essential in firms facing chaotic change: "You have to connect employees with the consequences of their work." One recent study suggests that the effect of making that connection can be dramatic. It found that TQM programmes which delegate responsibility for quality to individual shop-floor workers tend to be twice as likely to succeed as those which rely on "top-down" management (though the fad for teams brings problems too).

With slimmer resources, companies are also discovering that they must focus their total-quality efforts on what customers actually want. "In the 1980s we pushed quality too much for its own sake," says Mr LeVitt. So did Florida Power & Light (FP&L), an electrical utility which by the late 1980s boasted an 85-strong quality department and 1,900 quality teams—none of which seemed to bring about a significant improvement in its services. FP&L eventually scrapped most of its quality bureaucracy, and its service improved. Hewlett-Packard now treats TQM like any other investment: if a particular total-quality initiative doesn't show a quick return in terms of higher sales, lower costs or happier customers, it is redesigned or scrapped.

IBM, which has seen its workforce fall by half since 1986 (and this week underwent its latest management shake-up), is taking a similar tack. Big Blue no longer has formal, stand-alone TQM programmes; responsibility for quality has been pushed down to the factory floor; and it is trying to infuse every part of its corporate activities with the notion of quality. IBM's most ambitious goal, however, is to reconcile its massive re-engineering programme with its quality goals. And this, thinks Jim Patell of California's Stanford Business School, is where firms often trip up.

The dilemma facing managers is that whereas total-quality management emphasises continuous, step-by-step improvement, re-engineering relies on a radical, once-and-for-all scrapping of existing business processes. The tension between the two, says Mr Patell, can end up sabotaging a company's total-quality programme. Wilson Lowery, head of quality and re-engineering at IBM, says his company is now carefully monitoring its re-engineering programme to ensure, at the very least, that each bit of it improves, rather than worsens, quality. But this does not address the differing velocities of the two strategies. "We've a long way to go," says Mr Lowery.

Quality timed

Even if their total-quality schemes survive downsizing and re-engineering, many firms then find themselves facing another challenge: speed. Until recently, Xerox used to put dedicated teams together to implement total-quality practices for new products, a process that could take up to six months. Now, Xerox rotates teams of engineers and managers from existing products to new products, in an attempt to learn from its past total-quality errors and break out of "functional silos". This is tougher than it sounds, says Mr Motroni, because some TQM knowledge is invariably lost when teams are transferred.

Hewlett-Packard is taking a different approach to solving shaky quality in rapidly introduced products. Most glitches, says Mr LeVitt, arise during the transition from one product to its successor. In the past, Hewlett-Packard undertook what it calls "hard roll" product changeovers, in which production of the Mark 1 version of a product was replaced by the Mark 2 in one fell swoop. The result: a big initial dip in quality which had to be fixed before the new version could be put in the shops.

Hewlett-Packard is now experimenting with "soft" product changeovers. Once the specification of, say, a Mark 2 version is complete, the new features are incorporated, one by one, into selected production-runs of the Mark 1. The Mark 2 is officially launched—and the new features made visible to customers—only when this gradual roll-over has been finished successfully. As a result, says Mr LeVitt, the time taken to hit total-quality targets in new products is being slashed. And the new technique may also help the firm avoid the sort of gaffe—involving defective paper-rollers in 1.5m printers—it made public on January 9th.

As their product life-cycles collapse and price competition hots up, many firms are finding that the only way to maintain quality is to make their products simpler to manufacture. IBM's range of mass-market PCs are now built using fewer than 20 interchangeable modules; three years ago they were built from custom components. At Hewlett-Packard, "design

for reuse"—designing components for use not only in several products but also over several generations of those products—helps to improve quality while cutting costs. A drawback of this, concedes IBM's Mr Lowery, is that it can reduce customer choice—and satisfaction. But if TQM is to keep up with today's chaotic markets, firms must cut complexity.

Few companies are likely to give up the quality struggle, if only because—despite all the obstacles—TQM does seem to cut costs in the long run. And big cost savings, says Motorola's Mr Buetow, are the main reason why his firm will remain obsessive about TQM even beyond the point of perfection. Callers may not care if their Motorola carphone will work for a claimed 40–50 years before failing. But Motorola can at least rest easy that it should never have to dial up a costly recall.

The Economist, 14 January 1995
© *The Economist*, London (1995)

- *Performance.* Use the documentation as a working tool by doing everything that is written.
- *Verification.* Verify that in all cases the accepted written procedures are respected by all parties concerned.
- *Filing.* A written trace of all procedures should be retained, kept updated, and be available to all persons concerned.

Certification is by an independent third party. It can take up to two years to obtain certification and the total cost, including outside consultants' help, may run in excess of US$100 000. Adherence to the procedures is assessed annually by examiners accredited to the national standards-setting agency.

Modules in the ISO-9000 series

The ISO-9000 series is a detailed compendium of documented procedures covering, in the broadest sense, all of the operational aspects of a firm. The three main modules are ISO-9001, ISO-9002 and ISO-9003. In addition to these there are the guidance and vocabulary standards, ISO-9000, ISO-9004 and ISO-8402 which define and describe what is necessary to accomplish the requirements outlined in the main standards. These six modules are summarized below.

ISO-9001

ISO-9001 is the fullest and most complete standard. It is a module that defines all the elements necessary for conformity throughout the whole operating cycle from design through development, production, installation and servicing. Within the module are the 20 detailed sections as given in Table 4.2.[24]

ISO-9002

ISO-9002 is the module for quality assurance in production and installation and is the more common standard for manufacturers. It applies where there is already an established design or specification that constitutes the specified product requirement. With the exception of design, and design changes, this standard is very similar to ISO-9001.

ISO-9003

This is a model that applies to firms in a contractual situation which wish to demonstrate capabilities for inspecting and testing products. It covers document control, product identification and marking, control of products that do not pass specified tests, a handling and storage system, control of measuring and test equipment, statistical techniques and training.

ISO-9000

This explains fundamental quality concepts and provides guidelines for the selection and application of each standard.

ISO-9004

This is a guideline for the application of standards in quality management and quality systems.

ISO-8402

This is the 'pre-9000' module, which includes the vocabulary of quality management and quality assurance.

International firms

The following are a few examples of major international companies that have achieved ISO-9000 certifi-

Table 4.2 Sections in ISO-9001

1	Management responsibility	Defines how a company should draw up an organization chart to identify the responsibilities of all staff who manage, or carry out, work associated with the quality activity.
2	Quality system	Defines how a firm should establish and maintain procedures and instructions for a quality system to assure that products conform to specifications.
3	Contract review	Defines and documents how firms must establish, and maintain current, the requirements for contract review and contract differences between concerned parties.
4	Design control	Defines requirements and procedures to manage and verify product conception and design to ensure that defined specifications are achieved.
5	Document control	Establishes procedures for document control, including approval, availability, logging of manuals and diffusion to concerned parties.
6	Purchasing	Defines procedures to ensure that a purchased product conforms to specifications including evaluation procedures for subcontractors.
7	Purchaser-supplied product	Defines verification procedures for a supplier regarding storage and maintenance of purchased products.
8	Product/service identification and traceability	Describes, when appropriate, how a supplier for the purpose of traceability must establish and keep up to date identification procedures based on a product's original design specifications or other appropriate documents in all phases of production, delivery and installation.
9	Process control	Covers documentation of how a process should be carried out, including, where necessary, installation procedures. Written instructions must be given to the employee involved where appropriate and the process must be monitored.
10	Inspection and testing	Covers procedures necessary to assure that the product is neither used, or put into service, until it has been inspected and tested according to written specifications.
11	Inspection, measuring and test equipment	Covers requirements for using, standardizing and maintaining in good condition all inspection, measuring and test equipment.
12	Inspection and test status	Covers the status of inspection according to appropriate stamping, ticketing, markings, recording documents, follow-up instruction and the like.
13	Control of non-conforming product	Covers procedures in order to assure that a non-conforming product is not used or inadvertently installed. It covers identification procedures, documentation and isolation of the product.
14	Corrective action	Covers procedures for researching why a product does not conform, the corrective action necessary and to eliminate potential problems which might arise because of non-conforming products.
15	Handling, storage, packaging, and delivery	Covers procedures necessary for product handling to prevent damage, the type of storage areas and storage environment to prevent product deterioration or damage. It also includes detailed procedures for types of packaging, the packaging methods and delivery procedures to respect.
16	Quality records	Covers requirements to be established for the identification, collection, indexing, organizing and filing to keep up to date, or for destroying all records related to quality.
17	Internal quality audits	Covers procedures necessary for carrying out internal quality audits.
18	Training	Covers procedures to identify that appropriate training is available to all those persons who might in some way have an incidence on the quality operation of the firm.
19	Servicing	When after-sales service is identified in a contract, this section covers procedures to verify that the after-sales service is according to requirements.
20	Statistical techniques	Where appropriate, this section covers statistical procedures necessary to verify that a product or process is according to specifications.

cation: AT&T; Caterpillar; Digital Equipment; Dow Chemical; Eastman Kodak; Du Pont; Exxon Chemical; Fisher Controls; IBM; 3M company; Westinghouse Electric; Xerox.

Advantages of certification

Some of the reported advantages of ISO-9000 certification are as follows:

■ *Marketing muscle.* Companies that obtain ISO-9000 certification are permitted to display the appropriate certificate. As a result, in theory, a company that is certified is able to offer a superior product or service and this will give the company marketing muscle.

■ *Contractor selection.* If a company, say for example in Asia, is looking for a European subcontractor and it is not completely familiar with European business, it is more likely to select a partner that has the ISO certification.

- *Suppliers.* Selecting a new supplier can be time-consuming and costly (see Chapter 16 *Purchasing and Subcontracting*). If a potential supplier is ISO-9000 certified, then the selection process for a buyer firm can be considerably reduced. Suppliers in Europe, with European clients, are probably more likely to be selected if they have certification.

Criticism of certification

Obtaining certification is criticized by some as being:

- bureaucratic;[25]
- costly;
- no guarantee that a company that is certified provides a quality service or product.

Quality certification only provides a book of procedures and not necessarily better quality. Many companies such as Hewlett-Packard (computer products), C F Braun & Co. (engineering and construction), Suchard (chocolate and confectionery), Marks and Spencer (retail) long enjoyed a reputation for quality before certification. Strong opponents of ISO-9000 say that those who believe that achieving certification will result in the production of higher-quality products and services is somewhat like believing that giving people driving licences produces safer roads!

Within the organization, adhering strictly to the ISO certification is considered to be returning to the rigidity of Taylorism in the firm. (See also Chapter 8, *Human Resources in the System Design*). It demotivates people because it puts a block on individual initiative. Others say that the systematic controls and written procedures are considered as being unnecessary 'policing' of activity, the criticism thrown at the old quality control departments. On the employment side, when all procedures are written, it limits the hiring and the upward mobility of those unable to read.

EUROPEAN FOUNDATION FOR QUALITY MANAGEMENT (EFQM)

Background

The European Foundation for Quality Management (EFQM) was founded by the presidents of 14 major European companies, with the endorsement of the European Commission. Jacques Delors, the then President of the European Commission, signed the letter of intent to establish the EFQM in Brussels on 15 September 1988. The membership is now in excess of 550 organizations across 23 European countries, including multinational and national firms, research institutes and universities.[26]

The Mission of the EFQM

The mission of EFQM is twofold:

1 To stimulate and assist organizations throughout Europe to participate in improvement activities, leading ultimately to excellence in customer satisfaction, employee satisfaction, impact on society and business results.
2 To support the managers of European organizations in accelerating the process of making Total Quality Management a decisive factor for achieving global competitive advantage.

The EFQM model

The EFQM quality programme is based on a model containing nine elements, as illustrated in Figure 4.12, which can be used to assess an organization's progress towards excellence in business. Each of these elements examines *how* the organization is functioning and *what* the results are.[27]

The European Quality Award Programme

The European Quality Award, part of the EFQM programme, was developed in 1991 to recognize those companies that show a high level of commitment to quality. Entry for the award is through a cascade process involving national quality organizations from each of the European countries. The criterion for making the award is a point system, based on the EFQM model, which requires evidence of achievement in the nine model categories. The total possible points for the award are 1 000 and this breakdown, together with the required evidence or proof, is as described in the following sections.

Leadership

Leadership is how the behaviour and actions of the executive team and all other leaders inspire, support and promote a culture of Total Quality Management. This category has a maximum of 100 points, or 10 per cent of the total, and the evidence required is:

- How leaders visibly demonstrate their commitment to a culture of Total Quality Management.
- How leaders support improvement and involvement by providing appropriate resources and assistance.
- How leaders are involved with customers, suppliers and other external organizations.

Figure 4.12 The EFQM Quality Model.

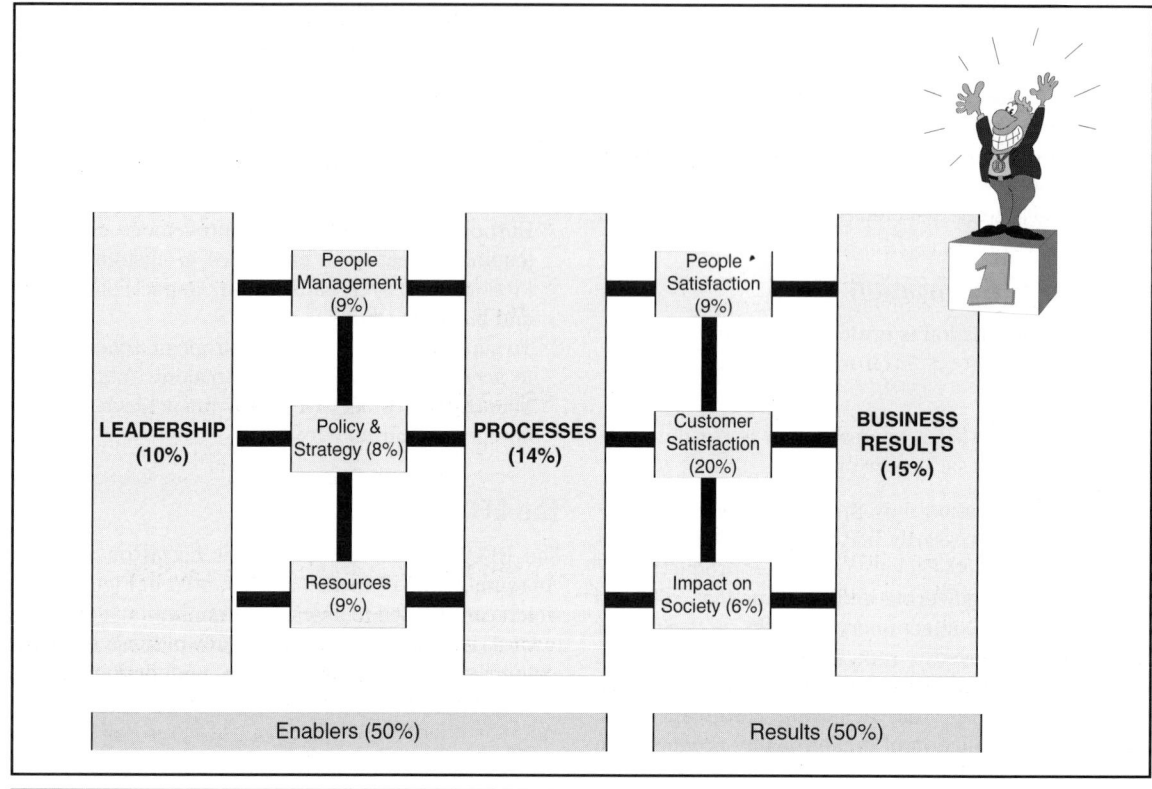

- How leaders recognise and appreciate people's efforts and achievements.

People Management

People Management is how the organization releases the full potential of its people. This category has a maximum of 90 points, or 9 per cent of the total, and the evidence required is:

- How resources for people are planned and improved.
- How people's capabilities are sustained and developed.
- How people are involved in targets and continuously review performance.
- How people are involved, empowered and recognized.
- How people and the organization have an effective dialogue.
- How people are cared for.

Policy and Strategy

Policy and Strategy is how the organization formulates, deploys and reviews its policy and strategy and turns these into plans and actions. The category has a maximum of 80 points, or 8 per cent of the total, and the evidence required is:

- How policy and strategy are based on information that is relevant and comprehensive.
- How policy and strategy are developed.
- How policy and strategy are communicated and implemented.
- How policy and strategy are regularly updated and improved.

Resources

Resources involves how the organization manages resources effectively and efficiently. This category has a maximum of 90 points, or 9 per cent of the total, and the evidence required is:

- How financial resources are managed.
- How information resources are managed.
- How supplier relationships and materials are managed.
- How buildings, equipment and other assets are managed.

- How technology and intellectual property are managed.

Processes

Processes is how the organization identifies, manages, reviews and improves its processes. This category has a maximum of 140 points, or 14 per cent of the total, and the evidence required is:

- How processes that are key to the success of the business are identified.
- How processes are systematically managed.
- How processes are reviewed and targets are set for improvement.
- How processes are improved, using innovation and creativity.
- How processes are changed and the benefits evaluated.

People Satisfaction

People Satisfaction is what the organization is achieving in relation to the satisfaction of its people. This category has a maximum of 90 points, or 9 per cent of the total, and the evidence is:

- people's perception of the organization;
- any other measurements relating to people satisfaction.

Customer Satisfaction

Customer Satisfaction is what the organization is achieving in relation to the satisfaction of its external customers. This category is the most important and has a maximum of 200 points, or 20 per cent of the total. The evidence required is:

- customers' perception of the organization's products, services and customer relationships;
- any other measurements relating to the satisfaction of the organization's customers.

Impact on Society

Impact on Society is what the organization is achieving in satisfying the needs and the expectations of the local, national and international community (where appropriate). This includes the perception of the organization's approach to quality of life, the environment and the preservation of global resources, as well as the organization's own internal measures of effectiveness. It includes the organization's relations with authorities and bodies that affect and regulate its business. This category has a maximum of 60 points, or 6 per cent of the total, and the evidence is:

- society's perception of the organization;
- any other measurements relating to the organization's impact on society.

Business Results

Business Results is what the organization is achieving in relation to its planned business objectives and in satisfying the needs and expectations of everyone with a financial interest or stake in the organization. This category has a maximum of 150 points, or 15 per cent of the total, and the evidence is:

- the financial measurements of the organization's performance;
- any other measurements relating to the organization's performance.

EFQM Quality Award Winners

The European Quality Award Winners, and other prize winners, since 1992 are given in Table 4.3.[28]

European Organization for Quality

The European Organization for Quality (EOQ), established in 1956 to facilitate information exchange among firms on quality theory and best practices, works with the EFQM on the quality awards programme. EOQ pays special attention to the needs of small and medium-size firms.

Table 4.3 The European Quality Award Winners, and other prize winners, since 1992.

Year	Category	Firm
1996	European Quality Award	Brisa, Turkey (manufacturing)
	Prize winners	BT
		Netas
		TNT Express (UK)
1995	European Quality Award	Texas Instruments Europe
	Prize winners	TNT Express (UK)
1994	European Quality Award	Design to Distribution (D2D)
	Prize winners	Ericsson SA
		IBM (SEMEA)
1993	European Quality Award	Milliken European Division
	Prize winners	ICL Manufacturing Division
1992	European Quality Award	Rank Xerox Ltd
	Prize winners	BOC Ltd, Special gases
		Industrias del Ubierna SA (UBISA)
		Milliken European Division

THE UK BEST FACTORY AWARDS

Background

The Best Factory Awards is a programme developed by *Management Today*, the leading UK management publication, in association with Cranfield School of Management, and in its present form has been run since 1992. Its purpose is to identify those manufacturing facilities in the UK that, in operational terms, are considered leaders in their field in quality, service, efficiency and cost. One of its aims is to promote manufacturing excellence in the UK.

Award categories

There are eight award categories, each of which is sponsored by a specific business:

1   Best Engineering Factory
2   Best Electronics Factory
3   Best Household Products Factory
4   Best Process Factory
5   Best Small Company Factory
6   Most improved Factory
7   Judges special award
8   Factory of the Year

Evaluation criteria

The evaluation criteria are comprehensive and evaluation is based on a 16-page questionnaire covering such operating criteria as:[29]

- Worldwide activity
- Customer lead times
- Product types
- Processing time
- Control elements
- Cost structure
- Profit margins
- Inventory levels/stock turns
- Employee characteristics (direct and indirect)
- Employee turnover
- Setup times and associated costs
- Customer network
- Supplier network
- Delivery frequency of materials
- Employee training provided
- New product innovation
- Management involvement
- Customer service

Timetable of the award process

The following is the timetable of the award process:

January–April	Participating firms carry out a self-administered audit.
May	Preparation of benchmark reports and selection of finalists.
June–July	Benchmarking reports distributed to all participants.
	Team of assessors make visits to the facilities of the finalists.
July	Selection of award winners.
November	Winners announced at a luncheon sponsored by *Management Today*.

Previous winners

Table 4.4 gives the winners for 1994[30], 1995[31] and 1996.[32]

European expansion of the programme

Since its inception, the Awards programme has been expanded to cover a broader European base. In 1996, with sponsors including Deutsche Bank, it was launched in Germany. In 1997 discussions began with SDA Bocconi, Milan, and Groupe ESC, E. M. Lyon, two business schools in Italy and France. Each of the four awards programmes will be based on the same questionnaire to select the Best Factories in the respective countries. Then, since the base criteria will be the same, country comparisons will be made.

MALCOLM BALDRIGE NATIONAL QUALITY AWARD

Malcolm Baldrige and the award

Malcolm Baldrige was the US Secretary of Commerce under President Reagan from 1981 until his death in a rodeo accident in 1987. In that year an award entitled, 'The Malcolm Baldrige National Quality Award' was established by Congress and signed into law on 20 August 1987 as Public Law 100-107. Its purpose is to raise awareness about quality management and to recognize US companies that have successful quality management systems.[33]

Background to the award

The award was established because of the analysis, studies, and criteria concerning US industry that are described in the following sections.[34]

US leadership

The leadership of the United States in product and process quality has been challenged strongly (and

Table 4.4 Winners of the Best Factories Awards

Year	Category	Company	Manufacturing activity	Challenge
1996	Factory of the Year	Van de Bergh Foods	Margarine manufacture	Low-cost, high-productivity production of brand foods to high quality
	Best Process Factory			Preventative maintenance, human resource management, continuous improvement
	Best Electronics and Electrical Factory	Sun Microsystems, Scotland	Computer manufacture	Circuit-board manufacture and assembly of hi-tech computers
	Best Engineering Factory	Pilkington, PE	Manufacture of electro-optical devices	Manufacture, assembly and test of hi-tech glass, plastics and metals to exacting tolerances and product specifications
	Best Household and General Products Factory	Walkers, Bradgate Bakery	Pre-prepared sandwich manufacture	Assembly and overnight delivery of pre-packed sandwiches to supermarket chains and petrol-station forecourts under strict temperature and hygiene conditions
	Best Small Company Factory	The Amtico Company	Vinyl flooring manufacture	Custom design and assembly of floors to tight cutting tolerances and short delivery times
	Most Improved Factory	Courtaulds Coatings' Wet Paint Supply Unit	Paint manufacture	Small-batch manufacture of high-performance coatings in a wide variety of packaging formats
	Judge's Special Award	Fujitsu Telecommunications	Telecommunications products	Design and assemby of telecommunication devices for telephone utilities and users
1995	Factory of the Year Electronics Industry Best Factory	Bonas Machine Co.	Jacquard weaving equipment	Manufacturing to exacting standards of quality, cost and lead times. Collaboration with unions to change work practices
	Best Small Company Best Household & General Products	W. H. Smith & Sons	Injection moulding and associated tool making	Just-in-time supply of high-quality, low-cost mouldings to demanding customers. Continuous improvement
	Best Process Industry Factory	Shell Lubricants	Lubricating oils	Blending/packaging of lubricating oils for retailers, workshops and bulk consumption. Process design
	Best Engineering Factory	Toshiba Consumer Products, UK	Air-conditioning equipment	Achieving Japanese levels of quality and efficiency. Preventative maintenance continuous improvement
	Most Improved Factory	Hoechst Trespaphan, UK	Multi-layer co-extruded oriented polypropylene film	Improvement of productivity; equipment utilization; preventative maintenance; cultural changes
	Judges Special Award	Honeywell	Electronic control devices	Low-cost, high-volume production using a range of technologies. Automation cellular manufacturing
1994	Factory of the Year Electronics Industry Best Factory	Design to Distribution	Printed-circuit boards	Just-in-time high-volume supply of circuit boards for companies like Hewlett-Packard, Dell, Madge Networks etc.
	Best Household Products Factory	Glaxo Wellcome Operations	Packaging of pharmaceutical products	Mixing, packaging and distribution in a variety of formats. Continuous improvement
	Best Engineering Factory Best Factory in Northern Ireland	Ryobi Aluminium Casting, UK	Aluminium diecasting	Just-in-time supply of automotive castings. Customer oriented culture; continuous improvement
	Best Process Industry Factory Best Factory in Scotland	Dexter Nonwovens	Specialist papers	Producing precision-engineered papers that sell on quality, price and delivery to a variety of customers

| Best Small Company | Kitchen Range Foods | Doughnuts and fruit pies for McDonald's | Achieving consistent standard of quality, cost and inventory availability |
| Judges Special Award | European Components Co. | Seat-belt assemblies for automobiles | Using a wide range of technologies, including steel pressing and plastic injection moulding in safety-critical products |

sometimes successfully) by foreign competition, and the nation's productivity has improved less than competitors over the last two decades.

Cost of quality

American business and industry are beginning to understand that poor quality costs companies as much as 20 per cent of sales revenues nationally, and that improved quality of goods and services goes hand in hand with improved productivity lower costs and increased profitability.

Strategic planning

Strategic planning for quality and quality improvement programmes, through a commitment to excellence in manufacturing and services, are becoming more and more essential to the well-being of the US economy and its ability to compete effectively in the global market place.

Manufacturing

Improved management and understanding of the factory floor, worker involvement in quality and greater emphasis on statistical process control can lead to dramatic improvements in the cost of quality of manufactured products.

All operations

The concept of quality improvement is directly applicable to small companies as well as large, to service industries as well as manufacturing and to the public sector as well as private enterprise.

Management-led and customer-oriented

In order to be successful, quality improvement programmes must be management-led and customer-oriented, and this may require fundamental changes in the way companies and agencies do business.

Other countries

Several major industrial nations have successfully coupled rigorous private-sector quality audits with national awards giving special recognition to those enterprises the audits identify as the very best.

Purpose of the quality award

It was considered that a national quality award programme in the USA would help improve quality and productivity in the following ways:

- Helping to stimulate American companies to improve quality and productivity for the pride of recognition, while obtaining a competitive edge through increased profits.
- Recognizing the achievements of those companies that improve the quality of their goods and services and providing examples to others.
- Establishing guidelines and criteria that can be used by business, industrial, governmental and other organizations to evaluate their own quality improvement efforts.
- Providing specific guidance for other American organizations that wish to learn how to manage for high quality by making available detailed information on how winning organizations were able to change their cultures and achieve eminence.

Award criteria

The award programme focuses on quality as a strategic integral part of business management and the award's criteria are widely accepted as the standard for quality excellence. They are designed to help companies deliver ever-improving value to customers and to improve overall company performance and capabilities. For many companies having quality as a strategic element, the result is better employee relations, higher productivity, greater customer satisfaction, increased market share, and improved profitability. (This further underscores why quality is a strategic component.)

The US Commerce Department's National Institute of Standards and Technology (NIST) manages the awards in close cooperation with the private sector. The examiners evaluate a company's quality management system by looking for achievements and improvements in the following seven areas.

Leadership

- Have the senior leaders clearly defined the company's values, goals and ways to achieve the goals?

- Are senior executives personally involved?
- Does this involvement include communicating quality excellence to groups outside the company?

Information analysis

- Is the information used to guide the company's quality management system reliable, timely and accessible?

Strategic planning

- How does the company plan strengthen its competitive position?
- How are these plans integrated into its overall business planning?

Human resource development and management

- How does the company develop the full potential of its work force?

Process management

- How are products and services designed?
- How are product and service production and delivery processes managed?
- How does the company assure that suppliers meet its performance requirements?

Business results

- How is the company performing in key business areas and what are its plans for improving?

Customer focus and satisfaction

- Is quality defined by the customer?

Figure 4.13 illustrates the various stages leading up to the award.

Award winners

Two awards may be given annually in each of the three categories: manufacturing, service and small business. The winners are given in Table 4.5.

ETHICS AND QUALITY

In Chapter 16, *Purchasing and Subcontracting*, ethics is discussed related to behaviour of some purchasing agents and their suppliers. Ethics is also an issue when it comes to quality control. Consider the report in Box 4.5 and the following situations for Lucas Industries and Philips.[35]

The incident recounted in Box 4.5 was not an isolated case. Numerous bolts holding Maverick missiles

have broken, either in mid-air or while the missiles were being loaded onto planes. The manufacturer of the bolts, United Telecontrol Electronics Inc. New Jersey has been charged in the US Federal Court with violating quality control regulations including:

- Using bolts with cracks, or lack of plating needed to guard against corrosion.
- Using other components with surface cracks that workers would grind off at night when inspectors were not around.
- Using parts that failed inspections, because workers manipulated computer-controlled measurements to produce passing reports.

Lucas Industries

A US unit of this British manufacturer pleaded guilty in US courts in 1995 to falsifying quality records for

Table 4.5 Malcolm Baldrige National Quality Award, 1988–1996

Year	Company
1996	ADAC Laboratories
	Dana Commercial Credit
	Custom Research Inc.
	Trident Precision Manufacturing Inc.
1995	Armstrong World Industries, Inc.
	Corning, Inc.
1994	AT&T Consumer Communications Services
	GTE Directories Corporation
	Wainwright Industries, Inc.
1993	Eastman Chemical Company
	Ames Rubber Corporation
1992	AT&T Network Systems Group/Transmission Systems Business Unit
	Texas Instruments, Inc. Defense Systems & Electronics Group
	AT&T Universal Card Services
	The Ritz-Carlton Hotel Company
	Granite Rock Company
1991	Solectron Corporation
	Zytec Corporation
	Marlow Industries
1990	Cadillac Motor Car Company
	Federal Express Corporation
	IBM Rochester
	Wallace Company
1989	Milliken & Company
	Xerox Corporation Business Products & Systems
1988	Motorola, Inc.
	Westinghouse Electric Corporation, Commercial Nuclear Fuel Division
	Globe Metallurgical, Inc.

Figure 4.13 Malcolm Baldrige Quality Award process.

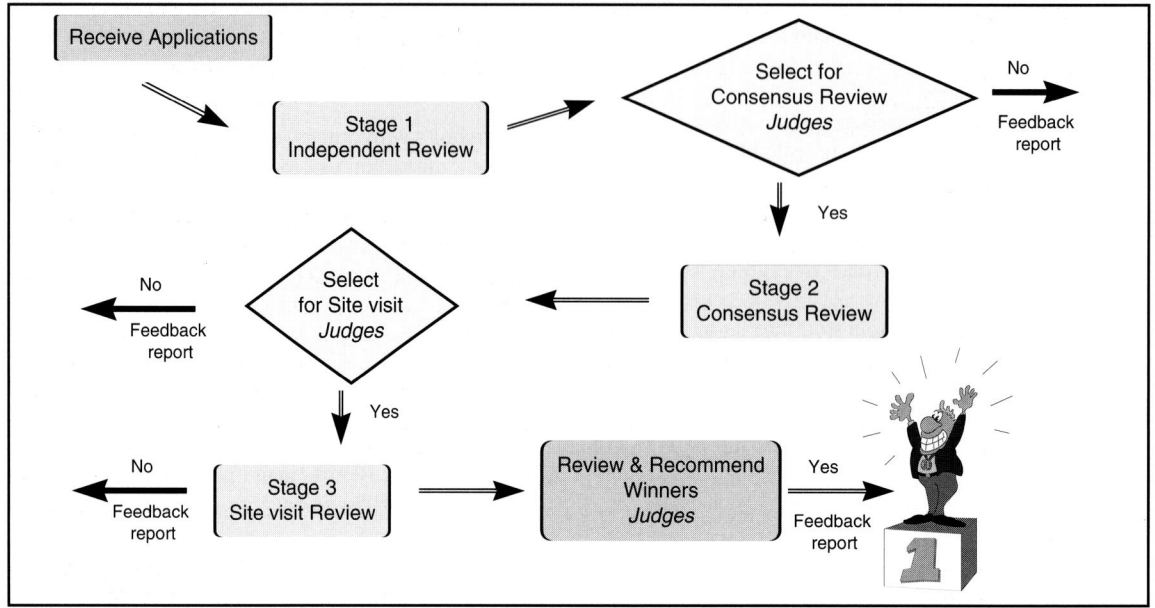

gearboxes that drive electrical oil and fuel systems on Navy F-18 fighters. Prosecutors said that when 150 of the gearboxes were taken apart, 100 per cent failed inspection. Faulty gearboxes were blamed for 71 emergency landings and several in-flight fires, as well as the loss of an F-18 during the Persian Gulf War.

Philips

A US unit of Philips Electronic NV pleaded guilty in 1995 to submitting false tests of resistors that control electric current in weapon systems. When resistors showed signs of failing, engineers would secretly replace them with fresh resistors to pass the tests.

Box 4.5 US military

While practising at 4 500 meters over Wisconsin, US says Lt Col. Richard Van Roo, his A-10 attack jet suddenly began 'bouncing and skidding' through the sky. One of the two bolts fastening a 225-kilogram Maverick missile to the wing had broken, leaving the missile swinging under the wing, attached only by the other bolt.

The pilot declared an emergency. Fire engines rushed to the runway. The pilot touched down and rolled to a safe stop with just 10 centimetres to spare between the dangling missile and the runway.

From *Wall Street Journal Europe* 4 March 1996

SUMMARY OF KEY ELEMENTS

- Quality problems often occur and the cause, usually deep rooted, can be traced to incorrect design and poor organization; it is usually related to people. Quality management involves long-term planning and organization and thus is a strategic issue.
- Customers judge quality. If a tangible product, or service, has a reputation for quality, customers will buy. And, all else being equal, the company will benefit.
- Providing a quality service or products gives a positive company image and improves competitive

ability and market share, which translates into improved profits.
- The International Standards Organization (ISO) defines quality as 'the totality of features and characteristics of a product, process, or service that bear on its ability to satisfy stated or implied needs'.
- A specification is the document that describes in detail the requirements which the product, process or service has to meet.
- Total Quality Management (TQM) is where attention to quality pervades the whole operation, and

not just one particular sector. The driving wheel of TQM lies in the word *Management* and more precisely, Top Management.

■ There exists a quality supply chain, analogous to a physical supply chain. A break in the link, including poor communication, can impact final quality.

■ Leading quality management authorities include Edwards Deming, Joseph Juran, Philip Crosby, Armand Feiggenbaum, Kaoru Ishikawa and Genichi Taguchi.

■ Quality-related costs include external and internal faults, the cost of non-quality and evaluation and prevention activities, which are considered as the cost of quality.

■ Quality control is all activities to satisfy quality requirements, including process monitoring and eliminating causes of poor performance at all stages in the supply chain. It is a non-value-added activity and, as such, a firm should have a TQM system in place to minimize the level of the quality control needed.

■ Practices to improve quality in an organization include Poka Yoke, Continuous improvement, Phantom customers, Taguchi methods, Activity Based Costing, Simple designs, Just-in-time, Benchmarking and perhaps Re-engineering.

■ ISO-9000 is a series of internationally accepted quality standards aimed at improving the quality of manufacturing and service organizations. The principal modules in the series are ISO-9001 which is the most complete, ISO-9002 and ISO-9003.

■ The EFQM has a quality model based on nine elements, which serve as a basis for an award programme that underscores the importance of the customer in quality issues.

■ Cranfield Business School has developed a Best Factory Award programme for quality for the UK. Similar programmes are operational in Germany, Italy and France.

■ The Malcolm Baldrige Award is a US programme to raise awareness about quality and to recognize US firms with successful quality management systems.

■ The difference between ISO-9000 and a quality award is that ISO is a way to improve quality, whereas an award is a once-only quality recognition.

■ Ethical issues are very often intertwined with quality problems.

REVIEW AND DISCUSSION QUESTIONS

1   **Service operation.** In your day-to-day life, you encounter some of the following operations:
   (a) business school;
   (b) shops;
   (c) post office;
   (d) medical office;
   (e) cinema;
   (f) bus company.
   What is your opinion of the quality of the services offered by these operations? Do you think improvements could be made? Describe.

2   **Quality and accidents.** Can you cite any illustrations when quality defects resulted in accidents, either minor or major, in operations and supply?

3   **Quality and value added.** For many quality is a non-value-added activity since the client does 'not see quality in a product or service'. Quality is expected by the client. Others believe quality is a value-added activity. Discuss, justifying your reasoning.

4   **Limit to quality design.** Discuss the 'idea of a limit to quality design'. Can you give illustrations where you believe there is too much quality in a product or a service offered.

5   **Quality chain.** Considering the operation from the start to the finish, develop a quality chain for:
   (a) a university or business school;
   (b) a hospital;
   (c) a restaurant;
   (d) a packaged ski trip;
   (e) a supermarket;
   (f) a flight from Paris to Los Angeles;
   (g) a case of wine;
   (h) an automobile;
   (i) a new house;
   (j) a bag of fertilizer.

6   **Quality is free.** Some management theorists believe that 'quality is free'. Do you believe in this axiom? Justify your reasoning.

CASE STUDY: WENTO COMPANY

Situation

Nicholas Carrias was feeling happy as he drove to work on the San Diego Freeway. He had realized his dream and was now living in Santa Monica, California, USA, not far from Los Angeles. He had been hired as manager of Quality Assurance at Wento Corporation, a company in Van Nuys that made electric motors for the operation of automatic venetian blinds, curtains and light aluminium doors. Wento was a company of some 1750 people and experiencing a period of rapid growth.

Nicholas was French. He was an engineer and had completed a Master's degree at the Lyon Graduate School of Business in France. During this programme, he had completed a six-month training assignment, covering the certification ISO-9002 for Somfy, a company in Cluses, in the French Alps, which also makes motors for sun blinds. Somfy subsequently hired Nicholas as Quality Coordinator, a post he held for two years.

Somfy is well known for the high quality of its products. Wento believed that, in hiring Nicholas, they would be able to improve the quality of their motors. It was not the first time that Wento had received complaints from clients because sometimes during operation the motors would cease operating for no apparent reason.

Nicholas went into his office and dropped his briefcase and hung up his coat. He had scheduled the whole of today for finishing a report on a quality management seminar he had attended in San Francisco and for contacting vendors regarding motor specifications. As he sat down, the door flew open and in strode a red-faced Bill Bates, the president of Wento.

'Nicholas, you have to sort out our quality problem. We have been having many complaints from clients about our new motor, reference DLW-1455. One incident was particularly embarrassing as the client was Disney Corporation. During the opening night of one of their presentations the curtains jammed half open. Michael Eisner was in the audience. He was really upset. I really don't know where the problem is, but, in my opinion, those people in production aren't very good. I haven't seen the production line for some time, but Mike Burton, the production manager, says his workers lack motivation. I'm putting the solution in your hands Nicholas.'

With that Bill dashed out, saying he would be gone for the rest of the week. Nicholas sighed. He decided he would have to visit the production line of Model DLW-1455. He put on his jacket, crossed the yard, passing the avocado and orange trees, towards the building that housed production of Motor DLW-1455.

'Boy, it's hot today' he thought, 'even for so early in the morning. It must be a Santa Ana condition.'

He entered the front door. The temperature wasn't much different from that outside. He went over to the office of Mike. He was in heated discussion with Sam Marchand, one of the superintendents on the line:

'Well, we had no choice,' Sam was saying, 'The copper wiring sent to us from our supplier was the wrong diameter, but we were able to work with it by modifying the connections somewhat. It wasn't easy but we met the requirements of the Master Schedule. The supplier of this copper wire is not very reliable. It is not the first time we have had material that is not according to specification. And, what's more, when it does arrive, it's not always on the date promised.'

Nicholas went into Mike's office.

'Hi Mike. I was talking to Bill Bates this morning and he tells me there have been some difficulties with the production of Model DLW-1455. I wonder if I might take a look around.'

Mike was fuming, obviously irritated by his conversation with Sam.

'Oh Bill Bates is a silly old fool. He's always complaining. There is nothing wrong here. Sure, once in a while, we have to shut down the line because machines malfunction, but we have always sufficient in-process inventory on hand to prevent a complete stoppage of the line. Yes, and its

true the components supplied by our suppliers are not always according to specification. You know our specs are quite rigid. However, my operators are very smart. They are always able to fix the faulty units. We always meet our demand requirements.'

'Do you mind if I take a look around?' said Nicholas.

'Well, you won't find anything wrong here. I'm not sure why they hired a manager of quality assurance. We can fix the problems ourselves,' Mike went on.

'Let me come with you.'

'No thanks, I would prefer to go alone,' said Nicholas.

Nicholas strolled down to upstream part of the operation, where the chassis were being drilled. He noticed that several chassis were sitting at the side of the drilling machine.

'What are these?' he asked the operator.

'Oh these are rejects,' said the operator. 'I've only been on the line for three days, I was transferred from the wiring section and I still have not mastered how to operate these drilling machines.'

'Can't your supervisor help?' enquired Nicholas.

'Oh he's no use. Besides, he's off sick today. Well, that's what I've heard.'

The cost of non-quality must be high and I wonder how they are using statistical process control, thought Nicholas. He wandered down further to where the controller unit for the motor was being assembled. This was a six-step operation performed by women whose function was to wire, solder and connect the appropriate joints. Between the third and fourth steps there was a pile of inventory. The fourth operator, a heavy lady in her fifties, seemed harassed trying to keep up with her operation. By, contrast the fifth and sixth operators seemed to have no problem in performing their work.

'Is Jidoka an accepted practice here?' Nicholas asked the last operator.

The lady looked at Nicholas with a weird look on her face. She was utterly confused and wondered what the heck he was talking about. Nicholas explained the concept to her. He didn't think it was worth asking her about Kaizen.

'What are these controller units in the red container?', asked Nicholas.

'Oh those are pieces that need redoing. Julie, the operator at post number 1 put the front panel on upside down,' said the operator.

'Have you talked to R&D about Poka-Yoke?' enquired Nicholas.

'Oh! those fellows think they are too educated for us. They don't have much to do with this assembly line,' she added.

Nicholas continued on further to the R&D department.

'Hi John, what are you doing?' he said to the head of R&D.

'Oh, we are just working on modifying the specification for the cam shaft of Model DLW-1455. We are not happy with the definitions and our suppliers for the raw materials are continually having problems meeting our requirements,' John said bluntly.

'Have you taken a look at applying the Taguchi concepts,' said Nicholas. 'That might help.'

Nicholas continued down the line to where the braking assemblies were being machined. On his way, he passed the office of Cindy Atkinson, responsible for planning and scheduling. He walked in. Cindy's office was a mess. On one corner of the desk was a computer terminal; any remaining space was covered with paper, order forms and charts.

'Good morning, Cindy, you look as if you are busy,' said Nicholas cheerfully.

'Oh! I'm struggling with the company-wide planning of all our products. I've developed what I thought was a reasonable aggregate plan, but our sales people keep modifying their requirements. First it's up, then it's down. I don't know whether we are coming or going. Each morning, when I consult our MRP system, I note some entries have been modified. Sometimes it's sales changes, but not always. This means that I have to keep modifying my written work orders to the operators.'

As she was talking, the phone rang. Cindy picked it up. The caller was speaking loud. He recognised the high-pitched voice of Mike Burton. Cindy talked for a while, then put the phone down.

'I have to dash,' said Cindy. 'Our number three milling machine is down.' With that, she was gone.

Nicholas glanced at his watch. It was close to lunchtime. He felt he had seen enough for the morning, so he set off at a steady pace to his office. He was glad to be away from the noise of the DLW-1455 production line.

Back in his office, Nicholas glanced at the half-finished quality management report sitting on his desk. The first thing he thought he would do for the problems with model DLW-1455 is to make an Ishikawa and Pareto analysis. Since he knew the Somfy corporation well, he also wondered about benchmarking.

Required

1   How would you asses the quality situation at Wento from a Total Quality Management point of view? What improvements would you suggest? (Note, some of the terms in this case are also discussed in Chapter 12, *Operations Planning*, Chapter 13, *Material Requirements Planning,* and Chaper 26, *Auditing Operations*).

NOTES AND REFERENCES

1. 'Jaguar factory tries to blend automation with best traditions of hand-crafted work'(1991) *Wall Street Journal Europe* 25 July.
2. *International Standards Organization.* (1994) ISO 8402: 1994. Quality management and quality assessment – vocabulary.
3. Millbank, D. (1994) 'New Competitor: East Europe's industry is raising its quality and taking on the west: Swift change in work habits yields exportable goods while costs remain low. A halt to drinking on the job', *Wall Street Journal Europe* 22 September.
4. 'Statecraft at Renault: Does state control always limit a manager? Renault's Louis Schweitzer has held the state at bay Until now' (1995) *The Economist* 27 May.
5. 'Cost cutting, how to do it right' (1990) *Fortune* 9 April: 28.
6. Deming, W. E. (1991) 'Philosophy continues to flourish', *APICS-The-Performance Advantage* 1(4): 20.
7. Deming, W. E. (1986) 'Out of the Crisis', MIT Centre for Advanced Engineering Study Cambridge, MA, USA.
8. Crosby, P. B. (1979) Quality is Free, New York, McGraw Hill, New York: (Also published by Cambridge University Press.)
9. Feigenbaum, A. V. (1983) *Total Quality Control: Engineering and Management*, New York: McGraw-Hill.
10. 'Never mind the buzzwords. Roll up your sleeves. The Feigenbaum brothers' advice is pragmatic, and it saves companies big bucks', (1996) *Business Week* 22 January: 50–51.
11. 'Vehicle Recalls in the US Surged to 11 million in 1993' (1994) *Wall Street Journal Europe* 24 February: 5.
12. 'Hotel lock failures may mean, No Exit. Key cards foil prowlers, and also guests' (1996), *Wall Street Journal Europe* 15 April: 4.
13. From a confidential study directed by Derek Waller.
14. 'On the line: Automotive suppliers in Germany take aim at years of inefficiency: Facing likely shakeout, plants try Japanese techniques to boost competitiveness. Catching up is common sense' (1996) *Wall Street Journal Europe* 6 February.
15. *Taguchi Methods: Selected Papers on Methodology and Applications* (1988) Dearborn, MI: ASI Press. USA.
16. 'The quality imperative' (1991) *Business Week* 2 December.
17. 'IBM discovers a simple pleasure' (1990) *Fortune* 21 May: 45.
18. 'An embarrassment of glitches galvanises Chrysler: With its vaunted turnaround threatened, No 3 gets serious about quality' (1995) *Business Week* 17 April: 58-59.
19. *Time* (1996) 15 January: 39.
20. 'The Straining of Quality: American companies are discovering what happens when total quality meets total chaos' (1995) *The Economist* 14 January.
21. Shipman, A. (1993) 'ISO 9000', *International Management* May:
22. Rothery, B. (1993) ISO 9000, Aldershot: Gower. (Includes Quality Manual Manufacturing and Quality Manual Services.)
23. *Interleaf Inc.* Prospect Place, 9 Hillside Avenue, Waltham, MA 02154, USA.
24. Norme Européene, Comité Européen de Normalisation, Brussels, Belgium.
25. 'A victim of its own success' (1993) *Financial Times* 21 July.
26. 'Histoire d'une adhésion', European Foundation for Quality Management, Brussels, Belgium.
27. 'Le Prix Européen de la Qualité', *Brochure d'information* (1997) European Foundation for Quality Management, Brussels, Belgium.
28. Taken from World Wide Web, URL: http://www.efqm.org/past.htm.
29. New, C. C and Szwejczewski, M. (1997) Best Factory Awards Audit, 1997, *Management Today*, Cranfield School of Management.
30. *Management Today's Guide to Britain's Best Factories* (1995) Department of Trade and Industry, Haymarket Business Publications.
31. *Management Today's Guide to Britain's Best Factories* (1996) Department of Trade and Industry, Haymarket Business Publications.
32. *Management Today's Guide to Britain's Best Factories* (1997) Department of Trade and Industry, Haymarket Business Publications.
33. National Institute of Standards and Technology, Route 270 and Quince Orchard Road, Administration Buillding, Room A537, Gaithersburg, MD, USA 20899-0001.
34. Findings and Purpose Section of US Public Law 100-107.
35. 'Bombs Away: US military contractor gets tough scrutiny for defective products: Missile bolt snaps in midair; Federal prosecutors find a high-level coverup. Other probes hit Lucas, Philips'. (1996) *Wall Street Journal Europe* 4 March.

FURTHER READING

'Managing for quality, costs. A bean-counter's best friend: This nifty, but unorthodox, accounting technique can unmask a company's hidden costs' (1991) *Business Week* 2 December: 38–39.

Akao, Y. (1990) *Quality Function Deployment: Integrating Customer Requirements into Product Design*, Cambridge, MA: Productivity Press.

Balkin, D. B. and Dolan, S. (1997) 'Rewards for team contributions to quality', *Journal of Compensation and Benefits* 13: 41–46.

Brown, M. G. (1997) 'Measuring up against the 1997 Baldrige criteria', *Journal for Quality and Participation* 20: 22–28.

Crosby, P. B. (1995) 'Thinking about the return of quality past', *Journal for Quality and Participation* 18: 97.

Dumond, E. J. (1995) 'Learning from the quality improvement process: Experience from U.S. manufacturing firms', *Production and Inventory Management Journal* 36: 7–13.

Eddy, D. M. (1997) 'Balancing cost and quality in fee-for-service versus managed care', *Health Affairs* (3): 162–73.

Ettlie, J. E. (1995) 'Quality is back', *Production* 107: 14–15.

Fredendall, L. D. and Robbins, T. L. (1995) 'Modelling the role of total quality management in the customer focused organisation', *Journal of Managerial Issues* 7: 403–19.

Giunipero, L. C., Brewer, D. J. (1993) 'Performance based evaluation systems under total quality management', *International Journal of Purchasing and Materials Management* 29: 35–41.

Griffin, A. and Hauser, J. R. (1993) 'The voice of the customer', *Marketing Science* 12: 1–27.

Heaphy M. and Gruska, G. (1995) *The Malcolm Baldrige National Quality Award*, Reading, MA and Wokingham: Addison Wesley Longman.

Hines, J. (1995) 'Delight makes the difference: The story of AT&T Universal Card', *TQM Magazine* 7(3): 6–11.

Juran, J. M. (1993) 'Made in the USA: A renaissance in quality', *Harvard Business Review* 71(4): 42–50.

Niehoff, B. P. and Whitney-Bammerlin, D. L. (1995) 'Don't let your training process derail your journey to total quality management', *SAM Advanced Management Journal* 60(1): 39-45.

Niven, D. (1993) 'When times get tough, what happens to TQM?', *Harvard Business Review* 71(3): 20–34.

Oakland, J. S. (1989) *Total Quality Management*, Oxford: Heineman Professional.

Pojidaeff, D. (1995) 'The core principles of participative management', *Journal for Quality and Participation* 18(7): 44–47.

Spreha, S. A. and Helms, M. M. 'ISO 9000: A struggle well worth the effort', *Production and Inventory Management Journal* 36(4) 46–52.

Weeks, B. Helms, M. M. and Ettkin, L. P. (1995) 'Are we ready for TQM? A case study', *Production and Inventory Management Journal* 36(4): 27–32.

5 | An environmental balance

Objectives and overview

Operations and supply-chain management functions with reference to the external environment, where resource depletion and pollution are concerns. The objective of this chapter is to underscore that operations management and environmental management are very closely linked. The chapter opens by presenting the broad environmental issues of organizations and then continues by summarizing the principal sources of environmental damage. After this, it discusses the concept of a product life-cycle analysis as a tool to manage environmental problems better from product conception through to disposal at the end of a product's useful life. The chapter then presents some of the considerations in minimizing environmental damage, including product packaging and possibilities for transportation systems. There is a section on cost/benefit analysis as a decision-making tool related to environmental programmes. The chapter then goes on to illustrate what firms might do to organize for sound environmental management, before concluding by reviewing the requirements of ISO-14000, the international environmental standard.

ENVIRONMENTAL ISSUES

The business firm is a system that interacts with the external environment. Among the many concerns in this external environment are economic use of natural resources, and pollution. Since operations is a subsystem of the business firm, then operations management responsibilities must take into account the environment in an ecological sense.

A strategic component

As with quality, environmental management issues are strategic. The decisions for a chemical firm to phase out the production of chlorofluorocarbons, for an airline company to invest in quieter, more fuel-efficient aeroplanes or the paper company to eliminate chlorine-based bleaching are long term, require significant capital investment and must have full top-management support. Like quality management, environmental issues have broad implications in operations. In the worst scenario, it is often as a result of poor operations management that environmental accidents occur.

Drivers for an environmental balance

As well as the extreme case of industrial accidents, other reasons that management needs to be concerned about the environment are that environmental controls in the European Union, in the USA and, to a certain extent, in Japan are becoming strict. There is also pressure from a growing environmentally conscious public, often fortified by the activities and discoveries of Greenpeace. Furthermore, many industry leaders believe that good environmental management makes long-term economic sense. Companies that score well on environmental programmes can become market leaders. Many consumers equate sound environmental products and/or processes with quality. Finally, every operations manager is a consumer and every top manager is a consumer. All business people live in society. Thus, from a moral, social and ethical point of view, environmental issues must be on a manager's agenda.

Environment and the supply chain

Environmental issues impact the entire operations supply chain. They are a consideration in plant location, raw-material purchases, product design, technologies employed, manufacturing processes, packaging, transportation, energy consumption, worker safety, marketing, sales, use and final product disposal.

Population is the environmental trigger

Population growth is the trigger of environmental matters, since more consumers demand more goods and services and the production, use and disposal of these leads to environmental damage, as illustrated in Figure 5.1. It is true that business, and particularly some industries such as oil refining, fertilizers, paper making and chemicals are directly responsibly for most environmental damage. However, the blame should not be heaped entirely on industry, because it provides goods and services at an economic price. Consumers are happy to use plastic wrapping, petrol for automobiles, refrigerators, computer products, throw-away nappies, etc.

Financial implications

If companies suffer an environmental disaster, the damage, both to the company image and in direct financial terms, can be high and can even lead to bankruptcy. Consider the following catastrophic operational situtations.

Sandoz

On 1 November 1986, there was a fire at the Sandoz (Novartis after the 1996 merger with Ciba-Geigy) production site near Basle, Switzerland. Some 15 000 m³ of water used to contain the fire flowed into the River Rhine, carrying with it over 1300 tonnes of agricultural chemicals, toxic insecticides and mercury compounds.[1] Hundreds of fish died, including 220 tonnes of eels, and drinking water for Swiss, French, German and Dutch communities was contaminated. The public reacted by boycotting the company's products and threats were made to the safety of executives. The estimated cost to the company was SF 60 million (US $50 million).[2]

Exxon Valdez

On the 24 March 1989, the oil tanker, *Exxon Valdez*, ran aground in the Prince William Sound, Alaska. Some 45 000 tonnes of oil was discharged along 1700 km of the coastline. Many species of fish and birds were destroyed. The fishing community suffered heavy losses. Again, people boycotted Exxon oil products, the stock price dropped and the president and officers of Exxon were lambasted in the press for their reactions to the disaster. The cost to Exxon was over US $1 billion.[3]

Three Mile Island

On 29 March 1979, the cooling system of Unit 2 of Metropolitan Edison's Three Mile Island nuclear power plant near Harrisburg, Pennsylvania, USA, failed to operate. By mistake, the safety cooling system was shut off and the reactor temperature system rose to a dangerous level. There was a threat of a meltdown, which could have released 100 tonnes of radiation into the atmosphere. All pregnant women and children within an 8 km radius were evacuated. To relieve system pressure, 1.5 million litres of lightly contaminated water was dumped in the Susquehanna River. Ten years afterwards, the cost of the accident was put at US $973 million, seven times the estimate made immediately after the accident. The nuclear facility will never reopen.[4]

Johns-Manville Corporation

Johns-Manville Corporation, Denver, USA was the world's largest producer of asbestos products. Asbestos is a fibrous material that is easily woven, does not burn and is a poor conductor of heat. As a result, it was used extensively in insulation of buildings and ships, for floor and ceiling tiles and for automotive brake linings. Subsequent research showed asbestos to be carcinogenic and many consumers filed expensive lawsuits against the company. Even though it was financially healthy, Johns-Manville filed for Chapter 11 bankruptcy on 26 August 1982 because of the litigation. Liability was of the order of $2 billion. The company (under a different form) re-emerged from bankruptcy, but Johns-Manville no longer exists.[5]

Global concern

Environmental concerns are not a local, regional or even a country issue. They are global. Consider the following:

- Toxic chemicals from the Sandoz accident spilled into the Rhine in Switzerland and then poisoned the drinking water for German, French and Dutch residents!
- Acid gases, emitted by British power plants, destroy the forests of Sweden![6]
- The explosion in the Soviet Chernobyl nuclear power plant in 1986 spewed radiation over much of eastern and western Europe and was even detected in the USA.[7]

Figure 5.1   The chain of environmental damage.

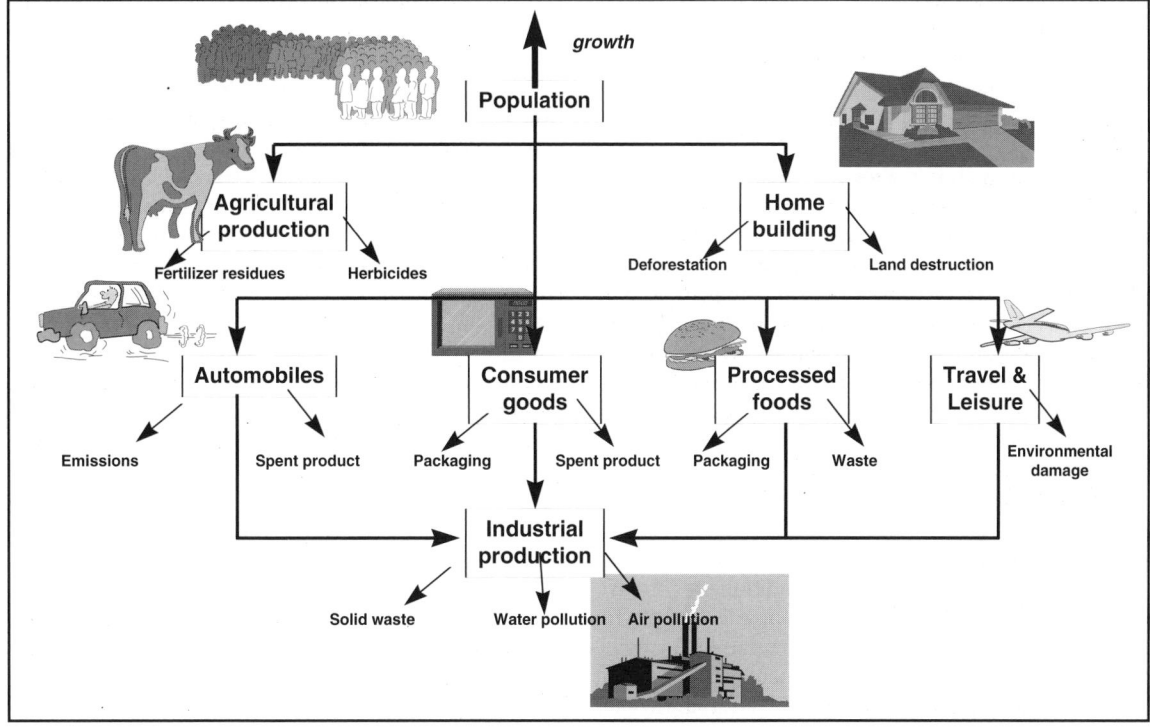

Sustainable development

Resources are limited. Sustainable development is the management of economic growth, avoiding irreparable damage to the environment. By balancing economic requirements with ecological concerns, the needs of people can be satisfied without jeopardizing the prospects of future generations.[8] The concept of sustainable development is illustrated by the practice of deforestation.

Deforestation

Trees are an inventory of oxygen and absorb carbon dioxide, a major greenhouse gas. Clear cutting, deforestation or destroying large swaths of forests, such as the Amazon rain forests, destroys wildlife (more than 90 per cent of the world's animals inhabit forests). Forests are also a source of raw materials for many drugs. Furthermore, destruction of trees reduces the ability of land to absorb rain, causing flooding. Cutting down trees enhances soil erosion and, in mountain areas, the natural barrier to avalanches is removed (often a problem in the European Alps). The practice of most logging companies, in recognition of sustainability, is now to plant at least the same number of trees as have been cut down.

SOURCES OF ENVIRONMENTAL DAMAGE

Environmental damage is air, water and solid-waste pollution and excess noise. The following sections summarize the principal causes.

Air pollution

Air pollution is caused by contaminants, or excess chemicals, in the air, which in humans lead to respiratory or other health problems. On structures and equipment it leads to corrosion. Air pollution also damages plant and animal life.

Acid rain

Fossil fuels, particularly oil and coal, produce sulphur dioxide and sulphur trioxide when burnt. These gases, dissolved in atmospheric moisture, constitute acid rain.

Acid rain kills plants by attacking foliage and roots. In rivers, it destroys marine life. On building structures, acid corrodes metal and degrades stone and paint. Figure 5.2 shows the concentration region of acid rain compared to other common liquids.

Fog

Coal, when burned, is reduced to fly ash, which, when airborne and mixed with moist air, produces fog. A notorious fog occurred in London, UK in 1950–1951 when between 4000 and 5000 people died owing to several foggy days as a result of coal combustion. This disaster led to tough clean-air laws in Britain, which among others forbids the open burning of coal. Today, fog is a problem in such areas as Eastern European countries, Turkey and China.

Chlorofluorocarbons

Chlorofluorocarbons (CFCs) are inert, non toxic, chlorine-based chemicals used in the manufacture of propellants for paint and deodorant in aerosol sprays, coolant in refrigerators and air conditioners (Freon), cleaning fluids for electronic circuit boards and plastic foam (Styrofoam) for packing cartons used for eggs, hamburgers and electronic components. CFCs, when exhausted to the atmosphere, react with ultraviolet light, which breaks down the CFCs into chlorine, which subsequently attacks the ozone in the atmosphere. The destruction of the ozone barrier in the stratosphere allows high concentrations of ultraviolet rays to reach the earth's surface, resulting in increased incidence of skin cancer, glaucoma, cataracts, weakened immune systems and crop damage as well as the disruption of the reproduction of plankton that anchor the marine food chain. As a result of the Montreal Protocol in September 1989, amended in June 1990 and November 1992, the production and use of CFCs, and halons, is being phased out.[9]

Halons

Halons are a group of chemicals containing bromine and are used in fire extinguishers. Bromine acts in a similar way to the chlorine of CFCs and attacks ozone. Although the production of halons is small compared to that of CFCs, bromine is considered more damaging to ozone than an equivalent amount of chlorine.

Smog

The action of sunlight on automobile exhausts and factory emissions, principally nitrous oxides, initiates a photochemical reaction that gives smog, of which ozone and NO_X (nitrous oxides) are the main con-

Figure 5.2 Acidity of certain products.

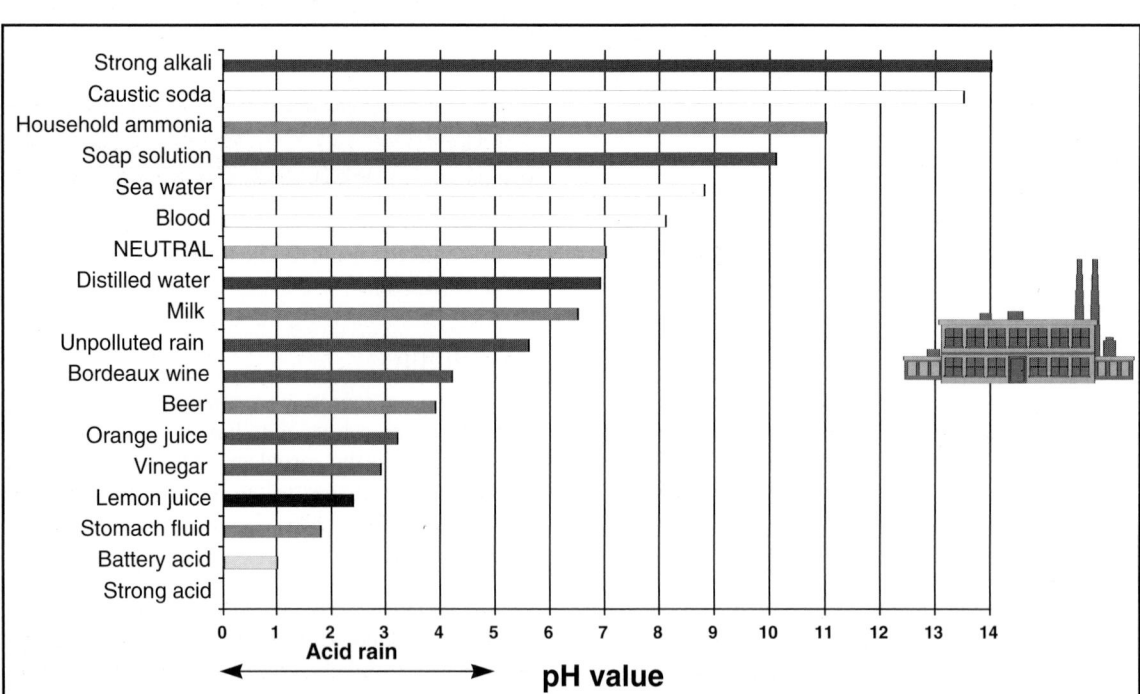

stituents. If an atmospheric inversion layer exists and conditions are still, then this smog is trapped at ground level, making respiration difficult. Los Angeles, Denver, Athens, Tokyo, Mexico City and Grenoble are cities that have chronic smog problems. As well as the respiratory effects on humans, smog attacks rubber in car tyres, windscreen wipers and gasket joints.

Lead oxide

Lead oxide is an additive used to upgrade gasoline (petrol). Vaporized lead in the atmosphere from automobile exhausts is highly toxic and can damage the brain. Its use in the USA has been phased out and Europe is heading in the same direction. However, leaded petrol is still used in Mexico, India and other developing regions.

Carbon dioxide

Carbon dioxide is an odourless, colourless gas under normal conditions and, though not toxic, contributes to the 'greenhouse effect'. Carbon dioxide is the product of the burning of any organic materials, including fossil fuels such as oil, gas, coal and wood. The theory of the greenhouse effect is that carbon dioxide, together with methane, are trapped in the upper atmosphere and their presence prevents the escape of heat. This causes the temperature of the earth's surface to rise, with a consequent impact on weather patterns and agriculture.

Radiation

Radiation is perhaps the most insidious of all pollutants. It is silent, odourless and invisible. High exposure is fatal and small doses can lead to cancer. Sources of radiation include nuclear power plants, nuclear weapons and associated manufacturing plants, nuclear testing sites and nuclear transportation systems such as submarines, aircraft carriers and rockets. Hospitals use radioactive iodine and cobalt for medical treatment. Radon also occurs naturally in the decay of uranium.

Water pollution

Water pollution is the discharge of toxic products, chemicals and other materials directly into rivers, lakes and the sea. It is also concerned with the dumping of such materials on land, because the toxic products can percolate into water sources.

Phosphates

Phosphates originate principally from detergents and their presence promotes the growth of algae. When algae blooms and spreads, it depletes oxygen and blocks sunlight, killing fish and other marine life.

Trichloroethylenes

Trichloroethylenes are the chemicals used in dry cleaning. They are toxic and, if not disposed of properly, find their way into drinking water systems.

Heavy metals

Heavy metals include lead originating from batteries, soldering operations and cans; chromium from stainless-steel products, cement, rubber and composition floor coverings; cadmium also originating from batteries; and mercury. Heavy metals are highly toxic and if dumped in waterways are consumed by fish, thus poisoning the food chain. Perhaps the most notorious example of heavy-metal poisoning is the Minamata Bay scandal in Japan in the 1960s. Mercury waste from a rubber and plastics maker was discharged into Minamata bay. More than 5400 people who ate fish caught in the bay died, were crippled or gave birth to deformed children.[10] A more recent instance of contamination by heavy metals occurred in April 1998 in Spain, near Seville when a reservoir, owned by Boliden Ltd, a Canadian-Swedish mining company, containing lead, zinc, arsenic, cyanide and other toxic materials, collapsed. Nearly 5.5 m^3 of waste escaped, contaminating farming land and a nature reserve and killing thousands of plants and animals.[11]

Sodium chlorate

Sodium chlorate is an oxidizing agent and bleach for making chlorine dioxide. It is used in paper manufacture, ore processing, herbicides, defoliants and pharmaceuticals.

Oil

Oil pollution originates from tanker or oil rig disasters, the illegal washing out of oil containers at sea and natural seepage.

Asbestos

Asbestos was used in the USA until the 1970s for pipe insulation, fireproofing, brake linings, roofing and flooring. It is now banned in the USA, but is still used in Europe and elsewhere in the world.

Arsenic

Arsenic occurs naturally in small amounts in food and is found in wood preservatives, paints and dyes. It is used in pesticides and solvents employed in the electronics industry.

Ethylene oxide

Ethylene oxide is used for sterilizing hospital surgical equipment, in the manufacture of solvents and lubricants and in the sweetening of petrol.

Vinyl chloride

Vinyl chloride is used in the manufacture of polyvinyl chloride for plastic, particularly beverage bottles, and in cigarette manufacture.

Benzene

Benzene is present naturally in some foods and occurs in petrol, oil, solvents and other petroleum-based products. It is found in cigarettes and is emitted in vehicle exhaust.

Solid waste pollution

Solid waste pollution in this context refers to the dumping of untreated commercial, consumer or industrial waste directly on land. In this case, besides being an eye-sore, the toxic products from this waste may eventually percolate into water sources. Alternatively, solid waste may be dumped into waterways; this then becomes a direct water pollution problem.

Human waste

This includes all untreated human waste, which is a great problem in large urban areas, particularly in developing regions.

Domestic waste

Domestic waste is all the packaging, newspapers, containers, etc. The quantity is enormous, as evidenced by the mountains that accumulate during a garbage collectors' strike.

Dioxins

Dioxins are a common name for a family of chemical compounds that have approximately 100 different structures. The most toxic is the chlorinated derivative 2,3,7,8-tetrachlorodibenzo-p-dioxin, usually referred to as TCDD. This chemical is the by-product of many chemical operations including chlorine bleaching of wood pulp. This bleaching process leaves traces of the dioxin in paper used in such products as coffee filters, toilet tissues, tampons, tea bags, nappies and kitchen towels. Dioxins are carcinogenic.

Farm waste

Farm waste is the solid waste from crop or animal farming.

Industrial waste

Industrial waste includes mine tailings from coal, copper, gold and silver mining and waste from paper and lumber mills.

Nuclear waste

A nuclear power plant uses rods of plutonium to generate heat. This in turn generates steam, which drives a power turbine. The plutonium, when spent, has to be stored and the only way to do this is in land repositories. Decay of the material to safe levels can take hundreds of years. Nuclear waste from hospitals has to be treated in the same manner.

Noise pollution

Noise is a pollutant, which in excess can impair hearing, reduce employee productivity and cause physical damage. Sound is measured in decibels and the addition of 10 decibels doubles the sound level. Experts indicate that about 85 decibels is the highest level considered safe for the uncovered human ear. Many urban areas and manufacturing plants have sound levels that are near to, or exceed, those levels. Table 5.1 gives some qualitative examples of various decibel levels.

Table 5.1 Some qualitative examples of various decibel levels

Decibels	Audibility	Example
2		Breathing
10		Private office
20	Faint	Average living room
40	Moderate	Vacuum cleaner
60	Loud	Food blender
80	Very loud	Power lawnmower
100	Deafening	Rock music
120	Painful	Smoke alarm, home alarm
140	Structural damage	Jet aircraft taking off

Natural pollution

Not all pollution is man made; some atmospheric pollution occurs naturally. For example:

- Particles in the atmosphere come from dust, forest fires and volcanoes.
- Plants decay and naturally give off chemicals.
- Sulphates from sea spray occur around coastal areas.
- Radiation comes from the sun.
- Radon is produced in the natural decay of materials.
- Sulphur comes from volcanoes.
- There is natural oil seepage, as for example off the coast of Santa Barbara, USA, causing both air and water pollution.

PRODUCT LIFE-CYCLE ANALYSIS

In view of the various kinds of pollution and because of the potential of environmental damage, one role of the operations manager (with others) is to consider a product life-cycle analysis (LCA). This is the evaluation of the life of a product from conception, through design, extraction of raw materials, purchasing, production, packaging, distribution and use to eventual disposal at the end of its life. The objective of a life cycle analysis is to minimize environmental damage, by paying attention to upstream activities, and to avoid 'end of pipe cleanup', or cleaning up after the product has caused environmental problems. Another terminology used is a life cycle assessment, or a cradle-to-grave approach, as illustrated in Figure 5.3. The following sections give some illustrations.

Product conception

In the development of new products (see also Chapter 6, *Design of the Product*) consideration should be given to deciding if the product is really needed. Does one really need electric can openers, petrol-driven leaf blowers, electric tooth brushes, potent herbicides, glues that also damage the skin, etc?

Product design

In product design attention should be paid to the following:

- Keeping the use and concentrations of toxic chemicals low. Polaroid in the late 1980s initiated a programme to reduce its use of toxic chemicals in the photographic industry.[12] Chemical companies have in place similar programmes related to the development of insecticides and herbicides.
- Developing new product formulations that are non-toxic, for example, using hydrogen peroxide instead of chlorine for bleaching, using water-based rather than oil-based paints, using lead-free paints and using enriched petrol rather than leaded petrol. Renault has indicated that by 1998 it will cease to use solvent-based paints at its factory in Douai in northern France.[13]
- Using recycled materials, such as paper in book publishing, plastic (PVC) in the construction industry and metals in tool making.
- Not designing with materials, or components, that are becoming extinct, such as ivory, exotic woods or animal skins.
- Designing products from renewable resources such as products from wood or cellulose-based-plastic, rather than petroleum-based plastic.

Figure 5.3   Life-cycle assessment: a cradle-to-grave approach.

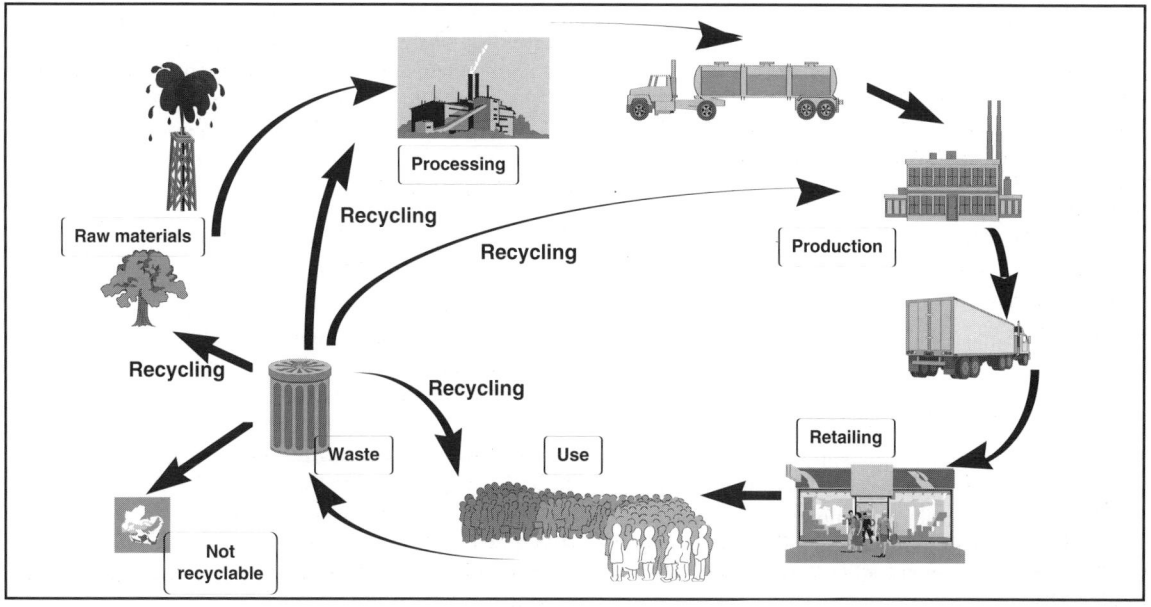

- Using less material and designing a process to minimize waste.
- Designing to ease disposal and recycling. Mobil Chemicals introduced biodegradable trash bags to replace the previous non-biodegradable products.[14] Furthermore, standardized materials are often easier to recycle. McDonald's designed a paper wrapping for hamburgers to replace the polystyrene clamshell packing.[15]
- Designing to avoid the use of heavy metals.
- Designing products that minimize harm to the environment, such as phosphate-free detergents or electric automobiles to replace those that are gasoline-driven in certain situations (baggage handling trucks at airports, postal delivery trucks, certain utility vehicles etc.)
- Designing products, such as automobiles, dishwashers, space heaters and aeroplanes that minimize the consumption of energy when in use.
- Designing products that can be reused, rather than discarded, when finished.
- Using rigid reusable plastic containers, rather than disposable cardboard.
- Designing using biotechnological means rather than requiring herbicides, e.g. for certain food products.

Purchasing

When purchasing from external suppliers, consideration should be given to:

- Using suppliers that respect environmental issues. The environment is a factor for Hewlett-Packard when selecting suppliers (see Chapter 16, *Purchasing and Subcontractors*).
- Using local suppliers, rather than imported materials, to minimize transportation. For example, local lumber rather than from the Far East, or chemicals produced in your own country, rather than in the Middle East.

Operations

Probably, the operations side of firms poses the biggest potential environmental threat.

Waste

- Use raw materials efficiently. For example, the paper industry, which once used half a tree and threw away the other half, now uses 90 per cent. It puts half the rest back on the land as part of reforestation and burns the final 5 per cent to produce energy.[16]

- In process and manufacturing operations, reuse wastewater rather than dumping it. Install catch basins to trap firewater; any scale, dirt, etc. can be collected and removed in special process units.
- Collect and recycle solvents, and the solid material they contain. Motor-vehicle manufacturers use cutting fluids or solvents to cool and lubricate the work piece in machining operations. They have installed filter systems that remove all iron filings and bur from the solvent, rather than letting it be discharged. This steel waste is sent back to the foundry and the solvents are reused.[17] Refining and chemical companies use a system of traps to prevent leaking oil and chemicals from going in to the sewer systems and this is also reused.

Energy

In the use of energy sources (electricity, coal, gas, or oil):

- Use new energy-efficient and non-polluting equipment and machinery.
- Develop cogeneration systems (using low-level heat) for electrical and thermal power.[18]
- Install energy-efficient lighting and heating.
- Automatic plant control usually uses less energy.
- Consider using cleaner fuels that do not contain polluting sulphur.
- Improve combustion by increasing the amount of oxygen in the combustion process or adding preheat. When the temperature of the combustion cycle is increased, fewer pollutants are formed.

Combustion gases

- Pass exhaust gases through mechanical equipment, such as filters, screens, cyclones and electrostatic precipitators, to catch the dust particles.
- Build tall chimney stacks – high enough to carry the pollutants away from urban areas and disperse them in the atmosphere.
- Use scrubbing systems, in which exhaust gases are passed through a stack and washed with water to remove acid gases.
- Use chemical treatment to reduce sulphur gases to elemental sulphur.
- Use catalytic converters, of the type used in car exhausts, for reducing automobile pollution.

Testing

Do not test products on animals. This is particularly the case for health and beauty products such as hair sprays, perfume and eye liner.

Packaging

In packaging the product:

■ Use just the amount necessary for protection. Reduced packaging reduces space and thus less storage area is needed. Also, less packaging reduces transportation costs, since more products can be carried in a truck.

■ Use packaging that is recyclable, reusable plastic packaging or packaging that is biodegradable.

Transportation

In deciding on the transportation and distribution part of the operation:

■ Plan and select in a manner to minimize environmental damage. For example, maximize the capacity of transport vehicles and plan that a vehicle makes the return journey loaded.

■ Use train transport rather than road transport where feasible.

Use

Educate consumers so that products or services are used in the most environmentally acceptable manner. In addition:

■ Encourage car pooling.

■ Where possible, use appliances, such as dishwashers, dryers and washing machines, in the evening or night when the overall energy demand is lower. This then reduces demands for new power plants.

■ Aeroplanes do not fly at night to/from urban areas.

Disposal

Manufacturers should cooperate in the collection, recycling and disposal of their products. Some recycling activities, such as paper for newsprint, bottles for reuse or pulverizing for making tiles, aluminium cans for melting and reuse, are quite common:

Motor vehicles

Motor vehicles represent a special case for disposal. More than eight million cars 'die' in the USA every year. Scrap yards have long made money by crushing and recycling the steel and other metals from junk cars, but this still leaves three million tonnes of rubber, glass and plastic, which are not easy to reuse. To compound the problem, the proportion of iron and steel in cars has dropped by some 20 per cent since 1997, whereas the proportion of plastics has risen some 36 per cent in the same period, as illustrated in Figure 5.4.[19]

There is pressure from governments, Germany is an example, to make the automobile manufacturer responsible for the cradle-to-grave or life cycle of vehicles.[20] This puts pressure on the producer to pay attention to the feasibility of recycling automobile materials, including not only the metal parts but plastic components, tyres, batteries, glass and paint.

Other factors include the following:

■ Car batteries are environmentally damaging because the lead and acid can leach into ground water supplies if the battery is simply dumped. Now, more than 80 per cent of batteries are recycled for reuse or recycled into such products as beverage containers and solar panels.

■ Automotive glass generally winds up in landfills. The glass contains plastic to prevent it from shattering in an accident and this glass–plastic combination is difficult to recycle.

■ Tyres pose a major difficulty in recycling. In the USA, about 240 million tyres are scrapped annually, with an estimated 85 per cent ending up in landfills. Some uses are being developed, such as fuel in the cement industry by Ciment Vicat, France and the Compagne Française des ferrailles,[21] and in the manufacture of sandals and other light shoes, for example by DejaShoes, Oregon, USA.[22]

■ Oil is recyclable. In the spring of 1991, Exxon Company, USA launched pilot programmes in Baton Rouge, Louisiana, and Richmond, Virginia, to collect and recycle used motor oil. Exxon has contracted with collection services in the two cities to pick up spent oil from service stations and recycle it into fuel for a variety of industrial uses.[23]

Advantages of a life-cycle analysis

In addition to minimizing the pollution impact of products, and the processes by which they are produced, companies can use life cycle analysis to justify claims made in product advertising and to avoid regulatory pressure from governmental agents. Furthermore, life-cycle analysis has shown that some products, processes and activities are more environmentally harmful than the considered alternatives, as discussed in the following sections.

Procter & Gamble

Procter & Gamble, together with Arthur D Little Consultants, after performing a life-cycle analysis on babies' nappies, concluded that the disposable vari-

Figure 5.4 Automobile ingredients (Source: *Wall Street Journal Europe* 6 May 1991).

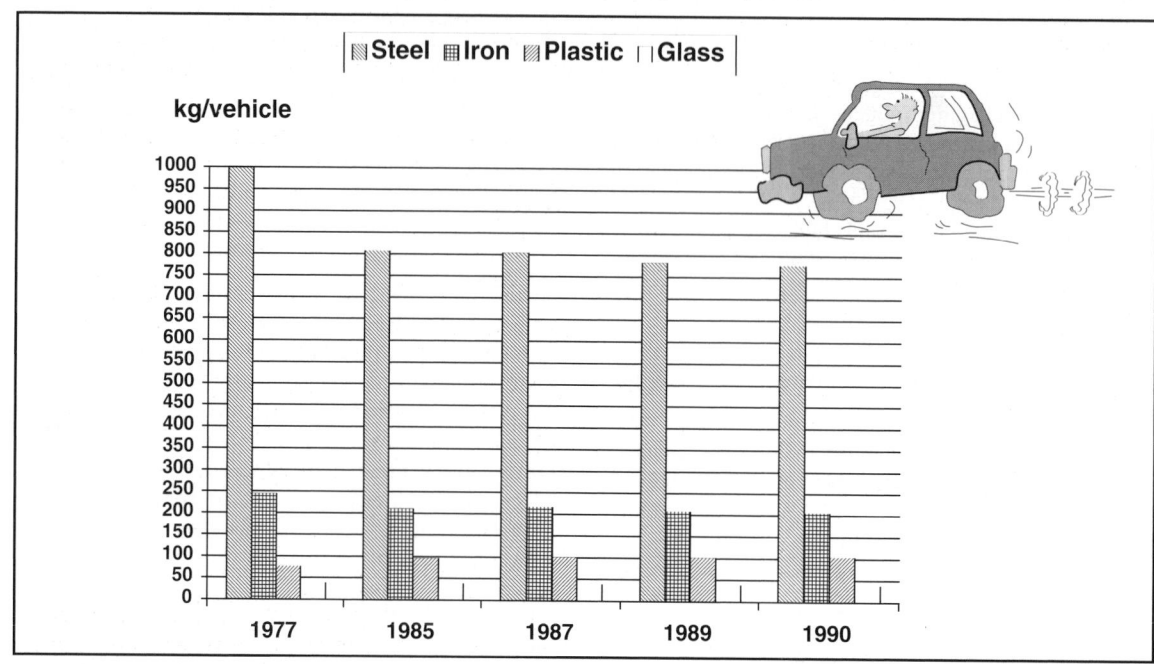

eties create less environmental impact on the environment than cloth nappies, which require a lot of water and energy to clean them for reuse.[24]

Paper cartons

Non-refillable paper cartons have less impact than bottles. Bottles occupy more space, use more energy for transportation and use a lot of water and energy for washing. Paper cartons also require less energy in refrigeration. When bottles are eventually disposed of in a landfill, they take up more space than paper and are not biodegradable.

Assumptions of a life-cycle analysis

A life-cycle analysis depends on the initial assumptions. Examples are:

- In the supply chain, over what distance are products transported? The conclusions may be different in a small country like Switzerland from, say, the USA.
- How many times will a bottle be used? The environmental impact may be less if the answer is 200 times rather than 10.

The BATNEEC principle

The BATNEEC principle, Best Available Technology Not Entailing Excessive Cost, is similar to the life-cycle analysis, except that it looks directly at cost. It is the response to the criterion, 'if the cost is affordable, and the product is more environmentally acceptable, then this would be the preferred technology'.[25] Some examples are:

- Design a photo copier unit that uses solvent free inks, and accepts paper that has been recycled (more dust is produced from some recycled paper).
- Develop fuel-efficient and quieter engines for aircraft and road vehicles.
- Design roll-on deodorants, or pump-action beauty products, instead of aerosol sprays containing chlorofluorocarbons.

The article in Box 5.1 illustrates what some chemical companies are doing to minimize pollution from their operations.[26]

PRODUCT PACKAGING

In the operations and supply chain, there is not only the product but the packaging. This consists of cardboard, corrugated fibreboard, wood, polystyrene foam, glass, paper, blister packs (transparent plastic packaging made from a matrix of air pockets) and other plastics. The primary objective of packaging is to protect

Box 5.1 Cleaning up. Chemical firms find that it pays to reduce pollution at its source. By altering processes to yield less waste, they make production more efficient. Dow reuses a toxic solvent. By Scott McMurray, Staff Reporter

The U.S. chemical industry's record on the environment has been a sorry one. Despite tougher regulation and pressure from public-interest groups, it still accounts for nearly half of all the toxic pollution produced in America.

Yet lately, a new force has been driving the industry to clean up its act: economics.

In a major shift, U.S. chemical companies are coming around to the view that waste is not an unavoidable result of the manufacturing process, it is a measure of its efficiency. The more unusable byproducts a process creates, the less efficient it is – and the more economic incentive there is for making it better.

That's what Du Pont Co. discovered at its Beaumont, Texas, plant, which makes products for plastics and paint. For years, the facility had been spewing out a staggering 55,000 tons of waste annually. Du Pont engineers argued that reducing the pollution would be too expensive.

Not Waste After All

But when they took a second look last year, they found just the opposite was true. By adjusting production to use less of one raw material, they were able to slash the plant's waste by two-thirds. Yields went up and costs went down. The savings: $1 million a year.

"When I heard about it, I just said: 'That's amazing,'" says Edgar Woolard, Du Pont's chairman and chief executive officer. He says the company now even sees waste reduction as a way to achieve a competitive advantage.

Environmentalists heartily support this view. Slashing toxic-waste production "is very similar to energy conservation in the 1970s: There is a potential for massive savings," says David Roe, a lawyer with the Environmental Defense Fund.

The entire U.S. chemical industry, says William Reilly, Environmental Protection Agency administrator, is "getting religion" about the benefits of cutting wastes. A number of European chemical companies as well, including the giant German chemical and plastics maker BASF AG, are pursuing similar projects to cut raw material and energy costs.

Other industries, from semiconductor makers in Silicon Valley to metal-processing companies across America's Rust Belt, also are beginning to focus on toxic-waste reduction as a way to cut costs, curb pollution and make operations more efficient. But it's the chemical industry that has the most to gain from waste-reduction savings simply because it churns out so much.

According to the EPA, in 1989, the last year for which figures are available, the U.S. industry produced nearly half of the 2.9 million tons of toxins generated in the country and tracked by the EPA. Officials at chemical companies say that, since then, the proportion has stayed roughly the same, though the total amount of toxins released in the U.S. is believed to have declined. Some environmentalists have argued, however, that the EPA significantly understates the amount of toxins discharged into the environment.

The Toxic Top Ten
U.S. companies ranked by the amount of toxic waste produced by their various facilities*

COMPANY	FACILITIES	TOXIC WASTE (in millions) of pounds)
Du Pont	85	348.40
Monsanto	33	293.83
American Cyanamid	29	202.09
BP America	18	123.66
Renco Group	2	119.08
3M	51	106.04
Vulcan Materials	2	93.15
General Motors	133	87.87
Eastman Kodak	23	79.48
Phelps Dodge	19	77.42

*1989 figures (latest available).
Source: Environmental Protection Agency

A Bigger Picture

Richard Mahoney, Monsanto Co.'s chairman and chief executive officer, estimates that there is $125 million worth of material that currently isn't recovered from the waste that leaves the company's plants. What's more, other costs associated with waste are rising. They include processing, disposal and cleanup, not to mention lawsuits and government fines when those jobs don't get done right.

Dow Chemical Co. recently spent $30 million building a waste incinerator and dump to handle toxic materials at its plant site in Midland, Michigan. And, earlier this year, Monsanto paid the state of Massachusetts $1 million to settle claims that its plant in Everett didn't report certain waste-water discharges. It also paid $192,000 to a trust fund that supports the cleanup of Boston harbor. Last year, the company paid out $27 million to clean other sites. And at year end, it had an accrued liability of $120 million on its balance sheet to cover certain future cleanup costs.

Chemical companies might have made substantial cuts in toxic emissions sooner had they recognized some of the potential economic advantages, such as lower materials costs. "One of the differences is that we're now putting some of our best people into this area," says Robert Luft, Du Pont's senior vice president, chemicals. "When you do that, you can start making some fast progress."

The Legacy of Bhopal

In the past, chemical companies used to focus merely on complying with federal and state pollution laws for specific chemicals or plants. They didn't pay much attention to the aggregate amount of waste they produced each year, or the future liability it represented. Waste disposal costs were low, and the typical approach to pollution often was the dilution solution: Dilute wastes in massive amounts of air up a smokestack or water out the end of a sewer pipe. More-permanent solutions were unattractive. They almost always involved adding equipment, which meant higher costs, and, thus, intense corporate resistance.

That began to change after the deaths of more than 3,800 people in Bhopal, India, following the release of a cloud of toxic gas at a Union Carbide Corp. subsidiary in 1984. The disaster led to U.S. legislation in 1986 directing the EPA to compile and publicize a survey of toxic emissions, which put pressure on big polluters to do more than just meet minimum government standards.

In the process, companies began to discover economic advantages, as well. Some advantages came from increasing production efficiency, while others came from finding other uses for some of the byproducts. Along the way, companies began to conclude that pollution was a sign of a bad manufacturing system. "When you make a lot of waste you know you don't have control of your operation," says Mr. Woolard, Du Pont's chairman.

Dow Chemical has been applying the same philosophy to its operations. For example, the company estimates that by recycling a toxic solvent used to make its Verdict herbicide it is now saving about $3 million a year, and halving the amount of solvent going out the door as waste.

At its Plaquemine facility near Baton Rouge, Louisiana, Dow spent $15 million on waste-reduction projects last year that it says already have saved $18 million in toxic waste disposal and raw-material costs. The company promotes these projects internally with the acronym WRAP: Waste Reduction Always Pays.

Monsanto says that its nylon-fibers plant in Pensacola, Florida, has cut its toxic air emissions about 90% since 1987, and saved a few million dollars a year in raw-materials expense. The plant is capturing a toxic solvent in a mineral-oil bath before it escapes up a smokestack. It then recycles the solvent back into the production process. The mineral oil isn't wasted either: It is returned to the plant, where it captures more solvent.

Capturing a Carcinogen

Monsanto says it's Sauget, Illinois, plant, across the Mississippi River from company headquarters outside St. Louis, cut its air and water emissions of PDCB, a carcinogenic chemical used in making mothballs, by 90%, or 500 tons. The company cooled the plant's waste vapor and captured the crystallized chemical for reuse before it was emitted. Loading the product directly into tank cars under sealed conditions cut vapor emissions even further.

In some cases, the industry is building plants that incorporate the latest waste-reduction technology. A new Du Pont herbicide plant, near Dunkirk, France, is expected to produce 90% less pollution than an existing facility. Among other things, it will distill and recycle solvents.

In other cases, chemical companies are tying together production processes at different plant sites to cut waste and save on raw-material costs. Last autumn, a Du Pont plant in Mobile, Alabama, that makes herbicides and insecticides began tapping into the waste stream leaving the plant, pulling out solvents and titanium byproduct that it once incinerated. The solvents get recycled into the plant's own operations, while the titanium is treated and shipped to a Du Pont plant in DeLisle, Mississippi, where it is used to make paint pigments. By integrating production this way, the Mobile plant cut its annual toxic emissions about 12,500 tons, nearly 20%.

Getting Along

Besides cutting costs, these waste-reduction programs help companies earn public good will, as well as meet demands from regulators and environmentalists. Arco Chemical Co. is using several waste-reduction processes to meet the stiff environmental standards that apply to the expansion of its Channelview, Texas, propylene oxide plant just east of Houston. The Arco Chemical plant, where 17 workers died in an explosion last July, is in an area of back-to-back oil and chemical plants that parallels the ship channel leading to the Gulf of Mexico.

"Roll down your car window and the aroma will knock you over," is how George Smith, of the Sierra Club's Houston chapter, describes the area.

The environmental group feared Arco Chemical's plant expansion would fill the air with an excessive amount of benzene, so it threatened to put the plan through a lengthy public hearing process. In response, Arco Chemical agreed to install a distillation process to recover benzene from liquid waste at the plant. The process keeps much of the benzene from reaching the plant's water-treatment unit, where it could partially evaporate into the air before decomposing.

Room for Improvement

As it turns out, the added cost of the distillation process is largely offset by savings from the benzene that's recycled, says John Evans, environmental superintendent for the plant. And when all waste processes are in place, including catalytic converters that break down hydrocarbons before they go up the smokestack, the expanded facility will emit substantially fewer toxic chemicals than the original plant, even though production will have increased 200%, Mr. Evans says.

Environmentalists say the U.S. chemical industry still has a long way to go before it gets unqualified praise. But chemical companies contend that both regulators and the public will continue to see a substantial reduction in their output of toxic wastes. Monsanto, Dow and Du Pont all say their emissions have declined 30% to 50% in the past four years. They add that the numbers will continue to drop in the years ahead. The EPA is providing additional incentive: Last month, the agency proposed extending the deadline for required pollution controls at plant sites if companies speed up voluntarily cuts in their emissions.

Even though some of the short-term costs for the new waste-reduction programs have been high – more than $200 million a year at the largest chemical companies – Monsanto's Mr. Mahoney says it is money well spent. "Our initiative and commitments to environmental protection will, over the long term, make us more efficient, more cost effective and more competitive," he predicts.

Wall Street Journal Europe, 14 June 1991
Reprinted by permission of *Wall Street Journal Europe*,

products in transport, either during transfer in the production processes or in shipping to final consumers. In some cases, such as food products (ketchup, yoghurt and breakfast cereals), detergents and beauty products, the packaging and the product are associated. It is a major element in the marketing mix as a medium for communicating product identity.[27]

Package redesign

Packaging cannot be eliminated, but waste, and costs, can be reduced by such changes as:

- redesign of packaging structure to eliminate one or more layers;
- modifying production and/or product design of existing packaging to reduce weight;
- eliminating a packaging type in favour of another more environmentally acceptable one, such as one that is biodegradable (paper, cardboard and to a certain extent some plastics).

Digital Equipment

Digital Equipment Corporation (DEC) of the USA, estimated that it spends $54 million annually on packaging. This translates into 27 000 tons or 127 500 m^3 of annual waste. DEC reduced packaging by redesign. Previously it would pack its computer mice in three layers of material – blister pack, polystyrene reinforcers and then a cardboard box. It reduced that to a redesigned single cardboard box. In addition to providing all product information on the outside, the box provided the strength and protection originally furnished by the original three packing layers.[28]

Table 5.2 shows quantitatively what Digital Equipment achieved in packing design for four computer products – mouse, software (including documentation), computer modules and computer cabinets.

Other companies, such as Procter & Gamble, McDonald's, Burger King, Gateway (UK supermarket chain) and Migros (Switzerland's biggest retailer) have all taken steps to modify, monitor or minimize packaging so that it is more environmentally friendly.

Technology and package weight reduction

Over the years, industry has made significant progress through technological modifications, such as redesign, reformulation or manufacturing changes, in reducing the unit weight of packing, as illustrated in Figure 5.5.[29]

Pouch technology

Pouch technology is a means of reducing packaging weight while at the same time maintaining strength. The idea originated in France several decades ago and is widely used in dry food packaging and has been adapted for liquid products. Here a typical pouch of 3 mm includes a polyolefin seal layer and uses polyester and nylon for the pouch construction. Weight and volume are reduced by between 60 and 90 per cent.[30]

Recycling ideas for packaging

The following are just a few of the products that can be made from waste packaging:[31]

- benches and anti-noise walls from plastic packaging (Limburgse Vinyl Maatschappij, Belgium);
- air-flow deflectors from polyurethane plastic scrap (Dow Chemicals and Mobay Corporation, USA);
- pig pens from old plastic bottles (Reko BV, The Netherlands);
- chipboard that can be turned into briefcases, wall clocks and vases from drink cartons (Tetra Pak, a Swiss–Swedish packaging company).[32]

TRANSPORTATION SYSTEMS

The supply chain in operations includes transporting goods, or people, by road, sea or air.

Road transportation

Road transport is particularly polluting and the current tax and charging system for road transportation does not take into account environmental damage.

Table 5.2 Packaging changes introduced by Digital Equipment

Product	Product volume (cm^3)	Package volume to product volume (before)	Package volume to product volume (after)	Reduction (per cent)
Mouse	216.96	8.62	0.94	89.1
Module	791.98	2.79	0.72	74.3
Software	181.90	15.17	1.79	88.2
Cabinet	900 472.00	0.36	0.25	31.0

Figure 5.5 Weight changes of various containers (Source: *The Economist* 13 April 1991).

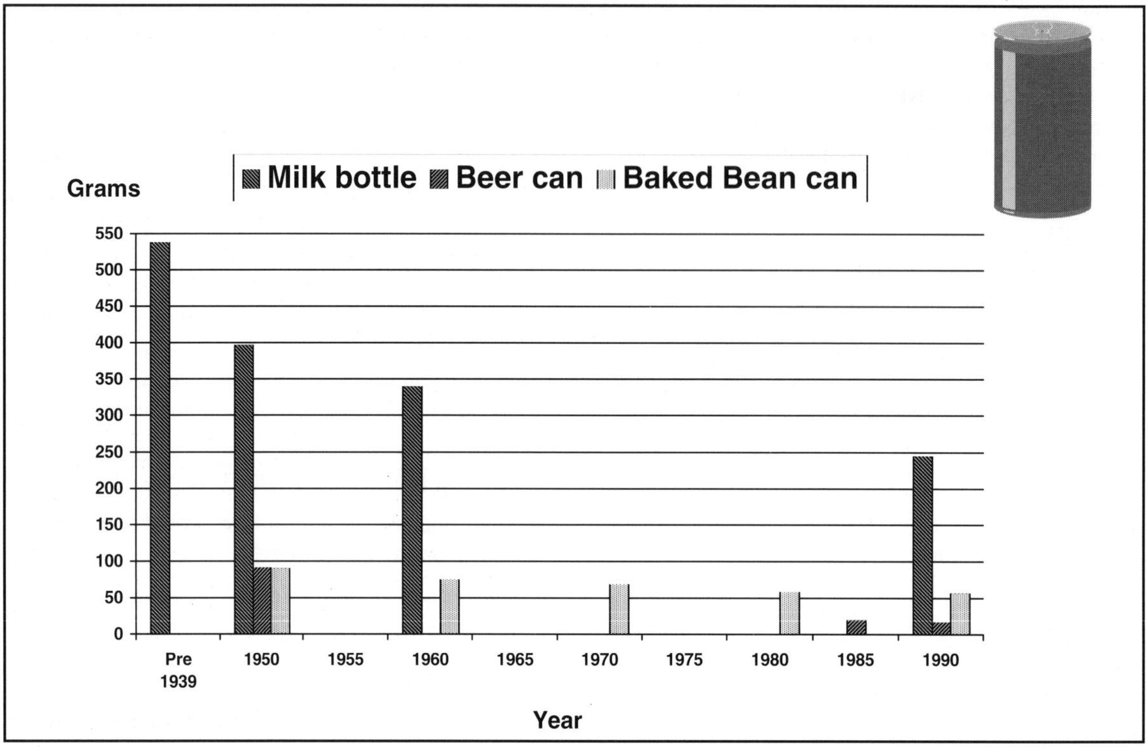

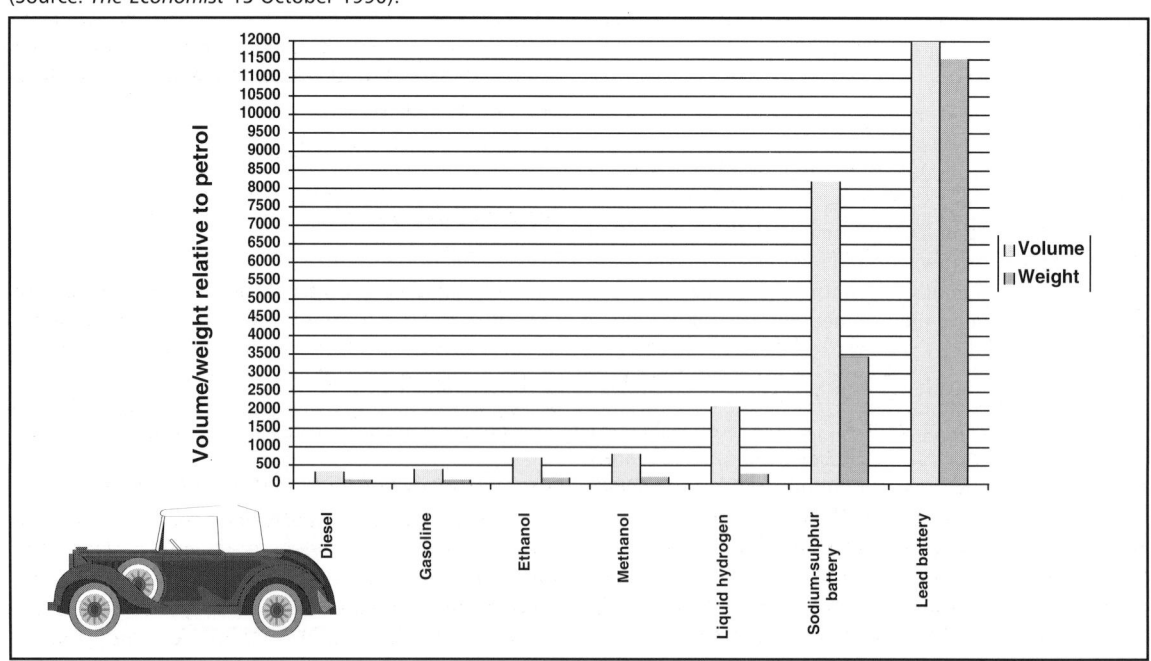

Figure 5.6 Storage volume and weight for fuels compared to petrol – petrol = 400 for volume and 100 for weight (Source: *The Economist* 13 October 1990).

Transferring road haulage to rail helps, but in many instances it is not cost-effective and neither is it compatible with just-in-time operations (See Chapter 15, *Lean Production and Just-in-Time*). Convenient rail links are not always available and outdated work practices on railroads make this transportation mode even more expensive. (See also Chapter 17, *Managing the Supply Chain*).

Pressure in Europe to pay more attention to transportation systems is coming from the European Union, which is advocating '*zero emissions from road vehicles*'. Initial proposals are asking that, by 2010, there is a 70 per cent reduction in carbon monoxide, volatile organic compounds and particulate matter and a 65 per cent reduction in total NO_x emissions.[33] Some considerations for reducing the environmental impact of transportation is given below and Figure 5.6 gives comparative data.[34]

Unleaded petrol

Lead-free petrol, with the same octane rating as previously, is produced by modifying the cracking operations in oil refineries. The US has been supplying lead-free petrol since 1978. Europe has been grossly slow in making the product available.

Petrol fuel reformulation

Petrol is a mixture of as many as 100 organic compounds obtained from the selective distillation of crude oil. Benzene, a major component, is carcinogenic and, with other hydrocarbons, is a contributor to ground-level ozone and photochemical smog. Oil companies (Arco, USA;[35] Neste Oy, Finland[36]) are experimenting with different types of less polluting petrol.

Lean-burning petrol engines

Lean-burning engines burn less fuel at lower temperatures and thus emit fewer oxides of nitrogen for similar engine performance. Automobile companies have long been working on this development.[37]

Catalytic converters for petrol engines

Catalytic converters, containing platinum compounds or other materials, are fitted immediately upstream of the tail pipe of motor vehicles to minimize emissions of carbon monoxide, nitrous oxides and unburned hydrocarbons. They have long been around in the USA and are becoming more common in Europe, where leaded petrol is still in use. (Lead in petrol 'poisons' the catalyst, making the converter unworkable). The technology of catalytic converters is not new. However, one of their drawbacks is that they only work at 260°C. Unfortunately, the largest quantity of emissions from an automobile occurs at start-up, when the catalytic converter is cold. These pollutants are not trapped. Companies are currently investigating the use of electrically heated converters, which would be immediately effective.

Methanol and ethanol

Methanol, made from natural gas or coal, and ethanol, made from corn, sugar cane or maize, do not contain all the hydrocarbon elements of petrol and, as such, their emissions are less polluting. However, engines that will use these as fuels are more expensive and the real cost of developing the fuel is considerably higher than that for petrol.[38]

Rape oil from colza

Rape oil from colza is another liquid substitute fuel for diesel or petrol that produces only marginally less power per litre than fossil fuel. Rape is a European herb, similar to the mustard plant and used as a forage crop for sheep and pigs. A strong impetus behind rape-oil fuel is that, with government-mandated cutbacks in farm production in Europe, farmers can use the idle land set aside to grow rape seed with government support.[39]

Electric vehicles

Electric vehicles are not new. Britain used hand-drawn electric vehicles for milk delivery in the 1960s, California uses electric wagons for mail distribution and airports use them for baggage movement. However, their use on a wide scale is limited because battery life restricts their range and the volume required for battery storage is large. However, all major automobile manufacturers have development programmes for electric vehicles with an eye on the California market, which has the severest environmental controls.[40]

Hydrogen-powered vehicles

Hydrogen-powered vehicles are an alternative providing a cleaner form of transport, though there are the following technology challenges:[41]

- On-board fuel storage volume is three times greater than petrol even if the hydrogen is in liquid form.
- The safety aspect of hydrogen; it is odourless and colourless and so difficult to detect.
- A viable hydrogen manufacturing and refuelling infrastructure would need to be established.

Electronic regulation of traffic movements

Electronic regulation of traffic movements involves systems where a vehicle driver, using computerized monitors, can see in advance such variables as road conditions, traffic hold-ups and weather patterns and thus make appropriate modifications for the journey. Automatic guidance systems make travelling efficient by reducing unnecessary travel distance and time with the secondary effect of fuel economy and reduced emissions. Many companies, including Nissan, Hitachi, Renault, Phillips, General Motors, Ford, Motorola and Intel, have electronic regulation development projects.[42]

Oil tankers

Oil spills are a major concern in water pollution and some considerations in oil-tanker design, which might avoid problems can be summarized as follows:[43]

- *Double hull*. A double hull gives more strength. The *Exxon Valdez* might have spilled 60 per cent less oil had it been double-hulled.
- *Catamaran design*. A catamaran design has wide ballast tanks that shield the oil cargo from collisions. A recessed tanker bottom reduces the chance of puncture in a collision (Shell International Marine).
- *Double tank*. In an ordinary tanker, pressure from oil above the waterline forces oil out of a hole in the bottom. With a double tank, the partition prevents leaks by eliminating that pressure (Mitsubishi).

Aeroplanes

Air transportation impacts the environment from a noise point of view, as those that live in the flight path of a major airport can testify. The noise problem is pushing manufacturers to build quieter aeroplanes. However, it is also putting pressure on authorities to ban, or reduce, night flying and not to permit the construction of additional runways. Airlines for their part claim that this is financially damaging to their business.

In addition to noise, airline exhaust emissions in the upper atmosphere cause extensive pollution, which is increasing rapidly with the growth of air travel. Air manufacturers are, however, developing more fuel-efficient and less polluting engines.

COST/BENEFIT ANALYSIS FOR ENVIRONMENTAL CONSIDERATIONS

A cost/benefit analysis is an analytical tool to decide whether expenditures for a certain project are greater or less than the financial benefits that would be obtained if the project was executed, or the operations were continued (see Chapter 22, *Decision Making and Risk Analysis*, for further considerations). A cost/benefit analysis is a useful tool where environmental situations are concerned, since very often the

battle is between those who think a project makes economic sense and others who think that it makes poor environmental sense. The following illustrates the broad concept.

Steel mill

Suppose a decision is to be made concerning keeping a steel mill operating. Elements to be considered in an environmental based cost/benefit analysis might be as given in the following sections.

Benefits

Over, say, an operating period of ten years the sum of the following total benefits is calculated:

- salaries paid to mill employees;
- social benefits to paid to employees and families;
- income generated by the firm's employees to the surrounding community (stores, real estate, service industries);
- taxes paid by the firm and employees at local and national levels;
- dividends to stockholders.

Environmental costs

Over the same period the environmental 'costs' are calculated.

Direct environmental costs are:

- installation of equipment to improve safety and minimize pollution.

Indirect environmental costs are:

- excess health costs as a result of unhealthy work environment;
- deaths (employees or town residents) above normal levels because of the mill;
- agricultural and plant damage from pollution;
- property damage from pollution (sulphur and acid rain);
- lost income from tourism (unattractive area);
- reduced quality of life in the town (unattractive living area).

On the basis of the cost/benefit criteria, if the benefits outweigh the cost, that is, the ratio is less than one, then the program should be continued. If not it, should be stopped.

Toll roads

Some countries, France and Italy for example, have an extensive motorway system controlled by toll booths as a means of recuperating direct costs. Other countries,

Germany, the USA and the UK, do not have tolls, but pay for the network through various tax mechanisms. Motor vehicles entering a toll road (taking a ticket) and leaving (paying) are idling. In idle mode, emissions of oxides of carbon and hydrocarbons increase by a factor of 2.5 compared to running at average speed. A cost/benefit analysis for using toll roads, taking environmental concerns into consideration, might therefore be developed as follows.

Revenues

These would be:

■ The total toll fees collected which represent benefits to authorities.

Direct costs to build

■ Construction cost of facilities, including entrance and exit roads and parking.
■ Cost of land for construction (not including motorway).
■ Salaries of all employees to build the facility.

Direct costs to operate

■ Maintenance costs.
■ Salaries of people to run the facility.

Annual accounted profit

This is basically the annual revenues less annual direct costs. In practice, the building costs would be depreciated over a certain time period, yielding an annual depreciated cost. This would be added to the annual operating costs to give a total cost.

Environmental costs

■ Cost associated with time lost approaching, waiting and leaving toll entrance
■ Cost associated with time lost approaching, waiting and leaving toll exit.
■ Pollution damage due to vehicle decelerating, idling and accelerating.
■ Additional vehicle cost due to vehicle decelerating, idling and accelerating.
■ Value put on environmental loss of land for booth and entrance/exit roads.
■ 'Irritant cost' due to waiting.
■ 'Costs' associated with accidents on other roads as drivers refuse to use toll roads because the direct cost to them is too high (motorways are safer than other highways).

When the environmental cost is considered in the profit equation, do the benefits outweigh the cost? That is, should the toll booths be eliminated and financing be arrived at by other means, such as taxation as is the case in Britain and Germany?

Real-world operating decisions

The following are real-world operating decisions where the environmental benefit obtained from a change has outweighed the cost.[44]

3M company

3M developed, at its pharmaceutical plant in California, a water-based medicine tablet coating replacing a solvent-based product. The cost of the change was $60 000, but this outweighed the need for pollution control equipment costing $180 000.

Proctor & Gamble

P & G, at one of its units in Germany, introduced Lenor concentrated fabric softener in a small and flexible refill pouch. This reduced packaging waste by up to 85 per cent with a corresponding cost saving to the company

Reynolds Metals

This company replaced solvent-based inks with water-based products in their packaging plants. This cut emissions by 65 per cent and saved $30 million in production equipment.

AT&T

AT&T redesigned their circuit board cleaning process, which resulted in an annual cost reduction of $3 million and the elimination of using toxic chemicals.

Xerox

Xerox instituted reuse of packaging and pallets based on standardized designs. This saved up to $15 million annually and reduced waste by 10 000 tons.

Criticisms of cost/benefit and the EPA

The US Environmental Protection Agency (EPA) often uses a cost/benefit analysis in assessing industry performance using uniform standards for emissions. If environmental costs outweigh the benefits, action has to be taken. Some of the criticisms of this approach are given in the following sections.

Evaluation

How does one reasonably assess the costs and benefits of clean air, water, health and life?

Technology

Industries, such as steel, that use different technologies are penalized. Those companies using older technology have to pay more to clean up effluent.

Small firms

Small companies cannot meet the cost and have to close down. Alternatively, small companies cannot afford temporary closure of a facility to install pollution abatement equipment.

High expectations

Expectations are sometimes unreasonable. The automobile industry claims that levels set for petrol for automobiles in California market are unobtainable. This has promoted the development of electric vehicles.

Sanctions

EPA regulations give no incentives for reducing pollution. All they do is provide sanctions. This is a 'stick', rather than the 'carrot' approach.

ORGANIZING FOR ENVIRONMENTAL MANAGEMENT

As for total quality management, top management must give 100 per cent support concerning environmental strategies, policies and operations. Some of the strategic and associated operational elements to consider in organizing for environmental management include the following.

Worker safety

Primordial is employee safety. Are employees being exposed to toxic chemicals, such as asbestos, sulphur compounds, mercury or benzene derivatives? Multiple chemical exposure, which is the exposure to a combination of chemicals that can interact and have a more pronounced – or perhaps a reduced – toxicity effect, needs to be considered.

Organizational changes

The Valdez Principle, named after the *Exxon Valdez* oil spill, calls on companies to make organizational changes and appoint an environmentalist to the corporate board, as well as to conduct an annual public audit of the company's environmental progress.

Compensation

Du Pont, USA, has made environmental criteria a part of determining a manager's compensation.

Internal cadre of environmentalists

An internal cadre of environmentalists includes having in place a crisis-management team to respond to any emergencies.

Research and development on environmental matters

In May 1987, Sandoz, after the disaster described earlier, set aside 10 million Swiss Francs for research and development related to the protection of the River Rhine.

Compensation for environmentally risky endeavours

Applied Energy Services, a power plant management firm, donated $2 million in 1988 for tree planting in Guatemala to compensate for a coal-fired plant it was building in Connecticut. The trees were intended to compensate for the carbon dioxide emissions from the coal facility that might contribute to global warming.

Overseas environmental practices

Ensure that environmental practices used in developing countries are the same as used in your own country. The equation is:

$$\text{Environmental practices overseas} = \text{Environmental practices at home.}$$

Gain environmental legitimacy and credibility

The Chief Executive Officer of Du Pont regularly delivers speeches on corporate environmentalism.

Collaborate with environmentalists

Work with, and inform, environmental groups when conducting an activity that will cause concern. Shell did not communicate properly on its proposed sinking of the Brent Spar Oil Rig in 1995 or its drilling in the oil-rich Niger delta, which resulted in the abuse of the Ogoni people in this Nigerian region.[45]

Prevent confrontation with governmental agencies

Inform, and collaborate with, the appropriate agencies before damaging activities are carried out. Comply early with regulations and take advantage of innovative compliance programmes.

Caterpillar Corporation

This US construction company defied a federal warrant by blocking inspection of its factory in York, Pennsylvania, where it was suspected that cadmium or perhaps other substances were causing health hazards. Caterpillar was threatened with fines and the imprisonment of two of its plant managers.[46]

Financing and accounting of resources

- Recognize that environmental damage is a cost and that true liability also includes environmental costs.
- Demonstrate that anti-pollution programmes pay and show the overall impact of the pollution-reduction programme.
- Gain the respect of the socially responsible investment community. As a corollary, a lending institution should consider environmental performance in assessing loans.

Provide the means

Provide the means to help consumers respect environmental practices. Two examples follow.

Carrefour

Carrefour, a major retail outlet in France, has implemented a recycling programme to treat glass, plastic, paper, clothing and metal, for which it has set-up collection areas. This is partly in recognition that as a service operator, it is indirectly responsible for much of the pollution problems.

Leclerc

In 1996 Leclerc, another major retailer in France, provided its customers with plastic bags for one franc. These bags could be exchanged at any time, at no charge, and Lerclerc takes the responsibility for recycling the old bags.

Human resources

- Recognize that, with the company, there are individuals who are environmentally conscious and that there may be pressure from these people, who are concerned about the company's image regarding environmental issues.
- Environmental performance and attitudes may be a consideration in attracting potential recruits.

- Work with Unions, because they are interested in safety and environmental issues.

Trading pollution rights

Manufacturing companies pollute and it has to be recognized that a minimum is unavoidable. Trading pollution rights is the process of buying and selling the right to pollute. This is a scheme proposed for minimizing the overall pollution level and it works as follows:[47]

- Specific pollution limits would be set for each company by government agencies or the local environmental control office.
- Companies able to reduce their pollution level below the established limit would receive credits in the form of permits. Those permits could be sold to other firms.
- Companies wishing to expand, or who could not comply with established limits, would have to buy the necessary credits from other similar companies who have credits to sell.
- Thus, all companies would have a financial incentive to keep pollution levels to a minimum.

Develop and expand environmental clean-up services

Building on the expertise gained in cleaning up its own plants, Du Pont has formed a safety and environmental resources division to help industrial customers clean up their toxic wastes.

Procedures

Have in place effective operating procedures before an accident occurs. The following example illustrates the necessity for this.

Three Mile Island

The Three Mile Island nuclear accident was in part the result of ineffective management communication procedures at Babcock and Wilcox (B&W), the firm that designed the plant. About 18 months before the accident, an engineer and a manager at B&W recommended changes in operator instructions at nuclear power plants designed by B&W. If the revised procedure had been followed by the operators at Three Mile Island, the accident could have been avoided. However, the instructions were never issued by B&W because poor management communication procedures obstructed timely decision making. In addition, B&W management had not established an appropriate communication environment and effective communication practices.[48] At the facility, even though a sophisticated information system existed, human and organizational factors limited its effectiveness.[49]

Environmental audits

Carry out a regular environmental audit. An environmental audit is a systematic, documented, periodic and objective evaluation of how well an organization, management and equipment perform on environmental matters. An audit facilitates management control of environmental practices and assesses compliance with internal company policies and external government regulations. It helps avoid accidents, legal action, bad publicity and even perhaps prison terms for employees.[50]

Steps and objectives

1. Define the scope: corporate, technical, design, plant operation.
2. Establish legal and policy requirements: emission limits, waste inventories.
3. Review actual performance against standards and policies.
4. Highlight positive aspects and principal achievements in performance.
5. Identify inefficiencies and problems. This may lead to cost reductions.
6. Indicate priorities for improvement.
7. Develop a list of action items, responsibilities and means of improvements, as well as a schedule for achieving modifications.
8. Publish a statement of achievements, performance and future strategy for internal and public access.
9. Use the statement to demonstrate to clients and the public the effectiveness of the company Environmental Management System.

European Union

The European Union is pushing for a proposal that would have companies do the following:

■ Undertake periodic self-assessment audits of their performance.
■ Have the self-assessments verified by an independent registered auditor.
■ Produce a statement of performance that would be public information.

Public affairs

Do not appear insensitive to environmental issues. If a company gives the public an impression that it is insensitive to environmental matters, the public may boycott that company's products, which can impact profits and

the company image. Some illustrations are given in the following sections:

Exxon

Exxon appeared insensitive to the *Valdez* incident because its reaction was defensive and antagonistic. In a survey after the accident, 41 per cent of Americans said that they would consider boycotting the company. Even after *Valdez*, on 1 January 1990, a pipeline owned by Exxon fractured on Staten Island New York and leaked into the Arthur Kill, a narrow waterway separating New York City from New Jersey. Exxon faltered again by taking too long to announce its eagerness to set things right. It apparently could not understand what the combination of bad luck, arrogance and ineptitude could do to its public image.[51]

The sinking of the Mont-Louis

On 25 August 1984 the French cargo boat, *Mont-Louis* collided with the British car ferry, *Olau Britannia*, about 20 km from Ostend, Belgium. The *Mont-Louis* sank in 15 m of water with 30 containers of 450 tons of toxic uranium hexafluoride in its holds. The last container of the gas was not retrieved from the wreckage until 4 October 1984. The maritime company was slow to admit that nuclear material was in the holds of the sunken vessel and the alert was given by the ecological group, Greenpeace. This insensitivity very much angered the public and, according to Greenpeace, was proof of the insecurity in the ways that toxic materials are transported by sea.[52]

Union Carbide

Union Carbide received high marks for its quick response to the Bhopal disaster. The accident occurred on Monday 3 December 1984. The same day, the company dispatched a team of experts, medical supplies, respirators, oxygen and a US doctor with an extensive knowledge of methyl isocyanate. Production of methyl isocyanate was immediately stopped at the company's other facility in Institute, West Virginia, USA. On Thursday 5 December Warren M. Anderson, the then Chairman and Chief Executive Officer of Union Carbide, flew to the plant site.[53]

AT&T

Another eloquent approach to an accident (not directly the result of environmental damage) occurred when a malfunctioning computer program led to a huge disruption of AT&T long-distance telephone services. An apology by the chairman, Robert E Allen, appeared across the country the next day in the press.[54] (See also Chapter 19, *Reliability and Maintenance*.)

ISO-14000 CERTIFICATION

Background

ISO-14000, the international environmental standard, came about because there were serious concerns among industry, government and the public about the development of a multitude of different local and national environmental standards and regulations. Many of these independent standards and regulations were viewed as potential barriers to trade and compliance with them placed an onerous burden on firms in tracking regulations and monitoring compliance, not to mention the cost. The ISO-14000 standard is an effort to level the field in terms of barriers to trade and competition and to ensure that organizations have a consistent environmental programme in place. It does not have the force of law, but companies will have to be certified ISO-14000 as a prerequisite for doing business in those countries that have adopted the standard.

Categories

There are six main areas in the ISO-14000 standard, broken down into two categories, organizational evaluation and product evaluation.[55] Within each of these two categories there are three sections.

The three sections under organizational evaluation are:

- Environmental Management System Standard;
- Environmental Auditing Standards;
- Environmental Performance Evaluation Standards.

Environmental Management System Standard

This requires that a company has a system that allows business units, divisions and plants to meet environmental goals without continuous oversight from a corporate environmental department. This means that in the company:

- A formal environmental policy and standards or specification are communicated and understood by all employees.
- Environmental measures, objectives and goals are developed and tracked.
- Legal requirements and compliance are monitored.
- Appropriate training is developed and implemented.
- Adequate documentation exists and is controllable.
- Emergency preparedness and response has been developed and implemented.

Environmental Auditing Standards

This section describes the general principles of environmental auditing, procedures for conducting environmental audits and auditor qualifications. Companies have to ensure that they have not only a corporate-level audit programme, but also an audit programme at the business unit/division and plant levels which requires periodic self-audit assessments to be performed regularly.

Environmental Performance Evaluation Standards

This requires a company to evaluate its environmental management system and the various operational systems that should be in place. Companies must develop measures and goals to assess environmental performance, such as the percentage reduction in air emissions, the hazardous waste generated, the reduction in energy, water and other natural resource consumption and the reduction in fines and penalties.

The three sections under the product evaluation category are:

- Environmental Labelling Standards;
- Life-Cycle Assessment;
- Environmental Aspects in Product Standards.

Environmental Labelling Standards

This section describes the general requirements for various environmental seal and other label programmes and deals with all environmental product claims, regardless of the media used. Companies using environmental product advertising, or making environmental claims for products would have to do so according to ISO standards. The objective of this section is to prevent false advertising and false claims.

Life Cycle Assessment

This section describes the principles and guidelines used to determine the impact of a product on the environment from the design stage through to disposal. This implies that firms should implement Design for the Environment (DFE) initiatives, including training and revised engineering processes to study how their products impact the environment. This addresses such issues as: finding benign or less hazardous substitutes for hazardous materials; redesigning manufacturing processes to use less energy, water or other natural resources, redesigning products and packaging for ease of disassembly and reuse and/or to use less materials that end up in landfills, and redesigning processes to reduce or eliminate discharges and waste.

Environmental Aspects in Product Standards

This section is a guide for standards writers. Its purpose is to incorporate environmental training into the development of product standards to prevent adverse impacts on the environment.

The development and the drive behind ISO-14000 has been strongly influenced by the British Standard BS 7750, the European Communities' Eco-Management and Audit Scheme (EMAS), the Chemical Industry Responsible Care, the International Chamber of Commerce (ICC), the Global Environmental Management Institute (GEMI), the Coalition for Environmentally Responsible Economies (CERES) and particularly the ISO-9000 Quality Standards (Chapter 4, *Quality Management*).

SUMMARY OF KEY ELEMENTS

- Environmental issues, although part of an organization's strategy, are important in the sound management of operations. They are triggered by population growth and impact the whole supply chain.
- Drivers for an environmental balance include the threat of industrial accidents, regulatory pressure from governments, an environmentally conscious public prompted by environmental organizations, economic advantages and simply the moral, social and ethical responsibility.
- Environmental issues are a global concern and all organizations in their operations should consider the concept of sustainable development, which is striking a balance between economic growth and environmental issues.
- Air pollution includes acid rain, fog, ozone damage by chlorofluorocarbons, smog, gaseous lead oxide from automobile exhausts, carbon dioxide as a component of the greenhouse gases and radiation from nuclear power plants.
- Water pollution is the discharge of toxic products, including chemicals, heavy metals and other materials, into rivers, lakes and the sea. It also concerns these materials being dumped on land, because the toxic products can percolate into water sources.
- Solid waste pollution is the dumping of untreated commercial, consumer or industrial waste directly on the land. Besides being an eye-sore, the concern is that toxic products from this waste eventually percolate into water sources.
- Noise is a pollutant, which in excess can impair hearing, reduce employee productivity and cause physical damage. Sound is measured in decibels and the addition of 10 decibels doubles the sound level.

- A product life-cycle analysis permits evaluation of the environmental impact of a product from its conception to its disposal at the end of its useful life.
- The BATNEEC principle, brings in the element of cost. The concept is to select the Best Available Technology Not Entailing Excessive Cost.
- Packaging contributes to solid-waste pollution, particularly relevant when packaging adds little value to the product. Package redesign, new technology and recycling or reuse of the packaging are ways to minimize the environmental impact.
- In operations, transportation in the supply chain contributes to environmental damage. Firms are investigating new technology as a way to reduce environmental damage, with the electric vehicle a key development in certain areas of road transportation.
- A cost/benefit analysis is a quasi-quantitative means of assessing the benefits of a project or operation when there are environmental issues to consider. On the basis of this approach, when the benefits exceeds the cost, the programme should proceed.
- Organizing for environmental management means setting up all the programmes, plans and resources necessary to avoid or minimize environmental problems. One key element is to have an environmental audit in place.
- The ISO-14000 standard, like the ISO-9000 quality standards, is a set of procedures to enable organizations to have a consistent programme to ensure that environmental problems do not occur. It is supported by the European Union.

REVIEW AND DISCUSSION QUESTIONS

1. **Environmental practices**. Consider operations with which you are familiar such as:
   (a) a university;
   (b) a medical centre;
   (c) a supermarket;
   (d) a library;
   (e) a firm where you may have done training.
   Suggest areas where you think the environmental practices could be improved.

2. **Environmental groups**. Environmental groups, most notably Greenpeace, are sometimes very harsh in attacking the activities of firms. For example, Shell Oil was castigated for its original decision to dump its Brent Spar oil platform in the Atlantic and then later in 1996 for its exploration activities in Nigeria, which were connected with the government's execution of Ken Saro-Wiwa, a political activist.[56,57] Sometimes the environmental groups' arguments are not too sound but the environmental groups usually convince the public. Do you believe that there is the right balance between environment and business operations in Europe? Discuss and justify.

3. **Life-cycle analysis**. Perform a product life cycle analysis on the following products:
   (a) the car you drive;
   (b) your household consumption during an average month (include food and non-food items, associated packaging and the way it is purchased);
   (c) the computer you use.
4. **Traffic reduction law**. In January 1997, a bill to reduce traffic and encourage cycling, walking and public transportation, passed its Second Reading in the UK House of Commons. It is hoped that it will become law by 1998.[58] List all the elements for a cost/benefit analysis for this situation.
5. **Economics and operations**. Some people believe that there should be an outright ban on the production of chlorofluorocarbons, oil-based paints, nuclear power and transporting nuclear waste. In distribution, forced use of train transportation instead of the truck is often advocated. This is all because of the environmental issues, even though the alternatives may not be economic. What is you opinion? Take into consideration any other operations that you consider 'marginal' in the environmental sense.
6. **Services and the environment**. Very often, one immediately thinks that it is the manufacturing firm that is responsible for environmental management. However, what do you believe the following service firms might do to improve their environmental management (consider the whole chain of activities):
   (a) Lufthansa Airlines;
   (b) Hilton Hotels;
   (c) Tesco supermarket;
   (d) London Business School;
   (e) local government.

CASE STUDY: IMPRIM

Situation

Imprim is a printing company, established in 1957 and based in Slough, England, with an operating area of some 10 000 m². Its product range includes:

- Newspapers
- Magazines
- Publicity brochures
- Catalogues
- Publicity packaging
- Folding boxes
- Calendars
- Administration and sales documents
- Labels
- Accounting forms.

It has diverse clients both from the service sector and from manufacturing and the company is one of the leading printers for the pharmaceutical and cosmetics industry.[59]

Imprim is principally an offset printer. In offset printing, an aluminium plate is etched according to the client requirements and mounted on a printing press. The image from this plate is then transferred to a second, rubber blanket, cylinder, as the cylinders rotate at high speed. The image is finally transferred to the printing paper as it is fed through the press. Imprim has the following sheet-fed presses:

- four offset presses that can print in five colours in a 71 × 102 cm format;
- one offset press that can print two colours in a 71 × 102 cm format;
- one offset press that can print one colour in format 45 × 64 cm.

All the offset presses are Heidelberg machines from Germany, which have built-in sensors to determine the paper feed rate, to detect the rate of ink flow and to monitor the image alignment. Imprim also has three web fed presses, where the paper, from large bobbins, is fed through the press at high speed. Web presses print at a higher rate than the sheet-fed presses, but the print quality is usually inferior.

The operation at Imprim is in three basic steps.

Preparation of the plate

Preparation of the plate involves engraving images onto the metal plates. This is a process which in silver, hydroquinine (an inhibitor in biological purifiers), chromium, copper and lead are expelled. The composite metal offset plates, which are discarded after use, produce hydrochloric acid and zinc chloride during the photo-engraving process. During the printing process the image from the metal plate is transferred to a composite rubber plate, which is cleaned after the printing process.

Printing

Paper, either sheet-fed (page by page), or web-fed (from bobbins) is fed through the printing press. In colour printing, pigments contain heavy metals, such as titanium, iron and copper plus inflammable solvents containing alcohol, acetone and esters. Other additives employed contain cobalt and volatile organic compounds (VOCs). Drying of the printed paper is by ultraviolet light and this produces toxic fumes and ozone products. In the printing process, the first few pages are a trial, which is discarded.

Once a printing operation has been completed, the machines, especially the rollers, must be cleaned with rapid drying solvents that are applied using cotton cloths.

Finishing

After the printing, depending on the product, the paper is cut to size and/or folded/trimmed on large guillotines. For those products that need binding, this is performed on machines where a resin of glue is applied mixed with solvents. After these operations the customer order is shipped out on wooden pallets.

Required

1 A print shop is a service function and individually they are small. However, if one considers Europe alone, there are literally thousands of printing firms. Discuss what you think are some of the environmental problems associated with printing, using the above information and your knowledge, as a consumer, of printed products. What needs be done to minimize environmental problems in this type of service operation?

CASE STUDY: THE BUSINESS TRAVELLER

Situation

Fred Seidel is in his London office in the Docklands preparing for a business presentation in Los Angeles. He rough-draughts his slides on PowerPoint and prints the 30 transparencies to see how they look. He then spends about a couple of hours going over them, making modifications in red ink. When he is satisfied, he goes back to his portable computer and makes the modification in his file marked 'LA Meeting'. When done, he prints off a master copy on white paper and then asks his secretary to make 20 copies each, plus a transparency set.

The next morning, Fred picks up the transparency package that his secretary has made for him and tosses it into his briefcase He hops into his BMW *en route* for Heathrow Airport. Fred's flight leaves at 12:00 and he arrives in good time to park and have a coffee and sandwich in the executive lounge. On the flight, Fred is offered a lunch of salmon and avocado salad. He picks at the plate, but after the sandwich at the airport he is not hungry and so he leaves most of the food and settles down to go over his presentation. When the next meal is offered, two hours before landing, Fred is fast asleep.

At Los Angeles International Airport, Fred picks up a rental car and drives to his hotel, a Hilton, close to Santa Monica, a beach city some 30 minutes drive from Los Angeles. On the way, not having eaten much on the plane, he stops at a McDonald's for a hamburger, French fries and Coke.

By the time Fred gets to the hotel it is 20:00. He checks in and takes the elevator to his room on the second floor. The room is cold from the intensity of the air conditioning. Unable to open the window, as it is permanently fixed, he turns off the air conditioning, drops his bags, and goes down to the hotel lobby for a drink.

The next morning, Fred, after a shower, goes down for the buffet breakfast. He leaves the hotel at 08:30 for his meeting in downtown Los Angeles. There are 15 people seated at the conference table and Fred, after giving each person a package of his transparencies, gives a very well received presentation. He is hosted for lunch at a restaurant at the nearby Bonaventure Hotel. After lunch, the team returns to the meeting room to go over some points on Fred's presentation and the meeting winds up at about 16:00. Feeling pretty tired from jet lag, Fred drives back to his hotel and takes a shower. Before dinner, he uses the hotel's copying machine and then drops some clothing off at the hotel cleaners. At the restaurant, he meets a colleague and they dine together. At noon the following day he has a flight scheduled for New York to make another presentation.

Required

1 Consider the business traveller, and there are thousands of them, using a host of services, from car rental agencies, airlines, restaurants, hotels, cleaning services, copying services, etc. What are some of the environmental issues that the operations of these services have to deal with? Where appropriate, consider their operations from a global perspective, taking a life-cycle approach.

NOTES AND REFERENCES

1. 'After the fire: How Sandoz dragged its corporate image from smoking ruins and rebuilt it' (1993) *Tomorrow* July: 10–15.
2. 'Le Rhin pollué par accident en Suisse' (1990) *Chronique du 20ème siècle*, Paris: Larousse: 1287.
3. 'Despite big cleanup, many Alaskans feel damage left by oil' (1991) *Wall Street Journal Europe* 5 September.
4. *Chronique du 20ème siècle* (1990) Paris: Larousse: 1175.
5. Steiner, G. A. and Steiner, J. F. (1988) 'Asbestos litigation bankrupts Manville, A case study', *Business Government and Society. A Managerial Perspective*, New York: Random House: 44.
6. Sawyer, J. (1989) '*Acid rain, and air pollution*', Geneva: World Wide Fund for Nature.
7. Medvedev, G. and Tauris, I. B. (1991) *Truth about Chernobyl*, London: Taurus; New York: Basic Books.
8. *ICC: The Brundtland Report, The Greening of Enterprise: Business leaders speak out on environmental issues* (1990) International Chamber of Commerce, June: 219–227.
9. 'Phasing out CFCs: The Vienna Convention and its Montreal Protocol' (1990) *Climate Change Fact Sheet* 224. World Wide Web URL http://www.unep.ch/iucc/fs224.html
10. 'Japan's green tinge' (1991) *The Economist,* 2 February: 50.
11. 'Breaking the toxic chain: Spain tries to limit damage at European marvel' (1998) *International Herald Tribune* 5 May.
12. 'Polaroid, Case study' (1997) Washington, DC: Management Institute for Environment and Business.
13. *Le Monde* (1995) 3 October.
14. 'Mobil Chemical Corp., Case Study, (1997) Washington, DC: Management Institute for Environment and Business.
15. 'McDonald's Environmental Strategy Case Studies' (1997) Washington, DC: Management Institute for Environment & Business.
16. 'Both ends of the pipe: The Economist Survey' (1990) *The Economist* 6 September: 15.
17. Renault VI, Lyon, France is an example.
18. 'Technology update, alternate energy' Texaco Co. report.
19. 'Automobile ingredients' (1991) *Wall Street Journal Europe*, 6 May.
20. 'Reporter's Question: Can Car Move? It's Blocking the Buffet' (1991) *Wall Street Journal*; 11 September.
21. 'Valerco propose une solution globale' (1991) *Lyon Fig-Eco* 18 February.
22. 'This walking shoe has one foot in the landfill' (1991) *Wall Street Journal Europe* 6 August.
23. 'Exxon launches pilot programs to recycle used motor oil' (1991) *Exxon News* September: 1.
24. 'Procter & Gamble, Case Study' (1997) Washington, DC: Management Institute for Environment and Business.
25. *Waste Minimisation Guide* (1992) Rugby: Institution of Chemical Engineers.
26. 'Cleaning up: Chemical firms find that it pays to reduce pollution at its source. By altering processes to yield less waste, they make production more efficient. Dow reuses a toxic solvent' (1991) *Wall Street Journal Europe* 12 July.
27. *Le Pack, Guide pratique du marketing de l'emballage produits de grande consommation*, (1987) BSN Emballage, CEP Communications, Paris.
28. Nielson, L. J. (1991) 'Measurement techniques in packaging waste management', *Proceedings of Corporate Environmental Management*, Washington, DC, 9–10 January.

29. *The Economist* (1991) 13 April.
30. Leaversuch, R. D. (1992) 'Pouch packaging', *Modern Plastics* 69(6): 64–65.
31. 'Bottled up: EC builds momentum for recycling plastics, but few are listening' (1991) *Wall Street Journal Europe* 15 October.
32. 'Waging war on waste' (1991) *International Management* November: 67.
33. White, D. (1996) 'On the road to zero emissions', *The Chemical Engineer* 25 July: 34–41.
34. *The Economist* (1990) 13 October.
35. 'Gee, Your Car Smells Terrific' (1991) *Time* 22 July: 38.
36. 'Auto-Industry Briefs, Nest Oy' (1991) *Wall Street Journal Europe* 17/18 May.
37. '55 Miles per gallon: How Honda did it' (1991) *Business Week* 23 September.
38. 'GM to sell green line of cars that can burn methanol, or gasoline' (1991) *Wall Street Journal*, 7 November.
39. 'Growing green fuel may be alternative to set-aside' (1992) *Financial Times* 15 September.
40. 'Renault and Peugeot plan to develop electric car' (1992) *Financial Times* July 29.
41. 'Hydrogen car moves on to the horizon' (1992) *Financial Times* July 8: 9.
42. 'A computer in every dashboard' (1997) *International Herald Tribune* 7 October.
43. 'Tankers designed to limit leaks' (1990) *Fortune* 16 July.
44. Gupta, M. C. (1995) 'Environmental management and its impact on the operations function', *International Journal of Operations and Production Management* 15(8): 34–51.
45. 'Can you be sure of Shell?' (1997) *The Chemical Engineer* 22 May: 11.
46. 'Can Cat keep out the watchdogs?' (1996) *Business Week* 6 May: 33.
47. 'Breathing easy: Want clearer skies? Just turn pollution into a commodity. US promotes the trading of emissions certificates in global-warming pact. Money going up the stacks' (1997) *Wall Street Journal Europe* 3–4 October.
48. Mathes, J. C. (1986) 'Three mile Island: The Management Communication Role'; *Engineering Management International* 3(4): 261–68.
49. Burns, C. (1985) 'Three mile Island: The Information Meltdown'; *Information Management Review* 1(1): 19–25.
50. *'Environmental Training for the Process Industries'* (1993) Rugby: Institution of Chemical Engineers.
51. Yagoda, B. (1990) 'Cleaning up a dirty image', *Business Month* 135(4).
52. *Chronique du 20ème siècle* (1990) Paris: Larousse, p. 1246
53. Steiner, G. A and Steiner, J. F. (1988) *Business Government and Society. A Managerial Perspective,* New York: Random House: 311.
54. 'The day that every phone seemed off the hook' (1990) *Business Week* 29 January: 23–24.
55. Tropea, L. C. (1996) 'An Opinion … ISO 14000 – A Corporate Perspective', *Global Environmental Services* AMP Inc., PO Box 3608, MS21-20, Harrisburg, PA 17105-3608, USA. (see also World Wide Web URL http://www.dep.state.pa.us/dep/deputate/pollprev/ISO14000/amp.htm)
56. 'Shellman says sorry: Royal Dutch/Shell faces a shareholder revolt over corporate ethics. Can its chairman come up with the right answer? (1997) *The Economist* 10 May: 73.
57. 'Can you be sure of Shell?' *The Chemical Engineer* p. 11–12.
58. 'UK traffic reduction law gets green light' (1997) *EEE May Bulletin*, Finland, January: 5.
59. Based on reports by Anne-Caroline Ulrich and Régis Laffont, Masters students, 1993/94, at the Lyon Graduate School of Business.

FURTHER READING

Billinghurst, K. (ed.) *Tomorrow: The Global Environment Magazine*, Published by Tomorrow Media, Stockholm.
Burke, T., Robins, N. and Trisoglio, A. (Editorial Board) (1991) *Environment Strategy Europe 1991: Including WICEM II Official Report*, Campden Publishing.
Cairncross, F. (1992) *Costing the Earth: The Challenge for Governments, the Opportunities for Business,* Boston, MA: Harvard Business School Press.
Charter, M. (ed.) (1992) *Greener Marketing; A Responsible Approach to Business*, Sheffield: Greenleaf Publishing.
Crick, M .J. and Linsley, G. S. (1957) *An Assessment of the Radiological Impact of the Windscale Reactor Fire*, National Radiological Protection Board, Chilton, Didcot, Oxfordshire OX11 0RQ.
Cunningham, A. M. (1989) 'Ten years after: Cleaning up Three Mile Island', *Technology Review* 92(3): 18–20.
Environment, Health & Safety Review (1990) Texaco Inc., 2000 Westchester Ave, White Plains, NY 10650, USA.
Environmental Progress Report, Dow Europe (1993) Dow Information Centre, PO Box 12121, 1100 AC Amsterdam Zuidoost, The Netherlands.
Environmental Projects: Badger, A Raytheon Company 16(2) The Badger Co. Inc., One Broadway, Cambridge MA 02142, USA.
Environmental Protection Bulletin (Quarterly) Institution of Chemical Engineers, Rugby, UK.
Fischer, K. and Schot, J. (eds) (1993) *Environmental Strategies for Industry: International Perspectives on research needs and policy implications*, Washington, DC: Island Press.
Gore, A. (1993) *Earth in the Balance: Ecology and the Human Spirit*, New York: Penguin.
Greener Management International: The Journal of Corporate Environmental Strategy and Practice (Quarterly), Interleaf Productions, Sheffield, England
Industry and Environment, (Quarterly), UNEP Industry and Environment Office, Tour Mirabeau, 39/43 quai André Citroën, 75739 Paris, France.
McKinsey & Co. (1991) *The Corporate Response to the Environmental Challenge*, Amsterdam.
Pearson, M. and Smith, S. (1990) *Taxation and Environmental Policy: Some Initial Evidence*, Institute for Fiscal Studies, No 19.
Porter, M. E. (1991) 'America's Green Strategy,' *Scientific American* April.
Schmidheiny, S. (1992) *Changing course: A Global Business Perspective on Development and the Environment*, Cambridge, MA: MIT Press (with the Business Council for Sustainable Development).
Willums, J.-O. (ed.) (1990) *The Greening of Enterprise: Business Leaders Speak Out on Environmental Issues.* Papers presented at the Industry Forum on Environment,

Bergen, Norway, 10–11 May 1990, Paris: International Chamber of Commerce.

Winter, G. (1988) *Business and the Environment: A handbook of Industrial Ecology with 22 Checklists for Practical Use*, New York: McGraw Hill.

'Cleaning up: Chemical firms find that it pays to reduce pollution at its source: By altering processes to yield less waste, they make production more efficient: Dow reuses a toxic solvent' (1991) *Wall Street Journal* 14 June.

'Corporate Quality/Environmental Management: The First Conference' (1991) 9–10 January 1991, Washington, DC: *Global Environmental Management Initiative*.

'Environmental technology: Muck and brass' (1996) *The Economist* 27 April: 93.

'Green warrior in gray flannel: Why business listens to activist Jeremy Legget' (1996) *Business Week* 6 May: 54–55.

'How clean is the plug-in car? After decades of false promises, electric cars will at last be introduced in the 1990s. But they will not be quite as environmentally friendly as once hoped' (1990) *The Economist* 13 October: 94–95.

'Nuclear power plant fire renews debate over safety' (1991) *Wall Street Journal* 2 May.

'Reed Beds' (1991) *The Chemical Engineer*, 14 March: 15.

'US Cities flunking ozone standards increase by 40 per cent in one year' (1989) *Los Angeles Times* 17 February.

United Engineers & Constructors, Today: Clean Air Programs, United Engineers & Constructors International, Inc., 30 South 17th St., PO Box 8223, Philadelphia, PA 19101, USA.

II | Part II.
Design in operations management

Operations is a system, part of a supply chain and an integral part of the organization in which it functions. Operations has to be effectively managed and designed so that it marches in harmony with the strategic objectives of this organization. The principal elements in the design of operations are the product; the process and the operations network; and the human resources. Together, they form a triangle signifying that one element cannot properly function without the other two. This part of the book then presents the nature of these three elements and how they interact. Chapter 6 concerns the product, or the finished unit or service destined for the customer, which in the business firm is the market force that drives the operation. Chapter 7 on process design and the operations network is how the product is effectively conceptualized, developed and produced. Finally, Chapter 8, on human resources, discusses the people who make it all happen.

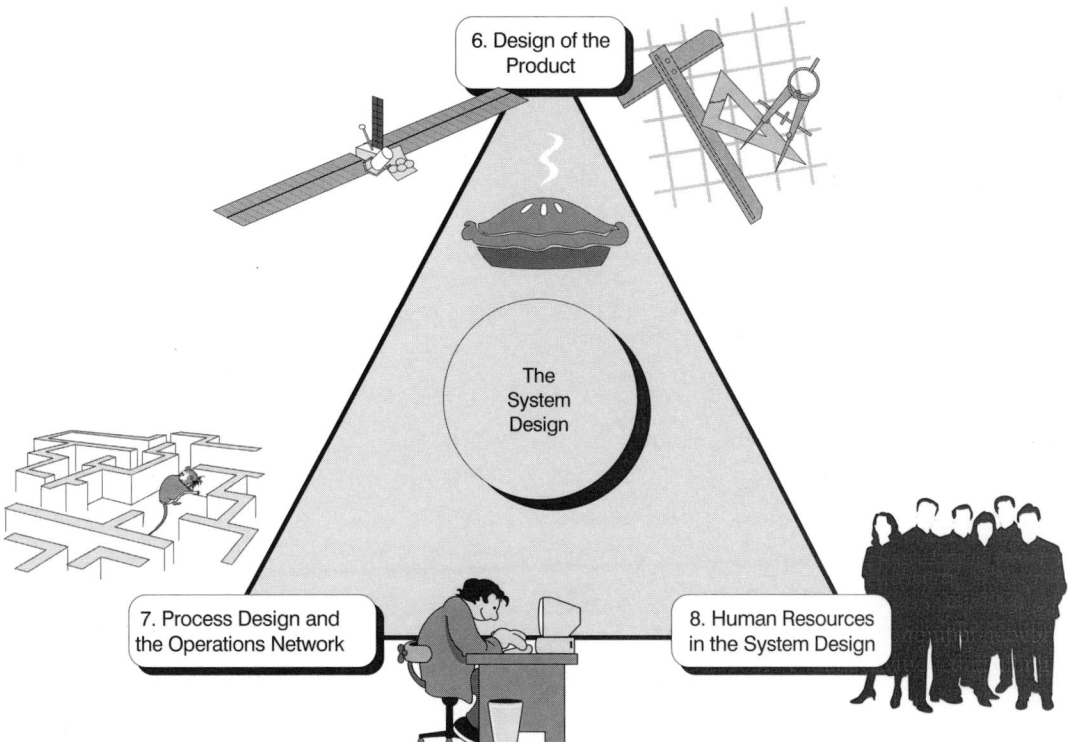

6 | Design of the product

Objectives and overview

Delivering the finished product is the end of the supply chain and one of the culminating activities of operations management. The objective of this chapter is to highlight characteristics that identify a product, and the development and analytical stages that the firm is involved in to put a product onto the market place. The chapter begins by characterizing service and manufactured products, and reviews projects in the context of a 'product'. There is then a section that gives the profile of the product life cycle and its relevance to the firm. The role of technology in product design is emphasized, from the materials employed to using computer-based systems in the conception of products. The chapter then goes into detail on the development stages of products from conception, to testing, to commercialization and introduces important analytical tools that are used to evaluate the viability of new products with reference to quality function deployment, value analysis and robust design. Finally, the chapter discusses flexibility in product design at both the customer level and the process design stage.

THE PRODUCT

The end product, when delivered or made available to the customer, represents the end, of either part or the complete integrated supply chain. The product is the culmination of an operation, or perhaps a project, and is what the firm, or organization, has been aiming to achieve. To arrive at this, perhaps lengthy and complex supply chains may have been involved. The product is designed to satisfy a certain need and normally is sold in a competitive environment and so the product's success is very much driven by market forces and must compete on cost, quality in the broad sense and delivery time. Products are services or tangible goods.

Products from service organizations

Products in services may be those provided by financial institutions, travel companies, hotel chains, telecommunications firms, universities or other educational institutions, etc. They may include:

■ a two-week vacation package in Tahiti;
■ a rail service between Paris and London;
■ the collection and disposal of your garbage;
■ a university MBA programme;
■ a hotel room with breakfast and dinner included;
■ a phone card which provides worldwide telephone access;
■ a financial product offering banking, credit-card service and stock transactions;
■ legal advice on a corporate merger programme.

Service products may also be a combination of products from various organizations. As an illustration, a holiday firm may offer a two-week vacation package in Tahiti including the round-trip air fare (subcontracted with the airline), accommodation (subcontracted with a hotel chain) and car rental (subcontracted with a car-rental agency).

Products from manufacturing firms

Tangible manufactured products can be classified into industrial products (sometimes referred to as intermediate goods) and consumer products. It is the consumer goods that are at the very end of the integrated supply chain, whereas generally industrial goods form intermediate parts of an integrated supply chain.

Industrial products

An industrial product is a finished item X made at Company A and then purchased by Company B. At Company B the product may be used as is, or used in the assembly of another product Y, which may then subsequently become a consumer product. Examples of industrial products are:

- sheet steel used in the manufacture of automobiles, washing machines and steel cabinets;
- copper wire used in electrical appliances, transmission cables and switch gear;
- starter motors used in the assembly of motorbikes, trucks and automobiles;
- glass bottles used for wine, beer and other beverages;
- extruded polypropylene used in the manufacture of plastic toys, container boxes and automobile components;
- flow meters used by power companies for measuring fluid flow;
- aeroplanes purchased by airline companies;
- oil drilling rigs purchased by firms like Esso, Texaco, Shell and BP.

Consumer products

Consumer products are items that are purchased through retail outlets or from a catalogue. Examples are:

- automobiles purchased through a dealer;
- washing machines, refrigerators and other kitchen appliances purchased though an electrical goods store;
- computers, printers, diskettes, paper and related items;
- yoghurt, chocolate bars, milk and bread from a supermarket.

For economic purposes, consumer products are also further classified into durable goods, such as automobiles, appliances and audio-visual products, and non-durable items, which includes food and clothing.

Standard products

A standard product is for the mass market and there is essentially no discernible difference between one product and the next. The following sections give illustrations.

Manufactured products

Examples include:

- refrigerators, televisions, washing machines and other durable consumer goods;
- a carton of milk, a roast chicken, a bottle of Heineken beer and other non-durable consumer goods;
- a roll of sheet steel, a 25 kg sack of extruded polyethylene, 200 metres of a textile and other industrial products.

Services

To categorize service operations as standard is difficult, because, by their very nature, they involve the client directly and each client will have their own particular needs. However, some almost standard service products are:

- a hamburger sold at a McDonald's restaurant;
- the train service between Brussels and London;
- the service provided at a Formula 1 hotel;
- an appendectomy at a medical centre (though there will be some differences depending on the patient's physique and health).

Characteristics in relation to the operating environment

Standard manufactured products exhibit a high degree of uniformity. In general, the following are some characteristics of standard products as opposed to customized products:

- They exhibit a low unit cost.
- They are produced in high volumes; conversely they have a low cycle or production time.
- They use standardized methods in their production.
- They are produced without receiving specific customer orders.
- They are *produced to stock* meaning from a planning point-of-view that a supply is kept in inventory.
- Since they are produced to stock, they are available *off the shelf* and have essentially zero delivery time, since an inventory of these goods is maintained by the supplier.

Services may not have the same characteristics, especially where inventory is not involved. However, they do, relative to customized products, have a low unit cost.

Customized products

Customized products are those that are specifically made to suit a certain customer's tastes, requirements or needs. Some examples are:

Manufactured products

- Durable consumer products would include, for example, an architect-designed house or a sofa made to a special size with a special fabric.
- Non-durable consumer goods might be a custom-made suit or a wedding dress.
- Industrial products would include an auxiliary back-up power system for a factory, a printing press or a construction Derrick.

Services

■ In medical services a face and nose change in plastic surgery.
■ A training programme developed for a certain firm.
■ The travel arrangements for the Prime Minister.
■ The repair of your automobile.
■ A firm's publicity brochure.

Characteristics in relation to the operating environment

Since customized products are produced to specific customer specifications, then, relative to standardized products:

■ They have a high unit cost.
■ They are produced in low volumes and thus have a high cycle time.
■ The production is planned only when a specific customer order is received.
■ They may require special production methods, or materials, in their manufacture.
■ They require a certain delivery, or lead time, between receipt of order and delivery of finished product to the client.
■ The orders appear on the producer's books as backlog.

PROJECT

A project is also a 'product', but is special in the sense that it is unique, or one-off. Thus, by this very definition it is a customized item. A project is not in the strict sense part of operations since it is not continuous. However, in carrying out a project many of the operations management functions come into play. To execute a project, certainly a major one, can involve very lengthy and complex supply chains. (See also Chapter 18, *Project Management*).

Major projects

The following are major projects that are most often performed by service-based firms. In both cases the characteristics of this type of project are that planning is complex, unique problems are encountered, the project is expensive, the completion time is long and usually highly qualified personnel are involved in work.

Construction projects

A construction project is a tangible 'product' designed according to certain specifications, for special needs and under unique conditions. Examples would include:

■ an oil refinery designed to process Arabian crude oil;
■ a dam across the River Rhône in France;
■ a factory to build BMW automobiles in the USA;
■ construction of the tunnel under the Channel between France and England;
■ construction of the TGV (*Train à grande vitesse*) terminus in Lyon, France;
■ construction of Los Angeles Airport, California;
■ the development of the Dockland region in East London, England.

Intangible projects

Intangible projects include:

■ the installation of a complex computer network to handle all the supply chain activities, the billing and sales activity of a firm;
■ the preparation of the hotel accommodation for Bill Clinton and his staff in Lyon in June 1996 for the G-7 meeting;
■ changing all the post office systems so that they can handle addresses with a numerical postal code;
■ changing all the computer codes in bank statements, credit cards and loan payments so that they accept the first two digits, 20 after the year 2000 rather than the present two digits of 19.

Study projects

A project may also be a specific activity, service or study for an operation, carried out internally by the manufacturing firm or service organization concerned. There may not be always be a tangible product at the termination of this type of project and usually these types of projects are of short duration and are not excessively expensive. For example:

■ a project to study reducing the setup times of a cutting machine;
■ a project to simplify the manufacture of a printer;
■ a project to reduce the lead time (time from order to delivery) of a particular manufactured product;
■ a project to study the best distribution network for a firm.

PRODUCT LIFE CYCLE

Products come and go. In industrial countries gone, or rapidly disappearing, are slide rules, coin telephone boxes, 33 rpm records, the typewriter, coal-fired engines, asbestos, DDT, leaded petrol and transatlantic passenger liners. All products are born and most eventually die, exhibiting a life-cycle profile similar to a human, although the time span may be different. The importance of the product life cycle to the firm is that management should be aware of when products are going to 'die' so that appropriate planning can be carried out to replace them.

Life-cycle phases

The principal phases in the product life cycle are as shown in Table 6.1. The profile for these phases is illustrated in Figure 6.1 and the characteristics are discussed below.

Table 6.1   The principal phases in the product life cycle

Stage	Phase	Human equivalent
1	Development	Conception and pregnancy
2	Birth or introduction	The new baby
3	Growth	Childhood through adolescence
4	Maturity	Adult phase through to retirement
5	Decline and death	Retirement to frail health and the end

Development

All products go through a development period prior to commercialization, as illustrated by the curve in Figure 6.1. In this development phase, the product is undergoing design, prototype tests and modifications prior to market launch. Principally, this phase would involve research and design personnel, although operations people would normally be involved to be sure that the product can be successfully manufactured. In this phase there are no revenues, only costs. The time for the development phase depends on the type of product. Searching for a successful AIDS vaccine is taking years, while the development of some computer programs may take just a matter of months. Further details of product development are presented in a later section.

Introduction

The introduction phase is when the consumer starts to see the product as it is commercialized and launched onto the market. From this point on, operations personnel are heavily involved in all the activities to produce the product to meet expected market demand, although initially sales may be slow as customers get used to accepting the product. Revenues start to be generated and these offset costs, which are now principally direct production costs, support costs for marketing and distribution, and for after-sales service.

Figure 6.1   Product life cycle (in terms of revenues, costs and profit).

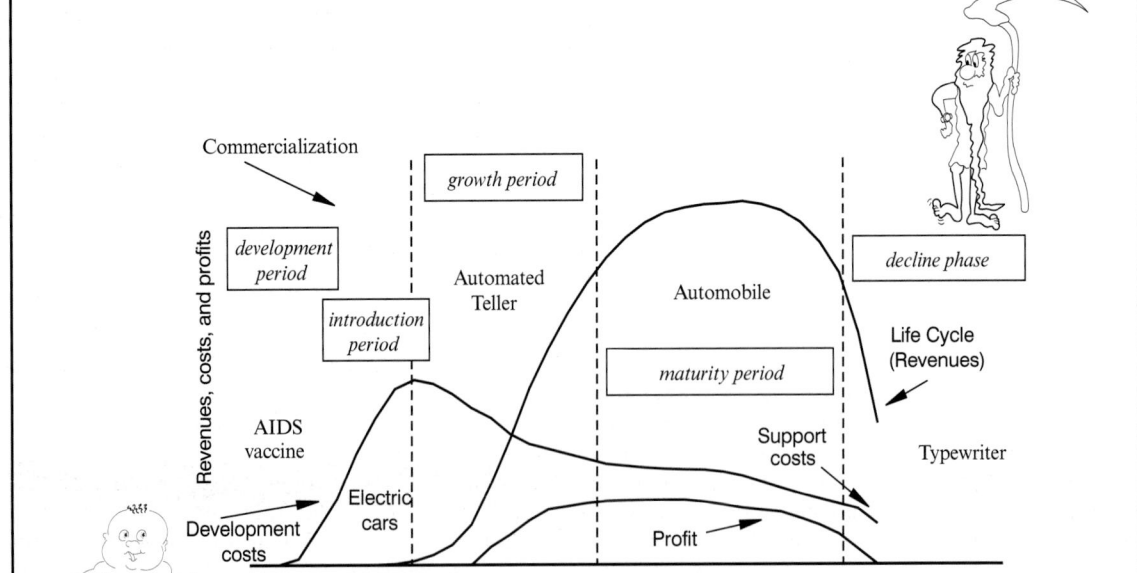

Some examples of products in the introduction phase might include electric cars, exotic vacations, videoconferencing, direct electronic banking and certain computer products.

Growth

The growth period is when the product is well accepted on the market, revenues are growing rapidly and support costs decline somewhat as the product becomes somewhat self-marketing. At some point in the growth period, total revenues will have offset the cumulated development costs and the successful product will start to show a profit. Operations management plays a dominant role in this phase, trying to keep production in pace with customer demand. Examples of products in this period are automated teller machines (ATMs), cruise vacations, compact discs, personal computers, bullet trains, snow surfing and Formula 1 type hotels.

Maturity

The product in the maturity phase is at a point where its existence is never given a second thought (though, for example, one might ask from time to time, 'How did we do without plastic bags!'). Products are most numerous in this phase. Profits continue to be generated here, though they are extremely affected by other competitive products in the market place. Operations management is dominant in this phase, although fluctuating demand may make planning somewhat complicated, leading to lean production periods. Examples of products in the maturity phase include automobiles, credit cards, radios, colour television, airline travel and fast-food services.

Decline and death

Decline and death is when the product reaches the end of its life and is eventually withdrawn. This may be because of technological innovations, for example 33 rpm vinyl records and cassette tapes being replaced by compact discs, the typewriter by the word processor, travellers cheques by the international credit card, the biplane by the single-wing aeroplane, and the motorbike and sidecar by small cars. Economics, perhaps modified by technological innovations, may herald the change, for example, the replacement of teller-assisted bank cash withdrawals by ATMs and transatlantic sea crossings by air travel. Similarly hotel valet services, such as porters opening car doors and carrying luggage and maids turning down the bed at night have disappeared in all but the most expensive hotels. Governments may step in and ban a product such as asbestos, oil-based paints, leaded petrol, chlorofluorocarbons, cotton nightdresses and DDT. Finally, changes in fad and fashion may herald a decline, per-

haps temporary; such was the case of the mini skirt in the 1960s and, more recently, alcohol-free beer.

In the decline phase, operations management activities essentially stop, although for manufactured products an inventory of parts is often maintained, usually for ten years, to service those products still in use. Not all products die or pass into the decline phase, but remain in the mature phase, perhaps as a result of continuous innovation, redesign or repackaging. Aspirin is one example that has been on the market for 100 years and is still the most widely sold over-the-counter drug. Similarly, the automobile, which has now been in existence for almost 100 years, is another classic example. The innovation and redesign of one model of automobile is illustrated in the article in Box 6.1.[1]

TECHNOLOGY IN PRODUCT DESIGN

Product design changes, new products, and the decline of existing ones have come about because of new technological developments, principally in the discovery of new materials and the development of computer-aided design systems.

Materials

Manufactured products have mushroomed because of the development of cheaper new materials, which sometimes have characteristics superior to the products that they have replaced. Service industries have been able to grow often as a result of new products, for example fibre-optic cables in telecommunications, inexpensive building materials in the hotel industry, durable plastics and the computer chip for banking and credit cards. The following sections highlight some of the principal new materials developed since the turn of the century. Appendix II gives further information on these technological developments.

Petrochemicals

Petrochemicals are the basis for almost all plastics. The world's first petrochemical, isopropyl alcohol, was discovered by the French chemist, Pierre Berthelot, in 1855 and was initially commercialized in 1920 by the Standard Oil Company of New Jersey (now Exxon). It was originally used as an additive in petrol, which was particularly important in the 1920s as Henry Ford was introducing his assembly-line-built Ford T automobile. The commercialization of isopropyl alcohol led to the rapid growth of the petrochemical industry, the products of which are used in clothes, cars, televisions, video cassette recorders

Box 6.1 Not your father's Corvette. It's being toned down and refined to take on European rivals

For decades, Corvettes, with their aggressive, low-slung styling and snarling V-8s, have been the ultimate in red-blooded American sports cars. Buyers, though, had to accept hefty trade-offs: a jolting ride, a cacophony of squeaks and rattles, and quarters so cramped that a GM executive once joked that when driving his 'Vette, he had to choose between riding with his wife or his golf clubs.

Chevrolet is counting on its first new Corvette in 14 years to change that image for good. Sure, the division's flagship car, which went into regular production at General Motor Corp.'s Bowling Green (Ky.) plant on Dec. 9, boasts 345 horses under the hood. But it also promises toned-down styling, more genteel road manners, and a comfier interior. Analysts and auto writers who have driven the car say its greater sophistication will attract new buyers from outside Corvette's macho circle. Says Ken Zino, *Road & Track*'s Detroit editor: "You no longer need a tattoo to buy one."

Even better, in Wall Street's eyes, is that GM accomplished all that on a relative shoestring. Although development of the Corvette dragged on for eight years and was frozen several times when capital ran low, the car stuck to its $250 million budget—$150 million for development and $100 million for tooling and equipment. Chevy is expected to price the new Corvette close to the outgoing model. That would mean sticker prices starting near $38,000, with well-equipped cars going for $42,000 or more. Independent auto consultant Christopher W. Cedergren figures GM will rake in gross margins as high as $8,000 on each new Corvette.

To get those kinds of profits, GM needs to sell 25,000 or 30,000 Corvettes annually, a substantial increase from the old model's 20,000-a-year volume. Getting there will be difficult. Corvette already owns 39% of what it calls the "high sport" market, which includes the Porsche 911, Toyota Supra, Acura NSX, and Dodge Viper. But Corvette faces stiff competition from a wave of new European sports cars now arriving: the Jaguar XK8, BMW's Z3 two-seater, Mercedes' SLK convertible, and Porsche's Boxster roadster.

LOW-TECH? Still, the new Corvette is better prepared for the fray than its predecessor. Engineers improved the ride and eliminated rattles and creaks by making the chassis four times more rigid. And they dropped the car's step-in height by four inches, making entry and exit far easier. Trunk space was doubled, making the Corvette more practical for hauling suitcases and grocery bags.

To keep the new Corvette affordable, Chevy's designers pinched pennies. According to James Schefter, author of *All Corvettes Are Red*, thrifty engineers borrowed parts and systems from other GM cars and used a traditional push-rod design in the aluminum V-instead of a more expensive multivalve, overhead-cam system. On the assembly line, the Corvette also will cost less. Its 34% fewer parts and more efficient design will knock assembly time from 64 hours down to about 45, cutting labor cost by about 28%, to $1,920 per car.

For all its improvements, the Corvette remains a hard sell for many fans of European cars. Bruce Wennerstrom, a Greenwich (Conn.) marketer and auto enthusiast, is dubious about Corvette's old-style push-rod engine. "We're turned on by overhead-cam engines and all the technological bells and whistles," he says. "GM has to get Corvette on the shopping list of people who buy imports."

GM has planned plenty of hoopla in hopes of snagging their attention. The Corvette will debut at the Detroit and Los Angeles auto shows in early January. Then, later this winter, the 400-plus high-volume Chevy dealers who get the first cars out of Bowling Green will hold special invitation-only unveilings for customers.

Of course, German auto makers will be touting the new Boxster and SLK on the auto-show circuit, too. The international contest is shaping up as a matchup worthy of Formula One racing. Says DRI/McGraw-Hill analyst Lincoln Merrihew: "It's classic American iron vs. European sophistication." Gentlemen, start your engines.

By Kathleen Kerwin in Detroit
Business Week, 23 December 1996

(VCRs), videotapes, surgical supplies, tyres, food packaging and plastics. Isopropyl alcohol is also used in pharmaceuticals, cleaning fluids, printing inks and thinners for paint and lacquers.[2]

Plastics

Plastic is a generic term for synthetic substances that are replacements for inorganic-based materials, such as metals, ceramics, cement and the like. Just about every product today contains some plastic component if it is not made entirely of plastic. Plastic development probably started at the time of the First World War, when the Germans, cut off from supplies of natural rubber, worked on the development of synthetic equivalents. In 1936 the firm of IG Farben presented the first synthetic rubber at the Berlin automobile show. About the same time Imperial Chemical Industries (ICI) in the UK, by the polymerization of ethylene, developed the first polyethylene, or polythene, widely used in packaging, moulded materials, pipes, electric wire insulation, metal coatings, upholstery, etc. In 1938, Du Pont of the USA commercialized Nylon, a polyamide discovered by W.H. Carothers. Parachutes during the Second War were one of the first nylon products made on a large scale and nylon is now used in all branches of the textile industry. In 1938 polystyrene was commercialized for use as insulation material in refrigerators and air conditioners, packaging, wall tiles and food utensils. Silicones, used in rubber and for surface treatment of glass and textiles, first appeared in 1943. In 1957 polypropylene, used for moulded automobile parts, appliances, cordage and bottles, started to be developed in large quantities. Today, the number of different plastics made from different chemical compounds is almost infinite.

Composites

Composites are combinations of materials that have properties superior to those of the individual constituents from which they are made. For example, fibreglass is made from a film of glass and a synthetic resin and it is more durable and does not shatter like the glass from which it is derived. A popular composite material is Kevlar, which is an aramide fibre, developed in 1965 by Du Pont and commercialized since 1972. Kevlar is very light, resists corrosion, does not burn and can be easily machined. It is used in making the shells of electrical cables, protective clothing and sailboat hulls and has significant use in the automobile, aeronautics and aerospace industries. A perhaps unexpected and growing market for Kevlar is for bulletproof vests for the police force. This material has proved so strong that it has saved the lives of police officers not only from bullets, but also from being struck by lightning, from being hit by shrapnel from a pipe bomb and from being run over by a Honda Accord automobile.[3]

Ceramic fibre composite materials play an important role in the electrical and electronics industry because of their insulating properties. Composite polymer materials are used in the automobile industry for bumpers, radiator grills and wheel hubs and in the computer industry for hardware. Carbon fibre material is used in the sports industry, notably for skis, tennis rackets, wheels of racing cycles and golf clubs. New metal alloys, for example aluminium–lithium, have been developed that are extremely light and are used in the space industry.

Computer-aided design

Computer-Aided Design (CAD) was developed in the 1970s. It is a special interactive graphic image system on computer terminals, which enables products, equipment and processes to be designed, and modified, in three dimensions. CAD provides for designers what word-processors give to writers, the freedom to make changes without having to remake the whole thing. The automobile, aeronautics and engineering and construction industries make extensive use of CAD.

DEVELOPMENT OF THE PRODUCT

Market growth

Technology changes rapidly, products die and thus, for firms to grow in terms of profit and/or market share, their strategy has to include continuous developing, innovating and bringing out new products. Firms like

General Electric, Minnesota Mining and Manufacturing (3M), Saatchi and Saatchi (advertising), Microsoft and British Airways are continually introducing new products or services, which make these firms leaders in their field. A classic example is General Electric, USA.

General Electric

General Electric (GE), currently with Jack Welch at the helm, is one of the world's most profitable companies with a market capitalization in 1997 of US $150 billion. Its growth has been based principally on using new technology to develop new products.[4] The precursor of GE was created by Thomas Edison in 1878 after the creation of the electric light bulb. Some of the milestones in its product development since that time are listed in Table 6.2.

Table 6.2 GE product development

1895	Built the world's biggest steam locomotive weighing 90 tonnes.
1905	Invented the electric toaster
1915	Development of the refrigerator
1932	Development of the dishwasher
1942	Production of the aircraft engine for the war effort
1954	Conception of the first turbine motor for the aeroplane
1978	Built the largest nuclear power station at Tokaï-Mura in Japan
1986	Developed television networking after acquiring RCA, which included NBC
1987	Launched into medical imagery after an exchange with Thomson, France

Today GE is the world leader in the following areas:[5]

- production of electric motors;
- construction of locomotive engines and railway stock;
- aircraft engines;
- medical instruments in imagery and diagnostics;
- turbine motors and nuclear and thermal power plants;
- industrial control systems;
- plastic products for various industrial sectors
- information network systems;
- television through NBC and the CNBC news network;
- credit leasing financial services.

In addition, General Electric is in second place for neon and incandescent lighting and for kitchen appliances, including washing machines, dishwashers and refrigerators

To grow continuously in the market, many companies have Product Development Departments and New Product Managers, who follow a product from conception to commercialization. The stages in new product development are summarized in Figure 6.2 and reviewed below.

Generation of new product ideas

As illustrated in Figure 6.3, companies, in order to start the process of developing new products, solicit opinions from:

- customers;
- sales staff;
- competitors;
- top management;
- product development teams.

Customers

Customers are an important source of new product ideas as they are the end user of the product. In particular, industrial customers 'know what they want'.

Sales staff

Company sales persons are continually in contact with clients and as such often have good notions of what type of new products would sell well in the market place. Sales people are motivated in this respect since, if they can persuade their company to develop new products to satisfy their customers, then one of their main objectives has been met.

Competitors

Often a competitor introduces a new product to the market (a proactive strategy) and another firm later introduces a similar product to the market (reactive strategy). For exampke, US automobile companies introduced compact cars following their successful Japanese introduction in the 1980s.

Top management

Top managers who have spent many years with the company, and also have many outside contacts, are another source for new product ideas.

Product development teams

Product development teams have the role of developing new products. As a starting point, they may use the technique of brainstorming for coming up with ideas. Brainstorming is a process where a small group of people in the company, often from different departments, meet and, without any inhibitions or preconceived notions, put forward their ideas for new products. In brainstorming:

- Participants should be free to express their thoughts and should not criticize others.
- Members of the group should be encouraged to come up with as many ideas as possible; the logic being that the greater the number of ideas, then the more likelihood that a workable one will be found.

Figure 6.2 Steps and activities in product development.

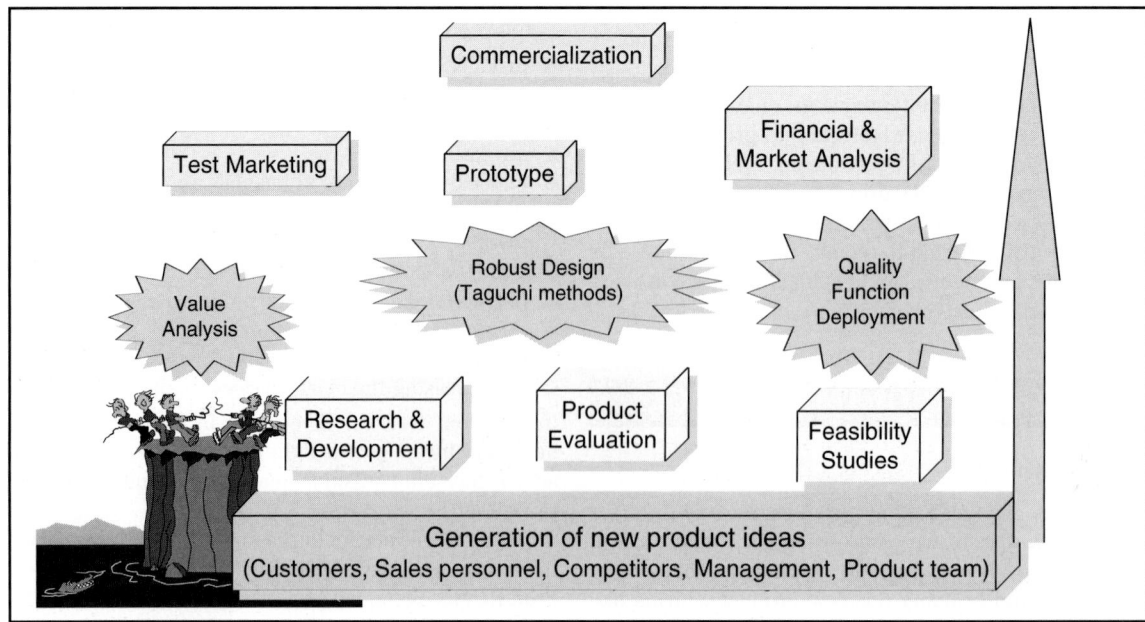

Figure 6.3 Generation of new product ideas.

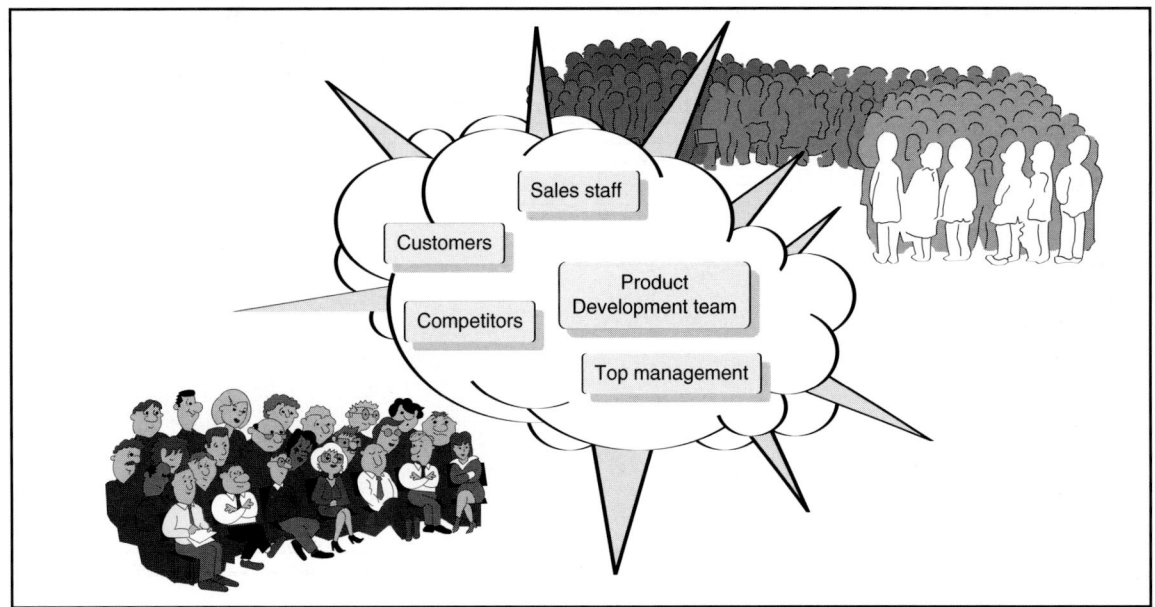

- Members should feel free to build upon each other's ideas. It is often the combination of inputs, particularly when members are from diverse backgrounds, that leads to the development of a new product.

Research and development

Many companies have research and development departments, which are continually testing new ideas or performing experimental work. Firms like Dupont have research departments that devote time to developing new concepts without at first necessarily having an immediate commercial objective; this comes later. Nylon, discussed in a previous section, was a classic example.

Product evaluation

The product evaluation step involves expanding upon the new product ideas, as well as eliminating those products that may not be viable in the long run or do not fit the company's strategic objectives. A product evaluation matrix, as illustrated in Figure 6.4, is an analytical tool that can be used for such an evaluation. In the matrix shown, a numerical weight is assigned to various criteria, as discussed below, considered important in the selection of the product.

Potential sales revenues

Companies are in business to make money. Thus, in bringing out new products the revenue-generating pos-

sibilities are perhaps one of the most important criteria and here this aspect has been assigned the highest value.

Competitive products

Whether there are competitive products on the market is also an important criterion. If competitors exist, it makes sales penetration more difficult, puts a constraint on gaining market share and, as such, makes marketing costs higher. Burger King, of the UK, pulled out of the fast-food market in Paris in 1997 since it said it could no longer compete with McDonald's (USA) and Quick (Belgium) restaurants that were in the same market sector.

Production costs

For a given market price, high production costs for the product will eat into profits and so this is an important criterion. However, if the product is almost unique and successful, a firm may be able to charge a high price to offset production costs and to recoup development costs. This was the case with Texas Instruments when they brought out their new electronic calculator in the 1970s. At the time, there were no real competing products and so initially they were able to charge a very high price.

Product life

The product life has to be a consideration since, if the life is short, there may not be time to generate suffi-

Figure 6.4   Product evaluation matrix.

	Weighting Importance	Product rating					Total	Maximum Possible	Percentage
		Poor 1	2	3	4	Excellent 5			
Potential sales revenues	8			X			24	40	60.00%
Competitive products	8		X				16	40	40.00%
Production costs	6				X		24	30	80.00%
Product life	6					X	30	30	100.00%
Time-to-market	5			X			15	25	60.00%
Environmentally friendly	5			X			15	25	60.00%
Patent possibilities	4					X	20	20	100.00%
Raw material availability	3				X		12	15	80.00%
Total							156	225	69.33%

cient revenues to make the product financially attractive to the firm.

Time-to-market

The time-to-market represents the elapsed time from product conception to when it is available to the consumer. This is important if, for example, there are competing products on the market, since the first one to appear will have a greater possibility of obtaining a larger market share. Automobile companies are very conscious of this and the classic example is the small automobile introduced by the Japanese into the US market in the 1970s. Competitive US companies (General Motors, Ford and Chrysler) were very slow to bring out competing models and as a consequence permanently lost market share.

Environmentally friendly

Environmentally friendly, discussed in more detail in Chapter 5, *An Environmental Balance*, is the criterion that will determine whether the product will be accepted, both in terms of government regulations and consumer acceptance. This may apply to herbicides, drugs, engines or other products that could pollute, but it will also include the safety element. Sears, a US retailer, withdrew a toy dart game from the market in the 1980s after a wrongly thrown dart injured a child.

Patent possibilities

Patent possibilities are a consideration when a new product is introduced, because a patent would give a certain amount of protection against competitive prod-

ucts. However, applying for a patent is expensive and fighting a patent infringement can be costly. The textile/clothing industry is notorious for copying ideas. Even though taking out a patent is possible, companies rarely do so because of the expense and often because of the short duration of clothing and fabric styles.

Raw material availability

This criterion is a consideration if the product uses raw materials or components that may one day be in short supply. With the globalization of markets, this is not often a problem, though from time to time can apply when suppliers of raw materials have planned their production capacity badly.

Once the criteria for product evaluation have been established, those involved in the product development, or other experts, will assign a score for each of the criteria. The weighted total score for each criterion is then determined and a total weighted average is calculated. In the matrix shown in Figure 6.4 the total points possible are 225, of which the score is 156 or 69 per cent of the maximum. Whether a product is accepted, or rejected, will depend on the policy of the company. For example, a company may be prepared to go ahead with those products that score, say, 65 per cent or more of the possible weighted average.

Feasibility studies

Feasibility studies in new product design examine the ease (or difficulty) of producing a product and its commercialization. They may include resolving such issues as:

- Are the necessary human resource skills available?
- Is there sufficient capacity in the present facility?
- Do we have the financial capability to invest?
- Can we incorporate the needed technology changes?

Quality function deployment (QFD)

Quality function deployment is an analytical method introduced in Japan in 1966,[6] and used by such companies as Toyota, Matsushita Electronics and Nippon Steel to ascertain that a new product or service meets customer requirements. Its objective is to develop a design aimed at satisfying the consumer, and then translating the customer requirements into design targets used throughout the development and production stages of the product. Quality function deployment is sometimes referred to as the 'House of Quality' because of its shape, or as the 'Voice of the customer', because of its purpose. The concept is illustrated in the following.

Electric weed trimmer

An electric weed trimmer is a gardening tool normally used for trimming weeds that are in places where a lawnmower cannot be used. The weeds are trimmed by a plastic thread, which spins at a high velocity and literally decapitates the weeds. There are several manufacturers and a model from Black and Decker is illustrated in Figure 6.5.[7]

A QFD diagram for this product is then illustrated in Figure 6.6 The left-hand column shows what the customer desires in the product in order of preference rating (comfortable to hold through to quiet operation). The top line above the matrix gives the firm's design proposals to meet the customer requirements. The strength of the correlations of these designs with the customer wants is then indicated in the body of the matrix. For example, there is a strong correlation between quiet operation and a sealed insulated motor. The roof of the house illustrates the relationship between the design capabilities of the firm. In this illustration, high-speed rotation has a medium correlation with an aluminium motor, a strong correlation with a sealed insulated motor and some correlation with the triangular cutting chord.

Robust design using Taguchi methods

As mentioned in Chapter 4, *Quality Management*, Taguchi methods are quality improvement techniques developed by Genichi Taguchi of Japan in the 1980s to improve the product, and also the process design, by attempting to make product designs production proof; this is done by building in tolerances for manufacturing variables known to be unavoidable. The argument is that missing the quality target in a consistent manner can be better than hitting it a few times with the rest being scattered all over the board. The following are the three basic concepts in the Taguchi Methods.[8]

Quality robustness

Quality robustness suggests that products can be produced uniformly and consistently in a variety of different manufacturing conditions. The idea is to eliminate the effects of adverse conditions, rather than removing their causes. This is often cheaper and more effective in producing a robust product. For example:

- Designing a product, the quality of which is not impaired by small changes in raw material quality, such as might be the case for clothing or paper.
- A product, the quality of which is not destroyed by small changes in process conditions, such as temperature, machines used or operators employed; for example, chemicals or plastic products.

Quality loss function

The quality loss function identifies all costs associated with poor quality and illustrates how these costs increase as the product deviates from what the client has ordered, or is expecting. The costs include 'cost' in terms of client dissatisfaction, warranty, service costs, internal inspection, repair and scrap costs, as well as 'costs' to society. The quality loss function is defined by the equation:

$$L = D^2 C,$$

where L is the loss, D is the deviation from the target value and C is the cost of avoiding the deviation.

Target specification

Taguchi's concept refuted the criterion that a product is acceptable if it falls within a certain tolerance. He felt that this was too simplistic and could give rise to quality problems. For example, if a bolt is at the extreme lower end of its outside tolerated diameter and the associated nut is at the extreme upper end of its inside tolerated diameter, then the fit will be sloppy. Target specification or target value is a philosophy of continuous improvement to bring the product exactly on target. This implies tighter and tighter tolerance limits, as illustrated in Figure 6.7.

Value analysis

Value analysis involves the examination of the product relative to its proposed price in order to see whether

Figure 6.5   The Black and Decker Electric Weed Trimmer (reproduced by kind permission of Black and Decker).

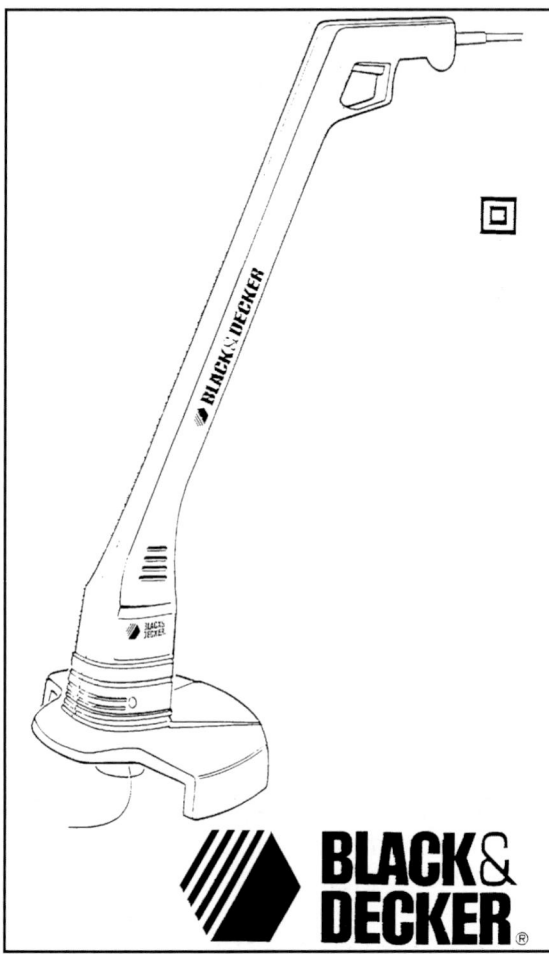

the consumer perceives that this product is going to give value for money. The concept was developed by Larry D. Miles at General Electric, USA between 1939 and 1945. Under wartime conditions, studies were continually made to see if alternative materials could be used for components and assemblies, because as often those in the design specifications were too expensive or difficult to obtain. The following tests for a product are based on ideas from General Electric:

- Does the use of the product by the client contribute value?
- Does the price correlate well with its usefulness to the client?
- Are all the features incorporated in the product necessary?

- Are there other products on the market that are better for the intended use of the product in question?
- Can any part of the product be made at a lower cost?
- Can a standard product replace the product in question?
- Do the material, labour, overhead and expected profit equal its total 'cost'?
- Can another dependable supplier provide it for less money?
- Is anyone else buying it for less?

The sections *Value Analysis* and *Value Engineering* in Chapter 16, *Purchasing and Subcontracting* give further details.

Financial and market analysis

A company develops a new product to be a success, to obtain a certain market share and, above all, to generate income for the company. Two ways of making an evaluation are to develop a break-even analysis or to produce a pro-forma income statement.

Break-even analysis

The break-even analysis determines what level of product units need to be sold in order that revenues are equal to total fixed and variable costs. Above this break-even point, the company would make a profit (see also Chapter 16, *Purchasing and Subcontracting*, for details of developing a break-even analysis.)

Pro-forma income statements

A pro-forma income statement is a financial model in which the revenues, costs and profit from the sale of the new product are estimated. A pro-forma income statement can sometimes be the deciding factor on whether to go ahead with the new product. The costs are the easiest part to estimate. Most difficult is to estimate sales. The presentation of the Hershey Co. strategic options (Chapter 2, *Strategy of Organizations*) is a type of pro-forma income statement.

Prototype

A prototype of a new product is a smaller-scale, or perhaps a full-scale, version of the final product (an automobile, a chemical plant, a turbine, a credit card) incorporating all its features. The purpose of a prototype is to see if the product performs as expected and whether it can be commercialized at an acceptable cost.

Figure 6.6 Quality function deployment of electric weed trimmer.

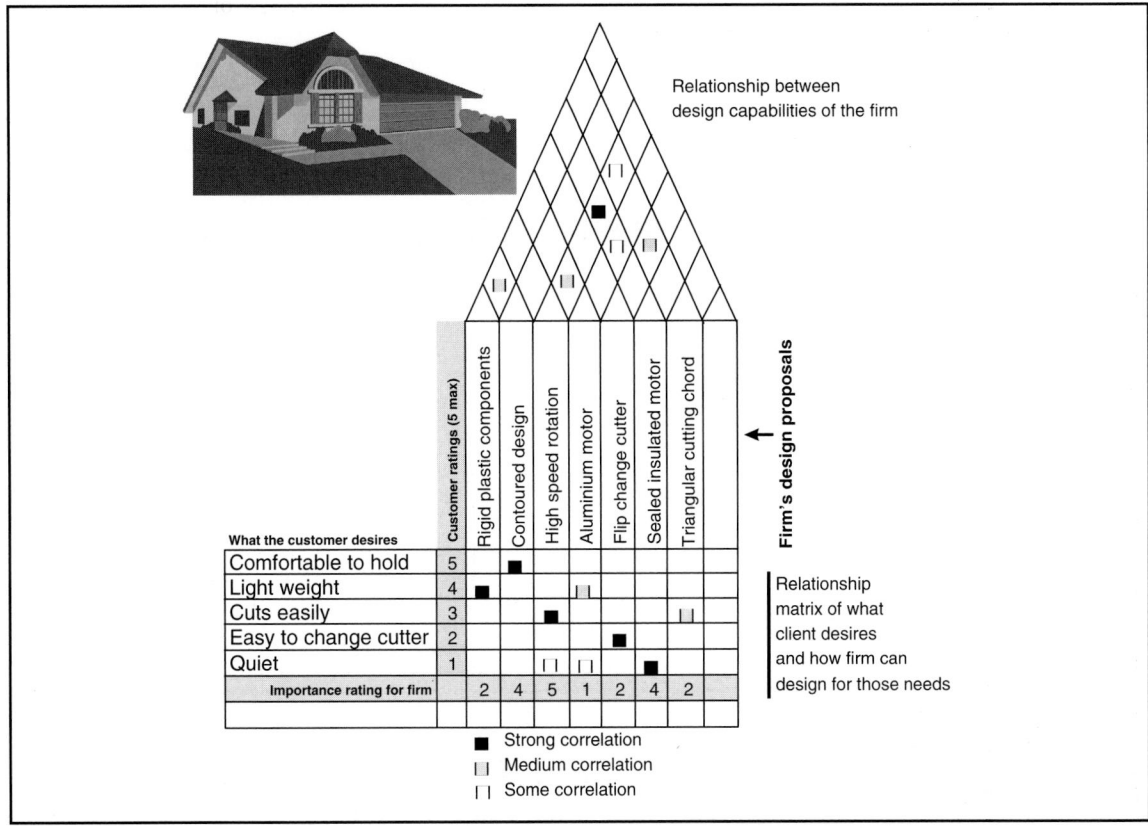

Test marketing

Test marketing involves introducing the product in a limited geographical market. For example, Sears USA tested a new credit card in the Chicago area. The objective of test marketing is to have a sample programme, which helps to minimize the risk of immediately commercializing a product nationwide. Chapter 23, *Statistical Quality Control*, gives more information on sampling.

Concurrent engineering

Concurrent engineering means having research and development personnel and design engineers work closely or in parallel (rather than in sequence) with production people to ensure that a product can be manufactured easily and cost-effectively. This avoids costly design changes at a later stage. Renault Automobile France believes that by bringing all its technicians under one roof, in order that they can work on a new design simultaneously, they can cut development time for vehicles from 58 months to 38 months. This would reduce the cost of designing each model by up to 1.5 billion French Francs or 20 per cent.[9]

Commercialization

Commercialization is the full-scale production of a product or service and its launch onto the national or international market.

Product success

At the beginning stage of searching for new product ideas, many suggestions may be thrown onto the table. However, as these ideas are analysed and studied in more detail, the 'successes' may be very limited. This process is illustrated in Figure 6.8. This illustrates that, after going through all the evaluation stages, the original 75 ideas were reduced to just one commercially viable product.

Figure 6.7   Taguchi methods for quality – target specification.

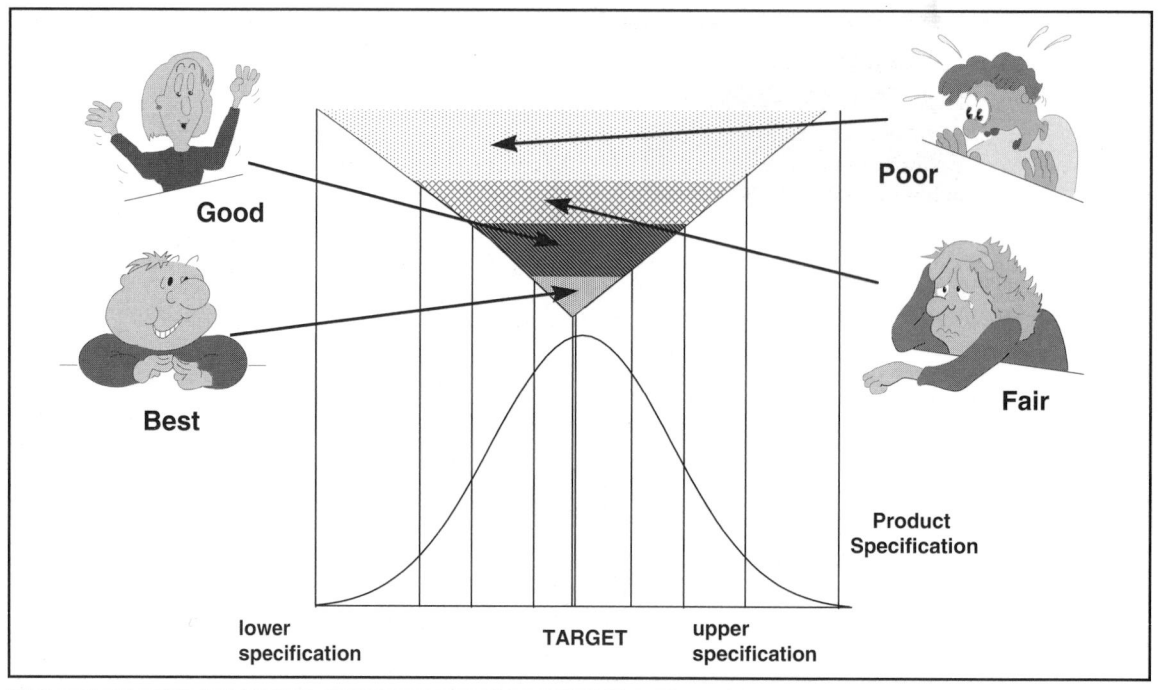

Figure 6.8   Product ideas and commercialization.

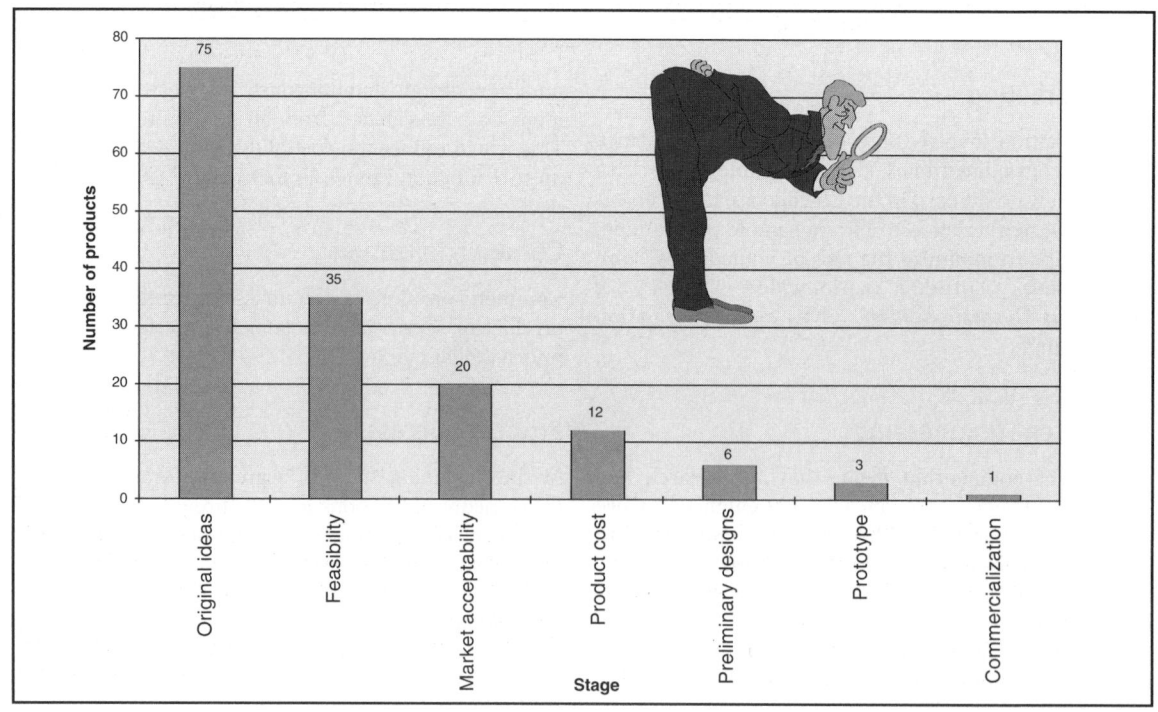

FLEXIBILITY IN PRODUCT DESIGN

Flexibility driven by the customer

Customers select products to suit their tastes, to be adaptable to the environment in which the products will be used and at a reasonable cost. Customers are different and, thus, for certain products firms need to build flexibility into the product design such that it will appeal to a broad range of clients. To develop a broad range of products, each with a completely different base design, would be so expensive to the firm that it would not be economic. Thus, to provide the flexibility demanded by the client, firms have a standard product design that can be modified, without excessive cost, to offer what the customer desires. Illustrations are:

- Kitchen appliances are available in a range of colours, with doors opening on the left or right to suit a customer's kitchen design. The interior is the same, but the outside is different.
- Colour tones of wood can be modified or fabric can be changed to give furniture a more personal appearance.
- A package holiday can be modified to include certain stopovers or special attractions to satisfy client requirements.
- A steak dinner can be prepared with the meat rare, medium or well done and it might be served with French fries, rice or a baked potato. Various other vegetables can also be made available.

A broader example of flexibility in product design is illustrated in the following example of the Honda motor company of Japan.[10]

Honda

Executives at Honda Motor Co. knew they had a problem on their hands the moment that they launched the sporty, re-styled Accord in 1993. It was too cramped for US drivers, but not stylish enough for the Japanese. The president, Nobuhiko Kawamoto, ordered a redesign of the vehicle and it cost tens of millions of dollars to build in flexibility to suit customer tastes. As a result:

- The new US Accord, launched in September 1997 for the US market, is 189 inches long and 70 inches wide. It has a raised roof to provide extra headroom and a roomy interior to accommodate a family.
- For the Japanese market the Accord is six inches shorter, four inches thinner and has a lower roof than its US cousin. It is a sporty compact, loaded with the high-tech options demanded by the Japanese customers.

- For the Europeans, the Accord for 1998 is designed with a short narrow body geared to the tiny streets and will have the stiffer, sportier ride that old-world drivers prefer.

Flexibility dictated by the process

In manufacturing, flexibility in product design declines as one moves through the production process (process design is one of the subjects of Chapter 7). The implication of this to the operations manager is that one has to be sure of market requirements before finalizing the production plans; otherwise, a producer may end up with finished goods for which there is a limited market. This flexibility constraint can be illustrated by using a VAT classification, which is grouping items according to the type of end product, and to a certain extent, according to the manufacturing process employed, as shown in Figure 6.9.[11]

V classification

The V classification is where from one, or a few, raw materials a variety of different end products can be produced. The base of the V represents the raw material and the top the end products. At the start point there is almost infinite flexibility as to what products can be produced from the raw material, but, moving through the production process, the degree of freedom declines. The following are examples:

- Crude oil by simple distillation can be turned into propane, butane, petrol, kerosene, fuel oil, diesel, asphalt, etc.
- Wood pulp can be turned into newsprint, paper of letter quality, book printing paper, cardboard, packaging, light building material, etc.
- Iron ore can be processed into sheet steel, wire, construction steel, nails, screws, stainless-steel cutlery, etc.

A classification

An A classification is the opposite to the V in that from a multitude of raw materials, parts and components (the bottom of the A) is made a single product (the apex of the A) or a few products. Very often for the A classification the end product is either a project or a customized product. Many of the component parts used in building the product are standard items that have uses in many types of products. However, as soon as they move through the production process, they become part of a sub-assembly and their flexibility for use elsewhere is lost. The following are illustrations:

Figure 6.9 VAT classification in manufacturing.

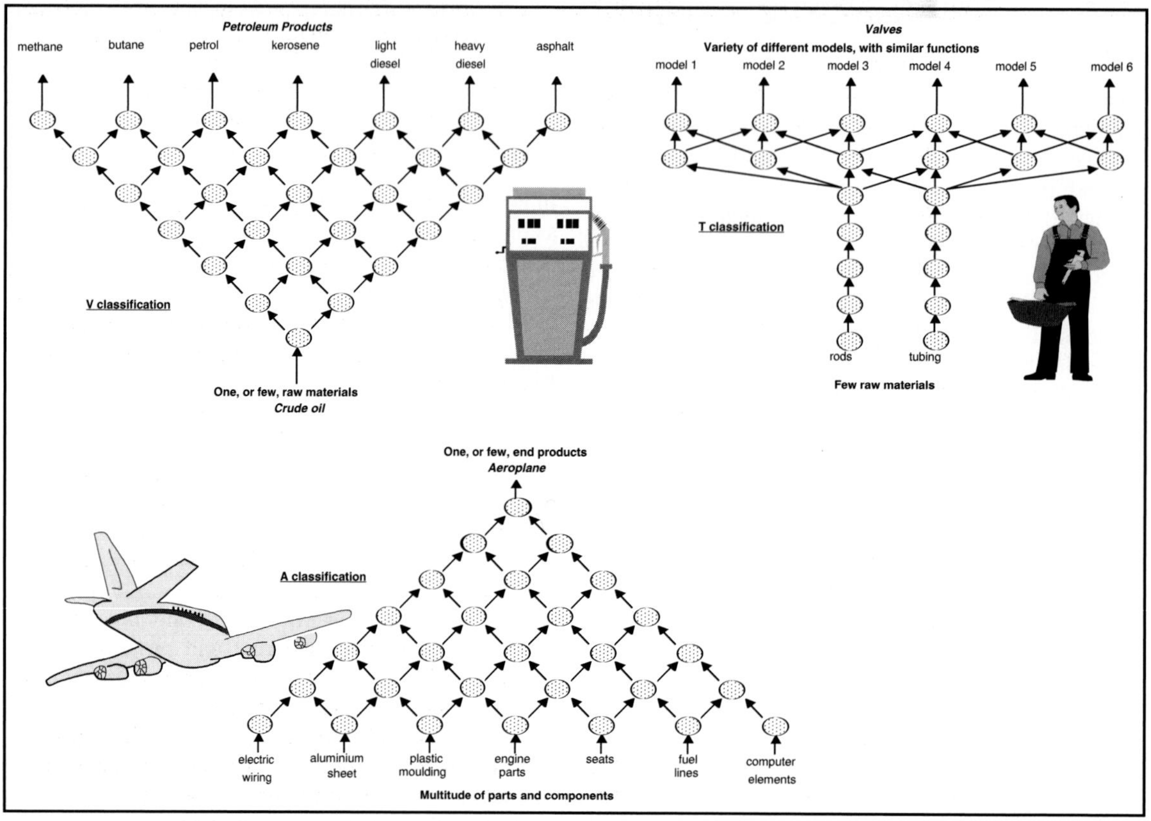

- A cruise ship is built from a multitude of standard parts, such as steel, plastic, wiring, engines, aluminium, fittings, paint, furniture, computer units, etc.
- A telecommunications satellite is a complex product, made from standard alloy material, computer components, electrical and electronic units, steel, plastic, etc.
- A Jumbo Jet, such as a Boeing 747 or an Airbus 300, has 250+ seats. It is built from a multitude of parts, including alloy and steel-frame assemblies, jet engine components, electronic sub-assemblies, interior fittings, etc.

T classification

In the T classification, products are similar in their functionality, but they are used in different services or applications. Components, parts and sub-assemblies may be common in each product, but, towards the end of the assembly as certain sub-assemblies are combined, specific products are produced, each having its own particular use. A T classification may be associated with a standard product that is modified to be 'customized'. It is the T-classification product that provides the flexibility to the customer discussed at the beginning of this section. Other than the household appliances already mentioned, T products would include:

- flow-control valves for water, gas and other fluids;
- measuring instruments;
- portable computers (internal cards can be added to modify the characteristics).

SUMMARY OF KEY ELEMENTS

- Manufactured products are either industrial goods for another firm or consumer goods. Consumer items are further classified into durable and non-durable goods. Service firms usually (but not always) provide non-tangible items.
- Standard products are destined for the mass market, unlike customized products, which are made according to specific customer specifications and, as such, are usually more expensive than standard items. A project is also a product, but by definition is customized to certain specifications.
- Most products exhibit a life cycle from development through introduction and growth maturity, to decline and death. Understanding the timing of the product life cycle is important in the development of new products or the modification of existing ones. Product development costs are usually recovered during the product growth period.
- New products or design changes are often driven by new technological developments, either in new materials or in design systems such as CAD. New product ideas may originate from customers, sales staff, competitors, top management or the product development team.
- Research and development is a step in new-product development, but at the beginning of the research no commercial venture may be identified.
- A product evaluation matrix can illustrate the potential of a new product. Evaluation criteria may include potential sales revenue, competitive products, production costs, estimated product life, time to market, how environmentally friendly it is, patent possibilities and raw-material availability.
- A feasibility study examines constraints on product commercialization, which may be related to plant capacity and human, financial and technological resources.
- Quality function deployment is an analytical method to verify that a new product or service satisfies customer requirements.
- Taguchi methods, or robust design, are techniques to ensure that product designs are production-proof by building in tolerances for variables known to be unavoidable.
- A value analysis evaluates a product to see if it provides value for money.
- A break-even analysis indicates the point at which profits might be generated from a new product. A pro-forma income statement gives an estimate of future revenues and costs for the new product.
- A prototype is a small- (or full-) scale version of the final product, which has the objective of testing the viability of the commercial version.
- Test marketing involves testing the product in a limited market so as to minimize the risk of immediate introduction on a large scale. The success rate of new product ideas may be only a small percentage of the products originally conceived.
- Product flexibility to the customer means tailoring the product to suit certain customer tastes. Flexibility in the use of raw materials and component products is reduced as one moves through the production chain.

REVIEW AND DISCUSSION QUESTIONS

1   **Life cycle of products**. Describe:
   (a) Some products that have disappeared from the market place. Give reasons why you believe they have 'died'.
   (b) Products that are nearing the end of their useful life.
   (c) Products that have been repackaged so that their maturity has been extended.
   (d) Products that are in the development phase.

2   **Technology**. What role do you think technology will play in the future of the following type of products? What will be the impact to the provider of these products:
   (a) food;
   (b) university degree programmes;
   (c) textiles and clothing;
   (d) sports equipment?

3   **Introduction of new products**. The text quotes General Electric of the USA as an example of a company that has been very successful in developing new products. Can you name other companies, in either manufacturing or services, that are leaders in product development?

4   **Quality function deployment**. Consider the following products:
   (a) the bus or train service you use to get to and from your work or school;
   (b) the writing instrument you use;
   (c) the car you drive;
   (d) the degree programme you are taking;
   (e) the meal that is served to you at lunchtime.

For each of these products apply the concept of quality function deployment. First, identify what you expect from these products. Then, analyse them to see if, in the context in which they are made or provided, they satisfy you as a customer or user. If not, what modifications would you propose to the producer that would make them meet your needs more closely.

5 **Value analysis**. Identify five products that you use on a regular basis, either tangible goods or services where you as a customer are satisfied that you are getting value for money. Then select another five products where you feel you are not getting value for money. Justify your reasoning.

6 **Robust design**. How would you apply the concept of 'Robust Design' to the following products:

(a) a university degree programme;
(b) a pair of shoes;
(c) the automobile you drive.

Describe the materials, processes, and customers that play a part in the robust design.

CASE STUDY: TYPEWRITERS AND SMITH CORONA

Situation

The typewriter first appeared commercially in 1875, when E. Remington and Sons made a machine called the 'Sholes & Glidden Type Writer', which printed only capital letters. In 1878 their 'Number 2 Type Writer' was introduced, which was able to print both upper- and lowercase letters. In 1895, the Underwood Co. introduced an improved machine, which used metal type bars that hit a platen in front. By 1900, most typewriters had inked ribbons and four rows of keys using the QWERTY format in the USA and England, the AZERTY format in France and some other European countries and the QWERTZ in yet other countries. These arrangements are still standard on current computer keyboards.

L. C. Smith and his brothers, gun makers in Syracuse, New York, USA, introduced their Smith Premier Typewriter Number 1 in 1889 and, in 1903, they started the L.C. Smith & Brothers Typewriter Co. In 1926 this company merged with Corona Typewriter Co., another firm that had been around since 1907. This merger was the beginning of the Smith Corona Co, which became a leading manufacturer of manual, then later electric, typewriters, personal word processors and fax machines. It was a name known and respected worldwide.[12]

In about 1994, the company's sales volume started to fall after its main competitor, Brother Industries Ltd, cut its prices on many of its models, a strategy that Smith Corona was not always able to match. During this year and 1995, Smith Corona began selling off its non-core businesses to focus on its typewriter and personal word-processor businesses. In May 1995, after reporting a loss of $12.1 million, or 40 cents a share, for its 3rd financial quarter, the company announced that it was suspending dividends. (In the same period the year before it had had a net income of $1.4 million, or 5 cents a share.) Also in May 1995, the company announced that it planned to cut its workforce by 26 per cent (about 750 jobs worldwide), which was expected to save $21 million annually after 1996.

On 5 July 1995, Smith Corona Corp. filed for bankruptcy protection reorganization under Chapter 11 of the US Bankruptcy Code in Wilmington Delaware. (This section of the bankruptcy code frees a company from creditors' lawsuits while it attempts to rework its financial situation.) In its filing, Smith Corona listed assets of US $207.9 million and liabilities of US $198.8 million. The company also noted 17 subsidiaries, none of which were part of the bankruptcy filing.[13]

In May 1996, Smith Corona, still in Chapter 11, announced a net income for its most recent quarter of $9.1 million. This was helped by the sale of its Singapore plant, although sales fell 36 per cent to $20 million from $31.4 million.[14]

In December 1996, the Pension Benefit Guaranty Corporation (PBGC) announced an agreement regarding the protection of the pensions of the 4700 workers and retirees of the Smith Corona Corporation. (PBGC is a federal corporation created under the Employee Retirement Income Security Act of 1974 to guarantee payment of basic pension benefits to American workers and retirees.) Under the agreement, Smith Corona would continue the pension plan for its salaried workers (the plan was underfunded by $14.5 million, with $39.7 million in assets and $54.2 million in liabilities). PBGC would take over and guarantee the plan for the hourly workers. (This plan was underfunded by $15.3 million, with $29.5 million in assets and $44.8 million in pension obligations.)[15]

Required

1 Why do you think Smith-Corona, once a market leader, allowed itself to fall into bankruptcy?
2 How do you think the company could have avoided this situation?
3 Where does the concept of 'management of technology' come into play.

CASE STUDY: FOUR PRODUCTS

Situation

The following describes some of the history, growth and current status of four products, two from service firms and two tangible products.

Airline travel

The worldwide air transport boom continues. In 1995 the number of passengers carried by airlines increased by almost 5 per cent to 2.2 billion over 1994, with demand particularly strong in Europe. which was up 6.8 per cent to 644 million, and the Asia–Pacific region, up 7.6 per cent to 358 million. Affordable prices and the expansion in world trade are both boosting the airline business. Air travel is likely to grow by an annual 5 to 6 per cent, doubling in volume over the next 15 years or so, while cargo traffic should also increase at an above-average rate. By far the strongest growth is expected for the Asia–Pacific countries. Air transport is already contending with serious constraints especially in

Europe, where roughly one in three flights arrives late as a result of delays on the ground or in the air.[16]

Aspirin

On 10 August 1897, Felix Hoffman, a research chemist in the employ of a German dyestuffs company called Bayer, managed to acetylate the phenol group of a compound called salicylic acid, developing acetylsalicyclic acid, better known as aspirin. Hoffman had develop the world's first truly synthetic drug, that is, not merely an artificial copy of a naturally occurring compound. Since the synthesis of aspirin, the product has gone from strength to strength. It was first marketed mainly as an anti-inflammatory, particularly for people suffering from rheumatism, but its popularity as a general-purpose painkiller followed quickly. It has not suffered proscription, as happened to its near contemporary, heroin. Nor has it been overtaken by more modern substances. Paracetamol and ibuprofen may have nibbled at its share of the over-the-counter (OTC) painkiller market, but aspirin still outsells them both. In Germany, for instance, half of the OTC market belongs to aspirin-based products and Bayer itself produces 11 billion tablets a year.[17]

The Hamburger

The rise of the hamburger is a metaphor for the rise of America. It came ashore with immigrants from Hamburg, who had long since acquired the habit of eating ground beef, raw with onion juice, from nomadic Tartar tribes. Like the immigrants themselves, the hamburger evolved in the new world. It was cooked, it was sheathed in bread. Then, sometime around 1920, a bun replaced the sandwich bread. In 1948, Richard and Maurice McDonald opened the first fast-burger joint. The food was prepared in advance and kept warm under infrared lamps. The pre-packaged hamburger, standard, efficient and cheap, fitted the mass American culture that emerged after the war.

Today, the average American eats three hamburgers a week, a collective effort that puts paid to 40 billion burgers annually. Despite cholesterol phobia, the number of hamburgers and cheeseburgers consumed in restaurants has jumped by nearly a fifth since 1990. By now, McDonald's has served 70 billion hamburgers, enough to reach to the moon and back 17 times over. The production of hamburgers has become as automated as Henry Ford's assembly line. McDonald's has opened restaurants in 103 countries, most recently in Tahiti and Cyprus. Like America, the hamburger has come to dominate the world. As with America, the question is: 'can the product last for ever?'[18]

Lladros Figurines

Lladros are the romantic porcelain figurines made by the company of the same name in Valencia, Spain. They have worldwide appeal because they deal with universal themes, very often based on the Victorian era, and they captivate people with their delicacy and romanticism. King Juan Carlos of Spain often gives the statuettes as gifts when on official state visits. And Lyn Cole, a long-time collector from Queensland, Australia, professed in a recent letter to Lladro that she feels 'moved by the beauty' of each of her 45 Lladro pieces. In fact, she says, Lladro has become 'an important part of my life'. In 1996, Lladro's sales stood at 14.8 billion pesetas (US $95.4 million), almost one third of that coming from the USA. There are 9700 stores that sell the ceramic products worldwide. Lladro has its own distribution company in the USA and a joint distribution venture in Japan.

Lladro was founded in 1933 by three brothers. When the brothers were teenagers, they worked on the family farm in eastern Spain during the day and studied painting and sculpture at a local school in the evening. Together they began to make their first ceramic figurines in the family backyard, 44 years ago. Each figurine is made by hand from a series of clay moulds at Porcelain City, as the Valencia factory is known. The pieces are fired separately and then melded together by hand with a special porcelain-based liquid. Each piece is hand-painted and fired once. The ceramic pieces range in price from about $30 for a Christmas Bell to $25 000 for the carriage of Cinderella drawn by four horses. Limited editions that sold for $70 in 1985 now go for as much as $16 000.[19]

Required

Examine these four products using the concepts presented in this chapter. From a product point of view how are they similar and how are they different? Look at their history, particularly the role of market forces on their growth rate. Where has technology played a role? Does technology have a future role? How would you apply the product life cycle to these four products? What about future development and flexibility? Finally, what do you feel is the future for airline travel, the aspirin, the hamburger and Lladro figurines. What events might modify sales either upwardly or in a downward fashion.

NOTES AND REFERENCES

1. Kerwin, K. (1996) 'Not your father's Corvette: It's being toned down and refined to take on European rivals', *Business Week* 23 December: 35.
2. McGhie, J. A. (1991) 'Birth of an industry: Petrochemicals made an unheralded debut 75 years ago in New Jersey', *The Lamp*, Exxon Corporation, Shareholders 77(3).
3. 'US armor makers have vested interest in survivors' stories: They say bulletproof attire fends off many dangers; Wounded buck stops here' (1996) *Wall Street Journal Europe* 1–2 March.
4. '1878–1997: La saga d'une entreprise qui a fait l'Amérique' (1997) *L'Expansion* 10–24 July: 30.
5. 'General Electric. Les secrets de la plus belle entreprise du monde' (1997) *L'Expansion* 10–24 July.
6. Akao, Y (ed.) (1990) *Quality Function Deployment: Integrating customer requirements into product design*, Cambridge, MA: Productivity Press.
7. *Users manual*, Black and Decker Products (with permission).
8. *Taguchi Methods, Selected Papers on Methodology and Applications* (1988) Dearborn, MI: ASI Press.
9. *The Economist* (1995) 27 May.
10. 'Can Honda build a world car?' (1997) *Business Week* 8 September: 38–44.
11. CHASE, R. B and AQUILANO, N. J. (1977) *Production and Operations Management: A Life Cycle Approach*, Homewood, IL: Irwin: 817.
12. King Features Syndicate, Inc. 1995 http://homarts.com/depts/home/kfkovee/19.htm.
13. *San Diego Daily Transcript* (1995) July.
14. *San Diego Daily Transcript* (1996) May.
15. Pension Benefit Guaranty Corp. (1996) Announcement 97, 11 December.
16. Commerzbank.
17. 'An aspirin a day keeps the doctor at bay: The world's first blockbuster drug is a hundred years old this week (1997) *The Economist* 9 August.
18. 'As hamburgers go, so goes America?' (1997) *The Economist* 23 August.
19. 'Lladro carves out global role for statuettes: Word 'Kitschy' doesn't deter the porcelain's collectors' (1997) *Wall Street Journal Europe* 29 July.

FURTHER READING

Adler, P. S., Mandelbaum, A., Nguyen V. and Schwerer, E. (1996) 'Getting the most out of your product development process', *Harvard Business Review* 74(2): 134–52.
Berg, T. L. and Schuman, A. (1963) *Product Strategy and Management*, New York; London: Holt, Rinehart, and Winston.
Bradbury, J. A. (1989) *Product Innovation: Idea to Exploitation* New York, Chichester: John Wiley & Sons.
Clark, K. B. and Fujimoto, T. (1991) *Product Development Performance: Strategy, Organisation, and Management in the World Auto Industry*, Boston, MA: Harvard Business School.

Deschamps, J.-P. (1995) *Products Juggernauts: How Companies Mobilise to Generate a Stream of Market Winners'* Cambridge, MA: Harvard Business School.

Ettlie, J. E. (1997) 'Integrated design and new product success', *Journal of Operations Management* 15(1): 33–55.

Frampton, R. (1997) 'Virtual designs get cars to market faster', *IEEE Spectrum* 34(11): 64–65.

Gabel, L. H. (1987) *Product Standardisation and Competitive Advantage*, North Holland.

Hadjincola, G. C. and Kumar, K. R. (1997) 'Factors affecting international product design', *Journal of the Operations Research Society* 48(11): 1131–43.

Hayes, R. and Wheelwright, S. (1984) *Restoring our competitive edge: Competing through manufacturing*, New York, Chichester: John Wiley & Sons.

Iansiti, M. and West, J. (1997) 'Technology integration: Turning great research into great products', *Harvard Business Review* 75(6): 69–75.

Leonard, D. and Rayport, J. F. (1977) 'Spark innovation through empathic design', *Harvard Business Review* 75(6): 102–8.

Lovelock, C. (1994) *Product Plus: How Product and Service: Competitive Advantage*, New York: McGraw-Hill.

Lunani, M., Nair, V. N. and Wasserman, G. S. (1997) 'Graphical methods for robust design with dynamic characteristics', *Journal of Quality Technology*, 29(3): 327–38.

Nayak, R. P. (1992) 'Measuring product creation effectiveness', *Journal of Business Strategy* 6: 48–52.

Romani, P. N. (1997) 'The resurrection of value engineering', *Manage* 49(1): 27–29.

Roy, R. and Wield, D. (1986) *Product Design and Technological Innovation*, Milton Keynes: Open University.

Tabrizi, B. and Walleigh, R. (1997) 'Defining next-generation products: An inside look' *Harvard Business Review* 75(6): 116–24.

Ulrich, K. T. and Eppinger, S. D. (1995) *Product Design and Development*, New York: McGraw-Hill.

Wasson, C. R. (1971) *Produce Management: Product Life Cycles and Competitive Marketing Strategy*, St. Charles, IL: Challenge.

7 Process design and the operations network

Objectives and overview

Tangible products, and services, need to be delivered according to customers' needs. The objective of this chapter is to highlight the elements and characteristics involved in the design of the process system and the operations network, part of the supply chain, to ensure that these requirements are met. The chapter opens by presenting typical process systems in both manufacturing and services and illustrating their correlation with product design. Capacity requirements of the process system are presented for manufacturing and services and then vertical integration, as a process design system strategy, is covered in detail and both the benefits and disadvantages are enumerated. There are three sections on technology in process design, including automation, the use of information technology and artificial intelligence systems. A section describes the use of an operations network flow chart as an aid to organizing process design. Finally, the concept of Business Process Re-engineering is described, with a real-world example.

DESIGN OF THE PROCESS SYSTEM

Chapter 6 was devoted to the design of the product. To produce and deliver the product as planned requires a well-organized process design system, complete with an integrated operations network (part of the physical supply chain), to ensure that material and information flow and transformation is smooth and efficient. There are a process system and an operations network in both manufacturing and services.

Manufacturing

In manufacturing the process system and the operations network form the supply chain, the complexity of which depends on the type of product, the volume produced, the size of the market, the final consumers, etc. As a minimum, the supply chain will include the delivery of the raw materials and components from suppliers, the manufacturing and assembly at one or several sites and then product distribution either directly, or via storage centres, to the client. Specific considerations for design of the process network include aspects discussed in the following sections. Most of them, as indicated, are covered in further detail elsewhere in the book.

Site location

Site considerations cover whether there is sufficient capacity to produce at an existing location or if it will be more feasible to build a new facility. In this case will the facility be built domestically, or internationally? (See also, Chapter 3, *Site Selection*)

Make or buy

Make or buy is an economic decision concerning whether a firm will manufacture the subassemblies and finished product itself, whether it will purchase from existing suppliers, or whether it will employ subcontractors to perform specific parts of the work. (See further, Chapter 16, *Purchasing and Subcontracting* for the make-and-buy calculation method).

Layout

The layout of the facility is very much a function of the type of product. If the production is expected to be small, then perhaps a batch-type operation with production in small lots would be appropriate. For high volumes, a continuous process would be a consideration that would involve a more rigid layout. Continuous flow might be appropriate for, say, liquid pharmaceutical products, or an assembly line operation might be better for mechanical pieces. Chapter 10, *Design of the Facility Layout*, treats this in detail.

Technology

What will be the extent of technology employed? Will the system be highly automated, involving a high capital investment? If so, what technological tools and machines will be employed? Alternatively, will there be significant manual input?

Distribution network

Issues to be resolved here include how the product will be delivered to the client. What storage areas will be necessary? What transportation systems will be the most economic? (See further Chapter 17, *Managing the Supply Chain*.)

Information systems network

This covers all the network systems for communicating between parties concerned. It would include the architecture for the computer links with purchasing, those within the manufacturing site and those concerned with distribution. This is addressed later in this chapter and also covered in Chapter 17, *Managing the Supply Chain*.

Services

Many of the elements in process design for manufacturing also apply to services. A particular differences with services is that the network is designed very much with the customer in mind in comparison with manufacturing, where customer convenience is really only a consideration at the end of the chain. Some specific considerations in services are as discussed in the following sections.

Air travel

For a major airline company, as a minimum, the physical process system consists of terminals to handle flight arrivals and departures, passengers, baggage handling, ticketing, restaurant services, etc. Then there is the information systems network for flight planning, weather reporting, operations planning, airline control, etc. Many airlines, for example British Airways, operate a hub-and-spoke system where Heathrow, London is a 'hub' for arrivals and departures of almost all of its flights. The 'spokes' extend worldwide into North America, Australia, Europe, Africa and Asia, covering some 165 destinations and handling over 36 million people.[1]

Rail travel

Rail companies have an elaborate network to service as well as possible the entire country. In some cases, for example the SNCF in France, the network also has stations that interconnect with airports, such as Paris, Charles De Gaulle, and Lyon, Satolas. Similarly, in Britain there are rail links to Heathrow and Gatwick airports. Again, in addition to the physical network, there is also an information systems network for route planning, ticketing, etc.

Telecommunications

Companies like BT (British Telecom), AT&T, USA and France Télécom, which provide telecommunications services worldwide, have complex system designs including networks of fibre-optic cables, satellites, undersea cables and computer tie-ups.

Consulting firms

Consulting companies like Mckinsey, Arthur D. Little and Arthur Andersen provide international consulting services. Their system design principally involves the offices, computer systems and the high-priced consultants. Virtual offices, dealt with in Chapter 10, *Design of the Facility Layout*, may replace physical ones.

Hotels

The system design includes location, room accommodation, restaurant service and communications links for the clients.

Correlation between the product and process design

The product type defines very much the process design system. Hayes and Wheelright[2] developed a correlation between product and process design, of which an adaptation is given in Figure 7.1. The horizontal bar at the top gives the characteristics of products ranging from low-volume, custom-designed products (Box A) through to very-high-volume standard products (Box D). The vertical bar on the left represents the process characteristics. At the top (Box 1) is functional layout or job shop, while at the bottom is completely continuous flow (Box 4). For these various categories the circles in the centre give examples of various product activities that fit these various categories. Flexibility, product volume and unit cost are the important elements of this correlation.

Flexibility

Products and process systems illustrated in Circle A-1 by the machine shop, consulting firm, hospital and car repair are relatively flexible as to the type of products or services they can produce or handle. To a certain extent, if the equipment is changed or modified, the service or product range can be quite large. On the

Figure 7.1 Correlation of the product and the process.

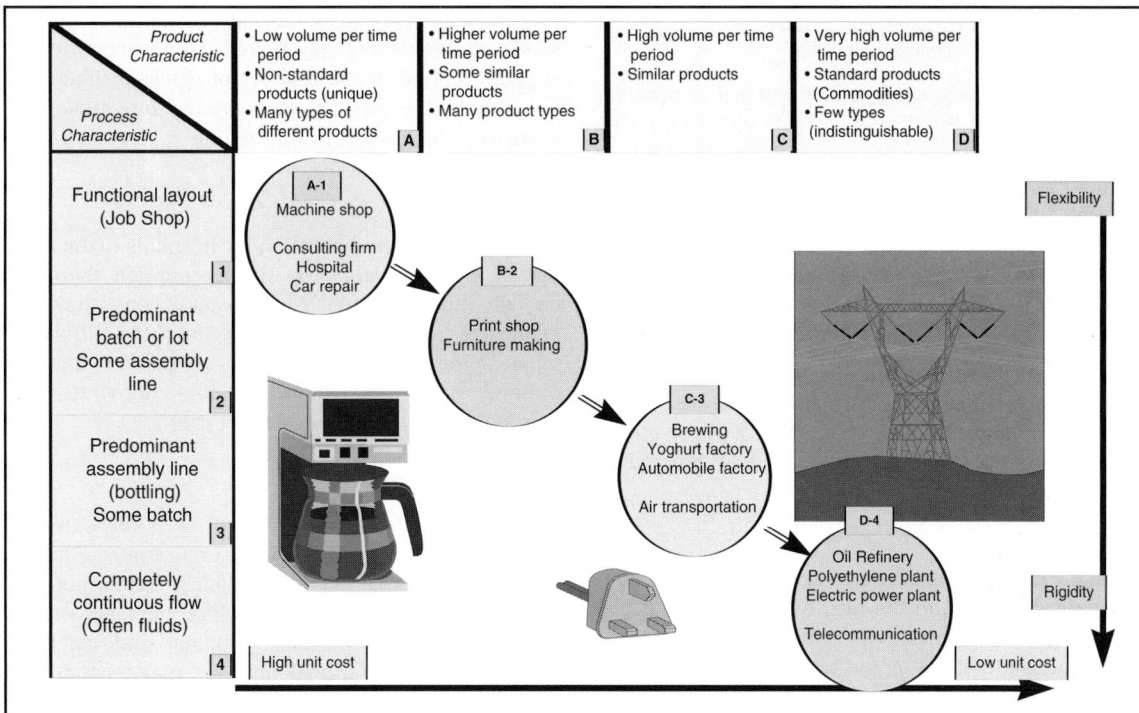

other hand, an oil refinery, polyethylene plant, electric power plant and telecommunications, illustrated in Circle D-4, are inflexible as to the range of products they can produce. Once a refinery or chemical plant is in place, to change the product types would involve significant re-engineering and layout modification.

Product volume

Those products, or services, of the type illustrated in Circle A-1 are produced in much lower volume, or have a longer cycle time, than those type of products exhibited by the Circle D-4. To repair one car might take three hours, but a barrel of diesel oil can be produced in minutes.

Unit cost

Products and processes represented by Circle A-1 have relatively high unit cost because each product is unique and also the educational or skills level of the personnel employed is high. On the other hand, those represented by Circle D-4 have a low unit cost. Compare the cost of a telephone call with that of a car repair!

Between the two extremes are given illustrations of other types of processes/products. The correlation is perhaps easier to conceptualize with physical products than with service-designed products.

THE CAPACITY OF THE PROCESS SYSTEM

A consideration in the design of the process system is determining what capacity should be developed in order that the products can be made, or the services can be offered, to meet the demand of customers, since, like many facets of operations management, capacity planning is market driven. System capacity involves a significant capital investment so that planning should be made carefully in order to optimize the utilization of financial resources in terms of the demand. Customers can quickly be lost if a firm's capacity is insufficient to meet demand. Alternatively, underutilized capacity can be very costly.

Defining capacity

Capacity is defined as the maximum possible output, or use, from a system under normal design, or planned conditions, in a given time period. The effective capacity, or capacity utilization, expressed as a percentage, is given by the ratio:

Effective capacity, or capacity utilization =

$$\frac{\text{Actual capacity used}}{\text{Design capacity.}}$$

The actual capacity used, under normal conditions, must be less than the design capacity. When, on average, this percentage starts to arise above about 90 per cent, then consideration should be given to adding additional capacity. If the capacity utilization hovers around 100 per cent during certain time periods, then on occasions there will almost certainly be bottlenecks or queues occurring.

Services

The capacity of many service firms is dictated by the physical arrangement of a capital facility whose utilization varies seasonally, weekly, or even daily. Some illustrations follow.

Transportation

Transportation systems, such as aeroplanes, trains, buses, ferry boats and the like, have a fixed capacity according to the number of seats available. Capacity utilization is measured by the ratio of number of seats filled to the number of seats available. At certain times of the day, such as morning and early evening, some transportation systems, such as inner-city buses and underground trains, are 'filled to capacity' with lines of people waiting. Because networks, such as runways or rail tracks, are fixed, transport firms are finding it difficult to increase capacity to accommodate this periodic demand. Some approaches are to use double-decker buses or trains on rail networks (as on the Paris–Lyon TGV line for example) or to use river transport (on the Seine in Paris or the Thames in London) to absorb some of this surface transportation. Similarly, road networks, again particularly around large urban areas, have a capacity that is saturated. Airline companies very often publish their average seat capacity in their annual reports as this is also considered a measure of efficiency.

Hotel industry

The capacity of the hotel industry is governed by the number of rooms available. Its capacity utilization is the ratio of the number of rooms used to those available. This ratio is very dependent on the period; for example, during holiday times many hotels operate close to capacity. Similarly in cities that accommodate the business traveller, hotels are heavily booked during the week. The utilization of hotels in a country is often an indicator of the success of its travel industry.

Theatres, cinemas, restaurants

The capacity of theatres, cinemas, restaurants or those services where clients are seated, as in transportation, is again limited to the number of places available. In restaurants, the capacity of the system has some flexibility as it depends both on the time a customer takes to eat and on the service time.

Hospitals

The major capacity limitation for hospitals is the number of beds available (on the assumption there are enough medical staff). New hospital construction is expensive, and often paid for by the State. Efforts to increase the capacity of hospitals are made by limiting patients' stay or, where feasible, moving from overnight treatment to outpatient care.

Manufacturing

The capacity of manufacturing firms is measured by the product output. All manufacturing systems have a nominal, or design, capacity, which is based, not only on the size of the physical facility, but also on the design throughput of the equipment and machines (with the non-operational time for maintenance and cleaning taken into account), the processing time necessary for each of the value-added activities, the flow of the raw materials and components from suppliers and all the labour necessary. Again, capacity design is market driven. This fact has been brought home sharply to the Boeing Aircraft Company, which in 1997 was caught off guard by the significant global customer demand in aircraft orders. It found its capacity insufficient as a result of insufficient labour and component parts, so that it was forced to freeze production of its 747 and 737 jetliners in October. This capacity-related problem had the additional impact of causing a drop in the price of Boeing's shares.[3]

Product and process design in the AIDS battle

Pharmaceutical companies are spending millions of dollars to develop an effective AIDS vaccine to meet a market demand that is soaring astronomically in most countries of the world, particularly Africa. One firm, Merck & Co., has brought out a new drug, Crixivan, which has shown a lot of promise, but the company is struggling to find the capacity to meet market demand. This interaction of market demand with capacity planning, together with new product development, system design, research and development, technology, prototype facilities, sub-contractors, mass production and competitive pressure is highlighted in the article in Box 7.1.[4]

Box 7.1 Short supply. Success of AIDS drug brings new concern: can Merck keep pace? Company Rushed Crixivan to market; now it faces a production bottleneck. Watching the patient count. By Elyse Tanouye, Staff Reporter

Merck & Co. has spent more than $1 billion over the past decade to create Crixivan, one of the most promising drugs ever to attack AIDS. It has paid off.

The drug won the fastest U.S. federal approval in regulatory history, is helping to restore health and hope to thousands of patients, and is soon expected to bring Merck a half-billion dollars in yearly revenue. After seven months on the market, it's outselling other new drugs in its class.

There's just one problem: The company has been struggling for months to keep ahead of demand.

One of the most closely watched numbers inside Merck these days is the weekly Crixivan patient count. About 90,000 patients world-wide already use the drug, but there is only enough supply for about 110,000. Demand could skyrocket as more states approve funding for the expensive therapy and more countries allow its sale.

As a result, Merck has been in a breathless race to rev up production and avoid a public-relations disaster: the prospect of running short of supply and having to turn away AIDS sufferers.

How did one of the world's most powerful drug makers get into this predicament?

Most Complex Drug

Merck created some of its own problems. Despite a world-wide abundance of production capacity, it pridefully chose to build its own plants rather than contract out all the work to a supplier. Then, upon learning that two rivals might beat it to market with similar therapies, Merck requested and got approval of Crixivan – the most complex drug it had ever tried to mass-produce – well before its plants were ready.

Much of the production crunch, however, is the unavoidable result of high-tech achievement, a pitfall of making ever-more-complex medicines. Merck's struggles illustrate the obstacles other companies will face as they pursue new AIDS therapies.

Competition to develop a new class of AIDS drugs began in 1989, when Merck published its discovery of the three-dimensional structure of the enzyme protease, a promising target for attacking the human immunodeficiency virus that causes AIDS. Protease acts like a scissors, cutting up a key HIV protein and enabling the virus to replicate.

Promising Candidates

The new drugs – dubbed protease inhibitors – would mimic part of the protein's shape, creating a decoy to lure protease away from the real protein and prevent it from fulfilling its duties.

About a dozen companies jumped in, and by the early 1990s a handful emerged with promising candidates: Merck, Roche Holding Ltd., Abbott Laboratories, Upjohn Co. (now Pharmacia & Upjohn Inc.), Vertex Pharmaceuticals Inc., and Agouron Pharmaceuticals Inc.

Merck began testing Crixivan in humans in early 1993, and that summer – long before even knowing whether the drug would work – top scientists met for lunch in the company cafeteria to chart how to mass-produce it. "We gulped. We didn't know how we were going to do this," recalls one of the scientists, Paul J. Reider.

Launching full-scale production of a new drug usually begins only after the drug is in advanced testing and has at least an 80% chance of success. The Crixivan effort, because of the AIDS crisis and competitive pressures, began far earlier – when the drug had only a 5% to 10% shot.

"The Water Kept Rising"

The effort was further hampered by the huge quantities of Crixivan that would need to be produced. Each patient must take six 400-milligram pills a day, every day, in combination with other AIDS drugs to achieve the desired effect of reducing HIV levels in the blood. Supplying just 90,000 patients with Crixivan is the equivalent of producing enough Vasotec, Merck's popular hypertension drug, for more than 21 million people.

Merck pushed other projects aside, assigned 400 employees to the Crixivan team and found ways to produce small quantities while rushing to build two factories – even before it knew exactly how the production lines would work. "We were always trying to get our heads above water, and every time we did, the water kept rising," says Dr. Reider, an ebullient, 45-year-old chemist who oversaw the design of the chemical process.

Most Merck pharmaceuticals are produced in about four steps over two weeks. Making a batch of Crixivan is a six-week process that requires 15 chemical steps. It takes about 35 kilograms of 30 raw materials to produce just one kilogram of the drug, enough to supply one patient for a year.

In late 1993, Dr. Reider's team began using a prototype production line at a plant in Rahway, New Jersey, which was able to turn out bigger batches but took up to four months to do it. Each time, only 15% of the volume of ingredients that went in emerged in the desired shape of the Crixivan molecule. Dr. Reider's team needed to cut the production time down to a month and a half and bring the yield up to 50%. Doing so in mass production – filling vats two stories high – would be far more difficult. That is because of Crixivan's terribly complex molecular structure.

A quick chemistry lesson: Many drugs are based on central hubs or "chiral centers," consisting of a carbon atom with four branches of various chemical atoms attached. These hubs usually are ready-made in nature; only in the past decade have scientists mastered the ability to create and link together multiple synthetic chiral centers.

Most medicines are based on just one or two naturally occurring chiral centers; Vasotec, by contrast, is far more complicated because it has three chiral centers, including a hard-to-create synthetic one. Crixivan goes further still: It has five central hubs, all of them man-made. The branches on the chiral centers can be manipulated chemically to form 32 different shapes, but only one creates the Crixivan molecule.

"A Humility Lesson"

One of the big problems with Crixivan's low yield lay in a crucial and especially troublesome step, in which a chemical reaction simultaneously creates two new hubs while fusing those atoms onto an already-joined pair of chiral centers. The resulting molecule kept "overcooking" because of high acidity in the process, ruining a large portion of the output. Four of Merck's best scientists tried to solve the problem but failed.

Then a 28-year-old chemist named Peter Maligres took a shot, adding a common chemical and mixing in some baking soda. He improved the yield from that step by 55%. "Sometimes kids come in and try the simplest things, and they work," Dr. Reider says. "It's a humility lesson." By November 1994, the team had designed the complete Crixivan process.

By now, Merck had to decide whether to pay an outside supplier to produce the drug or to build production from the ground up. Archrival Abbott Labs had confronted the same decision as it rushed to scale up production of its own protease inhibitor, Norvir. Abbott decided to strike deals with suppliers in Japan, Italy and France to handle up to 80% of production.

But Merck didn't entirely trust outsiders to handle the most complex chemistry experiment it had ever tried. Early on, the Crixivan team had hired a supplier to make 200 kilograms of a portion of the molecule for batches to be used in clinical trials. The supplier missed the deadline, threatening to set back the entire project, and Merck had to rush through a batch of its own.

High-Risk Gamble

So Merck restricted its outside dependence and relied on just two suppliers, Mitsui & Co. of Japan and DSM NV of the Netherlands, to handle seven early and less-complicated steps of the chemical process. Doing most of the work in-house would require Merck to commit several hundred million dollars to designing and building new production lines – even though Crixivan wasn't expected to go before regulators for another two years.

It was a big gamble, given that Crixivan thus far had delivered promising results in fewer than a dozen patients, who were taking it in combination with the older drug AZT. HIV's uncanny ability to develop resistance had already nixed one Merck drug candidate and had weakened Crixivan's effectivness when taken without other AIDS drugs. Clearly, Crixivan might eventually fail in clinical trials.

If Merck didn't proceed immediately, however, its new lines wouldn't be ready in time if Crixivan did work. Edward M. Scolnick, Merck's head of research and manufacturing, believed Crixivan would work, because one patient from an early trial persistently kept the virus at bay, even though all other patients relapsed.

"There was no way that patient could have been a fluke," Dr. Scolnick says now. As later tests combining Crixivan with AZT showed promise, "it provided enough assurance, at least internally, that we should go forward with the program."

Escape Clause

In late 1994, Raymond V. Gilmartin, who had just become Merck's chairman, agreed to get production up and running – provided Dr. Scolnick would pull the plug if the drug began to fail in clinical trials. The Merck board gave the go-ahead in February 1995, and frantic construction at two existing plants in Elkton, Virginia, and Albany, Georgia, began a month later.

Yet even as it was rushing to ramp up production, Merck was getting pummeled by AIDS activists, who accused it of dragging its feet on funneling Crixivan to patients. One group, led by Jules Levin, executive director of the U.S. National AIDS Treatment Advocacy Project, demanded that Merck allow an outside drug-manufacturing consultant to evaluate its production efforts.

In January 1995, the consultant met with Merck scientists, who explained in detail their difficulties. But Mr. Levin was unconvinced when the consultant told him Merck was doing all it possibly could. "I didn't believe him," Mr. Levin says. The activist continued to prod Merck to speed up its work and making supplies available on a "compassionate-use" basis, free of charge, to severely ill patients who didn't qualify for clinical trials.

Merck was supplying about 300 patients in trials at the time and needed to produce enough for 2,000 for late-stage trials that were getting under way in just three months. Given its manufacturing problems, Merck was hesitant about supplying hundreds more patients.

Growing Competition

But the activists' lobbying worked. It "reminded us in the middle of this to step back and think about how important every single life is ... and if we can find enough drug for one extra person, it makes a difference," Dr. Reider says. "Throwing caution to the wind," the chemist committed to supplying 1,400 patients on a compassionate-use basis, even before knowing whether Merck could deliver. "I was risking my career," he says.

By September 1995, competitive pressures were intensifying. Abbott reported that it had compiled impressive clinical data on Norvir. It was clear Abbott's drug would win quick U.S. federal approval. The same month Roche's Hoffmann-La Roche Inc. unit announced it had applied for U.S. Food and Drug Administration approval of its protease inhibitor, Invirase; by November, it had won an FDA panel's endorsement and FDA Commissioner David Kessler's promise of quick approval, which came the following month.

Under its original timetable, Merck was still a year away from launching Crixivan. But it was determined to get to market at the same time as its rivals. So its top researchers waged a pitched lobbying campaign to have Crixivan considered alongside Abbott's drug at a coming meeting of an FDA advisory panel. Never mind that Merck would have to file its FDA application by January 1996, eight months earlier than planned. And that its factories weren't ready.

Funneling the Supply

The FDA agreed, but had a principal concern: Could Merck produce enough Crixivan to meet initial demand? If too many patients started on the drug, they might find their pharmacies out when they went for refills. Patients who stop taking the drug even for a short time risk developing resistance to it.

Merck assured the FDA it could make enough Crixivan on its prototype line for up to 30,000 U.S. patients. To ensure a steady supply Merck would funnel most prescriptions through a single major distributor, a mailorder retailer named Stadtlanders Pharmacy in Pittsburgh, which is now majority owned by Counsel Corp. of Toronto. Merck could then control the number of patients on the drug, and bar new patients when demand matched supply. By contrast, Abbott planned to distribute Norvir to pharmacies nationwide.

Abbott's drug won FDA, approval on March 1 of this year and Merck's entry breezed through just 13 days later.

Soon, however, Merck encountered a torrent of protests over Crixivan's restricted distribution. AIDS activists accused the company of giving Stadtlanders a monopoly that let it price-gouge patients, and retail pharmacists decried getting cut out of the deal. Stadtlanders charges customers a 37% premium above what it pays Merck; but the pharmacy says most patients pay much less than the list price because of discounts under various insurance, government and other plans.

Mr. Levin, the activist, says that, in retrospect "it's obvious Merck does have a production problem."

The First Batch

Meantime, as Merck churned out small quantities of the drug at its prototype plant, construction proceeded at a furious pace at the 4,050-square-meter main plant in Elkton and the satellite in Albany.

Finally, on May 27, the big operation was ready. The first Crixivan batch entered the system at 9:30 a.m. For six weeks, Merck engineers and chemists crossed their fingers as 1,140 hectoliters of liquid trickled through 32 kilometers of pipes, vats, dryers, pressers and capsule- and bottle-fillers.

On July 6, the last of the batch's white capsules were in boxes, ready for shipment.

But demand for the drug had begun to pick up after the benefits of protease inhibitors received wide press coverage following an international AIDS conference that week. The Merck crew still had months of work ahead to bring the plants up to full production.

Slowly, more Crixivan "runs" are going on-line; the plants will eventually handle 18 batches at once, each lot producing two million capsules. The question now is whether Merck will get the operation up to full-scale production before demand overtakes it.

Outselling the Competition

Crixivan appears to be outselling Norvir and Invirase by a wide margin, according to IMS America Ltd., a Plymouth Meeting, Pennsylvania, market-research firm. Doctors and patients say they favor Crixivan because it has fewer side effects than Norvir and is more potent than Invirase.

Merck officials say they are confident they can keep pace. They estimate the new plants will be able to crank out enough Crixivan for 150,000 patients by the end of the year and 250,000 by early 1997.

"It wasn't humanly possible to be ahead of where we are, given the history of the project," Dr. Scolnick says. But he vows: "Merck isn't going to run out of this drug."

From *Wall Street Journal Europe*, 5 November 1996
Reprinted by permission of *Wall Street Journal Europe*,
© 1996 Dow Jones & Company, Inc.
All Rights Reserved Worldwide.

Capacity underutilization and flexibility

Many service systems are notoriously inefficient in the sense that the capacity utilization may be close to zero for long periods of the time. Schools and universities are often closed for up to three months during the year. Many hotel and holiday resorts are practically empty in the period from October to December. Transportation systems may be severely underutilized in the mid-morning and mid-afternoon periods, as are restaurants. Manufacturing facilities that provide seasonal products such as ski equipment, swimwear and winter clothing also have a fluctuating demand. Chapter 12, *Operational Capacity Planning*, discusses some possibilities that both service systems and manufacturing facilities might adopt to smooth out and increase their overall capacity utilization.

Capacity planning methods

Capacity planning requirements can be determined by forecasting the market demand. Quantitative forecasting methods in this respect are covered in Chapter 9, *Forecasting Customer Demand*, while Chapter 22, *Decision Making and Risk Analysis*, gives further

planning approaches for deciding on capacity levels and the risks involved. Finally, Chapter 25, *Financial Analysis*, goes into marginal analysis and the relationship between short-term and long-term capacity planning.

VERTICAL INTEGRATION

Vertical integration in the operations network is the combination under a single ownership of two or more stages of production and/or distribution in the supply chain of entities that are normally separate. Firms resort to integration because they deal in large volumes and believe it is more efficient and reliable to have control over suppliers and/or customers. Vertical integration can be backward integration or forward integration; alternatively the complete supply chain for the firm may form an integrated network.

Backward integration

Backward integration is when the firm owns some or all the activities upstream of its operation. This may be the raw materials, the suppliers of parts and components and perhaps even the transportation equipment used to deliver the raw materials. As an example, in mid-1981 for $7.3 billion, Du Pont, the US-based diversified chemical company acquired Conoco, which had interests in oil, gas and coal. The chairman of Du Pont stated that the merger would give the company 'a captive hydrocarbon feedstock source which would reduce the exposure of the combined companies to fluctuations in the price of energy and hydrocarbons'[5]. Dairy-producing firms represent a type of backward integration where, through a cooperative, the milk treating, cheese making and packaging firms own the dairy farms.

Forward integration

Forward integration is when the firm owns some or all of the activities upstream of its operation. For the manufacturing firm of finished products, this might include the distribution centres and retail outlets. For a manufacturer of raw materials or components, this might be the ownership of the manufacturing/assembly operation of the finished product. As an illustration, in the 1970s Texas Instruments of the USA, a producer of integrated circuits and electronic components, integrated forward into calculators, watches, and other electronic products. Delivery firms like UPS and Federal Express own the delivery vehicles, and even aeroplanes, so that they can completely control their schedules.

Complete integration

Complete integration is the control or ownership of the entire supply chain. Oil companies such as Texaco, BP, Shell or Exxon (Esso in Europe) are examples of a completely integrated firm. These firms first own and operate the oil refinery that distils the crude oil into petrol, aviation fuel, diesel and other products. They are backwardly integrated owning the upstream production activities for the crude oil, including the drilling platforms and pumping equipment that bring the oil to the surface. In addition, they own the pipelines for delivering the crude oil to port and the oil tankers that transport the oil to the oil refinery. Then they are forwardly integrated, owning the marketing activities, including the tanker trucks, or the tanker ships, that deliver the refined products to the distribution outlet and, in many cases, the petrol retail outlets themselves. This arrangement is illustrated in Figure 7.2. In some cases, oil companies go further and own downstream the chemical plants that produce a range of products based on petroleum feedstock.

Some US automobile manufacturing companies have a partially integrated network, since they own the facility that manufactures the component parts, as well as the dealer networks that sell the finished product.

Benefits of integration

Vertical integration can be of strategic importance to the operations manager, as it may provide possibilities for cost reductions, low levels of inventory and easier scheduling.[6]

Transaction costs

Vertical integration can reduce the buying and selling costs that are incurred when two separate companies own two stages of production and perhaps the physical distribution. When integrated, the marketing activities such as sales, advertising, promotion and market research can be eliminated.

Reliability of supplies

Vertical integration may be essential to ensure a supply of critical raw materials. This fact was made very evident in the 1970s during the oil crisis, when foreign owners of crude oil cut off supplies, thus reducing the availability of petrol supplies for automobile use as well as sharply increasing product costs.[7]

Captive customers

If a firm owns the upstream distribution centre and retail outlets, then to a certain extent it is creating a captive client base, for example an automobile company that owns a dealership or a paint manufacturer that owns a paint store.

Easier coordination

With vertical integration, coordination in the supply chain may be easier in terms of production and inventory scheduling between activities in the chain, since the flows in the supply and distribution networks are known with some certainty.

Technology

Another argument is that, with integration, companies are better equipped to use innovative technologies because they participate in many of the production and distribution activities where changes in innovations are likely to occur.

Entry barriers

The more vertically integrated a business, then often the greater the financial resources required for competitors to enter and compete in this market. Thus, ver-

Figure 7.2   Operations network for an oil company.

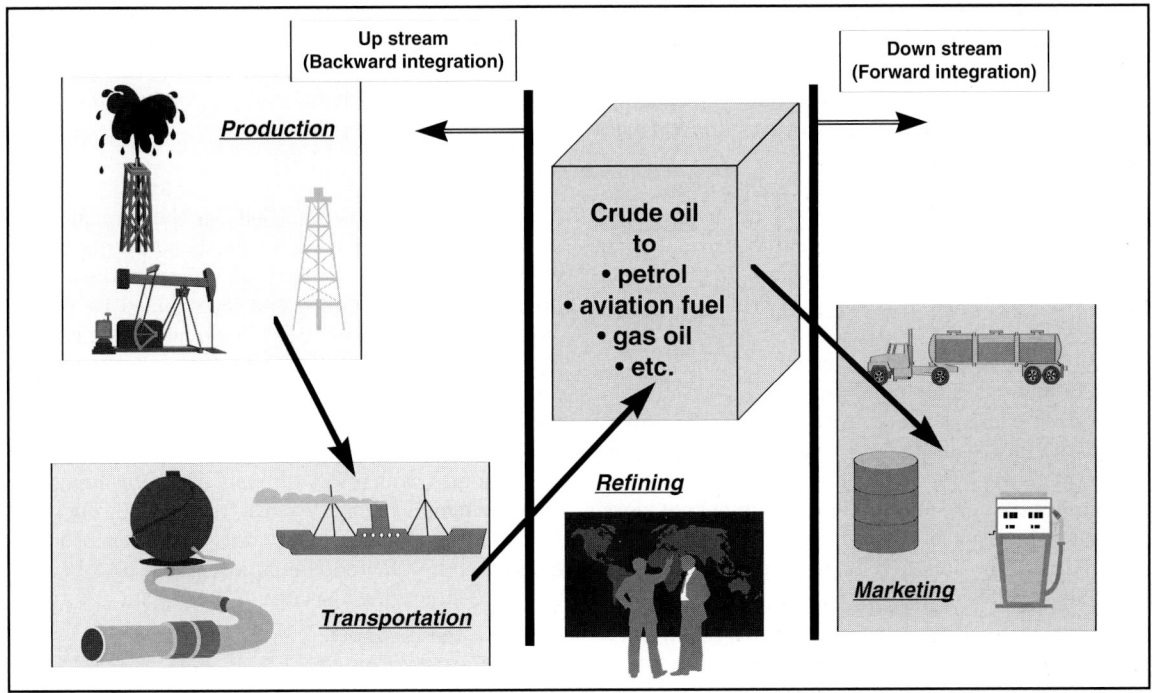

tically integrated companies have a certain monopoly that discourages competitor entry. (This fact is often used by regulatory agencies as an argument to break up companies because of their monopolistic powers.)

Disadvantages of integration

Disadvantages of integration include increased capital requirements, unbalanced throughput, reduced flexibility and loss of specialization.

Capital requirements

If a firm integrates either backwards or forwards, it needs to provide the capital that the newly acquired operation requires to be integrated successfully with the acquiring firm. In order for the combined firm to increase, or at least maintain, its profitability, the savings in the operating costs of the newly integrated organization must be substantially less than the capital investment required.

Unbalanced throughput

In combining the various stages of production, and/or distribution, the capacity of the units must be matched in order that cost reduction and efficiencies are obtained. For example, an automobile constructor

might acquire a component manufacturer, which has a capacity greater than the acquiring firm. To balance the system would mean that the automobile firm would have to produce more automobiles, which may not be feasible because of market constraints.

Reduced flexibility

When companies integrate vertically, they are accepting the work practices and operating methods of the acquired firm. If market conditions or technology change, then the controlling firm may not be able to compete effectively in the market place. This has occurred in the steel and textile industries, when firms purchased steel or textile mills which operated with old technology. When markets changed, these sites became obsolete, were closed down and charged as a write-off to the owner company.

Managerial style

Firms that acquire other firms sometimes impose their management style on the acquired firm and this may not correspond to the market, or environment, in which the acquired firm operates. In the past, major producing companies, such as paint firms, tyre producers and oil companies, have owned retail outlets. These new owners, whose mentality is producing, have not always had the flexible and customer-oriented marketing capabilities for the outlets to remain competitive. Today, for example, oil companies have given up direct ownership of some petrol stations and operate the retail outlets as a franchise. These franchise owners have maintained and increased their business by moving into food sales and other products for the traveller.

Another illustration related to management style occurred to C. F. Braun and Co., an independent California-based engineering firm that had a certain market niche and a good client base. In the 1980s Braun was purchased by Santa Fe, a drilling company, which wanted Braun to perform the upstream engineering work for them. The combined Braun/Santa Fe organization was later purchased by Kuwait Oil Co, which itself had an interest in Braun/Santa Fe providing all the upstream drilling, engineering design and construction work for its oil production, refineries and chemical plants. The network integration did not work, partially as a result of different objectives and corporate styles. Now, Santa Fe is again independent and Braun has essentially ceased to exist.

Japanese firms and *keiretsu*

Japanese manufacturing firms like Sony, Mitsubishi and Nissan avoid direct vertical integration, but have a middle-of-the-road approach and control their supply chain by having a vast network of suppliers who provide many of the components used in the assembly of the finished product. These suppliers are not strictly independent, in that many are financially supported by the manufacturing firm and become part of a network coalition known as *keiretsu*. Members of the *keiretsu* are assured long-term relationships and, as such, are expected to be reliable partners providing technical expertise and quality products on a continuing basis.

Disintegration

After vertically integrating their operations networks, some firms find that the economic gains are not as expected and that it is cheaper to purchase components and raw materials directly from independent suppliers, where they have more flexibility. These suppliers, having to fight for business, are sometimes able to produce at lower costs, with better quality, and provide more reliable delivery than the integrated supplier. In the latter case, the integrated supplier, knowing he has a guaranteed customer, provides a worse than expected service.

This idea of disintegration is evident in the non-profit sector, where local and state governments, who used to control all the municipal services such as cleaning, maintenance, landscaping etc., find it cheaper and

more efficient to subcontract out these services. On a larger scale, governments that privatize industries (British Rail, British Airways, BT, etc.) are finding the privatized firm, away from the government restrictions, is a more profitable entity. A high-profile example of disintegration is AT&T.

AT&T

AT&T was at one time 'Ma Bell', or the company that essentially controlled all of the local and telephone networks in the USA. As a result of an antitrust suit brought in 1974 by MCI, and later joined by the US Justice Department, the Bell telephone system monopoly was broken in the 1980s, so that smaller regional phone companies were created and the long-distance market opened to competitors. Then, in 1996, this new AT&T further disintegrated into three parts. Lucent Technologies, which was the part of the firm engaged in telecommunication systems, research through the Bell labs, microelectronics and consumer products evolved and NCR, the computing entity, also became independent leaving a smaller AT&T.[8]

Virtual companies

Having an integrated supply chain can be bureaucratic and reduce the flexibility for many firms, especially with changing markets, new technology and globalization. Virtual companies, also known as *hollow corporations* or *network companies*, are those that can be created or 'integrated' on demand to provide the services or network required. Virtual companies have flexible moving organizational boundaries that allow them to create a unique enterprise, providing services such as payroll, screening new hiring, designing products, providing consulting services, manufacturing components, conducting tests, or distributing products. The relationship may be short term and the participants may be true partners, or only collaborators, or even simply able suppliers and subcontractors. The advantages of virtual companies include specialized management expertise, low capital investment, flexibility and speed. Moreover, they can easily be disbanded when the service is no longer needed.[9]

AUTOMATION IN PROCESS DESIGN

Automation in process design is the replacement of labour with machinery, which today is almost all computer controlled. Computers saw their beginning in the 1950s with machines, developed by IBM, Burroughs and others, housed in air-conditioned rooms. Today the use and application of computers has mushroomed to

Figure 7.3   Profound statements relating to computer technology.

the control of equipment and machines, information exchange, printing, designing, material movement, financial transactions, etc. Even the 'experts' underestimated the dramatic growth and utilization of computer-based equipment as illustrated in Figure 7.3.

The range of automated equipment in manufacturing and services is vast. Examples are discussed in the following sections.

Mechanical aids

Mechanical aids do not necessarily involve computer control, but are often simple feed systems that avoid the operator performing the work. They result in more accurate operation and very often reduce the risk of injury. Some examples are:

- feed attachments for punching and drilling machines;
- centring and grasping devices for lathes;
- strip feeders for stamping machines;
- feeders that release precise quantities (either weight or volume) into containers.

Numerically controlled machines

Numerically controlled machines are those that have control systems that read instructions and translate these instructions into machine operations. Machines are preprogrammed with computer commands to perform a repeated cycle of operations, which replaces the manual changing of machine settings. They are available in such operations as: turning on lathes; drilling, boring and milling; assembly operations; printing; weaving; and quality control, such as is found in sensing on a bottling line.

Robots

Robots were introduced in the 1970s. They are used extensively in the automobile industry and in the manufacture of electrical appliances (television, radio, etc.). Robots enable repetitive work (such as soldering) to be performed more rapidly and with precision. They are useful in dirty environments, such as the paint spraying of automobile chassis, or in dangerous zones, such as in the nuclear and chemical industries. As a result of the incessant miniaturization of electronics and micromechanics, there are now also robot systems that can perform some kinds of brain and bone surgery.[10]

Figure 7.4 illustrates the growth of robots since 1990, with significant use in Japanese industry.[11] However, companies in Continental Europe are also investing heavily in robotic equipment as the article in Box 7.2 illustrates.[12]

Figure 7.4 Sales of industrial robots.

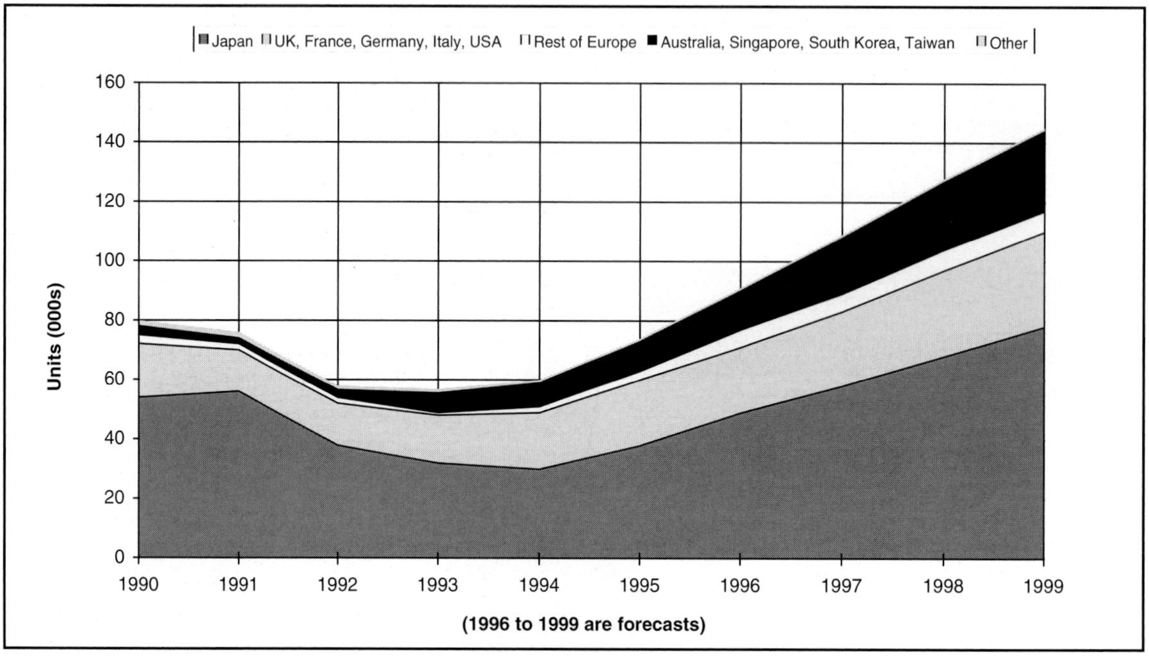

A drawback of robots is their high capital cost and they are not always as flexible as humans, even though they can work 24 hours per day. Furthermore, sometimes there is resistance to their use from labour unions as they result in a loss of personnel. An unusual application of robots in the food industry is illustrated by the article in Box 7.3.[13]

Computer-aided manufacturing

Computer-Aided Manufacturing (CAM) systems translate CAD information, discussed in Chapter 6, *Design of the Product*, into instructions for automated production machinery. This machinery performs the necessary production operations on the products with a minimum of direct worker involvement.

Flexible manufacturing systems

Flexible manufacturing systems (FMS) are clusters of computer-controlled machines, which produce a variety of products. Computers give instructions, robots handle materials and machine settings are automatically changed to produce the different products.

Automatic guided vehicles

Automatic Guided Vehicles (AGVs) are computer-driven vehicles that transfer material and machinery from one work zone to another. They are often used in the automobile and other heavy industries for transferring engines from one zone to another.

Automated storage and retrieval systems

Automated Storage and Retrieval Systems (AS&RS) are computer-controlled warehouses and storage systems. Here material and parts are automatically removed (picked) for shipping. Alternatively, components and raw materials are placed in the appropriate storage area after delivery. At the Lerclerc supermarket/hypermarket distribution centre in L'Isle d'Abeau France, there is an automatic storage and retrieval system in a warehouse zone that contains 8054 pallets of food products, stored 14 metres high, in seven alleys and managed by just three operators.

Computer-integrated manufacturing

Computer-integrated manufacturing (CIM) includes the entire system of production, incorporating the latest in high-tech production technology.

Virtual systems

Virtual systems are non-physical representations of the 'real thing', most often represented by computer-based simulations. In the operating environment, they are

Box 7.2 *Brave old world*. European business uses more robots and fewer people. High wages compel firms to invest in automation, even in service sector. This "crocodile" eats jobs. By Douglas Lavin, *Staff Reporter*

STUTTGART, Germany – On the fourth floor of the opulent Breuninger department store here, salesman Sven Kluge is explaining why the most technologically advanced shoe-selling device ever invented by man is, for the moment, kaput.

"This never happens," Mr. Kluge says, gesturing toward a massive robot arm hovering immobile over some 7,000 shoes stacked in a storeroom. "It's a software problem."

His hand-held computer features a bar-code scanner that's supposed to tell Mr. Kluge what sizes of black Fila Stand Out shoes are in stock – and allow him to order the robot to go fetch. Instead, the gizmo is flashing "transmission error."

Despite the inevitable bugs, companies throughout Continental Europe are investing heavily in automation. From Breuninger, which installed its system last autumn, to a Danish milk warehouse that went robotic this spring, companies large and small are replacing people with machines. The European market for automated systems has grown more than 10% this year alone – and shows no sign of letting up soon.

Growing Chasm

The reason for this expansion is simple. "I call it the crocodile gap," says Stelio Demark, president of ABB Asea Brown Boveri AG's flexible automation unit, the world's largest maker of robots. Sitting in his office in Zurich, Mr. Demark sketches the growing chasm between falling automation prices and rising West European labor costs (see chart). "It just keeps getting wider."

Mr. Demark estimates, for example, that it only costs about $10 an hour to operate an industrial robot, compared with $30 to $37 an hour for an industrial worker in Germany. As a result, his division expects between $1.6 billion to $1.8 billion in sales this year, up from $1.4 billion in 1996, mostly in Europe. "The market is bigger in Europe than in North America," he says, "and it is speeding up."

The development is something of a mixed blessing. At a time when near-record unemployment is already wracking the Continent, growth in the automation market could have disastrous effects on Europe's economy, particularly given that the boom is spilling out of heavy industry, automation's traditional base, and into the job-rich heart of tomorrow's economy: services. Yet if automation prices keep dropping, the trend could also spark a boom in productivity; and productivity growth, economists say, is the only real way to generate higher profits and, ultimately, higher wages.

In fact, the automation wave is already a prime reason why Western Europe has been able to remain competitive in the global marketplace despite its notoriously high labor costs. Automation alone, economists say, has allowed Europe to hold on to some of its sunset industries – glass and china in France, paper and wood products in Scandinavia and textiles in Italy – all of which today rely heavily on specialized machines, and in some cases, robots, to boost productivity.

At the Benetton Warehouse

Consider Benetton Group SpA's plants outside Treviso, Italy. They are tied via computer links directly to the Italian retailer's sales outlets and to an automated warehouse that employs only 19 people to handle 30,000 boxes a day – boxes that bundle precise orders for, say, blue sweaters and yellow slacks for direct shipment to stores. Without robots, the warehouse would need some 400 people, a Benetton spokesman says. "When the '92 recession hit, we had to do something," he adds. "It was either move production to the Far East – or invest massively in automation."

For many, the growth of automation on a Continent already riddled with high unemployment is disturbing. Some economists see it as a symptom of a sclerotic labor market so over-regulated that it discourages companies from hiring even when demand grows – and so full of worker-protection rules that some companies find it simpler to deploy robots instead of people.

"This could grow to be a very large wave if European labor markets aren't reformed," says Bill Lewis, head of the McKinsey Global Institute, in Washington, D.C., who warns of an "inexorable increase" in Europe's already punishing jobless rates – unless Europe's interventionist governments back off and deregulate massively.

But at a time when some European governments, like France's recently elected Socialists, are talking of cutting the work week to 35 hours from 39 hours without loss of pay, the automation wave is likely to swell. "Companies feel that automation is the only way they can survive," says Martin Haegele, head of the robotics department at Germany's most prominent think-tank for automation issues, the Fraunhofer Institut fur Produktionstechnik und Automatisierung, or IPA.

IPA is now developing a robotized system to clean the glass ceiling of Berlin's new train station, and it has previously developed systems that scrub Lufthansa jets, sort waste for recycling, and trim pork bellies. Most of these systems were designed for companies whose officers say automation is the only thing that has kept them from moving jobs abroad.

No wonder Europe's automation market – already about twice the size of the U.S. market, albeit smaller than Japan's – "is really booming," says Michael Hupf, a forecaster at IPA. Despite a languid domestic economy, Germany's automation trade group has reported record sales for its members last year, and some are forecasting that robot demand in Germany alone will surpass demand in the U.S. this year.

And much of that demand is in the new service economy. The French Formule 1 hotel chain, for example, is expanding its successful discount format built around prefabricated buildings and hotels that are unattended at night. Guests check in via an automated teller machine. Copenhagen Taxa, the Danish capital's largest taxi company, is expanding its system that directs a million cabs a year to a caller's address automatically – no dispatcher needed: The address automatically pops up on a small screen in the nearest available cab.

The Paris mass-transit authority, shut down by a strike in 1995, is building a new driverless subway line through the heart of the city; set to open next year, it will mimic a similar system already in operation in the northern city of Lille. Customers at a store near Nuremburg use a touch-screen to buy whole cases of cola or beer from what may well be the world's largest drink machine.

Then there's the Credit Agricole bank branch on Boulevard Montmartre in Paris, where the tellers' cash drawers don't contain a single check, franc or centime: All deposits and withdrawals pass through an array of seven specialized automated teller machines. Forget your bank card? A teller hands out a temporary one on the spot. The system inconveniences some, but it saves employees from the tedious job of counting and locking up money and allows them to concentrate on selling stock funds, insurance and credit.

"It cuts time spent on administration by 12%," says Jean-Pierre Soubie, head of quality programs at the bank. "It lets our workers concentrate on adding value."

Impact on Economy

The bank is expanding the automation program because the productivity improvements are well worth the expense of one million francs ($165,000) per branch. But it's far from clear whether Western Europe's automation boom is having a similar beneficial effect on the economy as a whole.

At first glance, the evidence would seem to suggest that it is. Labor productivity grew at an average annual rate of 2.2% in France and 1.1% in Germany between 1979 and 1996, compared with just 0.8% in the U.S., according to the Organization for Economic Cooperation and Development. Those increases stem partly from heavy capital spending on automation, economists say.

Even so, per capita gross domestic product remains higher in the U.S. than in Western Europe. So the recent increases in West European productivity suggest that the Europeans are merely catching up by borrowing U.S. business practices and technology, says William Baumol, a noted American economist.

Besides, an edge in automation doesn't always translate into a competitive advantage. The McKinsey Global Institute, for example, has found that U.S. retail banks are still more labor-efficient than their West European counterparts, despite huge automation advances in European banking. The reason? Hotly competitive markets in the U.S. force banks to pare their work forces, while European regulations and union agreements often limit competition and prevent banks from laying off workers.

More Reliable, Less Costly

Yet there's no doubt that more and more European firms are turning to automation in an effort to achieve productivity gains denied them by stiff labor costs and regulations. Real minimum wages have more than doubled in France and Germany over the past 25 years, even as they decreased moderately in the U.S. During the same period, automation has grown more reliable and less costly. A basic ABB robot arm – designed to do assembly-line work like welding or stacking – costs about $45,000 today, half the $90,000 it cost in the late 1980s.

The gains from automation aren't always immediately apparent, of course. Automation depends on advanced computer systems and, like those systems, it is complex and initially prone to hiccups. "You have to have respect for the learning curve," says Mr. Demark of ABB. "It's very slow."

That makes it easy to underestimate the cost of a new system, he says.

In the long run, however, automation offers the tantalizing prospect of second- and third-generation improvements at lower cost. A case in point is Denmark-based MD Foods Amba, one of Europe's largest dairies.

In 1992, MD Foods Amba paid 12 million kroner ($1.8 million) for a two-robot system that stacks orders for seven dairy products on pallets for supermarket delivery. Then, last year, the Danish government told the firm that it was violating worker-protection legislation by obliging 40 workers at a different warehouse to lift more than a total of 3,000 kilograms each during a 7.4-hour shift.

"I got an order from the Labor Ministry: either triple the number of employees or do something," says Mogens Rydiger, logistics director at the firm's distribution unit.

So he ordered a new 17-million-kroner ABB system that can stack twice as many goods in a day as the old one. It uses four robots to stack orders for 60 different types of creams, milks and yogurts received nightly from 800 supermarkets that are tied to the network electronically. "The first time one of my people will actually see an order is when the loaded pallet comes up and the system prints the order and slaps it on," Mr. Rydiger says.

Bugs and Shoes

Such complex robotized distribution systems have begun to spread throughout the Continent in the past four years, but are still rare in the U.S., says Mr. Hupf of the IPA. But all that complexity comes with new bugs.

The new ABB-designed system came in a year late and three million kroner over budget, Mr. Rydiger says. Still, the system enabled him to cut one third of his total work force. "Ultimately, we got the savings we wanted," he says, adding that he's convinced that future installations will be easier and will continue to boost his productivity. "Ten years from now, all our distribution centers will be automated."

And what about shoe stores? Back in Stuttgart, the robot starts working again – after a 45-minute pause and much muttering as shoe salesmen in the back room type in software commands dictated by hot-line technicians at Reis Robotics GmbH, which built the system.

Mr. Kluge, the salesman, says the robot has helped the department double sales since it was installed in October. That's partly because salesmen are no longer hidden in the storeroom looking for shoes – and partly because the robot, in a new plexiglass-enclosed storeroom, has become an attraction in itself.

The machine fetches a pair of Nikes and a pair of Filas for 12-year-old Florian Muenzmay. His mother rolls her eyes at all this alleged progress. "You can still never find a salesman when you need one," she says.

But Florian likes what he sees. "It's fast," he says. "It's cool."

Wall Street Journal Europe, 22 July 1997
Reprinted by permission of *Wall Street Journal Europe*,
© 1997 Dow Jones & Company, Inc.
All Rights Reserved Worldwide.

VIJFHUIZEN, the Netherlands – it wouldn't be accurate to say that Frank Miezenbeek's cows possess above-average intelligence. But his Holsteins have a talent shared by few of their breed: They can milk themselves.

As Mr. Miezenbeek watches proudly, the cows line up like so many customers in a post office. One at a time, Trijnte, Catie, Janke, Zoeki and the others march into the milking parlor without so much as a moo, deposit their milk and return to the herd.

The technological revolution has come to the barnyard. Thanks to the work of Dutch scientists, cows can milk themselves with the help of a computer. The high-tech bovine, wearing a computer chip in her collar for identification, approaches the machine whenever she feels the urge for a milking. A robot equipped with ultrasonic sensors does the rest. The farmer is alerted by beeper if anything goes wrong.

That Robot Touch

"It's a little impersonal, but the cows tend to like it," says Wim Nugteren, an executive of robot manufacturer Prolion Development.

So do farmers, who no longer have to get up with the cows. The robot saves them about four hours a day and reduces labor costs. Round-the-clock robotic milking allows cows to relieve their udders three times a day instead of the usual two, promoting an increase in milk production of 15%. It is also said by Prolion to reduce udder disease and to boost cow longevity. Though the machine can't handle the high volume of industrial farms, it could change the life of the family farmer with a herd of under 100 cows.

But farmers will feel squeezed to justify the machine's cost. The robotic three-stall milker sells for about $250,000, double the price of conventional milking machines, which are attached to the cow by hand.

"It's a very expensive machine, and I can't see how my boss will earn it back," says Mr. Miezenbeek, the farm manager. "I can't see the advantage that much." His new system is plagued by technological glitches. Mr. Miezenbeek's beeper goes off about 10 times a day, as early as 3:30 a.m. and often because of false alarms. "Socially, it's a disaster," he says. As he talks, his beeper sounds twice.

Dutch Obsession

Of the half-dozen companies developing or marketing self-milking machines, the two leaders are Dutch: Prolion and Lely Industries BV. That's not surprising in this dairy-obsessed land. Not far from Vijfhuizen resides Herman, who became a national celebrity as the first bull in the world to carry a human gene.

A cow enters the milking stall, usually encouraged by a sweet snack released if the computer (reading her ID chip) decides it is time for a milking. Once she's inside, gates close around the cow as the robotic milkmaid slides underneath, its sensors spinning like a ship's radar. It finds the "reference teat" first, then hooks to all four with a rubber pulsating vacuum.

The milking device washes the teats, checks for problems with the udders and milks, all within a few minutes. The robot will try five times to hook the machine to the cow; if it fails, the cow is sent into a separate chamber, and the farmer is alerted. Cows seem to learn the system after being pushed in two or three times. If they forget, some farms remind them with a moving electric fence.

Prolion, after 12 years of research, began selling its device in, 1992. There are now 15 farms with its device in Holland and others in Canada, France, Japan and Britain. Mr. Nugteren predicts 500 farms will have self-milking cows in five years. "Everyone knows this is going to be the future," he says. Prolion's machines are marketed under the "Liberty" brand name. Slogan: "Freedom for the cow. Freedom for the farmer."

Lely, which has sold 33 self-milking units since it began production last year, calls its system "the Astronaut," because the cow is tethered to the milking apparatus as if on a space walk. "The cow can move freely," says Marcel van Leeuwen, the Astronaut sales chief. "It can move and do a step forward and a step backward. The cows in our system feel free." Mr. van Leeuwen's system uses lasers to locate the cow's teats instead of ultrasound.

One of the world's largest agricultural-equipment firms, Alfa Laval Agri, says it plans to release a robotic milkmaid in three or four years, after it finds a way to lower costs. "It definitely will be a viable solution," says Hans Gisel-Ekdahl, executive vice president of the unit of Sweden's Tetra Laval Group.

It's hard to tell what cows think about all this, but Roger Shantz, manager of the dairy research center at Ontario's University of Guelph, says the system is "cow friendly." "We have cows who would come through 24, 36, 48 times a day if we let them," he says. Farmers Weekly concurs, suggesting cows might think "they are in some sort of bovine heaven."

Prolion hopes to win Washington's approval to sell in the U.S. within a year. But it may have some trouble in America, where the average farm is larger and receives less government support. The robotic milk machine is ideal for herds of 60 to 100 cows. But Robert Cropp, a professor of dairy marketing at the University of Wisconsin, says the trend in the U.S. is toward large farms of 500 cows. He thinks it could be difficult to target small farms. "I can't see how they can afford that."

European farmers are still waiting for the promised benefits. Gis van Veldhuizen, a Dutch farmer who has used the system for three years, has increased milking to three times a day. He has boosted output slightly and cut his farmhand's hours. His own alarm clock is set at 6:30 a.m. instead of 5:45. Yet he thinks it will be at least six more months before the bugs are worked out. "The system is OK, but there are still some software problems," says Mr. van Veldhuizen, who complains of frequent false alarms.

Robots have trouble milking cows with very big or low-hanging udders. Some animals kick and damage the machine. Prolion says about 10% of cows can't use the machine. Another problem comes in summer, when cows are at pasture and need to be herded into the barn to use the machine. Prolion says the glitches "will go away slowly."

If the company is correct, there could soon be a lot of idle farmers. But don't worry: They will have plenty of company. After it perfects the milking robot, Prolion plans to unveil a robot that cuts, wraps and delivers meat to a service window. "It ought to replace the butcher shop," Mr. Nugteren predicts.

Wall Street Journal Europe, May 1995

very often an extension of computer aided design. Two illustrations are given below.[14]

Virtual manufacturing

Virtual manufacturing is simulating the complete manufacture of a product, before any physical operation starts. This is what Boeing did when they built the 777 aircraft. Engineers, using data in digital form, which could be treated by other computer programs and which could be copied and shared by designers in any location, permitted collaboration on the same project. They used a system called CATIA, developed by Dassault Systèmes, a software company in France, to assemble an entire virtual 777. They were able to ensure that the hundreds of thousands of parts fitted, redesigning those that did not, before physically manufacturing the plane. As, a result when the first 777 was completed, it fitted together almost perfectly without additional machining modifications, which are sometimes necessary in normal manufacturing.

Virtual construction

Computer software systems, such as DMAPS, also by Dassault, and others by Tecnomatix Technologies, Herzlia, Israel can simulate an entire manufacturing facility. Engineers can calculate the most efficient route for a spray-painting robot to take around a car body, work out how quickly parts must be supplied, look for bottlenecks or even evaluate if a human worker's task is likely to give him backache. These simulations pick up many problems before construction of the manufacturing facility.

INFORMATION TECHNOLOGY IN THE PROCESS SYSTEM

Information technology in the broadest sense encompasses all the technological innovations to transmit information visually, by voice in written form on computer screens or downloaded onto paper. Figure 7.5 gives an illustration and the terms presented are discussed below.

Electronic data interchange

In its purest form, electronic data interchange (EDI) is paperless trading, or the transfer of structured data by agreed message standards from one computer to another, such as for purchase orders, shipping instructions, invoices and the like. Using EDI systems reduces transaction processing and lead times as it eliminates the preparation, sending and transfer of

hard copies. EDI has significant use, both in manufacturing and in the service sector, permitting the management of large operations. The following are two illustrations.

Siemens Nixdorf

Siemens Nixdorf, Germany, a major electronics firm, has extended EDI to manage the following:[15]

■ Finances, order processing, personnel, inventory control and traffic analysis at the Dallas/Fort Worth Airport, USA, which is used by over 52 million passengers per year.
■ Collection and billing of data for Belgacom, the Belgium public telephone system.
■ Logistics management of FZ Frischdienstzentrale, a German distributor of merchandise and food, including transactions, orders and billing.
■ Managing the payroll system for train crews on the French SNCF railroad.

River Hills West Health Care Centre

The River Hills West Health Care Centre in Pewaukee, Wisconsin has 245 residents. Each of the 245 residents receives multiple doses of up to 15 different medications a day. In the past, every time a doctor wrote a new order, it had to be transcribed by a secretary to a phone order, a pharmacy sheet and several other patient forms. These all had to be checked by nurses and then entered into a three-ring binder. Each month, nurses and secretaries spent about 64 worker-hours transferring records to new logbooks.

Now the routine has changed. Nurses write the first three letters of the drug's name on the screen of an electronic notepad called a CompuScriber. A list of choices appears on the screen, along with boxes to check off for doses and time of day. Once these items are entered, the network system sends the information to the River Hills network server. Records are instantly updated, eliminating about five stages of paper-work.[16]

Elements in information technology

Some key elements and terms in information technology are as follows.

Client/server

The client/server set-up is a method of computing in which one computer acts as a central repository for files and programs (server) that can be shared by a number of personal computers (clients) connected through a network. The client is the user in the system, working from either a desktop or laptop computer, or

Figure 7.5   A worldwide information network system.

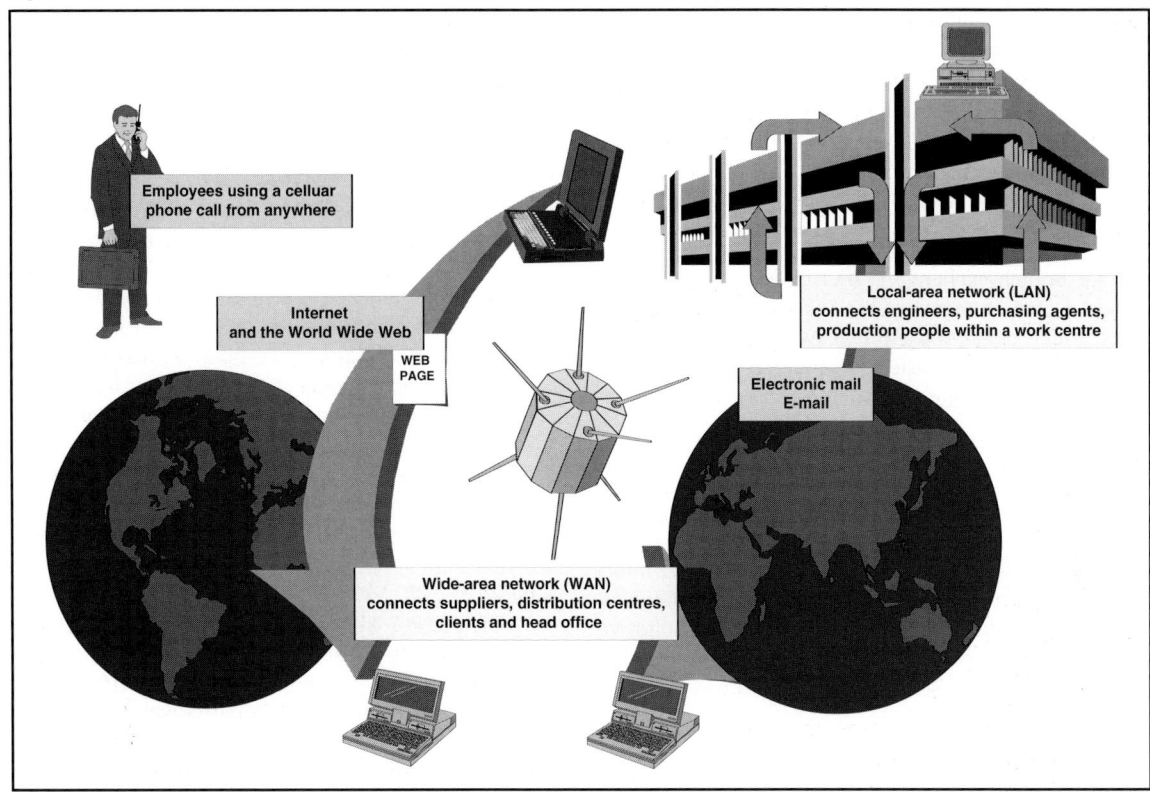

even from a mainframe so that he or she can retrieve data for analysis and reporting from the server. The server is usually a mainframe computer which stores data and also manages and controls access to shared databases. The client/server system replaces the previous mainframe centric arrangement.

Local-area network

A local-area network (LAN) is a network within a building, or limited area, that links computers and peripheral devices, permitting the sharing of information, programs and equipment such as printers or computer-controlled machines in a manufacturing environment. Most LAN systems connect within a 700 metre radius using their own communication channels.

Ethernet

The Ethernet is a set of local-area network (LAN) standards that allows networking products from different vendors to communicate. It was introduced in the mid 1970s by Xerox, Digital Equipment and Intel, and is perhaps the most widely used LAN technology. Other Ethernet systems include Apptalk from Apple Computer; Token Ring developed by IBM and Texas Instruments and ARCNet from Datapoint.

Wide-area network

The wide-area network (WAN) is an enterprise-wide communications network that allows signals to be transmitted from a LAN via public or private lines to other LANs in distant locations. A WAN may consist of a switched or dedicated line. The former is a telephone line that a user can access using his computer system where the information is switched to the appropriate destination. The dedicated line is one that is continuously available to the user. AT&T, MCI, France Télécom, Deutsche Telecom and British Telecom are some of the carriers for WAN systems.

Bridges and routers

A bridge is a device that links two local-area networks together so that they can share data.

A router, which is really a sophisticated bridge, is a device that connects local area networks that use different standards.

Asynchronous transfer mode

Asynchronous transfer mode (ATM) is a high-speed digital switching and transmission technology that allows voice, video and data signals to be sent over a single line at speeds ranging from 25 million to 1 billion bits per second (bps). For example, an analogue phone line transmits at about 2 million bps.

Frame relay

Frame relay is a transmission standard for sending data over public or private leased phone lines. Data is placed in frames, each the same size, for relaying.

Private branch exchange

Private branch exchange (PBX) is an automatic telephone switching arrangement for internal phone systems, which replaces the office switchboard. The PBX system can store, transfer, hold and redial telephone calls and also manage voicemail systems.

Integrated services digital networks

Integrated services digital networks (ISDN) are offered by local phone companies. ISDN is a protocol that turns a standard copper phone link into a high-speed digital link that can send voice, data, image and video information simultaneously. The system is international, developed in the late 1970s by the Consultative Committee on International Telegraphy and Telephony (CCITT) which represents over 150 countries.

The Internet

The Internet (the Net) is a sophisticated international network of smaller networks rather than one big network.

The Internet was born in the 1960s in the USA out of a concern of the US military, who were afraid that a nuclear attack would make their communication system ineffective. As a result of this, researchers connected up four small computers in a network between the University of California at Los Angeles and Stanford University, such that if one computer was out of action, the others were still able to function. That is, the intelligence of the system was not localized in one centralized supercomputer but distributed throughout the network.

Today information is sent through the network via telephone lines, fibre-optic cables, radio waves, satellites or undersea cables. Electronic mail (E-mail) is perhaps one of the most widely used functions on the Internet.

To use the Internet, three essential elements are needed:

- A personal computer with a minimum of 4 megaoctets available on the hard disk and 4 megaoctets of live memory.
- A modem or 'Black box', connecting the computer to the telephone line, enabling access to the Internet.

- A subscription to an Internet Service Provider.

Some of the following are terms used in literature on and about the Internet:

- *Cyberspace* is space without any geographic boundaries where the electronic information circulates.
- *TCP/IP* (Transmission Control Protocol/Internet Protocol) is a common computer language of the Internet developed by Vinton Cerf and Robert Khan. It was launched in 1972 by the Defence Advanced Research Projects Agency (DARPA) of the USA to help researchers link up computers. It is the oldest communication model on which the Internet is based and is still widely used in the USA, although in Europe other systems are favoured.
- *Netsurfers*, who are people who use the Internet.
- *World Wide Web* is a set of standards on the Internet for storing, retrieving, formatting and displaying information using client/server architecture. The Web employs graphical user interfaces for easy viewing and is based on Hypertext Mark-up Language (HTML) that formats documents and links documents and pictures in the same or remote computers. With these links, one is able to click on a key word or icon to be linked to information on another site, perhaps many kilometres away.
- *Web Page*, is a block of information, that can be called up across the Web. It is a way of organizing data on the Web and such pages are prepared by individuals, manufacturers, companies, advertisers, etc. as a way of announcing their activity and providing information.

The home page is the text and graphic screen display that explains the organization and leads the user to other Web pages, All of the pages constitute the Web Site. Companies, such as Usinor Sacilor, the French steel company are using Web pages on the Internet in its purchasing, sales and other activity to obtain a better and faster service and to increase its international reach.[17]

Business Use of Information Technology

The use of information technology is growing very rapidly. In a survey by the Management Centre Europe of 1055 senior managers, out of 15 business situations on the use of information technology an aggregate of two-thirds of the responses were positive. These 15 areas of utilization and the percentage responses are given in Figure 7.6.[18]

Figure 7.6 Business utilization of information technology.

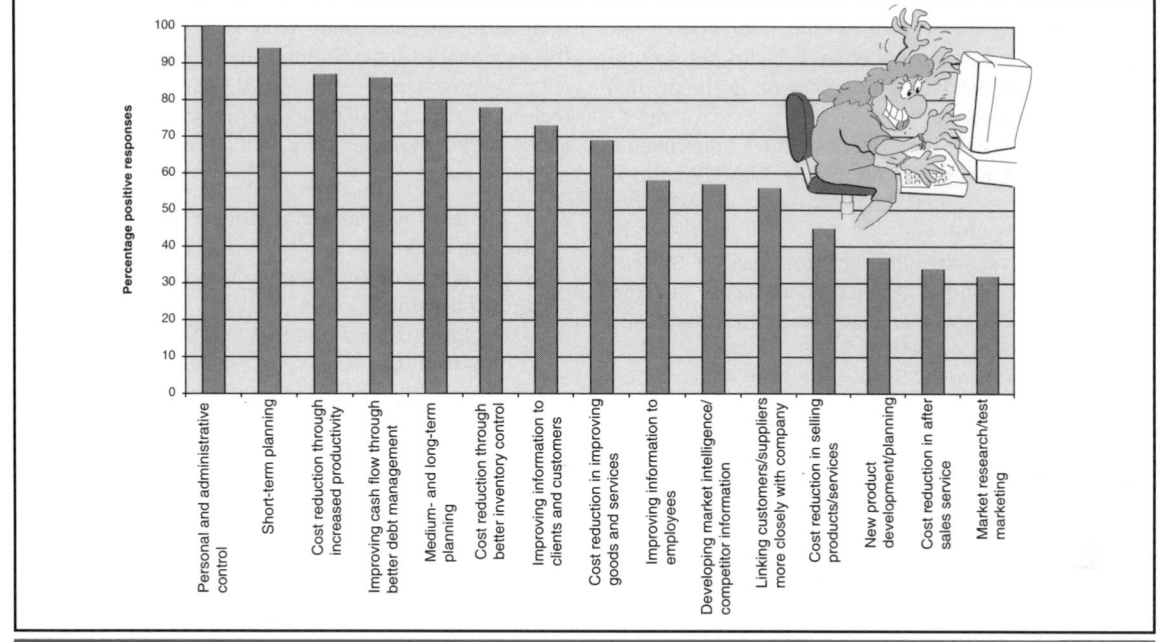

ARTIFICIAL INTELLIGENCE

Artificial intelligence is an aspect of information technology and is broadly the use of computers to mimic or copy aspects of human intelligence, such as learning languages, making decisions, and performing physical actions. Robots come under the definition of artificial intelligence where the robot is programmed to accomplish specific co-ordinated manual tasks. Three elements of artificial intelligence which has application in the design of processes include, expert systems, neural networks, and fuzzy logic.

Expert systems

Expert systems are knowledge-based systems that emulate expert thinking, or human logic, to solve complex problems in a particular domain. The difficulty with expert systems is the design of the 'system' so that it corresponds to the human brain. This means detailed programming so that every possible course of action is taken in to consideration.

Rule based

Expert systems are computer-based iterations and their main difference from neural networks is that they are rule based. This means that the expert system contains a predefined set of knowledge, which is used for all decisions. The system uses the predefined rules to produce results by using inference rules that are coded into the system. Depending on the kind of input, and the rules used, expert systems can be used either as quantitative or qualitative tools. A generic expert system will contain two main modules, the knowledge base and the inference engine.

The knowledge base

The knowledge base contains knowledge of the system regarding the specific domain, or area, for which it is designed to solve problems or make recommendations. For example, in the financial domain the knowledge base will include specific rules that the system contains (decisions concerning shares, price levels or margins).

The inference engine

The inference engine processes and combines facts related to the particular problem, case or question, using that part of the knowledge base which is relevant. The selection of the appropriate data in the knowledge base is performed according to various search criteria. Some examples of the process applications of expert systems are given in Table 7.1.

Neural Networks

Neural networks are computer hardware or software that attempt to copy the processing pattern of the biological brain. The brain has about 100 billion neurons and can operate at 100 hertz. This is slow by computer standards where an Intel 80486 chip operates at about 100 megahertz, or millions of cycles per second. Neural networks have found application in the medical field (for pap smear test that detect cervical cancer), prediction of securities ratings, stock purchasing, inspection and flaws in steel plates, classification of welding defects, sound analysis, and identification parts in a production line.

Neural networks are different from Expert Systems where here the human simulation is based on rules where neural networks emulate the human brain and are modelled from experience.

Fuzzy Logic

Computer systems basically rely on the exact binomial approach such as, open or closed, on or off, yes or no, right or wrong. Human thinking is not as precise. For example, is 4 km a long way to walk, or not very far? Is 32 °C hot, or a comfortable temperature? Is 10 kg too much to carry, or manageable? The response is inexact, or fuzzy and depends on a persons judgement, their physical make-up, and external conditions. Fuzzy logic is a rule-based development in artificial intelli-

gence which can be used to develop and solve certain problems. If the logic is expressed with some carefully defined impression, then fuzzy logic can be closer to the way people actually think that traditional IF-THEN rules. As an example, Ford Motor Co. developed a fuzzy logic application that backs a simulated tractor-trailer into a parking space. The application uses the following three rules:

1. IF the lorry is near jack-knifing, THEN reduce the steering angle.
2. IF the lorry is far away from the dock, THEN steer toward the dock.
3. IF the lorry is near the dock, THEN point the trailer directly at the dock.

Fuzzy logic is widely used in Japan in the design of home appliances such as refrigerators, vacuum cleaners, washers, dryers, rice cookers, and air conditioners.[19]

OPERATIONS NETWORK CHART

A process operations network can be designed, or later analysed, using an operations network chart (sometimes referred to as a process flow chart). If the process network has yet to be designed, the purpose of the chart would be to see 'what might occur'. If the network has already been designed, then the chart could be used to 'find out what is going on' and thence to establish ways of improving the process design.

Terms in the network chart

The heart of the flow chart lies in five symbols as shown in Figure 7.7. They are explained as follows.

O   Operation

An operation is any activity that transforms an element from one form to another, adding value during the operation. In services, this might be recording information, performing a treatment or making a transaction. In manufacturing, it would involve the transformation of a piece of inventory into something different, as might occur in cutting, drilling or assembly.

☐   *Inspection*

Inspection is an activity where a controller, a production manager or a client for example, is inspecting the service or material for quality, to see if it is according to specification, or simply to see if the right number of units are present. No change is taking place and thus no value is being added.

Table 7.1 Some examples of the process applications of expert systems

Subject area	Activity
Chemical compounds	Formulation of data about unknown chemical compounds
Infectious diseases	Diagnosing certain infectious diseases and proposing appropriate treatment
Credit cards	Validating user credit card access by financial firms
Consulting	Diagnosis or troubleshooting operations for consulting firms
Lung diseases	Diagnosis of the presence, and severity, of lung diseases and the production of reports
Engineering	Providing information on structural designs of buildings
Molecular biology	Design and simulation of experiments in molecular biology and genetic experiments
Mathematics	Development of new mathematical concepts and their associated proofs
Space travel	Diagnosing and proposing solutions related to spacecraft anomalies
Playing chess!	IBM's Deep Blue computer won a chess tournament against the reigning world champion, Gary Kasparov, in May 1997

Figure 7.7 Process flow chart.

Section								Operator	
Operation started									
Operation finished									
Summary		O	□	D	→	Δ			
Total actual									
Total expected									
Difference									

Description	operation	inspection	wait	transfer	store	quantity	time	frequency	distance	surface	lot size	Observations
1	O	□	D	→	Δ							
2	O	□	D	→	Δ							
3	O	□	D	→	Δ							
4	O	□	D	→	Δ							
5	O	□	D	→	Δ							
6	O	□	D	→	Δ							
7	O	□	D	→	Δ							
8	O	□	D	→	Δ							
9	O	□	D	→	Δ							
10	O	□	D	→	Δ							
11	O	□	D	→	Δ							
12	O	□	D	→	Δ							
13	O	□	D	→	Δ							
14	O	□	D	→	Δ							
15	O	□	D	→	Δ							

D *Waiting*

Waiting is simply that inventory or people are 'waiting' for someone to do something. This might be in a service centre, office, work centre, vehicle on a machine, etc. No change is taking place and thus no value is being added.

→ *Transfer*

Transfer is when materials, people, documents are being moved from one area to another. This might be from:

- one work area to another work area;
- a work area to storage;
- storage to a client;
- one office to another.

For materials, the transfer might take place by an operator carrying the units, on a moving belt or in a truck. For services, such as a hospital, it might be the transfer of a patient from one treatment zone to another. In an airport, it could be the transfer from one terminal to another. In a design office, it might be the transfer of written specifications from one building to another. Essentially, no change is taking place in the service operation or to the inventory material and so it might be argued that no value is being added. However, in both manufacturing and services, the patient, document, baggage or inventory is of no use

unless it is in the right place; thus, the fact of getting it to the right place is adding value. A Philips television set for example is of no value to a client at the factory in Eindhoven. However, it would be of value if it were on sale in a store in Amsterdam.

Δ *Storing*

Storing is when material is physically housed in an area devoted to that very purpose. For a finished consumer product, this might be the storage area of a supermarket, it might a distribution centre or it might be the warehouse for finished products at the production centre.

As shown on the chart for the five various activities, the quantity of units handled is entered, together with the time, frequency, distance, surface area involved and the lot size.

A completed network chart

A network chart that has been completed for an existing operation is illustrated in Figure 7.8. It illustrates the activity of components coming from storage through to delivery of the finished item to the final client. Each activity is connected by a line, so that the flow of material can be easily seen. The summary at the top of the chart gives the difference between actual times and expected times. Any differences would give rise to further investigation. Some observations from this chart:

- There is a significant difference between actual times and expected times.
- Non-value-added times (waiting, transfer and storing) are long.
- In two of the operation steps, fewer units leave than enter, suggesting that faulty parts have been found or that incorrect process work is being performed.

BUSINESS PROCESS RE-ENGINEERING

Defining business process re-engineering

Business process re-engineering (BPR) was an idea presented in 1990 by two Americans, James Champy and Michael Hammer. It is defined as the means by which an organization can achieve radical change, in performance (as measured by cost, cycle time, service and quality), by the application of a variety of tools and techniques that focus on the business as a set of related customer-oriented core business processes, rather than a set of organizational functions. Its primary objective is intended to boost competitiveness in the operations network through simpler, leaner and more productive

Figure 7.8   Completed process flow chart.

Section	Transformer mounting		Operators	
Operation started	Monday	8:15	Guillaume WALLER/Derek CUSIN	
Operation finished	Tuesday	17:48	Odette DUCREY/Cédric ACCARY	
Summary	O □ D → Δ			
Total actual	33:33	8:29 2:22 3:08 11:54 7:40 33:33		
Total expected	18:45	7:30 0:45 0:30 8:30 1:30 18:45		
Difference	14:48	0:59 1:37 2:38 3:24 6:10 14:48		

#	Description	operation	inspection	wait	transfer	store	quantity	time (a)	frequency	distance	surface	lot size	Observations
1	Component B-16	O	□	D	→	Δ	60	08:15			25,3		Storage area SA-25
2	Component B-16	O	□	D	→	Δ	60	08:45		5,5			By conveyor
3	Component B-16	O	□	D	→	Δ	60	09:48		9,0			Change of machine tools
4	Component B-16	O	□	D	→	Δ	60	14:52		6,1			Machining. Now ref C-18
5	Component C-18	O	□	D	→	Δ	58	16:12		5,7			Specifications checked
6	Component C-18	O	□	D	→	Δ	58	17:15		5,7			Trolleys not available
7	Component C-18	O	□	D	→	Δ	58	17:50		47,0			To adjacent work centre
8	Component C-18	O	□	D	→	Δ	58	18:52		10,3			No unloaders available
9	Component C-18	O	□	D	→	Δ	56	20:57		21,7			Assembly; Now ref DC-180
10	Component DC-180	O	□	D	→	Δ	56	21:59		9,3			Electric test for solder joints
11	Component DC-180	O	□	D	→	Δ	55	23:38		37,0			To storage area, SA-11
12	Component DC-180	O	□	D	→	Δ	55	07:18		56,8			In storage area, SA-11
13	Component DC-180	O	□	D	→	Δ	35	08:38		75,0			To packing zone
14	Component DC-180	O	□	D	→	Δ	35	09:58		34,0			Blister pack/wood boxes
15	Component DC-180	O	□	D	→	Δ	35	17:48					Shipped to client

(a) End of operation

processes. It has been applied in labour- and capital-intensive industries, such as automobile production, telecommunications and pharmaceuticals, and also in service sectors, such as insurance and banking. Business process re-engineering coins the phrase 'breaking the china', meaning that the firm is brave enough to ignore, or even destroy the process design activities that went on before, and start all over again.[20]

Real-world illustration

AT&T Power Systems in Dallas, Texas, produces custom switching power supplies in a very competitive market. The original process design process for each customer front proposal request to delivery of the finished product was identified as being made up of 42 different process activities, including 12 scheduled meetings as illustrated in Figure 7.9. A detailed analysis showed that the product could not continue to be competitive on costs. In addition, the product was taking on average 53 days to be delivered to the customer.

The company completely revamped the process design processes, creating multifunctional design teams and using standard designs where possible, yet still keeping the power supplies customized. By standardizing, the design teams were assured of parts availability in stock, since the same components were required for other standard subassemblies. In the new process design configuration, a number of the old activities were retained, but assigned to a design cell, which is a dedicated group comprising electrical, mechanical, test and quality engineers plus a model builder and the project manager who worked in close harmony to cut throughput time. Each team member was made responsible for his own work, avoiding cross-checking, reviews and formal meetings. As a result, 17 process design activities were eliminated, 10 were combined into cell activity, leaving only 17 formal steps and one meeting as illustrated in Figure 7.10. As a result, delivery time was reduced to five days or a reduction of 90 per cent on the original time.[21]

Figure 7.9 Formal design process for custom switching power supplies (before).

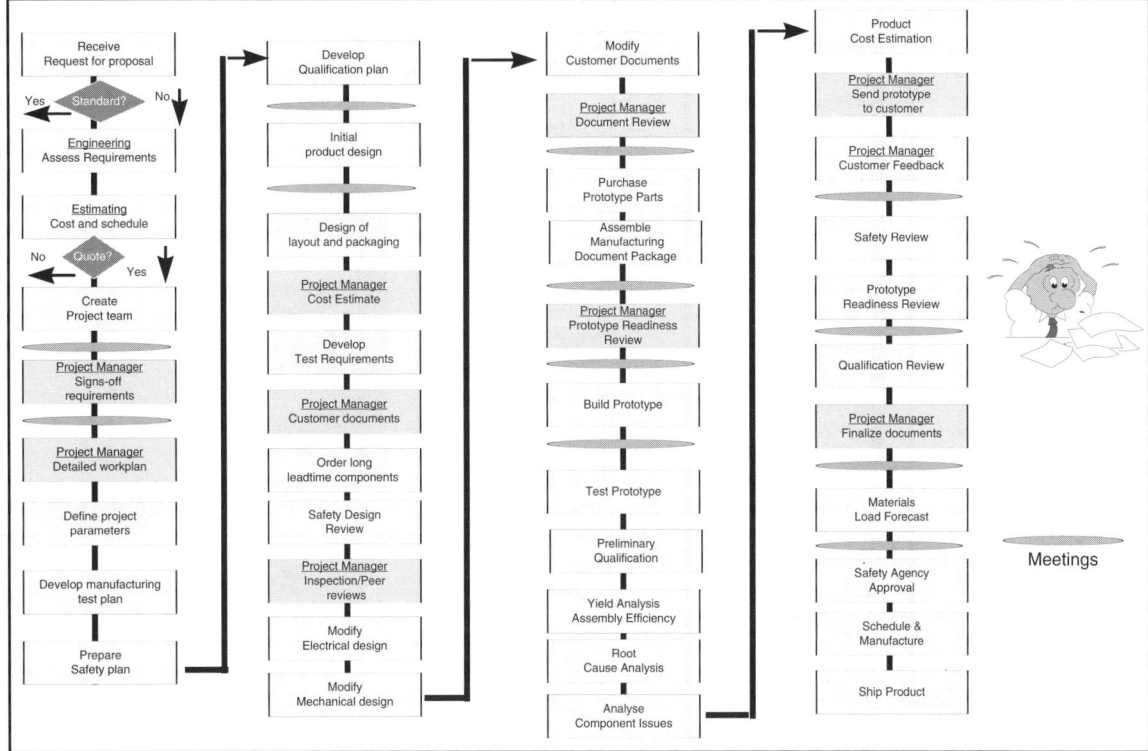

Does it always work?

In a study of more than 100 companies, Hall, Rosenthal and Wade from Harvard concluded that business process re-engineering is not always a success and they cite many instances where it has failed to achieve real business impact. They clarify that business process re-engineering is a 'top down' exercise and that, even with sufficient breadth and depth, a re-engineering project will fail without the full commitment of senior executives.[22] CSC Index, a consulting firm, after surveying 497 large companies in the United States and another 124 in Europe, stated that re-engineering is far from being a guarantee of corporate renewal. Fewer than half of the firms aiming at increasing market share achieved their market and some failed abysmally.[23]

As Chapter 4 on *Quality Management* highlighted, for many, business process re-engineering is a euphemism for downsizing, or terminating employees. The backlash to this has sometimes been lower quality from the de-motivated employees who remain with the firm.

Figure 7.10 Formal design process for custom switching power supplies (after).

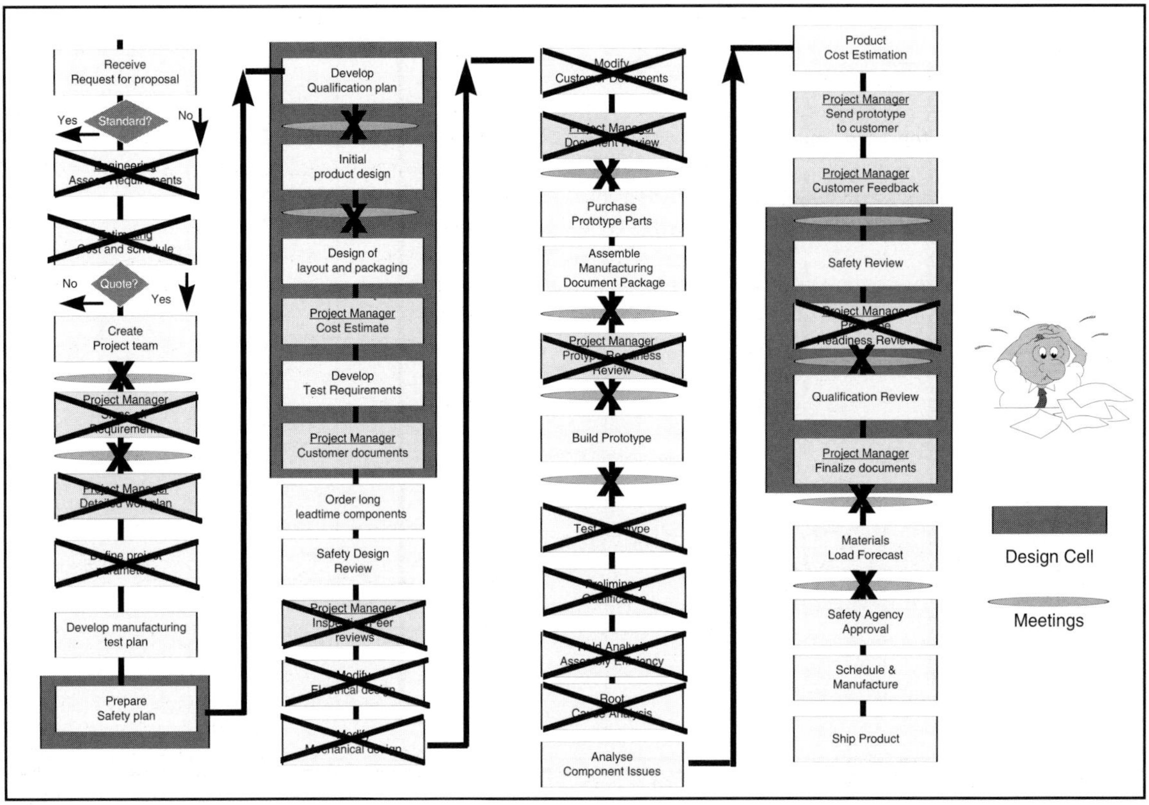

SUMMARY OF KEY ELEMENTS

- Design considerations of the process system include location, make or buy, facility layout, technology employed and the physical distribution and information systems network. In services the network is developed very much around the customer.

- Product types can be correlated with process design. Between the extremes of a job shop and continuous flow are differences in flexibility, volume and unit cost.

- In the process, system capacity planning, which is market driven, is a key design element. Capacity is the maximum output, or use of the system under normal conditions. Utilization is the ratio of the capacity used to the design capacity.

- Vertical integration is the combination under one owner of two or more stages of production and/or distribution. It can be backward, involving upstream activities, forward, involving ownership of downstream activities, or complete integration.

- Integration advantages may be found in transaction costs, supply reliability, captive customers, coordination, technology innovation and entry barriers to competitors.

- Disadvantages to integration may include high capital requirements, unbalanced throughputs, reduced operating flexibility and an incompatible managerial style.

- Japanese firms have a vast quasi-integrated network. Although they may not own suppliers and outlets, these are financially aided by the firm and become part of a network coalition known as *keiretsu*.

- There is a move in some organizations to disintegrate as the economic advantages and increased flexibility outweigh the advantages of integration.

- A virtual company is a type of vertical integration that has no physical structure. It can be disbanded when the service offered is no longer needed.
- Automated equipment in process design includes; numerical controlled machines; robots, computer aided and/or integrated manufacturing; flexible manufacturing systems; automatic guided vehicles; and automated storage and retrieval systems.
- Virtual systems are non-physical representations of the real thing. They are often an extension of CAD systems in simulating the process design network.
- Information technology is the electronic transmittal in visual, voice or document form. Its rapid increasing use vastly improves response in the process network.

- The Internet is an electronic data interchange facilitating communication. Web sites on the Internet increase the effectiveness of a firm in advertising its services.
- Artificial intelligence systems emulate human logic to solve complex problems and have application in process design in manufacturing and service operations.
- An operations network chart identifies the operation, inspection, waiting, transfer and storing activities. It is used to analyse the effectiveness of a process network.
- Business process re-engineering is a way to achieve radical change by focusing on customer-oriented business processes, rather than on organizational functions.

REVIEW AND DISCUSSION QUESTIONS

1 **Process system design**. Describe what is the process system design for the following:
   (a) a hospital;
   (b) an educational facility;
   (c) a restaurant;
   (d) a theatrical presentation.
2 **Hayes and Wheelright**. The scheme, based on Hayes and Wheelright, tries to put all manufacturing and service processes on the same continuum. Do you agree with this approach? Alternatively, do you feel that operations are so different that it is not very meaningful to create such a relationship? Discuss.
3 **Capacity**. Describe where innovation is employed to increase the effective capacity of the following service systems:
   (a) a university;
   (b) a hospital;
   (c) a restaurant;
   (d) a retail store.
   What are some of the advantages and disadvantages?
4 **Vertical integration**. Discuss what might be the advantages and disadvantages of vertical integration for the following organizations:
   (a) backward integration for an automobile company;
   (b) forward integration of a film producer with cinemas;
   (c) complete integration for the steel industry from raw materials through refining to manufacture of raw steel in sheet, wire or other forms.
   Consider all the elements in the integrated form.
5 **Automation in industry**. Unions traditionally oppose automation in industry, be it services or manufacturing. What are their concerns? Do you believe they are justified? How would you communicate with union people and explain the issues?
6 **The Internet**. The Internet and e-mail have greatly improved system design and simplified the circulation of information in business. However, there are those who believe that computer-based communication has reduced the personal contact, created misunderstandings, reduced the personal side of business and created more stress. What is your opinion? Justify your response with examples.
7 **Education and technology**. Information technology has improved the system design by facilitating the way to obtain information and reduced the need to do library research. Many computer-based products, covering geography, mathematics, languages, etc., have been developed in the field of education. Furthermore, at the level of higher education, distance learning for an MBA is possible. There are those who believe that these developments have depersonalized education and, in fact, are producing pupils and students who do not have the strengths of 'traditional students'. What do you believe? Justify your response with illustrations.
8 **Operations network chart**. Develop a process flow chart for the following:
   (a) Postal service from the preparation of a package in London, UK, to delivery in a small village some 50 km from Rome, Italy.
   (b) The manufacture, distribution and sales of ceramic gift items sold in a large department store.
   (c) Petrol sold at a petrol service station. Consider the flow from the raw crude oil to the finished product.
   (d) The manufacture of a custom-made suit from the raw textile to the shipment of the finished product.
   Develop the flow chart according to the various steps in the procedure. Make your best judgement on the times involved.
9 **Business process re-engineering**. What are some of the process activities in either business or day-to-day living that are, or have been, radically changed that one might say that the concept of business process re-engineering (BPR) has been applied even though during the transformation the concept of (BPR) was probably never used.

NOTES AND REFERENCES

1. Cooper, G., European Director of British Airways (1997) Presentation at the G7 Management Conference, 16 May, E. M. Lyon, France.
2. Based on Hayes, R. H. and Wheelright, S. C. (1979) 'Link Manufacturing Process and Product Life Cycles', *Harvard Business Review* January–February: 133–140.
3. 'Boeing shares drop on production crunch' (1997) *International Herald Tribune* 4–5 October.
4. Tanouye, E. (1996) 'Short supply: Success of AIDS drug brings new concern: Can Merck keep pace? Company rushed Crixivan to market: Now it faces a production bottleneck. Watching the patient count', *Wall Street Journal Europe* 5 November.
5. Buzzell, R. D. (1983) 'Is vertical integration profitable', *Harvard Business Review*, 61(1): 92–102.
6. Buzzell, R. D. (1983) 'Is vertical integration profitable', Harvard Business Review, 61(1): 92–102.
7. Teece, D. J. (1976) In E. J. Mitchell (ed.) *Vertical Integration in the Oil Industry*, Washington, DC: American Enterprise Institute: 105.
8. *AT&T Shareholders Report* (1996) September.
9. Heizer, J. and Render, B. (1995) *Production and Operations Management*, Englewood Cliffs, NJ: Prentice Hall: 534.
10. 'Robot Revolution' (1997) *National Geographic* July: 76–95.
11. United Nations (1996) *The Economist* 28 September.
12. Lavin, D. (1997) 'Brave old World: European Business uses more robots and fewer people. Higher wages compel firms to invest in automation, even in the service sector. This "Crocodile" Eats jobs', *Wall Street Journal Europe* 22 July.
13. Milbank, D. (1995) 'Unhand that cow, sir: Thanks to science, she can milk herself Barnyard breakthrough puts robot in charge of dairy; Using the reference teat', *Wall Street Journal Europe* 9 May.
14. 'Manufacturing technology: The immaterial world' (1997) *The Economist* 28 June: 104–106.
15. Siemons Nixdorf (1996) Advertising supplement.
16. 'Kiss that old patient logbook goodbye' (1995) Information Technology Annual Report, *Business Week* 26 June.
17. 'Europe Inc. starts to get wired: With U.S rivals outdistancing them, more companies join the information revolution' (1997) *Business Week* 17 March: 19.
18. 'Business utilisation of information technology' (1997) *Wall Street Journal Europe* 1/2 August.
19. Laudon, K. C. and Laudon, J. P. (1996) *Management Information Systems: Organization and Technology*, 4th edn., NJ, USA, Prentice Hall: 668.
20. 'Business Process Re-engineering' (1994) *International Management* May: 43.
21. Johansson H. J., McHugh, P., Pendlebury, A. J. and Wheeler III, W. A. (1993) *Business Process Re-engineering: Break Point Strategies for Market Dominance,* New York, Chichester: John Wiley & Sons: 65–79.
22. Hall, G., Rosenthal, J. and Wade, J. (1993) 'How to make re-engineering really work', *Harvard Business Review* November–December: 119-31.
23. 'Re-engineering reviewed: Re-engineering is the fad of the hour, as many re-engineered dole claimants know to their cost. But is it doing any good?' (1994) *The Economist* 2 July.

FURTHER READING

Abu-Hamdan, M.G. and El-Gizawy, A. S. (1997) 'Computer-aided monitoring system for flexible assembly operations', *Computers in Industry* 34(1): 1–10.

Armistead, C. and Rowland, P. *Business Process Re-engineering*, New York, Chichester: John Wiley & Sons.

Armistead C. and Rowland P. (1996) Managing Business Processes: BPR and Beyond, Wiley.

Bohez, E. L. J. and Thieravarut, M. (1997) 'Expert system for diagnosing computer numerically controlled machines', *Computers in Industry* 32(3): 233–48.

Davenport, T. H. (1993) *Process Innovation: Re-engineering Work through Information Technology*, Boston. Cambridge, MA: Harvard Business School.

Grover, V. and Malhorta, M. K. (1997) 'Business Process Re-engineering: A tutorial on the concept, evolution, method, technology and application', *Journal of Operations Management* 15(3): 193–213.

Hamilton, J. L. and Mqasqas, I. M. (1997) 'Direct vertical integration strategies', *Southern Economic Journal* 64(1): 220–34.

Hartley, J. L., Zirger, B. J. and Rajan R. (1997) 'Managing the buyer–supplier interface for on-line performance in product development', *Journal of Operations Management* 15(1): 57–70.

Iyer, S. and Nagi, R. (1997) 'Automated retrieval and ranking of similar parts in agile manufacturing', *IIE Transactions* 29(10): 859–76.

Karrer-Rueedi, E. (1997) 'Adaptation to change: Vertical and horizontal integration in the drug industry', *European Management Journal* 15(4): 461-69.

Khosrowpour, M. (ed.) (1994) *Information Technology and Organizations: Challenges of New Technologies,* Harrisburg, PA: Idea Group.

Kiely, T. (1997) 'Business processes: Consider outsourcing' *Harvard Business Review* 75(3): 11–12.

Lee, H. L. (1996) 'Effective inventory and service management through product and process redesign', *Operations Research* 44(1): 151–59.

Rajala, M., Savolaimen, T. and Jagdev, H. (1997) 'Exploration methods in business process re-engineering', *Computers in Industry* 33(2,3): 367–85.

Rohleder, T. R. and Silver, E. A. (1997) 'A tutorial on business process improvement', *Journal of Operations Management* 15(2): 139–54.

'Competition heats up in on-line banking' (1995) *Fortune International* 26 June.

'Design it yourself' (1989) *The Economist* 29 July.

'Is in-house design on the way out? US companies look more to outside firms and new technology' (1995) *Business Week* 25 September: 54.

'Japanese technology: Back to the drawing board' (1989) *The Economist* 2 December.

'The arrival of haute carture' (1989) *The Economist* 29 July.

'When GM's robots ran amok (Management Brief): In our second case study we examine the ambitious automation strategy pursued by General Motors in the early 1980s. Ten years and $80 billion later, it has failed. What went wrong?' (1991) *The Economist* 10 August.

8 | Human resources in the system design

Objectives and overview

The objective of this chapter is to illustrate the role of human resources in the system design, ultimately the entire organization, and their impact on the supply chain. The chapter opens by presenting a very brief history of working conditions and highlighting issues that exist today. It discusses extensively the contribution of management theorists, particularly in scientific management and human relations. The chapter then presents job design from specialization to the concept of empowerment and discusses some special considerations. Appropriate treatment of employees and attitudes in the work environment are reviewed, together with the approach managers should use in decision-making. Work measurement and standards are reviewed with an illustration of how a labour standard might be developed using time-and-motion studies. The learning-curve concept is treated in detail and its importance and role in real-world situations illustrated. The last section deals with people and change and stress in the work environment, what stress is and how it might be handled.

THE WORKING ENVIRONMENT

People

The third element in the system design is human resources, or people. In any part of the supply chain, people are the most important resource, but the most complex to manage. A motivated, well-trained and loyal work-force can make the company a market leader, financially strong and efficient. It is imperative to create and maintain a work environment where people feel comfortable, at ease, so that they can work as a team. Even with all the most up-to-date automated equipment and technology, a work-force lacking motivation, in a disagreeable work environment, will impede the efficiency and profitability of the organiza-

tion and an ineffective organization can disrupt the supply chain of which this organization is a part. The worst scenario is a breakdown in communications leading to a strike, which can have a disastrous effect on revenues and customer relations, as Box 8.1 illustrates.[1]

The past

At the end of the nineteenth century, and into the early twentieth century, factory conditions in manufacturing were appalling. The working hours were long, children were employed and management treatment of employees harsh. This environment, together with the absence of any meaningful dialogue with management, was the breeding ground for unionization. Many writers used

---

Box 8.1 Strikes

Union members struck a Renault engine plant in northern France in October 1991. The 22-day strike crippled Renault, forcing the company to close all but one of its French and Belgium car assembly plants for lack of engines and gear boxes. It cost Renault an estimated 1.4 billion French francs ($250 million) and wreaked havoc with profits at a company still recuperating from six years of heavy losses in the 1980s.

What upset the union leaders the most wasn't the money, but was the failure of Renault to build a new kind of labor system: A leaner more co-operative one that would help state-owned Renault survive rising Japanese competition. As a comparison, Japanese car makers in Britain have won virtual no-strike contracts from their unions.

From *Wall Street Journal Europe* 19 November 1991

the inhuman working conditions as a central theme in their books, as the following examples illustrate.

Charles Dickens

In his book *Hard Times*, published in 1854, Charles Dickens of Britain denounced capitalism and the way people were exploited.

Emile Zola

In 1885 Emile Zola of France published his work, *Germinal*, which addressed the harshness of working conditions in the coal mines and the brutal behaviour in a strike.

Upton Sinclair

The USA meat-packing industry was the subject of Upton Sinclair's book, *The Jungle*, published in 1906. This work concerned not only the working conditions, but also the lack of health standards in the food-processing industry.

The present

Today, in developed countries, there is certainly better attention paid to people. However, there are still human resource issues that surface. Some of these are described in the following sections.

Equal pay for equal work

Women, who in many cases do the same work as men, do not receive the same pay, as Figure 8.1 illustrates.[2]

Sexual harassment

Sexual harassment incidents against women (and sometimes against men) continually surface, especially in the USA. For example, a female employee of McKinsey Co., one of the world's biggest consulting firms, filed a sexual harassment suit in 1996 alleging discrimination in job promotion.[3]

Race relations

Texaco Corp. in late 1996 agreed to a hefty financial settlement, and dismissal of some of its management people, for poor treatment and racial slurs relating to some of its non-white employees.[4]

Sweatshops

In 1995 California officials freed 72 Thai immigrants from a sweatshop in El Monte, East of Los Angeles, where they had been forced to work for up to 17 hours a day. They were held captive in a razor-wired compound and were paid between $0.60 and $1.60 an hour at a time when the minimum wage was $4.25. Clothing made at this sweatshop was on sale at big retailers such as Montgomery Ward.[5]

Overseas

Often overseas, in some emerging economies, there is much to be done to improve the treatment of factory employees, as the article in Box 8.2, 'Keep the Heat on Sweatshops' illustrates.[6]

Salaried and non-salaried

Human resources by the strict definition include everyone from top management through to those persons who maintain the machines. However, very often when one is referring to human resources, the term applies only to hourly paid employees, rather than salaried people (those who receive a monthly salary regardless of whether they work 160 hours or 240 hours). Salaried workers generally have a higher level of education and have more flexibility in the work force than non-salaried workers. In this section, for the most part, human resources therefore refers to non-salaried employees. (In France there is a very strict separation of employees, *non-cadres* for hourly people and *cadres* for salaried persons whose treatment under the labour laws is sometimes different.)

MANAGEMENT THEORISTS

Way back in 1832, Charles Babbage, in his publication, *On the Economy of Machinery and Manufacturers*,[7] suggested that an axiom of the division of labour is that wages for a job should exactly match the skills required. If a job required only one skill, then only that skill should be recognized. However, if a job required several skills, then wages paid should be according to the highest skill level. Ever since then, management theorists, industrialists and researchers have tried to explain, modify, control and improve the human resources in organizations. Two significant phases have been scientific management and the human relations movement.

Scientific Management

Scientific Management was an early approach by management theorists or owners, whose objective was to treat the activity of workers in a logical, scientific way by using the study of time, motion and methods. The ultimate goal of this analytical approach was to

Figure 8.1 Men's and women's weekly earnings.

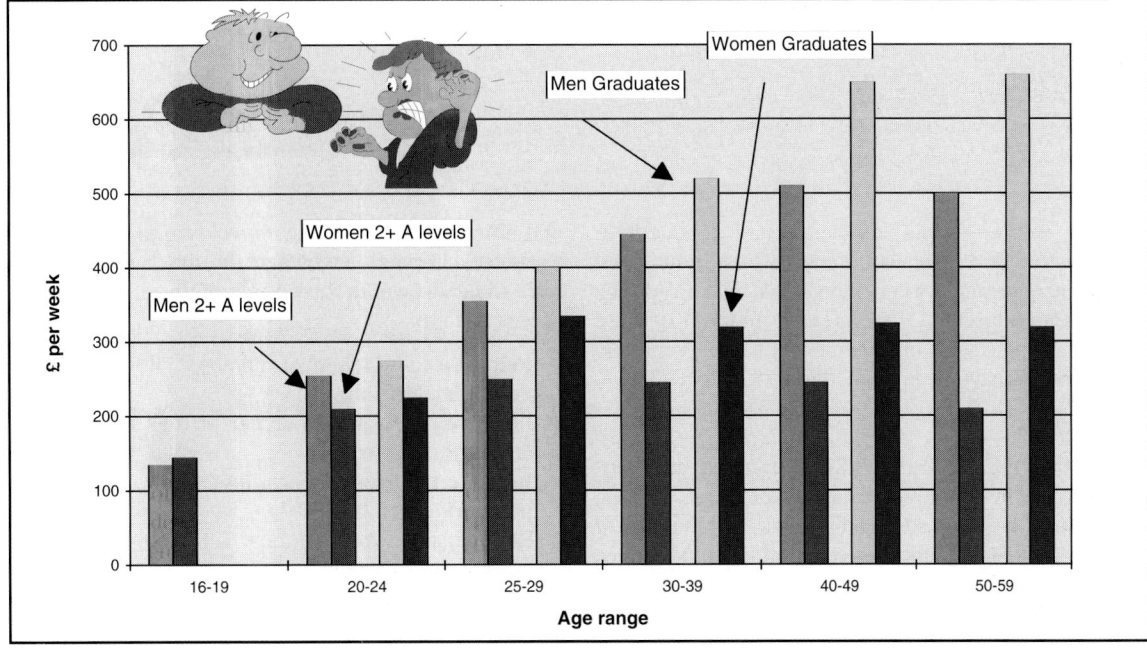

Box 8.2 Social issues. Commentary By Mark L. Clifford.
Keep the heat on sweatshops

It has been six months since the images of children stitching soccer balls in Pakistan, Haitian workers sewing Walt Disney Co. T-shirts, and Kathie Lee Gifford weeping brought the foreign sweatshop issue squarely into American living rooms. Now, it looks as if some of the U.S. companies accused are starting to take the issue seriously.

On Nov. 22, the World Federation of the Sporting Goods Industry pledged to try to eliminate child labor in their operations world-wide by 2000. In Pakistan, it expects to set up a pilot program for independent monitoring of soccer ball production early next year. Nike Inc. and Reebok International Ltd. are establishing 'stitching centers' that aim to deter piece-rate work done by children in homes.

A first. It was the first time a broad group of manufacturers voluntarily agreed to outside monitoring to end labor abuses. A few days earlier, 150 representatives from 50 companies, mostly U.S., met in Hong Kong to discuss everything from improving health and safety conditions to conducting internal audits at overseas contract factories. Sponsored by Business for Social Responsibility, it was the first gathering of its kind in Asia.

So far, so good. Such actions show that business is owning up to the problem. 'I think we've turned a corner', says Jeffrey Ballinger, director of Press for Change, a longtime Nike critic. Industry executives agree. 'Virtually every large retailer is asking for certification from vendors that they are complying with codes of conduct,' says Liv Hustvedt, vice-president of giftware importer Mid-west of Cannon Falls Inc.

Lets' hope the progress doesn't stop there. Too few executives understand that the clamor for ethical sourcing isn't going to disappear with the wave of a magic press release. They have protested, disingenuously, that conditions at factories run by subcontractors are beyond their control. Even now, many foreign and U.S. managers in Asia convey a condescending sense that workers are lucky to get a job at all, 'If you don't have a job, you're a prostitute, a beggar, a thief,' one expatriate Nike factory manager in Indonesia told me in July. Such attitudes won't wash any longer. Like it or not, U.S. and European companies, under fire from consumers and shareholders, are having to lead the way in setting standards for overseas manufacturing. Mostly, they don't like it: Improving conditions costs money and managers' time. Consumers want clothes made in decent factories offering decent pay— but they also want cheap goods. It's hard to give them both.

As the industry gropes for solutions, Nike will be a key company to watch. The world's largest footwear maker long has argued that providing jobs that meet or exceed local standards is contribution enough. But Nike now is stepping up enforcement of a 1993 code of conduct. In October, it set up a labor practices department to monitor its myriad subcontractors. Ernst & Young is finishing audits of Nike's factories, looking for evidence of underage workers or below-minimum pay.

Greed. How far should this go? Low-wage manufacturers likely won't raise pay or cut working hours, even though the added cost would represent a tiny portion of their products' retail price. But Nike is selectively releasing its audit data, while Reebok says it encourages activists to alert it to abuses. Further progress will require more openness to outside scrutiny. Companies, too, must consider broader issues, from the often rapacious methods contractors use to find labor to the food in factory canteens. In Pakistan, soccer ball makers increase worker output, efficiency and productivity, and thus to reduce production costs. The period of scientific management, when individuals like Frederick Taylor, the Gilbreths, Henry Gannt and Henry Ford coupled science with management ideas, is generally considered to have been from about 1875 to 1925.

Adam Smith

The Scottish Adam Smith (1723–1790) was a much earlier theorist in scientific management when, among other ideas, he suggested in his book *The Wealth of Nations* (1776) that labour specialization would reduce labour costs.[8] He based this idea on the fact that:

- Workers, by repeating their tasks, would increase their speed in that particular activity.
- If workers remained at the same task, then less time would be lost through job changing.
- Specialized tools could be developed for each task.

Frederick Taylor

Frederick Winslow Taylor of the USA (1856–1915) was the dominant theorist in scientific management. He rigorously examined the field of operations as a science, proposing to increase worker efficiency by job design.[9] His logic was that there was one best way to work and it was this way that should be developed and put into action. Taylor's work is illustrated by studies in the period 1900–1910 at Bethlehem Steel, USA, where he modified the jobs of employees whose sole responsibility was the shovelling of materials. He made assumptions that this task could be reduced to a science by first presenting the following questions:

1 Will a good employee do more work per day with a shovel full of 5, 10, 15, 20, 30, or 40 pounds?
2 What kinds of shovels work best, and with which materials?
3 How quickly can a shovel be pushed into a pile of material and pulled out properly loaded?
4 How much time is required to swing a shovel backwards and then throw the load a given horizontal distance and a given height?

As Taylor began formulating answers to these questions he developed ways to increase the productivity and efficiency by matching shovel size to such factors as men, materials, height and the distances materials were to be thrown. In three years of these experiments, he was able to:

- Reduce the number of persons shovelling from approximately 600 to 140.
- Increase the average number of tons moved/worker/day from 16 to 59.
- Increase the average earnings from $1.15 to $1.88 per worker/day.
- Reduce the average cost of shovelling from $0.072/ton to $0.033.

It is from Frederick Taylor that the concept *Taylorism* arises, which is considered to be synonymous with rigidity, excessive organization and lack of humanity in the management of people. Taylorism is very much scorned today as a managerial approach, although there are many work areas that have some foundations of Taylorism, such as the practice of just-in-time and use of ISO-9000 quality standards

The Gilbreths

The husband and wife team of Frank (1868–1924) and Lilian Gilbreth (1878–1973) of the USA analysed operations management as a science in the period 1900–1910. Their primary research tool was motion studies in order to reduce a job to its most basic movements. This research was used to establish performance standards and to eliminate unnecessary movements. Frank Gilbreth, himself an apprentice bricklayer, found that bricklayers could increase output by concentrating on some movements and eliminating others. His studies resulted in reducing the number of motions necessary to lay a brick by approximately 70 per cent, which resulted in tripling bricklaying production.

Henry Ford

Henry Ford (1863–1947) was the founder of the Ford Motor Company in Detroit, USA. Based on his observations of workers in a meat-packing operation, where carcasses were moved from one worker to another, each performing a particular task, he designed and put into operation the first assembly line (1890–1930) for automobile production. This operations layout embodied elements of scientific management, including standardized products, mass production, low unit cost, high volume, mechanized assembly lines, specialization of labour and interchangeable parts. A typical product example was the Model T Ford, only obtainable in the colour black. With this scientific approach in the assembly-line operation, production time of the Model T was reduced from 14 to less than 2 hours, which resulted in a corresponding reduction in price from US $850 to $265. In 1927 when production of the Model T ceased, over 15 million vehicles had been sold.

Human relations

The human relations approach to management was altogether different from scientific management, because its basic objective was to treat those in the workforce with respect and dignity. The human-relations period is considered to be from about 1925 to 1960. However, in many respects, the human-relations approach to management is an ongoing process. Notable theorists on the human motivation side of work include Elton Mayo and his colleagues, Henry Gantt, Abraham Maslow, Frederick Herzberg, Douglas McGregor and Peter Drucker.

Hawthorne studies

The Hawthorne studies, carried out by Elton Mayo, F. J Roethlisberger and William J Dickson between 1927 and 1932, were some of the earlier analyses of human relations in the work environment.[10] These studies examined the conditions of workers at the Hawthorne, Illinois Plant of Western Electric Co., USA. They originally investigated the effect of lighting on productivity and then went further by studying the human side. In conclusion, they found that the human elements and the role played by individuals was more important in productivity than physical elements such as the lighting.

Henry Gantt

Henry L. Gantt of the USA (1861–1919) was interested in both the human and scientific approaches to management. On the human side, his perception of managers was that they were slavedrivers, forcing workers to do jobs in which they had little interest, or desire to do, under poor conditions. He believed that a manager should not represent himself as a slavedriver and, when he asks workers to perform tasks, he should make it in their interest to accomplish them, being careful not to ask what is impossible or unreasonable. Furthermore, whereas Taylor had developed a wage system in which everyone was paid the same rate, Gantt proposed that workers should earn a bonus as an incentive, in addition to the piece rate, if they went beyond their daily production quota.[11]

Even though Gantt had a more human side than Taylor, he was still interested in increasing worker efficiency. His philosophy was that exact *scientific knowledge* of what could be done should always take precedence over the *opinion* of what should be done. He said that the best systems are those in which tasks are properly scheduled and this led to the development of the Gantt scheduling chart discussed in Chapter 14, *Operations Scheduling*.

Abraham Maslow

Abraham H. Maslow of the USA is best known for his 1943 publication, *A Theory of Human Motivation*, in which he theorized that people have five basic needs.[12] Using a pyramid approach and moving from the base to the apex of the pyramid, as illustrated in Figure 8.2, he described these need levels as shown in Table 8.1.

Table 8.1 Need levels according to Maslow

Needs	Definition
1 Physiological	Normal body requirements such as food and water, rest, sex and air. Until these needs are met, individual behaviour is aimed to satisfy them.
2 Security or safety	Needs people feel to keep themselves free from physical harm and economic ruin. Management can help in satisfying these needs with salaries, since with appropriate income employees purchase food and housing.
3 Social	These include the desire for love and friendship and reflect a person's desire to be accepted by others.
4 Esteem	These are the desire for self-respect, and respect for others.
5 Self-actualization	These ultimate needs are the desire to maximize a person's potential, for example a company manager who has a strong desire to become president.

Figure 8.2 Needs according to Abraham Maslow.

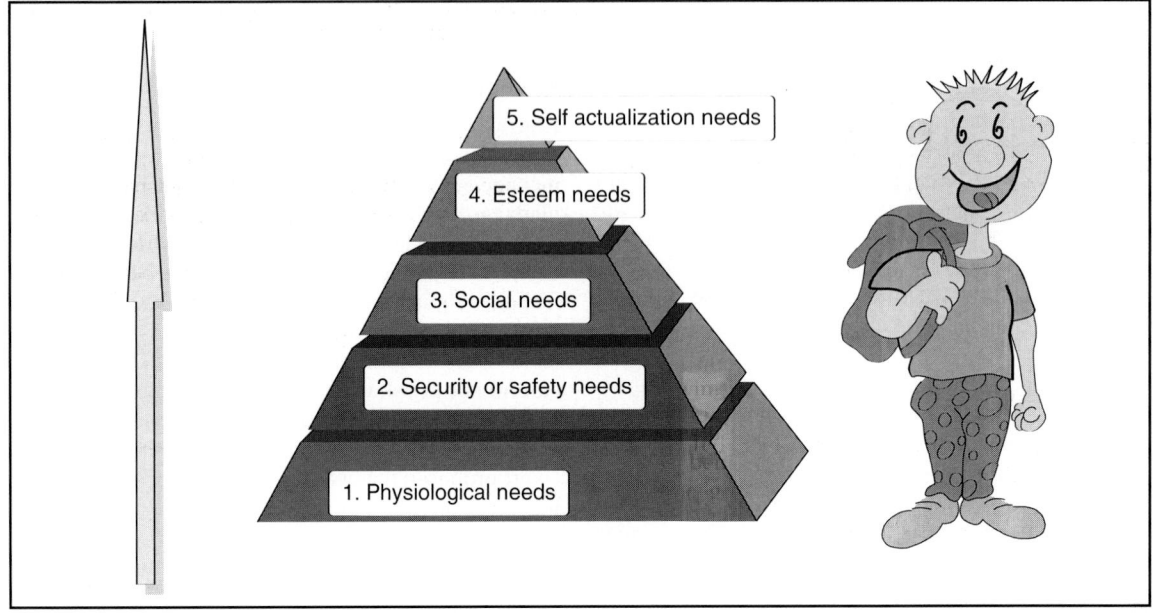

Maslow postulated that these needs are progressive. When Level 1 is satisfied, desires move upward until Level 5 is reached.

Frederick Herzberg

Frederick Herzberg concluded in his research on human motivation in the 1960s that there were two different variables that influenced people in an organization. They were hygiene, or maintenance factors that impacted job dissatisfaction, and motivating factors that influenced job satisfaction. Hygiene factors relate to the work environment and motivating factors are connected to the work itself.[13] Illustrations of these are presented in Table 8.2.

Douglas McGregor

Douglas McGregor developed a set of assumptions about people and said that they were either of Theory *X* type, who usually had negative assumptions about people, or Theory *Y*, who had positive ideas about people.[14] This theory could be used in a management environment, where the implication was that Theory *X* managers were bad and Theory *Y* managers were good and the better leaders. These assumptions are illustrated in Table 8.3.

Peter Drucker

Peter Drucker wrote very extensively on employee motivation and the role of management in organizations. He is responsible for establishing the idea of management by objectives in an organization and this has the following three basic characteristics.[15]

1 All individuals in an organization are assigned a set of objectives that they attempt to achieve during a reasonable time period. These objectives are established and agreed to mutually between the individual and the manager.

Table 8.2 Hygiene and maintenance factors according to Herzberg

Dissatisfaction: Hygiene or maintenance factors	Satisfaction: motivating factors
Company policies	Opportunity for achievement
Administration policies	Opportunity for recognition
Level of supervision	The work itself
Relationship with the supervisor	Level of responsibility
Relationship with peers	Possibilities of advancement
Relationship with subordinates	Opportunities for personal growth
Working conditions	Opportunities for learning new methods
Salary	Opportunities for working overseas

Table 8.3 The Theory *X* and Theory *Y* assumptions of McGregor

Theory *X* assumptions (negative)	Theory *Y* assumptions (positive)
The average person has an inherent dislike for work and they will avoid it if possible.	Physical and mental effort in work is as natural as play or rest.
People must be coerced, controlled, directed and threatened with punishment in order to get them to put forth adequate work efforts.	People will exercise self-direction and self-control in the objective of the organization. Commitment to objectives is a function of rewards associated with achievement.
People prefer to be directed, wish to avoid responsibility, and have little ambition,	The average person learns under proper conditions, both to accept and to seek responsibility.
The average person is only interested in security.	The capacity to exercise a relatively high degree of imagination, ingenuity, and creativity, is common among people.

2 Performance reviews are conducted periodically to determine how close the individual is to achieving these objectives.

3 Rewards are given to individuals on the basis of how close they are to reaching their objectives.

JOB DESIGN

Job design entails matching tasks or work activities to individuals or work groups. The ultimate objective is to increase the efficiency of an organization, with the parallel goal of making working conditions more agreeable. As illustrated in Figure 8.3, for some situations job design may be progressive moving from specialization to empowerment, concepts that are illustrated in the following sections.

Job specialization

Job specialization involves having people with certain skills who are dedicated to a certain activity in the operation. For example, specialization may involve:

- foundry workers responsible for pouring molten metal;
- intricate soldering on computer circuit boards;
- wiring electrical control boards;
- performing certain assembly-line jobs in automobile production.

As Frederick Taylor emphasized, job specialization should mean efficiency because people are performing work they know how to do well. However, the repetitive nature means that jobs can be boring to the point that people become sloppy; then quality suffers and costs rise. Job specialization is contrary to some philosophies of human resource management although it is sometimes difficult to find persons who are completely flexible. A

foundry worker may not have the dexterity to work on the same company's assembly line, for example.

Job rotation

Job rotation moves beyond specialization, so that people who have the required skills can rotate (say on a weekly basis) from one job to another to get away from the job specialization rut. For example, assembly line workers may work one week on engine mountings and then the following week on assembling dashboard components. Incorporating job rotation can help to reduce the monotonous aspects of the job.

Job rotation may not be desired for everyone, even though the necessary skills are in place. I once worked in a chocolate factory where there were several groups of women on the packing line, putting the various chocolate varieties in boxes. It was suggested that these groups changed periodically, both in their makeup and in the location where they worked. This idea was loudly rejected by the women, because they felt comfortable remaining with their group, whom they knew, and also in a job which required little additional thought.

Multiskills and plant flexibility

Job rotation implies multiskills in personnel. It is not only advantageous and motivating for the employee, but it also gives the employer the flexibility to adjust to client needs. If a customer increases the order requirement, modifies the product specifications or brings forward the delivery date, a production manager needs to have the facility to reassign personnel accordingly. For the company, this in turn means providing the appropriate training.

Job enlargement

Job enlargement is intended to avoid an employee being trapped in job specialization by trying to improve

Figure 8.3   Job design.

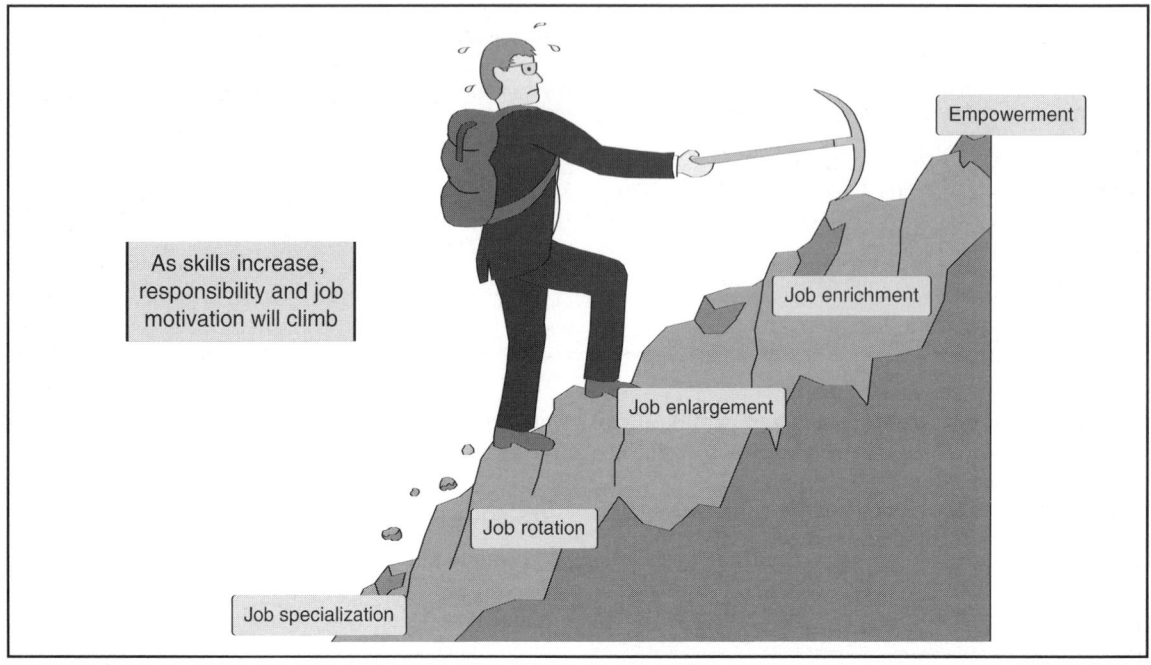

As skills increase, responsibility and job motivation will climb

Empowerment

Job enrichment

Job enlargement

Job rotation

Job specialization

the variety within a certain sphere of a person's ability and interest. Enlargement would mean expanding the tasks involved in a job. For example, a cutting operation could be enlarged by adding shaping and forming. This would be horizontal expansion of the job.

Job enrichment

Job enrichment means expanding the job vertically by adding design and planning elements. For example, a purchasing secretary whose basic job is the correspondence for a group of purchasing people could have the job enriched by planning the work assignments of the group, being an intermediate in customer contacts and maybe helping the evaluation of some proposals. That is, the secretary's job is enriched from becoming a secretary to being more an assistant. This is certainly the situation today when many of the classic secretarial duties are less required as more and more people have their own personal computer.

Empowerment

Empowerment is an extension of job enrichment by adding to it complete employee trust and responsibilities not originally associated with the job. Consider the two following examples, one in a service industry, the other in manufacturing.

Nordstrom

This US fashion retailer, based in Seattle, Washington, believes in empowering its workers. Its 'Employee Handbook' consists of a single sheet of paper urging people to set their goals high, stating the company's confidence in their ability to meet them and spelling out a single corporate rule 'Use your good judgement in all situations'. The employees respond by serving customers with an assiduousness that can extend to writing personal thank-you notes or pumping up flat tyres in the parking garage. Run at the top by the collective leadership of fourth-generation Nordstroms, the company devolves its merchandise-buying to the local level, in contrast to most department stores, which buy centrally.[16]

Chrysler

When Chrysler, the US-based automobile constructor, sets out to create a new model, or to revamp an old one, it forms a team of about 700 people from engineering, design, manufacturing, marketing and finance, including specialists of all kinds, or as Chrysler labels them 'a self-contained multidisciplinary group'. A vice-president acts as 'godfather' to the group, but all of the actual work is directed by leaders below that rank. Top management meet with the group to sketch out a vision for the vehicle and set aggressive goals for design, fuel economy and cost. Management works out a contract with the team, setting out objectives, after which the group is empowered to take on complete responsibility.[17]

Special considerations in job design

No matter at what level an organization is viewing job design, whether it be specialization or empowerment, the following are some other considerations which apply to all.

Women in the workforce

At the turn of the century, men pretty much dominated the workforce, principally in manufacturing. Women moving into the factories began in World War I. When war broke out, women filled the rôle of men who were on the war front and some remained when war ended. A similar situation occurred during World War II. Since the 1950s, the proportion of women in the work force has continued to rise, such that in Europe in 1994 women represented 41.4 per cent of the work force. This ranged from a high of 48.7 per cent in Sweden to a low of 34.0 per cent in Spain.[18] Data are similar for the USA and Japan and, in all three regions, the proportion of women working is increasing.

Thus, in job design the aptitudes and characteristics of women, compared to men, need to be considered. In assembly work involving activities like detailed soldering, mounting of sub-assemblies in motors, clocks or computers, women are considered to have more dexterity than men. Work involving physical strength, such as erecting scaffolding, building construction, etc., anatomically fits a man better. Although it is wrong to stereotype people in employment, there are jobs the design of which is such that they are better suited to women, and vice-versa. Even though women are replacing men in many forms of employment, their wages or salaries are still less than men (Figure 8.1). The argument that women perform better than men in activities, such as wiring, soldering or other detailed work, is sometimes hiding the fact that the company can pay them lower wages which reduces product costs!

Ergonomics

Ergonomics in job design pays attention to the equipment and machinery by balancing the work of the employee with the machine or the task at hand in order to minimize human effort and to make the work as comfortable as possible, for example:

- Renault VI has designed its buses so that assembly work on the roof of the bus can be performed at arm's length, rather than the operator straining at connecting elements that are above his or her head.

- Computer keyboards have been redesigned so that they are more comfortable to the operator.
- Cooking appliances in restaurant kitchens are, where possible, placed so that chefs do not have to do excessive bending. (Back and neck problems among restaurant kitchen staff are common.)

Basic skill level

In job design, even though an individual may be competent at performing the work, some basic skills may be lacking. For example, with globalization there is considerable movement of people whose language or other skills may not be sufficient. At the work-centre level, operators may not speak the native language. Thus in the job design, operating instructions need to be translated, or kept simple. It may be better to avoid figures and letters and use colours and symbols instead. Cashiers at McDonald's, Burger King, and Quick use symbol cash registers, which avoid the need for the cashiers to perform calculations.

Work schedules

All countries have a legal standard work schedule based on a certain number of hours per week. In Britain and the USA it is 40 hours and in France it is 39, with a proposal to go to 35 hours per week by 2000. It used to be that these times were spread out evenly over a five-day week. Now, many firms have flexible work schedules to suit both employee and employer. For example, it may be ten hours for four days rather than eight hours for five. Alternatively, if present for eight hours a day, the employee can start later and finish later, provided he is present during so-called core hours of the firm. A further option is that employees may work a 50-hour week when there is heavy customer demand and 30 or less hours per week when demand is slack. All this flexibility requires very close attention to scheduling, so that the competitiveness of the firm is not lost.

ATTITUDE TOWARDS EMPLOYEES

All operations involve members of management, or senior people, dealing with lower-level employees. The way these lower-level people are treated and addressed can have a significant impact on working relationships and on motivation, which have a direct bearing on productivity and cost. The following are some guidelines.

Communication

- Treat all people with respect, no matter what their level in the organization, from the person who cleans the washrooms upwards.

- Communicate with, and listen to, the employees. Let them know the positive side as well as the negative side of the business. Good communication minimizes the effect of 'corridor talk' and false rumours.
- Compliment employees when they do good work.
- Let employees know when their work is not as expected, but indicate mistakes in an objective manner and not a threatening one.
- Work any conflict through with people.
- Managers should often visit the work centre and talk directly with members of the workforce.
- Depend on people to do the job right and avoid 'breathing down their necks'.

Working environment

- Provide an atmosphere in which employees feel secure and confident.
- Provide an environment in which employees feel they are making a contribution to the progress of the firm.
- Create an atmosphere where there is trust and people are open with each other.
- Avoid special parking slots for those in senior positions.
- Keep workgroups as small as feasible, so that individuals can contribute.
- Emphasize team work.
- Everyone respects the rules of the organization. Just because one is a manager is no reason to arrive late for a meeting.
- Avoid segregation of eating areas.
- Use a first-name basis for employees at all levels. Allow lower-level employees to use first names for managers.
- Provide a physically clean, pleasant and safe work environment.
- Provide appropriate work tools, storage areas, toilets and washing facilities.
- Provide appropriate training for the employees, so that they are well trained for their job. Help them if they have problems.

Company objectives

- Provide clear and commons goals for the work force.
- Allow employees to share in the profits of the company.
- Provide opportunities for growth within the organization.
- Where possible, promote from within, rather than bringing in people from outside.

Management style and decision making

Managers spend much of their time making decisions. There are two extremes in the ways of making a decision, as illustrated in Figure 8.4.

The Best Way

Before a decision is made, discuss all the elements with those people who will be involved when the final decision is made. This will make it easy to implement the decision when the time comes. That is, take a bottom-up approach to decision making.

The Wrong Way

Avoid the top-down approach to decisions, where management makes the decision and pushes the new plan onto the workforce. This will make it much more difficult to put the decision into effect and will de-motivate the workforce.

The first approach will take longer to arrive at a final decision, but the long-term benefits will be more advantageous.

WORK MEASUREMENT

In order to plan effectively and control an operation, it is necessary to have standards and to be able to measure against these standards once they have been developed. The standard is the norm of work measurement, against which activity is compared.

Machine standards

A machine standard is usually the time per unit for a particular machine to perform a certain operation, for example the time per unit for a robot to paint-spray an automobile, the time to print one metre of cloth in the textile industry or the time per unit for a machine to fill and seal one box of cornflakes. Since machines are automatically controlled, they can perform the same repetitive action with little variation from unit to unit. Thus, machine standards are relatively easy to define.

Labour standards

A labour standard is the time for a worker with the appropriate training to perform a certain well-defined activity under normal conditions. This might be the time for the preparation of a hamburger at a McDonald's restaurant, the time per unit to load a pallet of items on a truck or the time per unit to enter information into a computer database.

Figure 8.4 Ways of decision making.

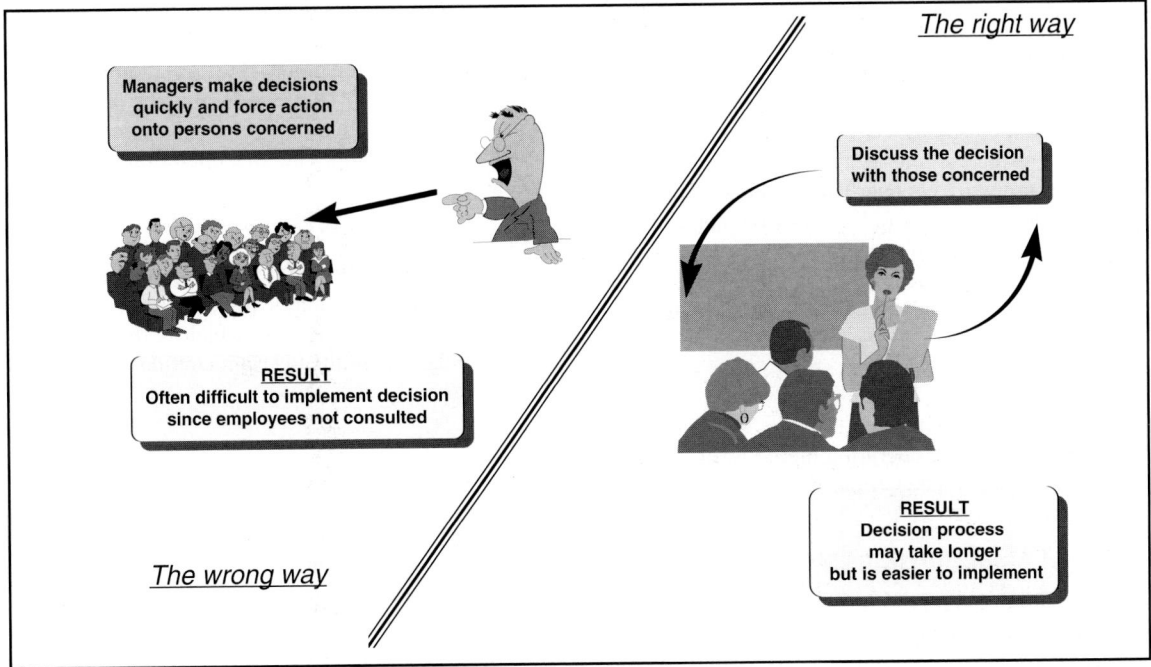

Labour standards are more difficult to establish than machine standards, since skill levels, physical ability and concentration levels vary between individuals. In addition to the standards, one has to take into consideration rest periods and the time of day. People may be faster in the morning and slower, say, at night. Two notable researchers on labour standards were L. H. C. Tipitt of England, who in 1934 performed work-sampling studies to develop production standards, and H. B. Maynard of the USA, who in 1948 developed time-measurement methods.

Reasons for standards

Work standards have the concept of Taylorism buried in them, but they are necessary for the following reasons.

Financial proposals

Business firms are in a competitive environment and often need to give financial estimates, or proposals, for performing work for clients. For example, a client might require a proposal for printing 10 000 copies of a publicity brochure. In order to develop the financial estimate, the following would be some of the elements:

- cost of paper required for 10 000 copies (quantity × unit cost);
- cost of ink for 10 000 copies (quantity × unit cost);
- preparation of printing plate (labour standard × cost/hour);
- machine cost for printing (machine standard per unit × cost per unit);
- operator cost (labour standard × unit cost).

Scheduling

For scheduling and planning purposes, a firm needs to know the labour and machine standards in order to be able to assign work to people and machines in the most efficient manner.

Cost control

For cost-control purposes a firm needs to know various standards for work in order that these costs can be accounted for and billed to the appropriate entity. For example, in the assembly of an automobile, the paint-spraying operation may be a cost centre for the production site. Using appropriate standards, these costs can be appropriately allocated to the complete production site.

Capacity planning

Knowing the various standards, a firm can plan for current and future capacity requirements. If necessary, appropriate steps can then be taken for subcontracting activity.

Budgeting

With standards, a firm can develop operating and capital budgets.

Bonus incentive

If standards are established and employees exceed the standards as far as the work output is concerned, employees can earn a bonus. This might be appropriate in say a sales environment, but probably not in a manufacturing centre. Employees who try to exceed standards might go too fast and compromise on product quality. The emphasis should be to 'work to quality' and not 'work to quantity'.

Comparing different operations

With appropriate standards, the cost of doing work according to different operating methods, or using different machines, can be compared.

Criticism of labour standards

Using labour standards in industry is very controversial and is often a source of conflict between management and labour. Labour unions often complain that labour standards are set too high, meaning that their members are continually under stress. Management on the other hand criticize them and say that they are set too low, so that product costs are high compared to competitors. This is particularly a criticism made when comparing Europe with Asian countries, whose labour standards are lower.

Time-and-motion study

A time-and-motion study is a way to analyse the time needed to perform a certain activity, to develop this into appropriate standards and then to translate this information into the output for a particular operation. In a time-and-motion study, a job is broken down into its individual elements and the time taken to perform each of these tasks for a certain sample size is measured. This information is then used to design the system.

The illustration of a simple time-and-motion study is given by the time and activities involved in preparing a hamburger. The information collected and the computations are shown in Figure 8.5.

Activities in the operation

The making of a hamburger is broken down into its individual elements. Here, there are eight given. First, the operator takes the two halves of the toasted hamburger bun from the toaster and replaces them with two fresh halves for the next hamburger. On the toast-

ed bottom part of the bun the operator then spreads mayonnaise sauce, places the cooked hamburger meat onto this and garnishes the meat with a piece of lettuce, tomato and an onion ring. The operator then spreads mayonnaise sauce onto the top half of the toasted bun and then closes the hamburger with this second part of the bun. The final operation is wrapping the hamburger.

Sample size

Here the operation is timed for a sample of 15 hamburgers. In practice, using statistics, one would determine the correct sample size, which is representative of the population within a certain confidence level, say 95 per cent.

Measurement

The operator times the activity on a continuous basis, noting only the time at the end of each activity. For example, for the first hamburger the operation starts at 9:45 and the stop watch is at zero. When the bun is taken from the toaster the reading is 5 seconds and this is also the activity time since the watch started at zero. The reading after a fresh bun has been put into the toaster is 7 seconds. Thus the activity time for putting the bun in the toaster is $7 - 5 = 2$ seconds. The time at the end of wrapping is 1:24 (1 minute 24 seconds) and the time at the end of closing the bun is 1:07. Thus the time to close the bun is 17 seconds (1:24 – 1:07). For the second hamburger the reading after the toasted bun has been taken from the toaster is 1:37 and thus the time to do this activity is 13 seconds (1:37 –1:24).

Cycle time

The cycle time is the total time for the eight activities, or the time to prepare one hamburger for a customer. The total of the cycle times for the 15 hamburgers is the last row on the principal table.

Average times

The average times for each activity and for the hamburger preparation are given in the column 'Average time'. These values are simple the total times divided by 15.

Rating factor

The rating factor shown in the column 'Rating factor' is a performance number estimated according to whether the determined time is considered to be above or below a real average value. It is a subjectively obtained number, based on the observer's analysis. A value greater than 1.0 means that, in the evaluation of the observer, the worker performed at a faster rate

Figure 8.5   Preparation of a hamburger.

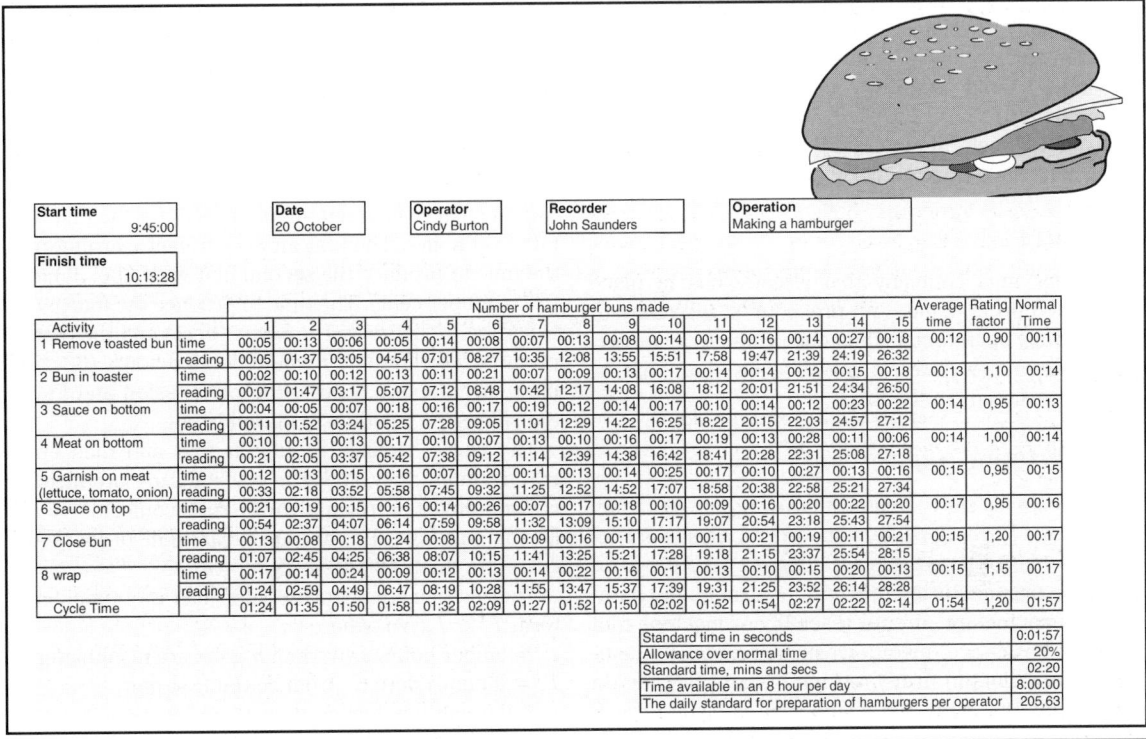

Start time	9:45:00
Finish time	10:13:28

Date	Operator	Recorder	Operation
20 October	Cindy Burton	John Saunders	Making a hamburger

Activity		Number of hamburger buns made															Average time	Rating factor	Normal Time
		1	2	3	4	5	6	7	8	9	10	11	12	13	14	15			
1 Remove toasted bun	time	00:05	00:13	00:06	00:05	00:14	00:08	00:07	00:13	00:08	00:14	00:19	00:16	00:14	00:27	00:18	00:12	0,90	00:11
	reading	00:05	01:37	03:05	04:54	07:01	08:27	10:35	12:08	13:55	15:51	17:58	19:47	21:39	24:19	26:32			
2 Bun in toaster	time	00:02	00:10	00:12	00:13	00:11	00:21	00:07	00:09	00:13	00:17	00:14	00:14	00:12	00:15	00:18	00:13	1,10	00:14
	reading	00:07	01:47	03:17	05:07	07:12	08:48	10:42	12:17	14:08	16:08	18:12	20:01	21:51	24:34	26:50			
3 Sauce on bottom	time	00:04	00:05	00:07	00:18	00:16	00:17	00:19	00:12	00:14	00:17	00:10	00:14	00:12	00:23	00:22	00:14	0,95	00:13
	reading	00:11	01:52	03:24	05:25	07:28	09:05	11:01	12:29	14:22	16:25	18:22	20:15	22:03	24:57	27:12			
4 Meat on bottom	time	00:10	00:13	00:13	00:17	00:10	00:07	00:13	00:10	00:16	00:17	00:19	00:13	00:28	00:11	00:06	00:14	1,00	00:14
	reading	00:21	02:05	03:37	05:42	07:38	09:12	11:14	12:39	14:38	16:42	18:41	20:28	22:31	25:08	27:18			
5 Garnish on meat (lettuce, tomato, onion)	time	00:12	00:13	00:15	00:16	00:07	00:20	00:11	00:13	00:14	00:25	00:17	00:10	00:27	00:13	00:16	00:15	0,95	00:15
	reading	00:33	02:18	03:52	05:58	07:45	09:32	11:25	12:52	14:52	17:07	18:58	20:38	22:58	25:21	27:34			
6 Sauce on top	time	00:21	00:19	00:15	00:16	00:14	00:26	00:07	00:17	00:18	00:10	00:09	00:16	00:20	00:22	00:20	00:17	0,95	00:16
	reading	00:54	02:37	04:07	06:14	07:59	09:58	11:32	13:09	15:10	17:17	19:07	20:54	23:18	25:43	27:54			
7 Close bun	time	00:13	00:08	00:18	00:24	00:08	00:17	00:09	00:16	00:11	00:11	00:11	00:21	00:19	00:11	00:21	00:15	1,20	00:17
	reading	01:07	02:45	04:25	06:38	08:07	10:15	11:41	13:25	15:21	17:28	19:18	21:15	23:37	25:54	28:15			
8 wrap	time	00:17	00:14	00:24	00:09	00:12	00:13	00:14	00:22	00:16	00:11	00:13	00:10	00:15	00:20	00:13	00:15	1,15	00:17
	reading	01:24	02:59	04:49	06:47	08:19	10:28	11:55	13:47	15:37	17:39	19:31	21:25	23:52	26:14	28:28			
Cycle Time		01:24	01:35	01:50	01:58	01:32	02:09	01:27	01:52	01:50	02:02	01:52	01:54	02:27	02:22	02:14	01:54	1,20	01:57

Standard time in seconds	0:01:57
Allowance over normal time	20%
Standard time, mins and secs	02:20
Time available in an 8 hour per day	8:00:00
The daily standard for preparation of hamburgers per operator	205,63

than he or she would under normal conditions. The reverse is true for a value less than 1.0. These factors are not easy to assess. An operator who knows he or she is being timed may be faster than normal, hoping to impress the recorder or management. Alternatively, if the operator expects salaries and output are going to be based on these results, he or she may be slow during the study, knowing that in practice he or she can exceed the rate and thus be considered a good employee. Thus assigning of realistic rating factors is difficult.

Normal Time

The normal time for each activity, given in the last column, is the product of the measured time and the rating factor. The normal cycle time for the preparation of a hamburger is the sum of all the normal activity times, which in this case is 1 minute 57 seconds.

Standard Time

To the normal time is added an allowance to arrive at the standard time. The allowance again is subjective and it is a factor to take into account stoppages, fatigue or interruptions. In this illustration an allowance of 20 per cent is given. Thus, the standard time is (normal time) × 1.20. In one eight-hour day there are 480 minutes, thus dividing the standard unit time into this gives the standard time per day. In this case, in Figure 8.5 it is 205 hamburgers per day per operator (rounded down rather than up to ensure that this figure is attainable).

Performing a time-and-motion study may at first seem straightforward, but it needs complete cooperation from the workers involved. In a factory or service environment people become very suspicious when they see management personnel arrive with a clip board and stopwatch and may do everything they can to disrupt the experimental work.

LEARNING AND THE EXPERIENCE CURVE

When anybody starts something new, there is a learning process before one arrives at one's optimum ability. In the life cycle, one learns to walk; one learns to talk; one learns to study; one learns in a professional environment. Some activities are harder to learn than others and some individuals are quicker to learn than others. The learning concept impacts productivity, costs and profit in all phases of the operations and supply chain.

New products

If a company develops a new product, or process, it takes time for engineers, operators and/or maintenance personnel to understand the process and the design fully and thus to be efficient regarding all the activities involved. As such, the operating and/or product costs at the early stages are higher than at later periods.

New hires

New hires, in a company that already has in place established programmes and procedures, take time to become fully operational. Thus, the productivity or output of these new hires is initially less than that of employees already in the firm.

Manufacturing and services

Some processes show greater improvement over time, or a definite learning curve, than others. This is particularly the case where there are complex labour operations in a manufacturing process, for example in automobile manufacture, aircraft assembly or machine-tool production. Service operations such as financial institutions, distribution firms, restaurants and the like do not exhibit the same trend and may in fact have a barely perceptible learning curve.

The curve

The experience, or learning, curve, sometimes called the manufacturing progress function, is a mathematical relationship between the cumulative production output and its cost, expressed either in financial terms or in production time. Studies have indicated that, for certain activities, production costs will decline by between about 10 to 30 per cent with the doubling of the cumulated output, illustrating that it takes time to learn fully new processes or new ideas. The concept of the learning curve is based upon the premise that the learning rate, as a percentage, is quite regular and its progression can be predicted. Research has shown that the more complex a system, the greater is the rate of learning. This learning can be illustrated by an exponential type curve, or a straight line if a logarithmic scale is used.

Mathematical representation

A mathematical learning curve can be developed by plotting production labour hours against the quantity of products produced. The curve decreases exponentially, showing that when a new production operation starts, as the number of units produced increases, the labour hours per unit decrease as operators become more familiar with the task. Learning curves are presented according to the learning rate, for example 75, 80, 85, or 90 per cent. Thus, an 80 per cent learning means that, as the quantity produced is doubled, the labour hours per unit decrease by 80 per cent.

The exponential 80 per cent learning curve

Assume that to manufacture a product for the first time takes 50 hours. Then, at an 80 per cent learning rate, the time to produce the second unit would be 40 hours (50×80 per cent). The time to produce the fourth unit would be 32 hours (40×80 per cent) and the time to produce the eighth unit would be 25.6 hours (32×80 per cent). Table 8.4 gives the progression and Figure 8.6 shows the relationship graphically.

The curve declines rapidly at first and then evens out, declining very slowly as new units are produced. It is this almost horizontal level that conforms to the labour standard for the particular item of work discussed in the previous section.

The mathematical relationship has the exponential form $T_n = T_1(n^b)$, where

T_n = labour hours/unit when n units are manufactured;
T_1 = labour hours to produce the first unit;
n = the unit number produced;
b = a constant representing the slope of the curve.

Logarithmic Analysis

The expression $T_n = T_1(n^b)$ can be converted to the logarithmic form to give the straight-line relationship:

$$\log_e T_n = \log_e T_1 + b \log_e n$$

The slope of the straight line is b and this can be rewritten as:

$$b = \frac{\log_e T_n - \log_e T_1}{\log_e n}$$

If the learning rate is denoted by L, the value of b can be determined by considering the time to produce the first and second units. The time to produce the second unit is given by, $T_1 \times L$ (by definition the learning process). Substituting this expression for T_n in the equation for b gives:

$$b = \frac{\log_e T_1 \times L - \log_e T_1}{\log_e 2}$$

$$= \frac{\log_e T_1 + \log_e L - \log_e T_1}{\log_e 2}$$

$$= \frac{\log_e L}{\log_e 2}$$

Table 8.4 The progression for an 80 per cent learning curve

Units produced	1	2	4	8	16	32	64	128	256
Hours per unit	50.0	40.0	32.0	25.6	20.5	16.4	13.1	10.5	8.4

For an 80 per cent learning rate, $L = 0.80$ and so:

$$b = \frac{\log_e L}{\log_e 2} = \frac{\log_e 0.80}{\log_e 2} = \frac{-0.2231}{+0.6931}$$

$$= -0.3219$$

The negative slope indicates that the time decreases as the number of units increases.

Alternatively, the value of b can be determined by using the information in Table 8.4. If one considers, say, the production time for the first and 16th unit and substitutes these in the equation for the slope b:

- labour hours to produce the 16th unit are 20.5;
- labour hours to produce the first unit are 50.0;
- unit number produced is 16.

Then in the equation for the slope b:

$$b = \frac{\log_e 20.5 - \log_e 50.0}{\log_e 16} = -0.3219$$

Substituting this value b in the exponential equation gives $T_n = T_1^{-0.322}$. From this the labour hours for any unit number can be determined. For example, the labour hours required to produce the 25th unit would be:

$$T_{25} = 50(25^{-0.322}) = 17.7 \text{ labour hours.}$$

Figure 8.7 is the alternative, logarithmic graph of the 80 per cent learning curve, which is a straight line given by the equation:

$$\log_e T_n = \log_e T_1 - 0.3219 \log_e n.$$

Similar calculations can be carried out and the corresponding graphs produced for other learning curves such as 70, 75, 85 and 90 per cent.

The worked example *Turbines*, on page 208, illustrates the principle of the learning curve.

Implications of the learning curve

For costs to decline and the learning-curve concept to apply, there has to be an increase in production volume. In the early stages, costs will be higher and decisions will have to be made on the pricing policy.

Figure 8.6 Exponential 80 per cent learning curve.

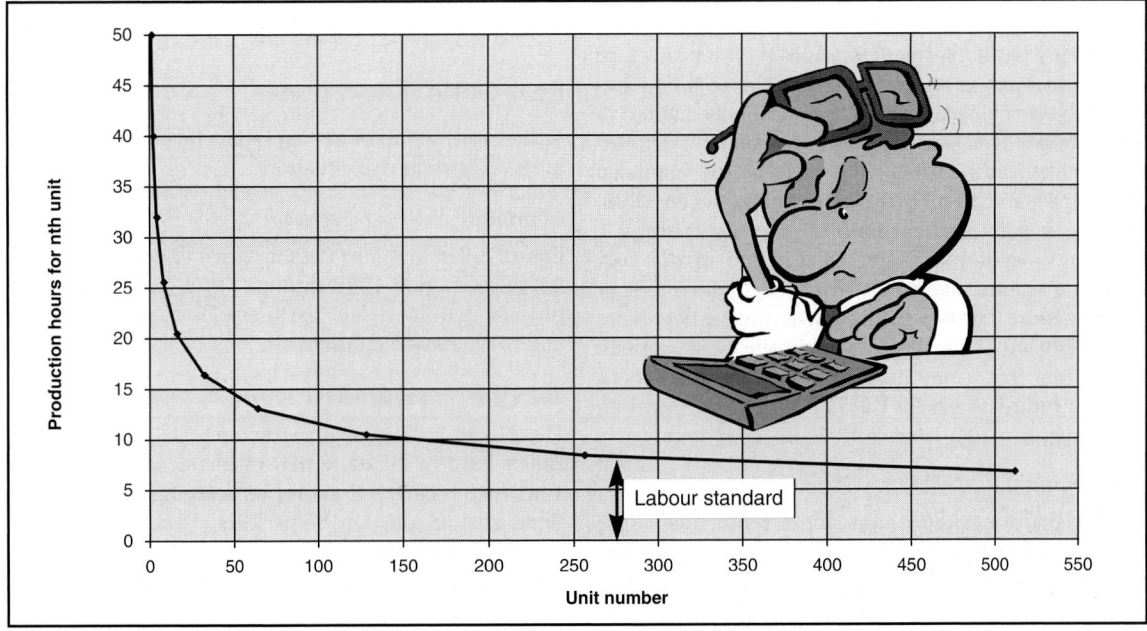

Figure 8.7 Logarithmic 80 per cent learning curve.

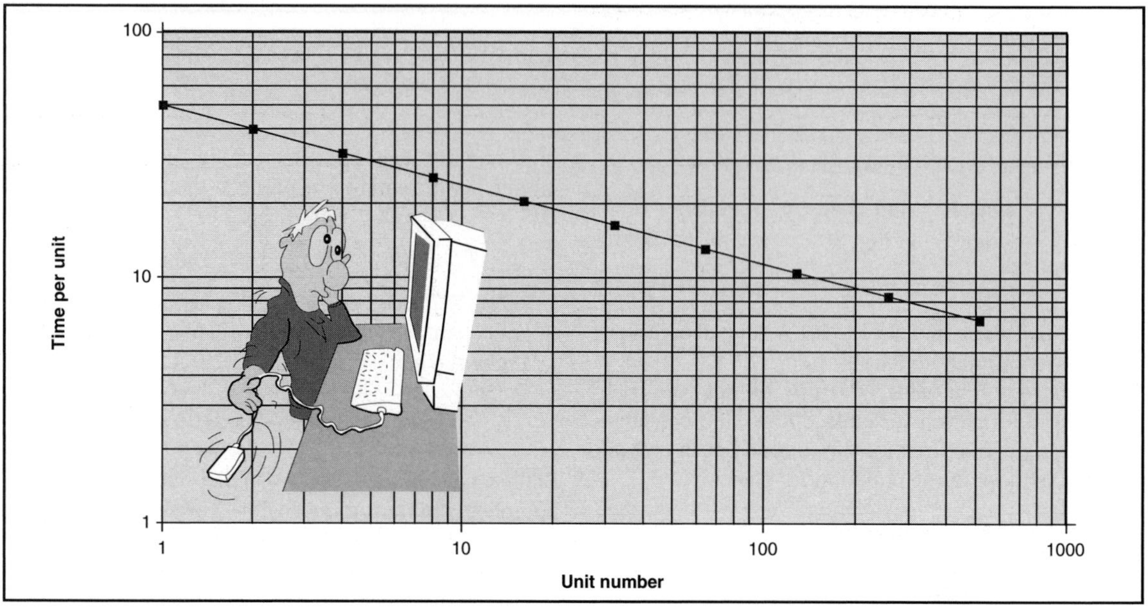

Producing a new product

The decision to be made at an early stage is whether to demand a higher product price to compensate for higher unit costs or to have an average cost and accept a lower margin at the beginning, which would rise with the progression of the learning curve. The production costs of new aeroplanes are higher and decline as the output increases.

Proposals

A company putting forward a proposal for a project, or for a new order, in an area in which the company has little experience, may price it accordingly higher to take into account learning. This may make it uncompetitive with other firms. Alternatively, the company may be prepared to take a lower margin, or even a loss, in order to gain experience for future projects or sales. Pratt and Whitney and General Electric of the USA were prepared to take a loss when they quoted to supply Singapore Airlines with engines for its new twin-engine Boeing 777s, as this would have been a prestigious order that would have provided learning experience for future orders for the 777 aeroplane. However, the Singapore order went to Rolls-Royce.[19]

Purchasing

Assume that a company approaches a potential supplier to purchase a product that the supplier has not furnished before, simply because the product is entirely new (military components, telecommunications equip-

ment or a new chemical compound) or because the product, although on the market, is new to the supplier. In this case, components supplied earlier will take longer to produce (and cost more) because new procedures and methods need to be employed. However, as more and more of the products are produced, the unit cost will decrease. From a purchasing point of view, this might mean that the client company pays more at the early stages of supply than later. That is, the client has to pay for the 'learning' process.

Real-world illustrations

In the past, the learning curve has been demonstrated in the following real situations.

Computer chip production

Figure 8.8 shows how the unit price of computer chips fell in the period 1978 through 1984. This experience process had the result that the price of personal computers decreased enormously.[20]

The Price of the Model T Ford

The Model T Ford was the automobile introduced by Henry Ford in the early part of this century (see page 194) and Figure 8.9 shows its learning curve with a slope of approximately 85 per cent.[21] The Model T Ford benefited from the experience curve for close to two decades, but an inflexible devotion to the vehicle proved the company's downfall when the car became obsolete.[22]

Other US industry

Table 8.5 gives other real illustrations of the learning curve concept.[23]

Figure 8.8   Seventy per cent experience curve for dynamics RAMs.

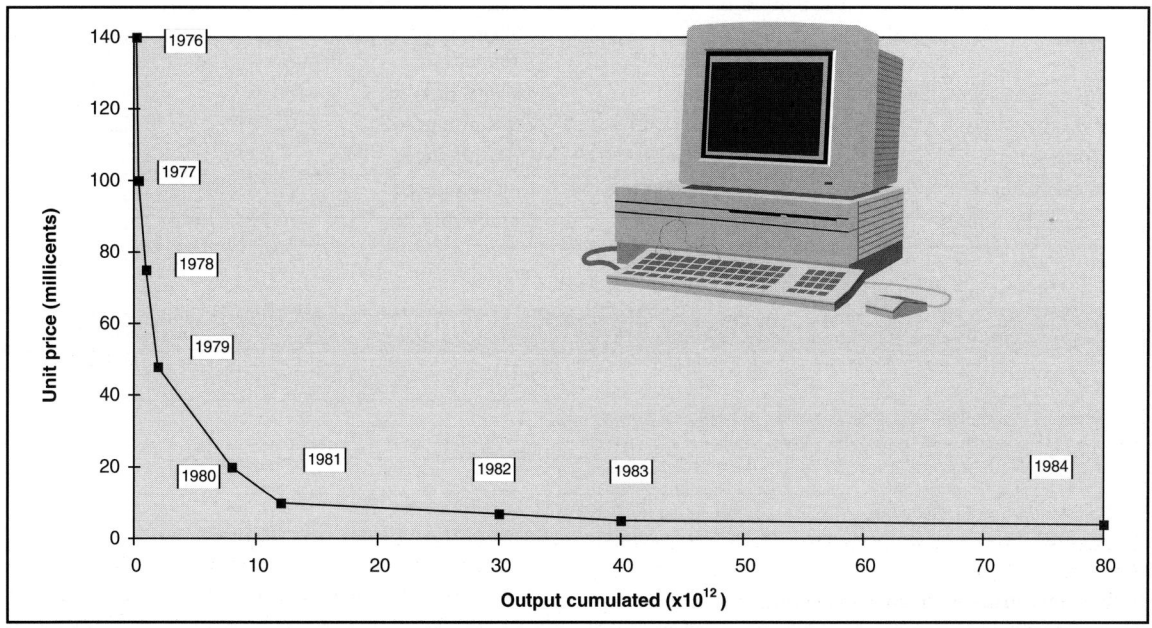

Figure 8.9   Price of a Model T Ford: 1909–1923 (average list price in 1958 $US).

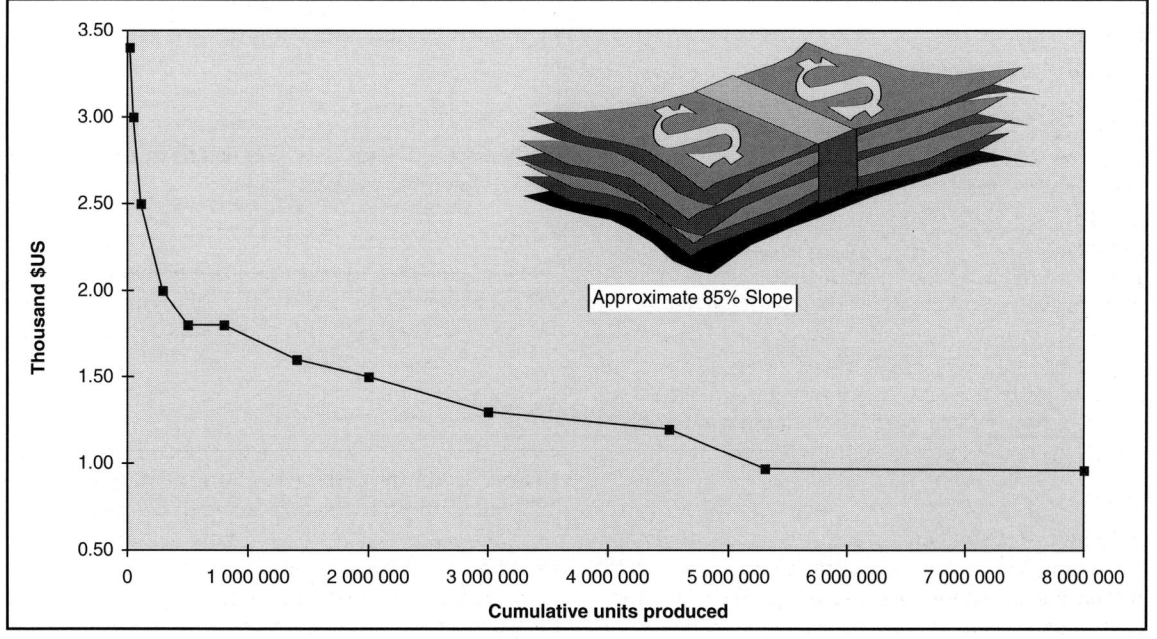

Table 8.5 Real illustrations of the learning curve concept

Operation	Parameter decreased	Cumulative	Rate (per cent)	Period
Aircraft assembly	Direct unit labour hours	Units produced	80	1925–1957
Equipment maintenance at GE	Average time to replace group of parts	Number of replacements	76	Around 1957
Oil refinery	Labour hours per barrel refined	Millions of US barrels refined	84	1860–1962
Electric power generation	Cost per kWh	Millions of kWh	95	1910–1955
Steel production	Production hours per unit	Units produced	79	1920–1955
Integrated circuits	Average price per unit	Units produced	72	1964–1972
Hand calculator	Average factory selling price	Units produced	74	1975–1978
Computer disk drives	Average price per bit	Number of bits	76	1975–1978

WORKED EXAMPLE: TURBINES

Situation

The Government of Saudi Arabia is developing a desalination and energy complex in the country. For this project a certain number of special turbines are needed to operate in a region where there are often sand storms. The Saudi Government has a contract with a manufacturer in Sweden to manufacture the turbines. The first turbine built for the first phase of the project took the manufacturer 18 000 labour hours to assemble. The Saudi Government has an option to purchase 20 similar turbines.

The average labour rate for the manufacturing company is US $32.00/hour. The cost of the product is calculated using this labour rate. Based on past experience, the company has a 75 per cent learning rate. In addition, it expects to make a 40 per cent margin on the sale of these turbines to the Saudi Government. This margin is calculated individually on each turbine, not averaged.

Required

1. Develop a learning curve for the turbine production in terms of labour hours up to a production of 20 turbines.
2. For five turbines, what is:
   (a) The average manufacturing time per unit?
   (b) The average cost per unit?
   (c) The average purchase price per unit that the Saudi Government expects to pay if it benefits from the learning curve concept?
   (d) The total profit to the manufacturing company?
3. If the Saudi Government exercised its option for all 20 units, then what is:
   (a) The average manufacturing time per unit?
   (b) The average cost per unit?
   (c) The average purchase price per unit that the Saudi Government expects to pay if it benefits from the learning curve concept?
   (d) The total profit to the manufacturing company?

Solution

1. Learning curve. Figure 8.10 gives all the required data for the turbine manufacture and Figure 8.11 shows the corresponding learning curve. The slope of the curve b is calculated from the relationship

Figure 8.10 Learning curve – turbines for Saudi Arabia.

Average labour rate, $/hr	32.00
Learning rate	0.75
Profit margin	0.40

Slope, b	−0.42

$$margin = \frac{price-cost}{price}$$

Turbine No.	Unit basis						
	Time/unit	Cost/unit	Price/unit	Profit	Total profit	Total price	Margin
1	18 000.00	576 000.00	960 000.00	384 000.00	384 000.00	960 000.00	0.40
2	13 500.00	432 000.00	720 000.00	288 000.00	672 000.00	1 680 000.00	0.40
3	11 409.04	365 089.44	608 482.40	243 392.96	915 392.96	2 288 482.40	0.40
4	10 125.00	324 000.00	540 000.00	216 000.00	1 131 392.96	2 828 482.40	0.40
5	9 229.41	295 340.99	492 234.98	196 893.99	1 328 286.95	3 320 717.38	0.40
6	8 556.78	273 817.08	456 361.80	182 544.72	1 510 831.67	3 777 079.18	0.40
7	8 026.48	256 847.36	428 078.93	171 231.57	1 682 063.24	4 205 158.11	0.40
8	7 593.75	243 000.00	405 000.00	162 000.00	1 844 063.24	4 610 158.11	0.40
9	7 231.46	231 406.77	385 677.95	154 271.18	1 998 334.42	4 995 836.06	0.40
10	6 922.05	221 505.74	369 176.23	147 670.49	2 146 004.92	5 365 012.29	0.40
11	6 653.58	212 914.61	354 857.69	141 943.07	2 287 947.99	5 719 869.98	0.40
12	6 417.59	205 362.81	342 271.35	136 908.54	2 424 856.53	6 062 141.33	0.40
13	6 207.89	198 652.58	331 087.64	132 435.06	2 557 291.59	6 393 228.97	0.40
14	6 019.86	192 635.52	321 059.20	128 423.68	2 685 715.27	6 714 288.17	0.40
15	5 849.93	187 197.70	311 996.17	124 798.47	2 810 513.73	7 026 284.33	0.40
16	5 695.31	182 250.00	303 750.00	121 500.00	2 932 013.73	7 330 034.33	0.40
17	5 553.80	177 721.53	296 202.55	118 481.02	3 050 494.75	7 626 236.88	0.40
18	5 423.60	173 555.08	289 258.46	115 703.38	3 166 198.14	7 915 495.34	0.40
19	5 303.25	169 703.89	282 839.81	113 135.92	3 279 334.06	8 198 335.15	0.40
20	5 191.54	166 129.30	276 882.17	110 752.87	3 390 086.93	8 475 217.33	0.40

	Unit basis				
	Time/unit	Cost/unit	Price/unit	Profit	Total profit
Avg for 5	12 452.69	398 486.09	664 143.48	265 657.39	1 328 286.95
Avg for 20	7 945.52	254 256.52	423 760.87	169 504.35	3 390 086.93

$$b = \frac{\log_e L}{\log_e 2} = \frac{\log_e 0.75}{\log_e 2} = \frac{-0.2877}{+0.6931} = -0.4150$$

The manufacturing time per unit for each unit is calculated from the relationship:

$$T_n = T_1(n^b),$$

where T_1 is 18 000 hours, and T_n is the time for the nth unit. Results are as follows:

■ The cost per unit is $32 \times T_1(n^b)$

Figure 8.11   Learning curve for turbine manufacture.

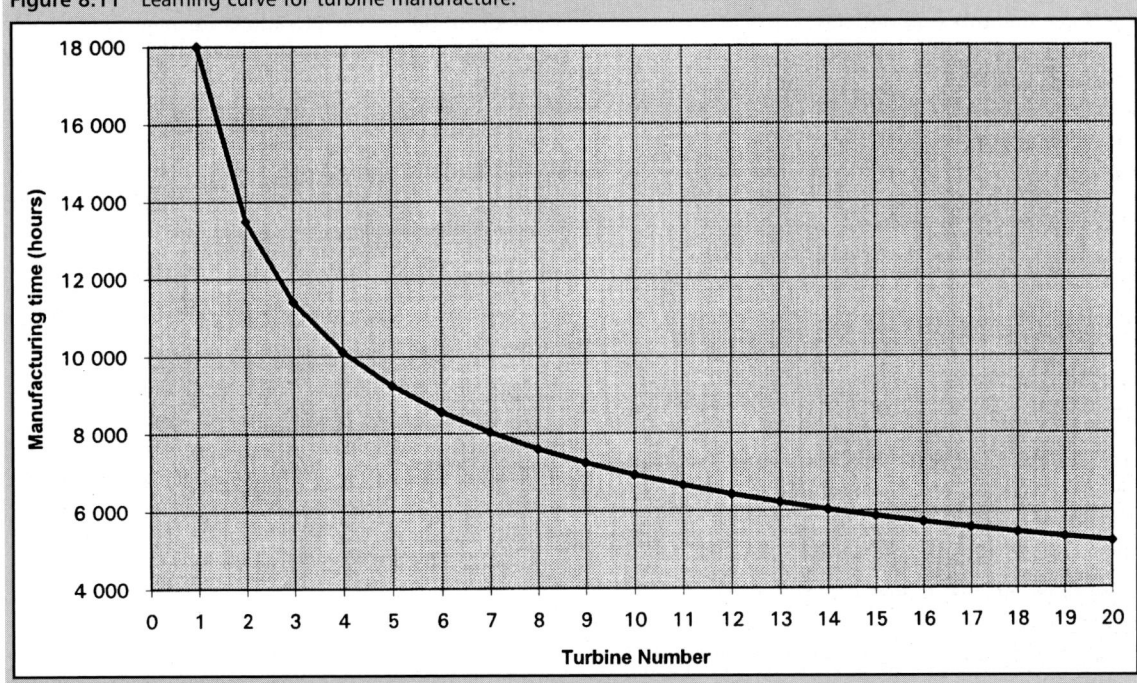

- The price per unit is $\dfrac{32 \times T_1\,(n^b)}{(1-0.4)}$ A 40 per cent margin is assumed for each unit.
- The margin is $\dfrac{(\text{Price} - \text{Cost})}{\text{Price}}$
- The total profit is (Price/unit – Cost/unit) × number of units.

2   For five turbines (figures are rounded up to nearest whole number):
   (a) The average manufacturing time per unit is 12 453 hours.
   (b) The average cost per unit is $398 486
   (c) The average purchase price per unit that the Saudi Government expects to pay if it benefits from the learning curve concept is $664 143.

   (d) The total profit to the manufacturing company is $1 328 287.

3   For 20 turbines (figures are rounded up to nearest whole number):
   (a) The average manufacturing time per unit is 7945 hours.
   (b) The average cost per unit is $254 257.
   (c) The average purchase price per unit that the Saudi Government expects to pay if it benefits from the learning curve concept is $423 761.
   (d) The total profit to the manufacturing company is $3390 087.

PEOPLE AND CHANGE

The business environment

The business environment is constantly in a state of change, which is sometimes very abrupt and unexpected. These changes can have a big impact on human resources in the firm. Some illustrations follow.

Re-engineering

Companies are re-engineering or re-organizing their operations (see Chapter 7, *Process Design and the*

Operations Network). This re-engineering often results in downsizing, the 1990s euphemism for layoffs.

Relocating

Firms are moving facilities away from home countries to overseas low-cost sites, resulting in closures or significant staff reductions domestically.

Technology

Information technology is replacing many elements of human labour in, for example, telecommunications companies, banking and purchasing. Heavy use of computer systems in business is meaning that people are having to retrain in order to use the new technology. Some find this very difficult.

Early retirement

Loyal employees are being offered retirement at the age of 55. Many are unprepared either financially or psychologically.

Mergers and acquisitions

Companies are being merged, or acquired by others. The resulting new organization often means that there is duplication of positions, so that these have to be trimmed.

Stress and change

Organizational changes have a physiological impact, not only on the people who lose their employment, but also on those that remain. Stress situations may be prompted by concerns such as the following:

- Will I be the next to lose my job?
- Will I have to relocate to another area?
- Will I have more work, which means working more hours?
- Will I have to do more travelling and spend significant time away from my family?
- Will I have to take on more responsibilities than I am able to handle?
- Will my responsibilities and decision-making functions be reduced?
- Will my old skills become obsolete?
- Will I be pushed to leave my friends?
- Will I be capable of working under the new organizational system?

Managing change

Employees sensing change, or 'hearing it through the grapevine', try, if possible, to resist. During the period in which change is 'in the air', motivation and productivity drop. Some considerations for managing people during this upheaval are considered in the following sections.

Eliminate surprise situations

Avoid springing the sudden changes on employees by keeping them informed of why the changes are necessary, what the likely impact will be, etc.

Reduce the fear of loss

Make efforts to turn the negative sides of the change into positive aspects, such as:

- Learning new technological skills will be an interesting challenge.
- The new location has advantages over the present location (skiing, cheaper housing, better schools, etc.).
- The new head of the department likes to delegate responsibilities.

Management should openly sell the change

Sometimes non-management employees have difficulty grasping reasons for reorganization, making them very resistant. Management at all levels should demonstrate a positive attitude towards proposed changes in order to give encouragement to others. Middle management openly criticizing top management's decisions can only exacerbate the company stress level.

Plant closure

Employees' sharp reaction to change was violently illustrated in March 1997 when Renault, facing big losses for 1996, unveiled plans to shut down its plant in Vilvoorde, Belgium, in July 1997 as part of a broad reorganization of its European production facilities. (Box 8.3)[24]

Box 8.3 Vilvoorde, Belgium

The closing at Vilvoorde, home of Belgian Prime Minister Jean-Luc Dehaene, provoked outrage in Belgium and across Europe because it appeared that Renault, though majority-owned by private investors since last summer when a further sale of shares dropped the government's stake to 46 per cent, was sacrificing Belgian jobs to save French ones, and violating European Union rules on worker consultation. Angry employees occupied the plant, taking hostage some 4,000 finished cars, and in March an estimated 70 000 union members from around Europe converged on Brussels to protest that European integration has failed to protect workers. Last week, Belgium Renault employees blocked a Eurostar train to London and a TGV to Paris claiming they were 'symbols of the Europe of capitalism'.[25]

SUMMARY OF KEY ELEMENTS

- People are key in system design and operation. The worst scenario in human relations is a breakdown in communications, leading to a strike that has disastrous effects on revenues, customer relations and working environment.

- Working conditions have evolved considerably this century, but issues still remaining include equal pay for equal work, sexual harassment, race relations and sweatshop work. Conditions in some emerging economies are still poor.

- The scientific-management period, from about 1875 to 1925, treated work in a logical and scientific way. Frederick Taylor was the most prominent contributor in this area and the concept of *Taylorism* developed.

- The human-relations period put a more human side to the management of people. Notables in this area were Elton Mayo, Henry Gantt, Abraham Maslow, Frederick Herzberg, Douglas McGregor and Peter Drucker.

- Job design entails matching job tasks to individuals or work groups. An objective is to increase the organizational efficiency, with the parallel goal of making working conditions more agreeable. Job design encompasses job specialization, job rotation, job enlargement, job enrichment and empowerment. It must take into consideration women, ergonomics, skill levels and work schedules.

- The correct attitude towards employees can have a positive effect on productivity and costs. Communications, a proper working environment and clear company objectives are elements of a smooth working environment.

- When management makes decisions involving personnel, it is better to discuss these with the persons involved, rather than pushing the decision onto the employees.

- Part of work measurement involves machine and labour standards. Standards are needed for proposal development, scheduling, cost control, capacity planning, budgeting, comparing different operating methods and perhaps bonus schemes.

- A time-and-motion study is used to develop labour standards. It involves breaking a work assignment into its various components and timing each one to come up with a total cycle time. A standard time is then developed using qualitative considerations.

- The learning curve is based on an exponential relationship illustrating that the time to perform an activity decreases as the number of units produced increases. An 80 per cent learning curve means that as output doubles, the required labour hours per unit decline by 80 per cent.

- The learning-curve concept is a consideration in new product development, hiring new employees, proposal preparation and purchasing.

- People in organizations are constantly under stress, brought about by such factors as re-engineering, firms relocating, technological changes, forced early retirement, plant closures and mergers and acquisitions.

- In managing change leaders should 'level' with employees by avoiding surprise situations, reduce the fear of loss and openly sell the change to those concerned.

REVIEW AND DISCUSSION QUESTIONS

1 **Unemployment**. In the USA and the UK unemployment is about half that in France and Germany, even though the skill levels and the potential market are very similar. Discuss why you believe this is so. What are the 'people' elements that help to explain these differences.

2 **Child labour**. In developing countries, child labour is often used in mining, the clothing industry and assembly plants. Products produced are then sold to the West (Europe, Japan and the USA). Some people abhor this idea and say that one should boycott all products of child labour and firms that sell these products. Other people say that, if the children were not used in the working environment, they would end up in prostitution, where they would be worse off. What is your opinion? What can be done?

3 **Technology**. What impact do you think technology has on the learning curve? Justify your response with examples.

4 **Your life**. Has the learning-curve concept had any impact on your life, your activities, or your education? Are you able to quantify the learning?

5 **Activity and learning rate**. Which activity, for persons starting the first time, do you think would have the greatest learning rate:
   (a) an operator using CAD to turn out a number of designs;
   (b) a cashier and the number of clients he or she is able to handle;
   (c) an operator manually wiring the inside of a telephone?
   What other elements come into play in considering the learning rate?

6 **Price and the learning curve**. Because of the concept of the learning curve, firms may price high at the early

stages of the introduction of a product and then lower the price later as the learning curve levels out. What are the dangers of applying this principle? What are some of the advantages?

7 **International differences in learning curves**. A firm that has identical manufacturing facilities in two different countries may have different learning rates for the same work being performed. Give your reasons why this might be the case. What impact does this have on international firms that are looking for facilities overseas? Based on the information provided in Chapter 3, *Site Selection*, can you identify those regions that might have a faster learning rate?

8 **Purchasing and the learning curve**. What impact does the learning-curve concept have on the relationship between the supplier and the client? If there is a high rate of learning, how might this benefit the client and/or the supplier? Conversely, if there is a low rate of learning, how might this benefit the client and/or the supplier?

9 **Services and the learning curve**. Why is the impact of the learning curve not as marked as in manufacturing? What are some of the characteristics of a service organization that make the principle of the learning curve more complicated than in a manufacturing environment?

10 **Time-and-motion study**. You work for a unionized textile company in Europe and the business is struggling

because of competition from overseas and rising operating costs. Your boss has suggested that you organize a time-and-motion study of the activity on the manufacturing floor to understand exactly what is happening and to see if the standards developed some time back are still meaningful. How would you carry out a time-and-motion study in a manufacturing situation?

11 **The Working Week**. In the middle of 1997 the governments of both France and Italy proposed a 35-hour working week, to come into force by 2000. One of their aims was to reduce the level of unemployment, at that time hovering around 12 per cent of the work force, by limiting the hours people work. What are your comments about this idea? Look at the impact on both the firm and the human resources.

12 **Services**. Carl Franklin Braun (1884–1954) founded a successful engineering design and construction company in California in 1909. This firm, in a campus-like setting, owned and operated its own restaurant and its own garden service, printed its own books and journals, maintained its employees' cars and had its own medical centre. What is different in firms today? Why do you think there are changes in the way companies manage this type of services? What has sometimes been the impact on human relations when this paternal employer–employee bond ceases to exist?

EXERCISE PROBLEM: CHAIRS FOR THE CHATEAU

Situation

A group of doctors bought a 16th century chateau in Clermond-Ferrand, France, which they planned to rent out for banquets, for weddings and as a conference centre. They wanted to refurbish the chateau exactly how it was when it was first constructed and so they searched for various artisans to manufacture the furniture. This was quite difficult because the number of artisans in the area was limited. They found one artisan who could make straight-backed wooden chairs with woven straw tops, an artisan who could make upholstered armchairs and an artisan who could make armoires. The labour cost for all the artisans was 38 FF/hour.

Required

1 The artisan for the straight-backed chairs took 20 hours for the first chair and 18 hours for the second.
   (a) What is the learning rate?
   (b) Develop a learning curve for the production of 120 chairs – the requirement of the chateau owners.
   (c) How long does it take to make the 20th chair?
   (d) What is the total cost for the full production of the chairs?
   (e) If the artisan wishes to make a margin of 10 per cent on each chair that is made, what would be the price of the total number of chairs to the chateau owners?
   (f) If the artisan wishes to make a margin of 10 per cent on the total lot of chairs, what would be the price to the chateau owners?

2 The artisan for the upholstered chairs took 35 hours for the first chair. His learning rate was 80 per cent.
   (a) Develop a learning curve for the production of 50 upholstered chairs – the requirement of the chateau owners.
   (b) How long does it take to make the 20th upholstered chair?
   (c) What is the total cost for the full production of the upholstered chairs?
   (d) If this artisan wishes to make a margin of 15 per cent on each upholstered chair that is made, what would be the price of the total number of chairs to the chateau owners?
   (e) If the artisan wishes to make a margin of 15 per cent on the total lot of upholstered chairs, what would be the price to the chateau owners?

3 The artisan for the armoires chairs took 40 hours for the second armoire. His learning rate is 85 per cent.
   (a) How long did it take to make the first armoire?
   (b) Develop a learning curve for the production of 20 armoires – the requirement of the chateau owners.
   (c) How long does it take to make the 20th armoire?
   (d) What is the total cost for the full production of armoires?
   (e) If this artisan wishes to make a margin of 20 per cent on each armoire that is made, what would be the price of the total number of armoires to the chateau owners?
   (f) If the artisan wishes to make a margin of 20 per cent on the total lot of armoires, what would be the price to the chateau owners?

EXERCISE PROBLEM: AEROPLANE ENGINES

Situation

A certain aeroplane manufacturer has developed a new twin-engine aeroplane. In parallel with the work, it offered a contract to an engine manufacturer to build a commercial prototype of a new aircraft engine. This commercial prototype of the engine took 55 000 labour hours. The airline company that is going to purchase this new plane has an option on 25 planes.

The average labour rate for the engine manufacture, including the design engineers, is $38.00/hour. The cost of the engine is calculated using this labour rate. Based on past experience, the engine company has an 80 per cent learning rate. In addition, it expects to make a 25 per cent margin on the sale of these engines to the aeroplane manufacturer. This margin is calculated individually on each engine, not averaged.

Required

1 Develop a learning curve for the engine production in terms of labour hours up to the maximum production expected if the airline company exercises its full option.

2 For 12 engines, what are the following:
   (a) Average manufacturing time per unit?
   (b) Average cost/unit?
   (c) Average purchase price/unit that the aeroplane manufacturer expects to pay if it benefits from the learning curve concept?
   (d) Total profit to the engine manufacturer?

3 If the airline company exercises its option for all 25 planes, then what are the following:
   (a) Average manufacturing time per unit?
   (b) Average cost/unit?
   (c) Average purchase price per unit that the aircraft manufacturer expects to pay if it benefits from the learning curve concept?
   (d) Total profit to the engine manufacturing company?

CASE STUDY: LAMSON & SESSION'S CO.'S PLASTICS FACTORY

Situation

The article in Box 8.4 illustrates a real-world situation in relationships with people.[26]

Box 8.4 *Life at the factory*. Full time, part time, temp – all see the job in a different light. Pay, loyalty and status vary in flexible work force in U.S., and strains show. Toolbox as emblem of power. By Timothy Aeppel, *Staff Reporter*

BOWLING GREEN, Ohio – There isn't supposed to be a seniority system in Lamson & Sessions Co.'s plastics factory on the outskirts of this college town. But don't try telling that to Robert Wendel.

His assignment today includes relieving co-workers at the various molding machines while they go to lunch. But as he tells one woman when he can cover for her, she snaps back that she decides when she eats. He rearranges his schedule.

"Did I mess up?" he asks, looking nervously at Dawnna DeVries, one of the plant's two full-time trainers and a sort of unofficial shepherdess for new hires.

Mrs. DeVries smiles and urges him to be tougher next time. "The one who wins around here is the one who doesn't back down," she says.

So much for workplace harmony.

Five Groups of Workers

Operating round the clock, the plant has five categories of workers, mostly women. It has about 90 full-time, permanent employees; approximately 40 of them stand in front of bus-size molding machines that thump out items such as the plastic boxes that hold the guts of light switches in walls. It

also has 40 temporaries, who operate the machines, too. In addition, it has 70 independent contractors who work outside the facility. And it has people who work only in summer and others who work part time.

Such flexibility is becoming more common in some types of manufacturing in the U.S., especially in fast-growing, nonunion plants such as this. It helps a company in a cyclical business meet ebbs and flows of demand. It also appeals to single mothers and college students. Lamson & Sessions considers the Bowling Green factory one of its best plants, even though such an arrangement complicates the dynamics of the work force and can generate conflicts.

Each group of workers views the job differently and feels varying degrees of loyalty. And even within a single group there are divisions, mainly among the full-time workers who have more invested in the job. Those who once held union jobs stick together in disputes over speeding up the molding machines. Those doing repetitive, tedious tasks clash with a small elite, the all-male technicians who change the molds and keep the machinery running.

Some Dissension

The Cleveland-based company strives to get all these people to mesh smoothly, but not always with complete success.

"We get a lot of people in here who act brain-dead," complains one permanent worker, Nancy Lein, tapping her forehead with a finger and referring to people standing at other machines less than seven meters away, doing the same work but employed as temporaries. "You got to keep that thing clear," Ms. Lein notes, pointing to a bin at the end of a conveyor belt at a nearby temp's machine. The bin is starting to overflow with parts.

Turnover among newcomers runs as high as 40% a month. As a result, workers such as Ms. Lein are constantly teaching new people tricks, such as picking up four parts in each hand simultaneously to examine them for faults. Turnover among permanent workers is under 1%.

The plant arrived at its present work-force structure through an often-bumpy evolution. When it opened in 1989, in the empty hulk of a former plastic-pipe plant, it had just one molding machine and 12 workers. It had no reason to call them permanent; employees were employees.

Several Advantages

After that, everyone who began working at the plant started out as a temporary despite having the same shifts and doing the same jobs. That system holds down costs because temps, as employees of an agency, don't get the same benefits or pay, and the managers can preview their skills before making a commitment to hire them. It also avoids layoffs of permanent workers when business slumps. But it sparks a classic us-vs.-them clash, of a kind usually dividing management and workers.

Involved most frequently in clashes are the temps. Although they make up half of the 80 operators, the core group that runs machines and packs boxes, and they work alongside the others, their pay is far lower. They get only $6.50 an hour, while permanent operators earn $8.60 to $11.19 an hour, plus benefits and a toolbox.

Toolboxes are emblems of power. When an operator wins permanent status, the company gives him or her a black plastic case stuffed with things such as Exacto knives and pliers. Many decorate the inside of the lids with pictures of their children and spouses, then prop them open on the edge of their workbenches so they can glance at them while working.

Moreover, permanent workers get something less tangible but more significant: They vote on which temps join their ranks. The system makes some sense. They work alongside the temps, see their work habits and attitudes and train them.

"That one over there's definitely going to make it, you can just tell," says Becky Clements, a 30-year-old permanent worker, pointing across the factory floor to a man holding a part up to the light and shaving off excess plastic with a knife.

Then she points down the corridor to a woman wearing a baseball cap and a dour expression. "That's the other extreme," she says. "She's got a bad attitude."

To do the job right, workers must learn a lot of tiny, repetitive tasks. Operators are assigned each day to one of 16 molding machines. The same machine may make different parts each day, depending on which mold is running in it.

"Most of the people in here aren't enjoying themselves; they're enduring," says Michelle Toney, a temp. Today, she is assembling cartons and pushing them to end of a conveyor belt, where parts plop directly into the boxes. When the boxes are filled, she drags them off and seals them for shipping. Unlike the woman next to her, Karen Diedrick, Mrs. Toney isn't hoping to graduate to a permanent slot; she is waiting for a job to open up at a unionized pudding factory nearby.

But Mrs. Diedrick wanted a permanent job, mainly for the extra money. She wanted it so badly that when she caught her hand in a bagging machine on one of her first days at work, she made a point of returning from the hospital to finish her shift. "Three hours in the emergency room," she says, holding up her hand to show a jagged scar. "The only tough part was working with my hand bandaged," adds the 34-year-old mother of two. Her dedication paid off: Last month, she became a permanent employee.

Futile Tactics

"Some people try to make it a popularity contest," comments Gary Keel, the plant's office manager. They offer to buy permanent workers coffee, for instance, or often volunteer for overtime. But Mr. Keel says such people seldom make it. "They're good at trying to be everybody's friend, but they can't make a part worth a damn, and the other people see that."

Plant managers acknowledge the difficulty of having so many temporaries, mainly because of rapid turnover. About half the temps leaving each month are told not to come back, because of poor attendance or inability to keep up with the work pace. In this area of Ohio, however, they can always go elsewhere: Local unemployment was only 4.7% in January.

The temps don't hurt product quality, says James Zechinati, the plant manager, because the work is double-checked.

But with less vested in the job, they sometimes create annoying glitches. Some newly hired temps have stalked out after a few hours or never come back after lunch. Others leave machines messy at the end of a shift or pocket expensive tools.

Temps themselves say they dislike the open-ended nature of their employment. They have no clear idea how long they may wait for a permanent slot to open up, and they may be nominated several times before making it – if at all. "You feel jerked around," says Lu Ann Welch, a 38-year-old permanent worker who spent 14 months as a temp before moving up.

Eva Harter, who recently found out that she is entering the promised land of permanent employment after five months as a temp, has bitter memories of her initiation. Shortly after starting as a temp, she was in the vending-machine room when a permanent worker – though once a temp herself – began talking loudly. "She went on and on about how temps make so many mistakes, they're dumb, the whole thing," the 56-year-old says. "She knew I was sitting there."

The Independent Contractors

Surprisingly, the issue of independent contractors, a source of much labor unrest elsewhere, stirs up less conflict. The plant started using them in 1995 to replace some bottom-rung employees who did tasks such as screwing together parts and putting them in bags.

One of the contractors is Carla Tiell, 26, the mother of two girls. She carts home boxes of parts, assembles them and brings them back a week later, earning about $100 for groceries. "I can do this at my own pace, while watching TV or between loads of laundry," she says. Because contractors aren't covered by the factory's insurance, she isn't allowed inside the plant but doesn't care and doesn't feel excluded.

Workers in the plant don't view contractors as interlopers, mainly because no one lost jobs to them. The people who did that work were promoted to better jobs as operators and ultimately earned more money. Because the plant is nonunion, there was no organized opposition to the change. And nepotism helps: Relatives of current workers get preference in obtaining outside assembly work.

Anyway, much of the friction occurs within the various groups. Permanent employees who need to go on part-time because of medical conditions often leave at midday, causing headaches for other permanent employees, who usually end up manning two machines for the rest of the shift. There is also a strong but largely unspoken division between those who support the notion of unionizing and those who don't. One pro-union worker, who resents the long work shifts and a program to speed up machines, keeps her anger to herself for fear of being fired or badmouthed by colleagues. "They would get rid of us and replace us," she says.

Another battle goes on between the operators, two-thirds of whom are women, and the crew of about 20 technicians, all men. (The plant once had two female technicians, but one left the company and the other switched to quality-control work because she wanted better hours.) The technicians, who change molds and keep the machines running smoothly, earn $11.59 to $12.70 a hour. They stride through the factory wearing headphones to talk to each other – adding to their aura of an exclusive fraternity.

Tension With Technicians

Many women complain that the technicians go out of their way to make them feel stupid when they call for help when a machine breaks down. The women also believe that because many technicians never worked as operators, they have no idea how difficult the job actually is.

Required

Discuss the situation presented in the terms of the product, the process and the people. Using the concepts presented in this chapter, present what you believe are improvements that could be made.

Suddenly, a bell goes off on the press Ms. Clements is operating. She tries unjamming it without success, then dials the intercom for help. When Erwin Szafraniec arrives, he sweeps past her without a word and fiddles with her press. He vanishes and comes back with more tools.

"Going to change the mold?" she asks.

"Yup," he says.

"Thanks for telling me," she replies, her voice thick with sarcasm.

However, Steve Holderman, another technician, says the operators sometimes ask for trouble by, for example, stuffing too many scraps of plastic into a grinder and jamming it. "Sure, I get frustrated and even swear sometimes," he says. "But I always look away so nobody can hear."

Plant managers say such tension is inevitable in any factory, especially when companies need different mixes of people to match changes in demand. Of course, management must be flexible itself in creating a flexible workplace.

About a year after the plant opened, it had 30 employees and was ready to go to a seven-day-a-week schedule. The company tried creating a separate, part-time class of workers just for weekends, assuming farmers' wives and college students would want the jobs. But the wives weren't interested, and the students were too undependable, especially when they wanted to go to a big dance or had exams. So the disastrous experiment was dropped, though the plant still hires a dozen or so college students in summer when demand for construction-related products soars.

"I forgot what I knew in college," says Mr. Keel, the office manager. "You party on the weekend. We're flexible, but even we couldn't deal with that."

Wall Street Journal, 19 March 1997
Reprinted by permission of *Wall Street Journal Europe*,
© 1997 Dow Jones & Company, Inc.
All Rights Reserved Worldwide.

NOTES AND REFERENCES

1. 'Challenge of the 1990s: Renault Strike shows the need to transform relations with labour. To compete with Japanese, Europeans have to learn to co-operate in factories. Of disruptions and disasters' (1991) *Wall Street Journal Europe* 19 November.
2. 'The Dearing Report' (1997) *The Economist* 4 October:11. Universities Survey.
3. *Business Week* (1996) 9 December.
4. *Business Week* (1996) 18 November.
5. 'Stamping out sweatshops: Dress code' (1997) *The Economist* 19 April: 54.
6. 'Keep the Heat on Sweatshops' (1996) *Business Week* 23 December.
7. Babbage, C. (1832) *On the Economy of Machinery and Manufacturers*, London [Modern editor (1993) London: Routledge/Thoemmes.].
8. Smith, A (1776) *An Inquiry in the Nature and Causes of the Wealth of Nations*, Adam Smith, London: A. Straham and T. Cadell. [Modern edition (1990) Chicago, London: Encyclopedia Brittanica.]
9. Taylor, F. W. (1911) *Principles of Scientific Management*, New York: Harper and Brothers. [Modern edition (with Shop Management) (1993) London: Routledge/Thoemmes]
10. Roethlisberger, F. J. and Dickson W. J. (1939) *Management and the Worker*, Cambridge, MA: Harvard University Press.
11. Certo, S. C. (1989), *Principles of Modern Management: Functions and Systems (4th edn)*, Boston, MA: Allyn and Bacon. pp 36-38. [Fifth edition: *Modern Management: Quality, Ethics and the Global Environment* (1992) Boston: Allyn and Bacon.]
12. Maslow, A. H (1943) 'A theory of human motivation', *Psychological Review*, 50: 370-96.

13. Herzberg, F, Mausner, B. and Snyderman B.B (1965) *The Motivation to Work*, New York: John Wiley & Sons.

14. McGregor D. (1960), *The Human Side of Enterprise*, New York: McGraw Hill.

15. Drucker, P., Smiddy, H., and Greenwood, R. G. (1981) 'Management by Objectives', *Academy of Management Review* 6 (April): 225.

16. *The Economist* (1997) 15 February: 49.

17. 'Empowerment that pays off. Chrysler gives power to its people, and the result is a string of hot cars and record earnings. But CEO Robert Eaton still isn't satisfied' (1995) *Fortune*, 20 March: 95.

18. 'Facts through figures' (1996) *Eurostat*, Luxembourg: Statistical Office of the European Community.

19. 'Aircraft engines: Rolls-Royce flies high', *The Economist* 28 June: 79.

20. Ghemawat, P. (1985) 'Building strategy on the experience curve', *Harvard Business Review* March-April: 143-49.

21. Abernathy, W. J. and Wayne K. (1974) 'Limits of the learning curve', *Harvard Business Review* September-October: 109-19.

22. 'Riding the experience curve', (1976) *Technology Review* March-April: 53-59.

23. Cunningham, J. A. (1980) 'Using the learning curve as a management tool' *IEEE Spectrum* June: 45.

24. 'Renault to axe Belgian plant, take $421.1 million charge' (1997) *Wall Street Journal Europe* 28 February/1 March.

25. 'A road to nowhere? Renault's troubles typify a European car-making industry where profits are low and problems high' (1997) *Time* 7 April.

26. Aeppel, T. 'Life at the Factory. Full time, part time, temp – all see the job in a different light'. (1997) *Wall Street Journal Europe* 19 March.

FURTHER READING

Armstrong, P. and Dawson, C. (1989) *People in Organisations*, Huntingdon: Elm.

Eisenhardt, K. J (1997) 'Effective training: Timing is everything', *Harvard Business Review* 75(3): 13-14.

Freeman, M. G. (1996) 'Don't throw scientific management out with the bathwater', *Quality Progress* 29(4): 61-64.

Frey, R. (1993) 'Empowerment or else', *Harvard Business Review* 71(5): 80-94.

Graham, H.T. (1992) *Human Resources Management*, London: Pitman.

Heifetz, R. A. and Laurie, D. L. (1997) 'The work of leadership', *Harvard Business Review*. 75(1): 124-34.

Karuppan, C. M. (1997) 'Advance manufacturing technology and stress: Technology and management support policies', *International Journal of Technology Management* 14(2,3,4): 254-64.

Li, G. and Rajogopalan, S. (1997) 'The impact of quality on learning', *Journal of Operations Management* 15(3): 181-91.

Malone, T. W. (1997) 'Is empowerment just a fad? Control, decision making, and IT', *Sloan Management Review* 38(2): 23-35.

Mazzola, J. B. and McCardle, K. F. (1997) 'The stochastic learning curve: Optimal production in the presence of learning-curve uncertainty', *Operations Research* 45(3): 440-50.

Niebel, B. (1993) *Motion and Time Study*, Homewood, IL: Irwin.

Megginson, L. C. (1968) *Human Resources: Cases and Concepts*, New York: Harcourt Brace and World.

Norman, R. and Presley-Noble, B. (1993) 'Reinventing labour: An interview with Union President, Lynn Williams', *Harvard Business Review* 71(4): 115-25.

Parnell, C. (1997/8) 'Teamwork: Not a new idea, but it's transforming the workplace', *Executive Speeches* 12(3): 35-40.

Peterson, P. B. (1986) 'Correspondence from Henry L. Gantt to an old friend reveals new information about Gantt', *Journal of Management* 12(3): 339–50.

Peterson, P. B. (1987) 'Training and development: The views of Henry L. Gantt (1861–1919)', *Advance Management Journal* 52(1): 20–23.

Pickard, J. (1997) 'A Yearning for Learning', *People Management* 3(5, 6): 34-35.

Schamp, J. (1997) 'North German operator uses learning curve to improve horizontal drilling techniques', *Oil and Gas Journal* 95(48): 69-85.

Strebel, P. (1996) 'Why do employees resist change?', *Harvard Business Review* 74(3): 86-92.

Sweeny, J. (1996) 'Give workers a voice', *Harvard Business Review* 74(5): 124.

Sweetman, K. M, Kahwajy, J. L. and Bourgeois, L. J. III (1997) 'How management teams can have a good fight', *Harvard Business Review* 75(4): 77-85.

Wasmuth, W. J., Simonds, R. H., Hilgert, R. and Lee, H. C. (1970) *Human Resources Administration: Problems of Growth and Change,* Boston: Houghton Mifflin.

'Jobs for life, why Japan won't give them up: When recession struck, Western doomsayers started writing obits for lifetime employment. But the system is stronger than ever. Here's why,' (1995) *Fortune* 20 March.

'The trouble with teams: Togetherness has its perils' (1995) *The Economist* 14 January.

Part III.
Planning, organizing, and control

Once the operation is in place, an important phase is the continuous planning, organizing and control of the system. This is the purpose of the third part of this book, which deals with some of the core functions of operations and the associated supply chain. It starts with Chapter 9, *Forecasting the Customer Demand*, the function which sets in motion the whole operations activity. Subsequent chapters deal with the importance of the design of the facility layout, inventory management, the complete operations planning activity, from determining capacity levels through to material requirements planning, and operations scheduling. There are chapters on lean production and just-in-time, purchasing and subcontracting and the management of the supply chain. Chapter 18 deals with project management and its relations with operations. The final chapter covers reliability and maintenance, illustrating the factors necessary to keep operations running smoothly.

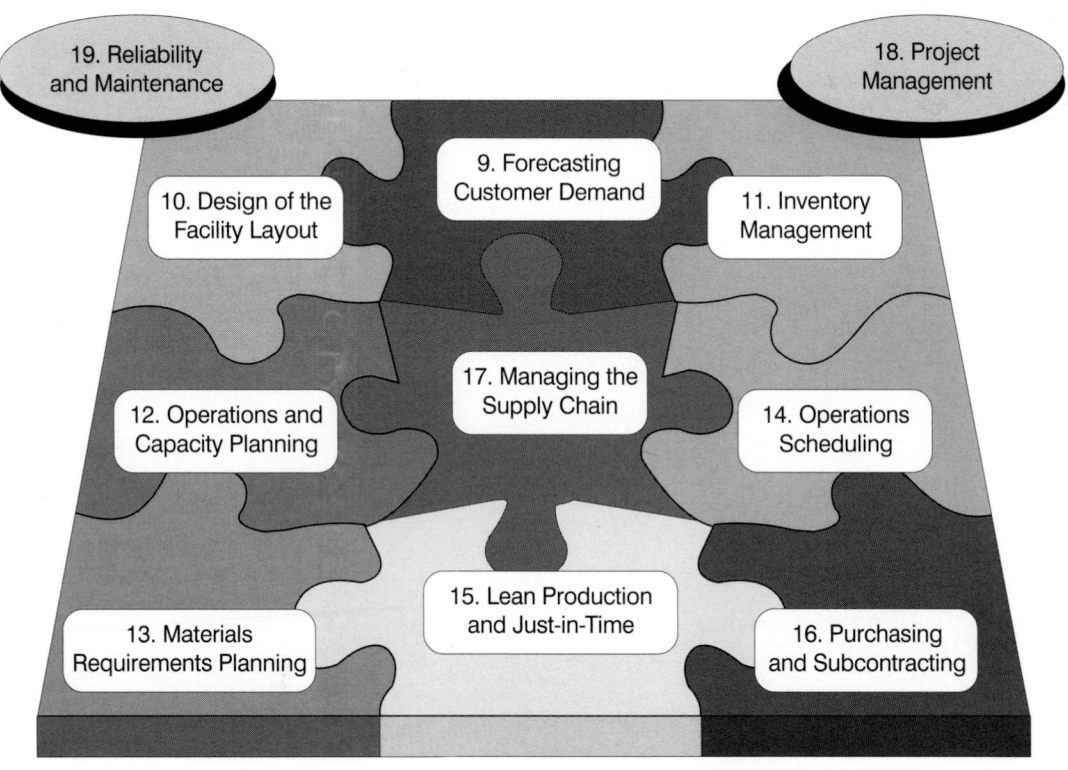

Part III Planning, organizing, and control

9 | Forecasting customer demand

Objectives and overview

The objective of this chapter is to describe the elements and importance of forecasting in the operations environment, which is the trigger that sets in motion the supply-chain activity. After the risks associated with forecasting, and the time horizons usually considered, the first half of the chapter is concerned with qualitative forecasting aspects. These include the roles played by top management, the sales force and purchasing agents. Then economic elements, which impact forecasts including leading indicators and macro- and micro-economic factors, are presented. Consumer surveys are then discussed. The second part of the chapter looks at some of the quantitative elements in forecasting, including time-series data and the components of interest. The chapter then considers forecasting models, including simple and weighted moving averages, exponential smoothing, simple linear regression with seasonal effects and linear modelling based on causal forecasting. The chapter closes by highlighting some of the elements that have to be considered in developing forecasting models.

THE CRITICAL NATURE OF FORECASTING

Forecasting in operations

Forecasting, or estimating, the demand for finished goods or services is the starting point for all operating activities. It is the trigger that sets the supply-chain in motion and includes the preparation of the following:

- capital budgets for plant and equipment and shorter term operating budgets;
- production plans;
- short-term operating cash requirements;
- personnel needs, full-time, part-time or perhaps on a contract basis;
- capacity levels of equipment, machines and buildings;
- purchase requirements of raw materials, components and services;
- plans for subcontractor requirements;
- transportation requirements for raw materials, finished goods and/or personnel.

Forecasting risks

Forecasting product or customer demand is probably one of the most inexact functions in management. One has to understand and evaluate the external environment, where there is considerable uncertainty, including the market, clients, and changing technology. Sloppy forecasting of client needs by the marketing department is often the reason for poor production planning and, as a result, contributes to friction between Marketing and Production personnel. In forecasting demand, one might be optimistic or make an estimate of demand higher than actually occurs. Alternatively, the forecast can be pessimistic, estimating a demand lower than actually occurs. In either case, there are risks and associated costs.

Optimistic forecast

A computer company estimates that it will sell 5 million units in one particular year. In reality, it only sells 3.5 million. The effect that this might have is:

- There is unnecessary inventory of finished goods and raw materials, together with associated high storage costs.

- Part of the inventory becomes obsolescent. Thus, the cost of the product cannot be retrieved.
- Plant capacity is used unnecessarily.
- The company is forced to sell the products at a marked down price, possibly below the marginal cost.

Pessimistic forecast

A computer company estimates that it will sell 5 million units in one particular year. In fact, it receives orders for 6.5 million. The impact is as follows:

- Stockouts occur, resulting in lost orders, which translates directly into lost profit and perhaps permanently lost customers.
- The production line is stopped, because there are insufficient raw materials.
- There are excessive costs from subcontracting, overtime and part-time labour as a result of trying to make up for the lost orders.

A situation like this happened in the computer industry in 1995. In January, analysts predicted that 1995 growth of personal-computer unit sales would slow to 15 per cent from the 20 per cent level in 1994. In fact, sales increased by as much as 30 per cent as consumers demanded more powerful machines to play the many new games that had appeared or to connect to or 'surf' the Internet. As a result, companies like Hewlett-Packard, Apple and Acer America Corporation fell short of components such as memory chips, CD-ROM drives and monitors, causing them to lose millions of dollars in sales and giving them a backlog of orders. Compaq Computer on the other hand had built up US$ 2 million in inventory and was largely able to satisfy its clients.[1]

Uncertainty

On balance, it is probably better to be optimistic with a forecast, rather than pessimistic. In the long term, continual stockout situations can cause clients to turn elsewhere for their products. Internally, repeated stockouts can be costly and employees can become demotivated.

TIME HORIZONS IN FORECASTING

Forecasts, or estimates, can be made over any time horizon. However, normally the shorter the period being considered, the more accurate is the forecast, since one is more certain of the variables involved. Illustrations of forecast elements over three time horizons would include short range, medium range and long range.

Short range

A short-range forecast is one for a time span of a few weeks, up to say about three months. It would include forecasting such items as:

- purchase transactions;
- cash requirements;
- work scheduling;
- workforce levels;
- job assignments;
- production levels.

Medium range

A medium-range forecast is one that covers between about three months up to one year. In this case it would include such items as:

- sales plans;
- production plans;
- capacity plans;
- operating cash budgets;
- management levels;
- subcontractor needs.

Long range

A long-range forecast is of about one to five years and would include:

- capital expansion plans;
- new investment;
- new product development;
- facility location;
- research and development programmes;
- strategic plans;
- implementing new technology;
- acquisitions.

The Delphi method

In 1948, the Rand Corporation, a consulting group of Santa Monica, California, developed the Delphi method for long-range forecasting. It was originally used to assess the potential impact of a nuclear bomb attack on the USA, but since has had uses in other long-range forecasting. In the Delphi approach there are three groups involved. There are the decision-makers, a group of five to ten experts, who prepare the final forecast. There are staff people, who assist the decision-makers by developing, diffusing, collecting and summarizing a set of questionnaires. The third group are the respondents, the people, often located in different places, whose judgements are valued and are being sought. This group provides inputs to the decision-makers before the final forecast is made. The state government of Alaska, USA, used the Delphi method to develop a long-range forecast for its economic future. The reason was that an enormous 90 per cent of the state budget is derived from 1.5 million barrels of oil pumped daily through the Prudhoe Bay oil pipeline.[2]

Variations of the time horizon

The category in which a type of forecast is placed very much depends on the type of industry and the country in which it is located. For example:

- It is easy to increase, or decrease, workforce levels in the USA and thus this element would be considered in a short-range horizon. However, in countries like Holland, France and Germany, it is more difficult to change workforce levels and so this would be considered in a medium-term horizon.
- A chemical company's time horizon is longer than that for, say, for a company that produces computer programs. Thus, time horizons for activities like purchasing, production or investment may be quite different.

QUALITATIVE FORECASTING

Qualitative, or judgemental, forecasting is forecasting based on assumptions, or intuitive estimates of those in the firm familiar with the market. This may include sales personnel, purchasing representatives or management people who all have close contact with the client. The accuracy of a qualitative approach depends on the good judgement, honesty and philosophy of the individuals concerned. Some considerations are discussed in the following sections.

Get to know the customer

Is the contact with, and the trust in, the client good? Qualitative estimates can be improved by working closely with the client. If clients can be encouraged to specify clearly their future needs, both parties win:

- Clients can be assured of obtaining their orders, on time, and perhaps at an attractive price.

- The supplier can plan his or her production needs better.

If the producer/supplier has several clients, perhaps some being overseas, a close association with all clients may not be possible. However, working closely with as many as possible would help to minimize the uncertainty, and therefore the corresponding risk.

Producing to demand

In terms of avoiding unnecessary inventory, producing to demand, that is setting up the production plan after the client has given his or her order, is less risky than producing to stock or making standardized products. However, firms producing to order need to be very flexible with their operations and to have low lead times in order to be competitive.

Sales bonus

The sales forecast may be skewed if the nature of the forecast impacts the remuneration of the individual. Consider a company that offers a bonus to sales people who exceed their sales quotas. For example:

- A bonus of five per cent is given above a certain base sales estimate.
- This base sales quota is established according to forecasts of expected sales. However, it is usually the sales people who have been involved in estimating expected sales, since it is part of their job!
- Thus, sales personnel may be pessimistic in making a forecast, because the lower the sales requirement, the easier it will be to obtain their base salary. In addition, the higher will be their bonus when the base sale is exceeded!

Understand the market

Markets can change rapidly and completely modify the demand for products. The sales of a product that has been performing well in the past may start to decline rapidly because of a change in 'fad', the desire of consumers or other events.

Hamburgers

McDonald's Fast Foods underestimated the impact of the health food movement in the USA in the 1970s. This fad drastically reduced the demand for beef, reducing the demand for hamburgers and pushed McDonald's to develop other meal choices, such as chicken nuggets, salads and fish.

Automobiles

The US 'Big-Three' automobile producers, General Motors, Chrysler and Ford, grossly underestimated the US demand for small automobiles in the USA in the late 1970s. This opened the door to Toyota, Nissan and others from the Asian countries, which sharply ate into the market of the Big Three.

Calculators

Manufacturers of slide rules, such as Faber Castell in Germany, underestimated the speed with which pocket calculators, initially introduced by Texas Instruments, would capture the market in the 1970s.

Tennis

The enthusiasm for tennis has waned for no really explainable reason. Thus, the market demand for tennis rackets, clothing, strings and products associated with the sport has declined.

Beef

The outbreak of bovine spongiform encephalopathy (BSE) or 'mad cow disease' in Britain in 1996 completely depressed the European demand for beef products.

Opinions of top management

Executives, senior managers and other business leaders have a prime interest in the business climate. They are responsible to their shareholders and need to respond to their employees regarding the outlook for employment conditions. They are also concerned to know at what level to increase, or decrease, capital expenditures. Since these executives are often in contact with other business leaders, or government representatives, they are in a good position to make general forecasts of future sales. In this respect Figure 9.1 illustrates the process of consolidation when vice presidents of various operating divisions have been in contact with the external environment.

Dun & Bradstreet of the USA makes regular quarterly surveys of business confidence. An example is shown in Figure 9.2, which gives the sales expectations of world business people for four consecutive quarters, starting from the third quarter 1993.[3] The figure shows the net percentage of business persons who expect higher sales (those expecting higher sales, less those expecting lower sales). In 12 of the 13 countries surveyed, the outlook for increased sales was positive. In the fourth quarter of 1994, Mexico's business persons were the most confident the optimists outnumbering pessimists by 82 per cent. For the same quarter,

Japan's business leaders were gloomy – the pessimists outnumbered optimists by 7 per cent.

The sales-force composite

The sales-force composite is a specific judgemental forecast for which opinions are solicited from line sales personnel at the regional level. The regional sales forecasts are then compiled at headquarters. This approach is illustrated in Figure 9.3, which shows how a company with headquarters in London, England would gather sales data from its country branches in England, France, and Germany. The country branches would themselves have collected data from their regional offices within the country concerned. Using the opinion of the sales force for compiling a forecast for future sales is:

- good in that line-sales are in touch with customers;
- misleading if used for salary/bonus system.

In addition, it may be difficult to break down the results on a product-by-product basis, since product models may be different for different countries.

Buyers' expectations

The use of buyers' expectations is when a manufacturer uses its sales people, or management staff, to solicit opinions from prospective purchasers about a new industrial product that is coming onto the market. This could be appropriate for such items as machine tools, haulage equipment, printing presses, computer programs or medical equipment. This type of forecasting is:

- easy if the firm has a good honest relationship with the customer (the purchaser of the product);
- not reliable in that it depends on the subjective feelings of the individual; is that person optimistic or pessimistic; in which case is the opinion representative of the entire company?

ECONOMIC INDICATORS IN FORECASTING

There are indicators in the economy that can be used to describe past, current or future macroeconomic conditions. The US government, for example, compiles leading, coincident and lagging indicators.[4]

Leading indicators

A leading indicator is one that reaches a high, or a low, before a related economic activity, as illustrated in Figure 9.4. As such, leading indicators can be important tools in forecasting. Examples follow.

Figure 9.1   Opinions of top management.

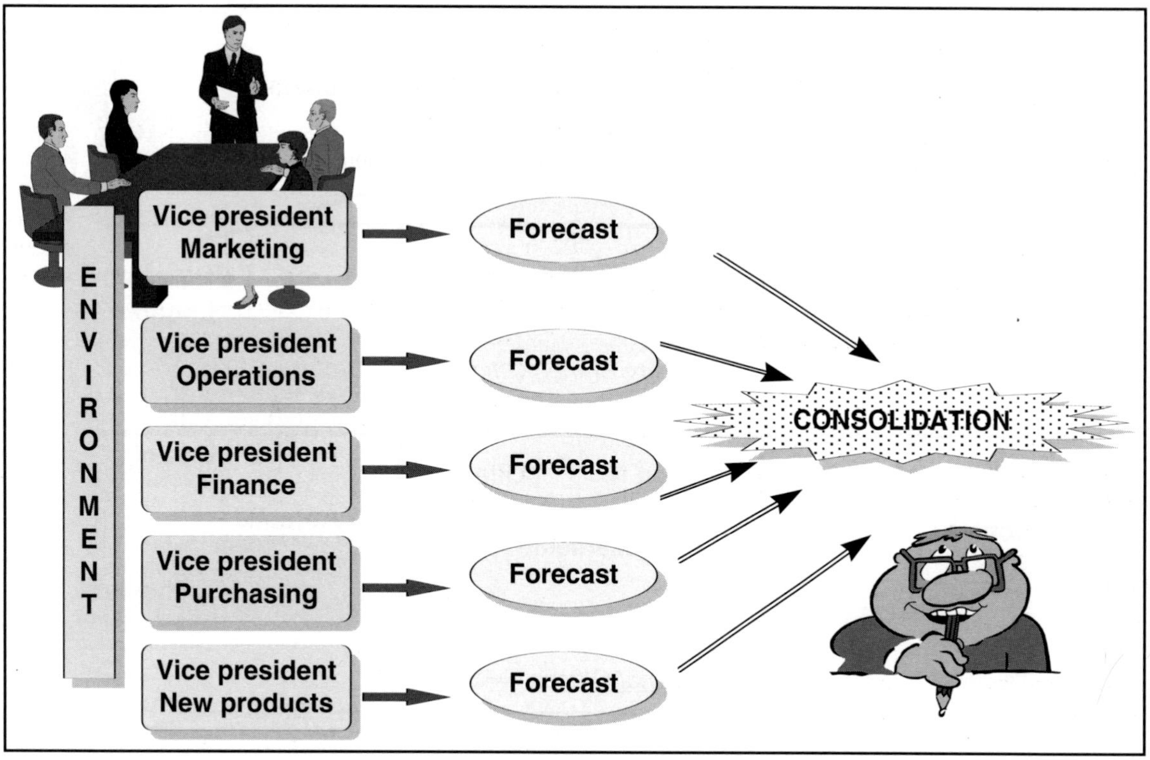

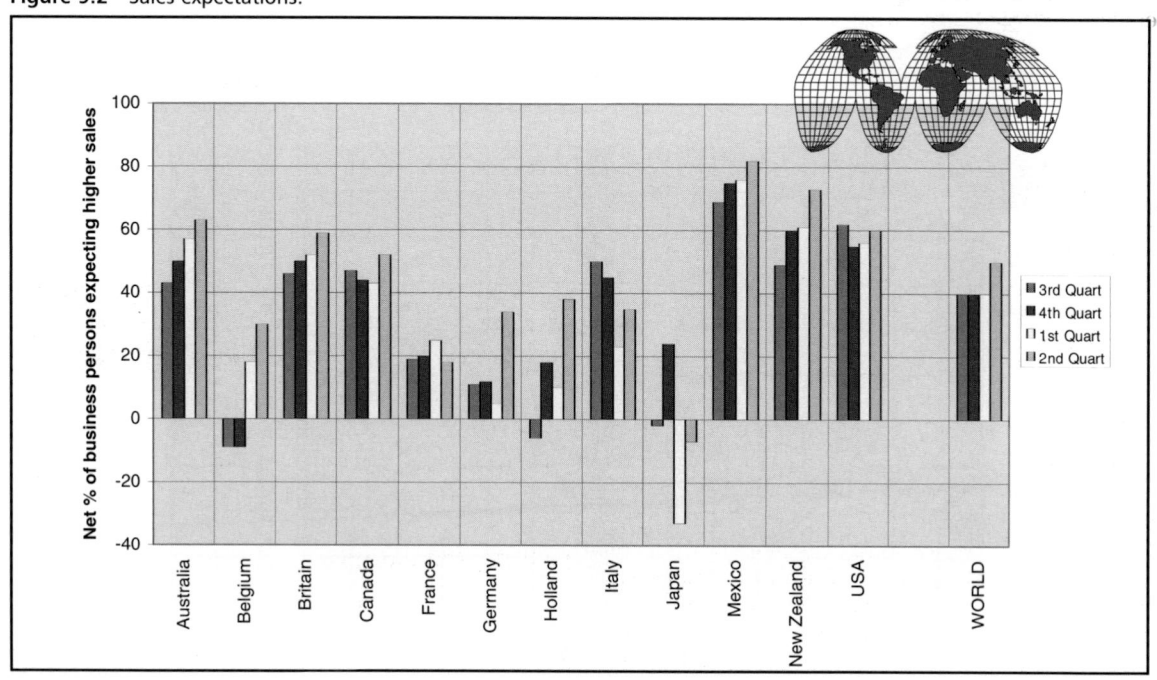

Figure 9.2   Sales expectations.

Figure 9.3 Opinions of sales force.

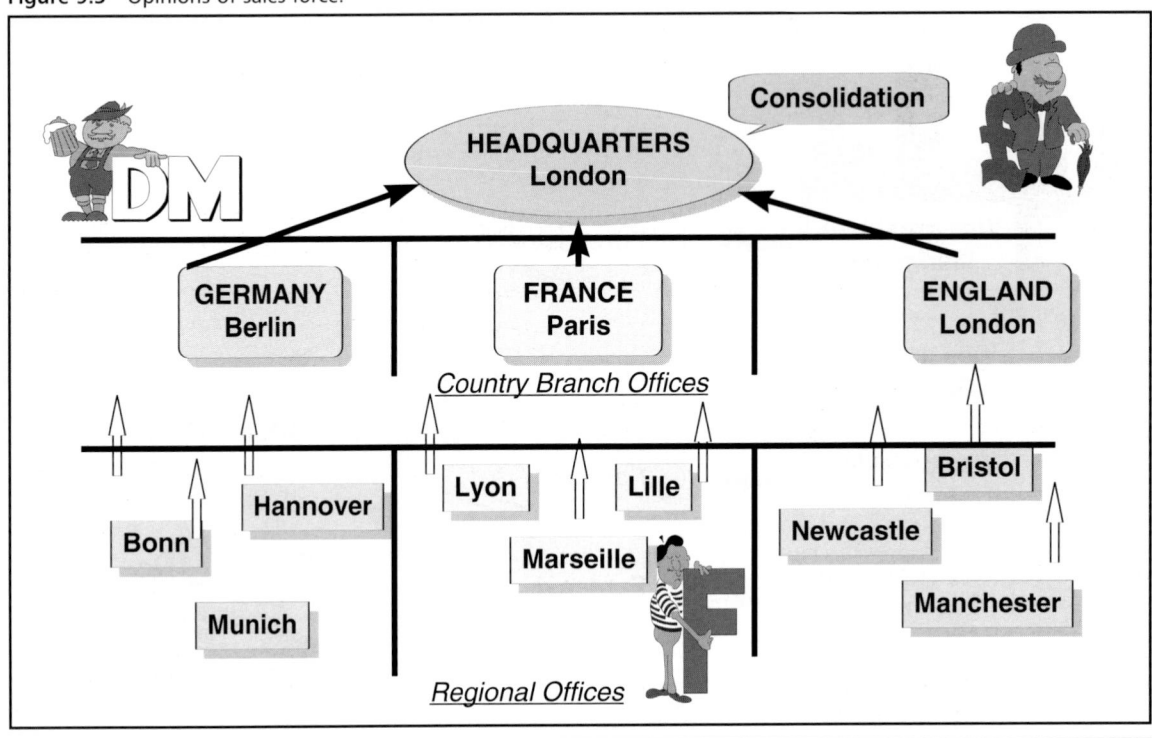

Figure 9.4 Leading economic indicators.

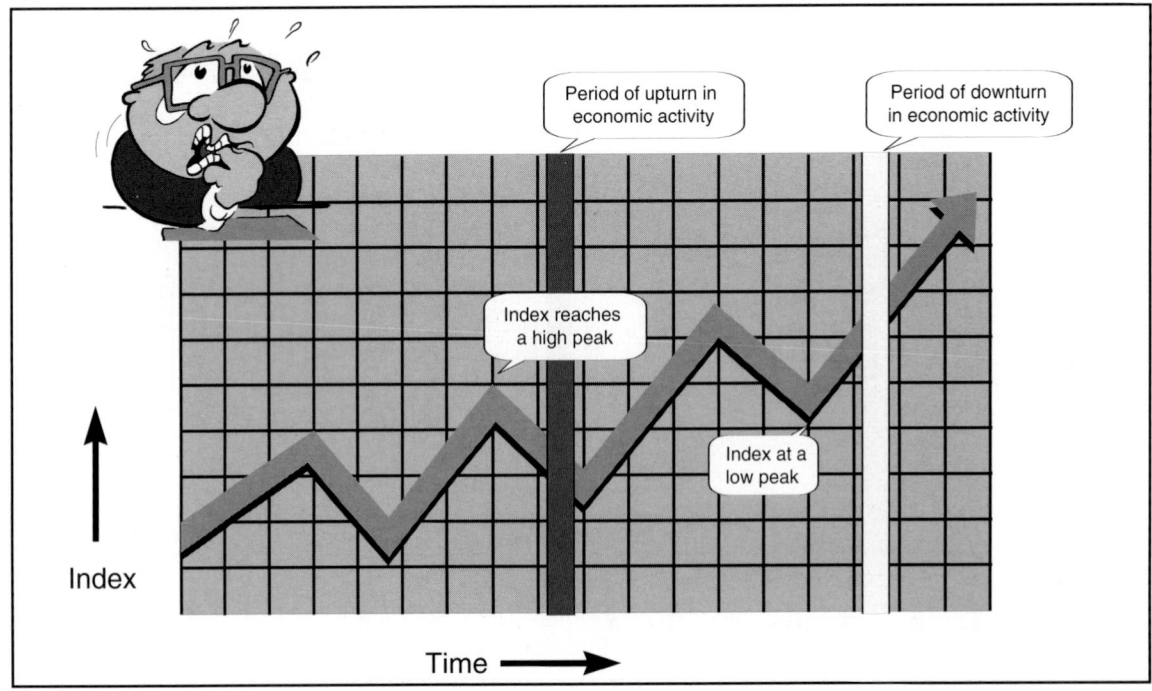

Construction contracts

New construction contracts awarded for industrial, commercial or residential facilities are a forecast of future needs for building materials such as lumber, cement and steel and also for electrical fittings, plumbing and furniture.

Plant and equipment

New contracts and orders for plant and equipment will forecast new demand for machines, tools, steel, fittings, etc., as well as an indicator of the growth of inventory levels.

Business incorporation

The number of new businesses that have been incorporated or have failed (the net change in business population) gives a forecast of future employment levels.

Capital appropriation

Newly approved capital appropriation will be a forecast of additional building and construction.

Inventory levels

A decrease in inventories is often a forecast of new manufacturing activity to replenish the decline in stocks. If inventories are increasing, and sales are sluggish, this would be a forecast of a decline in manufacturing activity.

Manufacturing orders

New manufacturing orders would be a forecast that new personnel are likely to be hired and that there will be an increase in demand for raw materials.

Coincident indicators

A coincident, or simultaneous, indicator is one that is in harmony with the associated economic activity. Coincident indicators have little use in forecasting since they are only indicating what is in fact happening now. Examples would include

- Gross National Product (GNP), which indicates the current economic health of a country;
- unemployment rate, which indicates the current employment climate;
- retail store sales, which are a record of what has been currently sold;
- index of industrial production.

Lagging indicators

A lagging indicator is one that reaches its high, or low, after the economic activity has occurred. Again, lagging indicators have little use in forecasting since

they are only indicating what has already happened. Examples include:

- labour cost per unit of production;
- commercial and industrial loans;
- book value of inventories.

MACROECONOMIC FACTORS

Macroeconomic conditions can enormously impact the forecast of future activity. Some examples are given in the sections that follow.

Interest rates

High interest rates suppress the demand for items where borrowing is involved, such as new homes, automobiles or capital appropriation for new research programmes.

Exchange rates

If the currency of a particular country is strong, it reduces exports from that country since goods are more expensive, it increases the capital flow into that country since investors have more confidence and it reduces tourism since it is more expensive for the overseas visitor.

Unemployment level

High unemployment reduces consumer purchases of items that can be deferred, such as new automobiles, eating out in restaurants or taking expensive vacations.

Demographic trends

The forecast of an increasingly elderly population forecasts the need for medical equipment and medical related services, retirement homes and package holidays.

Government regulations

Government laws, or the forecast of new laws, can impact other forecasts:

- Tax law changes in the USA concerning retirement plans gave rise to a forecast increase in money available for investment.
- Laws related to smoking have reduced the forecast of the demand for cigarettes in the USA and some European countries.

■ Regulations about the combustible nature of materials (clothing, and furniture) have increased the demand for non-flammable material.

Political climate

Changes in political parties can impact the forecast of economic activity. For example, the election of socialist governments after conservatives have been in power often decreases the forecast of economic activity because of the fear of government interference in business and often new taxes. (However, this was not the case when Tony Blair replaced John Major, the outgoing conservative leader, as UK Prime Minister in 1997).

Labour unrest

Strikes, or the fear of strikes, reduces the forecast of activity. For example, the continued threat of labour unrest by the dock workers in the port of Marseilles, France who are members of the CGT (*Confederation Générale du Travail*) has reduced the forecast of business at the port, but has increased the forecast of business at nearby Toulon and also at the port of Genoa in Italy.

Elasticity of demand

To some extent, forecasting product demand is a function of the product price. The higher the price of the product, the lower the demand. However, there is a varying degree in the change in the demand, which is a function of the 'elasticity' of the product.

Inelastic product

A product is considered to be inelastic if the quantity demanded does not change dramatically with price changes. For example, the demand for products such as bread, table wine, milk, rail tickets and computer paper does not change a great deal with price:

■ If the price increases, people will still buy in about the same amounts. These are essentially basic products, for which there is really little substitute.

■ If the price decreases, the amount consumed will not increase much either, because there is a limit to how much of these products can be consumed. The quantity demanded is effectively saturated for a given population.

Elastic product

A product is considered to be elastic if the quantity demanded by customers changes markedly with price

changes. The demand for products such as four-wheel-drive recreational vehicles, champagne, holidays at the Club Mediterranean and silk clothing changes considerably with price changes.

■ If the price increases, people will defer purchase of these products because there are substitutes, or they can live without them.

■ If the price decreases, the amount demanded increases as the products become more affordable. These are products, previously luxury items, that are now within price range of a large population. An example would be the sale of personal computers in the early 1990s.

Elastic products are usually expensive items, for which there may be substitutes, or they are not essential for a person's basic needs.

Figure 9.5, *Elasticity of Demand*, shows a simple relationship between price and quantity for inelastic, and elastic products. The phenomenon is important in long-range planning for both manufacturing or service organizations.

MICROECONOMIC FACTORS

Within a specific industrial sector, there are factors, what one might call microfactors concerning the organization or the product, that can impact a forecast. Examples follow.

Competition

A company's forecast of future sales depends very much on the extent of the competition. The following are illustrations.

IBM

When IBM introduces any new personal computer products on the market, it has to fight with competitors like Hewlett-Packard, Dell and Compaq.

Texas Instruments

When Texas Instruments, with little competition, introduced its scientific calculator in the early 1970s, it virtually cornered the market and was optimistic about future sales.

Boeing

When the demand for commercial aircraft is high, Boeing in Seattle, Washington, can be fairly optimistic about forecast sales. Its only major competitor is Airbus Industries, France.

Figure 9.5   Elasticity of demand.

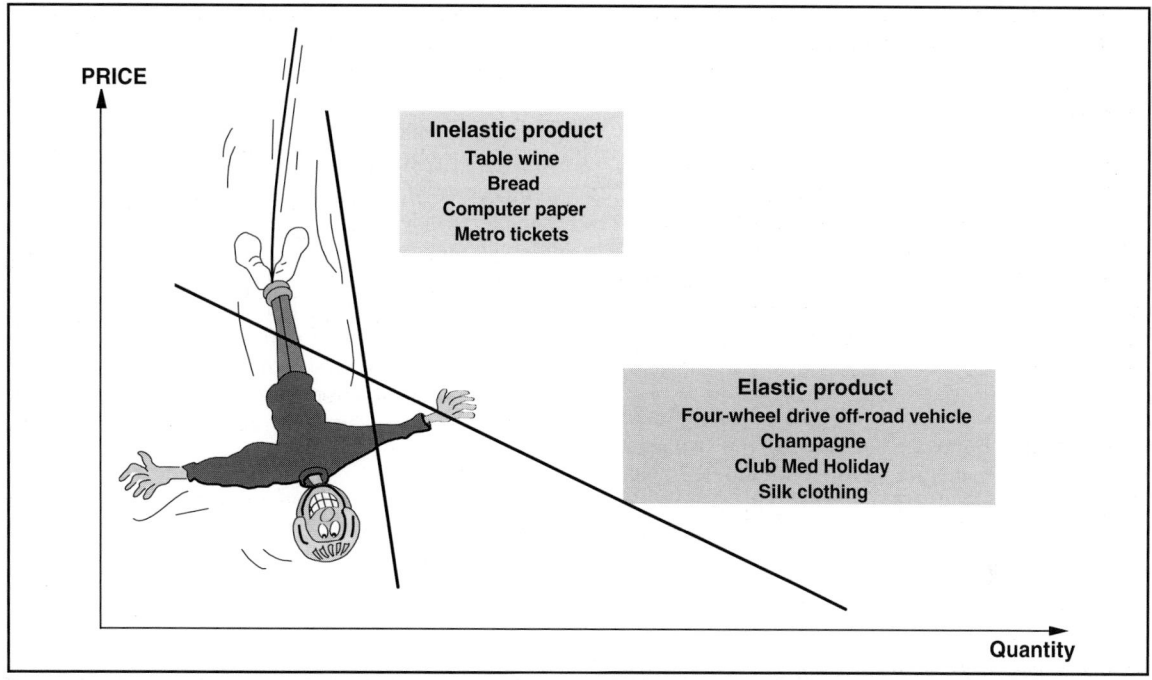

Reputation for quality

The quality image of a company, or the quality of past products, can impact a forecast, as shown in the following examples.

Marks & Spencer

Marks & Spencer, the UK-based retailer, has a reputation for high quality. Thus, generally, it has a favourable forecast for sales of its clothing and its food products.

Jaguar

The automobiles produced by Jaguar, UK, in the early 1980s had a terrible reputation for quality. As a result, the forecast of increased sales was quite poor. Now, under the present ownership of Ford of the USA, quality has improved somewhat.[5]

Price

Price levels always impact the forecast for future products. As a general rule, the lower the price, the higher the sales. However, products should not be priced too low in case consumers consider that they are of inferior quality.

Design

Knowing that a product is well designed enhances the forecast of sales, even though, on first appearance, the good design is not visible, as in the following examples.

Volkswagen

When it was in production, the Volkswagen Beetle from Germany had a reputation for quality. During good times for the sales of all automobiles its sales forecast was favourable. This was the case even though its style was not revolutionary. The same was true of Saab and Volvo automobiles from Sweden.

Heidelberg printing presses

Heidelberg printing presses from Germany are known for good design. Demand for their products is good in their particular market niche.

Delivery times

Manufacturers, suppliers and service industries that have a reputation for being reliable in delivery are more likely to have favourable forecasts than those who are not considered reliable.

Disasters

Companies that experience an unexpected disaster with one of their products can expect difficulties in the future, as the following examples show.

McDonnell-Douglas

In 1979 a DC-10 manufactured by McDonnell-Douglas crashed in Chicago because of a problem with the engine mounting. From that day on, the company had difficulty competing in the commercial airline market. Now it has been swallowed by Boeing. (For further reading, see Chapter 19, *Reliability and Maintenance*)

Ford Motor

Ford Motor USA used to manufacture a small automobile called the Pinto. In the early 1970s two people were killed when another motorist ran into the back of their Ford Pinto and it caught fire. The accident was blamed on poor shielding for the fuel tank. Sales of the vehicle began to fall and eventually Ford ceased manufacture of the Pinto.

CONSUMER SURVEYS

Consumer surveys are obtained by sampling in which responses related to certain subjects are solicited from individuals who are targeted at random, or selected according to a defined sampling plan. (For further reading, see Chapter 20, *Statistical Concepts.*) The survey information is prepared on questionnaires, which may be sent through the mail, completed over the telephone or distributed in person, either door-to-door or in areas, such as shopping malls, frequented by potential consumers. The survey data collected, or a sample, is then analysed and used to forecast or make estimates for the population from whom the survey was taken. Surveys are used in forecasting, for example to obtain ideas about a new product, because the required data is unavailable from other sources.[6]

Simple random sampling

Simple random sampling is surveying when each item in a population has an equal chance of being selected.

Systematic sampling

Systematic sampling is where people are selected from a population at a uniform interval in time, order or space. For example, in the USA, a population census is taken every 10 years of everybody, while every tenth residence receives a more detailed questionnaire that is delivered to each selected house.

Stratified sampling

Stratified sampling is an approach used in surveys, in which the population is divided into homogeneous groups or strata. Grouping may be according to age. For example, people in the 40-to-50 age group may have a different preference for a specific automobile (sports car, for example) than those in the 25-to-35 age group. Stratified sampling is used to reflect more accurately the characteristics of a target population and to avoid diluting these characteristics erroneously. It is used when there is a small variation within each group, but a wide variation between groups, for example teenagers between 13 and 19 and parents between 40 and 50.

Cluster sampling

Cluster sampling is the division of the population into clusters and sampling one or more clusters. Assume that Paris is targeted for preference of a certain consumer product. The city is divided into geographical clusters and then an appropriate number of clusters are selected for analysis. Well-designed cluster sampling can provide more accurate results than simple random sampling. Cluster sampling is used when there is considerable variation within each group (cluster) but groups are essentially similar, for example persons encountered in a shopping mall on Monday and those encountered on Tuesday.

The accuracy of consumer surveys

A well-designed sample survey can give quite accurate predictions of the requirements, desires or needs of a population. The accuracy lies in the phrase 'well-designed'. For example, in the US presidential elections in November 1948 the two candidates were Harry Truman, the Democratic incumbent, and Governor Dewey of New York, the Republican candidate. The *Chicago Tribune* was 'so sure' of the election outcome from the surveys that the headlines in their daily paper read 'Dewey elected president'. In fact, Harry Truman won![7]

The cost of surveys

Consumer surveys are expensive. There is the cost of designing the questionnaire such that it is able to solicit the correct response. There is the operating side of collecting the data, and then the subsequent analysis.

Outside consulting firms that specialize in surveying are often used by business.

Survey response

Soliciting information from consumers is difficult: 'everyone is too busy'. Postal responses have a very low response and their use has declined. Those people who do respond may not be representative in the sample. Telephone surveys give a higher return because voice contact has been obtained. However, again the sample obtained may not be representative, because those contacted may be the unemployed, retirees or non-working people; others are not available. Person-to-person contact gives a much higher response for consumer surveys.

TIME-SERIES DATA IN FORECASTING

A time series is historical data, representing a certain activity, that has been collected over a regular period of time. A time series might be used to illustrate the movement of such elements as sales revenues, cash flow, number of defective products, industrial accidents, shipments of raw materials, Gross National Product, Consumer Price Index, stock price, wage rates, etc. Economic indicators discussed in the previous section are a form of time-series data.[8]

A time-series analysis is usually presented in graphical form with the time variable plotted on the x axis, the abscissa or horizontal axis, and the variable of interest on the y axis, the ordinate or vertical axis. As an illustration, Figure 9.6 gives a time-series analysis of the sale of granular fertilizer, in thousands of tons, sold by a small chemical company over the last four years.

Components of a time series

Depending on the data being analysed, components in the time series may indicate a trend, a seasonal variation, a cyclical pattern, an irregular occurrence or random variations.

Trends

A trend in a time series can be either increasing or decreasing. Illustrations include,

- a steady increase in the consumer price index;
- an increase in population;
- an increase in annual salaries of top US executives;
- an increase in product sales;

- a decrease in the amount of alcohol consumed;
- an increase in the unemployment rate in Europe in the early 1990s;
- an increase in the average age of the population in Japan;
- a decrease in sales of cigarettes in the United States;
- a decrease in the fertility rate of Western women.

Seasonal variations

Seasonal variations in the time series are changes that occur as a result of seasonal impacts, for example:

- swimsuit sales are higher in the spring and summer;
- petrol consumption is higher in the summer;
- ski sales are higher in the autumn period;
- beer sales are higher in the summer;
- flu-related medicine consumption is higher in the winter;
- sales of school textbooks, pens and paper are higher in the autumn.

Business cyclical activity

Analysing long-term business activities indicates that there is cyclical activity, which seems to occur about every seven years (although there are indications in the 1990s that this may be changing). This cycle is an increasing wave-like pattern, which can be demonstrated by financial stock-market indicators such as the US Dow Jones Industrial Average, the UK *Financial Times* FT, or France's CAC 40. The indices are somewhat unpredictable, but there is evidence of repeat peaks and valleys of business activity, which have an effect on employment levels, capital investment and company profits.

Irregular occurrences

Irregular occurrences are unpredictable, such as:

- severe weather, like the rain-caused flooding in the USA in 1993, which disrupted industry and agriculture.
- labour problems, such as the 1984 UK coal strike, which reduced economic output.
- civil conflict, such as that in Northern Ireland, which reduced investment in that region, and the war in former Yugoslavia, which reduced tourism in that area but increased tourism in Spain and other countries in the Mediterranean basin.

Random variations

Random variations are those for which there seems to be no accountable reason and would include whatever is remaining after all other variations have been taken into account.

Figure 9.6 Sales of NKP fertilizer.

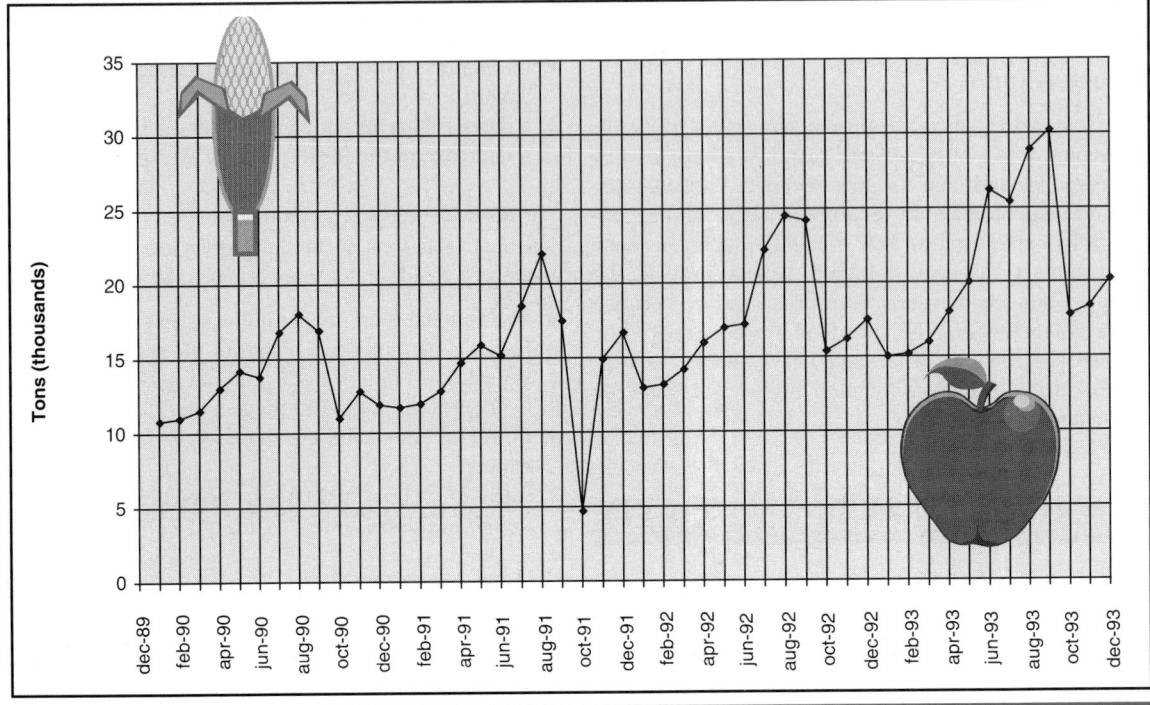

Figure 9.7 illustrates actual time-series data, showing the form of trend, seasonal, business-cycle and random-variation components.

Components of interest for forecasting

The components that are of principal interest in forecasting, and which occur in similar cycle periods, are trends, seasonal variations and random variations. Irregular occurrences are not included since, although they are of interest, they can probably be easily identified. For example, in production irregular occurrences might be effects due to operators' absences, equipment failures or stockouts of raw materials. In sales they might be due to a very strong promotional activity. Neither are business-cycle variations incorporated into the time-series analysis because such analyses are long-term relative to most forecast periods encountered in the operating environment.

MODELLING

Purpose of a model

Quantitative methods for forecasting use historical, or past, data to develop a mathematical model, which can

then be used to estimate future values. In addition to forecasting, mathematical models can be developed to simulate the supply chain, inventory movements or financial changes. The model is a representation of reality. As well as mathematical models, there are physical models to help in design, production or construction. Examples are a model of a nuclear reactor, a skyscraper or an aeroplane, the flight behaviour of which can be tested in a wind tunnel. Alternatively, the model might be a three-dimensional computer display using CAD systems, such as those used in automobile design. Whatever the type of model, its purpose is to provide a tool to help minimize risk, improve planning, reduce costs, expose potential problems and help make logical management decisions.

Time-series model

In forecasting, mathematical models are premised on the assumption that past events are a reasonable predictor of future activity. The models assume that the historical sales environment is representative of the future sales climate. If factors like advertising, competitor behaviour, product design, technology or needs of customers have changed, the developed model may not be representative of the future. Time-series data that have shown a trend in the past may not always be

Figure 9.7 Ten-year time-series data and its components.

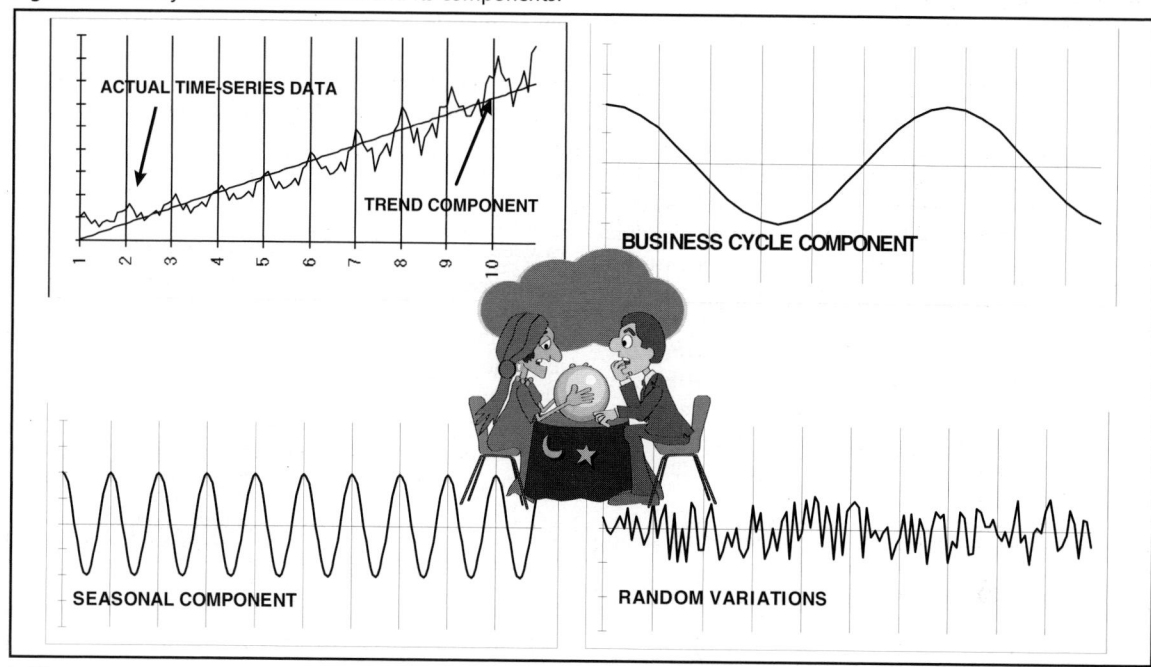

reliable for future forecasting, as the following illustrations show:

- oil prices in the 1990s compared to the 1970s;
- demand for large cars in the USA in the 1980s compared to the 1970s;
- demand for glass today compared to 15 years ago;
- demand for beef today compared to 15 years ago;
- demand for typewriters today compared to the 1970s;
- demand for cigarettes in the USA today compared to the 1950s.

Two models of interest to illustrate sales are a multiplication or an additive model.

Multiplication model

This is when the sales of, or demand for, a product, are a function of the mathematical product of various variables:

$$Y = T_f \times S_f \times C_f \times R_f.$$

Additive model

This is when the sales of, or demand for, a product are a function of the addition of various variables:

$$Y = T_f + S_f + C_f + R_f.$$

In both these models:

- Y is the sales or other activity.

- T_f is the trend over time on the assumption that no external events are intervening.
- S_f is a factor due to seasonal variations in the sales.
- C_f is a factor that modifies the sales according to the business cycle.
- R_f is a factor due to random occurrences.

Patterns in time-series data

To establish whether a particular set of time-series data is appropriate for developing a forecast model, the data is plotted to see how it has changed over time and to see if a pattern exists. For example, in the Figure 9.6 a pattern exists, from which the following observations can be made:

- The quantity of fertilizer sold shows an increasing trend.
- For any given year, the sale of fertilizer peaks during the third quarter, the months of July, August and September, and falls at about the end of the fourth quarter and in the first quarter. Thus the sales are seasonal.
- Something happened in October 1989, when sales dropped dramatically. In researching records, it was noted that there was a fire on the plant during that period, which cut down all activity for two weeks. This was an irregular occurrence.

Thus, this data can be used to develop a reasonably reliable forecast model.

Decomposing data

At first light, it may not be evident that past data can be developed into an appropriate forecasting model. As an illustration, Figure 9.8 shows the monthly sales in French Francs of the sales of filing cabinets manufactured by a manufacturer in Toulouse over the last four years. Initial observations are that sales appear to be erratic and that it is difficult to discern a pattern.

A further study of the data is made, this time presenting the information in terms of units, rather than using financial figures. In addition, sales are broken down into design types, as shown in Figure 9.9. This time, for two of the three models, there appears to be a discernible pattern:

- Unit sales of Design A are showing a steady increase.
- Unit sales of Design B remain quite steady (not rising above ten units per month).
- It is Design C that does not exhibit any pronounced pattern.

Thus, in decomposition of the data, different forecasting models might be applied. Linear regression models would be appropriate for Designs B and C and an averaging model for Design A. The regression models would be probably more reliable than the averaging model. Nevertheless, as a result of decomposing the information, the overall forecasting risk to the firm has been reduced from what it would have been if all the data had been taken together.

AVERAGE FORECASTING MODELS

Averaging models for a time series assume, with some exceptions, that there are no seasonal or trend effects. They only concentrate on the random factor and, when averaging methods are used, the past data is *smoothed*, or the random effect is nullified. This smoothed data is then to used as a predictor of future performance.

Naive averaging

The naive-averaging approach assumes that results from the immediately preceding period can be used to estimate needs for the next period. That is, the average is based on one piece of sample data. This model assumes that examination of historical data from period to period shows that the changes are not significant

Figure 9.8   Sales of filing cabinets – all design types.

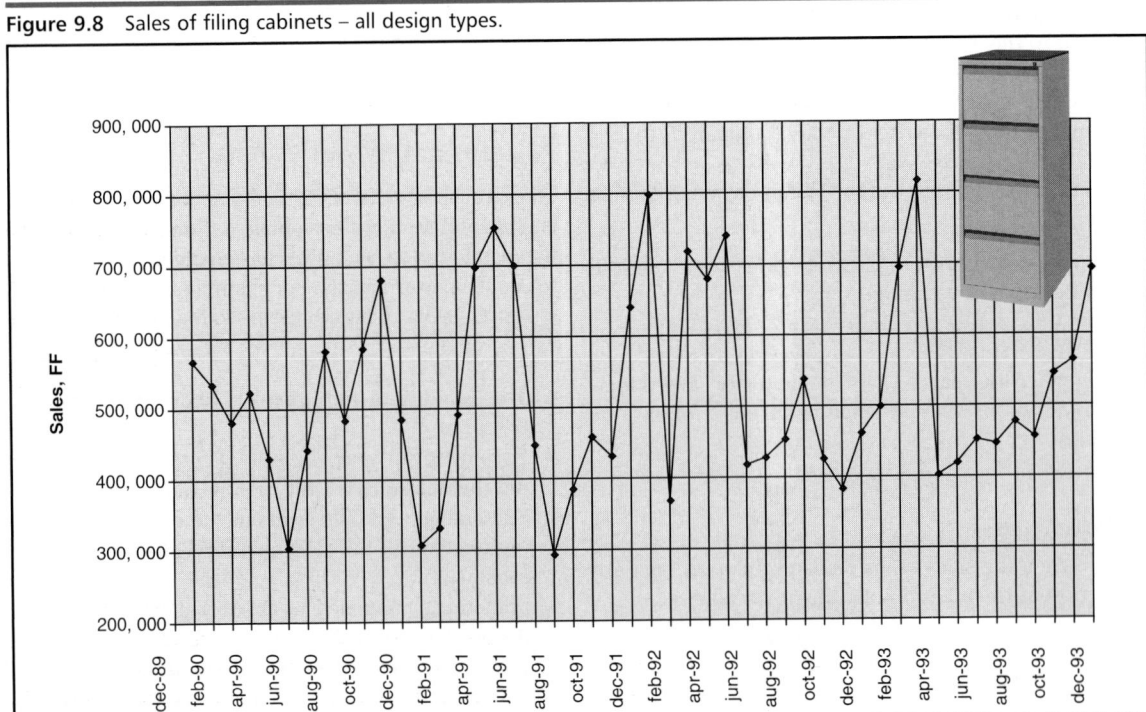

Figure 9.9 Sales of filing cabinets according to model design.

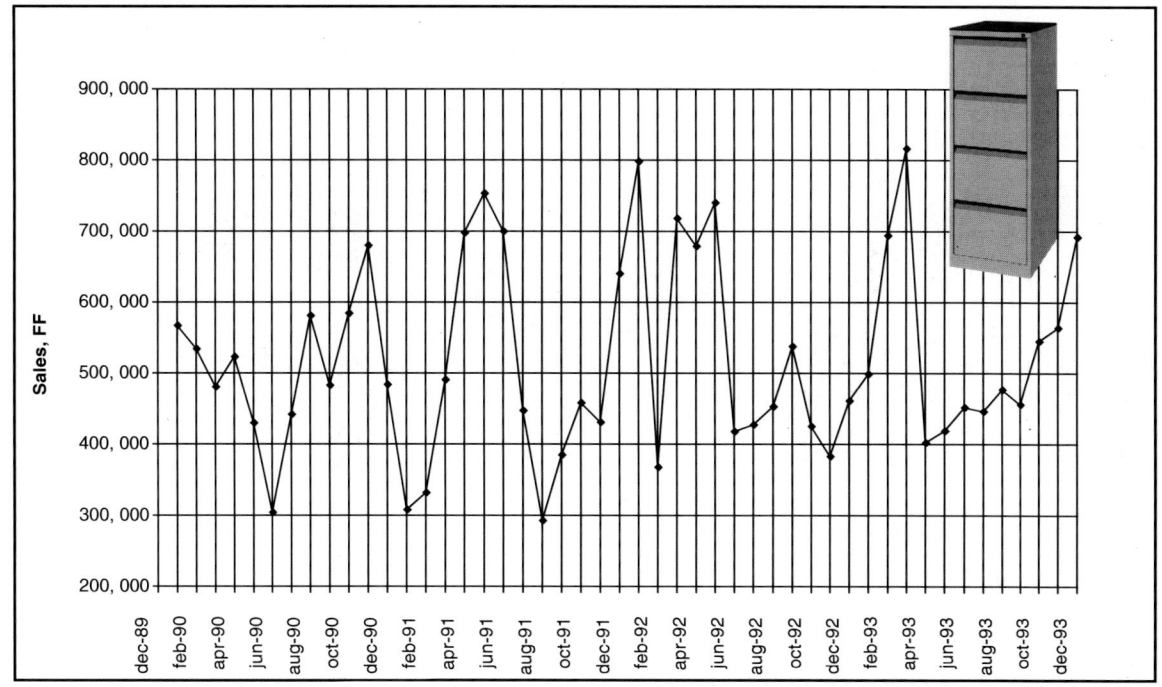

enough to be taken into consideration. The following are illustrations:

- Cash used in July was $17 500. Cash needs in August are estimated at $17 500.
- The number of personnel in work zone A-101 was 97 in January. Personnel needs in February are estimated at 97.
- Raw material costs in the first week of August were $24 500. Raw material costs in the second week of August are forecast at $24 500.

Straight moving averages

The straight, or simple, moving-averaging method uses the average of past-period data in a time series to forecast future activity. Assume that past sales of a particular product were as shown in Table 9.1. Then using a three-month moving average, the forecast for May would be the average of the sales for the three previous periods or, February, March and April:

$$\frac{(\$13\,500 + \$11\,500 + \$14\,000)}{3} = \$13\,000$$

When the actual sales results for May become available, the forecast for June is then calculated by using the average of the sales for March, April and May. That is,

one moves forward one period. Instead of a three-month moving average, other time periods can be used, such as four-month, five-month etc. The greater the number of periods, the greater is the smoothing effect.

Table 9.1   Example of sales over four months

January	£10 000
February	£13 500
March	£11 500
April	£14 000

Stock price movements

Figure 9.10 shows the use of a moving average to smooth the movements of the Dow Jones Industrial index.[9] It gives the actual data for 1994, together with a 200-day moving average. From this data, the trend in stock price movements is illustrated and this is then translated into an indicator of economic activity.

Weighted moving averages

The weighted-moving-average model is similar to the simple moving-average approach, except that, instead of the straight average of the data for each period, the periods are given different weights. That is, some

Figure 9.10 Dow Jones Industrial Average (Source: *Wall Street Journal* 9 January 1995).

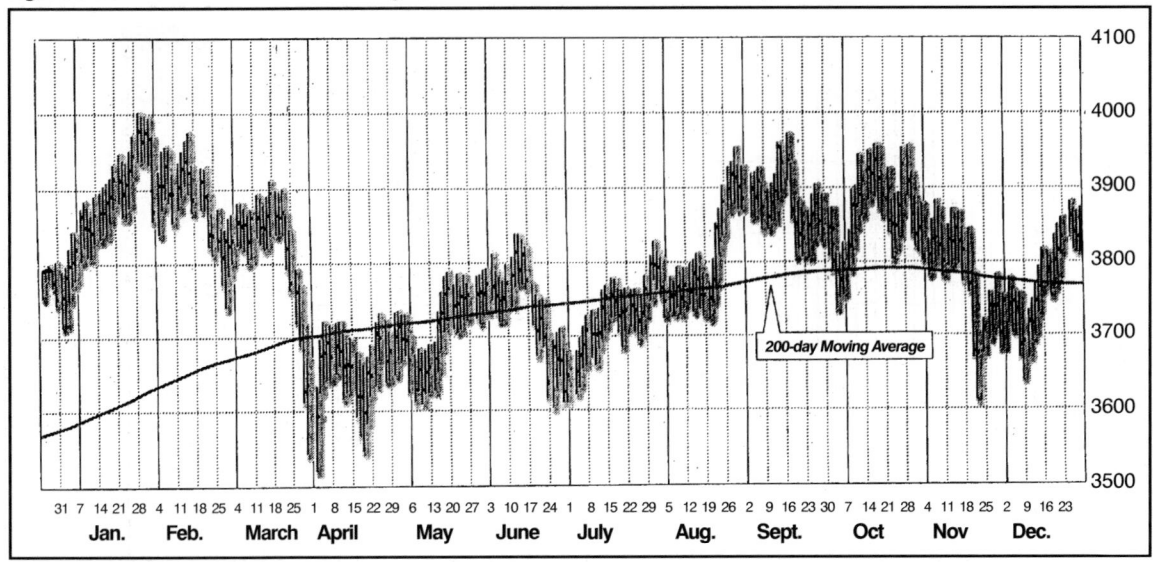

periods are considered more important than others. For example, assume past sales for a particular product were again as given in Table 9.1.

Assume that a model predicting the sales for the month of May is desired. Past experience has shown that a weight of 0.5 on the most recent period (the month of April), 0.3 on the month of March and 0.2 on February (the oldest period) is appropriate. Then, the forecast for May would be:

$$(0.2 \times \pounds 13\,500 + 0.3 \times \pounds 11\,500 + 0.5 \times \pounds 14\,000)$$
$$= \pounds 13\,150.$$

Whatever weights are used, the sum must equal unity. As for the straight moving average, when the data for May becomes available, this is used for the most recent period to forecast sales for June. The data for February is then dropped.

Considerations in the average models

In using straight, or weighted moving averages in forecasting, increases and decreases are balanced, thus smoothing the forecast. In theory, the number of periods used can range from two up to the number of data points in the series. In the extreme case, if all data points are considered in the forecast, then the resulting model would be just the mean value for all the data. Caution has to be exercised if a large number of periods are used and there is a trend, because the forecast is unreliable.

The greater the number of periods, the greater is the smoothing, or dampening, effect, as illustrated in Figure 9.11, which shows actual data in a time-series analysis, together with the forecast model for two, four and six periods. The smoothing effect is greater for six periods than for two periods. Also of interest is that none of the models reacts immediately to changing patterns, with the forecast lagging the actual data.

Model accuracy

When a forecasting model is developed by whatever method, it is important to know how well the model represents reality or how well the forecast compares to the actual data. If there are wide discrepancies, then the model used is not appropriate and another should be considered. It is rare that a forecast model will give perfectly accurate predictions all the time, but a good model should give good indications of reality. One simple way of testing the averaging model is by using the concept of the mean absolute deviation, or MAD, as presented below. Other methods for testing model accuracy are given in Chapter 21, *Additional Forecasting*.

Mean absolute deviation

The mean absolute deviation (MAD) is derived from the absolute deviation, which is the absolute value (the positive value) of the forecast error. The forecast error is the difference between the actual value Y and the forecast value $\hat{Y}$ in the same time period:

Figure 9.11 Moving-average forecasting.

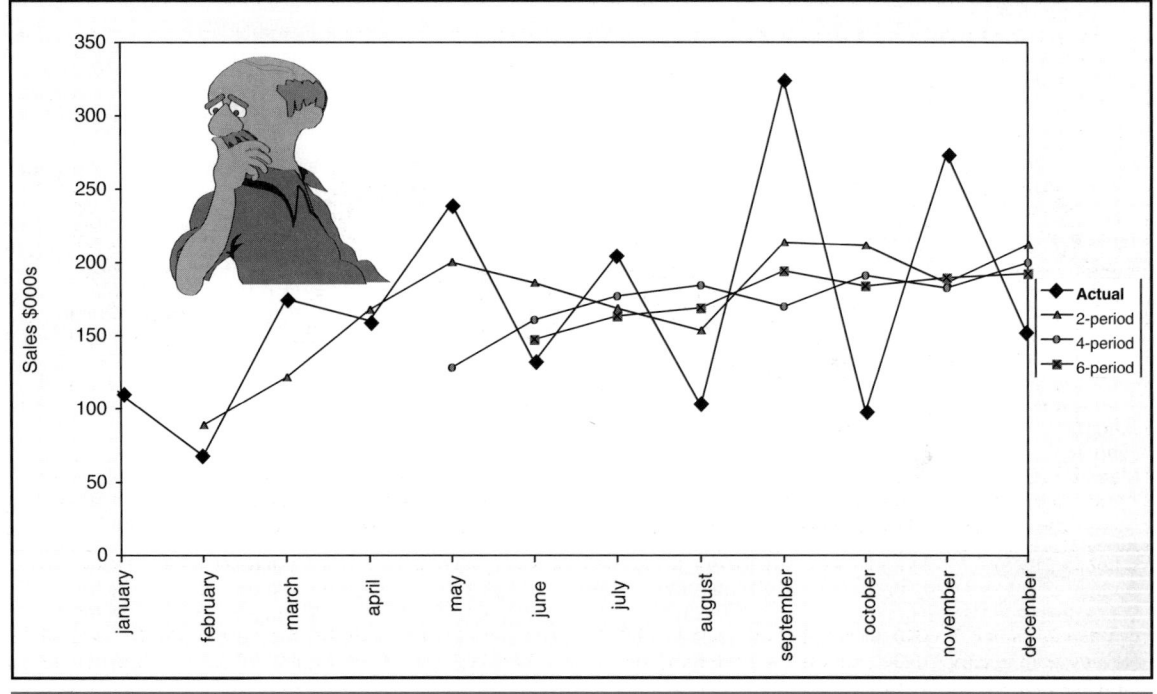

Absolute deviation $= |(Y - \hat{Y})|$.

The mean absolute deviation is then the sum of the mean absolute deviation divided by the number of data points in the series:

$$\text{Mean absolute deviation (MAD)} = \frac{\sum |(Y - \hat{Y})|}{n}$$

For each model that is developed the mean average deviation is calculated, and the model that has the lowest value of MAD would be the preferred model to use. This approach is developed in the following worked example, *Lube oil*, Part I.

WORKED EXAMPLE: LUBE OIL (PART I)

Situation

The Ipras Oil Refinery in Turkey has a processing unit for making lubricating oil (called lube oil in the business). Even though the production of lubricating oil requires a high capital investment, the profit margin from this product is higher than normal straight-run products such as petrol and diesel fuel. The production manager in the lube-oil plant needs to develop a simple forecasting model for estimating its blending requirements. Lubricating oil, unlike other refinery products, is not very seasonal. Table 9.2 gives the actual lubricating oil blended in a particular year.

Required

1 Develop a three-month simple moving-average forecasting model.
2 Develop a three-month weighted-moving-average model, using a factor of 0.6 for the most recent period, 0.2 for the next period and 0.2 for the oldest period.

Table 9.2 Lube oil blended on a monthly basis

Month	Actual oil used (000s litres)
January	10 000
February	12 000
March	13 000
April	16 000
May	19 000
June	17 000
July	11 000
August	22 000
September	31 000
October	18 000
November	16 000
December	14 000

3 Using the concept of the mean absolute deviation, determine which model is preferred
4 Use the preferred model to forecast the lube-oil requirements for the following January.
5 Plot the actual data and the two models.

Solution

The solution for this exercise is given in Table 9.3:

1 The simple moving average data is given in column 3 of the table.
2 The weighted moving average data is given in column 5 of the table.
3 The weighted moving average has the lowest MAD and so this is the preferred model.
4 The forecast requirements for the following January are 15 200 litres.
5 The data is given in Figure 9.12.

Table 9.3 Forecasting lubricating oil requirements with moving-average methods

1	2	3	4	5	6
	Actual	Simple moving average		Weighted moving average	
	oil used	Model	Absolute	Model	Absolute
	(1000 litres)		deviation		deviation
Month			from actual		from acutal
January	10 000				
February	12 000				
March	13 000				
April	16 000	11 666.67	4 333.33	12 200.00	3 800.00
May	19 000	13 666.67	5 333.33	14 600.00	4 400.00
June	17 000	16 000.00	1 000.00	17 200.00	200.00
July	11 000	17 333.33	6 333.33	17 200.00	6 200.00
August	22 000	15 666.67	6 333.33	13 800.00	8 200.00
September	31 000	16 666.67	14 333.33	18 800.00	12 200.00
October	18 000	21 333.33	3 333.33	25 200.00	7 200.00
November	16 000	23 666.67	7 666.67	21 400.00	5 400.00
December	14 000	21 666.67	7 666.67	19 400.00	5 400.00
January		**16 000.00**		**15 200.00**	
Mean Average Deviation, MAD			6 259.26		5 888.89

Note: Weights are 0.6 for the most recent period, 0.2 for the next period and 0.2 for the oldest period

Figure 9.12 Forecasting lubricating oil requirements.

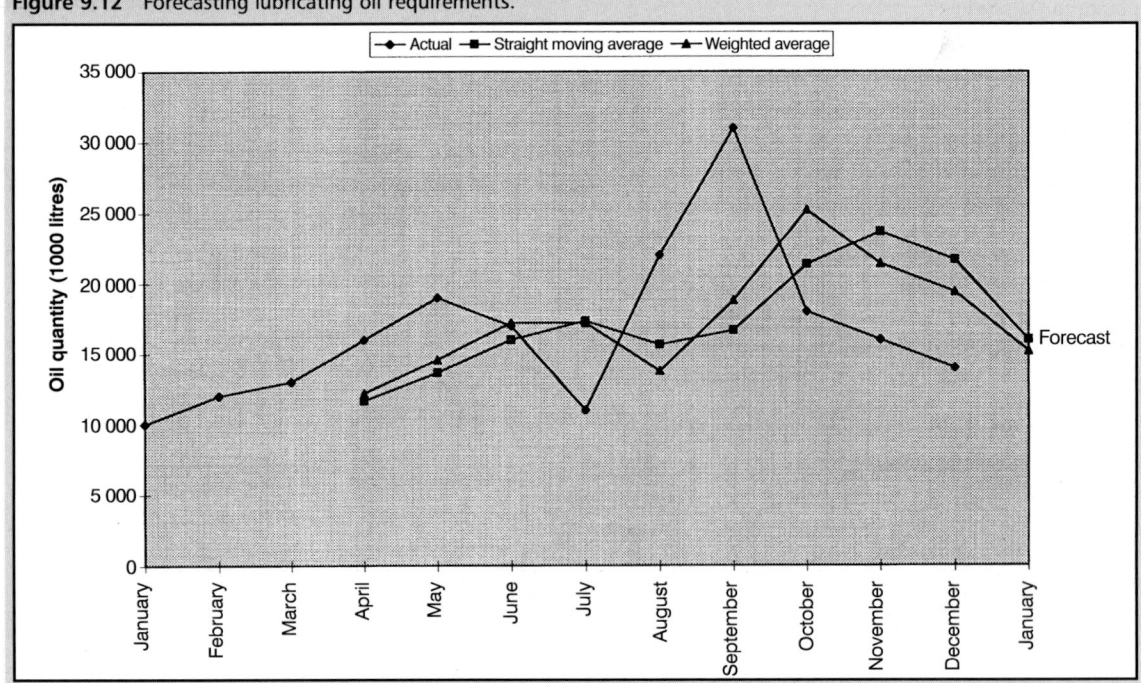

EXPONENTIAL SMOOTHING

Exponential model

Exponential smoothing is somewhat similar to the moving-averaging methods, but it eliminates some of the computational calculations.[10] It develops a model using a single weighting, or smoothing factor, called alpha (α), which takes a value greater than 0 but less than 1, to forecast the next period's activity. The mathematical model is: $F_{n+1} = F_n + \alpha(A_n - F_n)$ where F_{n+1} is the forecast for next period, F_n is the forecast for the current period, α is the assigned alpha factor and A_n is the actual data for the current period.

For example, assume that an automobile dealer predicted the sale of 23 000 vehicles for March in his region. The actual sales were 22 150. With an α factor of 0.40, the forecast vehicle sales for April would be:

$$F_{\text{April}} = 23\ 000 + 0.40(22\ 150 - 23\ 000)$$
$$= 22\ 660 \text{ vehicles.}$$

In exponential smoothing, the smaller the value of α, the greater is the smoothing or dampening effect since a smaller portion of the actual data appears in the forecast. This is illustrated in Figure 9.13, where the actual data and the model data for α values of 0.10, 0.50 and 0.90 is shown.

An alpha factor of Zero

If the smoothing factor $\alpha = 0$, then the forecast equation reduces to:

$$F_{n+1} = F_n + 0(A_n - F_n) = F_n.$$

This is the same as saying that the new forecast is equal to the previous forecast, which is meaningless.

An alpha factor of Unity

If the smoothing factor $\alpha = 1$, then the forecast equation reduces to:

$$F_{n+1} = F_n + 1(A_n - F_n) = A_n.$$

Thus, the new forecast is equal to the previous actual data, which is the same as the naive-averaging approach to forecasting.

Considerations in using exponential smoothing

Like the straight and weighted moving-average methods, the forecast values lag the actual data, as illustrated in Figure 9.13. Furthermore, the smoothing method can only predict one period in advance.

Figure 9.13   Forecasting using exponential smoothing.

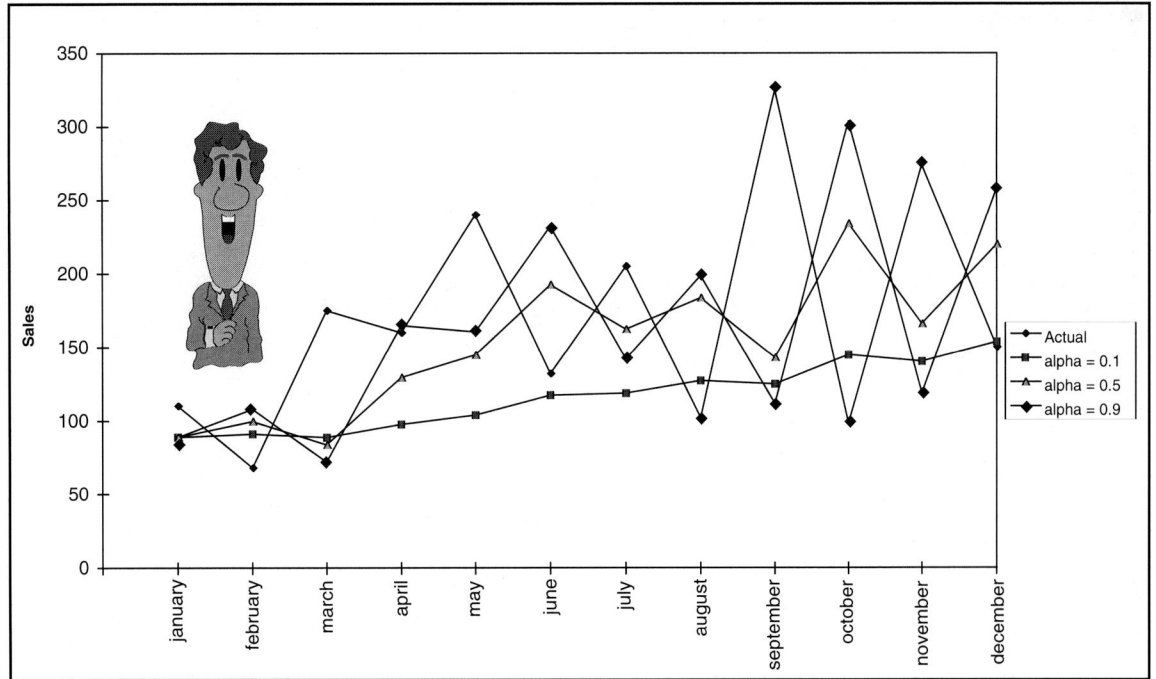

Model accuracy

The accuracy of the model developed by exponential smoothing can be determined in exactly the same manner as the averaging methods, using the criteria of the mean average deviation. This is illustrated in the following worked example.

WORKED EXAMPLE: LUBE OIL (PART II)

Situation

The situation is the same as presented in the previous worked example, *Lube Oil* (Part I).

Required

1 Develop an exponential smoothing forecast model using an α factor of 0.1.
2 Develop an exponential smoothing forecast model using an α factor of 0.5.
3 Use the concept of the mean absolute deviation, to determine which model is preferred.
4 Use the preferred model to forecast the lube-oil requirements for the following January.
5 Plot the actual data and the two models.

Solution

The two models are given in Table 9.4:

1 The model for an α factor of 0.1 is given in column 3.
2 The model for an α factor of 0.5 is given in column 5.
3 The exponential smoothing model for α = 0.1 has the lower MAD, so this is the preferred model.
4 The forecast for January is 15 683 litres (rounded).
5 The plotted data is shown in Figure 9.14.

Table 9.4 Forecasting lubricating oil requirements with exponential smoothing

1 Month	2 Actual oil used (1000 litres)	3 Exponential smoothing Model α = 0.10	4 Absolute deviation from actual	5 Exponential smoothing Model α = 0.50	6 Absolute deviation from actual
January	10 000	11 666.67	1 666.67	11 666.67	1 666.67
February	12 000	11 500.00	500.00	10 833.33	1 166.67
March	13 000	11 550.00	1 450.00	11 416.67	1 583.33
April	16 000	11 695.00	4 305.00	12 208.33	3 791.67
May	19 000	12 125.50	6 874.50	14 104.17	4 895.83
June	17 000	12 812.95	4 187.05	16 552.08	447.92
July	11 000	13 231.66	2 231.66	16 776.04	5 776.04
August	22 000	13 008.49	8 991.51	13 888.02	8 111.98
September	31 000	13 907.64	17 092.36	17 944.01	13 055.99
October	18 000	15 616.88	2 383.12	24 472.01	6 472.01
November	16 000	15 855.19	144.81	21 236.00	5 236.00
December	14 000	15 869.67	1 869.67	18 618.00	4 618.00
January		15 682.70		16 309.00	
Mean Average Deviation, MAD			5 342.19		5 822.83

Figure 9.14   Forecasting lubricating oil requirements: exponential smoothing.

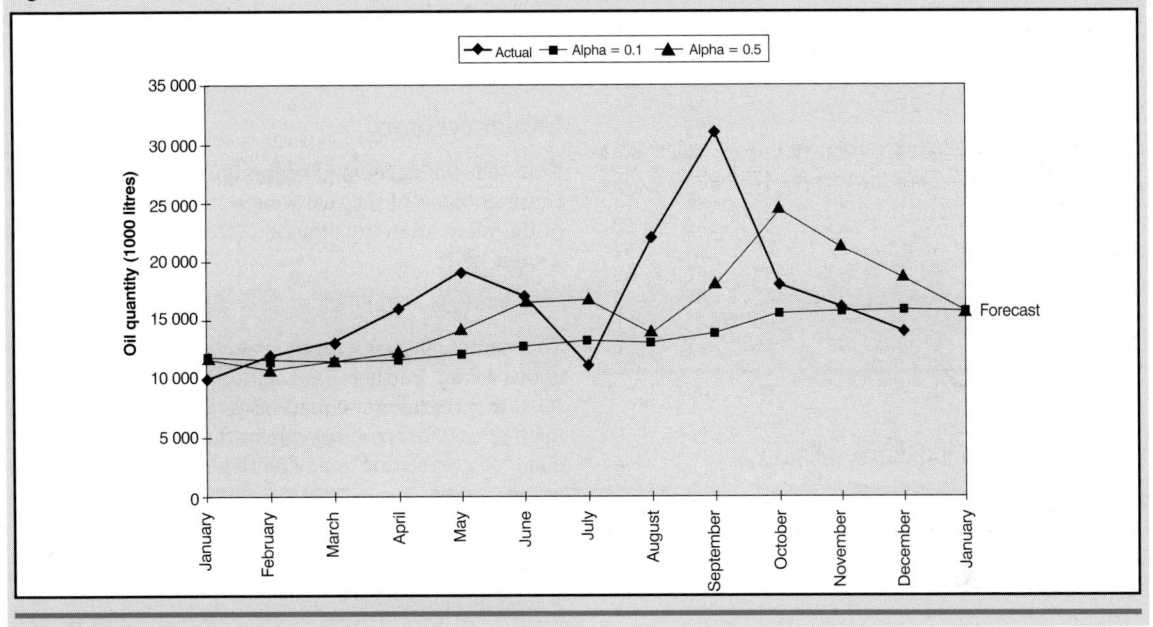

SIMPLE LINEAR REGRESSION IN A TIME SERIES

Simple linear regression in a time series is a useful tool for modelling when there is an increasing or decreasing trend in the data. The procedure involves the development of a linear relationship between a dependent variable of interest, such as sales revenues, profits, units sold, etc. and the time period or the independent variable. Time is always independent since, even if there is an earthquake, a fire or a business goes bankrupt, tomorrow will arrive and be another time period independent of any event.

Objective

The objective in simple linear regression is to develop a linear relationship of the general form:

$$\hat{Y} = a + bX,$$

where a is a constant, the intercept on the y axis, b is a constant, the slope of the line, X is the time, or the independent variable, and $\hat{Y}$ is the predicted value of the dependent variable.

When this equation is developed, for a given value of the independent variable X, the value of the dependent variable $\hat{Y}$ can be estimated. This would give a forecast, or estimate, for the corresponding value of X.

Derivation of the linear equation

To illustrate the derivation, and the use of the linear equation, Table 9.5 gives the data for the Design Type A of the filing cabinets presented earlier in Figure 9.9. The values of X represent the coded time period such that 1 is January 1990, 2 is February 1990, 3 is March 1990, etc. right up to 48, which is December 1993. The values Y are the numbers of units sold.

The linear equation can be developed by using the method of least squares illustrated in the Chapter 21, *Additional Forecasting*. The least-squares method determines the best fit by minimizing the difference (error) between the points estimated from the calculated line and the actual observed points that were used to draw the line. Computer packages, such as Microsoft Excel, have the regression functions built in and this avoids employing the tedious mathematics. Using the regression function in Microsoft Excel gives the following values for a and b:

- Intersect a is 14.3661.
- Slope b is 0.8541.

Inserting these values into the standard regression function gives the following equation:

Table 9.5 Data for sales of filing cabinets

X	Y	X	Y	X	Y	X	Y
1	13	13	26	25	32	37	42
2	17	14	27	26	38	38	43
3	15	15	23	27	40	39	47
4	19	16	28	28	39	40	44
5	14	17	30	29	42	41	48
6	18	18	31	30	43	42	51
7	21	19	33	31	42	43	50
8	23	20	31	32	45	44	52
9	19	21	35	33	44	45	53
10	24	22	34	34	42	46	54
11	26	23	37	35	40	47	57
12	25	24	36	36	45	48	56

$$\hat{Y} = 14.3661 + 0.8541X.$$

This then is the mathematical model that represents the sale of the file cabinets. This regression function is shown plotted with the actual sales data in Figure 9.15.

Using the model

Once the regression model has been developed, it can be used to forecast future sales. For example, suppose one is interested to know the sales in June 1994. The coded value for June 1994 is 52 and this is the value X.

Substituting this value in the regression equation gives a forecast value of:

$$\hat{Y} = 14.3661 + 0.8541 \times 52 = 60.4877 \text{ or } 61 \text{ units.}$$

Model accuracy

Note that the developed regression equation is a good representation of the real values. As a test, substitution of the value 48 in the equation (December 1993) gives a value of Y:

$$\hat{Y} = 14.3661 + 0.8541 \times 48 = 55.3631 \text{ or } 55 \text{ units.}$$

This compares well with the value of 56 units from the above table. Further information on model accuracy for linear regression equations is given in Chapter 21, *Additional Forecasting*, where the concepts of coefficient of correlation and coefficient of determination are discussed.

SEASONAL EFFECTS AND FORECASTING

In the previous example for file cabinets there was no apparent seasonal effect on the sales. For certain products, the activity is seasonal; for example, the demand for snow-ski equipment is higher in the late autumn

Figure 9.15 Sales of filing cabinets: design type A with regression line.

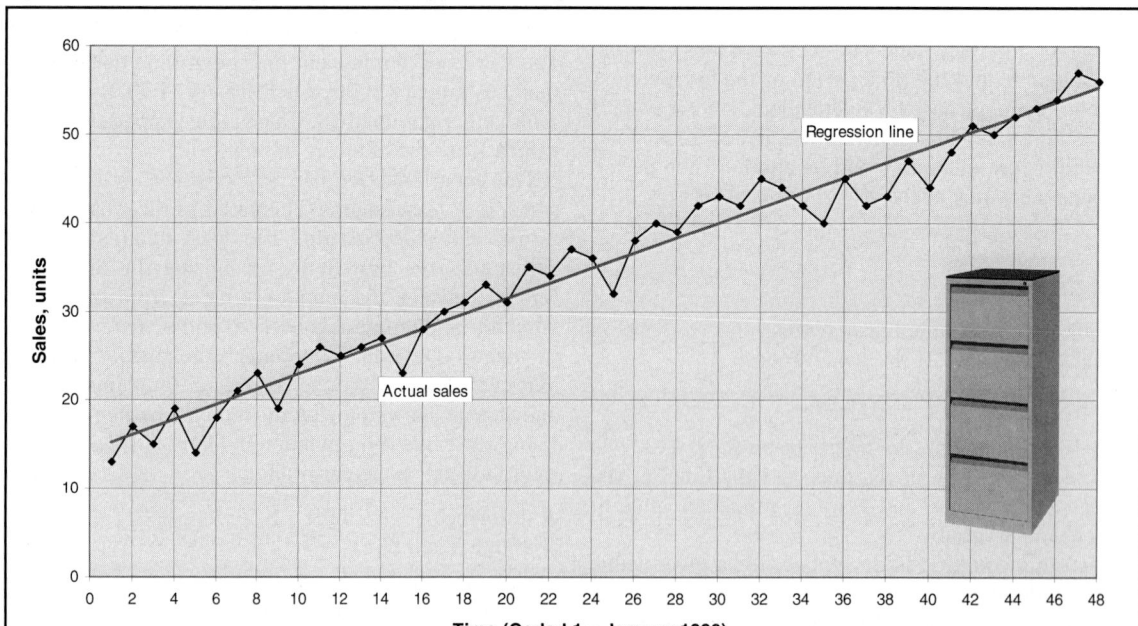

and winter months and the demand for swimwear is higher in the spring and summer months.

Seasonal models

In the section, *Modelling*, a time series was represented as a function of a trend, a seasonal factor, a factor according to the business cycle and random occurrences. The business-cycle factor can be ignored on the basis that its time span is much longer than the normal forecasting period. Furthermore, the random effect, if there is no seasonal effect, can be treated by averaging forecasting methods. In this case, the multiplication and additive models can be reduced to a simpler form:

- *Multiplication model*: $Y = T_f \times S_f$;
- *Additive model*: $Y = T_f + S_f$.

In both models:

- Y are the observed, or actual, values (sales for example).
- T_f is the sales trend over time on the assumption that no external events are intervening.
- S_f is a factor due to seasonal variations.

The objective of a seasonal analysis is to isolate the trend and the seasonal effect in order to forecast future sales.

Calculation procedure

To take into account the seasonal effects in a time series, the following procedure is followed:

1. The raw data is plotted to see if there is a trend or a seasonal effect. The latter will be apparent if there are peaks and valleys at regular seasonal periods.
2. A centred moving average is determined around the time period in consideration. The centred moving average covers the six months prior to the quarter in question and the six months after. In this way, by taking the average over a full-year, the seasonal effect is smoothed.

As an illustration, suppose one is considering the centred moving average around the summer. The middle of the quarter will be midsummer, or 15 August. Six months before this period will include the first half of summer, all of spring and one half of winter. Six months after will include the last half of summer, the autumn and one half of the winter in the following year. The calculation is given as:

$$\frac{0.5 \times \text{winter}(n) + \text{spring}(n) + \text{summer}(n) + \text{autumn}(n) + 0.5 \times \text{winter}(n+1)}{4},$$

where n is the data for a given year and $(n + 1)$ is the data for the following year.

3. Divide actual sales by the centred moving average for each quarter. This is the specific seasonal index SI for each quarter.
4. Determine an average seasonal index SI for each of the four seasonal quarters. For example, if there are four years being considered, then the average seasonal index for the summer would be the average of all the calculated SIs for the summer or:

$$\frac{(\text{SI}_{\text{Year 1}}) + \text{SI}_{(\text{Year 2})} + \text{SI}_{(\text{Year 3})} + \text{SI}_{(\text{Year 4})}}{4} \text{ for each summer}$$

5. Remove the seasonal effect from the actual sales. In the multiplication model this is done by dividing the actual sales Y by the corresponding index for each quarter. This procedure is arrived at from the rewritten model: $T_f = Y/S_f$.
   In the case of the additive model this would be arrived at from the rewritten expression, $T_f = Y - S_f$.
6. Perform a regression analysis on the deseasonalized sales for each quarter, using, if necessary, a code value corresponding to the quarter (in Excel the date is a numerical value and can be used in the calculation). Determine the value of the intercept a and the slope b.
7. Forecast deseasonalized sales for the next four quarters using the linear regression equation of the form, $\hat{Y} = a + b X$.
8. Determine the forecast seasonalized sales from the regression forecast data. For the multiplication model this is given by the expression $\hat{Y} = T_f \times S_f$. For the additive model this is given by the expression, $\hat{Y} = T_f + S_f$.
   The procedure is illustrated for the multiplication model by the worked example, *Garden Tools*, which follows.

Empirical approach

Another method for taking into account seasonal variations is an empirical approach in which a judgemental analysis is made of the available information. For example, assume that sales data for two successive years, Year 1 and Year 2, is available on a monthly basis. If there is a seasonal variation, then the following is an empirical approach to making a forecast:

1. Determine the difference in sales between similar months for Year 1 and Year 2.
2. Calculate average monthly differences for the complete 12 months.

3. Add the average difference between Year 1 and Year 2 to each month in Year 2 to obtain a forecast for Year 3.

This empirical approach is a way of treating the exercise problem, *British Gas*, given at the end of the chapter.

WORKED EXAMPLE: GARDEN TOOLS

Situation

The Mersey Store in Arkansas, USA is a distributor of garden tools. Table 9.6 shows the sales by quarter since 1987. All data is in $000s.

Table 9.6 Sales by quarter of garden tools

Year	Quarter	Sales ($000)	Year	Quarter	Sales ($000)
1987	Winter	11 302	1991	Winter	13 184
	Spring	12 177		Spring	14 146
	Summer	13 218		Summer	14 966
	Autumn	11 948		Autumn	13 665
1988	Winter	11 886	1992	Winter	13 781
	Spring	12 198		Spring	14 636
	Summer	13 294		Summer	15 142
	Autumn	11 785		Autumn	13 415
1989	Winter	11 875	1993	Winter	14 327
	Spring	12 584		Spring	15 251
	Summer	13 332		Summer	15 082
	Autumn	12 354		Autumn	14 002
1990	Winter	12 658	1994	Winter	14 862
	Spring	13 350		Spring	15 474
	Summer	14 358		Summer	15 325
	Autumn	13 276		Autumn	14 425

Required

1 Show graphically that the sales for Mersey are seasonal.
2 Use the multiplication model and predict sales by quarter for 1995. Show graphically the moving-average, deseasonalized sales, regression line and forecast.

Solution

The graphical data is given in Figure 9.16 and Table 9.7 gives the computed data. This information is explained as follows (the numbers correspond to the stages of the *Calculation Procedure* given above):

1 The actual data shows that there is a seasonal variation as there are peaks and valleys in the movement of sales. In addition, there is a trend as sales are increasing with time.

2 A centred moving average is calculated around each time period. For example, for summer 1987, the centred moving average is:

$$\frac{0.5 \times 11\ 302 + 12\ 177 + 13\ 218 + 11\ 948 + 0.5 \times 11\ 886}{4} = 12\ 234.$$

3 The centred moving average for each quarter is calculated in a similar manner (column 5 of Table 9.7).

4 The actual sales are divided by the moving average for each quarter (column 6). This ratio indicates the difference between the actual data and the average for the year. For example, in the summer of 1987, sales were 8 per cent higher than the yearly average.

Figure 9.16 Garden tools – multiplication model.

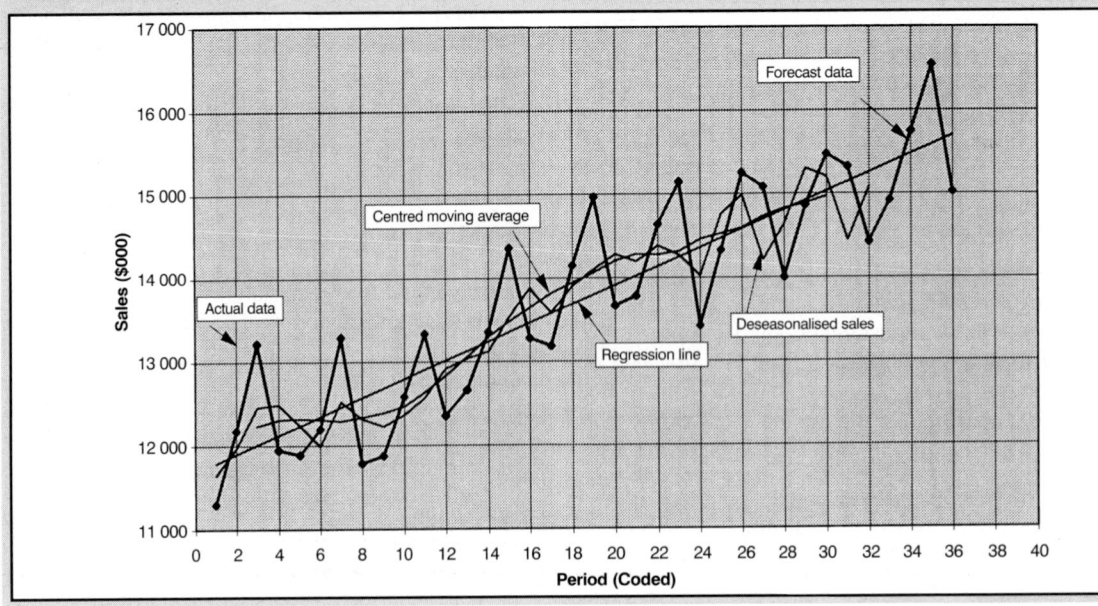

5 The average seasonal index for each quarter is determined. This is the average of the ratio of sales to the moving average for like quarters. For example, the seasonal index for the summer quarter is the average of the ratios for summer 1987 through summer 1993 (average of 1.08 + 1.08 + 1.06 + 1.07 + 1.06 + 1.06 + 1.02 or 1.06). Column 7 gives the average seasonal index for each quarter.

6 The seasonal effect from the actual sales is removed by dividing the actual sales by the corresponding index for that quarter (column 8).

7 A regression analysis on the deseasonalized sales is determined using the code value (column 3) corresponding to that quarter. This gives a value of 11 672 for a, the intercept on the Y axis, and 111.92 for b, the slope of the linear regression line.

Thus, the linear regression equation describing the deseasonalized sales is

$$\hat{Y} = 11\ 672 + 111.92X.$$

8 The deseasonalized sales for the next four quarters are calculated using the regression equation. This data is given in italics at the bottom of column 9.

9 The forecast seasonalized sales are calculated from the regression forecast data calculated in step 9. The seasonal sales is (predicted sales × seasonal index). This information is given in italics at the bottom of column 4, as the predicted data for periods 33 through 36.

Table 9.7 Forecasting: garden tools – multiplication model (all amounts in $000s)

1	2	3	4	5	6	7	8	9
Year	Quarter	Period	Actual sales	Centred moving average	Sales per moving average	Seasonal index (SI)	Sales/index (deseasonalized)	Regression line (predicted)
1987	Winter	1	11 302			0.97	11 640.18	11 784.48
	Spring	2	12 177			1.02	11 966.15	11 896.40
	Summer	3	13 218	12 234.32	1.08	1.06	12 455.36	12 008.31
	Autumn	4	11 948	12 309.91	0.97	0.96	12 489.33	12 120.23
1988	Winter	5	11 886	12 321.98	0.96	0.97	12 241.60	12 232.14
	Spring	6	12 198	12 311.03	0.99	1.02	11 986.58	12 344.06
	Summer	7	13 294	12 289.25	1.08	1.06	12 526.71	12 455.98
	Autumn	8	11 785	12 336.14	0.96	0.96	12 318.62	12 567.89
1989	Winter	9	11 875	12 389.23	0.96	0.97	12 230.33	12 679.81
	Spring	10	12 584	12 465.18	1.01	1.02	12 366.00	12 791.72
	Summer	11	13 332	12 634.20	1.06	1.06	12 563.09	12 903.64
	Autumn	12	12 354	12 827.87	0.96	0.96	12 913.39	13 015.56
1990	Winter	13	12 658	13 051.86	0.97	0.97	13 036.90	13 127.47
	Spring	14	13 350	13 295.31	1.00	1.02	13 118.99	13 239.39
	Summer	15	14 358	13 476.26	1.07	1.06	13 529.58	13 351.30
	Autumn	16	13 276	13 641.47	0.97	0.96	13 877.03	13 463.22
1991	Winter	17	13 184	13 816.94	0.95	0.97	13 578.32	13 575.14
	Spring	18	14 146	13 941.55	1.01	1.02	13 901.17	13 687.05
	Summer	19	14 966	14 064.81	1.06	1.06	14 102.34	13 798.97
	Autumn	20	13 665	14 200.68	0.96	0.96	14 283.72	13 910.88
1992	Winter	21	13 781	14 283.96	0.96	0.97	14 193.16	14 022.80
	Spring	22	14 636	14 274.74	1.03	1.02	14 382.73	14 134.72
	Summer	23	15 142	14 311.80	1.06	1.06	14 268.35	14 246.63
	Autumn	24	13 415	14 456.96	0.93	0.96	14 022.43	14 358.55
1993	Winter	25	14 327	14 526.27	0.99	0.97	14 755.99	14 470.46
	Spring	26	15 251	14 592.10	1.05	1.02	14 986.88	14 582.38
	Summer	27	15 082	14 732.30	1.02	1.06	14 211.49	14 694.30
	Autumn	28	14 002	14 826.97	0.94	0.96	14 636.01	14 806.21
1994	Winter	29	14 862	14 885.23	1.00	0.97	15 306.59	14 918.13
	Spring	30	15 474	14 968.52	1.03	1.02	15 205.77	15 030.04
	Summer	31	15 325			1.06	14 440.79	15 141.96
	Autumn	32	14 425			0.96	15 078.16	15 253.88
1995	*Winter*	*33*	*14 919*			*0.97*		*15 365.79*
Prediction	*Spring*	*34*	*15 750*			*1.02*		*15 477.71*
	Summer	*35*	*16 544*			*1.06*		*15 589.62*
	Autumn	*36*	*15 021*			*0.96*		*15 701.54*

Regression			Slope	**111.916**	**11 672.565**	Intercept on Y-axis
				6.0389127	114.18177	
	Coefficient of determination			0.9196685	315.41398	Standard error of estimate
				343.45261	30	
				34168719	2984579.3	

CAUSAL FORECASTING

Causal relationships

Causal forecasting is when sales or other activity, is related to, or *caused* by, some other event. For example:

- The forecast sale of compact discs (CDs) increases as the sale of CD players increases.
- There is a reduced demand for dairy products as a result of a correlation between cholesterol (present in dairy products) and heart ailments.
- The demand for smaller automobiles increases as the price of petrol rises.
- There is an increase in the use of public transport as city congestion increases.
- There is an increase in the incidence of skin cancer with increased exposure to the sun.

Although time is not a direct correlating factor, some causal events do occur over a changing time period.

The scatter diagram

A scatter diagram is a two-dimensional graph showing the x and y coordinates of various observations. The lines between successive data points are not shown, and the diagram appears simply as a series of data points. The purpose of the scatter diagram is to examine visually if there appears to be a relationship, or pattern, between the two sets of data. If so, perhaps it can it be used for forecasting, or estimating, future activity. In a scatter diagram the variable believed to be dependent on another observation is plotted on the y axis and the other, independent, variable is plotted on the x axis. The objective is to see if there is a causal effect of the independent variable on the dependent variable. The approach is similar to the time-series analysis, except that in the time series the independent variable is the time.

Figure 9.17 is a scatter diagram for the number of equivalent personnel days absent per month and the number of defective units discovered in that same month for an assembly operation. The number of defective components is plotted on the y axis and the employees absent per week plotted on the x axis. The purpose is to see if there is a relationship between defective units, and operator absenteeism, a dependency of the former on the latter. From the graph, it does appear that a dependency exists, in that the number of

defective units increases with absenteeism. In this case, the question is posed 'Is the rate of absenteeism a cause of product defects?'.

Linear regression equation

The data in Table 9.8 is that from which Figure 9.17 has been developed. In calculating absenteeism, two people absent for four days and one person absent for three days would be considered as 11 days.

Table 9.8 The data used to create Figure 9.17

Employees absent (days), X	Defective products (units) Y	Employees absent (days), X	Defective products (units) Y
15	45	12	13
13	35	16	41
12	19	14	25
11	17	20	59
13	23	21	62
9	9	15	35

As for a time series, the objective is to develop a linear equation of the form,

$$\hat{Y} = a + bX,$$

where X is the absenteeism, $\hat{Y}$ is the predicted value of the number of defective components, a is a constant, the intercept on the y axis, b is a constant, and the slope of the curve.

Using the regression function in Excel gives values of $a = 35.6182$ and $b = 4.7393$. These values, when substituted into the regression equation, give the following.

$$\hat{Y} = a + bX = -35.6182 + 4.7393X.$$

This regression line is shown plotted on the scatter diagram Figure 9.18. The line is such that the vertical distance between the observed Y value and the predicted value $\hat{Y}$ from the regression equation balance out. In other words, the Y values above the regression line, cancel out the Y values below the line.

Prediction

Once the regression equation has been determined, it can be used to predict other values of $\hat{Y}$, given the corresponding value of X. For example, if 18 employees

Figure 9.17 Absenteeism and defective components scatter diagram.

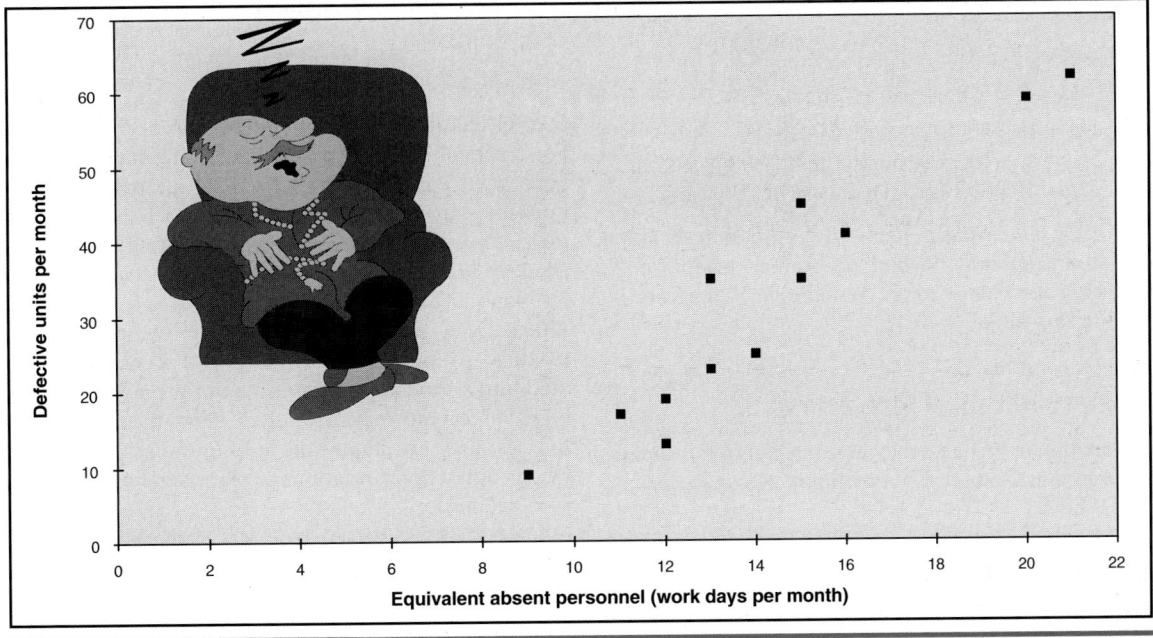

Figure 9.18 Absenteeism and defective components scatter diagram with regression line.

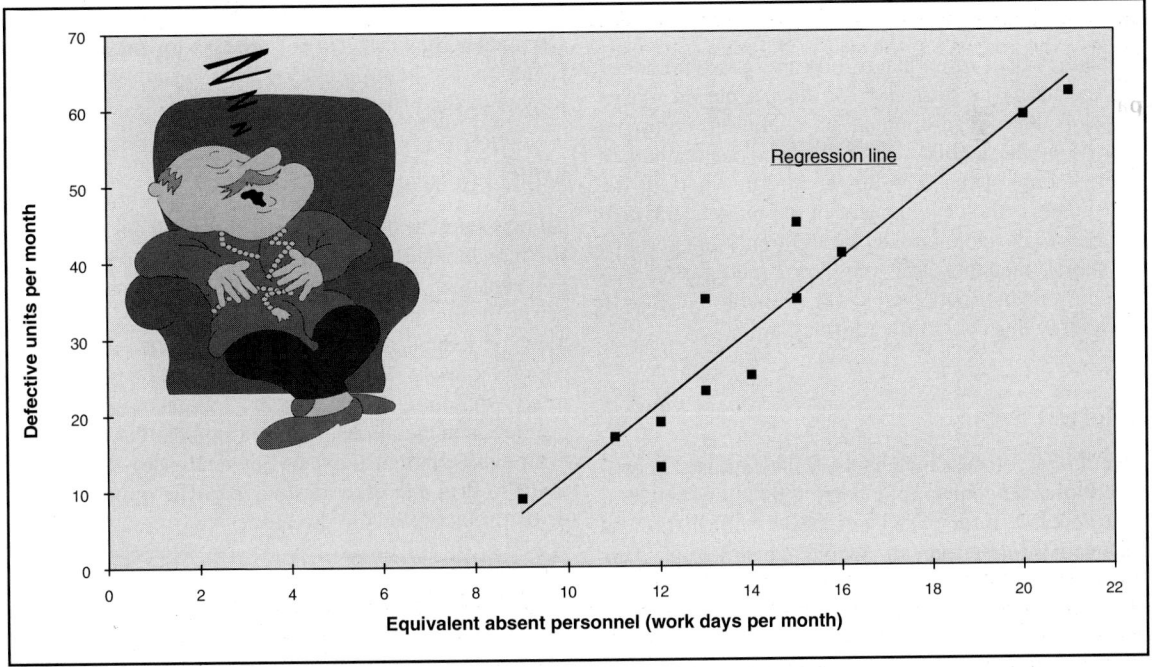

are absent, the estimate of defective parts can be calculated from the regression equation:

$$\hat{Y} = a + bX = -35.6182 + 4.7393X,$$

where:

$X = 18;$
$\hat{Y} = a + bX = -35.6182 + 4.7393 \times 18;$
$\hat{Y} = 49.6892$ (or an estimate of 50 parts).

One must be careful in using the regression equation not to extrapolate beyond the values given for X, because such values for X, which give Y, may not be valid in this range.

Accuracy of causal forecasting

Information on the accuracy in using causal forecasting is covered in Chapter 21, *Additional Forecasting*.

CONSIDERATIONS IN FORECASTING

The following are some elements to consider when developing a forecast model.[11]

Time horizons

Managers would often like a forecast to extend as far into the future as possible. Too long a period makes selection and development of a model complex, because of the inability of methods to accommodate different time spans. The longer the time period, the more costly is the development of the model. One possibility is to develop a model for different time periods, say short-, medium- and long-term, recognizing that the shorter-time-span model will probably be able to provide the most accurate information.

Collected data

Quantitative forecast models use collected data to estimate future outcomes. In collecting data it is better to have detailed, rather than aggregate, information as aggregate information can camouflage situations. This principle was illustrated in the sale of filing cabinets, where the detailed data in terms of units sold was shown to be more useful than the aggregate data in terms of revenues generated. In addition to the distortion caused by aggregating design types, revenues as a variable can be distorted by market events. It is better

to aggregate data after the forecast model has been developed, rather than before.

Market changes

Market changes should be anticipated in forecasting. For example, in the past steel requirements might have been correlated with the forecast sale of automobiles. However, as illustrated in Chapter 6, *An Environmental Balance*, plastic is rapidly replacing steel, so this factor would distort the forecast demand for steel if the old forecasting approach was used. Alternatively, more and more uses are being found for plastics, so this element would need to be incorporated into a forecast for the demand for plastics. These types of events may not affect short-term planning but certainly are important in long-range forecasting when capital appropriation for plant and equipment is a consideration.

Models are dynamic

A forecast model must be made a dynamic working tool with the flexibility to be updated or modified as soon as new data becomes available that might impact the outcome of the forecast. For example, an economic model for the German economy had to be modified with the fall of the Berlin Wall in 1989 and the fusion of the two Germanys. Similarly, current models for the European Economy are being modified to take into account the impact of the proposed single currency.

Model accuracy

All managers want an accurate model. The accuracy of the model, whether it is estimated at 10, 20 or, say, 50 per cent, can only be within a range bounded by the error in the collected data. Furthermore, accuracy must be judged in the light of the control a firm has over resources and external events. As well as accuracy, what is also of interest in a forecast is when turning points in situations might be expected to occur, for example a marked increase (or decrease) in sales so that the firm can take advantage of the opportunities, or be prepared for the threats.

Selecting the best model

It is difficult to give hard and fast rules for selecting the best forecasting model. Selecting a model and testing it against actual data or opinions may be a trial-and-error process. If a quantitative forecast model is used, there needs to be consideration of subjective input, and vice-versa. Models can be complex. In the early 1980s, I worked on developing a forecast model for world crude-oil prices needed to estimate financial returns from oil drilling and exploration and refinery and chemical plant operation. The basis for forecasting was a multiple regression model using economic data, including changes in GNP, interest rates, energy consumption patterns, chemical use, demographics, taxation, capital expenditure, seasonal effects and also country political risk. Throughout the development the model was tested against known situations.

SUMMARY OF KEY ELEMENTS

- Forecasting, or estimating the demand for finished goods or services, is the trigger for all operating activities in the supply chain.
- Forecasting is not an exact science. An optimistic forecast can result in higher than normal inventories, increased storage costs and plant capacity used unnecessarily. A pessimistic forecast may result in lost orders, lost clients and/or idle production through insufficient raw materials.
- Time horizons in forecasting can be short (up to about three months), medium (three months to one year) and long range (one to five years).
- Knowing the customer and knowing the markets are important qualitative aspects of forecasting.
- Forecasts, developed when employee bonuses are involved, risk being distorted.
- Forecasts from top management consolidate opinions of future activity from senior members of the organization.
- A sales-force composite is a consolidated judgmental forecast from the sales force.
- Buyers' expectations in forecasting mean soliciting opinions from prospective purchases of products.
- Leading economic indicators, including new contracts, purchase orders, inventory levels, capital appropriation and business incorporation, are tools for forecasting.
- Macroeconomic factors, including interest levels, exchange rates, unemployment, demographics, regulations, political climate and labour stability, can impact forecasts.
- The demand for elastic products, which are usually high priced and for which there are substitutes, changes sharply with price. The demand for inelastic products does not.
- Microeconomic factors for a firm, such as level of competition, product quality, price, design, delivery and accidents, are considerations in forecasting.
- Consumer surveys, help to forecast demand for products, but are expensive to carry out and their design needs to be such that they are representative of the population.
- A time series is historical data that may exhibit a trend, seasonal variation, irregular occurrences, a business cycle component and random variations.
- Straight moving-averaging models use the simple average of time periods. Weighted-moving-average models apply different weights for different time periods.
- Exponential smoothing uses an alpha factor (α) which takes a value between 0 and 1.
- Simple linear regression is the development of a linear equation model for forecasting; this takes the general form $\hat{Y} = a + bX$.
- Many products exhibit a seasonal effect on sales. The seasonal effect can be taken into account by determining a seasonal index and applying this to the actual data.
- Causal forecasting is when sales, or other activity, are caused by or dependent on another variable. This can be analysed by using a linear regression equation.
- In a forecast model the following are important: the time horizon, accuracy of collected data, market changes, model flexibility and accuracy, including turning points.

REVIEW AND DISCUSSION QUESTIONS

1 **Forecast risks**. In the long range, is it better to be optimistic or pessimistic in a forecast? Are the risks less for some firms than for others? Justify your reasoning.
2 **Level of forecast**. What are the costs involved if one is pessimistic, or optimistic, in the forecast sales of the following:

(a) food products;
(b) automobiles;
(c) restaurant meals?

3 **Sales remuneration**. Some companies give a bonus to sales staff according to the level of sales they make. The argument is that this motivates the sales people. Other firms do not agree with giving a bonus, because they argue that selling is a team effort and involves others in the company. What do you believe? Are there some products when a sales bonus is appropriate and others when it is not?

4 **Demographics**. Illustrate situations where demographic changes have modified the forecast of the sales of goods and services.

5 **Consumer surveys**. At some stage you have probably been confronted with responding to a survey, even maybe as an evaluation of a professor for a teaching programme. What do you think are the dangers of surveying? What are the advantages?

6 **International**. What are some of the international changes that have an impact on the sales of goods and services?

7 **Club Mediterranean**. Club Mediterranean, or Club Med, is a French-based travel group originally known for its 'sex, sea and sun' orientation towards vacations. It was once a rapidly growing business, but now its forecast for growth is not so strong. What are some of the factors you think might be affecting the changing forecast growth for this company?

8 **Time horizons**. In developing forecasting models, would you expect the model to be more accurate in the strategic time frame or in the operating time frame? Justify your reasoning.

9 **Causal factors**. What are some of the causal factors that impact the forecast of the following:
   - PVC piping;
   - ski vacations;
   - utilization of public transport;
   - pharmaceutical products;
   - golf clubs;
   - urban growth;
   - private education;
   - marriage;
   - automobiles;
   - fish for consumption;
   - increase in environmental laws;
   - alcohol consumption.

Consider both increasing and decreasing senses.

10 **Seasonal forecasting**. Name some products, either tangible or service-related, which are *not* subject to seasonal variations.

EXERCISE PROBLEM: BRITISH GAS

Situation

In a particular remote area of Northern Scotland, British Gas is considering adding new distribution networks in order to supply its customers with North Sea gas. In order to take some decisions, it needs to develop a forecast of consumption in 1995 on a month-by-month basis. Historical data of consumption is available for the previous two years as given in Table 9.9.

Required

1 Develop an appropriate forecast model using an empirical approach. Use the model to estimate gas demand for next year on a month-by-month basis.

Table 9.9 Gas consumption data

	Gas volume (millions of cubic feet)	
	Actual 1993	Actual 1994
January	29.9	57.2
February	33.8	53.3
March	27.3	42.9
April	19.5	29.9
May	15.6	33.8
June	18.2	22.1
July	6.5	22.1
August	7.8	18.2
September	13.0	26.0
October	16.9	29.9
November	23.4	39.0
December	19.5	49.4

EXERCISE PROBLEM: EXXON CORPORATION

Situation

Mark Atkinson has shares in Exxon Corporation, the US-based oil company in his investment portfolio. He bought a round lot (100 shares) in September 1984 for $40.156 per share. Since that date, Mark has participated in Exxon's reinvestment programme, which meant that he reinvested all quarterly dividends into the purchase of new shares. In addition, from time to time, he made optional cash investment in new shares.

The share price, and the number of shares held by Mark, at the end of each quarter since the time of the initial purchase up to the third quarter of 1996, are given in Table 9.10. Note that between June and September 1987, there was a two-for-one stock split which explains the drop in share price in that period.

Table 9.10 Mark's shares in Exxon Corporation

Date (end of quarter)	Price US$	Number of shares
Sep. 84	40 156	100.00
Dec. 84	44 593	101.91
Mar. 85	49 334	103.66
Jun. 85	51 244	105.38
Sep. 85	52 055	107.10
Dec. 85	51 025	108.99
Mar. 86	53 914	110.81
Jun. 86	59 183	112.50
Sep. 86	67 950	113.99
Dec. 86	70 174	115.45
Mar. 87	82 002	116.71
Jun. 87	88 410	117.90
Sep. 87	47 602	249.02
Dec. 87	39 291	262.71
Mar. 88	42 236	278.85

Date (end of quarter)	Price US$	Number of shares
Jun. 88	46 206	282.17
Sep. 88	45 015	296.90
Dec. 88	44 994	300.53
Mar. 89	45 026	304.21
Jun. 89	44 161	307.99
Sep. 89	44 913	311.49
Dec. 89	50 452	315.20
Mar. 90	46 264	319.28
Jun. 90	48 305	334.01
Sep. 90	50 935	337.94
Dec. 90	49 952	342.47
Mar. 91	56 549	355.37
Jun. 91	57 998	359.48
Sep. 91	58 809	363.57
Dec. 91	57 228	376.57
Mar. 92	55 876	381.08
Jun. 92	62 702	385.46
Sep. 92	63 160	389.85
Dec. 92	59 927	394.54
Mar. 93	64 149	398.97
Jun. 93	65 946	418.13
Sep. 93	65 077	422.76
Dec. 93	62 528	427.63
Mar. 94	65 507	432.33
Jun. 94	61 520	437.39
Sep. 94	59 665	442.66
Dec. 94	60 539	448.15
Mar. 95	63 969	453.40
Jun. 95	70 975	458.19
Sep. 95	70 416	463.07
Dec. 95	80 033	467.41
Mar. 96	80 978	471.74
Jun. 96	84 740	482.29
Sep. 96	83 704	486.85

Required

1 Illustrate with a time-series scatter diagram for the asset value (value of the portfolio) that there is a reasonable linear relationship.
2 What information indicates quantitatively the accuracy of the asset value and time for this model?
3 From the linear regression equation, what is the annual growth rate of the asset value of the portfolio?
4 Show the linear regression line on the scatter diagram.
5 Mark plans to retire at the end of December in the year 2000 (fourth quarter 2000). Using the linear regression equation, forecast the value of Mark's assets in Exxon stock at this date.
6 Compute an approximate 95 per cent confidence level for the value of the assets at the end of December 2000. (see Chapter 21, *Additional Forecasting*.)
7. What occurrences or events could affect the accuracy of forecasting the value of Exxon's asset value in 2000?
8. Qualitatively, would you think there is a great risk of Mark finding that the value of his assets is significantly reduced when he retires? Justify your response.

EXERCISE PROBLEM: HOUSES

Situation

San Marino is a reasonably affluent area in the north east of Los Angeles, California. A study was made to see if there was a relationship between the price of a house and its surface area. The surface area of the land was not included.

Table 9.11 gives a sample of 14 houses, together with their market price in $000s.

Required

1 Plot a scatter diagram to demonstrate whether or not there is a relationship between surface area and house prices.
2 Develop a linear estimating equation for this data.
3 Show the linear regression line on the scatter diagram.
4 How would you interpret the slope of the regression line?
5 What is the coefficient that demonstrates the strength of the relationship and what is its value?
6 If a home owner with a property of 1600 square feet was considering putting his or her home on the market, what would be a reasonable estimate of the market price?
7 Develop a 90 per cent confidence interval for the house price for a house that has a surface area of 1600 square feet.
8 What is the predicted market price for a house of 800 square feet? What are your comments about this value?
(See Chapter 21, *Additional Forecasting*, to respond to Questions 5 and 7.)

Table 9.11 A sample of 14 houses together with their market price

Area (Square feet)	Price ($000)
900	250
1550	400
1600	590
2200	900
3200	2100
1820	750
1710	684
1000	680
950	175
3100	2800
2300	1100
4000	5200
3750	3550
3500	3750

EXERCISE PROBLEM: MARINO CO.

Situation

The Marino company in Ventura County, Southern California sells swimming pool equipment. The sales for swimming pool motors in Southern California over the last 13 months are given in Table 9.12.

Required

1 Develop a forecasting model using a three-month simple moving average. Plot this model together with the original data. What is an estimate of demand for motors for next February?
2 Using a three-month weighted moving average, estimate the demand for swimming pool motors for next February. Use 1, 2, and 3 for the weights, with 3 being the weight for the most recent period, and 1 the weight for oldest period. Plot the model together with the original data.
3 Using the criteria of the mean average deviation, which of the methods in Requirements 1 and 2 would seem the most appropriate?

Table 9.12 Sales for swimming pool motors in Southern California over the last 13 months

Month	Sales (US $)
January	11 000
February	14 000
March	16 000
April	10 000
May	15 000
June	17 000
July	11 000
August	14 000
September	17 000
October	12 000
November	14 000
December	16 000
January	11 000

EXERCISE PROBLEM: PARKAS

Situation

The Hapsburg family is a distributor of Parkas in Vienna, Austria. This item of clothing is sold to both domestic and foreign clients. Sales for 1990, 1991, and 1992 are given in Table 9.13.

Required

1 Establish that there is a seasonal variation in the sales of parkas.
2 Develop a forecast by quarter for 1993.

Table 9.13 Sales of Parkas for 1990, 1991, and 1992 in thousands of units sold

	1990	1991	1992
January	65	69	87
February	52	57	69
March	43	51	62
April	39	45	57
May	31	39	47
June	33	42	49
July	23	31	41
August	19	23	27
September	17	23	28
October	67	72	90
November	69	75	93
December	72	79	97

CASE STUDY: WINE SALES

Situation

The Manzio family own a small premium winery in the Florence area of Italy. The volume of wine sold during 1992, 1993, and 1994 is given in Table 9.14.

Required

Based on this information, the owner is interested in developing a forecast model to estimate future sales.

Part I

Using the data for the full 36 months, develop forecasting models using three-month, four-month, and six-month moving averages. Which is the best model? Using this, what is an estimate of January 1995 wine sales?

Table 9.14 Volume of wine (in thousand litres) sold during 1992, 1993, and 1994

	1992	1993	1994
January	530	535	578
February	436	477	507
March	522	530	562
April	448	482	533
May	422	498	516
June	499	563	580
July	478	488	537
August	400	428	440
September	444	430	511
October	486	486	480
November	437	502	499
December	501	547	542

Part II

Can you improve upon the three-month moving average model if you use weighting factors of 0.4, 0.3 and 0.3, where 0.4 is for the most recent period? Justify your response.

Part III

Using the data for the full 36 months, develop forecasting models using the exponential smoothing method with α values of 0.1, 0.3 and 0.5, and using 500 000 litres for the starting point of the model. Which is the best model? Using this, what is an estimate of January 1995 wine sales?

Part IV

1 Is a regression analysis appropriate for forecasting if the independent variable is the time period? Plot a scatter diagram to justify your response.
2 What conclusions would you draw from calculating the coefficient of determination?
3 If regression is appropriate, use the regression equation to determine the best estimate of January 1995 sales.

The Manzio family noted that most of their wine sales were to tourists or to people who normally lived outside the wine growing area. Many of these people stayed in the numerous hotels and guest houses around Florence. Through a market survey of hotel accommodation, the data in Table 9.15 was compiled of the number of persons booked into hotels and guest houses during the periods for which wine sales are given in Table 9.14.

4 Does there appear to be a reasonable relationship between hotel occupancy and wine sales? Explain your analysis with the aid of a scatter diagram and a regression curve.

5 What conclusions would you draw from determining the coefficient of determination?
6 According to the tourist board, the hotel bookings are 31 000 for January 1995 and 25 000 for February 1995. Using this information, what is your best estimate of wine sales for these months using the regression equation?
7 Discuss the variables and other environmental factors that play a role in forecasting this type of product. Include macro- and micro-economic factors.
(See Chapter 21, *Additional Forecasting*, concerning the Co-efficient of Determination.)

Table 9.15 Numbers of people booked into hotels and guest houses in 1992, 1993 and 1994

	1992	1993	1994
January	28 700	29 800	30 800
February	23 200	25 200	28 000
March	29 000	28 000	31 000
April	23 500	26 000	28 400
May	21 900	25 000	27 500
June	25 300	31 000	32 000
July	26 000	25 550	31 000
August	20 100	23 200	22 000
September	22 300	24 100	26 000
October	25 100	25 100	27 000
November	22 600	27 000	28 000
December	27 000	31 900	30 200

NOTES AND REFERENCES

1. 'PC Makers aren't complaining, but ... with demand booming, components are scarce' (1995) *Business Week* 19 June: 33.
2. Heizer, J. and Render, B. (1996) *Production and Operations Management*, Englewood Cliffs, NJ: Prentice Hall: 161–62.
3. Dun & Bradstreet (1994) *The Economist* 4 June.
4. Byrns, R. T. and Stone, G. W. (1987) 'NBER Classification System', *Economics* (3rd edn), Glenview, IL: Scott Foresman: 146.
5. 'Have you driven a Jag, lately? Ford bags the carmaker as GM backs away' (1989) *Newsweek* 13 November: 49.
6. Alreck, P. L. and Settle, R. B. (1985) *The Survey Research Handbook*, Homewood, IL: R.D. Irwin.
7. *Chicago Daily Tribune* (1948) 3 November.
8. Box G. E. and Jenkins G. (1990) *Time Series Analysis: Forecasting and Control*, San Francisco, CA: Holden Day.
9. *Wall Street Journal Europe* (1995) 9 January.
10. Gardner E. S. (1985) 'Exponential smoothing: The state of the art', *Journal of Forecasting* 4(March).
11. Georgoff, D. M. and Murdick, R. G. (1986) 'Manager's guide to forecasting', *Harvard Business Review* January/February: 110–20.

FURTHER READING

Chase, C. W. Jr (1997) 'Selecting the appropriate forecasting method', *Journal of Business Forecasting Methods and Systems'* 16(3): 2,23.

Chen, C. (1997) 'Robustness properties of some forecasting methods for seasonal time series: A Monte Carlo study', *International Journal of Forecasting* 13(2): 269–80.

Geurts, M., Lawrence, K. D. and Guerard, J. (1994) *Forecasting Sales*, Greenwich, CT: JAI.

Guerts, M. D. and Whitlark, D. (1996) 'Improving sales forecasts by improving the input data', *Journal of Business Forecasting Methods and Systems* 15(3): 15–18.

Guadagno, A. (1995) 'Mastering the magic of sales forecasting', *American Salesman* 40(11): 16–23.

Kahn, K. B. and Mentzer, J. T. (1995) 'Forecasting in consumer and industrial markets', *Journal of Business Forecasting Methods and Systems'* 14(2): 21–28.

Kirkpatrick, R. and Gaynor, P. (1994) *An Introduction to Time Series Modelling and Forecasting for Business and Economics*, New York: McGraw Hill.

Makridakis, S. and Wheelwright, S. C. (1989) *Forecasting Methods for Management*, New York, Chichester: John Wiley & Sons.

Makridakis, S. G. (1990) *Forecasting Planning and Strategy for the 21st Century,* New York, Free Press.

Metcalfe, M. and Horrocks, J. (1995) 'Looking back at forecasting', *Journal of General Management* 21(1): 62–70.

Morrison, J. S. (1995) 'Life-cycle approach to new product forecasting', *Journal of Business Forecasting Methods and Systems* 14(2): 3–5.

Pecar, B. (1994) *Business Forecasting for Management,* New York: McGraw Hill.

Rosas, A. L. and Guerrero, V. M. (1994) 'Restricted forecasts using exponential smoothing techniques', *International Journal of Forecasting* 10(4): 515–27.

Rosati, A. M. (1996) 'Forecasting at Segix, Italia: A pharmaceutical company', *Journal of Business Forecasting Methods and Systems* 15(3): 7–9.

Sanders, N. R. and Manrodt, K. B. (1994) 'Forecasting practices in US corporations: Survey results', *Interfaces* 24(2): 92–100.

Shahabuddin, S. (1994) 'Forecasting: Is it a technique or a random walk?' *International Journal of Management* 11(4): 889–97.

Shays, M. E. (1997) 'Forecasting backlog', *Journal of Management Consulting* 9(4): 26–29.

Smith, S. A., Mcintyre, S. H. and Achabl, D. D. (1994) 'Sales forecasting in two stages: Improved support for retail decision-making', *Stores* 76(8): RR8–RR9.

Wisner, J. D. and Stanley, L. L. (1994) 'Forecasting practices in purchasing', *International Journal of Purchasing and Materials Management* 30(1): 22–29.

Zellner, A. (1994) 'Time-series analysis, forecasting and econometric modelling: The structural econometric modelling, time-series analysis (SEMTSA) approach', *Journal of Forecasting* 13(2): 215–33.

10 Design of the facility layout

Objectives and overview

The objective of this chapter is to illustrate the importance of design of the layout of the operating facility in order that the supply chain functions at its optimum. The chapter opens with an illustration of the fundamental differences between the layouts of manufacturing and service facilities. It then goes on to describe functional, cellular, assembly line, flexible-manufacturing and fixed-position layouts in operations that produce tangible goods. For service systems, it reviews layouts for retail stores, restaurants, airports and offices. It addresses the tendency towards open-plan office design and particularly the concept of 'hoteling' or reserving office space as needed. The chapter concludes by giving some methods for designing facility layout, including using two-dimensional templates, load–distance analysis, contact–distance analysis, systematic layout planning and line balancing.

DEFINING FACILITY LAYOUT

Chapter 7, *Process Design and the Operations Network*, addressed the conceptual steps involved in designing the process for delivering tangible products or services to a customer. This chapter details that part of the process design involving the physical layout, or arrangement, of all machines, equipment and workstations used in the operating environment. For supply-chain considerations, the design of the layout is important, because a poorly organized facility can delay the flow of materials or information and thus impact on timely delivery of the goods or services to the client. Facility layout applies to both manufacturing and service firms as discussed in the following.

Manufacturing

A manufacturing site is established to transform raw materials or components into finished goods destined for consumer or industrial use. Here, a facility layout would include the organization of:

- machines used in cutting, drilling, printing, packaging, filling, painting, etc.;
- workstations for individuals, teams of operators or robot controlled systems;
- storage areas for raw materials, purchased components, packaging, and finished products;

- offices for all the service-related functions.

Service organization

Many service facilities offer direct client contact and so the facility layout is heavily influenced by the need to provide maximum customer convenience. The layout depends very much on the service offered and might include:

- aisle and shelving arrangement in retail stores;
- reception areas for clients in a bank, insurance broker, or accounting firm;
- offices for personnel in consulting, engineering, purchasing, etc.;
- repair bays in an automobile repair shop;
- operating rooms, treatment areas and patient beds in a medical centre;
- loading and unloading docks for the transportation vehicles in a distribution centre;
- storage zones for finished products in a wholesaling operation.

Material and information flow

Any firm includes some, or all, flow streams of material, people, transfer equipment and information. The global objective of any facility layout is efficiency such that:

- It uses a flow pattern that is the most cost-effective.

- It optimizes utilization of space.
- It facilitates the installation of an information systems network.
- It conforms to health regulations.
- It respects safety rules.
- It takes into consideration the comfort and well-being of employees.
- It is the most agreeable for customers.

Facility access

Whatever the facility, it should offer easy access to transportation routes, adequate parking for utility, customer and employee vehicles. In addition, there should be escalators and/or lifts if work or service areas are on several floors.

The cost of the facility layout

The preparation and implementation of a facility layout is costly, in terms of labour, materials and time. In addition, to reorganize an existing arrangement is doubly costly, because of the expense of curtailing operations during the changeover. For this reason, careful consideration has to be given to deciding on a facility layout, because the arrangement is normally long lasting. Nonetheless, with changing markets, needs or new technology, all firms modify layouts from time to time.

Site selection and layout

In locating a new facility, discussed in Chapter 3, *Site Selection*, the prospect of additional space for facility expansion always needs always to be taken into consideration.

LAYOUT IN MANUFACTURING

Manufacturing steps

A manufacturing operation is a network involving the movement of materials, adding value at each step in the activity.

1 Raw materials, components and packaging are delivered to the manufacturing site.
2 The material is unloaded, inspected for conformity and placed into storage.
3 Material is taken from storage as needed for the production process.
4 In-process inventory on the shop floor is transferred from one workpost to another.

5 Finished products are taken from the last workpost and put into a storage area.
6 Finished goods are taken from storage and dispatched to the client.

Factors in the layout

The layout will depend on the type of production operation, the size of the organization, and the number of different components handled. Some considerations will include those discussed in the following sections.

Types of materials

- For solid materials, the volume, weight and fragility. A firm may be dealing with iron castings that are heavy but may crack on impact, glass or ceramic materials that break easily or plastic components that are light but can be easily scored.
- Sterile zones may be required, for example, in the production of pharmaceutical products, syringes and other medical equipment.
- Refrigerated areas may be needed for food, vaccines or other perishable items.
- Some products may be affected by humidity, so dehumidified zones need to be incorporated.
- Computer components and nuclear-related products need areas that are free from dust and electrostatic charge.

Building construction

- The building used to house the facility should be such that walls, ceilings and floors have sufficient structural strength for machines and heavy equipment, for example stamping presses, furnaces, robots, overhead cranes, etc.
- If the facility is in an earthquake zone, such as Southern California, Japan or Mexico, the building structure needs to take this into consideration.
- Insulation from noise and vibration should be such that other areas are not affected if there is noise or vibration in one or more particular areas.

Environment and safety

For personnel working at the facility, environmental and safety regulations need to be respected:

- Noise levels should be kept to an acceptable level and lighting, heating and air conditioning should be adequate.
- Flammable liquids, such as petroleum products, cleaning fluids or paints, should be kept in an appropriate area away from personnel.
- Storage silos for fine solid materials, such as grain, chemical products or coal, should be far away from

personnel areas as they could explode under adverse conditions. (In Bordeaux, France in 1997 a grain silo exploded and killed people in an office building located nearby).

Working area

▨ The area should be comfortable and agreeable for employees and customers who visit the site.

▨ There should be sufficient room to carry out necessary maintenance procedures. In a chemical plant, for example, maintenance people need to be able to clean out heat exchangers, change fluid pumps or work on furnace equipment.

▨ There should be sufficient space for people and mobile equipment, as well as for delivery vehicles to manoeuvre around the area.

Meeting rooms

▨ Meeting rooms for operators to discuss improvements, quality aspects, etc. should be available near the production area.

Functional layout

A functional layout, also known as a job-shop, batch or process layout, is where different types of products are subjected to different process operations, such as cutting, welding, drilling, milling, cleaning, painting, heat treatment and the like, as illustrated in Figure 10.1.

If the company is a small business, and the volume of any one type of product is small, then the type of layout shown in Figure 10.1 is perhaps the best arrangement. The facility is organized according to the process operation employed, rather than the products themselves, and materials may not pass directly through the facility. The workforce is often specialized in a certain process operation and these people remain in the department concerned.

In the functional layout illustrated in Figure 10.1, the Numbers, 1, 2, 3 and 4 represent a group of different families of products, which pass through the various process centres of the job shop. For example they might be as shown in Table 10.1.

Table 10.1 Products used in various process centres

Reference number	Material
1	Copper units for electrical use
2	Aluminium units for impeller blades
3	Carbon-steel flanges
4	Stainless-steel cog wheels

With this layout there are waiting periods while operators are working on a particular reference group. For example, if, in the Cutting area, work is currently proceeding on reference group 1, then any components in groups 2 to 3 are waiting. A similar situation would occur in the other functional areas.

Jewellery manufacture

A functional layout for the manufacture of costume jewellery is shown in Figure 10.2. This is a family-owned business near Annecy, France which employs about 50 people and exports its products worldwide. From the basic raw materials of chain, stones and gold or silver for coating it makes several hundred different models of rings, earrings, necklaces, bracelets, pendants and brooches. The functional areas are: receiving and storage of the raw materials; cleaning, cutting and forming; casting and de-burring; soldering; mounting; hand and machine polishing; surface treatment; quality control; packing; and dispatching. In each of the functional areas are persons specialized in that particular operation.[1]

Cellular layout

The inconvenience, and certain inefficiency, arising from the functional layout can be considerably minimized if the work centre is organized according to the product, rather than functional activity, as illustrated in Figure 10.3. In this scheme, the reference group illustrated in Figure 10.1, now flows directly from one process operation to another as equipment is dedicated to a particular product line or cell. If the system is correctly balanced, there will be essentially no waiting time. In this arrangement, operators have to be multiskilled so that they can work on any process operation and concentrate on the product flow. With cellular layout there is less movement of parts, waiting time is reduced, the volume of in-process inventory is reduced and, if properly designed, the productivity of the operation is increased.

Cellular layout provides greater flexibility in manufacturing. However, it involves a bigger capital investment in machinery, equipment and, normally, surface area. In addition, it will only work if operators are multiskilled, although, in any event, multiskilled employees are often more motivated and are more useful to an organization. Before an organization restructures its workcentre into a cellular layout, it needs to be clear that there will be continued future work and a financial analysis needs to be made to be sure that the additional investment is justified. Some alternatives to consider are discussed in the following sections.

Figure 10.1 Functional layout.

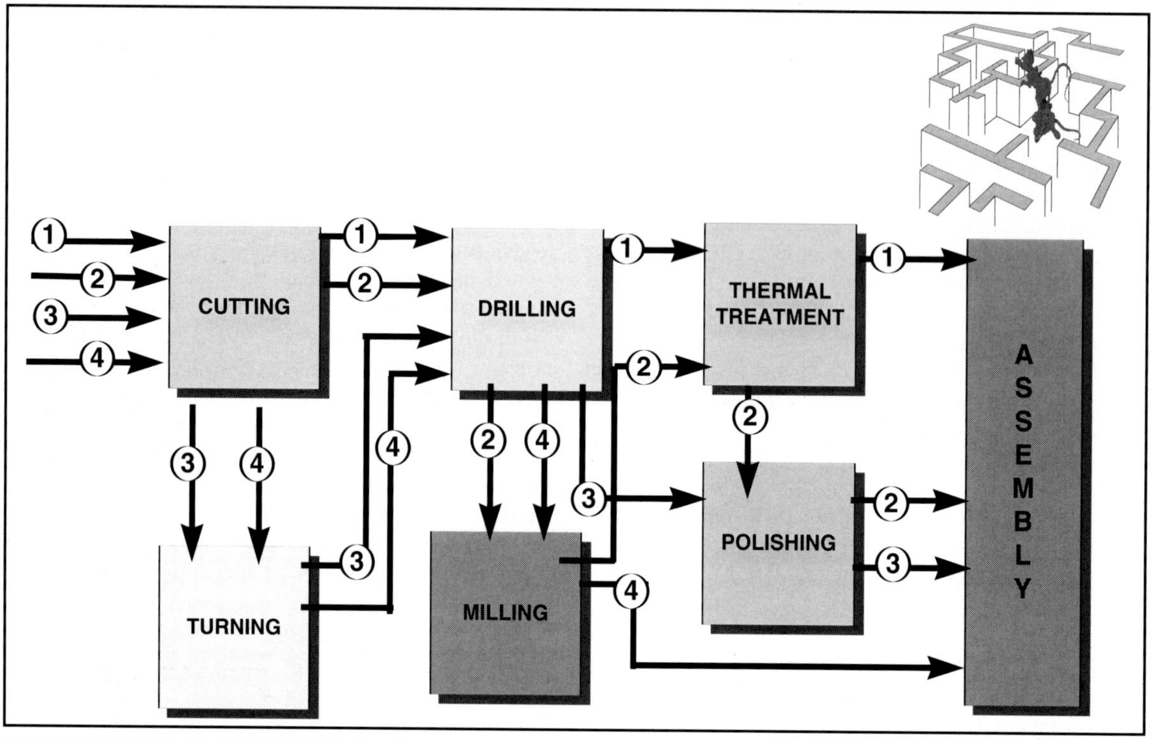

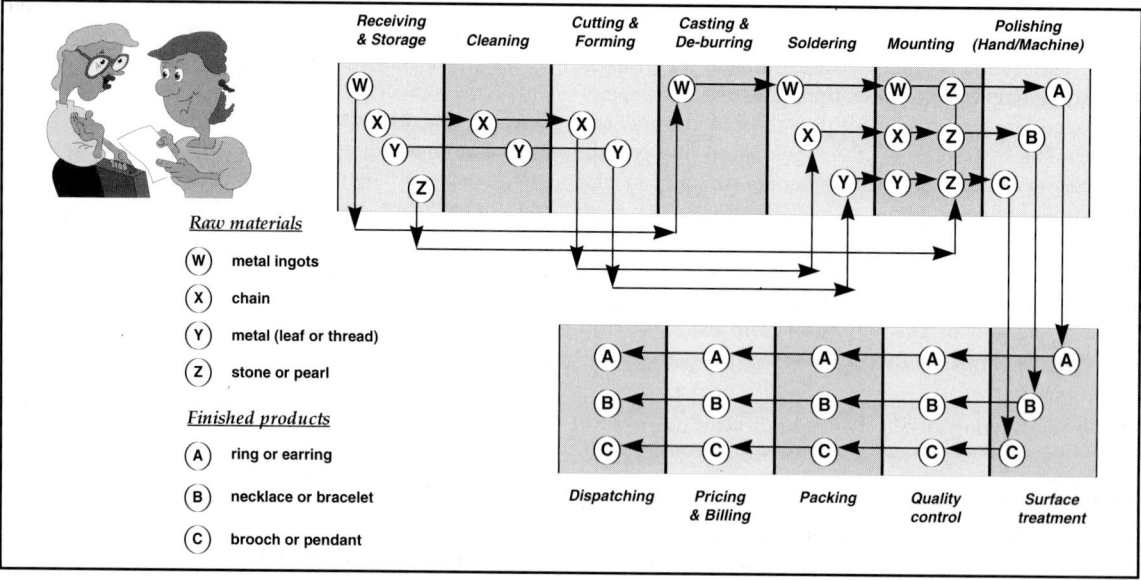

Figure 10.2 Process layout of a costume jewellery company (Trenel SA, ZI des Césardes, 7400 Seynod, France).

Figure 10.3 Cellular manufacturing.

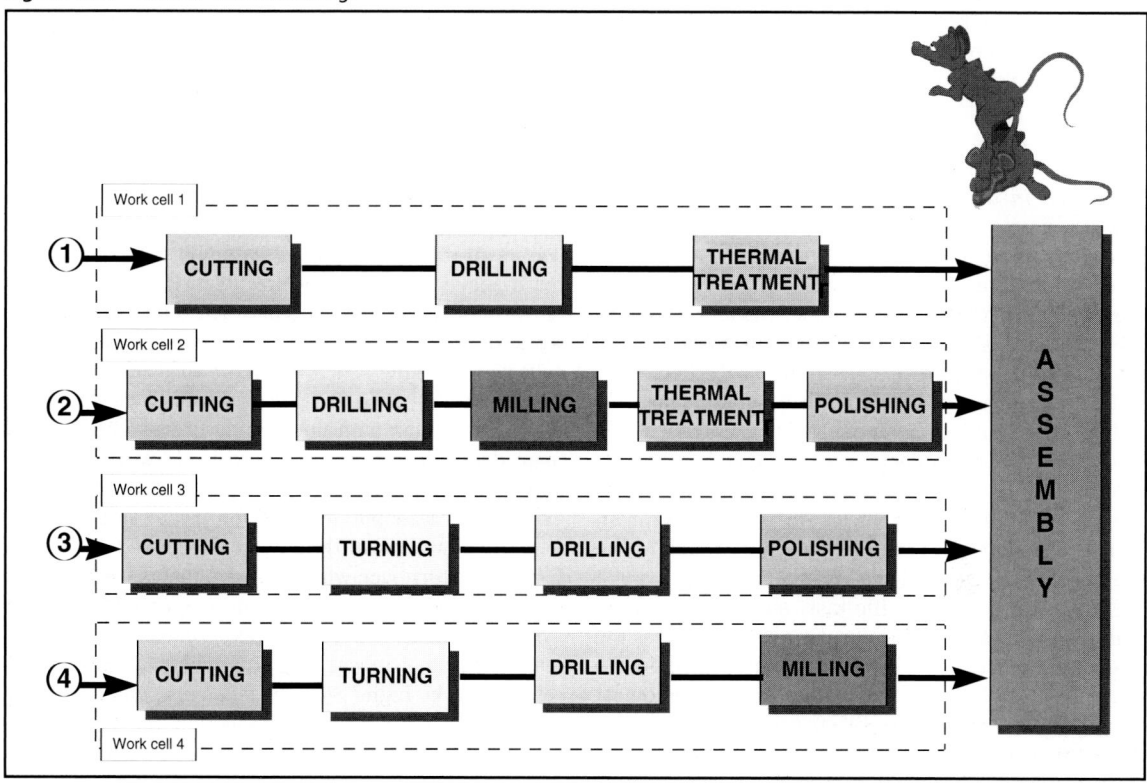

Mobile equipment

One way of minimizing the investment is to have equipment that is mobile and can be transferred from one product line to another, according to demand. Small drilling, cutting or sewing machines can be made mobile by mounting them on wheeled trolleys. Large heavy, automated equipment, however, is difficult to relocate.

Subcontracting

For small firms, which do not have the necessary financial or human resources, a cellular organization can be used if part of the work is subcontracted (Chapter 16, *Purchasing and Subcontracting*). For example, the firm might be able to use its available resources to establish a cellular layout for the principal products and then subcontract products for which the production volume is smaller.

Multiple operating sites

Companies that have several operating sites, performing similar work, may be able to reorganize their facil-

ities by dedicating each site to a particular product line using cellular manufacturing at each site as illustrated in Table 10.2

Assembly-line layout

The assembly-line layout is an arrangement to accommodate mass-produced products, such as computers, automobiles, washing machines or other relatively standardized products produced in large quantities. It is the product that moves in this layout and each

Table 10.2 Reorganization using a cellular layout.

Site	Products made before with functional layout	After with cellular layout
1	A, D, E, F, G, K	A, D, E
2	A, E, G, K, L, X	G, K, X
3	A, D, F, K, L, M	F, L, M

operator remains basically in the same area, performing a specific task. An assembly line is an inflexible arrangement, involving high capital cost, and is designed to allow the best possible direct material flow through the facility. The concept is often attributed to Henry Ford in the 1920s with his facility layout for the production of Ford T automobiles (Chapter 8, *Human Resources in the System Design*). Another notable illustration was during World War II when Charles Sorenson of the USA designed a facility layout called 'The Willow Run Assembly Line', which was able to produce one B-24 Liberator bomber plane every hour.

Figure 10.4 shows schematically an assembly-line layout, where the raw materials arrive at the beginning of the line and each operator performs a particular task, adding the required components or subassemblies, before the finished product leaves at the end of the line. Figure 10.5 illustrates the layout for a truck axle, as assembled in a heavy-vehicles factory (Caterpillar, Renault VI, Mercedes). The axle casing arrives at the beginning of the assembly line on a conveyer belt. Each operator performs a specific task, such as bolting on brake assemblies, fluid lines or differential units, as the axle casing moves linearly down the line. Components and subassemblies are positioned in chronological order at the side of the line. Electric tools such as drills, wrenches and screwdrivers are positioned overhead for the maximum convenience of the operators and to avoid encumbering the work area. The axles are positioned at about waist height for the operators so that excessive bending or reaching is avoided.

The Volvo experiment

In 1987 Volvo, Sweden, embarked on an experiment to mass-produce its Volvo Model 740, in which it did not use its previously employed assembly line. Instead, it put in place a cellular-type arrangement using seven to ten workers in a team, who performed all the assembly work necessary to produce four cars per shift. The cells were designed such that more than 80 per cent of the assembly could be performed in a comfortable working position with no bending or stretching. Each team determined how long they would work on a car and took the responsibility for fixing defects. Volvo's experiment was put in place to try to improve the monotonous work of the operators and reduce absenteeism and turnover, which in Volvo plants were around 20 per cent and 30 per cent respectively. At the Uddevala plant, where this experiment was put in place, absenteeism was only 8 per cent and morale was reported to be high.[2] Sony, of Japan also changed from assembly line to cellular production for its camera

Figure 10.4   Assembly-line layout.

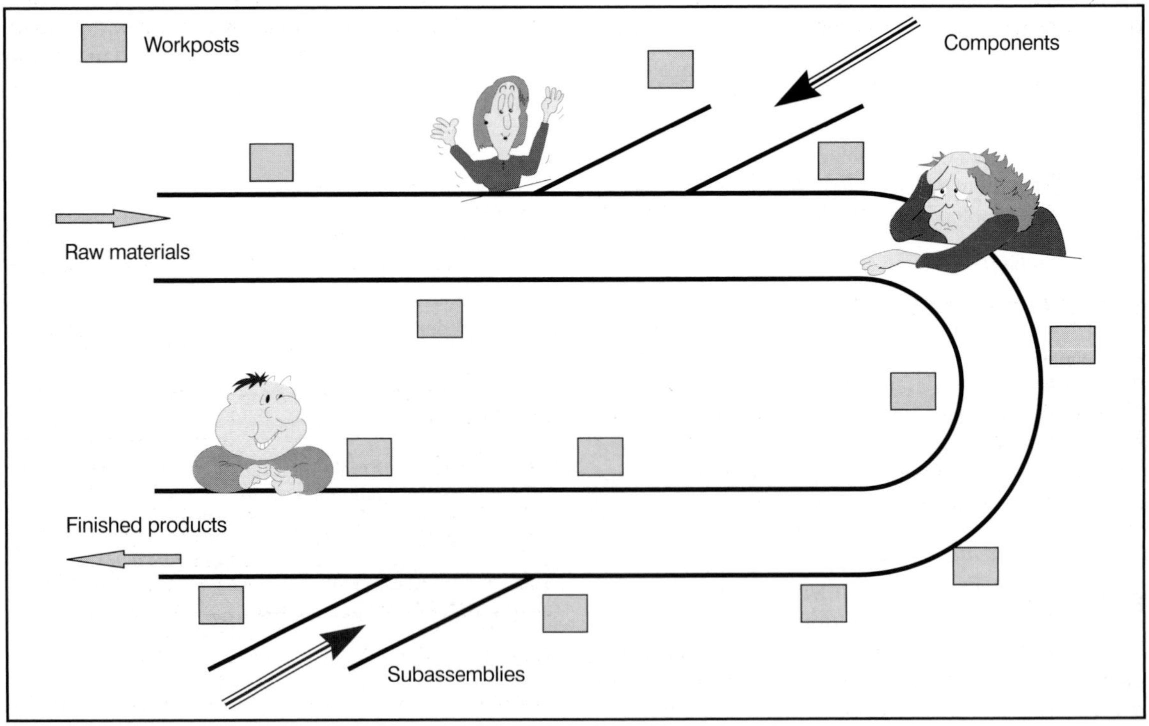

Figure 10.5   Assembly-line flow.

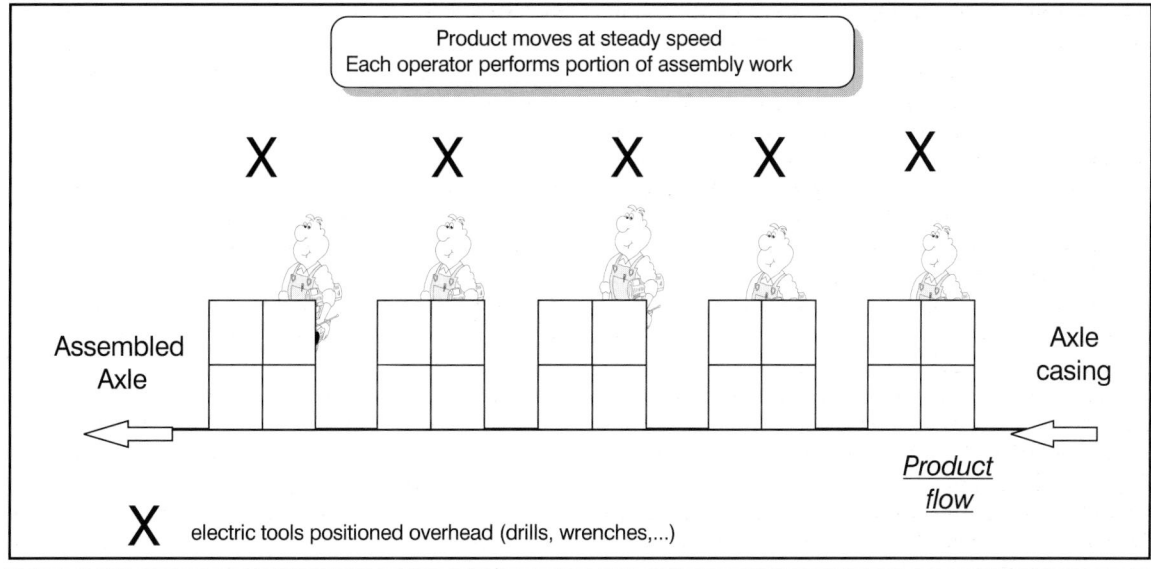

units and found that output was 10 per cent higher than in a conventional assembly line.[3]

Flexible manufacturing systems

Flexible manufacturing implies a single assembly facility that can build a wide assortment of models and types of products on one assembly type layout. The traditional assembly line with the rigid conveyor system does not permit this and so in flexible manufacturing, the conveyor is replaced by automatic guided vehicles (AGVs), which transfer parts to various work areas according to specific computer commands. The concept of flexible manufacturing is illustrated in the article in Box 10.1[4]

Layout and throughput

In general terms, the differences between the three layouts, functional, cellular, and assembly line can be illustrated by an exponential curve of the type shown in Figure 10.6. This correlates the layout with volume throughput, and product variation. Table 10.3 compares the assembly line and the functional layout. A cellular layout is intermediate between these.

Fluid flow

Fluid flow layouts apply to continuous manufacturing operations, such as oil refineries, chemical facilities, pharmaceutical plants and parts of some food opera-

tions (brewing, soft drinks, wine, etc.). Processing steps may include heating, distillation, catalytic transformation, cooling, mixing or fermentation. This type of layout incorporates pipelines, reaction vessels and heat exchangers and is often limited to a very narrow range of products. The layout is rigid, has a high capital investment and, once in place, is difficult to change. The workforce is limited to a few personnel, who manage the facility operations from a control room incorporating a sophisticated network of automatic process control systems.

Fixed position layouts

A fixed-position layout applies either to large product units that are difficult to move during the early stages,

Table 10.3 Comparison of the assembly line and the functional layout

Assembly line	Functional layout
Unit throughput is high	Unit throughput is low
Capital cost for equipment is high	Capital cost for equipment not excessive
Layout is rigid	Flexibility with type of products handled
Labour employed is low	Labour employed is high
High proportion of automation	Low proportion of automation
Number of different products is low	Number of different products is high

Box 10.1 Nissan takes the mass out of production to increase flexibility at its 'dream factory' By Clay Chandler and Joseph B. White, Staff Reporters

Kazutaka Kobatake has declared war on the conveyor belt.

For years, Mr. Kobatake and members of a key production-engineering team at Nissan Motor Co. struggled to design a "flexible-manufacturing system" – a single assembly facility that could build a wide assortment of models and types of cars at high speed on one assembly line. One big problem was the conveyor; it held every vehicle on a line hostage to the progress of the car that took longest to build. What to do?

Mr. Kobatake's answer is now coming to life at a new, hospital-clean factory at Kanda-Cho, Kyushu, the southernmost of Japan's five main islands. Nissan managers call it the "Dream Factory." Inside, instead of a conveyor, is a convoy of "intelligent motor-driven dollies," little yellow platforms that tote cars at variable speeds down the production line, sending out a stream of computer-controlled signals to coach both robots and workers along the way.

Mr. Kobatake's dolly line highlights what experts say is the next big challenge for auto makers. With the global vehicle market fragmenting into a thousand niches, car makers face increasing pressure to make their factories and robots not just efficient, but highly flexible.

Adding Flexibility

The goal, which could cost billions to achieve, is for each assembly line to handle not just two or three variations of the same basic chassis, but five or six or more different vehicles. That way, the factory stands a better chance of running profitably if one model doesn't sell.

That's a big change from so-called mass-production systems, where tools and conveyors are set up to turn out 240,000 copies of the same basic car.

On the surface, it appears the Japanese are running ahead of U.S. auto makers in developing the first generation of flexible-production lines. With a few exceptions, most North American factories of the Big Three automakers are still tooled to build just one chassis.

"The U.S. is still in mass production, working on lean production. The Japanese are farthest along the curve," says Len Allgaier, a GM manufacturing expert who's worked on a study of flexible-manufacturing strategies.

Honda Motor Co. assembles three different models on the same line at plants in both Japan and the U.S. Mazda Motor Corp. has been producing cars, trucks and minivans on the same line at its plant in Hofu, Japan, for nearly a decade. Nissan officials say the Kyushu plant – the first to eliminate the conveyor belt in all stages of the production process – outdoes both Honda and Mazda, and is more sophisticated than archrival Toyota Motor Corp.'s new plants. When fully operational, the new Kyushu facility will be capable of building four models in as many as eight different body types at a rate of about 240,000 vehicles annually, company officials say.

All Down the Line

"We can send almost anything down this line," Mr. Kobatake declared as he toured the new factory with a group of foreign journalists last month.

For Nissan and other auto makers, the rewards for perfecting truly flexible-manufacturing systems promise to be great. But so, say analysts, are the risks.

In the 1980s, General Motors Corp. learned the hard way that increasing the number of robots on an assembly line doesn't necessarily translate into production savings or increased sales. GM struggled to debug robots that spray-painted one another rather than cars, and some GM factories even sidelined robots, including self-guiding dollies, to go back to a more basic approach.

Today's robots are "smarter" and less prone to bugs than the earlier generation models that gave GM so much trouble. But they still cost plenty to buy and maintain.

Nissan's new Kyushu plant "is great from the engineers' point of view," says Koji Endo, an auto analyst at S.G. Warburg Securities Ltd. in Tokyo. "But I'm not sure yet how much it will contribute right away for the company as a whole."

Nissan executives say the new Kyushu plant is 30% more productive than any of their other factories, and will save them a bundle in the long run. But with its 100 billion yen ($804.5 million) cost, the facility may make it harder for Nissan to achieve its ambitious short-run goal of reducing assembly costs by 10% a year over the next three years.

Real Test Coming

For now, all those versatile machines aren't doing Nissan nearly as much good as they could, because the Kyushu plant is manufacturing only one model, the relatively easy-to-assemble Pulsar car, in three body types. "The real test will come when Nissan adds other models to the Kyushu line," says Noriyuki Matsushima, an automobile analyst at the research affiliate of Nikko Securities Co. Nissan won't say when that will be, but Mr. Matsushima guesses it won't happen for another year.

"Nissan designed this plant when business was booming," he cautions. "It's got more equipment than they need."

Mr. Kobatake is among the first to acknowledge that combining automation and flexible-manufacturing techniques isn't easy. Production at the new Kyushu plant is still at about 170 cars daily, slightly behind schedule, and engineers are finding that it takes more time than expected to work bugs out of robots' software. A number of the devices supposedly being demonstrated for visitors recently operated sporadically or not at all.

Still, Japan's No. 2 car maker has high hopes that the flexible-manufacturing techniques at the new Kyushu plant will give it a jump on rivals. It's a jump Nissan badly needs. The company's sales and profits are slumping, and its factories, both in Japan and the U.S., trail rival Toyota's in productivity.

Meeting Changing Demand

The primary goal of the new flexible techniques, Nissan officials say, is improving the company's ability to respond quickly and efficiently to consumer demands. Mr. Kobatake says shifting to production of a completely new model will take less time at Kyushu-style plants because there's no need to replace the jigs on robots used there. In conventional Japanese car plants, retooling for production of a new model usually requires at least 10 months. But he says such as ships, aircraft or locomotive engines, or, to buildings, bridges or dams, which simply cannot be moved. The latter are unique items, or projects (Chapter 18, *Project Management*). In a fixed-position layout, materials, machines and subcontractors move to and from the product, or work site, as required by the project plan, as shown in Figure 10.7. There are situations in aircraft manufacture at Airbus, Toulouse, France, or Boeing, Seattle, Washington, USA, where, at some stage of the production operation, the product, does move in an assembly-type operation on a conveyor arrangement.

Movement of materials

Manufacturing involves a lot of handling and movement of materials. In the design of the facility layout, best efforts should be made to ensure the following:

- Materials flow through the system in a linear flow pattern in order to minimize zigzagging and backtracking.
- The production processes are arranged to facilitate the direct flow of material.
- Workposts are positioned such that material movement is minimized.
- Storage areas are located near the usage area to minimize movement of operators.
- Equipment is positioned such that operators working with material are at their normal standing or sitting level to avoid bending, stretching, and reaching.
- Heavy physical activity, such as lifting or carrying loads, is avoided by using automatic systems including robots.
- Heavy or bulky materials are moved the shortest distance and only then with mechanical equipment.

Figure 10.6 Nature of layout configurations.

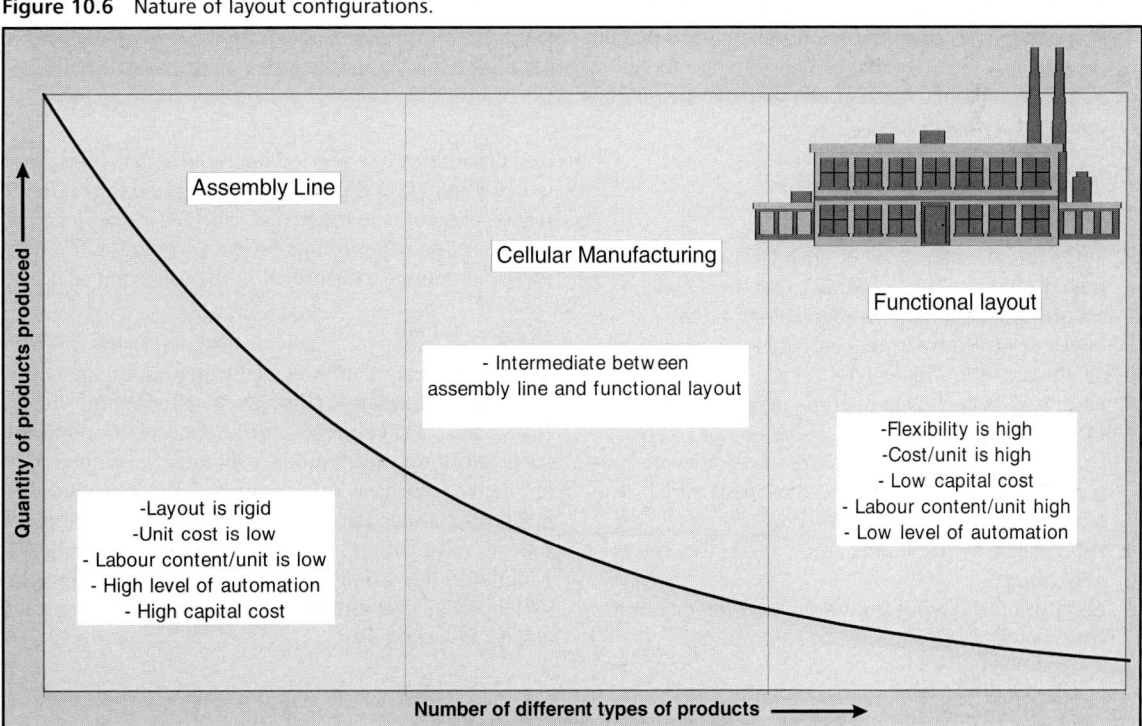

Figure 10.7 Fixed-position layout.

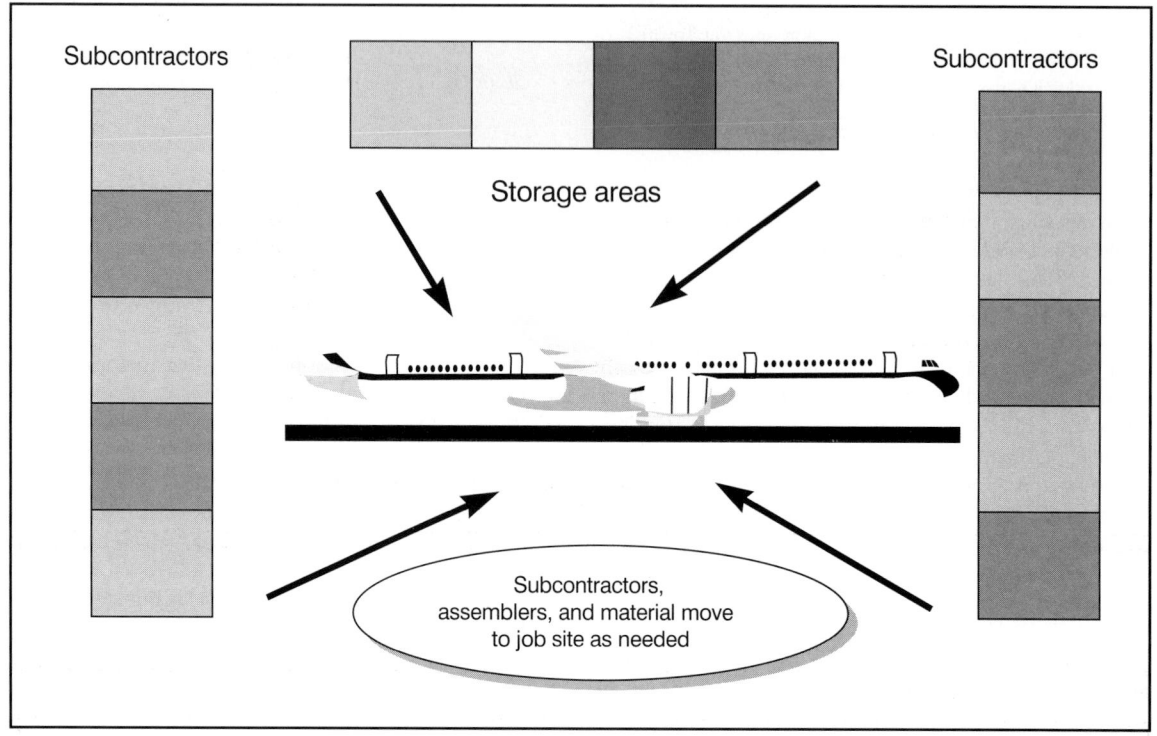

Subcontractors

Subcontractors

Storage areas

Subcontractors, assemblers, and material move to job site as needed

- The number of times any material is moved is minimized.
- Mobile equipment that is used to move material is operated at capacity.

Materials-handling equipment

Types of materials handling facilities include:

- automatic transfer devices, such as robots and automated guided vehicle (AGVs) that move materials according to specific computer commands;
- operator-driven trolleys, front-end loaders or trucks, as illustrated in Figure 10.8;
- overhead or moveable operator-controlled cranes;
- moving carpets, conveyors, belts, chains or rotating carousels or turntables (Figure 10.9 gives an illustration of a rotating table used in firms which manufacture automobile components);
- rigid plastic boxes, hand carts, pallets, tote boxes or wire bins;
- elevators for moving from floor to floor, or to move from one storage platform to another.

RETAIL FACILITIES

Types

Retail facilities are service operations that offer products for sale directly to the consumer and they differ in terms of products they sell, surface area, location, sales service offered and product price. Some of the most common are described in the following sections.

Hypermarkets

A hypermarket, common in France and some other European countries (though less common in the USA), sells a diverse selection of products including food, clothing, automobile products, large electrical appliances such as refrigerators, washing machines, small appliances like toasters, coffee percolators and razors, and other consumer goods. Harrods, in Knightsbridge, London, is a very special hypermarket which sells 'everything' though everything may not always be on display.

Figure 10.8   Equipment for material transfer.

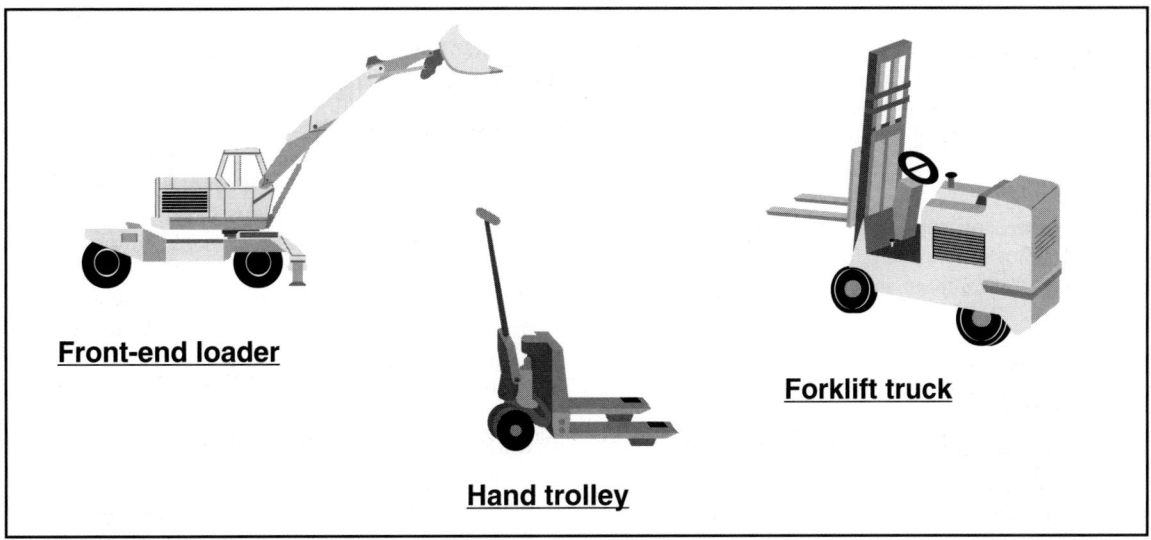

Figure 10.9   Layout: rotating table.

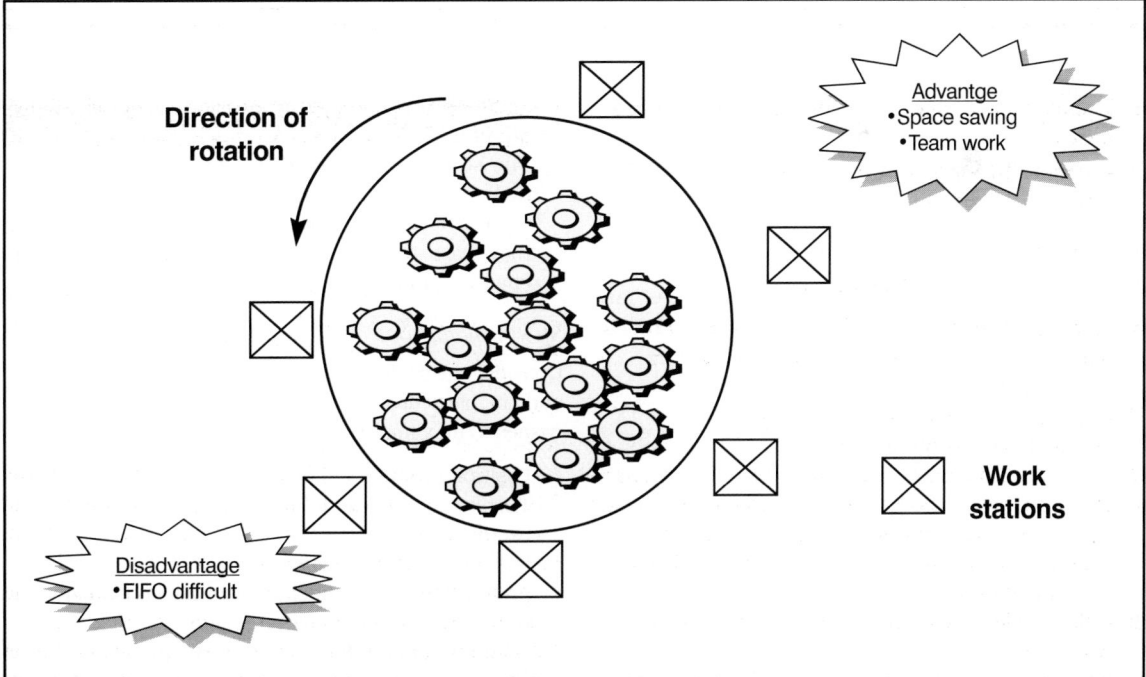

Supermarkets

A supermarket principally sells food and drink items and other products related to the household, such as paper goods, cleaning fluids and plastic items. Depending on the surface area, it may also sell a limited amount of clothing, books and toys.

Grocery stores

A grocery store, or 'superette', has a small surface area and sells almost exclusively food and household products. They are common in the villages and towns of Europe.

Petrol station convenience stores

Petrol convenience stores, run by such oil firms as Esso, Mobil, BP and Elf, sell travel-related items including packaged food, automotive products, reading material, etc. This is now an important part of petrol stations' business.

Speciality stores or boutiques

Speciality stores sell specific ranges of items such as jewellery, clothing, sporting goods, hi-fi equipment, etc.

Warehouse discount stores

Warehouse stores are those that sell a range of items at a discount if products are bought in bulk. Often there is minimal display of the products. They are common in the USA and Canada.

Department stores

A department store sells a wide range of goods including clothing, furniture, home appliances, garden equipment, travel goods, etc. Very often they have one or more restaurants in the facility. Examples are Selfridges in England and Galerie Lafayette in France.

Objectives of a retail outlet

A retail outlet is a profit centre and its principal objective is to maximize sales. Stores that belong to a chain are very often compared, or 'benchmarked', according to their sales volume during similar periods. One element in maximizing sales is the layout or physical location of the goods in the store. For example, many department stores will have men's items close to the entrance and often on the ground floor to make it easy for men to shop, because in general it is not one of their preferred pastimes! For retail outlets selling food and related items, the layout is principally a merchandising function where the location of products in the store, and their positioning on shelves strongly influences their sale. The following are considerations.

Aisle arrangement

Figure 10.10 shows schematically the layout of a grocery store or supermarket. Some of the criteria for the aisle arrangement are:

- Frequently sold items, such as milk, bread and cheese, are located at the end of the store. This obliges consumers to pass through the entire store, increasing the probability that other articles will be purchased on impulse as they pass other displayed items.
- Related products, such as tea, coffee, and sugar, are grouped together so that the purchase of one may help to trigger the purchase of another.
- High-margin items, such as beauty products and pet foods, are located in the most frequently used aisles, which are often the first and last in the store.
- Long continuous aisles, rather than short broken ones, are installed, which again forces customers to walk through the whole length of the store.
- Promotional goods or high-margin items are located at the end of shelves.
- Items that are purchased frequently, such as wine, bread, milk, cheese, meat and paper goods, are dispersed in different locations as again this obliges customers to traverse other departments.
- Spontaneously purchased items, such as chewing gum, sweets, and magazines are placed at the check-out.
- Shelves are positioned to provide for impulse buying of articles.
- The store layout should be changed from time to time. This confuses customers, who are obliged to 'search again' for products. During their search, they pass through aisles and make impulse purchases of items.

Shelf layout, and merchandising

Consider the shelf position as illustrated in Figure 10.11 and, in particular, product X, the sales of which one wishes to maximize over and above competing products:

- Position product X about 1.60 metres from the floor. This is visually where the consumer can best see the product.
- Position competing brands, which have a higher price, close to product X, so that consumers can easily make the price comparison.
- Position products that have lower prices, or lower profit margins, near floor level. where consumers are less likely to see them.
- Make the face of product X large, with a bigger surface area or bright colours, so that it draws the attention of the customer.
- Give product X an eye-catching design.

Figure 10.10   Layout of a grocery store.

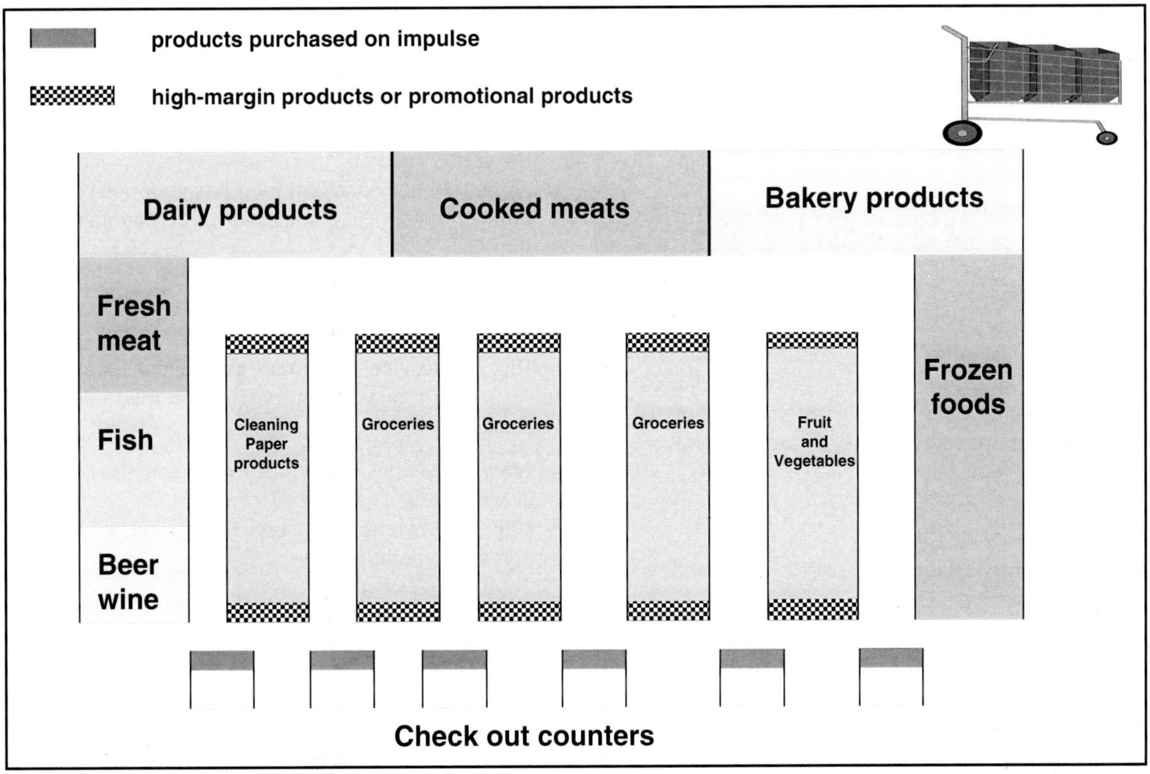

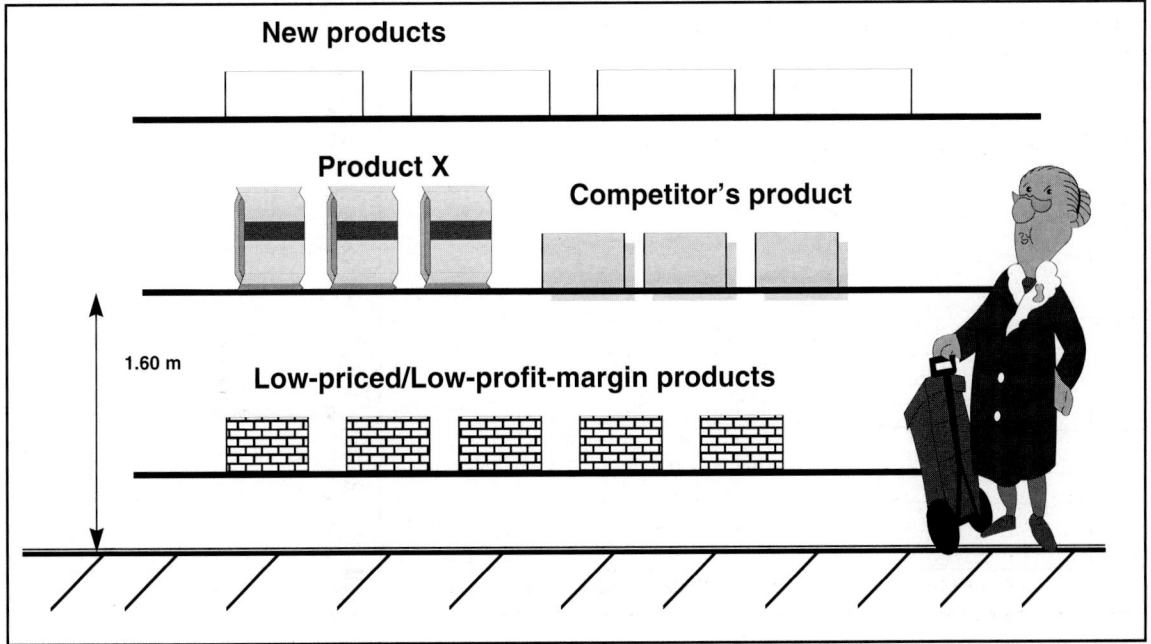

Figure 10.11   Layout: shelf positioning.

In addition to the customer-oriented layout aspects for retail outlets, aisles and shelves need to be positioned in stores so that they can be easily restocked from the warehouse. Externally, parking zones need to be planned so that they provide easy access for customers and there must be adequate space for delivery vehicles.

RESTAURANTS

Restaurants are service firms that, in general, can be divided into three principal categories, full service, self service and fast food. This qualitative nature can be presented in an exponential-type curve, similar to that used in manufacturing, as illustrated in Figure 10.12. The following are some relative characteristics.

Full-service restaurant

The full-service restaurant provides a complete waiter or waitress service:

- The layout enables effective flow of servers between the food preparation area and clients.
- Layout and decor provide a pleasant eating/social environment.
- Total labour costs are high.

- Meal prices are high.
- Food-preparation surface area relative to client area is high.
- Variety of meal choices is high and customized (e.g. a well-done, medium or rare steak).
- Clients remain in place during service of food and the servers move.
- Cycle time (service and food consumption) is long.
- Some full-service restaurants offer banquet possibilities.

Self-service restaurant

In the self-service restaurant the clients help themselves to the food. Operators clean up the tables after the meal:

- Layout provides efficient flow of clients past a food service area.
- Clients move during service of food, operators/servers remain in place.
- Total labour costs are average.
- Meal prices are medium.
- Food preparation surface area relative to client area is average.
- There is a limited variety of meal choices.
- Cycle time (service and food consumption) is average.

Figure 10.12 Comparison of eating establishments.

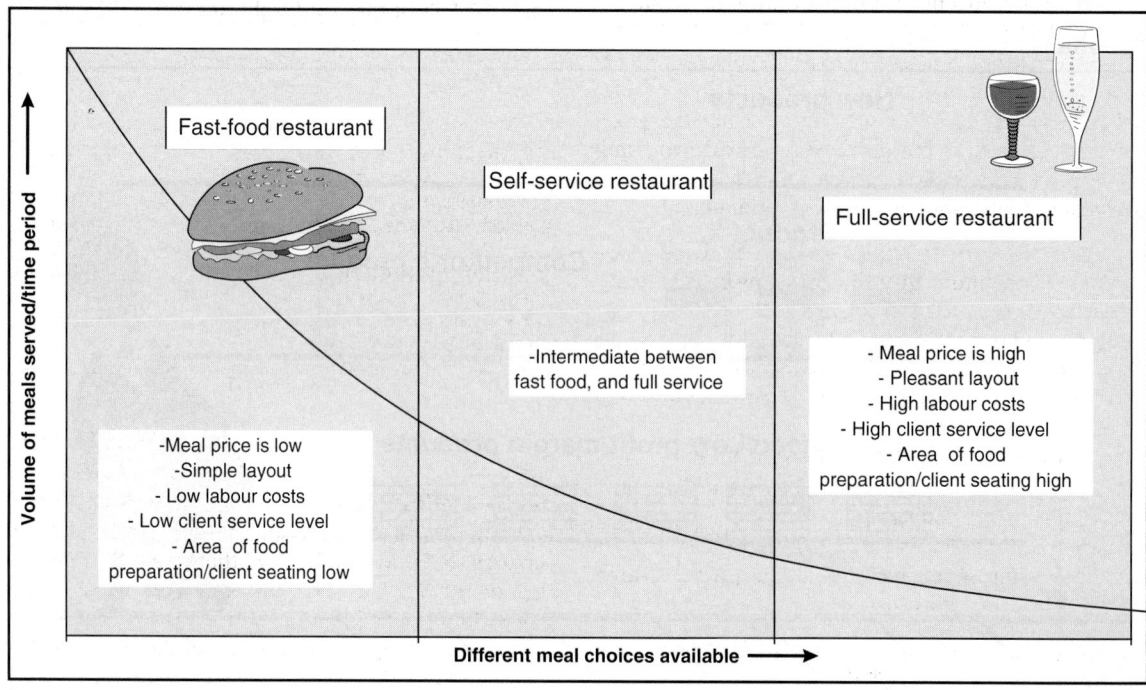

Fast-food restaurant

Self-service restaurant

Full-service restaurant

-Intermediate between fast food, and full service

- Meal price is high
- Pleasant layout
- High labour costs
- High client service level
- Area of food preparation/client seating high

-Meal price is low
-Simple layout
- Low labour costs
- Low client service level
- Area of food preparation/client seating low

Volume of meals served/time period

Different meal choices available

Fast-food restaurants

A fast-food restaurant is at the opposite end of the scale to a full-service restaurant. Here, the principal objective is to provide fast customer service:

- The layout provides a seating area for customers and a service counter.
- Layout and decor are simple with inexpensive furnishings.
- Total labour costs are low.
- Meal prices are low.
- Food preparation surface area relative to client area is low.
- Variety of meal choices is very low – standardized products.
- Operators remain in place during service of food; clients move.
- Clients clean up after the meal.
- Cycle time (service and food consumption) is short.

McDonald's

McDonald's, founded by the late Ray Kroc in the early 1960s, is the largest of the fast-food restaurant chains, with franchise outlets worldwide. There is an enormous amount of standardization in McDonald's restaurant, including the food, preparation times, restaurant decor, packaging, food preparation equipment and uniforms worn by the operators. There are some differences from country to country – the price, and beer is served in the French McDonald's but not in the USA! A floor plan for a small McDonald's is illustrated in Figure 10.13. The area is small but efficient, so that employees do not have to move distances. During peak periods, principally lunchtime, there is a team of three persons at the counter, one each at the grill and fryer and two jointly on the toaster, preparation of vegetables and onions and packaging. Preparation is closely programmed:

- Toaster time for hamburger buns is slightly less than one minute to give them a sunny brown texture and make them slightly crusty.
- The hamburger 'assembly' operation is lay out toasted bottom, spread mayonnaise, add grilled beef, top with lettuce and onions, close with toasted top and package.
- Preparation time for a hamburger is 90 seconds.
- French fries must only remain in storage for a maximum of seven minutes
- Prepared food that is packaged can only remain for a maximum of ten minutes in the prepared area. After that, it is discarded.

For those at the service counter their programmed instructions are:

1. Welcome the customer with a smile.
2. Take the order.
3. Collect and prepare the order on a tray.
4. Present the order.
5. Take the payment.
6. Thank the client and invite them to return.

In McDonald's, like other fast-food chains, the cash register has icons of the item purchased rather than figures. This facilitates completing the bill for the food purchased and minimizes errors.

For all eating establishments kitchen appliances are positioned so that staff do not have to do excessive bending or stretching. Nonetheless, a common ailment with chefs is neck problems associated with bending over the cooking area (as already highlighted in the section on Ergonomics in Chapter 8, *Human resources in the system design*).

AIRPORT

Characteristics

An international airport is perhaps the single biggest service operation and supply chain, the layout of which is a complex system handling a vast number of clients and a huge volume of freight. Some passenger and freight statistics for seven of the worlds biggest airports in 1991 are given in Table 10.4.

Table 10.4 Passenger and freight statistics (1991) for seven of the world's biggest airports

Airport	Passengers (millions)	Freight (million tons)
Chicago, O'Hare, USA	59.9	754.3
Dallas-Fort Worth, USA	48.2	387.1
Los Angeles, USA	45.7	993.7
London, Heathrow, UK	40.2	661.0
Kennedy, New York, USA	26.3	1 168.0
Paris, Charles de Gaulle, France	22.0	588.4
Schipol, Amsterdam, The Netherlands	16.5	629.9

The surface area of airports is enormous. Paris, Charles de Gaulle, covers 3113 hectares (1260 acres) and the world's biggest in surface area, King Khaled International in Ryad, Saudi Arabia, covers 22 100 hectares (8950 acres). In 1990 there were 37 739 civil airports, of which 45 per cent were in the USA, 6 per cent in Europe, and less than 1 per cent in Japan.[5]

A distinguishing operating aspect of the airport is that the inside layout is concentrated very much on the con-

Figure 10.13 Layout of food preparation area for a small McDonald's fast-food restaurant.

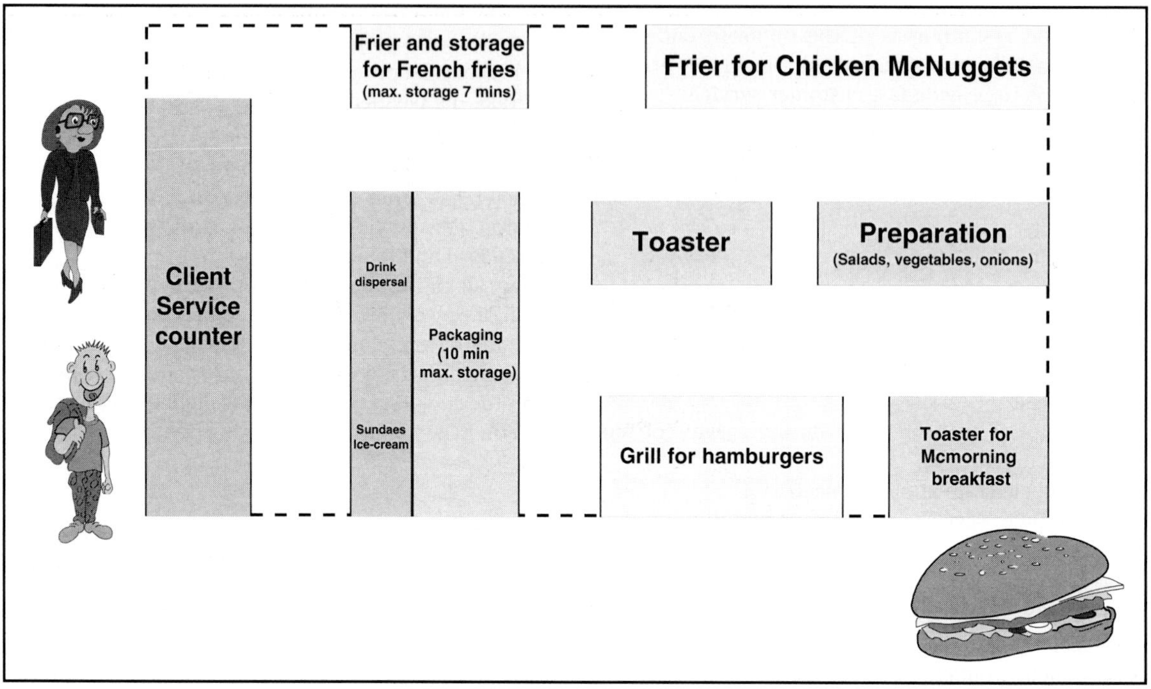

veyance of the clients (the passengers); whereas the outside layout is very much concerned with the operational aspects of the arrival and departure of the aircraft.

Hub and spoke type arrangement

The physical layout of most major airports is designed as a hub-and-spoke type arrangement, the basic form of which is illustrated in Figure 10.14. Each hub-and-spoke system constitutes a terminal and, depending on the size of airport, there may be more than one terminal. London's Heathrow currently has four terminals, one each for International, European, Domestic and British Airways.

Hub

The hub houses the passenger services, which will include amenities for ticket sales, shops, restaurants, arrival and departure lounges, transfer equipment such as carousels and moving carpets for baggage, escalators and people movers for passengers, and security systems.

Spokes

The spokes outside are the arrival and departure gates for the aeroplanes. Inside, they provide the departure lounges for passengers and are connected to the hub by long corridors, which in some cases have moving carpets for the passengers.

Surrounding the airport terminals are the control towers and runways, which in major airports permit up to a combined total of 35–40 take-offs and landings per hour. In addition, there are facilities for parking and some airports, such as London Heathrow, Paris Charles de Gaulle and Lyon Satolas, have rail connections to major European Networks. (This physical layout of a 'hub and spoke' is not to be confused with the 'hub and spoke' worldwide operations network presented in Chapter 1, *Positioning Operations Management*, where, for example, London might be a hub for the spokes in South Africa, New York and Argentina.)

Technology

An airport has some of the most up-to-date technological equipment. Apart from the aeroplanes themselves with their complex material construction and sophisticated controls, the airport has ground to air communication, computerized ticketing, complex flight-scheduling systems, weather-forecasting equipment, security networks, etc.

Environment

Environmental constraints are high on the development and operation of an airport. The site itself swallows up a large area of land. Then, the noise of landing/takeoff of aeroplanes causes environmental con-

Figure 10.14 Hub and spoke system of an airport.

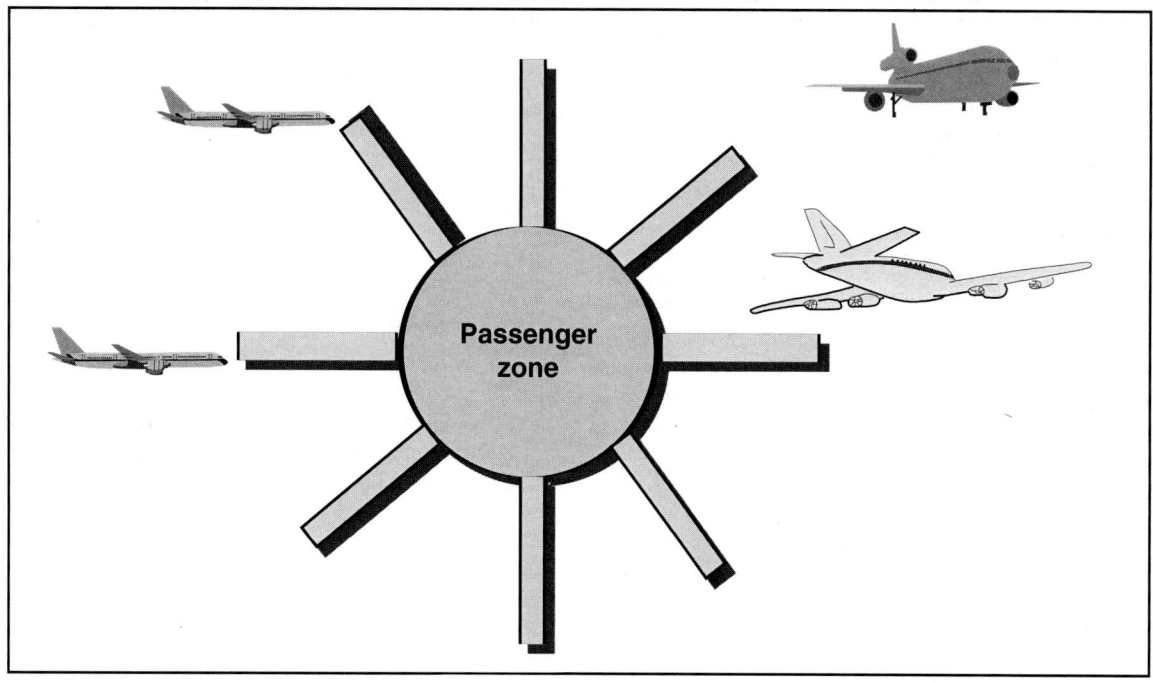

cerns for neighbouring communities, while the road networks leading to and from the facility add to road congestion.

ENGINEERING, CONSULTING OR DESIGN OFFICE

Every organization, be it a service or a manufacturing business, has offices. A pure service such as a bank (Barclays), a consulting organization (McKinsey) or the headquarters of a major organization (IBM) consists of just offices. A manufacturing site (Renault VI, Venniseux, France) also has office areas for the engineers, purchasing, accounting, etc.

Cellular offices

Historically, most corporate offices had a cellular layout, in which office departments that had the most contact with one another were located close together. Employees had their own individual enclosed area (the decor depending on position), with desk, telephone and bookcase, as in the following illustration.

Braun

In the 1970s and 1980s I worked with C. F. Braun & Co. an engineering and construction company in Los Angeles, California. It was called the 'campus'. The gardens were immaculate, with trees and plants from all over the world. Every employee had their own cellular carpeted office, with telephone, an upholstered desk chair and two matching chairs for visitors. For those low in the hierarchy, the desks were metal with a Formica top. When a promotion came you were awarded a solid wooden desk and upholstered chairs of a more pleasing hue. Project and department managers graduated to a very sturdy wooden desk with more efficient storage areas. Vice-presidents had even more attractive wooden desks, and a bigger office area. Office layout, furniture and location were a status symbol.[6]

Open plan offices

The office concept has changed as many companies, such as Hewlett Packard (computers), Unisabi (pet foods) and Valéo (automobile components), have adopted open-plan layouts where employees are totally exposed to their co-workers. Privacy is replaced with productivity, hierarchy is being replaced with teamwork; and status is being replaced with mobility. To minimize interruptions, meeting rooms are available. The open-plan layout has reduced cost in terms of space and increased ease of human contact, but (according to some) reduced efficiency because of the noise of phones, adjacent conversations, and passing footsteps.

After salaries, office space is the next biggest expense for many companies. With the ease of telecommunications, white-collar workers can, in theory, work at home and communicate by telephone, fax, modem, electronic mail and the Internet. As a result, some companies are trying to move away from the concept of the one-desk rule and adopting the policy of 'hot desking' where desks are shared. However, unless jobs are very specific and can be properly scheduled, desk sharing can be complicated. Besides, most people have their own files, documents, books and the like. A compromise on this is locker trolleys that can be wheeled to a free desk.[7]

Hoteling

Hoteling is the open-plan office at its very extreme and is being adopted by sales- and service-based companies, such as IBM, AT&T, Arthur Andersen and other major accounting and consulting firms. Private offices are eliminated in place of hoteling, which is a system in which temporary space is provided for employees when they are on-site. This saves money on rent and gets employees out spending more time with customers.[8] The following describes how it works.

Reservation

An employee phones in advance, or probably makes contact with the aid of his personal computer to indicate the length of time he or she needs an office. A space is allocated, equipped with appropriate connections for telephone and computer. When the employee arrives, even after normal hours, he or she can access the space by the insertion of a magnetic card. Space is allocated in a first-come-first-served basis (so the first gets a better place).[9]

Layout

The office plan is open space, which allows working alone or in groups. Filing cabinets on wheels, containing employees' documents and the like, can be located where necessary. Coffee drinking areas are available where employees can relax.

Closed offices

These are available for a limited time when an employee needs to work in isolation, or to have meetings with others. The number of these offices is limited to be sure that they are used to the maximum.

Conference rooms

These are available on reservation.

Office management

A concierge is present on the site full time to organize reservations and to be sure that things run smoothly.

See also Box 10.2 with Dilbert's view of hoteling.[10]

METHODS FOR FACILITY LAYOUT

The following are some methods for developing a facility layout. They are considered as heuristic methods in that they may not give the optimum solution, but there is a certain logic to their development and the layout obtained is pragmatic.

Two dimensional templates

With the two dimensional template approach, first the room area, where equipment is to be located, is measured and the surface area and shape are drawn to scale. Then, two-dimensional forms called templates are made of the plan view of the equipment, machines or furniture on the same scale as the floor plan. These cut-outs are then arranged as desired on the facility plan. Where the floor plan already exists, the use of two-dimensional templates is a simple way of planning a layout for offices, small machinery areas and at home.

Load–distance analysis

Load–distance analysis is a method that can be employed in a manufacturing organization when material is being transferred from one location to another. The objective of the layout is to develop a plan for which the sum of the products of the material movement and the distance is a minimum. Mathematically, this is represented as:

$$\sum_{i=1}^{n} \sum_{j=1}^{n} Q_{ij} D_{ij}$$

Where n is the number of work centres or departments, i, j are the individual departments, Q is the quantity of material moved from department i to department j, and D is the distance between department i and department j.

This method is illustrated with the worked example, *Guillaume Co.*

Contact–distance analysis

A contact–distance analysis is a layout method that might be employed in a service function when there is contact with various functional departments (accounting, purchasing, sales, etc.) The objective of this approach is to adopt a department layout where the product of the total number of physical contacts and distance travelled is a minimum. The logic is similar to that of load–distance analysis, except that material flow is not involved. This idea is illustrated with the worked example *Justin Co.*

Systematic layout planning

In the contact–distance approach, no importance is given to closeness of the groups being considered. Systematic layout planning, developed in the early 1960s by Richard Muther, is a variation on the contact–distance approach that allows qualitative inputs on the desirability of departments being closely located.[11] The approach can be described as follows.

Relationship table

A relationship table is developed between departments, or workcentres, according to the necessity, or otherwise, of these being closely located. This relationship table is presented in a hierarchical form, from categories such as 'essential' to 'avoid', each one being given a code. This is illustrated in Table 10.5 for a small manufacturing firm that has departments and work areas for purchasing, storage of raw materials, machining, assembly, storage of finished products, maintenance, sales and accounting as well as loading and unloading areas.

The criteria for being close might be:

- Constant communication is important.
- Departments share the same personnel, such as secretaries or assistants.
- The same equipment is used (photocopying machine, computer terminal, printer).
- Next sequence in the work flow.
- Perform very similar work.

The criteria for avoiding proximity might be:

- Working conditions are unpleasant (printing inks, dyes or cleaning fluids).
- Confidential information is processed.
- There is excessive noise.

Relationship diagram

A diagram showing schematically the relationship between each department is then developed as illustrated in Figure 10.15. In such a diagram the closeness relationship is identified by a line code of different

Table 10.5 A relationship table for a small manufacturing firm

	Purchasing	Storage-RW	Machining	Assembly	Storage-FP	Maintenance	Sales	Accounting	Loading	Unloading
Purchasing		I	A	A	N	A	E	V	N	N
Storage RW	I		V	I	A	N	N	N	A	E
Machining	A	V		E	N	V	A	A	N	N
Assembly	A	I	E		E	V	A	A	N	N
Storage FP	N	A	N	E		N	I	N	E	A
Maintenance	A	N	V	V	N		A	A	I	I
Sales	E	N	A	A	I	A		V	I	N
Accounting	V	N	A	A	N	A	V		N	N
Loading	N	A	N	N	E	I	I	N		A
Unloading	N	E	N	N	A	I	N	N	A	

Note: The relationships and their codes are: Essential E; Very important V; Important I; Not important N; Avoid A.

colour or density. Only the Essential, Very Important and Avoid are shown on this diagram.

Layout

By trial and error a layout is identified by respecting the closeness criteria. The layout is then positioned in the total space available for the facility, as is illustrated in Figure 10.16. As a result of all the possible combinations, it may not always be possible to respect to the letter every relationship and some adjustments may need to be made. For this example, the criterion was to avoid putting sales, purchasing and accounting offices next to the production areas. A complete separation was not possible and the requirement was accommodated by separating the offices from the production area by a wide corridor.

Assembly-line balancing

The line-balancing approach is the grouping of work teams in a manufacturing assembly-line operation to maximize product throughput and to minimize worker idle time. To balance the assembly line, the following information is necessary.

1. The tasks necessary to complete the finished product.
2. The time necessary to perform each task in the assembly line.
3. A division of the tasks among the workforce.
4. The production rate needed to meet client demand.
5. The cycle time, or elapsed time, within which products must leave the line in order to maintain the required production rate.
6. The permitted way tasks can be combined to form a compatible work group. When this is established specific jobs are allocated. For example:
   - Tasks are grouped that use common materials in order to reduce the amount of material travel and the number of inventory storage locations.
   - Tasks are grouped according to safety requirements. A welding operation would not be combined with one that uses cleaning fluids.
   - Tasks are grouped that are adjacent to each other in the assembly sequence.
   - Tasks are grouped that have similar operating environments. Greasy or dirty tasks would not be combined with those requiring a clean room environment.

Figure 10.15 Systematic layout planning I.

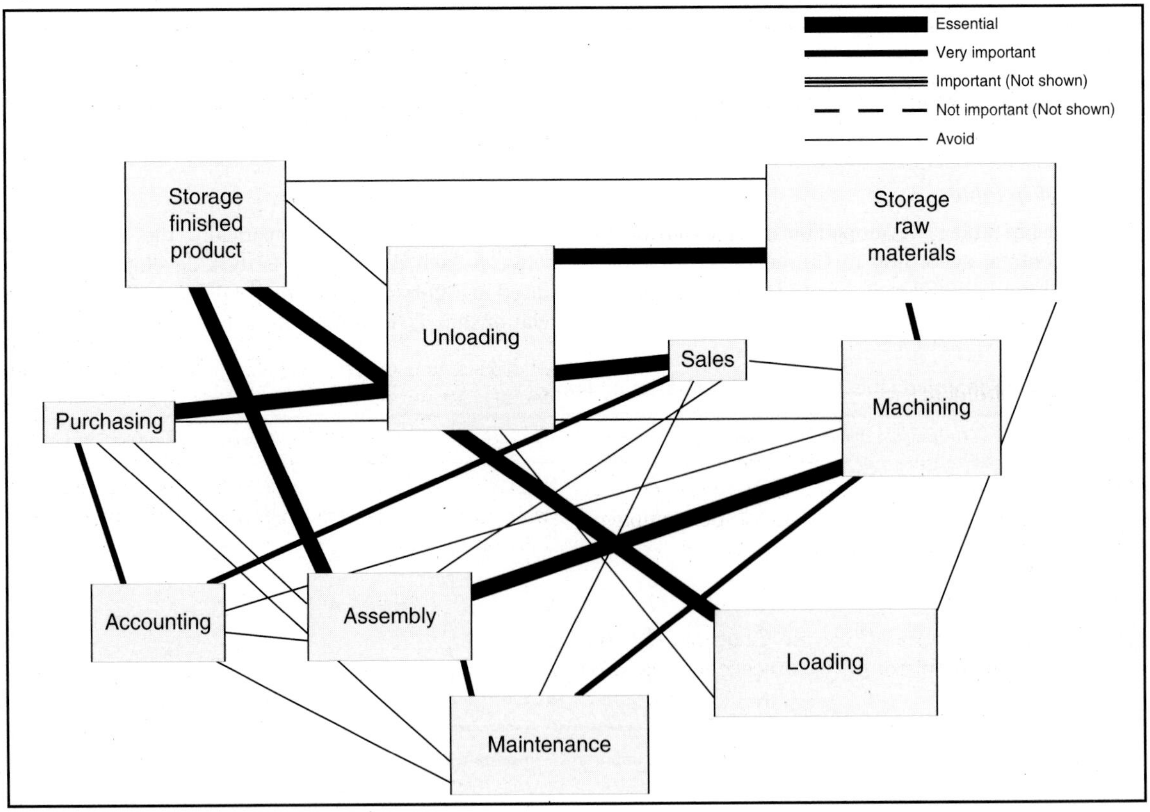

Figure 10.16   Systematic layout planning II.

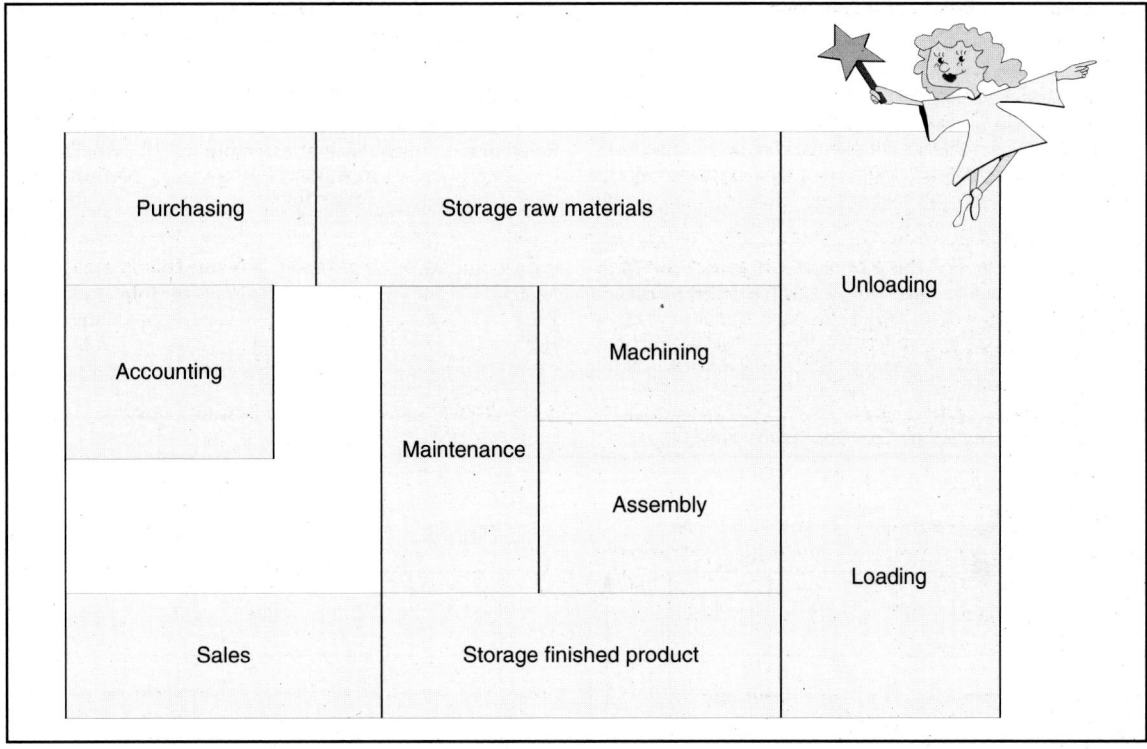

Tasks are grouped that use the same machines and equipment.

Tasks are grouped that require the same level of labour skill.

The line balancing procedure can be analysed by two approaches

most tasks following;

longest time to complete.

Most tasks following

The operations performed first are those that have the largest number of operations that follow afterwards. However, precedence has to be taken into account, which means that an activity cannot be completed unless a prerequired activity has been completed.

Longest time to complete

The operations performed first are those that take the longest time to complete. Again, precedence has to be taken into account.

The worked examples *Dorf Co.* gives an illustration of the line-balancing technique.

Computer aids in facility layout

When a facility is large and there are many constraints, manual design of a facility layout is complicated. As with any design approach, there are many computer programs, as developed by IBM, General Electric USA, Microsoft and others, available to assist in optimizing facility layouts according to needs[12]. A well-known program for facility layout is CRAFT (Computerized Relative Allocation of Facilities Technique).[13] There also exist computer programs that will optimize the way retail shelves are stocked with the objective of maximizing sales.

WORKED EXAMPLE: GUILLAUME CO.

Situation

The Guillaume Co. manufactures transformer units, which are sold to electricity companies throughout Europe. The company is considering relocating its plant from the centre of Grenoble, France to a location outside the city. The company has nine operating departments coded 1 to 9. Two possible L-shaped layouts for the new facility, indicating where the departments would be located, are given in Figure 10.17. The company produces five basic products whose reference numbers are L-32, B-41, N-65, P-25, and H-95. Each of these products is assembled differently and the operating departments which handle these products, together with the weekly production rate, are given in Table 10.6. The sequence means, for example, for product L-32, that the assembly operation starts at Department 1, moves to Department 3, then to Department 6, then Department 8 and finally Department 9. The average distance in metres between departments, measured between the centres of the working areas is given in Table 10.7.

Table 10.6 Handling of products at Guillaume Co.

Reference	Sequence of assembly operation by department					Weekly production units
L-32	1	3	6	8	9	250
B-41	2	7	6	5	4	385
N-65	4	9	5	2	6	190
P-25	6	9	2			565
H-95	7	1	8	4		420

Figure 10.17 Guillaume Co – floor plans available.

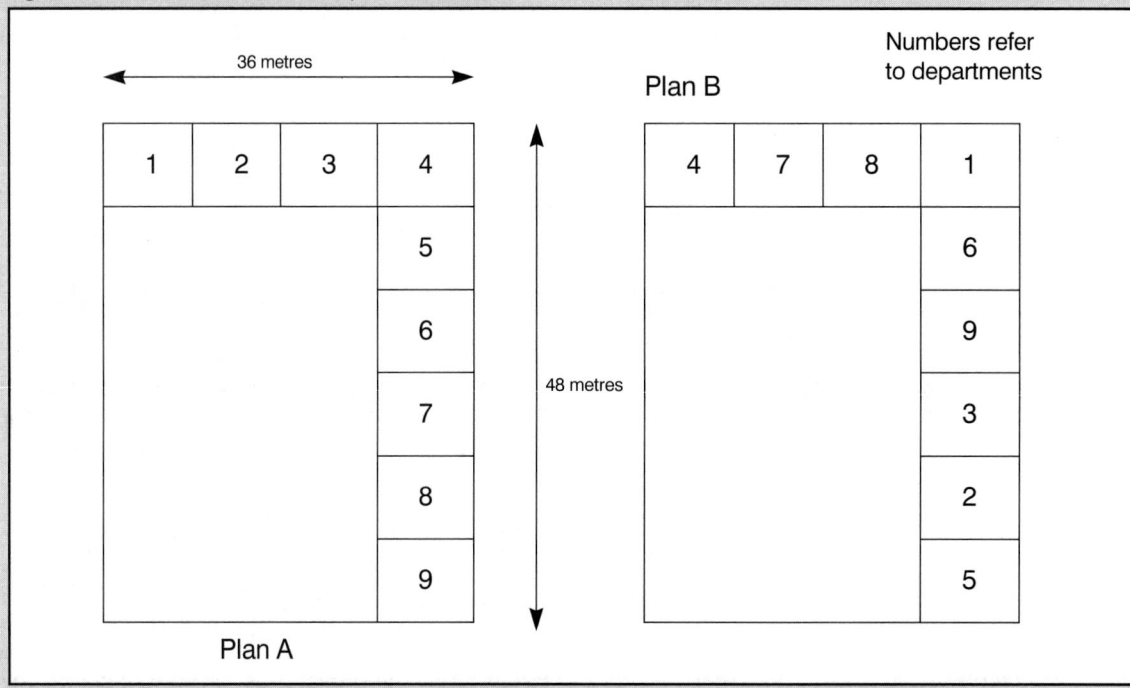

Plan A

Plan B

Numbers refer to departments

36 metres

48 metres

Table 10.7 Average distances between departments at Guillaume Co.

From department	To department	Distance Plan A (m)	Distance Plan B (m)	From department	To department	Distance Plan A (m)	Distance Plan B (m)
1	3	26.00	33.00	9	5	41.00	33.00
3	6	21.32	25.00	5	2	22.58	17.00
6	8	25.00	14.52	2	6	26.56	33.00
8	9	17.00	21.32	6	9	33.00	17.00
2	7	32.63	39.58	9	2	46.95	25.00
7	6	17.00	22.58	7	1	38.60	26.00
6	5	17.00	41.00	1	8	44.42	17.00
5	4	17.00	50.95	8	4	41.00	26.00
4	9	49.00	34.00				

Required

Determine which of the layouts would be the optimum for the Guillaume Co.

Solution

The solution is given in Table 10.8.

- First, the total distance travelled for each product is calculated for Plan A and Plan B.
- Next, the production quantity is multiplied by the distance to give the unit–distance measure. These values are summed for Plan A and Plan B.
- The smallest total unit–distance would be the preferred plan. In this case it is Plan B. (Differences in the unit × distance column are due to rounding.)

Table 10.8 Facility layout for Guillaume Co

Reference		Department operating sequence				Reference	Weekly production units
L-32	1	3	6	8	9	L-32	250
B-41	2	7	6	5	4	B-41	385
N-65	4	9	5	2	6	N-65	190
P-25	6	9	2			P-25	565
H-95	7	1	8	4		H-95	420

	From	To	Distance Plan A	Distance Plan B	Total distance Plan A	Total distance Plan B	unit × distance A	unit × distance B
L-32	1	3	26.00	33.00				
	3	6	21.32	25.00				
	6	8	25.00	14.52				
	8	9	17.00	21.32	89.32	93.84	22 329.00	23 459.20
B-41	2	7	32.63	39.58				
	7	6	17.00	22.58				
	6	5	17.00	41.00				
	5	4	17.00	50.95	83.63	154.12	32 197.49	59 335.28
N-65	4	9	49.00	34.00				
	9	5	41.00	33.00				
	5	2	22.58	17.00				
	2	6	26.56	33.00	139.14	117.00	26 437.08	22 230.00
P-25	6	9	33.00	17.00				
	9	2	46.95	25.00	79.95	42.00	45 170.63	23 730.00
H-95	7	1	38.60	26.00				
	1	8	44.42	17.00				
	8	4	41.00	26.00	124.02	69.00	52 090.10	28 980.00
Total							178 224.30	**157 734.48**

WORKED EXAMPLE: JUSTIN CO.

Situation

The Justin Co. writes and distributes computer software for small companies in France, Belgium and French-speaking Switzerland. The company has its headquarters in a small office block in the centre of Beaune, France. However, demand for its product has grown and it is planning to relocate to one floor of a large building in Dijon. The proposed office plan is given in Figure 10.18 and the average distances between each room measured from centre to centre in metres is given in Table 10.9. Justin has six departments, which are listed in Table 10.10. Finally, Table 10.11 is the average number of contacts each week made by personnel in each department, based on past data. This means, for example, that Consulting and Design have 90 total contacts per week where either personnel go from Consulting to Design or vice-versa.

Table 10.9 Distances between rooms at Justin Co.

	A	B	C	D	E	F
A		90	140	45	95	145
B			90	95	45	95
C				145	95	45
D					90	140
E						90
F						

Figure 10.18 Justin Co. – proposed office plan.

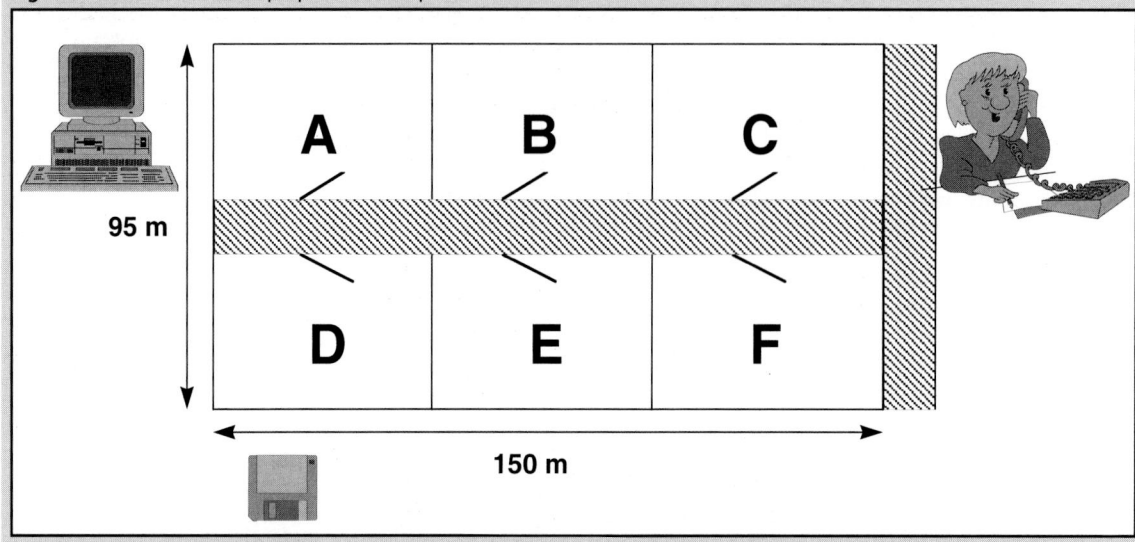

Table 10.10 Departments at Justin Co.

Code	1	2	3	4	5	6
	Development	Consulting	Design	R & D	Computing	Administration

Table 10.11 Average number of contacts per week at Justin Co.

	Development	Consulting	Design	R & D	Computing	Administration
Development		90	25	23	11	18
Consulting			8	5	10	16
Design				10	25	7
R & D					4	2
Computing						3
Administration						

Required

Optimize the layout, keeping Administration in area A as this is closest to the entrance and is thus the most convenient for receiving clients and suppliers.

Solution

A trial-and-error solution is produced by locating the departments in each of the office spaces, but always keeping Consulting and Development in adjacent offices since they have the maximum number of contacts. The distance is multiplied by the number of contacts and the distance–contact total was calculated for each proposed layout. (The total is divided by two to nullify the double accounting.) The optimum solution is given in Figure 10.19.

Figure 10.19   Justin Co. – office layout calculations.

OPTION 4 DISTANCE		A	B	C	D	E	F
A		0	90	140	45	95	145
B		90	0	90	95	45	95
C		140	90	0	145	95	45
D		45	95	145	0	90	140
E		95	45	95	90	0	90
F		145	95	45	140	90	0

Average contacts/week between departments

CONTACT	Develop	Consult	Design	R & D	Computing	Admin
Develop	0	90	25	23	11	18
Consult	90	0	8	5	10	16
Design	25	8	0	10	25	7
R & D	23	5	10	0	4	2
Computing	11	10	25	4	0	3
Admin	18	16	7	2	3	0

Layout

A Admin	B Consult	C Computing
D R & D	E Develop	F Design

DISTANCE		A Admin	B Consult	C Computing	D R & D	E Develop	F Design
A	Admin	0	90	140	45	95	145
B	Consult	90	0	90	95	45	95
C	Computing	140	90	0	145	95	45
D	R & D	45	95	145	0	90	140
E	Develop	95	45	95	90	0	90
F	Design	145	95	45	140	90	0

CONTACT		A Admin	B Consult	C Computing	D R & D	E Develop	F Design
A	Admin		16	3	2	18	7
B	Consult	16		10	5	90	8
C	Computing	3	10		4	11	25
D	R & D	2	5	4		23	10
E	Develop	18	90	11	23		25
F	Design	7	8	25	10	25	

Contacts x distance

CONTACT		A Admin	B Consult	C Computing	D R & D	E Develop	F Design	Total
A	Admin	0	1 440	420	90	1 710	1 015	4 675
B	Consult	1 440	0	900	475	4 050	760	7 625
C	Computing	420	900	0	580	1 045	1 125	4 070
D	R & D	90	475	580	0	2 070	1 400	4 615
E	Develop	1 710	4 050	1 045	2 070	0	2 250	11 125
F	Design	1 015	760	1 125	1 400	2 250	0	6 550
	Total	4 675	7 625	4 070	4 615	11 125	6 550	38 660

Divide by 2 to avoid double accounting   19 330

WORKED EXAMPLE: DORF COMPANY

Situation

The Dorf company is a small manufacturing concern in Belgium that assembles high-quality walking and talking dolls. All the raw materials and components are imported from Hong Kong. At the present time, the facility layout is rather haphazard and the company is having difficulty in reaching its output objective of 50 dolls per day. This target is based on the market demand within Europe. The Production Manager, Michael Dorf, is considering modifying the facility layout in order to increase the production level to the desired objective. The assembly consists of 11 operations, which, together with the estimated time for completion, are given in Table 10.12. The company works eight hours a day, five days a week.

Table 10.12 Operations at Dorf Company

Step	Operation	Time	Operation immediately preceding
A	Preparation of electronic parts	2 min 40 sec	None
B	Preparation of body components	3 min 40 sec	None
C	Assembly of packing boxes	5 min 00 sec	None
D	Tuning/assembly of voice box	2 min 40 sec	A
E	Assembly movement with limbs	2 min 00 sec	A, B
F	Sewing	2 min 20 sec	B
G	Soldering	3 min 00 sec	D, E
H	Pressing	4 min 40 sec	F
I	Final assembly	1 min 00 sec	G, H
J	Final painting	4 min 20 sec	I
K	Packing	2 min 40 sec	C, J

Required

Determine the optimum assembly-line arrangement, showing a flow scheme with work stations, and calculate the theoretical efficiency. Use two approaches:

1. Perform those operations that have the largest number of operations needed to be completed afterwards (*most tasks following* method). Precedence has to be taken into account. For example, sewing [F] cannot be performed until the body component operation [B] has been performed.
2. Perform those operations that take the longest to complete (*Longest task method*). Precedence has to be taken into account.

Solution

Figure 10.20 illustrates the layout with the precedence relationship.

- The cycle time is determined on the basis of the required production rate. It is given by the time available divided by the customer demand rate and is the rate at which a finished product will come off the assembly line. The cycle time is 576 seconds. $\left(\dfrac{8\times60\times60}{50}\right)$

1. The *Most task following* calculations are given in Figure 10.21 and the flow scheme is shown in Figure 10.22:
   - Elapsed time for doll assembly = 2304 seconds.
   - Actual time used = 2040 seconds.
   - Dead time = 264 seconds.
   - Efficiency is 88.54 per cent.
   Four work stations are required:
   - Workstation 1: Tasks B, A and D.
   - Workstation 2: Tasks F, E and H.
   - Workstation 3: Tasks G, I and J.
   - Workstation 4: Tasks C and K.
2. The *longest-task* calculations are given in Figure 10.23 and the flow scheme is shown in Figure 10.24:
   - Elapsed time for doll assembly = 2880 seconds.
   - Actual time used = 2040 seconds.
   - Dead time = 840 seconds.
   - Efficiency is 70.83 per cent.
   Five work stations are required:
   - Workstation 1:   Tasks C and B.
   - Workstation 2:   Tasks A, D and F.
   - Workstation 3:   Tasks H and E.
   - Workstation 4:   Tasks G, I and J.
   - Workstation 5:   Task K.

Figure 10.20   Dorf – flow scheme.

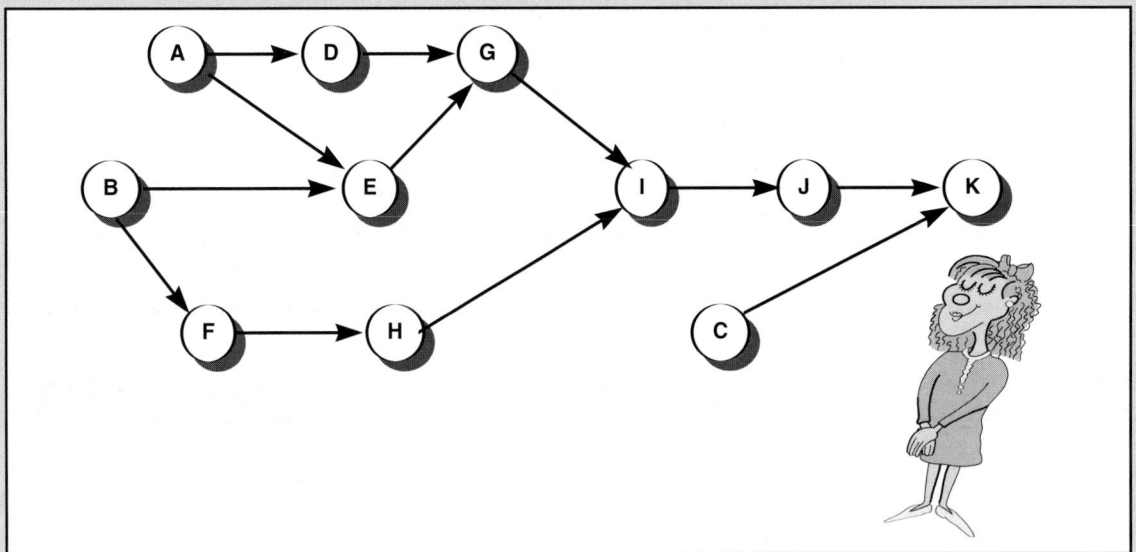

Figure 10.21 Dorf – facility layout calculations for 'most tasks following'.

Information		Source or calculation
Production rate, units /day	50	given
Hours per day	8.00	given
Cycle time, secs/unit	576.00	secs per day/production rate
Theoretical workgroups	3.54	Operating time/cycle time

t

Task	Operating time (secs)	Number of tasks following		Task	Longest time secs
A	160	6		C	300
B	220	7		H	280
C	300	1		J	260
D	160	4		B	220
E	120	4		G	180
F	140	4		A	160
G	180	3		D	160
H	280	3		K	160
I	60	2		F	140
J	260	1		E	120
K	160	0		I	60
Total	2 040			Total	2 040

Grouping according to *Most tasks that follow*

Task	Tasks following	Time	Time left	Dead time	Group	
B	7	220	356			
A	6	160	196			
D	4	160	36	36	1	
F	4	140	436			Place before E because longest time
E	4	120	316			
H	3	280	36	36	2	Place before G because longest time
G	3	180	396			
I	2	60	336			
J	1	260	76	76	3	
C	1	300	276			
K	0	160	116	116	4	
Total				264		

Number of workstations required	4

Operating time per doll, secs	2040	
Elapsed time per doll, secs	2304	Operating time + dead time
Efficiency (Operating time/elapsed time)	88.54%	

Figure 10.22 Dorf – low scheme for 'longest task'.

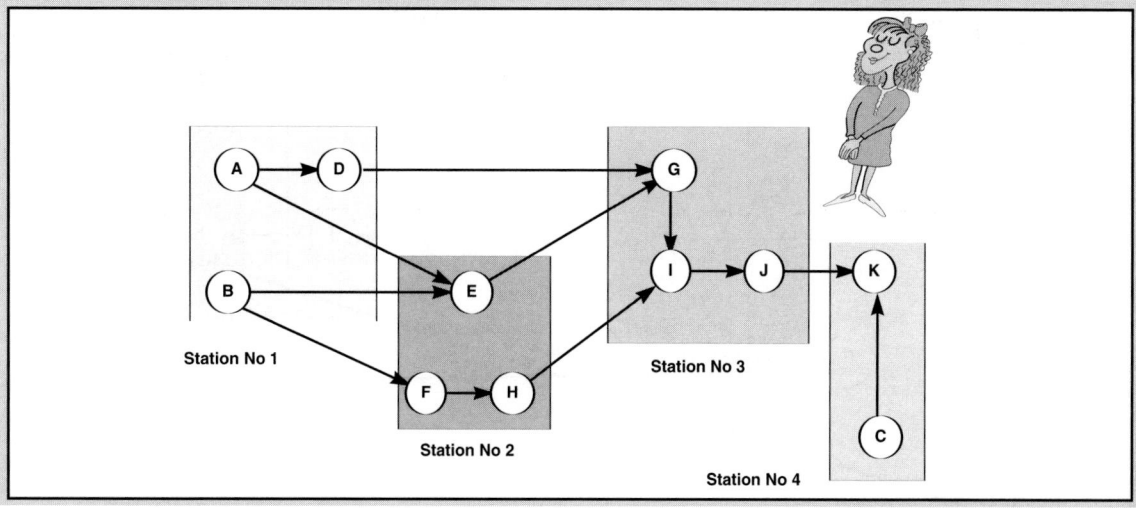

Figure 10.23   Dorf – facility layout calculations for 'longest task'.

Information		Source or calculation
Production rate, units /day	50	given
Hours per day	8.00	given
Cycle time, secs/unit	576.00	secs per day/production rate
Theoretical work groups	3.54	Operating time/cycle time

Task	Operating Time (secs)
A	160
B	220
C	300
D	160
E	120
F	140
G	180
H	280
I	60
J	260
K	160
Total	2,040

Longest Time Task	secs
C	300
H	280
J	260
B	220
G	180
A	160
D	160
K	160
F	140
E	120
I	60
Total	2,040

Grouping according to Longest Task

Task	Operating Time (secs)	Time left	Dead Time	Group
C	300	276.00		
B	220	56.00	56.00	1
A	160	416.00		
D	160	256.00		
F	140	116.00	116.00	2
H	280	296.00		
E	120	176.00	176.00	3
G	180	396.00		
I	60	336.00		
J	260	76.00	76.00	4
K	160	416.00	416	5
Total			840	

Number of work stations required	5

Operating time per doll, secs	2,040	
Elapsed time per doll, secs	2,880	Operating time + dead time
Efficiency (Operating time/elapsed time)	70.83%	

Figure 10.24   Dorf – flow scheme for 'longest task'.

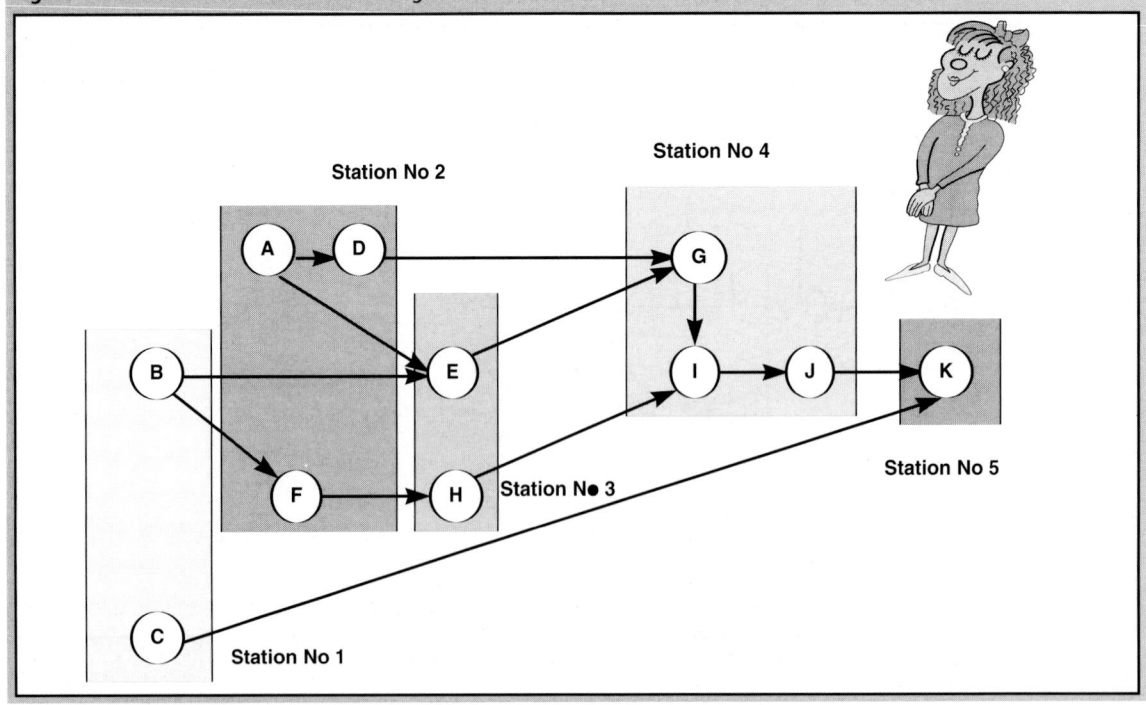

SUMMARY OF KEY ELEMENTS

- Facility layout is the arrangement of all physical resources used in operations.
- A good layout establishes cost-effective flow patterns, optimizes space utilization, facilitates installation of an information systems network, conforms to regulations and takes into account the comfort and well-being of employees and customers.
- A functional, or job-shop, layout is organized according to specific activities. Throughput is low, labour is specialized and inventory often accumulates.
- In a cellular layout operators work as a team, concentrating on the product as opposed to just the function. Employees are multi-skilled and more motivated.
- The constraint of capital investment in a cellular layout may be overcome by using mobile equipment, subcontracting or dedicated product lines at different sites.
- An assembly-line layout in mass production is where the product moves through the facility with workers remaining in the same area performing repeat operations.
- Companies, notably Volvo, have experimented with turning assembly lines into cellular manufacturing to boost employee motivation and to increase productivity.
- A flexible manufacturing system is where one facility can produce different products. Computer-controlled AGVs transfer material to appropriate work areas.
- The layout for a continuous fluid-flow operation involves a series of transfer pipes, exchanges and reaction vessels. It is completely automatically controlled.

- In fixed-position layouts the product does not move and the operating functions, work teams and storage areas are organized around the product.
- Materials-handling equipment includes robots, elevators, AGVs, trolleys, front-end loaders, trucks, cranes, moving conveyers, hand carts and containers.
- The layout of a retail facility is a merchandizing function, where aisle arrangement and shelf layout have an impact on the volume of products sold.
- Restaurants are either full-service, self-service or fast-food. Layout is concentrated on providing a pleasing customer environment with efficiency for the operators.
- Airports are hub-and-spoke arrangements to provide efficiency for aeroplane movements, passenger convenience and ease of baggage handling.
- Open-plan layouts are replacing cellular offices to reduce cost. Hoteling, the extreme open-plan layout, is where office space is reserved as needed.
- Two-dimensional scaled templates may be used in the layout of small surface areas.
- The load–distance layout method minimizes the total movement of products.
- The contact–distance layout method minimizes the total of the personnel contact distance.
- The systematic layout planning method takes into consideration the desirability of workcentres or departments being close together.
- The line-balancing method in assembly-line layouts creates groups of work teams to maximize throughput and minimize idle time.

REVIEW AND DISCUSSION QUESTIONS

1 **Current facility layouts**. Of the following layouts analyse those with which you are familiar:
   (a) University;
   (b) Grocery store;
   (c) Car repair operation;
   (d) Your house or living accommodation.
   Do you think the layout is efficient, and pleasing? If not, what changes would you propose? Justify your reasoning.
2 **Accommodating the sexes**. In the new UK Labour Government, there are more women than ever before. The House of Commons does not have sufficient washroom facilities for ladies. Are there are other establishments with which you are familiar which you believe are similarly poorly designed for both sexes?

3 **Cost and productivity**. List and discuss all of the elements in a poor facility layout that can reduce productivity in a manufacturing or service firm.
4 **Technology**. What impact do you believe technology will in the future have on the organization and layout of the following entities:
   (b) retail store;
   (c) medical centre;
   (d) distribution centre;
   (e) automobile manufacturer;
   (f) consulting company's office;
   (g) hotels?
   Justify your arguments.
5 **Floor plan of a house**. You have purchased a piece of land of 2000 m² on which you plan to build a house. The living area of the house will be 200 m². You are married with two teenage children and you currently have two cars and two large dogs. What are some of the con-

siderations you think are important in arranging the floor plan of your house?

6 **Assembly line layout**. Discuss what you believe are the positive and negative aspects of an assembly-line lay-

out. Consider the impact on investment, productivity and human resources.

EXERCISE PROBLEM: BAIRD

Situation

The Baird Engineering Co. has been awarded a design and engineering contract. The project team, to be led by a Project Manager, will consist of persons from the following departments:

- Purchasing
- Accounting
- Scheduling
- Civil Engineering
- Process Engineering
- Design Engineers
- Plant Modelling

- Piping Engineers
- Mechanical Engineers
- Chemical Engineers.

In addition, there will be customer representatives working with the project team.

The complete project team will work in an open plan office space, with sound proof partitions, according to Figure 10.25. The length of each office space is 9 metres and the distance between each space is given in Table 10.13. In addition, based on experience with past projects, the average contacts per week between functional groups are given in Table 10.14.

Figure 10.25 Baird – office layout.

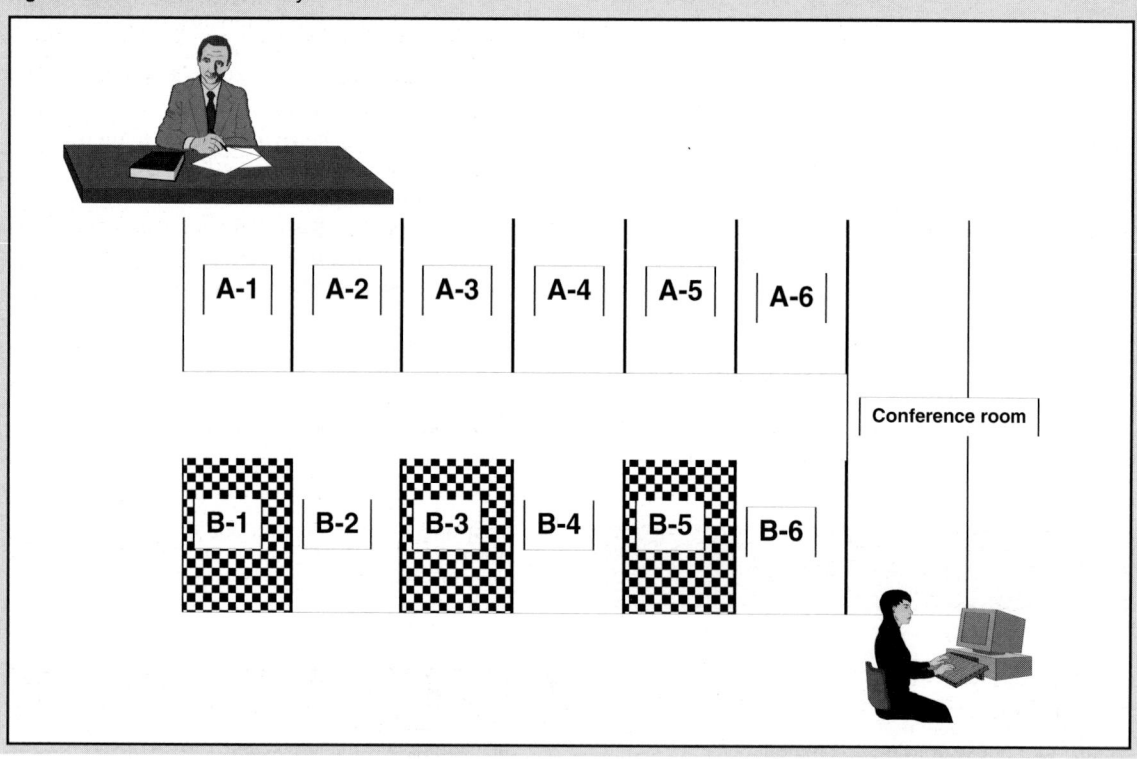

Table 10.13   Distance in metres between each office space

Length of office space, metres

Distance	A-1	A-2	A-3	A-4	A-5	A-6	B-1	B-2	B-3	B-4	B-5	B-6
A-1		9	18	27	36	45		9	18	27	36	45
A-2	9		9	18	27	36	9		9	18	27	36
A-3	18	9		9	18	27	18	9		9	18	27
A-4	27	18	9		9	18	27	18	9		9	18
A-5	36	27	18	9		9	36	27	18	9		9
A-6	45	36	27	18	9		45	36	27	18	9	
B-1		9	18	27	36	45		9	18	27	36	45
B-2	9		9	18	27	36	9		9	18	27	36
B-3	18	9		9	18	27	18	9		9	18	27
B-4	27	18	9		9	18	27	18	9		9	18
B-5	36	27	18	9		9	36	27	18	9		9
B-6	45	36	27	18	9		45	36	27	18	9	

Table 10.14   Average contacts/week between departments

Distance	Purchasing	Accounting	Scheduling	Civil Eng	Process	Design	Customer	Modelling	Piping	Project Mn	Mechanical	Chemical
Purchasing		12	24	8	2	1	15	1	1	25	8	8
Accounting	12		8	5	2	16	8	5	17	21	2	7
Scheduling	24	8		7	8	14	9	2	12	15	7	3
Civil Eng	8	5	7		10	14	5	12	19	12	15	15
Process	2	2	8	10		12	6	5	8	6	21	23
Design	1	16	14	14	12		6	18	22	21	25	15
Customer	15	8	9	5	6	6		2	5	32	5	7
Modelling	1	5	2	12	5	18	2		22	9	18	6
Piping	1	17	12	19	8	22	5	22		10	15	8
Project Mng	25	21	15	12	6	21	32	9	10		12	8
Mechanical	8	2	7	15	21	25	5	18	15	12		27
Chemical	8	7	3	15	23	15	7	6	8	8	27	

Required

Optimize the layout of the office space by considering the contacts and the distance between partitions. Assume that distances travelled to opposite spaces is the same. For example, a person in Space A-1 would have the same distance to go to Space A-4 and Space B-4.

As the Project Manager organizes many meetings, he will have a space next to the Conference Room (either A-6 or B-6).

EXERCISE PROBLEM: CHIC

Situation

Chic is a large clothes cleaning operation, which serves individuals and hotels in the region. The principle functions are:

- dry cleaning
- pressing
- wrapping
- hanging
- washing machines (water)
- delivery bay (hotel deliveries)
- customer service desk (individuals).

The relationship requirements for each function and the criticality codes are given in Table 10.15.

Chic is considering moving into new space which currently is divided up according to the scheme shown in Figure 10.26.

Table 10.15 Chic Systematic layout for a cleaning/washing operation

Department Code		1. Relationship requirements							2. Criteria	
		1	2	3	4	5	6	7		Criticality Code
		Dry cleaning	Pressing	Customer desk	Washing machine	Hanging	Wrapping	Delivery bay		
1	Dry cleaning		A	D	C	A	B	C	Necessary	A
2	Pressing	A		D	A	A	B	C	Desirable	B
3	Customer desk	D	D		D	D	B	C	Not important	C
4	Washing machines	C	A	D		A	C	C	Not desirable	D
5	Hanging	A	A	D	A		A	C		
6	Wrapping	B	B	B	C	A		B		
7	Delivery bay	C	C	C	C	C	B			

Figure 10.26 Chic's new space arrangements.

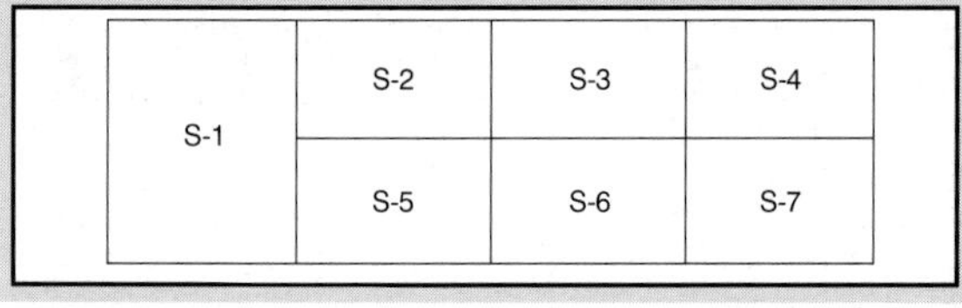

Required

1 Using the concept of systematic layout planning, decide on an appropriate layout for the cleaning operation.

EXERCISE PROBLEM: DAWSON

Situation

An engineering and construction company has been awarded a contract to perform the process design, engineering and construction of a chemical facility in the Middle East. The key personnel on this project will be the Project Manager, Design Engineers, Process Engineers, Purchasing, Model Shop, Estimators and Scheduling. In addition, the client will be resident on site. The facility available for the project is shown in Figure 10.27.

As for all projects, finishing on schedule, and within budget is critical; thus the project manager needs always to be kept informed of the situation. Furthermore, although it is important for the client and project manager to be in contact, it is not desirable to have the client involved in the day-to-day activity of the work as this will impede progress. The desired relationship for office departments is given in Table 10.16.

Figure 10.27 Facility available for Dawson Middle-East project.

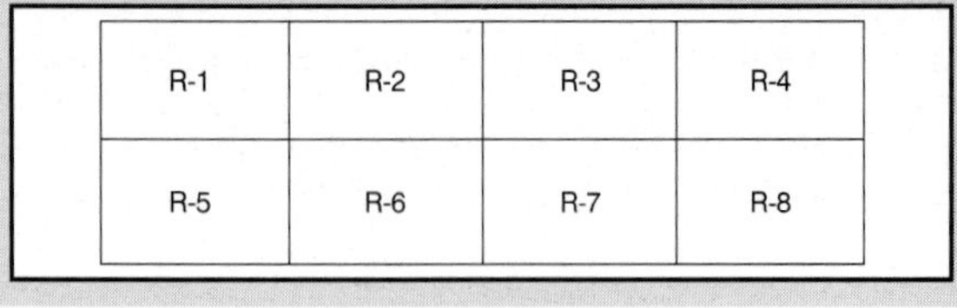

Table 10.16 Desired relationships between office departments in the Dawson Middle-East Project

Department Code		1	2	3	4	5	6	7	8
		PM	DE	PE	PU	MS	ES	SC	CL
Project manager (PM)	1		C	D	C	D	A	A	A
Design engineers (DE)	2	C		A	B	B	A	D	E
Process Engineer(PE)s	3	D	A		E	E	D	C	F
Purchasing (PU)	4	C	B	E		E	C	B	F
Model shop (MS)	5	D	B	E	E		D	D	E
Estimators (ES)	6	A	A	D	C	D		C	E
Scheduling(SC)	7	A	D	C	B	D	C		C
Clients (Cl)	8	A	E	F	F	E	E	C	

Note: Codes have the following meanings: A Critical; B Very important; C Necessary; D Desirable; E Unimportant; F Not desirable.

Required

Using the concept of systematic layout planning, decide on an appropriate room arrangement for the project team.

EXERCISE PROBLEM: MILKY CANDY COMPANY

Situation

The Milky Candy Company produces all types of chocolate candy, which are boxed before being sent to the retail outlets.

After the chocolate has been poured, the candy production goes though all types of operations from adding fillers, shaping, decorating, coating and the like, before being put into boxes, wrapped, and put into cartons. This production/assembly operation operates for five days a week, eight hours a day. Each week there is a demand for 3000 boxes of the chocolates.

Production/packaging consists of 13 operations. These, together with the estimated time for completion, are given in Table 10.17.

Table 10.17 Milky Candy Co's production/packaging operations

Operation	Time (s)	Operation immediately preceding
1	6	—
2	8	1
3	9	2
4	11	2
5	12	2
6	14	3, 4, 5
7	9	1
8	5	7
9	12	7, 8
10	8	9
11	9	6
12	12	10, 11
13	9	12

Required

1 Draw the process flow sheet, taking precedence relationships into account.
2 What are the theoretical number of groupings?
3 What would be the workstation groupings and the operation efficiency calculated on the basis of the *Most tasks following* heuristic rule?
4 What would be the workstation groupings, and the operation efficiency calculated on the basis of the *Longest task* heuristic rule?
5 How would the assembly-line arrangement change if the weekly demand doubled?

EXERCISE PROBLEM: TEMPLATE

Situation

An office in a service centre is 3 by 5 metres. On one of the smaller sides is a window of 1.25 metres width. At the end of one of the long walls is a door of 70 cm in width.

In the office it is proposed to put in the following furniture, whose surface dimensions are given in centimetres

- Desk 75 × 160
- Table 77 × 152
- Table 100 × 60
- Two roller cabinets 44 × 60
- Book shelving 44 × 140
- Book case 37 × 87
- Chair 50 × 45
- Chair 43 × 47.

Required

1 Using templates drawn to scale, develop an appropriate office layout.

CASE STUDY: INTERMARK

Situation

Intermark, a food retailer, is planning a new distribution centre close to London in the UK for its private-label and brand-named products. Its function will be to receive the products in bulk quantities, put them into storage and then distribute products according to the requirements of the retail stores. The principal products it handles are classified into the ten groupings given in Table 10.18 and the proposed warehouse storage zones with the linear distance between each is shown in Figure 10.28.

Table 10.18 Intermark product groupings

Dry goods	Vegetables, rice, sugar, cereals, etc.
Health/beauty products	Deodorants, dental, products, soap, etc.
Paper goods	Towels, toilet paper, serviettes, plates
Frozen foods	Meats, pre-cooked meals
Non alcoholic beverages	Cola, orange, water
Canned goods	Preserves, vegetables, fruit
Alcoholic beverages	Wine, beer and spirits
Animal-related products	Dry/moist food for cats and dogs, miscellaneous
Household	Cups, plates, cutlery, brooms, mops, etc.
Soaps/Detergents	Washing powders

There are three proposals for using the storage area, as shown in Table 10.19.

Figure 10.28 Proposed storage zones at the Intermark distribution centre.

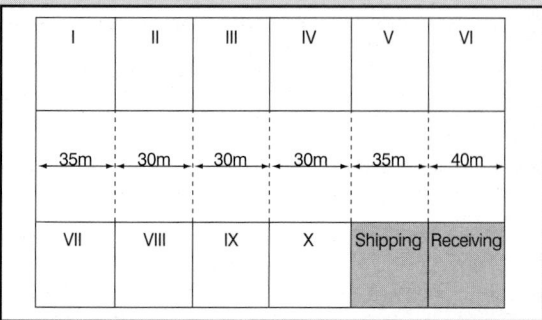

Table 10.19 The three proposals for using the storage area at the new Intermark distribution centre

Zone	Proposal 1	Proposal 2	Proposal 3
I	Dry goods	Frozen foods	Non-alcoholic beverages
II	Health and beauty products	Canned goods	Household
III	Paper goods	Health and beauty products	Dry goods
IV	Frozen foods	Paper goods	Health and beauty products
V	Non-alcoholic beverages	Non-alcoholic beverages	Animal-related products
VI	Canned goods	Alcoholic beverages	Frozen foods
VII	Alcoholic beverages	Animal-related products	Alcoholic beverages
VIII	Animal-related products	Dry goods	Soaps/detergents
IX	Household	Household	Canned goods
X	Soaps/ detergents	Soaps/ detergents	Paper goods

All products received go into storage and remain there from 4 to 14 days. The rotation depends on the items. Non-alcoholic beverages are faster moving than household products. When orders are received by the retail outlets, the products are taken from storage (picking) to the shipping area, from where they are dispatched to the retail outlet. Based on historical data, Table 10.20 shows the average monthly number of journeys made by trolley handlers from reception to storage, and from storage to shipping. Numbers are always low for the receiving part since products arrive in bulk, whereas for shipping products demanded are always of smaller quantities.

Table 10.20 Intermark: average movements in one month

	Receiving to storage	Storage to shipping
Dry goods	270	1 230
Health/beauty products	40	850
Paper goods	120	630
Frozen foods	300	1 000
Non alcoholic beverages	650	2 100
Canned goods	250	1 800
Alcoholic beverages	120	980
Animal-related products	230	1 645
Household	175	1 775
Soaps/detergents	80	1 270

In order to calculate the distance travelled by a handler the following formulas are used:

$$\text{Receiving to Storage} = 0.5 \times (\text{Length of receiving dock})$$
$$+ (\text{Sum of lengths of other storage zones traversed})$$
$$+ 0.5 \times (\text{Length of storage zone used});$$

$$\text{Storage to Shipping} = 0.5 \times (\text{Length of storage zone used})$$
$$+ (\text{Sum of lengths of other storage zones traversed})$$
$$+ 0.5 \times (\text{Length of storage zone used}).$$

For example, in proposal 1, movement of dry goods would mean distances travelled as follows:

$$\text{from Receiving to Storage} = 0.5 \times 40 + (35 + 30 + 30 + 30)$$
$$+ 0.5 \times 35 = 162.50 \text{ m};$$

$$\text{from Storage to Shipping} = 0.5 \times 35 + (30 + 30 + 30)$$
$$+ 0.5 \times 35 = 125.00 \text{ m}$$

while, for non-alcoholic beverages, the distances travelled would be:

$$\text{from Receiving to Storage} = 0.5 \times 40 + 0.5 \times 35 = 37.50 \text{ m};$$

$$\text{from Storage to Shipping} = 0.5 \times 35 = 17.50 \text{ m}.$$

Required

1 Based on using the load–distance analysis for layout, which of the three proposals should be chosen?
2 What are other considerations in the facility layout of a distribution centre such as the one described here?

NOTES AND REFERENCES

1. Information provided by the owner, Mr Trenel, in 1995.
2. 'Volvo's radical new plant: The death of the assembly line?' (1998) *Business Week* 28 August: 54.
3. 'Back to the past: Some plants tear out long assembly lines, switch to craft work', (1994) *Wall Street Journal Europe* 25 October.
4. Chandler, C. and White, J.B. (1992) 'Nissan takes the mass out of production to increase flexibility at its dream factory', *Wall Street Journal Europe*, 10/11 July.
5. Frémy, D. and Frémy, M. (1993) *Quid*, Paris: Editions Laffont: 1561–62.
6. *Organisation for Engineering* (1969) C F Braun & Co. Alhambra, CA: 96
7. 'White-collar factories: Good office design can sound like a fancy indulgence or a marginal extra. But managers neg-

lect it at their peril' (1995) *The Economist* 25 November: 95–96.

8. 'The new work place: Walls are falling as the office of the future finally takes shape' (1996) Business Week, 6 May: 56B-E to 56H-E.

9. 'Vie quotidienne des sans-bureau-fixe,' *L' Expansion* July: 14.

10. Adams, S. (1996) 'Dilbert's Management Handbook', *Fortune* 13 May: 53-54.

11. Muther, R. (1973) *Systematic Layout Planning*, Boston, MA: Cahners Publishing Company.

12. Francis, R. L., McGinnis, L. F. and White, J. A. (1992) *Facility Layout and Location*, Englewood Cliffs, NJ: Prentice Hall.

13. Buffa, E.S., Armour, G.S. and Vollman, T.E. (1964) 'Allocating facilities with CRAFT', *Harvard Business Review*, 42, 2: 136-159

FURTHER READING

Askin, R. G. Mitwasi, M. G. (1992) 'Integrating facility layout with process selection and capacity planning', *European Journal of Operations Research* 57, (2): 162–73.

Bozer, Y. A., Meller, R. D. (1997) 'A reexamination of the distance-based layout problem', *IIE Transactions*, 29, (7): 549–60.

Bozer, Y. A., Meller, R. D. (1994) 'An improvement-type layout algorithm for single and multiple-floor facilities', *Management Science* 40, (7): 918–32.

Brookman, F. (1993) 'Drug emporium unveils new store layout with cross aisles', *Drug Topics*, 137, (13): 54.

Butler, T., Karwan, K. R., Sweigart, J. R. (1992) 'Multi-level strategic evaluation of hospital plans and decisions', *Journal of the Operational Research Society* 43, (7): 665–75.

Cimikowski, R. and Mooney, E. (1995) 'Heuristics for a new model of facility layout', *Computers and Industrial Engineering* 29, (1– 4): 273–77.

Eley, J. and Marmo, A. (1995) *Understanding Offices*, London: Penguin.

Harshell, J. and Dahl, S. (1988) 'Simulation model developed to convert production to cellular manufacturing layout', *Industrial Engineering* 20, (12): 40–45.

Houshyar, A. and White, B. (1993) 'Exact optimal solution for facility layout: Deciding which pairs of locations should be adjacent', *Computers and Industrial Engineering*, 24, (2): 177–87.

Kusiak, A. and Heragu, S. S. (1987) 'The facility layout problem', *European Journal of Operational Research* 29, (3): 229–51.

Leung, J. (1992) 'A new graph-theoretic heuristic for facility layout', *Management Science*, 38, (4): 594–605.

Meller, R.D, Gau, K. Y. (1996) 'The facility layout problem: Recent and emerging trends and perspectives', *Journal of Manufacturing Systems* 15, (5): 351–66.

Rosenblatt, M. J. and Golany, B. (1992) 'A distance assignment approach to the facility layout problem', *European Journal of Operations Research* 57, (2): 253–70.

Rowh, M. (1994) 'Designing an office that works', *Office Systems* 11, (6): 43 – 46.

Savsar, M. (1991) 'Flexible facility layout by simulation', *Computers and Industrial Engineering* 20, (1): 155 –65.

Shafter, S. M., and Charnes, J. M. (1993) 'Cellular versus functional layouts under a variety of shop operating conditions', *Decision Sciences* 24, (3): 665 –81.

Urban. L. (1989) 'Combining qualitative and quantitative analyses in facility layout', *Production and Inventory Management* 30, (3): 73–77.

Vischer, J (1995) 'Strategic work-space planning', *Sloan Management Review*, 37 1: Fall 1995: 33 – 42.

Ziai, M. R. and Sule, D. R. (1989) 'Computerized materials handling and facility layout design', *Computers and Industrial Engineering* 17, (1–4): 55 – 60.

'Re-engineering offices;' (1995) *The Economist* 25-November: 95.

11 | Inventory management

Objectives and overview

The objective of this chapter is to detail the concepts related to inventory management, one of the key physical variables in the supply chain. The chapter opens by presenting the types of inventory encountered, the difference between independent and dependent demand inventories, the reasons firms hold more than the normal level of inventory and why in-process inventory accumulates in a manufacturing operation. The chapter then discusses costs associated with inventory management including carrying, purchasing and stockout costs. There is a section covering ordering inventory in fixed quantities and in fixed time periods, including an illustration of the corresponding inventory profiles that would be expected with these policies. The chapter then presents in detail the concept of economic order quantity models, starting with the basic form and then going on to the continuous supply and usage model, the production model and models modified for quantity discounts. Setting order points and customer service levels are presented and highlighting the concept of demand during lead time, the criteria for holding safety stocks and the risks associated with stockouts. The fixed order period model is then presented as a way of estimating the time between orders and the chapter closes by presenting the requirements for good inventory management, including the ABC Pareto method for inventory classification.

INVENTORY AND THE SUPPLY CHAIN

In the supply chain one of the key variables that has to be managed is inventory. The inventory includes a vast spectrum of material that is being transferred, stored, consumed, produced, packaged or sold in one way or another during a firm's normal course of business. Inventory has a financial value, which for accounting purposes is considered to be a short-term asset, and one goal in operations is to keep the level of inventory in the supply chain as low as possible, thus freeing up funds for other purposes. Another goal is to move the inventory, in its continually changing form, as fast as possible through the supply chain, for delivery to the final client, in order to realize the gains in the value added. In contrast to inventory, there are capital goods, or long-term assets, shown on a balance sheet as a depreciated item, and these may include machines, equipment, vehicles and buildings used for operating the business, including transforming, delivering and storing the inventory. Capital goods are not consumed in the same way as inventory and may have a practical life of many years.

Every business, be it service or manufacturing, handles, consumes, or moves inventory of one sort or another and good inventory management is a critical part of the operations. Some types of material that come under the global concept of inventory are as discussed in the following sections.

Services

- A restaurant has an inventory of raw food, an in-process inventory of the food being cooked and the finished meal itself. In addition, there is wine, bread, sauces and everything else that goes with preparing a meal.
- A retail outlet will have a finished-goods inventory, which is waiting to be purchased by customers.
- Offices, such as law firms and consulting companies, have consumable supplies of inventory, such as paper, pencils, computer diskettes and the like.
- Distribution companies that provide storage and transport may have inventory of finished goods, such as clothing, household or office equipment. The inventory might be raw material such as cocoa

beans, animal carcasses or paper pulp, or it might be industrial goods destined for another firm, such as engine parts, plastic moulds or cut lumber for construction.

- Pharmacies, and particularly hospitals, hold a large inventory of, often very expensive, pharmaceutical products.
- Computer software companies such as Microsoft have an 'inventory' of intellectual property, the computer programs.

Manufacturing

Inventory is what production in the manufacturing sector is all about, with its global supply chain being made up of the purchasing, transformation, transfer, storage and packaging of pieces, parts and sub-assemblies. As illustrated in Figure 11.1, inventory associated with manufacturing include the following:

Raw materials

Raw materials are the starting elements for any production process. In their lowest level form, raw materials in the process industries may include iron ore, lumber, crude oil, wheat, water, paper pulp, etc. For some firms, the raw materials may be purchased parts or an intermediate chemical, because for them, this is the 'start point' of their operation.

Purchased parts

Purchased parts or components are products made by Company B that are used by Company A in its production operation. Such items may, for example, include engine parts, tyres and lights used by automobile companies.

Work in process

Work in process, goods in process or semifinished goods are the pieces that are moving though the production operation. At each stage, the pieces are being modified and value is being added. All inventory between raw materials and finished goods constitutes work in process. This type of inventory is sometimes referred to as WIP (Work In Process). The term work in progress is equivalent.

Finished goods

Finished goods are the products that have reached the end of the production line within a certain manufacturing organization. However, they may not necessarily be the finished goods that are used by the final consumer. Automobiles from Citroën, televisions from Thompson

Figure 11.1 Inventory types.

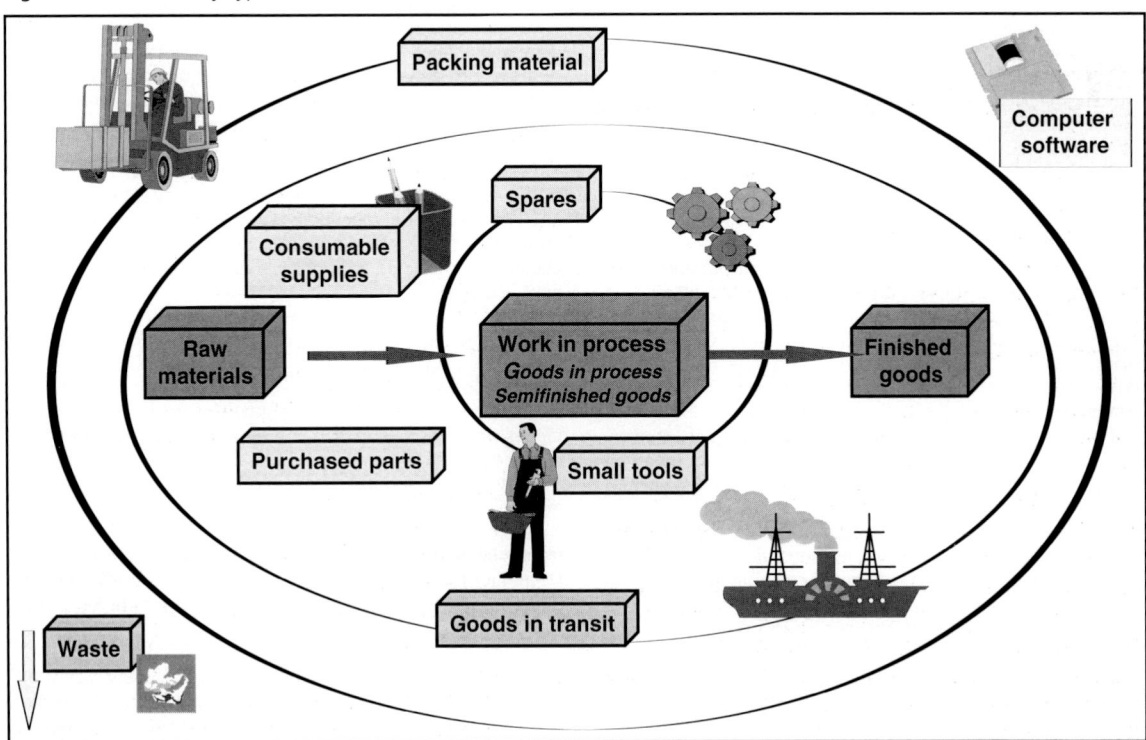

or computers from Dell are finished products for which the next destination after the distributor is the customer (consumer goods). Starter motors for automobiles made by Valéo, meters for gas pipelines, made by Schlumberger or polypropylene for plastic products, made by Rhône-Poulenc, are all finished goods destined for another firm (industrial goods). The article in Box 11.1 illustrates the impact finished goods inventory might have on a company's strategy[1]

Goods in transit

Goods in transit are products that are being transferred from one location to another. The term could, for example, refer to raw material such as crude oil being shipped from the Middle East to an oil refinery in Southampton, England, vanadium metal being shipped from South Africa to a tool firm in Germany or lumber from Norway being shipped to a construction firm in Spain. Goods in transit may be finished consumer items, such as Volkswagen's automobiles assembled in Mexico and being shipped to consumers in Europe,

clothing made in Hong Kong being shipped to consumers in France or televisions made in Japan being shipped to consumers in the USA. Alternatively, goods in transit may be industrial goods for another firm.

Spare parts

Spare parts are inventory items that are kept in store for repair purposes. Piston rods, cog wheels or springs would be spare parts kept for machinery. Wheels, chains or brake blocks would be spare parts kept by a retailer for customers needing to repair their bicycles. Spare parts are a special type of finished goods.

Small tools

Small tools are items that are used in a manufacturing or construction organization and are considered inventory because they are used up, maybe lost or perhaps stolen. Wrenches, screwdrivers, drills, work gloves, and overalls would be considered as small tools in these industries. All manufacturing companies have tools as an inventory, as do construction companies.

Box 11.1 GM faces lots of troubles as its car inventories grow. By Rebecca Blumenstein and Gabriella Stern, Staff Reporters

DETROIT – With its growing inventory of unsold cars now the highest of the U.S. Big Three auto makers, General Motors Corp. is under mounting pressure to follow its competitors by cutting production or launching aggressive rebate campaigns.

GM's supply of cars on dealer lots Jan. 31 was enough to last 106 days at current selling rates, according to Ward's Automotive Reports, a trade publication. By contrast, Ford Motor Co.'s inventories stood at 83 days and Chrysler's at 97 days.

The industry considers no more than a 60 to 65 day supply to be ideal. A month earlier, GM had an 83-day supply of cars on dealer lots, compared with 81 days for Ford and 91 days for Chrysler.

Its rising inventories put GM in a bind as it pursues a new marketing strategy it calls "value pricing," under which the focus is on giving customers simplified and relatively low prices with a minimum of marketing gimmicks. GM's marketing chief, Ronald Zarrella, has said repeatedly that GM's strategy is to try to avoid offering heavy rebates and incentives.

Even so, deteriorating market conditions are expected to prompt the No. 1 auto maker to join its rivals in stepping up its sales-incentive programs to trim down its bloated car stocks. For now, people close to the situation say GM wants to avoid cash-on-the-hood incentives and is probably more inclined to boost sales using leasing subsidies and dealer incentives. Big production cuts could come later in the winter or in early spring, they say, if GM determines that January's mixed sales results weren't just a reflection of severe winter weather.

In fact, aggressive marketing campaigns by Ford and Chrysler have already prompted GM to offer rebates on a few vehicles, including some of its 1996 models, although the programs are far less extensive than those offered by the competition, according to a GM spokesman.

At GMC, where inventories of the Jimmy sport-utility vehicle at the end of last month were enough to last a discouraging 104 days, a spokesman said that as the spring selling season opens, "we are going to have some aggressive marketing initiatives – ways to move the product." He declined to elaborate.

At the same time, a GM spokesman cautioned that company officials are taking a wait-and-see attitude toward piling on any across-the-board marketing incentives or making any extensive production cuts based on January's mixed sales results. "February becomes a very important month for us to look at," the spokesman said.

Ford and Chrysler in the past few weeks have responded to their own rising inventory levels by cutting production and launching retail incentives. Chrysler is offering a minimum $1,000 rebate on most cars and Ford is offering a choice of a $600 rebate or 4.8% financing on almost all of its light vehicles.

"GM does come in with very attractive, affordable prices. But the market determines what the price is," says Susan Jacobs, of Jacobs & Associates Forecasting & Strategic Planning in Rutherford, New Jersey. "And in this current market, the softness is suggesting that everyone's prices are higher than the consumer is willing to pay." Ms. Jacobs observes that GM's inventories are so high that the company is likely to have to both cut production and offer more marketing incentives.

There are even signs of weakness in the market for light trucks, such as sport-utility vehicles and pickups. From December to January, GM's supply of light trucks shot up to 87 days from 65 days, while Ford's rose to 88 from 84, and Chrysler's to 72 from 59 days.

Wall Street Journal Europe, 15 February 1996
Reprinted by permission of *Wall Street Journal Europe*,
© 1996 Dow Jones & Company, Inc.

Typically, in making a proposal for building a process unit such as a refinery or a chemical plant, a construction company will consider in the cost something like 2 per cent for small tools.

Consumable supplies

Oil and cleaning fluids would be considered as consumable supplies. In addition, as in a service company, there would also be office-type materials such as pens, paper, files, envelopes, computer diskettes, etc.

Packaging

Packaging covers all the material used to protect finished goods or to display items for marketing purposes. Cardboard boxes, corrugated paper and rubber sheeting are packaging materials for protection. Fancy perfume bottles are also packaging, but their shape, and the associated wrapping, is also a marketing aid. Packaging represents finished goods to the producer of the packaging, while to users such as Proctor and Gamble, Hewlett Packard and Unilever packaging is a special inventory item.

Waste products

Waste products are all the discarded products from a business and may in some instances have value (albeit a small amount), for example:

- Scrap metal from a firm making sheet steel, rod, girders and other metal products can be sent back to a foundry for re-processing.
- Scrap meat from a food-processing factory can be sold as animal feed.
- Wood scraps and sawdust from a lumber company can be reprocessed into chipboard for furniture manufacture.

A special waste, which represents a cost (and danger) is radioactive material, principally from nuclear power plants. This inventory has to be stored in repositories for many years. It essentially has no value.

Dependency of inventory

All inventory can be divided into two broad groupings according to its dependency on other items.

Independent demand inventory

Independent inventory includes those items that are not dependent on other parts. This means that they are the ultimate finished products destined for the final consumer (automobiles, cans of beer, washing machines, etc.). Demand for them depends solely on the requirements and demand of the consumer. Managing these inventory items requires forecast information on consumer needs.

Dependent demand inventory

Dependent inventory includes items that are usually assemblies or parts used in the manufacture of the final consumer product. For example, in the manufacture of a bicycle, as illustrated in Figure 11.2, there are one frame, one saddle, one pair of handle bars and two wheels. For each wheel there are 36 spokes (depending on the model), one tyre, 24 bearings, etc. Except for components used for spare parts, the quantity of inventory of these components depends on the demand for the finished product. As these inventory items have a dependency, they can be effectively managed using a material requirements planning system (MRP), as presented in Chapter 13, *Material Requirements Planning*.

REASONS FOR HOLDING INVENTORY

Inventory has a value, so keeping a store of goods costs money. However, as summarized in Figure 11.3, and discussed below, there are many valid reasons why firms keep in storage a certain amount of inventory and often more than is required in the next immediate period.

Finished goods held by a distributor or retailer

Retailers (Marks and Spencer, Safeway, Carrefour) or wholesale distributors to retail outlets always have a certain amount of inventory on hand for reasons such as those given in the following sections.

Variation in customer demand

Customers' demands vary from period to period and, as it is not always easy to forecast these needs, extra supplies are kept in order so as always to be able to satisfy the client (i.e. provide a high level of service). In addition, it is often more economic to hold inventory rather than place emergency orders for clients. Furthermore, backordering of standard products may be unacceptable to the customer, who will purchase elsewhere.

Display of products

Holding inventory allows display of products to aid the sale. In some cases, it may not be possible to sell products after they have been used for display purposes. Alternatively, they will be sold at a marked-down price. For example, clothing pinned to mannequins is difficult to sell as the pinning may damage the fabric and sunlight falling on goods in a window may fade the material.

Figure 11.2 Product structure for a bicycle.

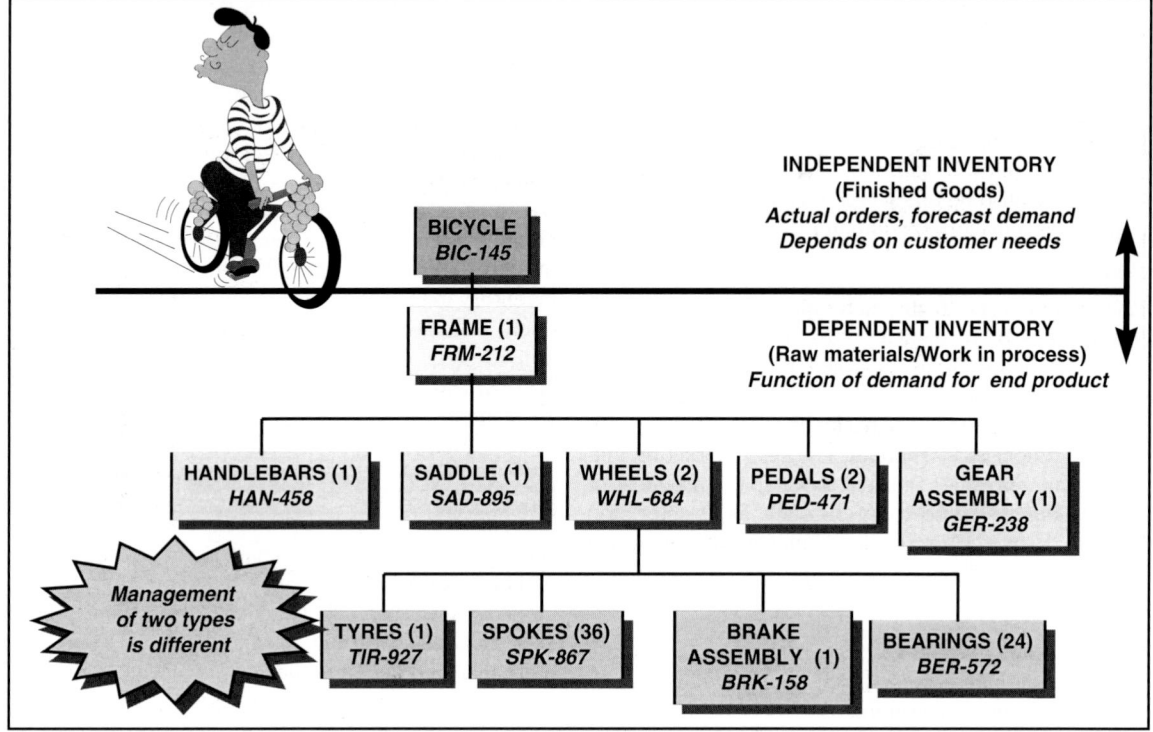

Price discounts

If finished products are purchased in bulk, discounts are often available. Thus, it is more economic to take advantage of lower unit prices and store what is not immediately required.

Favourable exchange rates

Exchange rates between countries fluctuate and, sometimes, taking advantage of these when they are beneficial to the buying party is a reason for buying more goods than is immediately necessary, for example:

■ German-made Mercedes cars sold in California;
■ French perfume sold in New York;
■ Japanese televisions destined for the US market.

Anticipated price increases

Finished goods may be held in anticipation, or forehand knowledge, of price increases. For example, an increase in value added taxes announced by the government or tax increases on petrol cause consumers or retailers to stock up on the finished product.

Finished goods held by a producer

Manufacturing concerns strive to work just-in-time (Chapter 15, *Lean Production and Just-in-Time*). Even so, some level of finished inventory is held to allow the producer more flexibility in production scheduling, and also to supply clients when there is unplanned demand. A special case for holding finished goods inventory is described the following.

Milk

Candia, France, a Sodiaal subsidiary, has a 'quarantine' of four days on the finished-product milk that it has pasteurized and put into cartons. This four-day holding period is to allow the quality control laboratory to perform required tests to be sure that the milk is fit for consumption. The inventory is stored on pallets stacked 27 metres high in warehouses that have automatic placement and withdrawal systems.[2]

Raw materials

Raw materials are held in inventory by manufacturing companies for reasons such as those described in the following sections.

Figure 11.3   Reasons for holding larger than normal inventory.

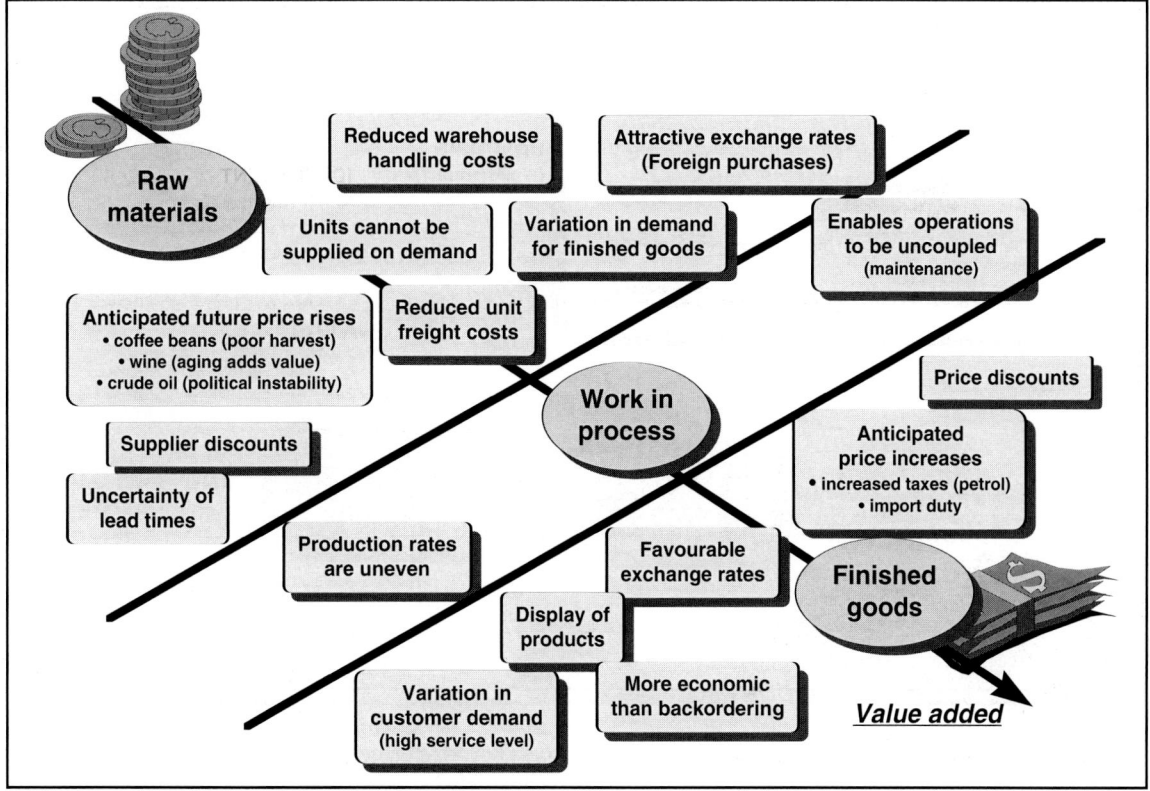

Immediate delivery is not feasible

Supplies of crude oil, iron ore and coal cannot always be supplied immediately on demand and so the producer needs a certain level of inventory to permit reasonable production planning.

Variation in the demand for finished goods

If the demand for finished goods varies, then this snowballs back along the production supply chain and creates a variation in demand for the raw materials.

Anticipated price rises

Price rises of raw materials, such as green coffee, crude oil or wheat, may be anticipated. In this case, the user of this raw material may choose to purchase larger than normal inventories. Often, rather than taking physical control of the inventory, futures contracts of these types of raw materials are purchased (See Chapter 16, *Purchasing and Subcontracting*).

Unit price discount

Buying in large quantities allows favourable unit pricing. This is the case for crude oil, steel, fabric and extruded plastic, for example.

Reduced freight costs

Buying in bulk (one train load, one truck load or one ship load) can reduce unit transportation costs.

Lower warehouse costs

If materials are purchased in bulk, then the handling charges per unit in a warehouse or storage zone may be lower since labour and machines are all used in one assigned time period.

Uncertainty of lead times

Uncertainty in lead time (time between ordering and delivery) because of political instability such as strikes, the weather or tight supply situations may result in holding higher than normal inventory.

Work in process inventory

Work in process inventory arises principally because of waiting or delays of one type or another in the production 'pipeline'. This pipeline scheme is illustrated by Figure 11.4, which shows a flange connection used in fluid-flow operation. Consider two workcentres.

Figure 11.4 Material flow of work in progress.

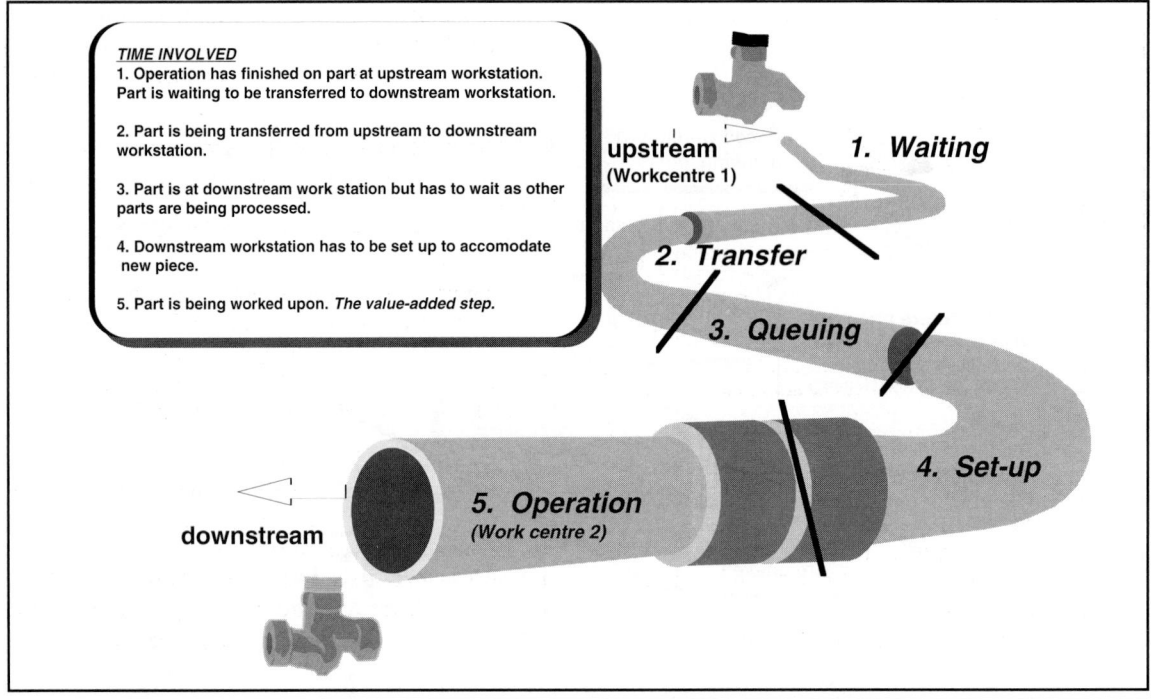

TIME INVOLVED
1. Operation has finished on part at upstream workstation. Part is waiting to be transferred to downstream workstation.

2. Part is being transferred from upstream to downstream workstation.

3. Part is at downstream work station but has to wait as other parts are being processed.

4. Downstream workstation has to be set up to accomodate new piece.

5. Part is being worked upon. *The value-added step.*

upstream (Workcentre 1)

1. *Waiting*
2. *Transfer*
3. *Queuing*
4. *Set-up*
5. *Operation* (Work centre 2)

downstream

- upstream, Workcentre 1, where the left side of the flange is completed;
- downstream, Workcentre 2, where the right side of the flange is completed.

The pipeline can be considered broken into five zones:

1 Workcentre 1 where the left side is finished, and the semifinished flange is waiting to be transferred to Workcentre 2.
2 The semifinished flange is being transferred to Workcentre 2.
3 At Workcentre 2 there are other jobs being worked upon as the system is unbalanced. Thus, there is queuing time for this particular flange.
4 Setup time. At Workcentre 2 the machines have to be adjusted to the specifications required by the flange in question.
5 Setup is finished and the last stage is the time taken to do the operation. This is the only value-added step.

Actual delay times vary according to firm, industry and the operation being carried out. However, to illustrate the point, Figure 11.5 gives the relative magnitudes of the various zones where inventory is being held. What is important is that for about only 5 per cent of the total time is value being added to the inven-

tory. For 95 per cent of the holding time, no value is being added.

The argument of production managers for keeping work-in-process inventory is that production rates are uneven and uncoupling of operations can give more flexibility. The counter-argument to this is that the production rate should be balanced, allowing a smooth flow right through the operation.

COSTS ASSOCIATED WITH INVENTORY MANAGEMENT

Three categories of costs in inventory management are carrying costs, ordering costs and stockout costs.

Inventory carrying costs

Inventory carrying costs are those costs associated with keeping inventory in a storage area. They might include:

- Investment in the inventory:
  - borrowing costs associated with obtaining the funds to purchase the inventory;

Figure 11.5 Proportion of time spent as work in progress.

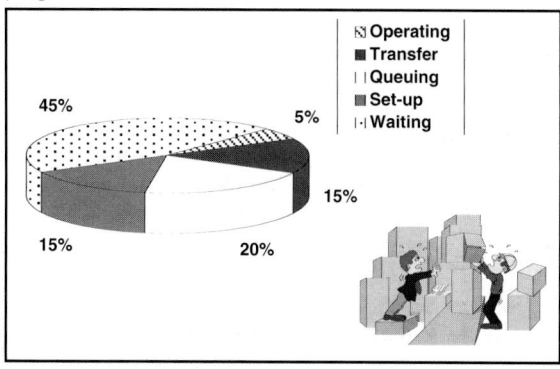

- opportunity costs, or financial returns that could be realized from investments other than purchasing the inventory.
■ Warehousing:
  - property taxes on the facility;
  - rental, or purchase, of the facility, which thus incurs a depreciation charge;
  - insurance on the warehouse facility for fire or other hazard;
  - energy or utilities, which can be especially high for refrigeration for perishable goods.
■ Holding costs:
  - insurance on the inventory;
  - spoilage that might occur with fresh foods;
  - Obsolescence, which is a risk associated with clothing, text books and high-technology equipment;
  - security costs;
  - loss due to fire, theft, or damage.

Inventory carrying costs can be up to a third of the value of the inventory. It is often the borrowing costs, or the opportunity costs associated with the inventory purchase, that are the highest proportion of the carrying costs. Although holding costs here are identified as a part of carrying costs, holding costs is sometimes the term used interchangeably with carrying costs. Carrying costs are expressed either as a percentage of the cost of inventory (say 25 per cent) or given as the actual cost to carry material for a defined period.

Inventory ordering costs

Inventory ordering costs are those costs associated with procuring the inventory. They are expressed as cost per order and do not include the purchase cost of materials. The inventory might be acquired externally or internally.

Externally obtained inventory

Inventory might be purchased from an external source, for example the purchase of sheet steel for a manufacturing plant. In this case, the ordering costs would include:

■ salary of purchasing staff or those persons involved in a proposal analysis, preparing and sending the order;
■ salary of accounting staff involved in paying for purchased goods;
■ Communication costs including postage, telephone, fax, electronic mail or an Internet connection;
■ expediting the goods if they do not arrive as planned;
■ warehouse costs associated with receiving, handling, separating lots, classifying and inspection.

Internally obtained inventory

The inventory might be produced by the same company. For example, Workcentre B orders some engine assemblies from Workcentre A. Both are cost centres and Workcentre A would charge Workcentre B for ordering the inventory in addition to the price of the inventory itself. Inventory ordering costs in this case would include:

■ preparation of production orders;
■ preparation of materials, tools and needed labour;
■ setup of machines.

In most instances, the various inventory ordering costs are associated with the salary or wages of operating personnel.

Inventory stockout costs

Inventory stockout costs are those costs associated with not having sufficient inventory to satisfy client demand. These costs may be related to the finished product that is sold to clients or to a production system that uses the inventory in its operation. When orders are placed for replenishment, smaller quantities do result in average lower inventory levels but, since stockouts usually occur during lead time (the time between order and delivery) the likelihood of stockouts is increased when smaller orders are placed. Furthermore, with small orders, more inventory cycles per year are needed (more inventory ordering). Stockout costs are hard to quantify directly and would not appear on an income statement. However these 'costs' would include the following for finished goods and the production system:

■ Finished goods:
  - lost profit on customer orders that cannot be filled;

- loss of clients who went elsewhere for the products;
- additional costs to satisfy an order, such as sub-contracting, overtime or direct purchase from another source;
- if the customer accepts backlogging, additional costs from extra paperwork, special handling of orders and expediting;
- additional transportation costs to finally satisfy the demand.
- Production system:
  - shutdown costs due to insufficient raw materials;
  - machines underutilized;
  - labour underemployed;
  - reduced employee moral, which can lead to a decline in productivity;
  - expediting necessary articles;
  - startup costs, such as the preparation of orders and preparing machines.

Quantifying the value of a stockout

To quantify how much inventory to carry, a company needs to determine the expected cost, or how much money it would lose if a stockout does occur. This is not easy to determine exactly, but might be estimated as follows on the basis of historical data and the weighting of that information. Assume that when a product is out of stock:

- For 55 per cent of the time this results in preparing a backorder for the client. Backordering reduces the profit margin by $5.
- For 25 per cent of the time this results in a lost sale for the product. This means a $50 loss in profit margin.
- For 20 per cent of the time this results in a lost customer. This means a $500 loss.

Thus, the expected loss is:

$$0.55 \times \$5 + 0.25 \times \$50 + 0.20 \times \$500$$
$$= \$115.25$$

This amount represents the average value of incurring a stockout. Thus, a company should carry additional inventory to avoid stockouts, providing that on the average the cost of carrying this additional stock does not exceed $115.25 per unit. (Chapter 22, *Decision Making and Risk Analysis* gives more detail on this concept.)

Safety stocks

In selling, in production or in purchasing operations there is uncertainty:

- Customers may increase an order.
- There may be a strike.
- Machinery may breakdown.
- Suppliers may be unable to deliver when promised.

To attempt to avoid stockouts resulting from these uncertainties, an organization might keep a safety stock 'just in case'. This safety stock is dead inventory; it provides a safeguard, but adds to inventory carrying costs.

Value added to inventory

As raw material and components move through the production chain, they are modified in one way or another (for example, sheet steel is cut, drilled, shaped and dipped). These operations add value to the material. As a result of adding value, finished goods are the inventory which represents the highest value to the business. At the end of the production line, the maximum amount of value has been added. Thus, if there is a choice, it is preferable to hold raw materials, which have a lower value, than finished goods, which have a higher value. In addition, as explained in Chapter 17, *Managing the Supply Chain* as one moves through the production pipeline, flexibility with the inventory is lost.

ORDERING DECISIONS FOR INDEPENDENT DEMAND INVENTORY

Two decisions to be made in ordering finished goods, or independent inventory, are:

1 *The quantity of goods to order.* These may come from an outside supplier or from a production department within the same organization.
2 *When, or at what date, to place the order.* This would depend on the lead time – the time between when the order is placed and when the order is received.

Ordering in fixed order quantities

Here, as illustrated in Figure 11.6, purchase orders are placed for the same quantity of material in each inventory cycle (the period between successive inventory ordering activities). The order quantity Q is constant and it is assumed this quantity is delivered in one single lot. When this inventory arrives, the level in storage increases to around a pre-established maximum level. As inventory is taken out of storage for use or sale, the level falls until it reaches a critical level, the order point. At this level, another order is placed. The level of

Figure 11.6 Inventory movements and ordering using a fixed order quantity (T1 ≠ T2 ≠ T3 ≠ T4).

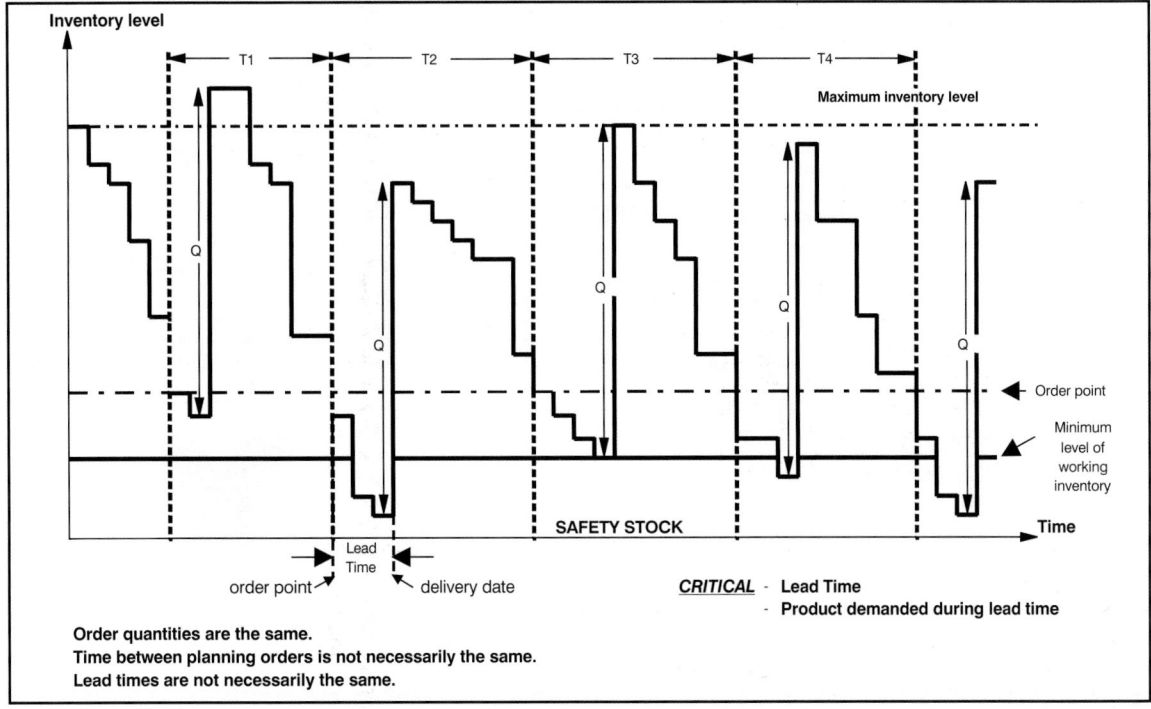

this order point is determined by estimating the expected usage of inventory during lead time, plus perhaps a safety stock. During this lead time, as illustrated, inventory is still being consumed and may or may not eat into the safety stock. (At worst, a stockout may occur.)

Two-bin system

A two-bin system is a special form of a fixed ordering system, which can be used for bulk products such as fertilizer, cattle feed, cement, chemical materials, oil, etc. Inventory of material is kept in two silos, or holding tanks, A and B as shown in Figure 11.7. A is much larger than B and is the feed receptacle from which material is normally withdrawn. If the inventory is solid, then at the bottom of bin A there may be a preprinted requisition for another order of material. This requisition is sent to purchase another lot. In the mean time, while the new order is awaiting delivery, material is used out of container B. Container B is sized to hold enough material to last until the next inventory replenishment (the demand during lead time plus a safety stock). If the inventory is a liquid, a level gauge fitted with an alarm system will indicate when container A is empty and a new order needs to be placed.

Just-in-time production (Chapter 15, *Lean Production and Just-in-Time*) is often implemented using a two-bin system. At a workpost, an operator uses components on the principle, 'One container empty, one full'. At the operator post there is always one container (bin) full of component parts and one container (bin) from which pieces are being used. When the latter container is empty, the operator replaces it with a full container, meanwhile work continues using parts from the container that was originally full.

Ordering using a fixed order period

Here, as illustrated in Figure 11.8, purchase orders are placed at preset time intervals. At these time intervals, the existing inventory level is measured and orders are placed to bring inventory levels back to some predetermined level. Thus, order quantities may be unequal but order intervals are equal.

Small grocers or retailers might use this type of system. Inventory levels would be measured at the end of the week and the required order quantities placed.

Since there is uncertainty between the ordering times (customer demand might be unusually high), the fixed order system requires more safety stock to accommodate the increased risk of stockouts.

Figure 11.7 Two-bin inventory system.

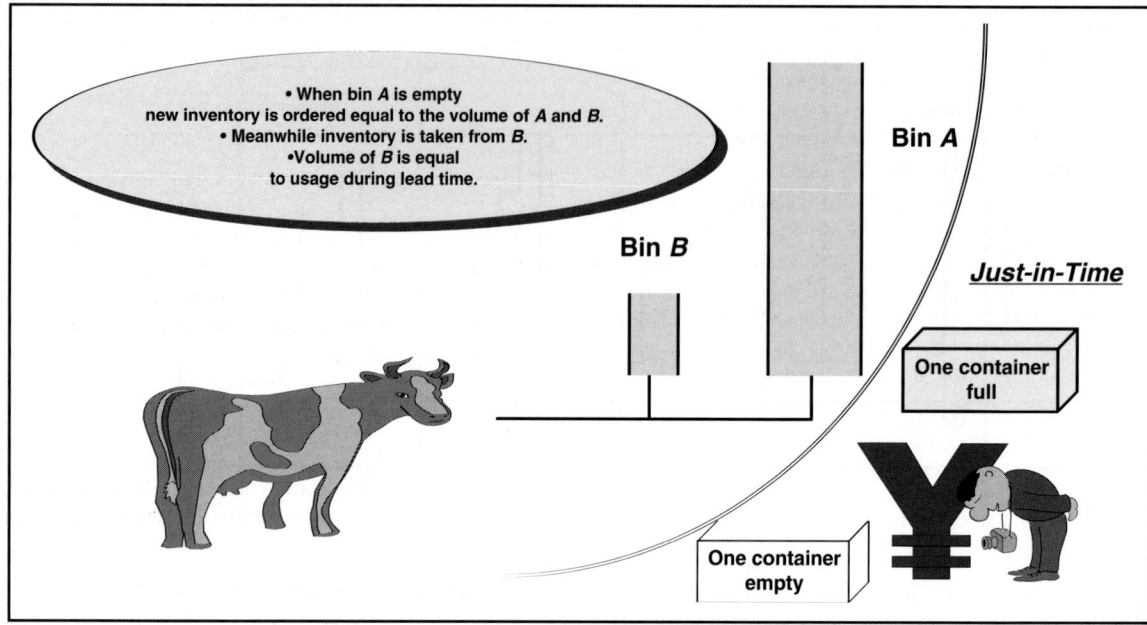

- When bin *A* is empty
new inventory is ordered equal to the volume of *A* and *B*.
- Meanwhile inventory is taken from *B*.
- Volume of *B* is equal
to usage during lead time.

Bin *A*

Bin *B*

Just-in-Time

One container
full

One container
empty

Figure 11.8 Inventory movements and ordering using a fixed order period (Q1 ≠ Q2 ≠ Q3 ≠ Q4 ≠ Q5).

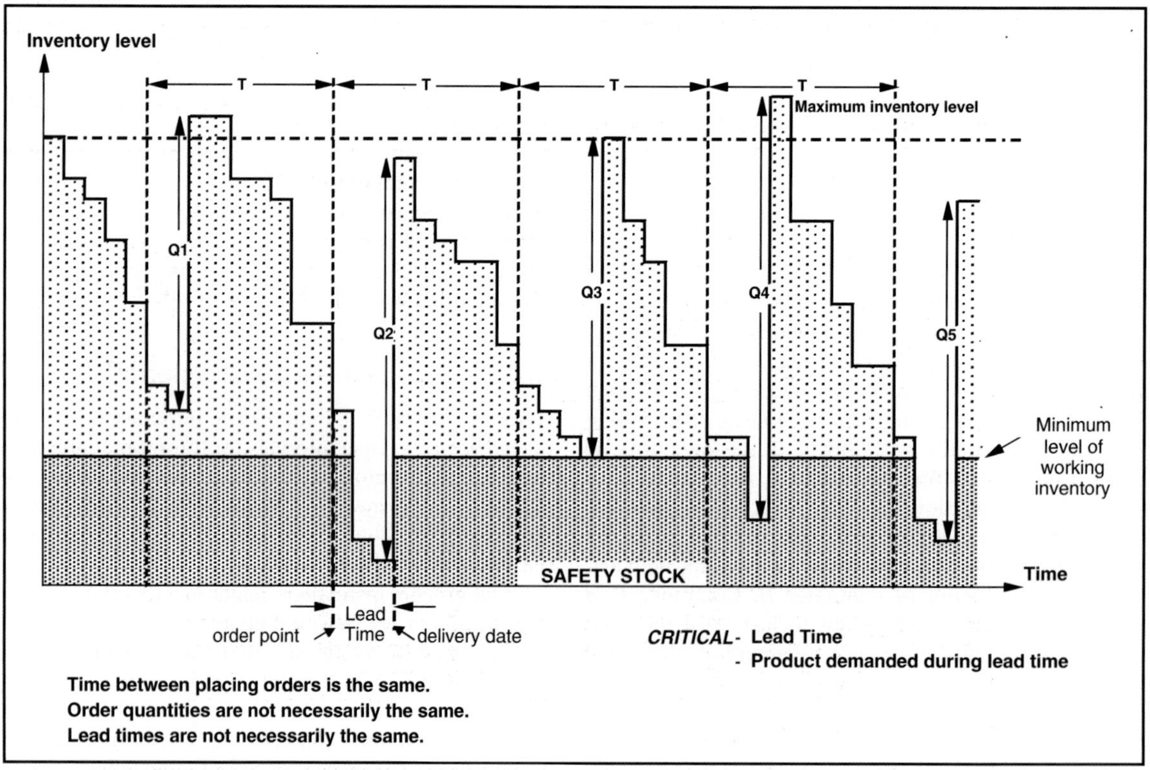

Inventory level

T — T — T — T

Maximum inventory level

Q1

Q2

Q3

Q4

Q5

Minimum
level of
working
inventory

SAFETY STOCK

Time

order point ↗ Lead
Time ↖ delivery date

CRITICAL - Lead Time
- Product demanded during lead time

Time between placing orders is the same.
Order quantities are not necessarily the same.
Lead times are not necessarily the same.

Butcher's shop

As an illustration, when the author was a student, he was employed for five years in a butcher's shop near London. Every Friday afternoon he would work in the cold storage counting the carcasses of beef, lamb and pork and the number of chickens and turkeys. This inventory listing he gave to the butcher, who then called the slaughterhouse on Saturday morning to make an order for meat to bring his inventory up to a predetermined level. This order was delivered from the slaughterhouse on Monday morning. On occasions, the butcher would have a stockout of beef, for example, on a Thursday as the weather had turned cold and people were cooking more steak and kidney pie. Then, the butcher had to call the slaughterhouse and have a special order delivered.

Bar codes

A barcode is a way of uniquely identifying a product including the price. The code is a series of wide and narrow strips, or bars, stamped onto the product label. Symbols, letters and numbers are used to identify the product and the barcode can be read by a computer scanner. This system greatly improves the management and ordering of inventory at the retail level and also in production systems. When a customer, or user, takes a product, the item is scanned, recorded and automatically deducted from inventory. Thus, management has a continuous reading of inventory levels.

Inventory levels and order quantities

An objective in inventory management is to keep inventory-related costs to a minimum. The quantity ordered in each cycle can impact the average inventory level and thus the investment in this inventory. Consider a situation in which there is a certain daily demand for inventory and to support this demand there are two inventory ordering choices.

1 Every five days a fixed quantity of 100 units of inventory is delivered, an average quantity of 20 units/day.
2 Every day, a fixed quantity of 20 units of inventory is ordered, an average quantity of 20 units/day, as in the first situation.

The movement of inventory for these two situations is illustrated graphically in Figures 11.9 and 11.10. In the case of the larger order, the average inventory level is over 50 per cent higher, which results in higher holding costs. However, ordering costs would be lower, so there would be a trade-off between large and small orders. This analysis has considered no safety stocks.

Figure 11.9   Inventory movement (large quantities delivered less frequently).

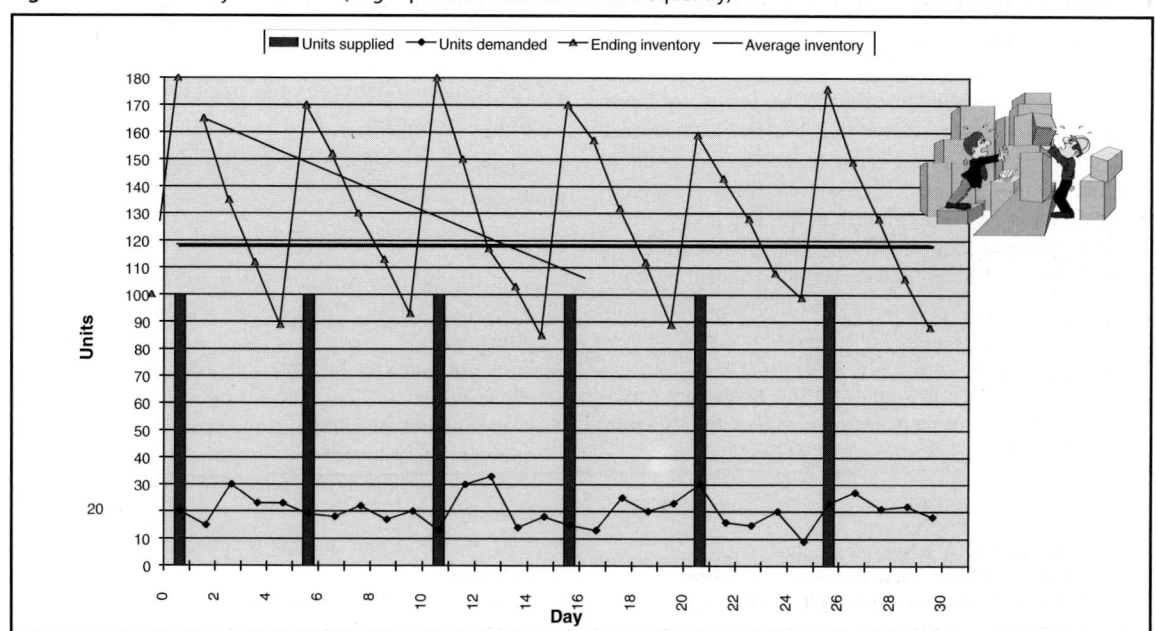

Figure 11.10 Inventory movement (small quantities delivered less frequently).

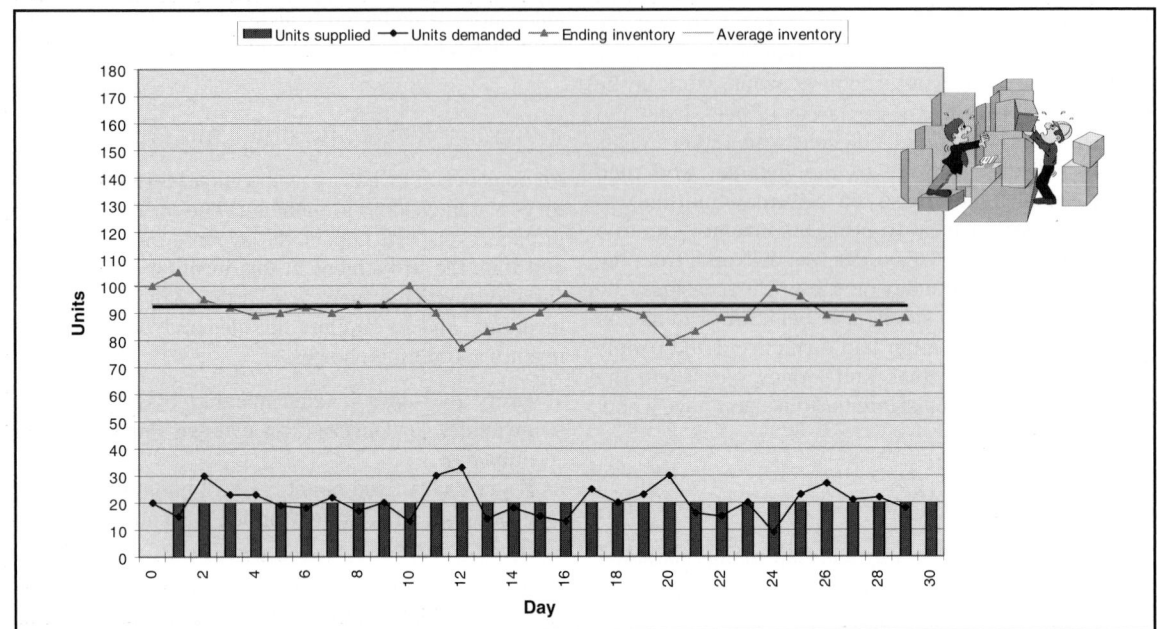

If safety stocks were held, this would additionally increase the holding cost.

ECONOMIC ORDER QUANTITY MODELS

Inventory models have been developed to determine an economic order quantity for independent inventory.[3] The Economic Order Quantity, EOQ, is the optimum amount of material to order that has the least overall cost with carrying costs, ordering costs and stockout costs taken into account. If large quantities of material are ordered at any one time, then the inventory ordering costs per unit, and the probability of stockout, will be low. However, inventory carrying costs will be high. Thus, there are costs that tend to decrease (ordering cost and 'stockout cost') and a cost that tends to increase (carrying cost). The total cost is the sum of the inventory carrying costs and the inventory ordering costs; the economic ordering cost is when this total cost is a minimum.

Model I. Basic EOQ

The assumptions for ordering and using inventory are:

■ Inventory of quantity Q is delivered in one lot according to an ordering schedule.

■ Delivered inventory is used at a uniform, or linear rate.

■ When the last item of inventory is used, a new lot arrives immediately.

■ There is no safety stock, as it is not needed for the conditions of this model.

■ Unit price of inventory is the same regardless of the quantity ordered. That is, there are no quantity discounts.

■ The lead time between ordering and delivery is constant and known.

Figure 11.11 gives the profile of the inventory movement.

Terms

■ D is the annual demand for material in units/year (though the time could be weeks, months or some other period).

■ Q is the quantity of material ordered in units/purchase order.

■ C is the cost of carrying one unit in inventory for one year ($/unit/year).

■ S is the average cost of placing a purchase order ($/order).

■ TSC is the total annual inventory stocking cost ($/year).

■ Values of D, C and S can be precisely determined and remain constant.

Figure 11.11 Inventory management.

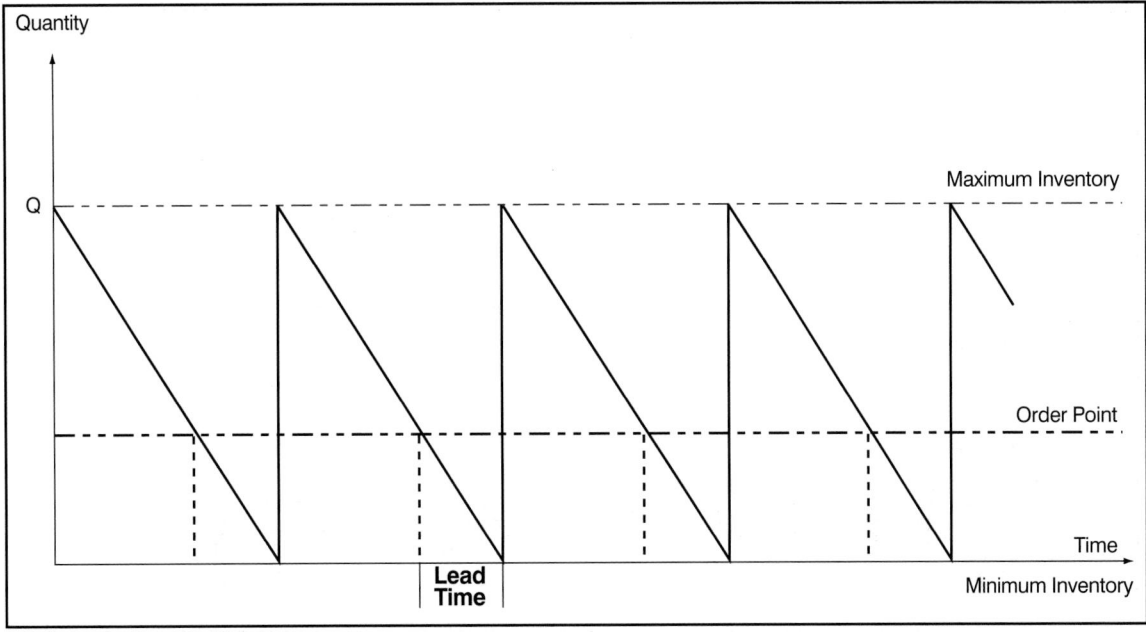

Model development

Since the assumption is that all the inventory is used up before the next order quantity arrives, then the minimum value of inventory is 0 and the maximum is Q. Therefore:

- The average inventory is one half the maximum and minimum inventory or = $Q/2$
- The annual stocking cost is the (average inventory) × (unit stocking cost) = $QC/2$
- The number of orders made per year is the (annual consumption)/(order quantity) = D/Q
- The annual ordering cost is the (number of orders) × (ordering cost) = DS/Q

The total cost associated with inventory handling is the sum of ordering and stocking cost:

$$\text{TSC} = \frac{Q}{2}C + \frac{D}{Q}S.$$

This shows that one cost is increasing with the increase in the value of Q (the stocking cost) and the other is decreasing with the value of Q (the purchase cost). Thus the total costs are a minimum when the total stocking costs and the purchasing costs are equal:

$$\frac{Q}{2}C = \frac{D}{Q}S.$$

Reorganizing to make Q the subject of the equation:

$$Q = \text{EOQ} = \sqrt{\frac{2DS}{C}}.$$

This is the economic order quantity (EOQ) or the quantity to order to make inventory-related costs a minimum.

Alternatively, this result can be arrived at by using calculus and differentiating the total cost equation with respect to Q:

$$\frac{\partial(\text{TSC})}{\partial Q} = \frac{C}{2} - \frac{DS}{Q^2}.$$

This value will have a minimum when $\dfrac{\partial(\text{TSC})}{\partial Q} = 0$, or:

$$\frac{C}{2} - \frac{DS}{Q^2} = 0.$$

Solving this equation for Q gives:

$$Q_2 = \frac{2DS}{C}$$

$$Q = \text{EOQ} = \sqrt{\frac{2DS}{C}}$$

or the same as before.

Figure 11.12 shows the graphical relationship between inventory carrying costs, inventory ordering costs and total costs. The inventory carrying costs increase linearly with the quantity Q, the ordering

Figure 11.12 EOQ model I: cost curves.

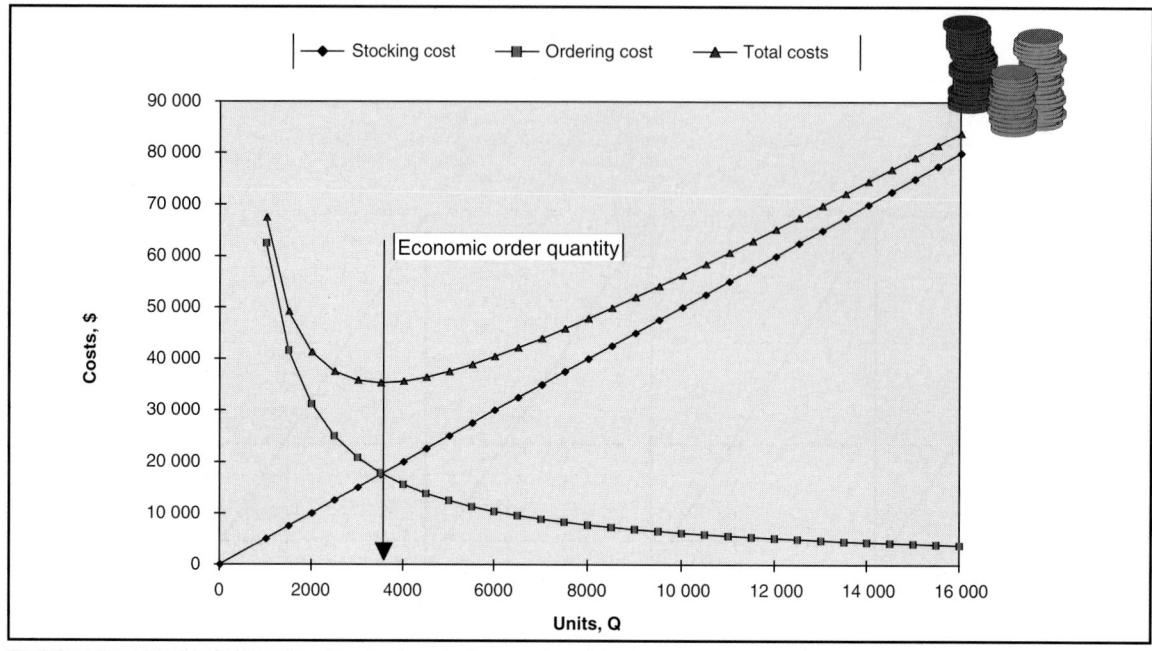

costs decline with Q and the total costs exhibit a minimum. These curves are obtained by calculating the various costs for different inventory quantities.

Range of economic order quantity

In calculating the value of the EOQ there is mathematically only one precise value. However, there are a range of order quantities around the EOQ for which the total stocking cost does not change significantly. This is illustrated in Figure 11.13, where the mathematically calculated EOQ is 3536 units, giving a total stocking cost of $35 355. However, if EOQ values in the range of 2800 to 4400 (a difference of 43 per cent) are considered, the total stocking cost at both of these quantities is about $36 000. This is a difference of only ±2 per cent from the mathematically calculated EOQ. This illustrates that an economic order quantity for a practical application is flexible and, although the model is academic, it can be applied in practice as a tool in inventory management.

Model II. Simultaneous supply and usage

This type of model might be applied when:

1 In distribution, inventory items are being delivered to a distribution centre and put into storage. Simultaneously during delivery, items are being withdrawn from this stockpile.
2 In production, upstream workpost No. 1 is producing units destined for the adjacent downstream

workpost No. 2. Workpost No. 2 is using the inventory items at the same time they are being delivered, as illustrated in Figure 11.14.

Maximum inventory

In contrast to the basic model, the inventory level never reaches the maximum value of Q, but a smaller level given by:

$$\frac{(p-d)}{p}.Q,$$

where p is the delivery rate and d the usage rate. The derivation of this relationship is illustrated by considering a crude-oil storage tank, into which oil can be pumped and from which it can be withdrawn, as shown in Figure 11.15. At the entrance and the exit of the storage tank there is a shutoff valve. Assume that:

■ The tank is initially empty.
■ The volume of oil pumped into the tank is Q litres.
■ The inlet flow rate is p litres/hour.
■ The outlet flow rate is d litres/hour.
■ The volume of the tank is Q litres.

There are three feasible situations:

1 The outlet valve is closed so that there is no oil leaving and $d = 0$. The volume of oil in the vessel when pumping stops is Q litres.
2 The outlet valve is open and the outlet flow is considered equal to the inlet flow or $d = p$. The volume of oil in the vessel when pumping stops is 0 litres.

Figure 11.13 EOQ model I: range is large for small change in total cost.

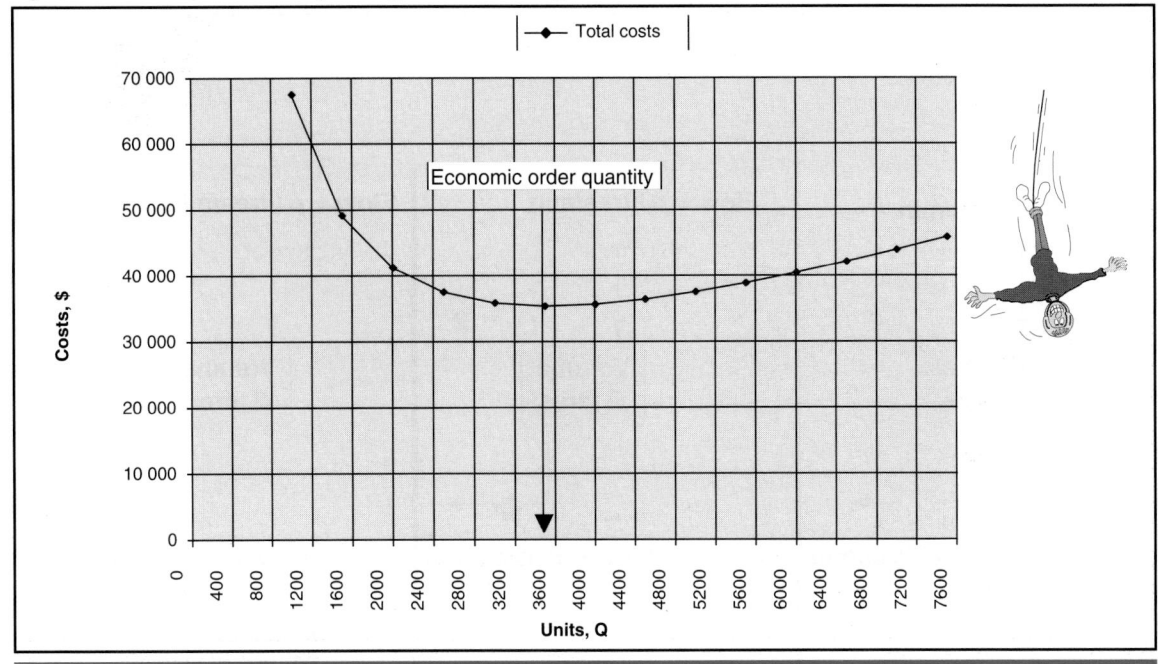

3 The outlet valve is partially open and here the outlet flow d is less than the inlet flow p, such that:

- The build-up rate of crude oil is $(p-d)$ litres/hour.
- The time for crude oil flows into tank is Q/p hours.
- The maximum oil level is $(p-d)\,Q/p$.

Distribution

Here inventory is being delivered and used at the same time and the profile for this model is given in Figure 11.16. The assumptions are essentially the same as for Model I, except that terms p and d appear:

- D is the annual demand for material in units/year.

Figure 11.14 Inventory model II: inventory usage at adjacent workstations.

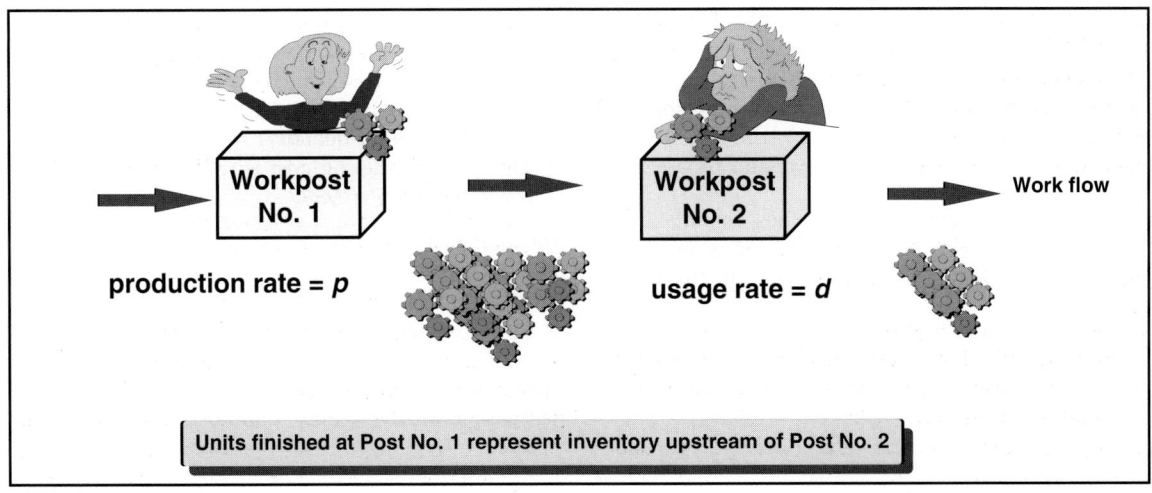

Figure 11.15 Inventory build-up for gradual delivery and usage.

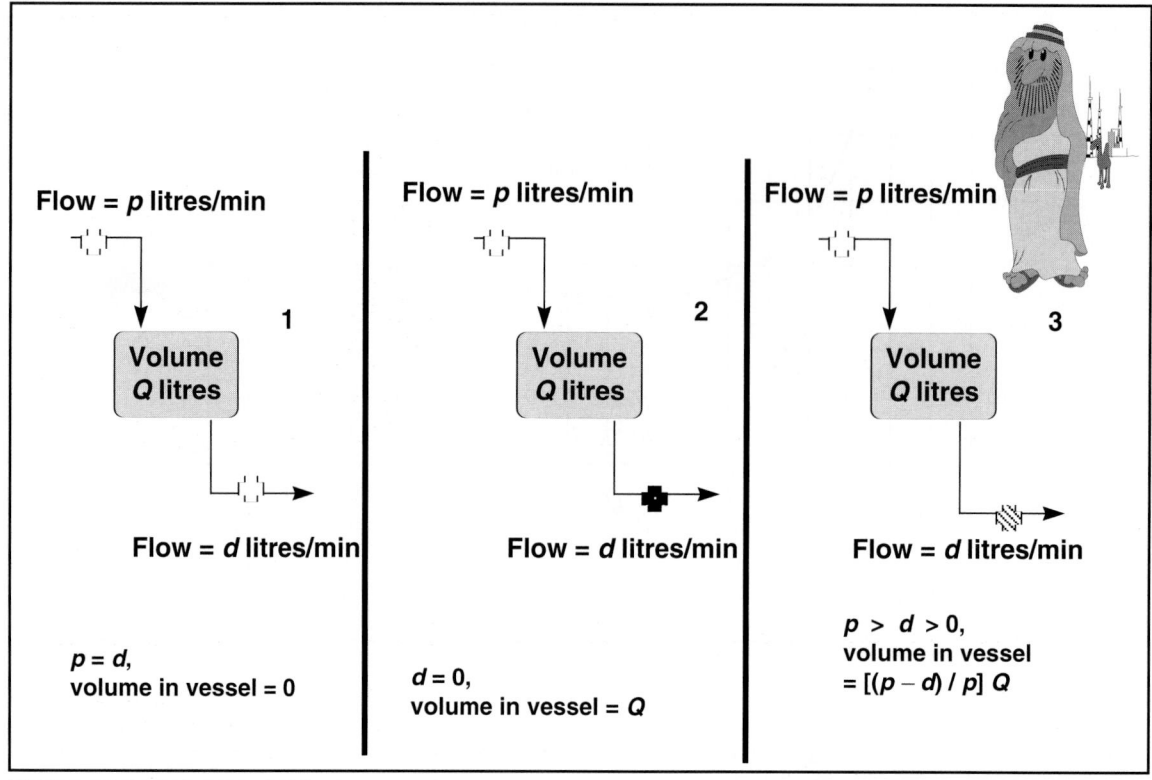

- Q is the quantity of material ordered in units/purchase order.
- C is the cost of carrying one unit in inventory for one year ($/unit/year).
- S is the average cost of placing a purchase order ($/order).
- d is the usage rate of the material in units/hour (or other time period).
- p is the delivery rate of the material in units/hour (or other time period). The value of p is always greater than d; otherwise there would be a stockout.
- TSC is the total annual inventory stocking cost ($/year).
- Values of D, C, p and d are known and are constant.

The inventory level never reaches the maximum value of Q, the quantity delivered, but a maximum value given by the relationship $[p - d)/p]Q$. In the two extreme cases:

- When the value of $d = 0$ (the inventory is not being used), the maximum value is Q; or the same as for Model I.

- When the value of $d = p$ (supply is equal to demand), then there is zero inventory or a completely balanced system (see also Chapter 15, *Lean Production and Just-in-Time*).

As before, the minimum inventory level is 0. The other variables are as follows:

- The average inventory is the mean of the maximum and minimum inventories = ½ $(p - d)$ Q/p.
- The annual stocking cost is (average inventory) × (unit stocking cost) = $[(p - d)/2p]$ QC.
- The number of orders made per year is (annual consumption)/(order quantity) = D/Q.
- The annual ordering cost is (number of orders) × (ordering cost) = DS/Q.

The total cost associated with inventory handling is the sum of ordering and stocking cost:

$$TSC = \frac{(p - d)}{2p} QC + \frac{D}{Q}S.$$

Again, one cost is increasing with Q and the other is decreasing with Q. Thus, total costs are a minimum

Figure 11.16 Inventory movement for model II.

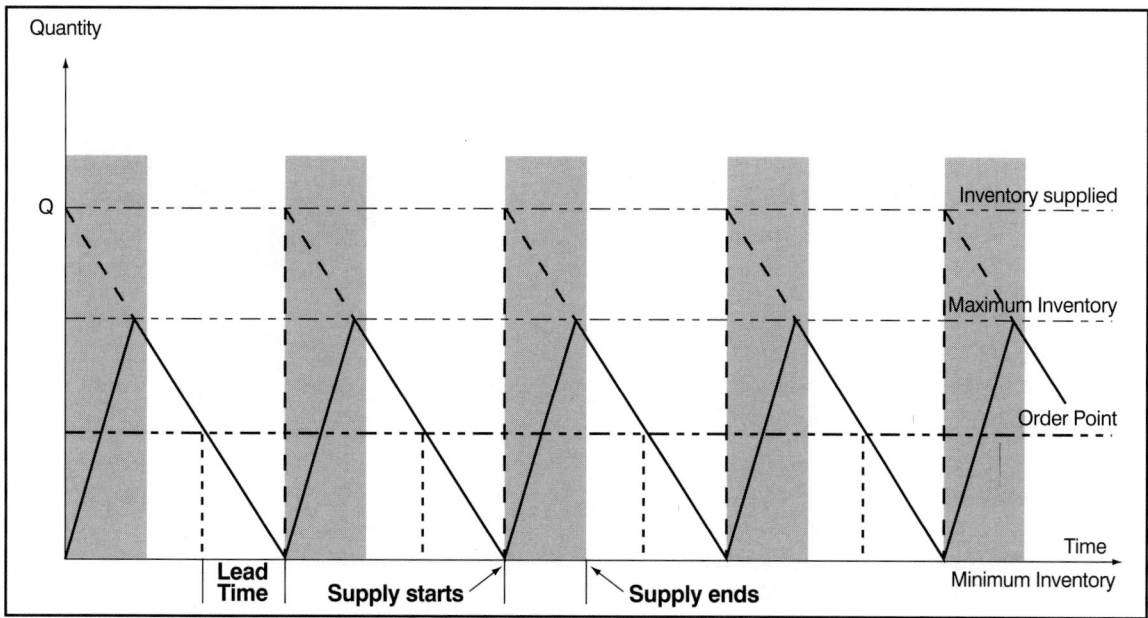

when the annual ordering costs are equal to the annual carrying costs:

$$\frac{(p-d)}{2p}\, QC = \frac{D}{Q}\, S.$$

Making Q the subject of the equation gives:

$$Q = \sqrt{\frac{2DS}{C}\left(\frac{p}{p-d}\right)}$$

and this is the economic order quantity (EOQ).

Alternatively, this can be arrived at by differentiating the total cost equation with respect to Q:

$$\frac{\partial(\text{TSC})}{\partial Q} = \frac{(p-d)}{2p}\, C - \frac{D}{Q^2}\, S.$$

This value will have a minimum when $\dfrac{\partial(\text{TSC})}{\partial Q} = 0$ or:

$$\frac{(p-d)}{2p}\, C - \frac{D}{Q^2}\, S = 0,$$

which, rearranged, is:

$$Q^2 = \frac{2p}{(p-d)}\, DS,$$

giving:

$$Q = \text{EOQ} = \sqrt{\frac{2DS}{C}\left(\frac{p}{p-d}\right)}$$

the same as before.

Figure 11.17 shows the relationship between the costs and order quantities for gradual deliveries and usage. The profile is similar to that for the fixed order quantity model.

Economic production run size

In a situation where an upstream workcentre is producing units used by a downstream centre, the EOQ analysis can be used to identify an optimum run size. There are three possible situations:

1 If usage (demand) and production rate are equal, there will not be a build-up of inventory and the question of run size is irrelevant.
2 If the demand rate (usage rate) d exceeds supply rate p, then there will be a stockout.
3 If production p exceeds demand d, then the EOQ analysis can be applied:
   - As long as production occurs, inventory continues to build.
   - It will be at a maximum when production ceases.
   - Demand occurs over the entire cycle. When inventory is exhausted, then production will begin again.
   - Since the firm makes the product itself, the ordering costs are now the machine setup costs and other associated preparation activities.
   - Setup costs are considered independent of run (lot) size.

Figure 11.17 EOQ model II: cost curves.

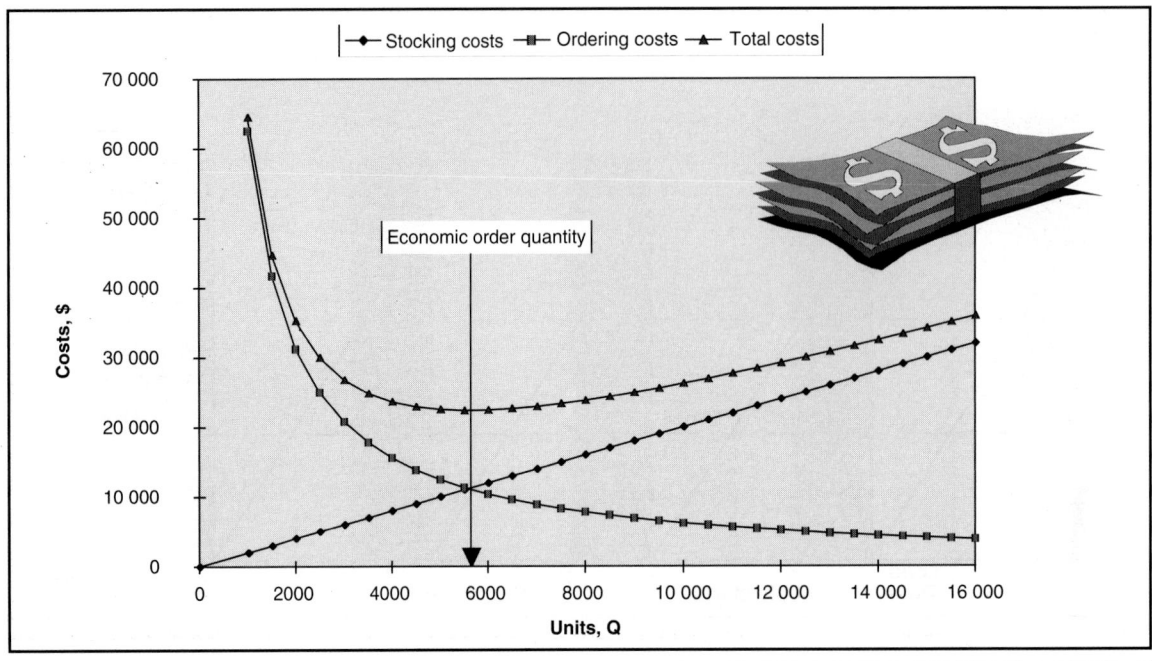

This profile is illustrated in Figure 11.18. The total setup and carrying costs are given by the relationship:

$$\text{TSC} = \frac{(p - d)}{2p} QC + \frac{D}{Q} S.$$

TSC is a minimum when Q, the lot size, is the economic order quantity:

$$Q = \text{EOQ} = \sqrt{\frac{2DS}{C} \left(\frac{p}{p - d} \right)}.$$

Figure 11.17 shows the identical profile for a production operation. The only difference is that one is for ordering outside, or a purchase cost, and the other is for ordering inside, or a setup cost. The cycle time, Tc, the time between starting one production run and the start of the next, is a function of the run (lot) size, and the demand or usage rate and is given by $\text{EOQ}/d = Q_E/d$, where $Q_E = \text{EOQ}$.

The production run time, Tp, is a function of the run (lot) size and the production rate and is given by $\text{EOQ}/p = Q_E/p$.

Balancing the run size

This EOQ formula for a production run can be rewritten as:

$$Q = \sqrt{\frac{2DS}{C \left(\frac{p - d}{p} \right)}} = \sqrt{\frac{2DS}{C \left(1 - \frac{d}{p} \right)}}.$$

This can be interpreted as saying that the closer the demand rate d approaches the production rate p, the greater becomes the value of the lot size Q. In other words, the greater is the production run. This would be the case for an assembly-line operation where the production of the upstream workpost is equal to the usage (demand) of the downstream workpost; the posts are in balance. In an assembly operation in which p is greater than d, inventory starts building up. When d becomes greater than p, stockouts occur. In a similar manner, two workstations, one upstream of the other, use Kanbans to achieve the balance of the supply and demand of components (Chapter 15, *Lean Production and Just-in-Time*).

EOQ models with quantity discounts

In inventory situations, quantity discounts may be possible if a greater quantity of material is ordered:

- In purchasing products from an outside supplier, quantity discounts are offered because there are economies in transportation and order preparation.
- Similarly, in a production operation, the greater the lot size, or production run, the lower is the unit cost because there are fewer set ups.

In this situation, in addition to taking into account the stocking and ordering costs, the total cost of the inven-

Figure 11.18 Economic production run size.

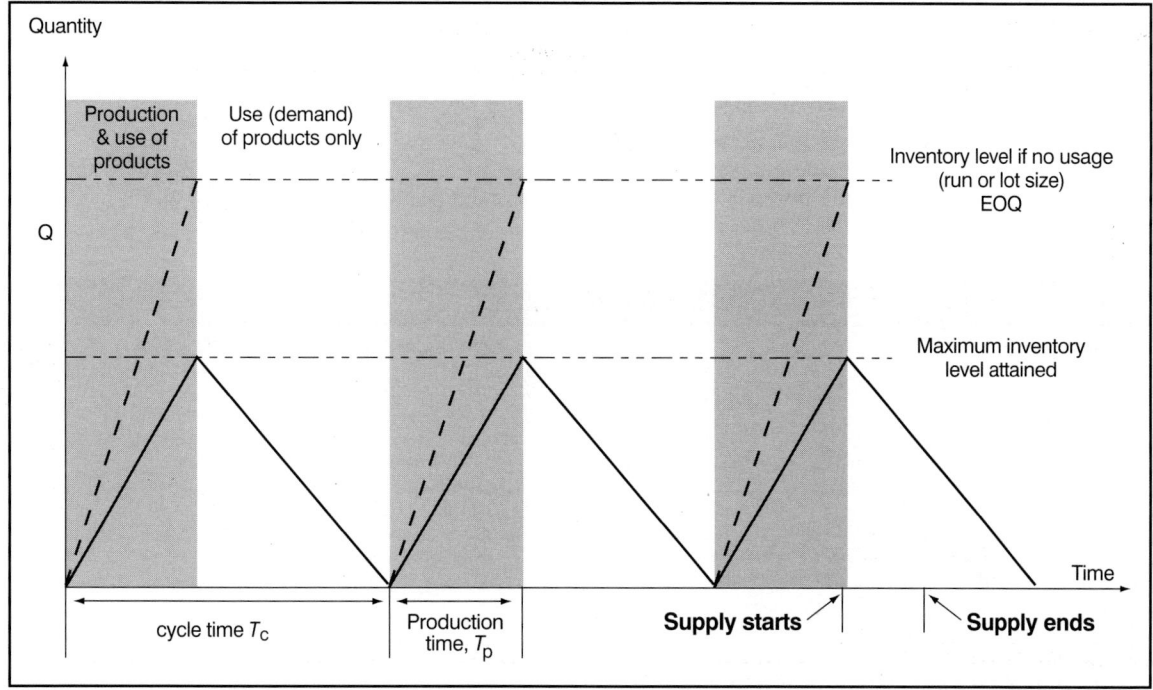

tory should be considered, since it will vary depending on the unit cost. There may be a savings in buying in bulk because of the lower unit cost, even though inventory stocking costs will be higher.

Model development

All the terms and assumptions of Models I and II apply with the addition of two others:

■ *P* is the price per unit of product (inventory) in $/unit.
■ TCP is the total of the price paid for the product, the inventory carrying costs and the ordering costs.

The total purchase cost of the material is the price times annual demand or $P \times D$, where P is now a variable. Thus, for either Model I or Model II:

$$\text{TPC} = \text{TSC} + DP.$$

The economic order quantity now occurs when the total product costs (total inventory-related costs plus total price paid) are a minimum.

Model IIA

Here delivery is immediate and so:

$$\text{TPC} = \frac{Q}{2}C + \frac{D}{Q}S + DP.$$

Model IIB

With continuous supply and usage:

$$\text{TPC} = \frac{Q}{2}\left(\frac{p-d}{p}\right)C + \frac{D}{Q}S + DP.$$

Calculation procedure

1 The model EOQ is computed using each of the sales prices for either Model I or Model II. *C*, the stocking cost, is usually a function of sales price. For example, stocking cost can be 20 per cent of the sales price and thus the EOQ will change as *P* changes.
2 The feasible EOQ from step 1 is determined, that is, the EOQ in the quantity range for the given price. In some cases, it may not make sense to purchase the quantity *Q* at the unit price given. In other cases, it may not be possible to purchase the quantity *Q* at the unit price given.
3 The total annual product cost TPC is computed for each feasible EOQ. In addition, values of TPC are calculated for purchase quantities that may not have been derived from the EOQ relationship, but at which level a new lower unit price is possible.
4 The order quantity with the lowest total annual product cost TPC is now the economic order quantity. This value may have no relationship to a model EOQ.

EOQ inventory models and management

The EOQ theory illustrates that, no matter what the situation, for every material held in inventory there is an optimal order quantity where total costs are a minimum:

- Although the models are academic in their development they are a reasonable attempt to present the inventory situation in organizations.

- Because of assumptions made, they are not a panacea for inventory management.
- However, in modelling inventory movement, management is forced to examine closely holding costs, ordering costs and stock-out costs associated with inventory.

The use of these inventory models is illustrated by the worked example, *Arbrelle*.

WORKED EXAMPLE: ARBRELLE

Situation

The Arbrelle Co., located in Chimilin, France is a service organization that packages and distributes automobile components and accessories to retail outlets throughout the Rhône-Alps region. The automobile components arrive in bulk at Chimilin, where they are sorted, packaged automatically in display boxes, ticketed with a bar code and then put into shipping cartons.

One product of particular interest is a security lock, reference SL-200. The estimated consumption (demand from the retail outlet) of this product is 10 000 units per year. The base price for purchasing the security lock from the manufacturer is 142.00 FF. If more than 1000 units are purchased, then there is a discount of 2.5 per cent per unit on the base price. If more than 3000 units are purchased, then there is a discount of 5 per cent per unit of the base price. Ordering costs from the manufacturer are estimated at 950.00 FF per order.

Arbrelle works 250 days per year and the inventory storage cost for the security lock is estimated at 35 per cent of purchase price from the manufacturer.

Required

1. If the security lock is purchased at the base price and the units are delivered in one lot from the manufacturer, determine the economic ordering quantity using the basic model.
2. If the security lock is purchased at the base price and the units are delivered at a rate of 100 units per day from the manufacturer, determine the economic ordering quantity using the gradual usage and delivery model. Assume that the packaging (usage rate) of the model is the average of the annual demand.
3. Determine the annual savings in inventory-related costs between the gradual usage and delivery model (Question 1) and the basic model (Question 2).
4. If the price discounts are taken into consideration, determine the economic order quantity using the base model.

5. Determine the annual savings in inventory related costs between using the basic model with no price discounts (Question 1) and the basic model using price discounts (Question 4).
6. If the price discounts are taken into consideration, determine the economic order quantity using the gradual delivery and usage model with the same delivery rate of 100 units per day.
7. What are the annual savings in inventory-related costs between using the gradual delivery and usage model with no price discounts (Question 2) and the gradual delivery and usage model using price discounts (Question 6).

Solution

The calculation sheet shown as Table 11.1 gives the solutions for this exercise. The given data is inserted into the formula for the single lot as follows:

$$\text{TSC} = \frac{Q}{2}C + \frac{D}{Q}S$$

$$Q = \text{EOQ} = \sqrt{\frac{2DS}{C}}$$

$$\text{TPC} = \frac{Q}{2}C + \frac{D}{Q}S + DP;$$

and for simultaneous supply and usage as follows

$$\text{TSC} = \frac{(p-d)}{2p}QC + \frac{D}{Q}S$$

$$Q = \sqrt{\frac{2DS}{C}\left(\frac{p}{(p-d)}\right)}$$

$$\text{TPC} = \frac{Q}{2}\left(\frac{p-d}{p}\right)C + \frac{D}{Q}S + DP.$$

Table 11.1 Calculation sheet for the Arbrelle worked example

	Security Lock SL-200	Comments
Question 1		
Base price p (FF)	142.00	
Stocking cost, fraction	0.35	
Annual demand D (units)	10 000	
Ordering cost s (FF/unit)	950.00	
EOQ	618.30	
TSC (FF)	30 729.46	
TPC (FF)	1 450 729.46	

Question 2

Delivery rate p (units/day)		100
Working days/year		250
Usage rate d (units/day)		40.00
$(p - d)/p$		0.60
EOQ		**798.22**
TSC (FF)		23 802.94
TPC (FF)		1 443 802.94

Question 3

TSC(1) – TSC(2)	**6 926.52**

Question 4

	From	To		
Price $P1$ (FF)	1	999	142.00	
Price $P2$ (FF)	**1 000**	2 999	138.45	
Price $P3$ (FF)	3 000	greater	134.90	
EOQ @ $P1$			618.30	Only feasible
EOQ @ P2			626.18	Not possible
EOQ @ P3			634.36	Not possible
TPC @ price P1 and EOQ-1 (FF)			1 450 729.46	Possible
TPC @ price P1 and EOQ-2 (FF)			1 414 842.92	Not valid
TPC @ price P1 and EOQ-3 (FF)			1 378 951.38	Not valid
TPC @ price P2 and supplier minimum			**1 418 228.75**	Possible–best
TPC @ price P3 and supplier minimum			1 422 989.17	Possible

Question 5

TPC (1) – TPC(4)	**32 500.71**

Question 6

	From	To		
Price P1 (FF)	1	999	142.00	
Price P2 (FF)	1 000	2 999	138.45	
Price P3 (FF)	**3 000**	greater	134.90	
EOQ @ P1			798.22	Only feasible
EOQ @ P2			808.39	Not possible
EOQ @ P3			818.96	Not possible
TPC @ price P1 and EOQ-1 (FF)			1 443 802.94	Possible
TPC @ price P1 and EOQ-2 (FF)			1 408 003.52	Not valid
TPC @ price P1 and EOQ-3 (FF)			1 372 200.24	Not valid
TPC @ price P2 and supplier minimum			1 408 537.25	Possible
TPC @ price P3 and supplier minimum			**1 394 660.17**	Possible–best

Question 7

TPC(2) – TPC(6)	**49 142.77**

1 Economic ordering quantity using the basic model:
- The given data is entered into the EOQ formula to give a value of 618.30 (say 618 units).

2 Economic ordering quantity using the gradual usage and delivery model:
- The average usage rate is given by the annual demand divided by the effective days per year or a value of 40 units/day.
- The given data is entered into the EOQ formula to give a value of 798.22 (say 798 units).

3 Annual savings in inventory-related costs between the gradual usage and the basic model:
- This is the difference between the total stocking costs for the two situations and the value is 6927 FF. (Since the purchase price is the same, a similar value will be obtained using the TSP values.)

4 Economic order quantity using the base mode and price discounts:

- With the price discounts given the price levels are:
  - 142.00 FF as the basic price;
  - 138.45 FF as the first discount price;
  - 134.90 FF as the second discount price.
- The EOQ is calculated for each price level. The value changes because the value of C changes as it is a function of the price.
- Only the first EOQ value is feasible. EOQ levels for the other two do not fit with the quantity range.
- The total purchase cost, TPC, is determined for the valid EOQ figure.
- Since the supplier offers discounts above a certain level, the TPC can be determined for these quantity breaks (1000 and 3000), even though they do not fit the EOQ model.
- The 'EOQ' value is the quantity that gives the lowest TPC, in this case a purchase quantity of 1000 units.

5 Annual savings in inventory-related costs between using the basic model with no price discounts (Question 1) and the basic model using price discounts (Question 4):
  ■ This is the difference between the TPCs for the two situations.
6 Economic order quantity using the gradual delivery usage model with the same delivery rate of 100 units per day and taking into account price discounts:
  ■ The EOQ is calculated for each price level. The value changes because the value of C changes as it is a function of the price.
  ■ Only the first EOQ value is feasible. EOQ levels for the other two do not fit with the quantity range.

  ■ The total product cost, TPC, is determined for the valid EOQ stocking figure.
  ■ Since the supplier offers discounts above a certain level, the TPC can be determined for these quantity breaks (1000 and 3000), even though they do not fit the EOQ model.
  ■ The 'EOQ' value is the quantity that gives the lowest TPC, in this case a purchase quantity of 3000 units.
7 Annual savings in inventory-related costs between using the gradual delivery and usage model with no price discounts (Question 2) and the gradual delivery usage model using price discounts (Question 6):
  ■ This is the difference between the TPCs for the two situations.

ORDER POINTS AND SERVICE LEVELS

In addition to knowing how much inventory to order, it is also necessary to know the order point, or the date at which to place the purchase order for a new quantity of inventory. This quantity would normally be when the level of inventory currently being used has fallen to a certain minimum, level as illustrated in the already presented Figure 11.6. This order point is based on the lead time (the time between placing the order and receiving shipment) and the estimated amount of inventory that is going to be consumed or demanded during this lead-time period. For example, while a grocery store is waiting for a new shipment of corn flakes, there are still customers purchasing corn flakes. The value of this demand is critical. If it is higher than expected, there would be the risk of stockouts. Thus, how much cushion, or safety stock, should be held? If demand is low, inventory levels would be high with the associated high stocking costs.

Demand during lead time

The demand during lead time (DDLT) is derived from two components. One the customer demand, the other the supplier's lead time.

Supplier

Suppliers may be extremely reliable and always deliver when promised. In this case, the lead time will not be a variable and the demand during lead time is an estimate of customer requirements during this known lead-time period. However, there may be times when the weather is bad, which delays delivery, or at the supplier's facility machines may break down or operators may be absent, either of which will increase the time to complete the order. For these cases, the lead time is longer than planned and so consideration should be given to having a safety stock on hand to cover these unexpected situations.

Customers

Customers are not always predictable in that their daily demand for material varies. Alternatively, there may be external occurrences that change demand; for example, a sudden hot spell increases the demand for beer and an unseasonably wet period increases the demand for umbrellas. Thus, determining safety stock levels may not be straightforward.

Order point

The order point OP, the level of the present inventory at which a new order is placed, is given by the sum of the expected (or average) demand during lead time EDDLT plus a safety stock SS:

$$OP = EDDLT + SS.$$

Increasing the safety stock for a material reduces the probability, and the cost, of a stockout during the lead time, but it has the disadvantage of increasing carrying costs. When there are uncertainties both in the customer demand and in the supplier lead time, then the expected demand during lead time EDDLT can be estimated by:

$$EDDLT = (\text{Average inventory used per day}) \times (\text{Average supplier lead time}).$$

Customer service levels

The customer service level in inventory situations is for clients that proportion of orders that can be completed by using existing inventories of finished goods. Similarly, in the case of production, it is that proportion of production department orders that can be filled by using existing raw-materials inventories. Thus, the customer may be the end user of the finished product, a downstream work centre or a factory in the next town. In any event, the reason for keeping inventories is to satisfy this downstream customer, taking into consideration uncertainties of the operation (manufacturing or service). If inventories are too low, stock-outs could occur. A stockout situation is particularly critical during the lead time and, if the customer is not satisfied, there will be repercussions on the business; see Figure 11.19.[4]

Service levels are given as a percentage. Thus, a 95 per cent service level means that on average, 95 per cent of customers' orders are filled out of current inventory. The other 5 per cent of customers' orders will not be filled from current inventory because a stockout is experienced. This other 5 per cent of orders will have to be filled at a later date.

Stockout risk

Since there is a cost associated with holding (carrying) inventory, or a safety stock, the risk of a stockout must be traded off against the cost of carrying inventory. The objective is to carry the optimum level of inventory. The more inventory that is carried, then the lower is the probability or risk of a stockout. However, the greater is the holding cost. The more the variability in either customer demand or supplier lead time, then the greater the amount of safety stock required to achieve an established service level. The stockout risk is the complement of the service level:

Stockout risk = 100 – percentage service level.

Payoff tables for order point

Payoff tables can be used to optimize between carrying too little and carrying too much safety stock. In payoff situations there are two cost-related terms, long cost and short cost.

Long cost

The long cost is the cost of stocking one unit that is not demanded during the lead time. That is, the unit is in inventory but there is no customer demand. This cost is usually associated with carrying costs, the cost of special handling and other expenses involved in carrying a unit from one period to another.

Short cost

The short cost is the cost of not stocking a unit that is demanded during lead time. That is, there is a customer demand but that unit is not in inventory. This cost is ordinarily associated with stockout costs, such as lost revenue and special handling and expediting to satisfy the customer.

The worked example *Coffee* illustrates the use of payoff tables for order points.

Distribution of demand during lead time

If historical data for an operating system exists, then frequency distribution curves can be developed for the

Figure 11.19 Customer service: the hard facts (Source: US Government Office of Consumer Affairs).

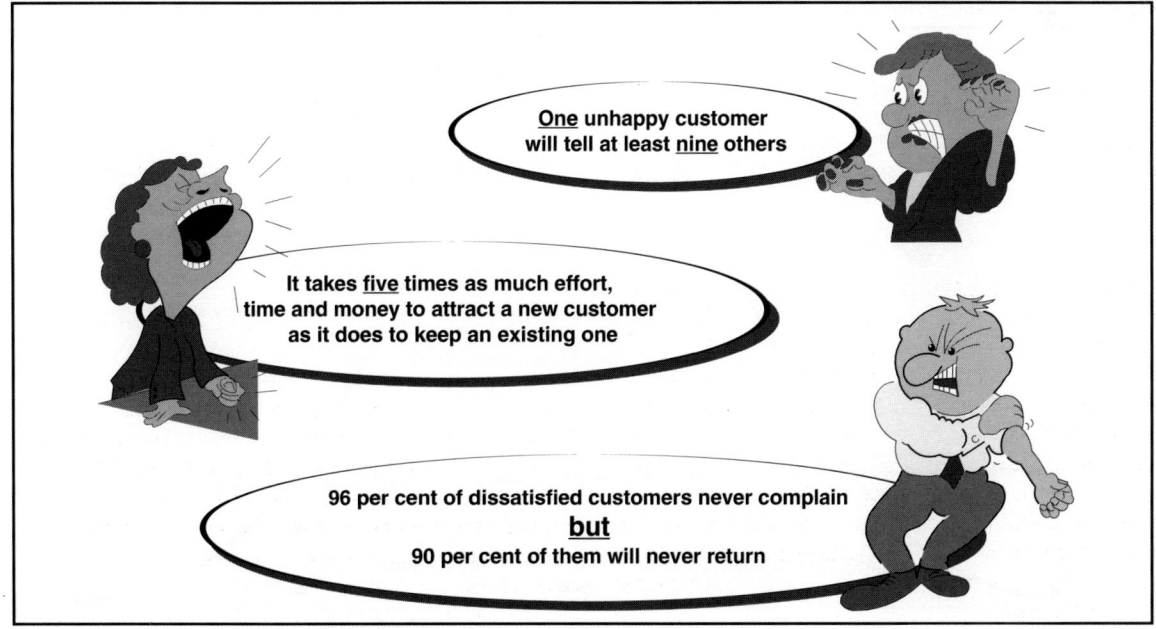

inventory quantity demanded during the lead time. Then, using this frequency distribution, safety stock inventory levels during lead times can be estimated. The frequency distribution may be a continuous distribution (in the case of petrol demanded from a service station) or a discrete distribution (in the case of boxes of chocolates demanded in a supermarket). However, whatever the situation, the inventory demand can be approximated by a normal distribution as shown in Figure 11.20. (Chapter 20, *Statistical Concepts* gives more on frequency distributions and the normal distribution).

The average point in the curve is the most likely occurring quantity of inventory demanded and is the expected demand during lead time (EDDLT). It implies that, for 50 per cent of the time, the inventory demanded is less than the average, EDDLT and for 50 per cent of the time it is higher than average. The second situation is the more critical and thus to avoid stockouts, a cushion or safety stock needs to be held. As an illustration, a safety stock of 45 per cent of the EDDLT, as shown in Figure 11.20, would give a service level of 95 per cent. If this was an acceptable service level, then this would be the order point at which a new order is placed. As a corollary, the probability of a stockout is to the right of the order point and in this case would be 5 per cent. If statistical data is available for the operating system, then:

$$\text{Order point} = \text{EDDLT} + \text{SS}$$

$$\text{Order point} = \text{EDDLT} + z\sigma_{\text{DDLT}}.$$

Here is the σ_{DDLT} standard deviation of the demand during lead time or a measure of how the demand during lead time is distributed about the mean or the EDDLT. The value z is the number of standard deviations the demand is from the mean.

Known lead times

If it is difficult to obtain DDLT, then demand-per-day data might be used. In this case, a constant lead time would be assumed. Supplier lead times are more controllable than the variable nature of independent customer daily demand. In this case, the frequency distribution curve is the average daily customer demand. The expected demand during lead time EDDLT is now given by the constant lead time (LT) multiplied by the average daily demand $\bar{d}$:

$$\text{EDDLT} = \text{LT} \times \bar{d}.$$

In addition:

$$\sigma_{\text{DDLT}} = \sqrt{\text{LT}(\sigma_d)^2}$$

where σ_d is the standard deviation of the daily demand. In this case, the order point can be calculated by:

$$\text{Order point} = \text{EDDLT} + \text{SS}$$

$$\text{Order point} = \text{EEDLT} + z\sigma_{\text{DDLT}}$$

$$\text{Order point} = \text{LT} \times \bar{d} + z\sqrt{\text{LT}(\sigma_d)^2}.$$

Figure 11.20   Inventory demanded during lead time.

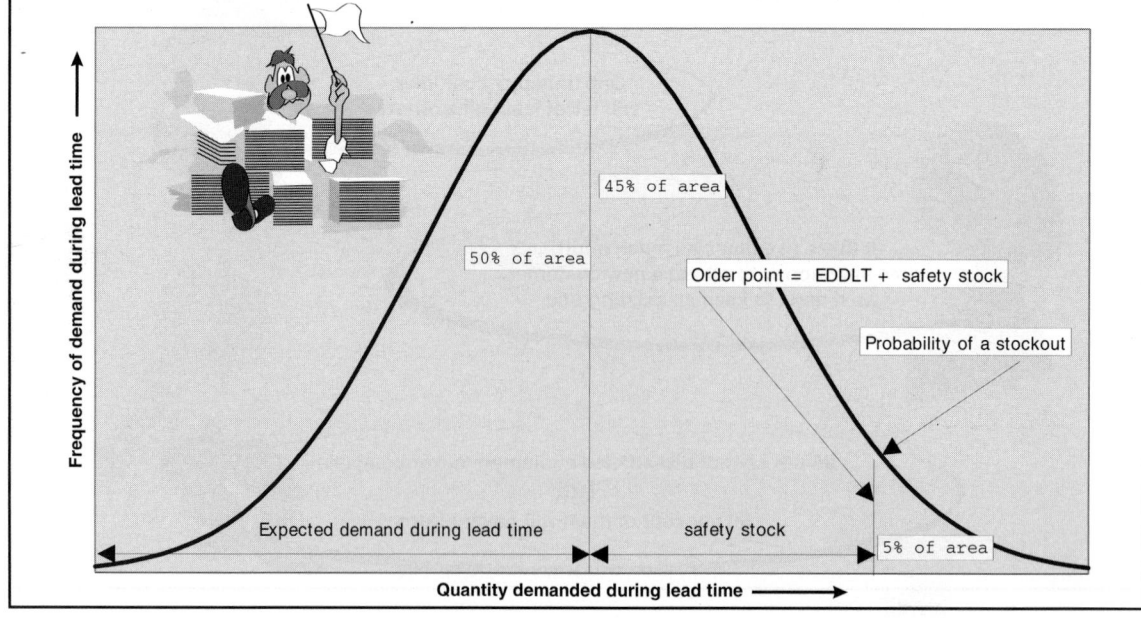

Arbitrary methods for order points

If reliable statistical data is not available for lead times or inventory demands, then the following are two arbitrary approaches for establishing order points.

Percentage Approach

Here the order point is based on a percentage or a fraction of the estimated quantity demanded during the supplier lead time:

$$\text{Order point} = \text{EDDLT} + k \times \text{EDDLT}.$$

Here, k is a percentage factor that varies according to the experience of the firm and how critical the situation would be if a stockout occurred. As an illustration, consider an electrical manufacturer that uses the six classes of components in Table 11.2, which have been attributed a value for k according to how severe the situation would be if a stockout occurred.

Assume that the expected demand during lead time for items in class 3 is 700 kg. Then the order point is given by:

$$\text{Order point} = 700 + 700 \times 20 \text{ per cent} = 840 \text{ kg.}$$

Classifications such as these would be custom-designed for a firm's inventory system and uniformly applied to most materials in finished-goods and raw-materials inventories.

Square-root method

Here the safety stock is calculated as the square root of the expected demand during lead time to give the following relationship for the order point level.

$$\text{Order point} = \text{EDDLT} + \sqrt{\text{EDDLT}}.$$

As an illustration, suppose the EDDLT was 5, 25, 200 or 1000 units. Then, with the square root method, Table 11.3 gives the corresponding safety stock SS, the order point OP, and the ratio of the safety stock to the EDDLT. This method gives safety stock levels that are large relative to EDDLT when EDDLT is small. However, safety stocks are relatively small when EDDLT is large.

The worked example *Miko* illustrates developing order points using the normal distribution and arbitrary methods.

Safety stocks and EOQ

Safety stocks have little effect on the economic order quantity EOQ in a fixed-order-quantity inventory system. However, total annual stocking costs would change because:

- There would be increased annual carrying costs as the safety stocks are dead stocks.
- There would be lower annual stockout costs because a safety stock is held. (In the economic models, the basic EOQ calculation does not include an allowance for stockout costs. While methods do exist, it is difficult to make accurate estimates).

Table 11.2 Classes of components for an electrical manufacturer

Class	Factor k (%)	Material	Reasoning
1	5	Packaging	Not essential. Many suppliers
2	10	Cleaning fluids	Essential. Many suppliers
3	20	Polypropylene	Essential. Limited suppliers
4	50	Special fasteners	Critical. Few suppliers with company specifications
5	100	Copper for lining	Extremely critical. Limited sources at quality level
6	200	Vanadium rods for tooling	Extremely critical. Single source overseas

Table 11.3 Variables with the square-root method (see text for definitions)

EDDLT	SS	OP	SS/EDDLT (%)
5	2.236	7	44.7
25	5.000	30	20.0
200	14.142	214	7.1
1000	31.623	1032	3.2

WORKED EXAMPLE: COFFEE

Situation

The raw material for producing ground coffee is green coffee. A producer, who purchases the green coffee from a local distributor, makes an estimate of the number of pallets of green coffee used per day over an 80-day period. Long costs and short costs are estimated respectively at $30 and $70 per pallet. This information is given in Table 11.4.

Table 11.4 Estimates for the Coffee worked example

Pallets demanded	Days this level occurred
20	15
40	20
60	12
80	10
100	23
Total days	80

Required

Determine the optimum number of pallets of green coffee to purchase in order to minimize the cost.

Solution

Tables 11.5 and 11.6 show the frequency calculation and the calculation for optimizing the number of pallets to purchase.

- The number of pallets demanded and the number of days on which this level was demanded are converted into a frequency distribution

by dividing this number of days by the total number of days (Column 3, Table 11.5). (See also Chapter 20, *Statistical concepts*.)
- A payoff table (Table 11.6) is constructed whose framework shows the pallets demanded, the pallets to order and the frequency of occurrence.
- In each cell, the cost is developed using the long and short costs. For example:
  - If 80 pallets are demanded and 40 pallets are stocked, the cost is $(80 - 40) \times \$70 = \$2,800$.
  - If 20 pallets are demanded and 80 pallets are stocked, the cost is $(80 - 20) \times \$30 = \$1,800$.
- The expected cost is given by the sum of the probabilties × individual cost.
- The expected cost is a minimum when 80 pallets are ordered.

Table 11.5 Data for green coffee inventory calculations

Pallets demanded	Days occurred	Frequency (%)
20	15	18.75
40	20	25.00
60	12	15.00
80	10	12.50
100	23	28.75
Total	80	100.00

Table 11.6 Pay off table for green coffee; each cell gives the cost ($)

	Pallets stocked	Pallets demanded					Expected cost ($)
		20	40	60	80	100	
Order	20	0	1 400	2 800	4 200	5 600	2 905
point	40	600	0	1 400	2 800	4 200	1 880
(number of	60	1 200	600	0	1 400	2 800	1 355
pallets)	80	1 800	1 200	600	0	1 400	**1 130**
	100	2 400	1 800	1 200	600	0	1 155
Probability (per cent)		18.75	25.00	15.00	12.50	28.75	100.00

WORKED EXAMPLE: MIKO

Situation

The Miko company uses polypropylene pellets, supplied in 50 kg sacks, in its moulding machines for making plastic toy components. Based on past data and on supplier delivery time of the polypropylene pellets, the excepted usage during lead time (EDDLT) of 50 kg sacks is 450 sacks. This usage is based on the customers' demand for toy products.

Required

1. If the usage of polypropylene pellets can be considered as normally distributed with a standard deviation of the demand of 35 sacks, determine the level of safety stock for the pellets and the corresponding level of inventory at which Miko should place orders. Assume a client service level of 98 per cent.

2 Using the arbitrary method of percentage of expected demand during lead time, with a factor k of 20 per cent, determine the level of safety stock for the pellets and the corresponding level of inventory at which Miko should place orders.

3 Using the arbitrary method and the square root of expected demand during lead time, determine the level of safety stock for the pellets and the corresponding level of inventory at which Miko should place orders.

Solution

The solution is given in the calculation shown in Table 11.7. The method of using k factors gives the greatest security, whereas the square root method gives the least (see Chapter 20, *Statistical concepts* for the method for Question 1).

Table 11.7 Calculation for the Miko worked example

Question 1 (Normal distribution)	
EDDLT	450
Standard deviation	35
Service level	0.98
z	2.0537
Safety stock = σz	71.88
Safety stock (rounded)	72
Order point	**522**
Question 2 (Percentage approach)	
EDDLT	450
Safety stock policy (value k)	20
Safety stock	90
Order point level	**540**
Question 3 (Square root method)	
EDDLT	450
Safety stock	21
Order point level	**471**

SYSTEMS WITH A FIXED ORDER PERIOD

Situation

In a system with a fixed order period, the objective is to select an optimal time period between times when new orders are placed. There are two extreme situations.

Frequent orders

In this situation, orders are made very frequently, an activity which involves high ordering costs and more frequent handling for putting the material in storage. However, it reduces the probability of stockouts.

Less frequent orders

In this situation, materials are ordered less frequently, which reduces total ordering costs, but may increase the risk of stockouts.

Model III. Economic order period

As for the models for economic ordering quantity, a mathematical model can be developed to arrive at an optimum time period for ordering materials. The model balances carrying costs against ordering costs to give an optimum time interval.

Assumptions

The assumptions are similar to models for economic order quantity:

- D is the annual demand for material (units/year).
- Q is the quantity of material ordered (units/purchase order).
- C is the cost of carrying one unit in inventory for one year ($/unit/year).
- S is the average cost of placing a purchase order ($/order).
- T is the time between orders (fraction of a year).
- TSC is the total annual stocking cost ($/year).

For these assumptions:

- Values of D, C and S can be precisely determined and remain constant.
- No safety stock is used.
- Lead time (time between placing an order and receipt) is known and is constant.
- Orders are received at once in a single lot.
- Material is entirely used up by the time the next order arrives.
- There are no stockout costs.
- There are no quantity discounts.

Development

- If orders are made once a year then average inventory is $0.5D$
- If orders are made every six months, then average inventory is $0.25D$
- If orders are made every three months, then average inventory is $0.125D$

The average inventory is given by:

(annual demand) × (0.5 time between orders)

$$= D\frac{T}{2}.$$

The annual carrying cost is:

$$(\text{average inventory}) \times (\text{carrying cost}) = \frac{DTC}{2}.$$

Orders per year is the reciprocal of the order period = $1/T$ and annual ordering cost is the order cost times the number of orders per year = S/T. The total annual stocking cost (TSC) is the sum of the annual ordering costs and the annual stocking costs:

$$\text{TSC} = \frac{S}{T} + \frac{DTC}{2}.$$

Ordering costs decrease with T and stocking costs increase with T. The total annual stocking cost will be a minimum when these costs are equal:

$$\frac{S}{T} = \frac{DTC}{2}.$$

Rearranging gives

$$T = \sqrt{\frac{2S}{DC}}.$$

Alternatively, using calculus and differentiating total stocking costs with respect to the variable T:

$$\frac{\partial(\text{TSC})}{\partial T} = -\frac{S}{T^2} + \frac{DC}{2}.$$

The minimum value is when the derivative, $\dfrac{\partial(\text{TSC})}{\partial \text{T}} = 0$ or

$$-\frac{S}{T^2} + \frac{DC}{2} = 0$$

which give $T = \sqrt{\dfrac{2S}{DC}}$, the same as before.

Order quantity

When the time between orders has been established the next target is to determine the order quantity. This is calculated by the following relationship:

Order quantity = Maximum inventory target
– inventory level + EDDLT.

The following worked example, *Maps*, illustrates the use of the economic period model and the calculation of the order quantity.

WORKED EXAMPLE: MAPS

Situation

A tourist office in France, which is open six days a week, 50 weeks a year, supplies, among other items, maps of the local area. It wants to establish a time period between orders to the printer that supplies the maps. Table 11.8 gives estimated data concerning this item.

Table 11.8 Estimated data for the Maps worked example

Annual demand (units/year)	500 000
Stocking cost (FF/unit/year)	0.65
Ordering cost (FF/order)	250
Lead time from ordering to receipt (days)	5
Maximum inventory desired	30 000

Required

1. Using the modelling approach of fixed-order-period systems, develop a graph illustrating the total cost, the ordering cost, and the stocking cost.
2. Determine the optimum time between orders using the above information.
3. When the inventory level was reviewed at a certain time period (say period 0), the number of maps in inventory was 9500. Determine the quantity that should be ordered from the supplier.
4. Using Question 3 as the start period, develop a profile of inventory movements for the first 40 days for the tourist office. For simplification, assume an average usage of maps each day.

Solution

1. Development of a graph:
   - An arbitrary time period of 1 to 42 is chosen (Column 1) of Table 11.9.
   - The days are converted into a fraction of a year by dividing by 300 (50 × 6 days) (Column 2).
   - The average inventory is calculated by applying the relationship $0.5DT$ (Column 3).
   - Total stocking cost is calculated by multiplying average inventory by the unit stocking cost (Column 4).
   - Ordering cost is calculated from the relationship S/T (Column 5).
   - The total cost is the sum of the ordering cost and the stocking cost (Column 6).
   - The graph is shown in Figure 11.21. From this graph the minimum total cost lies for an ordering period between 10 and 15 days.
2. Optimum time between orders:
   - Substituting the values in the relationship $T = \sqrt{2S/DC}$ gives a value of T of 11.77 days (say, make the orders every 12 days).
3. Order quantity:
   - The average demand per day is the total per year divided by 300 or 1666.67.
   - Lead time is five days. Thus average demand during lead time is 8333 (5 × 16666.67).
   - Order quantity = Maximum inventory target – inventory level + EDDLT:

$$30\,000 - 9500 + 8333 = 28\,833.$$

■ This data is shown in Table 11.10 (without the rounding). The
inventory movements are illustrated in Figure 11.22.

Table 11.9 Work sheet for the Maps example (Questions 1 and 2)

Questions 1 and 2	Symbol	Value	Units	Source
Annual demand	D	500 000	units/year	Given
Stocking cost	C	0.65	FF/unit/year	Given
Ordering cost	S	250	FF/order	Given
Days/week		6		Given
Weeks/year		50		Given
Open days/year		300		Calculated
Optimum time	T	11.77	days	Calculated

Time (Days)	Time (years)	Average inventory	Stocking cost	Ordering cost	Total cost
0	0.0000		0.00		
1	0.0033	833.33	541.67	75 000.00	75 541.67
2	0.0067	1 666.67	1 083.33	37 500.00	38 583.33
3	0.0100	2 500.00	1 625.00	25 000.00	26 625.00
4	0.0133	3 333.33	2 166.67	18 750.00	20 916.67
5	0.0167	4 166.67	2 708.33	15 000.00	17 708.33
6	0.0200	5 000.00	3 250.00	12 500.00	15 750.00
7	0.0233	5 833.33	3 791.67	10 714.29	14 505.95
8	0.0267	6 666.67	4 333.33	9 375.00	13 708.33
9	0.0300	7 500.00	4 875.00	8 333.33	13 208.33
10	0.0333	8 333.33	5416.67	7 500.00	12 916.67
11	0.0367	9 166.67	5 958.33	6 818.18	12 776.52
12	0.0400	10 000.00	6 500.00	6 250.00	12 750.00
13	0.0433	10 833.33	7 041.67	5 769.23	12 810.90
14	0.0467	11 666.67	7 583.33	5 357.14	12 940.48
15	0.0500	12 500.00	8 125.00	5 000.00	13 125.00
16	0.0533	13 333.33	8 666.67	4 687.50	13 354.17
17	0.0567	14 166.67	9 208.33	4 411.76	13 620.10
18	0.0600	15 000.00	9 750.00	4 166.67	13 916.67
19	0.0633	15 833.33	10 291.67	3 947.37	14 239.04
20	0.0667	16 666.67	10 833.33	3 750.00	14 583.33
21	0.0700	17 500.00	11 375.00	3 571.43	14 946.43
22	0.0733	18 333.33	11 916.67	3 409.09	15 325.76
23	0.0767	19 166.67	12 458.33	3 260.87	15 719.20
24	0.0800	20 000.00	13 000.00	3 125.00	16 125.00
25	0.0833	20 833.33	13 541.67	3 000.00	16 541.67
26	0.0867	21 666.67	14 083.33	2 884.62	16 967.95
27	0.0900	22 500.00	14 625.00	2 777.78	17 402.78
28	0.0933	23 333.33	15 166.67	2 678.57	17 845.24
29	0.0967	24 166.67	15 708.33	2 586.21	18 294.54
30	0.1000	25 000.00	16 250.00	2 500.00	18 750.00
31	0.1033	25 833.33	16 791.67	2 419.35	19 211.02
32	0.1067	26 666.67	17 333.33	2 343.75	19 677.08
33	0.1100	27 500.00	17 875.00	2 272.73	20 147.73
34	0.1133	28 333.33	18 416.67	2 205.88	20 622.55
35	0.1167	29 166.67	18 958.33	2 142.86	21 101.19
36	0.1200	30 000.00	19 500.00	2 083.33	21 583.33
37	0.1233	30 833.33	20 041.67	2 027.03	22 068.69
38	0.1267	31 666.67	20 583.33	1 973.68	22 557.02
39	0.1300	32 500.00	21 125.00	1 923.08	23 048.08
40	0.1333	33 333.33	21 666.67	1 875.00	23 541.67
41	0.1367	34 166.67	22 208.33	1 829.27	24 037.60
42	0.1400	35 000.00	22 750.00	1 785.71	24 535.71

Question 3	Value	Units	Source
Lead time	5	days	Given
Max inventory	30 000	units	Given
Usage/day	1666.67	units/day	calculated
EDDLT	8333.33	units	calculated
Inventory level	9500	units	Given
Order quantity	28 833	units	calculated

End of day	Inventory at end of period	Use during period	Order at beginning of period	Arrive at end of period
0	9 500.00			
1	7 833.33	1 666.67	28 833.33	
2	6 166.67	1 666.67		
3	4 500.00	1 666.67		
4	2 833.33	1 666.67		
5	30 000.00	1 666.67		28 833.33
6	28 333.33	1 666.67		
7	26 666.67	1 666.67		
8	25 000.00	1 666.67		
9	23 333.33	1 666.67		
10	21 666.67	1 666.67		
11	20 000.00	1 666.67		
12	18 333.33	1 666.67		
13	16 666.67	1 666.67	20 000.00	
14	15 000.00	1 666.67		
15	13 333.33	1 666.67		
16	11 666.67	1 666.67		
17	30 000.00	1 666.67		20 000.00
18	28 333.33	1 666.67		
19	26 666.67	1 666.67		
20	25 000.00	1 666.67		
21	23 333.33	1 666.67		
22	21 666.67	1 666.67		
23	20 000.00	1 666.67		
24	18 333.33	1 666.67		
25	16 666.67	1 666.67		
26	15 000.00	1 666.67		
27	13 333.33	1 666.67	20 000.00	
28	11 666.67	1 666.67		
29	30 000.00	1 666.67		
30	28 333.33	1 666.67		
31	26 666.67	1 666.67		20 000.00
32	25 000.00	1 666.67		
33	23 333.33	1 666.67		
34	21 666.67	1 666.67		
35	20 000.00	1 666.67		
36	18 333.33	1 666.67		
37	16 666.67	1 666.67		
38	15 000.00	1 666.67		
39	13 333.33	1 666.67		
40	11 666.67	1 666.67		
41	30 000.00	1 666.67		
42	28 333.33	1 666.67		

Figure 11.21 Maps – optimum time period between orders.

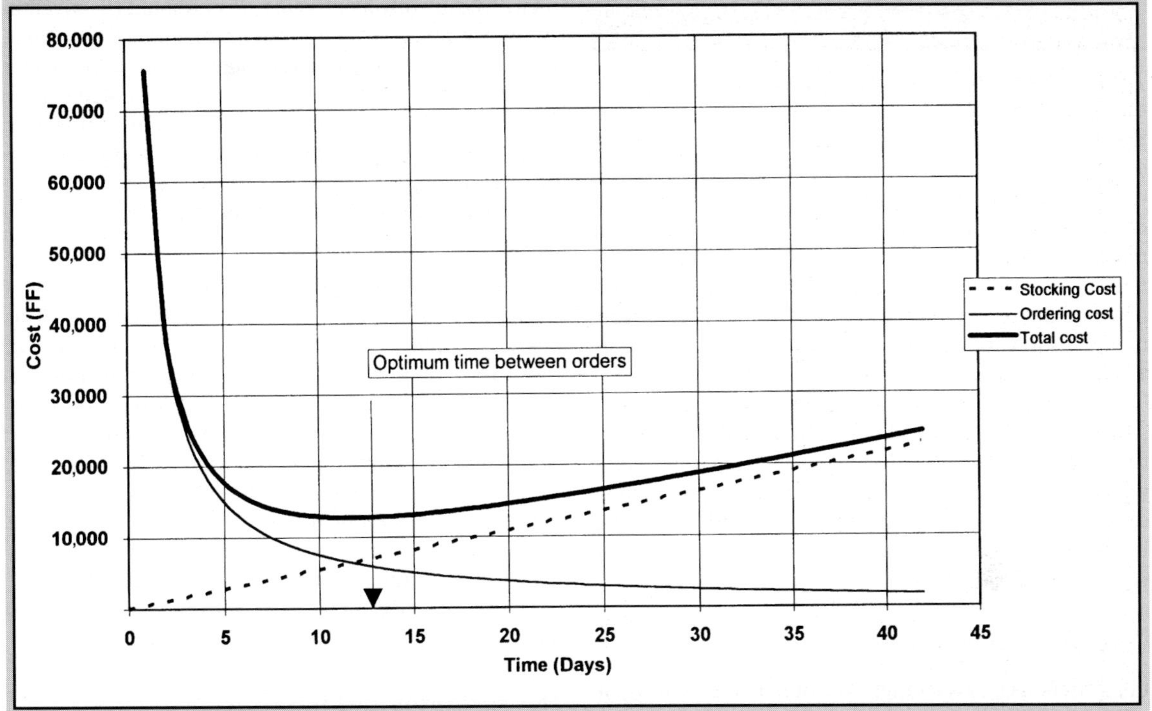

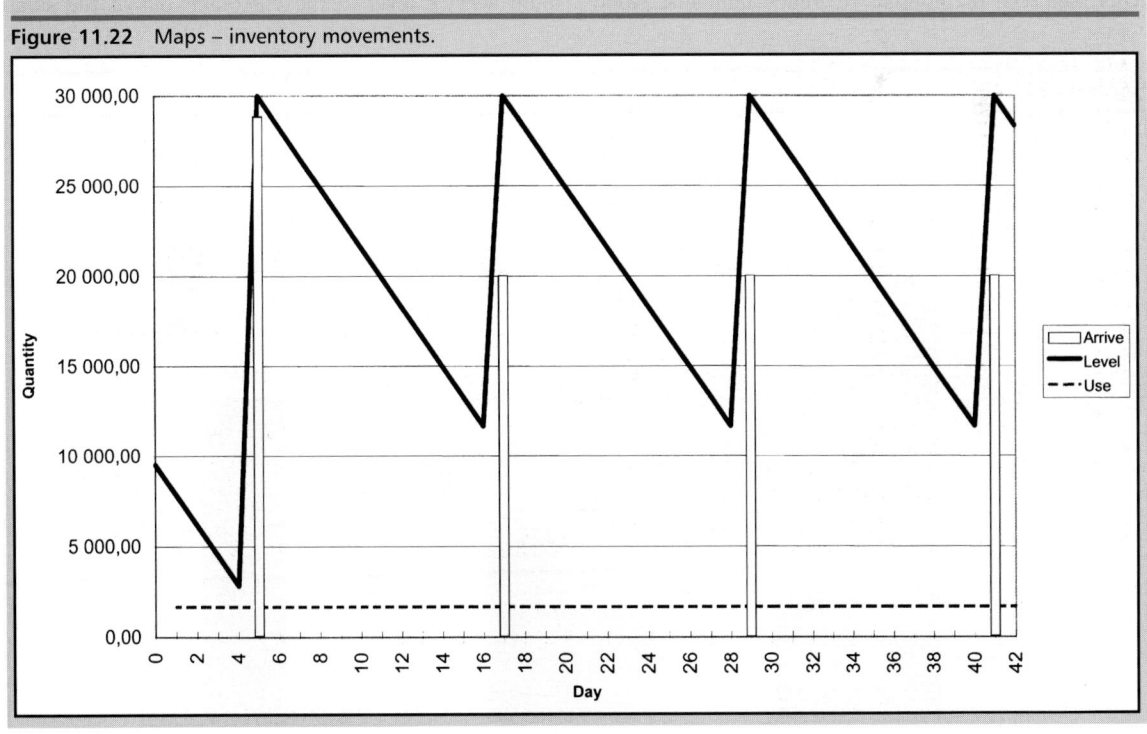

Figure 11.22 Maps – inventory movements.

REQUIREMENTS FOR GOOD INVENTORY MANAGEMENT

The roots of good inventory management lie in knowing the customers and understanding their requirements, so that more accurate forecasts can be prepared. Once an accurate forecast is established, production planning can be organized better. Another step is then to work closely with suppliers and aid them to improve, and respect, delivery times so that no 'insurance' stocks need be held. With a well-organized supply chain just-in-time and Kanban systems can be put in place, which further helps to eliminate excessive inventory (see Chapter 15, *Lean production and just in time*).

With regard to the inventory itself, managers should be aware of all the costs that make up inventory carrying costs, ordering costs from purchases made outside and set-up or other transfer costs when orders are made within the firm. In addition, the implementation of a classification system for inventory helps management.

Classification of inventory

In a warehouse, or a storage area of a manufacturing or service organization supplying finished goods inventory, there are often numerous inventory items with perhaps hundreds of different reference numbers. Good inventory management means turning over this inventory as frequently as possible. How should the inventory be classified? Which is the most important? Often, when one observes a large quantity of a particular material, an inclination is to manage these items more closely because they 'are the most visible'. However, these may not be the items that contribute to the highest investment. One way of organizing and managing inventory is to use an ABC classification.

ABC inventory management

An ABC classification, developed by H. Ford Dickey of the USA in 1951, is a type of Pareto analysis. This analysis applies the 80/20 rule and, in the case of inventory, observations have shown that approximately 80 per cent of the quantity of inventory represents 20 per cent of the cost. Conversely, 20 per cent of the quantity contributes to 80 per cent of the cost, as illustrated in Figure 11.23. Here class A shows approximately 80% of the value and 20% of the cost whilst the combined classes B and C shows approximately 80% of the quantity and 20% of the value.

The Worked Example, *EDF*, illustrates the development of ABC analysis for classifying inventory.

The customer and the risks

Good inventory management means providing the optimum service level to the customer, but at the same

Figure 11.23 ABC analysis as a histogram.

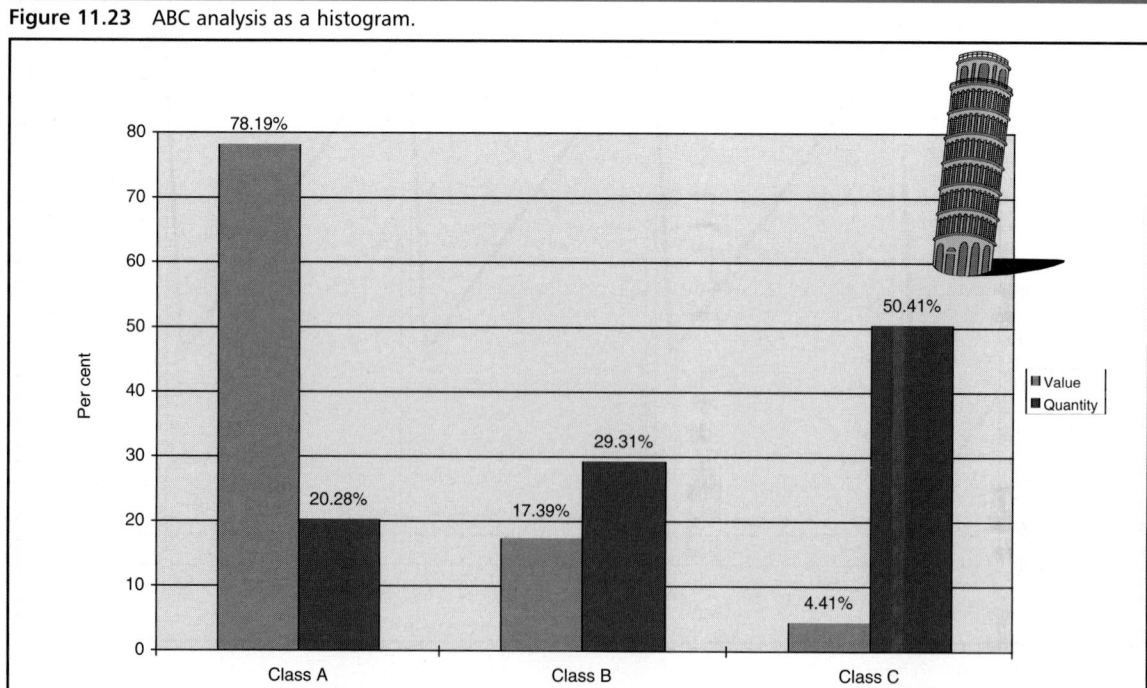

time keeping associated inventory costs to a minimum. Inventory carrying costs can be estimated, but it is difficult to measure the cost of a stockout. If there is a stockout, the customer may at least accept having the product put on back order. However, it may be that an individual sale is lost or, if the customer is very inconvenienced, he or she may be permanently lost. At the very worst, the customer talks to colleagues and a whole group of customers is lost. If in doubt, always organize to satisfy the customer.

WORKED EXAMPLE: EDF, ABC ANALYSIS

Situation

EDF (*Electricité de France*) is the state-owned electricity supply company in France. One of its branches, just east of Lyon, provides repair, modification and emergency services in the Rhône-Alps region. In its large warehouse it keeps spares such as tyres for emergency trucks, copper cable, insulating joints, steel bars, lubricating oil, plastic tubing, switches, electric contacts, etc. Alarmed about the financial investment in the inventory, the regional manager asked for an analysis of the material used. The Controller, with the help of the Warehouse superintendent compiled the data shown in Table 11.10.

Table 11.10 Analysis of the EDF inventory

Product reference	Units used per year	Cost per unit (FF)
D-56981	3200	2.75
D-9865	1600	0.75
F-4589	800	45.80
F-4598	1500	17.20
F-5892	3200	11.00
G-5698	4000	2.25
H-4562	800	3.75
K-8592	1225	12.40
M-7895	400	152.50
M-85941	300	52.80
N-8591	850	12.70
Q-8594	800	45.00
S-1485	700	15.80
S-4985	2400	0.50
T-7852	1200	13.00

U-6821	1500	144.00
W-4561	1600	37.00
X-5986	2500	2.10
Z-5642	1100	96.00
Z-9876	775	280.00

Required

1. Develop an ABC analysis of the given inventory items. Show the information graphically. Which items would go into the classifications of A, B and C?

Solution

The ABC analysis is given in Table 11.11 and is calculated as follows:

- This annual usage is translated into a percentage of the total quantity used.
- From the average unit cost of each item, the total cost of each product used in one year is determined.
- The items investigated are sorted in decreasing order of the total annual cost.
- The total cost of each unit used is translated into a percentage of the total cost of all the units investigated.
- The percentage quantity, and the percentage cost, are further translated into cumulative percentages.
- The cumulative percentages are plotted as a curve (Figure 11.24). From this curve, or from the table, an ABC classification is made. Here about 60 per cent of the value is classed A, about 10 per cent classed C and 30 per cent classed B. The break point is not rigid; for example, item M-7895 could have gone into the A classification. What is important is a logical classification.

Table 11.11 ABC analysis for EDF

	Product reference	Units used per year	Cost per unit (FF)	Total cost (units × cost/unit)
1	D-56981	3200	2.75	8 800.00
2	D-9865	1600	0.75	1 200.00
3	F-4589	800	45.80	36 640.00
4	F-4598	1500	17.20	25 800.00
5	F-5892	3200	11.00	35 200.00
6	G-5698	4000	2.25	9 000.00
7	H-4562	800	3.75	3 000.00
8	K-8592	1225	12.40	15 190.00
9	M-7895	400	152.50	61 000.00
10	M-85941	300	52.80	15 840.00
11	N-8591	850	12.70	10 795.00
12	Q-8594	800	45.00	36 000.00
13	S-1485	700	15.80	11 060.00
14	S-4985	2400	0.50	1 200.00

15	T-7852	1200	13.00	15 600.00		
16	U-6821	1500	144.00	216 000.00		
17	W-4561	1600	37.00	59 200.00		
18	X-5986	2500	2.10	5 250.00		
19	Z-5642	1100	96.00	105 600.00		
20	Z-9876	775	280.00	217 000.00		
Total				889 375.00		

	Product reference	Cumulative percentage of product references	Units used per year	Cost per unit (FF)	Total cost FF	Percentage of total cost	Cumulative percentage of total cost	
		0					0.00	
1	Z-9876	5	775	280.00	217 000.00	24.40	24.40	A
2	U-6821	10	1500	144.00	216 000.00	24.29	48.69	A
3	Z-5642	15	1100	96.00	105 600.00	11.87	60.56	A
4	M-7895	20	400	152.50	61 000.00	6.86	67.42	B
5	W-4561	25	1600	37.00	59 200.00	6.66	74.07	B
6	F-4589	30	800	45.80	36 640.00	4.12	78.19	B
7	Q-8594	35	800	45.00	36 000.00	4.05	82.24	B
8	F-5892	40	3200	11.00	35 200.00	3.96	86.20	B
9	F-4598	45	1500	17.20	25 800.00	2.90	89.10	B
10	M-85941	50	300	52.80	15 840.00	1.78	90.88	C
11	T-7852	55	1200	13.00	15 600.00	1.75	92.64	C
12	K-8592	60	1225	12.40	15 190.00	1.71	94.34	C
13	S-1485	65	700	15.80	11 060.00	1.24	95.59	C
14	N-8591	70	850	12.70	10 795.00	1.21	96.80	C
15	G-5698	75	4000	2.25	9 000.00	1.01	97.81	C
16	D-56981	80	3200	2.75	8 800.00	0.99	98.80	C
17	X-5986	85	2500	2.10	5 250.00	0.59	99.39	C
18	H-4562	90	800	3.75	3 000.00	0.34	99.73	C
19	D-9865	95	1600	0.75	1 200.00	0.13	99.87	C
20	S-4985	100	2400	0.50	1 200.00	0.13	100.00	C
Total					889 375.00	100.00		

Figure 11.24 EDF — ABC analysis.

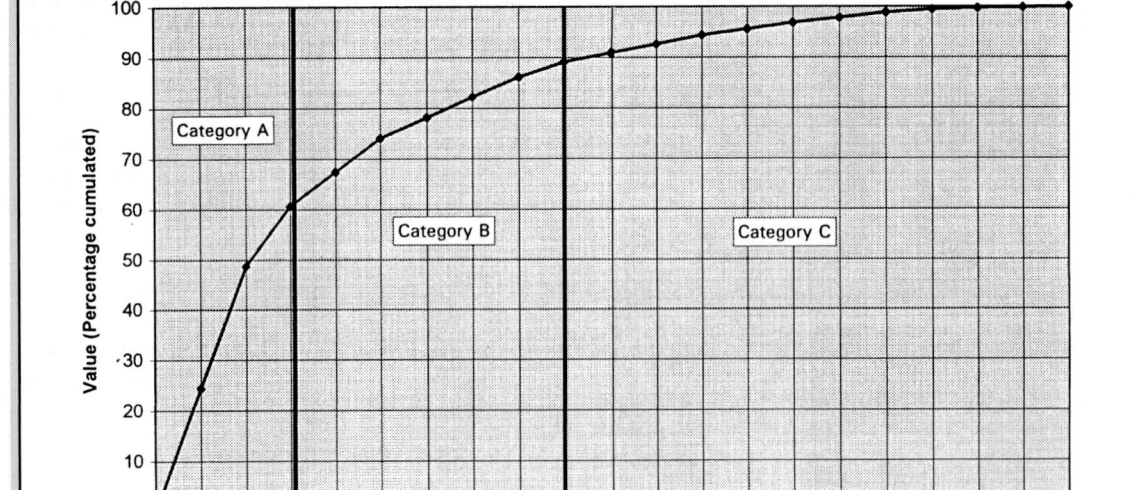

SUMMARY OF KEY ELEMENTS

- Inventory is a store of goods, accounted for as a short-term asset and consumed during the normal course of business. All firms use inventory of some sort.
- In manufacturing, inventory includes raw materials, purchased parts, work in process, finished goods, goods in transit, spare parts, small tools, consumable supplies, packaging and waste material.
- Independent inventory is essentially finished goods for which the demand depends on the requirements and needs of the customer.
- Dependent inventory is material that is usually a subassembly or component of another product. Management of dependent inventory is by MRP systems.
- High levels of finished goods inventory may be held because of uncertainty in customer demand, display purposes, price discounts, favourable exchange rates or anticipated price increases.
- High levels of raw materials may be held because immediate delivery on demand is not feasible or because there are variations in the demand for finished goods, anticipated price rises, unit price discounts, lower warehouse costs or uncertainty in lead times.
- Work-in-process inventory arises because of waiting, transfer, queuing, set-up and operating times. Operating time is the only value added activity and may be just 5 per cent of the total waiting time.
- Costs associated with inventory include carrying costs (investment, warehousing, holding), ordering costs (purchasing externally or set up internally) and stockout costs.
- Safety stocks are dead stocks, held for uncertainty, and the cost of these adds to carrying costs.
- The basic questions in ordering inventory are: When? and What amount?
- Fixed-order-quantity purchasing is ordering the same quantity each time an order is placed, not necessarily at the same time interval. A two-bin system is a special example of fixed order quantity.
- Fixed order period means ordering perhaps different amounts at the same time intervals. This ordering approach has a higher risk of a stockout.
- Ordering large quantities less frequently, as opposed to small quantities more frequently increases the carrying cost but reduces the probability of a stockout.
- The models of the economic order quantity EOQ determine the optimum order quantity to balance total carrying costs against total ordering costs.

- In the basic model, Model I;

$$\text{TSC} = \frac{Q}{2} C + \frac{D}{Q} S \text{ and } Q = \text{EOQ} = \sqrt{\frac{2DS}{C}}.$$

- The EOQ model is robust in the sense that a large change in the EOQ value may not significantly change the total stocking cost TSC.
- In Model II:

$$\text{TSC} = \frac{(p - d)}{2p} QC + \frac{D}{Q} S$$

$$\text{and EOQ} = \sqrt{\frac{2DS}{C} \left(\frac{p}{p - d} \right)}.$$

- In Model II, when supply equals demand, the system is balanced. When supply is greater than demand, inventory accumulates. When demand is greater than supply, there is a stockout.
- When quantity discounts are offered, the EOQ models take into account the total amount paid for inventory and the total inventory cost becomes:

Total product cost equal to TSC
+ (Unit price × Annual demand).

- The quantity demanded during lead time for inventory is a function of the customer's demand and the supplier's lead time.
- The expected demand during lead time, EDDLT, is the average inventory per day multiplied by the average supplier lead time. It is also the order point plus the safety stock.
- A service level of 95 per cent means that 95 per cent of the time customers' orders can be filled from current inventory. It also implies that the risk of a stockout is 5 per cent.
- In payoff tables for inventory calculation, the long cost is associated with holding too much inventory and the short cost is associated with stockouts.
- If a normal distribution can represent the quantity of inventory demanded during lead time, then the order point is given by the relationship

Order point = EDDLT + $z\sigma_{\text{DDLT}}$.

- If the lead time is considered constant, then the distribution becomes the quantity demand during a fixed lead time (LT) and the order point can be rewritten as:

Order point = $\text{LT}\bar{d} + z \sqrt{\text{LT}(\sigma_d)^2}$.

- The percentage approach to arbitrary order point determination, applies a factor k that is dependent on the critical nature of the material and its ease of supply.

■ The square-root method approach for arbitrary order-point determination considers that the safety stock is the square root of the expected demand during the lead time.

■ The fixed order period Model III gives the optimum time between placing orders as.

$$T = \sqrt{2S/DC}:$$

Order quantity = Maximum inventory
– inventory level + EDDLT.

■ The ABC analysis of inventory classification is based on the Pareto approach that a small quantity of inventory contributes to the highest cost, and vice versa.

REVIEW AND DISCUSSION QUESTIONS

1 **Production and inventory**. The Block Company manufactures fuel injection systems for aeroplanes. One particular assembly, Code AMB-1487, made from aluminium, passes through a drilling process where seven holes of three different dimensions are drilled into the unit. The immediate next operation is polishing. During these two operations a significant quantity of in-process inventory is generated. Give possible reasons:
   (a) Why there might be a high level of in-process inventory.
   (b) Why a high inventory level is cause for concern.
   (c) Suggest ways that in-process inventory might be minimized.

2 **Changing inventory levels**. Sometimes in the press one reads that inventories of finished goods are increasing or decreasing. Discuss the impact of changing inventories on industrial activity.

3 **Higher than normal inventories**. Discuss the reasons why, when and in what circumstances inventories may be higher than normal for the following:
   (a) a food distribution firm;
   (b) an automobile component parts manufacturer in Germany or France;
   (c) a petrol station;
   (d) a sweet factory;
   (d) a stationery store or the stationery department of a departmental store.

4 **Inventory management costs**. For the following situations, how in practice would one determine inventory carrying costs, inventory ordering costs and inventory stockout costs:
   (a) a retail store;
   (b) a production centre.

5 **In-process inventory**. What can be done to reduce the level of in-process inventories in a production operation?

EXERCISE PROBLEM: BRICKS

Situation

A building supplier in southern England supplies, among other things, bricks for house construction. The bricks are ordered on pallets from three suppliers. The company is interested in establishing a time period within which to order pallets of bricks. Table 11.12 gives the estimated data concerning the firm and its usage of bricks.

Table 11.12 Usage of bricks

Annual demand for bricks (pallets/year)	245 000
Stocking cost (£/pallet/year)	150
Ordering cost (£/order)	5000
Lead time from ordering to reception (days)	3
Maximum inventory desired (pallets)	12 000
Open days per week	6
Operating weeks per year	50

Required

1 Using the modelling approach of fixed order periods develop a graph illustrating the total cost, the ordering cost and the stocking cost.

2 Determine the optimum time between orders, using the above information.

3 When the inventory level was reviewed at a certain time period (say period 0), the number of pallets of bricks in inventory was 12 000. Determine the quantity that should be ordered from the supplier.

4 Using Question 3 as the start period, develop a profile of inventory movements for the first 15 days.

EXERCISE PROBLEM: CAKES

Situation

A bakery calculates that, on average, the marginal profit for the sale of Black Forest gateau (chocolate cake) is £1.50 and the marginal loss is £2.50. The average demand per day, based on past sales, is given according to Table 11.13.

Table 11.13 Probability of demand for Black Forest gateau

Demand (units)	Probability of this demand
0	0.02
1	0.04
2	0.06
3	0.10
4	0.15
5	0.15
6	0.25
7	0.10
8	0.05
9	0.05
10	0.03

Required

Using marginal analysis, how many cakes per day should the bakery make first thing in the morning to optimize the inventory situation? (See Chapter 22, *Decision making and risk analysis* for the method of marginal analysis).

EXERCISE PROBLEM: CASSIS CO.

Situation

The Cassis Co., located on the shores of Lake Michigan, is a manufacturer of automobile engines. Table 11.14 gives historical data on the typical annual usage of component parts for one of its six-cylinder engines. The cost of the finished engine has been increasing by about 5 per cent per year. This is principally due to approximately the same increase in the cost of the component parts.

Table 11.14 Historical data for typical annual usage of component parts for a six-cylinder engine

Part number	Annual quantity	Unit Cost ($)
111D	32 000	1.00
128H	50 000	0.50
196G	7 490	22.40
205Y	3 000	270.00
216U	3 060	12.80
217J	3 500	122.40
228G	840	98.40
235D	64 000	1.80
249E	14 000	6.30
258L	2 200	62.40
261K	20 000	1.20
272J	5 000	9.00
324H	22 000	1.50
333C	2 280	15.40
334U	8 000	24.00
352S	13 000	19.20
391J	2 200	51.60
421A	4 500	9.60
432S	4 890	7.60
436S	75 000	0.25
452F	3 800	13.50
462R	4 000	16.80
463H	3 000	132.00
478L	27 140	1.20
521I	3 000	13.80
532Q	1 200	144.00
610B	30 000	5.10

Required

1 Examine the inventory usage data using the concept of the ABC analysis. Show the results graphically.
2 What is a reasonable grouping in categories A, B and C. What part numbers are in category A?

EXERCISE PROBLEM: FLOUR

Situation

Boulanger is a medium-sized baker. Based on past data and on supplier delivery time, the expected usage during lead time (EDDLT) of flour is 7000 kg.

Required

1 If the usage of flour can be considered normally distributed with a standard deviation for the demand of 100 kg, determine the level of safety stock Boulanger should keep for the flour. What is the corresponding level of inventory at which Boulanger should place orders? Assume a client service level of 99.5 per cent.
2 Using the arbitrary method and percentage of expected demand during lead time, with a factor k of 15 per cent, determine the level of safety stock for the flour and the corresponding level of inventory at which Boulanger should place orders.
3 Using the arbitrary method and the square root of expected demand during lead time, determine the level of safety stock for the flour and the corresponding level of inventory at which Boulanger should place orders.

EXERCISE PROBLEM: PAPER

Situation

A company purchases cartons of paper, which are then sold for photographic printing. It has looked at usage of paper for the last month in terms of boxes sold. This information is as given in Table 11.15.

Table 11.15   Demand for paper

Cartons demanded	Days on which demand occurred
15	1
35	2
45	9
55	4
70	8
100	6

Further, it estimates the long cost for stocking the inventory of paper as £5.00 and the short cost as £12.00.

Required

Determine the optimum number of cartons of paper to purchase in order to minimize the cost.

EXERCISE PROBLEM: SPARKY

Situation

The Sparky Co. is a service organization that distributes electric components throughout the Rhône-Alps region in France. The distribution centre is located in Annecy.

Henry Wohler, the Purchasing Manager, is meeting with Agnes Mira, his assistant. The object of the discussion is to establish a stocking policy for certain products that are stored in, and distributed from, the warehouse in Annecy. There are three principal products at the warehouse, which can be classified according to an ABC analysis:

■ *Transformer (Part No TRA-100)*. This is considered a Class A product as it represents about 20 per cent of the quantity of inventory in stock and about 75 per cent of the total value. The basic cost of the transformer to Sparky is 299.00 FF. Annual demand is estimated at 105 000 units per year and the ordering cost at 2000.00 FF per order.
■ *Armature winding (Part No INT-137)*. This is considered a Class B product as it represents about 30 per cent of the quantity of inventory in stock and about 20 per cent of the total value. The basic cost of the transformer to Sparky is 138.00 FF. Annual demand is estimated at 15 000 units per year and the ordering cost is estimated at 1000.00 FF per order.
■ *Switches (Part No BOU-1455)*. This is considered a Class C product as it represents about 50 per cent of the quantity of inventory in stock, and about 5 per cent of the total value. The basic cost of the transformer to Sparky is 75.00 FF. Annual demand is estimated at 6500 units per year and ordering cost at 400.00 FF per order.

The Sparky Co. works 250 days a year and the inventory storage cost for all products is estimated at 35 per cent of product cost.

Required

1 If transformers are delivered in fixed lots to Sparky, how many transformers would be ordered under the basic economic order quantity conditions?
2 If transformers are delivered to the warehouse at an average rate of 450 units/day, what would be the new economic order quantity?
3 What is the saving in annual cost between Questions 1 and 2?
4 If armature windings are delivered in fixed lots to Sparky, how many would be ordered under the basic economic order quantity conditions?
5 If armature windings are delivered to the warehouse at an average rate of 150 units/day, what would be the economic order quantity?
6 What is the saving in annual cost between Question 4 and Question 5?
7 The supplier of the transformer indicates he is able to offer the discounts shown in Table 11.16. Under these conditions, what is the optimal ordering quantity, assuming that the other information in Question 1 remains unchanged.

Table 11.16   Quantity discounts on purchase of transformers

Order quantity	Unit cost (FF)
1 to 999	299.00
1000 to 3999	297.00
4000 and over	296.00

8 For the transformer, what is the difference in total costs between the situation when price discounts are offered and the case when there are no price discounts using the basic model?
9 If the transformers are delivered at the average rate of 450 units per day, then using the price discount situation, what would be the economic order quantity?
10 What are the costs savings between Question 9 and Question 2?
11 The supplier of the armature windings indicates he is able to offer the discounts shown in Table 11.17. Under these conditions, what is now the optimal ordering quantity?

Table 11.17   Quantity discounts on purchase of armatures

Order quantity	Unit cost (FF)
1 to 999	138.00
1000 to 1999	137.00
2000 and over	136.40

12 For the armature windings, what is the difference in total cost between the situation when price discounts are offered and the case when there are no price discounts?
13 What is the economic order quantity for the switches?
14 What are your criticisms of just using models to manage inventory?

EXERCISE PROBLEM: STANFORD

Situation

The Stanford Co. in Newcastle-upon-Tyne suppliers meter components to the British Gas company. At the present time the inventory of component parts is badly organized. Some pieces are kept on the shop floor, some in the receiving dock and some in the warehouse. The Production Manager has been advised by the Financial Manager that the company needs to have better management of the inventory.

The Production Manager, with the aid of a Master's student, makes an analysis of the quantity of units used over a three-month period, together with their unit cost based on the purchase price. This is given in Table 11.18.

Table 11.18 Quantity of units used over a three month period, together with their unit cost

Reference number	Quantity used each quarter	Unit price (£)
a-123	27	56.00
d-145	17	127.00
e-459	200	2.54
f-1254	120	2.61
f-458	55	14.80
f-598	21	41.90
g-58	56	47.80
g-789	540	0.75
h-124	45	32.70
h-154	605	4.58
j-124	98	38.70
j-457	805	1.00
k-2654	89	14.00
k-7892	256	3.70
r-5698	298	3.54
r-654	1189	0.28
x-253	140	0.98
y-789	35	63.80

Required

1. Examine the inventory usage data using the concept of the ABC analysis. Show the results graphically.
2. What conclusions can you draw from the classification?

CASE STUDY: FORTNEX

Situation

Fortnex is a subsidiary of a French company in the Czech Republic and assembles small household appliances, including coffee makers, toasters and food mixers. These products are sold principally in the European Union and some of the eastern European countries.

About 65 per cent of the components used in the assembly operation are purchased from suppliers in lots and this leads to a considerable amount of raw material inventory in the workcentre. In addition, the layout, scheduling, line balancing and the fact that assembly is performed in lot sizes of 150 units engenders a certain amount of in-process inventory. The parent company of Fortnex has been concerned about the rising product cost of the finished products, which has led to reduced profit margins. (Household appliances are very competitive and increasing prices is not a viable option.) One of the demands of the parent company has been to review the inventory management practices of Fortnex.

Two options that Fortnex is currently investigating are economic order quantity purchasing and ABC analysis.

Purchasing EOQ

At present the company purchases copper wire for a certain appliance under economic order quantities based on the information given in Table 11.19.

Table 11.19 Information for EOQ purchasing of copper wire

Annual demand for copper wire (kg)	12 000.00
Price per kg (FF)	12.25
Order cost (FF/order)	50.00
Carrying cost (percentage of price)	20.00

The supplier of copper wire is proposing a discount of 5 per cent if Fortnex purchases in lot sizes of 1000 kg, rather than the calculated EOQ.

ABC analysis

For a particular series of referenced products, Table 11.20 shows the number of units used per year, together with the unit cost.

Table 11.20 Product usage

Product reference	Units used per year	Unit cost (FF)
B7894	700	5.50
C1289	875	1.80
G235	50	102.00
G458	250	42.00
Q4587	110	125.00
Z5892	375	12.00

Required

1. Discuss some of the requirements that would help improve inventory management in this assembly situation. Consider all the elements in the supply chain from purchasing, through assembly, to storage and distribution of the finished product.
2. In the case of the purchase of the copper wire, should Fortnex take advantage of the price discount? Justify, by calculation, your response.
3. What would be the impact on the company if it set up activities under a just-in-time operation?
4. In the referenced inventory items indicated, to which two should Fortnex give maximum management attention? Which should be given the least?

NOTES AND REFERENCES

1. Blumenstein, R. and Stern, G. (1996) 'GM faces lots of troubles as its car inventories grow', *Wall Street Journal Europe* 15 February.
2. Author's visit to Sodiaal, Vienne, France, 7 April 1997.
3. Plossl, G. W. and Wight, O. W. (1967) *Production and Inventory Control*, Englewood Cliffs, NJ: Prentice Hall.
4. US Government of Consumer Affairs.

FURTHER READING

Arnold, J. R. T. (1996) *Introduction to Materials Management*, London: Prentice Hall International.

Barry, C. (1993) 'Developing an inventory strategy', *Catalog Age* 10(11): 125–30.

Blatherwick, A. (1997) 'Inventory Management – The state of the art', *Logistics Focus* 5(8): 2–5.

Bonney, M. C. (1994) 'Trends in inventory management', *International Journal of Production Economics* 35(1–3): 107–14.

Charnes, J. M. Marmorstein, H. and Zinn, W. (1995) 'Safety stock determination with serially correlated demand in a periodic-review inventory system', *Journal of the Operational Research Society* 46(8): 1006–13.

Cobbaert, K. and Van Oudheusden, D. (1996) 'Inventory models for fast moving spare parts subject to "sudden death" obsolescence', *International Journal of Production Economics* 44(3): 239–48.

Ernst, R., Guerro, J.-L., Roshwalb, A. (1993) 'A quality control approach to monitoring inventory stock levels', *Journal of the Operational Research Society* 44(11): 1115–27.

Grant, M. R. (1993) 'EOQ and price break analysis in a JIT environment', *Production and Inventory Management Journal* 34(3): 64–69.

Henig, M., Gerchak, Y., Ernst R. and Pyke, D. F. (1997) 'An inventory model embedded in designing a supply contract', *Management Science* 43(2): 184–89.

Inman, R. R. (1993) 'Inventory is the flower of all evil', *Production and Inventory Management Journal* 34(4): 41–45.

Kok, T. de and Inderfurth, K. (1997) 'Nervousness in inventory management: Comparison of basic control rules', *European Journal of Operational Research* 103(1): 55–82.

Krupp, J. A.G. (1997) 'Safety Stock Management' *Production and Inventory Management Journal* 38(3): 11–18.

Lau, H.-S., Zhao, L.-G. (1993) 'Optimal ordering policies with two suppliers when lead times and demands are all stochastic', *European Journal of Operational Research* 68(1): 120–33.

Moinzadeh, K. and Aggarwal, P. (1997) 'An information based multiechelon inventory system with emergency orders', *Operations Research* 45(5): 694–701.

Moore, T. and Roy, C. (1997) 'Manage inventory in a real-time environment', *Transportation and Distribution* 38(11): 93–97.

Ribar, T. R. (1997) 'Just get it right! Measure it and fix it: The only sure route to 98-percent inventory record integrity', *Hospital Material Management Quarterly* 19(1): 56–62.

Seetharma, L. N. and McLeavey, D. W (1995) *Production Planning and Inventory Control*, Englewood Cliffs, NJ: Prentice Hall.

Sox, C. R., Thomas, L. J. and McLain, J. O. (1997) 'Co-ordinating production and inventory to improve service', *Management Science* 43(9): 1189–97.

Thomas, A. B. (1980) *Stock Control in Manufacturing Industries*, Farnborough, UK: Gower.

Vujosevic, M., Petrovic, D. and Petrovic, R. (1996) 'EOQ formula when inventory cost is fuzzy', *International Journal of Production Economics* 45(1–3): 499–504.

Waters, D. C. (1992) *Inventory Control and Management*, New York: John Wiley & Sons.

12 Operations and capacity planning

Objectives and overview

The objective of this chapter is to discuss the concept and the role of operations and capacity planning in the firm and its importance in the smooth functioning of the supply chain. The chapter first presents the time horizons in planning and the linkage of aggregate planning, master production scheduling and the material requirements plan. The development of the aggregate plan is given in detail and then various options for adjusting the short-term capacity of the system to meet customer demand are described. The chapter then presents various ways of modifying demand to impact the capacity of the facility and, particularly, describes how this applies to service industries. The concept of level and synchronized production in manufacturing is described and the role played by inventory. A similar presentation is given for the service industries, with a description of what possibilities are available to smooth out the production level. Finally, the chapter presents in detail the master production schedule (MPS). After an explanation of the role of the MPS, the concept of rough-cut capacity planning is discussed, how the MPS is finalized, rigorous management using time fences, how the MPS is updated, and the length of the planning horizons.

DEFINING PLANNING

The term 'planning' covers all those activities required for desired objectives to be met. In business, the planning process generally has its roots in the strategic, or long-range, plan, which is then broken down into a more detailed operating plan. As discussed in Chapter 2, *Strategy of Organizations*, a strategic plan has a nominal time horizon of about five years, though it may be longer or shorter depending on the industry. On the other hand, the horizon of the operations plan is about a year, although for some firms it may be up to 18 months. The objective of the operating plan is to enumerate in detail all the activities necessary in order to produce end-products, or to provide the required services for a customer in a timely manner.

Operations plan

An operations plan itself may further comprise short-term and medium-term components, as illustrated in Figure 12.1.

Short-range plans

A short-range plan would cover less than three months, maybe one week, or even one day. Activities might include.

- scheduling production programmes;
- establishing work assignments;
- organizing deliveries of raw materials;
- organizing shipments of finished goods;
- hiring or termination of employees where flexibility exists in countries like the USA. (In the US management model, minimal social laws do not impede changing work-force levels. 'US firms can fire, so they hire. Japanese and German firms can't fire, so they don't hire,' says C. Fred Bergsten, Director of the Institute for International Economics.[1]

Within the short-range period just-in-time management methods are used, as indicated in Figure 12.1. Just-in-time is discussed in detail in Chapter 15, *Lean Production, and Just-in-Time*.

Medium-range plans

A medium-range plan would cover the period between three months and 12 or 18 months and some of the activities would include:

Figure 12.1 Operations planning horizons.

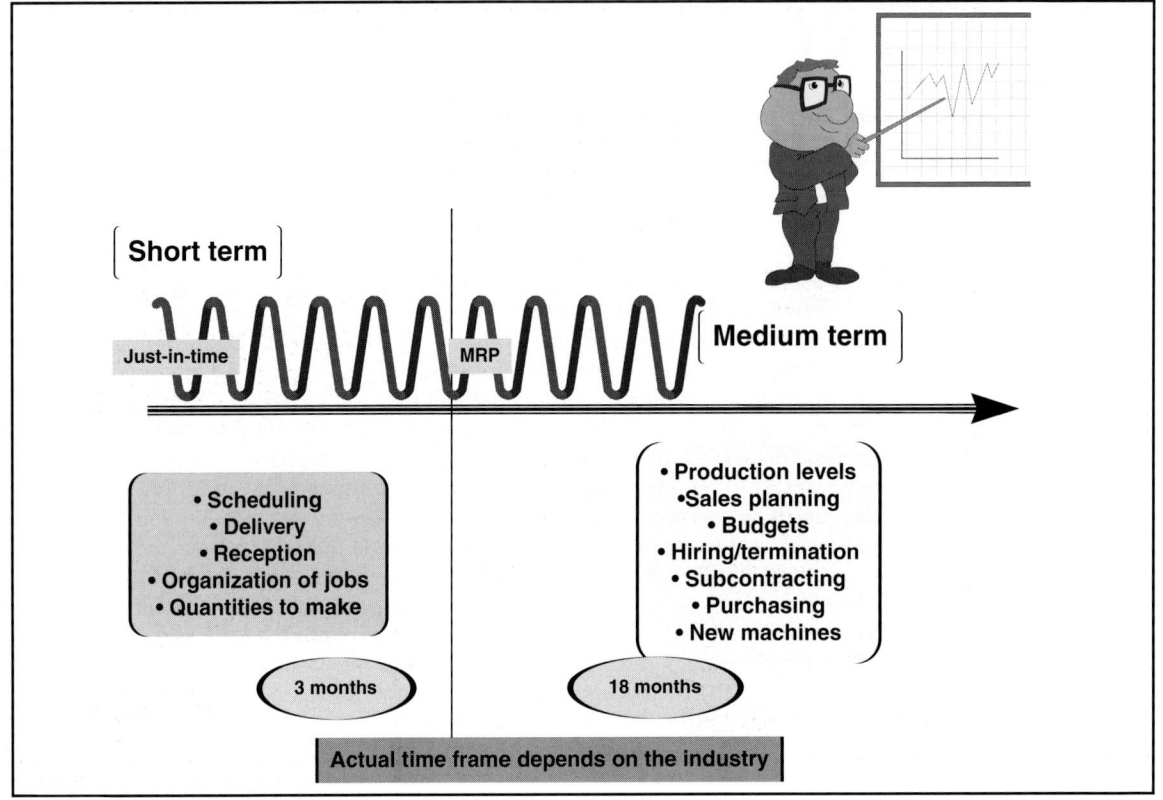

- sales planning;
- hiring, or termination, of employees (in most of the European Community);
- budgets (usually budgets are prepared for the year);
- selecting new subcontractors or suppliers;
- selecting, and installing, new machines and equipment (this may be part of the long-range plan for large expensive capital equipment);
- production plans.

The operations plan is driven by customers' firm orders or by forecast demand and then developed from three component plans, the aggregate plan, where short-term capacity adjustments are made, the master production schedule and the material requirements plan. When these are established, then operations scheduling proceeds, as illustrated schematically in Figure 12.2. Aggregate planning, capacity adjustments and master production schedule are presented in this chapter. *Material Requirements Planning* and *Operations Scheduling* are reviewed in Chapters 13 and 14 respectively.

The operations plan, encompassing the aggregate plan, the master production schedule and the material requirements plan, are closely linked, most often by

computer-integrated systems, and changing any one variable will change other variables and options in the plan. Further, like the strategic plan, the operations plan is dynamic and often in a state of flux because of variations in the external environment or customer requirements. As such, those responsible for planning must be reactive, particularly to the customer, or, as Tom Peters and Robert Waterman bluntly stated in their book, *In Search of Excellence: Lessons from America's Best Run Companies.*[2]

> In too many companies, the customer has become a bloody nuisance, whose unpredictable behaviour damages carefully made strategic plans, whose activities mess up computer operations, and who stubbornly insist that purchased products should work!!

The supply chain and planning

Evidently, rigorous attention to operations planning is critical for the smooth functioning of the supply chain. Poor scheduling in the reception of raw materials, in production programmes or in the delivery of finished goods can all lead to delays and dissatisfied customers.

Figure 12.2 Planning stages in operation.

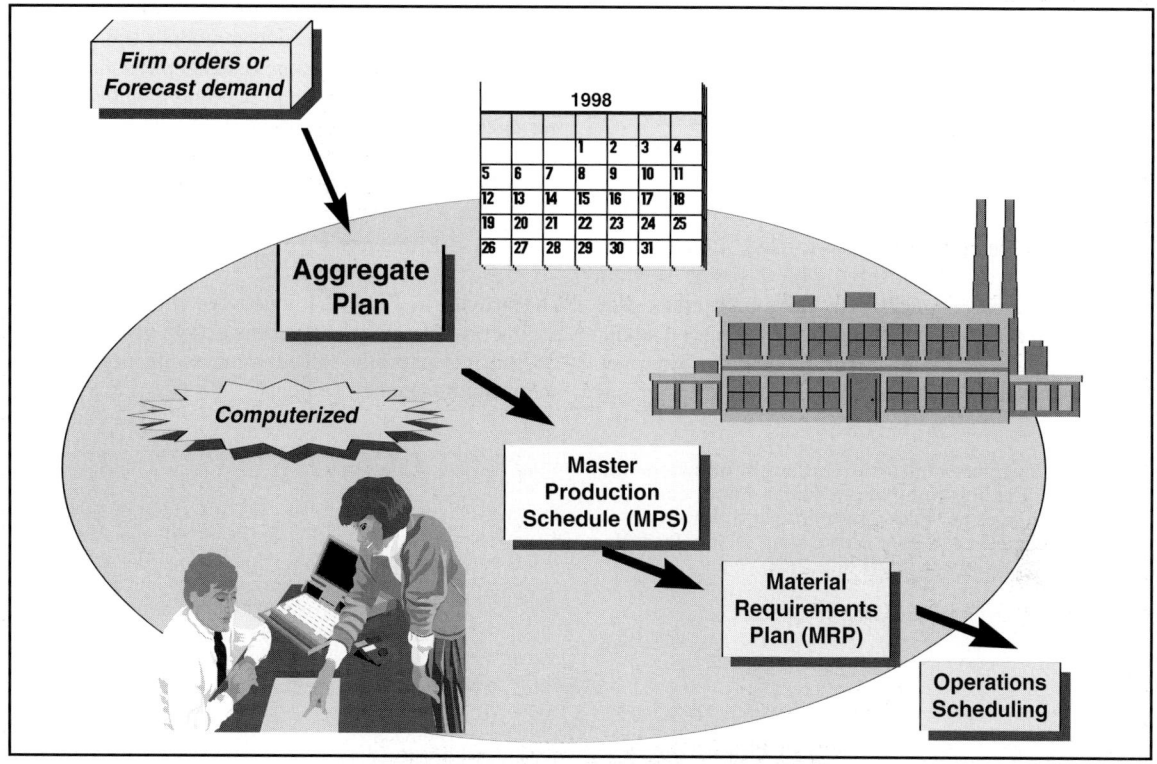

Similarly, poor planning requirements for labour, machines or subcontractors can diminish capacity availability, meaning that products cannot be produced and delivered when promised.

AGGREGATE PLANNING AND CAPACITY

Formulating an aggregate plan

The starting point for the aggregate plan is the development of an estimate of future needs of end-products. This estimate, derived with input from Marketing, may be firm orders from clients, anticipated orders 'promised' but not yet booked or pure forecasts. When this estimate is established, all the end products are totalled or aggregated into a demand for the production facility. For production to convert this into capacity requirements, the aggregate demand is translated into resource requirements of material quantities, labour hours and machine hours using appropriate standards. (Labour standards have been considered in Chapter 8, *Human Resources in the System Design*.)

The conversion of an aggregate demand into production units is relatively straightforward for a company that produces just one product, closely allied products, products that are reasonably homogeneous or products that use few component parts, for example:

- a cement factory;
- a coal mine;
- a shoe manufacturer;
- an oil refinery;
- a polyvinyl chloride plant;
- a ski company.

However, for facilities that produce a diverse set of products, such as furniture, medical instruments or household appliances, the development of an aggregate plan is more complex. This concept of converting demand quantities into production factors is illustrated in the worked example, *Attaché cases*. In this example, the capacity of the facility in terms of labour hours is illustrated and compared with the actual capacity required, or the load demanded.

Capacity utilization

Aggregate planning in the manufacturing or service sector involves deciding on how resources will be used to meet the forecast or actual client demand cost-effectively within the constraints of the capacity of the facility. This means deciding on the requirements for and use of:

- the existing labour force within the company;
- machines and equipment already in the facility;
- raw materials and components that need to be purchased;
- outside labour services, including subcontracting.

Ideally a company would like to have a plan that is repetitive and can be effected with a steady rhythm, such as producing similar quantities of materials each week, using the same machines and using a level labour force. All this would make organizing simple. However, client requirements are rarely constant and there may be peaks of high demand and troughs of low demand. Thus, a well-conceived aggregate plan should provide for orderly production to accommodate the high and low demands, but at the same time keep resources such as machines, work teams and building facilities operating close to capacity, avoiding overloading and excessive underloading or permitting resources to be idle. The efficiency of the aggregate plan is expressed by:

$$\text{Efficiency} = \frac{\text{Actual output}}{\text{Facility capacity}}.$$

The article, in Box 12.1 illustrates the challenges of production planning.[3] Since this article was published, Boeing has partially solved some of its problems by acquiring McDonnell Douglas.

Box 12.1 Sleepless in Seattle. Onslaught of orders has Boeing scrambling to build jets faster. Boom comes at tricky time as company is overhauling the way it makes planes. Lead over Airbus may widen. By Jeff Cole, Staff Reporter

SEATTLE – After years of drought at Boeing Co., the new orders for airliners are finally coming. They are arriving from all around the world – and not in a trickle but almost in a torrent.

For Boeing, oddly enough, that isn't unalloyed good news.

The problem is that Boeing is right in the midst of a huge revamping of its engineering processes. Yet the Seattle-based company – which invited new business during the lean years with its first-ever broad discounts of up to 10% – is in no mood to turn away any orders now that they are finally arriving, even if they are so huge they threaten to overwhelm its current capacity.

So the world's largest airliner manufacturer finds itself struggling with an uncharacteristic run of factory snarls. And despite the rush of orders, its profitability is under pressure. That's because airlines remain so frugal – and so willing to refurbish and retrofit old planes – that Boeing has no choice but to keep its own costs and prices to a minimum, demand surge or no.

Redoing a Wing

The problems are evident in the assembly line for the 777, a hot-selling model. The line producing wings for the plane has fallen badly behind schedule. Three weeks ago, one of the huge wings had to be pulled back up the line for a weekend of costly reworking after harried mechanics misdrilled a main connection.

On the 747 line, meanwhile, Boeing has been running out of some wing panels. And in a mini-glitch, some new staff machinists unwittingly repainted sets of tools that were color-coded.

The problems, which Boeing says it is correcting as they arise, are symptomatic of an unusually fast ramping up of production rates. Officials won't disclose their production outlook, but suppliers and others familiar with the strategy say the company plans to more than double its rate of production by 1999, to 46 or more airliners per month – which figures out to 552 a year. Boeing's one-year record is 446 planes, in 1992.

The Job Outlook

The surge in demand is likely to increase Boeing's lead over its main rival, Europe's Airbus Industrie, although Airbus also is seeing orders grow. In the first six months of this year, Airbus won 143 orders, more than it achieved in all of 1995, when the European consortium fell behind both Boeing and McDonnell Douglas Corp. At the end of June, the consortium had an order backlog of 651 aircraft, or 73 more than it had at the beginning of the year.

For Boeing, the new orders should easily safeguard the 113,000 jobs that remain following losses of some 30,000 jobs during the dry years. In fact, the orders are expected to create thousands of new openings. Still, Boeing is trying to meet demand with a minimum of new hires, and the fast production step-up is leading to new strains in labor relations just months after a 69-day machinists' strike.

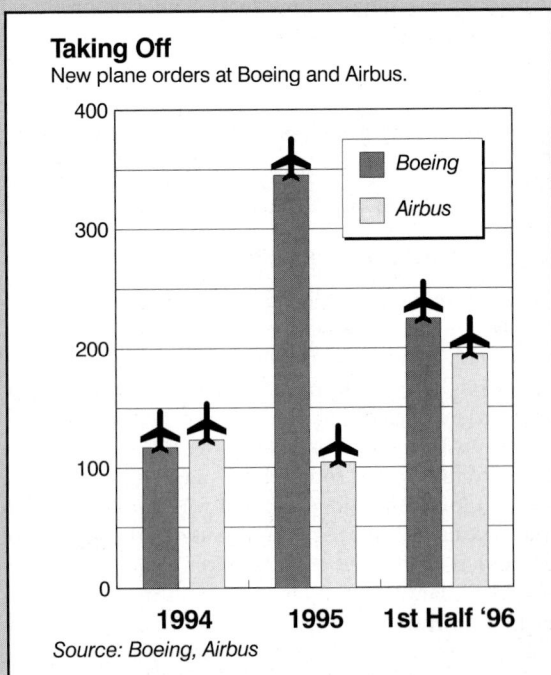

Taking Off
New plane orders at Boeing and Airbus.

Source: Boeing, Airbus

While Boeing executives are delighted with the order upturn, they admit it makes it harder to carry out the big re-engineering program under way. The overhaul of production software and systems aims to simplify the process of assembling jets with millions of parts, leading to lower labor and handling costs.

For several years, top management has been searching for ways to smooth out the jerky boom-bust cycles that traditionally plagued the company and played havoc with the work force. The company is only half to two-thirds of the way through the $1 billion engineering changeover, and jacking up production at this stage risks long delays in this program.

Quick Pace

"In an ideal world, I wish this ramp-up would have started a couple of years from now," says Ronald Woodard, head of the commercial-airplane group, who says the burst of orders is arriving "far faster" than he had expected.

The race toward faster production "is hurting this [re-engineering] program" and risking a slower implementation, says Dave Auer, vice president of strategic accounts for Cimlinc, a Chicago manufacturing-services house hired by Boeing to guide essential elements of the changeover. The flood of orders pleases Boeing, he says, but it's happiness "with a lot of pain in it."

Boeing executives don't dispute such assessments. Having encouraged an upturn that was too long in coming, the company can only "be responsive" to carriers now demanding planes, says Philip Condit, who assumed the chief executive's job from Boeing Chairman Frank Shrontz in April. "You would love to have everything all organized. I would love to take a year off. That'd be great," Mr. Condit says. "It doesn't work that way. You've got to keep the highway open."

One issue that arises is whether the company can increase its efficiency quickly enough to make money on all those planes being sold at lower prices. "That's a real good question," Mr. Woodard allows. But he says Boeing will remain profitable despite price pressure.

Part of what's bringing Boeing all the new business is simply that airlines, after holding off ordering in recent years, now badly need new jets. Demand has been surging in fast-growing Asian markets. And in the U.S., noise-control rules are taking effect, requiring that old jets be upgraded or replaced.

In this year's first six months, Boeing logged orders for 225 planes, valued at $17.6 billion – nearly double the total for all of 1994. Many big operators have been weighing in with huge new orders in recent months. Last month, Singapore Airlines signed agreements to buy as many as 77 of Boeing 777s, a deal valued at up to $12.7 billion. United Airlines is poised to place a $3 billion order for more 777s and 747s, while British Airways is expected to place orders valued at more than $4 billion for 30 planes. Asiana Airlines of South Korea and China's carriers are poised to order billions of dollars more in the months ahead.

Last Friday, Boeing confirmed it had received its first new-aircraft order from China in 19 months, $510 million for three 747s. With U.S.-China trade tensions easing, Boeing hopes China will approve prenegotiated orders valued at $4 billion or more.

The Production Rate

Boeing won't say how fast it intends to crank up production. Mr. Woodard says only that "we are definitely ramping up

substantially." The company already has said that today's 19-jets-a-month rate will increase to 34 by early 1998.

Some suppliers and others familiar with Boeing's strategy believe that is just the beginning. They say Boeing is readying its factories to produce as many as 24 of its smallest 737 jets a month. They expect each of three other models to increase to five or more a month, and the 777 to top out at seven planes monthly, compared with fewer than four today.

Of the production snafus Boeing faces, those on the 777 line appear to be worst. In a memo to wing-shop employees this month, a senior manager warned of production problems "that have plagued our program" and knocked the schedule 25% off its target. Starting two weeks ago, workers there were ordered to stay on the job for 10-hour shifts over 19-day stretches, and an annual two-week August shutdown has been canceled to try to get production back on track, the memo says.

To speed the 777s along, workers are being borrowed from 747 and 767 production lines, although machinists on those programs also report delays and complications stemming from the quickening pace.

The large-scale lending of employees and the hiring reminds some company officials of the late 1980s, when a host of design and manufacturing problems beset production and delayed deliveries of the first 747-400s. This time, there is an added twist: Boeing workers are still tense after last December's strike and are emboldened by having successfully drawn the line with management. The strike ended after the union won concessions in pay and job-security rules.

Proud and Fuming

Rancorous union machinists are fuming about the drive for greater productivity. They are proud to be making Boeing planes, they say, but the company asks too much and morale is sagging. "We're struggling already," says Ray Baumgartner, a 777 line worker who doubles as a union safety official. "What's it going to be like," he asks, "if the production rate on the jet doubles?"

Satisfying workers is a tall order. Some, including machinists who aren't active in union matters, are unhappy with the confusion caused by taking on new workers. Other line workers fault the jet maker for not hiring enough new help.

Bill Johnson, president of the 27,000-member Machinists Union District 751, says wounds from the strike are still healing, and members' expectations of the company and the union "are probably higher than they've ever been." He adds that while he backs members' complaints, "our biggest problem is right here at home, getting our members to realize that we've got an excellent agreement, excellent wages, excellent benefits and a really bright future."

Restraining employment is an essential aspect of the company's hopes of controlling costs in the reheated jet market. So far, Boeing has announced plans to add just 8,800 employees, less than a third of the total cut through layoffs and attrition since 1992. Boeing brass say they are determined to avoid the sort of mass hiring that would inevitably end in widespread layoffs once the boom cycle subsides, probably around the year 2002.

Fighting Airbus

But even as it seeks to limit payroll growth, Boeing is trying to stay one step ahead of its main rival, Airbus. To do so, it is considering developing two new variants of the 747, at a cost of $4 billion to $5 billion. They would be long-haul and high-capacity versions fitted with a new wing. Boeing is under pressure to go ahead with the new models because Airbus is planning a new plane, the A3XX, that would have at least the same range as Boeing's planned long-haul 747 and could ultimately contain more seats. If Boeing decides this year to proceed, it could get a two-year head start on Airbus, which is now seeking risk-sharing partners for its proposed new jumbo, which carries a development cost estimated at between $7 billion and $12 billion.

The European consortium, which is also under pressure to increase production, plans to ramp up more gradually than Boeing. Airbus expects to deliver 200 jets annually in 1998 and 1999; its high was 163 in 1991.

Boeing faces other concerns as the orders flow in. The cost of lightweight titanium has jumped 80% in a year, and long delivery delays have emerged because of increasing demand. Metal producers have been balking at the lower prices fixed in Boeing's long-term contracts.

Dance Floors

A more immediate supply problem involves a two-week-old strike of 870 workers at a Boeing plant in Winnipeg,

Manitoba, cutting off the flow of large upper-wing surfaces – "dance floors" in factory jargon – for the 747.

Boeing had advised customers in Saudi Arabia, Germany and elsewhere to replace those parts on existing planes. But some of the airlines that responded with orders – and scheduled major maintenance stops for installation – have found Boeing can't deliver on time. Internal memos show that the panels have been diverted to keep Boeing's production line going. Last week, convoys totaling 70 trucks from Winnipeg began arriving at Boeing's Auburn, Washington, fabrication center with an emergency load of tools and parts-in-progress to be set up to keep the lines running, employees and company managers acknowledge.

Boeing's race to boost output is worrying some suppliers, which are already struggling to cope. "It's like Boeing is already at 35 airplanes a month," says the president of one important subcontractor, requesting anonymity. "I think there's a freight train coming."

Staff Reporter Charles Goldsmith contributed to this article.

WORKED EXAMPLE: ATTACHÉ CASES

Situation

A small company in the Czech Republic makes leather attaché cases, which it exports worldwide. Much of the work is performed by hand. At the start of a planning period, the production manager had the demand in units as given in Table 12.1, for four of its major models over an eight-week planning period.

Table 12.1 Demand in units as given in Table 1.1, for four major models over an eight-week planning period

	Product			
Week	A	B	C	D
1	110	440	325	180
2	170	450	300	185
3	100	480	410	180
4	150	470	385	175
5	140	410	510	145
6	90	390	345	190
7	80	385	325	185
8	120	425	320	270

From its labour standards, the company needs the following labour hours per unit to produce these four different products:

- Product A: 3.25 hours;
- Product B: 2.05 hours;
- Product C: 4.28 hours;
- Product D: 3.85 hours.

Required

1 Develop the workforce loading data for the four products. Show the results graphically.

2 If the company has a permanent work force of 80, who work 40 hours per week, then illustrate the labour loading for the company.

Solution

1 The units demanded are multiplied by the unit labour hours and totalled for the whole production centre. For example, for product A in week 1 the units demanded are 110 and this multiplied by 3.25 gives 357.50 labour hours. The data for the four products is given in Table 12.2 and plotted in Figure 12.3.

Table 12.2 The data for the four products

	Product				
Week	A	B	C	D	Total
1	357.50	902.00	1391.00	693.00	3343.50
2	552.50	922.50	1284.00	712.25	3471.25
3	325.00	984.00	1754.80	693.00	3756.80
4	487.50	963.50	1647.80	673.75	3772.55
5	455.00	840.50	2182.80	558.25	4036.55
6	292.50	799.50	1476.60	731.50	3300.10
7	260.00	789.25	1391.00	712.25	3152.50
8	390.00	871.25	1369.60	1039.50	3670.35

2 A labour force of 80 people represents 80×40 or 3200 hours per week. Thus, if this figure is compared with the total column, there will (except for week 7) be insufficient capacity to satisfy demand. The company will have to adjust capacity by using overtime or part-time labour or by subcontracting some of the work. Figure 12.4 illustrates the aggregate loading.

Figure 12.3 Attaché cases: aggregate plan for four products.

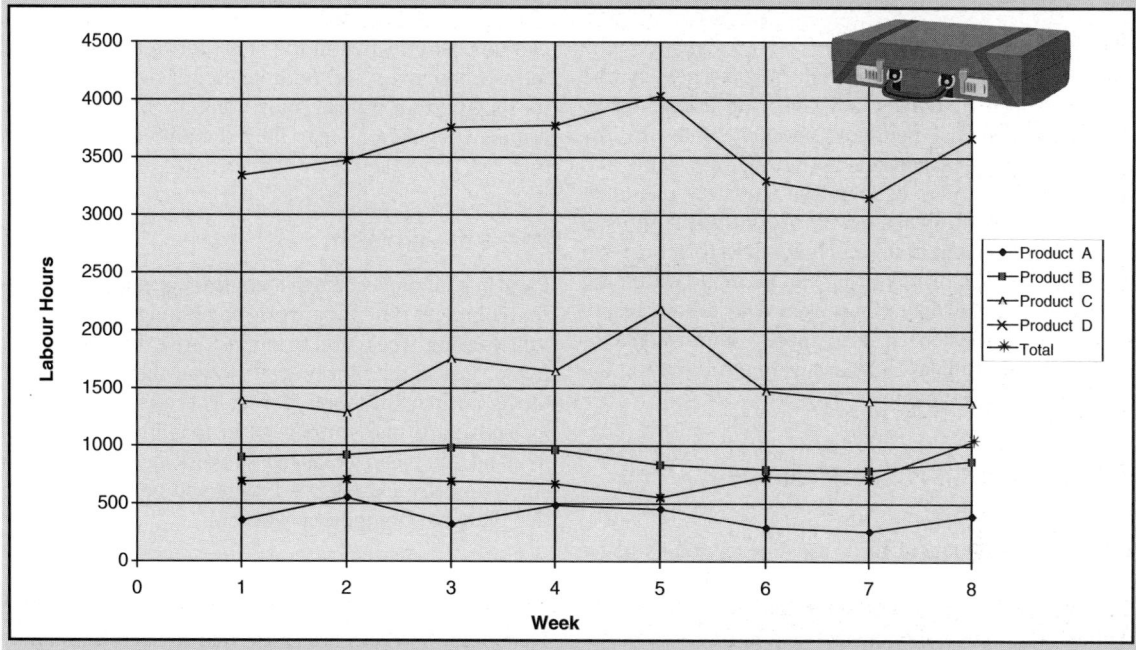

Figure 12.4 Attaché cases: aggregate loading for labour.

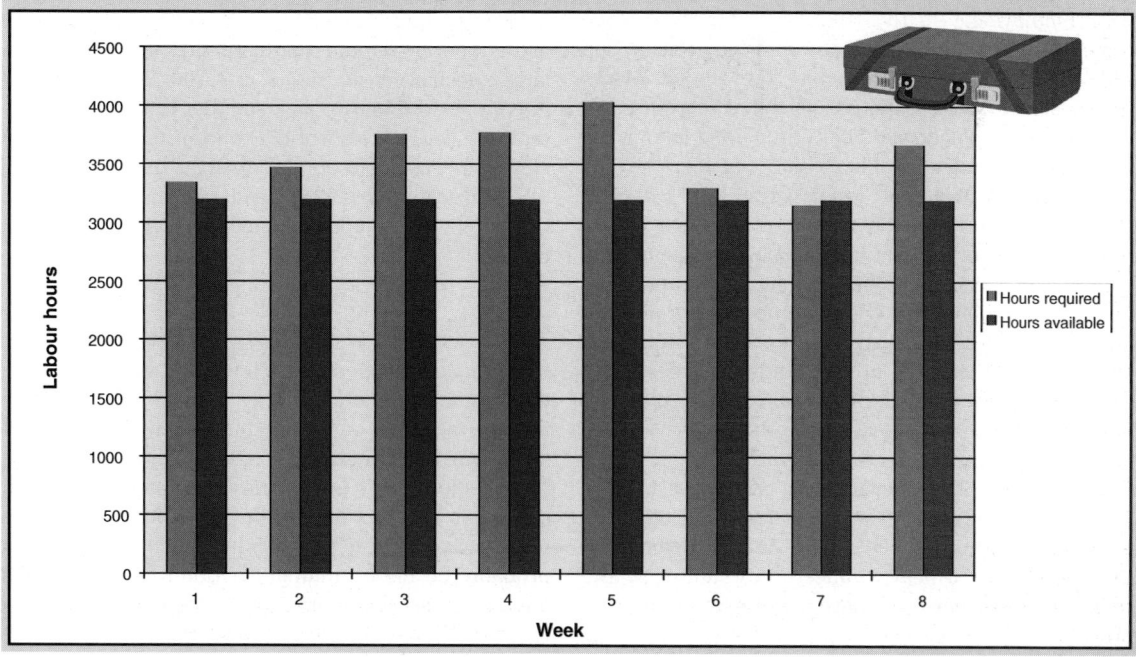

CAPACITY ADJUSTMENT TO MEET DEMAND

The capacity of an organization is governed by the physical space (buildings and land) the labour force, financial resources, materials and machines. In the short term, physical space is not normally variable and is considered as part of long-term capacity planning, which is covered in Chapter 25, *Financial Analysis*. Capacity adjustment in this context refers to short-term capacity changes, or those that can be made within the framework of the operations plan. The following are some of the ways to make capacity adjustments to accommodate demand increases without increasing the size of the physical plant.

Hiring and termination of the permanent workforce

The needs of the labour force are determined by using labour standards or the ratios that indicate how much time is needed to complete a certain task or to make a certain unit. Increasing, or decreasing, the level of the permanent workforce can be modified by hiring or termination, although the firm's flexibility to do the latter may be limited by union contracts or government regulations. These vary from country to country, so that, for example, it is easier to hire people and terminate their employment in the USA than in France. (See Chapter 3, *Site Selection*). In addition, for certain skills, it may be difficult to hire the labour locally. Hiring personnel of course assumes that there is sufficient space in the current facility. In adding labour, the operations manager should take into consideration the changes in marginal costs. (See Chapter 25, *Financial Analysis*, for further details).

The costs involved in hiring include advertising, perhaps the use of outside hiring agencies, interviewing and initial training. In addition, new hires are not immediately as productive as current employees because of the learning process and so, at first, they are more costly in their production output than the more experienced employees (see the section on the learning curve in Chapter 8, *Human Resources in the System Design*). In terminating employees, costs involved may include severance benefits. In addition, when a firm terminates the employment of members of the workforce, it leaves uncertainty amongst the remaining staff, which can have a downward impact on productivity. This has been a real problem in Germany and France in the 1990s.

Overtime

The current labour force can be put on overtime. This can be cost-effective in the short term, but in the long term productivity can be impacted if overtime is used for long periods. Furthermore, labour contracts or government regulations may limit the amount of overtime that can be worked.

Part-time workers

Part-time employees have a contract or agreement with the company that they work something less than the full working week, for example three days instead of five or just in the morning. However, they are still part of the permanent labour force. There is some flexibility with part-time employees in that in times of high demand, they can be asked to work more hours and, since they are experienced, they will be more productive than, say, temporary workers.

Temporary workers

Temporary workers are those that are hired on an 'as needed' basis. This policy can be cost-effective during peak demands. Retail stores and the post office use temporary labour during the Christmas season and vacation resorts use temporary labour during the peak summer period, or the winter period in ski resorts. In periods of heavy demand, manufacturing companies use temporary labour for tasks that are not particularly specialized. In the secretarial field the 'Kelly Agency' is well known as a supplier of temporary secretaries. One of the world's top ten temporary agencies is the Pasona Group in Japan, as the article in Box 12.2 illustrates. In 1994 it had 120 000 people on its books, 28 000 company clients, and revenues of $840 million.[4]

An extra shift

If a company is operating one or two shifts per day, a third shift can be added. This will take time to implement in the sense of finding and training the appropriate labour, and negotiating required union agreements. As a result of these initial costs, the company needs to be certain that this third shift can be kept operational for a period of time to make it economic. This would probably be for a minimum period of three months, but, of course, it depends on the product and the type of work. Experience has shown that the third shift (usually at night) is less productive than day shifts.

Box 12.2 Pasona non grata. Japan's workplace is changing, and Yasuyuki Nambu, cyclist, entrepreneur and friend of the great, is leading the way

THE boss of Japan's Pasona Group is a man of many virtues, but modesty is not one of them; certainly not modesty about his connections with leading politicians. The walls of Yasuyuki Nambu's Tokyo office are covered with photographs of him schmoozing with the global political elite: Margaret Thatcher (several times), Ronald Reagan, Bill Clinton, Mikhail Gorbachev, Prince Charles (again, several times), to name but a few. Strikingly, none of these pictures is of a Japanese politician.

It is Mr Nambu's entrepreneurial drive that seems to have caught foreign leaders' attention. He started his first company, a Buddhist kindergarten, while he was at university, employing fellow students as teachers. Noticing, on graduating, that Japan had lots of bored mothers with nothing to do and lots of frustrated companies with too few staff to meet surges in demand, he started Japan's first temporary-employment agency: the Pasona Group. Though it is not doing as well as it was in the days of the bubble economy (see chart), the business now has 120,000 people on its books, 28,000 company clients, and revenues in 1994 of $840m. That is enough to turn Mr Nambu into a billionaire; and his company into one of the world's top ten temp agencies.

As well as temporary employment, Mr Nambu has expanded into more than 100 other lines of business, including credit cards, child care, consulting, job placements for the handicapped and advice on computers. Three years ago he plunged into discount stores. Designers Collezione, his chain of ten stores, sells western designer clothes for prices one-third below those of most rivals, a feat it manages by bypassing Japan's network of trading companies and distributors. Mr Nambu's latest venture is to buy American luxury cars from American dealers and sell them direct to Japanese consumers, at 20% below normal prices.

All this has endeared him to bargain hungry consumers; but not to Japan's bureaucrats, who hate the fact that Mr Nambu's ventures get such friendly press comment. Even worse, Mr Nambu relishes being a maverick. He wears flashy suits, surrounds himself with pretty secretaries and loves talking about himself, particularly about his encounters with the famous. (Ask him how he got to know Prince Charles, and he replies that Ronald Reagan introduced them.) And he bicycles to work in scarlet cycling shorts.

Mr Nambu's main mission, however, is to demolish a cornerstone of Japanese society: lifetime employment. He sees a future of short-term contracts, just-in-time workers and down-to-earth relations between bosses and employees. In fact, the future is already arriving: temporary and part-time workers now make up more than a quarter of Japan's workforce. But the labour ministry is unenthusiastic. It has blocked a scheme of Mr Nambu's for helping to move middle managers from big firms, which want to slim, to small ones, which would like to expand but cannot afford high salaries, by getting big companies to subsidise smaller ones' wage bills. More seriously, the ministry allows temps to work in only 16 categories of job, which exclude nurses, telephone marketers, receptionists and caretakers, who are the stalwarts of most western temporary manpower agencies.

Handywork

At Pasona, Mr Nambu is consciously experimenting with new organisational structures in a country long dominated by big, hierarchical firms. His firm resembles western organisations, anatomised by Charles Handy, a British management guru, that have a core of full-time workers and a reserve of temporary workers who can be placed wherever they are needed. Yet Mr Nambu is sensitive to worries about the fragmentation of society, and is keen to refashion corporate paternalism, not destroy it.

As a talented manager himself, he is keen that Pasona should be the sort of democratic, fashionable company that young people compete to work for. He has set up a junior executive board, elected from among younger staff, to generate ideas and offer him advice. Every year, on the anniversary of the company's creation, he holds a "challenge day", when all employees are encouraged to suggest new ideas. He has designed his offices and furniture himself, making copious use of pine, glass and primary colours. It is not necessary to be a big company to give workers a feeling of "affluence", he argues.

To ensure that temporary workers feel that they too belong to Pasona, senior managers have their desks in the middle of the company's giant open-plan offices, so that they meet the temps when they collect their pay-cheques. Mr Nambu sends out 30 or so "herograms" a day: elegant, handwritten notes that express his appreciation for outstanding work. Much of the top floor is devoted to a stylish cafe, where workers can socialise, and a health centre, where they can get a check-up or a $3 massage.

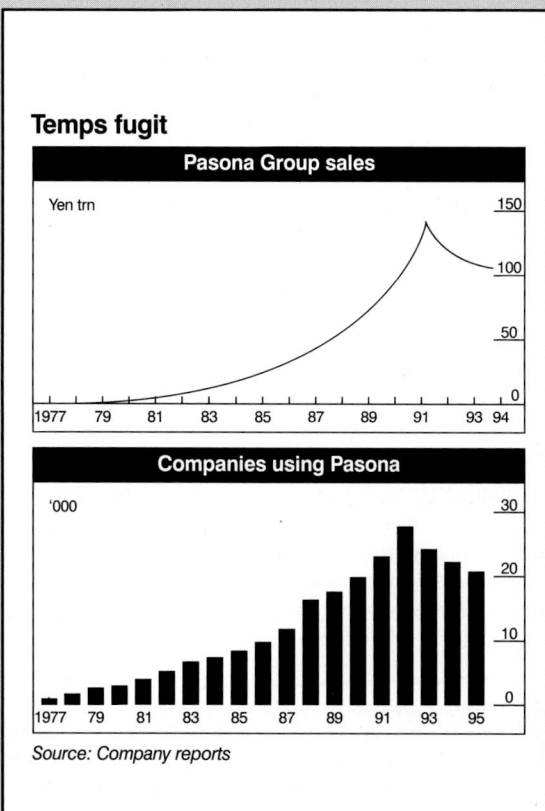

Temps fugit

Pasona Group sales

Yen trn

Source: Company reports

Mr Nambu clearly enjoys tweaking the establishment: he showers visitors with newspaper articles about his battles with the Japanese bureaucracy. But as the photographs on the wall suggest, he also yearns to be embraced by the establishment. A native of Kobe, he has given generously to the city's rebuilding fund. A keen patriot, he thinks that Japan's only chance of succeeding lies in getting rid of its hidebound business methods. A good test of claims that the Japanese establishment has become more open to outside ideas may be when Pasona's boss adds a Japanese politician to his gallery.

The Economist, 10 February 1996
© *The Economist*, London 1996

Weekend work

Another way of increasing output is to work at weekends. This again depends on union contracts and government regulations. Some stores in Europe are at present not allowed to open on Sundays (in France and Germany, for example), even though it is felt that there is customer demand.

Machines

Machine capacity is limited by the fact that machines can only operate 24 hours per day. Additional machine output requires purchasing new machines, leasing or subcontracting and these alternatives often require a long lead time. Planning, purchasing, installing and training operators on expensive equipment such as robots, printing presses and bottling lines would not normally be feasible in the time frame of one period of the operating plan. However, smaller mobile machines can be moved in and out of the operating area to modify capacity.

Purchased materials

Supplies of raw materials or parts can be adjusted up and down relatively easily if the supplier is well known, the product is unsophisticated (screws, sheet metal or plastic mouldings) and the supplier is close at hand. However, for more sophisticated items, computer chips, vanadium and carbon fibre, there may not be the same flexibility. When new sources of supply are developed, there may be additional costs payable to the new supplier.

Adjusting inventory levels

In manufacturing or warehouse/distribution, when demand is slack, inventories are allowed to increase by continuing production at some pre-established level. These can be used to satisfy demand at a future period. This approach has to be balanced against the cost of carrying inventory (see Chapter 11, *Inventory Management*).

Demands on backorder

Backordering means booking the customer's order and indicating that delivery will be made at some future date. On the company's books the orders then become backlog, noted in unit quantity, labour hours or financial terms. Backordering may be appropriate for custom-made products. However, clients may not accept backordering for standard items, which to the supplier firm could result in lost orders and/or permanently lost customers.

The concept of backlog is commonly used in service companies like engineering and construction firms. For these companies, the end product is a unique project. Work only begins when the company has received a contract from a client, and often up-front funding. The backlog is recorded as the number of hours reported as necessary to complete the work and is also converted into revenues based on the average rate for the hours on backlog. Changes in backlog indicate the growth, or contraction, of the firm. As an illustration, Figure 12.5 gives backlog data from the annual report for Fluor Construction a major engineering and construction firm based in Los Angeles, California.[5]

Subcontractors

Subcontractors provide flexibility to the client company in terms of capacity and often can produce the products cheaper than the client firm. This is one reason subcontractors are used, although a make-or-buy analysis would be appropriate first to see which is the more cost-effective approach (see Chapter 16, *Purchasing and Subcontracting*). However, in using subcontractors, the client company loses some control over the product quality and delivery date of the required items. In addition, it may be required to share company technical know-how that could be later used by the subcontractor to establish itself as a competitor to the client company. These concerns can be improved by careful selection, long-term relationships, and creating a climate of confidence between the client company and the subcontractor.

MODIFYING DEMAND TO ACCOMMODATE CAPACITIES

Another aggregate planning approach is to attempt to modify the demand at the customer level in order to impact capacity utilization or consumption patterns.

Figure 12.5 Backlog: Fluor Construction.

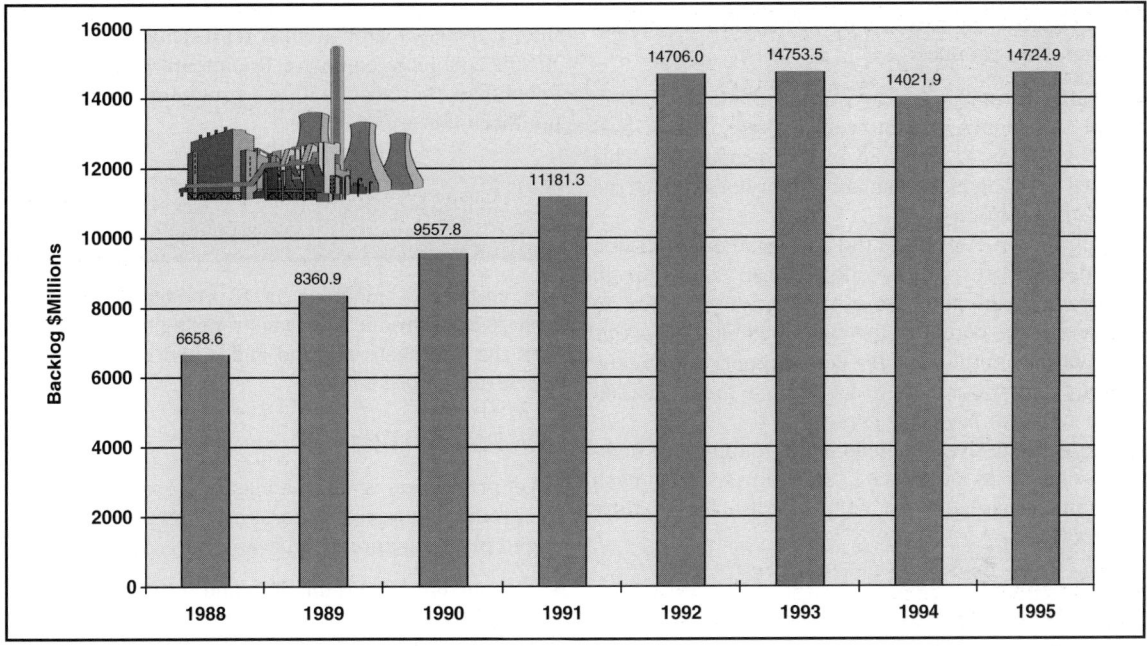

This might be because surplus capacity exists in the firm or because governments, for various reasons, wish to modify demand. Modifying customer demand is not as easy to implement as changes in production capacity, because it involves the hard-to-control external environment and customer habits. Further, the success of adjusting the demand is to a certain extent a function of whether the product is elastic or inelastic (see Chapter 9, *Forecasting Customer Demand*). Some approaches to modifying the external demand include the following.

Reduction in product price

A reduction in product price is common in the service sector when fixed capacity exists. The objective of the price reduction is to increase demand during slack periods to soak up some of the unused capacity. If customers can be encouraged to switch from periods of normally heavy demand to these slack periods, new capacity investment can be avoided. Examples include:

■ lower airline, train or ferry boat fares during off-peak periods;
■ cheaper electricity between 22:30 and 06:30, which is the case in France;
■ lower telephone rates between 12:00 and 14:00 or at nights and weekends;
■ lower cinema prices mid-afternoon or before 17:00;
■ restaurants before 12:00 for lunch or before 17:00 for dinner;
■ lower vacation package prices during off-season periods;

■ lower toll road fees in off-peak hours.

In manufacturing or distribution firms, lowering prices in sales or special promotions is also a way of reducing cumulated inventories.

Taxation and fees

Government taxation is used to modify consumer consumption for various reasons. This has an indirect impact on capacity utilization. For example:

■ Increased taxes on automotive fuels (as a means of reducing global warming) reduce the demand for these products and increase the capacity utilization of public transport.
■ Increased parking fees and road-user fees also increase the effective utilization of public transport.
■ Increased taxes on tobacco and alcohol reduce the consumption of these products and indirectly reduce the effective capacity of firms producing them.

Advertising

Advertising is a powerful way of modifying demand. Again, if as a result of this modification of the demand, the capacity utilization of the producer firm is changed:

■ health warnings on cigarettes to reduce demand;
■ sales advertising to increase the demand for end-of-line items.

Cash payments

Cash payments by firms or governments can modify demand. For example:

- The European Union gives cash grants to farmers not to produce certain crops or rear certain live-stock, in order to avoid excess production. This does not change the demand, but it does reduce the effective capacity.
- In France in 1994/1995 the government of Balladur, and then later Juppé, offered cash incentives to encourage the purchase of new cars in an effort to increase the output of the automobile industry. This artificial distortion had the correct impact during the grant period, but there was a slump in the car market when the car payments ceased.
- Firms themselves, such as kitchen appliance mak-ers and car producers, sometimes offer cash grants, or rebates, to enhance the sale of their products.

Creating a new demand

Here again, the objective is to make use of a fixed capacity that is normally underutilized in the period in question:

- Many business schools and universities are closed in the summer months, which means maybe the facil-ity is not used for up to a quarter of the year. Creating summer programmes can provide revenue without any increased in fixed costs (depreciation on the building).
- Similarly, at the high school level, adding teaching in high schools in the summer to create year-round schooling (Los Angeles, USA) will avoid building new schools.
- Buses can be used for tourist use during off-peak periods.
- Ski shops become year-round sports suppliers by dealing in surf boards (water), sail boards and swim wear in the summer months.
- Hotels can be used as conference centres during the day.
- Holiday centres can be used for seminars during off-peak holiday seasons; this is done by the Club Mediteranée, as the following extract illustrates.

Club Mediteranée

Although still famous for its image of sun and fun, nowadays Club Mediteranée SA increasingly spells commerce. On the French Riviera, near Nice, people from Ista, a French computer distributor, are getting an update on new IBM computer products, another meet-ing room is jammed with people from Babolat, a Lyon-based manufacturer of tennis equipment, while other business groups include Belgium's floor-tile company Inter Carrelages and German representatives from the Epson computer company. Rooms are equipped with telephones that accommodate computer modems, and fax machines are available.[6]

AGGREGATE PLANNING CHOICES IN MANUFACTURING

The choices of planning in a production operation include level production, synchronizing the production with the aggregate demand and a hybrid of level and synchronized production.

Level production

Level production is when a plan is prepared such that the production rate is uniform over time. This is a pre-ferred planning approach because:

- Labour hiring, termination, and overtime are mini-mized.
- Supervision is simplified as the operation is smoother.
- Resource planning is less complicated.
- Scrap rates are lower because of few production rate changes.
- Quality is usually higher as a result of the smoother production rate.
- Scheduling of maintenance programmes is simplified.
- Labour and material costs are reduced because start-ups and shutdowns are minimized.

Seasonal demand

When the product demand is seasonal, as for skis, sum-mer clothing, fertilizer, etc., a level production plan may be established based on the estimated total demand for a certain period (the whole year for exam-ple) and then this amount is averaged on a weekly or monthly basis to create a level production plan. In these situations there will be sharp inventory changes. When demand is low, inventory builds up and with it the associated inventory holding cost. When the demand is high, inventory levels are drawn down and this may be a critical period with the risk of stockouts. This situation is illustrated in Figure 12.6. Here the total requirement for the year is 21 000 units and this is broken down to a level production of 1750 units per month. There are periods in the winter months when demand is low, which results in a build up of inventory. In the summer months the demand increases, which makes the inventory level very low in August and September. If the demand is more than estimated, the firm will be in a stockout situation.

Figure 12.6 Level production and seasonal demand.

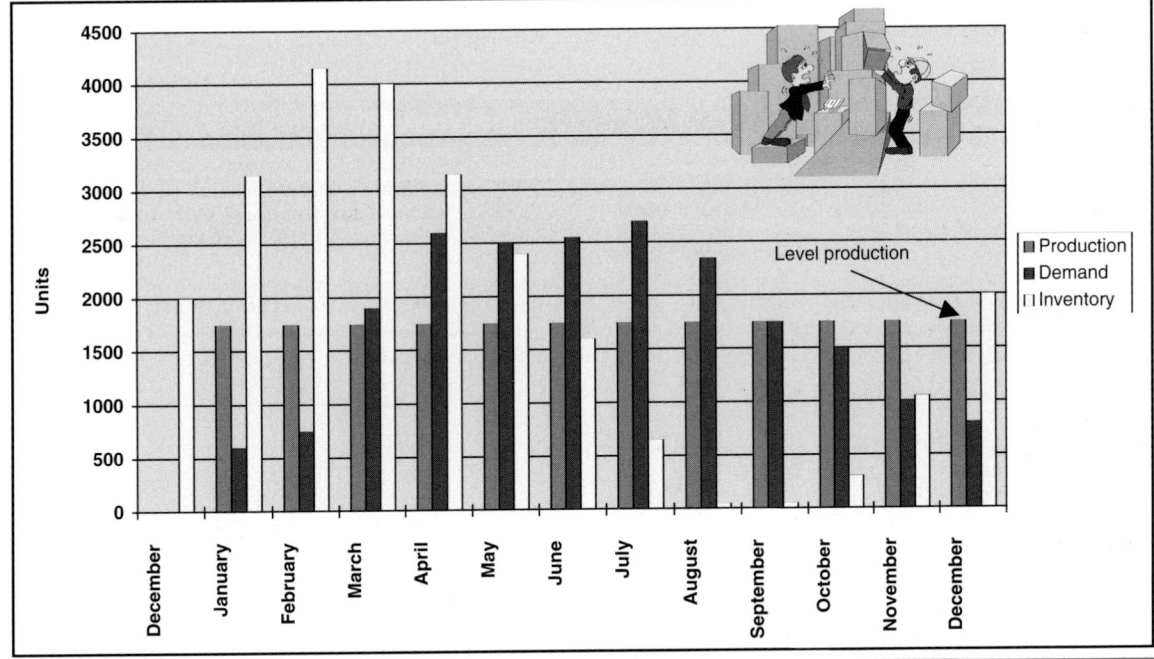

Produce-to-stock

Produce-to-stock operations will be the case for standard products, such as processed foods, industrial chemicals, appliances, etc. Although the demand for the products may not be seasonal, there is a certain fluctuation of demand. When level production is used, the finished goods inventories buffer differences between demand and production from period to period. Again, when demand is high, inventory is drawn down, and when demand is low, the inventory is built up. Thus during slack demand a level production plan results in higher inventories with the associated high carrying costs. The buffering action of inventory for a produce-to-stock situation is illustrated by the worked Example, *McCrea Co.* Question 1.

Produce-to-order

When goods are produced to order for customized items, finished goods cannot be used as an inventory buffer, since production does not begin until customer orders are received. This might be the case for furniture, where there is a large choice of upholstery available, tailor-made clothing or computer equipment for specific customer requirements. In this case, when a level-capacity aggregate plan is used, it is the backlog of customers' orders that buffers the difference between level production capacity and variable demand. The buffering action of a backlog for a pro-

duce-to-order situation is illustrated by the Worked example, *McCrea Co.*, Question 2.

Synchronized capacity with aggregate demand

Synchronized capacity with aggregate demand is the production of just the amount required to satisfy demand for any given time period. In this case the finished goods inventory is almost non-existent and so inventory carrying cost are low. However, synchronizing capacity with demand is not easy to operate, because labour, machine and material requirements will change frequently, which, apart from making planning difficult, increases production costs. Further, many firms do not have the flexibility to adjust labour needs up and down. The just-in-time method, discussed in Chapter 15, *Lean Production and Just-in-Time*, is an approach whose goal is to synchronize capacity with aggregate demand.

Hybrid of level and synchronized production

A hybrid of a level and synchronized production plan would be where a firm establishes a base-level production plan. Then, swings in customer demand, either up or down, would be handled by using temporary labour or overtime as necessary to accommodate customer needs.

The worked example, *Blackbird Co.* (Part I), illustrates the development of an aggregate plan using some of the variables discussed.

WORKED EXAMPLE: McCREA CO.

Situation

The McCrea Co., situated outside Edinburgh, Scotland, has a manufacturing operation for making office furniture. There are two work centres, Zone A, which is dedicated to producing standard items, and Zone B, which is reserved for customized items. In both work centres McCrea works according to a level production plan. For one particular planning period McCrea has the same quarterly demand for standard items as for customized units. This demand is as shown in Table 12.3.

Table 12.3 Quarterly demand (in units) in Zones A and B at McCrea Co.

Quarter	Zone A, (Produce-to-stock)	Zone B, (Produce-to-order)
1	30 000	30 000
2	40 000	40 000
3	50 000	50 000
4	35 000	35 000

At the start of the planning period, there are 4000 units of standard products in inventory and 10 000 units of customized products in the backlog on the company's books.

Required

1 Develop an aggregate planning schedule, by quarter, for Zone A of McCrea Co. Show the demand, production and inventory changes graphically. In establishing the production plan, use the average of the new annual demand for developing the production by quarter; that is, do not deduct the initial inventory.
2 Develop an aggregate planning schedule, by quarter, for Zone B of McCrea Co. Show the demand, production, and backlog changes graphically. In establishing the production plan, use the average of the new annual demand for developing the production by quarter. That is, do not deduct the initial backlog.

Solution

1 The quarterly demand is totalled to give the annual demand of 155 000 units. This amount, divided by 4, gives the quarterly production level.

Excess inventory over demand is added to inventory. A shortfall of demand over production is taken from inventory. The demand per quarter, the production level and the inventory levels by quarter are given in Table 12.4. The movement of material is illustrated in Figure 12.7.

Table 12.4 Demand per quarter, production level and inventory levels by quarter for Zone A of McCrea Co.

Quarter	Demand (units)	Production (units)	Inventory (units)
			4 000
1	30 000	38 750	12 750
2	40 000	38 750	11 500
3	50 000	38 750	250
4	35 000	38 750	4 000
Total	155 000	155 000	

2 The quarterly demand is totalled to give the annual demand of 155 000 units. This amount is divided by 4 to give the quarterly production level. Orders received are added to backlog. This backlog is worked off according to the level-production amount. The demand per quarter, production level and inventory levels by quarter are given in Table 12.5. The movement of material is illustrated in Figure 12.8.

Table 12.5 Demand per quarter, production level and inventory levels by quarter for Zone B of McCrea Co.

Quarter	Demand (units)	Production (units)	Backlog (units)
			10 000
1	30 000	38 750	1 250
2	40 000	38 750	2 500
3	50 000	38 750	13 750
4	35 000	38 750	10 000
Total	155 000	155 000	

Figure 12.7 McCrea: zone A, produce to stock.

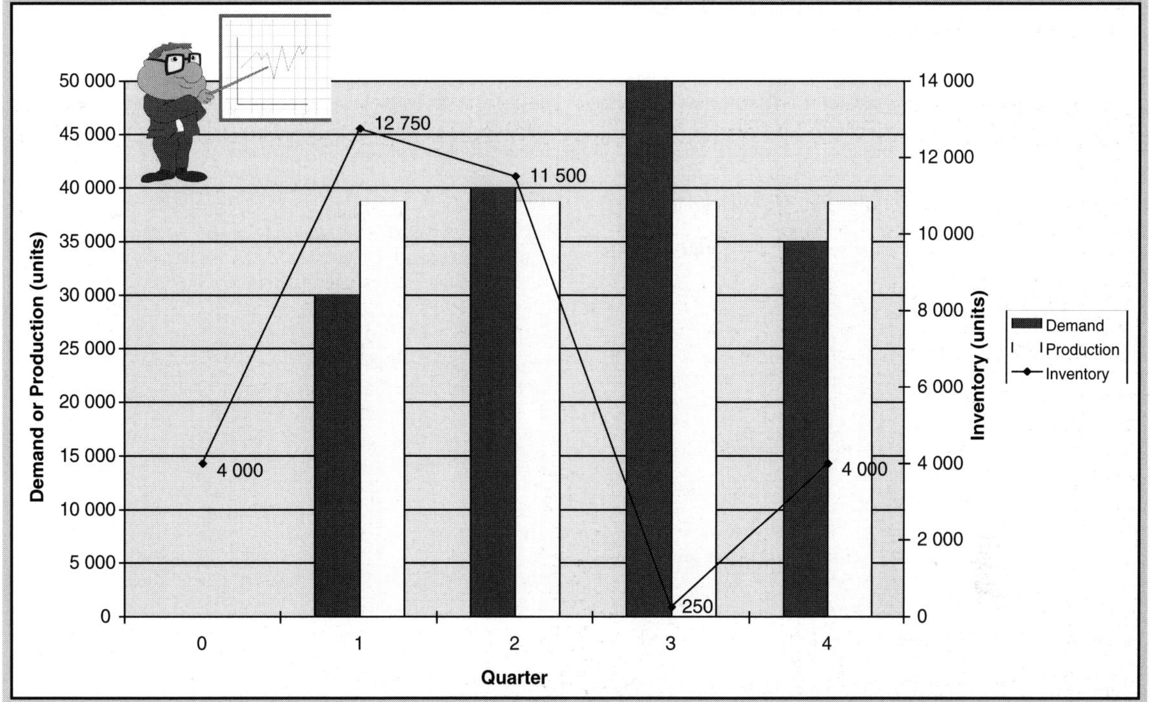

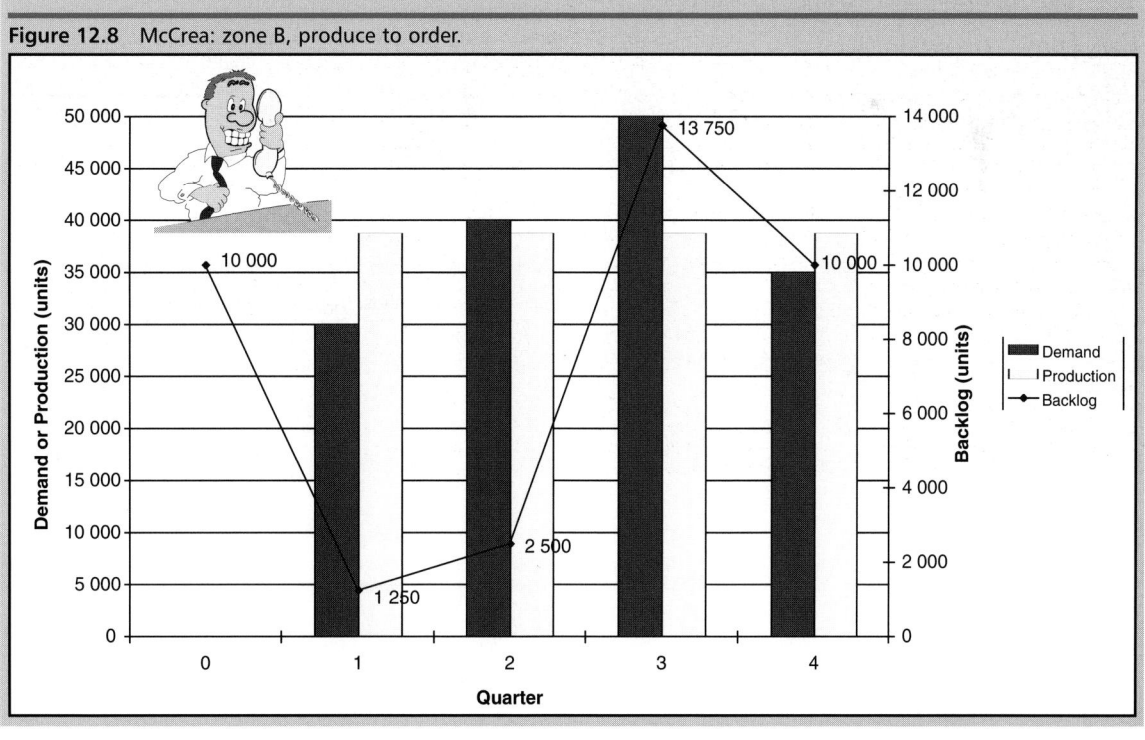

Figure 12.8 McCrea: zone B, produce to order.

WORKED EXAMPLE: BLACKBIRD ENTERPRISES (PART I)

Situation

Blackbird Enterprises, near Bristol, UK, manufactures and assembles telecommunication units, principally for BT (British Telecom). The month is now December and the company has developed the demand shown in Table 12.6 for finished products for the next calendar year.

Table 12.6 Demand at Blackbird Enterprises for finished products for the next calendar year

January	2700
February	3500
March	4700
April	1800
May	1500
June	3245
July	4250
August	3875
September	2975
October	1875
November	2500
December	1100

This month (December) the production level is 1800 units and there is exactly the workforce necessary to produce this quantity on the basis of a normal working week, without recourse to overtime or subcontracting. The ending inventory for December has been calculated as 250 units. Other operating data for the company is given in Table 12.7.

Table 12.7 Operating data for Blackbird Enterprises

Ending December inventory (units)	250
Stockout costs per unit	£35.00
Holding costs per unit per week	£2.50
Hiring cost per employee	£350.00
Termination cost per employee	£275.00
Labour cost per hour	£8.00
Overtime cost per hour	£12.00
Subcontracting cost per unit	£35.00
Labour hours per unit	3.20
Production December (units)	1800
Working week (hours)	40
Maximum overtime per week (hours)	10
Weeks per month	4

Required

Develop, as follows, two aggregate plans and indicate which is the preferred plan on the basis of the given costs. In developing the plans, round staff levels up or down to the nearest whole number. Take into account the inventory at the beginning of the plan period.

Plan A

Plan A is a synchronized aggregate plan where employees are hired or terminated as needed in order that exactly the amount required for the month in question can be supplied. Overtime is not an option in this plan.

Plan B

Plan B is to produce internally at a monthly rate equal to the minimum quantity demanded for the year, using only normal working hours, and to subcontract out production for the rest of the units. Workforce adjustments are to be made in January and the appropriate charges recorded for that month. Overtime is not an option in this plan.

Solution

Plan A

This is shown in Table 12.8:

- Production level in units is the amount demanded less the amount in inventory at the beginning of the period.
- Labour hours is the production level times labour hours/unit.
- Staff level is labour hours divided by hours in the month (160). If there is a fraction, numbers are rounded (up or down) to the nearest whole number.
- Actual production in units is the staff (rounded to the nearest whole number) times hours in the month, divided by labour hours per unit. Normally this is the same as the production level in units except where the staff level has been rounded up, (that is, the production level is slightly higher).
- Hiring is the amount needed to make up the deficit. Termination is when there is an excess of labour.

Plan B

This is developed with the same logic as Plan A and is given in Table 12.9.

From the two plans, A would be the preferred on the basis of total cost.

Table 12.8 Blackbird Enterprises: aggregate planning – Plan A production = demand (hire, and terminate accordingly). Production cost calculated by staff × hours/month. Assumption is staff produce maximum quantity. If only exact requirements were produced, holding costs would be lower. Aggregate demand is given in Table 12.6 and other data in Table 12.7

Month	December	January	February	March	April	May	June	July	August	September	October	November	December	Total
Demand	1 800	2 700	3 500	4 700	1 800	1 500	3 245	4 250	3 875	2 975	1 875	2 500	1 100	34 020
Labour														
Production, units	1 800	2 450	3 500	4 700	1 800	1 500	3 245	4 245	3 870	2 945	1 870	2 470	1 070	33 665
Labour hours	5 760.00	7 840.00	11 200.00	15 040.00	5 760.00	4 800.00	10 384.00	13 584.00	12 384.00	9 424.00	5 984.00	7 904.00	3 424.00	107 728
Staff	36.00	49.00	70.00	94.00	36.00	30.00	64.90	84.90	77.40	58.90	37.40	49.40	21.40	673
Staff (rounded)	36	49	70	94	36	30	65	85	78	59	38	50	22	676
Actual production	1 800	2 450	3 500	4 700	1 800	1 500	3 250	4 250	3 900	2 950	1 900	2 500	1 100	33 800
Hiring		13	21	24	0	0	35	20	0	0	0	12	0	125
Termination		0	0	0	58	6	0	0	7	19	21	0	28	139
Inventory														
Beginning	250	250	0	0	0	0	0	5	5	30	5	30	30	
Ending		0	0	0	0	0	5	5	30	5	30	30	30	
Average	125.00	125.00	0.00	0.00	0.00	0.00	2.50	5.00	17.50	17.50	17.50	30.00	30.00	
Stockouts	0	0	0	0	0	0	0	0	0	0	0	0	0	
Costs (£)														
Production		62 720.00	89 600.00	120 320.00	46 080.00	38 400.00	83 200.00	108 800.00	99 840.00	75 520.00	48 640.00	64 000.00	28 160.00	865 280.00
Hiring		4 550.00	7 350.00	8 400.00	0.00	0.00	12 250.00	7 000.00	0.00	0.00	0.00	4 200.00	0.00	43 750.00
Termination		0.00	0.00	0.00	15 950.00	1 650.00	0.00	0.00	1 925.00	5 225.00	5 775.00	0.00	7 700.00	38 225.00
Carrying		1 250.00	0.00	0.00	0.00	0.00	25.00	50.00	175.00	175.00	175.00	300.00	300.00	2 450.00
Stockouts		0	0	0	0	0	0	0	0	0	0	0	0	0.00
TOTAL		68 520.00	96 950.00	128 720.00	62 030.00	40 050.00	95 475.00	115 850.00	101 940.00	80 920.00	54 590.00	68 500.00	36 160.00	949 705.00

Table 12.9 Blackbird Enterprises: aggregate planning – Plan B (Production at minimum demanded, remainder subcontracted). Aggregate demand is given in Table 12.6 and other data in Table 12.7

Month		January	February	March	April	May	June	July	August	September	October	November	December	Total
Demand	1 800	2 700	3 500	4 700	1 800	1 500	3 245	4 250	3 875	2 975	1 875	2 500	1 100	34 020
Production														
Units	5 760.00	1 100	1 100	1 100	1100	1 100	1 100	1 100	1 100	1 100	1 100	1 100	1 100	13 200
Labour hours	36.00	3 520.00	3 520.00	3 520.00	3 520.00	3 520.00	3 520.00	3 520.00	3 520.00	3 520.00	3 520.00	3 520.00	3 520.00	42 240
Personnel	36	22.00	22.00	22.00	22.00	22.00	22.00	22.00	22.00	22.00	22.00	22.00	22.00	264
Personnel (rounded)		22	22	22	22	22	22	22	22	22	22	22	22	264
Hiring		0	0	0	0	0	0	0	0	0	0	0	0	0
Termination		14	0	0	0	0	0	0	0	0	0	0	0	14
Subcontract		1 350	2 400	3 600	700	400	2 145	3 150	2 775	1 875	775	1 400	0	20 570
Inventory														
Beginning	250	250	0	0	0	0	0	0	0	0	0	0	0	
Ending		0	0	0	0	0	0	0	0	0	0	0	0	
Average		125.00	0.00	0.00	0.00	0.00	0.00	0.00	0.00	0.00	0.00	0.00	0.00	
Stockouts		0	0	0	0	0	0	0	0	0	0	0	0	
Costs (£)														
Production		28 160.00	28 160.00	28 160.00	28 160.00	28 160.00	28 160.00	28 160.00	28 160.00	28 160.00	28 160.00	28 160.00	28 160.00	337 920.00
Hiring		0.00	0.00	0.00	0.00	0.00	0.00	0.00	0.00	0.00	0.00	0.00	0.00	0.00
Termination		3 850.00	0.00	0.00	0.00	0.00	0.00	0.00	0.00	0.00	0.00	0.00	0.00	3 850.00
Subcontracting		47 250.00	84 000.00	126 000.00	24 500.00	14 000.00	75 075.00	110 250.00	97 125.00	65 625.00	27 125.00	49 000.00	0.00	719 950.00
Carrying		1 250.00	0.00	0.00	0.00	0.00	0.00	0.00	0.00	0.00	0.00	0.00	0.00	1 250.00
Stockouts		0	0	0	0	0	0	0	0	0	0	0	0	0.00
TOTAL		80 510.00	112 160.00	154 160.00	52 660.00	42 160.00	103 235.00	138 410.00	125 285.00	93 785.00	55 285.00	77 160.00	28 160.00	1 062 970.00

AGGREGATE PLANNING IN SERVICES

The difference between many aggregate planning options for service firms and manufacturing is that in services there is little or no inventory to act as a buffer between customer demand and production. As such, the aggregate planning function is closely interwoven with scheduling. The following are some planning considerations and then Chapters 14, *Operations Scheduling* and Chapter 24, *Waiting Lines*, give more on the subject.

Restaurants

Almost all restaurants operate in a synchronized production mode, only preparing meals when there is customer demand and, because of the perishable nature of their products, scheduling periods are very short. The fast-food industry, such as McDonald's, Burger King or Kentucky Fried Chicken, which have relatively standardized products, often keep a small amount of finished products in anticipation of customer demand, although for most of these the inventory is held for a maximum of about seven minutes. Self-service restaurants prepare some of the food in advance so that it is on display when customers are in the service line. Full-service restaurants prepare a lot of the food on demand, except in the case of vegetables and desserts. Customers have the flexibility to go elsewhere if a particular restaurant is filled to capacity.

Consulting, accounting and design firms

Consulting and design firms have a fixed capacity and this is the staff. The work, by its very nature, is customized and so they work in a synchronized production mode, starting work when a contract is signed and putting other work on backlog when demand is higher than production capacity. Very often a firm's ability to start work immediately is a strong factor in being awarded a contract. The flexibility of these firms to meet high demand comes from working overtime and weekends, because here there are usually no regulations governing the amount of overtime these persons can work. When demand is low, the employees in these firms spend their 'non-revenue' producing time in prospecting for new work or updating their various standards.

Hospitals and medical services

Hospitals for in-patient care have a fixed capacity, limited by the number of beds available. Hospital out-patient care and doctors' offices are capacity limited by the staff availability. Production and demand are smoothed by using appointment schedules. Where feasible, hospitals are turning more and more to out-patient care for small surgical procedures (the patient comes in in the morning and is discharged in the evening) so as to be able to provide more bed space for longer-term patients. For emergency services, usually at the weekends when there are more accidents, hospitals may have extra staff or have a corresponding hospital where patients can be sent in the case of an overload.

Retail outlets

Most retail outlets, except for special orders, provide goods on demand. Their buffer between supply and demand is the inventory they keep in their storage area. When their wholesaler or distribution depot is close, they may have the flexibility to restock within a half day. When there are high demands in the evenings, or at weekends, stores increase their staff loading. Some retail outlets, Tesco in Britain is an example, are experimenting with using the Internet to permit customers to place orders and then have the products delivered. When this approach becomes popular, it will enable smoother planning for the retail outlet.[7]

The travel industry

Airline companies and railways use planning schedules to increase capacity during periods of high demand in the mornings and evenings, although this has its limitations at airports because of the limited number of landing slots and aeroplanes. Similarly, with railways, there are capacity limitations due to rolling stock and track availability. In periods of high demand customers have the flexibility to switch from one airline company to another, use a different route or take a later train. Furthermore, in Europe one has the flexibility to switch from plane to train, or vice-versa.

MASTER PRODUCTION SCHEDULE

Definition

The *Master Production Schedule*, MPS, is a key planning tool, with a time horizon in weeks or months (depending on the firm), indicating what end items need to be completed. These might be:

- finished products or consumer goods, to be shipped directly to the client;
- finished products to be placed in inventory;

- intermediate goods, or industrial products, to be dispatched to another firm;
- intermediate goods to be transferred to another section of the same firm.

The MPS is the pilot for all work centres and, as shown in Figure 12.2, it is the bridge between the Aggregate Plan and the Material Requirements Plan. In many instances, the MPS is a computer-driven tool linked to other modules of the planning function. It is planning that should be prepared in collaboration with the managers of production, sales and perhaps finance and is established considering the capacity constraints, the demands of clients and the financial means of the firm. The objective of the MPS is to develop a schedule of end items to be completed, when promised, so that client delivery dates are respected. It should also avoid overloading or underloading the production facility so that the system is optimized.

Rough-cut capacity plan

The master production schedule is developed from firm, or expected, customer orders, forecasts, inventory status reports and production capacity information. The most urgent orders are placed in the first available open slot of the MPS and, as all the orders are slotted, a rough-cut capacity plan emerges that shows the load of the production work centre in relationship to the available capacity. The load may equal the capacity, it may be underloaded or it may be overloaded. As an illustration, the demand data shown in Table 12.10 is for a manufacturing firm.

This data shows the scheduled units to be finished each week, in a time horizon of 13 weeks, according to whether they are committed (that is there is a firm order), expected (not a firm order but fairly definite) and forecast based on sales estimates. This tabular data is shown transposed into an MPS bar-chart in Figure 12.9 which shows the capacity of the facility, fixed by machine and labour availability, as 240 units each week.

Underloading

Underloading is the situation where, in the initial MPS, not enough production has been scheduled so that the facility is not fully loaded. In Figure 12.10 the facility is underloaded in Weeks 1, 2, 6, 9, 10, 12 and 13.

Overloading

Overloading is where too much production capacity has been scheduled. In Figure 12.10 this is the case for weeks 3, 4, 7, 8 and 11.

Balancing the master production schedules

The purpose of the rough-cut capacity plan is to see where adjustments can be made to balance the MPS. For the situation given, production units have been shifted from one time period to another to balance the load with capacity and thus create an optimized MPS, as shown in Table 12.11 and illustrated in the new MPS, Figure 12.10, which shows that the total units for each category have not changed but the system is completely balanced and the excess load is left for period 13. This final MPS is shown broken down into four time zones, or fences. This is something firms may do, depending on the rigidity of their planning programme.

Frozen

The frozen period here is shown for the first two weeks and is the schedule for all committed units. The implication is that definite plans have been made in terms of using staff, machines and materials; any changes within this time frame would seriously disrupt operations. As such, modifications in this period are usually prohibited because it would be costly to alter plans. Changes would only be made under extraordinary circumstances and then only with authorization from the highest level such as the vice president in charge of manufacturing

Fixed

This second stage of the MPS, shown here as covering weeks 3 through 5, is the programme for the remaining committed and some planned units. This time frame is considered as fairly rigid, though less than for the first two weeks. Plans may be modified in this section, but only under exceptional circumstances and any changes would be resisted as much as possible.

Full

This is the third stage of the MPS, shown here covering weeks 6 through 9 for planned and forecast units. Here, all the available production capacity has been allocated but changes might be made without an excessive increase in production costs. However, any effect on customer satisfaction is uncertain at this point.

Open

This is the fourth stage of the MPS, shown here covering weeks 10 through 13. Not all production capacity has been allocated in period 13 and this is where any new orders would be slotted.

Table 12.10 Demand data for a manufacturing firm

Week	1	2	3	4	5	6	7	8	9	10	11	12	13
Committed	220	180	160	45									
Planned			105	230	240	190	275	190	150	100	30	10	
Forecast								80	60	115	230	170	140
Total	220	180	265	275	240	190	275	270	210	215	260	180	140

Rigidity of the MPS

It may be felt that a firm is being very inflexible if it adopts the time-fence approach to planning and is not accommodating last minute changes for the customer. This is true, in that the schedule, once established, is not flexible in the early periods. However, this drives home that it is important for effective supply chain management that Production, Sales and Finance should be closely involved in the preparation of the master production schedule and should all make the commitment to support it once an agreement has been reached. Any last-minute changes in the MPS represents a cost to the firm, of which Production will probably bear the brunt, but in reality Sales and Finance departments belong to

the same organization so unnecessary costs are also their problem. Boxes 12.3 to 12.5 give real-world illustrations related to rigorous planning.

Updating of the MPS

The master production schedule is a dynamic (moving) tool and is usually updated weekly. When one week is finished, that week is deleted from the front, and a week is added to the end. The demands for the whole MPS are then re-estimated, with any changes taken into account, and if necessary the MPS is rebalanced. Accuracy of the data in the later part of the schedule is not as reliable as the early weeks, which are usually

Figure 12.9 Master production schedule: rough cut.

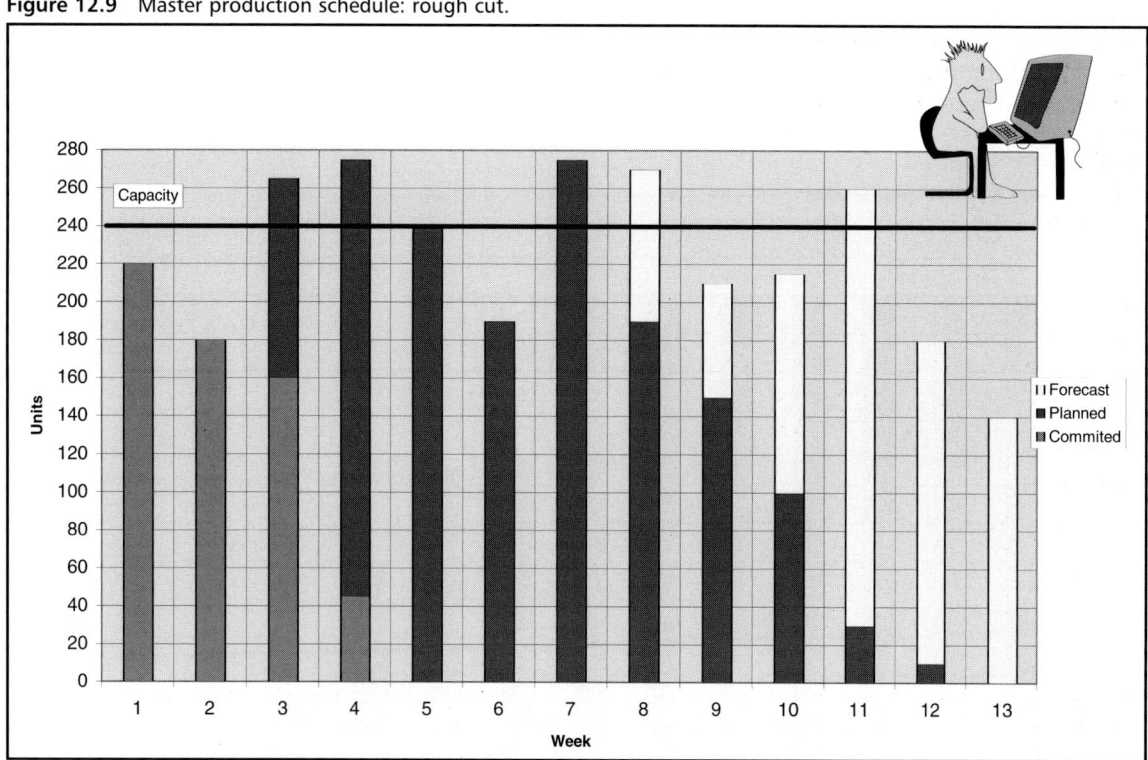

Table 12.11 Load data with balanced capacity

Week	1	2	3	4	5	6	7	8	9	10	11	12	13
Committed	240	240	125	0	0								
Planned	0	0	115	240	240	240	240	155	150	100	30	10	
Forecast	0	0	0	0	0			85	90	140	210	230	40
Total	240	240	240	240	240	240	240	240	240	240	240	240	40

dominated by firm customers' orders, whereas the latter weeks are dominated by forecasts.

MPS in produce-to-order

In a produce-to-order firm, it is the customers' specific orders that dominate demand management in the MPS. Scheduling work is from backlog and product forecasts may never be used. In updating the MPS, orders in backlog are assigned open production slots and the lot size (the number of products to produce in an order) is usually determined by the customer requirements. If a customer orders 1000 desks for example, ordinarily 1000 of these desks will be produced for that order. This approach to lot sizing is called lot-for-lot. (Chapter 13, *Material Requirements Planning*, gives more information on lot sizing.) Since produce-to-order firms

have many product designs, the number of product references that have to be placed in the MPS may be large.

MPS in produce-to-stock

In updating the MPS in produce-to-stock firms, product orders may come from the warehouse within the company or from the firm's own distribution centre. These orders are based on forecasts of future demand and thus accurate forecasting plays an important part in demand management in produce-to-stock situations. In the early part of the MPS, these warehouse orders, which were based on forecasts, may be backed up by actual customer orders. Lot sizes in produce-to-stock firms are a matter of economics. Small-size lots increase the set-up costs and large lot sizes increase carrying costs.

Figure 12.10 Master production schedule: balanced.

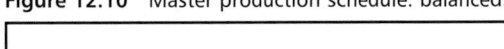

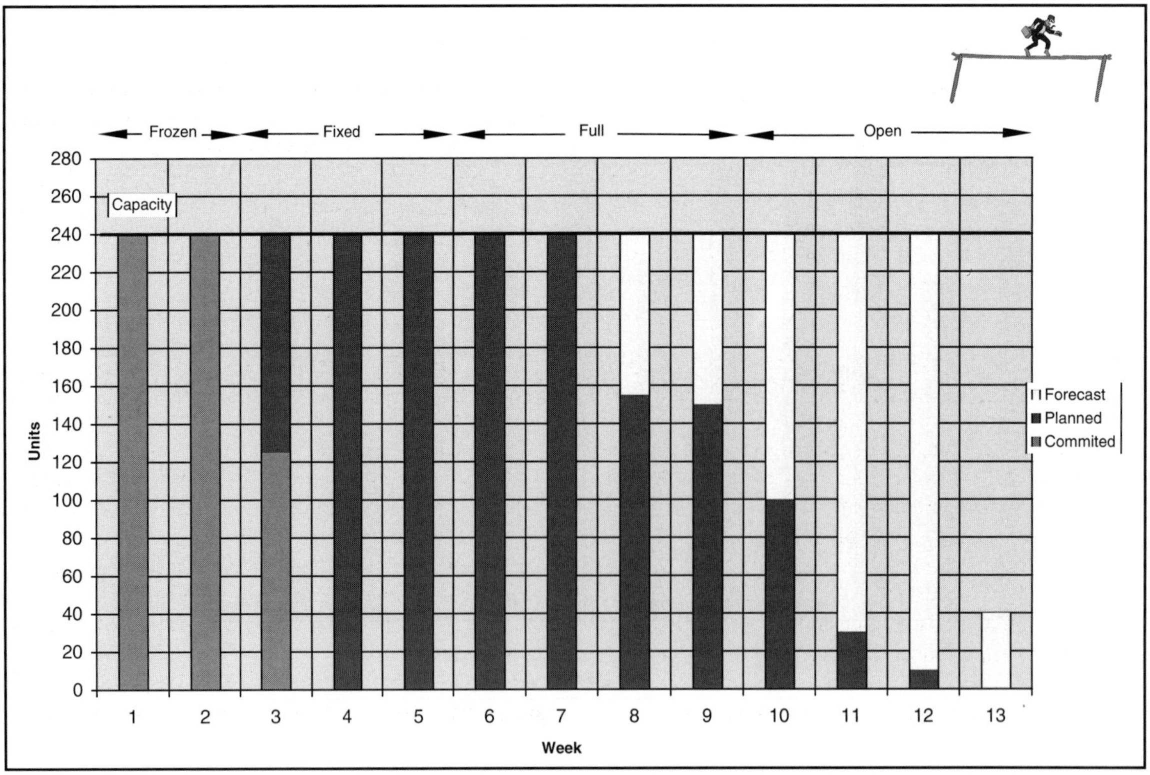

Box 12.3 Paint company

A small paint company prepared cans of paint of various colours for retail outlets. The company had three processing vessels, which it used to mix the various paints. It would set its MPS covering a two-week period. There were occasions when, in the middle of mixing, it received an urgent order from its biggest client for an order of paint. In these cases often it would stop the preparation in process, discard the paint, clean the vessel and restart the mixing operation for its major client. That is, it would interrupt its MPS in the first part of the time fence, rather than allocating new orders to the end. It was costly! The firm eventually went out of business.[8]

Box 12.4 Scandinavian Airways

Airline companies often illustrate the quality of their service by the percentage of on-time arrivals and departures. In the 1980s, Scandinavian Airways (SAS) had an advertisement on the radio touting the punctuality of its service. The advert went something like this:

There was a daily scheduled flight on a Boeing 747 that left Los Angeles around midday, direct for Copenhagen. A certain David Carlson, the president of a prestigious Swedish company, used this particular flight every week. One day, Mr Carlson called from his car phone while on the Santa Monica Freeway (the route that connects downtown LA with the airport) to say that he was going to be late. He didn't say in as many words, but the fact that he called the airline was an implicit request to delay the flight until he arrived. The SAS flight left as scheduled on time and Mr Carlson missed the flight. SAS booked Mr Carlson on an American Airlines flight to New York, and then on an SAS flight direct from New York to Copenhagen. The airline company did not want to hold up 450 or so passengers for just one person. What SAS was implying that it was not prepared to modify its MPS once it was put into action. A plane that leaves late will arrive late, and then be late for its next destination. That is, changing the plans has a costly snowballing effect.

Box 12.5 Business meetings

The time frame of an MPS can be likened to the conduct of a business meeting. The project management meeting is scheduled for 11:00. It starts at 11:00 with 19 of the 20 invited in attendance. Then, 15 minutes late, a senior executive enters. The project manager stops and repeats the events of the last 15 minutes so that the executive does not miss anything. That is, the project manager 'modifies his MPS' at the last minute. There is a significant cost related to the time wasted of those who arrived at the meeting on time!

MPS planning horizon and the supply chain

The planning horizon for the master production schedule can be from upwards of a few weeks to months. While it depends on the industry, the horizon should be at least equal to the longest cumulative end-item lead time. The cumulative end-item lead time is based on the length of the supply chain and is the amount of time to obtain materials from suppliers, produce all parts and assemblies, assemble items, pack and ready them for shipment and then deliver to customers. It is the end item with the greatest cumulative lead time in the supply chain that determines the span of the planning horizon, though, in practice, planning horizons are usually greater than this minimum.

SUMMARY OF KEY ELEMENTS

- An operations plan may have a time span of 18 months, depending on the firm. It is driven by customers' orders or forecasts and comprises an aggregate plan, a master production schedule and a material requirements plan.
- The aggregate plan is developed by converting the needs of end products into production resource requirements using labour and machine standards.
- Aggregate planning involves deciding how to select the most efficient mix of labour, machines, raw materials and outside labour services.
- Short-term capacity can be modified by hiring or termination, overtime, part-time or temporary workers, an extra shift, weekend work, using mobile machines, adjusting inventory levels, backorders or using subcontractors.
- Backorders is a concept usually related to custom products. When a client makes an order, this is a backorder to the client and represents a backlog on the firm's books.
- Product demand can be modified, impacting capacity utilization, by price changes, taxation and

fees, advertising, cash payments and creating a new demand.

- Level production is when the production rate is uniform over time. This mode is the easiest to plan, and probably the most cost-effective in manufacturing.
- Seasonal demand can be accommodated using level production. Inventory is built up in periods of slack demand and drawn down during periods of high demand.
- Level production is appropriate for produce-to-stock companies, as inventory can be built up or drawn down. The inventory acts as a buffer between demand and production.
- Produce-to-order firms normally do not keep an inventory of products. It is the backlog of the company that acts as the buffer between demand and production.
- Synchronized capacity with aggregate demand is producing just what is required. It is hard to plan as it means constantly changing the level of production resources.
- A hybrid of level and synchronized production is using a base-level production programme and accommodating changes by using temporary labour or overtime as needed.

- In aggregate planning in services there is usually no inventory to act as a buffer. Appointment schedules might be used to level out demand requirements.
- The master production schedule (MPS) indicates the quantity and timing of end-products. It is the bridge between the aggregate plan and the material requirements plan.
- The rough-cut capacity plan indicates the extent of underloading and overloading in production. A balanced MPS will optimize the production system.
- A well-developed MPS should be able to be used to respect frozen, fixed, full and open time fences to avoid unnecessary production costs.
- The MPS is a dynamic tool updated weekly. In produce-to-order firms it is the backlog that is used to make the updates and in produce-to-stock firms it is the forecast.
- The MPS planning horizon should be at least equal to the greatest cumulative total lead time in the supply chain from raw materials through to product delivery.

REVIEW AND DISCUSSION QUESTIONS

1 **Planning horizons**. An integrated oil company such as Texaco, BP or Shell might be involved with the following:
(a) searching for new oil fields;
(b) drilling for oil;
(c) building an oil refinery;
(d) refining the oil;
(e) delivering the oil from a domestic refinery to petrol stations in the same country.
(f) In addition, the petrol station has a retail store, which sells food items, maps, books, compact discs, maps and automobile accessories. The owner is responsible for purchasing these sale items.
What are likely to be estimated time horizons of each of the above activities? Which would fit into the long-, medium-, and short-range plans? Discuss.

2 **Part-time workers**. In both Europe and the USA, the number of part-time workers is increasing compared to those in full-time employment. Discuss some of the reasons for this situation.

3. **Adding a third shift**. Adding a third shift at night is an option in aggregate planning to increase capacity. However, experience has shown that quality of work and productivity on this shift are lower than during the day. What do you think are some of the reasons for this?

4 **Taxation**. Governments in Europe believe that one way to reduce the demand for petrol (and thus environmental pollution) is to increase taxes. What are some of the fallacies with this economic policy? What is its impact?

5 **Seasonal consumption**. What are the risks involved in the production, and inventory storage of:
(a) summer clothing;
(b) skis;
(c) beer?

6 **French Riviera**. In the months of July and August, the population of the French Riveria explodes with tourists, principally from other European countries. How does this 'demographic' change impact the aggregate planning of a food distribution centre that serves the retail outlets in the coastal towns?

7 **Time fences**. The time fences (frozen, fixed, full and open) in a master production schedule make sense from an internal planning point-of-view. Discuss the constraints these time fences would have on the operation of:
(a) a medical centre;
(b) a small business serving big clients;
(c) a consulting firm performing projects for big industrial firms;
(d) a farm that produces agricultural products and rears animals.

8 **Produce-to-stock/produce to order**. In developing a master production schedule, what are the advantages and disadvantages between produce-to-stock and produce-to-order?

9 **Technology**. What impact does new technology have on operations planning? Consider information technology, new products and processes.

EXERCISE PROBLEM: BLACKBIRD ENTERPRISES (PART II)

Situation

The situation for the firm Blackbird Enterprises as the same as given in the worked example, *Blackbird Enterprises* (Part I), earlier in this chapter.

Required

Develop two aggregate plans as follows to satisfy the client demand. Indicate which is the preferred plan on the basis of the given costs. In developing the plans, round staff levels up or down to nearest whole number. Take into account the inventory at the beginning of the plan period. Compare these two plans with the ones developed as a worked example.

Plan C

Plan C is to produce at a monthly rate equal to the average quantity demanded for the year. Workforce adjustments are to be made in January and the appropriate charges recorded for that month. Use inventory movements as a buffer between supply and demand. Overtime is not an option in this plan.

Plan D

Plan D is to establish a base level, using normal hours to produce at a monthly rate equal to the unit production level of the previous December. To meet additional demands, overtime is to be used up to the maximum permitted for this base rate. If this is insufficient, the rest of the requirements should be subcontracted out.

EXERCISE PROBLEM: GABRIEL JOB SHOP

Situation

The Gabriel Job Shop, in Watford, England, manufactures pumps and cooling units for oil refineries, chemical plants, oil-field processing units and other types of chemical plants.

The demand for the company's products can be divided into domestic orders for facilities in the UK, intercompany orders to Gabriel's subsidiaries in France and Spain (for European clients) and export orders to countries outside the European Union.

Gabriel develops its master production plan on a weekly planning schedule, using a time horizon of 12 weeks. The input data for the master production schedule for both the pump assembly and the cooling unit for Gabriel is given in Tables 12.12 and 12.13. The demand includes firm orders for domestic, export and intercompany clients. There is also a forecast demand developed by the company's marketing department.

Table 12.12   Gabriel Job Shop – Demand for the pump assembly

	Firm orders			
Week	Domestic	Export	Intercompany	Forecast
1	30	10	8	1
2	28	7	0	0
3	34	15	20	20
4	19	0	20	15
5	24	4	0	45
6	5	0	0	50
7	2	0	0	55
8	0	0	0	50
9	10	0	0	50
10	0	0	0	40
11	0	0	0	40
12	0	55	0	40

Table 12.13   Gabriel Job Shop – demand for the cooling unit

	Firm orders			
Week	Domestic	Export	Intercompany	Forecast
1	30	0	17	0
2	30	0	0	5
3	10	30	0	15
4	20	20	0	15
5	10	10	20	20
6	10	20	0	20
7	0	0	5	20
8	5	15	15	15
9	0	0	20	15
10	0	0	30	15
11	0	0	15	15
12	0	0	0	15

The company has an operating programme of producing the pump assemblies in lot sizes of 100 and cooling units in lot sizes of 75. In addition, it has a policy of keeping a safety stock of a minimum of 20 units for the pump assembly and 15 units for the cooling unit. The initial inventory at the beginning of the planning cycle is 80 units for the pump assembly and 50 units for the cooling unit.

Required

1   Develop a separate master production schedule for Gabriel, for the two products. A suggested plan outline is given in Table 12.14.
2   During week 1 the marketing department receives the following notification of order changes from clients:
■   a fax from its client in Saudi Arabia cancelling all the export orders for pump assemblies and cooling units originally demanded in week 3;

- a telephone call from its subsidiary in France cancelling all the intercompany cooling units originally demanded for weeks 7 and 8;
- a fax from a client in Kuwait cancelling all the export orders for cooling units originally demanded in week 8.

With only these changes, develop the new master production schedule for the two products and the composite master production schedule. What impact do these changes have on the production planning operation of Gabriel?

Table 12.14 Gabriel Job Shop – plan outline

Week	1	2	3	4	5	6	7	8	9	10	11	12
Client orders (domestic)												
Client orders (export)												
Intercompany orders												
Forecast												
Gross demand												
Stock available												
MPS												
Lot size												
Safety stock												

EXERCISE PROBLEM: KAYAK MANUFACTURE

Situation

A small family-owned business in Kajaani, Central Finland makes hand-made kayaks. One of its models, the Acirema, is sold exclusively through a distributor in the United States. For this reason, all the production costs are denominated in dollars. The production manager is developing her aggregate plan for the coming year. Through her US distributor she has obtained the forecast demand for the next year as 2570 units, broken down on a monthly basis as shown in Table 12.15

Table 12.15 Monthly breakdown of the next year's demand for Acirema Kayaks

Month	Forecast demand (units)
January	190
February	230
March	260
April	280
May	210
June	170
July	160
August	160
September	220
October	250
November	260
December	180

The demand is seasonal. Activity is heaviest in February, March and April to meet the summer season. In addition, activity in September, October and November is relatively heavy to meet the holiday season. The workshop currently employs 20 full-time people, each of whom can pro-duce 10 kayaks per month at a cost of $600 per unit. Inventory carrying costs are $50.00 per unit per month. Backlog costs are $100.00 per unit per month. At the start of the planning period in January the inventory level of kayaks is zero. From the forecast demand, it can be seen there will be a shortfall of 170 units. (Annual demand is 2570 units; maximum capacity is 12 months $\times$ 10 units/month $\times$ 20 workers = 2400 units.)

Required

Develop the following three aggregate plans, and select the least expensive.

Plan A

This plan involves hiring two additional people to commence working in January. One would only be on a temporary basis, working through May. Hiring costs are $1000 per employee and termination costs are $750 per employee.

Plan B

This plan involves hiring only one worker full time, at an additional cost of $1000. Any shortfalls are made up using subcontracting at $700 per unit. Maximum subcontracting allowed is 20 units per month.

Plan C

In this plan no new workers are hired. Any shortfalls are made up using subcontracting alone. Maximum subcontracting allowed is 20 units per month.

Since there is plenty of competent labour in the area, a new hire will have the same productive output as the current employees, so that there is no learning curve consideration.

EXERCISE PROBLEM: TRENEL

Situation

The Trenel Company, at St Bonnet, east of Lyon, France, manufactures fireplaces. The key components of the product are the hearth manufactured in cast iron and a glass window. The hearth is made in a foundry and the window is assembled by hand.

For one of its models, the Radiant 700, the company has firm orders for the first quarter of 1997 and a forecast demand for the remainder of the year. The number of these units is as given in Table 12.16.

Table 12.16   Trenel – demand for the 'Radiant 700'

January	190
February	230
March	260
April	280
May	210
June	170
July	160
August	160
September	220
October	250
November	270
December	180

Stocking costs for the Radiant 700 are estimated at 45.00 FF/unit/month. If an order is put on backorder there is a cost of 95.00 FF/unit/month due to additional paperwork and an estimated amount for loss of potential customers. The production cost is 1000.00 FF per unit. In addition, to

increase the production level from one month to another, there is a cost of 85.00 FF per unit. For a decrease in production, there is a cost of 75.00 FF per unit. These costs are due to machine adjustments and reorganizing the workshop. The company only changes its production levels at the beginning of a month.

For planning purposes, assume that the demand in January 1998 is 190 units. The demand in December 1996 was 180 units and the inventory at the end of 1996 was zero.

Required

1. Normally the production manager operates the manufacture of the fireplaces with a level production plan such that monthly production is an average quantity based on the yearly demand. Changes in demand are accommodated by adjusting inventory levels or using backorders. On this basis, what is an estimate of the annual production cost?
2. A consultant has suggested operating the factory by synchronizing production with demand to avoid accumulation of inventory. On this basis, what would be an estimate of the annual production costs? Besides just the cost, what are the disadvantages of operating a factory under these conditions?
3. Is there a less expensive aggregate plan using a combination of synchronized and level production on the basis that production is in lots of multiples of 5 (for example, 180, 185 or 190, but not 181, 186 or 192)?

For each of the three production plans, show graphically the monthly demand and production amounts. This would be a planning schedule.

EXERCISE PROBLEM: VEATCH CO.

Situation

Veatch Co. is a manufacturer of light aircraft components in Arkansas, USA. The company always prepares a nine-month aggregate plan to decide what is the optimum way to determine requirements for planning purposes, though this is modified when the demand requirements change. The estimated demand for a particular unit for the period January through September is given in Table 12.17. The current workforce is based on the production level in the previous December. Operating data is given in Table 12.18.

Table 12.17   Veatch Co. – Estimated demand for a particular unit for the period January through September

January	1785
February	1850
March	2100
April	1975
May	2300
June	2550
July	2100
August	1750
September	1500

Table 12.18   Operating data for Veatch Co.

Initial inventory (units)	400
Stockout costs per unit	$125
Holding cost per unit per month	$25
Hiring cost per unit	$70
Termination cost per unit	$85
Subcontract cost per unit	$85
Production units the previous December	1500

Required

Develop the following aggregate plans.

Plan A

In this plan the workforce level is varied to meet exactly the demand requirements. There is no sub-contracting. In January the beginning inventory should be used to reduce production requirements.

Plan B

In this plan production is at a constant rate of 2000 units per month. Subcontracting should be used to meet a 100 per cent service level every month.

Plan C

In this plan production is at a constant rate equal to the average demand for the planning period. Subcontracting should be used to meet a 100 per cent service level every month.

Plan D

In this plan production is at a constant rate equal to the minimum quantity demanded for the year. Subcontracting should be used to meet a 100 per cent service level every month.

Based purely on costs, which is the preferred plan? What other non-financial considerations might be taken into account?

EXERCISE PROBLEM: WHIRL

Situation

The Whirl company in Hamburg Germany makes microwave ovens for sale in Europe. The forecast sales data for one particular model in France, Britain, Scandinavia, Italy, and the German domestic market is given in Table 12.19. The holding cost for finished units is estimated at 4.50 DM per unit and there are 1500 units in inventory at the start of the planning period.

Required

1. Develop a master production schedule for Whirl on the basis that the company produces in lot sizes of 2500 units and that it has a policy of keeping a safety stock of 250 units. What is the impact on holding cost and set-up times? Show the MPS on a bar chart.
2. Develop a master production schedule for Whirl on the basis that the company produces in lot sizes of 2000 units and that it has a policy of keeping no safety stock. What is the impact on holding cost and set-up times? Show the MPS on the same bar chart as for Question 1.
3. Which do you believe would be the better policy for the company? Justify your reasoning.

Table 12.19 Whirl forecast sales data for France, Britain, Scandinavia, Italy and the German domestic market

Week	1	2	3	4	5	6	7	8	9	10
France	350	450	240	650	780	560	240	430	220	380
Britain	120	220	175	210	300	420	225	250	185	325
Scandinavia	80	45	85	95	125	140	220	145	75	50
Italy	45	75	85	125	45	0	95	125	150	220
Domestic	520	55	560	650	725	625	550	450	250	780

CASE STUDY: SCHUTZ CO.

Situation

Schutz Co., in Graz, Austria, is a small company of 50 people that manufactures control systems. The company was created in 1971 by three engineers who perfected a simple security device adaptable to private homes, hotels, banks and other businesses. The product was very successful and sold well in Austria, Switzerland and Germany. In the early 1980s Schutz received a large capital infusion from a private investor and a local bank, which enabled it to enlarge its manufacturing site in Graz. The increased capacity was necessary as a result of increased demand for the security systems and the addition of two new products, one for space heating and the other for restaurants. In parallel with that expansion, Schutz hired some very competent computer specialists and four commercial people to expand its market beyond its former territory.

All the products manufactured by Schutz are very high-tech and the technology employed is constantly being updated. The security devices operate by electronic sensing into a small central computer, which can activate alarms, flashing lights and a message to the local police station or other central area and also firmly lock doors and windows. The space-heating system, for gas or electric appliances, use somewhat similar controls and programming devices, which switch on or off according to need. In addition, a simple control card, together with peripheral devices controls the raising or lowering of sun blinds according to ambient temperatures. The other new product programs cooking/baking units for restaurants.

Schutz's business is now growing very fast. With Austria's entry into the European Union, it now has markets in all the 15 member countries. In addition, thanks to some clever marketing and to flexible systems, it has penetrated the North American market where, among other things, the increase in the crime rate has provided a profitable niche. Demand for the company's products is somewhat seasonal; there is a higher demand in the spring months for security devices (businesses and homes are sometimes closed during the summer period) and the space-heating and restaurant control products are more in demand during the winter period.

At the present time, Schutz is quite well integrated regarding the manufacturing and assembly of the units. All the electronic components, sensing units, frames, cases, computing cards and connecting devices are made by Schutz. It is these parts that were developed by the company and are very strategic to the finished product. Almost the only parts that Schutz purchase are various screws and fixation pieces, plus some plastic mouldings. The company has several patents on the various units it has developed, but some of these patents are beginning to expire. Competitors are becoming more and more dominant, particularly from Britain which can more easily penetrate the North American market.

With the expansion of its product demand, Schutz is considering changing its policy towards manufacturing and assembly. At the present time all the 50 employees are full time. However, labour costs in Austria are very high and the company is toying with the idea of subcontracting out about 25 per cent of its operation to a small firm in India, which is very competent in the high-technology field. The alternative to this is to further expand the facility in Austria and increase employment levels.

Required

Schutz needs to establish a new planning policy regarding anticipated growth. Discuss the advantages and disadvantages of the following long-term and medium- to short-term planning options.

Long-term options

1 Expansion of the Graz facility by adding new manufacturing capability.
2 Subcontracting 25 per cent of its business to India.

Medium- to short-term options

3 Using temporary hires during the periods of peak demand.
4 Building up inventories during slack periods for expected sales during peak demands.
5 Buy, rather than make, a larger proportion of the components on the European market.
6 Limit production to stock by putting orders on backorder.

NOTES AND REFERENCES

1. 'Dynamic Model: US Economy shows foreign nations ways to grow much faster. Denver may offer Europe, Japan lesson in the value of flexible capital, labour' (1997) *Wall Street Journal Europe* 20/21 June.
2. Peters, T. J. and Waterman R. H. (1982) *In Search of Excellence: Lessons from America's Best Run Companies*, New York: Harper and Row.
3. Cole, J. (1996) 'Sleepless in Seattle. Onslaught of orders has Boeing scrambling to build jets faster', *Wall Street Journal Europe*, 25 July.
4. 'Pasona non grata,' (1996) *The Economist* 10 February.
5. Fluor Corporation (1995) Annual Report.
6. 'Swinging singles grow up: Club Med mixes work and play: French resort company displays a more mature image' (1996) *Wall Street Journal Europe* 3-4 May.
7. 'No lines at Britain's first on-line grocery', (1997) *Wall Street Journal* 25/26 July.
8. Based on the author's work in the Los Angeles Basin in the 1980s.

FURTHER READING

Barman, S. and Tersine, R. J. (1993) 'Comparing two aggregate planning models', *Omega*, 21(5): 511–7.
Buxey, G. (1993) 'Production planning and scheduling for seasonal demand', *International Journal of Operations and Production Management* 13(7): 4–21.
Buxey, G. (1995) 'A managerial perspective on aggregate planning', *International Journal of Production Economics* 41(1–3): 127–33.
Ciarallo, F. W., Akella, R. and Morton, T. E. (1994) 'A periodic review, production planning model with uncertain capacity and uncertain demand: Optimality of extended myopic policies', *Management Science* 40(3): 320–32.

Claassen, G. D. H. and van Beek, P. (1993) 'Planning and scheduling packaging lines in food industry', *European Journal of Operational Research* 70(2): 150–58.
Das, S. K. and Sarin, S. C. (1994) 'An integrated approach to solving the master aggregate scheduling problem', *International Journal of Production Economics* 34(2): 167–77.
Dobres, I. (1996) 'Aggregate planning with continuous time', *International Journal of Production Economics* 43, Iss. 1, 1 May 1996: 1–9.
Erkut, E. and Ozen, U. (1996) 'Aggregate planning for distribution of durable household products', *Journal of Business Logistics* 17(2): 217–34.
Gferer, H. and Zappel, G. (1995) 'Hierarchical model for production planning in the case of uncertain demand', *European Journal of Operational Research* 86(1): 142–61.
Gilgeous, V. (1988) 'A functional objective search approach to aggregate planning', *International Journal of Operations and Production Management* 8(1): 48–62.
Goddard, W. E. (1995) 'Try master scheduling by capacity', *Modern Materials Handling* 50(9): 29.
Gupta, T. and Gali, T. R. (1993) 'Design and implementation scheme for an alternate process planning system', *Computers in Industry* 22(1): 15–23.
Kadipasaoglu, S. N. (1995) 'The effect of freezing the master production schedule on cost in multilevel MRP systems', *Production and Inventory Management Journal* 36(3): 30–36.
Kamien, M. I. and Li, L. (1990) 'Subcontracting, co-ordination, flexibility, and production smoothing in aggregate planning', *Management Science* 36(11): 1352–63.
Kuik, R., Salomon, M., and van Wassenhove L. N. (1994) 'Batching decisions: Structure and models', *European Journal of Operational Research* 75(2): 243–63.
Lewis, H. S., Sweigart, J. R. and Markland, R. E. (1992) 'Master scheduling in assemble-to-order environments: A capacitated multiobjective lot-sizing model', *Decision Sciences* 23(1): 21–43.
Lin, N.-P., Krajewski, L., Leong, G. K. and Benton W. C. (1994) 'The effects of environmental factors on the design of mas-

ter production scheduling systems', *Journal of Operations Management* 11(4): 367–84.

Macleod, K. R., Reeves, G. R. (1992) 'An application of the AXIS solution framework to multiple objective aggregate production planning', *Decision Sciences* 23(6): 1315–32.

Matt De, R. and Miller, T. (1993) 'A note on the growth of a production planning system: A case study in evolution', *Interfaces*, 23(4): 116–22.

Metters, R. D. (1993) 'A method for achieving better customer service, lower costs, and less instability in master production schedules', *Production and Inventory Management Journal* 34(4): 61–65.

Migliorelli, M. and Swan, R. J. (1988) 'MRP and Aggregate Planning', *Production and Inventory Management*, 29(2): 42–45.

Pan, L. and Kleiner, B. H. (1995) 'Aggregate planning today', *Work Study* 44(3): 4–7.

Ronen, B. and Pass, S. (1992) 'Manufacturing management information systems require simplification', *Industrial Engineering* 24(2): 50–53.

Scramm, W. R. and Freund, L. E. (1993) 'Application of economic control charts by a nursing modelling team', *Industrial Engineering* 25(4): 27–31.

Sridharan, V. and Laforge, R. L. (1994) 'A model to estimate service levels when a portion of the master production schedule is frozen', *Computers and Operations Research* 21(5): 477–86.

Tadei, R., Trubian, M., Avendano, J. L., Della Croce, F. and Menga, G. (1995) 'Aggregate planning and scheduling in the food industry: A case study', *European Journal of Operational Research* 87(3): 564–73.

Venkataraman, R. and Nathan, J. (1994) 'Master production scheduling for a process industry environment: A case study', *International Journal of Operations and Production Management* 14(10): 44–53.

Walker, W. T. (1991) 'Master planning simulator provides real-time feedback on plan effectiveness', *Production and Inventory Management Journal* 32(1): 54–61.

Wang, P. P., Wilson, G. R. and Odrey, N. G. (1994) 'An on-line controller for production systems with seasonal demands', *Computers and Industrial Engineering* 26(3): 565–74.

Zhao, X. and Lee, T. S. (1993) 'Freezing the master production schedule for material requirements planning systems under demand uncertainty', *Journal of Operations Management* 11(2): 185–205.

13 Material requirements planning

Objectives and overview

The objective of this chapter is to present in detail material requirements planning (MRP), its importance in the supply chain and how it is used in both operations and the global business environment. The chapter first presents the basic requirements for MRP-I, from product structure, master production schedule, inventory records file and lead times for product release and reception. The chapter then presents criteria related to lot sizing, a consideration in MRP, and discusses four methods: lot-for-lot, economic order quantity, periodic order quantity and part-period balancing. The last section of the chapter presents the closed-loop manufacturing resource planning systems, MRP-II, and how they integrate the whole planning function of the firm from the business and marketing plan, through to the production plan and shop floor planning and control. Finally, commercial enterprise resource planning (ERP) systems, for managing the entire organization, are reviewed.

MATERIAL REQUIREMENTS PLANNING I

The concept of material requirements planning (MRP) was developed and refined by Joseph Orlicky at IBM and Oliver Wight, a consultant, in the 1960s and 1970s[1]. It is a mathematical modelling tool for determining the needs of dependent components, such as raw materials, parts and sub-assemblies in a manufacturing or warehousing/distribution environment. An MRP system is computer based and companies may have their own developed system or have purchased one of the many commercial packages that are available.

Objectives of the MRP and the supply chain

The MRP is driven by the master production schedule (presented in detail in Chapter 12, *Operations and capacity planning*), the basic purpose of which is to indicate:

- what types of material, have to be ordered from outside, and in what quantities, taking into account current inventory levels;
- what types of material need to be manufactured internally, and in what quantities, taking into account current inventory levels;
- when to place these orders, either for purchases from outside or for manufacturing inside, taking into account the lead times for materials.

As a planning tool, the MRP provides precise control for operations personnel regarding the amounts and timing of deliveries of materials necessary to produce end-items, as indicated by the master production schedule. This control helps to avoid inventory stock-outs, to minimize excessive levels of inventory and to optimize the utilization of labour and machines. The MRP system is one of the major planning tools for supply-chain management linking the purchasing and manufacturing activities. When the MRP is coupled to a distribution requirements planning type system (discussed in Chapter 17 *Managing the Supply Chain*) the combination serves to manage the supply chain as a complete integrated operation.

Inputs/outputs for a material requirements plan

In order for the MRP to provide an accurate programme of material requirements, the following inputs are necessary:

- master production schedule;

- product structure on bill of materials;
- inventory file.

Master production schedule

The master production schedule is the driving wheel for the MRP. Early periods of the MPS are frozen such that operations departments can depend on this information. Middle periods are fixed, later weeks are full and then open. The MPS is dynamic, dropping a period once the operation is completed.

Product structure or bill of materials

The product structure, or bill of materials, is a diagram, an engineering drawing or a listing of all materials and quantities required to produce one unit of finished product, or end item. Every product in a work centre would have its own product structure. As an illustration, Figure 13.1 shows an engineering diagram, or product structure, of all the components that go into making a Bosch Electric Hand Drill.[2]

A product structure is often exhibited in a hierarchical relationship showing components and materials at various levels. The end product would be at the highest level (denoted level 0 or 1) and then components which go into making the end product at the lower levels. An example is shown in Table 13.1.

Table 13.1 A typical product structure

Part	Level
Finished product	0
Assemblies	1
Sub-assemblies	2
Raw materials	3

A product structure in a hierarchy form is illustrated in Figure 13.2. Rather than a hierarchical form, a product structure may also be presented in an indented form. For example, the hierarchical product structure, given in Figure 13.2, may be presented as shown in Figure 13.3 where the indentation corresponds to the next level.

Inventory file

The inventory file is a complete record of the quantity of each material held in inventory. A detailed file would show transactions, receipts, disbursements, scrapped materials, planned orders, order releases, projections of delivery dates, quantities of each materials to order and when to place orders. Also within the inventory file would be the lead times, or the time required to produce a production lot in-house or to receive a lot purchased from a supplier. To take into account the lead time, a requirement in one time period will necessitate the release of the order in some earlier period according to the established delay period.

When the inputs have been established, then the MRP will generate the outputs, which would be the purchasing requirements for products obtained from outside and production requirements for those materials produced internally. The input/output relationship is illustrated in Figure 13.4. The MRP is interrelated with all these element, so any errors in one can snowball throughout the system. This framework represents the original concept of materials requirements planning, or MRP I, an open system with no feedback loops between inputs and outputs.

Terms in materials requirement planning

Use of a materials requirements plan is widespread. However, because there are many commercial products on the market, the terminology used is often different although the meanings are similar. The following are some generally accepted terms.

Gross requirements

Gross requirements are the total quantity of material needed to satisfy demand in a time period. Some of the gross requirements may be satisfied by units already in inventory.

Available, or on-hand, inventory

Available, or on-hand, inventory, is material available for use during a corresponding time period. It may include units in storage left from previous periods, safety stock or scheduled receipts expected to arrive during the time period in question.

Allocated Inventory

Allocated inventory is material that is in storage, but is destined for purposes other than the material requirements plan being developed. Other purposes might mean spares or another production operation.

Safety stock

Safety stock is inventory that is not normally available for the operation in question. In this case, the material that can be used for the MRP programme would be determined from the relationship:

Inventory on-hand − Inventory allocated
− Safety stock.

Scheduled receipts

Scheduled receipts are inventory that is expected to be received from suppliers at a defined time period as a

Figure 13.1 Diagram of a Bosch Electric Hand Drill (reproduced by permission of Robert Bosch Ltd).

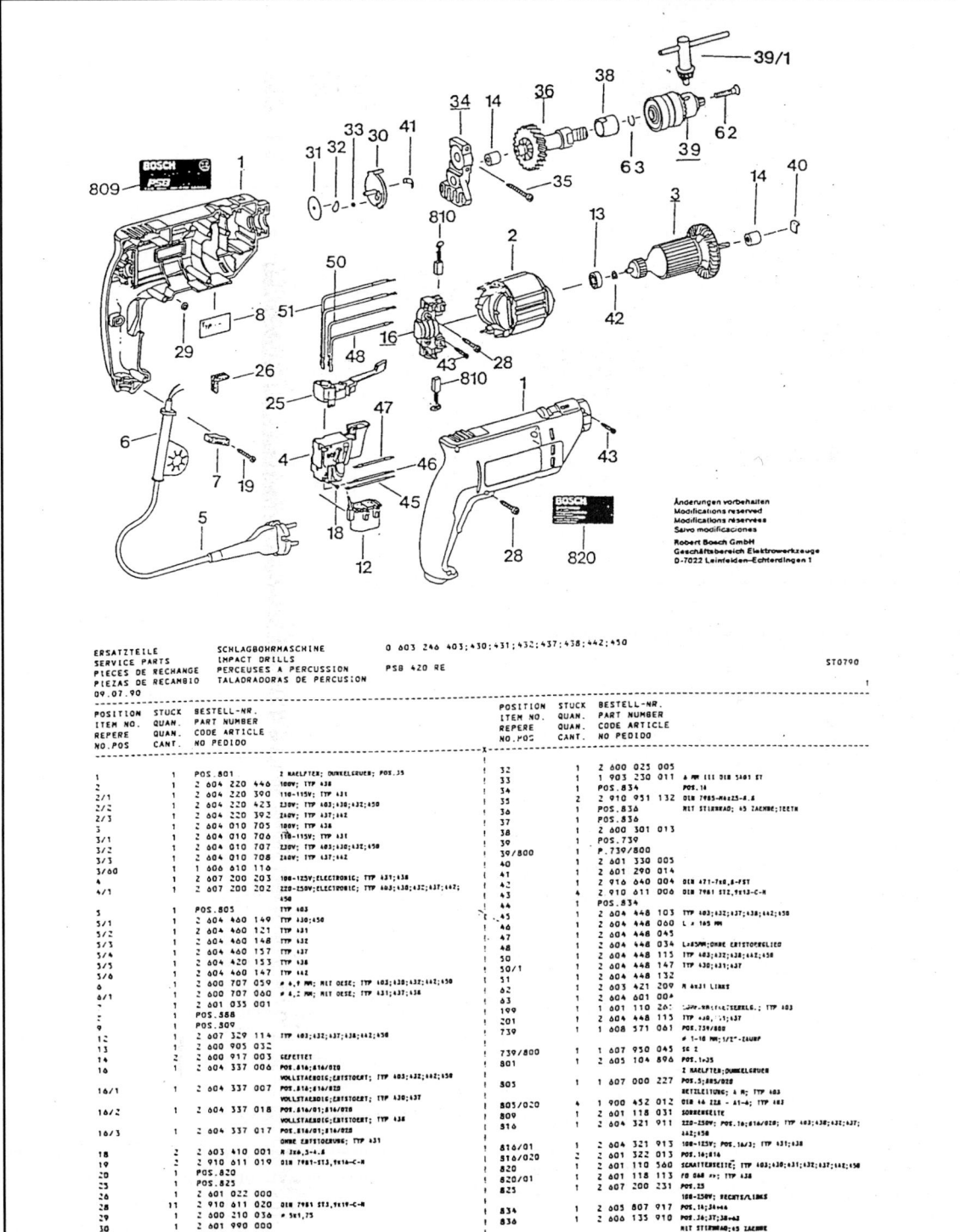

Figure 13.2 Product structure in hierarchical form.

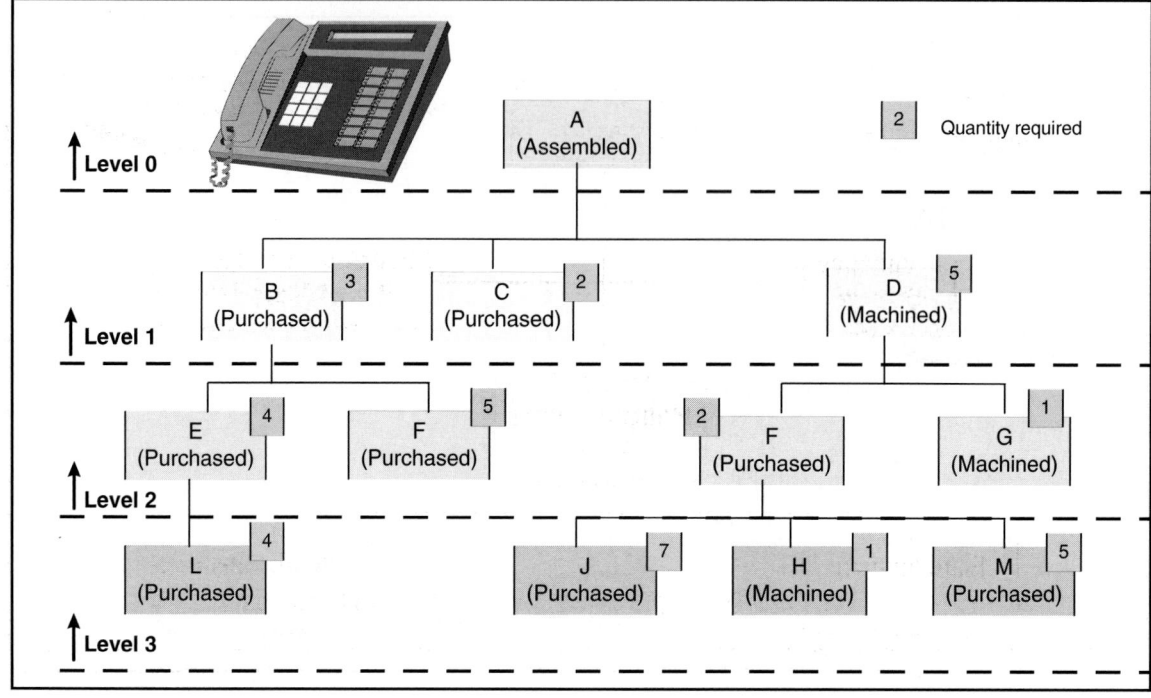

Figure 13.3 Product structure in indented form.

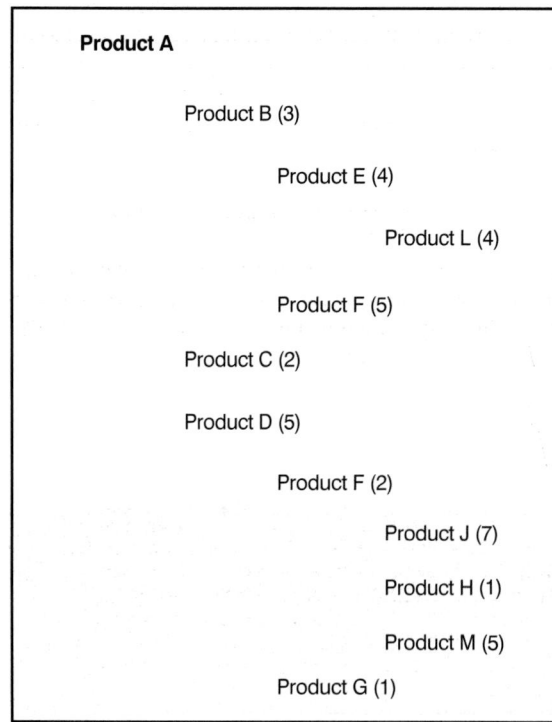

result of orders already placed, for example through open orders. Scheduled receipts are often assumed to be available for use during the time period in question. Scheduled receipts are not the same as planned ordered receipts.

Net requirements

Net requirements are the quantity of material needed to meet the scheduled demand:

$$\text{Net requirements} = \text{Gross requirements} - \text{Inventory available.}$$

Planned ordered releases

Planned ordered releases are the quantity of units that must be planned to be released in a certain time period, so that they are available to meet planned ordered receipts at a future date. The lead time is the time difference between planned ordered releases and planned ordered receipts.

Planned ordered receipts

Planned ordered receipts are the quantity of material planned to be received in order to meet the net requirements. There may be a lot-size limitation resulting in planned ordered receipts being greater than net requirements. In this case, excess inventory goes into storage for the next period.

Figure 13.4 Needs and output of a material requirements plan (MRP 1).

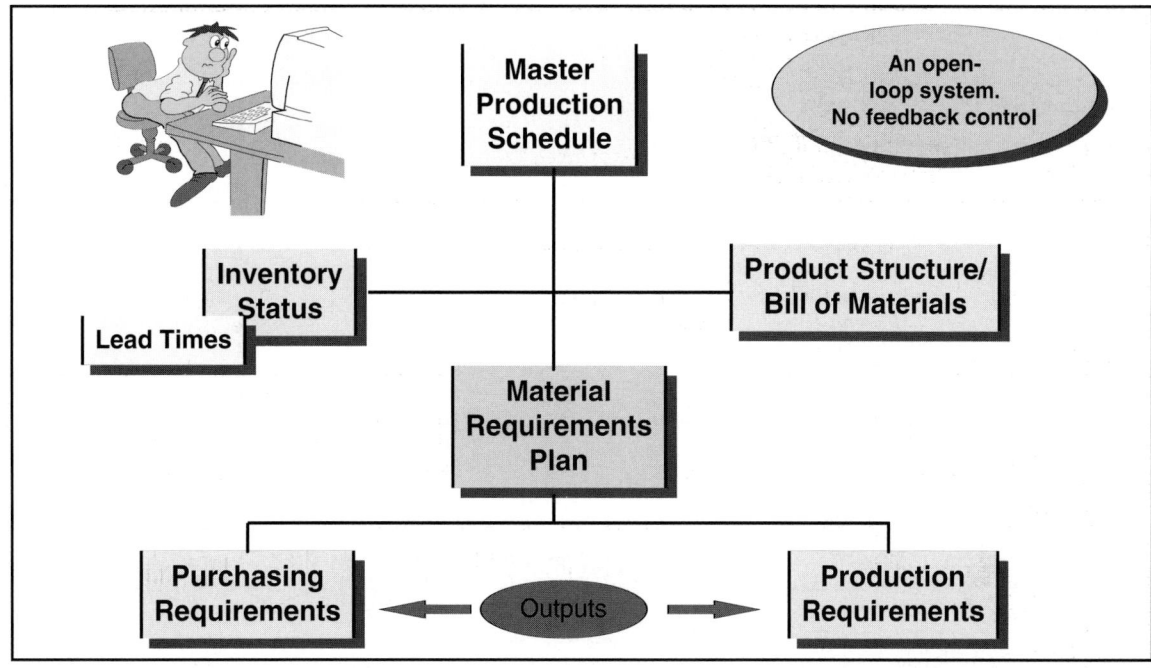

Yield rate

Ideally, when a product is made from components and raw materials, it is hoped that 100 per cent of the required materials are used. However, this may not be the case, because some parts may not be according to specification, they may be damaged in the work centre or there may be waste. In this case, the yield of components needed at a higher level will be less than actually put into operation at the lower level. The yield rate is the percentage of starting material that actually ends up in the product. It takes into account the proportion of material that does not conform to requirements and, as such, is unusable.

The yield rate needs to be known when calculating lot sizes since, if material is lost during an operation, the actual order quantity will need to be greater than net requirements. Actual order quantity Q is given by the relationship:

$$Q = \frac{\text{net requirements}}{100 - \text{scrap percentage}}$$

where $(100 - \text{scrap percentage})$ is the yield rate.

For example, if the net requirements of a subassembly unit in a lot-for-lot ordering system are 800 units and the estimated loss is 4 per cent, then the actual quantity to be ordered is (converting the percentages to proportions):

$$Q = \frac{800}{1.00 - 0.04} = 834 \text{ units (rounding up)}.$$

The development of a material requirements plan, illustrating the concepts discussed is demonstrated with two following worked examples, *Plastic Products Co.* (Part 1) and *Farley Co.*

WORKED EXAMPLE: PLASTIC PRODUCTS CO. (PART I)

Situation

The Plastic Products Co., located near Glasgow, Scotland, is a manufacturer of plastic products including industrial and consumer rubbish containers and large rigid PVC packing boxes. An exploded diagram of one of its models is given in Figure 13.5. The structure of this model is given in Figure 13.6. The company receives an order for 280 of the rubbish containers from the City of Manchester to be delivered from the production site at the end of week 7. In addition, it receives an order from the City of Newcastle for 350 units to be ready at the end of week 8. The bill of materials, component source and current inventory levels are given in Table 13.2.

Table 13.2 Plastic Products Co. – The bill of materials, component source and current inventory levels

Description	Reference	Units in product	Level	Source	Lead time	Inventory on hand
Waste container	WDC-1455	1	0	Asembled	1	25
Body	BDY-137	1	1	Injection mould	1	19
Cover	COV-10	1	1	Injection mould	1	17
Clips	CLP-74	4	2	Purchased	2	80
Front pivot wheel assembly	PIV-958	2	2	Assembled	1	54
Rear brake wheel assembly	BRK-452	2	2	Assembled	1	12
Stirrup assembly	STP-589	1	2	Assembled	1	56
Plug assembly	PGA-45	1	2	Assembled	1	21
Axle rods	AXL-21	4	2	Purchased	2	68
Wheel	WHF-85	1	3	Purchased	2	69
Screws	SCW-326	4	3	Purchased	1	250
Bracket	BKF-991	1	3	Purchased	2	17
Wheel	WHR-98	1	3	Purchased	2	25
Bracket	BKR-891	1	3	Purchased	3	23
Steel bar	STB-56	1	3	Purchased	3	6
Rivets	RVT-486	11	3	Purchased	2	5
Plug	PLG-142	1	3	Manufactured	1	2
Gasket	GSK-78	1	3	Manufactured	1	5

Figure 13.5 Plastic Products Co. – diagram of industrial waste container WDC-1455.

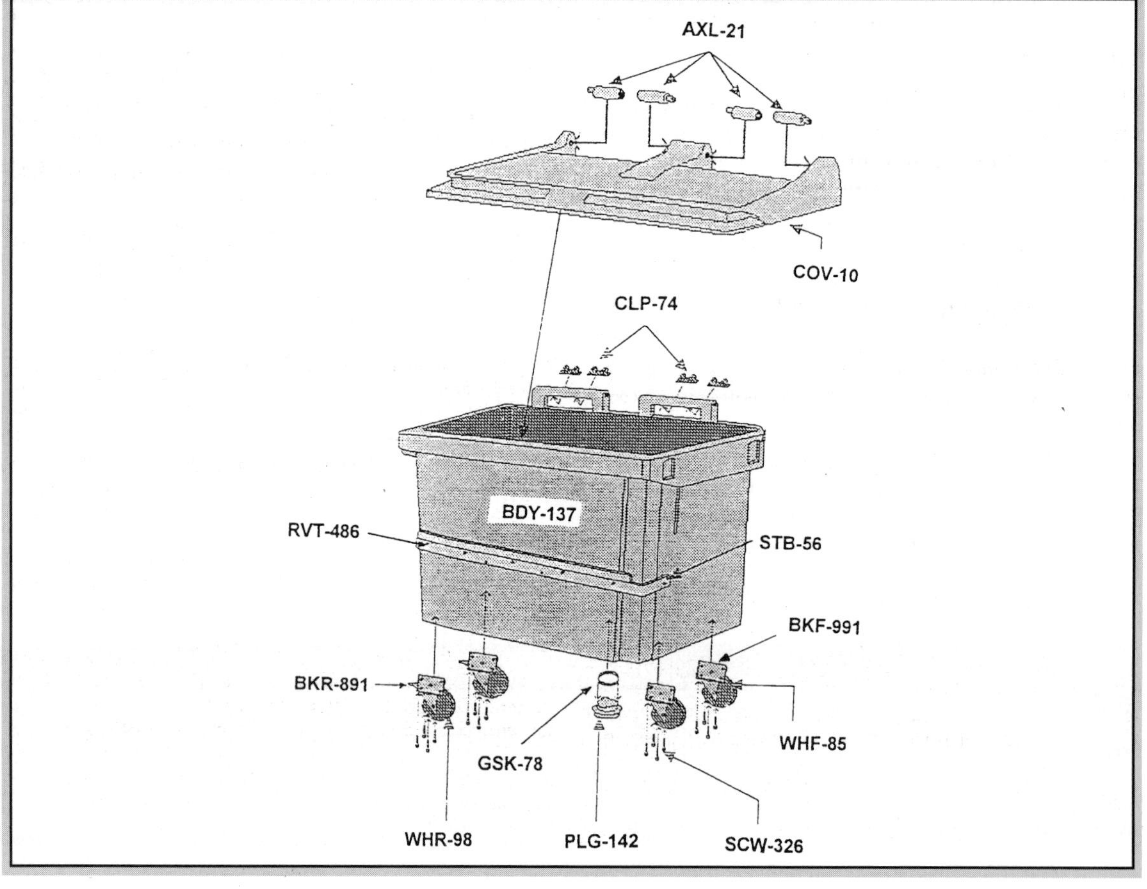

Figure 13.6 Structure of an industrial waste disposal container.

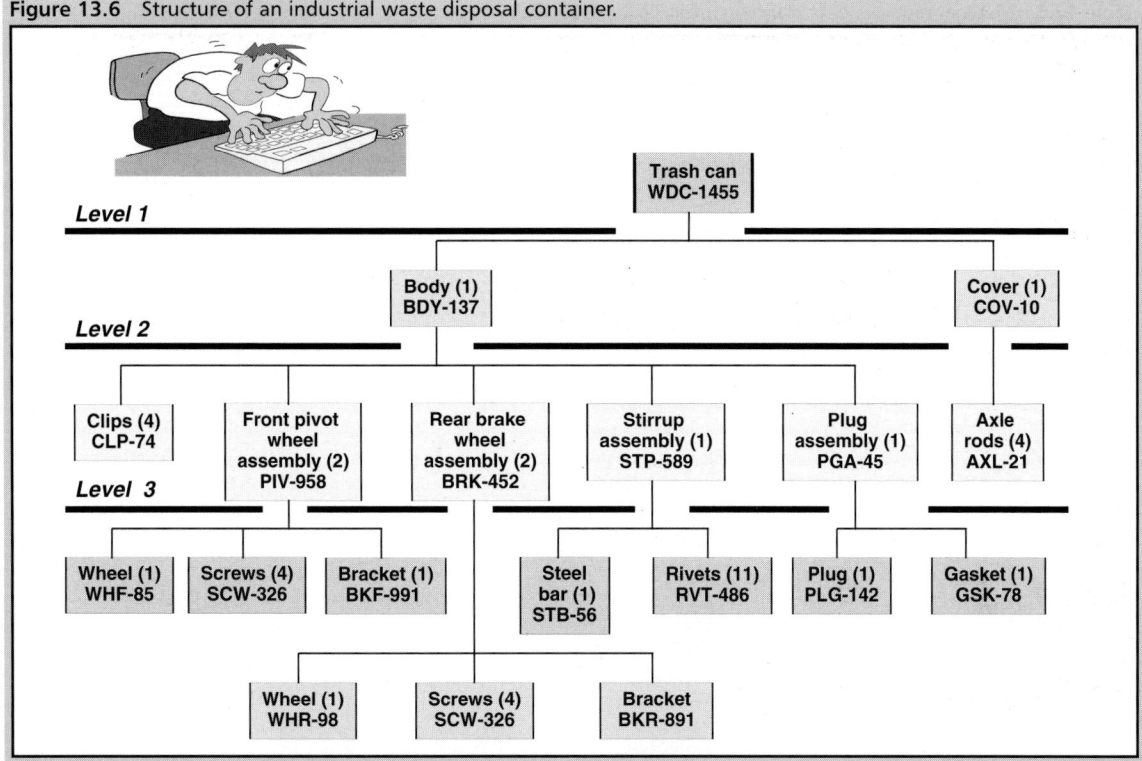

Required

Develop a material requirements plan showing a schedule to meet the final product demand.

Solution

The Material Requirements Plan is given as Table 13.3. The explanations of three of the schedules is given below.

Waste Container, WDC-1455

- Gross requirements are 280 in week 7 and 350 in week 8, as required by the client.
- Inventory available in week 7 is 25 units.
- Net requirements in week 7 are 255 (280 − 25).
- Planned order receipts in week 7 are 255 (lot-for-lot) demand.
- Planned order releases in week 6 are 255 (1 week lead time).
- Planned order releases are 350 in week 7 (inventory has been used up and there is one week lead time).

Body, BDY-37

- In week 6 gross requirements are 255 and 350 in week 7. (This quantity is driven by the end product, the Waste Container; there is one body for each container.)
- There are 19 units in inventory, so net requirements in week 6 are 236 (255 − 19). Net requirements in week 7 are 350, the same as the gross requirements.
- Planned ordered receipts are 236 in week 6 and 350 in week 7 (lot-for-lot).
- Planned ordered releases are 236 in week 5 and 350 in week 6 (with one week lead time)

Rear brake wheel assembly, BRK-452

- In week 5 gross requirements are 472 (this quantity is driven by the Body and there are two Rear brake wheel assemblies per Body 2 × 236 = 472).
- In week 6 gross requirements are 700 (2 × 350 = 700).
- There are 12 units in inventory, so net requirements in week 5 are 460 (472 − 12) and net requirements in week 5 are equal to the gross requirements (no inventory available).
- Planned ordered receipts are 460 in week 5 and 700 in week 6 (lot-for-lot).
- Planned ordered releases are 460 in week 4 and 700 in week 5 (one week lead time).

Screws, SCW-326

- In week 4 gross requirements are 3512 and 5600 in week 5 (this quantity is driven by the Rear brake wheel assembly, where four screws per assembly are needed, and the front pivot wheel assembly, which also needs four screws per assembly. Planned ordered releases of BRK-452 are 460 in week 4 so 1840 (4 × 460) screws are needed. Planned order releases of PIV–958 are 418 in week 4 so 1672 (4 × 418) screws are needed. Thus, the total number of screws needed is 3512. Similar calculations apply to week 5.
- There are 250 units in inventory, so net requirements in week 4 are 3262 (3512 − 250) and net requirements in week 5 are equal to the gross requirements (no inventory available).
- Planned ordered receipts are 3262 in week 4 and 5600 in week 5 (lot-for-lot).
- Planned ordered releases are 3262 in week 3 and 5600 in week 5 (one week lead time).

Table 13.3 Material requirements planning – for Plastic Products Co

Description	Reference	Quantity	Week	1	2	3	4	5	6	7	8
Waste container	WDC-1455	0	Gross requirements							280	350
			Inventory available	25	25	25	25	25	25	25	0
			Net requirements	0	0	0	0	0	0	255	350
			Planned ordered receipts	0	0	0	0	0	0	255	350
			Planned ordered releases	0	0	0	0	0	255	350	0
Body	BDY-137	1	Gross requirements	0	0	0	0	0	255	350	0
			Inventory available	19	19	19	19	19	19	0	0
			Net requirements	0	0	0	0	0	236	350	0
			Planned ordered receipts	0	0	0	0	0	236	350	0
			Planned ordered releases	0	0	0	0	236	350	0	0
Cover	COV-10	1	Gross requirements	0	0	0	0	0	255	350	0
			Inventory available	17	17	17	17	17	17	0	0
			Net requirements	0	0	0	0	0	238	350	0
			Planned ordered receipts	0	0	0	0	0	238	350	0
			Planned ordered releases	0	0	0	0	238	350	0	0
Clips	CLP-74	4	Gross requirements	0	0	0	0	944	1400	0	0
			Inventory available	80	80	80	80	80	0	0	0
			Net requirements	0	0	0	0	864	1400	0	0
			Planned ordered receipts	0	0	0	0	864	1400	0	0
			Planned ordered releases	0	0	864	1400	0	0	0	0
Front pivot wheel assembly	PIV-958	2	Gross requirements	0	0	0	0	472	700	0	0
			Inventory available	54	54	54	54	54	0	0	0
			Net requirements	0	0	0	0	418	700	0	0
			Planned ordered receipts	0	0	0	0	418	700	0	0
			Planned ordered releases	0	0	0	418	700	0	0	0
Rear brake wheel assembly	BRK-452	2	Gross requirements	0	0	0	0	472	700	0	0
			Inventory available	12	12	12	12	12	0	0	0
			Net requirements	0	0	0	0	460	700	0	0
			Planned ordered receipts	0	0	0	0	460	700	0	0
			Planned ordered releases	0	0	0	460	700	0	0	0
Stirrup assembly	STP-589	1	Gross requirements	0	0	0	0	236	350	0	0
			Inventory available	56	56	56	56	56	0	0	0
			Net requirements	0	0	0	0	180	350	0	0
			Planned ordered receipts	0	0	0	0	180	350	0	0
			Planned ordered releases	0	0	0	180	350	0	0	0
Plug assembly	PGA-45	1	Gross requirements	0	0	0	0	236	350	0	0
			Inventory available	21	21	21	21	21	0	0	0
			Net requirements	0	0	0	0	215	350	0	0
			Planned ordered receipts	0	0	0	0	215	350	0	0
			Planned ordered releases	0	0	0	215	350	0	0	0
Axle rods	AXL-21	4	Gross requirements	0	0	0	0	952	1400	0	0
			Inventory available	68	68	68	68	68	0	0	0
			Net requirements	0	0	0	0	884	1400	0	0
			Planned ordered receipts	0	0	0	0	884	1400	0	0
			Planned ordered releases	0	0	884	1400	0	0	0	0
Wheel	WHF-85	1	Gross requirements	0	0	0	418	700	0	0	0
			Inventory available	69	69	69	69	0	0	0	0
			Net requirements	0	0	0	349	700	0	0	0
			Planned ordered receipts	0	0	0	349	700	0	0	0
			Planned ordered releases	0	349	700	0	0	0	0	0
Screws	SCW-326	4	Gross requirements	0	0	0	3512	5600	0	0	0
			Inventory available	250	250	250	250	0	0	0	0
			Net requirements	0	0	0	3262	5600	0	0	0
			Planned ordered receipts	0	0	0	3262	5600	0	0	0
Bracket	BFK-991	1	Gross requirements	0	0	0	418	700	0	0	0
			Inventory available	17	17	17	17	0	0	0	0
			Net requirements	0	0	0	401	700	0	0	0
			Planned ordered receipts	0	0	0	401	700	0	0	0
			Planned ordered releases	0	401	700	0	0	0	0	0

Description	Reference	Qty									
Wheel	WHR-98	1	Gross requirements	0	0	0	460	700	0	0	0
			Inventory available	25	25	25	25	0	0	0	0
			Net requirements	0	0	0	435	700	0	0	0
			Planned ordered receipts	0	0	0	435	700	0	0	0
			Planned ordered releases	0	435	700	0	0	0	0	0
Bracket	BKR-891	1	Gross requirements	0	0	0	460	700	0	0	0
			Inventory available	23	23	23	23	0	0	0	0
			Net requirements	0	0	0	437	700	0	0	0
			Planned ordered receipts	0	0	0	437	700	0	0	0
			Planned ordered releases	437	700	0	0	0	0	0	0
Steel bar	STB-56	1	Gross requirements	0	0	0	180	350	0	0	0
			Inventory available	6	6	6	6	0	0	0	0
			Net requirements	0	0	0	174	350	0	0	0
			Planned ordered receipts	0	0	0	174	350	0	0	0
			Planned ordered releases	174	350	0	0	0	0	0	0
Rivets	RVT-486	11	Gross requirements	0	0	0	1980	3850	0	0	0
			Inventory available	5	5	5	5	0	0	0	0
			Net requirements	0	0	0	1975	3850	0	0	0
			Planned ordered receipts	0	0	0	1975	3850	0	0	0
			Planned ordered releases	0	1975	3850	0	0	0	0	0
Plug	PLG-142	1	Gross requirements	0	0	0	215	350	0	0	0
			Inventory available	2	2	2	2	0	0	0	0
			Net requirements	0	0	0	213	350	0	0	0
			Planned ordered receipts	0	0	0	213	350	0	0	0
			Planned ordered releases	0	0	213	350	0	0	0	0
Gasket	GSK-78	1	Gross requirements	0	0	0	215	350	0	0	0
			Inventory available	5	5	5	5	0	0	0	0
			Net requirements	0	0	0	210	350	0	0	0
			Planned ordered receipts	0	0	0	210	350	0	0	0
			Planned ordered releases	0	0	210	350	0	0	0	0

EXERCISE PROBLEM: FARLEY CO.

Situation

Farley Co. is a small private company, near Amsterdam, Holland, that makes specialized bicycles for sale throughout Europe. The company principally performs assembly of the bicycles from components purchased in Nottingham, England, although it does have a machine shop where it produces the frames and handlebars. Much of this work is hand crafted. Details of the product (simplified) are given in Figures 13.7 and 13.8.

Farley receives an order for 2700 bicycles, all of one model, from a French distributor. Of these, 900 are to be ready in week 6, and 1800 are to be ready in week 10. Inventory data for all of the components is given in Table 13.4. The explanation of this information is as follows.

Description, reference, quantity in product, and level

This information is identical to the structure information given in Figure 13.8.

Source

This indicates the origin of the components. If units are assembled, or machined, this is done in house by Farley. All the purchased parts are from outside suppliers.

Table 13.4 Farley Co. – component data (no minimum lot size indicates that policy is lot-for-lot)

Description	Reference	Quantity in product	Level	Source	Lead time (weeks)	Minimum lot size	Safety stock	Inventory allocated	Inventory level (Week 1)	Scheduled receipts	
										Quantity	Week
Bicycle	BIC-145		0	Assembled	1		0	0	0		
Frame	FRM-212	1	1	Machined	1		0	0	5		
Handlebars	HAN-458	1	2	Machined	1		0	0	20		
Saddle	SAD-895	1	2	Purchased	2		0	0	0		
Wheels	WHL-684	2	2	Assembled	1		0	30	60		
Pedals	PED-471	2	2	Assembled	1		20	10	70		
Gear assembly	GER-238	1	2	Purchased	3		0	0	0		
Tyres	TIR-927	1	3	Purchased	2	2 000	100	0	120	4 000	1
Spokes	SPK-867	36	3	Purchased	2	60 000	1 750	19 000	1 900	60 000	1
Brake assembly	BRK-158	1	3	Purchased	2		0	20	80		
Bearings	BER-572	24	3	Purchased	2	50 000	15 000	1 500	1 250	50 000	1

Figure 13.7   Bicycle assembly.

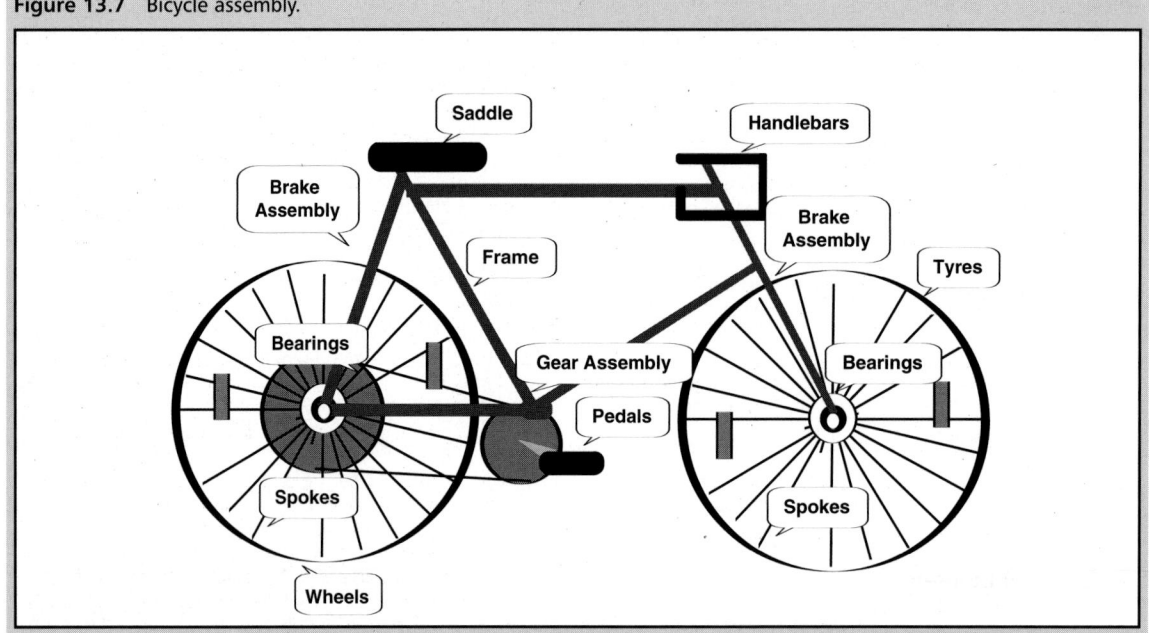

Figure 13.8   Product structure for a bicycle.

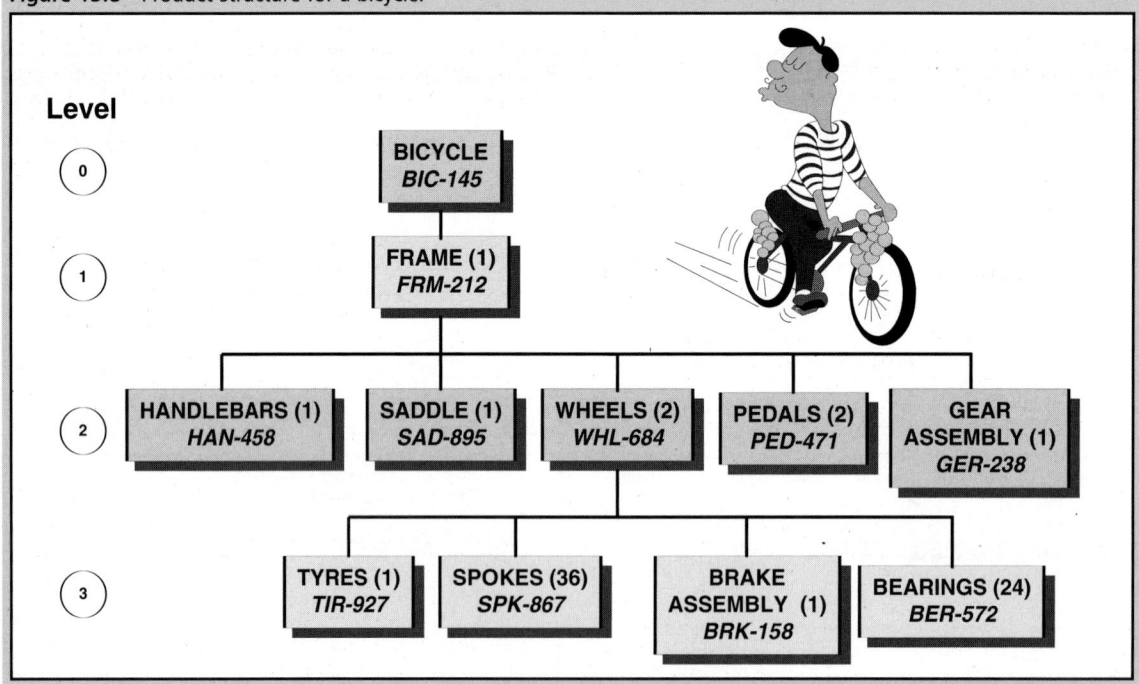

Lead time

This is the elapsed time between ordering a part (either externally or internally) and its receipt ready for use in the workcentre.

Minimum lot size

Here, this applies to the purchased tyres, spokes and bearings and is the minimum lot ordered, based on economic criteria.

Safety stock

For some components, Farley keeps a safety stock in the firm for use in emergency situations to supply key customers. This safety stock is not available for use for other planning purposes.

Inventory allocated

This is the inventory allocated for spare parts for identified clients. It is not available for normal planning purposes.

Inventory level, (Week 1)

This is the total inventory in stock. Total amounts are always recorded by Farley as this information is used by the Finance Department for determining inventory investments.

Scheduled receipts

These are items that are delivered periodically on a blanket order basis. They are those items that are held in safety stock to satisfy rush orders for clients. The information shown is the scheduled receipts due to be delivered in week 1. They are available for use in that week and are available for the MRP.

Required

Develop a weekly-period material requirements plan for Farley based on the information given. Use the grid shown as Table 13.5 for the development of the MRP.

Solution

The Material Requirements Plan is given as Table 13.6. The explanations of four of the schedules are as follows:

Bicycle, BIC-145

- Gross requirements are 900 in week 6, and 1800 in week 10, as demanded by the client.
- There is no on-hand inventory. Thus net requirements for both weeks are 900 and 1800 respectively.
- Planned order receipts are 900 in week 6 and 1800 in week 10, equal to net requirements since there is no minimum lot size.
- There is a one-week lead time and so planned ordered releases are 900 in week 5 and 1800 in week 9.

Frame, FRM-212

- Gross requirements are 900 in week 5, and 1800 in week 9, as the frame requirements depend on the bicycle (one frame for each bicycle). It is the period, and the quantity of the planned ordered releases for the bicycle, that drive the frame requirements.
- There are five units of inventory on hand and so net requirements in week 5 are 895 (900 – 5). Net requirements in week 9 equal gross requirements (no inventory on hand).
- Planned order receipts are 895 in week 5 and 1800 in week 9, equal to net requirements since there is no minimum lot size.
- There is a one-week lead time and so planned ordered releases are 895 in week 4 and 1800 in week 8.

Wheels, WHL-684

- Gross requirements are 1790 in week 4, and 3600 in week 8, as the wheel requirements depend on the frame (two wheels for each frame). It is the period, and the quantity of the planned ordered releases for the frame, that drive the wheel requirements.
- There are 60 units of inventory on hand and, of this, 30 have been allocated. Thus inventory available is 30 (60 – 30). Thus, net requirements in week 4 are 1760 (1790 – 30). Net requirements in week 8 equal gross requirements (no inventory on hand).
- Planned order receipts are 1760 in week 4 and 3600 in week 7, equal to net requirements since there is no minimum lot size.
- There is a one week lead time and so planned ordered releases are 1760 in week 3 and 3600 in week 7.

Bearings, BER-572

- Gross requirements are 42 240 in week 3, and 86 400 in week 7, as the bearing requirements depend on the wheel (24 bearings for each wheel). It is the period, and the quantity of the planned ordered releases for the wheel, that drive the bearing requirements.
- There are 1250 units of inventory on-hand, 1500 have already been allocated and there is a safety stock requirement of 15 000. Thus, inventory 'available' in week 1 is –15 250 (1250 – 1500 – 15 000). However, in week 1 there are 50 000 bearings of scheduled receipts to arrive. Thus, for use in week 3 (when they are required) 34 750 (50 000 – 15 250) are available.
- Net requirements in week 3 are 7490 (42 240 – 34 750).
- Planned order receipts are 50 000 in week 3 as this is the minimum lot-size requirement, even though only 7490 units are required.
- Carried over to inventory in week 4 are 42 510 units of inventory (50 000 – 7490) and this appears in the inventory file until week 7, when it is needed.
- Net requirements in week 7 are 43 890 (86 400 – 42 510)
- There is a two week lead time, so that in week 1 there are 50 000 units of planned ordered releases and in week 5 there are 50 000 units.
- There are 6100 units of inventory carried over to week 8 and beyond (50 000 – 43 890).

Table 13.5 Grid for the development of the MRP

Description	Ref.	Quantity	Week	1	2	3	4	5	6	7	8	9	10
			Gross requirements										
			Scheduled receipts										
			Inventory available										
			Net requirements										
			Planned ordered receipts										
			Planned ordered releases										

Table 13.6 Material requirements planning for Farley Co.

Description	Reference	Quantity	Week	1	2	3	4	5	6	7	8	9	10
Bicycle	BIC-145	0	Gross requirements	0	0	0	0	0	900	0	0	0	1 800
			Scheduled receipts	0	0	0	0	0	0	0	0	0	0
			Inventory available	0	0	0	0	0	0	0	0	0	0
			Net requirements	0	0	0	0	0	900	0	0	0	1 800
			Planned ordered receipts	0	0	0	0	0	900	0	0	0	1 800
			Planned ordered releases	0	0	0	0	900	0	0	0	1 800	0
Frame	FRM-212	1	Gross requirements	0	0	0	0	900	0	0	0	1 800	0
			Scheduled receipts	0	0	0	0	0	0	0	0	0	0
			Inventory available	5	5	5	5	5	0	0	0	0	0
			Net requirements	0	0	0	0	895	0	0	0	1 800	0
			Planned ordered receipts	0	0	0	0	895	0	0	0	1 800	0
			Planned ordered releases	0	0	0	895	0	0	0	1 800	0	0
Handlebars	HAN-458	1	Gross requirements	0	0	0	895	0	0	0	1 800	0	0
			Scheduled receipts	0	0	0	0	0	0	0	0	0	0
			Inventory available	20	20	20	20	0	0	0	0	0	0
			Net requirements	0	0	0	875	0	0	0	1 800	0	0
			Planned ordered receipts	0	0	0	875	0	0	0	1 800	0	0
			Planned ordered releases	0	0	875	0	0	0	1 800	0	0	0
Saddle	SAD-895	1	Gross requirements	0	0	0	895	0	0	0	1 800	0	0
			Scheduled receipts	0	0	0	0	0	0	0	0	0	0
			Inventory available	0	0	0	0	0	0	0	0	0	0
			Net requirements	0	0	0	895	0	0	0	1 800	0	0
			Planned ordered receipts	0	0	0	895	0	0	0	1 800	0	0
			Planned ordered releases	0	895	0	0	0	1 800	0	0	0	0
Wheels	WHL-684	2	Gross requirements	0	0	0	1 790	0	0	0	3 600	0	0
			Scheduled receipts	0	0	0	0	0	0	0	0	0	0
			Inventory available	30	30	30	30	0	0	0	0	0	0
			Net requirements	0	0	0	1 760	0	0	0	3 600	0	0
			Planned ordered receipts	0	0	0	1 760	0	0	0	3 600	0	0
			Planned ordered releases	0	0	1 760	0	0	0	3 600	0	0	0
Pedals	PED-471	2	Gross requirements	0	0	0	1 790	0	0	0	3 600	0	0
			Scheduled receipts	0	0	0	0	0	0	0	0	0	0
			Inventory available	40	40	40	40	0	0	0	0	0	0
			Net requirements	0	0	0	1 750	0	0	0	3 600	0	0
			Planned ordered receipts	0	0	0	1 750	0	0	0	3 600	0	0
			Planned ordered releases	0	0	1 750	0	0	0	3 600	0	0	0
Gear Assembly	GER-238	1	Gross requirements	0	0	0	895	0	0	0	1 800	0	0
			Scheduled receipts	0	0	0	0	0	0	0	0	0	0
			Inventory available	0	0	0	0	0	0	0	0	0	0
			Net requirements	0	0	0	895	0	0	0	1 800	0	0
			Planned ordered receipts	0	0	0	895	0	0	0	1 800	0	0
			Planned ordered releases	895	0	0	0	1 800	0	0	0	0	0
Tyres	TIR-927	1	Gross requirements	0	0	1 760	0	0	0	3 600	0	0	0
			Scheduled receipts	4 000	0	0	0	0	0	0	0	0	0
			Inventory available	20	4 020	4 020	2 260	2 260	2 260	2 260	660	660	660
			Net requirements	0	0	0	0	0	0	1 340	0	0	0
			Planned ordered receipts	0	0	0	0	0	0	2 000	0	0	0
			Planned ordered releases	0	0	0	0	2 000	0	0	0	0	0
Spokes	SPK-867	36	Gross requirements	0	0	63 360	0	0	0	129 600	0	0	0
			Scheduled receipts	60 000	0	0	0	0	0	0	0	0	0
			Inventory available	−18 850	41 150	41 150	37 790	37 790	37 790	37 790	0	0	0
			Net requirements	0	0	22 210	0	0	0	91 810	0	0	0
			Planned ordered receipts	0	0	60 000	0	0	0	91 810	0	0	0
			Planned ordered releases	60 000	0	0	0	91 810	0	0	0	0	0
Brake assembly	BRK-158	1	Gross requirements	0	0	1 760	0	0	0	3 600	0	0	0
			Scheduled receipts	0	0	0	0	0	0	0	0	0	0
			Inventory available	60	60	60	0	0	0	0	0	0	0
			Net requirements	0	0	1 700	0	0	0	3 600	0	0	0
			Planned ordered receipts	0	0	1 700	0	0	0	3 600	0	0	0
			Planned ordered releases	1 700	0	0	0	3 600	0	0	0	0	0
Bearings	BER-572	24	Gross requirements	0	0	42 240	0	0	0	86 400	0	0	0
			Scheduled receipts	50 000	0	0	0	0	0	0	0	0	0
			Inventory available	−15 250	34 750	34 750	42 510	42 510	42 510	42 510	6 110	6 110	6 110
			Net requirements	0	0	7 490	0	0	0	43 890	0	0	0
			Planned ordered receipts	0	0	50 000	0	0	0	50 000	0	0	0
			Planned ordered releases	50 000	0	0	0	50 000	0	0	0	0	0

LOT-SIZING IN PRODUCTION PLANNING

In operations planning in manufacturing, warehousing/distribution or purchasing, decisions need to be made about how much material, or what size of lots, to prepare. Lot-sizing is an important part of MRP planning and, depending on the lot size, ordering components in the MRP by lots results in a pattern of periods of high inventory when material arrives, interrupted by longer periods of decreasing inventory as the material is being consumed. The following are considerations related to lot sizing.

Units produced to order

In units produced to order the products are only made when a customer order has been received. Thus, if feasible with the resources available, the lot size is equal to the size of the order. For example, a furniture maker receives an order for 45 oak filing cabinets. The order quantity made is thus 45.

Units produced to stock

In units produced to stock the product is standard and the size of the lot is based on the economic size that is feasible and the expected sale of the product.

Large lot sizes

If large lots are produced at any one period, then:

- The cost of machine set-up per unit is less.
- Carrying costs are higher. Further, carrying costs for finished goods are higher than for raw materials because of the value-added activity.

Small lot sizes

If smaller lots are prepared (see Chapter 15, *Lean Production and Just-in-Time*, then there will be:

- larger set-up costs;
- lower carrying costs;
- a reduced risk of obsolescence.

The size of a production run

Manufactured products may be produced on individual machines or on a complete production line. Although products may be similar in nature and function, distinct differences may exist. For example:

- In a plastic moulding plant, blue plastic wash basins are produced followed then by the production of red wash basins.
- In a printing operation, the printing machine first runs off the TV Guide and this is then followed by the Sunday Review.
- In the textile industry, a roll of white cotton cloth is printed in a red Tartan design. This is then followed by the printing of synthetic fabric with a blue country design.

In each case, after each identifiable product has been produced, machines need to be shut down, cleaned, readjusted and possibly retooled, in order to be adapted to the next product. During this changeover time, there is 'lost' production and a certain amount of inventory, downstream of the machine in question, has to be kept in order to maintain production. The longer the set-up time, the greater the amount of this inventory needed. If set-up costs are high (usually determined by the number of labour hours involved) production managers may decide on long production runs, to minimize these changeover costs, even though product demand is less than the lot size (production run).

Production costs

In a production operation assume that the following conditions exist:

- Variable costs are $15.00 per unit and this includes the labour, materials and associated overhead. This cost does not change with the quantity of units produced.
- The set-up cost is estimated at $275.00 and is considered fixed, regardless of the quantity of pieces manufactured. This cost would include principally labour, but possibly also new machine tools, new moulds, cleaning fluids etc.

Then for lot sizes ranging from 5 to 500 units, Table 13.7 gives the total cost per lot, equal to the set-up cost plus the total variable cost, and the average production cost per unit determined by the total cost divided by the lot size.

This information is shown graphically in Figure 13.9. This curve illustrates that the unit cost drops sharply at first, then evens out. Thus, given this data, for standardized products or those produced for stock, there is a clear argument for large production runs. However, for non-standardized products, such as those made to customer order, setting a production run exactly equal to the demand is more economic. If more

Table 13.7   Lot sizes and costs

Lot size (units)	Total variable cost ($)	Set-up ($/set up)	Total cost ($)	Average cost, ($/unit)
5	75	275	350	70.00
10	150	275	425	42.50
15	225	275	500	33.33
30	450	275	725	24.17
50	750	275	1025	20.50
100	1500	275	1775	17.75
175	2625	275	2900	16.57
200	3000	275	3275	16.38
250	3750	275	4025	16.10
350	5250	275	5525	15.79
450	6750	275	7025	15.61
500	7500	275	7775	15.55

are produced than demanded by a particular client, there is no guarantee that the excess will be sold. One of the reasons why custom products are more expensive is that a producer cannot take advantage of large production runs.

The curve in Figure 13.9 also illustrates that for small lot sizes, the set-up cost is a high proportion of total cost. This underscores why companies strive to reduce set-up times (and hence cost) so that they have more flexibility in their operations and are not always constrained to produce in large lot sizes. This is the basis of SMED (Single Minute Exchange of Die), which is presented in more detail in Chapter 16, *Lean Production and Just-in-Time*.

Lot sizes of purchased materials

When raw materials, components or parts are purchased from an external source, then the quantity (lot size) may depend on price discounts available at certain quantity levels, as discussed in the following.

Supplier price discounts

A company may require 4000 units of an article. The unit purchase price is $2.50 per unit. However, the supplier offers a 10 per cent discount on quantities over 5000 units, or a unit cost of $2.25/unit. Since the purchaser anticipates using the extra 1000 units at some future date, he takes advantage of the price discount. The supplier is able to offer these discounts because his total costs are a function of his set-up costs which are lower. (see also Chapter 11, *Inventory Management*).

Transportation costs

Purchasing in large lots may provide lower unit costs because of lower transportation costs. If a client purchases a truck load of goods, rather than, say, half a truck load, his unit-price shipping cost is usually less.

Figure 13.9   Unit production costs and lot sizes.

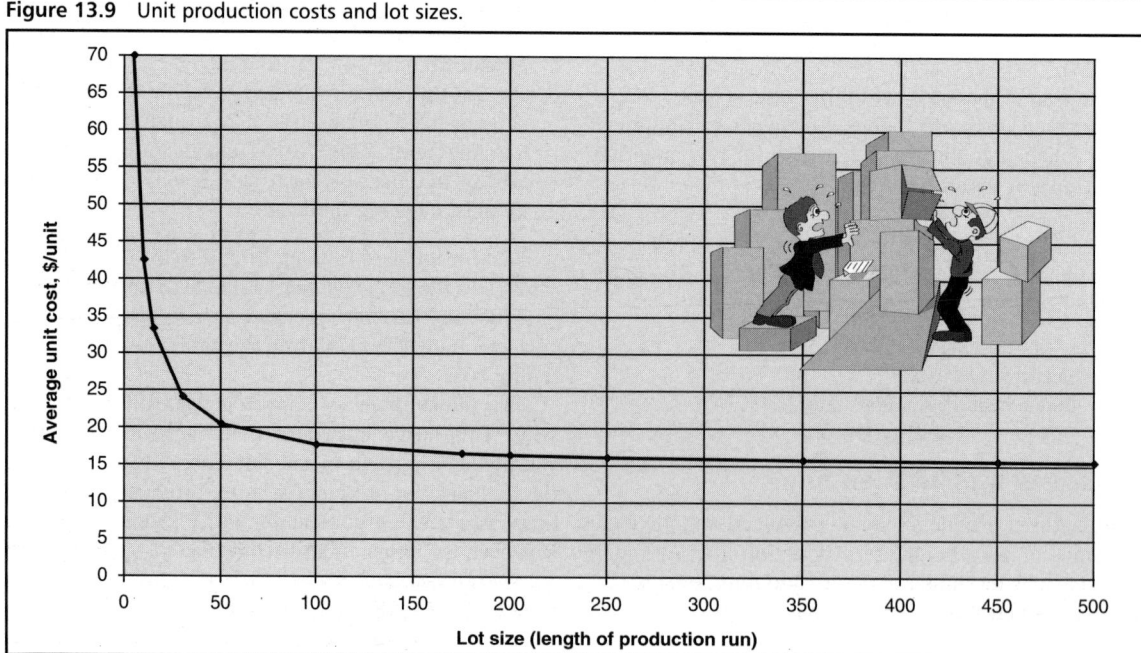

Methods for calculating an optimum lot size

Methods for calculating the optimum lot size generally depend on balancing the set-up costs with holding costs. Thus, for lot-sizing calculation methods to be appropriate, it is necessary that these costs are known with some reliability. The following are some quantitative methods for determining lot size.[3]

Lot-for-lot

In the lot-for-lot (LFL) approach, the lot size manufactured or purchased is equal to the net requirements at that particular time period. Using this method minimizes inventory holding costs and avoids the risk of obsolescence. However, it means that set-up costs are incurred for each operation. Also, if the lot sizes vary greatly from period to period, it makes planning more complicated.

Economic ordering quantity

Economic order quantity (EOQ) models, already presented in Chapter 11, *Inventory Management*, may be used for optimizing the lot size. This approach assumes that the demand is quite stable from period do period (which may not be the case) and also price discounts are not taken into account in the basic models.

Period order quantity method

In the period order quantity (POQ) method, a certain quantity of material or parts is produced at a regular period, say every week or every 10 days. In this way planning is somewhat simplified, since set-up requirements for the installation are known with regularity.

Part-Period Balancing

The part period balancing (PPB) approach, like the economic order quantity method, balances the set-up costs with holding costs, with the exception that it is dynamic in that it reflects requirements for future demand requirements.

The worked example, *Benoit Co.*, illustrates these four methods for calculating lot size.

WORKED EXAMPLE: BENOIT CO.

Situation

The Benoit Co., outside Lille, France, makes a variety of plastic moulded components used in the automobile industry. The components are made in a variety of colours and, before a new production run is started, the presses have to be cleaned, the appropriate type mould has to be installed and the equipment has to be pre-heated. Data indicates that the set-up time (order cost) for producing a new lot is FF 480.00. Carrying costs for the finished products are estimated at FF 0.50/unit/week and there is no initial inventory. Carrying costs for raw materials are not taken into consideration. For the next 10 weeks the gross requirements for the end product are as shown in Table 13.8.

Required

1 Develop a plan for lot sizing using the criteria lot-for-lot. Determine the carrying costs, holding costs and the total plan concept using this method
2 Develop a plan for lot sizing using the criteria of economic order quantity. Determine the carrying costs, holding costs and the total plan concept using this method
3 Develop a plan for lot sizing using the criteria of periodic order quantity. Determine the carrying costs, holding costs and the total plan concept using this method.

4 Develop a plan for lot sizing using the criteria of part period balancing. Determine the carrying costs, holding costs and the total plan concept using this method.
5 Which is the preferred plan?

Solution

1 Table 13.9 gives the planning schedule for the lot-for-lot criterion.
   ■ Production lots are made each week according to the gross requirements. Each time production takes place, a set-up, ordering cost is incurred.
2 Table 13.10 is the plan schedule for the EOQ criterion.
   ■ Each time the inventory level falls below the economic order quantity, a production equal to the EOQ is made.
   ■ Average inventory is the mean of the beginning and ending inventories.
   ■ Carrying cost is the sum of the average inventory times the inventory carrying cost.
   ■ Ordering cost is the number of set-ups made during the planning period times the set-up cost.
3 Table 13.11 is the plan schedule for periodic order quantity criterion.
   ■ The economic order quantity (EOQ) is calculated as before.
   ■ The orders made during the planning period are calculated as the total requirements in the planning period divided by the EOQ.

Table 13.8 Benoit Co. – Gross requirements for the end product

Week	1	2	3	4	5	6	7	8	9	10
Gross requirements	340	310	350	220	150	0	280	330	180	220

Table 13.9 Benoit Co., Lot-for-lot

Order cost, FF/order	480
Carrying cost, FF/unit/week	0.50
Lead time, weeks	0
Beginning inventory on-hand	0

Week	1	2	3	4	5	6	7	8	9	10	Total
Gross requirements	340	310	350	220	150	0	280	330	180	220	2 380
Beginning inventory	0	0	0	0	0	0	0	0	0	0	
Production lots	340	310	350	220	150	0	280	330	180	220	2 380
Ending inventory	0	0	0	0	0	0	0	0	0	0	0
Average inventory	0	0	0	0	0	0	0	0	0	0	

Carrying cost, FF	0
No, of orders made	9
Ordering costs, FF	**4 320**
Total costs, FF	**4 320**

Table 13.10 Benoit: Economic order quantity EOQ $= \sqrt{2DS/C}$

Order cost, FF/order	480
Carrying cost, FF/unit/week	0.5
Lead time, weeks	0
Beginning inventory on-hand	0
Demand during planned period, D	2 380
Carrying cost in plan period, (FF)	5.00
EOQ	675.99
EOQ (rounded)	676.00

Week	1	2	3	4	5	6	7	8	9	10	Total
Gross requirements	340	310	350	220	150	0	280	330	180	220	2 380
Beginning inventory	0	336	26	352	132	658	658	378	48	544	
Production lots	676	0	676	0	676	0	0	0	676	0	2 704
Ending inventory	336	26	352	132	658	658	378	48	544	324	
Average inventory	168	181	189	242	395	658	518	213	296	434	

Carrying cost, FF	1 647.00
No. of orders made	4
Ordering costs, FF	**1 920.00**
Total costs, FF	**3 567.00**

- The periodic order quantity (POQ) is the weeks in the planning period divided by the number of orders.
- This number is rounded.
- Thus for each POQ a production lot is made to equal the demand for that period.

4 Table 13.12 gives the plan schedule for the part period balancing criterion.

- The economic part period (EPP) is calculated as the ratio order costs/divided by carrying costs. This value means that if this number of units were held in inventory for one week, it would have a carrying cost equal to the ordering cost. Thus the concept is to find the cumulative part period that corresponds to the EPP.

- First, a lot size equivalent to the gross requirements of period 1 is calculated. In this case the number of excess units produced is zero. The period (weeks) that this number of units is carried is also zero. Thus, the cumulative part period is zero.

- Next, a lot size equal to the requirements for first two weeks is assumed to be produced in week 1. In this case, the number of excess units produced is the requirements for the second week. This amount is carried for one week. Thus the part period (quantity × time) is calculated.

- Next, a lot size equal to the requirements for weeks 1, 2 and 3 is assumed. The number of excess units, over and above the requirements for weeks one and two is the requirements for the third week. This amount is carried for two weeks. The part period

Table 13.11 Benoit Co. – periodic order quantity EOQ = $\sqrt{2DS/C}$

Order cost, FF/order	480
Carrying cost, FF/unit/week	0.5
Lead time, weeks	0
Beginning inventory on-hand	0
Demand during planning period, D	2 380
Carrying cost in plan period, (FF)	5.00
EOQ	675.99
EOQ (rounded)	676.00
Orders during planning period, D/EOQ	3.52
Period order quantity is:	
weeks in planning period/orders	2.84
POQ (rounded)	3

Week	1	2	3	4	5	6	7	8	9	10	Total
Gross requirements	340	310	350	220	150	0	280	330	180	220	2 380
Beginning inventory	0	660	350	0	150	0	0	510	180	0	
Production lots	1 000	0	0	370	0	0	790	0	0	220	2 380
Ending inventory	660	350	0	150	0	0	510	180	0	0	
Average inventory	330	505	175	75	75	0	255	345	90	0	

Carrying cost, FF	925.00
No. of orders made	4
Ordering costs, FF	1 920.00
Total costs, FF	2 845.00

Table 13.12 Benoit Co. – Part period balancing

Order cost, FF/order	480
Carrying cost, FF/unit/week	0.5
Lead time, weeks	0
Beginning inventory on-hand	0
Economic part period, EPP, is:	
Order costs/carrying costs	960

Periods combined	Lot size (trial)	Excess units Quantity	Excess units Periods carried	Part period	Cumulative part period	
1	340	0	0	0	0	
1 and 2	650	310	1	310	310	
1, 2 and 3	1 000	350	2	700	1 010	Closest to economic part period
4	220	0	0	0	0	
4 and 5	370	150	1	150	150	
4, 5 and 6	370	0	2	0	150	
4, 5, 6 and 7	650	280	3	840	990	Closest to economic part period
8	330	0	0	0	0	
8 and 9	510	180	1	180	180	
8, 9 and 10	730	220	2	440	620	No following period

Week	1	2	3	4	5	6	7	8	9	10	Total
Gross requirements	340	310	350	220	150	0	280	330	180	220	2 380
Beginning inventory	0	660	350	0	430	280	280	0	400	220	
Production lots	1 000	0	0	650	0	0	0	730	0	0	2 380
Ending inventory	660	350	0	430	280	280	0	400	220	0	

Average inventory	330	505	175	215	355	280	140	200	310	110
Carrying cost, FF	1 310.00									
No. of orders made	3									
Ordering costs, FF	1 440.00									
Total costs, FF	2 750.00									

is the quantity multiplied by the number of periods for which that quantity is carried. A cumulative amount is then calculated. This figure of 1010 is close to the EPP of 960 and so a lot size equal to the requirements of the first three weeks is made.

- The steps are repeated for the subsequent weeks, stopping each time when a cumulative part period is found that is closest to the EPP.
- The planning schedule for lot sizes is then developed as in the other cases.

5 In summary the total costs are
- Lot-for-lot   FF 4 320.00
- Economic order quantity   FF 3 567.00
- Periodic order quantity   FF 2 845.00
- Part period balancing   FF 2 750.00

Thus, the part period balancing approach gives the lowest overall cost.

MANUFACTURING RESOURCE PLANNING, MRP-II, AND BEYOND

Evolution

MRP I was a planning tool important in the 1970s. As an isolated unit, it applies to a relatively small part of the manufacturing function and has the disadvantage that, because it is an open system there are no feedback loops between inputs and outputs. The basic MRP-I system thus evolved considerably into so-called MRP-II systems, or Material Resource Planning, and beyond this to business applications software systems that manage a company's entire business. These are referred to as Business Resource Planning (BRP) or Enterprise Resource Planning (ERP) systems.[4]

Feedback

In the MRP-II type of system, elements of the business plan are relayed through to the sales plan to the production plan, and then to the master production schedule. In these modules are feedback loops that provide information so that previous plans can be adjusted if resources are insufficient. The master production schedule then provides data for the material requirements plan, the capacity plan of the facility, purchasing requirements and shop floor activity. As earlier, there are feedback loops that make it possible to adjust, or propose modifications to, earlier plans if resources are insufficient.[5] Thus the whole system is a closed loop. This scheme is illustrated in Figure 13.10.

MRP-II systems require that every employee, including the operator, analyst, quality inspector, sales person, purchasing agent, planning staff and even account staff, be thoroughly and strictly disciplined about entering current data into the system. Managers can calculate the requirement of every part or subassembly, week by week, and track in advance possible delays or material shortages. People in inventory control can then plan the release dates and meet promised deliveries. At the business level, MRP-II verifies the marketing and production plans so that the availability of resources can be determined. Then, by combining the business plan with production goals, it considers what is in inventory, the time it takes for vendors to deliver, the cash flow and that dates when the product can be delivered to the customer.[6]

Commercial ERP systems

Commercially, there are numerous complex ERP-type business applications software systems for aiding management in either manufacturing or service-related activities. The software systems are generally compiled in series of modules, each one covering particular functional elements of the firm such as:

- sales;
- manufacturing;
- accounting;
- inventory management;
- distribution;
- transportation;
- payroll management;
- project management.

Modules can either be stand-alone products or be combined with other modules to give a complete integ-

Figure 13.10 Manufacturing resource planning (MRP-II).

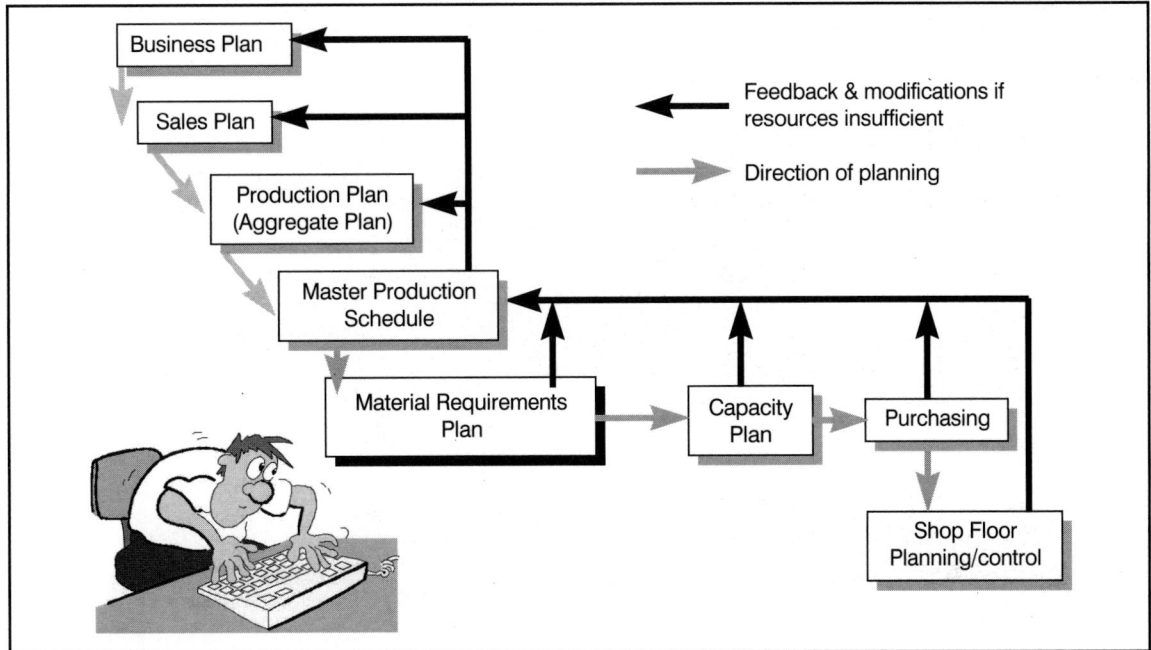

rated system and are usually able to operate on Microsoft, UNIX or IBM AS/400 systems. Figure 13.11 gives a general presentation of what companies can offer.

Commercial products are different in their application. They might apply to process industries, such as refining and chemicals, assembly operations such as electronics or automobiles, or the food industry, where menus replace the product structure for assembled products. Some modules might be available from one company and not from another. Support service may be better in one case than another and commercial terms will probably be different. Five of the principal suppliers of this type of client/server software are J.D. Edwards, Oracle, Peoplesoft, Baan and SAP from Europe[7]. A brief description of two big European based companies is given below.

Baan

The Baan company was founded in 1978 and has dual headquarters in Barneveld in the Netherlands and Menlo Park in California.[8] Its clients include Hitachi Ltd., Mercedes Benz US International Inc., Philips Medical Systems Nederland BV, and the Boeing Co., USA. Baan produces Enterprise Resource Planning software that provides supply-chain management at every operating level, using the Baan IV product line. This has five main components:

1 BAAN Orgware
2 Desktop computing
3 Internet
4 Applications including Manufacturing, Finance, Project, Service, and Transportation
5 Technology.

SAP

SAP, Walldorf, Germany,[9] is the biggest European company for client/server applications. SAP (for Systems Applications and Products) was started in 1973 by former IBM employees, including Hasso Plattner, the current head of the company. The Group sales in 1995 were DM 2696.4 million with a net profit of DM 404.8 million.[10] Clients include Shell (and other European refiners) and Unisabi (the pet food subsidiary of Mars). In July 1996 SAP signed a contract with Coca-Cola Co., which is potentially one of the company's best-ever customers because of Coca-Cola's global reach. Also in 1996, SAP won a contract with the city of Cologne, one of Germany's biggest municipalities.[11] In 1996 a contract was signed with the chemical company Hoechst of Germany for a project to handle the logistics aspects of their hazardous materials.[12]

Figure 13.11 Module arrangement of commercial business applications software systems, for example Oracle, SAP-R/3 Baan, J.D. Edwards and Peoplesoft.

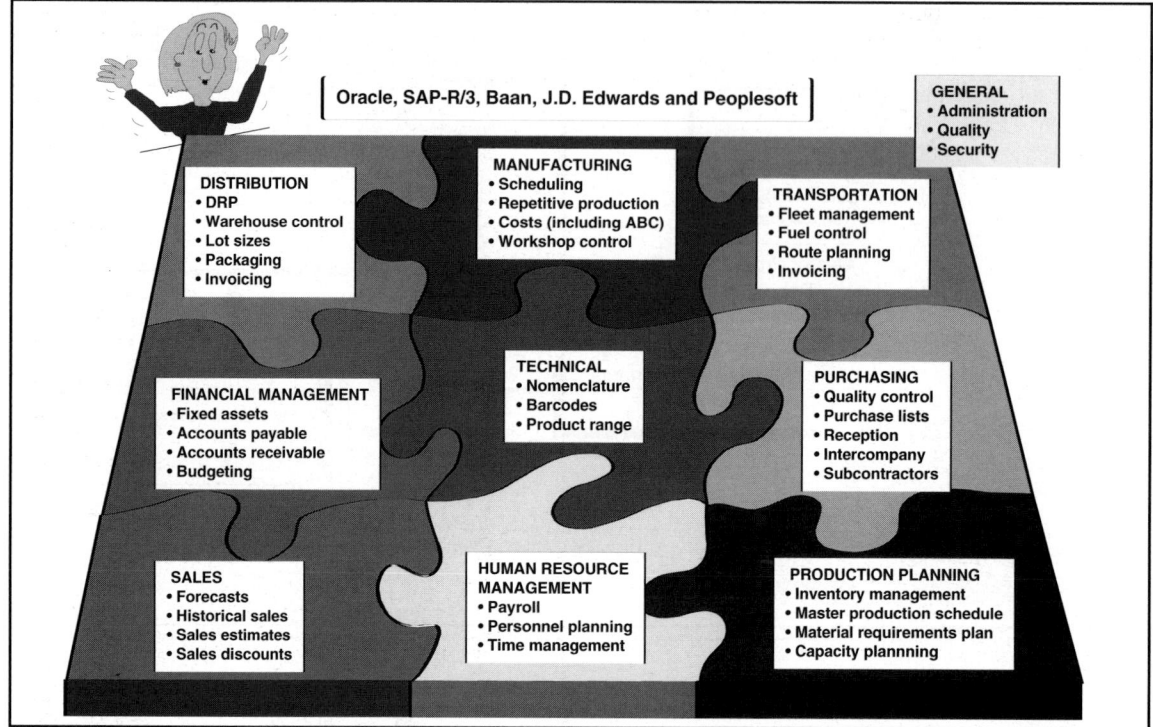

SAP's principal product is the R/3 system, which provides data-processing solutions for all areas of business. The various integrated modules include:

- sales and distribution, SD;
- materials management, MM;
- production planning, PP;
- quality management, QM;
- plant maintenance, PM;
- human resources, HR;
- financial accounting, FI;
- controlling, CO;
- fixed assets management, AM;
- project system, PS;
- workflow, WF;
- industry solutions.

The article in Box 13.1 illustrates the explosive growth of the Enterprise Resource Planning client/server software, giving particular reference to the Baan and SAP products.[13]

Box 13.1 Out of Nowhere: Dutch software firm gives Germany's SAP much to worry about. Baan charts explosive growth in the client/server niche with quality and flexibility. Waiting for a sweater day. By Silvia Ascarelli, Staff Reporter.

EDE, Netherlands – When Boeing went shopping for new computer software to help halve its production time, Germany's SAP was a prime candidate. The world's largest aerospace manufacturer had even begun installing the software in a Wichita, Kansas, plant.

But SAP AG had to withdrew its bid, saying it couldn't meet the deadline because of other big commitments and couldn't meet some of Boeing's specialized demands right away. Enter little-known Baan NV.

Nearly 18 months later, Boeing is set to start using Baan software at one site Feb. 19. The $20 million contract –

Baan's largest to date – has helped the Dutch company take off as rapidly as one of Boeing's jets.

Dramatic Ascent

Baan is now one of SAP's toughest challengers in the exploding market for client/server software. Although only one-tenth the size of the German company, Baan is competing with Oracle Corp. of the U.S. for the No. 2 spot world-wide behind SAP in the market niche known as enterprise resource planning, or ERP. Baan is rapidly expanding in the U.S. and is expected to grow even faster than SAP, a growth phenomenon in its own right.

Baan's dramatic ascent from nowhere to just about everyone's short list reflects a high-quality product, a few prominent orders and savvy promotion, as well as plain luck and perseverance. Through no fault of its own SAP's dominance was due to ebb as more competitors entered the market. But the popularity of these two companies in an industry that has been dominated by American firms shows how the growing globalization of industry is opening up opportunities for Europeans, where multicurrency thinking and cross-border sites are a way of life.

"I would call [Baan] extremely fierce competition" for SAP, says Mike Riffle, technology analyst with New York brokerage firm. Arnhold & S. Bleichroeder Inc. who strongly recommends the company. "I'm sure SAP is looking in the rear-view mirror."

How Results Match Up

Both firms posted 1995 earnings Wednesday. Sales at Baan, which is listed both on the Amsterdam Stock Exchange and Nasdaq, surged 76% to $216.2 million from $122.9 million in 1994. Net profit jumped more than 12-fold to $15.3 million from $1.2 million. Per-share earnings of 34 cents slightly exceeded market forecasts, and analysts say they could hit 58 cents this year.

At SAP, sales jumped 47% to 2.7 billion marks ($1.81 billion), outstripping a 44% increase in net profit to 405 million marks. Analysts put the results at the lower end of expectations, but were withholding final judgment until today's meeting with company officials. Nevertheless, the share price fell 4.4% in the final 3½ hours of electronic trading to 217.50 marks.

Baan clearly has targeted SAP and rarely mentions other competitors. "No. 1 is the biggest; No. 2 is the best," Paul Baan, vice chairman and managing director for business development, is fond of saying. "If we are not better than SAP, then why should people buy from Baan?"

Low total cost, speed and flexible software are Baan's major selling points. SAP counters that it offers a broader product range. "If you want complex, detailed mission-critical support, you'd have to go with SAP," says Mr. Riffle, the broker. "Baan offers a lot less complex solution in a lot less time."

When the two do go head-to-head, Baan tends to win the manufacturing software deals, says Bruce Richardson, vice president of research at Advanced Manufacturing Research, a Boston-based consultancy. SAP has the edge with suppliers, and generally wins if financial operations are the focus.

"Business Process Re-Engineering"

Neither company has a shortage of customers, thanks to the buzzword of the 1990s, "business process re-engineering." As part of that drive for leaner operations, ERP software helps users, often manufacturers, with everything from better sales forecasting to reducing inventory and quickly spotting parts shortages. The programs are more flexible than older software systems that generally involved customized packages based on mainframe computers where even minor changes can be full of headaches.

The world-wide ERP market, already valued at $2.5 billion, is growing more than 20% annually, estimates Chris Jones, research director for manufacturing applications at the Gartner Group. At that pace, it could be a $7.5 billion industry by 1999, not even counting costly consultant fees. Others say it's even bigger. Baan and SAP's piece of the pie – open systems and client/server setups – is doubling every

two years, and that kind of growth means there are likely to be several winners.

"Saturation is a long ways off," Mr. Jones says. "There's a tremendous amount of pent-up demand. There are a lot of systems out there that are 15, 20 years old that are constraining people's business."

Of course, Baan's not a sure bet. There's no sign of a price war yet, but the size and unpredictable timing of Individual contracts make earnings lumpy, and deals can be delayed if the overall economy sours. Any short fall in revenue, however temporary, can drop straight to the bottom line. Moreover, there's an industrywide shortage of experts who can get these kinds of systems up and running, which could constrain Baan's growth.

Wall Street Impressed

So far, though, Baan has impressed Wall Street. Since the company went public in May, the share price on Nasdaq has rocketed about 160%, and earnings forecasts have been steadily pushed higher. (SAP's share price has risen slightly less than 50% during the same time). While SAP shares have been downgraded to neutral by many analysts, who say it can't maintain its breakneck growth, Baan's share price is expected to rise faster than the German firm's and is on many buy lists.

Baan is also sustaining its astonishing corporate growth. Less than two years ago, it was selling its Triton-brand software primarily to Dutch clients, and the average purchase was only $70,000, Mr. Richardson, the AMR consultant, says. But after landing the Boeing deal, Baan has won contracts with blue-chip clients such Northern Telecom Ltd., Weyerhaeuser Co. and Mercedes-Benz U.S. International Inc. The average sale now is $1.2 million.

"We estimate they sold more than 500 licenses last year," Mr. Richardson says. "That would only put them behind SAP in terms of new business."

For 1996, company officials predict another year of rapid growth. They plan to release in the second quarter a new version of their Triton software, which will be called Baan IV, and which will include the first transportation and process applications. "The pipeline for the first quarter has some very exciting names," says Madhavan "M.R.", Rangaswami, the company's marketing chief.

An Unlikely Pair

To folks in Silicon Valley, founder and chief executive officer Jan Baan, 49, and his brother Paul, 44, must seem like an unlikely pair of software millionaires. For one thing, neither is a programmer by trade. Rather, they come from the same world as their customers. Jan Baan used to earn his money as a financial consultant and received his first computer, an 8086 model with 64 kilobytes of memory, as payment from a cash-strapped client in 1979. He wanted to use it for work but had to ask friends to write the software he needed.

At the same time, Paul Baan was working his way up in the housing-construction industry to become his employer's youngest management board member. Today he describes himself as the more customer-oriented of the two, and his brother as the more entrepreneurial and technically minded.

The ebullient duo have been working together since 1982, when Paul joined his brother's four-year-old company. They are now next-door neighbors in Barneveld, a town of 45,000

Chasing Number One   Sales for the top three ERP software vendors in 1994

SAP	$723 million
Baan	$120 million
Oracle	$113 million

Source: Advanced Manufacturing Research

about 15 kilometers away from Baan's secluded headquarters. They even take their large broods – they have 19 children between them – on joint vacations.

Both eschew the glamorous life. Paul Baan recently returned from a family skiing vacation in northern Germany; jetting off to Switzerland wouldn't be as much fun, he says. And just before taking Baan public, the pair sold 24 million shares to the Baan Investment BV foundation for about $30 million, a price far below the then market value. The foundation, which they control, is to do charitable activities in the Third World.

"The meaning of life is not money," Paul Baan says. Adds his brother: "I'm not a big spender. I like to have a nice dinner, but I do not like to spend my money for nothing."

Stumbling Along the Way

It took more than a decade before the Baan brothers could even dream of billions. For a long time, the company grew rapidly but quietly in Europe. It didn't even set up a formal marketing department until last year, when sales had already exceeded $100 million.

Early attempts to break into the U.S. market were flops. It opened an office in Grand Rapids, Michigan, in the late 1980s. Barely anyone noticed. A 1992 distribution deal with the ASK Group collapse over legal problems two years later. Then the Baan brothers lured away a big-spending executive from Oracle to get sales going. That didn't work either. In 1993, the U.S. operation was still a money loser.

In fact, it was only after Boeing that Baan began announcing a string of attention grabbing deals. Now it makes almost every short list and is in talks to supply software to a leading Japanese auto maker and one of the U.S. Big Three.

Baan is adding high-powered U.S. executives to help manage that growth. The biggest catch is Tom Tinsley, an 18-year veteran of international consultancy McKinsey & Co. who became Baan's president and chief operating officer in November. In his consultant days, he sat on the boards of three information-technology companies when they were booming – Electronic Data Systems Corp., Compaq Computer Corp. and Microsoft Corp. Like the Baan brothers, he's not much of a software writer. Still wearing his McKinsey uniform of a blue pinstriped shirt and tie, he's waiting for the moment to suggest that Baan allow managers the occasional sweater day.

Selling With ORGWare

For Baan customers, a product called ORGWare has become a big selling point. It is a set of software tools that can convert data from a company's older software systems and uses a set of generic components to create 450 business functions. By comparison, SAP's software requires customers to painstakingly work their way through 10,000 items. Moreover, Baan's system can be reconfigured to change with the company more easily than SAP's.

"They have a better manufacturing product, and the product generally goes in faster and cheaper," says AMR's Mr. Richardson. "The one area where SAP has always been vulnerable is on the time and cost of the installation."

Baan officials claim that for every dollar spent on their software, a customer spends only $1 to $2 on consultants who then make the software work. SAP and others say SAP's software can cost $5 to $10. An SAP spokesman declines to comment directly on the cost differences but said customers are more concerned about corporate solidity and continual improvements to the software. "It's very infrequent that a customer tells us that we aren't being selected because we're too expensive," he says.

SUMMARY OF KEY ELEMENTS

- A material requirements plan determines the need-for dependent components, taking into account lead times. MRP-I is an open system with no feed-back loop.
- The inputs for the material requirements plan come from the master production schedule, the product structure and the inventory records file.
- The gross requirement is the amount needed to satisfy demand in a certain period.
- On-hand inventory is available for use during a corresponding period. Allocated inventory is for purposes other than the MRP, such as spare parts. Safety stock is inventory not normally available for the MRP. Thus, inventory for the MRP is inven-

tory on hand less both inventory allocated and safety stock.
- Scheduled receipts are inventory expected to be received from suppliers in a defined time period as a result of orders already placed, such as through open orders.
- Net requirements are the quantity of material needed to meet the scheduled demand. They are the gross requirements less the inventory available.
- Planned ordered releases are the quantity to be released in a specific time period, to satisfy planned ordered receipts at a future date. The time difference is the lead time.

- Planned ordered receipts are to satisfy net requirements, although lot-size limitations may result in planned ordered receipts being greater than net requirements.
- The yield rate is the percentage of starting material that actually ends up in the product. It takes into account the proportion of unusable non-conforming material.
- With large lots, unit set-up costs are less, but carrying costs are high. Finished-goods carrying costs are higher than for raw materials because of the value added.
- If lots are small, then unit set-up costs are high, but inventory carrying costs are lower and there is a reduced risk of obsolescence.
- With high set-up costs, large lot sizes are more economic. However, this constraint underscores the drive to reduce set-up times to give more plant flexibility.
- Firms may purchase in large lots to take advantage of supplier discounts or reduced unit transport costs.

- The lot-for-lot (LFL) method of lot sizing calls for lots equal to the net requirements. This minimizes carrying costs and avoids the risk of obsolescence.
- The economic order quantity (EOQ) method for lot sizing balances set-up costs with carrying costs.
- In the period order quantity (POQ) method for lot sizing a certain quantity of material or parts is produced in a regular period.
- The part period balancing (PPB) method for lot sizing balances set-up costs with holding costs but takes into consideration requirements for future periods.
- MRP-II is an expansion of MRP-I and is a closed-loop system to manage a firm's entire supply chain by integrating business, marketing and production plans. It determines resources, inventory, lead times, cash flow and client delivery dates.

REVIEW AND DISCUSSION QUESTIONS

1 **Product structure**. Prepare a product structure for:
  (a) a dining-room chair;
  (b) a brief case or attaché case;
  (c) a pair of skis (one ski);
  (d) a bed;
  (e) the lock on a door (both sections);
  (f) a portable computer;
  (g) a trolley basket used in a supermarket;
  (h) major sections of an aeroplane;
  (i) an electric guitar.
2 **Safety stock**. Discuss the advantages and disadvantages of keeping safety stock.

3 **Yield Rate**. If a firm is using the concept of yield rate, what does this imply? What suggestions might you propose?
4 **Lot sizing**. Discuss the reasons why firms might produce in large or small lots. What are the advantages and disadvantages of these two modes of operation. Consider the type of products that are being produced.
5 **ERP systems**. The installation of enterprise resource planning systems is a fast growing business. What advantages are there to a firm to have in place an ERP system such as supplied by Baan, Oracle or SAP? What impact does it have on the personnel? What might be some of the disadvantages?

EXERCISE PROBLEM: BELECOM

Situation

The Belecom company in Montpellier, France, manufactures car telephones. One product, Model J-610, comprises two subassemblies F-956, two assemblies N-458 and one purchased component X-459. Each assembly N-458 is manufactured from three subassemblies P-891 and two components G-587. Each subassembly P-891 is made from three components M-897, two components J-953 and three components D-896.

Table 13.13, gives the inventory records file including lead times for the final product and all its components. Table 13.14 gives the master production schedule for the finished product for a six week planning horizon.

Required

As director of production, prepare a material requirements plan for the finished product J-610 and all its components.

Table 13.13 Inventory records file

Reference number	Minimum lot size	Lead time (weeks)	Quantity in stock	Safety stock (week 1)	Stock already assigned	Scheduled receipts in week 1
J-610	500	1	300	200	50	100
F-956	700	1	250	100	0	3 000
N-458	4 000	1	1 000	200	0	3 000
X-459	1 500	1	500	100	300	1 500
P-891	25 000	2	800	50	0	20 000
G-587	18 000	2	1 000	40	120	13 000
M-897	250	3	1 500	100	40	80 000
J-953	50 000	2	400	120	75	60 000
D-896	85 000	1	800	400	55	80 000

Table 13.14 The master production schedule for the finished product for a six week planning horizon.

Reference	J-610	Week	1	2	3	4	5	6
		Gross requirements	0	1 500	2 250	1 750	4 000	5 000

EXERCISE PROBLEM: BEWDLEY

Situation

The Bewdley company in Shropshire, England makes automobile components for Ford Motor Co. Two major products are steering wheel assemblies. There are two models of the steering wheels, A-0137 and H-1455 and the indented product structure for the two products is given in Figure 13.12. In this product structure there is a one-for-one basis for component requirements. The inventory records file is given in Table 13.15 and the gross requirements in Table 13.16.

Required

1 Given the above information, develop a material requirements plan for the two finished products and all the components.
2 Redo the material requirements plan assuming the following:
   - Assembly from level 2 to level 1: there is a yield rate of 92 per cent.
   - Assembly from level 1 to level 0: there is a yield rate of 96 per cent.

Figure 13.12 Bewdley – Indented product structure.

A-0137	H-1455
B-1365	J-8954
D-1865	E-4789
E-4789	F-0265
C-1258	K-6957
F-0265	E-4789
G-1285	F-0265
	C-1258
	F-0265
	G-1285

Table 13.15 Inventory records file

Reference number	Minimum lot size	Lead time (weeks)	Inventory on hand
A-0137	0	1	10
B-1365	0	2	100
C-1258	50	2	50
D-1865	0	1	50
E-4789	0	1	600
F-0265	200	2	1 500
G-1285	0	1	75
H-1455	0	1	45
J-8954	300	3	100
K-6957	0	3	100

Table 13.16 Gross requirements

Week	1	2	3	4	5	6	7	8	9	10	11	12
A-0137	0	0	0	0	0	200	150	200	250	50	50	150
H-1455	0	0	0	0	300	250	150	50	100	200	50	100

EXERCISE PROBLEM: BURTON CO.

Situation

Burton Co. in England produces subassembly motor units for refrigerators, which are shipped to various clients. One particular subassembly, reference CAT-1892 is made on special equipment. Past data indicates that the set-up time (order cost) for producing a new lot of the subassembly units is a high £3000 as a result of special adjustments to the equipment. Carrying costs for the finished products are estimated at £1.75/unit/week. Carrying costs for raw materials are not taken into consideration.

For the next ten weeks the gross requirements for the end product are as shown in Table 13.17. Initial inventory is 1750 units.

Required

1 Develop a plan for lot sizing using the lot-for-lot criterion. Determine the carrying costs, holding costs and the total plan concept using this method

2 Develop a plan for lot sizing using the economic order quantity criterion. Determine the carrying costs, holding costs, and the total plan concept using this method

3 Develop a plan for lot sizing using the periodic order quantity criterion. Determine the carrying costs, holding costs and the total plan concept using this method.

4 Develop a plan for lot sizing using the part period balancing criterion. Determine the carrying costs, holding costs and the total plan concept using this method.

5 Which is the preferred plan?

Table 13.17 Burton Co. – the gross requirements for the end product for the next ten weeks

Week	1	2	3	4	5	6	7	8	9	10
Gross requirements	1100	1570	1550	1750	1050	1250	1180	450	1150	1250

EXERCISE PROBLEM: PLASTIC PRODUCTS CO. (PART II)

Situation

The operating data for the Plastic Products Co. is the same is in the worked example (Part I) except that now, based on historical data, 4 per cent of the purchased wheels are unusable in the assembly operation. This means that the planned ordered receipts have to be adjusted accordingly. Assume that those wheels in inventory have already been inspected and are suitable for the assembly operation.

Required

1 Develop a material requirements plan showing a schedule to meet the final product demand.

EXERCISE PROBLEM: SPRINKLER

Situation

Anedrag company has a patent on garden sprinklers, a product that it sells directly to garden and horticultural stores. Anedrag purchases all of the components from suppliers and its only work is the assembly of the finished product. The product structure for two particular models, AA-010 and BB-020, is given in Figure 13.13. A particular customer has put in a firm order for 10 000 units of model AA-010 and 20 000 units of model BB-020. At the time of the order, inventory data for the two products is given in Table 13.18. There are no minimum lot-size constraints, no safety stock is held and the initial inventory of all the components, and the finished product, at the beginning of the operation is zero.

Table 13.18 Inventory data for the two sprinkler products

Reference	Quantity in product	Source	Lead time (weeks)
AA-010		Assembled	2
BB-020		Assembled	2
AA-116	1	Purchased	2
BB-117	1	Purchased	2
AA-223	1	Purchased	2
BB-224	1	Purchased	1
AB-225	1	Purchased	1
AA-338	1	Purchased	3
BB-339	1	Purchased	4
AB-340	1	Purchased	2
AB-341	1	Purchased	2
AB-540	1	Purchased	1

Figure 13.13 Product structure for two sprinkler models.

AA-010	BB-020
AA-116	BB-117
AA-223	BB-224
AA-338	BB-339
AA-340	AB-340
AB-340	AB-340
AB-225	AB-225
AB-341	AB-341
AB-540	AB-540

Required

1 Based on the information provided, in how many weeks could the firm promise the order quantity of the two finished products to the client? Show the material movements on a complete material requirements plan.

2 If Anedrag were able to negotiate with its suppliers to have the delivery lead time for all components reduced to one week and, further, it was able to put in another shift so that the assembly of the finished products could also be reduced to one week, then what delivery lead time for the complete order would Anedrag be able to promise to its client? Justify your response on a modified material requirements plan.

3 What impact might the changes proposed in requirement 2 have on the operation of the firm?

NOTES AND REFERENCES

1. Orlicky, J. (1975) *Material Requirements Planning*, New York: McGraw-Hill.
2. Robert Bosch handrill, with permission (14 November 1997).
3. Heizer, J. and Render, B. (1996) *Production and Operations Management: Lot sizing*, 4th edn: 662–66.
4. Waldron, D. (1992) 'What follows MRP II? Enterprise Resource Planning', *Professional Engineering*, 5(5): 22–23.
5. Groussaud, G. (1993) 'La méthode MRP II clé de voute d'une GPAO', *L'informatique professionnelle*, No 119 (Décembre).
6. Johnson, A. (1986) 'MRP II? MRP? OPT? CIM? FMS? JIT? Is any system lettter-perfect?', *Management Review* (September): 22–27
7. 'The best software business Bill Gates doesn't own' (1997) *Fortune*, 29 December.
8. Head Offices, Zonneoordlaan 17, PO Box 250, 6710 BG Ede, The Netherlands.
9. Headquarters, SAP Aktiengesellschaft, PO Box 1461, D-69190 Waldorf, Germany
10. SAP Annual Report (1995).
11. 'SAP expects pretax profit to grow by 45 per cent this year' (1996) *Wall Street Journal Europe* 26–27 July.
12. 'New Formula for Hoechst' (1997) *Information Strategy* 2(5): 40–43.
13. Ascarelli, S. (1996) 'Out of nowhere: Dutch software firm gives Germany's SAP much to worry about: *Wall Street Journal Europe* 1 February.

FURTHER READING

Abad, P. L. (1996) 'Optimal pricing and lot-sizing under conditions of perishability and partial backordering', *Management Science* 42(8): 1093–1104.

Bruker, H. D., Flowers, G. A. and Peck, R. D., 'MRP Shop-Floor Control in a job shop: Definitely Works', *Production and Inventory Management Journal* 33(2): 43–46.

Cosgrove, W. J,. Westerman, R. R. and Knox, J. E. (1993) 'Optimal discrete lot sizing: A convenient approach', *Production and Inventory Management Journal* 34(3): 14–19.

Davis, D. (1994) 'Profit found in MRP II, execution integration', *Manufacturing systems* 12(7): 16–20.

Estep, J. A. (1996) 'Tailoring your MRP system to meet your needs', *IEE Solution* 28(9): 36–39.

Franca, P. M., Armentano, V., Berretta, R. E. and Clark, A. R. (1997) 'A heuristic method for lot-sizing in multi-stage systems', *Computers and Operations Research* 24(9): 861–74.

Gardiner, S. C., Blackstone, J. H. Jr (1993) 'The effects of lot sizing and dispatching on customer service in an MRP environment', *Journal of Operations Management* 11(2): 143–159.

Gregory, A. (1995) 'Capitalise on MRP II for better cost reporting', *Works Management* 48(2): 36–39.

De Groote, X. (1994) 'Flexibility and product variety in lot-sizing models', *European Journal of Operational Research* 75(2): 264–74.

Gumaer, R. (1996) 'Beyond ERP and MRP II', *IIE Solutions* 28(9): 32–35.

Hariga, M. (1994) 'The inventory lot-sizing problem with continuous time-varying demand and shortages', *Journal of the Operational Research Society* 45(7): 827–37.

Hasin, M. A. and Pandy, P. C. (1996) 'MRP II: Should its simplicity remain unchanged?', *Industrial Management* 38(3): 19–20.

Hecht, B. (1997) 'Choose the right ERP software', *Datamation* 43 (3): 56–58.

Jacobi, M. A. (1994) 'How to unlock the benefits of MRP II and just-in-time', *Hospital Materiel Management Quarterly* 15(4): 12–22.

Lagodimos, A. G. (1993) 'Models for evaluating the performance of serial and assembly MRP systems', *European Journal of Operational Research* 68(1): 49–68.

Lee, W. J., Kim, D. and Cabot, A. V. (1996) 'Optimal Demand Rate, lot sizing, and process reliability improvement decisions', *IIE Transactions* 28(11): 941–52.

Lee, Y.-Q and, Shin, H.-J. (1996) 'CIM implementation through JIT and MRP integration', *Computers and Industrial Engineering* 31(3): 609–12.

Lunn, T. (1994) 'Integrating MRP into modern business', *Hospital Material Management Quarterly* 15(4): 6–11.

Luscombe, M. (1994) 'Customer-focused MRP II', *Logistics Information Management* 7(5): 22–29.

Nakagiri, D. and Kuriyama, S. (1996) 'A study of production management systems with MRP', *International Journal of Production Economics* 44(1, 2): 27–33.

Piszczalski, M. (1997) 'Lessons learned from Europe's SAP users', *Automotive Manufacturing and Production* 109(1): 54–56.

Sum, C.-C., Ang, J. S. K. and Yeo, L.-N. (1997) 'Contextual elements of critical success factors in MRP implementation', *Production and Inventory Management Journal* 38(3): 77–83.

Sum, C.-C., Png, D. O.-S. and Yang, K.-K. (1993) 'Effects of product structure complexity on multi-level lot sizing', *Decision Sciences* 24(6): 1135–56.

Ulusoy, G. and Uzsoy, R. (1992) 'Computer-aided process planning and Material Requirements Planning: First steps towards computer-integrated manufacturing', *Interfaces* 22(2): 76–86.

14 Operations scheduling

Objectives and overview

The objective of this chapter is to present operations, or short-term scheduling, which is a planning decision in operations management critical to the smooth flow of goods and services in the supply chain. The chapter opens by defining scheduling and giving some typical illustrations. It then presents the Gantt or bar chart as a scheduling tool; what it is, how it is used and its advantages in short-term scheduling. The chapter then goes on to discuss order sequencing and its importance in optimization. Quantitative techniques are presented for optimizing the scheduling function, including Johnson's Method for two or three workcentres, the Assignment Method, the Run-out Method and the Line of Balance Technique. The chapter then presents the nine rules of Optimized Production Technology before concluding with scheduling of personnel.

THE SCHEDULING ACTIVITY

Scheduling is the function that involves the preparation of a timetable for work that needs doing to meet client-need dates, or for activities to achieve some desired objective. In the supply chain, effective management of the scheduling activity is important to avoid bottlenecks, to optimize the utilization of equipment, labour and machines, and at the same time to ensure the smooth flow of goods or services to customers. Operations scheduling covers those activities that are normally repetitive in nature and have a relatively short-term time frame of hours, days, weeks or perhaps a few months. Illustrations for certain industries are given below.

Print shop

This might include scheduling the following activities to publish a sales catalogue:

1. Making the film
2. Mounting
3. Preparation of the plates
4. Printing
5. Binding
6. Trimming
7. Packaging
8. Shipping

Foundry

This might include scheduling the following activities to make a bronze impeller blade for a boat:

1. Making the sand mould
2. Pouring liquid metal into the mould
3. Cooling of the mould
4. Separation of casting from mould
5. Removing burrs and joints
6. Cleaning and polishing the casting

Chocolate manufacture

This might include scheduling the following activities to produce an order of milk chocolate bars:

1. Roasting cocoa beans
2. Making cocoa paste
3. Adding milk
4. Crushing
5. Moulding
6. Cooling
7. De-moulding
8. Wrapping
9. Packaging
10. Delivery

Railway company

This might include scheduling the following activies for the use of rolling stock:

1. Departure and arrival timetables
2. Equipment (express, buffet car)
3. Personnel (drivers & ticket controller)
4. Food/drink for restaurant and bar
5. Cleaning
6. Maintenance

Business school

This might include scheduling the following activities for the preparation and delivery of classes:

1 Programme
2 Instructors
3 Classrooms to be used
4 Teaching material (computer, TV)
5 Exam schedule
6 Marking exams

Medical facility

This might include scheduling the following activities for the effective treatment of patients:

1 Consultations
2 Timetable for surgical procedures
3 Use of beds
4 Staff requirements – nurses and doctors
5 Delivery of medical supplies
6 Rehabilitation treatment

Food distribution centre

This might include scheduling the following activities to meet the needs of retail outlets:

1 Warehouse personnel
2 Reception dates of bulk products
3 Storage areas to be used
4 Preparation of client pallets (picking)
5 Organizing delivery vehicles
6 Drivers necessary

In contrast to operations scheduling, which is short term, is project scheduling, which is long term involving the development of a timetable for a unique activity where the project-completion time frame may be several years. This type of scheduling is presented in more detail in Chapter 18, *Project Management*.

GANTT CHART

The engineer Henry L. Gantt of the USA (1861–1919), developed the Gantt chart, commonly known as a bar chart, in 1916 to provide managers with an easily understood summary of what work is scheduled for certain time periods, how much of the scheduled work is completed according to plan and what function performed the work. An example of a Gantt chart for a printing operation is given in Figure 14.1. This is explained in the following.

A printing operation

Activities

The activities to be performed are on the left-hand side of the chart:

■ making a film;
■ mounting the film;
■ preparation of the final plates;
■ printing on an offset printing machine;
■ binding the printed documents;
■ packing finished product to deliver to the client.

Time

The time frame is given on the top of the chart:

■ It runs from Monday through Saturday morning.
■ Each day is broken down into hours from 08:00 to 17:00. Production stops for lunch between 12:00 to 13:00 (this time is not shown).

Jobs

The job references are shown on the bars:

■ There are seven jobs, A, B, C, D, E, F and G, that start this particular week.
■ There are six jobs, M, N, W, X, Y and Z, that were started in a previous period.

Planned schedule

■ The unshaded horizontal bars give the start and finish for a particular activity for a certain job.
■ The light-shaded area is the set-up time required to adjust the machine and to do all that is necessary to prepare for the next job.
■ The dark-shaded area is the idle time when no activity is planned.

All this information would have been prepared prior to the start of the week, say Friday evening or early Monday morning. As the actual time proceeds, the status of the activity, for each job, is marked on the Gantt chart with the thick black horizontal line on the bottom of the bar.

Update to operations manager

Suppose the time period is now Thursday morning at 08:00 as shown by the vertical line in Figure 14.1. Then Table 14.1 gives the status from the Gantt chart at this time.

Using a Gantt chart, an operations or production manager can see if resources can be modified to ensure that activities are kept on schedule. In this example, Printing is behind schedule, which then risks delaying the following jobs, A and B. If this happens, this will have repercussions in the downstream operations of

Figure 14.1 Gantt chart for a printing operation.

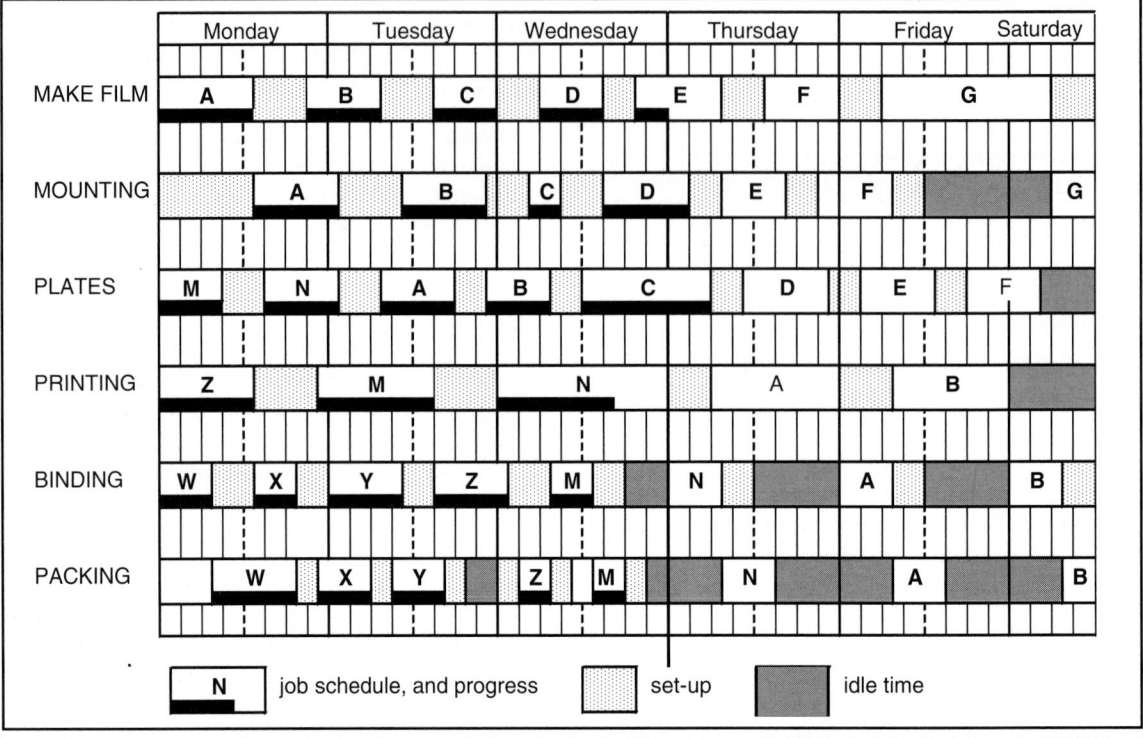

Table 14.1 The status of the Gantt chart at 08:00 on Thursday

Activity	Status
Making a film	Job E is on schedule
Mounting the film	Job D is ahead of schedule. This job is finished, although it was not scheduled to be finished until 09:00 Thursday morning.
Preparation of the final plates	Job C is ahead of schedule. This job is finished, although it was scheduled to be finished at 10:00 Thursday morning.
Printing on an offset printing machine	Job N is behind schedule. This job was scheduled to be finished by Wednesday at 17:00. It is 2½ hours behind schedule.
Binding the printed documents	Activity is on schedule. Binding of product N is ready to begin.
Packing finished product	Activity is on schedule. At the present time there is no activity.

Binding and Packing, putting jobs A and B behind schedule.

Advantages of the Gantt Chart

With the Gantt chart the following questions can be asked:

■ Since mounting and preparation of plates is ahead of schedule, can personnel from here assist in printing?
■ There is idle time in packing. Can people here be used in printing?
■ Can the printing time for A and B be reduced to avoid delays?

■ Can the set-up time in printing between jobs N and A be reduced to avoid delays in printing?

The Gantt chart is a useful tool to help a production manager monitor the activities of a production operation. In addition, in presenting activities according to a time scale, a manager can see if operation improvements can be made. In the example here, the chart shows that set-up times are long in comparison to operating time. There is considerable idle time in binding and packaging. Perhaps scheduling can be reorganized to avoid this situation. In order to have the flexibility to transfer personnel from one operation to another, the workforce must be multiskilled. Hence the importance of training in order to be able to meet client needs or to have flexibility when operations do not proceed according to plan.

ORDER SEQUENCING

Resources such as labour, machines and time are limited in any production or service operation. Order sequencing is to decide in which sequence to process jobs or people that are waiting upstream. These might involve:

- machining operations in a manufacturing concern;
- assembling machined parts;
- trucks waiting to depart to deliver goods to clients;
- packaging of finished goods;
- serving a customer at a service centre, such as a store, bank or insurance firm.

A particular operating sequence might be more acceptable than another in terms of overall costs. Some sequencing rules are discussed in the following sections

First come, first served

First come, first served (FCFS) means that the next job to be processed is the one that arrived first in the waiting line. This would be a fairness approach, particularly if one is dealing with people. In inventory management it is synonymous with FIFO (first in first out), meaning the first piece of inventory to arrive at a storage area is the first to be used.

Earliest due date

The earliest due date (EDD) means that the next job to be processed is the one that has the earliest (closest) date when the finished job is promised to the client. This criterion is important to avoid irritating, and perhaps losing, the customer.

Shortest processing time

The shortest processing (SPT) time means the next job to be processed is the one that has the least time necessary to complete. The philosophy here is to get the smallest jobs over quickly, which gives a physiological impression that one is being more productive. The problem with this approach is that large jobs, which might be more urgent, get pushed behind.

Longest processing time

The longest processing (LPT) time means that the next job is the one that has the longest processing time. The logic here is to get the biggest jobs over with first. In practice, if jobs have long processing times it is often better to try and break them down into two or more smaller ones. Scheduling works best when one is dealing with jobs that require roughly equal processing time or resource requirements.

Last arrived, first processed

The last arrived, first processed (LAFP) means that the next job to be processed is the one that arrived last. This is probably illogical, and is sloppy management, but it means that the last job that is put on the top of the pile, is then processed first!

Least slack time

The least slack time (LST) means that the next job is the one that has the least amount of slack time. The slack time, sometimes referred to as the float time, is the difference between the date or time when the job is promised and the processing time to complete that job.

Critical ratio

The critical ratio (CR) means that the next job to be processed is the one that has the lowest critical ratio, which is defined as follows:

$$\text{critical ratio} = \frac{\text{time to the due date}}{\text{remaining process time}}.$$

If the critical ratio is less than unity, it means that the job will be finished after the promised delivery date. In this case, effort should be made to utilize other resources, such as overtime, part-time labour, etc., to reduce the overall processing time, in order that the critical ratio is increased to greater than unity. In this way the client will be satisfied.

Least changeover cost

The least changeover cost means that the next job is one that involves least machine changeover, or set-up, time; that is, try to minimize the cost of changeover by treating those jobs that have similar machine settings. For example, a machine shop is currently processing rectangular mouldings in red plastic. The jobs waiting upstream are rectangular mouldings in blue plastic and a cylindrical moulding in red plastic. It may be more cost-effective to produce the red cylinder moulding next since this will avoid cleaning the machine (a procedure which would be necessary if the blue moulding was the next job processed).

Non-quantifiable sequencing rules

Other sequencing rules that are normally not planned, but nevertheless exist in real life include the following.

Client who shouts the loudest

Sometimes in the real world clients who are very persistent put verbal pressure on their suppliers in order to get preferential treatment for their job.

Best client

Sequencing rules may be adopted to satisfy those clients who pay the highest price, have the highest margin or purchase in large quantities. Thus, the best go first.

Emergency situations

In the medical profession, patients who have a life-threatening situation are treated first. Also, when emergency supplies, such as medical products, raw materials are needed because of a plant shutdown, food after an earthquake for example, schedules may be completely revamped.

Criteria for comparing sequencing rules

If processing times and delivery dates are known with some certainty, then the following criteria might be used to compare sequencing rules.

Average flow time

The average flow time is the average amount of time each job stays in the workcentre. It is calculated by the total flow time (the total time each job stays in the workcentre, including processing time and non-active time, calculated from the start of the first job) divided by the number of jobs being handled. In a sense, average flow time represents the 'average inventory' of jobs.

Average number of jobs in the workcentre

The average number of jobs in the workcentre is the total flow time (the total time each job stays in the workcentre from the start of the first job) divided by the total production time.

Number of jobs late

The number of jobs late is the number of jobs that are not completed according to the date promised to the client.

Average jobs late

The average jobs late is the number of jobs that were finished after the promised due date, divided by the total number of jobs processed in the workcentre.

Number of days late

The number of days late is the total number of days that jobs are delivered after the date promised to the client.

Average days late

The average days late is the total days late divided by the number of jobs processed.

Changeover cost

The changeover cost is the total cost of making all of the machine changeovers for a group of jobs.

The preferred sequence method

There is not necessarily one method that is optimal, because it really depends on the circumstances, but the following are some considerations.

Respecting delivery dates

An important management criterion is to satisfy the client. Thus, those sequencing rules that respect delivery dates, or at least minimize delays, would be the best. These sequencing rules include:

- critical ratio;
- earliest due date;
- least slack time.

First-come-first served

The first-come-first served rule does give customers sense of satisfaction, and is fair when dealing with people. However, from a planning or cost point of view it is not necessarily optimal.

Shortest processing time

Using this means that, at the beginning, more jobs will be completed, which gives some psychological satisfaction of achievement. The disadvantage is that long-duration jobs may be continuously pushed back in the schedule in favour of the short-duration jobs.

Longest processing time

This provides the satisfaction of getting 'the worst out of the way'. However, it certainly may not be optimum.

Changeover costs

The least changeover costs is an important criterion to take into consideration, providing that in applying this rule, client jobs are not delayed. Under ordinary circumstances, jobs that require similar machine set-ups should follow each other at a workcentre. However, to minimize the importance of changeover costs, attention should be given to implementing a SMED system (see Chapter 16, *Lean Production and Just-in-Time*).

The worked example, *Carver* Part I, illustrates the use of some of the sequencing rules for various operating times and delivery dates.

WORKED EXAMPLE: CARVER (PART I)

Situation

Carver and Son operate a small print shop in the Chico area of Northern California, USA, where they have one offset press to perform work for customers. By scheduling of the personnel, they are able to operate the print shop seven days per week at eight hours per day. The eight hours is for printing jobs. Set-up time for changeover of jobs is performed on overtime, either in the evening or early in the morning. Orders received are put on backlog until current scheduled work has been completed. At 24 February (day 55) the jobs waiting to be processed are as shown in Table 14.2.

Table 14.2 Carver – Jobs waiting to be processed on 24 February (day 55)

Job	A	B	C	D	E	F
Process time	9	11	8	12	7	5
Date received	39	42	47	48	37	55
Date Due	71	81	75	98	86	108

Required

1 Develop for this situation the sequencing rules

(a) first come, first served;
(b) earliest due date.

Prepare a Gantt chart for these two rules and determine:
■ total elapsed flow time (time to process all jobs from day 55);
■ average flow time/job, or average completion time/job (total flow time/number of jobs in system);
■ average jobs in system (total flow time/total processing time);
■ number of jobs late;
■ average days late (total days late/total number of jobs).

Solution

1 With a 7-day work schedule, and the assumption that there are no vacation days, there is sufficient time to process all the jobs by the end of the last due date:
■ total processing time necessary: $(9 + 11 + 8 + 12 + 7 + 5) = 52$ days;
■ processing time available: $(108 - 55 + 1) = 54$ days.

However, because of due dates for specific jobs, some may be finished late when sequencing rules are considered. The solutions are shown in Tables 14.3 and 14.4 with the respective Gantt charts in Figures 14.2 and 14.3. The explanation of the terms are as follows:

Table 14.3 Carver – First come, first served; the Gantt chart is shown in Figure 14.2

Today's date	55						
Job	**E**	**A**	**B**	**C**	**D**	**F**	**Total**
Process time	7	9	11	8	12	5	52
Date received	37	39	42	47	48	55	
Date due	86	71	81	75	98	108	
Flow time (time in centre)*	7	16	27	35	47	52	184
Date finished	62	71	82	90	102	107	
Days late	0	0	1	15	4	0	20

	FCFS	
Number of jobs processed	6	
Total flow time	184	
Average flow time	30.67	(Total flow time)/(Number of jobs processed)
Average jobs in system	3.54	(Total flow time)/(Total process time)
Number of jobs late	3	
Average number of jobs late	0.5	(Number of jobs late)/(Numer of jobs processed)
Number of days late	20	
Average days late	3.33	(Number of days late)/(Number of jobs processed)

* After the schedule has been developed, not from when the order has been received.

Figure 14.2 Gantt chart for first come, first served (Table 14.3).

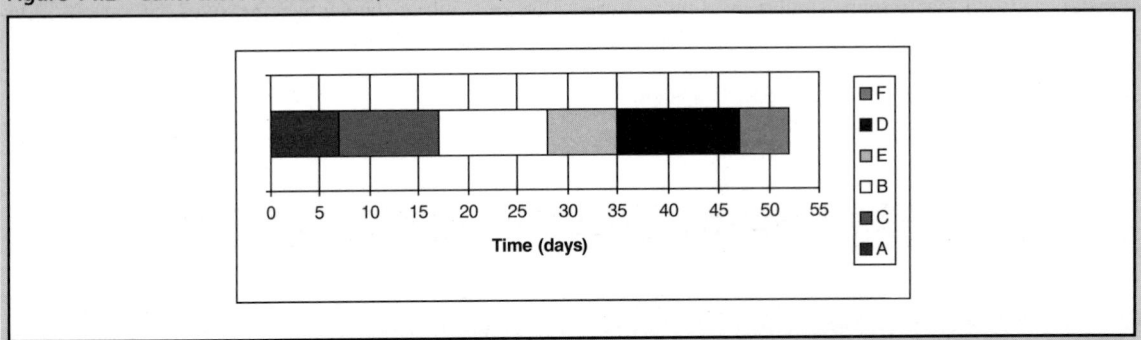

Table 14.4 Carver – Earliest due date; the Gantt chart is shown in Figure 14.3

Today's date	55						
Job	A	C	B	E	D	F	Total
Process time	9	8	11	7	12	5	52
Date received	39	47	42	37	48	55	
Date due	71	75	81	86	98	108	
Flow time (Time in centre)*	9	17	28	35	47	52	188
Date finished	64	72	83	90	102	107	
Days late	0	0	2	4	4	0	10

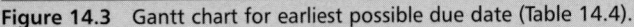

	EDD	
Number of jobs processed	6	
Total flow time	188	
Average flow time	31.33	(Total flow time)/(Number of jobs processed)
Average jobs in system	3.62	(Total flow time)/(Total process time)
Number of jobs late	3	
Average number of jobs late	0.5	(Number of jobs late)/(Number of jobs processed)
Number of days late	10	
Average days late	1.67	(Number of days late)/(Number of jobs processed)

* After the schedule has been developed, not from when the order has been received.

Figure 14.3 Gantt chart for earliest possible due date (Table 14.4).

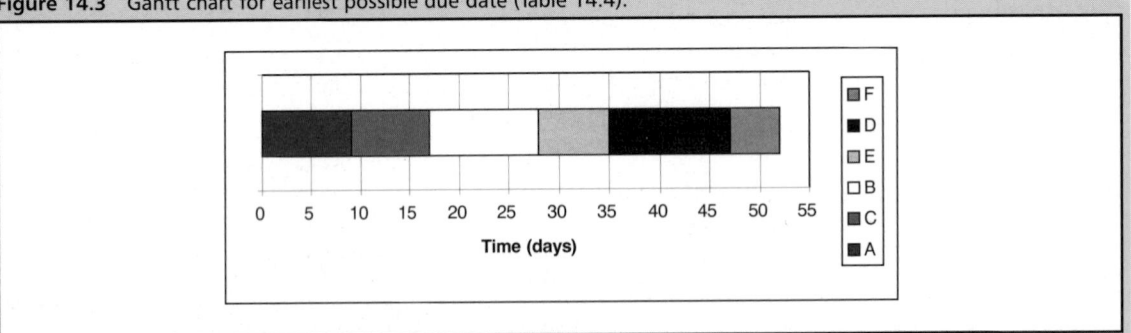

Production time

This is the time needed to complete each of the six jobs.

Flow time

This represents the time that the jobs stay in the centre based on the start date of day 55. It is equivalent to a measure of the *inventory* of jobs that stay at the centre.

Need time

This is the date when the job is promised to the client.

Date finished

This is the start date of the job plus the processing time.

Days late

This is the difference between the date promised and the date finished. If the value is positive, then the days late are zero.

JOHNSON'S RULE

Johnson's rule is a scheduling technique developed by S. M. Johnson of the USA in 1954 for job-shop scheduling. It is used when several jobs need to be processed successively through two workcentres. With more than two workcentres the method is more complex, but if certain criteria apply, it can be developed for three centres.[1]

Two work centres

The method establishes the best sequence, which will be the same for both centres and will optimize the use of resources and minimize the total processing time. Work centres might include:

- forged components that must first pass through a drilling operation, before going to milling;
- a book-binding operation, where books must first pass through binding before going to trimming;
- finished products that must pass through inspection before going to packing;
- a medical centre where patients must be seen by a doctor before passing onto the X-ray department.

In applying Johnson's rule to these situations, the assumption is that there is only one resource available at each workcentre, such as one drilling machine, one milling machine, one binding unit, one trimmer, one inspector, one packer, one doctor, one specialist for example.

Procedure

Assume there are two processing areas, Work Centre 1 and Work Centre 2. There are six jobs to be processed, A, B, C, D, E and F.

1 Select the shortest processing time for all the operations for all jobs in both work centres. Assume that the shortest processing time is for job D.

2 If the shortest processing time occurs at Work Centre 1, then schedule job D first at Work Centre 1; Job D would then also be first at Work Centre 2. If the shortest processing time occurs at Work Centre 2, then schedule job D last at Work Centre 1 and also last at Work Centre 2.

3 Eliminate further consideration of job D.

4 Select the shortest processing time for the jobs remaining. Repeat Steps 2 to 3 assigning a schedule either from the front (Work Centre 1) or the back (Work Centre 2) until all jobs have been allocated a schedule position.

5 If a tie for the shortest processing time occurs in different work centres, there is no problem in determining the job sequence. However, if a tie occurs in the same work centre, the competing two job sequences need to be evaluated by comparing cumulative processing times. The lowest cumulative processing time first would be the recommended sequence.

6 Johnson's rule is based on the assumption that the optimum sequence is the same in Work Centres 1 and 2. This implies that work cannot be carried out simultaneously on the same job in both work centres.

The use of Johnson's Rule for two work centres is illustrated with the worked example, *Kneier*.

Three work centres

Three work centres would include an extension of the operations given above, for example:

- forged components that must pass through a cutting, drilling, and finally milling;
- a book-binding operation, where books pass through printing and binding before going to trimming;
- finished products that pass through polishing and inspection before going to packing;
- a medical centre where patients see a doctor, pass onto X-ray and then consult a specialist.

Johnson's rule can be applied if either of the following two criteria apply:

- The smallest time at the first processing operation is at least as great as the largest duration at the second processing operation.
- The smallest duration at the third processing operation is at least as great as the largest duration at the second operation

Procedure

To apply Johnson's for three work centres, for calculation purposes the three centres are reduced to two by combining the times of each job in Work Centres 1 and 2 to give a 'Work Centre 1A' and those in Work Centres 2 and 3 to give a 'Work Centre 2B'. The situation shown in Table 14.5 becomes that shown in Table 14.6. Then Johnson's rule is applied, treating the situation as two workstations. This method is illustrated by the worked example, *Serre Co.*

Table 14.5 Jobs in three work centres

Job	Work Centre 1 time (hs)	Work Centre 2 time (hs)	Work Centre 3 time (hs)
A	X_1	X_2	X_3
B	Y_1	Y_2	Y_3
C	Z_1	Z_2	Z_3

Table 14.6 Jobs in Work Centres 1, 2 and 3 after combining the times

Job	Work Centre 1A time (hs)	Work Centre 2B time (hs)
A	$X_1 + X_2$	$X_2 + X_3$
B	$Y_1 + Y_2$	$Y_2 + Y_3$
C	$Z_1 + Z_2$	$Z_2 + Z_3$

WORKED EXAMPLE: KNEIER

Situation

The Kneier company near Freiberg, Germany, is a small family firm that manufactures custom items of wood furniture. Raw lumber arrives at the factory, where it is cut to length, turned and shaped according to customer specifications in Work Centre A. From Work Centre A jobs pass to Work Centre B, where the components are assembled and finished. Assembly involves mounting the components, either by using tongue and groove joints or by gluing. Finishing is the final sanding, polishing and/or varnishing. The staff is limited and work crews can only work on one job at a time. On one particular Monday morning, the jobs waiting to be processed were as given in Table 14.7.

Table 14.7 Kneier – Jobs waiting to be processed on Monday morning

Item	Order of arrival	Work Centre A job time (hrs)	Work Centre B job time (hrs)
Small chair	1	1.50	0.50
Armchair	2	4.00	1.00
Coffee table	3	0.75	2.25
Magazine rack	4	1.00	3.00
Lamp standard	5	2.00	4.00
Rocking chair	6	1.80	2.20

Required

1 Using the sequence rule, first come, first served, develop a planning schedule for Work Centre A and Work Centre B:
   (a) What is the total time for each operation?

(b) What is the total elapsed time?
   (c) Present the sequence on a Gantt chart showing operating times and dead times.
2 Use Johnson's method to develop a schedule:
   (a) What is the total time for each operation?
   (b) What is the total elapsed time?
   (c) Present the sequence on a Gantt chart showing operating times and dead times.
3 Compare the schedule produced under first come, first served with that produced with Johnson's rule.

Solution

1 First come, first served
   Figure 14.4 gives the Gantt chart under the first come, first served rule, together with a summary of the processing times.
2 Johnson's method
   Figure 14.5 gives the Gantt chart using Johnson's method, together with a summary of the processing times.
3 If the two rules are compared, using Johnson's rule means that:
   - Total elapsed time has been reduced from 17.95 hours to 13.70 hours or by almost 24 per cent (23.68 per cent).
   - Dead time in Work Centre A has been reduced from 6.90 hours to 2.65 hours or by almost 62 per cent (61.59 per cent).
   - Dead time in Work Centre B has been reduced from 5.00 hours (1.50 + 3.50) to 0.75 hours or by 85 per cent.
   - Total dead time for the whole operation has been reduced from 11.90 hours to 3.40 hours or by about 71 per cent (71.43 per cent).

In practice, with proper planning, for both schemes the dead time at the end of Work Centre A can be allocated to work on other assignments.

Figure 14.4   Kneier – first come, first served.

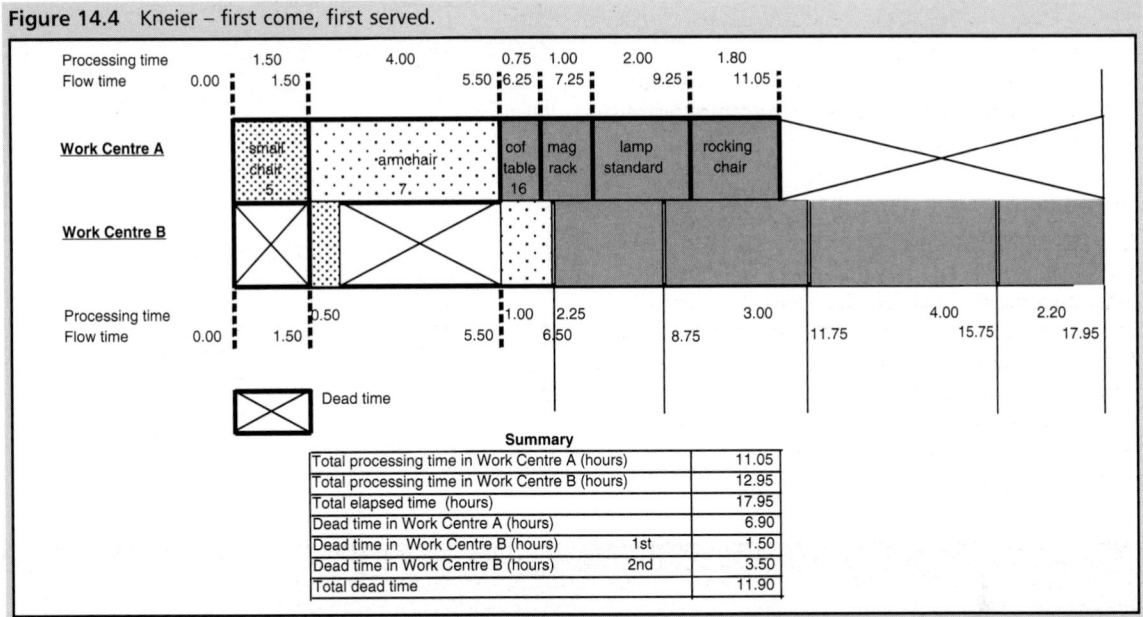

Figure 14.5   Kneier – Johnson's rule.

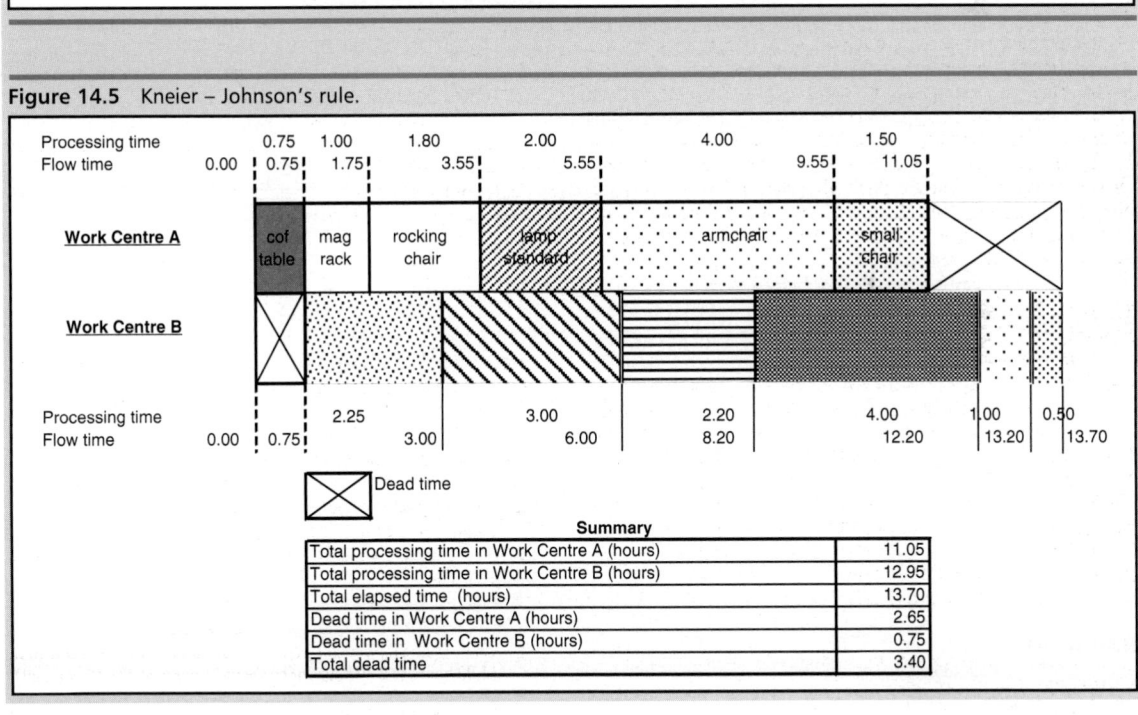

WORKED EXAMPLE: SERRE CO.

Situation

The Serre Co. is a small job shop outside Exeter, England, which manufactures custom-made heating units for farms in the area. There are three principal operations in the manufacture of the heaters: cutting, drilling and milling. Serre has only one each of the cutting, drilling and milling machines. On one particular morning, six jobs arrive for Serre. These jobs and the time for each operation are given in Table 14.8. The jobs arrived in the scheduling office in the order given.

Table 14.8   Serre – jobs for scheduling

Job	Cutting (min)	Drilling (min)	Milling (min)
A	12	7	18
B	18	14	24
C	9	17	25
D	22	9	21
E	14	12	21

Required

1 Develop a planning schedule for these five jobs using a first come, first served operation. Present the results on a Gantt chart. What is the total elapsed time for completing all of the five jobs?
2 Redo the schedule using Johnson's rule. Show the results on a Gantt chart. What is the new elapsed time for completing all of the five jobs?
3 Compare the planning schedules produced in requirements 1 and 2

Solution

1 First come, first served operation
   Table 14.9 presents the operating data for the first come, first served sequencing rule. Here the jobs are handled by each of the three machines in the same sequence. There is dead time at some periods while an operation is being carried out on a particular job on a previous machine:

   ■ At the beginning, there is dead time of 12 min on Drilling while an operator is working on Job A in Cutting (operating time is 12 min). There is 19 min dead time on Milling while Cutting and Drilling is being carried out on Job A (12 + 7 min).
   ■ When Job A is finished in cutting, work starts immediately in cutting on Job B. This is finished after 30 min have elapsed.
   ■ In drilling, Job A is finished after 19 min have elapsed. However, there is dead time in Drilling while the operator waits for Job A to be finished in Cutting.
   ■ In Milling Job A starts after 19 min have elapsed and finishes at time 37 min. However, since Drilling is still working on Job B, there is a dead time of 7 min in Milling.
   ■ There is dead time of 8 min in Drilling while the operator is performing Cutting on Job E.

Figure 14.6 gives the Gantt chart, which shows the start and finish of each job, together with the corresponding dead time. The total elapsed time to finish all jobs is 135 min. Total dead, or inactive, time is 54 min.

Table 14.9   Serre Co. – first come, first served

Initial Data

Job	Machine 1 Cutting	Machine 2 Drilling	Machine 3 Milling
A	12	7	18
B	18	14	24
C	9	17	25
D	22	9	21
E	14	12	21
Total	75	59	109

	Job	Cutting	Drilling	Milling
		Activity time (mins)		
Start	A	0	12	19
Finish	A	12	19	37
Start	B	12	30	44
Finish	B	30	44	68
Start	C	30	44	68
Finish	C	39	61	93
Start	D	39	61	93
Finish	D	61	70	114
Start	E	61	75	114
Finish	E	75	87	135

Activity	Job	Cutting	Drilling	Milling	Total
	Dead	0	12	19	31
Job	A	12	7	18	37
	Dead	0	11	7	18
Job	B	18	14	24	56
	Dead	0	0	0	0
Job	C	9	17	25	51
	Dead	0	0	0	0
Job	D	22	9	21	52
	Dead	0	5	0	5
Job	E	14	12	21	47
Operating time	Total	75	59	109	243
Dead time	Total	0	28	26	54
Elapsed time	Total	75	87	135	297

2 Schedule using Johnson's Rule
   First a test is made to see if Johnson's rule can be applied to the three workstations:
   ■ Is the shortest time on Machine 1 greater than the longest time on Machine 2? – No; (9 is less than 17)
   ■ Is the shortest time on Machine 3 greater than the longest time on Machine 2? – Yes. (18 is greater than 17)
   Thus, Johnson's rule can be applied and thus combining machines the new arrangement is as shown in Table 14.10.

Figure 14.6 Serre Co. – first come, first served.

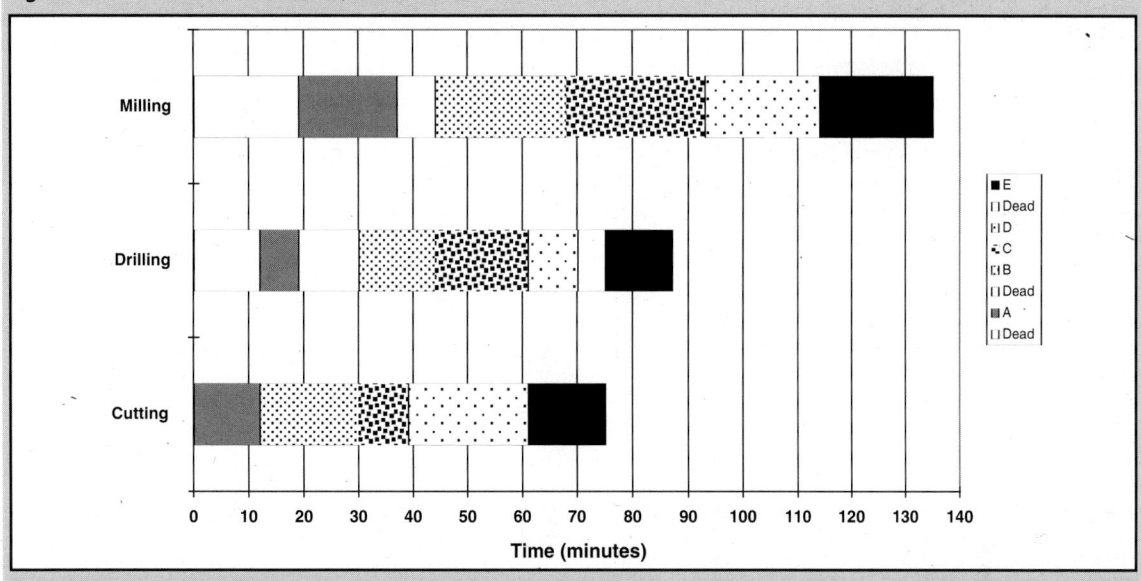

Table 14.10 Serre – Combination of job times for Johnson's rule

Job	Machine	Machine
	X	Y
A	19	25
B	32	38
C	26	42
D	31	30
E	26	33

Tables 14.11 and 14.12 give the modified schedule after applying Johnson's Rule and Figure 14.7 gives the Gantt chart illustrating the start and finish of each job, together with the corresponding dead time. The total elapsed time to finish all jobs is 129 min. Total dead, or inactive, time is 45 min.

Table 14.11 Serre – Applying Johnson's rule to the combination. Schedule order is putting C before E since the times are the same

Job	Machine X	Machine Y
A	19	25
C	26	42
E	26	33
B	32	38
D	31	30

Elapsed time

	Job	Cutting	Drilling	Milling
Start	A	0	12	19
Finish	A	12	19	37
Start	C	12	21	38
Finish	C	21	38	63
Start	E	21	38	63
Finish	E	35	50	84
Start	B	35	53	84
Finish	B	53	67	108
Start	D	53	75	108
Finish	D	75	84	129

Time in minutes

Activity	Job	Cutting	Drilling	Milling	Total
	Dead	0	12	19	31
Job	A	12	7	18	37
	Dead	0	2	1	3
Job	C	9	17	25	51
	Dead	0	0	0	0
Job	E	14	12	21	47
	Dead	0	3	0	3
Job	B	18	14	24	56
	Dead	0	8	0	8
Job	D	22	9	21	52
Operating time	Total	75	59	109	243
Dead time	Total	0	25	20	45
Elapsed time	Total	75	84	129	288

Table 14.12 Applying Johnson's rule to the combination. Schedule order is putting E before C since the times are the same

Job	Machine X	Machine Y
A	19	25
E	26	33
C	26	42
B	32	38
D	31	30

		Elapsed time		
	Job	Cutting	Drilling	Milling
Start	A	0	12	19
Finish	A	12	19	37
Start	E	12	26	38
Finish	E	26	38	59
Start	C	26	38	59
Finish	C	35	55	84
Start	B	35	55	84
Finish	B	53	69	108
Start	D	53	75	108
Finish	D	75	84	129

		Time in minutes			
Activity	Job	Cutting	Drilling	Milling	Total
	Dead	0	12	19	31
Job	A	12	7	18	37
	Dead	0	7	1	8
Job	E	9	17	25	51
	Dead	0	0	0	0
Job	C	14	12	21	47
	Dead	0	0	0	0
Job	B	18	14	24	56
	Dead	0	6	0	6
Job	D	22	9	21	52
Operating time	Total	75	59	109	243
Dead time	Total	0	25	20	45
Elapsed time	Total	75	84	129	288

3   Compare the planning schedules of requirements 1 and 2. The elapsed time has been reduced by 6 min (about 4 per cent) and inactive time by 9 min (about 17 per cent).

Figure 14.7   Serre Co. – Johnson's rule.

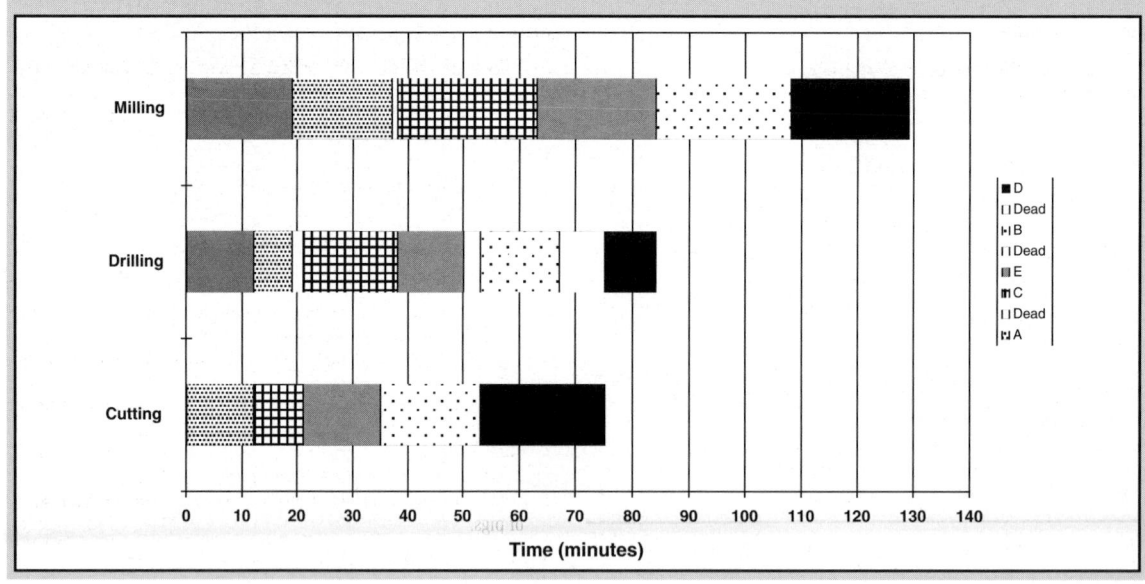

ASSIGNMENT METHOD OF JOB ALLOCATION

Criteria

The assignment method of job allocation is a way of assigning tasks when there are several possibilities, for example:

- There are several jobs waiting to be processed that can be assigned to one of various work centres.
- There are drilling jobs waiting to be processed that can be assigned to one of several numerically controlled drilling machines.
- There are many engineers in a design department who can be assigned to one of several design projects.
- There are several sales persons who can be assigned to one of several sales territories.

Objective

The objective of the assignment method is either to minimize the cost or to maximize the profit, depending on the situation being considered. In the assignment method for job allocation the assumption is that a job can be correctly processed in any work centre. In the assignment method for personnel, the assumption is that each individual is multiskilled and can perform any of the tasks (design or sales function) to which they would be assigned. Further, it is assumed that there are n assignments which need to be assigned to n work centres.

The worked example, *Biodecta*, illustrates the situation where the Excel 'Solver' has been used to optimize the solution.

WORKED EXAMPLE: BIODECTA

Situation

The Biodecta Company in Birmingham, England, performs research and development on genetic recombination. The manager of the research division, Jacques Enorme, has identified five biotechnology programmes for the forthcoming year. These are:

- the improvement of the production of wheat;
- the modification of the growth of tomatoes;
- a new blood testing technique;
- a biodegradable plastic;
- a perfume made from the sweat of pigs.

There are five teams at the Centre managed by John Jordan, Sally Stock, Mandy Mooner, Brian Brains and Lucia Label. Each of the five teams is relatively multiskilled, such they are able to work on any of the five projects. The manager has estimated the costs for the first phase for each research project, according to which team carries out the work and these are shown in Table 14.13.

Table 14.13 Estimates of the costs (in £000s) for the first phase for each research project, according to which team carries out the work

Project Team	Wheat	Tomatoes	Blood	Plastic	Perfume
Jordan	624	1440	228	468	828
Stock	588	1428	252	456	876
Mooner	780	1380	216	444	804
Brains	660	1404	264	480	828
Label	600	1464	240	432	816

Required

Considering only the above costs, what would be the optimum way to schedule these projects? What is the corresponding minimum cost?

Solution

Optimum way to schedule these projects
Figure 14.8 gives the two possible solutions for this project.

Alternative 1

- Sally Stock would be assigned to the improvement of the production of wheat.
- Mandy Mooner would be assigned to the modification of the growth of tomatoes.
- John Jordan would be assigned to the new blood testing technique.
- Lucia Label would be assigned to a biodegradable plastic.
- Brian Brains would be assigned to a perfume made from the sweat of pigs.

The total (minimum cost) for the five projects is £3 456 000.

Alternative 2

- Sally Stock would be assigned to the improvement of the production of wheat.
- Brian Brains would be assigned to the modification of the growth of tomatoes.
- John Jordan would be assigned to the new blood testing technique.
- Lucia Label would be assigned to a biodegradable plastic.
- Mandy Mooner would be assigned to a perfume made from the sweat of pigs.

The total (minimum cost) for the five projects is £3 456 000.

Setting up the framework

The framework for the two alternatives is set up in the following way (see Figure 14.8):

- The upper table (rows 1 to 8) gives the set up for the job assignments. The variables to be solved are in the matrix (B-2) ... (F-6). Before starting the simulation these values are given a value of 0.

Figure 14.8 Biodecta – job assignments using Excel Solver.

	A TEAM	B Wheat	C Tomatoes	D Blood	E Plastic	F Perfume	G Total
1	TEAM	Wheat	Tomatoes	Blood	Plastic	Perfume	Total
2	Jordan	0	0	1	0	0	1
3	Stock	1	0	0	0	0	1
4	Mooner	0	1	0	0	0	1
5	Brains	0	0	0	1	1	1
6	Label	0	0	0	0	0	1
7							
8	Total	1	1	1	1	1	5
9							
10	Cost (minimum is shown for alternative 1)						
11	TEAM	Wheat	Tomatoes	Blood	Plastic	Perfume	
12	Jordan	624	1440	228	468	828	
13	Stock	588	1428	252	456	876	
14	Mooner	780	1380	216	444	804	
15	Brains	660	1404	264	480	828	
16	Label	600	1464	240	432	816	
17							
18	Cost	588	1380	228	432	828	3456
19							
20	Assignment (alternative 1)						
21	TEAM	Wheat	Tomatoes	Blood	Plastic	Perfume	
22	Jordan	0	0	228	0	0	
23	Stock	588	0	0	0	0	
24	Mooner	0	138	0	0	0	
25	Brains	0	0	0	0	828	
26	Label	0	0	0	432	0	
27							
28	Cost	588	1380	228	432	828	3456
29							
30	Assignment (alternative 2)						
31	TEAM	Wheat	Tomatoes	Blood	Plastic	Perfume	
32	Jordan	0	0	228	0	0	
33	Stock	588	0	0	0	0	
34	Mooner	0	0	0	0	804	
35	Brains	0	1404	0	0	0	
36	Label	0	0	0	432	0	
37							
38	Cost	588	1404	228	432	804	3456

- The centre table (rows 11 to 18) gives the matrix for the job costs established for the problem.
- The bottom tables (rows 21 to 28 for Alternative 1) and (rows 31 to 38 for Alternative 2) gives the allocation of job assignments.
- The objective is to minimize the cost. In Solver, the value in Cell (G-28 for Alternative 1, and Cell (G-38) for Alternative 2) is set to be a minimum.
- For Alternative 1, Cell (G-28) contains the formula (B-28) + (C-28) + (D-28) + (E-28) + (F-28).
- For Alternative 1, Cell (B-28) contains the formula (B-2)*(B-12) + (B-3)*(B-13) + (B-4)*(B-14) + (B-5)*(B-15) + (B-6)*(B-16).
- For Alternative 1, Cells (C-28), (D-28), (E-28) and (F-28) contain a similar formula to that in (B-28) for the corresponding column.

The constraints for the problem are that the defined variables have a value:

- greater or equal to 0;
- less than or equal to 1;
- are a whole number.

This effectively means that they either take on the value 1 or 0:

- Cell (B-8) is given the constraint that it is equal to 1. This cell contains the formula for the sum of column Cells B-2 through B-6. The constraint and formula is similar for Cells (C-8) through (F-8).
- Cell (G-2) is given the formula for the sum of Cells (B-2), (C-2), (D-2), (E-2) and (F-2).
- Cells (G-3) through (G-6) are assigned a similar formula.

Thus, in the set-up arrangement for Solver, when 1 appears in a variable cell it means that the corresponding job has been assigned. When a zero appears, it indicates that no job has been assigned.

RUN-OUT METHOD OF SCHEDULING

Application

The run-out method of scheduling is a way of scheduling:

- standard products as opposed to those that are custom made to order;
- products that go into inventory awaiting delivery to clients;
- when there is limited production capacity such that each product is produced in a batch quantity on the same assembly line or in the same processing unit.

Two approaches

The run-out method, which does not try to optimize inventory storage costs, assumes that the product demand rate can be reasonably well estimated. There are two approaches:

- Products are produced in fixed inventory quantities.
- The aggregate run-out time method

Products produced in fixed quantities

This approach assumes that products are produced in fixed inventory quantities, determined as a result of equipment limitations, customer requirements or economic lot size. Run-out means determining which product's stock would be depleted first (run-out of stock) if production was stopped. It is this product which is scheduled next for production. The run-out of stock is given by the relationship:

Run-out time for product X =

$$\frac{\text{Current inventory of Product X}}{\text{Customer demand for Product X.}}$$

In order to apply the method for a series of products, there must be sufficient inventory available of each product to satisfy customer demand while production of other products is in operation. Requirement 1 of the worked example, *Toubon Co.*, illustrates the application of the run-out method when there are fixed inventory quantities.

Aggregate run-out time

The aggregate run-out-time approach assumes that lot sizes are not fixed, but can be varied according to requirements. It considers all the products together, as an aggregate, and determines the aggregate time that all products will be depleted. A schedule is then developed in consideration of this time. The key steps involve:

- determining the equivalent processing time in current inventory;
- determining the equivalent processing time in product demand.

Then:

Aggregate run-out time (ART) =

$$\frac{\text{Total equivalent processing hours available}}{\text{Total equivalent processing hours required}}$$

$$= \frac{\text{Equivalent processing time in aggregate inventory} + \text{Processing time in processing period}}{\text{Processing time need by client demand.}}$$

The processing time in the processing period could be say, 40 hours, or the work week for the production operation. Requirement 2 of the worked example, *Toubon Co.*, illustrates the use of the aggregate run-out-time method.

WORKED EXAMPLE: TOUBON CO.

Situation

The Toubon Co., just outside Namur in Belgium, is a family-owned operation that makes its own named-brand chocolate bars. The company has a steady business, but limited production capacity. Toubon's most popular chocolate bars are milk, black, brandy-filled, nut and cherry-filled and these can only be manufactured on one production line. Producing the bars basically involves mixing the chocolate, adding the ingredients, moulding, cooling, wrapping and packaging. On one particular Friday evening the following was the operating data available for the five varieties of chocolate was as shown in Table 14.14:

Table 14.14 Toubon – operating data available for the five varieties of chocolate (units of 100 gram bars)

	Run size (lot size)	Production time (hours)	Demand per week	Current inventory
Milk	24 000	30.00	10 000	30 000
Black	20 000	18.00	8 000	19 000
Brandy filled	18 000	24.00	4 000	9 000
Nut	15 000	25.00	6 000	11 000
Cherry filled	17 500	21.00	3 200	7 500

- Run size was the number of 100 gram bars of chocolate produced each time the equipment was set up. Differences were generally due to the limitations of the mixing equipment available.
- Production time was the time from mixing to final wrapping of the bars.
- Demand per week was the estimated demand from the work centre to the various distribution centres in Belgium.
- Current inventory was the quantity of wrapped 100 gram chocolate bars in final product storage at the Toubon production centre.

Required

1. Using the run-out method for fixed lot sizes, develop a production schedule for the next five weeks. Show the production schedule on a Gantt chart. Assume 40 hours of production time per week.
2. Using an aggregate run-out time method (lot sizes are not fixed) develop a production schedule for the next five weeks. Show the production schedule on a Gantt chart. Assume 40 hours of production time per week.

Solution

1. Production schedule using the run-out method for fixed lot sizes
   The solution is given in Figures 14.9 and 14.10. These are developed as follows:

- The run-out time is calculated for each type of chocolate bar calculated by the ratio:

$$\text{Run-out time (hours)} = \frac{\text{Current inventory}}{\text{Demand per week}/40}.$$

- Production is scheduled first for that product which has the least run-out time. For the first production load this is the nut chocolate [Cell (F-7)].
- Production time is 25.00 hours. During production of nut chocolate, inventory is being used according to the demand rate.
- Ending inventory at the end of production is given in Cells (E-16) through (E-20).
- The run-out test is repeated after the first production load. In this case it is the brandy-filled chocolate that must be scheduled [Cell (F-18)].
- The planning schedule is thus developed each time making the run-out test after a production run.

  The five week planning schedule is given in the matrix (A-113) ... (C-125) of Figure 14.9 and illustrated as a Gantt chart in Figure 14.10.

2. Using an aggregate run-out time method
   The solution is given in Figures 14.11 and 14.12. These are developed as follows.

Figure 14.9 Toubon Chocolate – products produced in fixed inventory quantity.

	A	B	C	D	E	F
1	**Start**	Run Size	Production time	Demand per week	Current Inventory	Runout time
2			(hours)			(hours)
3						
4	Milk	24 000	30.00	10 000	30 000	120.00
5	Black	20 000	18.00	8 000	19 000	95.00
6	Brandy-filled	18 000	24.00	4 000	9 000	90.00
7	Nut	15 000	25.00	6 000	11 000	73.33
8	Cherry-filled	17 500	21.00	3 200	7 500	93.75
9						
10	Min runout time	73.33				
11	Schedule	Nut				
12	Production time	25.00				

	A		C	D	E	F
14	**First Production load**		Inventory remaining	New Prodn	Total Inventory	Runout Time
16	Milk		23 750	0	23 750	95.00
17	Black		14 000	0	14 000	70.00
18	Brandy-filled		6 500	0	6 500	65.00
19	Nut		7 250	15 000	22 250	148.33
20	Cherry-filled		5 500	0	5 500	68.75
21						
22	Min runout time	65.00				
23	Schedule	Brandy-filled				
24	Production time	24.00				

	A		C	D	E	F
26	**Second Production load**		Inventory remaining	New Prodn	Total Inventory	Runout Time
28	Milk		17 750	0	17 750	71.00
29	Black		9 200	0	9 200	46.00
30	Brandy-filled		4 100	18 000	22 100	221.00
31	Nut		18 650	0	18 650	124.33
32	Cherry-filled		3 580	0	3 580	44.75
33						
34	Min runout time	44.75				
35	Schedule	Cherry-filled				
36	Production time	21.00				

	A		C	D	E	F
38	**Third Production load**		Inventory remaining	New Prodn	Total Inventory	Runout Time
40	Milk		12 500	0	12 500	50.00
41	Black		5 000	0	5 000	25.00
42	Brandy-filled		20 000	0	20 000	200.00
43	Nut		15 500	0	15 500	103.33
44	Cherry-filled		1 900	17 500	19 400	242.50
45						
46	Min runout time	25.00				
47	Schedule	Black				
48	Production time	18.00				

	A		C	D	E	F
50	**Fourth Production load**		Inventory remaining	New Prodn	Total Inventory	Runout Time
52	Milk		8 000	0	8 000	32.00
53	Black		1 400	20 000	21 400	107.00
54	Brandy-filled		18 200	0	18 200	182.00
55	Nut		12 800	0	12 800	85.33
56	Cherry-filled		17 960	0	17 960	224.50
57						
58	Min runout time	32.00				
59	Schedule	Milk				
60	Production time	30.00				

63	**Fifth Production load**		Inventory remaining	New Prodn	Total Inventory	Runout Time
65	Milk		500	24 000	24 500	98.00
66	Black		15 400	0	15 400	77.00
67	Brandy-filled		15 200	0	15 200	152.00
68	Nut		8 300	0	8 300	55.33
69	Cherry-filled		15 560	0	15 560	194.50
70						
71	Min runout time	55.33				
72	Schedule	Nut				
73	Production time	25.00				

76	**Sixth Production load**		Inventory remaining	New Prodn	Total Inventory	Runout Time
78	Milk		18 250	0	18 250	73.00
79	Black		10 400	0	10 400	52.00
80	Brandy-filled		12 700	0	12 700	127.00
81	Nut		4 550	15 000	19 550	130.33
82	Cherry-filled		13 560	0	13 560	169.50
83						
84	Min runout time	52.00				
85	Schedule	Black				
86	Production time	18.00				

89	**Seventh Production load**		Inventory remaining	New Prodn	Total Inventory	Runout Time
91	Milk		13 750	0	13 750	55.00
92	Black		6 800	20 000	26 800	134.00
93	Brandy-filled		10 900	0	10 900	109.00
94	Nut		16 850	0	16 850	112.33
95	Cherry-filled		12 120	0	12 120	151.50
96						
97	Min runout time	55.00				
98	Schedule	Milk				
99	Production time	30.00				

101	**Eighth Production load**		Inventory remaining	New Prodn	Total Inventory	Runout Time
103	Milk		6 250	24 000	30 250	121.00
104	Black		20 800	0	20 800	104.00
105	Brandy-filled		7 900	0	7 900	79.00
106	Nut		12 350	0	12 350	82.33
107	Cherry-filled		9 720	0	9 720	121.50
108						
109	Min runout time	79.00				
110	Schedule	Brandy-filled				
111	Production time	24.00				

	Product	Time (hours)	Time (hours)
113/114			
115	Nut	25	0.63
116	Brandy-filled	24	0.60
117	Cherry-filled	21	0.53
118	Black	18	0.45
119	Milk	30	0.75
120	Nut	25	0.63
121	Black	18	0.45
122	Milk	30	0.75
123	Brandy-filled	24	0.60
124			
125	Total	215	5.38

Figure 14.10 Toubon Chocolate Gantt chart – run-out method: production in fixed inventory quantities.

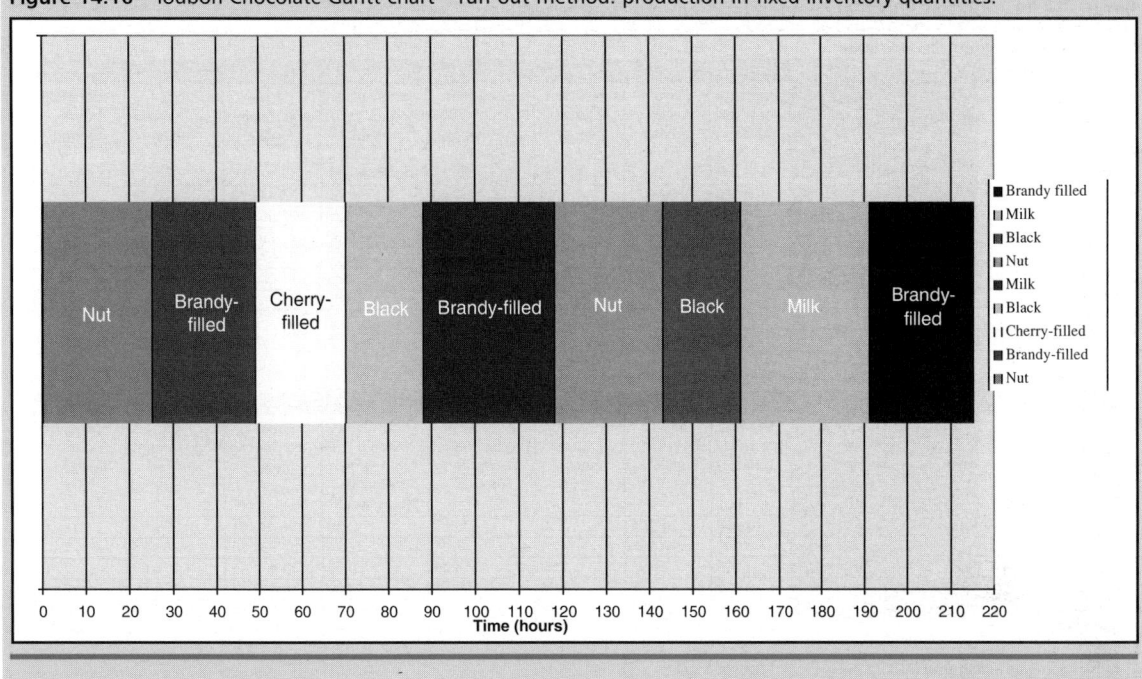

The first section of the spreadsheet in Figure 14.11, entitled 'Start and schedule for first week' gives the initial data and the development of the aggregate run-out time:

- Columns B, Run size, and C, Production time for lot, are not considered in this scheduling method, but are used to calculate Column F, Production time per unit:

$$\text{Production time per unit} = \frac{\text{Production time for lot}}{\text{Run size}}.$$

- Equivalent production time in inventory (Column G) is the amount of processing time represented by the inventory:
  - Equivalent production time in inventory = Current inventory × Production time\unit.
  - This is calculated for each product and then totalled [Cell (G-11)].
  - Equivalent production time in weekly demand (Column H) is the amount of processing time represented by the weekly demand.
  - Equivalent production time in weekly demand = Weekly demand × Production time\unit.
  - This is calculated for each product and then totalled [Cell (H-11)].
- Aggregate run-out time, ART, in weeks is calculated by:

$$\frac{\begin{array}{c}\text{Equivalent processing time in aggregate inventory}\\ + \text{ Processing time in processing period}\end{array}}{\text{Equivalent processing time needed by client demand.}}$$

  - Equivalent processing time in aggregate inventory is the value in Cell (G-11).
  - Equivalent processing time needed by client demand is the value in Cell (H-11).

- Processing time is 40 hours for the week.
- The aggregate run-out time means that if the chocolate production is left operating for one week (40 hours), then the current inventory, plus the inventory produced during one week, will be depleted in 3.4454 weeks.
- Lot sizes are then determined based on the aggregate run-out time.
- Gross requirements, Column I, for each product during the aggregate run-out time of 3.4454 weeks are then calculated by:
  - Gross requirements = Demand per week (Column D) × ART.
  - Net requirements = Gross Requirements (Column I) – Current inventory (Column E).
  - Production hours needed (Column K) = Net requirements (Column J) × Production time/unit (Column F).
  - Total production hours needed [Cell (K-11)] are the hours available during the production (processing) period (40 hours in this case). These times represent the amount of time processing that must be spent on each type of product during the week. This is given in the Gantt chart for Week 1 (Figure 14.12).

The second section of the spreadsheet entitled 'After one week and schedule for second week' gives the development for the second week:

- Current inventory is now the Gross requirements from the previous week less the demand for that week. For example for milk chocolate:
  - Cell (E-22) = Cell (E-6) – Cell (D-6) + Cell (J-6)
  - Similarly for all the other products.
- Thus there is a new value for the Equivalent production time in inventory [Cell (G-27)]. Using this gives a new value of ART of 3.4744 weeks [Cell (D-29)].

Figure 14.11 Toubon Chocolate – aggregate run-out time scheduling.

Start and schedule for first week

	A	B	C	D	E	F	G	H	I	J	K
		Run Size (units) [not used]	Production time for lot (hours	Demand per week (units)	Current Inventory (units)	Production time/unit (secs)	Equivalent Product'n time in inventory (hours)	Equivalent Product'n time in weekly demand (hours/week)	Gross Requirements (units)	Net Requirements (units)	Production hours needed
Milk	24 000	30.00	10 000	30 000	4.50	37.50	12.50	34 453.78	4 453.78	5.57
Black	20 000	18.00	8 000	19 000	3.24	17.10	7.20	27 563.03	8 563.03	7.71
Brandy-filled	18 000	24.00	4 000	9 000	4.80	12.00	5.33	13 781.51	4 781.51	6.38
Nut	15 000	25.00	6 000	11 000	6.00	18.33	10.00	20 672.27	9 672.27	16.12
Cherry-filled	17 500	21.00	3 200	7 500	4.32	9.00	3.84	11 025.21	3 525.21	4.23
Total						93.93	38.87			40.00

Aggregate runout time (ART)	3.4454 weeks

After one week and schedule for second week

	A	B	C	D	E	F	G	H	I	J	K
		Run Size (units) [not used]	Production time for lot (hours	Demand per week (units)	Current Inventory (units)	Production time/unit (secs)	Equivalent Product'n time in inventory (hours)	Equivalent Product'n time in weekly demand (hours/week)	Gross Requirements (units)	Net Requirements (units)	Production hours needed
Milk	24 000	30.00	10 000	24 454	4.50	30.57	12.50	34 743.61	10 289.83	12.86
Black	20 000	18.00	8 000	19 563	3.24	17.61	7.20	27 794.89	8 231.86	7.41
Brandy-filled	18 000	24.00	4 000	9 782	4.80	13.04	5.33	13 897.44	4 115.93	5.49
Nut	15 000	25.00	6 000	14 672	6.00	24.45	10.00	20 846.17	6 173.90	10.29
Cherry-filled	17 500	21.00	3 200	7 825	4.32	9.39	3.84	11 117.96	3 292.75	3.95
Total						95.06	38.87			40.00

Aggregate runout time (ART)	3.4744 weeks

After two weeks and schedule for third week

	A	B	C	D	E	F	G	H	I	J	K
		Run Size (units) [not used]	Production time for lot (hours	Demand per week (units)	Current Inventory (units)	Production time/unit (secs)	Equivalent Product'n time in inventory (hours)	Equivalent Product'n time in weekly demand (hours/week)	Gross Requirements (units)	Net Requirements (units)	Production hours needed
Milk	24 000	30.00	10 000	24 744	4.50	30.93	12.50	35 033.44	10 289.83	12.86
Black	20 000	18.00	8 000	19 795	3.24	17.82	7.20	28 026.75	8 231.86	7.41
Brandy-filled	18 000	24.00	4 000	9 897	4.80	13.20	5.33	14 013.38	4 115.93	5.49
Nut	15 000	25.00	6 000	14 846	6.00	24.74	10.00	21 020.07	6 173.90	10.29
Cherry-filled	17 500	21.00	3 200	7 918	4.32	9.50	3.84	11 210.70	3 292.75	3.95
Total						96.19	38.87			40.00

Aggregate runout time (ART)	3.5033 weeks

After three weeks and schedule for fourth week

	A	B	C	D	E	F	G	H	I	J	K
		Run Size (units) [not used]	Production time for lot (hours	Demand per week (units)	Current Inventory (units)	Production time/unit (secs)	Equivalent Product'n time in inventory (hours)	Equivalent Product'n time in weekly demand (hours/week)	Gross Requirements (units)	Net Requirements (units)	Production hours needed
Milk	24 000	30.00	10 000	25 033	4.50	31.29	12.50	35 323.27	10 289.83	12.86
Black	20 000	18.00	8 000	20 027	3.24	18.02	7.20	28 258.62	8 231.86	7.41
Brandy-filled	18 000	24.00	4 000	10 013	4.80	13.35	5.33	14 129.31	4 115.93	5.49
Nut	15 000	25.00	6 000	15 020	6.00	25.03	10.00	21 193.96	6 173.90	10.29
Cherry-filled	17 500	21.00	3 200	8 011	4.32	9.61	3.84	11 303.45	3 292.75	3.95
Total						97.31	38.87			40.00

Aggregate runout time (ART)	3.5323 weeks

Figure 14.11   Continued.

	A	B	C	D	E	F	G	H	I	J	K
63	**After four weeks and schedule for fifth week**										
64	A	B	C	D	E	F	G	H	I	J	K
65–69		Run Size (units) [not used]	Production time for lot (hours	Demand per week (units)	Current Inventory (units)	Production time/unit (secs)	Equivalent Product'n time in inventory (hours)	Equivalent Product'n time in weekly demand (hours/week)	Gross Requirements (units)	Net Requirements (units)	Production hours needed
70	Milk	24 000	30.00	10 000	25 323	4.50	31.65	12.50	35 613.10	10 289.83	12.86
71	Black	20 000	18.00	8 000	20 259	3.24	18.23	7.20	28 490.48	8 231.86	7.41
72	Brandy-filled	18 000	24.00	4 000	10 129	4.80	13.51	5.33	14 245.24	4 115.93	5.49
73	Nut	15 000	25.00	6 000	15 194	6.00	25.32	10.00	21 367.86	6 173.90	10.29
74	Cherry-filled	17 500	21.00	3 200	8 103	4.32	9.72	3.84	11 396.19	3 292.75	3.95
75	Total						98.44	38.87			40.00
76											
77	Aggregate runout time (ART)			3.5613	weeks						

Schedule summary: Production hours used

	Week 1	Week 2	Week 3	Week 4	Week 5
Milk	5.57	12.86	12.86	12.86	12.86
Black	7.71	7.41	7.41	7.41	7.41
Brandy-filled	6.38	5.49	5.49	5.49	5.49
Nut	16.12	10.29	10.29	10.29	10.29
Cherry-filled	4.23	3.95	3.95	3.95	3.95
Total	40.00	40.00	40.00	40.00	40.00

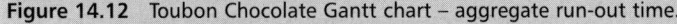

- With the new ART new net requirements are determined and thence a new schedule, Cells (K-22) through (K-26).
- Similar schedules are developed for the third and subsequent weeks.

A five-week schedule plan has been developed assuming no changes in the weekly demand. If demand changes during the course of operations, then the schedule will be adjusted accordingly.

Figure 14.12   Toubon Chocolate Gantt chart – aggregate run-out time.

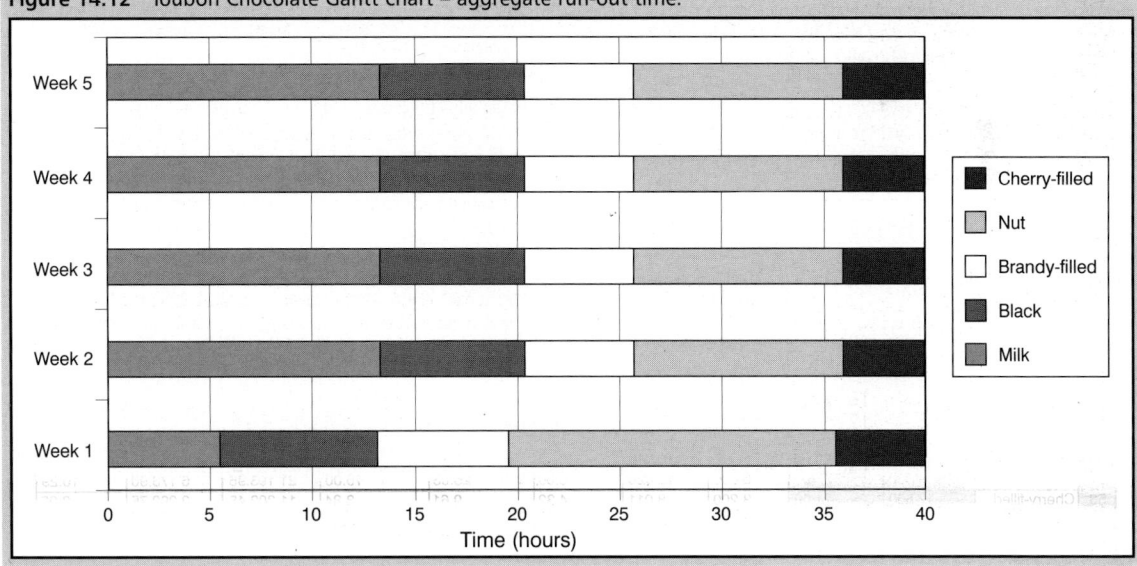

LINE OF BALANCE TECHNIQUE

The line of balance technique is a useful scheduling tool when there is a fixed quantity of a customized product that is to be delivered to a client over a period of time. The purpose of the technique is to check, at various reporting periods, if the various operations in producing the final product are on schedule. That is, is the actual operation in 'balance' with the scheduled operation? Elements of the line-of balance technique include the following.

Delivery schedule

The delivery schedule includes the timing when the units of product are scheduled to be delivered to the client. A point delivery schedule is converted to a cumulative delivery schedule to serve as a control tool.

Assembly/lead-time chart

This is a diagram illustrating the various activities in the assembly of the product, together with the lead times. On the assembly chart are various control points indicated by a circle, square or other symbol, showing the start or finish of an activity. These control points are analogous to the activity start or finish points in a network diagram, discussed more fully in Chapter 18, *Project Management*.

Progress at a given time

Inventory levels are indicated on a histogram, showing the status at any given point so that the production manager can ascertain progress.

The line-of-balance technique is illustrated by the worked example, *Circuit breakers*.

WORKED EXAMPLE: CIRCUIT BREAKERS

Situation

The Linmer Niger Co. in France is a constructor of electrical transformers, switch gear and circuit breakers for clients worldwide. It has been awarded a large contract by a south-east Asian client to supply 200 industrial circuit breakers for medium-power electrical transmission. A large portion of the work for these circuit breakers is subcontracted, with some major machining work performed by Linmer Niger. Other activities for Linmer Niger are to test some key components before final assembly and final test. The elapsed time for the activity for Linmer is 8 weeks. This includes a two-week delivery schedule from France to the client. Figure 14.13 gives the control points, and the lead time for Linmer.

The client has contracted with Linmer to deliver the units according to the schedule shown in Table 14.15.

Table 14.15 Linmer – delivery schedule

Week	Units delivered on site	Week	Units delivered on site
1		14	9
2		15	10
3		16	11
4	1	17	11
5	2	18	11
6	2	19	12
7	3	20	12
8	4	21	12
9	5	22	13
10	6	23	13
11	6	24	14
12	7	25	14
13	8	26	14

Required

Linmer is at week 12 of the schedule. Table 14.16 shows the status of the units at the 15 control points of the assembly schedule. The lead time in weeks is taken from the assembly/lead-time chart and the units are either finished or semifinished products:

1 Using the line-of-balance technique, for the portion of the supply chain shown in Figure 14.13 (that is from receipt of purchased parts to delivery of finished units on site) should Linmer be satisfied with the operation? If not, what action might be considered?

Solution

- In the line-of-balance technique, the weekly delivery schedule is converted into a cumulative delivery schedule. This data is given in Table 14.17 and shown graphically in Figure 14.14. Week 12 is indicated with a solid vertical line.
- The actual units either finished units, as at control points 1, 2 and 3, or semi-finished units at the control points 4 through 15 are shown on Table 14.18 and as the dark bars in Figure 14.15.
- The scheduled units or semi-finished units, which must be in inventory at each control point, are given as the light bars in Figure 14.15. The derivation of these numbers and the status, line of balance with actual and scheduled, is given below. The scheduled units are interpreted from Table 14.17.

Control point 1

At week 12 the cumulative units that should be at the site are 36. Actual units on site are 36. Thus, as far as finished products are concerned, delivery is on schedule, or there is a line of balance as illustrated by the two bars on the histogram for control point 1.

Control point 2

This is the end of the final test. After this point there is a two-week delivery time. Thus, the quantity of units that must be at control point 2 at Week 12 must be that quantity of units given on the cumulative delivery schedule two weeks ahead of Week 12, at Week 14. This is because, when two weeks have elapsed, these units will arrive at the delivery site at week 14. From the cumulative delivery schedule this number should be 53 units. Actual units are 55, either from Table 14.17 or the Figure 14.15. There is not a 'line of balance'. Production is ahead of schedule at this

Figure 14.13   Assembly/lead-time chart for circuit breakers.

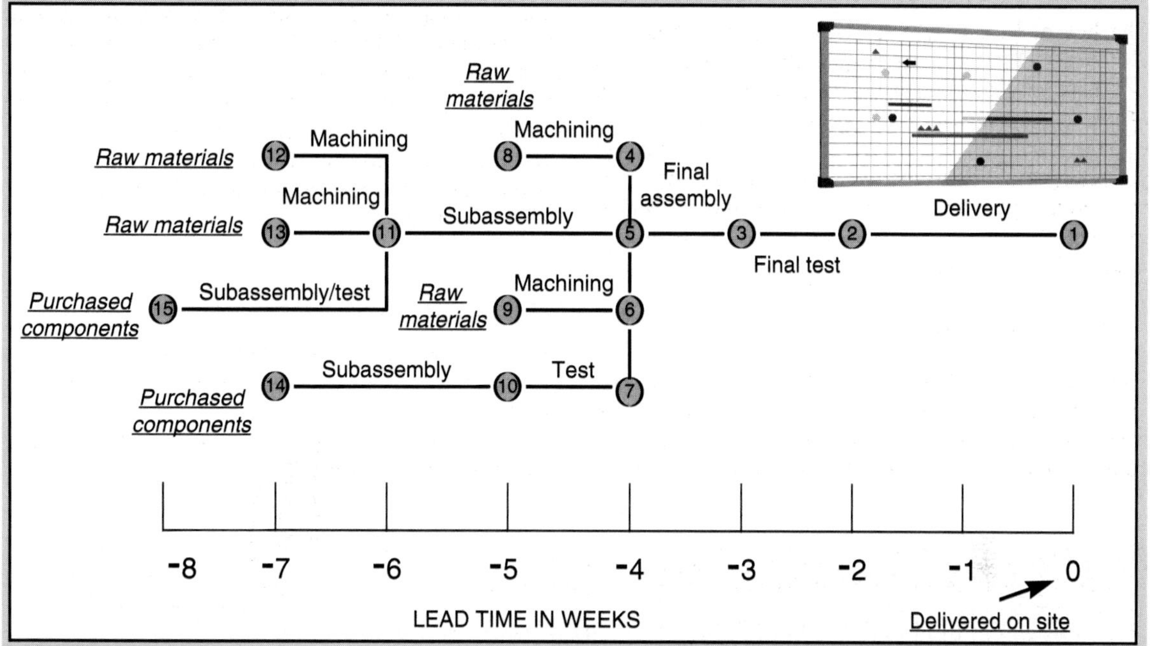

Table 14.16   Linmer – Status of units at week 12

Control point	1	2	3	4	5	6	7	8	9	10	11	12	13	14	15
Lead time	0	2	3	4	4	4	4	5	5	5	6	7	7	7	8
Units	36	55	67	72	70	76	78	82	80	79	90	100	108	110	120

Table 14.17   Linmer – circuit breaker delivery schedule

Week	Units delivered on site	Cumulative units on site
0		
1		
2		
3		
4	1	1
5	2	3
6	2	5
7	3	8
8	4	12
9	5	17
10	6	23
11	6	29
12	7	36
13	8	44
14	9	53
15	10	63
16	11	74
17	11	85
18	11	96
19	12	108
20	12	120
21	12	132
22	13	145
23	13	158
24	14	172
25	14	186
26	14	200

Table 14.18   Inventory situation after week 12

Control Point	Lead time (weeks)	Scheduled units	Acutal units
1	0	36	36
2	2	53	55
3	3	63	67
4	4	74	72
5	4	74	70
6	4	74	76
7	4	74	78
8	5	85	82
9	5	85	80
10	5	85	79
11	6	96	90
12	7	108	100
13	7	108	108
14	7	108	110
15	8	120	120

point so there is unnecessary inventory and therefore unnecessary inventory storage costs.

Control point 3

This is the end of the final assembly. After this point there is a three-week period before the units must be at the site. Thus, the quantity of units which must be at control point 3 at Week 12 must be that quantity of units given on the cumulative delivery schedule three weeks ahead of Week 12, at Week 15. This is because, when three weeks have elapsed, these units will arrive at the delivery site at Week 15. From the cumulative delivery schedule this number should be 63 units. Actual units are 67 either from Table 14.17 or Figure 14.15. Thus, production is ahead of schedule at this point so there is unnecessary inventory and therefore unnecessary inventory storage costs. There is not a 'line of balance'.

Control point 4

This is the end of machining. After this point there is a four-week period before the units that must be at the site. Thus, the quantity of units that must be at control point No 4 at Week 12 must be that quantity of units given on the cumulative delivery schedule four weeks ahead of Week 12, at Week 16. From the cumulative delivery schedule this number should be 74 units. Actual units are 72. Thus, production is behind schedule at this point. There is not a 'line of balance'.

The status at all the other control points in interpreted in the same manner. A summary of all is presented in Table 14.19.

The production manager needs to pay attention to those control points where production is behind schedule. Is it possible to:

- Transfer resources from those activities that are ahead of schedule of those that are behind schedule?
- Use overtime?
- Use additional labour?

It is important now to make attempts to 'balance the line' in order not to break the supply chain and fall behind with deliveries.

Figure 14.14 Cumulative delivery schedule for circuit breakers.

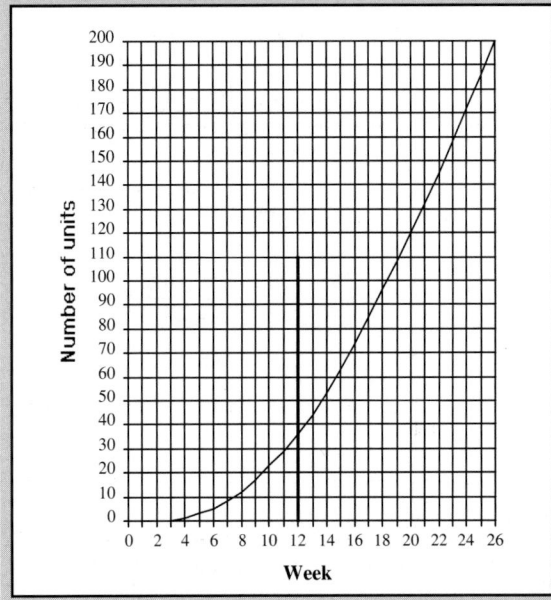

Figure 14.15 Line of balance for delivery schedule.

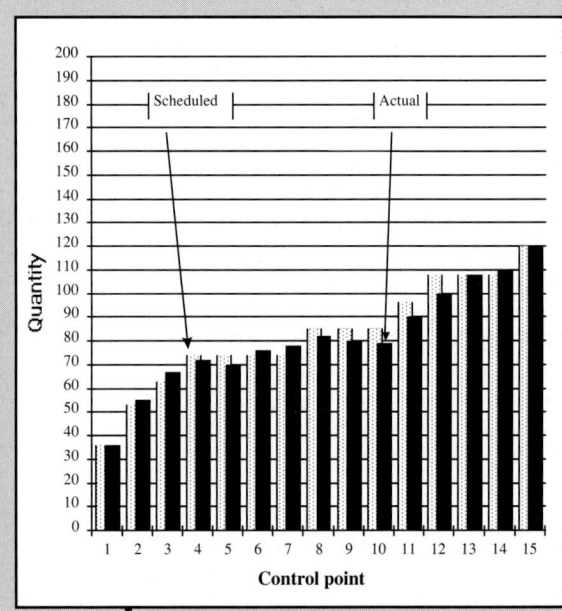

Table 14.19 Linmer – The status at all the control points

Control point	Activity	Scheduled units	Actual units	Status
1	At client's site	36	36	On schedule
2	End of final test	53	55	Ahead of schedule
3	End of final assembly	63	67	Ahead of schedule
4	End of machining	74	72	Behind schedule
5	End of subassembly	74	70	Behind schedule
6	End of machining	74	76	Ahead of schedule
7	End of test	74	78	Ahead of schedule
8	Start of machining	85	82	Behind schedule
9	Start of machining	85	80	Behind schedule
10	End of subassembly	85	79	Behind schedule
11	Start of subassembly	96	90	Behind schedule
12	Start of machining	108	100	Behind schedule
13	Start of machining	108	108	On schedule
14	Start of subassembly	108	110	Ahead of schedule
15	Start of subassembly/test	120	120	On schedule

OPTIMIZED PRODUCTION TECHNOLOGY

Optimized production technology (OPT), also called management by the theory of constraints (TOC), is a computerized production planning and scheduling tool developed in 1979 by Creative Output of Milford, Connecticut, USA. It is useful for coordinating engineering, manufacturing and marketing operations in a job shop, or a work centre where there is repetitive manufacturing.[2] The OPT software gives a detailed description of the network, defining variables of the resources used such as set-up times, production run times, inventory levels, lot sizes, lead times, order quantities and due dates.

Optimized production technology is based on a set of nine related rules, which principally revolve around the concept of bottlenecks. In an operations context, a bottleneck is a resource such as a work centre, machine or labour force, where the capacity of this resource is less than the downstream demand, as illustrated in Figure 14.16. Indications of a bottleneck in an operation would be the accumulation of inventory, people waiting or vehicles queuing.[3] The nine rules of OPT are as follows.

Rule 1: Balance material flow through a system, rather than the capacity

Each work centre in a manufacturing operation is subjected to different random occurrences, such as machine breakdowns, absentee operators or materials that do not conform to specification. These random occurrences will lead to delays. This first rule, Figure 14.17, stresses that efforts should be made to create a smooth flow of material through the system, adapted to the downstream market, rather than to try and keep all resources fully occupied. When there are fluctuations in demand, a smooth flow might be achieved by using operators who are multiskilled.

Rule 2: Use of a non-bottleneck is determined by other constraints in the system

In a production system two types of resources can be considered:

- a bottleneck resource (capacity is less than downstream demand);
- a non-bottleneck resource (capacity is greater than or equal to the downstream demand).

The throughput of any system is always governed by the capacity of the bottleneck resource, as illustrated in Figure 14.18. In the scheme, Post No. 2 (non-bottleneck) cannot operate at its full potential, or capacity, because Post No. 1 (bottleneck) is unable to absorb all the flow, and the inventory level would increase.

Rule 3: Utilization and full employment of a resource are not synonymous

In the scheme in Figure 14.19 the capacity of Post No. 4 is 250 units/h. However, it can only be utilized at a rate of 150 units/h because of the constraints of the

Figure 14.16 Bottleneck situation.

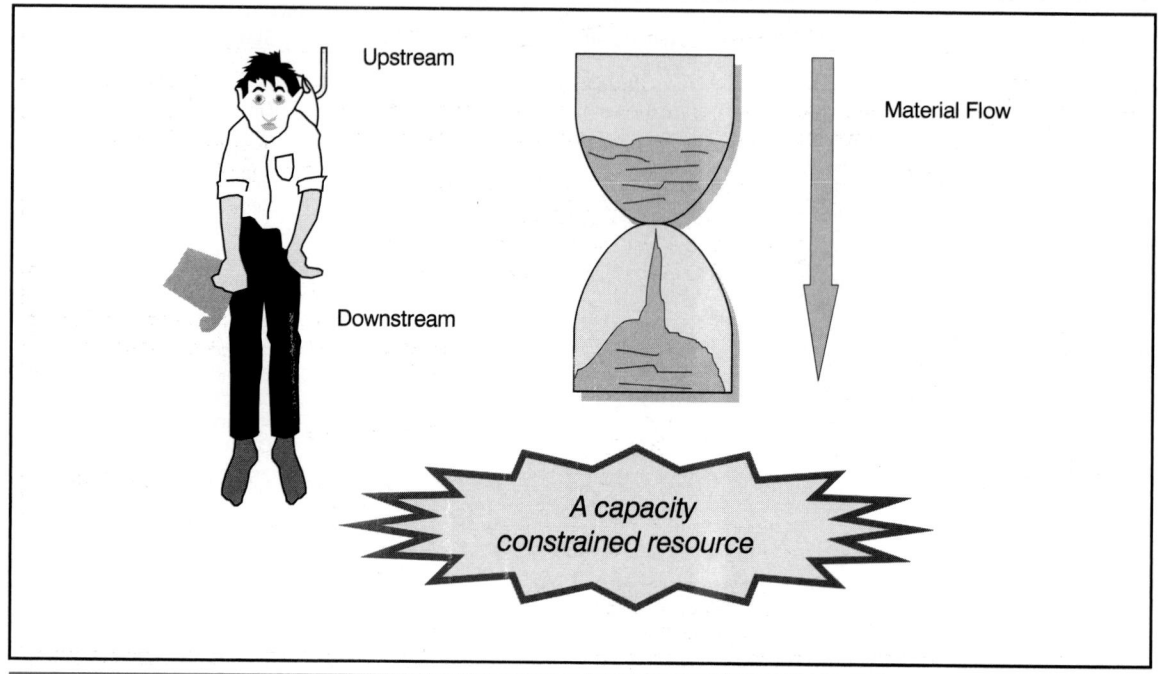

Figure 14.17 Optimized production technology: Rule 1.

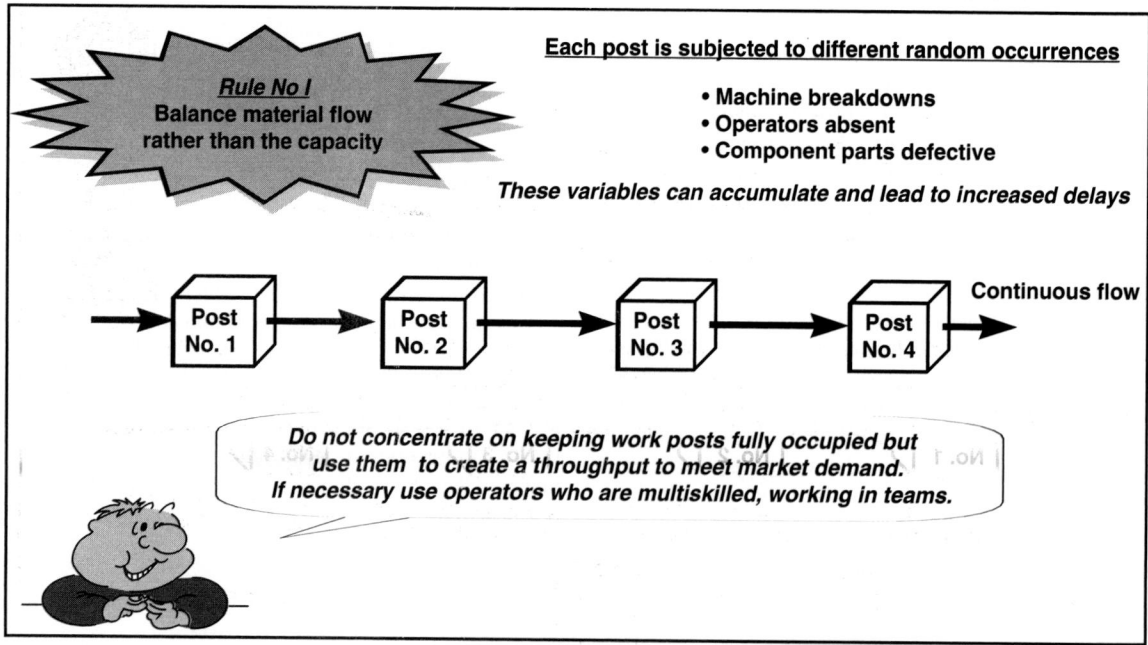

Figure 14.18 Optimized production technology: Rule 2.

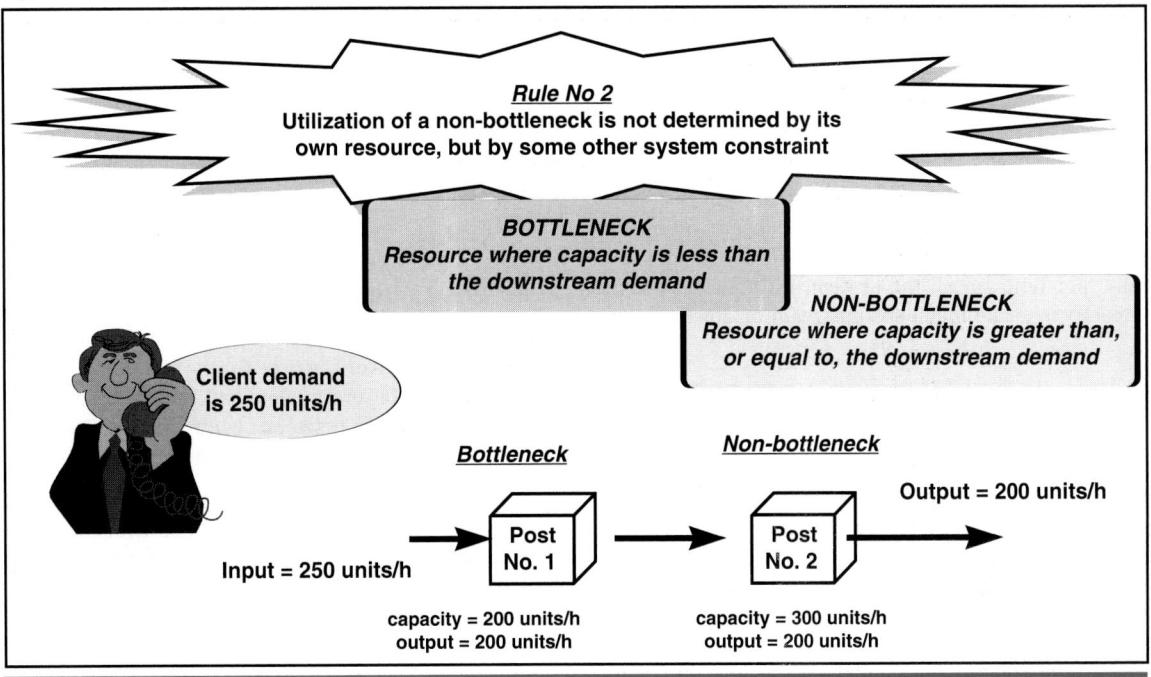

Figure 14.19 Optimized production technology: Rule 3.

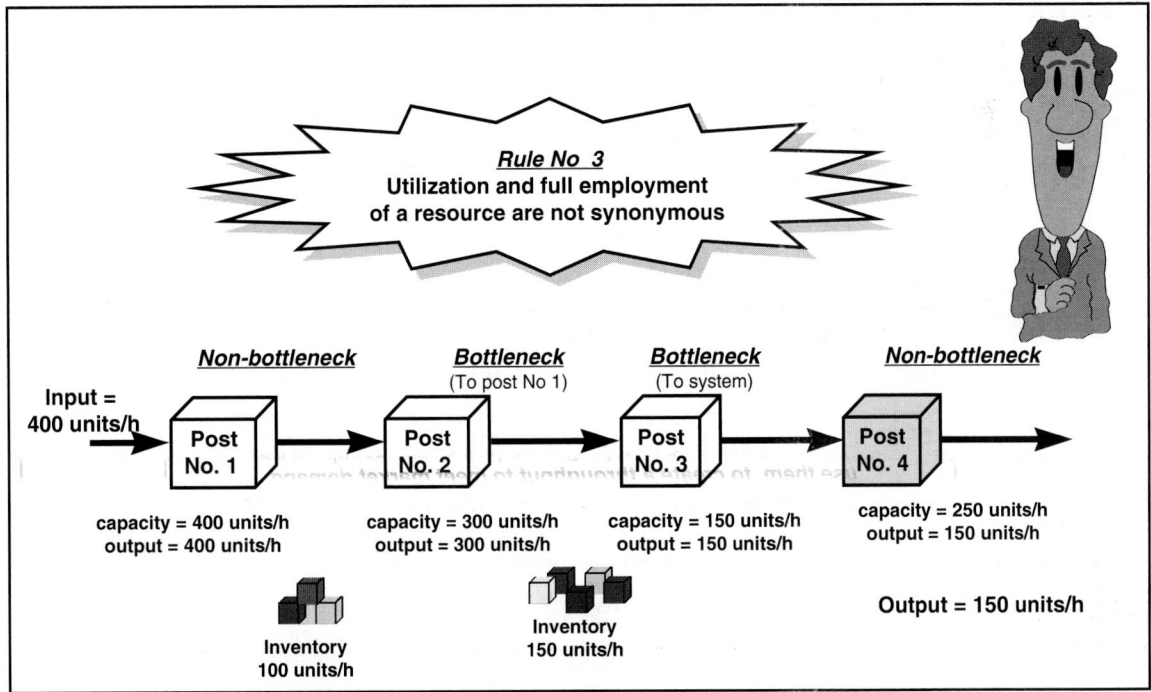

upstream Work Post No. 3. Work Post No. 2 is a bottleneck to Work Post No. 1, but it is No. 3 that is the principal constraint.

Rule 4: An hour lost on a bottleneck resource is an hour lost on all the system

In the scheme in Figure 14.20 if machine No. 3 can only produce 130 units per hour because of an operating problem, then production on the line is only 130 units per hour on all the system, no matter what the capacity is of the machines upstream or downstream.

Rule 5: An hour saved on a non-bottleneck resource is just a mirage

Since the capacity of the system is governed by the bottleneck resource, saving time on a non-bottleneck resource does nothing for the throughput in the whole system. In Figure 14.21 the upper diagram gives the system before any modifications. Assume the set-up time of Post No. 2 can be reduced, thereby enabling the production rate to be increased to 280 units per hour. The production rate does not change as it is always limited by the bottleneck resource.

Rule 6: Bottlenecks govern both throughput and the accumulation of inventory

In the scheme in Figure 14.22 the production rate of the system is 150 units/h, or the capacity of the bottleneck. As a result, inventory accumulates at a rate of 250 units/h.

Rule 7: The size of transfer batch does not need to be equal to the process batch

The transfer batch is the quantity of material transferred from one work centre to another, whereas the process batch, or production lot, is that quantity of material produced between each machine set-up. Consider the situations in Figure 14.23:

- An operator waits until all the lot has been produced at Post No. 1, before the units are transferred to Post No. 2. In this case there is an accumulation of a maximum of 1000 units of in-process inventory sitting just downstream of Post No. 1.
- Assume a quantity of 200 units is transferred each time from Post No. 1 to Post No. 2. Then the in-process inventory between the two is limited to a

Figure 14.20 Optimized production technology: Rule 4.

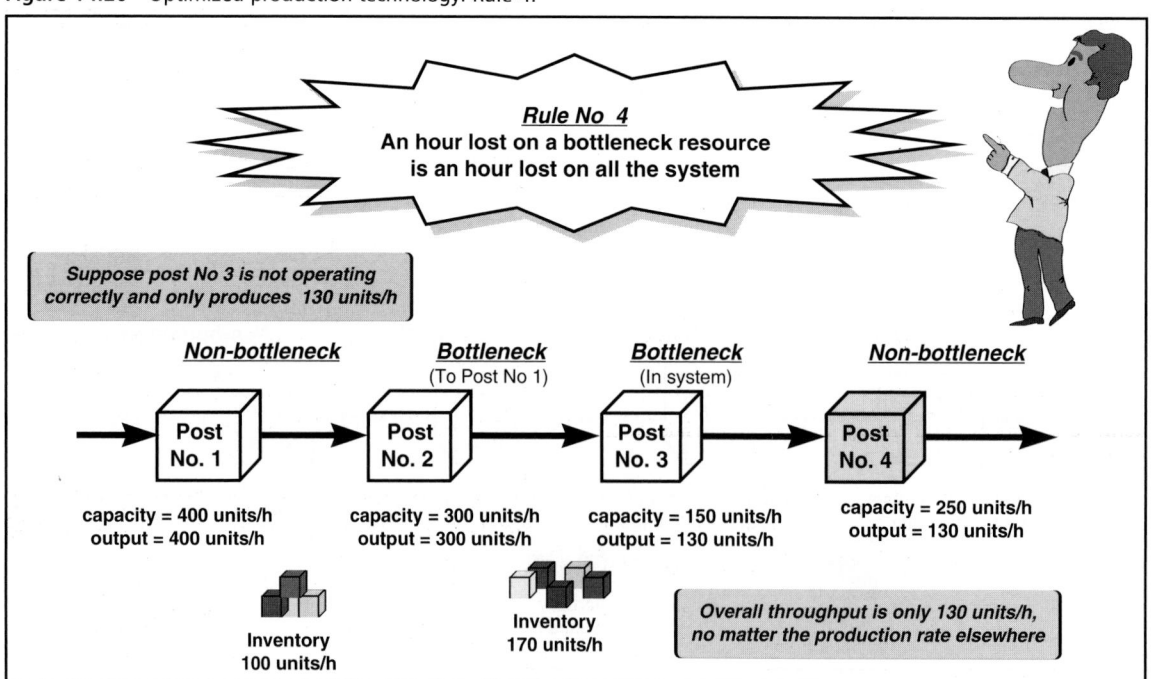

Figure 14.21 Optimized production technology: Rule 5.

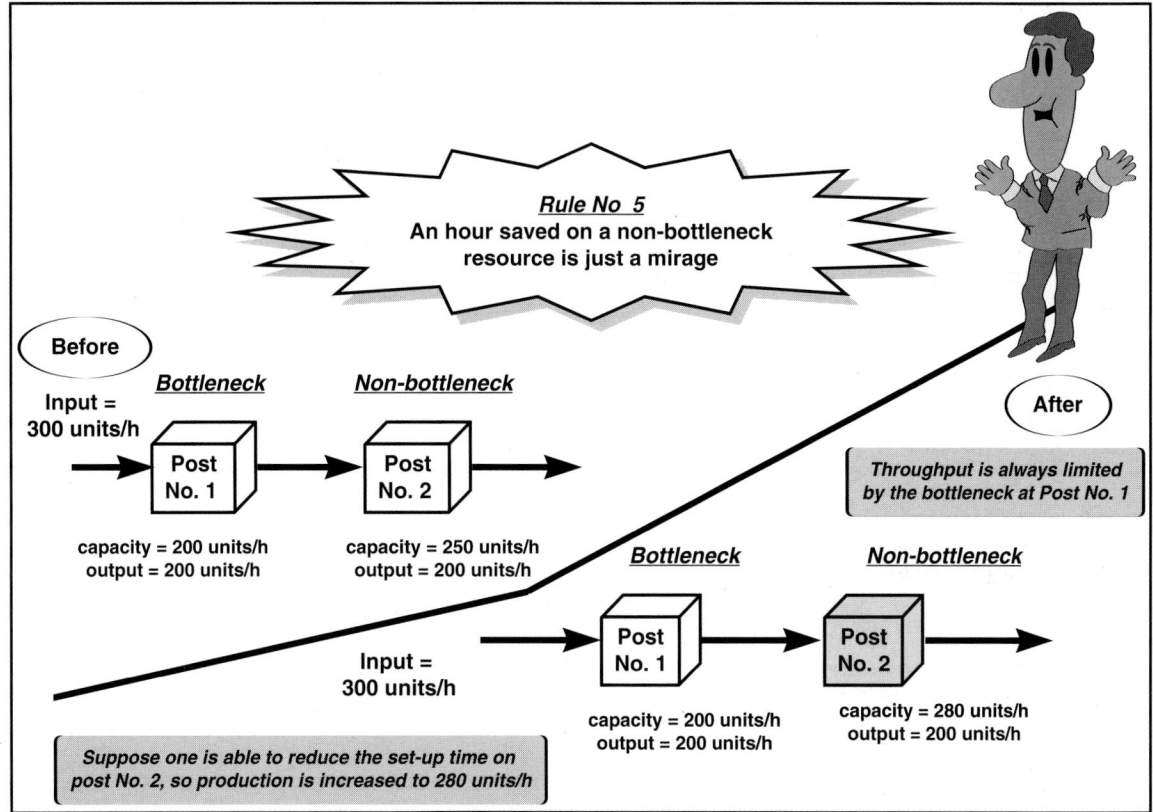

maximum of 200 units. In addition, depending on the availability, work can begin on those pieces transferred over to Post No. 2.

Rule 8: Lot sizes should be variable and not fixed

The lot sizes in optimized production technology are a function of the schedule and thus should not be fixed over time, or from operation to operation. When different components are manufactured on different machines, the lot size should be varied in order to achieve a smooth, and timely, flow of materials to the customer.

Rule 9: Schedules must be established by taking into account all system constraints

In a production process, delays are often a function of scheduling and cannot always necessarily be predetermined. For example.

■ An MRP system presumes that the delays are known beforehand, and fixed.

■ In OPT management, delays are flexible.

Consider the scheme in Figure 14.24:

■ Suppose that component A has to be worked on Post No. 1 and Post No. 2, Component B on Post No. 1 and Post No. 3.

■ In this case, it would appear that the delay for component A is 15 hours. The delay for component B is 19 hours.

■ However, if one starts working with component A, the delay will be 15 hours and 28 hours for B.

■ If one starts with component B, the delay will be 19 hours and 20 hours for component B.

PERSONNEL SCHEDULING

Service function

Personnel scheduling is a planning activity in all organizations. Service operations, such as the airline industry, a full service restaurant, highway toll booths, government offices and supermarket check-outs, are by their very nature heavily people-oriented and

Figure 14.22 Optimized production technology: Rule 6.

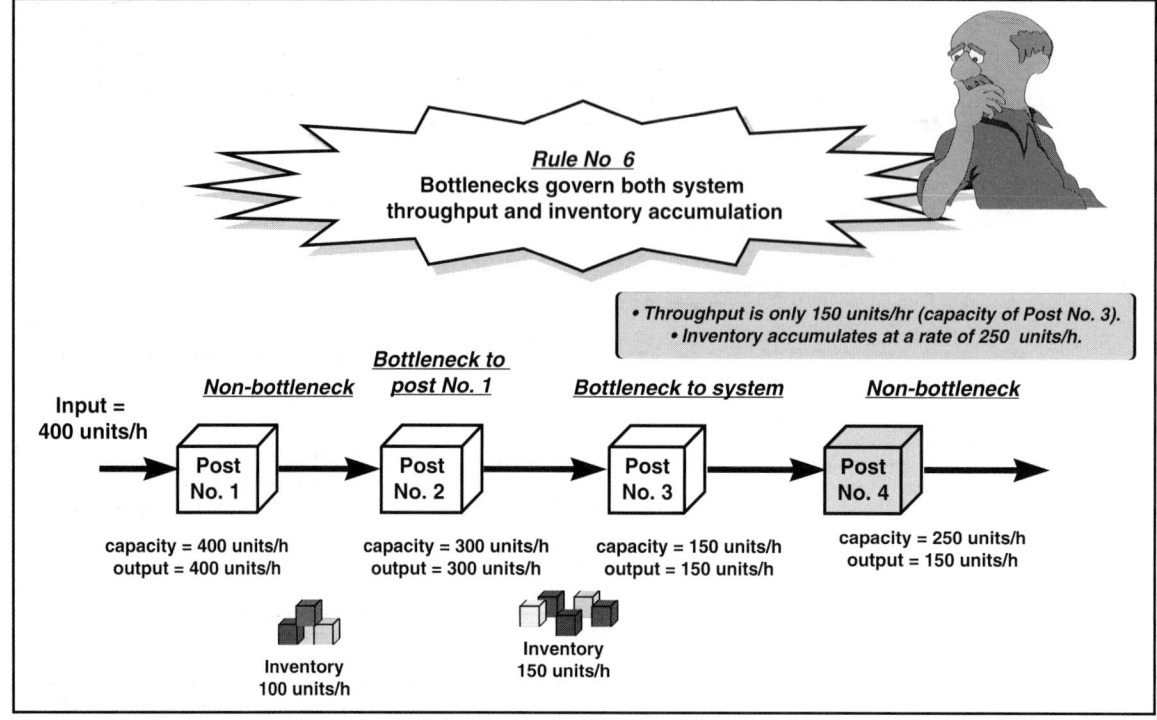

scheduling is a major activity. In manufacturing firms, as well as the functions that deal with tangible goods, there are support services involving personnel scheduling, such as the employee restaurant, the medical centre, customer billing, computer services and the printing department.

Since the operation of a service function is heavily labour intensive, one challenge is to optimize labour costs, although that is not to say that service industries with heavy capital investment, such as airlines, leisure cruises, and hotels, should not have a first priority to maximize facility utilization. In the service function the demand often varies according to the time of day, time during the week or season of the year. And, unlike manufacturing, there is not a buffer of inventory to smooth out fluctuations.

Scheduling possibilities

Some scheduling possibilities for personnel include the following.

First come, first served

Using the first come, first served scheduling sequence relies on waiting lines to buffer the difference between demand and the system capacity. From a scheduling point of view, this will permit a uniform system capacity from period to period, as might be the case in a supermarket, toll booth or a doctor's waiting room; the medical profession is notorious for putting a high value on doctors' time and a low value on patients' time.

This type of scheduling, often used, is advantageous to the operation of the service because it facilitates planning and costs can easily be predetermined. However, it may be unacceptable to the client if they have to wait. In a competitive situation (supermarket for example), clients may choose to go elsewhere.

Appointment schedules

Appointment schedules to level demand would be an option in the medical profession, when patients who want to visit a doctor, dentist or other specialist make an appointment for a certain time period to satisfy the capacity of the service (number of doctors or dentists available). However, even scheduling does not always avoid the waiting-line situation.

Priority system

A priority system in scheduling might be applied to emergency medical care or large orders for a good client.

Figure 14.23 Optimized production technology: Rule 7.

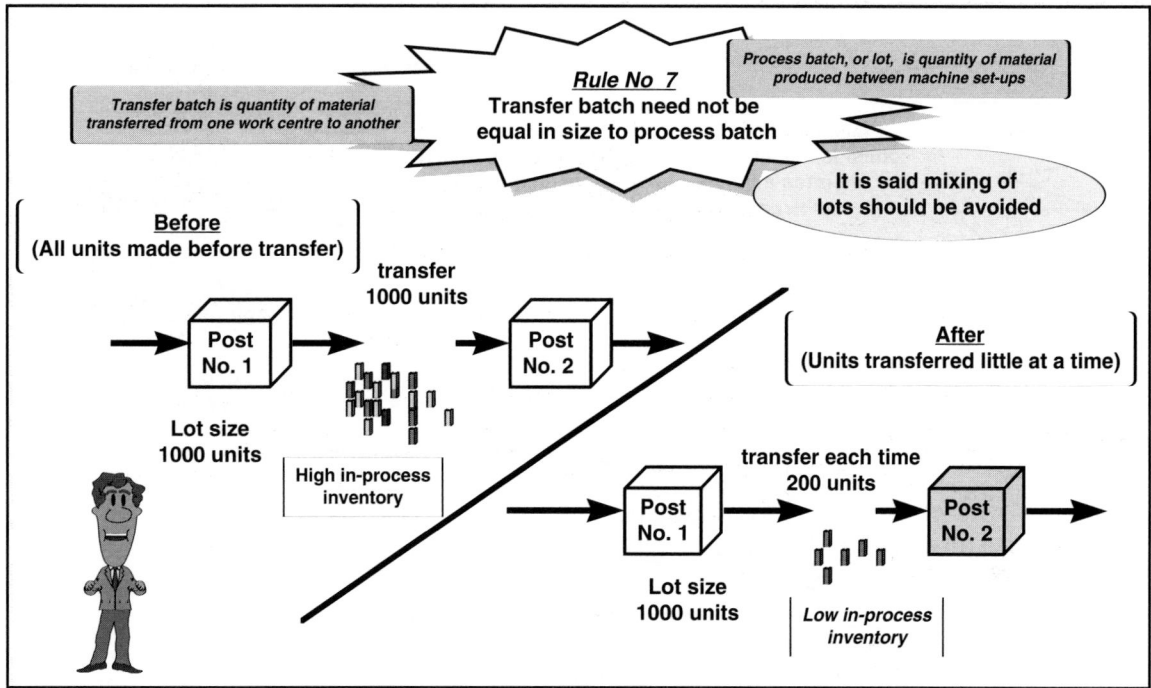

Adjusting capacity

To satisfy the needs of clients better, and to avoid excessive capacity when not needed, companies strive to adjust schedules to balance the system. This often means putting more personnel in the system when demand is high and vice versa; if part time personnel can work alongside full-time personnel, this helps to avoid idle time. Some examples are:

- On the toll roads in France, there are more toll booths open during holidays, weekends and other heavily used periods.
- Cashiers in a hyper- or supermarket are more numerous in the lunch period and early evening when demand is heavy.
- Hospitals schedule more emergency medical staff on Friday and Saturday evenings when demand is heavy (more drunks, fights, and other 'accidents').
- There are more truck drivers on a Monday morning to supply inventory demand run down from the weekend.

- Many US banks use part-time tellers during peak hours.

Emergency services

Emergency services, such as fire departments for a city or an oil refinery complex, ambulance crews, police and similar services, provide a 24-hour full-crew coverage. During periods of low demand if the crews are multiskilled they can perform other tasks such as maintenance, office work, cleaning, etc. During peak demand, off-duty personnel, services from other communities or even other countries may be called in. This might be in the case of forest fires, earthquakes, rail disasters or similar emergencies.

The worked example, *Moopick*, illustrates the development of personnel scheduling using Excel.

Figure 14.24   Optimized production technology: Rule 9.

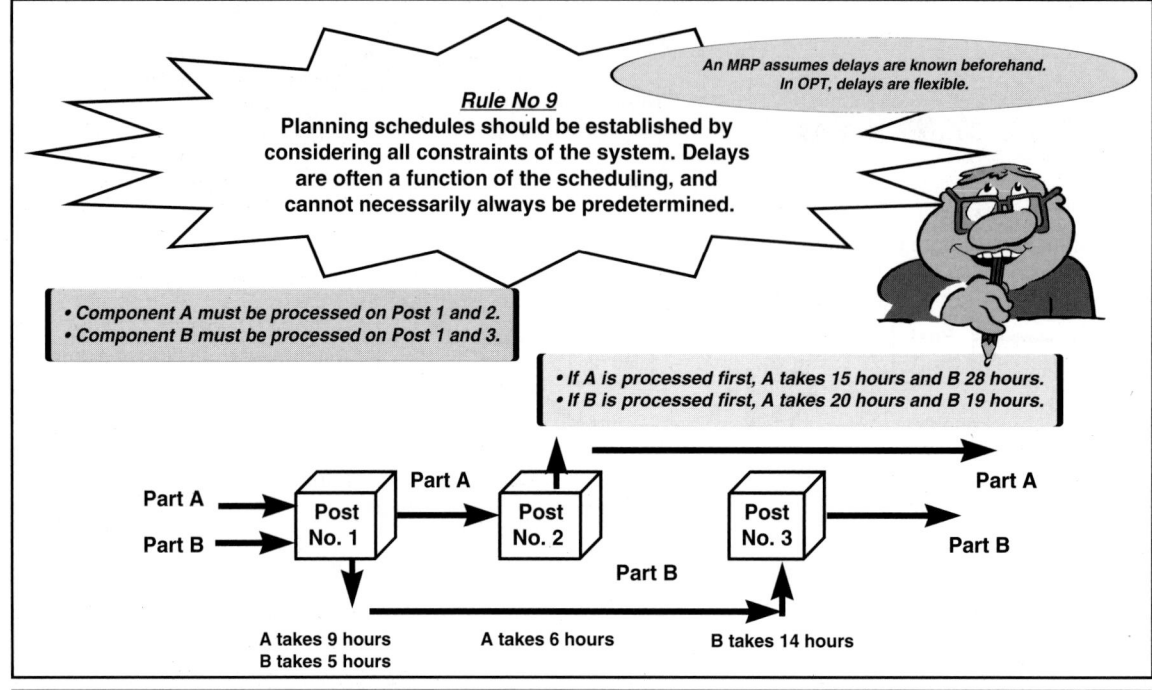

WORKED EXAMPLE: MOOPICK

Situation

The Moopick Co. operates a chain of restaurants that serve the motorways in Switzerland. On one of its outlets near Zurich, Moopick needs to determine staffing needs per week. Based on historical data of occupancy at the restaurant, it knows that the scheduled personnel, needed are as shown in Table 14.20. According to regulations it has to give each employee two consecutive days off during the week. And, all its staff are permanent such that on any one day, the staff are either working, or they are on their day off.

Required

Develop a planning schedule showing the staffing for Moopick in a week.

Solution

Planning schedule for Moopick

Figure 14.25 gives a planning schedule for Moopick, which has been developed using Excel Solver. This is developed as follows:

Figure 14.25   Staff scheduling for Moopick.

	A	B	C	D	E	F	G	H	I
1					Day working				
2	Time off	Staff off	Mon	Tue	Wed	Thu	Fri	Sat	Sun
3	Monday, Tuesday	2	0	0	1	1	1	1	1
4	Tuesday, Wednesday	7	1	0	0	1	1	1	1
5	Wednesday, Thursday	4	1	1	0	0	1	1	1
6	Thursday, Friday	8	1	1	1	0	0	1	1
7	Friday, Saturday	3	1	1	1	1	0	0	1
8	Saturday, Sunday	1	1	1	1	1	1	0	0
9	Sunday, Monday	1	0	1	1	1	1	1	0
10									
11	Total scheduled	26	23	17	15	14	15	22	24
12									
13	Total required		23	17	13	14	15	22	24
14									
15	Total paid staff		26	26	26	26	26	26	26

- Cells (A-3) through (A-9) are the possible combinations of days off for employees.
- In each row 3 through 9 are the working days for the employee. A value of 1 indicates that the employee works. A value of 0 indicates that the employee has a day off.

Table 14.20   Staff needed by Moopick

	Monday	Tuesday	Wednesday	Thursday	Friday	Saturday	Sunday
Total required	23	17	13	14	15	22	24

- Cells (C-13) through (I-13) in row 11 are the required staff set by Moopick.
- The objective is to have the minimum staff. Cell (B-11) is the objective function, the value of which is set to a minimum.
- The formula in Cell B-11 is the sum of Cells (B-3) through (B-9) in column B.
- Variables in the solution are Cells (B-3) through (B-9).
- Constraints in the system are:
  - cells (B-3) through (B-9) in column B are greater than zero;
  - cells (B-3) through (B-9) in column B are integer numbers;
  - cells (C-11) through (I-11) in row 11 are greater or equal to cells of line (C-13) through (I-13) of row 13.
- The formula in Cell (C-11) is (B-3)*(C-3) + (B-4)*(C-4) + (B-5)*(C-5) + (B-6)*(C-6) + (B-7)*(C-7) + (B-8)*(C-8) + (B-9)*(C-9).
- The formula in Cell (D-11) is (B-3)*(D-3) + (B-4)*(D-4) + (B-5)*(D-5) + (B-6)*(D-6) + (B-7)*(D-7) + (B-8)*(D-8) + (B-9)*(D-9).

- The formula in Cell (E-11) is (B-3)*(E-3) + (B-4)*(E-4) + (B-5)*(E-5) + (B-6)*(E-6) + (B-7)*(E-7) + (B-8)*(E-8) + (B-9)*(E-9).
- The formula in Cell (F-11) is (B-3)*(F-3) + (B-4)*(F-4) + (B-5)* (F-5) + (B-6)*(F-6) + (B-7)*(F-7) + (B-8)*(F-8) + (B-9)*(F-9).
- The formula in Cell (G-11) is (B-3)*(G-3) + (B-4)*(G-4) + (B-5)*(G-5) + (B-6)*(G-6) + (B-7)*(G-7) + (B-8)*(G-8) + (B-9)*(G-9).
- The formula in Cell (H-11) is (B-3)*(H-3) + (B-4)*(H-4) + (B-5)*(H-5) + (B-6)*(H-6) + (B-7)*(H-7) + (B-8)*(H-8) + (B-9)*(H-9).
- The formula in Cell (I-11) is (B-3)*(I-3) + (B-4)*(I-4) + (B-5)* (I-5) + (B-6)*(I-6) + (B-7)*(I-7) + (B-8)*(I-8) + (B-9)*(I-9).
- Cells (C-15) through (I-15) of row 15 show that on any day there are 26 staff members on the payroll. This includes those in the restaurant and those on their day off.

Figure 14.26 is a bar chart illustrating the minimum staff scheduled and the actual staff scheduled.

Figure 14.26 Moopick – staff scheduling.

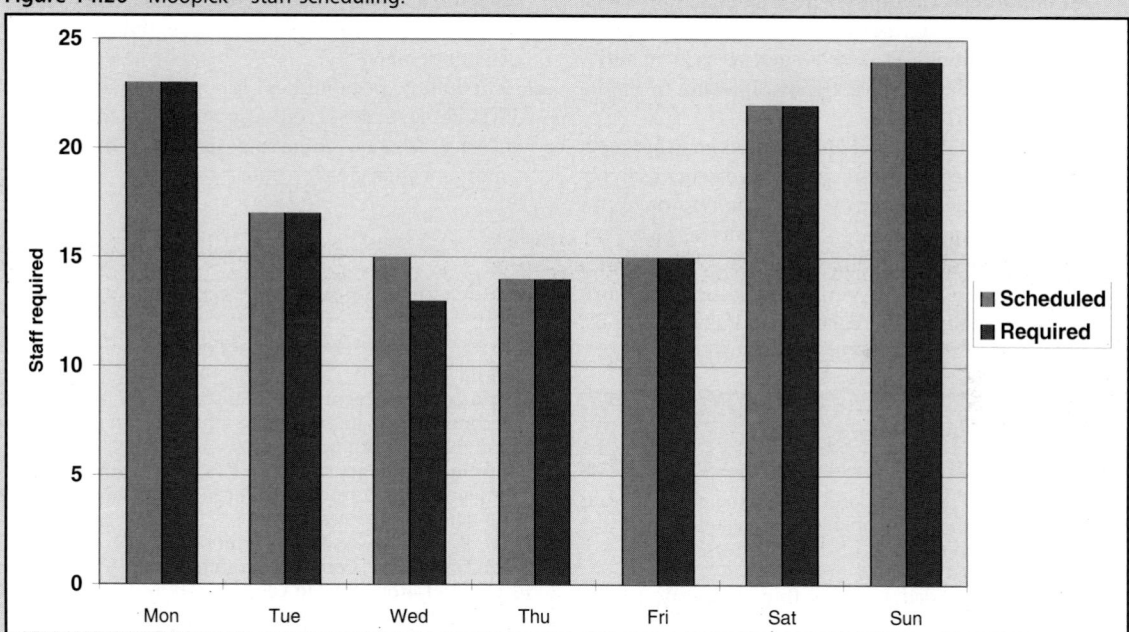

COMPUTERIZED SCHEDULING PLANS

Large, and even medium-sized, organzations have computerized scheduling programmes, which might be a part of an MRP-II system, a stand-alone scheduling programme or an optimized process technology type system. These work well, provided the input data regarding delivery times, inventory levels and client delivery dates is correct – which is not always the case!

Small companies that have limited resources, either for the purchase and installation of computerized scheduling systems or for the knowledgeable personnel to operate them, may rely on calculators, rule of thumb and rudimentary Gantt charts developed on a week-to-week basis.

In the US, many scheduling packages can be purchased in the $100 to $500 price range. More professional packages (Primavera for example) cost up to $5,000 and are perhaps more appropriate for project management scheduling (see Chapter 18, *Project Management*).

SUMMARY OF KEY ELEMENTS

■ Scheduling involves the preparation of a timetable for work that needs doing to meet client need dates or for activities to meet some desired objective.

■ A Gantt, or bar, chart is a tool that indicates work scheduled for certain time periods, how much is completed according to plan and who performed the work. Using a Gantt chart, an operations or production manager can see if resources can be modified to ensure that activities are kept on schedule.

■ Order sequencing is deciding the optimum order in which to process jobs or people. Sequencing rules include: First come, first served; Earliest due date; Shortest processing time; Longest processing time; Last arrived, first processed; Least slack time; Critical ratio; and Least changeover cost where set-ups are involved.

■ An important criterion is client satisfaction. Thus, those sequencing rules that respect delivery dates, or at least minimize delays such as critical ratio, earliest due date and least slack time, are often the most appropriate.

■ Johnson's rule is a scheduling method when several jobs need to be processed successively through two work centres. If certain criteria apply, it can be adapted to three work centres.

■ The assignment scheduling method is to assign personnel or jobs to certain activities, or work posts, to minimize the cost or maximize the profit.

■ The run-out method of scheduling determines which product to process next in order to avoid running out of stock. There are two approaches, one considering fixed inventory quantities, the other the aggregate run-out time.

■ The line of balance technique is a scheduling tool used when there is a fixed quantity of a customized product to be delivered over a period of time. The technique checks, at various reporting periods, if operations producing the final product are on schedule, that is, whether the actual operation is in 'balance' with the scheduled operation.

■ Optimized production technology is a computer-based scheduling tool with a set of nine rules revolving around the concept of bottlenecks. In an operations context, a bottleneck is a resource such as a work centre, machine or labour force, where the capacity of this resource is less than the downstream demand.

■ Scheduling possibilities for personnel include: First come, first served; Appointment schedules; A priority system; Adjusting capacity; and Using emergency services.

REVIEW AND DISCUSSION QUESTIONS

1 **Gantt Chart**. Prepare a Gantt scheduling chart for your activities for the forthcoming month. Indicate on the schedule which are:
(a) value added activities;
(b) non-value-added activities (but necessary, eating, sleeping, etc.);
(c) idle time.
After the Gantt chart has been prepared, analyse and see if any improvements can be made to increase the proportion of value-added activities.

2 **Bottleneck situations**. In the following, what would raise a red flag to indicate that bottlenecks were occurring:
(a) retail food store;
(b) restaurant;
(c) highway;
(d) a machine shop producing automobile parts;
(e) border control.
If bottlenecks are occurring, what steps could be taken to reduce them?

3 **Information technology**. Discuss how information technology has improved the scheduling in both service and manufacturing industries?

4 **Unplanned occurrences**. What are some of the unplanned occurrences that can upset the scheduling for some companies such as:
(a) British Airways (transportation);
(b) Ford Motor Company (automobiles);
(c) The Hilton Hotel in London;
(d) Norbert Dentressangle (storage and distribution in Europe – particularly France and Britain);
(e) Production at Glaxo–Wellcome (drugs);
(f) Royal Free Hospital (a major medical centre in Hampstead, North West London)?

5 **Supply chain**. Discuss the repercussions in the intgrated supply chain of poor scheduling for firms such as:
(a) Benetton (clothing);
(b) Boeing (aircraft manufacturer);
(c) British Steel (steel products);
(d) Nestlé (food products).
Consider both the operating firm and the clients.

EXERCISE PROBLEM: CARVER (PART II)

Situation

The Carver print shop, and the scheduling conditions, are the same as presented in the worked example, *Carver Part I*.

Required

1 Use the following sequencing rules:
   (a) shortest processing time;
   (b) longest processing time;
   (c) last arrived, first processed;
   (d) least slack time;
   (e) critical ratio.

Determine:
- total elapsed flow time (time to process all jobs from day 55);
- average flow time/job, or average completion time/job (total flow time/number of jobs in system);
- average jobs in system (total flow time/total processing time);
- number of jobs late;
- average days late (total days late/total number of jobs).
Illustrate each sequence on a Gantt, or bar, chart.

2 What is the preferred sequencing rule for this situation, including the first come, first served and the earliest due date presented in the worked example, *Carver* (Part I)?

EXERCISE PROBLEM: FROST

Situation

Frost is a small print shop in Chorleywood, England, which does print work for publicity brochures, catalogues and company documents. There are three principal operations in the print shop, printing, binding and trimming. Frost has only one each of the printing, binding and trimming machines.

On one particular morning, six jobs arrive for Frost. These jobs, and the time in hours for each operation, are given in Table 14.21. The jobs arrived in the scheduling office in the order given.

Table 14.21 Frost – jobs for scheduling

Job	Printing (h)	Binding (h)	Trimming (h)
A	4.25	3.75	2.75
B	5.00	4.00	2.25
C	5.25	4.00	3.00
D	5.50	3.50	6.25
E	4.75	3.00	5.50

Required

1 Develop a planning schedule for these five jobs using a first come, first served operation. Present the results on a Gantt chart. What is the total elapsed time for completing all of the five jobs?
2 Redo the schedule using Johnson's rule. Show the results on a Gantt chart. What is the new elapsed time for completing all of the five jobs?
3 Compare the planning schedules of requirements 1 and 2.

EXERCISE PROBLEM: HYPERMARKET

Situation

A hyper-market store is open from 08:00 until 22:00 six days a week. Based on historical data, it knows that the scheduled cashiers needed at the store on Mondays through Fridays are as shown in Table 14.22 (Saturday is different as it is quite busy throughout the day). The cashiers work eight hours per day and, to accommodate this, the store gives its cashiers three consecutive two-hourly periods off during the day. All its cashiers are permanent employees such that on any one day, the staff are either working or they are off.

Required

1 Develop a planning schedule showing the cashiers required for Monday through Friday.

Table 14.22 Requirements for hypermarket cashiers

Time period	08–10	10–12	12–14	14–16	16–18	18–20	20–22
Total required	12	20	30	18	25	35	16

EXERCISE PROBLEM: KILN

Situation

Annie Sabatier runs a gift shop in the South of France. In addition, she has a single pottery kiln in which she bakes pottery items for many clients around the area. When she runs the kiln, she separates items into lots according to the clients. The time needed for baking is a function of the clay and the glazing employed. Generally each client always uses the same type of clay and glazing compound, though these materials vary from client to client. Mrs Sabatier only runs the kiln eight hours a day, five days a week. There is an automatic shutoff of the kiln for any lots which take more than 8 hours to bake.

On one particular early Monday morning, Mrs Sabatier has the six lots shown in Table 14.23 waiting to be baked. This information gives the processing time for the lot, the order it was received and the time required by the client. Eight hours corresponds to Tuesday, 16 at Wednesday, 24 hours to Thursday, 32 to Friday and 40 to Saturday, each at 08:00).

Required

1 Use the following sequencing rules;
   (a) first come, first served;
   (b) earliest due date;
   (c) shortest processing time;
   (d) longest processing time;
   (e) last arrived, first processed;
   (f) least slack time;
   (g) critical ratio.
Determine:
■ total elapsed flow time (time to process all jobs from time 0);
■ average flow time/job, or average completion time/job;
■ average jobs in system;
■ number of jobs late;
■ average hours late.
Illustrate each sequence on a Gantt, or bar, chart.
2 What is the preferred sequencing rule for this situation?

Table 14.23 Job lots that Mrs Sabatier has to schedule

Job lot	A	B	C	D	E	F
Process time (hours)	7	3	4	5	6	8
Order received	1	2	3	4	5	6
Time due	16	8	8	32	24	24

EXERCISE PROBLEM: NEOSERVICE

Situation

Neoservice[4] is a company in France that designs, manufactures and assembles food trolleys. These are the types used in hotels and restaurants for displaying desserts, in businesses for delivering tea (principally the British market) and also externally for ice cream.

The products are handcrafted out of wood. In the workshop there are two work centres, 1 and 2. The first is the preparation of the wood and varnishing and the second is assembly and finishing. The time taken to perform these various activities is given in Table 14.24 for the six principal models produced by the company. In addition, the order of arrival for the order is indicated.

Required

1 Develop the schedule according to the arrival time, that is, first come, first served, for Work Centre 1 and Work Centre 2. Determine the total time for each operation, the total elapsed time to finish the six products, including both work centres. Present the sequence on a Gantt chart, showing operating times and dead times.
2 Repeat the scheduling procedure using Johnson's Rule for Work Centre 1 and Work Centre 2. Determine the total time for each operation, the total elapsed time to finish the six products, including both work centres. Present the sequence on a Gantt chart, showing operating times and dead times. What is the percentage of time saved?

Table 14.24 Neoservice – processing time for the principal models

	Paris	Tahiti	Savoie	Pose P	Loire	Glace
Order of arrival	1	2	3	4	5	6
Work Centre 1 Total time (min)	306	345	322	330	303	371
Work Centre No 2 Total time (min)	294	309	306	288	352	371

EXERCISE PROBLEM: SOFTWARE

Situation

Software is a computer-products company based in Palo Alto, California, which plans to establish European sales offices, specifically in France, Germany, Norway, Benelux, Italy and Spain. There will be a sales manager at each of these branches. Software performed a market survey for each of these countries and then asked its prospective managers to make an estimate of the first year's annual sales revenues that might be generated based on the market survey, their particular knowledge of the country, their language ability and their sales experience.

The estimated first yearly sales revenue for each of the six countries, estimated by each of the six prospective managers, Julia, Andy, Fred, John, Alice and Joan, is given in Table 14.25. The estimated first-year fixed costs for these branches and, the annual salaries for the six managers are also shown in Table 14.25.

Required

1   Using the assignment method, which would be the optimum way to schedule the assignments for these sales personnel if the objective was to maximize profit?
2   Software is somewhat uncertain of the success of this venture. If the annual operating costs for each site are estimated as the sum of the fixed costs and the annual salary of the sales manager, what would be the best way to schedule the location of the sales personnel if the criterion is to minimize cost?
3   Which assignment schedule would you propose based on the information given? (See also Chapter 22, *Decision Making and Risk Analysis*.)

Table 14.25   Software estimated first-year sales revenue, fixed costs and managers' salaries (all figures in $000)

	France	Germany	Norway	Benelux	Italy	Spain	Manager's salary
Estimated first yearly sales revenue							
Julia	700	700	925	1025	1200	425	120
Andy	900	850	450	1010	950	525	80
Fred	500	900	525	950	875	946	75
John	800	1000	945	525	950	850	60
Alice	625	750	825	850	850	650	110
Joan	525	955	675	590	725	725	90
Estimated first year fixed costs							
	250	200	350	200	100	150	

EXERCISE PROBLEM: STAMPING

Situation

Stamping Inc., near Coventry in England, is a firm that makes metal frame assemblies destined for the electricity, automobile and construction industries. One of its stamping presses is dedicated to the production of six frame assemblies, A-654, B-498, C-325, D-785 and E-458. Because of the set-up time involved for the stamping press, Stamping makes the assemblies in lot sizes. This information, together with the production time, customer demand per week and the current inventory at the beginning of the week is given in Table 14.26.

Required

1   Using the run-out method for fixed lot sizes, develop a production schedule for the next five weeks. Show the production schedule on a Gantt chart. Assume 40 hours of production time per week.
2   Using an aggregate run-out time method (lot sizes are not fixed), develop a production schedule for the next five weeks. Show the production schedule on a Gantt chart. Assume 40 hours of production time per week.

Table 14.26   Stamping – lot sizes, production time, customer demand and current inventory

	Run size (units)	Production time (h)	Weekly demand (units)	Current inventory (units)
A-654	800	12.00	350	200
B-498	600	8.00	200	160
C-325	250	15.00	125	240
D-785	750	20.00	180	230
E-458	250	10.00	200	100

NOTES AND REFERENCES

1. Johnson, S. M. (1954) 'Optimal and Three Stage Production Schedules with Set-up times included', *Naval Research Logistics Quarterly*: 61–68.
2. Goldratt, E, M. (1985) 'Devising a coherent production, finance, and marketing strategy using OPT rules', *BPICS Control* April/May: 7–12
3. Goldratt, E. M. and Cox, J. (1986) *'The Goal: A Process of Ongoing Improvement'*, New York: North River Press. (Also published in French: *'Le but: Un processus du progrès permanent'*, AFNOR.)
4. Based on a study by Benoit Stos and Sidney Grünbergy, students ESC Lyon (1997).

FURTHER READING

Ashby, J. R. and Uzsoy, R. (1995) 'Scheduling and order release in a single-stage production system', *Journal of Manufacturing Systems* 14(4): 290–306.

Ashcroft, S. H. (1989) 'Applying the principles of optimized production technology in a small manufacturing company', *Engineering Costs and Production Economics* 17(1–4): 79–88.

Bailey, J. E. (1986) 'Personnel scheduling with flexshift: A win/win scenario', *Personnel* 63(9): 62–67.

Bart, H. and Kroon, L. G. (1996) 'Variants of the two machine flow shop problem connected with factorization of matrix functions', *European Journal of Operational Research* 91(1): 144–59.

Bassett, G. and Todd, R. (1994) 'The SPT priority sequence rule', *International Journal of Operations and Production Management* 14(12): 70–78.

Bechtold, S. E. and Brusco, M. (1995) 'Microcomputer-based working set generation methods for personnel scheduling', *International Journal of Operations and Production Management* 15(10): 63–74.

Brusco, M. J. and Jacobs, L. W. (1993) 'Developing flexible personnel schedules using a microcomputer', *Work Study* 42(5): 5–8.

Brusco, M. J. and Jacobs, L. W. (1995) 'Cost analysis of alternative formulations for personnel scheduling in continuously operating organisations', *European Journal of Operational Research* 86(2): 249–61.

Brusco, M. J., Jacobs, L. W., Bongiorno, R. J., Lyons, D. V. and TANG (1995) 'Improving personnel scheduling at airline stations', *Operations Research* 43(5): 741–51.

Brusco, M. J., Jacobs, L. W. and Johns, T. R. (1995) 'Improving the dispersion of surplus labor in personnel scheduling solutions', *Computers and Industrial Engineering* 28(4): 745–54.

Cheng, T. C. E. (1991) 'Optimal assignment of slack due-dates and sequencing of jobs with random processing times on a single machine', *European Journal of Operational Research* 51(3): 348–53.

Cheng, T. C. E. (1996) 'Due-date assignment and single machine scheduling with compressible processing times', *International Journal of Production Economics* 43(2,3): 107–13.

Cheng, T. C. E. (1992) 'Efficient implementation of Johnson's Rule for the n/2/F/Fmax scheduling problem', *Computers and Industrial Engineering* 22(4): 495–99.

Coughlan, P. and Darlington, J. (1993) 'As fast as the slowest operation: The theory of constraints', *Management Accounting – London* 71(6): 14–17.

Creech, D. B. and Whitehouse, G. E. (1987) 'Development, operation, and testing of a heuristic line balancing program for a microcomputer,' *Computers and Industrial Engineering* 13(1–4): 153–55.

Deckro, R. (1989) 'Balancing cycle time and workstations', *IIE Transactions* 21(2): 106–11.

Heck, M. (1994) 'Milestones etc. offers a quick, simple path to Gantt charts', *InfoWorld* 16(40): 75–78.

Huisman, H. H., Polderman, G. L. and Weeda, P. J. (1990) 'Maximizing throughput in some simple time constrained scheduling situations', *Engineering Costs and Production Economics* 18(3): 293–99.

Hwang, H. and Song, J. Y. (1993) 'Sequencing picking operations and travel time models for man-on-board storage and retrieval warehousing systems', *International Journal of Production Economics* 29(1): 75–88.

Jayson, S. (1987) 'Goldratt and Fox: Revolutionizing the factory floor', *Management Accounting* 68(11): 18–22.

Jones, C. V. (1988) 'The three dimensional Gantt chart', *Operations Research* 36(6): 891–903.

Karacapilidis, N. I., Pappis, C. P. (1993) 'Optimal due date determination and sequencing of *n* jobs on a single machine using the SLK method', *Computers in Industry* 21(3): 335–39.

Lundrigan, R. (1986) 'What is this thing called OPT?', *Production and Inventory Management* 27(2): 2–12.

Martello, S. and Toth, P. (1986) 'A heuristic approach to the bus driver scheduling problem', *European Journal of Operational Research* 24(1): 106–17.

Meleton, M. P. Jr (1986) 'OPT – Fantasy or breakthrough?', *Production and Inventory Management* 27(2): 13–21.

Milas, G. H. (1990) 'Assembly line balancing . . . Let's remove the mystery', *Industrial Engineering* 22(5): 31–36.

Neely, A. D. and Byrne, M. D. (1992) 'A simulation study of bottleneck scheduling', *International Journal of Production Economics* 26(1–3): 187–92.

Parker, S., Malstrom, E. M., Irwin, L. M. and Ducote, G. (1994) 'A decision support system for personnel scheduling in a manufacturing environment', *Computers and Industrial Engineering* 27(1–4): 185–88.

Prabuddha, D., Ghosh, J. B. and Wells, C. E. (1991) 'Optimal delivery time quotation and order sequencing', *Decision Sciences* 22(2): 379–90.

Rahbar, F. F. and Rowings, J. E. (1992) 'Repetitive activity scheduling process', *American Association of Cost Engineers Transactions* 2: 51–58.

Ronen, B. and Starr, M. K. (1990) 'Synchronized manufacturing as in OPT: From practice to theory', *Computers and Industrial Engineering* 18(4): 585–600.

Starkweather, T. (1993) 'Optimization of sequencing problems using genetic algorithms', unpublished PhD Thesis, Department of Computer Science, Colorado State University, USA.

Vollman, T. E. (1986) 'OPT as an enhancement to MRP II', *Production and Inventory Management* 27(2): 38–47.

Wheatley, M. (1986) 'How to beat the bottlenecks', *Management Today*, October: 84–86.

Wheatley, M. (1989) 'OPTimising production's potential', *International Journal of Operations and Production Management* 9(2): 38–44.

Yenradee, P. (1994) 'Application of optimized production technology in a capacity constrained flow shop: A case study in a battery factory', *Computers and Industrial Engineering* 27(1–4): 217–20.

15 Lean production and just-in-time

Objectives and overview

The objective of this chapter is to describe the elements of lean production in the supply chain and to highlight just-in-time operation, which is a key component. The chapter opens by presenting pull and push systems, illustrated by a detailed analysis of a production operation. Balancing a production operation, to be in harmony with client demands, is discussed with emphasis on multiskilled operations and cellular design. The Kanban system is detailed; how it works, how to calculate the number of Kanbans in circulation and how to establish priority systems in situations where several components are produced at one workstation. Good inventory management is again highlighted and the concepts of Single Minute Exchange of Die (SMED) and Overall Equipment Effectiveness for improving added value are presented. The Japanese Five S rules, for being efficient and rigorous, are described, as are the five zeros in just-in-time. The last part of the chapter underscores the importance of quality and the application of just-in-time in services. The chapter then concludes by illustrating the risks associated with just-in-time.

CONCEPTS

Lean production

Lean production has its roots in the Toyota Automobile Co. of Japan, where waste was to be avoided at all cost: the waste in time caused by having to repair faulty products, the waste of investment in keeping high inventories and the waste of having idle workers. Elements of lean production include:

■ To consider the organization in terms of a supply chain of value streams that extends from suppliers of raw materials, through transformation, to the final client.
■ To organize workers in teams and to have everybody in the organization conscious of their work.
■ To produce products of perfect quality and to have continuous quality improvement as a goal.
■ To organize the operation by product, or cellular manufacturing, rather than using a functional layout (see Chapter 10, *Design of the Facility Layout*).
■ To operate the facility in a just-in-time mode.

The article in Box 15.1 illustrates the challenge of lean production for a new European manufacturing facility.[1]

Just-in-time

A key element of lean production is just-in-time (JIT), conceived by Taiichi Ohno, the former president of Toyota Motor Co. of Japan, in the 1980s. It was later perfected by other Japanese manufacturing and service companies and is now a philosophy adopted by firms worldwide. The Japanese manufacturing success, with increased productivity, low product cost and often superior quality products, can very much be attributed to just-in-time (JIT) manufacturing methods. JIT means:

■ producing the quantity of units that is needed, no more and no less;
■ producing them on the date and at the time required, not before and not after;
■ that a supplier delivers the exact quantity demanded, at the scheduled time and date.

Any deviations from these requirements mean that either resources are being unnecessarily wasted or that clients' needs are not being respected. There is really no technological sophistication with JIT. It is simply an acronym for being efficient, organized and rigorous, having the ability to be flexible, with an ultimate objective of satisfying the client, respecting delivery times,

Box 15.1 GM's new Opel plant is to adapt methods from around the globe to eastern Germany. By Timothy Aeppel, Staff Reporter

EISENACH, Germany – The opening of a new car factory is usually a pretty sedate affair.

But there's little about General Motors Corp.'s new plant in this gritty eastern German town that's usual. "All of Europe is looking to Eisenach," said Louis Hughes, GM Europe's president, who came to Eisenach to help open the facility, "because this is where they can see the future."

"Eisenach will be our most productive facility in Europe," GM President John F. Smith Jr. told the crowd, which included most of the plant's current work force of 650, at Wednesday's factory opening. Chancellor Helmut Kohl praised GM for investing in Eisenach and urged other companies to follow the auto maker's example. Mr. Kohl also used the opportunity to speak out against the continuing attacks against foreigners in Germany.

Borrowing the Best Ideas

The factory is GM's answer to the Japanese auto makers' mounting invasion of Europe – a plant that takes the best ideas from factories around the globe and adapts them to eastern Germany. If it succeeds, Eisenach will help GM revamp its other European operations and send a jolt through the European auto industry, which often argues that some methods, particularly those borrowed from Japan, are impossible to implement in Europe.

In some ways, GM's plunge into eastern Germany reflects the very different conditions that existed when the decision was made to build the plant two years ago. European car sales were booming, especially in Germany. But now, many European car makers, including Ford Motor Co., are cutting production in the face of a deepening European recession. GM officials insist they still need the capacity of the Eisenach plant.

The plant also carries special significance for Germany. GM's one billion-mark investment was one of the first and largest single investments by a western company in the region. With unemployment in eastern Germany now soaring and Germany as a whole on the brink of recession, the factory opening provided one of the few glimmers of business confidence seen in recent months.

Slow Start-Up Process

But even GM officials admit they still face the toughest test – getting the plant to work as envisioned. The opening was only an official start for a slow start-up process that will stretch into next year. When it reaches full capacity, the factory will employ 2,000 people and produce 150,000 cars annually.

The philosophy at Eisenach is to integrate "lean production" techniques into the plant from the start. These techniques include just-in-time parts deliveries, continuous quality improvement, and workers organized in teams. Mr. Hughes, who recently took over as president of GM's European headquarters in Zurich, spearheaded the development of Eisenach in his previous job – as chairman of Adam Opel AG, GM's German subsidiary.

When it comes to lean production, Mr. Hughes is a true believer. In the factory, he points at a blue table just off the assembly line, where two workers fasten hoses and wires onto a gas tank. "In a normal factory, this would be a mess," says Mr. Hughes. "There would be huge inventories of tanks waiting to be installed in the cars on the line." In Eisenach, the tanks are subassembled just before they are inserted in the cars – drastically cutting the amount of space and materials needed for the operation.

Comprehensive Philosophy

Even the workers' uniforms are dictated by the philosophy. All Eisenach employees, including top managers, wear grey slacks and white, button-down shirts. Ties are not allowed. "We see it as a form of communication," says Juergen Gebhardt, the plant's managing director. "It shows that we're all sitting in the same boat – and that we need to talk openly to one another."

But the factory also stirs skepticism. Bob Barber, an auto analyst at James Capel & Co. in London, says Eisenach's relatively small projected capacity means it will be less than 10% of GM's total European output of about 1.6 million. "This is quite small, in the context of a major European producer," he says.

Mr. Barber says GM's challenge will be to integrate the ideas from Eisenach in its older factories. "Every other car manufacturer in Europe is trying to do the same thing in new facilities," he says, "so the goal posts keep moving; that's the nature of the business."

Wall Street Journal Europe, 24 September 1992
Reprinted by permission of *Wall Street Journal Europe*,
© 1992 Dow Jones & Company, Inc.
All Rights Reserved Worldwide.

having the specified quality and producing at minimum cost.

Requirements

For just-in-time to work effectively, stable and level production schedules are desirable. Ideally, the same products are produced in the same sequence, in the same quantities and in similar time periods (for example each week). Just-in-time works best with smaller and more-focused work centres, as small specialized centres are easier to manage. The method requires reduced lot sizes, a reduction in inventory levels and the communication between work posts using Kanbans, or cards.

Enforced problem solving

The just-in-time mode of operation presents a system of enforced problem solving. There are are no safety factors because:

- Every item of material is expected to meet quality standards.
- Every component and part must arrive at the right place, at the right time.
- Every worker is required to work productively.
- Every machine must function without breakdowns.

It is not to say that just-in-time is easy, or does not have other problems, as in the words of an official of R. V. Industriels, France (a manufacturer of trucks, buses and other heavy vehicles).[2]

> We have put in place a system of just-in-time in all our work areas including the foundry, pressing and stamping, machining and assembly. We have succeeded in reducing inventory. We have reduced costs. We have increased our competitiveness. We have improved product quality. And, we have increased the stress level of our operators!!

MRP 'push' and just-in-time 'pull'

Analogies are often made between just-in-time, which is a flexible pull system, and the MRP, which is a rigid push system. As discussed in Chapter 13, *Materials Requirement Planning*, the MRP is driven by the master production schedule, which is based not only on firm orders, but also on forecasts, so that when the planning system is set in motion some products are being pushed through the pipeline, Figure 15.1.

A pull system

Just-in-time is a pull system, because it is the client's order that triggers a demand. This demand *pulls* the required product through the supply chain from distribution, manufacturing, back to purchasing. As an illustration, in European automobile manufacturing, at any given time (Citröen's automobile facility at Aulnay-sous-bois, France is one example) sequentially, on the same assembly line, are semi-finished vehicles of various colours, of different models, some with steering wheels on the right (for the UK) and some with steering wheels on the left. Each one of these is being pulled through the production line by a specific customer order placed through a dealer.[3]

Push system

The strict *push* concept is where products are manufactured and pushed through the supply chain, where it is then up to the sales personnel to find clients. For example, in 1977, I purchased a sports car in Los Angeles. I wanted white, with black interior and certain options. I was unable to order in advance and had to visit various car dealers in the area to see if the model I wanted was available. At each dealership, sales persons tried to convince me to purchase another colour/design, offering each time an 'attractive' price. They were 'pushing' their products onto a prospective client. Now, as the previous paragraph has illustrated, if one purchases an automobile, one is able to give the exact specifications to a dealer (colour, interior fit-

Figure 15.1 MRP (push) and JIT (pull) systems.

tings, options, etc.) and this order is transmitted to the manufacturer. In about four to six weeks (depending on production levels) the required vehicle is ready.

That is not to say that automobile manufacturers are entirely producing on the 'pull' system. In the USA, Longo Toyota in El Monte, California, the world's biggest car dealer, 'pushes' its products onto the clients. At this dealership there is an enormous parking lot where clients can purchase a vehicle on the spot to suit their requirements. The dealership is open 364 days per year (25 December is the exception), from 07:00 until 22:00. In 1995, 21 000 vehicles were sold.[4]

The analogy of push and pull

An analogy of the *pull* and *push* systems can be demonstrated in the way two different cultures purchase and consume a staple commodity, bread.

The Americans

There are few individual bakeries in the USA and bread is usually purchased in supermarkets. The most popular bread is sliced and contains food preservatives that give it a relatively long life of seven to 14 days if kept in a freezer until it is required. The following is the purchase and consumption process:

- As in the MRP, a shopper estimates household bread consumption between two successive trips to the supermarket. This quantity, plus a safety stock, is purchased and stored in the freezer. At the time of the purchase, inventory is high and then, as in the MRP system, declines during the consumption period until the next purchase.
- Bread consumption is unplanned and erratic (unlike in France, it is not eaten with every meal). Thus, inventory decline is not predictable.
- More loaves are purchased at the next shopping cycle according to the inventory remaining in the freezer.

This can be likened to a push system. Inventory of bread stored in the freezer is *pushed* to the user as consumption is desired. The cycle time is long, up to two weeks, and the turnover of bread is low.

The French

The French only eat fresh bread and very often a baguette that is only good for the day of purchase. Bread is usually purchased at the local bakery, fresh, every day. (A baker starts work at 04:00). The purchase and consumption process is as follows:

- A baguette (one or several according to that day's estimated needs) is purchased in the morning. At this point, after the purchase, inventory level is at a maximum.
- Bread is consumed with most meals, and always with cheese.
- Inventory of bread at night, after the last meal, is zero (or near zero).
- In the morning, the bread container is empty, (or that remaining is hard as baguettes contain few preservatives), so another baguette, or several, is purchased.
- The cycle is repeated.

This is a pull system. Zero bread inventory in the morning 'pulls' another baguette through the household pipeline. The cycle time is short (one day). A given unit of bread remains at most one day in inventory. Thus, inventory turnover is high.

The supply chain and integration of MRP and JIT

Although it might at first seem that MRP and JIT are incompatible since they function differently and have different time horizons (JIT operates in a much shorter time frame than MRP), the two systems can be effectively combined to give an integrated planning tool for the entire supply chain. As an illustration, a major manufacturing company in Europe, which produces a wide range of consumer products, operates as follows:

- The manufacturing site obtains the sales forecast for Europe for about the next 18 months and this becomes the company-wide sales plan.
- This sales plan is broken down into an aggregate plan covering a three-month period.
- The aggregate plan is reduced to a master production schedule and a MRP system covering a six-week time horizon.
- The MRP is the driver for the daily just-in-time operation, using Kanbans in the manufacturing centres.

ANALYSIS OF A TRADITIONAL PUSH SYSTEM

Consider a simple production operation with three work posts and one operator at each post.

Production quantities

In the traditional push system, as illustrated in Figure 15.2, each operator works at his own rhythm, disre-

Figure 15.2 Traditional approach in production (operators work at their own pace trying to maximize output).

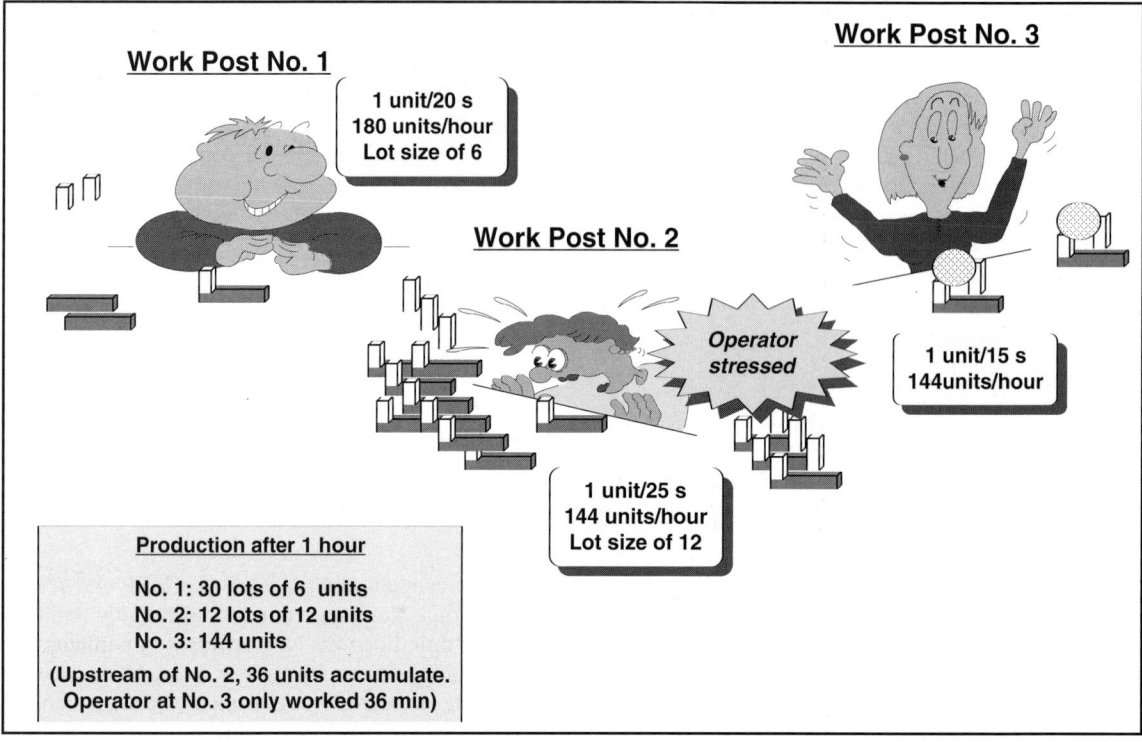

garding what is going on upstream or downstream. Table 15.1 gives the operating conditions. Under these conditions, the situation after one hour would be as shown in Table 15.2.

Table 15.1 Operating conditions in a push system

Post	
1	Time taken to complete one unit is 20 s, or 180 units/hour. Operator makes a lot of six units before transferring, or 'pushing' them, to the next post. Lots of six are made because the distance between two work posts makes it more economic to transfer six units, rather than one at a time. Under normal operation, hourly production is 30 lots.
2	Time taken to complete one unit is 25 s, or 144 units/hour. Operator produces a lot of 12 units before transferring them to the next post. Again, units are transferred in lots because it is more economic. Under normal operation, hourly production is 12 lots.
3	Time taken to complete 1 unit is 15 s. Production rate per hour is 240 units.

Table 15.2 Situation after one hour of operation

Post	
1	180 units have been produced, or 30 lots of six units. These units have been passed along to work post No. 2.
2	12 lots of 12 units have been produced (144 units in total). 36 units accumulate upstream of this post (180 – 144). The presence of these in-process units stresses the operator and the operator's efficiency drops.
3	144 units have been produced. Operator uses only 36 minutes of the hour in actually producing (144/240)×60. Thus, there is 24 min/hour of unproductive time.

As time proceeds, the situation deteriorates. After four hours for example, assuming the operator at Post No. 2 is able to maintain her output, 144 units accumulate upstream of the post. In four hours, operator at Post No. 3 has 96 min of unproductive time.

Flow times

Consider that the operation has been running for one hour with the accumulation of units as given in Table

15.2. After this first hour a new unit, Piece A, arrives upstream of Work Post No. 1, as shown in Figure 15.3. Table 15.3 presents the new situation.

Table 15.3 Situation after the first hour of operation (into the second hour)

Post

1   It takes 20 s to work on piece A.
    Operator then makes five more units (lot of six units) before sending to these to Post No. 2. Thus, operator at post No. 2 must wait 2 min (6 × 20 s) before he receives piece A.
2   At the start of the second hour there are 36 units waiting up-stream of post No. 2.
    In the 2 min that Operator at Post No. 1 is working on the first lot, Operator at Post No. 2 completes 4.8 of the 36 units (2 × 60s/25)
    Operator at Post No. 2 needs another 13 min (36 − 4.8)×25 s to complete the remaining units upstream. Thus, Post No. 2 cannot work on piece A until 15 min have elapsed (2 + 13).
    Operator at Post No. 2 takes 25 s to work on piece A. He then makes another 11 (lot of 12) before passing them to Post No. 3.
    Thus, piece A rests at Post No. 2 for an additional 5 min (12×25 s) before being sent to Post No 3.
    Work Post No. 3 receives piece A when 20 min have elapsed.

3   It takes operator at Post No. 3, 15 s to work on piece A.
    Thus, elapsed time for piece A to be finished is 20 min 15 s or 1215 s.

The situation can be summarized as follows.

Waiting time

The waiting time is 19 min 15 s (20 min 15 s – 1 min) or 95.06 per cent of the elapsed flow time!

Value added

The actual operating time during which value is being added is one minute (20 + 25 +15 s) or just 4.94 per cent of the total elapsed time.

This analysis underscores the inefficiency of waiting time as presented in Figure 11.5 in Chapter 11, *Inventory Management*.

Reasons for low productivity in traditional production

This illustration shows the quantitative inefficiencies in a traditional approach to production. Other qualitative aspects to take into consideration are given in Table 15.4.

Figure 15.3 Flow time in traditional approach in production (operators work at their own pace trying to maximize output).

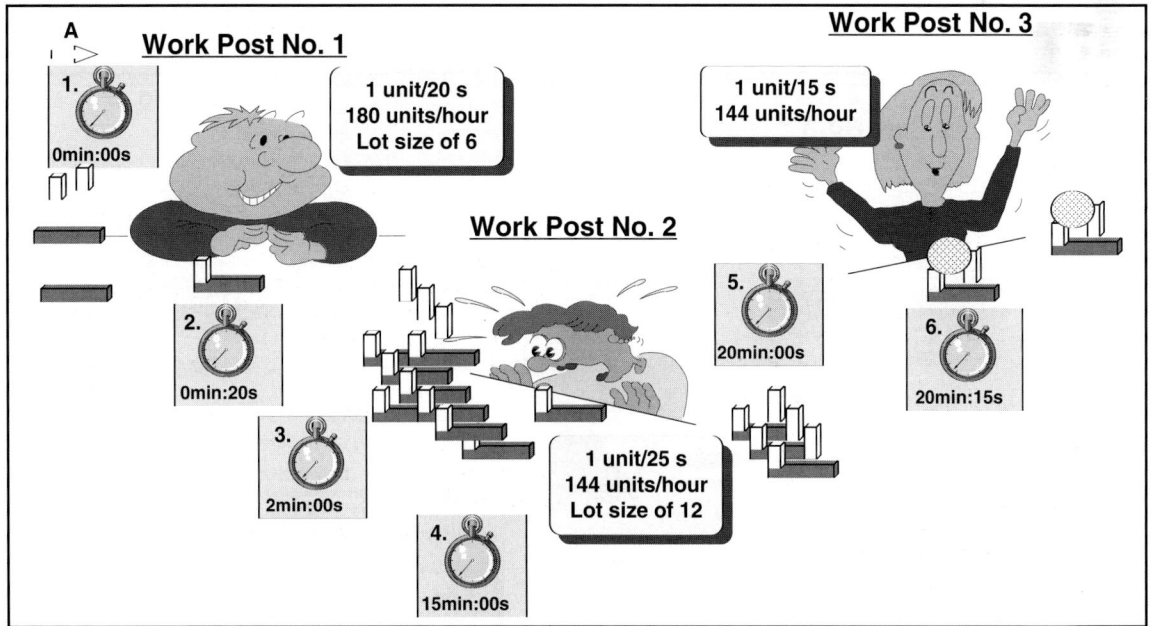

Table 15.4 Qualitative problems of the traditional approach to production

Criterion	Reasons/outcome
Operators poorly trained	Do not fully understand task
Poor product design	Complex manipulations for operators
Work stations unbalanced	Rate upstream greater than downstream
Operators stressed	Inventory build-up upstream creates 'panic'
Communication	Poor communication creates imbalance
Learning curve	Time needed to assimilate task
Idle time	Operators not fully occupied, de-motivated
Poor job design	Operators unsuitable for task

Table 15.5 The situation after one hour in a just-in-time system

Post	
1	144 units have been produced with a pause of 5 s between each unit.
2	144 units have been produced under a non-stressful situation.
3	144 units have been produced with a pause of 10 s between each unit.

Although production of Post No. 1 has been reduced, the output from Post No. 3 has not changed. However, in-process inventory has been virtually eliminated and the operator at Post No. 2 has not been intimidated by the accumulation of inventory upstream of his post.

Flow times

Again, consider that the operation has been running for one hour, Figure 15.5. At the beginning of the second hour, a new unit, Piece A, arrives upstream of Post No. 1. The situation now is as shown in Table 15.6.

The situation can be summarized as follows:

Waiting time

The actual waiting time for Piece A is 5 s at Work Post No 2 or just 7.69 per cent of the elapsed flow time!

ANALYSIS OF A JUST-IN-TIME PULL SYSTEM

Production quantities

Here, just-in-time is a unit-by-unit operation where the operator upstream waits until the immediate downstream post needs a unit before producing it, as illustrated in Figure 15.4. Under these conditions, the situation after one hour would be as shown in Table 15.5.

Figure 15.4 Just-in-time approach in production (upstream operator waits until downstream post needs a unit before producing).

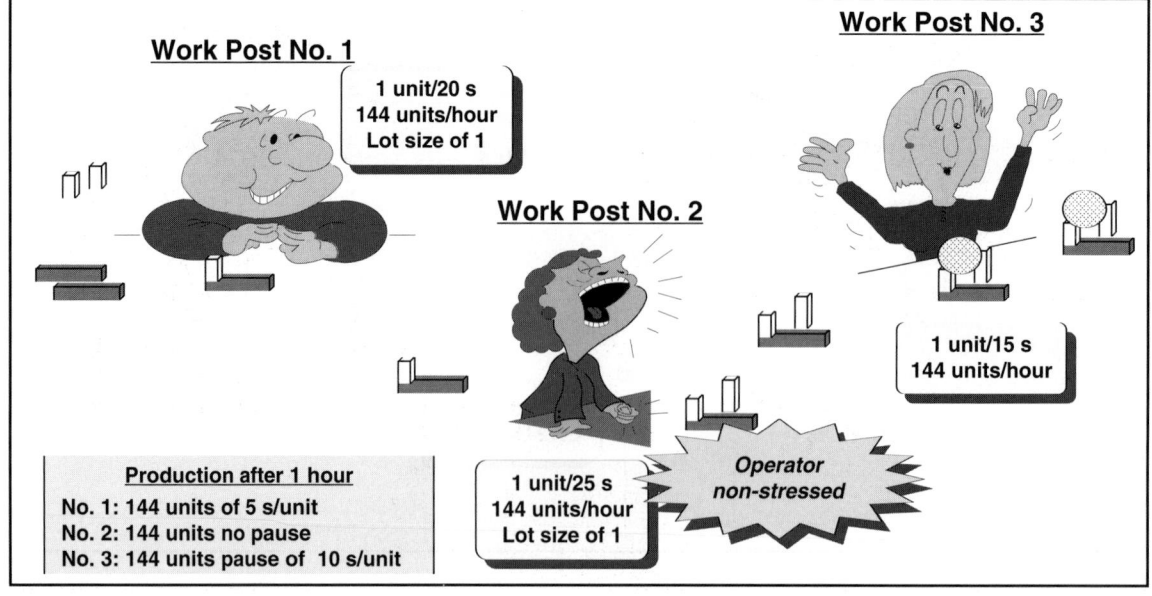

Value added

The actual operating time where value is being added is one 1 min (20 + 25 +15 s) or 92.31 per cent of the total elapsed time.

Because of the imbalance in operating times between posts, the operator at post No. 1 waits 5 s before starting another piece. The operator at Post No. 3 waits 10 s before starting another piece.

BALANCING A PRODUCTION LINE UNDER JUST-IN-TIME

Cycle time

Cycle time is the rate at which units are being produced on a production, or assembly, line. To be efficient, and to avoid building up unnecessary inventory, the cycle time should be equivalent to the client's demand rate.

Cycle time analogous to '*Takt* time'

An analogy of the cycle time, is *Takt* time. *Takt* is a German word meaning rhythm, where an orchestra plays slow or fast according to the requirements of the conductor. In production, the conductor is the client. Thus, the production team should be working at the

Table 15.6   Situation after the first hour of operation (into the second hour)

Post	
1	It takes the operator 20 s to work on this unit. He then passes this unit to Post No. 2.
2	There are no units waiting at Post No. 2. However, the operator is working on the previous piece, which takes another 5 s to finish (25 – 20 s). It then takes the operator 25 s to work on piece A. When finished, he passes Piece A onto Post No 3. Elapsed time for completing piece A is 50 s (20 + 5 + 25).
3	There are no units waiting and it takes the operator 15 s to work on Piece A. Total elapsed time for piece A is 1 min 5 s (50 + 15 s).

same rhythm, or cycle time, demanded by the client. Consider the following.

Situation No. 1

The client demands 4320 units per day. Assume there are three shifts producing a product, with three operators per shift, Figure 15.6:

- Each shift works 8 h/day. Thus, total production time is 86 400 s.
- Cycle time, or rate at which units must be produced, is 20 s (86 400/4320).
- Work Post No. 1 needs 20 s to produce one unit, or at the client cycle (*Takt*) time.

Figure 15.5   Flow time in just-in-time approach in production (upstream operator waits until downstream post needs a unit before producing).

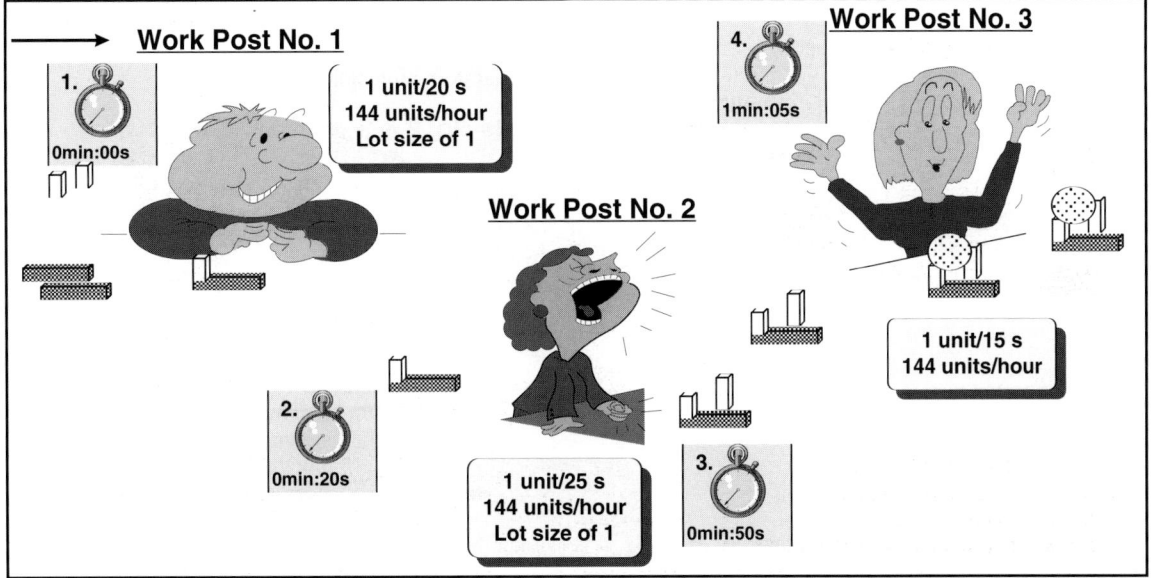

- Currently, Post No. 2 requires 25 s/unit, and Post No. 3 requires 15 s/unit with a 10 s pause.
- If operators at Post Nos 2 and 3 are multiskilled such that they can do either task, then the combined time per unit for Post No. 2 and Post No. 3 is 40 s (25 + 15). Now, operator at Post No. 2 performs task for Post No. 2 and then continues on same unit for task originally performed at Post No. 3.
- The line is balanced and the operators work at the same rhythm (*Takt* time) as the client demands.

Situation No. 2

Client demand drops to 2880 units per day from the original 4320 units per day. Assume again there are three shifts, Figure 15.7:

- Each shift works 8 h/day. Thus, total production time available is 86 400 s.
- Cycle time (rate at which units must be produced) is 30 s (86 400/2880)
- If operators are completely multiskilled (they can perform the tasks originally performed at the three work posts), then each operator takes 60 s to complete a piece (20 + 25 + 15).
- Thus, only two operators per shift are needed to meet the client's demand, or *Takt* time. Each operator produces 480 units or 960 units/shift. This is a total of 2880 units per day for three shifts.
- The third operator can be redeployed elsewhere.

If this arrangement was adopted, then to minimize movement of the operator, the machines should be positioned around this person, or in a cellular arrangement. If necessary, in order to make appropriate adjustments, equipment or machines can be removed and redeployed elsewhere. This can be facilitated by having machines on trolley-type arrangements (see Chapter 10, *Design of the Facility Layout*).

KANBAN

Definition

Kanbans are the heart of just-in-time production. Kanban is a Japanese word meaning card and these cards are the means of communicating within, to and from a work centre. Kanbans effectively replace all written work orders, move tickets and routing sheets. No parts can be moved, produced or used without an appropriate Kanban. Parts, and components are transferred from one work area to another in rigid plastic containers. These containers are just large enough to hold a small, and fixed, quantity of units of the same component reference. Different parts are not put into the same container.

Kanban forms

The physical form of Kanbans depends on the organization, and on the particular work centre within that organization. They may be magnetic strips, which can

Figure 15.6   Flexibility in just-in-time operation with multiskilled operators.

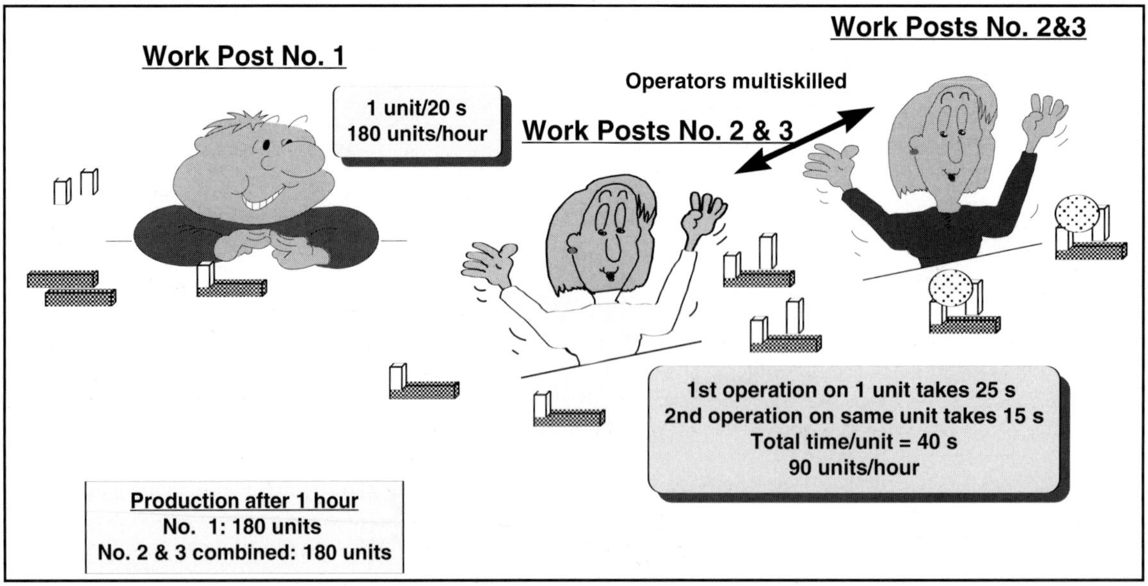

Work Post No. 1

1 unit/20 s
180 units/hour

Work Posts No. 2&3

Operators multiskilled

Work Posts No. 2 & 3

1st operation on 1 unit takes 25 s
2nd operation on same unit takes 15 s
Total time/unit = 40 s
90 units/hour

Production after 1 hour
No. 1: 180 units
No. 2 & 3 combined: 180 units

Figure 15.7   Just-in-time operation: two operators completely multiskilled.

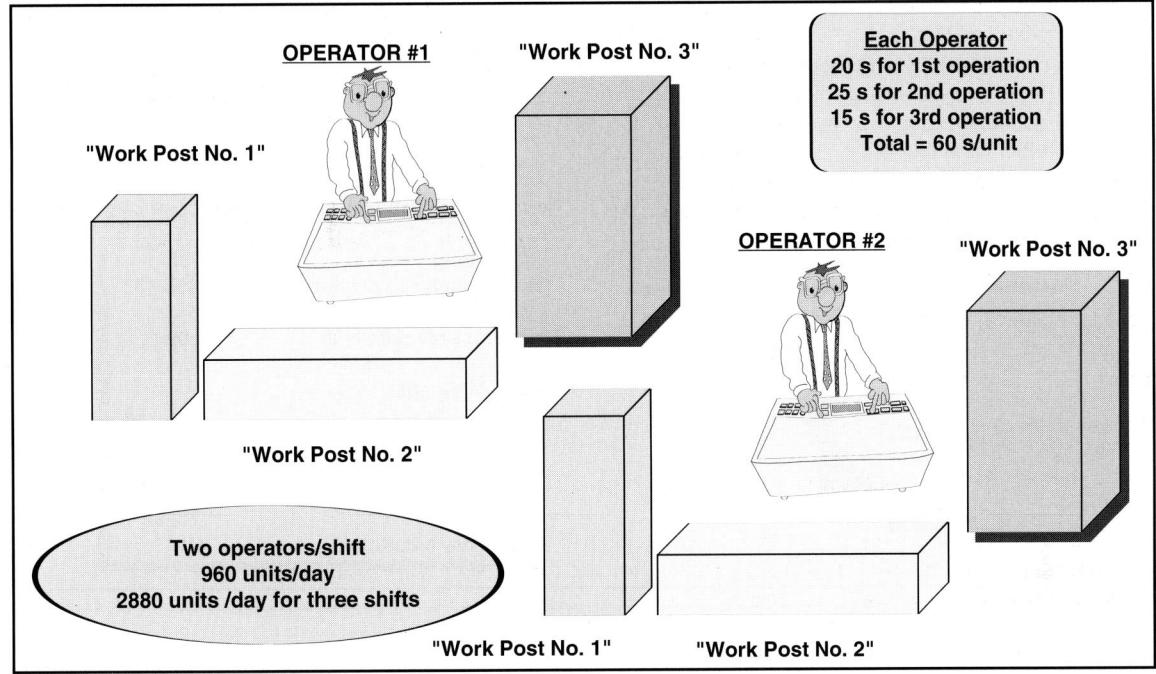

be affixed to a board adjacent to a work post, they may be cards that are put into the containers containing the products, or the containers themselves may be the Kanban. Hewlett Packard, Valéo, and Renault VI of France all use combinations of these types of Kanban.

Written on the Kanban is information concerning the part. This will include the reference number, storage areas and associated work centres. Figure 15.8 illustrates the type of information that would be found on two types of Kanbans, the Conveyance Kanban and the Production Kanban. In practice now, many companies using Kanbans have the information written in barcode form.

Production Kanban

Figure 15.9 illustrates the use of Kanbans with one type of card, the Production Kanban:

- An operator at the downstream Work Post No. 2 has an empty container, containing a production Kanban, K_p. The fact that the container is empty is the authorization to the operator to obtain additional components.
- The operator goes either to the storage area containing the parts (if a dedicated storage area exists) or to the upstream Work Post No. 1, where the needed parts are being machined.

- The operator exchanges the empty container for a full container containing the required parts, in which there is also a K_p Kanban.
- The production Kanban that was contained in the empty container is posted at the upstream work centre. This is the authorization for the upstream Work Post No. 1 to produce another container of parts.
- The operator returns to Work Post No. 2 to continue production.

Production and conveyance Kanban

Figure 15.10 illustrates the use of Kanbans with two types of card, the Production Kanban and the Conveyance Kanban:

- An operator at the downstream Work Post No. 2 has an empty container, containing a conveyance Kanban, K_w. The fact that the container is empty is the authorization to the operator to obtain additional components.
- The operator goes to the storage area containing the parts. He takes a full container of parts, which also contains a production Kanban, K_p. The operator replaces the K_p Kanban with the K_w Kanban that was in the empty container.

Figure 15.8   Information contained on Kanbans.

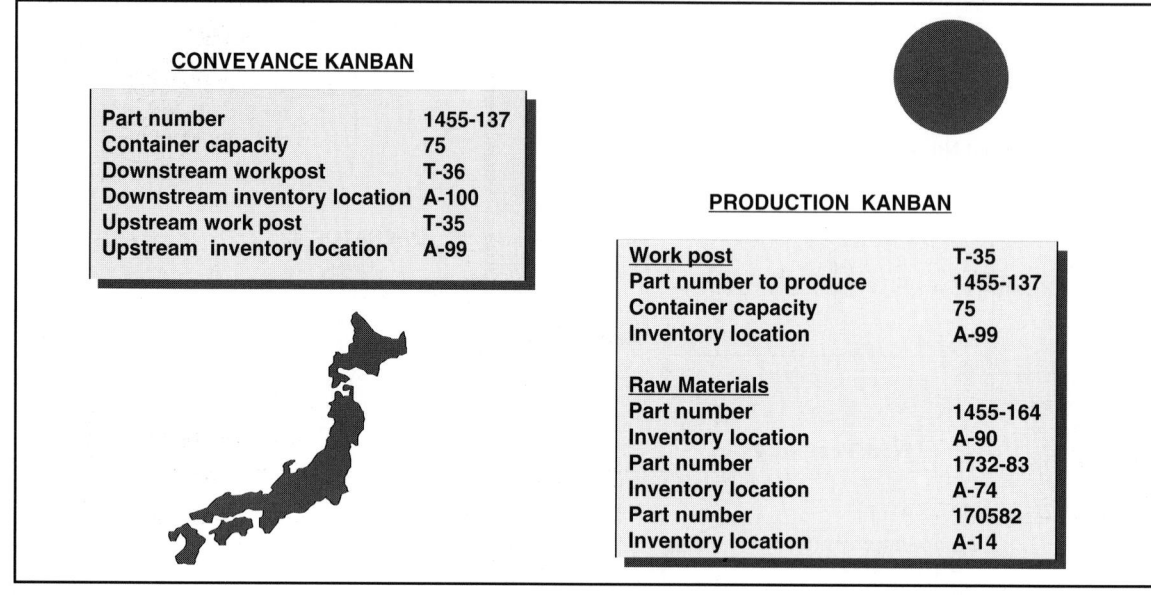

- The K_p card is posted at Work Post No. 1. This is the instruction for personnel at Work Post No. 1 to produce a container of parts.
- The operator returns to Work Post No. 2 and continues producing.

With the two-card system the conveyance cards circulate around the downstream Work Post, No. 2, and the production cards circulate around the upstream Work Post, No. 1. If additional inventory of a product is needed, such as for example another work post

Figure 15.9   Kanban system (one card).

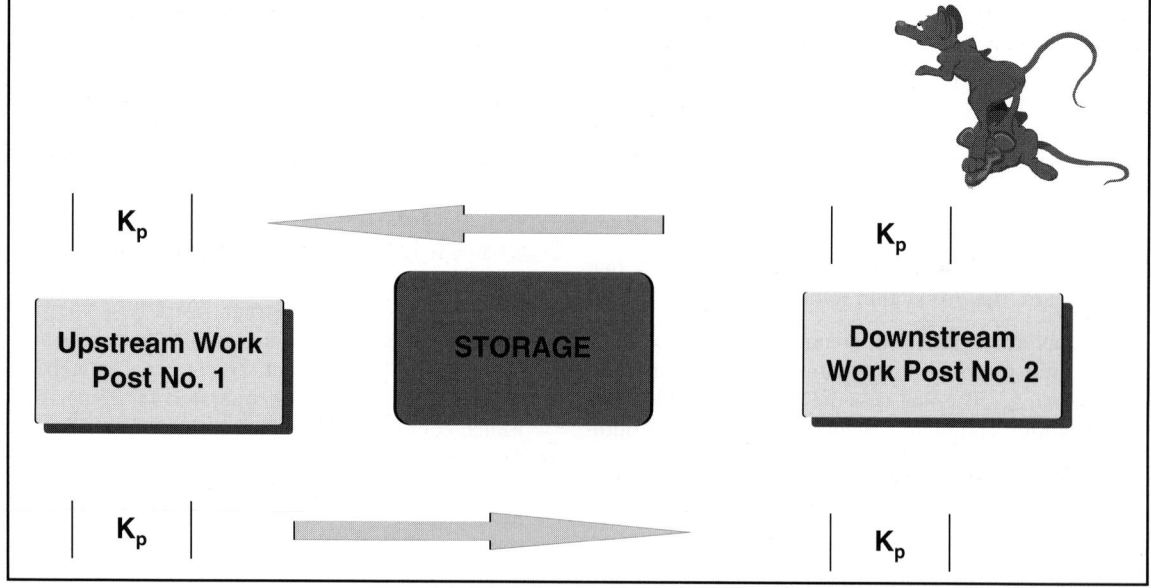

Figure 15.10 Kanban system (two cards).

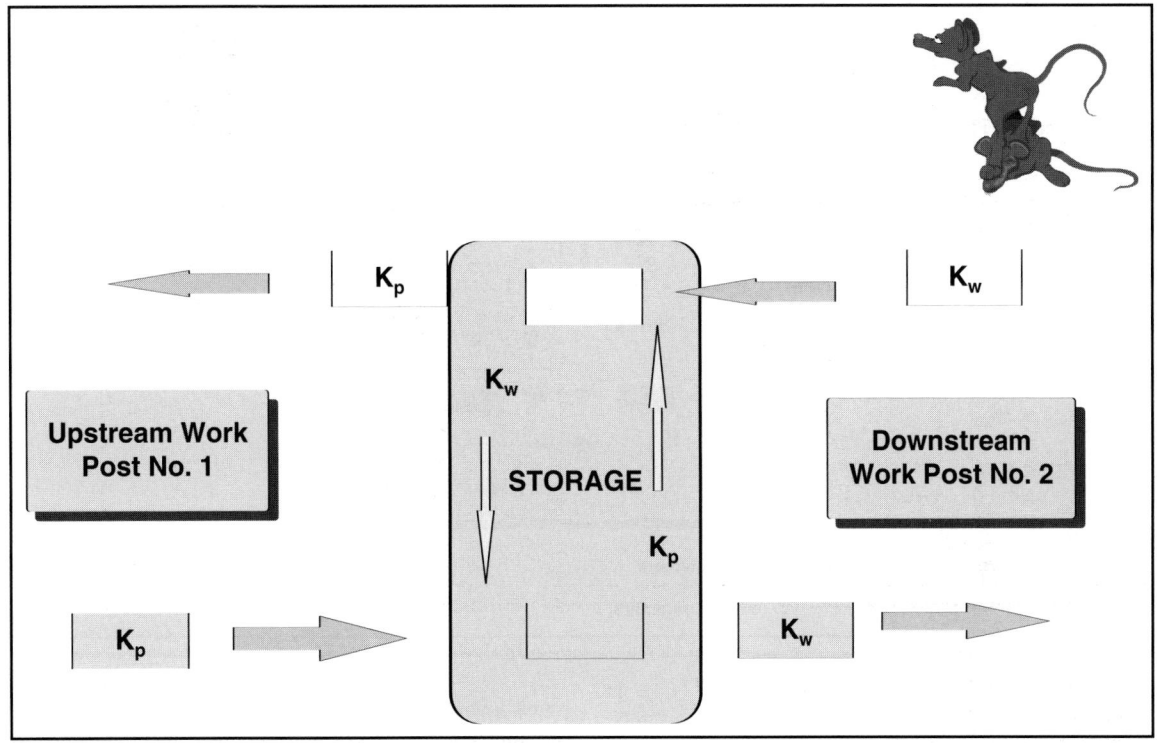

requires the same parts, it would be sufficient to have more K_p cards in circulation than K_w cards.

With either type of card system some industries operate on the principle, 'one container full, one empty'. That is to say, at the downstream work post there are two containers for a product with the same reference number. When one of the containers is empty, the operator goes to collect a new container of parts. In the meantime, the machine is working from the full container (if the machine has an automatic feeder, then the operator can leave the work post while the machine is producing).

Kanbans outside the work centre

The principle of using Kanbans can be extended to the supplier, and the client, as illustrated in Figure 15.11:

- From the supplier, full containers of component parts are delivered to the work centre. With a good working relationship with the client, the supplier can deliver the component parts directly to the storage area of the work centre without passing through a reception area or quality control.

- Empty containers, with Kanbans, are removed by the suppliers; the Kanbans are the instructions to the supplier to provide additional parts. This is the communication, or information, flow.
- In the work centre, the components and cards flow through the four work areas (Machining-1, Machining-2, Assembly and Packaging)
- The finished products are delivered to the client's delivery vehicles in the Kanban containers. The empty containers that are returned are the instructions to the work centre to provide more finished components.

Determining the number of Kanbans

The number of Kanbans to put into circulation might be determined by calculation or empirically.

Calculation

The number of Kanbans is determined from the formula:

$$N = \frac{R(T_p + T_d)(1 + X)}{C}$$

Figure 15.11 Kanbans between supplier, work centre and client.

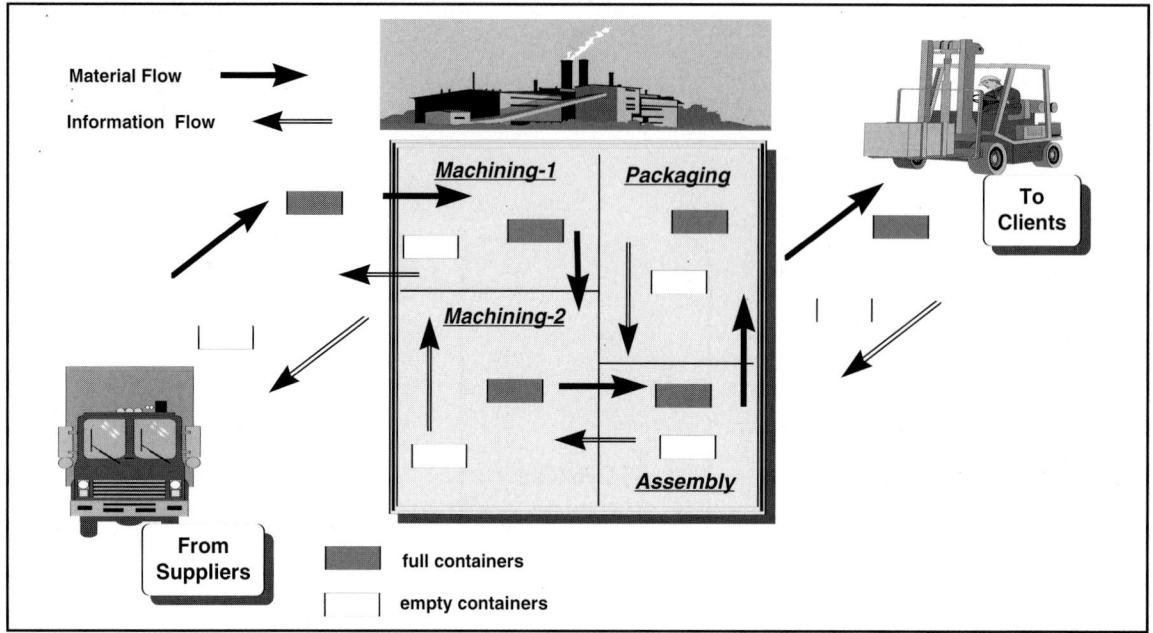

where, for example

- R is the rate of utilization of components, say 400 units/h;
- T_p is the production time, say 1.5 min per unit;
- T_d is the delivery or transfer time of a container, say 2.5 min;
- C is the capacity of the container in units, say 45;
- X is a variation in the demand rate, say 5 per cent.

Then

$$N = \frac{R(T_p + T_d)(1 + X)}{C}$$

$$N = \frac{\dfrac{400}{60}(45 \times 1.5 + 2.5)(1 + 0.05)}{45}$$

$$= 10.89 \text{ or } 11 \text{ Kanbans.}$$

Empirical

It is the number of Kanbans in circulation that determines the amount of products that can be produced, used or transferred. One way of deciding on the number of Kanbans is first to make a rough estimate of the number necessary by analysing operating rates and utilization at all of the work posts involved. This number of Kanbans is put into circulation. Afterwards, the movement of inventory is analysed. If there is too

much inventory of a particular product reference, then the number of Kanbans is gradually reduced in order to obtain a smooth flow. If stockout situations start to occur for a particular reference, then the number of Kanbans is increased.

See also Fukukawa and Hong, 'The determination of the optimal number of Kanbans in a just-in-time production system'.[5]

Priority work when using Kanbans

When several products are being produced at a work post, a question always arises which reference should be made next, or what is the priority? The following are three methods.

Method 1

Assume that a work centre is producing four different components, A, B, C and D, as given in Figure 15.12. The status of the Kanbans is as shown in Table 15.7. Thus, from this information, the priority for the operator is to produce product, reference C, since there are no full containers of these parts in the work centre.

Method 2

Another approach, used by a manufacturer of automobile components, is illustrated in Figure 15.13. For the particular workstation shown there are four components

Table 15.7 Status of Kanbans

Product reference	A	B	C	D
Kanbans in circulation	7	9	4	5
Number of Kanbans posted	4	4	4	4
Number of full containers in work centre	3	5	0	1

Table 15.8 Status of Kanbans

Reference	586769	186354	186527	184892
Zone present	orange	green	red	orange
Status	Soon required	None required	urgent	Soon required

being produced, with reference Nos. 586769, 186354, 186527 and 184892. Each reference has an area where the Kanbans are posted. Above each posting area the zone is marked green (far left), orange (centre), and red (far right). If there are Kanbans posted in the red zone this means that these products have a high priority for being produced. If they are in the green zone then this is a low priority. For the situation illustrated the status is shown in Table 15.8 Thus the next component to be produced would be No. 186527. As components are being used in the work centre, the Kanbans will be returned to this display board. Thus, the Kanbans now in the orange zone would move to the red zone, and so these components would have a high priority for production.

Method 3

This approach is used by a manufacturer of a variety of consumer products as illustrated in Figure 15.14. Like Method 2, there are three zones for three situations:

- Zone 1 (green): Production stopped.
- Zone 2 (orange): Production possible.
- Zone 3 (red): Production required.
- If there are Kanbans posted in Zone 3 (as is the case for product reference A), then production is necessary immediately.
- If there are no Kanbans posted in Zones 2 or 3 (as is the case for product reference B) then production is stopped. (The absence of Kanbans means that in the work area there are containers of product reference B.)
- For product references C and D production is possible and would depend upon the resources available.

Kanban zones for large objects

When large components, such as automobile engines, pumps, or furniture items, are being handled, the card

Figure 15.12 Priority board for using Kanbans: method 1.

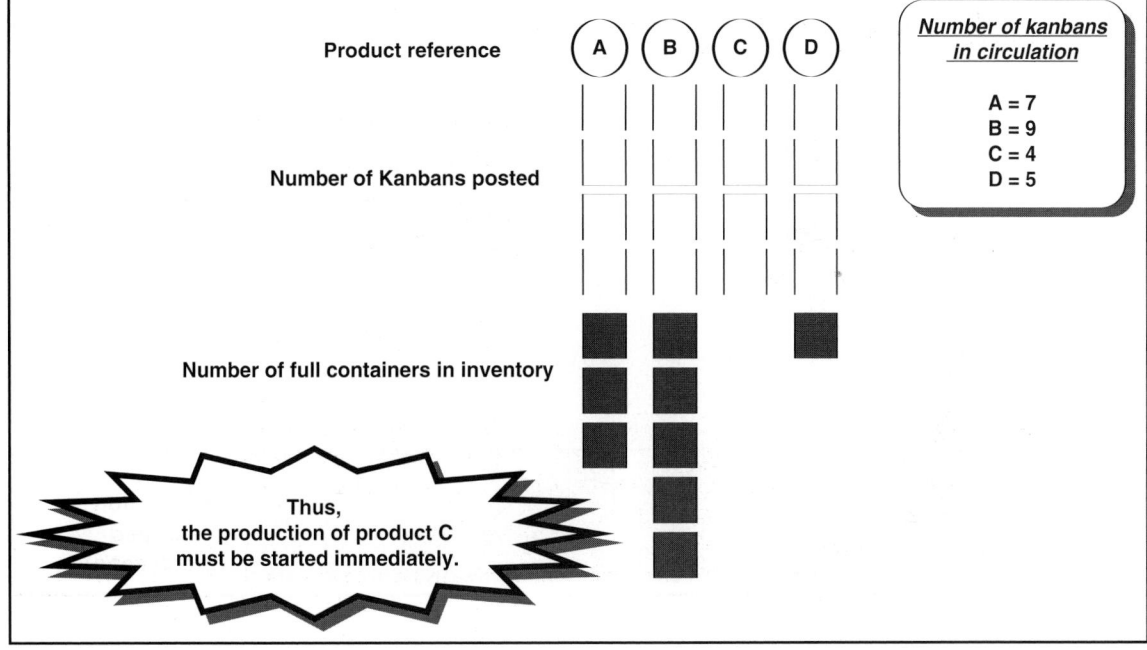

Figure 15.13 Priority board for using Kanbans: method 2.

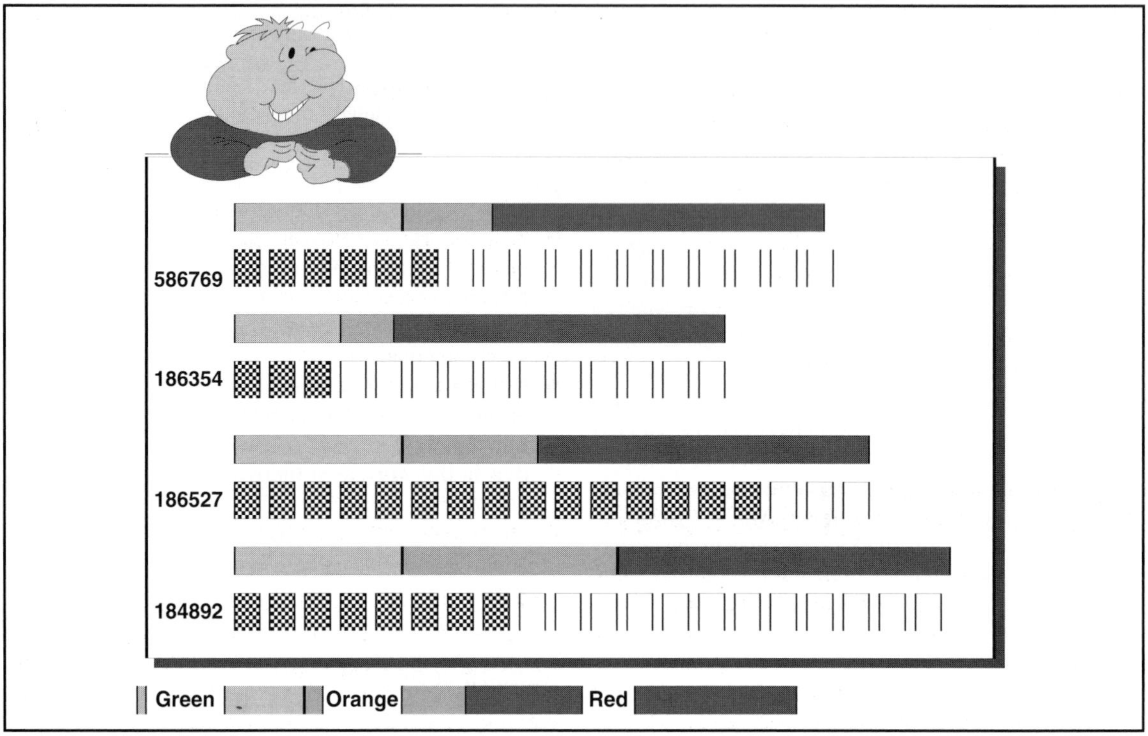

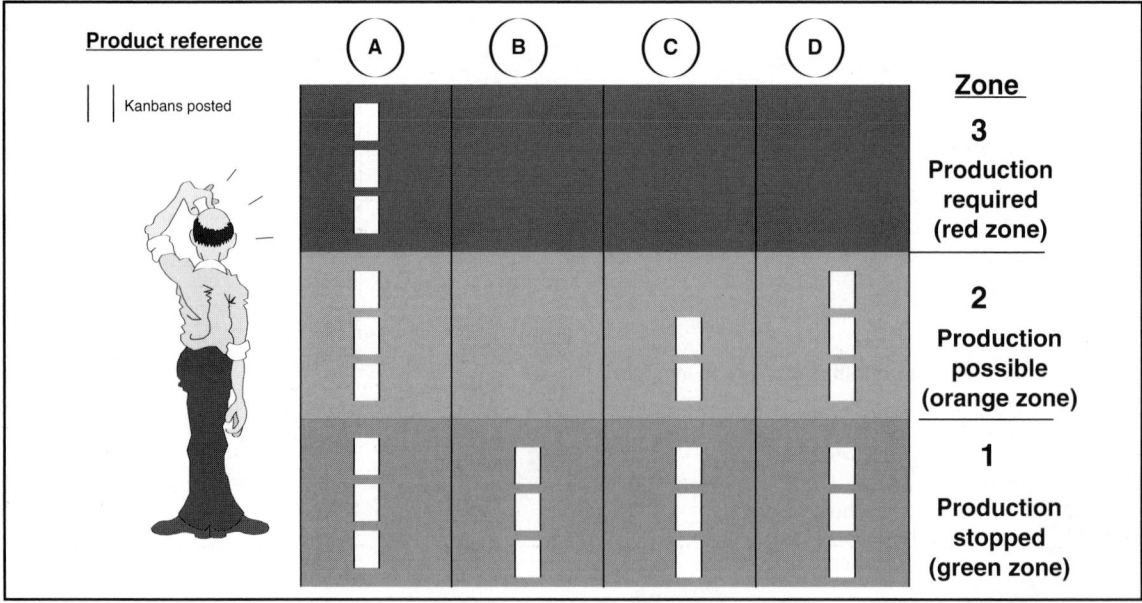

Figure 15.14 Priority board for using Kanbans: method 3.

system can be replaced by holding Kanban zones marked out on the work-centre floor, as illustrated in Figure 15.15. Here the zone is a rectangle marked out by a yellow tape. This zone is sized to contain the maximum number of components. When the zone is not completely filled, this is the authorization for operators immediately upstream of this storage area to produce another component. When the zone is full, no production is necessary.

An alternative organization for the Kanban zones is to colour code them in green, orange and red, similar to the display board. When the red zone is uncovered this means that production requirements take a high priority. The reverse would be when the green zone is uncovered.

INVENTORIES IN LEAN PRODUCTION

In lean manufacturing the ideal situation is to have zero inventory thus keeping waste of resources to a minimum. In practice, this is probably impossible because it would mean that the entire purchasing, production and distribution function is finely tuned. However, it is desirable to have the minimum amount of inventory to keep costs low, and at the same time maintain a smooth production operation.

High inventories

If there is a high level of raw material, in-process and finished goods inventories, it may not be immediately critical if:

- suppliers are late delivering;
- material is off specification;
- machine set-up times are long;
- a machine malfunctions;
- production lots are large;
- employees are absent;
- orders are modified;
- designs are changed;
- production orders change often;
- scrap rates are high;
- information flow is slow;
- work pauses are long.

A high level of inventory of raw materials, components and finished products in the form of 'safety stock' is a buffer against these uncertainties. However, all this 'safety stock' represents a large financial investment that can be put to better use elsewhere.

Figure 15.15 Kanban zones for large objects.

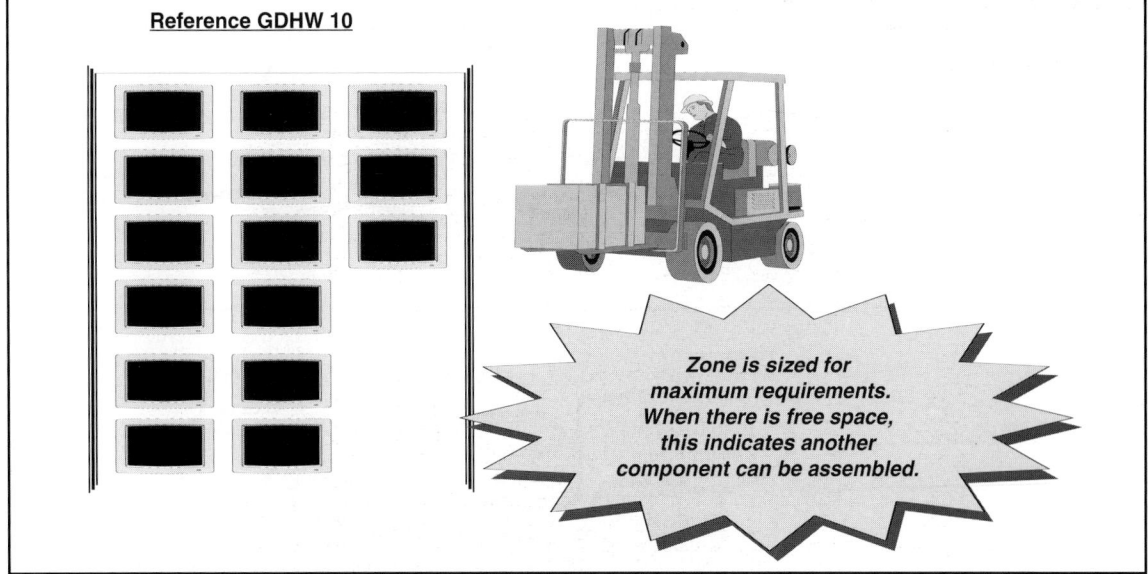

Low inventories

A part of the just-in-time philosophy is to keep minimum inventories. To do this, scrupulous attention has to be paid to all aspects of operations including:

- reducing machine set-up times;
- eliminating last minute design changes;
- preventative maintenance of all equipment and machines;
- motivation of the workforce to reduce absenteeism;
- reducing lot sizes;
- a close working relationship between Sales and Operations to minimize last-minute order modifications;
- working with suppliers so that they respect delivery schedules – if they do not, engage other suppliers (it is a competitive world!);
- enforcing attention to quality to avoid off-specification material.

If attention is not paid to these aspects and inventory is reduced, then problems will occur preventing production to meet client demands.

Analogy

The high-inventory situation can be compared to the situation of rocks at the bottom of a river. In the springtime, when the river is running high, there is no problem to the oarsman out for his daily row, Figure 15.16. However, in the autumn, when the river level has fallen to a low level, the rocks become closer to the surface, or are even exposed. In this case, the situation becomes critical and dangerous to river users, Figure 15.17. This is likened to the situation when the customer demand increases rapidly. The producing organization reaches a crisis situation and is unable to respond to the customers' needs.

MACHINE SET UP TIMES, AND SMED (SINGLE MINUTE EXCHANGE OF DIE)

The logic revolving around producing in lots is because of set-up times. If the set-up and adjustment time is long (high cost), then more products should be produced in one batch in order to reduce the set-up cost per unit. Operating like this has the effect of creating more inventories. Practical situations of set-up include the following:

Pharmaceutical industry

Many pharmaceutical products are made in batch processes. For example, for a certain antiseptic cream, the solid active ingredient is dissolved in water to give

---

Figure 15.16 Inventory is analogous to rocks in a river – high water.

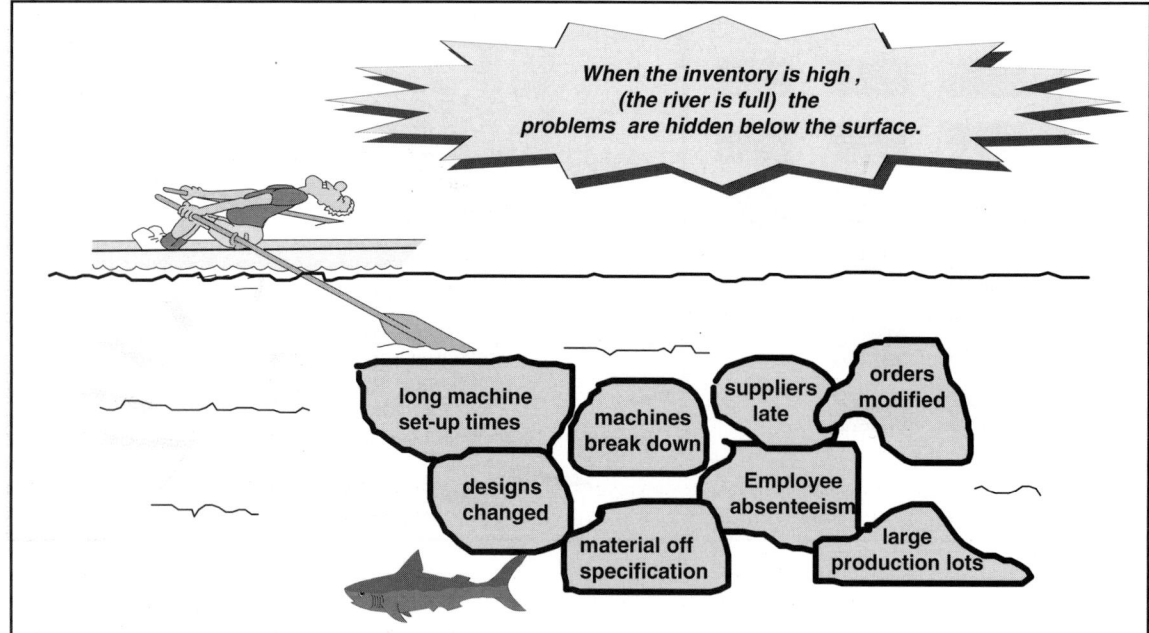

Figure 15.17 Inventory is analogous to rocks in a river – low water.

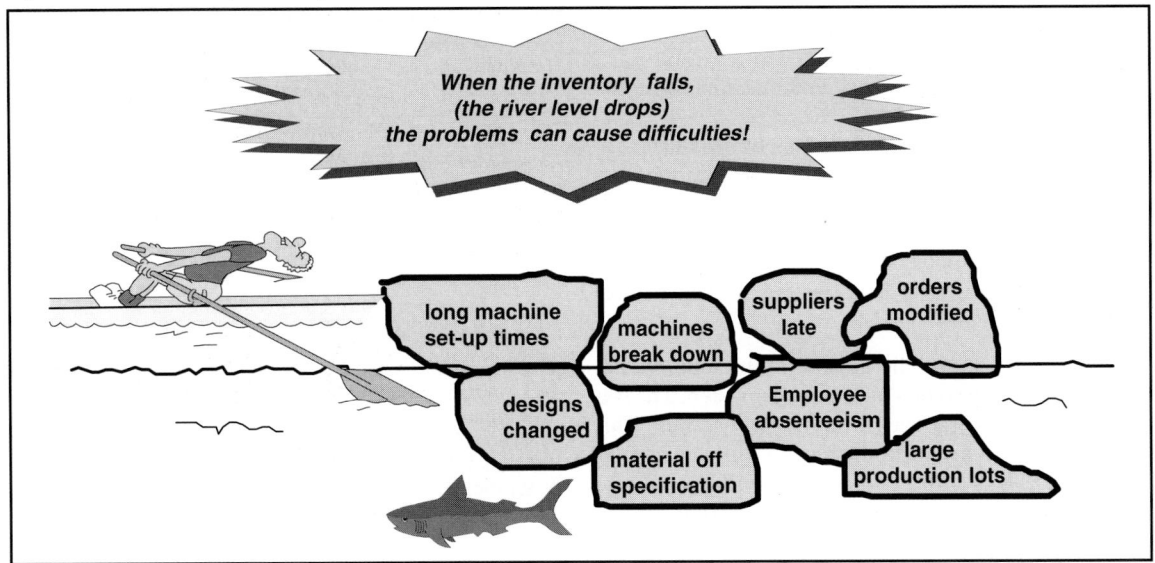

Implementation of SMED

JIT systems concentrate on reducing the cost of setting up machines to avoid the negative aspects of producing small lot sizes. The principle is known as SMED (Single minute exchange of die). SMED evolves from the work in the 1980s of Shigeo Shingo, of Toyota Motor Co., Japan, who spent some 19 years rigorously analysing the set-up procedures related to automobile manufacture.[6] The ultimate objective was to change a machine tool in less than ten minutes (hence the expression, *single minute* exchange of die). The idea comes from Formula I motor racing, where the rapid pit change of wheels, oil, etc. can enormously enhance the chance of a driver winning a race.

To effect SMED procedures, the logic is to establish the distinction between:

- External set-up: Machine is running
- Internal Set-up: Machine is stopped.

To maximize efficiency, where possible, the set-up procedures should be performed while a machine is running *(external set-up)*; that is, the activity is being performed in parallel with actual production time. Only those set-up procedures that cannot be performed unless the machine is stopped *(internal set-up)* should be carried out at this time. For example, the transfer of machine tools, moulds or dies to the storage area should only be performed while a machine is running. The actual changing of a die or a mould can normally only be performed while the machine is stopped.

an aqueous solution. This solution is then transferred to another stainless-steel mixing vessel, where it is mixed with lanolin or other grease materials in order to make a cream formula (creams are better absorbed by the skin). This resulting batch is then unloaded to the filling area, where the cream is filled into tubes. Assume that the next production run for the two vessels is a mosquito cream, for which the formula is quite different from the previous antiseptic cream. In this case the vessel's inlet and outlet lines have to be completely steam cleaned before the next production run can be made. This cleaning is the set-up time and may take between two and four hours depending on the operation. In order that the filling line has a continuous feed, an upstream inventory of semi-finished goods has to be maintained.

Injection moulding in the plastics industry

Consider the plastic crates that are used for transporting merchandize. These are produced in large injection moulds. The master mould, from which the plastic item is produced, is often steel, quite heavy and has to be bolted onto the injection machine. The set-up in this instance includes the changing of the mould for different formats. Further, if the colour of the object changes, then the feed lines have to be thoroughly cleaned so that the colour just used does not contaminate the colour about to be used. A problem arises in making yellow objects after red. It is very difficult to remove 100 per cent of the red and so the first yellow items that are produced contain red speckles and have to be scrapped.

If preheating of a machine is necessary, perhaps this can be performed while the machine is operating. In general, set-up times can be reduced by:

■ locating required inventory and machine tools closer to the operating area;
■ standardizing the set-up functions of machines;
■ improving the procedures for tool preparation;
■ eliminating unnecessary machine adjustments;
■ synchronizing operator jobs;
■ automating set-up procedures, using computer control – only do this if it is less costly than manual adjustments.

Figure 15.18 shows the impact on the total operating time when a system SMED is implemented. The set-up time has been reduced from 2.5 h to 8 min. This allows the total production time for producing four products, A, B, C and D, to be reduced from 23 h to 13 h 32 min, or by some 41 per cent. The reduction in set-up time translates into a reduction in cost and a gain in productivity of resources. Tables 15.8 and 15.9 give some industrial examples.[7]

Average unit production cost

In Chapter 11, *Inventory Management*, the average unit production cost was shown when the set-up cost was $275.00/unit and the unit variable cost $15/unit.

Table 15.9 Presses and Plastic forming machines – reductions in set-up time with SMED

Company	Set-up time (before)	Set-up time (after)	Reduction factor
Presses			
Arakawa Auto Body Industries	1 h 40 min	7 min 46 s	13
Matsushita Electric	2 h 10 min	7 min 25 s	18
Sharp Electric	1 h 20 min	5 min 45 s	14
I Metals	50 min	2 min 48 s	18
Toyota Manufacturing	4 h 0 min	4 min 18 s	56
Plastic Forming Machines			
M Manufacturing	6 h 40 min	7 min 36 s	53
N Rubber	2 h 0 min	4 min 18 s	28
N Chemicals	40 min	3 min 45 s	11
D Plastics	50 min	2 min 26 s	19
Y Synthetics	40 min	2 min 48 s	14

This curve is repeated in Figure 15.19. Assume that with the implementation of SMED the set-up cost is reduced to $2.75/unit, keeping the same $15/unit variable cost. The average unit production cost is recalculated and shown in Figure 15.20; note the different scale of the vertical axis. From this new figure the average unit production cost changes very little with lot size (Table 15.10).

Figure 15.18   Single minute exchange of die (SMED).

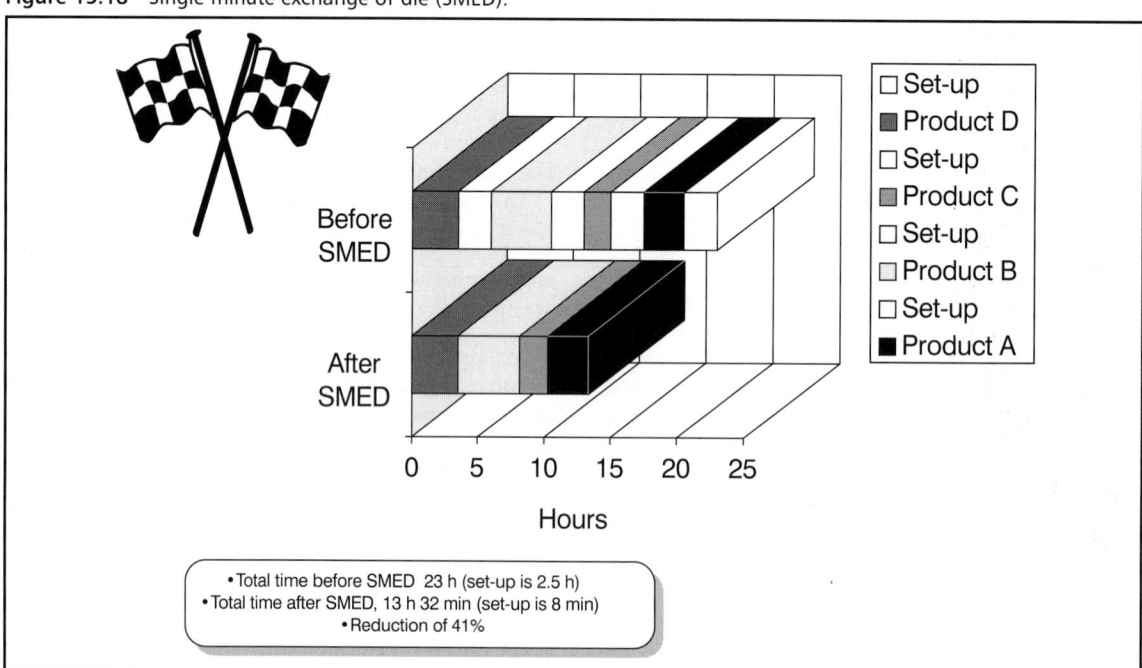

- Total time before SMED 23 h (set-up is 2.5 h)
- Total time after SMED, 13 h 32 min (set-up is 8 min)
- Reduction of 41%

Figure 15.19   Lot size and average unit cost (before SMED).

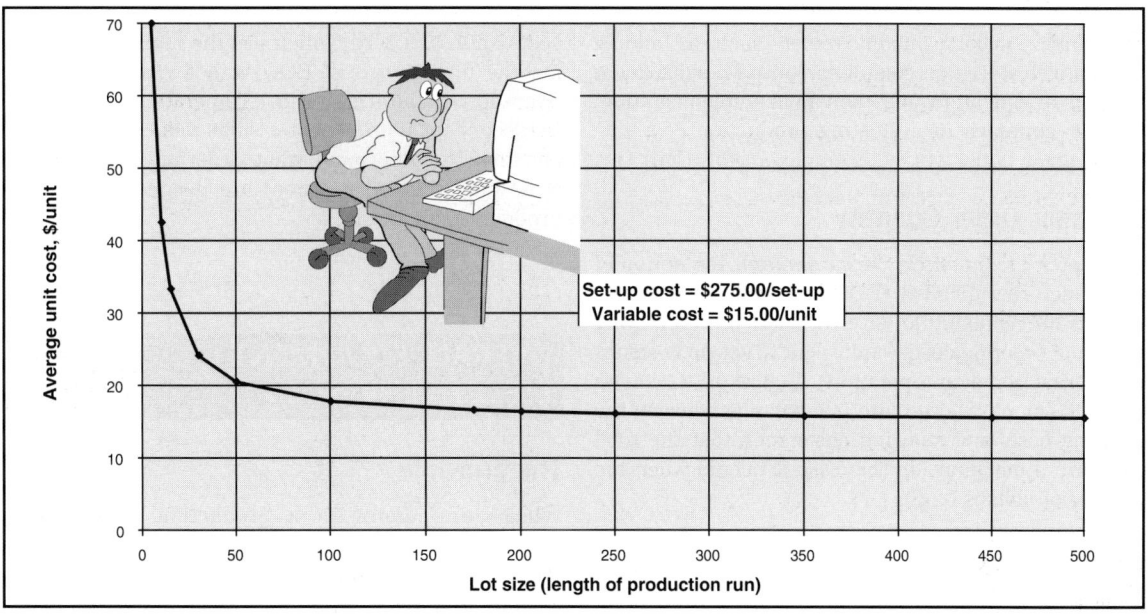

Table 15.10   Unit production costs before and after implementation of SMED

Lot size (units)	5	500	Change (%)
Cost after SMED ($/unit)	15.55	15.01	3.47
Cost before SMED ($/unit)	70.00	15.55	77.78

Thus the advantages in implementing SMED are:

■ Smaller lot sizes can be produced without a significant difference in overall cost.
■ There is more flexibility in the production operation.

Figure 15.20   Lot size and average unit cost (after SMED).

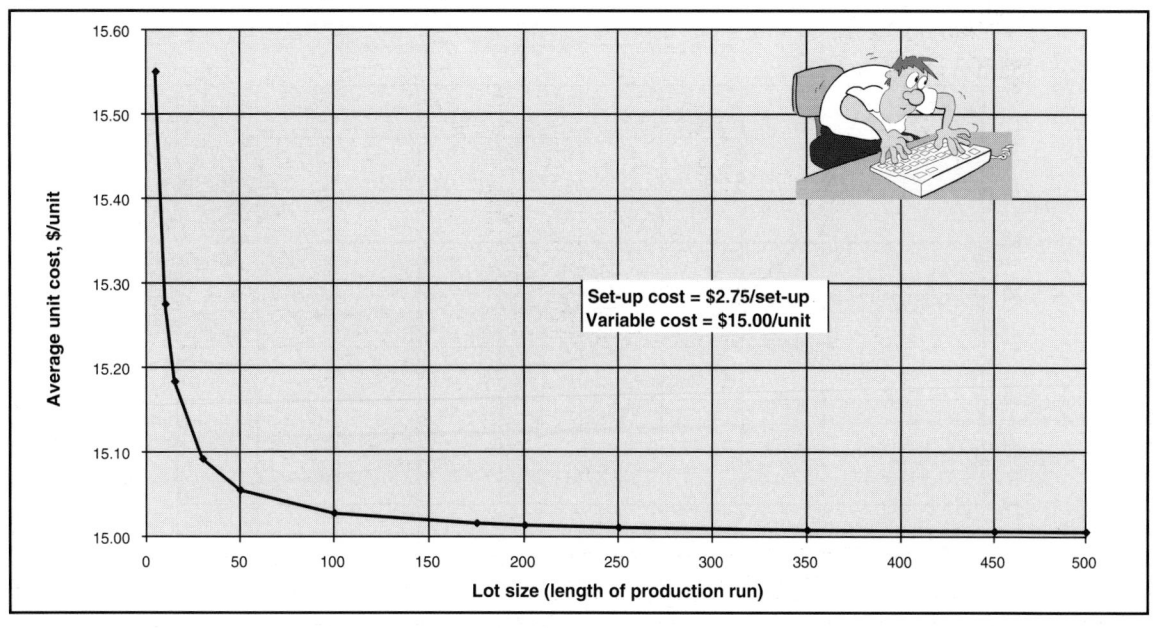

Implementing the SMED approach does not happen overnight. It takes a long time of studying the set-up procedures, making modifications, such as adding automatic features or computer controls, subsequent training of operators and then final implementation. Another approach to evaluating production cost savings is given in the worked example, *Panels* (Part I).

Economic Order Quantity

In Chapter 11, *Inventory Management*, the notion of economic order quantity (EOQ) was discussed, where there is an economic lot size to balance the carrying costs and ordering costs (equivalent to set-up costs for an internal company operation). Figure 15.21 shows the EOQ curve, where there is a balance between the ordering costs and stocking costs such that the total costs are a minimum. In this case it occurs when the number of units is 3536.

Applying SMED

Applying the SMED principle to reduce the set-up time (thus reducing the ordering costs) has the effect of decreasing the number of units to balance ordering costs and stocking costs. This is illustrated in Figure 15.22, where the ordering costs have been reduced by a factor of ten. In this case the EOQ quantity is now 1118 units.

Going further by decreasing the ordering costs by yet another factor of ten to $1.25/order (Figure 15.23) results in an EOQ quantity of 354 units.

Thus, in applying the SMED principle the economic production lot size approaches zero as the set-up costs approach zero, which has the impact of nullifying the importance of EOQ with a real just-in-time operation. An alternative in JIT operation in using the EOQ concept is to accept a small value for the EOQ and then to determine what ordering costs (set-up costs and thus set-up time) are needed in order to produce small lot sizes.

OVERALL EQUIPMENT EFFECTIVENESS

The principle

When an operator in a production operation is assigned to a work post, such as running a lathe, a cutting machine or a drilling machine, the just-in-time philosophy requires that the time spent should be maximized to working on the part in question, or adding value. If a large proportion of time is occupied by non-value activities, then productivity is low. An analysis of machine utilization can be performed by determining the overall equipment effectiveness. The bar chart in Figure 15.24 illustrates the overall equipment effectiveness analysis and the terms are discussed in the following sections.

Figure 15.21   EOQ: stocking and ordering cost (ordering = $125.00 per order).

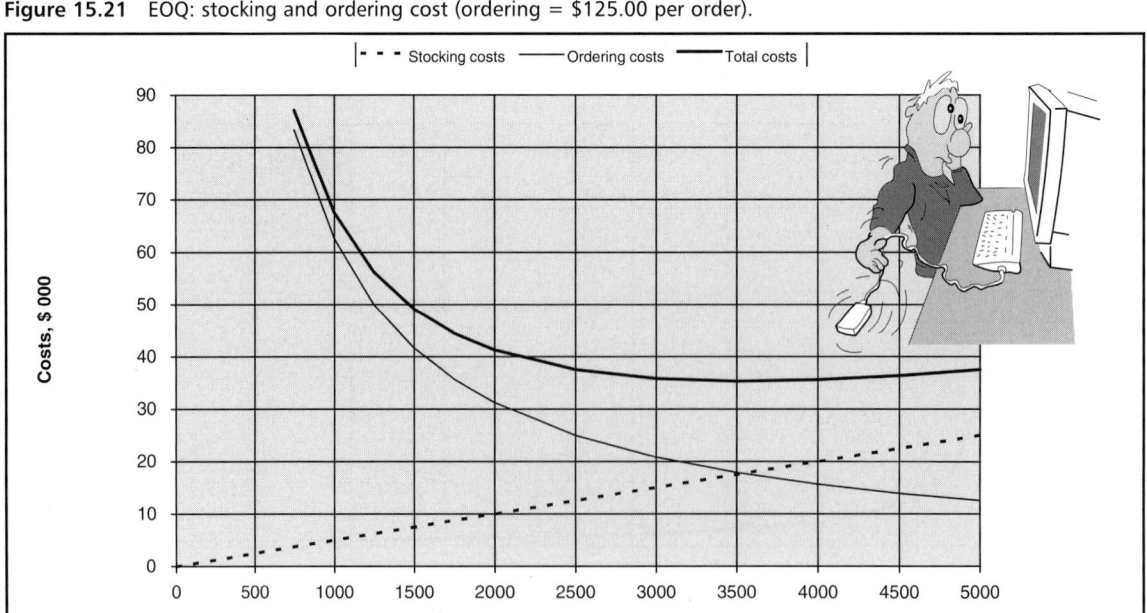

Open time

The open time is the total time per day that an operator has available to work on a machine. This is normally eight hours, or 100 per cent.

Operator pause

Operator pauses includes time that an operator stops for coffee, to go to the bathroom or just to 'chat'. In the example given, the time for breaks in any one day is considered to be five minutes every hour, or 40 min in one day. This reduces the effective time to 92 per cent of the open time.

Machine breakdowns

Machine breakdowns cover the time when a machine stops running or has to be shut down because of unforeseen mechanical problems. In this case, 35 min has been assumed. This reduces the effective time to 84 per cent of the open time.

Unplanned interruptions

Unplanned interruptions include the time lost because the part jams up the machine or the machine has to be modified slightly in order to accept the piece because it is too large or too small. Here, 24 min has been assumed, which drops the effective time of the machine to 79 per cent of the open time.

Machine set-up

Machine set-up is the time taken to readjust the machine so that it can work on a different product. Here 70 min has been assumed, which drops the machine effectiveness to 65 per cent of the open time.

Low performance

Low performance is the machine throughput being less than design. This may be because the machine has been badly maintained and is not running correctly or because the operator is not correctly trained for running the machine. Here, 62 min has been assumed, which drops the effective operating time to 52 per cent of the open time.

Scrap products

Scrap products represent the time spent on producing parts that are not according to specification and have to be scrapped. Here 12 min has been assumed, which has reduced the effective time to 49 per cent. This final figure is then the overall equipment effectiveness.

Thus, unless careful attention is paid to the operation of a machine, the effective usefulness can drop rapidly. If this is the case, in-process inventory needs to be maintained upstream of each machine or workstation to take into account operating inefficiencies.

Figure 15.22 EOQ: stocking and ordering cost (ordering = $12.50 per order).

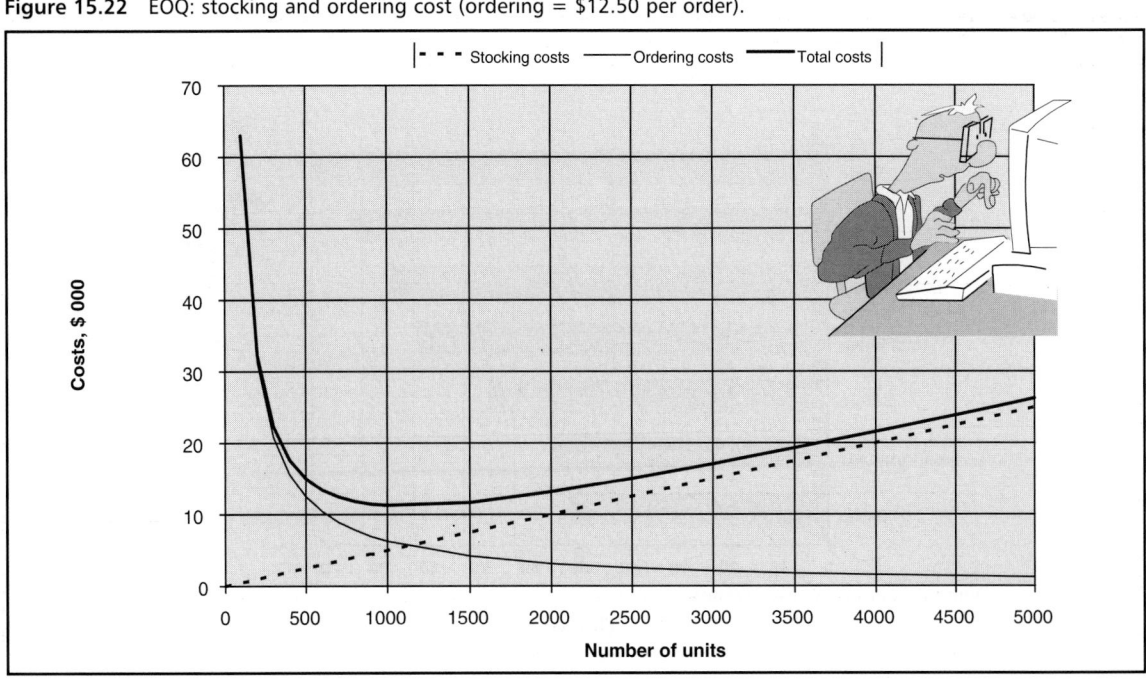

Figure 15.23 EOQ: stocking and ordering cost (ordering = $1.25 per order).

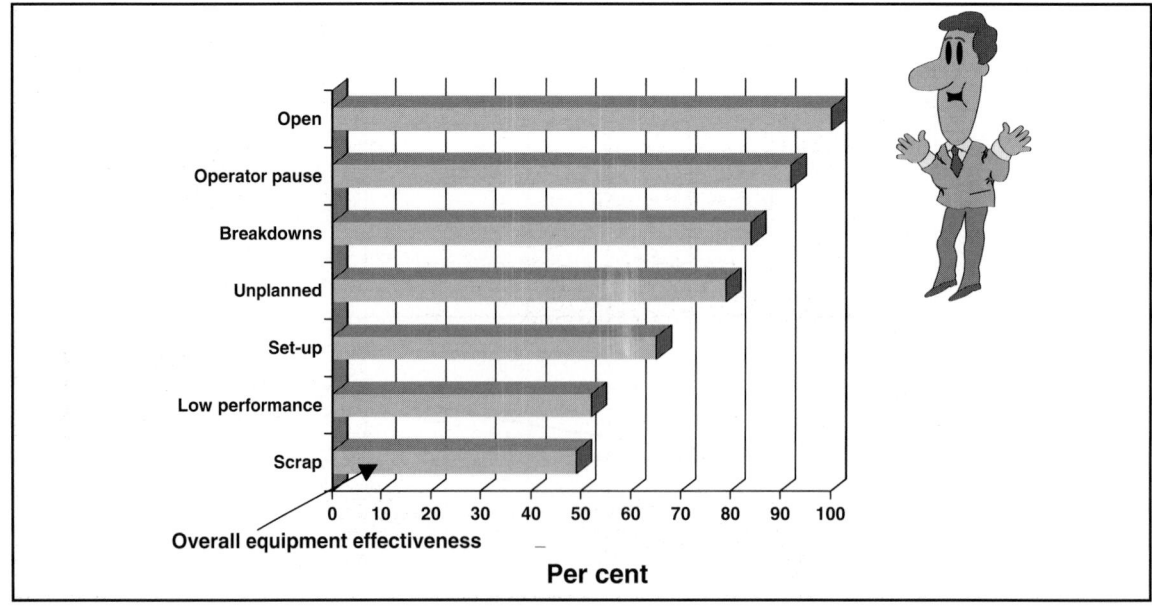

Improving machine effectiveness

Considerations that can bring the overall equipment effectiveness closer to 100 per cent are:

- Operators take breaks when machines are running.

- Machine breakdowns are minimized by rigorous preventative maintenance.
- Unplanned operations are minimized by having a quality assurance system to maximize the probability that all parts are of specification quality.

Figure 15.24 Overall equipment effectiveness.

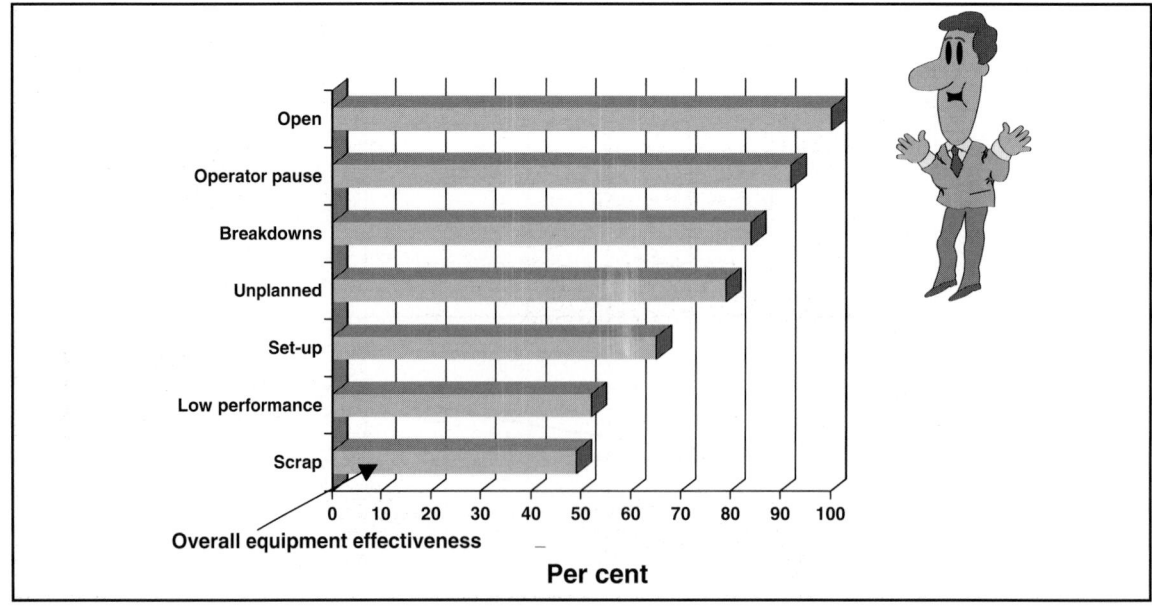

Machine set-ups are reduced by implementing a SMED study.

If the speed is less than design, it will be necessary to examine the operating parameters of the machine or examine how the operator is running the machine and modify as necessary.

Scrap products can be reduced by better operator training, improving quality procedures upstream of the machine in question or ensuring that suppliers always provide materials of specification quality.

THE FIVE S RULES

Lean production incorporating just-in-time implies being rigorous, organized and efficient. The Japanese have five expressions for this, as illustrated in Figure 15.25.

Seiro – remove

Here the philosophy is to remove from the work area any unneeded work tools, materials, equipment or paperwork. The idea is that if you don't need it, don't have it cluttering the operating area, because it may get in the way and slow down your activity. This applies equally to an operator in a production centre and to a person working in an office, where, if you receive clients, a cluttered desk gives the impression that you are a cluttered worker. In the 1970s and the 1980s I worked for an engineering services company. We had instructions to have only one design sheet on our desk at any one time. Any more and it was considered that we 'were not organized'.

Seiton – organize

This means to organize all materials, tools, pencils, papers, computer diskettes, and documents that are used in the operation. An effective classification of all work items documents and files will help to reduce the time spent searching for these when they are needed. Are files best placed on the right or left? Where on the desk should the phone be placed? Where should the wrenches be located? In a service environment, it is embarrassing when a client stops by, or telephones, and one is unable to find the correct information.

Seiso – keep clean

In a manufacturing environment, keeping the working area clean is appropriate from a health-and-safety point of view. If machines are being used, this means removing excess oil, dirt, water, etc. In the food industry it goes without saying that the work environment should be kept clean. In the office, keep desks clean and computer equipment free of grease. A clean working area not only looks better, but it aids in doing quality work (at least psychologically) and gives a good

Figure 15.25 The five S words.

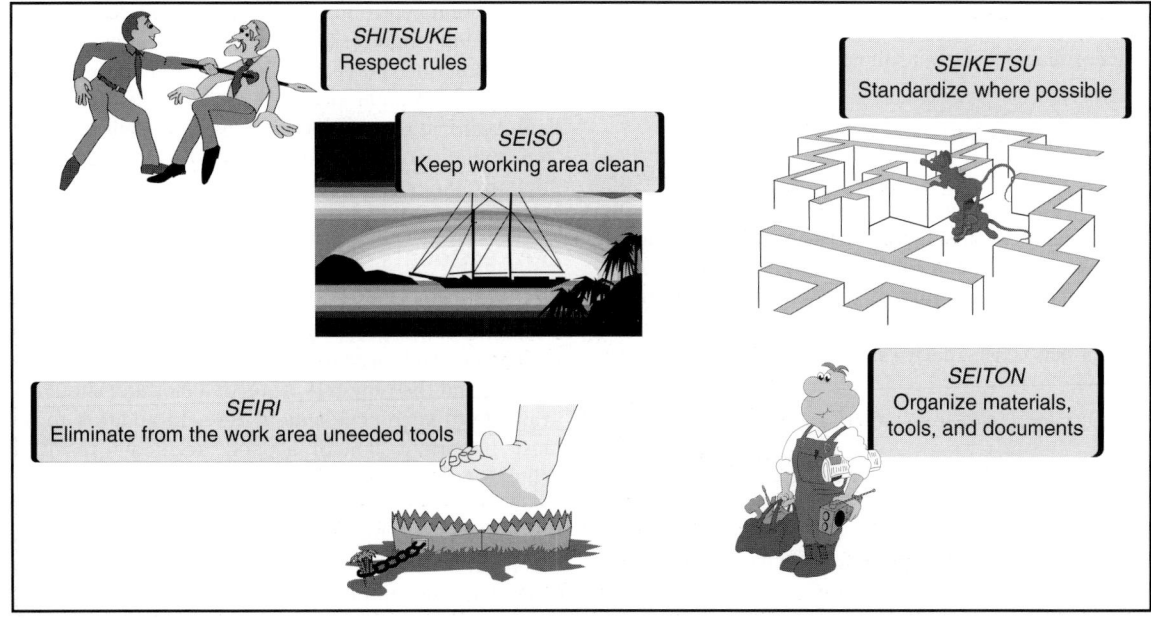

impression to clients, co-workers or supervisors who might stop by the office.

Seiketsu – standardize

Where possible, standardize operations and activities so that, whoever is at the work centre, the job in hand is performed in the same manner and with the same materials. Standards should be set for how a job is to be performed, how a design is to be executed, when machines should be cleaned or overhauled and where material should be filed, etc. When standards have been established, they should be made visible and accessible to all those concerned in the organization. Setting standards for the operations is one of the criteria for ISO-9000 Quality standards, which are discussed in Chapter 4, *Quality Management.*

Shitsuke – respect the rules

Organizations, firms and society all function through teamwork and cooperation, which involves respecting rules. Specific rules may apply to procedures for machine cleaning or adjustment, or to materials to use. In addition, there may be general rules related to safety, arriving or leaving at the correct time, smoking only in the designated areas, etc. Respecting rules avoids stressful situations among teams and enhances efficiency.

THE FIVE ZEROS

For a perfect, ideal operation there are five zeros and (by corollary) a sixth, as illustrated in Figure 15.26.

Zero breakdowns

Zero Breakdowns means that all equipment, tools and machines are in perfect running order during production. To achieve this, there has to be a regular schedule of preventative maintenance. A printing press, a numerically controlled drilling machine or an air compressor that malfunctions during production will result in unnecessary costs, delays and probably irritated clients.

Zero defects

Zero Defects implies that all raw materials, component parts and finished products are faultless. This means that suppliers respect all specifications and quality control before delivering their products. Plant operators upstream verify the quality of their work before passing it along to the downstream post. The key is 'quality at the source'.

Zero delays

Zero Delays implies that all delivery dates are respected. A supplier delivers his components when promised, an operator finishes his work when scheduled, a manager completes his report on time. To achieve this, schedules that are prepared must be realistic, and all those implicated in the work must be aware of, and agree to, the planning.

Zero inventory

Zero Inventory means that stocks of raw material, in-process parts and finished goods are zero. In practice, this is impossible and probably not desirable. However, the philosophy is to keep stocks to as near zero as possible, while keeping the operation functioning smoothly. Unnecessary inventory means idle investments, space used unnecessarily and risk of obsolescence. Of course, less than zero inventory is more of a problem since this implies stockouts and production shutdowns – and/or dissatisfied clients.

Zero paper

The use of Kanbans as a method of communication reduces paper orders and instructions. Paper instructions can be misinterpreted (especially if badly written). Also, it has to be recognized that some persons in a production centre may not have a good command of the working language and thus may be unable to interpret instructions correctly. Electronic data interchange and other computer transfers also reduces the paper flow. Again, at the moment, it is hard to envisage a real 'zero paper' world. However, again the command is to minimize the quantity employed.

Zero accidents

Zero Accidents is the corollary of a well-managed operation. Machines properly serviced and protected, the workplace well organized and clean, the necessary training and the required protective clothing should be available to keep accidents at zero. In addition to the most important human aspect, accidents result in delays, cost and damage to the company image.

Except perhaps for inventory and paper usage, the other 'zeros' are attainable with good management and control systems in place.

Figure 15.26   The five (and even six) zeros.

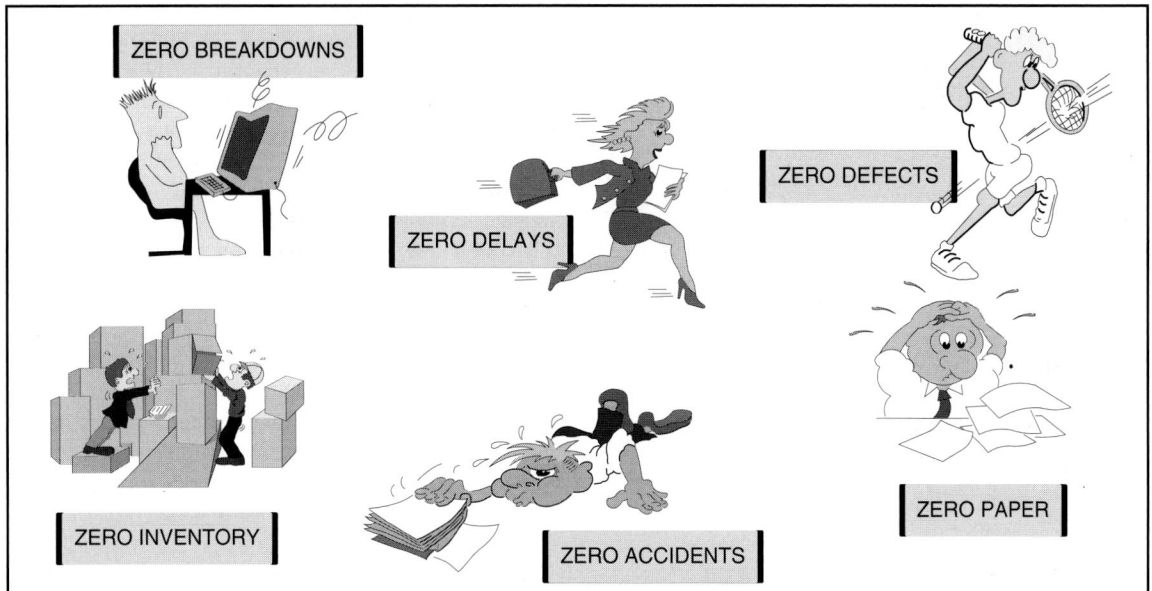

QUALITY

Lean production enforces adherence to quality work at all levels, (see also Chapter 4, *Quality Management*). The following summarizes some of the quality elements and the in role in lean production.

Quality at the source

Quality at the source means putting all employees in the driver's seat as far as the responsibility for the quality of their work is concerned.

Control station

Every operator is also a quality control station. In addition, for machining, assembling or other task, the worker is responsible for inspecting his own work, identifying any defects, reworking them and correcting any cause of defects.

Stopping production

Each worker is given the right to signal, by pressing an alarm bell, the stoppage of a production line if a problem is encountered. Then, others on the chain should work as a team to resolve the problem.

Work groups

Workers and line managers are given facilities to organize themselves into work groups to analyse problems or to discuss production improvements. These work groups are informal and kept small (seven to nine persons). For example, in the motor assembly area of Renault VI in Lyon, France, there are eating areas positioned very close to the assembly line. Experience has shown that workers feel more comfortable discussing work on the spot, rather than being taken away to another location. Also, time is not wasted in looking for a meeting place. These work groups are also known as quality circles in Japanese manufacturing organizations.

Inventories

With a reduction in inventories, there is no safety margin. If there are stoppages due to machine problems or defective components, production has to stop until the problem has been fixed. For example, if components are defective because of a machine fault, the fact that there are low inventories means that only a few parts are affected and the cost involved is small. Since production is stopped until the problem is corrected, attention is then on solving the quality problem, so that it will not be repeated.

Well-trained employees

In just-in-time, products of a similar type are produced every day. With well-trained employees, job assignments are well understood, workers are familiar with their task and this aids in improving product quality.

Purchasing

Just-in-time companies strive to have a small number of suppliers, and supplier networks, which can be relied upon to deliver parts of perfect quality (*quality at the source*). As illustrated in Figure 15.11, suppliers use the replacement principle of Kanban, in which small, standard-size containers are used both to ship supplies frequently to customers and give suppliers the authority to delivery components directly to the production line without going through inspection (see also Chapter 16, *Purchasing and Subcontracting*).

Automated equipment

The use of automated equipment and robots goes a long way in helping to manufacture parts of superior quality. Automated machines produce a consistent output in such areas as soldering, painting and stamping.

Preventative maintenance

To avoid production interruptions, intensive preventative maintenance programmes should be in place to adjust machines and equipment before they break down. Machines constantly in adjustment produce parts that are within quality standards (see also Chapter 19, *Reliability and Maintenance*).

Statistical quality control

The use of statistical quality control techniques (see Chapter 23, *Statistical Quality Control*) are used to monitor the quality of parts produced at each workstation. Further, easy-to-understand charts and graphs are used to communicate progress to workers and managers.

JUST-IN-TIME IN SERVICES

Toyota's just-in-time approach was originally conceived for a manufacturing organization. However, since JIT is strongly focused on organization, processes and repetitive activities, service firms operate very much in a just-in-time mode. The following are some illustrations.

Fast-food restaurants

Fast-food outlets like McDonald's, Burger King and Quick Restaurants operate with many just-in-time characteristics. Here there are standard products, low inventories of finished goods and repetitive processes in the food preparation (fries, hamburgers, coffee, etc.) and the way it is served (tray on the counter, ask for order, ring up the order, place the food on the tray and take the money). There is rigorous organization and design of the food preparation facility (see Chapter 10, *Design of the Facility Layout*) and even the cash registers with their icons, rather than numbers, speed up the efficiency of serving the client. Furthermore, the addition of a drive-in service means that clients can be served 'just-when-needed'. McDonald's recently announced that they will go further with their just-in-time service by installing computer-monitored machines to make the fries, robots to prepare drinks and computer systems to 'sense' traffic, so that orders can be prepared in advance and to perform an analysis of how many employees are needed on any particular day.[8]

Delivery services

Delivery services such as Federal Express and UPS offer a just-in-time approach for collecting and dispatching packages, providing almost worldwide next-day deliveries. These services, of course, came about when government-run postal services were unable, or unwilling, to provide reliability in their services.

Transportation

Many modern transportation systems are designed to offer almost immediate or continuous service analogous to just-in-time. For example, on the bullet trains in Japan or France, which travel at 300 km/h, a service can be offered every three or four minutes. (The distance separating the trains is a minimum of seven kilometres and they need three kilometres to stop from the maximum speed.) Metro or underground rail offers services every minute. Even international airports can allow up to about 40 planes per hour to land or take off on the same runway. At the airports there is careful synchronization and planning between connecting flights, baggage handling and passenger changes.

Entertainment

In the entertainment field, theme parks, Disneyland being a prime example, operate using the criteria of lean production, certainly at least when it comes to the five S terms. The attraction parks are clean, staff have standard procedures, preventative maintenance of equipment is well planned and attractions are synchronized to permit the maximum number of clients to visit during the day.

News emissions

Television stations offering news programmes, such as CNN or BBC World News, operate on a just-in-time operation, where the presentations provide immediate 'just happened events'. In fact CNN is credited being better than the US government in providing up-to-date information!

RISKS IN LEAN MANUFACTURING

Lean manufacturing involves rigorous organization, a disciplined workforce, few suppliers and minimum inventories; that is, no fat. This involves risks that can be very costly when there are unplanned occurrences, as the two articles, Boxes 15.2 and 15.3 illustrate concerning Toyota (the originator of lean manufacturing and just-in-time).[9,10]

Box 15.2 Not quite in time

When he was dreaming up Toyota Motor Corp.'s famous "just in time" inventory system, Taiichi Ohno never factored in 7.2 on the Richter scale. Toyota, whose system of "lean production" has revolutionized the auto industry worldwide, does not have a plant in the Kansai region, yet still has serious problems because of the quake. Two suppliers of Toyota's – makers of car radios and brake calipers – do have plants near Kobe, and both suffered damage severe enough to halt production. But just-in-time means what it says: parts are to be delivered precisely when the customer needs them. So critical is this system to Toyota's operations that the loss of those two suppliers forced the company to shut down all 12 of its Japanese assembly plants last week, and by Friday a company spokesman conceded that management was still unsure when production would resume. It was a problem experienced by hundreds of companies throughout Japan and abroad that depend on parts and components from the workshops of Kansai, which accounts for 12.2 percent of Japan's industrial production. Still, a smoothly running just-in-time system is such a competitive weapon that, earthquake or not, Toyota is not about to rethink. "You can't run your business based on acts of God," said a senior Toyota executive in Tokyo last week. "This is a problem for now, but we'll fix it."

From *Newsweek*, 30 January 1995
© 1995, *Newsweek*, Inc. All Rights Reserved.
Reprinted by permission.

Box 15.3 Fire at parts supplier's factory forces Toyota to shut down production in Japan. By Valerie Reitman, Staff Reporter

TOKYO – Production at Toyota Motor Corp.'s plants in Japan – which build 16,200 vehicles a day – has virtually ground to a halt after a fire at a parts maker's factory cut off supply of three small brake and clutch parts.

Many of Japan's No. 1 auto maker's lines may not reopen for up to a week as the company scrambles to find alternative parts suppliers, Toyota said.

Toyota said it will have halted all but one of its 30 assembly lines in Japan by today, after suspending over two-thirds of the lines Monday amid shortages of the parts that Toyota had bought from just one supplier, affiliate Aisin Seiki Co. That supplier's factory in Central Japan was destroyed in a fire early Saturday.

Toyota said it hoped to gradually restore production lines and be running at full tilt by next Monday. But it isn't clear if that could be accomplished.

Serious Disruption

"It's very serious for the Toyota group," said an industry official familiar with the disaster. "I think it will be several days and there is no assurance even then."

Toyota's U.S. and European assembly plants aren't expected to be affected, since they apparently source those parts locally, said Toyota spokesman Tetsuo Kitagawa.

However, some Toyota plants in Asia that assemble car-kit exports could be halted as well, he said.

That a fire in the factory of just one supplier could virtually shut down mighty Toyota's assembly lines shows the flip side of the auto maker's vaunted cost-cutting efforts over the past few years.

Toyota used to contract at least two suppliers for each part prior to heavy cost-cutting initiated in the past few years, said Peter Boardman, an auto analyst with UBS Securities Ltd. But some suppliers began offering volume discounts if Toyota sourced certain parts solely from them, he said. "It's a sign that Toyota cut some edges," he said.

Toyota's trouble shows the continuing vulnerability of Japan Inc.'s much-heralded just-in-time inventory systems. As recent as two years ago, the Kobe earthquake brought to light the system's weaknesses when production of key parts was interrupted. (Under just-in-time manufacturing, suppliers deliver parts as often as hourly so the manufacturer doesn't have to store them in expensive facilities.

"Even three days of inventory is a failure to Toyota" and its group parts makers, said Tatsuo Ushijima, senior research associate at Mitsubishi Research Institute, a think tank in Tokyo.

Sourcing Arrangement

Toyota's shutdown also points to the weakness in Japan's *keiretsu* system, in which companies still depend on affiliates for much of their sourcing. Aisin Seiki is about 28%

owned by Toyota and another Toyota affiliate, Toyoda Automatic Loom Works.

The production shutdown comes at a key time for Toyota, whose Japanese plants are striving to keep pace with brisk domestic sales and strong U.S. demand for popular exports such as the RAV4, Lexus, and 4-Runner sport-utility models. Though shortages of those models may loom, most U.S. dealers shouldn't suffer immediately, given an average 20-day inventory.

With the roughly 300,000 yen ($2,470) profit Toyota makes on an average car, Mr. Boardman of UBS estimated that the shutdown is costing Toyota about 4.9 billion yen a day. However, the company should be able to recoup some of the lost production by running its factories on the weekends, albeit at overtime rates, he said.

The Saturday fire destroyed an Aisin Seiki plant in Kariya, near Toyota's headquarters, which sells 80% of its products to Toyota. None of Aisin's 12 other factories in Japan produces the parts and it isn't clear if any of its overseas factories makes them.

The destroyed factory produced master cylinders, which pump hydraulic fluid, for brakes and clutches in Toyota vehicles, as well as parts called proportioning valves, which regulate hydraulic fluid in brake lines.

Wall Street Journal Europe, 4 February 1997
Reprinted by permission of *Wall Street Journal Europe*,
© 1997 Dow Jones & Company, Inc.
All Rights Reserved Worldwide.

SUMMARY OF KEY ELEMENTS

- Eliminating waste is an objective in lean production, the waste of time in repairing faulty products, in the investment of high inventories and of having idle workers.

- Just-in-time is producing, or having delivered, exactly that quantity of units demanded, on the correct date and at the right place. It is a system of enforced problem solving with no safety factors. All material must meet quality standards, every worker must be productive and there should be no machine malfunctions.

- Just-in-time is a pull system, where client orders pull material through the supply chain. This is as opposed to systems in which producers push material through the pipeline.

- JIT and MRP systems can be effectively integrated in an operating environment.

- Insufficient training, poor product design, unbalanced workstations, poor communication, idle time and poor job design are reasons for low productivity.

- Designing a system in a just-in-time mode can enormously increase efficiency in terms of the value-added time.

- If operators are multiskilled, then changes up or down in customer demands can be accommodated by balancing the system with cellular-type arrangements.

- A Kanban is a card used for communicating between work centres. Modifying the number of Kanbans in circulation can change the volume of products produced.

- In Kanban systems, colour-coded priority boards can be used to indicate which units should be the next in production.

- For large objects, Kanban zones can be marked out on the floor of a work centre.

- SMED is a study to reduce set-up times, which will reduce unit production costs. To implement SMED, distinctions must be made between External set-ups, when the machine is running, and Internal set-ups, when the machine is stopped.

- If the SMED principle is applied, this has the impact of nullifying the impact of the economic order quantity in production situations.

- The overall equipment effectiveness involves an analysis of machines, or work posts, to increase the value-added time of an operation. It analyses breakdowns, operator pauses, non-quality of materials and set-up times.

- Adopting the five S rules, *Seiro* (Remove), *Seiton* (Organize), *Seiso* (Keep clean), *Seiketsu* (Standardize) and *Shitsuke* (Respect rules) aid operation efficiency.

- The five zeros in JIT are: zero breakdowns; zero defects; zero delays; zero inventory; zero paper; if practised these give the sixth corollary of zero accidents.

- Quality in lean production pertains to quality at the source, reduced inventories, trained employees, few suppliers, automated equipment, preventative maintenance and the use of statistical quality control.

- Just-in-time can apply to services where there are repetitive operations and standard products, such as in fast-food outlets, delivery services, transportation, theme-park attractions and news delivery.

REVIEW AND DISCUSSION QUESTIONS

1   **Environmental concerns**. In a manufacturing firm what are some of the positive aspects of just-in-time where the environmental impact is considered? What are some of the negative aspects? Consider the complete supply chain from purchasing, through manufacturing, to product distribution. Refer also to Chapter 5, An *Environmental Balance*.

2   **Human impact**. A company has had very sloppy management practices with loose planning and organization. After, a change of ownership and an injection of capital investment, lean manufacturing and just-in-time procedures are put into practice. Discuss what you believe might be the positive and the adverse effects on the employees.

3   **Overall equipment effectiveness**. Analyse the following activities and apply the principle of 'Overall Equipment Effectiveness':
    (a) studying;
    (b) working at your job;
    (c) gardening;
    (d) looking after your child?
    How efficient are you? Could you make any improvements, or are you convinced that you are 100 per cent efficient?

4   **SMED**. Analyse the activities of the following individuals:

(a) your co-worker (or member of your group);
(b) your spouse;
(c) your room mate.
Apply the SMED principle. Are there any improvements that you might propose?

5   **The five S words**. Again, analyse the following activities;
    (a) studying;
    (b) working at your job;
    (c) gardening;
    (d) looking after your child.
    Do you practise the elements presented in the five S words? If not, what improvements do you believe could be made?

6   **Quality at the source**. One of the elements of lean production is quality at the source. Consider the following operations with which you are familiar:
    (a) university or business school;
    (c   supermarket, or hypermarket;
    (c) government office (mayor's office, immigration, tax office, etc.).
    Do you consider that quality at the source is practised. If not, what improvements might you propose.

7   **Uncertainty in just-in-time**. In any activity there is always uncertainty and risk; see Chapter 22, *Decision Making and Risk Analysis*:
    (a) Examine a manufacturing operation and look at some of the possible risks and the outcome when just-in-time is practised.
    (b) Do the same for a service organization.

EXERCISE PROBLEM: ASSEMBLY

Situation

An automobile company has an assembly operation for the components of the gear box. The company uses Kanbans for the operation and the operating details for one part of the assembly operation are given in Table 15.11.

Table 15.11 Operating details for parts of the gearbox assembly operation

Rate of utilization of components (h)	350
Production time/unit (min)	2.75
Delivery time of a container (min)	2
Capacity of the container (units)	60
Variation in the demand rate (%)	3

Required

1   Using the calculation procedure, determine how many Kanbans would be needed for this operation.

2   The layout of the operation is changed, such that it takes 20 minutes for delivery of the container from the storage area. In this case, now calculate the number of Kanbans required.

3   Assume that the variation in demand rate increases to 25 per cent, and all the other conditions of requirement 2 remain the same. How many Kanbans would be required?

EXERCISE PROBLEM: LATHE

Situation

A company in Latvia makes drive-shaft assemblies for propeller motors used on boats. The principal equipment used for this operation is a 1950s lathe machine, which is adjusted by hand. The set-up data and other information for a typical annual demand of 20 000 units is given in Table 15.12

Table 15.12 Set-up data and other information for a typical annual demand of 20 000 units.

Annual demand, D (units)	20 000
Stocking cost (£/month)	4
Set-up time (min)	125
Persons needed for set-up	2
Average wage cost (£/h)	10.50

The company was having financial difficulties and was being considered for purchase by a British firm, which was planning to inject new capital into the firm, including putting in automated controlled machines.

Required

1 Under the old operation, what would be the economic lot size to balance stocking costs with set-up costs (ordering costs). Illustrate the ordering costs, stocking costs and total costs on an economic lot size curve, highlighting the minimum value of total costs (the EOQ quantity).

2 With the proposed new equipment the personnel to perform the set-up could be reduced to one. What would have to be the set-up time if the economic lot size required was 20 units? Illustrate the new costs (ordering costs, stocking costs and total costs) on an economic lot size curve that would show the economic lot size as 20 units.

EXERCISE PROBLEM: PRESS

Situation

Press Co. is engaged in making rigid plastic storage containers from PVC in a variety of colours. The production operation basically involves injecting the heated plastic into a mould housed in a hydraulic press. After cooling, the item is ejected, the rough edges are cleaned and metal brackets are attached. Press makes the containers in lot sizes multiples of 20 (20, 40, 60, etc.).

The following is the initial operating data for making the containers: the variable unit cost of £4/unit includes the plastic material and operating labour; the set-up cost is £150.00/set-up. Production costs can be estimated as the sum of the set-up cost and the variable unit labour cost.

Required

1 Develop an average unit product cost curve for the operation for lot sizes ranging from 20 to 400.

2 At what lot size does the average unit cost drop below 10 per cent of the variable unit cost?

3 After what lot size does the change in average unit cost from one lot size to another fall below 1 per cent.

4 Press implements a SMED operation, which reduces the set-up cost by a factor of 20. Redo the average cost curve again for lot sizes from 20 to 400 in multiples of 20.

5 After SMED, at what lot size does the average unit cost drop below 10 per cent of the variable unit cost?

6 After SMED, after what lot size does the change in average unit cost from one lot size to another drop below 1 per cent.

7 What is the impact on the firm, on its pricing policy and/or on its margin if it implements a SMED programme?

Chapter 25, *Financial Analysis*, may be helpful in this question.

CASE STUDY: FABRIX

Situation

Fabrix is a manufacturer of medical instruments in Idaho, USA. The company was started by the Fabrix family in 1938 and had been very innovative in the types of instruments that it put onto the market. The employees were very faithful to the company and many had been with the firm for all their working lives. The average age was 46. In 1996, the family was approached by a large German competitor to purchase the Fabrix facility. Since the Fabrix family had no children who were willing to continue the business, the family sold in January 1997. The acquiring company agreed to keep the Fabrix name, but no guarantee was to given regarding the employment situation of the present personnel.

Fabrix had been reasonably profitable in early years, but as little new investment had been made since the 1970s, profit margins had declined, primarily due to increasing operating costs. In addition, new products developed by the company did not have the performance as some competitor products.

At the time of the purchase, the physical facilities of Fabrix included two manufacturing/assembly buildings called ABO-1 and ABB-2, plus a small building, ABX-3, for management personnel, accounting, purchasing and a sales meeting room. There were five key products manufactured and assembled by Fabrix, called Models A, B, C, D and E. The first four of these (Models A, B, C and D) were machined and assembled in building ABO-1. The layout of the production operation showing the process flow of these four models is illustrated in Figure 15.27. All of the models pass through final assembly to test, before packaging. Building ABB-2 was similar in surface area to ABO-1 and contained the machining and component assembly of the fifth product line, Model E. Final assembly, test and packaging for Model E was carried out in Building ABO-1 (flow line indicated on Figure 15.27). In addition, Building ABB-2 was used for rework of defective units and for the storage of some obsolete components. In both of the manufacturing buildings there was a considerable quantity of inventory items.

After the purchase, an audit team from the acquiring company analysed the details of Fabrix Operation with the objective of incorporating lean manufacturing and injecting whatever investment necessary to achieve these goals.

Required

1 What are your comments on the Fabrix operation as it is currently presented?

2 What are some of the changes you might propose for the Fabrix operation to incorporate the idea of lean manufacturing?

3 Within your analysis, where would you propose to incorporate some of the logic of optimized production technology? (See Chapter 14, *Operations Scheduling*.)

Figure 15.27   Fabrix – Layout of Building ABO-1 (scale 1 cm = 3.4m).

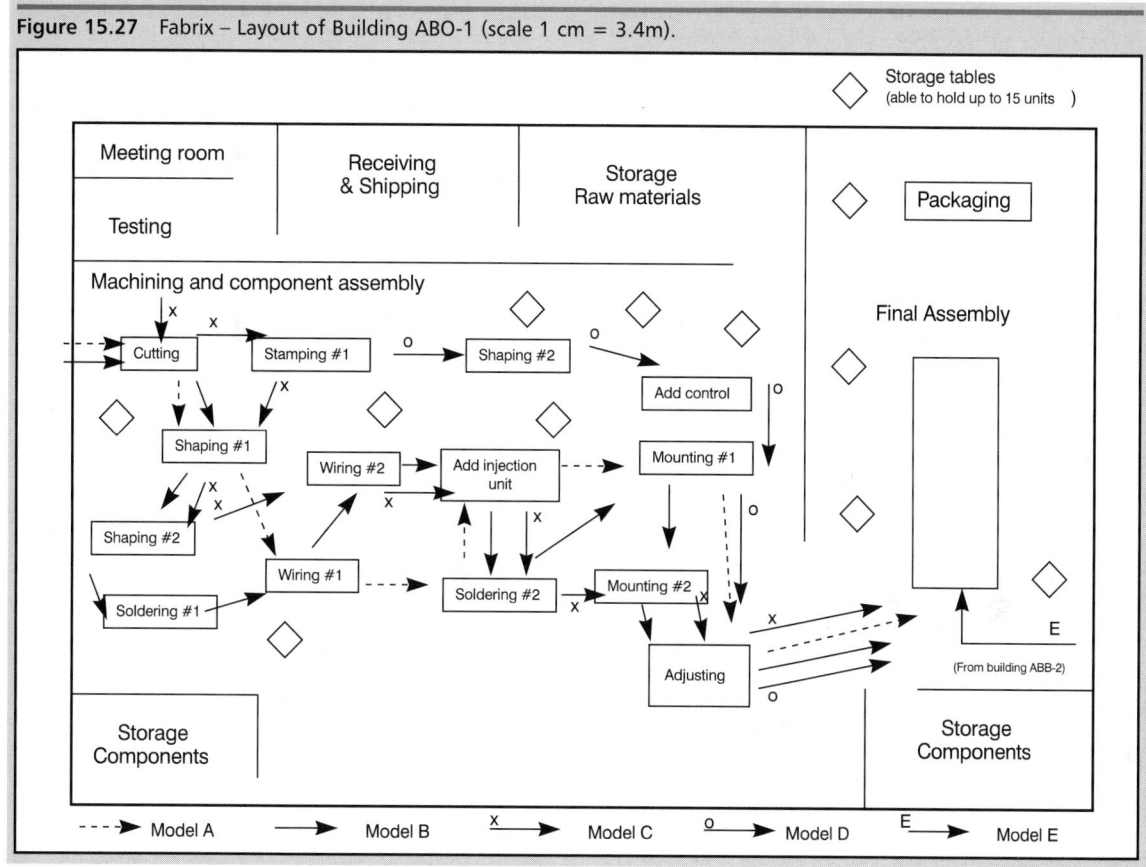

NOTES AND REFERENCES

1. Aeppel, T. (1992) 'GM's new Opel plant is to adapt methods from around the globe to Eastern Germany', *Wall Street Journal Europe* 24 September.
2. Renault official at Vennisseux, France, March 1995.
3. Operations visit to the Citroën facility at Aulney sous Bois, France, 6 December 1993, organized by Marc Gourisse and Mr Monsieur Da Silva of Design Development.
4. 'La Plus grande concession du monde, La concession Toyota d'El Monte, près de Los Angeles, écoule 5,000 voitures de plus par an que les 110 concessionnaires Toyota éparpillés dans toute la France!' (1996) *L'auto journal* No 447, 26 September: 118 [Translation: The world's biggest car dealer, Toyota at El Monte, near Los Angeles sells, 5000 more automobiles per year than all the 110 car dealers throughout all of France!].
5. Fukukawa, T. and Hong, S.-C. (1993) 'The determination of the optimal number of kanbans in a just-in-time production system', *Computers and Industrial Engineering* 24(4): 551–9.
6. Shingo, S. (1983) *A Revolution in Manufacturing: The SMED System* Cambridge, MA: Productivity Press.
7. Shingo, S. (1983) *A Revolution in Manufacturing: The SMED System*, Cambridge, MA: Productivity Press, 114–15.
8. 'McDonald's Robot: Fries. With. That?' (1997) *International Herald Tribune*, 13 November: 12.
9. 'Not Quite in Time' (1995) *Newsweek* 30 January: 26
10. Reitman, V. (1997) 'Fire at parts factory forces Toyota to shut down production in Japan', *Wall Street Journal Europe* 4 February.

FURTHER READING

Ardalan, A. (1997) 'Analysis of local decision rules in a dual-kanban flow shop', *Decision Sciences* 28(1): 195–211.
Black, G. (1993) 'UK manufacturers adopting JIT technology just-in-time', *Software Magazine* 13(15): 111–14.
Chen, S. and Chen, R. (1997) 'Manufacturer–supplier relationship in a JIT environment', *Production and Inventory Management Journal* 38(1): 58–64.
Clarke, B. and Mia, L. (1993) 'JIT manufacturing systems: Use and application in Australia', *International Journal of Operations and Production Management* 13(7): 69–82.
Cook, R. L. and Rogowski, R. A. (1996) 'Applying JIT principles to continuous process manufacturing supply chains', *Production and Inventory Management Journal* 37(1): 12–17.

Germain, R. Droge, C. and Spears, N. (1996) 'The implications of just-in-time for logistics organization management and performance', *Journal of Business Logistics* 17(2): 19–34.

Ham I., Hitomi, K. and Yoshida T. (1985) *Group Technology* Hingham, MA: Kluwer Nijhoff Publishing.

Hutchins, D. (1988) *Just in Time*, Gower.

Jin, H., Hartman, S. J. and Bondi, P. J. (1994) 'How do JIT systems affect human resource management?', *Production and Inventory Management Journal* 35(1): 1–4.

Josa, D. G. (1996) JIT demands faster set-ups', *Manufacturing Engineering* 116(1): 112.

Kazazi, A. and Keller, A. Z. (1994) 'Benefits derived from JIT by European manufacturing companies', *Industrial Management and Data Systems* 94(10): 12.

Keller, A. Z., Kazazi, A. and Carruther, A. (1992) 'Impact of implementing just-in-time in a European manufacturing environment', *International Journal of Quality and Reliability Management* 9(7): 54–63.

Kochan, T. A. and Lansbury, R. D. (1997) 'Lean production and changing employment relations in the international auto industry,' *Economic and Industrial Democracy* 18(4): 597–620.

Kasonen, K. and Buhanist, P. (1995) 'Customer focused lean production development', *International Journal of Production Economics* 41(1–3): 211–16.

Lee, C. Y. (1997) JIT adoption by small manufacturers in Korea', *Journal of Small Business Management* 35(3): 98–107.

Levy, D. L. (1997) 'Lean production in an international supply chain', *Sloan Management Review* 38(2): 94–102.

Markey, M. (1996) 'Examining a Kanban material acquisition system', *Industrial Management* 38(3): 22–26.

Di Mascolo, M. (1996) 'Analysis of a kanban system with a general arrival process of demands', *European Journal of Operational Research* 89(1): 147–63.

Mazany, P. (1995) 'A case study: Lessons from the progressive implementation of just-in-time in a small knitwear manufacturer', *International Journal of Operations and Production Management* 5(9): 271–288.

Mclachlin, R. 'Management initiatives and just-in-time manufacturing', *Journal of Operations Management* 15(4): 271–292.

Minahan, T. (1997) 'Dell Computer sees suppliers as key to JIT', *Purchasing* 123(3): 43–48.

Minahan , T. (1997) 'Toyota continues quest for true JIT excellence', *Purchasing* 123(3): 42–43.

Mould, G. and King, M. (1997) 'Just-in-time implementation in the Scottish electronics industry', *Industrial Management and Data Systems* 95(9): 17–22.

Nilsson, T. (1996) 'Lean production and white-collar work: The case of Sweden', *Economic and Industrial Democracy* 17(3): 447–472.

Oliver, N., Delbridge, R. and Lowe, J. (1996) 'Lean production practices: International comparisons in the auto components industry', *British Journal of Management* 7(Special Issue March): S29–S44.

Procter, S. J. (1995) 'The extent of just-in-time manufacturing in the UK: Evidence from aggregate economic data', *Integrated Manufacturing Systems*, 6(4): 16–25.

Sarker, B. R. and Balan, C. V. (1996) 'Operations planning for kanbans between two adjacent work stations', *Computers and Industrial Engineering* 31(1): 221–224.

Schneiderjans M. J. (1993) *Topics in Just-in-Time Management*, Boston, MA: Allyn and Bacon.

Stank, T. P. and Crum, M. R. (1997) 'Just-in-time management and transportation service performance in a cross-border setting', *Transportation Journal* 36(3): 31–42.

Tanabe, M. (1992) 'Making JIT work at NCR Japan', *Long Range Planning* 25(5): 37–42.

'The Right Stuff: Does US industry have it? GM's new Saturn is a bold venture to show that with teamwork and new ideas, American manufacturers can still compete' (1990) *Time* 29 October.

Trinkhaus, J. Dannenbring, D. and Nathan, J. (1996) 'A JIT-type stocking system for hospital pharmacies: The stockless method', *Hospital Material Management Quarterly* 17(4): 1–13.

Venjara, Y. (1996) 'Set-up savings', *Manufacturing Engineering* 117(1): 96–102.

Warnecke, H. J. and Huser, M (1995) 'Lean production', *International Journal of Production Economics* 41(1–3): 37–43.

Whitson, D. (1997) 'Applying just-in-time systems in health care', *IIE Solutions* 29(8): 32–37.

Womak, J. P and Jones, D. T. (1994) 'From lean production to the lean enterprise', *Harvard Business Review* 72(2): 93–103.

Womak, J. and Jones D. (1996) *Lean Thinking*, New York: Simon & Schuster.

Zayko, Mathew J., Broughman, Douglas J., Hancock, Walton M., 'Lean manufacturing yields world-class improvements for small manufacturer', IIE Solution, Vol. 29, Iss., April 1997: 36–40.

'Just in time is becoming just a pain: The system clogs Japan's roads, fouls its air, and boosts prices' (1991) *Business Week* 17 June.

'Lean, mean and through your windscreen' (1991) *The Economist* 23 February.

'Manufacturing management: For JIT read jitters' (1991) *The Economist* 19 February.

'The Celling out of America: Across America factories are scrapping assembly lines and replacing them with numerous 'cells' of workers' (1994) *The Economist* 17 December.

16 Purchasing and subcontracting

Objectives and overview

The objective in this chapter is to present the different aspects of purchasing and its role in operations and the supply chain. The chapter opens by defining the purchasing function and addressing the international aspects including sourcing, the impact of exchange rates, commodities, hedging and some of the barriers to international purchasing. The chapter then presents how purchasing departments might be organized, from a decentralized to a centralized organization, or a hybrid of the two. The activity of buyers is presented and then there is a section covering ethics in purchasing, giving an overview of governing laws in various countries. Suppliers in the purchasing activity are discussed, together with the role of checklists in selection and the use of an ABC Pareto-type analysis. The steps in the purchasing process are detailed, starting from purchase requisition through to final payment for the service or product. The chapter then moves on to review the concept of value analysis, or value engineering, and just-in-time as it applies to purchasing. There is a section on subcontractor selection as a purchasing function and the final section in this chapter covers the decision of make or buy for a firm and presents the quantitative approach of a break-even analysis.

THE PURCHASING ACTIVITY

Purchasing is the buying of materials or services from an outside source, thus involving the transfer of goods from one distinct entity to another. The purchasing activity is the start of the supply chain and is set in motion by the client's demand for finished goods. A client's requirements are negotiated with Marketing; this establishes the basis for production plans and then Production decides what needs to be purchased. In order to ensure an unbroken supply chain, Purchasing, Marketing and Production must work in tandem to ensure that delivery dates are met. Purchased products might include those listed in Table 16.1

Magnitude of purchasing operations

Purchasing represents a significant part of a company's business. Food firms such as Danone and Nestlé, appliance manufacturers and automobile constructors have reported that between 60 and 70 per cent of their manufacturing costs is for purchased materials. In 1994, Ford Motor Company spent $50 billion on

Table 16.1 Examples of purchased products

Purchased product	Examples
Raw materials	Crude oil, green coffee beans, sheet steel, paper pulp
Parts	Nuts and bolts, plastic tubing, impeller blades
Subassemblies	Computer frames, electrical armature windings, truck axles
Assemblies	Pumps, compressors, automobile lights
Machinery and equipment	Printing presses, computers, numerically controlled drilling machines
Packaging	Cardboard, bottles, aluminium cans, tops
Office supplies	Paper clips, pencils, paper, printing cartridges, diskettes
Services	Restaurant, payroll, medical, rental of vehicles, rental of buildings and additional land, travel service for personnel, temporary staff – Kelly Girls
Finished goods	Clothing, sports equipment, household appliances
Subcontractor services	Electrical installations, building extensions

purchased parts and services. Jose Ignacio Lopez, the former head of purchasing at General Motors, before he defected to Volkswagen in 1993, reportedly saved the company an estimated $1 billion on purchased materials.

According to *La compagnie des acheteurs Français* (French Purchasing Organization), who surveyed 130 French companies, the value of purchased components relative to revenues was:

- about 45 per cent in the 1980s;
- about 70 per cent in 1995.

It is expected to rise to about 90 per cent by the year 2000.

Purchasing function

Purchasing departments maintain a database of available suppliers covering such aspects as the types of products supplied, quality, price and delivery times. It is Purchasing which normally makes the ultimate buying decisions, though not without prior consultation with and recommendations from other departments, such as Research and Development, Manufacturing, Marketing, Finance, Engineering, etc.

Purchasing managers' index

Purchasing activity is directly related to manufacturing operations. A high level of purchasing signals an increase in manufacturing, and vice versa. In the USA, the National Association of Purchasing Management compiles a monthly index that measures factory activity, as illustrated in Figure 16.1. This index means that a value above 50 per cent indicates an expansion of activity in US production centres, while a reading below 50 per cent measures a decline. In Figure 16.1 the index fell to 46.1 per cent in May 1994, from 52 per cent the previous month. This drop was attributed to a decline in consumer purchases.[1]

PURCHASING IS INTERNATIONAL

For most companies, purchasing is an international operation. Raw materials may be purchased from abroad because that is the only source, for example coffee from Brazil and the Ivory Coast, oil from Kuwait and Iran, or uranium from the USA and Russia. Alternatively, raw materials are purchased internationally because they are less expensive or of better

Figure 16.1 Purchasing Managers Index.

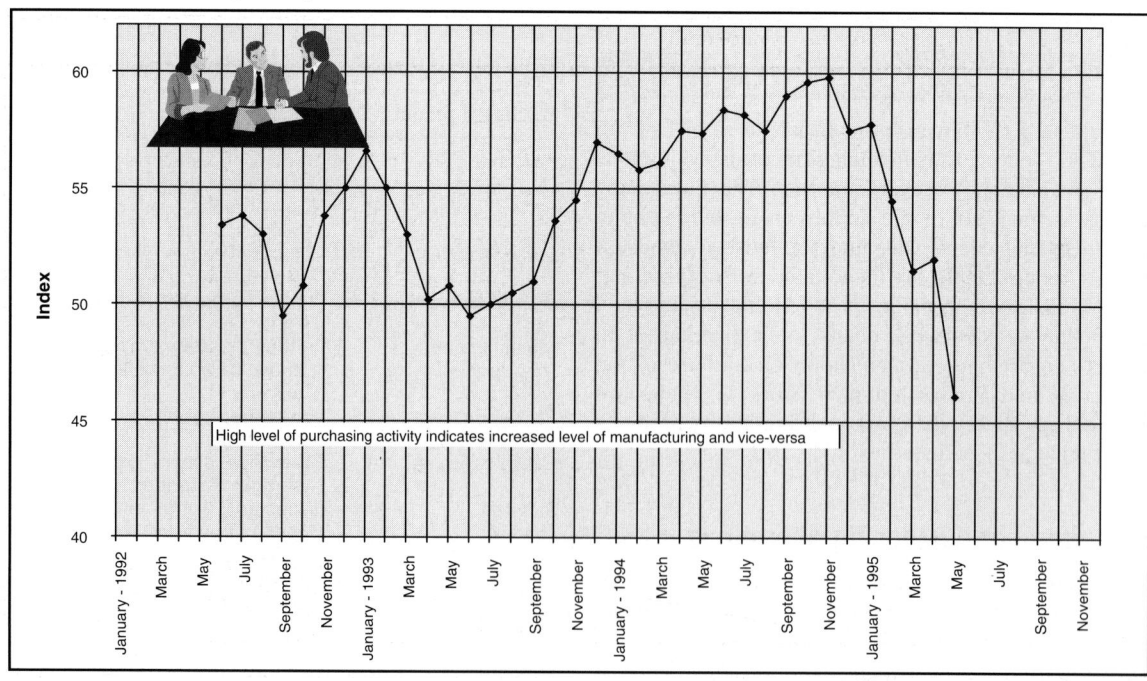

quality. This might apply to textiles, computer chips or steel, for example.

Sourcing

Sourcing is the activity of searching for a supplier (a source) of raw materials or products that presents the best ratio of quality to price, as illustrated by Figure 16.2, in no matter what country of the world. Companies may operate their own sourcing activity, although, since covering the globe requires tremendous resources of personnel, contacts, money and time, firms are apt to use services that specialize in sourcing. For example, major European retailers use the services of sourcing agents based in Hong Kong. There is considerable risk in using sourcing agents because qualities may not conform to specifications and price levels may change as a result of fluctuating exchange rates.

Exchange rates

Table 16.2 gives exchange rates for some emerging economies in units per $US.[2]

For some areas there is a wide fluctuation. Consider the following.

Table 16.2 Exchange rates and variations for some developing countries

	Currency	December 1994	December 1993	Change %
Argentina	Peso	1.00	0.99	−1.00
Brazil	Cruzeiro	0.86	0.09	−89.53
Chile	Escudo	388.00	413.00	+6.44
China	Yuan	8.51	5.79	−31.96
Czech Republic	Koruna	28.30	29.80	+5.30
Greece	Drachma	243.00	244.00	+0.41
Hong Kong	Dollar	7.73	7.72	−0.13
Hungary	Forint	110.00	98.30	−10.64
India	Rupee	31.40	31.10	−0.96
Indonesia	Rupiah	2 188.00	2 102.00	−3.93
Israel	Pound	2.95	2.90	−1.69
Malaysia	Dollar	2.56	2.55	−0.39
Mexico	Peso	3.45	3.10	−10.14
Philippines	Peso	24.10	27.30	+13.28
Poland	Zloty	23 074.00	19 995.00	−13.34
Portugal	Escudo	161.00	174.00	+8.07
Russia	Ruble	3 275.00	1 229.00	−62.47
Singapore	Dollar	1.46	1.60	+9.59
South Africa	Rand	3.56	3.36	−5.62
South Korea	Won	791.00	809.00	+2.28
Taiwan	Yuan	26.30	26.60	+1.14
Thailand	Baht	25.10	25.40	+1.20
Turkey	Pound	36 655.00	13 961.00	−61.91
Venezuela	Bolivar	203.00	102.00	−49.75

Figure 16.2 Sourcing: optimize quality/price ratio.

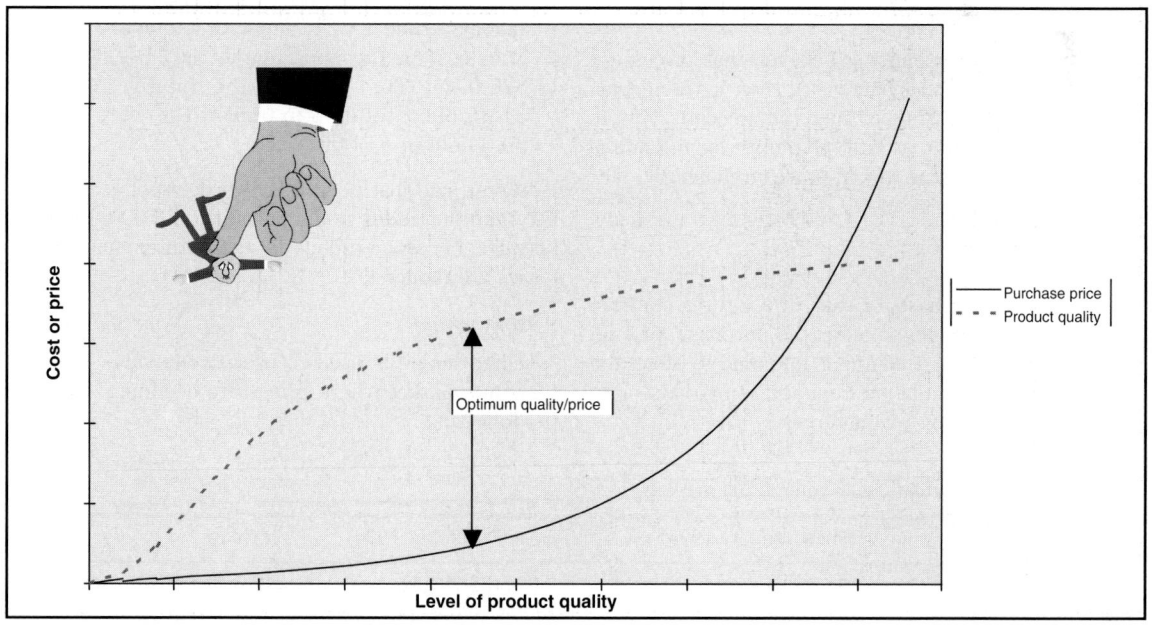

Case A. Downside risk

- A US company purchases 10 000 computer assemblies from the Philippines in December 1993 at a unit price of 480 pesos (local currency).
- Total price paid is 4 800 000 pesos or US $175 824 (4 800 000/27.30).
- If the company purchased the same quantity of assemblies in 1994, at the same unit price in pesos, then the cost would be US $199 170 (4 800 000/ 24.10).

Case B. Upside risk

- A US company purchases 50 000 metres of textile from China in December 1993 at a price of 4 yuan (local currency) per metre.
- Total price paid is 200 000 yuan or US $34 542 (200 000/5.79).
- If the company purchased the same quantity of textiles in 1994, at the same unit price in yuan, then the cost would be US $23 502 (200 000/8.51).

Forward buying

If a company that produces its accounts in US $ believes that prices are rising, as in Case A (downside risk), then it would purchase in large quantities to lock in the favourable price. This is sometimes referred to as forward buying and, in this case, the purchasing company would incur the associated stocking costs.

Hand-to-mouth buying

Alternatively, if the company believes that prices are falling, as in Case B (upside risk), then it would purchase just that quantity of material needed. This is sometimes referred to as hand-to-mouth buying and is somewhat equivalent to just-in-time purchasing.

Hedging

Hedging is the purchase, or sale, of a futures contract of a specific commodity to offset the purchase, or sale, of a cash commodity. Hedging is intended to offset the risk occurred in fluctuating commodity markets or to guarantee a source of raw materials.

Commodities

Commodities may be raw materials for food companies, such as livestock (cattle and hogs) or agriculture products like corn, soybeans, wheat, cotton, orange juice, coffee, sugar and cocoa. Commodities may be metals, such as gold, copper and silver, for the electrical, electronic, jewellery and photographic industries or they may be liquid products, such as crude oil and refined petroleum products for the refinery and chemical industry. Commodity market prices can fluctuate widely as illustrated in Table 16.3.[3]

Hedging is like an insurance policy. An insurance policy protects against loss by paying a cash sum at the end of a predetermined period or when there is a certain loss. The premium represents the cost of receiving the cash payment in return.

Buying hedge

A buying hedge protects against price fluctuations when a fixed-price sale is made now, for delivery at a future date. Consider the transaction of crude oil as a commodity:

- In June an oil producer sells 20 000 barrels of crude at $19.00/bbl, or a total of $380 000 on the spot (cash) market. He buys on the futures market 20 000 bbl of January crude at $20.50/bbl or a total of $410 000.
- In November he buys 20 000 bbl of crude at $20.30/bbl, or a total of $406 000 on the spot market. He sells on the futures market 20 000 barrels of January crude at $21.75/bbl, or a total of $435 000.
- The loss on the spot market is $1.30/bbl (total $26 000). The gain on the futures market is $1.25/bbl (total $25 000). The net loss is $0.05/bbl or $1 000.

If trading had just been done on the spot (cash) market, then the trader would have lost $26 000. However, because he also traded on the futures market, his losses are reduced.

Selling hedge

A selling hedge is used to protect the value of inventory in a market where prices are declining. Consider the following:

Table 16.3 Price fluctuations in commodity markets

Product	Price (January 1993)	Price (December 1994)	Increase
Polypropylene	3.2 FF/kg	5.5 and 5.7 FF/kg,	78 per cent
Copper	$1 767.5/ton	$3 088/ton	75 per cent
Rubber (Kuala Lumpur)	220 Malaysian cents/kg	450 Malaysian cents/kg	105 per cent

■ In June an oil refiner owns 20 000 barrels of crude at $20.50/bbl (total value $410 000). He sells 20 000 bbl of January crude on the futures market at $21.50/bbl, or a total of $430 000.

■ In November he refines and 'sells' 20 000 bbl of crude at $19.00/bbl (total value $380 000). He buys 20 000 barrels of January crude on the futures market at $20.05/bbl (total value $401 000).

■ The loss on refined oil is $1.50/bbl (total value $30 000). The gain on futures market is $1.45/bbl (total value $29 000). The net loss is $1 000.

Without trading on the futures market, the refiner would have lost $30 000.

Completely knocked down

Completely knocked down (CKD) is the term used for companies that export their products (sell to purchasers) in a disassembled, or kit, form. Renault, France, operates part of its business in this manner, where automobile parts or subassemblies are exported to such countries as Turkey, Morocco, Argentina, Columbia, Venezuela and Thailand 'completely knocked down'. CKD purchasing usually means that:

■ The product can be purchased at a lower price.

■ Shipping costs are less because the product can be packaged more compactly (less wasted space).

■ Customs duties are less as there is often a lower tariff on components than on finished goods.

The CKD approach to selling may often be the requirement of the buying country as it wants to use local labour in the assembly of the finished good. That is, importation of the finished product will not be permitted. Weighing against the CKD approach is the time and labour necessary in unpacking and assembly of the products. In addition, the expertise of those assembling in the country of purchase may not be equivalent to those who manufactured the product. Thus product quality could suffer.

Barriers to international purchasing

In addition to the financial risk, other barriers to international purchasing include the following.

Language

Negotiating prices and specifications of products in another language is difficult if the purchasing agent is not fluent. English is more and more the language of transaction. However, if the purchaser is unable to converse correctly he/she may not get the best deal. In Europe, purchasing personnel are at least trilingual.

Culture

Performing transactions in India, Taiwan or Columbia is not the same as in Germany, the USA or Britain. If the latter are the buyer countries, patience has to be used because negotiating is not always as blunt and straightforward as it is in Anglo-Saxon and some European countries.

Customs duty

Duty, or taxes payable on imported goods, can sharply increase prices if there are no reciprocal trade agreements. However, with the North American Free Trade Agreement (NAFTA) between Canada, the USA and Mexico (Chile began formal negotiations to join on 7 June 1995) and the European Union, some customs duties are on their way to being eliminated.

Quotas

Countries sometimes have quotas on the amount of products that can be imported into a country. This has been the case for Japanese cars imported into France.

Specifications and norms

Design specifications and codes differ across the globe. There are specifications in the British measuring system and others in metric. Electric wiring and electrical codes are different. Paper sizes are different. Building specifications are not the same. Environmental regulations covering car emissions are very strict in California and much less so in other areas. The list is enormous. The International Standards Organization, ISO, is making inroads into standardizing the multitude of specifications. (see Chapter 4, *Quality Management*, on ISO-9000 and Chapter 5, *An Environmental Balance*, on ISO-14000.)

Local laws

Laws in foreign countries vary enormously. The relatively clearly stated laws in Europe or the USA make it relatively easy for firms to do business in these regions. However, in Asia, the Middle East and South America local laws are more complicated. Thus, if there is a contract problem with a purchase (for example, regarding quality, quantity or delivery times) in countries where litigation is onerous, obtaining an equitable solution may be time consuming and costly. Thus, the advantage obtained in price may be completely lost because of legal problems. Some companies refuse to do business with certain countries because they perceive the legal risk to be too high.

Political risk

Having supply contracts with countries that are politically unstable (see Chapter 3, *Site Selection*, Figure

3.9) can pose a risk of a cut off of supplies if war or civil strife breaks out. South Africa (under apartheid), Iran, Nigeria, Iraq and Cuba have in the past presented problems.

ORGANIZATION OF PURCHASING DEPARTMENTS

For organizations that have several manufacturing sites, the purchasing activity may be either completely centralized or decentralized, the two extreme cases, or a hybrid of the two approaches.

Centralized purchasing

Centralized purchasing means that all purchased items for every division are centralized through one department, or operating site. This has the following advantages:

- Buying in larger quantities usually means that it is possible to obtain more attractive prices from suppliers.
- Purchasing in large quantities often means that the supplier is more attentive to the order (more clout with the supplier).
- Centralized purchasing permits a standardization of purchased products and thus guarantees a constant quality throughout the organization. This is especially important where food products are concerned (Nestlé, Switzerland; Danône, France; General Mills, USA).
- Having larger purchasing departments, as a result of ordering for many manufacturing sites, means that company can afford greater staff specialization, for example a group concentrating on piping, one on valves, one on steel, etc. This can lead to greater purchasing competence and lower material cost.
- Combining small orders reduces administrative costs, the time taken to negotiate orders, billing time, customs procedures, where appropriate, and thus overall cost.
- Relations with the suppliers are simplified, since there are fewer interlocutors.
- There is reduction of transportation costs because orders are shipped in larger quantities.

Decentralized purchasing

This means that every division within the organization makes its own purchasing decisions. This has the following advantages:

- There is a much quicker response than using a centralized operation (less bureaucratic).
- Transportation costs may be lower if the supplier is located close to the division making the purchase.
- Sometimes local purchasing is more responsive to the needs of the particular operation. (The taste requirements for, say, wheat in a division in France may not be the same as for a division in Britain, because of differences in consumer tastes.)
- Decentralized purchasing reduces inventory costs since divisions only purchase the quantity needed. (In centralized purchasing larger quantities are purchased.)
- The risk is reduced in buying in smaller quantities. For example, consider a food company with six operating companies, which purchases a large quantity of sugar from Cuba for all the operating companies. If the exchange rate suddenly changes, or there is a problem with quality or delivery dates, the risk to the purchasing company can be high. However, if all the operating companies have a decentralized purchasing policy and individually purchase their required quantities of sugar from Europe, Australia, South Africa, Brazil, Mexico and Cuba, the risk arising from currency exchange, quality or delivery is minimized.

Hybrid of purchasing functions

A mixed purchasing organization (hybrid of centralized and decentralized) may be established, depending on the items to be purchased:

- Small or rush orders, or those specific to site needs, are purchased locally (decentralized).
- High-cost capital equipment, high-volume material, standardized products that are used for several operating companies, goods with a high technical content or those from overseas are purchased by the head office (centralized).

Organization chart

The type of organization chart for a purchasing department depends on the size of the organization, the activity of the firm, and whether the company is decentralized or centralized. Figure 16.3 gives the basic structure. There is a purchasing vice president, who reports to the president (for large companies, where purchased products represent a significant proportion of a company's activity). Below the vice president are purchasing managers, who are responsible for particular products. Reporting to these managers are buyers. It is the buyers who have the direct contact

Figure 16.3 Organization chart for a purchasing department.

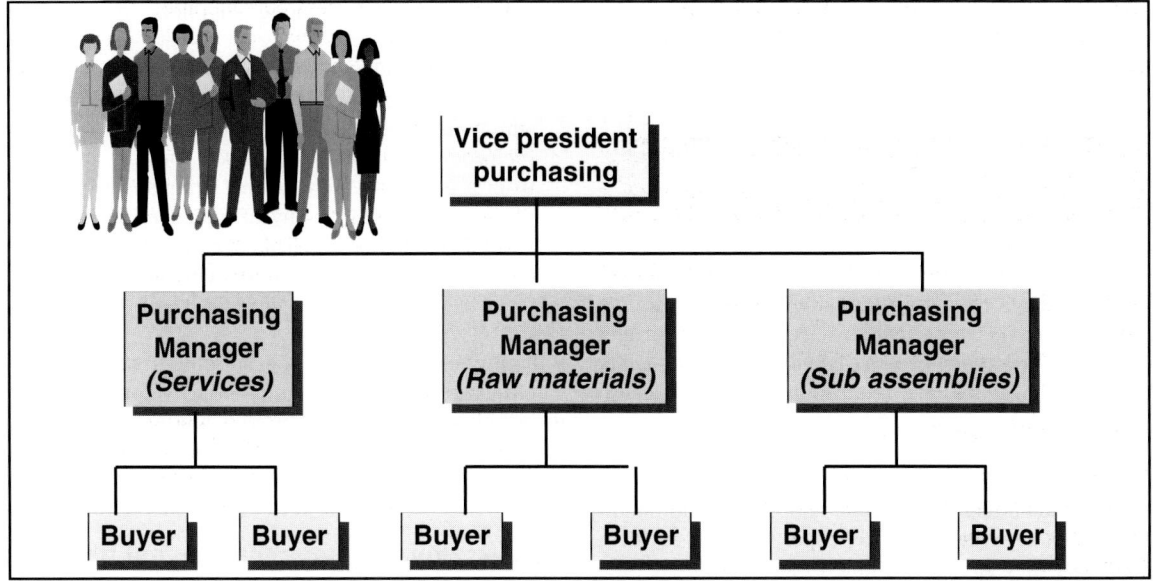

with the supplier organization. Table 16.4 is an illustration of how two European firms organize their purchasing activities. Both have seven departments.

Table 16.4 Organizational purchasing activities in two European firms

Industrial electrical equipment	Ship construction firm
Services	Hull construction material
Raw materials	Interior fittings and air conditioning
Mechanical components	Energy (propulsion) and lubricating fluids
Electrical components	Paint, subcontracting and customs
Electronic components	Safety equipment and office material
Other industrial components	Quality control of suppliers
Insulation material	Receiving and quality control of all supplies

In some companies, particularly centralized organizations where products are purchased in large quantities, the buyers might be few, or even non-existent. In this case, purchasing is done directly by negotiation with the purchasing manager.

Buying

Buying is performed by the buyers in the purchasing departments. Buyers are usually specialized according to a commodity, such as copper, steel, valves, livestock, etc. This specialization allows buyers to become experts at purchasing their particular commodity. In addition, their quality is enhanced by being knowledgeable in the following areas.

Company

Buyers should have a good understanding of their own company, including manufacturing process, products, sales and other company policies. They should be cost and value conscious so that they can negotiate the best contract terms for their company.

Price structure of purchased product

Buyers should know the market and the going price of the commodity available. This includes being aware of the cost structure of the purchased product. For example, consider a buyer for a food company who purchases steel cans from a supplier, which are used for canning fruits and vegetables. The buyer should be able to estimate how much the supplier includes in the price of the purchase product for material cost, labour and profit margin. Understanding this breakdown, the buyer will be better able to negotiate a price.

The price structure of end product

In addition to the purchased product, buyers should be aware of the cost structure of the finished products sold by their company. Again, consider a can of vegetables, for which the buyer purchases the steel cans.

The buyer should know what proportion of the cost price of the finished product (a can of vegetables) is represented by the cost of the can. If the proportion is low, then the buyer should exercise less effort, and less time, in his negotiations for the purchase, than if the proportion is high.

Laws

Buyers should be knowledgeable of the laws that govern their areas of responsibility, such as contract law, misrepresentation and fraud, infringement of patent rights, damage claims against suppliers and shipping regulations. This also includes legislation governing security of transport, product labelling, product safety and specific regulations, regarding, say, pharmaceuticals or foods.

Human relations

Buyers should feel comfortable and behave diplomatically when interviewing sales people, who call on them daily, and they must to be able to schedule their time well so that sales people do not use excessive time. They should be good at dealing with people, including negotiating internally with their own company, as well as externally with the supplier company. Furthermore, senior buyers should be able to manage and lead a team of buyers when it comes to particular projects or when negotiating multiple contracts.

Companies often only permit their buyers to remain, say, for two years on a particular purchasing activity. If they stay longer than this, they become too familiar with the supplier and thus may lose their objectivity for their employer company.

ETHICS IN PURCHASING AND BUYING

Unethical practices?

Sales persons deluge buyers with free lunches, gifts, etc., which open the door to unethical situations. Buyers may feel obligated to sales persons who have given them gifts and may not act in the best interest of their own firm. At what point is the gift giving too much? Some companies limit the annual gifts to no more than $25, or to no single gift exceeding $25. The following are questionable, unethical or illegal buying practices:

- taking advantage of obvious clerical or computational errors in quotations;
- fixing prices;

- collusion among bidders;
- playing favourites among suppliers in awarding orders;
- failing to respect personal obligations;
- upgrading product samples, with the intention of supplying lower-grade products;
- reciprocity, which is purposely buying products from a company because that company buys your product – the philosophy of 'you scratch my back and I'll scratch yours'. This occurs not infrequently and is often ignored as far as being unethical.

Who is the competition?

Willingly, or unwillingly, the supplier's sales person can be the source of 'confidential' information. In proposal work, when competitive bidding is involved, suppliers have been known to divulge the nature of the competition.

US laws governing purchasing and buying

In the USA, the purchasing/buying activity is governed by the following laws.

Sherman Act

The Sherman Act of 1890 prohibits:

- price fixing among competitors;
- group boycott by competitors or agreeing not to buy from a supplier;
- allocation of customers or markets;
- agreement between a manufacturer and customers that they will not buy a competitor's products.

Clayton Act

The Clayton Act of 1914 extended coverage under the earlier Sherman Act and prohibits:

- price discrimination, or charging different prices to different buyers for identical articles;
- tying clauses, requiring the purchase of another item, with the purchase of the desired item;
- exclusive dealing, meaning prohibiting buyers from carrying products of other manufacturers;
- full-line forcing, or requiring buyers to buy the entire seller offering and not just selected items.

Federal Trade Commission Act

The Federal Trade Commission Act of 1914 gave the Federal Trade Commission (FTC) the power to pursue companies that engage in unfair competition or deceptive practices. In the USA, all proposed corporate mergers must withstand the FTC test of unfair competition.

Robinson–Patman Act

The Robinson–Patman Act is the 1936 Amendment to the Clayton Act and governs conditions under which it is lawful to charge different prices to different buyers:

- quantity discounts for large orders;
- lower prices on the end-of-season products (sale items);
- goods that are in danger of deteriorating;
- private-label brands, as opposed to named items;
- charging the same prices as competitors prices in good faith, for example with the slogan 'we will not be undersold'.

Foreign Corrupt Practices Act

The Foreign Corrupt Practices Act of 1997 makes it illegal to bribe foreign clients in order to obtain contracts. It was enacted after Lockheed, the US aerospace company, was found guilty in 1976 of bribing government officials in Europe, Japan and Latin America to purchase its military equipment.[4] Prince Bernhard of the Netherlands was accused of having received $100 000 and Tanaka of Japan, Strauss of Germany and the Italian Andreotti were also mixed up in the scandal.[5] Lockheed Corporation bribery of Japanese government officials brought down the Tokyo government and harmed the reputation of the Netherlands royal family.

The following article given as Box 16.1 illustrates an unethical purchasing practice related to a US firm.[6]

German Law

Compared to US rules, the German law regarding ethics is inconsistent.[7]

Kickbacks

It is illegal to demand and accept kickbacks, but it is essentially legal to pay them. German companies are allowed to deduct such payments from their tax bills as a business expense. The law has been somewhat changed since 1996 and now says that the payments become taxable as soon as they become the subject of a criminal complaint.

Prosecution

Prosecutors can open an investigation involving public officials on the basis of an anonymous tip, but they are prohibited from probing private-sector kickbacks unless someone lodges a formal complaint. Prosecution of public-sector corruption is given a high priority and can result in stiff penalties. However private-sector corruption is considered a problem that companies should solve themselves. Penalties, which are rare to begin with, often amount to a slap on the wrist.

In early 1996, the Opel Germany unit of GM launched an internal investigation into charges that an official at its Bochum plant took bribes of 3 million Marks ($2 million) from its supplier, Pagid AG, an Essen-based company that makes brake linings, in exchange for orders.[8]

Box 16.1 Deals on the side. How a Penney buyer made up to $1.5 million on vendors' kickbacks. But the products he bought sold well, and U.S. store ignored some red flags. "Hard-nosed view" at Harrods. By Andrea Gerlin, Staff Reporter

DALLAS – As a buyer for J.C. Penney Co., Jim G. Locklear earned $56,000 a year. But he controlled the spending of millions of dollars a year, and in 1988 he started peddling that influence.

He admits he sold crucial information to some suppliers and manufacturers' representatives, such as the amount of their competitors' bids. To others, he flat-out sold the promise of large orders. In exchange, some vendors handed him cash; others wrote checks to front companies he set up. Over four years, he supplemented his salary with as much as $1.5 million in bribes and kickbacks.

The story of Mr. Locklear's graft emerged in a federal-court case here that prosecutors describe as unusual. "For a retail buyer to be prosecuted ... is definitely rare," says Assistant U.S. Attorney Michael Uhl.

However, corruption among retail buyers isn't so rare – a fact that image-conscious retailers have kept secret by not going to court. "There are many big cases where the buyers pay back the retailers and there's no publicity," says Herbert Robinson, a New York attorney who has represented retailers

in dozens of bribery cases. "The companies sweep a lot of these cases under the rug."

Acceptable Practices

Unlike kickbacks to government buyers, retail bribery hurts customers, not taxpayers. But because customers can shop around, it doesn't stir much outrage. Indeed, some in the retail industry don't even realize it's illegal. "We've had people calling us and telling us that these practices are just accepted" in the industry, Mr. Uhl says.

Yet the cost to customers runs into millions of dollars a year. Although the exact total can't be calculated, experts say Sam Walton considered it significant. Striving to make his Wal-Mart Stores Inc. the lowest-price retailer, Mr. Walton established the industry's toughest conflict-of-interest policy. He prohibited buyers from accepting as much as a cup of coffee from vendors.

"The Wal-Mart policy is black-and-white, it leaves no room for interpretation, and it's probably a factor in helping them keep costs down," says Sidney Doolittle, a Chicago retail consultant and a former manager at Montgomery Ward & Co.

Some of the major European retailers also maintain strict policies to prevent buyers from accepting any gifts that might be construed as kickbacks, or at most only those of nominal value. "We have a very hard-nosed view on this," says a spokesman for Harrods department store in London. "The acceptance of almost everything is forbidden."

Harrods requires its chief buyers to regularly remind their staff not to accept personal gifts, vouchers, trips, services or entertainment. The store's conflict-of-interest regulation also forbids buyers and their families from investing in supplier companies or doing outside work for them without written approval from Harrods.

At German retailer Kaufhof AG, employees may not accept presents worth more than 50 marks ($32.60). Rival department store chain Karstadt AG has written a ban on accepting gifts into buyers' contracts; violators are fired. Both retailers say they haven't had any problems with suppliers in recent years.

If problems do arise, however, stores prefer to resolve them out of courtroom, a Kaufhof spokesman says. "I'm sure [unethical conduct] will always exist, but companies tend to settle such things in-house," he says. "They don't exactly help the image."

U.S. Typically Not Strict

Other than Wal-Mart, U.S. retailers typically let buyers accept meals, small gifts, even trips. The policy that Penney produced in a lawsuit in 1994 stated that as long as buyers anticipated a chance to reciprocate, they could accept "dinners, theater tickets, golf dates, fishing or hunting trips."

Retail experts say temptations and opportunities for scams are inevitable, with big retail chains' buyers deciding how to spend millions of dollars and thus able to make or break a supplier or manufacturer's representative. And if a buyer does cross the line, catching him or her can be difficult. Often, the racket is detected only when someone tattles. "One guy who worked for me went through a divorce, and his wounded wife turned him in," Mr. Doolittle says. "She'd built a file on all the gifts he'd taken that he shouldn't have.

Mr. Locklear declines to comment, saying he promised his silence as part of a plea agreement with the U.S. Attorney's Office in Dallas; he is helping it gather evidence for possible use against those who paid him off. But documents in the government's criminal case against Mr. Locklear, as well as in Penney's civil case against him, offer a rare glimpse into the temptation – and lackadaisical policing – of buyers.

When Mr. Locklear joined Penney in late 1987, he was a 38-year-old swamped with trouble. He had four children from four marriages, child-support payments of $900 a month, a nearly half-million-dollar house that would soon go into foreclosure and, at that time, four years of probation remaining on a charge of indecency with a minor to which he had pleaded guilty.

Among retailers, however, he was known as a first-rate housewares buyer with an eye for fashion and a knack for negotiating low prices. After 10 years at a Dallas retail chain then owned by Federated Department Stores Inc., he joined Allied Stores Corp.'s Jordan Marsh chain in Boston in 1987 at an annual salary of $96,000, according to an employment application filed with the Collin County District Court in Penney's suit against him.

But he got homesick for his native Texas. So, after only three months at Jordan Marsh, he applied at Penney, which was about to move its New York headquarters to Dallas. Penney offered him a way home, but at a base salary of $56,000 a year – a $40,000 pay cut. He accepted, and in late 1987 he joined Penney as a buyer of housewares.

Growing Suspicions

A little more than a year later, Penney officials received complaints about Mr. Locklear. A cutlery supplier, Lifetime Hoan Corp., of Dayton, New Jersey, told a Penney personnel director that Mr. Locklear was taking kickbacks, according to a March 1989 internal Penney memo filed with Dallas County District Court in a related lawsuit. An assistant buyer at Penney told company executives that he was suspicious of Mr. Locklear's choice of suppliers.

In May 1989, Penney, unbeknownst to Mr. Locklear, hired an outside firm to investigate him. The firm, Floyd E. Purvis & Associates of Dallas, uncovered his financial woes but no proof of bribery.

One reason Mr. Locklear may have still seemed trustworthy: his sparkling performance. Theoretically, a buyer influenced by kickbacks would perform poorly, compared with one seeking solely to satisfy customer demand. But Mr. Locklear showed skill in predicting and shaping customer tastes. Under him, Penney's annual sales of tabletop merchandise soared, at one point rising to $45 million from $25 million, according to an estimate by HFN, a housewares trade publication. Three times, in 1989, 1990 and 1991, Penney named Mr. Locklear a buyer of the year.

A Creative Bent

He didn't just buy fast-selling goods; he also created new lines. One was Penney's solid-color Home Collection, comprising coordinated dinnerware, flatware and glassware and described by HFN as producing "a cohesiveness not seen before in a tabletop department of such size."

Suppliers loved him. "He could spot a trend and jump on it quickly and be the first to do it," said Glenn Simon, vice president of marketing for Sakura Inc., a New York dinnerware company that hasn't been linked to any kickbacks.

In July 1992, however, an anonymous letter informed Penney officials of a "special relationship" between Mr. Locklear and Charles A. Briggs, a Dallas manufacturer's representative from whom Mr. Locklear later admitted taking $200,000 in bribes and kickbacks. Penney launched a second investigation, discovered Mr. Locklear's front companies and fired him. Mr. Briggs, according to his lawyer, didn't break any laws; neither man would comment further.

Prosecutors say Penney might have acted more quickly than it did. They note that it wouldn't have taken a genius to figure out that Mr. Locklear was spending more than $56,000 a year. He splurged on a lifetime membership in a country club, vacations at resorts, a luxury car and securities accounts. "It's like the Aldrich Ames case, where this guy is living above his means and the CIA should have known about it," Prosecutor Uhl says.

Penney apparently received reports as early as 1989 that Mr. Locklear was living beyond his means. But Henry J. Rusman a Penney spokesman, says it didn't know – or in any case couldn't prove – that he was taking kickbacks.

Detailed Admissions

But in his confession to federal authorities, Mr. Locklear admitted accepting and soliciting bribes and kickbacks almost from the start of his stint at Penney. He told of selling information on competitors' bids to Christopher Boyhan, an appliance manufacturers' representative at Global Marketing Co. in Parsippany, New Jersey. Mr. Boyhan, who didn't respond to numerous requests for comment, signed checks that turned over to Mr. Locklear at least $39,000 over the next four years, according to Mr. Locklear's confession and records filed in Penney's civil suit.

Mr. Locklear also told prosecutors about attending a trade show in San Francisco and receiving $10,000 in cash from Felix Amar, president of Westly Forge, a cutlery maker in Norfolk, Virginia. The money represented a percentage of every cutlery set that Westly sold to Penney. In all, Mr. Locklear admitted taking $161,000 from Roger Barker of Dallas, an independent sales representative for Wesley Forge. Mr. Amar couldn't be reached, and Mr. Barker declined to comment.

To get kickbacks from manufacturers' representatives, Mr. Locklear threatened to take the business away and award it to their competitors, according to a lawsuit filed against Penney by David Buckley of Plano, Texas, and other reports. Of 10 accounts known to have produced kickbacks for Mr. Locklear, as many as eight involved manufacturers' representatives.

For them, lining Mr. Locklear's pocket became a matter of survival, according to Mr. Buckley, a representative of small-appliance makers, who says he paid $25,000 to Mr. Locklear when Mr. Locklear demanded it. "If I had not paid him and he pulled the line as he had threatened, I'd have gone out of business," Mr. Buckley says. He also noted in a deposition that he didn't go to Penney because "it was my word against the buyer of the year, the shining star."

"No Reason to Suspect"

Some suppliers say they participated in the scam unknowingly. Norman Ng, president of a Berkeley, California, wok and coffee-maker supplier called Taylor & Ng, says his independent sales representative told him to pay $100,000 in commissions and advertising money to a company that, unbeknownst to Mr. Ng, the Penney buyer owned. "We had no reason to suspect that there was anything wrong," Mr. Ng says.

But Penney didn't treat participants in the scam as victims. In the case of Mr. Buckley, it sent letters to his suppliers, saying it would no longer do business with any company associated with him. Mr. Buckley's suit, filed in Dallas County District Court, charges that the company put him out of business and seeks unspecified damages.

Penney discontinued its orders from Mr. Ng's company – a step that it unsuccessfully tried to get reversed last year. Far from deserving punishment, Mr. Ng says, "we have been damaged by the conduct of J.C. Penney's corrupt buyer and should be seeking redress for that."

Prosecutors here express no sympathy for suppliers and manufacturers' representatives who knowingly gave kickbacks to Mr. Locklear. They say plenty of other vendors turned down Mr. Locklear and faced no retribution from him while still managing to sell to Penney.

Today, Mr. Locklear is selling insurance while awaiting sentencing. He faces up to five years in prison and a maximum fine of twice his financial gain or twice the loss to Penney, whichever is greater. He also owes Penney a portion of a $789,000 judgment that the company obtained in its civil suit against him.

Despite the problems, Penney says it doesn't plan to tighten its ethics code beyond revisions made last April that included prohibiting gifts of hunting and fishing trips. "We do think that our ethics requirements are stringent enough," Mr. Rusman says. He says the revisions weren't in response to the Locklear case.

Cacilie Rohwedder contributed to this article.

Wall Street Journal Europe, 9 February 1995
Reprinted by permission of *Wall Street Journal Europe*,
© 1995 Dow Jones & Company, Inc.
All Rights Reserved Worldwide.

French law

In France the regulations governing payments to foreign governments to ensure contracts, 'pots-de-vins', are very fluid. Companies that make such payments may deduct the amount from taxes under the rubric of 'commercial expenses for export purposes'. The company has to justify the amount paid and it should not be excessive compared to the profits reported.[9]

SUPPLIERS

Suppliers are those companies that furnish goods and services to buyer operations. Good management and control of suppliers is necessary to keep production costs at the appropriate level.

Supplier selection

Criteria for the selection of an appropriate supplier include those shown in Table 16.5.

Global cost structure

For some companies it is not sufficient to negotiate strictly on price, but also to understand how a particular product will perform in a manufacturing operation. For example, paper for a printing operation may be purchased at a low price. However, if it continually tears during the printing operation, causing several shutdowns, what is gained in the price of the raw material is lost during the processing operation? Similarly, raw meat purchased for a food company may be at a low price, but, if during processing there is a high loss, it might be advantageous to purchase pre-cooked meat, even though it costs more, because there is less loss during processing.

Checklist for supplier selection

Companies often use checklists, with weighting criteria, in order to evaluate suppliers. Each criterion graded (Very good to Very poor, for example) and the criteria themselves are weighted according to their importance

Table 16.5 Some criteria for the selection of an appropriate supplier

Criterion	Includes
Product price	Unit price, price for large quantities and discounts available
Quality of material	Does supplier have quality certification such as ISO-9000 or is it certified by the buying company?
Reliability	Supplier's history of meeting delivery dates
After-sales service	Services such as replacement of defective parts, instructions on equipment use, repairs or update of products
Supplier location	This can impact delivery time, transportation costs and response time for rush or replacement orders. Where feasible, firms may choose to buy locally to create goodwill, improve the buying company's image or to improve the local economy. With the same logic, firms may chose to purchase in the country in which they operate, rather than overseas.
Inventory availability	Does the supplier always have sufficient supplies available?
Supplier flexibility	Willingness to respond to changes in demand, design, or order quantities
Financial stability	How long has it been in business? What are its profit and debt levels? Is the supplier a 'going concern' and one that will be around in the years to come?
Technical capability	Capacity of the supplier in research and development. Does the supplier have facilities to continually develop and improve products?
Product range	Ability to supply a wide range of products. For example, if a food company needs to purchase food additives, it would be better to find a supplier who can supply a wide range of additives, rather than the food company having to negotiate with several different suppliers. Having a single, or a few suppliers, is less costly.

to the buying company. A sample evaluation checklist is given in Figure 16.4.

This rating sheet evaluates both the product and the supplier company. The evaluation criteria for the product cover quality through warranty conditions and the evaluation criteria for the supplier cover technical capability through environmental awareness. The buyer firm assigns an importance factor from 1 to 5 to the various criteria, arranged in descending order of importance. The criteria themselves have a quantitative rating of 5 (Excellent) to 1 (Terrible). The last column is the product, Weighting × Importance factor. For example, if a supplier has a product whose quality (factor = 5) is judged fair (weighting = 3), then the score would be 15 (5 × 3). If a supplier whose management competence is being evaluated (factor = 3) is given a rating good (weighting = 4), then the score would be 12 (3 × 4).

The use of a supplier check sheet is illustrated with the worked example, *Stainless Steel*.

Reducing the number of suppliers

Over the years, well established companies build up large databases of suppliers that they either use frequently or hardly at all. In order to reduce cost, companies have, or are in the processing of, reducing the number of suppliers that are used by the organization. The reasons for this is that, with fewer suppliers (Figure 16.5):

- Administrative costs are lower.
- When a supplier knows that it is one of a few suppliers, and furnishes a large proportion of product to a purchasing company, then the purchaser can exercise more power over the supplier regarding contract terms.
- It facilitates management of the purchasing function.
- A buyer company is able to reduce its number of purchasing staff.

ABC analysis of suppliers

If one wants to reduce the number of suppliers, questions to ask are who to keep and who to let go. A first approach might be to make an ABC analysis of the suppliers according to the monetary volume purchased, and the number of suppliers. As an illustration, the division of a textile company near Lyon, France, which purchased a wide range of fabrics, solvents, plastic film, paper, netting and other material, had 110 suppliers in its database. In performing an ABC analysis it established that almost 80 per cent of the monetary volume purchased was from 20 per cent of the total number of suppliers, whereas 60 per cent of the total number of suppliers only furnished 5 per cent of the monetary value of the supplied material (Figure 16.6).[10]

Thus, a first step in reducing the number of suppliers after an ABC analysis has been carried out is to start elimination in category C, moving through B and eventually category A. Rating sheets are also used to evaluate the best suppliers.

Figure 16.4   Supplier rating sheet.

	Weighting	Excellent 5	Good 4	Fair 3	Poor 2	Terrible 1	Factor Max=5	Weighting × factor
PRODUCT								
Quality							5	
Price							4	
Delivery reliability (time)							3	
Delivery reliability (conditions)							2	
Warranty conditions							1	
Total							15	
SUPPLIER								
Technical capability							5	
Financial strength							5	
Quality certification							4	
Flexibility with buyer							4	
Profit consistency							3	
Labour relations (unionized)							3	
Capacity available							3	
Management competence							3	
Knowledegable sales staff							3	
After-sales service							3	
Location relative to buyer							2	
Human rights (emerging economies)							1	
Environmental awareness							1	
Total							40	
Total: Product and Supplier							55	

Figure 16.5   Reducing the number of suppliers.

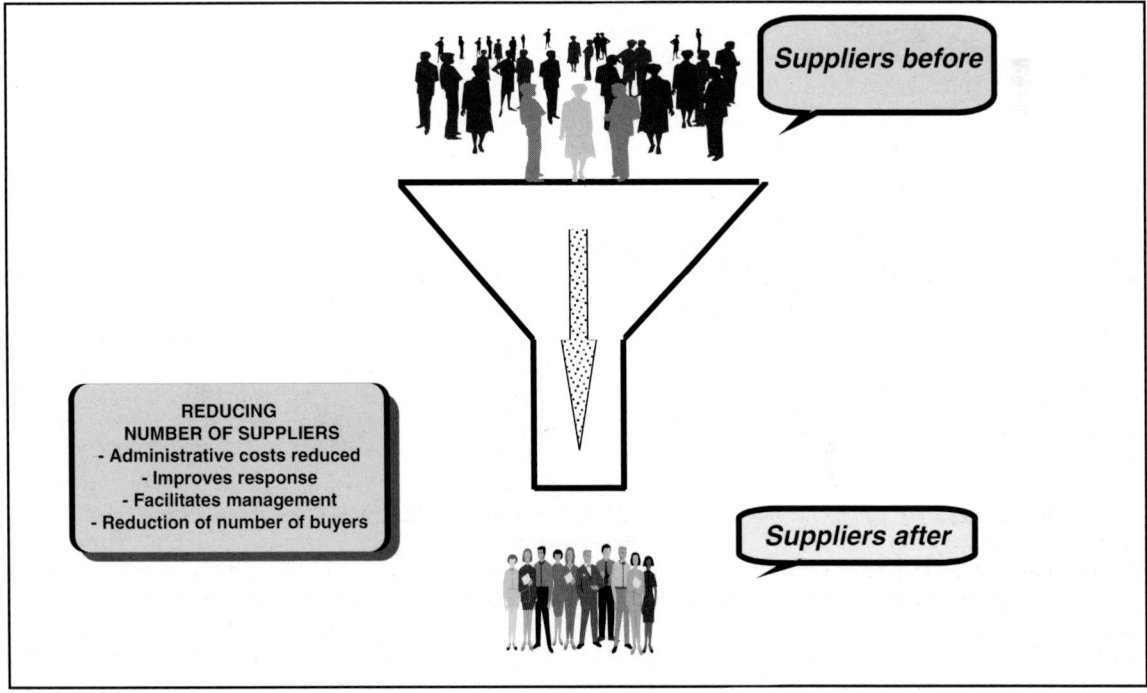

Figure 16.6 ABC analysis for supplier evaluation.

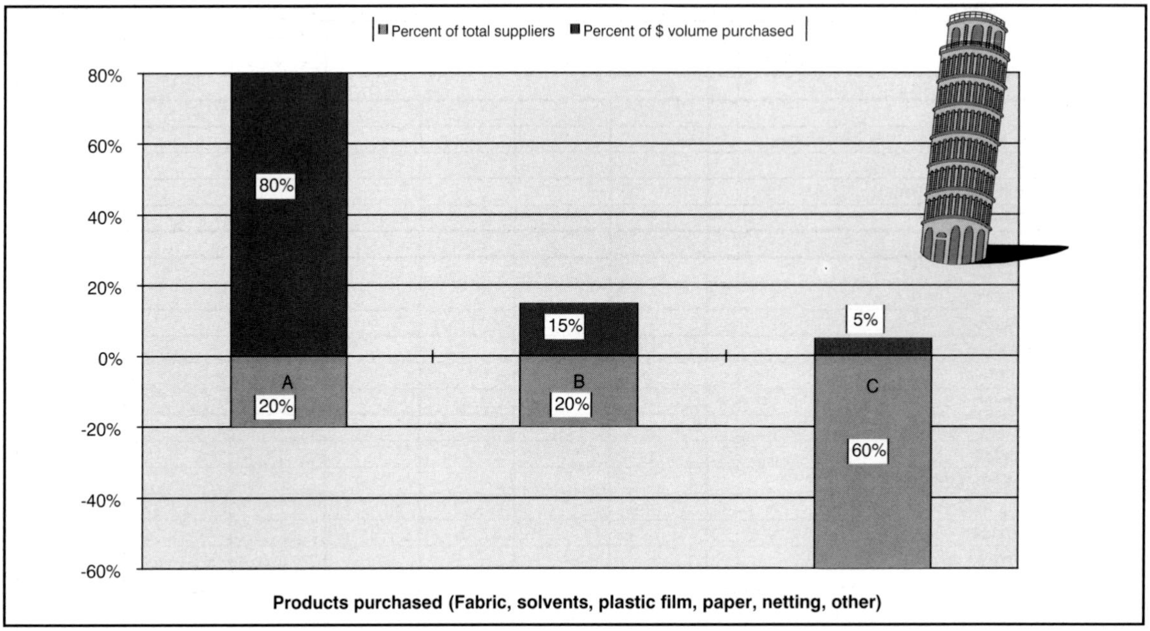

Products purchased (Fabric, solvents, plastic film, paper, netting, other)

Ford USA

Ford, USA, has set a goal to hold its overall costs at 1995 levels through to the end of the decade and, to this effect, has asked its 250 biggest suppliers world-wide to join in a 'collaborative effort' to cut costs of parts 5 per cent a year from 1996 through 1999.[11] The major thrust of this cost-cutting effort is to reduce complexity by reducing the number of alternative components used on vehicles, for example:

■ reducing the number of types of car horns from 30 to 3;
■ reducing the number of types of batteries from 40 to 14;
■ reducing the number of types of steering wheels from 50 to 11;
■ using a single material and colour for trunk carpeting in all vehicles instead of the present half dozen materials and colours. This is expected to reduce costs by 7 per cent.

WORKED EXAMPLE: STAINLESS STEEL

Situation

The Purchasing department at the Chirac plant in Colmar, France, is looking for a new supplier of stainless-steel tubing, sheet and wire. There are three suppliers being considered:

■ Sheffield, England;
■ Karlsruhe, Germany;
■ Mulhouse, France.

The purchasing department has evaluated the proposals from the three locations and completed checklists for each supplier. These are given in the matrices of Figure 16.7 (Sheffield), 16.8 (Karlsruhe) and 16.9 (Mulhouse).

Required

Based on these ratings which is the preferred supplier?

Solution

The completed rating sheets are given in Figure 16.10 (Sheffield), 16.11 (Karlsruhe) and 16.12 (Mulhouse). The overall scores for product and supplier are:

■ Sheffield, England – 203;
■ Karlsruhe, Germany – 180;
■ Mulhouse, France – 160;

Thus, based on these evaluations, Sheffield would be the preferred supplier.

Figure 16.7 Supplier rating sheet – Sheffield, England.

	Weighting	Excellent 5	Good 4	Fair 3	Poor 2	Terrible 1	Factor Max=5	Score Wt x factor
PRODUCT								
Quality		X					5	
Price (high price = low score)					X		4	
Delivery reliability (time)			X				3	
Delivery reliability (conditions)		X					2	
Warranty conditions				X			1	
Total							15	
SUPPLIER								
Technical capability			X				5	
Financial strength			X				5	
Quality certification			X				4	
Flexibility with buyer				X			4	
Profit consistency			X				3	
Labour relations (unionized)			X				3	
Capacity available					X		3	
Management competence		X					3	
Knowledgeable sales staff			X				3	
After-sales service				X			3	
Location relative to buyer				X			2	
Environmental awareness		X					1	
Total							39	
Total: Product and Supplier							54	

Figure 16.8 Supplier rating sheet – Karlsruhe, Germany.

	Weighting	Excellent 5	Good 4	Fair 3	Poor 2	Terrible 1	Factor Max=5	Score Wt x factor
PRODUCT								
Quality			X				5	
Price (high price = low score)		X					4	
Delivery reliability (time)				X			3	
Delivery reliability (conditions)			X				2	
Warranty conditions				X			1	
Total							15	
SUPPLIER								
Technical capability					X		5	
Financial strength			X				5	
Quality certification					X		4	
Flexibility with buyer					X		4	
Profit consistency			X				3	
Labour relations (unionized)			X				3	
Capacity available				X			3	
Management competence		X					3	
Knowledgeable sales staff			X				3	
After-sales service					X		3	
Location relative to buyer					X		2	
Environmental awareness			X				1	
Total							39	
Total: Product and Supplier							54	

Figure 16.9 Supplier rating sheet – Mulhouse, France.

Weighting	Excellent 5	Good 4	Fair 3	Poor 2	Terrible 1	Factor Max=5	Score Wt x factor
PRODUCT							
Quality		X				5	
Price (high price = low score)			X			4	
Delivery reliability (time)			X			3	
Delivery reliability (conditions)		X				2	
Warranty conditions		X				1	
Total						15	
SUPPLIER							
Technical capability				X		5	
Financial strength			X			5	
Quality certification				X		4	
Flexibility with buyer				X		4	
Profit consistency			X			3	
Labour relations (unionized)					X	3	
Capacity available			X			3	
Management competence		X				3	
Knowledgeable sales staff		X				3	
After-sales service				X		3	
Location relative to buyer	X					2	
Environmental awareness					X	1	
Total						39	
Total: Product and Supplier						54	

Figure 16.10 Supplier rating sheet – Sheffield, England – with weighted score.

Weighting	Excellent 5	Good 4	Fair 3	Poor 2	Terrible 1	Factor Max=5	Score Wt x factor
PRODUCT							
Quality	X					5	25
Price (high price = low score)				X		4	8
Delivery reliability (time)		X				3	12
Delivery reliability (conditions)	X					2	10
Warranty conditions			X			1	3
Total						15	58
SUPPLIER							
Technical capability		X				5	20
Financial strength		X				5	20
Quality certification		X				4	16
Flexibility with buyer			X			4	12
Profit consistency		X				3	12
Labour relations (unionized)		X				3	12
Capacity available				X		3	6
Management competence	X					3	15
Knowledgeable sales staff		X				3	12
After-sales service			X			3	9
Location relative to buyer			X			2	6
Environmental awareness	X					1	5
Total						39	145
Total: Product and Supplier						54	203

Figure 16.11   Supplier rating sheet – Karlsruhe, Germany – with weighted score.

Weighting	Excellent 5	Good 4	Fair 3	Poor 2	Terrible 1	Factor Max=5	Score Wt x factor
PRODUCT							
Quality		X				5	20
Price (high price = low score)	X					4	20
Delivery reliability (time)			X			3	9
Delivery reliability (conditions)		X				2	8
Warranty conditions			X			1	3
Total						15	60
SUPPLIER							
Technical capability				X		5	10
Financial strength		X				5	20
Quality certification				X		4	8
Flexibility with buyer				X		4	8
Profit consistency		X				3	12
Labour relations (unionized)		X				3	12
Capacity available			X			3	9
Management competence	X					3	15
Knowledgeable sales staff		X				3	12
After-sales service				X		3	6
Location relative to buyer				X		2	4
Environmental awareness		X				1	4
Total						39	120
Total: Product and Supplier						54	180

Figure 16.12   Supplier rating sheet – Mulhouse, France – with weighted score.

Weighting	Excellent 5	Good 4	Fair 3	Poor 2	Terrible 1	Factor Max=5	Score Wt x factor
PRODUCT							
Quality		X				5	20
Price (high price = low score)			X			4	12
Delivery reliability (time)			X			3	9
Delivery reliability (conditions)		X				2	8
Warranty conditions		X				1	4
Total						15	53
SUPPLIER							
Technical capability				X		5	10
Financial strength			X			5	15
Quality certification				X		4	8
Flexibility with buyer				X		4	8
Profit consistency			X			3	9
Labour relations (unionized)					X	3	3
Capacity available			X			3	9
Management competence		X				3	12
Knowledgeable sales staff		X				3	12
After-sales service				X		3	6
Location relative to buyer	X					2	10
Environmental awareness					X	1	1
Total						39	103
Total: Product and Supplier						54	156

STEPS IN A PURCHASING PROCESS

The procedure for securing a purchased item or service differs from company to company, and the monetary volume of the purchase. Nevertheless, the general procedure used for, say, a quantity of mechanical components is illustrated in Figure 16.13 and the following sections detail the steps.

Purchase requisition

A purchase, or material, requisition is issued by Production and sent to Purchasing. This document is a request to buy an item. This requisition will include:

- identification of the item to be purchased;
- quantity to be purchased;
- delivery date or schedule;
- account to which purchase order is to be charged;
- delivery location.

Request for quotation (RFQ)

Purchasing, with the aid of Production, prepares a Request for Quotation (RFQ), which is a document defining the item for prospective suppliers. This RFQ would include:

- description of the item to be purchased;
- detailed specification (materials to be used, dimensions, etc.);
- diagram of the item.

Out for bidding

The RFQ would be sent out to several vendors or suppliers (three is often a number used) for quotations, which would include price and delivery time, if not specified by the buying company. This is competitive bidding. Depending on the size of the order, purchasing personnel may go out and visit the prospective suppliers.

Reception of quotations

Proposals are sent from the prospective suppliers to the buying company. Suppliers may deliver their quotations personally to the buying company.

Figure 16.13 The purchasing process.

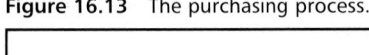

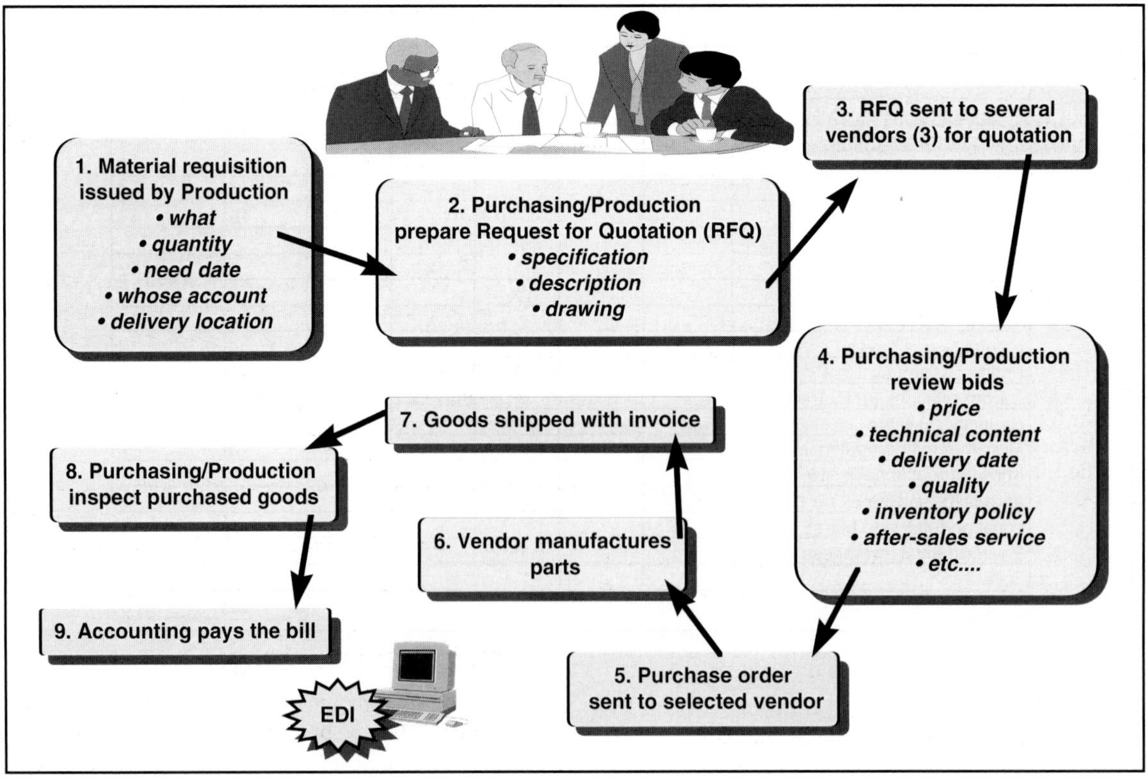

1. **Material requisition issued by Production**
   - *what*
   - *quantity*
   - *need date*
   - *whose account*
   - *delivery location*

2. **Purchasing/Production prepare Request for Quotation (RFQ)**
   - *specification*
   - *description*
   - *drawing*

3. **RFQ sent to several vendors (3) for quotation**

4. **Purchasing/Production review bids**
   - *price*
   - *technical content*
   - *delivery date*
   - *quality*
   - *inventory policy*
   - *after-sales service*
   - *etc....*

5. **Purchase order sent to selected vendor**

6. **Vendor manufactures parts**

7. **Goods shipped with invoice**

8. **Purchasing/Production inspect purchased goods**

9. **Accounting pays the bill**

EDI

Supplier (vendor) selection

Purchasing, with the aid of Production, and perhaps Research & Development or other technical departments, will review the proposal documents. Then Purchasing, and maybe Production, personnel may visit the vendors to review the proposal in more detail. The best supplier will be selected based on such criteria as price (or global cost), delivery time, quality, availability of spares, after-sales service and the like.

Purchase order

The Purchasing department sends out a purchase order to the selected vendor.

Supplier manufactures

The selected vendor sets in motion the production of the required components.

Shipping

Goods are shipped to the buyer with invoice.

Inspection

The buying company inspects all (or a sample) of the goods to verify that they are according to specification.

Payment

When payment is made for a purchased item depends on the terms offered by the supplier of the goods, and also on the size, in financial terms, of the order.

Credit terms

A supplier firm may, for example, offer the terms 2/10, net 30. This means that the customer is able to deduct 2 per cent from the bill when paying within the first 10 days. If the discount is not taken, the customer must make full payment within 30 days. Not taking the discount can be costly.

Assume that the bill for a purchase order is £100.00 with the terms 2/10, net 30. This means that the supplier can pay £98.00 up to the tenth day or £100.00 at 30 days. If the cash discount is not taken, it means having the use of £98.00 for 20 days, at a £2.00 fee. This is equivalent to an annual cost of 36.72 per cent, calculated as follows.

$$\text{Cost of not taking cash discount} = \frac{\text{Discount (\%)}}{(100 - \text{discount})} \times \frac{360}{(\text{Final due date} - \text{discount period})}.$$

For this example the cost of not taking the cash discount is:

$$\frac{2}{(100-2)} \times \frac{360}{(30-10)} = \frac{2}{98} \times \frac{360}{20}$$
$$= 2.04\% \times 18$$
$$= 36.72\%.$$

At this high rate it would be better to take the discount and borrow money elsewhere.

There may be no credit terms offered and the buyer pays for goods after say 60 days from receipt of invoice. In the food industry in France, payment terms are 30 days for perishable food and 20 days for live animals and fresh meat.

Large purchased items

For large items it may be that the buyer gives money up front to the supplier before his production starts. Alternatively, progress payments might be made, for example:

- 10 per cent of the cost is paid before fabrication starts;
- 50 per cent is paid halfway;
- 85 per cent is paid on completion.

A holdback of, say, 15 per cent (common in the construction industry) is held by the buyer until it is sure the item(s) conform to specifications.

Other types of purchase orders

Two other approaches to purchasing include the use of the following instruments.

Blanket purchase order

When materials are purchased in high volume and continuously – steel pipe, fittings, glass and the like – a purchaser issues a blanket purchase order, which may cover a year. When the materials are needed, a release order is sent to the supplier. This procedure allows organizations to tie up suppliers for long-term arrangements.

Open purchase orders

For small purchases or consumable supplies like paper, pencils or work gloves, these are often purchased from the petty cash of the department using open purchase orders.

Electronic Data Interchange

More and more companies are using Electronic Data Interchange (EDI) in purchasing. Order transactions are made by computer linkup between client and supplier. See further Chapter 17, *Managing the Supply Chain*.

VALUE ANALYSIS OR VALUE ENGINEERING

Companies are continually examining ways to reduce purchasing costs and value engineering, or value analysis, has this ultimate objective. It is a study of the function of purchased materials to see whether, without impairing use or performance, specifications can be modified in order to reduce cost. The concept of value analysis was developed during World War II by Larry D. Miles of General Electric. Under wartime conditions, studies were continually made to see if alternative materials could be used for components and assemblies because those specified were either expensive or difficult to obtain (see also Chapter 6, *Design of the Product*).

Function of a product

Value analysis attacks two aspects of a product:

- the use function, or the ability of the product to perform according to specifications;
- the aesthetic function, or the appearance or style of the product.

Value analysis is easier to apply to industrial products because the client is principally interested in the product performing correctly, rather than its appearance. In contrast, consumer products (foods, household appliances, automobiles) are often purchased according to their appearance, where the aesthetic function is a marketing tool. Even though changing the aesthetic function may dramatically lower the cost, it may also markedly reduce the sale. (Who would buy Chanel perfume in a simple plastic bottle?)

Considerations for a value analysis

Purchasing people work alongside technical personnel in carrying out a value analysis. Points to be considered, as illustrated in Figure 16.14 might include:

- Could a cheaper part or material be used (for example, plastic instead of metal)?
- Can the component be eliminated without impairing the operation of the assembled unit (for example, replacing the corner window in automobiles with a single window)?

- Is the function necessary?
- Could the function of two or more parts or components be performed by a single part at a lower cost (for example, one flexible tube in a vacuum cleaner, instead of several steel tubes that have to be 'sleeved' together)?
- Is the cost of the part in line with its function? (For example, would carbon steel be suitable in place of more expensive stainless steel?
- Can the part be simplified?
- Could product specifications be relaxed so that the part can be produced at lower cost?
- Could standard parts be substituted for custommade parts (for example, a standard automobile injection system to serve many types of engines)?
- Can the weight be reduced by redesign, or by using different materials? This would reduce not only production costs, but also transportation costs.
- Can the packaging volume be reduced, for the same protection of the item?

Steps in carrying out a value analysis

Conducting a value analysis would proceed as follows:

1 Establish the objectives (the ultimate aim is to reduce the cost of the purchased product).
2 Constitute a multidisciplinary team from Marketing, Sales, Production, Cost control, Suppliers and Purchasing; the last would be the team leaders.
3 Analyse the production process of the supplying company. This would include decoupling the cost price at each step of the production process.
4 Analyse the use of the product at the purchaser's company, phase by phase.
5 Decompose and analyse the various characteristics of the purchased product, applying a weighting coefficient to each according to its importance. Characteristics would include physical (size, shape, form), chemical composition, use, taste (in the case of food) and preparation.
6 Hold a creative brainstorming session to explore all alternative possibilities, with the team having no preconceived ideas.
7 Sort the ideas and establish the cost of each.
8 Select the best alternative.
9 Develop a plan for implementing the change.

Increasing use of plastics

Comparison of today's products with those of earlier periods shows that there has been a significant increase in the purchase of plastic components to replace metal,

Figure 16.14 Value analysis.

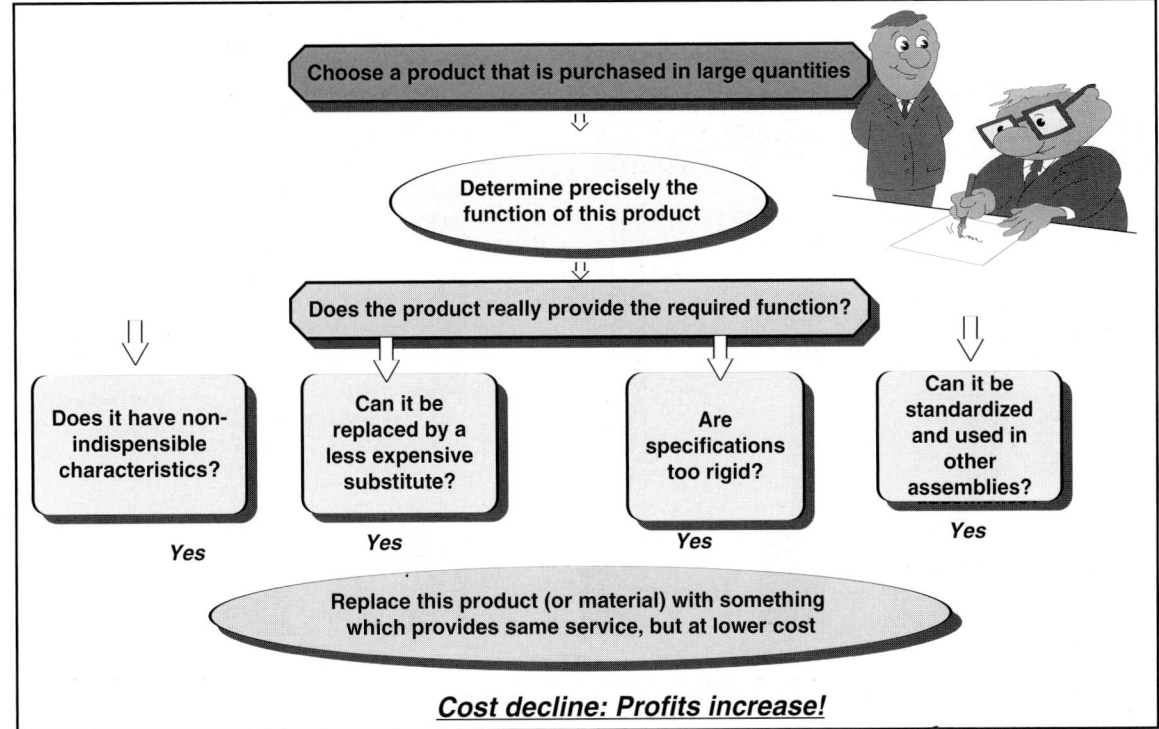

Choose a product that is purchased in large quantities

Determine precisely the function of this product

Does the product really provide the required function?

Does it have non-indispensible characteristics?

Can it be replaced by a less expensive substitute?

Are specifications too rigid?

Can it be standardized and used in other assemblies?

Yes   *Yes*   *Yes*   *Yes*

Replace this product (or material) with something which provides same service, but at lower cost

Cost decline: Profits increase!

glass and wood. Plastic is cheaper, lighter and often easier to mould and shape. As Figure 16.15, already presented in Figure 5.4 in Chapter 5, *An Environmental Balance*, shows, plastic use has increased to the detriment of steel. A typical product example is the automobile petrol filler cap, which is most often now made of one-piece plastic. Previously, it was steel, with a metal shaft, steel spring cap and rubber gaskets.

Weight reduction

Even where materials cannot be replaced, there has been a significant improvement in the technology to reduce the unit weight of material. For example, glass is still used for wine, milk, beer and other food products, but, as Figure 16.6 illustrates, the weight of glass in bottles is now some 45 per cent of the weight in a similar product before 1939.[12]

Frequency of a value analysis

Technology is constantly changing and companies need to make a periodic value analysis for their manufactured and purchased products. Every year is a time frame used by several European companies.

JUST-IN-TIME PURCHASING

Essential elements

If a company is operating in a just-in-time (JIT) mode (see Chapter 15, *Lean Production and Just-in-Time*), then JIT must apply to purchasing. Essential elements of purchasing, in order for just-in-time to be effective are the following.

Long-term relationships

Firms develop a network of long-term contracts with a few suppliers rather than short-term contracts with many suppliers. The Japanese call these subcontractor networks, and refer to suppliers as co-producers. Having few suppliers keeps ordering costs low and the networks build trust between buying and supplying firms, as well as providing dependable supplies of raw material and parts. Repeat business is awarded to the same suppliers, with competitive business normally limited to new parts. A buying firm continually evaluates the suppliers, so that they keep competitive, and any vertical integration with a supplier is avoided. The suppliers are encouraged by the buying company also to operate under just-in-time and to extend JIT methods to their own suppliers.

Figure 16.15 Automobile ingredients.

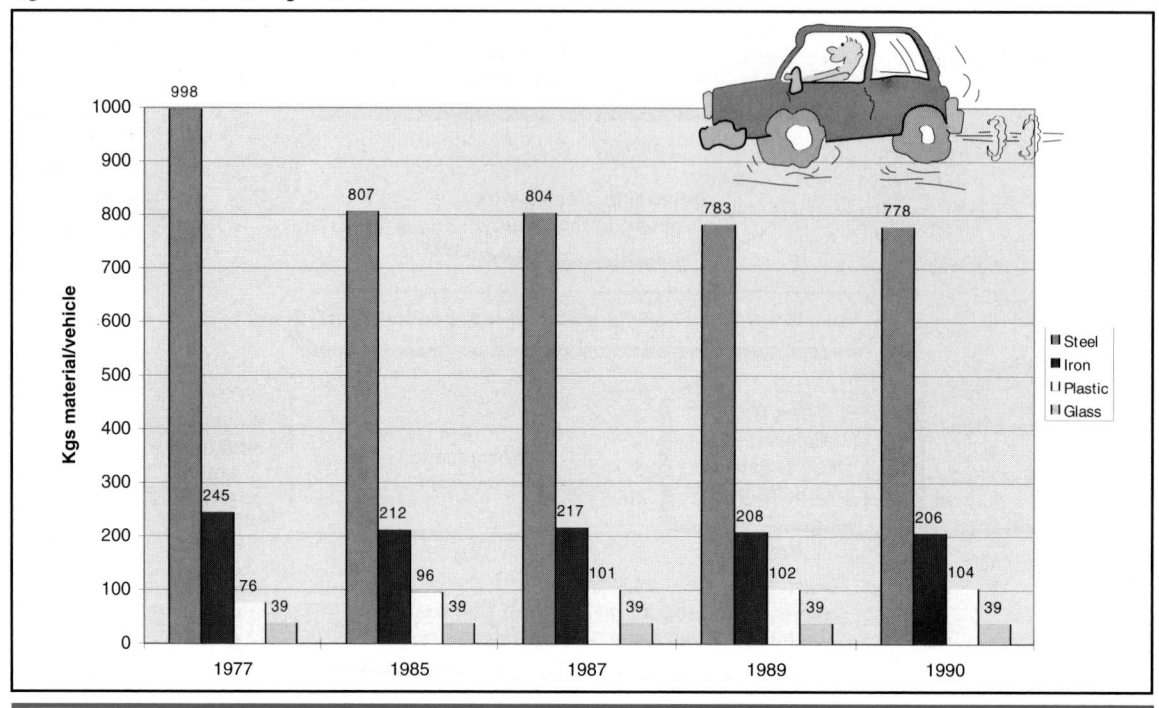

Figure 16.16 Weight of a glass milk bottle.

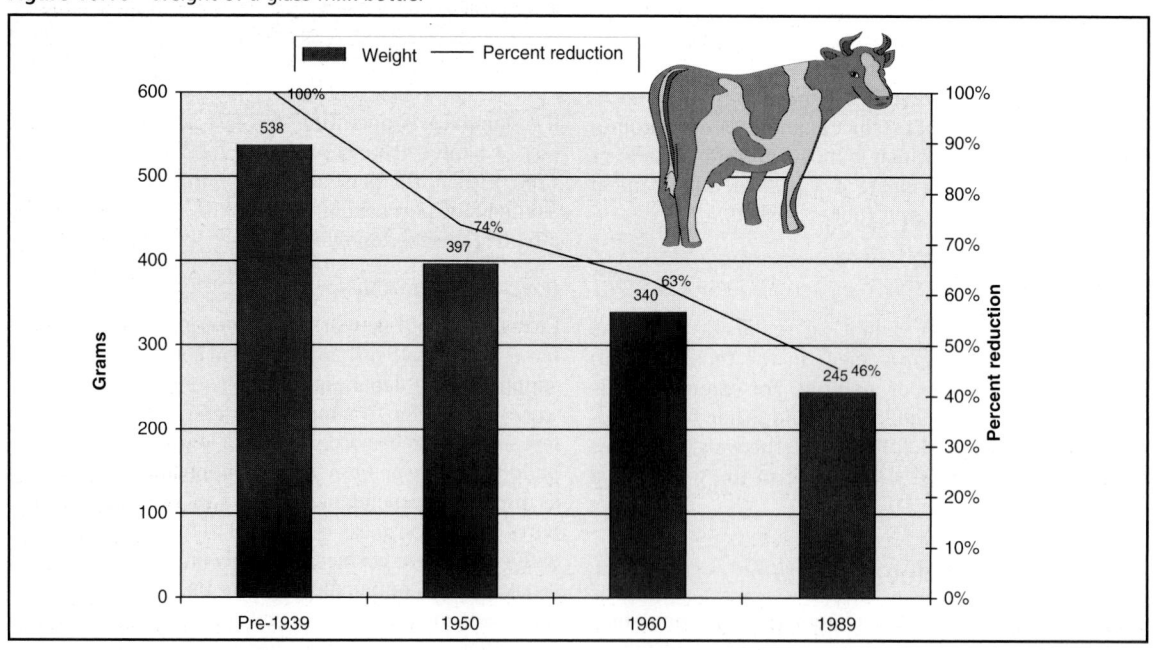

Proximity

To manage just-in-time purchasing better, companies may have a policy that suppliers must be located near the buying firm's factory so that they can deliver small orders throughout the production day; thus, lead times are shorter and more reliable. Parts, in exact quantities, are delivered in small standard-size containers with a minimum of paperwork. This keeps inventories low. At Renault, France, 60 per cent (in value) of the purchased items are delivered daily. However, for some companies proximity may not be a requirement. In this case, the company would analyse the risk in having a 'distant' supplier and develop an appropriate inventory policy.

Quality

Since suppliers have a long-term relationship with the buying firms, and because parts are delivered in small lots, quality of purchased materials tends to be high. The buying firm should work closely with the supplier to improve quality and should impose just the necessary product specifications. Further, the suppliers should be encouraged to use statistical process control rather than inspection of lots and to use company-owned or contract transport, rather than common carriers, to permit easy control of the material.

Risk

Companies need to analyse the risk involved in implementing a just-in-time policy. For example, with just-in-time in place, what would be the outcome on production if purchased parts were late as a result of accidents, strikes or supplier equipment malfunctions?

Responsibility

In just-in-time it must be clear who is responsible for initiating the delivery of the purchased product – the production centre or the buyer. Without clear delineation of responsibility the supply chain can be broken. The article given in Box 16.2 illustrates how far some companies are extending their purchasing activities to a just-in-time operation.[13]

SUPPLIERS AS SUBCONTRACTORS

The line differentiating a supplier and a subcontractor is not always evident for organizations. Generally a subcontractor is a third party who produces a customized product, or a service, for a firm and there is a specific contract between the two parties, detailing the work, the delivery date and price. For example, Rolls Royce is a subcontractor to Airbus for an Airbus 300 aircraft engine. A supplier, on the other hand, often supplies standard products to firms and there may be no contract, just a purchase requisition. For example, Guilbert, a European supplier of office material, provides diskettes, paper and office supplies to Airbus.

Employing subcontractors can be considered a purchasing function, since one is purchasing the services of a third party. Selection of the right subcontractor is important, as poor quality subcontracted work can have a negative client perception on the quality of the final assembled product.

Evaluating subcontractors

Firms use checksheets to evaluate subcontractors, similar to those for suppliers. Table 16.6 gives examples of the criteria in a checksheet used by Hewlett Packard, a manufacturer of computer components, where the subcontractor evaluation is made jointly by engineers and those in purchasing.[14] The criterion, Environment is one of the factors that is becoming more important for firms in subcontractor selection.

Table 16.6 Examples of criteria used in evaluating subcontractors

Criterion	Definition
T – Technology	Ability of the subcontractor to provide the necessary technical expertise
Q – Quality	The level of the quality of the work performed
R – Responsiveness	Is the subcontractor a viable concern in the long term?
D – Delivery	Ability of the subcontractor to accept, and respect, delivery dates
C – Cost	Cost, or the price, of the services performed
E – Environment	Verification that the subcontractor respects environmental regulations and uses non-toxic materials where possible; also that products are recyclable.

Proportion of work performed by subcontractors

Judgements are often made that a subcontractor, or supplier, to a client should limit the proportion of his business with any one entity to, say, 20 per cent. The reason is that if the figure is higher than this, the subcontractor, or supplier, becomes too dependent on one client, in which case the buyer can put pressure on the subcontractor to reduce his price if he wants to retain the buyer's business. Furthermore, if the client goes out of business, then the subcontractor will be in a difficult situation.

Box 16.2 Strange bedfellows. Some companies let suppliers work on site and even place orders. Both sides can save money but run serious risks of conflicts of interest. Much data no longer secret. By Fred R. Bleakley, Staff Reporter.

In the brave new world of procurement, some customers are treating their suppliers almost like their own employees.

Vendor sales representatives have desks next to the factory floor. Their badges let them roam wherever they choose, attend production-status meetings, stop by the research lab and click computers onto sales forecasts. Then, they can write a sales order for which the customer is billed.

It's called JIT II, the 1990s version of just-in-time inventory control. The original just-in-time practice can stir up hostility by putting pressure on suppliers; JIT II is designed to create harmony and efficiencies for both sides. Based on sharing of previously guarded data, such as up-to-the-minute sales forecasts, JIT II relies heavily on trust since the companies could face serious conflicts of interest.

Significant Risks

However, if not done right, it can cause many problems, says Lance Dixon, director of purchasing at Bose Corp. He should know. While at the Framingham, Massachusetts, maker of high-fidelity systems in the late 1980s, he fathered the idea. He also has helped set up JIT II programs at other companies, including International Business Machines Corp. and Ingersoll-Rand Co.

Most JIT II relationships go through a rocky period because traditional mistrust and hard-nosed negotiations over price and bulk purchases linger on. Other attempts don't get off the drawing board; customers and suppliers alike worry about releasing too much confidential information or technology.

In Europe, JIT II hasn't yet taken off as a new management fad – and it may never take off. Contrary to many U.S. manufacturers, European companies have stuck to close, long-term relationships with their suppliers.

JIT II "isn't felt to be necessary over here," says Hans Van der Hoop, a consultant in logistics and procurement based in Rotterdam. "Here we tend to keep our suppliers – sometimes too long – but it works," he says. In the U.S., he points out, manufacturers switch suppliers far more easily and links between parties aren't seen as much as a business partnership.

Improved Logistics

Instead of JIT II, many companies with operations in Europe – and global U.S.-based companies in particular – are currently focusing their efforts on improved logistics to cut down costs and boost efficiency. Rather than work more closely with their suppliers, Mr. Van der Hoop says, European-based manufacturers are seeking to work more closely with the transporters who ship the parts to the assembly plant, even inviting them to set up offices in-house.

As a result, hundreds of corporations in the past few years have established so-called European logistics centers, giant warehouses that combine distribution with manufacturing, marketing and other activities. Most of these logistics centers are located in the Netherlands, Belgium or Western Germany, within a hundred kilometers or so of the major harbors of Rotterdam or Antwerp to speed up delivery times and cut back on inventories.

In the U.S., however, JIT II is coming into its own – though it's not without its critics.

Karen Dale, who oversees $180 million of orders as manager of central purchasing of office supplies for Honeywell Inc., didn't like the idea of in-house suppliers when her boss first suggested it two years ago. "My concern was how to keep things confidential," she says. "They might overhear conversations about their competitors' prices or go to someone's desk at night and sift through their papers." But she now has five suppliers working with her 20 buyers and says her only problem was with one of her own buyers, who, concerned about his job security, looked for ways to show an in-plant supplier was uncompetitive. He eased up after being given other responsibilities.

Suppliers' Hazard

Suppliers also can be at risk because they may be asked to reveal their costs. "All of a sudden, a supplier can be at the mercy of its customer trying to squeeze his profit margin," says Patrick Byrne, a management consultant at A.T. Kearney Inc. of Chicago.

But despite all the potential pitfalls, Michael Hammer, who recently co-authored a bestseller on corporate "re-engineering," believes that JIT II is more than a passing fad because it can be highly effective. He views it as the next wave of re-engineering, which broke down barriers between departments. Now, he says, barriers to outside suppliers are falling as well.

Bose's Mr. Dixon came up with JIT II to make his procurement department more productive. By allowing suppliers into the plant to order from themselves, he saw the potential to reduce inventories, eliminate redundant purchasing agents and get cost-saving tips from having suppliers more familiar with Bose. Because suppliers are expected to treat their own vendors in the new way, they help form a supply chain that cuts costs all along the line.

Suppliers such as G & F Industries Inc., which makes plastic components, were initially leery about dedicating a full-time employee to Bose. But, says John Argitis, G & F's president, "Lance promised he wouldn't hire him away, and he told us we'd get more business." JIT II suppliers at other companies say that they also get a better bead on their own competitors and that such information can be used in customer relationships elsewhere.

But Mr. Dixon, who has written a new paperback, 'JIT II: Revolution in Buying and Selling," warns that buyers should forget about cost savings from low inventory when a supplier isn't geared to produce in sync. Such a situation can turn into just a shell game of who holds the goods, he says. Or suppliers might try to give preferred service to more customers than it can handle. And if a supplier's goods become outmoded, it isn't as easy to end a JIT II relationship as one that is at arm's length.

To protect against all the things that can go wrong, Mr. Dixon screens in-plant suppliers and makes them sign confidentiality agreements and agree to guidelines. Purchases over a certain amount need Bose approval. Only once in seven years has a supplier's representative exceeded the limit without authority; he was replaced at Bose.

Mr. Hammer also says companies should be wary. A supplier may decide to ship a lot of goods to improve its numbers for the quarter, he says, "or you could turn over continuous replenishment to a clown who ships the wrong stuff or is out of stock." Too often, he adds, "Senior guys hug and kiss, but purchasing managers still feel suppliers are there to get kicked and to negotiate price."

Severing Ties

Indeed, some partnering relationships that resemble JIT II have collapsed. Ball Corp. always knew just how many jars to make for the baby-food factories of Gerber Products Co. in Asheville, North Carolina; with its jar plant next door, workers from both companies were in each others' space every day. But the relationship ended last year after Gerber shopped around for a cheaper world-wide source (Ball served only the U.S. operations). Without Gerber as its main customer, Ball shut down its plant and laid off most of the 350 workers.

The U.S. General Electric Co.'s appliance division also ran into problems. It reverted to competitive bidding after finding that some preferred suppliers that had inventory on consignment weren't offering the lowest prices. A spokesman says GE won't discuss its purchasing policies.

At IBM, some suppliers operate under the mistaken notion that their willingness to commit a full-time person to a plant gives them a lock on the business, says Edward O'Donnell, manager of purchasing at the company's mid-Hudson Valley, New York, plants. "They can't understand why we are still seeking quotes on his business," he says.

Recently Mr. O'Donnell called Jack Laufer, president of North American Bolt & Screw Co., one of the in-plant suppliers. "I told him we have to test the market on pricing and he was uncomfortable with that notion," Mr. O'Donnell said. However, Mr. Laufer denies he was troubled by Mr. O'Donnell's call. "We've been their supplier for 38 years, and they test the market periodically," he says.

A Factory's System

At Honeywell's Minneapolis headquarters, even Ms. Dale and her boss, Eugene Haistings, don't go as far as their counterparts at the company's big factory 14 kilometers away at Golden. Valley, Minnesota, where thermostats and other building controls are made. Some in-plant suppliers there, such as Standard Register Co., a maker of business forms, and Packaging Corp. of America, a corrugated-box company, are permitted to place orders on Honeywell's behalf with their own competitors. At headquarters, however, "we have not reached the comfort level of placing orders outside a contract because we don't know if we will get the best price," says Mr. Haistings, the director of corporate materiel services.

Golden Valley now has on hand 15 representatives from 10 suppliers, ranging from printed materials to metals to electronics, who have their own cubicles just off the production floor. Some are technicians working on new product designs. But most are overseeing purchases for existing products, and they think more like a Honeywell employee and look around for ways to trim costs. Honeywell's payoff so far has been inventory levels measured in days rather than weeks or months, 25% fewer purchasing agents, and tips on ways to standardize some parts so they are cheaper to make.

Handling metals purchases for the plant is Tom Nord of Jos. T. Ryerson & Son, a unit of Inland Steel Industries Inc. He was recently on the phone at Honeywell contacting other suppliers to buy a single four-foot (120-centimeter) bar that his customer needed. "It might save Honeywell some money by not having it specially cut," he says. He also recently suggested a switch to a different grade of aluminum available for weekly deliveries instead of one that had to be ordered every six months and stockpiled.

Danger of Abuse

On routine business, Mr. Nord says, "It's my call what to order, when and from whom." But he and the other in-plant suppliers know that if they abuse the privilege, they and their company could lose not only Honeywell's business but their reputation in the industry.

"Someone could pull something over on us, but it wouldn't be easy," says William Grimes, head of procurement and logistics at the factory. At first, he says, he was skeptical of JIT II, but "you can't get improvement anymore simply by negotiating a better price and showing suppliers half the cards. Something else has to change."

Other companies, however, don't want their suppliers underfoot. When Apple Computer Inc. set up partnering deals with suppliers last year to reduce inventories, it gave them production and forecast data they previously didn't have. But "too many people running around would filter information they wanted to hear and get mixed signals," says Shaun Connolly, who designed the system and now is a KPMG Peat Marwick consultant.

So instead of giving suppliers space at its Fountain, Colorado, plant, Apple built a warehouse 19 kilometers away and arranged for a third party to manage it. The warehouse keeps suppliers' inventory on consignment and tracks shipments on the move, so that Apple has one system to contact if it wants to schedule a production change. Otherwise, Mr. Connolly says, "everyone has different ways of showing and receiving numbers. We'd have to have five people managing five suppliers." His system, which is saving the plant $10 million a year in inventory costs, will be rolled out at other Apple factories as well, he says.

Despite the growing pains, some companies are pushing the frontiers even further. In one version that could be dubbed JIT III, more than 100 hospitals now rely on Baxter International Inc., the drug company, to replenish virtually all of the hospitals' supplies from itself and other companies. Around the clock, Baxter personnel take products to each ward, using hand-held scanners to inform an off-site warehouse that inventories should be replenished.

Some consultants warn about expecting too much of such systems. "This isn't a magic-bullet installation," says Harold Sirkin of Boston Consulting Group Inc. "It has to be an evolutionary process that relies on a number of changed relationships."

Already, Mr. Dixon says, "many companies are using JIT II more aggressively than we who invented it." He expects that before long a buyer will inadvertently reveal next year's technology to a supplier whose parent company is a direct competitor somewhere else. "One of these days there's going to be a horror story about missing technology or missing money," he says. "It's bound to happen."

Martin du Bois in Brussels contributed to this article

Wall Street Journal Europe, 16 January 1995
Reprinted by permission of *Wall Street Journal Europe*,
© 1995 Dow Jones & Company, Inc.
All Rights Reserved Worldwide.

However, each industry should be looked at individually before percentage values are criticized or specified. In many cases, performing considerably more than 20 per cent of one's business with the same client may not be unreasonable. The following are possible reasons:

■ A client (buyer) who has developed a good long-term relationship with a subcontractor will not let this subcontractor go so easily.
■ Assume a subcontractor has 80 per cent of its business with one client, and the supplied product is strategically important to the client. In this case the client would be more willing to work closely with the subcontractor and provide assistance, such us evaluating production methods, to ensure that subcontractor quality is maintained. A client would not be prepared to do this if its subcontractor also provides component parts to other companies (some of whom may be competitors to the client).
■ A subcontractor who is aligned with a reputable client, such as a food producer to Marks and Spencer, may be happy to have a high proportion of his business, perhaps close to 100 per cent with the client. This particular client has a strong reputation for quality and provides attractive profit margins to the subcontractor. However, a supplier would need to carefully analyse the risk in its association with the client.

Closer working relationship with subcontractors

Historically, US and European companies have kept their suppliers/subcontractors at arm's length. Relationships have often been adversary and some clichés often used are:

■ 'Give them only the information you need to know'.
■ 'Be careful, they will tell the competition'.
■ 'Don't trust them'.

Now the climate has changed somewhat. Japan has for a long time had close contacts with suppliers/subcontractors and European and US companies are finding that close supplier relationships are cost-effective, lead to innovative ideas and decrease supply time, as the following two examples illustrate.[15]

Ford Motor Co.

When this US automobile manufacturer built a paint-finishing plant in Oakville, Canada, it developed an alliance with Asea Brown Boveri (ABB), rather than going through the normal bidding process. ABB's effort reduced the cost to 75 per cent of the expected amount and correspondingly reduced completion time.

Marks and Spencer

By creating an alliance with a knitwear supplier, this British retailer was able to reduce delivery from 14 weeks to a few days.

The article given as Box 16.3 illustrates how the form of working relationship is changing for some companies.[16]

Although this form of strategic alliances has its benefits, it is not to say that all companies are creating such cosy relationships with their suppliers or subcontractors. In Germany, for example, there is a tendency for the reverse approach, where Volkswagen and Opel have agreed to dismiss fewer workers in return for greater flexibility on wages and working practices and this is resulting in less subcontracting as the retained workers have to be given something to do. Instead of 'outsourcing (subcontracting) these companies are 'insourcing' (doing the work themselves). Insourcing tasks for Opel include the development of plastic parts. Volkswagen restarted the production of power-steering systems and axles.[17]

MAKE-OR-BUY

One decision for a manufacturing firm is whether to make all the components of a product completely in-house, or to purchase some assemblies or sub-assemblies from outside. It may be that the company's production department can make parts for less cost, with better quality and with faster delivery, than suppliers. Alternatively, in some cases, it may be more cost-effective to purchase the components from outside, if reliable suppliers are available.

Criteria for making

Some of the detailed reasons for making a product within the firm might include:

■ It is cheaper to manufacture within the company rather than to purchase outside.
■ The confidence in the suppliers concerning delivery time, quality and price is low.
■ There is better quality control, that cannot be obtained from suppliers.
■ There is excess capacity in work centres and making in-house will contribute to fixed costs.
■ The particular part is strategic to the company, which is concerned about divulging technology and know-how to outsiders as this may impair competitiveness.

The next manufacturing revolution is under way, and U.S. companies are bringing airplanes, cars, even kitchen stoves to market faster and cheaper by leaning on their suppliers to help engineer and bankroll new projects.

This revolution goes far beyond the changes of the 1980s, when manufacturers attacked their high labor costs by shifting production to suppliers with lower labor costs. Now, manufacturers are slashing product-development expenses by farming out the tasks to suppliers – in essence, evolving from manufacturers to orchestrators that harmonize their suppliers work.

Meanwhile, the suppliers, which once did little more than bang out parts as cheaply as possible, are hiring hundreds of engineers to staff new research-and-development departments.

Many Success Stories

Using the new approach, Whirlpool Corp. is cooking up its first gas range without hiring engineers to create the gas-burner system; instead, the design work is being done by Eaton Corp., a supplier that already makes gas valves and regulators for other appliance manufacturers. Whirlpool expects to get its new range to market several months sooner this way.

McDonnell Douglas Corp. is trimming $300 million off the $500 million cost of developing its new 100-seat jetliner by having suppliers kick in up-front tooling and development costs and by subcontracting assembly of the plane. Smiths Industries PLC of the U.K. forked out its own R&D money for a control system on Boeing Co's newest jetliner.

Chrysler Corp.'s skillful use of parts suppliers to design everything from car seats to drive shafts has enabled it to spend consistently less money than its competitors do to develop new vehicles. And increasing the role of the supplier is crucial to Volkswagen AG's cost-cutting drive, spearheaded by J. Ignacio Lopez de Arriortua, the flamboyant purchasing chief who jumped to VW from General Motors Corp. in early 1993.

The latest revolution has important implications for the U.S. economy. Just as Japan's economic potential blossomed with the help of its *keiretsu* system, which strengthens ties between manufacturers and suppliers, the sea change in the U.S. will increase American companies' international competitiveness.

Some Problems

It also makes some rough waves, however. Industrial secrets shared with other companies are more likely to slip away. Farming out more work reduces factory and engineering jobs at the manufacturers, riling their employees. And while some suppliers, adapting to a new era, are booming, many are losing business.

But with manufacturers saving money and enhancing product development, the trend looks irreversible. "In the future," says Thomas Stallkamp, Chrysler's purchasing chief, the new alliances "will still be the most important thing."

To succeed in this new world, big companies are abandoning some cherished assumptions. Absolute control is no longer paramount, and the common practice of pitting suppliers to bid against each other is being abandoned in favor of longer-term commitments to single suppliers. Manufacturers are also bringing suppliers on board much earlier in the design process, at times even inviting them to help dream up a new product.

"We now realize that the people who make these components know a lot more about it than we do," says Ronald Woodard, president of commercial-airplane production for Boeing. "It's hard to believe," he adds with a laugh.

An Obvious Truth

In one way, American industry has awakened to a truth that seems obvious in hindsight: The maker of a part should be able to conceive a new one more cheaply than the final assembler, which is responsible for the entire product. Using suppliers for engineering also enables manufacturers to get more products out the door without themselves adding engineers. And because a supplier can sell parts to an entire industry, the system becomes a vehicle for transferring new techniques from one manufacturer to another.

In the Detroit research center of Johnson Controls Inc., a major supplier of automotive seats, a computer-operated shaking machine subjects the seats to the bumps and bangs encountered on a test track. In a nearby room, one Johnson team is devising seats for Chrysler's next generation of midsize cars – while teams in other rooms are doing the same job for Ford Motor Co., GM, Toyota Motor Corp. and the Mercedes-Benz unit of Daimler-Benz AG, often without any of the manufacturers' employees present. All that is a big reason Johnson Controls' automotive sales soared to $2.87 billion in its fiscal year ended Sept. 30 from just $1.24 billion in fiscal 1991.

The downside: As a result of Chrysler's consolidation of its suppliers, the auto maker dropped Douglas & Lomason Co., a Johnson Controls rival, as a supplier of finished seats. The increased use of suppliers has also roiled the United Auto Workers union, precipitating short strikes by UAW-represented engineering workers last June at Chrysler's and GM's engineering centers near Detroit. "We feel the suppliers are taking our jobs," says Mike VanAcker, a UAW official who represents Chrysler technical workers.

Much the same has happened in the airliner industry. Seattle-based Boeing recently said Rockwell International Corp. would produce large wing sections for its newly upgraded 737 jetliners.

Unionized machinists at Boeing – their ranks already decimated by more than 24,000 job cuts at the company in recent years – angrily protested the contract. Boeing's union engineers generally favor efficiency gains that are good for the company, says Charles Bofferding, president of the 24,200-member Seattle Professional Engineering Employees Association, though they are wary of potential job losses and "loading-up design work on the information highway and trucking it" to other companies and countries.

For Rockwell, the contract will bring more than 300 factory jobs to its Tulsa, Oklahoma, aircraft-parts operation, which has lost about 1,000 jobs in the past five years as commercial-airplane orders weakened. To land the $450 million contract, Rockwell engineers spent months in Seattle co-designing the parts.

Breakthrough Project

The roots of Rockwell's new intimacy with Boeing were put down four years ago when Boeing began developing its all-new 777. The 300-passenger airliner, designed entirely on computers, is the first commercial jet devised by Boeing "design-build teams" that included suppliers and airline managers.

Britain's Smiths Industries, a longtime supplier to the U.S. aerospace industry, contributed a high-tech control system that cuts down on Boeing's overall construction costs and makes its planes cheaper to fly. In return for its R&D investment in developing a unique product, Smiths gets a captive customer in Boeing and enjoys relatively high margins for a troubled industry.

When the first 777 came off the assembly line last year, parts snapped together so neatly that its nose-to-tail measurement was off less than 23/1000 of an inch from design goals. Boeing believes it has eliminated up to half the costly parts "rework" that, in the past, has plagued new planes. And suppliers note that many key parts are being built in half the order-to-delivery "cycle time" of earlier Boeing models.

This progress was achieved not simply because of the computer links but because of the "mutual respect" and "trust" of those who pulled the plane together, says Boeing's John Marchese, who oversees ties with 500 suppliers on the 777 program. "The way everybody attacks a problem is unprecedented," he adds.

Boeing has applied the same principle to its military work, including its development of the F-22 fighter with Lockheed Corp. Not only have subcontractors Westinghouse Electric Corp. and Texas Instruments Inc. been deeply involved in designing the F-22's advanced radar systems, they also have been entrusted with keeping the U.S. air force up to speed on progress instead of having Boeing and Lockheed "reserving that role for themselves," says Lew Miller, who oversees a $640 million radar contract for Westinghouse.

Under the old, "hierarchical" system, Mr. Miller adds, the subcontractors would simply have been "given a specification and monitored." The new arrangement "makes us feel like part of the team."

Reducing the Bills

Of course, manufacturers are betting that this esprit de corps will translate into real savings. Manufacturers that properly incorporate suppliers into their product-development process can cut their bills for purchased parts and services by as much as 30%, according to A.T. Kearney Inc., a Chicago consulting firm. That's a huge savings, for purchased parts and services typically account for 50% to 70% of manufacturers' total costs.

A major reason suppliers can make parts more cheaply is that they can spread their engineering costs much more efficiently than a final assembler.

For example, a car maker might have a handful of engineers to make universal joints, the flexible couplings that link together segments of a drive shaft. But Dana Corp., a major supplier of truck axles, has an entire 60-engineer laboratory near Toledo dedicated to U-joints. Using a computer-aided design system hooked up to a vast database of some 18,000 existing U-joint parts, Dana can design new U-joints cheaply and quickly, often using off-the-shelf parts. "We can build a prototype in a matter of hours," says Leon W. Valencic, director of engineering for Dana's universal-joint division.

Saving time is a top priority for Mr. Lopez at VW, which also is focusing on reducing the number of its suppliers while increasing the depth of services performed by the suppliers. The emphasis is on getting suppliers to become "system-suppliers," who provide not just parts but fully-assembled units. Indeed, Mr. Lopez's "dream factory" concept, in which a car can be assembled in as little as six hours, hinges on smart use of system suppliers who would deliver major pre-assembled portions of the car.

At Mercedes-Benz AG, Chairman Helmut Werner has made it a corporate goal to reduce the amount of the car manufactured in-house in an effort to close the price gap between Mercedes and its Japanese competitors. Mr. Warner says he has reduced the portion of a car produced in-house to 40% from 45% and will continue to cut it.

Deluxe sports-car maker Porsche AG is applying much of the same supplier philosophy. When its new model generation goes into production in 1996, the number of suppliers will be slashed to just 300 from around 900.

A New Risk

Despite the cost savings, however, supplier partnerships present a new risk to manufacturers: Sensitive information on such subjects as pricing, profit margins and market strategies must be shared from the outset.

This summer, Ford got so irritated about leaks from its suppliers about future products that it fired off a letter warning newspapers that any information given to them about Ford was confidential. "It's very easy to reveal confidential information innocently," Ford wrote, "that ultimately causes damage."

A.T. Kearney counsels companies to think long and hard before turning to suppliers for engineering help. "Before doing any of that, you've really got to look inside the company and say, 'What's the core thing we do and how do we distinguish ourself from our competitors?'" says Tom Slaight, an A.T. Kearney efficiency expert. "If you give it all away, you pretty much have no edge in the marketplace."

He cites one cost-cutting move that backfired miserably: In the 1960s, the then-dominant U.S. television industry gave the technology to build picture tubes to low-cost Asian suppliers; a few years later, the Asians began manufacturing entire TV sets, and the U.S. industry nearly went out of business.

Fears of such a fate permeate engineering and machinist ranks at Boeing, which for the past decade has let Japanese suppliers get steadily closer to its fuselage-design practices on such wide-body jets as the twin-engine 767 and the newer 777. Boeing has long advocated the partnerships as a way to keep a grip on the Japanese while encouraging airliner sales in Japan, but machinists fear that Boeing is helping rev up an Asian aircraft industry. Privately, some Boeing engineers concede as much – and note that they monitor incidents in which they think Japanese engineering trainees in Seattle are doing too much snooping through design documents.

St. Louis-based McDonnell Douglas, which historically has limited its overseas supplier relationships, followed Boeing's lead in setting up the supply chain for the new MD-95 it hopes to produce by 1998. The plane maker signed Korean, Japanese, Italian and British companies to build much of the aircraft in hopes of winning more orders from the countries' carriers. In the end, says McDonnell Douglas's new chief executive, Harry Stonecipher, "I'm going to play in more markets because of whom I chose as suppliers."

McDonnell Douglas also took supplier reliance a step further: It cut its $500 million share of development costs for the jet to just $200 million by requiring suppliers to cover their own tooling costs and other up-front expenses. And it tapped Dalfort Aviation Inc., a Dallas subcontractor, to put the plane together, for the first time sending the work outside its own layoff-wracked factories in Long Beach.

That move angered local and state politicians, and Mr. Stonecipher moved to soothe them by saying the company is still committed to California" for lead engineering and for assembly of other planes.

Yet the bottom line is that the Dalfort contract will save McDonnell Douglas $40 million to $50 million. Moreover, Mr. Stonecipher says, the contract suggests "we could build the whole airplane that way."

Brian Coleman and Audrey Choi contributed to this article.

- Purchasing would involve layoffs within the organization, which would have a negative impact on the labour force.
- There is concern about supplier collusion (even though illegal) regarding price, specifications, delivery of product and firm's business.
- Purchasing the product would involve eliminating specialized know-how, meaning that in the long run the firm would lose its competitiveness.
- Excessive time is needed to find a supplier, work with him and make initial tests, in order to obtain the desired product.
- There is a concern about legal problems if the supplied part does not meet specifications. (In the USA legal ramifications can affect the whole supply chain, even if a company did not make the part, but used a purchased part in an assembly.)

Criteria for purchasing

The criteria for purchasing, some of which are obviously the antithesis of the criteria for making, are as follows:

- It is overall less expensive to purchase outside than to make within the company.
- There is a high confidence in the reliability of the suppliers.
- It is not possible to produce in-house because the product is protected by patent rights.
- There is insufficient machine and labour capacity in-house to manufacture.
- To make would mean adding additional capacity in terms of labour, machine and surface area and the long-term need for this additional capacity is uncertain.
- By purchasing, the investment in inventory is reduced and the firm's policy is to have the supplier

hold inventory until it is needed (just-in-time for the firm).

- There will be more flexibility with the production operation when demand requirements are unclear. Flexibility is increased if there are several suitable suppliers.
- The supplies of raw materials to make the necessary part are not readily available.
- Purchasing enhances the company's cash position, enabling it to enact other strategies, such as acquisitions, capital improvements and increase dividend payments.
- The product is relatively simple and producing within the company would add very little value to the operation.

Opposite policies

Two European companies that manufacture electrical related products have opposite policies regarding make and buy.

Merlin Gerin

Merlin Gerin in Grenoble, France, (a subsidiary of the Group Schneider) manufactures industrial electrical transformers, distributors and circuit breakers. It purchases most of its components from outside and Merlin Gerin performs the assembly work, which it considers is the strategic activity for the product. The company has over 10 500 suppliers. Its policy is that by resorting to sub-contractors, and suppliers it maintains a liquid base for acquisitions if necessary.

Le Grand

Le Grand in Limoges, France, makes plugs, switches, fuses and other electrical products for home and industrial use for sale throughout Europe. It has a policy of machining, manufacturing and assembling the products itself.

Break-even analysis

A quantitative method for deciding whether to make or buy is to use a break-even analysis. This approach determines at what quantity of units the total cost to purchase is equal to the cost of producing, or the break-even quantity. Below this break-even value it is cheaper to purchase and above it is cheaper to produce. Table 16.7 gives a simple illustration.

Table 16.7   Example of break-even analysis

Units are purchased	
Price per unit (no price discounts)	$20.00
Units are made	
Variable cost per unit (materials, labour)	$15.00
Fixed cost (machines, buildings, overhead)	$20 000
Level of units required is x	
Production cost for x units is sum of	
fixed and variable cost	20 000 + 15x
Purchase cost for x units	20x

There is a break-even point when total production cost equals total purchase cost:

$$20x = 20\,000 + 15x$$
$$5x = 20\,000$$
$$x = 4000.$$

That is, the break-even point is at 4000 units. Thus, based strictly on this quantitative analysis, the decision would be to purchase when less than 4000 units are needed and produce when more than 4000 units are needed. If only variable costs were considered, then in this situation it is always cheaper to produce than to buy with a difference of $5 per unit. However, this is not the case when fixed costs are added and it is only at 4000 units that the total difference between purchase price and production cost that fixed costs are absorbed. Figure 16.17 shows how the cost-curve picture changes according to the number of units required.

Caution

The analysis has to be treated with caution since, if a firm already has in place some fixed capacity that is available for production, yet it purchases from outside, there is no contribution to the cost of this fixed capacity (see also Chapter 25, *Financial Analysis*). And, of course, a break-even situation only occurs if variable costs per unit are less than the purchase price per unit.

A new product

Assume that a company is considering a introducing a new product onto the market and a make-or-buy analysis indicates that making is less expensive. However, this may not be the best strategy because the new product may not succeed. If the company has invested in

Figure 16.17   Break-even point.

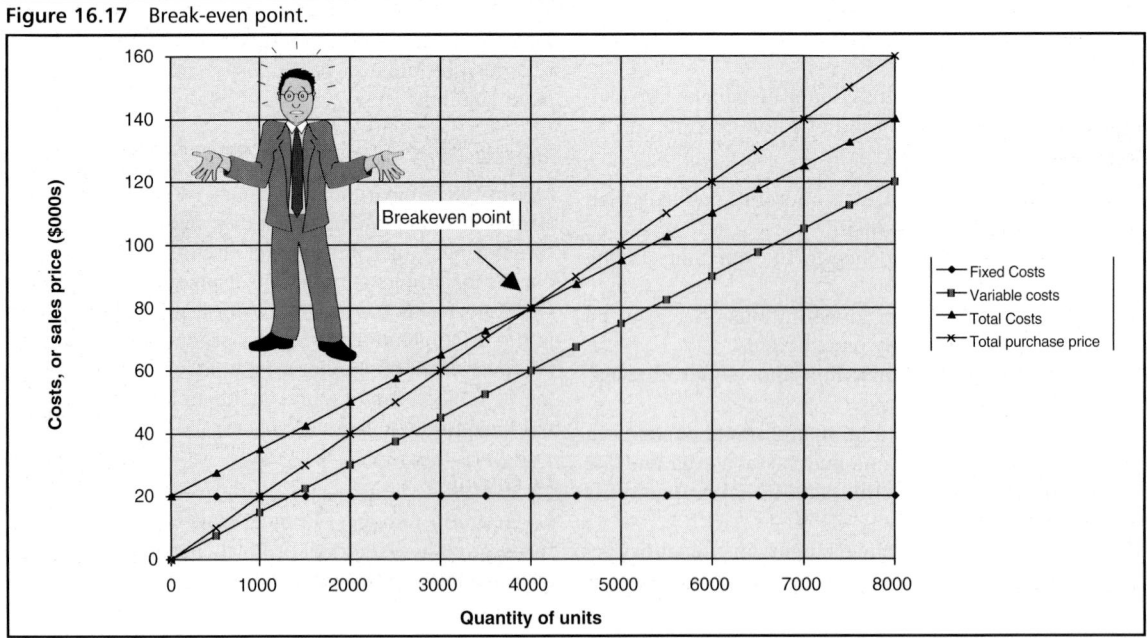

new production equipment, it can be costly. A better strategy might be:

- Initially to buy (even though the price is higher, there is less long-term financial risk).
- See if the product is successful on the market place.
- If successful, make the necessary investment to be able to make.

Food company

This was the type of strategy adopted in 1991 by a major European food company which wanted to introduce a new food product on the market. Its approach was as follows:

- It negotiated a contract with a company in England to supply the purchased products over two years.

- In the contract, the supplier company furnished the product for two years. And, for two years after that, it had the option to supply the client company exclusively.
- After it was proven that the product was a success, the food company invested in the necessary equipment to make the product itself.

The danger with this type of strategy is that a supplier company, at the end of the contractual period, could become a competitor.

The following worked example, *Pistons*, gives a more detailed calculation of a make or buy decision incorporating many of the individual costs related to manufacturing.

WORKED EXAMPLE: PISTONS

Situation

The Brulschmerg company, in the Paris region of France, manufactures industrial meters for gas distribution. One of the subassemblies for these meters is an aluminium piston that rotates in a cast bronze cylinder. In each piston there are eight rubber flanges, and 16 small steel screws. Brulschmerg wishes to analyse the cost associated with producing a quantity of 15 000 pistons in-house or purchasing this same quantity from a reliable supplier. The unit cost to purchase outside is FF52.20.

The following is the production data available for the work centre:

- The work centre operates on three shifts.
- Four operators work in the operation (cutting, turning, polishing and finishing).
- The four operators can produce 20 pistons per hour.

The costs are given in Table 16.8. The fixed overhead allocated to this operation is FF95 000 regardless of the production level. This includes administrative costs, sales cost, taxes, insurance, preventative maintenance costs and depreciation of equipment,

Table 16.8 Brulschmerg – Internal costs for the break-even analysis

Labour costs	
Labour rate per hour (FF)	70.00
Employer social charges (per cent)	18.50
Material costs	
Aluminium tubing (FF/m)	10.50
Rubber flanges (FF/unit)	0.75
Steel bolts (FF/unit)	0.05
Variable overhead	
Energy cost for work centre (per shift)	400.00
Work centre supervision (FF/shift)	2500.00
Tool centre charges (FF/shift)	1250.00
Warehousing (percentage of total material costs)	2.00

Cutting/lubricating fluids (FF/finished unit)	0.15
Other (FF/unit)	0.25

Design information for pistons	
Aluminium tubing (m/unit)	0.55
Rubber flanges (per unit)	8
Steel bolts (per unit)	16

Required

1 Based on the data provided, which would be the preferred strategy for Brulschmerg?
2 What are other consideration before a final decision is made?
3 Is there any production level at which the strategy might change?

Solution

1 Preferred strategy for Brulschmerg
The calculations, together with the procedures, using Excel, are given in Figure 16.18. At a quantity of 15 000 pistons it would be cheaper to buy from outside (FF783 000 to purchase as opposed to FF931 310 to produce).
2 Other considerations before a final decision is made:
- Fixed costs have been allocated to this production (they have to be absorbed whether the pistons are produced or not). Thus, even though purchasing is cheaper, producing in-house contributes to fixed overhead. It may not always be meaningful to consider fixed overheads in decision-making such as this.
- Production employs four people in the work centre. What would happen to these people if pistons were purchased? Is there other work, or would they be idle?
- To produce assumes that there is sufficient capacity available. If the work centre is heavily loaded with work then this might strengthen a decision to purchase
3 Production level at which the strategy might change
There is no break-even level. It will always be cheaper to purchase (Figure 16.19).

Figure 16.18 Brulschmerg – piston manufacture.

	A	B	C	D
			Calculation method	*Value*
1		**Variable Labour Costs**		
2		Labour rate per hour, FF	given	70.00
3		Employer social charges, %	given	18.50
4		Total labour rate	(D-2)+(D-2)*(D-3)	82.95
5				
6		**Variable Material Costs**		
7		Aluminium tubing, FF/meter	purchase cost	10.50
8		Rubber flanges, FF/unit	purchase cost	0.75
9		Steel bolts, FF/unit	purchase cost	0.05
10				
11		**Variable Overhead**		
12		Energy cost for work centre, per shift	from past data	400.00
13		Work centre supervision, FF/shift	from past data	2 500.00
14		Tool centre charges, FF/shift	from past data	1 250.00
15		Warehousing, % of total material costs	from past data	2.00
16		Cutting/lubricating fluids, FF/finished unit	from past data	0.15
17		Other, FF/unit	from past data	0.25
18				
19		**Allocated Fixed Overhead**	allocated	95 000.00
20				
21		Purchase price, FF/unit	given	52.20
22		Quantity required	client needs	15 000
23				
24		**Design information**		
25		Aluminium tubing, metres/unit	given	0.55
26		Rubber flangers, per unit	given	8
27		Steel bolts per unit	given	16
28				
29		**Material cost/unit**		
30		Aluminium tubing	(D-11)*(D-25)	5.78
31		Rubber flanges	(D-12)*(D-26)	6.00
32		Steel bolts	(D-13)*(D-27)	0.80
33		*Total cost/unit*	(D-30)+(D-31)+(D-32)	12.58
34		**Total Material Cost**	(D-33)*(D-26)	188 625.00
35				
36		**Production**		
37		Operators per unit	given	4
38		Production rate, units/hour	given	20
39		Time for production, hrs	(D-22)/(D-42)	750.00
40		Shifts for production (8 h/shift)	(D-39)/8	93.75
41		Time for production, days (3 shifts)	(D-44)/3	31.25
42		Direct labour cost	(D-4)*(D-37)*(D-39)	248 850.00
43				
44		**Variable Overhead Costs**		
45		Energy cost for work centre	(D-12)*(D-40)	37 500.00
46		Work centre supervision	(D-13)*(D-40)	234 375.00
47		Tool centre charges	(D-14)*(D-40)	117 187.50
48		Warehousing	(D-15)*(D-34)	3 772.50
49		Cutting/lubricating fluids, FF	(D-16)*(D-22)	2 250.00
50		Other, FF/unit	(D-17)*(D-22)	3 750.00
51		**Total Variable costs**	sum[(D-45)..(D-50)]	398 835.00
52				
53		**Summary of production costs**		
54		Material cost	(D-34)	188 625.00
55		Direct labour	(D-42)	248 850.00
56		Variable Overhead	(D-51)	398 835.00
57		Allocated fixed overhead	(D-22)	95 000.00
58		**Total production costs**	sum[(D-54)..(D-57)]	931 310.00
59				
60		**Purchase price**		783 000.00
64		Purchase price per unit	D-60/15 000	52.20
65		Production cost per unit	D-58/15 000	62.09

Figure 16.19   Brulschmerg – pistons make or buy.

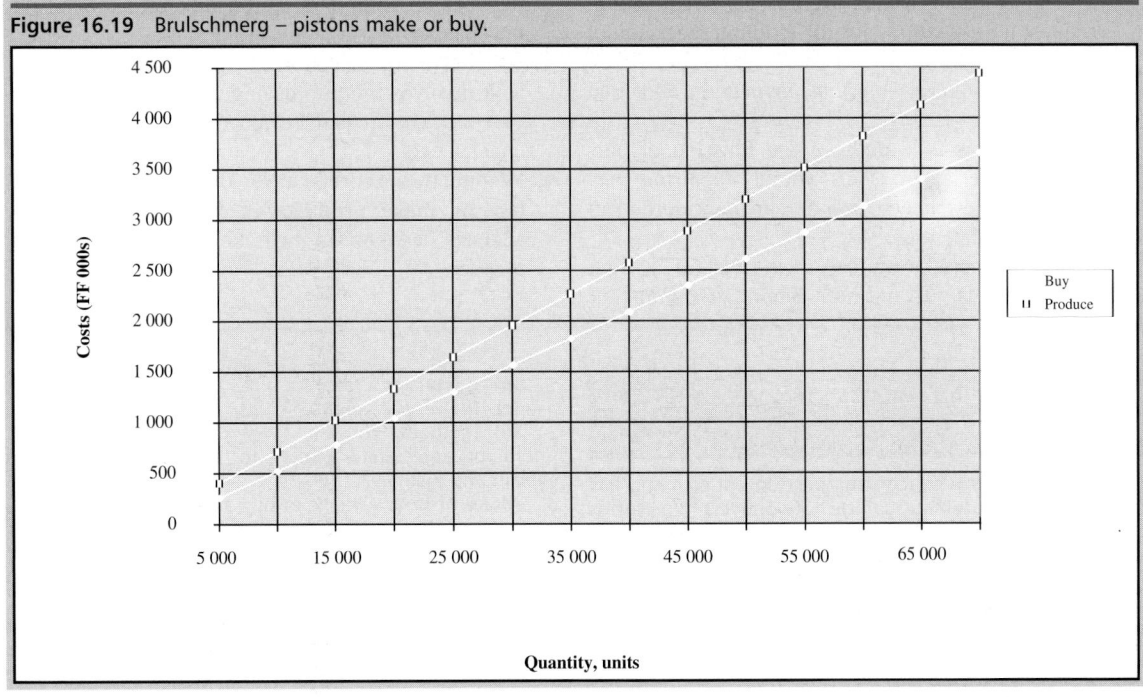

SUMMARY OF KEY ELEMENTS

- Purchasing is the buying of materials or services from an outside source. Upwards of 60 per cent of the cost of goods in manufactured products can come from purchases.
- Purchased products include raw materials, parts, subassemblies, machinery, equipment, packaging, supplies, finished goods and subcontractor services.
- A purchasing managers' index is directly related to manufacturing. An index above 50 per cent indicates an increase of manufacturing and below 50 per cent means a decline.
- Sourcing is the activity of searching worldwide for a supplier (a source) of raw materials or products that presents the best ratio of quality to price.
- Fluctuating exchange rates are a risk in international purchasing. Forward buying for increasing prices, or hand-to mouth buying for declining prices, can offset risk.
- Hedging is the purchase, or sale, of a futures contract of a commodity to offset the purchase, or sale, of a cash commodity. It is used to offset the risk occurred in fluctuating commodity markets or to guarantee a source of raw materials.

- Completely knocked down (CKD) is the term used for companies that export their products (sell to purchasers) in a disassembled, or kit, form.
- Barriers to international purchasing include language and cultural differences, customs requirements, quotas, specifications, local laws and political risk.
- For organizations that have several sites, the purchasing activity may be centralized, decentralized or a hybrid of the two.
- Buyers usually specialize in a specific commodity. Buyers should be familiar with their company, price structures and laws and be good at human relations.
- Unethical buying practices may include taking advantage of quotation errors, price fixing, collusion, playing favourites, upgrading of product samples and reciprocity.
- Criteria for supplier selection include product price, quality, reliability, after-sales service, supplier location, inventory policy, flexibility, financial stability, technical capability and extent of product range.
- With few suppliers, administrative costs are lower, a purchaser has more clout with suppliers and purchasing staff can be reduced.

- The steps in purchasing are purchase requisition, request for quotation, out-for-bidding, reception of quotations, supplier selection, purchase order, supplier produces, shipping, inspection and final payment.
- Value analysis is a study of the function of purchased materials to see, without impairing performance, how specifications can be modified in order to reduce cost.
- If a firm operates under just-in-time (JIT), then purchasing is just-in-time. Having a competent network of suppliers, physically close, aids JIT purchasing.
- Subcontractor selection is a purchasing function as it involves the purchasing of services of a third party. Selection can be aided by using weighted checksheets.
- Manufacturing firms make decisions whether to buy or make products. A financial break-even analysis between the two choices is useful in this respect.

REVIEW AND DISCUSSION QUESTIONS

1 **Suppliers versus subcontractors**. Close-It company has a patent on automatic garage door openers. It performs a limited amount of manufacturing, but about 80 per cent of its activity is the assembly of the units from components. The door openers include:
   (a) screws, bolts, springs, and other fasteners;
   (b) a complex control mechanism of a specification written by Close-It;
   (c) a timer;
   (d) standard plastic covers;
   (e) cardboard cartons for packaging of the assembled product.
All of these components are obtained from outside sources. Which of the above parts do you believe might be obtained from suppliers and which would be subcontracted? Justify your reasoning. Discuss the difference between a supplier and a subcontractor.

2 **Value analysis**. Examine the following:
   (a) the car you drive;
   (b) the bus you take;
   (c) the bicycle you use;
   (d) the books you use.
Could you apply value analysis to these products? Discuss, explain and justify.

3 **Make-or-buy**. A make-or-buy analysis is strictly a comparison between costs. What other considerations should be taken into account, not necessarily quantitative aspects? Consider both a manufacturing and a service organization.

4 **International purchasing**. More and more developed nations (the USA, Europe and Japan) are purchasing raw materials and services in developing countries. Firm owners think that this is the only way to stay competitive. Employees, and often governments (particularly in Europe), do not always agree. Discuss the merits of purchasing from overseas.

5 **Just-in-time purchasing**. Japan has no trouble in applying just-in-time purchasing. Europe, however, has difficulty in applying the same concepts. Why do you think this is so? Do you feel that some European countries are better than others?

EXERCISE PROBLEM: CHIPS

Situation

The Purchasing department at a computer manufacturer in California is evaluating the suppliers of computer chips. There are three suppliers being considered in different locations:

- USA;
- Japan;
- Hong Kong.

The purchasing department has evaluated the proposals from the three locations and completed checklists for each supplier. These are given in the three rating tables (Tables 16.9, 16.10 and 16.11).

Required

1 Based on these ratings which is the preferred supplier?

Table 16.9 Ratings for the US chip supplier

Weighting	Excellent 5	Good 4	Fair 3	Poor 2	Terrible 1	Factor Max=5
Product						
Quality		X				5
Price (high price = low score)				X		4
Delivery reliability (time)		X				3
Delivery reliability (conditions)	X					2
Warranty conditions		X				1
Supplier						
Technical capability			X			5

	Excellent	Good	Fair	Poor	Terrible	Factor
Financial strength	X					5
Quality certification		X				4
Flexibility with buyer			X			4
Profit consistency	X					3
Labour relations (unionized)					X	3
Capacity available				X		3
Management competence		X				3
Knowledgeable sales staff			X			3
After-sales service			X			3
Location relative to buyer	X					2
Environmental awareness			X			1

Table 16.10 Ratings for the Japanese chip supplier

Weighting	Excellent 5	Good 4	Fair 3	Poor 2	Terrible 1	Factor Max=5
Product						
Quality	X					5
Price (high price = low score)				X		4
Delivery reliability (time)	X					3
Delivery reliability (conditions)	X					2
Warranty conditions		X				1
Supplier						
Technical capability		X				5
Financial strength	X					5
Quality certification		X				4
Flexibility with buyer				X		4
Profit consistency			X			3
Labour relations (unionized)	X					3
Capacity available				X		3
Management competence	X					3
Knowledgeable sales staff			X			3
After-sales service				X		3
Location relative to buyer			X			2
Environmental awareness				X		1

Table 16.11 Ratings for the Hong Kong chip supplier

Weighting	Excellent 5	Good 4	Fair 3	Poor 2	Terrible 1	Factor Max=5
Product						
Quality		X				5
Price (high price = low score)	X					4
Delivery reliability (time)			X			3
Delivery reliability (conditions)		X				2
Warranty conditions			X			1
Supplier						
Technical capability				X		5
Financial strength		X				5
Quality certification				X		4
Flexibility with buyer				X		4
Profit consistency		X				3
Labour relations (unionized)		X				3
Capacity available			X			3
Management competence	X					3
Knowledgeable sales staff		X				3
After-sales service				X		3
Location relative to buyer				X		2
Environmental awareness		X				1

EXERCISE PROBLEM: COMFORT

Situation

Comfort company makes space heating systems. The control units for these are housed in steel cabinets, Reference No. A-10. The control units, Reference No. B-20, consist of three parallel on/off units made of copper and insulation bars. The control unit is bolted into the cabinet. For every control unit made, a cabinet is required, and vice versa. The combined Cabinet/Control Assembly has the Reference AB-30.

Comfort wants to know whether it is better to purchase these components from outside, or to manufacture them itself. It has the option shown in Table 16.12. If Comfort selects buying any unit at a certain level, it would buy all the units at this level. Similarly, if it decides to make a unit at a certain level, it would make all the units at this level. Table 16.13 gives the relevant financial data on which decisions are made.

Table 16.12 Comfort's options

	Cabinet A-10	Control Unit B-20
Option 1	Make	Make
Option 2	Buy	Buy
Option 3	Make	Buy
Option 4	Buy	Make

Table 16.13 Comfort – financial data

	Variable cost (£/unit)	Fixed costs (£)	Purchase price (£/unit)
Steel cabinets, A-10	6.00	2000	8.55
Switching Units, B-20	11.00	3000	12.00

Required

1 If Comfort has an order of 500 for Assembly AB-30, which would be the optimum Option for this size order? Justify your reasoning.
2 If Comfort has an order of 1000 for Assembly AB-30, which would be the optimum Option for this size order? Justify your reasoning.
3 If Comfort has an order of 3000 for Assembly AB-30, which would be the optimum Option for this size order? Justify your reasoning.
4 Show the alternatives on appropriate break-even cost curves.

EXERCISE PROBLEM: TIMING

Situation

A company is proposing to make a timing assembly unit in Work Centre A for electric circuit breakers. This unit is essentially made from a stainless-steel rod, springs and steel caps. When finished, this unit assembly unit will then be sent to Work Centre B, where it will be incorporated into the final circuit breaker. The company wants to make a decision whether to purchase the timing unit or to manufacture it itself. The operating data is given in Table 16.14.

Table 16.14 Date for make-or-buy analysis for timing unit

Variable labour costs	Value
Labour rate (£/hour)	6.00
Employer social charge (%)	12.00
Variable material costs	
Stainless-steel rod (£/metre)	0.75
Steel caps (£/unit)	0.15
Springs (£/unit)	0.05
Variable overhead, Centre A	
Energy cost for work centre (£/shift)	35.00
Work-centre supervision (£/shift)	175.00
Tool centre charges (£/shift)	95.00
Warehousing (% material cost)	0.95
Cutting/lubricating fluids (£/finished unit)	0.15
Other (£/unit)	0.10
Allocated fixed overhead, A (£)	7 500.00
Purchase information	
Purchase price (£/unit)	6.00
Quantity required (unit)	14 000
Design information	
Stainless-steel rod (metres/unit)	0.35
Steel caps (Number/unit)	6
springs (Number/unit)	20
Production, Work Centre A	
Operators (Number/unit)	3
Production rate (units/h)	30

Required

1 Based on the quantity required, should the company make or buy?
2 Is there any quantity level at which the make-or-buy decision might change? Show your analysis on cost curves for making or buying.
3 What other considerations need to be taken into account in this type of a decision?

CASE STUDY: BOEING CO.

Situation[18]

Boeing Aircraft Co., based in Seattle, Washington, USA, is the world's largest commercial airline manufacturer. Its recent acquisition of McDonnell Douglas catapulted Boeing into a giant competitor to European Airbus. In addition to commercial planes, it competes in the defence and space markets (Navy, Air Force, Army, NASA and foreign militaries). It is also develops high-technology data-processing and computer services.

After years of drought, new orders for airlines are exploding. They are arriving from all around the world. In the first six months of 1996 Boeing logged orders for 225 planes valued at $17.6 billion. In June 1996 Singapore Airlines signed an agreement to buy as many as 77 Boeing 777s and other orders have been received from British Airways, United Airlines and carriers in South Korea and China. Later in 1997, it was expected that the production level will be up to 40 planes a month, rising to 46 or more in 1999. This will include a large proportion of 737s as well as the 747, 757, 767 and the new 777.

Boeing aeroplanes are made up from literally thousands of different raw materials, parts, components, subassemblies and assemblies. Lightweight titanium is a key material and the cost of this increased some 80 per cent in 1996, coupled with long delivery delays. In addition to inventories used in the original aeroplane assembly, Boeing is the only aeroplane manufacturer that offers next-day shipment of routine spares. It has inventories of key components stocked around the world.

Required

1   Why is the purchasing function of Boeing such a key operational (and strategic) element of the firm?
2   To a certain extent, the purchase of McDonnell Douglas has added to the vertical integration of Boeing. From a purchasing point-of-view, what are the advantages and disadvantages of vertically integrated companies?
3   Why would the learning-curve concept play an important role in the purchasing and other operational activities of Boeing? (See also section on Learning Curve in Chapter 8, *Human Resources in the System Design*.)
4   What are some of the policies that Boeing should have towards suppliers? What are some of the tools that might be used in analysis? What are some of the key elements in the analysis of suppliers?
5   What are some of the considerations Boeing might use regarding inventory management related to purchased components? Where would just-in-time purchasing play a role?

NOTES AND REFERENCES

1. 'Latest data in US signal slowdown in manufacturing' (1995) *Wall Street Journal Europe* 2–3 June.
2. *The Economist* (1994) 10 December (with additions).
3. 'Futures Options' *Wall Street Journal Europe*, Money & Markets section.
4. Sturdivant, F. D. (1985) Chapter 'Business Ideology and Ethics', *Business and Society*, Homewood, IL: Irwin: 114.
5. 'Le scandale qui a tout déclenché' (1997) *L'Expansion* 10–24 July, No. 553: 44. [Translation: The Scandal which broke all].
6. Gerlin, A. (1995) 'Deals on the side: How a Penny buyer made up to $1.5 million on vendor's kickbacks', *Wall Street Journal Europe* 13 February.
7. *Wall Street Journal Europe* (1997) 9 April.
8. 'General Motors Corp: Opel unit confirms official is facing bribery charges' (1996) *Wall Street Journal Europe* 1–2 March.
9. 'Europe-Etats-Unis: le choc des pots-de-vin: Comment sont payés les intermédiares" (1997) *L'Expansion* 10–24 July, No. 553: 44. [Translation: Europe–USA: The shock of under-the-table payments. How intermediaries are financed].
10. Study at the Groupe ESC Lyon (1993).
11. 'Ford says goal is to keep costs at 1995 levels' (1995) *Wall Street Journal Europe* 10 May.
12. *The Economist* (1991) 13 April.
13. Bleakley, F. R. (1995) 'Strange bed fellows. Some companies let suppliers work on site and even place orders', *Wall Street Journal Europe* (1995) 16 January.
14. With permission from Hewlett Packard, 1 June 1998.
15. 'Holding the hand that feeds: More and more companies are forming cosy partnerships with their suppliers. Such relationsips can be risky' (1995) *The Economist* 9 September: 71.
16. Templin, N. and Cole, J. (1994) 'Working together. Manufacturers use suppliers to help them develop new products', *Wall Street Europe* 22 December.
17. 'DIY in Germany'. *The Economist* 2 March 1996.
Based on Boeing Annual Reports and *Wall Street Journal Europe* (1996) 25 July.

FURTHER READING

Barnett, H., Hibbert, R., Curtiss, A. and, Scolthorpe-Pike, M. (1995) 'The Japanese system of subcontracting', *Purchasing and Supply Management* December: 22–26.
Bleil, R. (1993) 'Increasing competitiveness through better supply management', *Electronic Business Buyer* 19(11): 72–74.
Brown, D. (1992) 'Outsourcing: How corporations take their business elsewhere', *Management Review* 81(2): 16–19.
Burnes, B. and New, S. (1997) 'Collaboration in customer–supplier relationships: Strategy, operations and the function of rhetoric', *International Journal of Purchasing and Materials Management* 33(4): 10–17.
Choi, T. Y. and Hartley, J. L. (1996) 'An exploration of supplier selection practices across the supply chain', *Journal of Operations Management* 14(4): 333–43.
Cook, R. L. (1992) 'Expert systems in purchasing: Applications and development', *International Journal of Purchasing and Materials Management* 28(4): 20–27.
Cruz, C. (1997) 'Global economy pushes purchasing offshore', *Purchasing* 122(6): 20–21.
Cruz, C. (1997) 'Long term supplier relationships are the key to successful management', *Purchasing* 123(1): 127.
Dowlatshahi, S. (1992) 'Purchasing's role in a concurrent engineering environment', *International Journal of Purchasing and Materials Management* 28(1): 21–25.
Ellram, L. M. and Pearson, J. N. (1993) 'The role of the purchasing function: Toward team participation', *International*

Journal of Purchasing and Materials Management 29(3): 3–9.

Farmer, D. (1987) *Purchasing Management Handbook*, Aldershot: Gower.

Farrington B. and Waters, D. W. F. (1994) *Managing Purchasing: Organizing, Planning and Control*, London, New York: Chapman & Hall.

Fawcett, S. E., Birou, L. and Taylor, B. C. (1993) 'Supporting global operations through logistics and purchasing', *International Journal of Physical Distribution and Logistics Management* 23(4): 3–11.

Fitzgerald, K. R. (1995) 'Cost: Suppliers help trim the fat', *Purchasing* 119(8): 43–47.

Florsheim, R. and Paderon, E. S. (1992) 'Purchasing practices in a hospital environment: An ethical analysis', *Hospital Materiel Management Quarterly* 13(4): 1–10.

Frear, C. R., Metcalf, L. E. and Alguire, M. S. (1992) 'Offshore sourcing: Its nature and scope', *International Journal of Purchasing and Materials Management* 28(3): 2–11.

Germain, R. and Droge, C. (1997) 'Effect of just-in-time purchasing relationships on organizational design, purchasing department configuration, and firm performance', *Industrial Marketing Management* 26(2): 115–125.

Goldhar, D. Y. and Stamm, C. L. (1993) 'JIT practices in manufacturing firms', *Production and Inventory Management Journal* 34(3): 75–79.

Heinritz, S., Farrell, P. V., Giunipero L. and Kolchin M. (1991) *Purchasing – Principles and Applications*, Englewood Cliffs, NJ: Prentice Hall.

Houshyar, A. and Lyth, D. (1992) 'A systematic supplier selection procedure', *Computers and Industrial Engineering*, 23(1–4): 173–176.

Landry, S., Duguay, C. R., Chausse, S. and Themens, J.-L. (1997) 'Integrating MRP, Kanban, and bar-coding systems to achieve JIT procurement' *Production and Inventory Management Journal* 38(1): 8–13.

Lee, H. and Wellan, D. M. (1993) 'Vendor survey plan: A selection strategy for JIT/TQM suppliers', *International Journal of Physical Distribution and Logistics Management* 23(7): 39–41.

Lyons, B. R. and Bailey, S. (1993) 'Small subcontractors in UK engineering: Competitiveness, dependence, and problems', *Small Business Economics* 2(June): 101–09.

Morris, J. and Imrie, R. (1993) 'Japanese style subcontracting: Its impact on European industries', *Long Range Planning* 26(4): 53–58.

Muhhopadhyay, S. K. (1995) 'Optimal scheduling of just-in-time purchase deliveries', *International Journal of Operations and Production* 15(9): 59–69.

O'Reilly, J. (1992) 'Subcontracting in banking: Some evidence from Britain and France', *New Technology Work and Employment* 7(2): 107–15.

Palaniswami, S. and Lingaraj, B. P. (1994) 'Procurement and vendor management in the global environment', *International Journal of Production Economics* 35(1–3): 171–76.

Presutti, W. D. Jr (1992) 'The single source issue: US and Japanese Sourcing Strategies', *International Journal of Purchasing and Materials Management* 28(1): 2–9.

Raia, E. (1992) 'Value analysis: Taking out cost', *Purchasing* 112(10): 42–43.

Riedel, J. C. K. H., Lewis, J. and Pawar, K. (1992) 'Make or buy: The strategic product design choice', *Integrated Manufacturing Systems* 3(2): 9–14.

Scheuning, E. E. (1989) *Purchasing Management*, Englewood Cliffs, NJ: Prentice Hall.

St John, C. H. and Heriot, K. C. (1993) 'Small suppliers and JIT purchasing', *International Journal of Purchasing and Materials Management* 29(1): 11–16.

Stevens, J. (1995) 'Global purchasing in the supply chain', *Purchasing and Supply Management* January: 22–25.

Sweetman, K. J. (1966) 'Procurement', *Harvard Business Review* 74(6): 11–13.

Thoburn, J. T. and Takashima, M. (1993) 'Improving British industrial performance: Lessons from Japanese subcontracting', *National Westminster Bank Quarterly Review* February: 2–12.

Turner, G. B., Taylor, G. S. and Hartley, M. F. (1994) 'Ethics policies and gratuity acceptance by purchasers', *International Journal of Purchasing and Materials Management* 30(3): 43–47.

Williams, A. J., Lacy, S. and Smith, W. C. (1992) 'Purchasing's role in value analysis', *International Journal of Purchasing and Materials Management* 28(2): 37–42.

Wood, G. (1995) 'Ethics at the purchasing/sales interface: An international perspective', *International Marketing Review* 12(4): 7–19.

Zenz, G. (1994) *Purchasing and the Management of Materials*, Chichester: John Wiley.

'Foreign aid: Japanese auto makers help part suppliers become more efficient. Toyota drills an Illinois Firm in fine points of building bumpers faster, cheaper. How Valeo is benefiting, too' (1991) *Wall Street Journal Europe* 10 September.

'VW puts suppliers on production line: Argentina cost-cutting bid may alter industry' (1996) *Wall Street Journal Europe* 23/24 February.

17 Managing the supply chain

Objectives and overview

The objective of this chapter is to underscore supply-chain management as the critical integrated activity in operations management. The chapter begins by presenting in detail the supply chain and then discusses supply-chain modelling as an aid to management for analysing the value-added components in the network. The concept of pipeline mapping is discussed as an approach to determining the reactivity and flexibility of a firm and then the distribution requirements planning (DRP) tool is developed using an illustrative example. The role of electronic data interchange, including the Internet, is reviewed and its application is illustrated by the reference to the retail food industry. Transportation means are discussed in detail and the current status of transportation modes in Europe presented. International considerations are discussed, with reference to trade restrictions sometimes enforced by host governments, which impede the viability of the supply chain. The organization of the supply chain function is then presented, including a description of specific activities of a logistics or supply-chain manager. Finally, the chapter presents some ideas of how costs might be reduced in the supply chain and how some firms are resorting to subcontracting for this very reason.

THE SUPPLY CHAIN

The concept of the supply, or logistics, chain has already been developed in Chapter 1, *Positioning Operations Management* (The section *Model of operations*), and in Chapter 7, *Process Design and the Operations Network* (the section *Design of the Process System*), as being the integrated process operations network in place to provide tangible goods or services to a client. In manufacturing, this supply chain is the linkage for the physical movement of all materials from suppliers, through transformation, and then as finished goods for the customer. In service concerns, such as retail stores or a delivery service like UPS or Federal Express, the supply chain is distribution, where the start point is the finished product that has to be delivered to the client in a timely manner. For a pure service operation, such as a financial services firm or a consulting operation, the supply chain is principally the information flow. However, whatever organization is concerned, within the supply chain there is always an information flow back from the customer to the provider of the service.

Activities in supply-chain management

Management of the supply chain involves rigorous attention to quality, cost and lead or delivery times. It implies teamwork, cooperation and effective coordination throughout the entire organization. Some key management activities (already presented in earlier chapters) include:

- Site selection as where best to locate a facility to achieve the most rapid response. This includes not only the manufacturer's facility but also the supplier's factory, service centres, offices, warehouse and distribution centres (Chapter 3).
- Forecasting the demands for customers, which is the activity that sets into motion planning and the material flow in the supply chain (Chapter 9).
- Development of an operations plan that corresponds to the sales needs. This includes all the integrated activities, such as development of the master production schedule, the material requirements plan and the operations schedule (Chapters 12, 13 and 14).
- Management of raw-materials inventories, work in process and finished goods, such that there is suffi-

cient not to have stock-out situations, but not too much so that costs are unnecessarily high. This activity will almost certainly involve just-in-time management practices (Chapters 11 and 15).

■ Layout of the facility, so that material goods can flow smoothly through the system, be it a storage area, manufacturing or a retail outlet (Chapter 10).

■ Purchasing to ensure that the right materials, of the expected quality, are delivered at the right location on the specified date (Chapter 16).

■ Distribution requirements route planning, and transportation for finished products (this chapter).

An integrated supply chain

The concept of an integrated supply chain is illustrated in Figure 17.1. Raw materials, or parts from suppliers, are delivered and stored in a raw-materials warehouse at the production centre. From here material is withdrawn as needed by the production centre, which in this illustration comprises three work centres.

Work Centre No. 3

Here the raw materials are transformed into subassemblies, which are sent through the chain to Work Centre

No. 2. Work Centre No. 3 also prepares semi-finished goods, which are sent to Work Centre No. 1.

Work Centre No. 2

Work Centre No. 2 transforms its raw materials from storage, plus the subassemblies received from Work Centre No. 3, into semifinished foods, which are passed onto Work Centre No. 1.

Work Centre No. 1

Work Centre No. 1 produces the finished products from the semifinished goods it receives from Work Centre No. 2 and Work Centre No. 3. Finished goods from here are put into Finished Product storage.

From storage, the finished goods are delivered to the distribution centres (here five are shown) by some form of transportation. This may be by truck, as illustrated, but it could be by rail and later by ship or air, depending on the location. From the distribution centre the products are then sent to the clients, which may, in the case of consumer goods, be simply retail outlets. All this activity represents the physical flow of material. In the reverse sense, as illustrated, is the information flow from the client going back to the suppliers.

Figure 17.1 The supply chain.

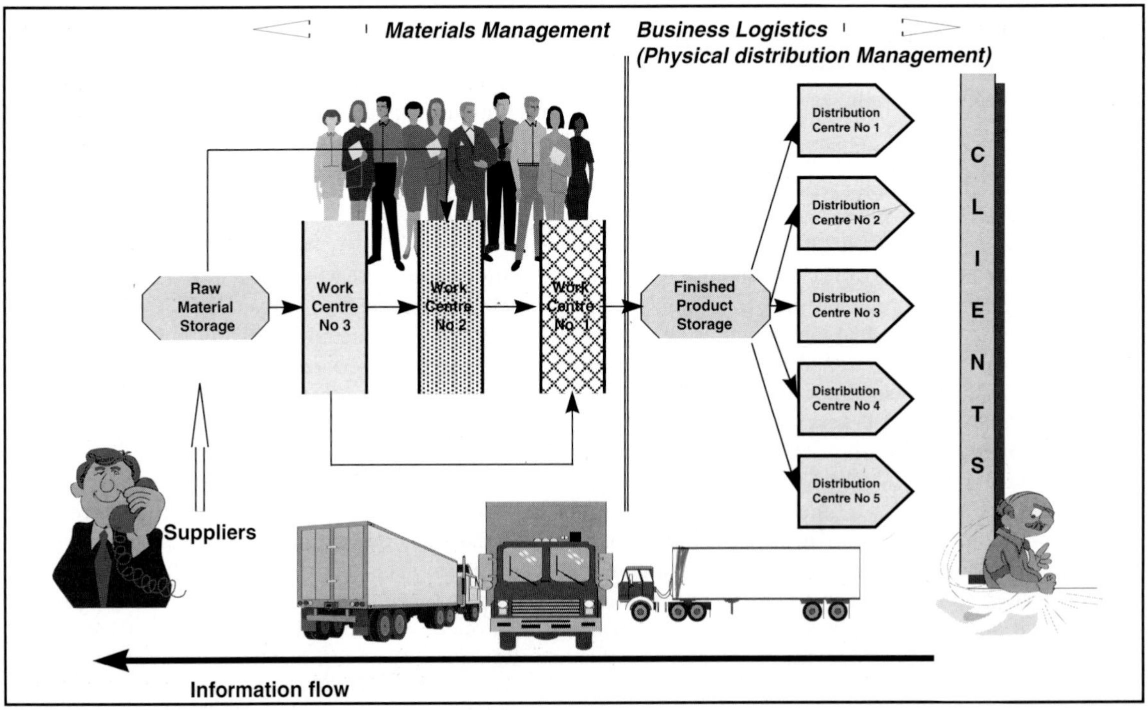

Lead times

To satisfy the customer, products need to be delivered according to schedule. The operations manager, or logistics manager, needs to be sure that the supply chain is not broken. Further, lead times or the time to complete an activity are critical to planning customer needs. For example, assume in Figure 17.1 that the lead times, or durations for various activities are as given in Table 17.1.

Table 17.1 Lead times for the activities in Figure 17.1

Activity	Lead time or duration
Delivery of raw materials	4 weeks
Reception, control and storage of raw materials	3 days
Production in Work Centre No. 3	1 week
Production in Work Centre No. 2	1 week
Production in Work Centre No. 1	4 days
Control, storage of finished goods	4 days
Delivery of finished goods to distribution centre	3 days
Total lead time	**8 weeks**

Then the minimum lead time from ordering raw materials to delivery of a specific order to the distribution centre is eight weeks. Any delays in any activity will of course add to the total lead time and result in finished goods being delivered late.

Supply chain in two parts

From a management viewpoint, organizations sometimes consider the supply chain as two distinct activities, Materials Management and Physical Distribution Management, rather than as a complete integrated network, as illustrated in Figure 17.1.

Materials management

Materials management is the upstream part of the chain. It covers purchasing of raw materials, components and packaging, their storage and the production or transformation phases, including internal transfer within the work centre. This phase might be effectively managed by a material requirements plan, as already discussed in Chapter 13, *Materials Requirements Planning*.

Physical distribution management

Physical distribution management, sometimes called Business Logistics, is the downstream portion of the chain and covers the storage and inventory control of the finished products, order processing, distribution planning, order picking (removal from the storage centre), transportation of the finished products to the distribution centres and then to wholesalers and retailers. This part of the chain can be managed by a distribution requirements plan. For retail outlets this may be the only logistics phase, since their activity involves transporting the finished products from the warehouses and distributing them to stores for final sale.

Even though the supply chain may be two parts, belonging to separate organizations, many kilometres apart, maybe in different countries, for effective management the supply chain has to be considered as an integrated network, since a problem in one part can impact the other, and vice-versa.

Distribution network

The distribution network in the supply chain covers the complete delivery zone for the finished products and an illustration is shown in Figure 17.2 Here, there is a production centre at Namur, Belgium, and five distribution centres at Ettelbruck in Luxembourg, Arnhem in the Netherlands, Metz in France, Hof in Germany, and St. Gallen in Switzerland. The distribution centres might be:

■ wholesalers, from where the product goes further to retailers;
■ a holding centre for component parts manufactured by a supplier, where the client draws on these component parts as needed. For example, Valéo, a manufacturer of automobile parts for companies such as Renault, General Motors or Citröen, manages large distribution centres located close to the client. Valéo owns this inventory until at such time the parts are withdrawn by the client.

Considerations in planning the supply chain

The client demand triggers an order, which triggers production, which triggers purchasing of those components and materials that are not made in-house. All along the supply chain are planning factors that need to be considered to avoid missing the client delivery date. Figure 17.3 lists some of the elements that need to be taken into account.

Supply chain management is critical

Supply chain management is a critical activity in serving the customer. Consider a manufacturer of washing machines, such as Brandt in Europe, whose products are sold through specialized chains and hypermarkets. The simplified activities and events of one particular

Figure 17.2 Distribution network in Europe.

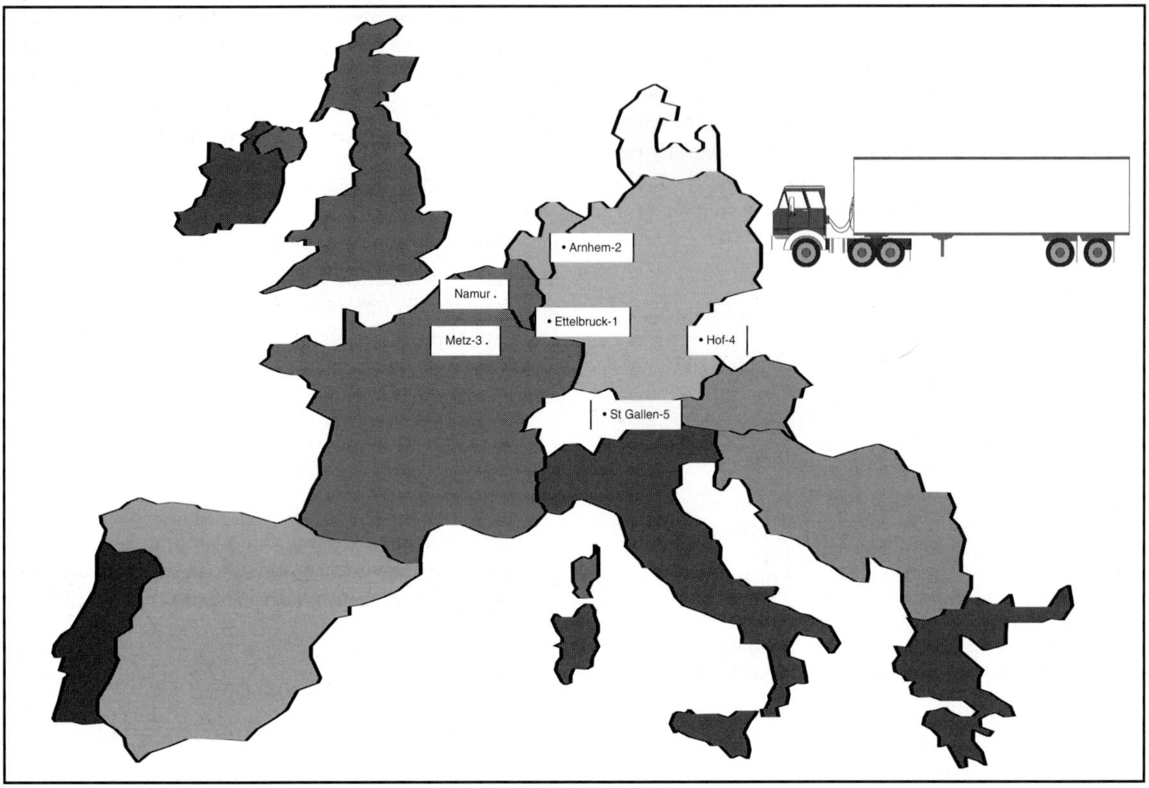

Namur .

• Arnhem-2

• Ettelbruck-1

Metz-3 .

• Hof-4

• St Gallen-5

Figure 17.3 Considerations in planning the supply chain.

PURCHASING

- ● Has lead time for raw materials been considered in client delivery dates?
- ● If several purchased components, have their delivery dates been considered in scheduling production?
- ● Have times for unloading, controlling and storage of raw materials been taken into account in planning?
- ● When must payment of raw materials be made? Has the timing, and amount been taken into consideration in production cost?

- ● Is the labour sufficient in each work centre for production?
- ● Have set-up times between each product been considered in planning?
- ● Is labour multiskilled such that it can be transferred between sites?
- ● Is hiring necessary to meet the planned production level?
- ● Have inventory storage costs been considered in production costs?
- ● Is production capacity sufficient?
- ● If normal capacity is tight, what overtime possibilities exist?
- ● What is labour cost?

PRODUCTION

DISTRIBUTION

- ● Is the truck volume sufficient?
- ● Is the truck weight sufficient?
- ● Is there enough delivery time to meet client due dates?
- ● Has loading and unloading time been taken into consideration?
- ● Is there sufficient transportation?
- ● Is the capacity of the warehouse sufficient?

top-loading model, reference BB-40, are illustrated in Figure 17.4:

- Brandt subcontracts out the manufacture of the tumbler section, article T-489, of model BB-40.
- Usinor-Sacilor, the supplier of the sheet steel for the tumbler, delivers a bad lot to the subcontractor.
- The subcontractor has insufficient safety stock of this particular steel and so tumbler production stops until a new supply of steel is received.
- The interrupted supply of the tumbler to Brandt delays the final assembly of washing machine, BB-40.
- Carrefour, a hypermarket, temporarily runs out of stock of model BB-40.
- A Carrefour customer finds the washing machine she would like is not in stock.
- An efficient sales person convinces the customer to purchase a washing machine manufacture by Whirlpool, a Brandt competitor. Thus, Brandt has lost a sale and the associated profit margin!

Global operations

Multinational firms, say producing automobiles, aeroplanes or computers, have multiple players and the logistics chain can be very complex. Raw materials may come from any of the five continents and the subassemblies may originate from Mexico, Ireland and Singapore. The final product is then assembled in the USA before being exported to Europe. As a result, the following are situations that are driving firms to improve the management of their supply:

- increasing pressure from overseas manufacturing competitors;
- manufacturing sites that are geographically very dispersed and often in low-cost labour countries in Asia and Central and South America.
- cut-throat marketing channels such as independent dealers;
- maturing of world economies increasing demand for locally made products;
- increasing pressure to provide quick reliable delivery of finished products.

MODELLING THE SUPPLY CHAIN

If a supply chain is broken down into smaller elements or modelled, understanding, and thus management, can be significantly improved. The concept is illustrated as follows.

Figure 17.4 Supply-chain management is critical.

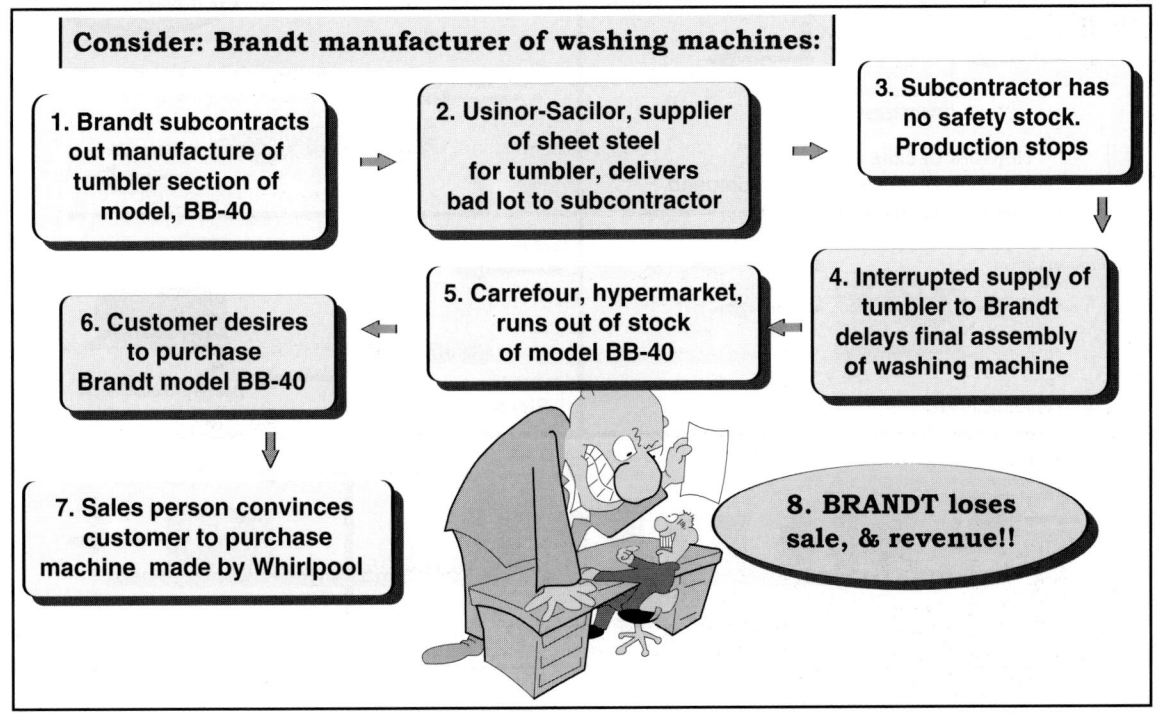

Value-added cells

The various operating stages in the supply chain can be represented by a simple model of a material-transformation processing cell, where value is added to the upstream component to produce something of a higher value at the downstream end.[1] At each processing cell there is a supply and a demand, and this model applies at any level as illustrated in Figure 17.5.

Manufacturing

In automobile assembly this could be the paint spraying of the chassis. The supply is the bare steel chassis, the transformation is the painting and the demand is the downstream work centre.

Warehousing

In a warehouse, products arrive in bulk on a truck or train and this is the supply. The products are unloaded and sorted into smaller units, which is the transformation. The demand is the client who takes the smaller units.

Packaging

In the packaging of beer or soft drinks into cases, the separate cans of the beverage are the supply. The packaging process of putting a ring of plastic over six cans would be the transformation. The demand would be the pallet waiting to stack the 'six packs'.

Distribution

The distribution of a product from a warehouse to a retail outlet is a value-added step. Even though the product's characteristics do not change, the fact that a customer is able to find the product in the store adds value in the customer's eyes. It has no value to the customer if it is sitting in a warehouse some 150 km away. As a value-added cell, the supply is loading the product onto a truck and the demand is the retail outlet. The value-added step is represented by the cost of the service activity or the physical distribution.

An integrated supply chain can thus be considered as a network of material-processing cells, as illustrated in Figure 17.6. The supplier may be a third party supplying purchased parts, a subcontractor or an internal unit

Figure 17.5 Modelling of the supply chain.

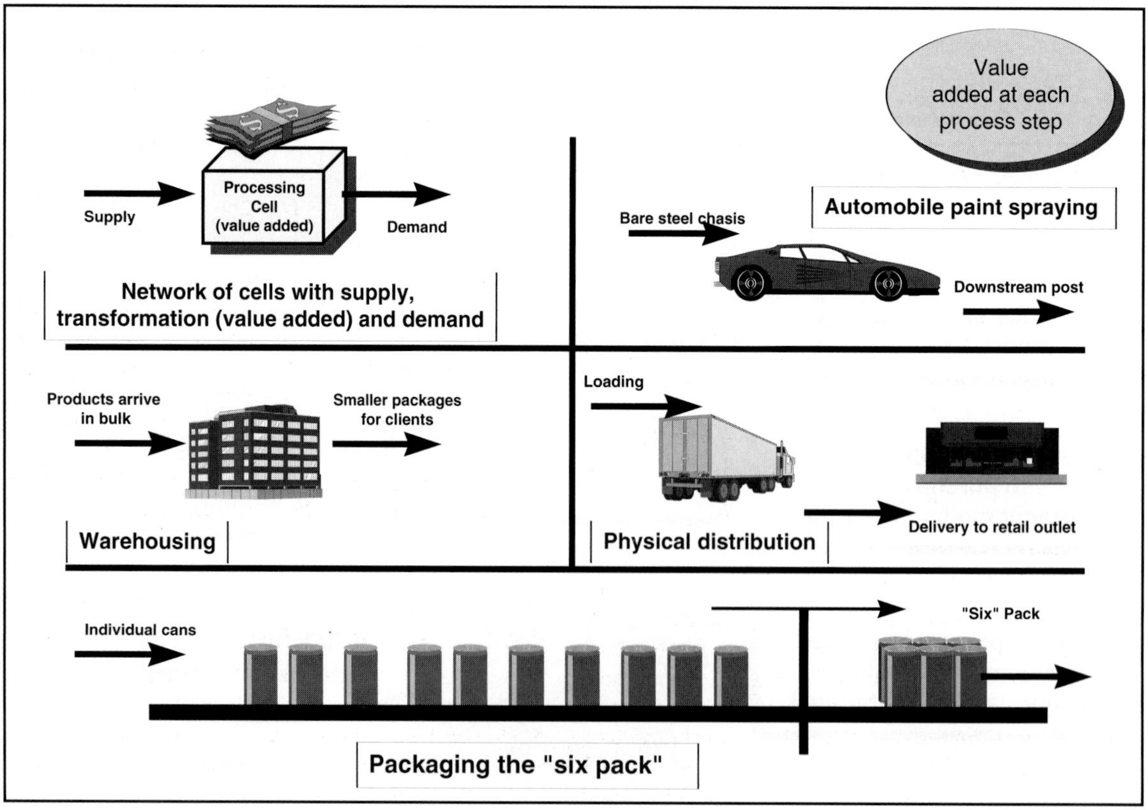

Figure 17.6   Supply chain in a production operation.

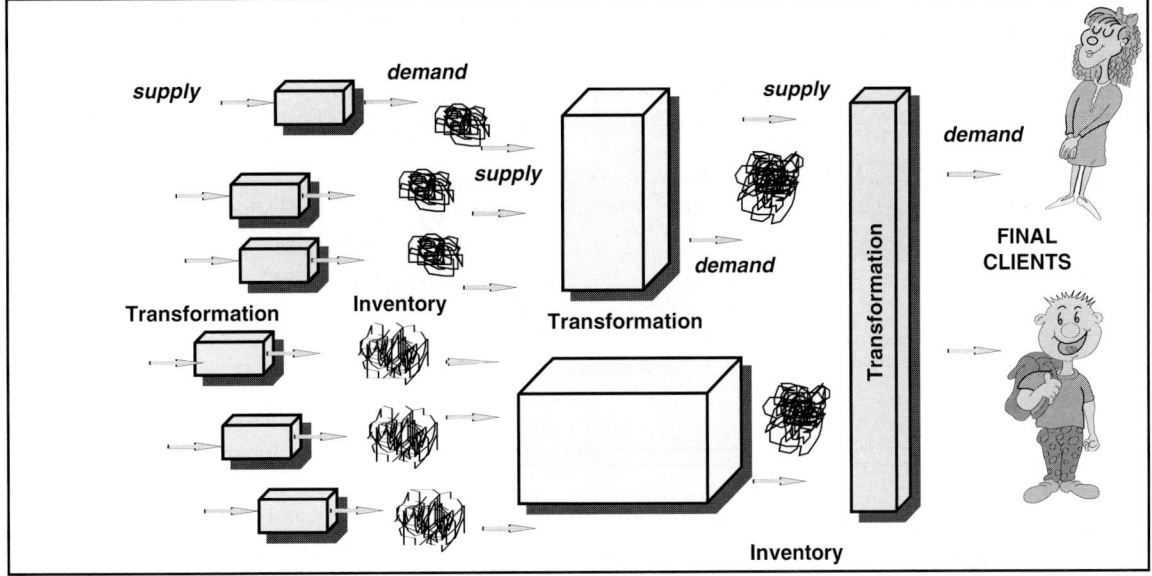

in the manufacturing organization. The downstream demand may be the next work centre, or the final client.

Supply-chain costs

Supply-chain costs are high and so, the greater the value added in each processing cell, the more efficient is the supply chain. Figure 17.7 gives a breakdown of the supply-chain costs according to the various steps, from supply of raw materials to delivery of finished goods.[2] Studies indicate that, on average, of the total supply-chain costs, upstream activity accounts for about 29 per cent, transformation 7 per cent, and downstream cost 64 per cent. The biggest logistics cost is the transportation of the finished goods (32 per cent), which varies, of course, depending on the form of transportation. For example, in Japan in 1993, the cost per ton of transportation from Tokyo to Kyushu, a distance of some 1200 km, was 12 000 yen ($100) for sea and 150 000 yen ($1,250) for air.[3]

Inventory in the supply chain

In the supply-chain model, uncertainty exists, which is one reason why inventory, or safety stock, is kept both upstream and downstream of the cells. A critical decision of the logistics chain is to decide how much raw materials, work in process or finished-goods inventory to hold. Even companies using just-in-time approaches to operations management carry some inventory, and

with it comes the associated costs. This inventory is insurance against uncertainty which might arise for several reasons.

Uncertainty of the on-time delivery of suppliers

- The supplier quotes a delivery date, but he is late.
- There was a truck drivers' strike.
- The packaging equipment broke down.
- Two of the machine operators were sick.
- A ferryboat sank. (True experience of the author.)
- One of the suppliers was late in delivering the assembly screws.

The more unsure one is of the on-time delivery of the supplier, the more safety stock is held. Long lead times also add to uncertainty. If companies purchase complex components or raw materials, such as vanadium pumps, silicon chips or special pistons, the lead time may be long, say nine months. In this case the company contracts nine months ahead or more before these will reach the input to the transformation cell.

Uncertainty in manufacturing

During the production, or transformation, operation uncertainty may arise because:

- Another project tied up a key worker.
- The machine went out of alignment.
- One of the operators was injured on the shop floor.
- The subcontractor's components were not up to specification.

Figure 17.7 Supply-chain costs.

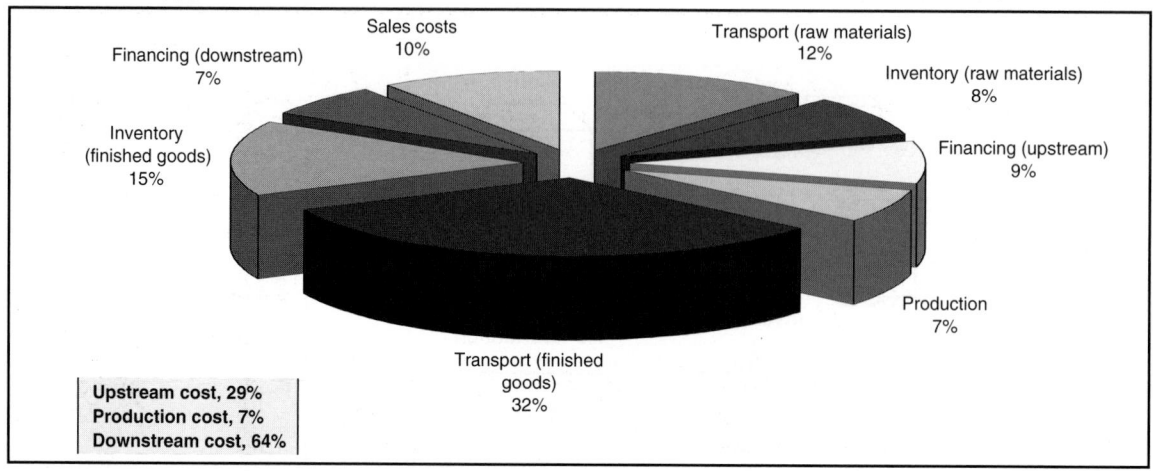

Financing (downstream) 7%

Sales costs 10%

Transport (raw materials) 12%

Inventory (raw materials) 8%

Inventory (finished goods) 15%

Financing (upstream) 9%

Production 7%

Transport (finished goods) 32%

Upstream cost, 29%
Production cost, 7%
Downstream cost, 64%

The more variable, or more uncertain, the operation, the more inventory is held. The more unreliable is the process operation, or the more lax is the preventative maintenance, the more safety stock is held.

Uncertainty of the client's real needs

- The client changes his mind at the last minute.
- The demand forecast was too low.
- 'Our clients are fickle'.
- The customer's customer cancelled his order.

The more fickle is the customer, or the more uncertainty in the forecasting technique, the larger is the inventory of finished products so that the customer can be satisfied from completed orders as needed.

To manage inventory better, firms need to audit performance to see what is happening with inventory movement, with the objective of making improvements. Better control of the uncertainties is critical as all inventory is safety stock to cover the uncertain world! See also Chapter 26, *Auditing Operations*.

PIPELINE MAPPING

A pipeline map is an analytical tool to monitor inventory movements and operating activity as an aid in supply-chain management. The pipeline map is a linear flow scheme of the supply chain, highlighting each operation in terms of the processing time and also the holding time that material stays in the supply chain. The object of the pipeline map is to expose clearly all the activity times and, when this has been done, improvements can be proposed to minimize these times and thus improve

throughput.[4] The concept and development of a pipeline map applies to any type of organization and here it is illustrated by the analysis of a small European foundry.

Foundry description

The foundry makes a wide variety of non-ferrous alloy products, such as rings, bearings, flange bearings, nuts, gears, impellers, pumps, valve bodies and slide bars for the automobile industry, chemical industry and other manufacturing firms. The alloys include tin–bronze, lead–bronze, aluminium–bronze, electrolytic and chrome copper, lead and its alloys, white metal, cupro-nickel and other aluminium alloys. Foundry customers include Valéo, Alsthom Atlantique, Pont-à-Mousson, Péchiney, Renault Vehicles Industriel, Mobil Oil and Rhône-Poulenc.

Processing steps

The simplified processing scheme is given in Figure 17.8 and the steps are detailed below.

1 Using the customer's blueprint design, a subcontractor makes a pre-mould casing in wood to serve as the sand mould for the alloy product. It takes two half sections of a mould to make one complete unit.
2 At the foundry, filler tubes of asbestos are embedded in the mould to allow for the pouring of the metal.
3 A mixture of sand (15 per cent new and 85 per cent recycled) and resin is poured into the pre-mould casing to form a compact mould for pouring the metal.
4 The mould is left so that the resin–sand mixture dries and hardens to take the exact form of the product.

Figure 17.8   Processing steps in a foundry.

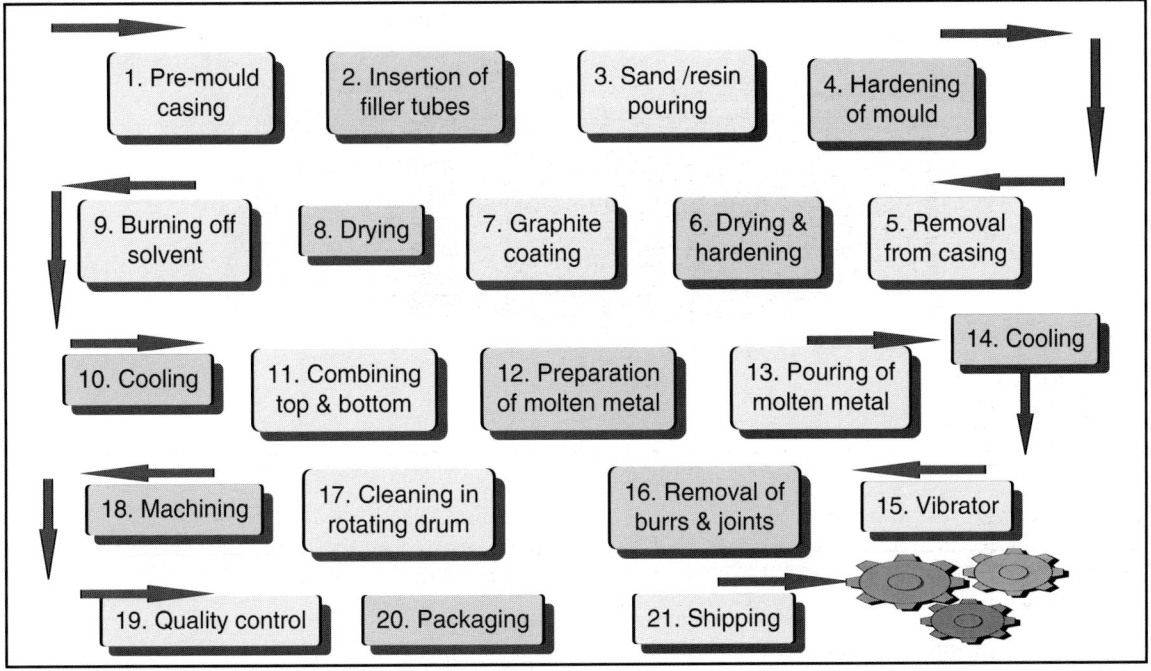

5   The sand mould is removed from the wooden casing.

6   The mould, free of the casing, is further allowed to dry and harden.

7   The mould is coated with a graphite and alcohol solvent mixture to smooth the surface of the sand.

8   The mould is left to dry, allowing the excess solvent to evaporate.

9   The mould is ignited, which burns off the alcohol solvent leaving a smooth surface around the mould. This will give a smooth finished to the metal product.

10   The mould is left to cool.

11   The two sections of the mould are united (bottom and top make a complete mould). The joint is sealed with a sand–resin mixture similar to that used for preparation of the mould.

12   The molten metal is prepared.

13   The molten metal is poured into the mould.

14   The mould is allowed to cool.

15   The mould is dumped onto a vibrator where it is broken and the sand falls off. The sand from the mould is sent to a regenerating vessel, where fines are removed. Regenerated sand is reused.

16   Burrs and moulding joints are cut from the metal product.

17   Forged pieces are cleaned in a rotating vessel, which contains small metal beads to rough-polish the surface.

18   Machining – the machine shop contains numerically controlled machines and operations include drilling, turning and polishing.

19   Quality control for dimension, surface finish and inspection of any irregularities in the metal.

20   Packaging – this involves wrapping the products in bubble packing for protection and then boxing in cardboard cartons.

21   Shipping – this involves preparing the shipping documents and contacting the shipping agent.

Pipeline map

The pipeline map developed for the foundry is given in Figure 17.9. The numbers on the x-axis correspond to the steps in Figure 17.8. Here, the vertical bars represent the time when the product is waiting before and after the process operation. This time may include cooling periods or just 'waiting'. The horizontal lines represent the time for each processing step

Pipeline length

The pipeline length is the sum of all the horizontal lines and is equivalent to the total processing time. This is

Figure 17.9 Pipeline map for a foundry.

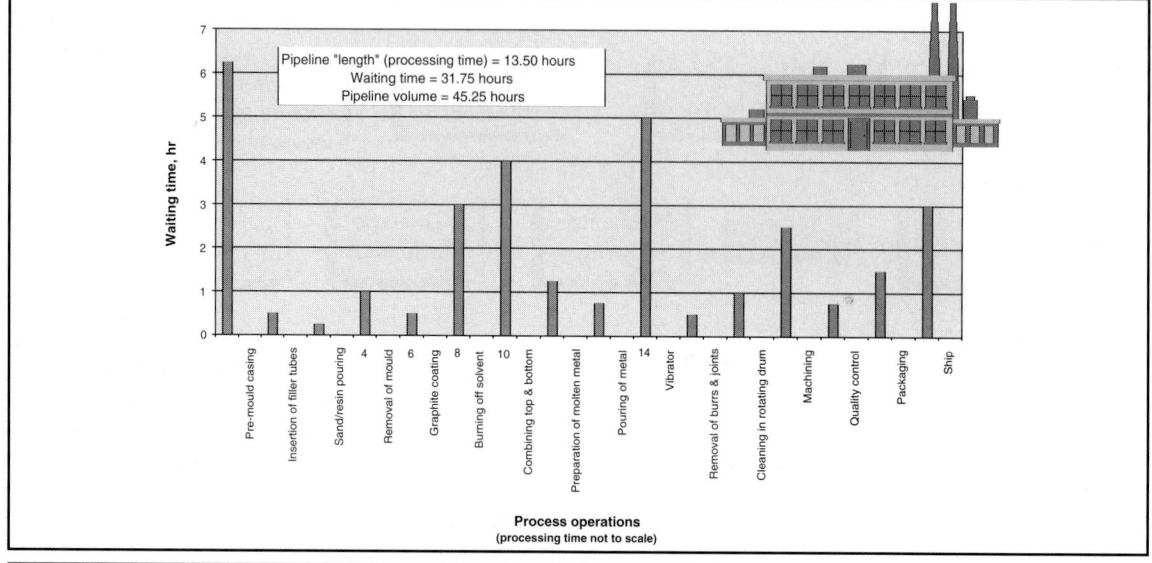

Process operations
(processing time not to scale)

Pipeline "length" (processing time) = 13.50 hours
Waiting time = 31.75 hours
Pipeline volume = 45.25 hours

the time taken to respond to the increase in demand, or the lead time to pull the end product through the pipeline, if current inventory levels are unchanged. In this example the pipeline length is 13.50 hours.

Pipeline height

The pipeline height is the sum of all the vertical bars and is representative of all the waiting time, or principally non-value added activities. In this example the pipeline height is 31.75 hours.

Pipeline volume

The pipeline volume is the sum of all the vertical and horizontal lines and is equivalent to the time required to respond to a decrease in demand. It is the time required to 'drain' the complete supply chain at the current rate of throughput. In this example the pipeline volume is 45.25 hours.

An objective of a pipeline map is to identify where either the vertical or horizontal lines can be reduced. If such reductions are possible, then inventory costs can be lowered and also customer response time can be improved. Often, if the horizontal lines, representing the process time, can be reduced, then the vertical lines representing the inventory holding time can also be reduced. For example, if a production manager is able to pull a product through four hours quicker, then he would be inclined to hold a correspondingly smaller inventory. In addition, reducing set-up times would help in reducing the vertical lines or the waiting time.

Complexity

In the complete logistics chain, the pipeline map is more complicated than the simpler linear production line. More likely, it will be tree-shaped, involving all the suppliers of different materials, including packaging, and the various distribution arms. However, breaking down the pipeline map into smaller manageable sections will help to identify the critical path in the logistics chain. The critical path would be that portion of the pipeline which has the largest volume.

When the pipeline map covers several organizations, such as suppliers, subcontractors, manufacturers, distribution centres, retail outlets and the like, tall vertical lines may be observed at the beginning and end of the organizational boundaries of the pipeline map. These represent the high level of inventory of delivered material or finished goods waiting to be shipped to customers. All organizations, such as the supplier or the manufacturer, are ensuring against uncertainty, one in supply, the other in demand. Through better communication and sharing of information, it should be possible to reduce the length of, or even eliminate, at least one of the vertical lines.

Usefulness of a pipeline map

Using a pipeline map will help to uncover potential problems as:

■ inventory in unmanaged areas;

- disjointed flows as a result of uncoupled production processes;
- employees not having the same objective because of different performance measures, conflicting strategies or a poor organization;
- interface difficulties with players such as sloppy suppliers, manufacturing overproducing for fear of stockouts or sales overforecasting for fear of not having enough products for clients;
- integrated operating problems, such as lack of management support, unreliable suppliers, quality of raw materials sometimes being low, poor communication throughout the supply chain, poor customer forecasts, unreliable data, motivation levels low, etc.

The client is King. An optimized supply chain is customer-focused, always meeting internal and customer schedules. It helps to build teamwork within the organization and develop partnerships externally with clients and suppliers. In the long term, a well-managed supply chain will help to increase market share, reduce costs, increase profits and increase quality. This is where a pipeline map is useful.

The variety funnel

A variety funnel can be developed and used in conjunction with the pipeline map. The variety funnel shows the reduction of flexibility with materials as the operation moves through the supply chain. A variety funnel is illustrated in Figure 17.10, showing that, with the increase of added value to the product moving through the chain, there is less flexibility with components, or in this case ingredients, the further one moves downstream. The variety funnel has similarities to the VAT analyses presented in Chapter 6 *Design of the Product*.

DISTRIBUTION REQUIREMENTS PLANNING

Distribution requirements planning (DRP) is the planning process in the supply chain to help ensure that finished goods destined for a client reach the right location, on the right date and in the right quantity. The supply chain covering the DRP may be from the manufacturer, through the various distribution centres, to the retailer, or it may just be from the distribution centres to the retailers in a service firm, for example a large grocery store moving finished goods from the distribution centre to the retail stores.

Integrated distribution requirements plan

A more complex and complete DRP would be a module interconnected with the master production schedule and other planning activities of the production organization, as illustrated in Figure 17.11. Here a production centre is located in Lyon, France, and there are two distribution centres, one in Strasbourg, France, and the other in Toulouse, France. Retail outlets are in Brussels, Belgium, and Amsterdam, Holland, served by the distribution centre in Strasbourg, and Bordeaux, France, and Madrid, Spain, served by the distribution in Toulouse. Physical flow is from the production centre to the distribution centres and finally the retail outlets. The flow of information, by electronic data interchanged if the network is established, is from the retail outlets to the distribution centres, and then from the distribution centres to the production centre. The production centre in Lyon, with the required client information, then develops its master production schedule, and thence the material requirements plan. The distribution requirements plan might be a pull or a push system.

Pull system

A pull system is the most common type of planning approach and for many it is the only distribution requirements plan. A pull system is when the outlet at the lowest level, or end, of the distribution network, usually the retailer, initiates the order. The retailer 'pulls' the products through the distribution, or supply-chain, network. The retailer has its own ordering policy and the supplier only makes a delivery when a specific order has been made.

Client demands

The only independent demand is from the retail outlets. The other demands are dependent demands. This is analogous to the MRP system. In MRP, the independent demand is the finished product. The dependent demands are the components that go into making the finished product.

Master production schedule

The demand from each of the retail outlets imposes a master production schedule (MPS) on the manufacturer, which may not be optimum. The manufacturer loses some control of his planning process and has to be flexible to accommodate customer demands. In some instances the pull system may impose a MPS on the manufacturer that is not feasible, when, for example, insufficient resources are available. If a just-in-time

Figure 17.10   Chocolate manufacture: variety funnel.

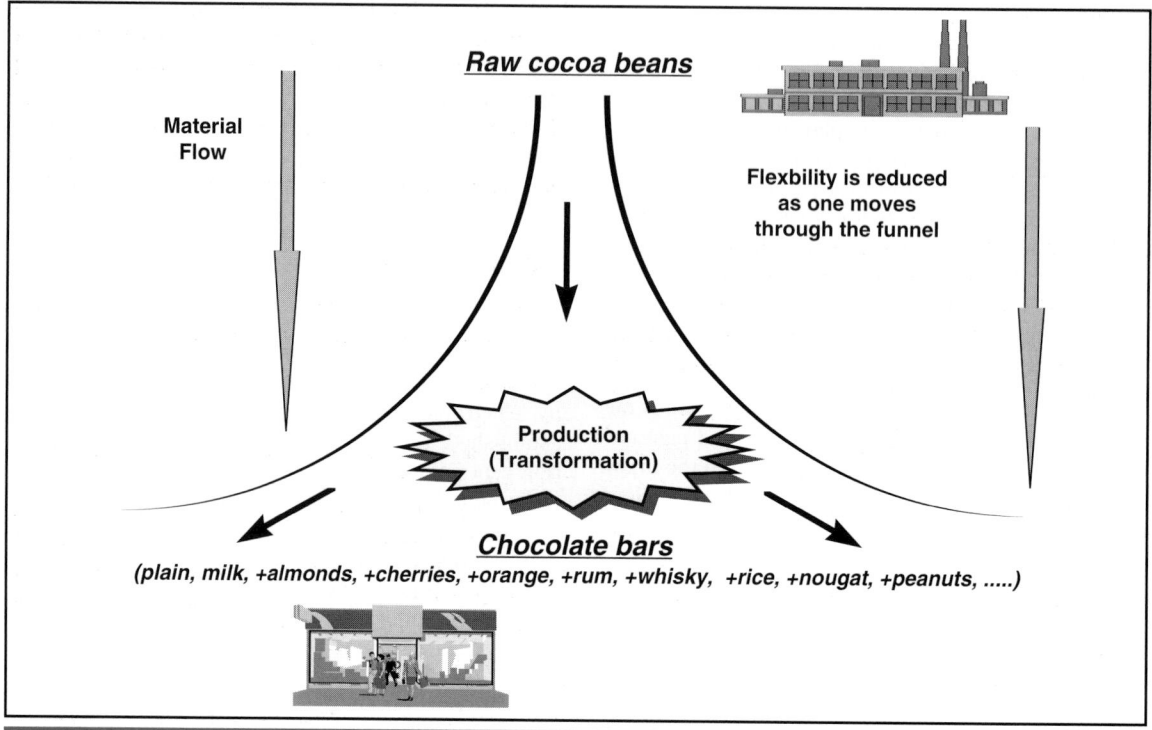

Figure 17.11   Integrated distribution and manufacturing.

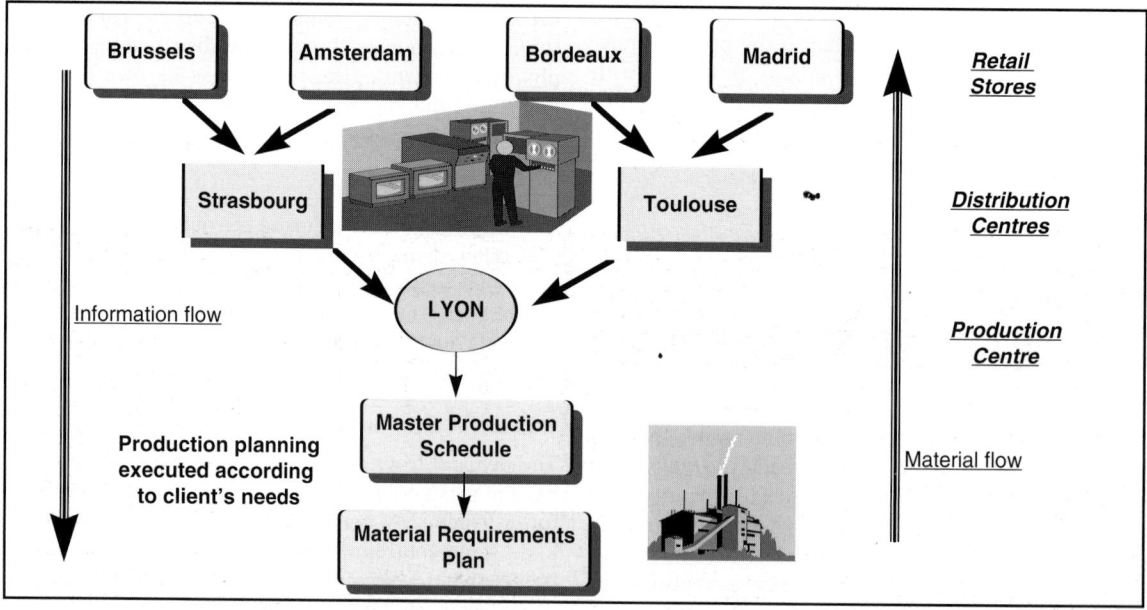

system is in place, the manufacturer will have more flexibility.

The development of the pull system DRP is shown by the worked example, *Chianti Wine* (Part I).

Push system

In the push system, the supplier at the beginning of the network, usually the manufacturer, produces the finished products according to his own master production schedule (MPS). This MPS would have been established according to estimates of clients demands and then modified to suit the company's resources available at the manufacturing site. Material is pushed through the distribution channel when the products are ready. The flow of material may not necessarily be in harmony with the needs of the final retail outlet. As a result, the retailer accumulates too much stock or, worse, he runs out of inventory. This was a situation in the 1970s in the US, when automobile companies would manufacture cars, push them through the supply chain, and they would then end up on a dealer's lot waiting to be sold. The development of the push system is the exercise problem, *Chianti Wine* (Part II).

Hybrid of the pull and push system

A hybrid of the push and pull systems in distribution requirements is to use the distribution centre as the inventory buffer. In the scheme presented in Figure 17.11, Lyon develops its master production schedule to suit its own resources. Finished products are then 'pushed' out to the distribution centres at Strasbourg and Toulouse. The retail outlets in Brussels, Amsterdam, Bordeaux and Madrid 'pull' their product

requirements as needed from the corresponding distribution centre. It is the distribution centres that are the buffer and incur corresponding storage costs. To avoid stockouts (assuming that the gross amount produced by Lyon is sufficient), then either Lyon increases its distribution to Strasbourg and reduces it to Toulouse, or vice-versa. Alternatively, Strasbourg and Toulouse have the possibility of exchanging inventory as needed.

Alternatives to DRP

Some simple alternatives to a distribution requirements plan network might be the following.

Base-stock system

A base-stock system is where an organization maintains a base, or minimum, stock of a certain product. The ordering policy is that each time an item is sold, an order is placed for a new item. This type of ordering, a sell-one, buy-one approach, is a form of just-in-time. It might be an approach used for large items, or for retail outlets that have limited space for inventory such as refrigerators or other large household appliances.

Reorder-point system

In a reorder-point system, or replenishment system, the inventory policy of the outlet is to maintain a certain level, which is considered as full stock. When the inventory level falls to some predetermined low level, the inventory is replenished. To take into account demand during the lead time, a certain amount of minimum inventory is maintained. (See also Chapter 11, *Inventory Management.*)

Both these two cases are pull systems, since it is the lowest level of chain that initiates the order.

WORKED EXAMPLE: CHIANTI WINE (PART I)

Situation

A small winery in Milan, Italy, produces, among its many products, Chianti wine. This is bottled in one-litre green bottles with a colourful cork and has the traditional Italian raffia around the bottle. The winery has two distribution centres, one in Zurich, Switzerland, and the other in Torino, Italy. The centre in Zurich supplies three retail outlets in Baden, Zug and St

Gallen. The centre in Torino supplies retail outlets in Como, Piancenzo and Bergamo. The network for the system is shown in Figure 17.12.

The average quantity of wine demanded (sold) by each retail outlet, the current inventory on-hand, and the quantity ordered from the distribution centre each time an order is made are given in Tables 17.2. All the data is in cases of wine. Delivery time from the distribution centre to the retail outlet is one week.

Table 17.2 Data for the Chianti retail outlets

Switzerland				Italy			
Retail outlet	Weekly demand	Inventory on hand	Order quantity	Retail outlet	Weekly demand	Inventory on hand	Order quantity
Baden	8	12	15	Como	15	18	25
Zug	9	14	20	Piancenzo	18	21	35
St Gallen	12	19	15	Bergamo	22	32	30

Figure 17.12 Distribution network: Milan winery and its outlets.

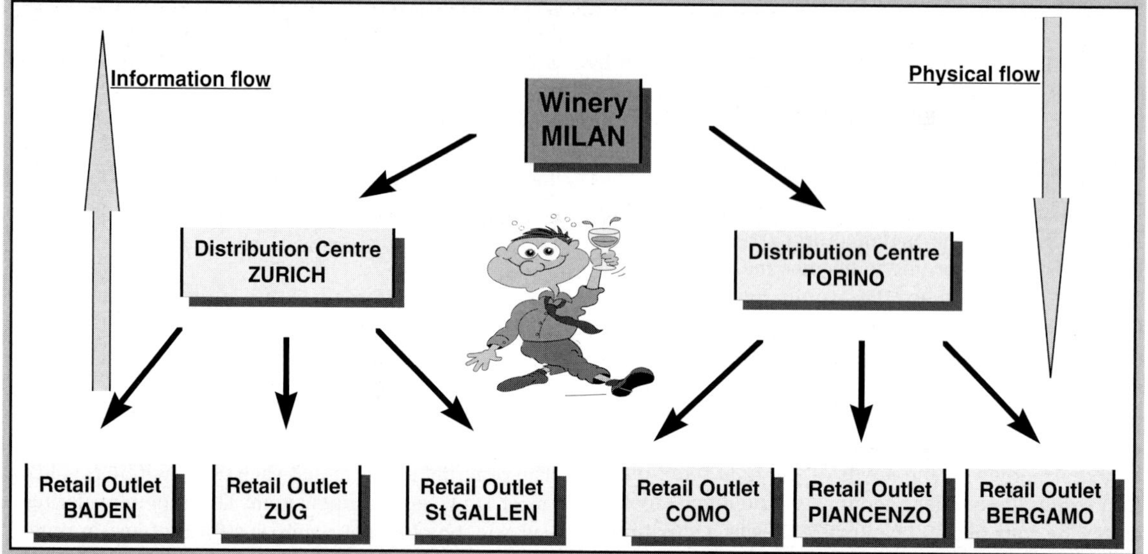

Information flow

Weekly demand

This is the average amount sold per week based on past data. The weekly forecast could be different if the retailer had a more sophisticated planning model.

Inventory on hand

Inventory on hand is that quantity of cases of wine in the store available for sale.

Order quantity

This is the amount of cases ordered by the retail outlet according to its purchasing policy. This would be an economic quantity based on the inventory storage cost, space available and transportation costs.

Similar data for the Distribution Centres are given in Table 17.3, which shows the current inventory on hand and the quantity ordered by each distribution centre from the winery each time an order is placed. All the data is in cases of wine. Delivery time from the winery to the distribution centre is one week.

Table 17.3 Data for the Chianti distribution centres

Distribution centre	Inventory on hand	Order quantity
Zurich, Switzerland	65	50
Torino, Italy	105	70

Inventory on-hand

This is that quantity of cases of wine in the distribution centre available to be shipped to the retail outlets.

Order quantity

This is the amount of cases ordered by the distribution centre according to its ordering policy. This would be an economic quantity based on the inventory storage cost, space available and transportation costs.

Finally Table 17.4 gives the inventory on hand at the winery and the production lot each time an order is made. The production lot represents the cases of wine bottled and packaged. Normally the wine is stored in bulk in large fermenting-type vessels and only bottled when needed. It takes one week to bottle and package the wine.

Table 17.4 Data for the Milan winery

	Inventory on-hand	Production Lot
Milan	80	160

Inventory on-hand

This is that quantity of cases of wine in the winery available to be dispatched to the distribution centres.

Production lot

This is that quantity of cases that the winery prepares each time for shipping to the distribution centres. As already noted, the Chianti wine is stored in large container vessels and is only bottled and packed when needed by the distribution centres.

Required

1 Develop a 'pull' distribution requirements plan over an eight week period using the weekly demand from each retail outlet as the independent demand that pulls the product through the network.
2 Calculate the average inventory each week at the six retail outlets.

Solution

1 The distribution requirements plan, preceded by the initial data, is illustrated in Table 17.5. (Week 9 is included in order to complete the planning schedule.) The DRP plan was generated automatically from the initial data using Microsoft Excel. Each retail outlet only generates a demand when the inventory level is insufficient to satisfy the

Table 17.5a   Chianti wine: pull system (initial data)

	Weekly demand	Inventory on hand	Order Quantity
Supplied from Distribution Centre at Zurich (Delivery time from Zurich to retail outlet is one week)			
Baden	8	12	15
Zug	9	14	20
St Gallen	12	19	15
Supplied from Distribution Centre at Torino (Delivery time from Torino to retail outlet is one week)			
Como	15	18	25
Piancenzo	18	21	35
Bergamo	22	32	30
Supplied from Milan winery (Delivery time from Milan to distribution centre is one week)			
Zurich	65	50	
Torino	105	70	

	Inventory on-hand	Production Lot
Milan winery	80	150

Table 17.5b   Chianti wine: pull system

		(Inventory on hand at end of week)								
	0	1	2	3	4	5	6	7	8	9
Retail Stores – Switzerland										
Baden										
Gross requirements		8	8	8	8	8	8	8	8	8
Inventory on hand	12	4	11	3	10	2	9	1	8	0
Planned receipts		0	15	0	15	0	15	0	15	0
Planned orders	0	15	0	15	0	15	0	15	0	15
Zug										
Gross requirements		9	9	9	9	9	9	9	9	9
Inventory on hand	14	5	16	7	18	9	0	11	2	13
Planned receipts		0	20	0	20	0	0	20	0	20
Planned orders	0	20	0	20	0	0	20	0	20	0
St Gallen										
Gross requirements		12	12	12	12	12	12	12	12	12
Inventory on hand	19	7	10	13	1	4	7	10	13	1
Planned receipts		0	15	15	0	15	15	15	15	0
Planned orders	0	15	15	0	15	15	15	15	0	15
Retail Stores – Italy										
Como										
Gross requirements		15	15	15	15	15	15	15	15	15
Inventory on hand	18	3	13	23	8	18	3	13	23	8
Planned receipts		0	25	25	0	25	0	25	25	0
Planned orders	0	25	25	0	25	0	25	25	0	25
Piancenzo										
Gross requirements		18	18	18	18	18	18	18	18	18
Inventory on hand	21	3	20	2	19	1	18	0	17	34
Planned receipts		0	35	0	35	0	35	0	35	35
Planned orders	0	35	0	35	0	35	0	35	35	0
Bergamo										
Gross requirements		22	22	22	22	22	22	22	22	22
Inventory on hand	32	10	18	26	4	12	20	28	6	14
Planned receipts		0	30	30	0	30	30	30	0	30
Planned orders	0	30	30	0	30	30	30	0	30	30

	Inventory on hand at end of week									
	0	1	2	3	4	5	6	7	8	9
Distribution Centres										
Zurich										
Gross requirements	0	50	15	35	15	30	35	30	20	30
Inventory on hand	65	15	0	15	0	20	35	5	35	5
Planned receipts		0	0	50	0	50	50	0	50	0
Planned orders	0	0	50	0	50	50	0	50	0	30

	Number dispatched in week									
Zurich routing to:										
Baden	0	15	0	15	0	15	0	15	0	15
Zug	0	20	0	20	0	0	20	0	20	0
St Gallen	0	15	15	0	15	15	15	15	0	15
Total	0	50	15	35	15	30	35	30	20	30

	Inventory on hand at end of week									
Torino										
Gross requirements	0	90	55	35	55	65	55	60	65	55
Inventory on hand	105	15	30	65	10	15	30	40	45	60
Planned receipts	0	70	70	0	70	70	70	70	70	70
Planned orders	0	70	70	0	70	70	70	70	70	0

	Number dispatched in week									
Torino routing to:										
Como	0	25	25	0	25	0	25	25	0	25
Piancenzo	0	35	0	35	0	35	0	35	35	0
Bergamo	0	30	30	0	30	30	30	0	30	30
Total	0	90	55	35	55	65	55	60	65	55

	Inventory on hand at end of week									
Manufacturing Site – Milan										
Gross requirements	0	70	120	0	120	120	70	120	70	30
Inventory on hand	80	10	50	50	90	130	60	100	30	0
Bottled/ready		0	160	0	160	160	0	160	0	0
Planned production	0	160	0	160	160	0	160	0	0	0

	Number dispatched in week									
Actual shipping from Milan to:										
Zurich	0	0	50	0	50	50	0	50	0	
Torino	0	70	70	0	70	70	70	70	70	
Total	0	70	120	0	120	120	70	120	70	

	Average inventory at retail levels, week $[n + (n + 1)]/2$								
Baden	8.00	7.50	7.00	6.50	6.00	5.50	5.00	4.50	
Zug	9.50	10.50	11.50	12.50	13.50	4.50	5.50	6.50	
St Gallen	13.00	8.50	11.50	7.00	2.50	5.50	8.50	11.50	
Como	10.50	8.00	18.00	15.50	13.00	10.50	8.00	18.00	
Piancenzo	12.00	11.50	11.00	10.50	10.00	9.50	9.00	8.50	
Bergamo	21.00	14.00	22.00	15.00	8.00	16.00	24.00	17.00	

demand. All inventory data is that for the end of the week. For example, considering the Baden retail outlet.

Baden retail outlet

- In week 1 there is sufficient inventory on hand of 12 cases to satisfy the demand (of eight cases) for that week.

- Inventory level at the end of week 1 drops to four cases given by (12 − 8).

- The four cases at end of Week 1 will be insufficient to supply the demand for Week 2, and so an order is made in week 1 of 15 cases according to policy. This quantity arrives in week 2.

- At end of week 2 there are 11 cases of wine on hand (15 + 4 − 8).

- The movement of inventory continues in the same manner for the eight-week planning schedule.
- At week 8, the ending inventory is 8 (15 + 1 − 8), so there is sufficient for the ninth week on the assumption that the demand requirements are the same.
- For the planned ordered cells, a logic function (an *if* clause) is used to generate the value. For example for Baden, Week 1, the test is:
    If the inventory on hand at the end of week 1 is less than the demand, then order the required amount (15 cases); if not the value is 0.

Zurich distribution centre

All the planned orders for the three retail outlets in Switzerland are totalled to give the demand required from the corresponding distribution centre. For example:

- The total demand for the Switzerland retail outlets at week 1 is 50 cases (15 +20 + 15). This is the gross requirement for week 1 for Zurich.
- At the start of week 1 there are 65 cases, at the end there are 15 cases (65 − 50).

Italy – retail outlet and distribution centre

The same calculation is made for the all the retail outlets and the distribution centre in Italy.

- In Torino, at the start of week 1 there are 105 cases, at the end there are 15 cases (105 − 90). The 90 cases is the total ordered by the retail outlets in Italy at the end of week 1. These will arrive in Week 2 as planned receipts.

Milan winery

- The gross requirement for Milan at Week 1 is 70 cases. This is triggered by the planned orders from the distribution centres at Week 1 (0 + 70).

- The gross requirement for Milan at Week 2 is 120 cases. This is triggered by the planned orders from the distribution centres at Week 1 (50 + 70).

Plan period

- The distribution resource plans are generated for the eight-week period. It is assumed that the demand for the ninth week is the same is for the eighth, so that in some cases a planned order is triggered.
- The average inventory for each retail site is shown at the end of Table 17.5. It is based on the average of the inventory at the end of one week and the inventory at the end of the following week.

Comments

- The only independent demand is from the retail outlets. The other demands are dependent demands based on these quantities. This is analogous to the MRP system, where the independent demand is the finished product. The dependent demands are the components that go into making the finished product.
- The demand from each of the retail outlets imposes a master production schedule (MPS) on the manufacturer, which may not be optimum. The manufacturer loses some control of his planning process and has to be flexible to accommodate customer demands. In some instances, the pull system may impose a MPS on the manufacturer that is not feasible.
- All the retail outlets hold a certain amount of stock, but there is never a stockout situation.
    (Note: week 9 is included to complete the planning schedule.)

ELECTRONIC DATA INTERCHANGE

A supply chain works in two directions. There is the physical flow of goods from purchasing, through manufacturing, to delivery of the finished product to the client (upstream to downstream). Then there is the information flow from the client to the retail outlet, back to the distribution centre, to the manufacturing centre and to the suppliers of raw materials or components (downstream to upstream). The speed with which the products are delivered depends very much on the effectiveness of communication in the supply chain and this is where Electronic Data Interchange (EDI) plays a significant role.

EDI is the transfer of information from a computer at one site to another computer at a different location using transmission through the telephone, or other network, system. (See also Chapter 7, *Process Design and the Operations Network*). Information sent using EDI might include such things as customer orders, purchase requests, delivery orders, shipping instructions, manufacturing requests and the like. EDI replaces the paper documents that are exchanged between organizations and is described as 'paperless trading'. A simple scheme illustrating a supply chain in which EDI is used is given in Figure 17.13.

Before EDI

Regular mail was the alternative before electronic communication. It could take an average of eight days for an order to get from a customer to a supplier, where the activity involved included the following:

- The customer writes out the order.
- The customer encloses the order in an envelope.
- The customer puts the order in the mail.
- The postman delivers the letter to the supplier.
- The supplier opens the envelope.
- The supplier logs in the order requirements.

With EDI

Using electronic data interchange, the time to communicate an order may be as little as a few minutes:

Figure 17.13 EDI and the supply chain.

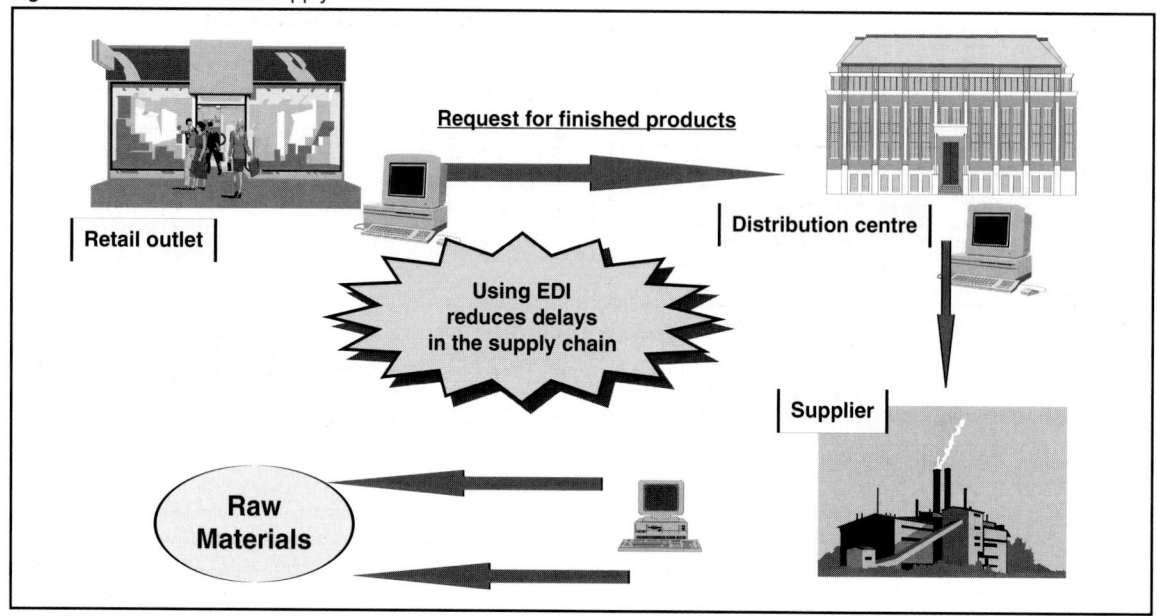

- The customer types in his order on his computer terminal.
- The order is transmitted electronically to the supplier's computer.
- The supplier does not have to record invoice details as these are already in his computer file.

Advantages of EDI

Some of the advantages of EDI include:

- There is quicker response as there is real-time customer service.
- It eliminates paper and thus reduces costs.
- It is inexpensive because there are fewer people involved in sending the message.
- There is better-quality service as there are fewer administrative mistakes.
- The order status is always available, so it is easy to track orders.
- The inventory management is more effective as there is quicker update of units in stock.
- It provides a 'closeness' with customers or suppliers, promoting more cooperation with the possibility of creating partnerships or alliances.

EDI standards

Agreed message standards have to be used with EDI in order that messages sent are in an acceptable format for the receiver. The simple example in Figure 17.14

indicates that the current message format of a customer does not correspond with the format of the supplier.

If only two firms are involved then they can agree on a data structure. However, in the automobile industry, companies like Citröen, Ford and Mercedes Benz have thousands of suppliers. In this case, it is necessary to have an agreed standard. The Organization for Data Exchange by Telephone Transmission in Europe (ODETTE) is a group within the Society of Motor Manufacturers (SMMT) that has created EDI message standards for the automobile industry. Another, created by the United Nations, is EDIFACT or Electronic Data Interchange for Administration, Commerce and Trade.

Drawbacks of EDI

Some of the drawbacks of EDI are:

- The initial set-up costs are high as they can include purchase of computer hardware, software, cabling and training of personnel.
- Users have to agree to message standards.
- Whether EDI messages are acceptable as legal documents.
- It reduces the human contact between the parties concerned.

The World Wide Web and the supply chain

An extension of EDI including catalogue shopping, ordering, delivery and invoicing, using the World Wide

Figure 17.14 EDI formats that do not match.

Customer's Format	Supplier's Format
CUSTOMER ADDRESS	PRODUCT REFERENCE
CUSTOMER NAME	PRICE
PRODUCT REFERENCE	SUPPLIER NAME
PRICE	SUPPLIER ADDRESS
SUPPLIER ADDRESS	CUSTOMER NAME
SUPPLIER NAME	CUSTOMER ADDRESS

Web over the Internet is illustrated in Figure 17.15. This supply chain network operates as follows:

1 A customer browsing the Web sees an article he or she would like and places the order electronically to the supplier.
2 The order is electronically received.
3 The supplier checks electronically to see if there is sufficient inventory in stock, and also checks the profile of the customer regarding his or her credit rating.
4 The order is verified and accepted.
5 Necessary shipping instructions are sent to the warehouse.
6 At the warehouse, the item is physically located, packaged and sent to the customer.

7 The Accounting department is notified of the order.
8 Customer is billed electronically.

All the transactions have been carried out by electronic interchange, with the only physical flow being the delivery of the item. The lead time for this sort of purchasing is of the order of five days. The extract of the article given as Box 17.1 illustrates how Fruit of the Loom (textiles) uses the World Wide Web for its selling activity.[5]

THE RETAIL FOOD INDUSTRY

The retail food industry, a service organization, represents a special supply chain in that food products, and especially fresh foods, have to be shipped rapidly through the network. There is no value-added process operation as found in manufacturing; instead the 'value-added' step is getting the products, of the right size and of the correct brand, to the desired place on the expected date.

Product variety

In the retail food industry there are numerous different types of products handled (fruit and vegetables, meat

Figure 17.15 Using the Internet in the supply chain.

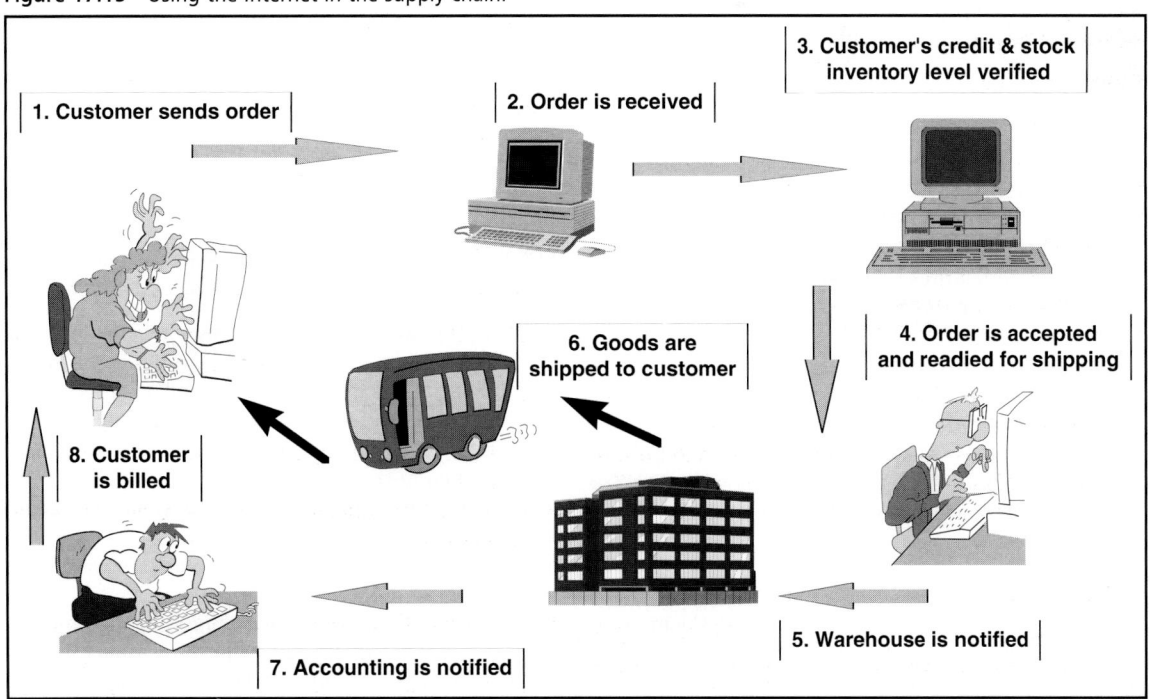

1. Customer sends order
2. Order is received
3. Customer's credit & stock inventory level verified
4. Order is accepted and readied for shipping
5. Warehouse is notified
6. Goods are shipped to customer
7. Accounting is notified
8. Customer is billed

Box 17.1 Fruit of the Loom

In the meantime, some companies are already rigging E-commerce systems (electronic business systems for purchasing, distribution and invoicing) on the Net. Fruit of the Loom Inc., until recently a self-confessed technology laggard, is using the Net to make up for lost time. Led by computer executives hired away from Federal Express Corp. and elsewhere, the apparel maker is using the Web to one-up Hanes Cos. and other brands in the market for blank T-shirts and other items sold through novelty stores and at special events.

Fruit depends on some 50 wholesalers nationwide to ship its goods in bulk to thousands of silk-screen printers, embroidery shops and similar outfits. And now, it's offering to put those wholesalers on the Web, at virtually no charge to them. Fruit's plan is to give each one a complete computer system, called Active On-line, that's programmed to display collar catalogues, process electronic orders 24 hours a day and manage inventories.

One of Fruit's major goals is to avoid losing customers when a wholesaler is out of stock. If, for instance, a silk screener needs 1000 black T-shirts in a hurry for a Megadeth concert and the wholesaler is low, Fruit's central warehouse can be notified to ship the shirts directly to the customer. 'We'll make Fruit's inventory a virtual inventory for our wholesalers,' says Charles M Kirk, Fruit's chief information officer.

Until now, it would have taken years to build a rich E-commerce system – even if it were possible on the closed, mainframe-based EDI networks run by companies such as GE and IBM. But for Fruit of the Loom, Connect Inc.'s software called OneServer, and a catalogue program from Snickleways Interactive, helped to get it on-line in just a few months. And its retailers need only an ordinary PC with a modem and Web-browsing software.

Business Week, 10 June 1996

---

and fish, dry foods such as rice, beans and sugar, canned foods, beverages, paper goods, etc.). In hypermarkets (common in Europe), as well as food items, there is a complete range of consumer goods such as washing machines, computers, school items, etc. Some goods are standard, others are very specialized. Some are from local suppliers; some are national; others come from foreign suppliers. Proper management of inventories, especially for fresh-food stocks that have a short life, and the logistics chain is the key to success of the organization. As an illustration of size, the following are some 1994 statistics of Casino, a major food and consumer goods retailer based in St Etienne, France.

Casino

- Annual turnover of FF70 billion ($14 billion)
- 109 hypermarkets, whose surface area ranges between 5000 and 17 000 m^2
- 491 supermarkets
- 2318 grocery stores (supérettes), with on average a surface area of about 180 m^2
- 224 cafeterias
- 14 warehouses with 490 000 m^2 of storage area
- 600 000 daily deliveries
- logistics network computer-integrated
- 2000 Casino own-label products in addition to brand names
- Over 50 000 employees and agents

Distribution

The logistics for retail food companies like Casino represents a significant cost, estimated at up to 25 per cent of the turnover. The industry attempts to operate in a just-in-time mode, keeping inventory levels to a minimum, and the use of transportation is optimized. Lorries may serve one or a very few stores, delivering a variety of different products so that a driver only has to drive to one urban area and park. The alternative would be one lorry serving many stores with the same product. In this case there is a lot of dead time as the lorry has to negotiate traffic at several locations, park and unload. The larger the number of delivery sites, the greater is the amount of 'non-added-value time' due to delays as a recent study illustrates.[6] For one delivery site, the extra delay over the planned schedule was 30 min, for two sites it was 90 min and for three sites 210 min. In addition, towards to end of the route the lorry is half empty and waiting time of the lorry at a location has to be paid for by the retail outlet.

Fresh foods

Figure 17.16 illustrates a typical supply chain network for perishable items like fruit and vegetables:

- At 07:00 Monday the store communicates, by computer network, its requirements to the head office.
- The head office aggregates similar orders from other stores and relays this to the supplier at 07:30 Monday. At the same time, the retailer's warehouse is notified of the arrival of a pending order.
- The order is shipped from the producer (supplier) between 10:30 and 14:30 Monday.
- The order is received at the producer's warehouse between 14:30 and 18:30 Monday
- The order is broken down according to retailer's requirement and shipped from the supplier's warehouse between 17:30 and 21:30 Monday.

- The order is received at the retailer's warehouse between 20:30 Monday and 00:30 Tuesday.
- The order is dispatched at 03:30 Tuesday and is received by 06:30 Tuesday.

Times depend on the locations of the various sites, loading and unloading times and travel times. However, the object is to ensure that the store receives the produce the day after it is ordered. For fresh food, attention is given to using local producers and conveniently located warehouses.

Dry and canned foods

Figure 17.17 illustrates the logistics management chain for these types of goods. The principle is the same as for fresh foods, although the objective here is to have the products delivered within two weeks of order.

Selecting a distribution centre

The following are some considerations in establishing or selecting a distribution centre or warehouse:

- First, is the distribution centre really needed? Costs may be reduced by minimizing the number of distribution centres.

- Would it be more cost-effective to subcontract the physical distribution rather than operate it yourself? Unisabi pet foods, a subsidiary of Mars, operates in this way, where it subcontracts all the storage and distribution of both the raw materials and finished products.
- How close is the facility to final clients? Is the site in an optimum location? (See Chapter 3, *Site Selection*.)
- What about security, particularly from theft?
- What handling equipment will be necessary? What would be the cost to fully automate the facility, including the packing?
- What are the overall operating costs, including labour, equipment and capital cost of the facility?
- What is the inventory holding cost?
- What is the profit margin from the facility?
- Is there ease of access to the centre? Is it close to major transportation arteries?
- How close is it to production centres or suppliers?
- Is the layout of facility suitable for efficient operation?
- Will it be operated at close to capacity?
- What is the maximum capacity? Is there room for expansion?

Figure 17.16 Supply chain for fresh food.

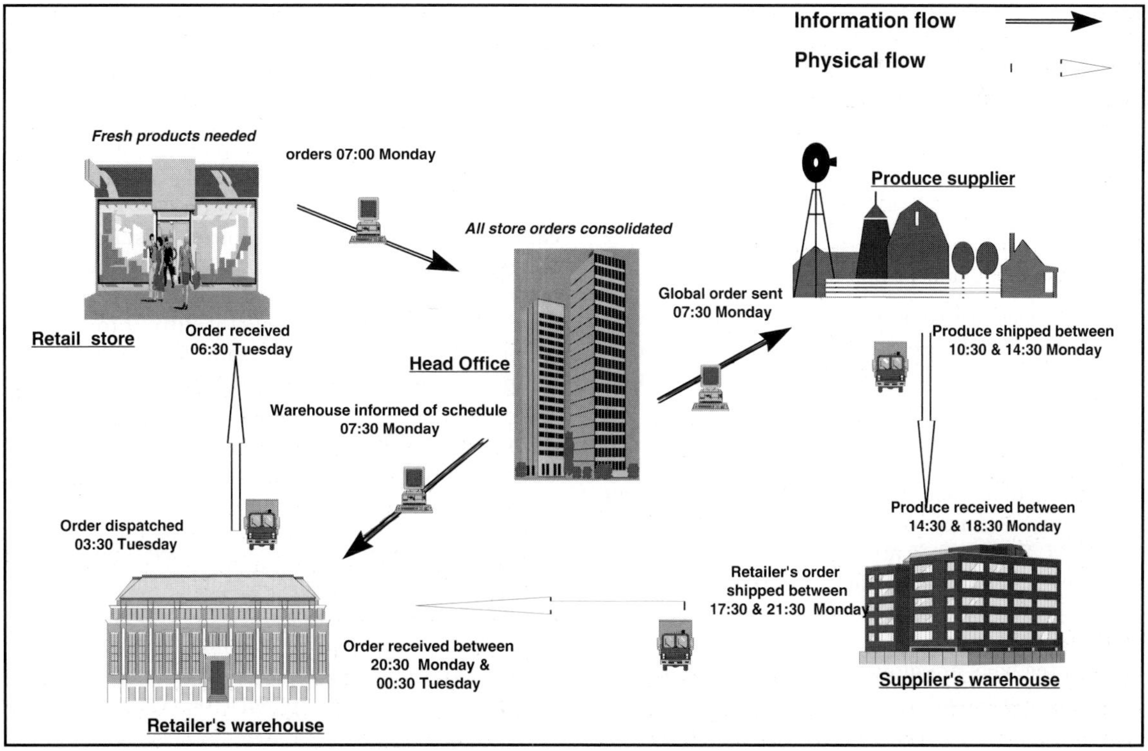

Figure 17.17 Supply chain for dry and canned goods.

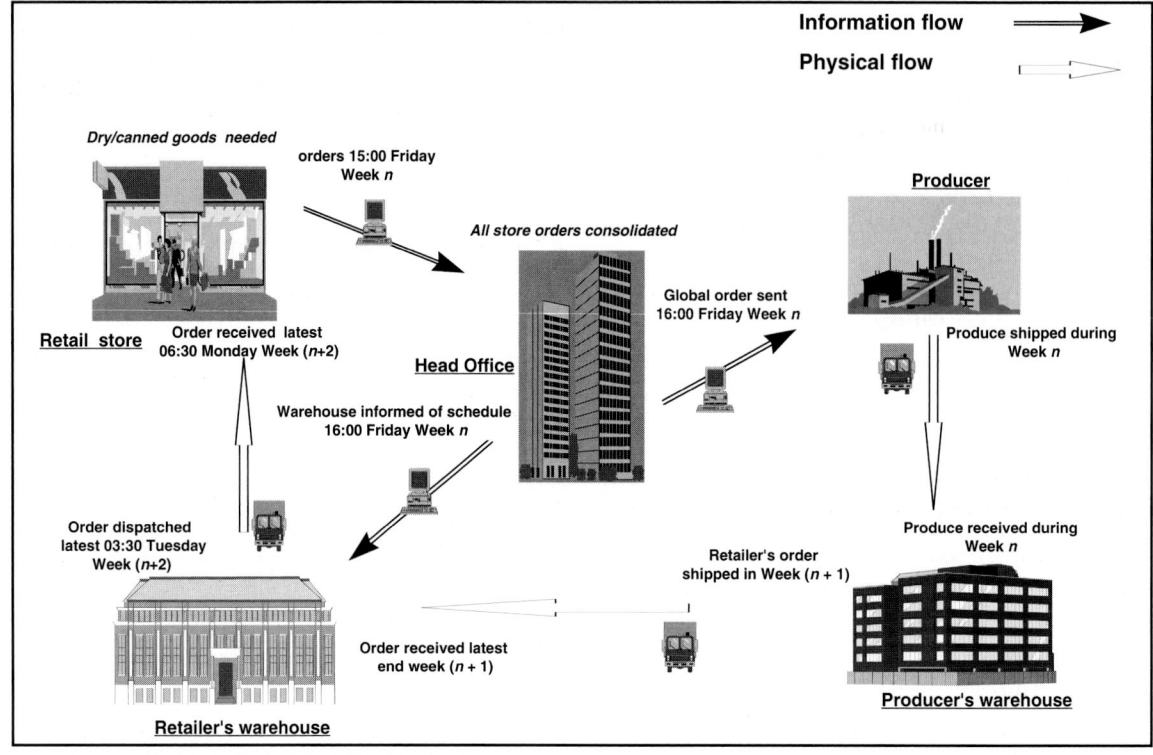

General management of the warehouse facilities

In addition to the computer-controlled network planning of the distribution for retail foods, warehouse management plays an important roll in keeping an efficient supply chain. The following are some considerations.

Crossdocking

When products arrive at a regional warehouse from a centralized warehouse, they normally have to be unloaded from the truck, logged in, broken down into smaller units, or units specific for a customer need, and then loaded onto another truck. All of these operations take time, involve labour and increase inventory holding time. In total, they add to the logistics cost. To minimize this, a policy of crossdocking is sometimes employed. When goods arrive, every effort is made so that they just 'cross the docks'. This principle is to avoid opening large containers, logging products in and breaking down packages into smaller units. Instead, the units are directly relocated to their corresponding dispatching truck.

Computer control

Some warehouses have a computer control system, which manages the arrival of the products from the warehouse and the preparation of the orders for individual retail stores. For the preparation of the order, the computer software produces the required label, indicating quantity and the location where each article can be found in the warehouse. Most software is able to present the labels in both alphanumeric and barcode form. Once the articles have been retrieved from the picking area the label is affixed to the customer order, which is thus ready for shipping. The computer labels are a form of Kanban card with the same objective as in a manufacturing operation, to reduce written or verbal instructions and to smooth material flow.

Combining warehouses

Historically, fresh produce and dried and canned goods have been treated separately as their handling, storage, and inspection requirements are quite different. However, this resulted in a duplication of loading, shipping and unloading. To avoid this duplication, a concept has been put forward of combining fresh food and dry unit warehouses (Casino calls this the Pump).

Benchmarking

To compare and challenge the productivity within a distribution network, some companies develop an internal benchmarking policy. Some elements compared in benchmarking are:

- stocking costs per type of product per m² of storage area;
- the number of packages prepared per unit of time;
- the number of trucks loaded and unloaded per day.

Chapter 26, *Auditing Operations*, presents more on benchmarking.

TRANSPORTATION

Once products are finished in a work centre, they have to be shipped to their next destination, either an industrial user, the final client, a distribution centre or a retail outlet. The next destination may be national, or international. Transportation is a key element in the supply chain. Products may be manufactured according to schedule, be of acceptable quality and be at the right price, but if the correct transportation is not available, resulting in late delivery and/or arrival in a damaged state, the client will be irritated. Transportation, depending on the type of product, point of departure and point of arrival is by road, rail, air, sea, inland waterways or, in certain cases, pipeline.

Selection criteria

The criteria of selection for transportation include:

- Does a network exist? Can the delivery routes be easily optimized?
- The distance to be travelled.
- The speed with which products can be delivered to the client. Will they arrive on time?
- Volume limitations on the transportation mode.
- Weight limitations on the transportation mode.
- Security and the safety of the products during shipment.
- Regulations that govern shipping. Some toxic products may not be allowed to be shipped by truck, for example.
- What are the costs including per kilometre, per hour, and for overtime?
- Unloading times.

Transportation types

Table 17.6 illustrates the transportation systems available, giving their advantages and disadvantages. The Table states that air transportation is limited by the product size, but as the article in Box 17.2 indicates, this is not necessarily the case.[7]

Transportation in the European community

Although not evenly spread, the European Union (Belgium, Denmark, Germany, Greece, Spain, France, Ireland, Italy, Luxembourg, Netherlands, Austria, Portugal, Finland, Sweden, UK) has, on average, has one of the world's densest transport networks.[8]

Rail

As illustrated in Figure 17.18, Germany and France have one of the longest rail networks, whilst Germany, Belgium and Luxembourg have the densest at about 110 km per 1000 km. Italy, France, the Netherlands, the UK and Denmark have a rail density about half that amount. Rail density in other Member States is lower.

Road

Germany, France and Italy, in that order, have the longest motorway networks, as shown in Figure 17.19, whilst Germany, the Netherlands, Luxembourg and Belgium have the densest motorway networks at between 30 and 55 km per 1000 km. The figure is about 10 to 20 km per 1000 km in Italy, France, the UK and Denmark, and very sparse in other member states. Also, France and Germany have the longest non-motorway road networks.

Inland waterways

The river Rhine, navigable for 1000 km, is the backbone of Europe's inland waterway network. Major canals link it to the Meuse, the Scheldt, the Elbe and, since 1992, to the Danube. However, France and the Netherlands have the longest inland waterway networks used principally for pleasure purposes.

Sea transport

The bulk of Europe's sea transport is concentrated in some 60 ports, each of which handles upwards of 10 million tonnes per year. The six largest, handling more than 50 million tonnes a year are Rotterdam, the largest in the world, with 290 million tonnes in 1991, Antwerp, Marseille, Hamburg, Le Havre and London. Except for Marseille, these all lie on North Sea or Atlantic Ocean coastlines.

Table 17.6 Transportation means

Advantages	Disadvantages
Rail	
Piggy-backing (using loading and off-loading direct to trucks)	Often three journeys necessary if factory supplier does not have a rail spur; factory to station, station to station, station to delivery location
Containerization possible (liquids, gas, automobiles)	Limited to at least one wagon load, or even one train load; thus not effective for just-in-time operation
Reasonably fast	
Good for bulk products – coal, chemicals, steel	
Relatively low cost for long journeys	
Truck (lorry)	
Relatively low cost	Weather conditions can affect delivery times
Cheaper than train over short distances	Affected by labour unrest (France)
Accessibility. Only a single journey necessary: supply site to demand location	Circulation difficult on some routes due to traffic conditions
Flexibility regarding size, and time for departure	
Pipeline	
Relatively low cost	Only suitable for products in liquid or gaseous form – petroleum and chemical products and coal in the form of a slurry
Continuous flow	Only feasible where pipeline exists
Can cross any terrain	
Sea transportation	
Only economic means for country to country delivery	Usually three journeys necessary: factory to dock, port to port, port to delivery location
Containerization possible	Only feasible where ports exists
Useful for bulk products	
Usually no size limitations for products	
Inexpensive relative to air transport	
Inland waterways	
Relatively inexpensive	Limited to where there is an inland waterway network
Useful for bulk products – coal	Usually three journeys necessary: factory to dock, port to port, port to delivery location
Environmentally friendly	Slow
Air transport	
Fast	High cost
Useful for perishable products, or those required	Three journeys necessary: factory to airport, airport to airport
urgently, such as medical supplies	airport to delivery location
Useful for inaccessible locations in, say, Africa, central Australia, Central America	Limit to size of products that can be transported.

Box 17.2 The mighty Antonov is only way to fly your locomotive. Soviet military relic carries anything; despite quirks, behemoth does the job. By Douglas Lavin, Staff Reporter

How do you get a 21 meter-long diesel locomotive or a 77-ton Pepsi-Cola bottling line across the Atlantic quickly?

By Antonov, obviously.

For $250,000 a load – about $11,000 per flying hour – you can hire an Antonov 124, one of the biggest planes aloft. It comes with everything – a score of chain-smoking, sleep-deprived Russians, jet engines prone to burning out, and a cargo bay big enough to haul almost anything almost anywhere.

A yacht to California, 230 ostriches to England, oil rigs to Azerbaijan, helicopters (five at a time) to Somalia, and a 200-year-old, 19-meter cactus to Spain. All of these things have flown Antonov.

Peace Dividend

The mighty Antonov 124 was designed to carry 165 tons of Soviet ammunition, trucks and tanks into battle, and it is now available to consumers – an odd peace dividend of the former Cold War.

Federal Express and Flying Tiger aren't sweating this competition, however. The Antonov is an inefficient fuel guzzler, and a primitive one at that. It uses about 900 gallons (3,420 liters) of jet fuel just to taxi onto a runway.

Consider what happened recently when a flight bound for the Mexican city of Guadalajara carrying eight semitrailers full of new Pepsi bottling equipment stopped in Shannon,

Ireland, for refuelling after just a three-hour hop from Italy: The Russian navigator pulled out a slide rule to help calculate the next, trans-Atlantic, leg. An exhausted pilot napped. And Anatoly, a technician, climbed a ladder to tighten three screws that help hold a Russian jet engine on the right wing.

Clearly, these planes have few advantages apart from their size. Too crude and costly to compete with Western air freighters for the bulk of air cargo, they work the fringes of world trade in outsized stuff.

Antonovs can handle loads too big to be flown by any other means, and there is enough of that sort of business to keep two East-West joint ventures flying as many as 10 Antonovs in round-the-world, round-the-clock marathon service for Western clients. Air Foyle Ltd. of Luton, England, operates with the Antonov Design Bureau of Kiev, Ukraine, HeavyLift of Stansted, England, works with Volga-Dnepr Airlines of Ulyanovsk, Russia.

On the Air Foyle/Antonov Design Bureau flight to Guadalajara, the 124 carries 19 crewmen. Most of them apparently have less to do with *flying* the plane than with tending to its many needs – checking vital signs and making slightly unnerving repairs. In the cockpit, four engineers operate the radio, navigate and monitor the engines and the hydraulics. There are two pilots.

Design Flaw

The engines are a problem. 'Our domestic-manufactured engines are not so good,' concedes Vladimir M. Sudorgin, a flight manager for the design bureau. Some have been scrapped after just 1,000 hours' use. Jet engines manufactured in the West typically last 8,000 to 10,000 hours before major maintenance is required.

Not much about being a passenger on this particular cargo plane is comforting. There are no magazines and no movies. Everyone smokes, no one wears seat belts. Carry-on bags are not stowed beneath the seat in front of you. Cartons of mineral water, spare parts and the crew's luggage litter the floor of the flight deck. But then, these planes, like the U.S. military's C5, were designed for tanks, not tourists.

Thanks to earlier maintenance problems, the flight I am on, bound for Guadalajara, is two days late to Bologna, in Italy, where the bottling equipment is picked up. Most of the crew works all night loading, with only an hour's rest before returning for a 7 a.m. departure.

The takeoff is smooth as can be. The heavy load makes for a stable ride. Despite the deafening roar of the four jet engines, most members of the all-male crew are soon fast asleep, with the aircraft lumbering along at a slow 475 miles (760 kilometers) an hour.

Three hours into the flight, we land gently in Ireland for refuelling. A technician in the cockpit pops open electronic controls and fixes warning switches. Two other technicians are similarly engrossed.

A Difference of Opinion

"Minor technical adjustments," says Mr. Sudorgin, the only fluent English speaker among the Russian and Ukranian crew. Martin Holliday, Air Foyle's representative on board, is reassuring: "Same thing happens on a Boeing 747, you just don't see it." (A Boeing spokesman later says that isn't true.)

The Antonov, primitive as it is, is an amazingly flexible machine. The Air Foyle crew tells of the pressurized flight carrying those 230 live, caged ostriches from Namibia to England for breeding. Unable to make the flight in a single hop, the plane landed in Cairo to refuel. That posed the ticklish problem of how to prevent the big birds from being baked alive as the midday 38-degree Celsius heat turned the Antonov into a very big oven. What to do?

The plane's crew parked with the nose into the wind, dropped down the tailgate and lifted open the nose cone. That left the ostriches in a huge, shaded, open tunnel.

Then there was the time, in the summer of this year, that production delays at General Motors Corp.'s locomotive division jeopardized a big Irish railroad order. GM hired Air Foyle, rolled a four-meter-high, 108,000-kilo diesel locomotive into an Antonov and flew it across the Atlantic. The U.S. military's C5 isn't available for commercial loads, and the feat couldn't have been accomplished by a Boeing 747 with cargo space bifurcated by a floor and with access limited to shipments no more than three meters high.

En Route to Gander

After the refuelling stop in Shannon, we are in the air again, bound for Gander, Newfoundland, a flight that takes six hours, covers 3,840 kilometers and burns 83,600 liters of fuel. When our Antonov arrives in snowy Gander, two other Antonov-124s are on the tarmac. Both are operated by the competing joint venture of HeavyLift and the Volga-Dnepr airline.

Over drinks, a member of the HeavyLift crew (the pilots aren't drinking), Gerald Hearne, says HeavyLift is making a special run of Volkswagen parts from Germany to Mexico. He has reassuring words about the aircraft: Both AirFoyle and HeavyLift have accident-free safety records.

But Mr. Hearne lets something else slip. He says one reason the Antonov is so safe is that it has *three* pilots on board. So, a disquieting question comes to mind: Why is *my* Antonov risking it with a mere two pilots at the controls? The next morning, after takeoff, Mr. Sudorgin, the flight manager, has the answer. "Normally three pilots," he says. "This is smaller crew. We have only two pilots."

Fortunately, our short-handed flight crew seems up to the challenge. Another takeoff, nine more hours and 5,520 kilometers, and Guadalajara beckons. All told, our journey from Bologna takes two days, 18 flying hours and 254,600 liters of fuel. The latest 747400 cargo jet can fly the same weight nonstop in about 11 hours, burning just 144,400 liters, Boeing says. But that is beside the point: The 747 couldn't handle machines four meters tall.

Landing in Mexico

In Guadalajara, Enrique Nunez Gomez, head of purchasing for the local Pepsi bottling plant, is at the airport with his wife and daughter and eight semitrailer trucks.

The new 1,200-cans-a-minute bottling line the Antonov has delivered will go into operation at least a month earlier than would be possible had it been transported by ship.

Outside, greeters from the tourist board wave hello, and smiling policemen pose for snapshots in front of the plane.

Inside, nine members of the crew are huddled around the engine-monitoring desk. They are in animated, angry

How Two Flying Behemoths Compare

Antonov An-124

Lockheed C-5B

	Antonov An-124	Lockheed C-5B
Wingspan	240′ 5¾′′	222′ 8½′′
Overall Length	226′ 8½′′	247′ 10′′
Overall Height	68′ 2¼′′	65′ 1½′′
Maximum Payload	330,693 lbs.	261,000 lbs.
Maximum Fuel	507,063 lbs.	332,500 lbs.
Maximum Takeoff Weight	892,872 lbs.	837,000 lbs.
Range with Maximum Payload	2,795 miles	3,434 miles

Note: The C-5B is not commercially available   Source: Janes's All the World's Aircraft

discussion, and a technician is running up from the cargo hold with tools. But when a newspaper reporter walks in, conversation stops. What's wrong? he wonders. "Minor technical problem," says Mr. Sudorgin.

In 1979 almost 30 per cent of the world's merchant fleet tonnage belonged to the European Union (EUR 12 – the 12 Member States at that date). In 1992 this figure fell to 15 per cent (with a corresponding loss of jobs in this sector), partly as a result of an increase in the number of ships sailing under the open shipping register, or flag of convenience. For example, in the same period, the number of ships registered in Liberia, Panama, Cyprus, the Bahamas and Malta increased from 16 to 35 per cent, even though some of these registrations belonged to European Union ship owners.

Container transport has expanded strongly. Some 8 per cent of the total tonnage carried by sea in 1991 and 13 per cent of the tonnage leaving European ports was in containers. In Rotterdam, container goods accounted for 17 per cent of total tonnage.

Air traffic

Air traffic is most dense in the London–Paris–Frankfurt triangle. Spain, France, Italy and the UK each have over 20 airports with a traffic volume of over 200 000 passengers a year. Germany and Greece have 10 to 20

Figure 17.18 European rail network in 1992.

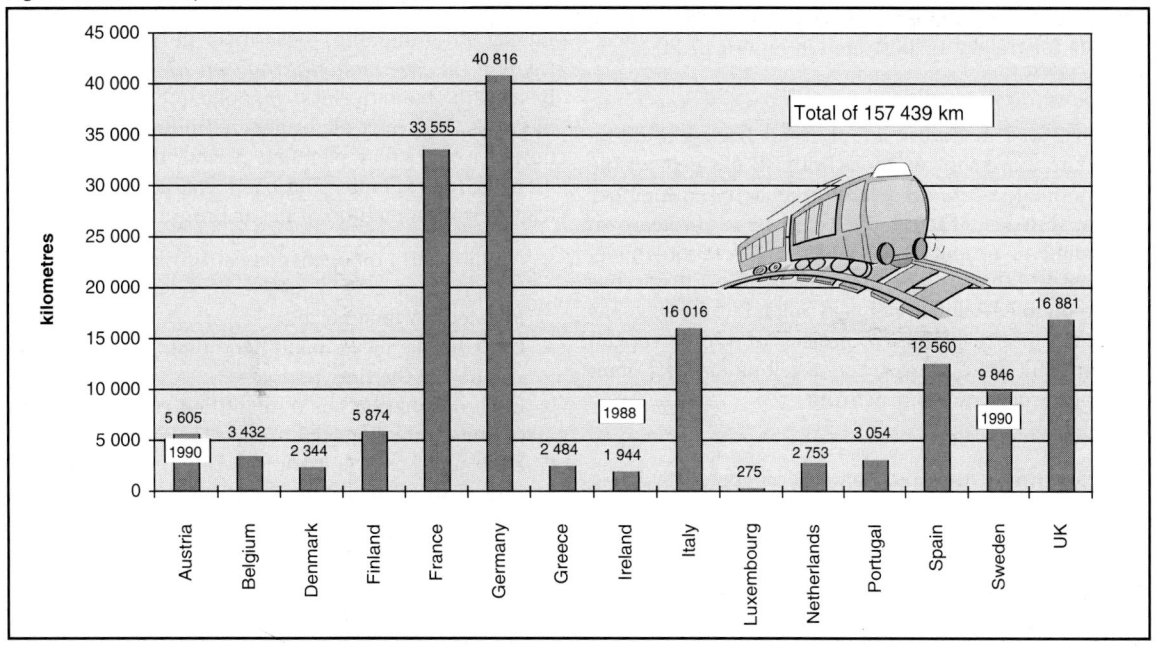

Figure 17.19 European Union motorway network in 1992.

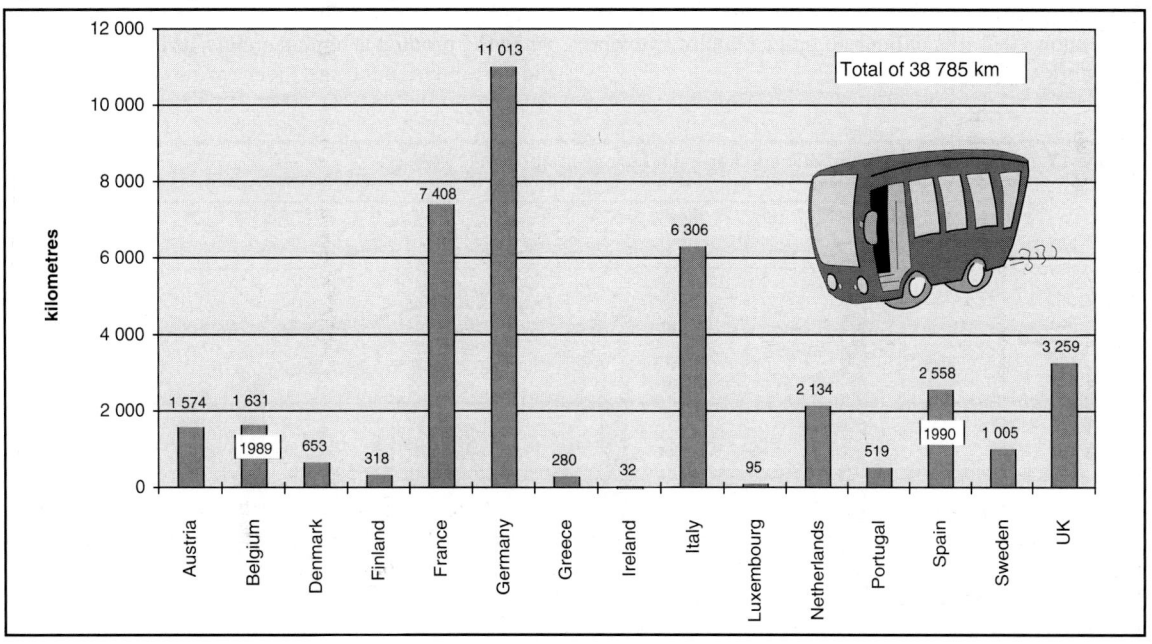

and the remaining Member states fewer than 10 each. The airport in Frankfurt, Germany, is the biggest in Europe for freight as illustrated in Figure 17.20.

Transportation employed

As illustrated in Figure 17.21, road transport dominates the movement of goods with 38 per cent of the total tonnage of goods transported between Member States. Further, Figure 17.22 gives a breakdown according to product type and transportation mode. Relative to 20 years ago, road haulage in Europe has about doubled whilst, rail and inland waterway has remained pretty stable. A project of the European Government is to increase the development of a combined rail/road transport network.

Trucking costs

A breakdown of the costs, as a percentage, for using road transport are given in Figure 17.23. The wages/costs for the driver are about 46 per cent of the cost, followed by 23 per cent for the fuel cost.[9] The fuel cost is quite significant, so that fuel-tax increases weigh heavily on the total transportation costs. Trucking companies, such as Norbert Dentresangle (France and Britain), use their trucks on average 150 000 km per year and try to have a 24-hour-a-day utilization. This is not easy to manage as it requires having two drivers all the time in the cabin and experience shows that it is difficult to find a team of two who can work together.

Optimizing a transportation network

Linear programming, described in more detail in Chapter 22, *Decision Making and Risk Analysis*, can be used to obtain the least-cost plan for the distribution of goods from multiple origins to multiple destinations during a particular planning period, daily; weekly or monthly for example. The basic characteristics of the transportation method of linear programming are:

- A finite and homogeneous set of discrete units are shipped from several sources to several destinations in a certain time period.
- Each source has a quantified number of units to be shipped in the time period.
- Each destination has a quantified required number of units to be received in the time period.
- Each unit has a unit transportation cost from each source to each destination. The unit cost remains constant regardless of the quantity shipped.
- There is only one transportation route between source and destination.
- The variables in the linear program are the number of units to be shipped from each source to each destination during the time period.
- The objective is to minimize the total transportation cost for the time period.

Linear transportation methods are very appropriate when the product is homogeneous, as in the case of liquid products such as beer, wine and petroleum

Figure 17.20   Goods loaded and unloaded at main European airports (1992).

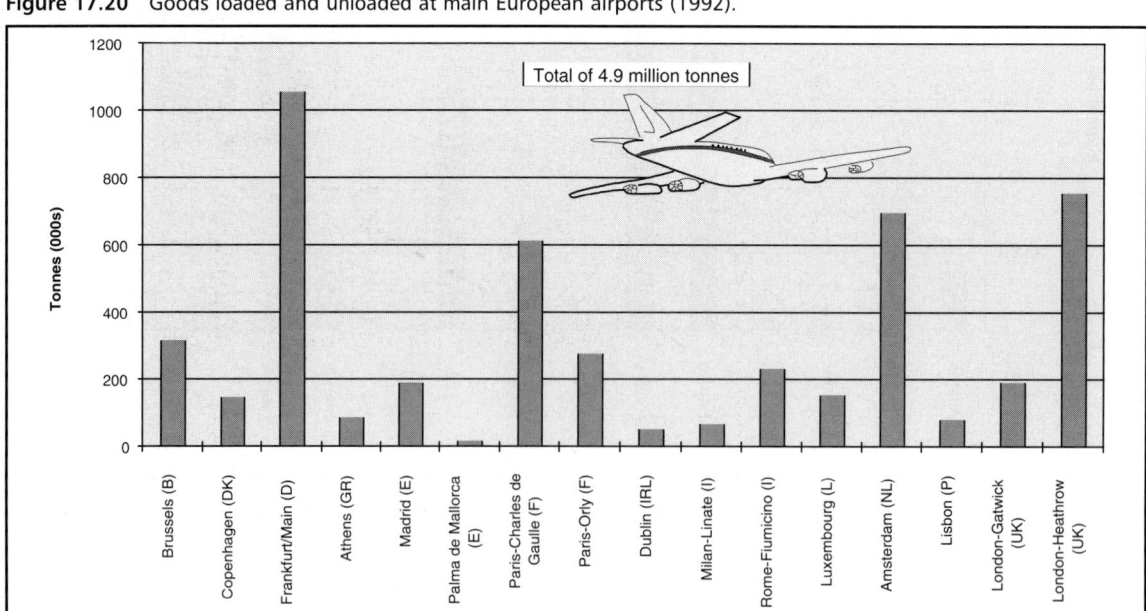

Figure 17.21 Mode of transport used in the European Union (1991).

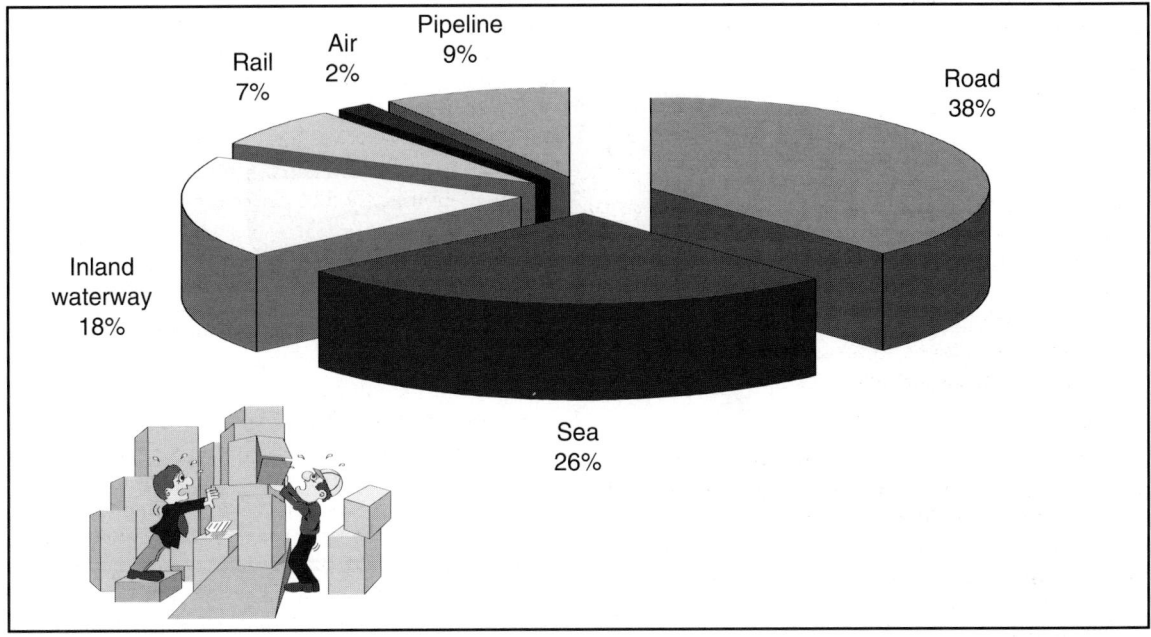

Figure 17.22 Goods and mode of transport in the European Union (1991).

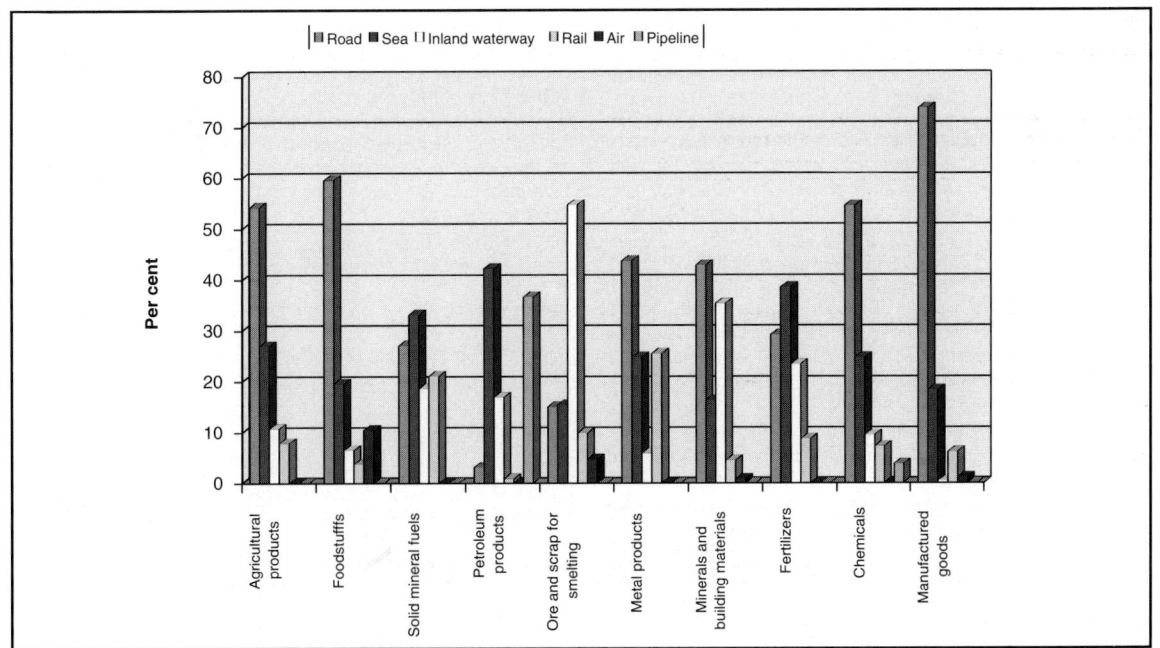

Figure 17.23 Breakdown of costs for a 30 ton vehicle.

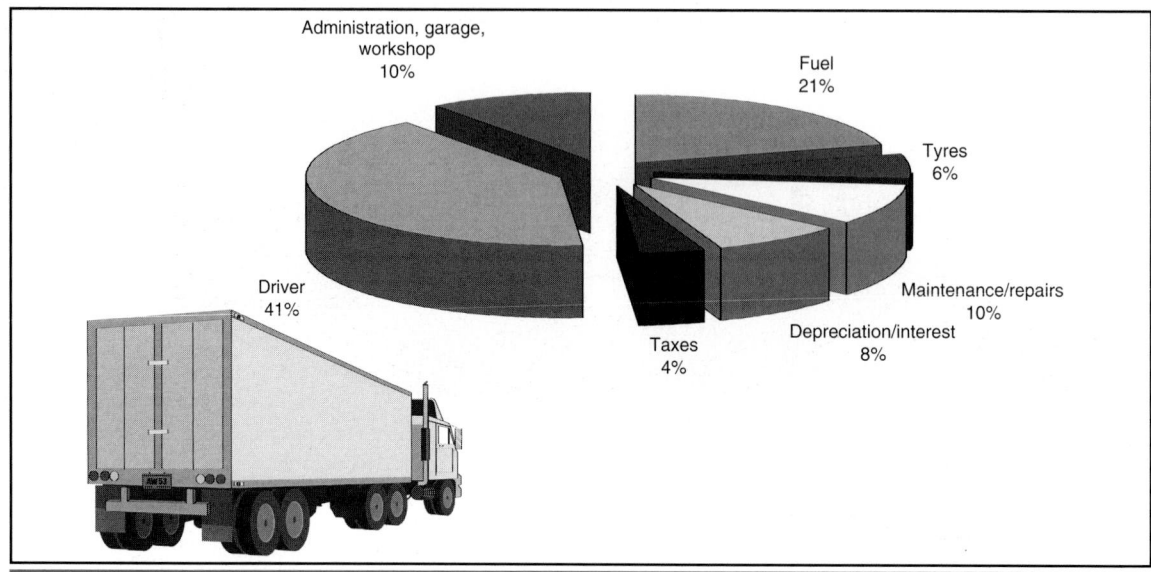

products. If there are several different products to be shipped, then an average shipping cost per unit can be determined. The transportation method using the linear program of Microsoft Solver is illustrated in the worked example, *Machine Tools* (Part I). The heart of many of the software packages available for transportation route planning is linear programming.[10]

WORKED EXAMPLE: MACHINE TOOLS (PART I)

Situation

A company, which manufactures machine tools, has production centres in Liverpool, England, Toulon, France, and Hamburg, Germany. These production centres supply four distribution centres located in Lyon, France, London, England, Frankfurt, Germany, and Barcelona, Spain. The distribution network for this operation is given in Figure 17.24.

Table 17.7 gives the production rates at each of the three production centres and the quantity demanded at each of the distribution centres. In this situation, the total quantity demanded is balanced with the total quantity produced. The shipping costs for this transportation network in German Marks per unit are presented in Table 17.8. As an example, the cost to transport from Toulon to Frankfurt, is 8 DM/unit.

Table 17.7 Production rates at each of the three production centres and the quantity demanded at each of the distribution centres

Factory	Production rate (units/day)	Distribution centre	Daily demand (units/day)
Liverpool	150	Lyon	180
Toulon	275	London	150
Hamburg	325	Frankfurt	185
Total	**750**	Barcelona	235
		Total	**750**

Table 17.8 Shipping costs

	Lyon	London	Frankfurt	Barcelona
Liverpool	5	7	7	1
Toulon	12	4	8	9
Hamburg	8	11	15	5

Required

Develop the optimum transport network.

Solution

The optimum distribution network is solved by using the Macro 'Solver' in Excel and Figure 17.25 gives the framework and the solution, which is described below.

Value to optimize

Here the aim is to minimize the total distribution costs for all the sites, (Cell G-16). This cell contains the formula:

$$(G\text{-}16) = (G\text{-}11) + (G\text{-}12) + (G\text{-}13)$$

and

$$(G\text{-}12) = (C\text{-}3)*(C\text{-}12) + (D\text{-}3)*(D\text{-}12) + (E\text{-}3)*(E\text{-}12) + (F\text{-}3)*(F\text{-}12)$$

Figure 17.24 Distribution network for machine tools.

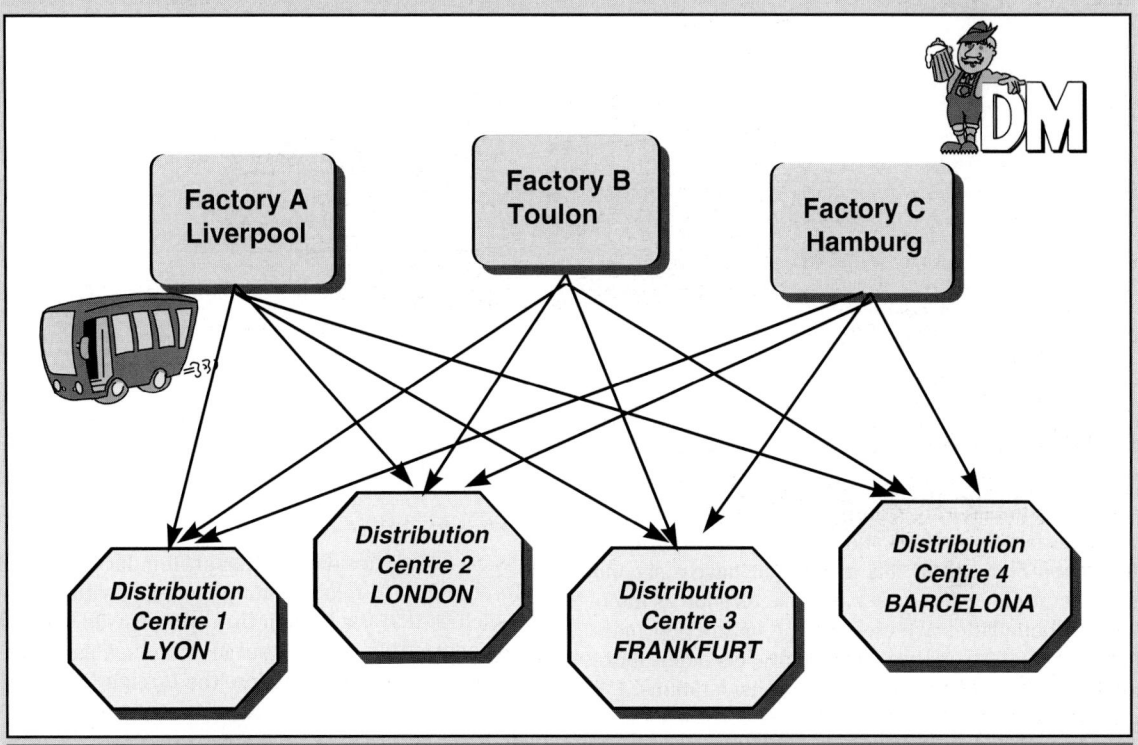

Figure 17.25 Distribution network for machine tools. Supply is equal to demand (solution by Microsoft Solver). Constraints are: 1 Variables are greater than or equal to zero; 2 Amount supplied is less than or equal to the supply; 3 Amount delivered is greater than or equal to the amount demanded.

	A	B	C	D	E	F	G
1	*Units*		Distribution Centre				
2	**Factory**	Supply Max	Lyon	London	Frankfurt	Barcelona	TOTAL
3	Liverpool	150	0	0	60	90	150
4	Toulon	275	0	150	125	0	275
5	Hamburg	325	180	0	0	145	325
6	TOTAL	750	180	150	185	235	750
7							
8	Quantity demanded		180	150	185	235	750
9							
10	*Costs*		Unit transportation costs, German Marks				TOTAL
11	**Factory**		Lyon	London	Frankfurt	Barcelona	COST
12	Liverpool		5	7	7	1	510
13	Toulon		12	4	8	9	1600
14	Hamburg		8	11	15	5	2165
15							
16	Total Cost		1440	600	1420	815	4275

$(G-13) = (C-4)*(C-13) + (D-4)*(D-13) + (E-4)*(E-13) + (F-4)*(F-13)$
$(G-14) = (C-5)*(C-14) + (D-5)*(D-14) + (E-5)*(E-14) + (F-5)*(F-14).$

Variables to calculate

These are 12 values contained in the shaded matrix from Liverpool–Lyon (Cell C-3) to Hamburg–Barcelona (Cell F-5).

System constraints

- The values of the variables (Cells C-3 through F-5) must be greater than or equal to zero. Before starting the iteration, these cells should be given an arbitrary value of 0.
- The totals of the quantity demanded for each distribution centre (Cells C-8 through F-8) must be greater than, or equal to, the quantity delivered (Cells C-6 through F-6).

- The total supplied (Cells G-3 though G-5) must be less than or equal to the given maximum supply (Cells B-3 though B-5).

Optimum network

Here the minimum cost is DM4275, with the following distribution:

- 60 units shipped from Liverpool to Frankfurt;
- 90 units shipped from Liverpool to Barcelona;
- 150 units shipped from Toulon to London;
- 125 units shipped from Toulon to Frankfurt;
- 180 units shipped from Hamburg to Lyon;
- 145 units shipped from Hamburg to Barcelona.

INTERNATIONAL CONSIDERATIONS

The supply chain of many organizations is international. A manufacturing firm in Germany might import raw materials from China and export finished goods to the United States. And this firm might have a second manufacturing facility in, say, Nigeria. As soon as international boundaries are crossed, the nature and management of the supply-chain activity becomes more complex.[11] The following are some considerations.

Trade restrictions

Many countries are parties to the WTO, the World Trade Organization (formerly GATT, the General Agreement on Tariffs and Trade), which has an objective of breaking down trade barriers between nations and facilitating the movement of goods. However, as the following illustrates, there still exist many anomalies in trade, or foreign government policies that can severely add to the costs involved in the supply chain.

Tariffs

Tariffs are charges applied by foreign governments to products imported into that country, with the primary purpose of protecting local activity. When tariffs are added to the price that one must charge to cover all costs to earn a profit, they may make a product non-competitive with similar locally made products.

Subsidies to local firms

In this case, subsidies are financial inputs by governments to national industries. Subsidized firms can afford to earn less in their home markets. This means that even if real costs are similar to, or higher than, those of imported goods, they can price below imported products. Alternatively, on foreign markets subsidized firms can price lower than local firms which are not subsidized, making it difficult for these non-subsidized firms to compete. This is an on-going problem in agriculture.

Subsidies to foreign firms

In this case, the subsidies are financial inducements to the foreign firm to relocate in that country with objectives such as that the foreign firm will provide needed employment. (This is discussed in detail in Chapter 3, *Site Selection*). In this situation, the foreign firm benefits and may decide initially to price lower in order to create a market.

Product standards

Product standards and other rules relating to safety, health and the environment are mandated by governments. Many of these are legitimate as governments have the right and obligation to ensure that imported products do not harm their citizens. However, such requirements have the effect of excluding imports. The US Federal Drug Administration (FDA) makes it very hard for foreign firms to import drugs or pharmaceutical products. Also, Europe is not open about importing genetically altered vegetables from overseas.

Patents and copyright

Firms take out patents and copyright on their products, which are valuable assets. However, if governments, through neglect or lack of enforcement, make it easy for nationals to infringe property protection rights, then competitiveness is lost. This has been the case with clothing, music recordings and high-tech products in Asian countries.

Investment restrictions

Investment restrictions in a foreign country can range from the outright prohibition of foreign involvement in a specific industry to severe limitation on what a foreigner can do with the money earned within that country.

Shipping regulations

When a company's supply chain extends beyond national boundaries, there are shipping regulations with corresponding documention, which has to be submitted to authorities in the country concerned, either before or during shipment of goods. Even with the most sophisticated supply-chain network in place, without the correct documentation, raw materials for a production operation or finished goods for a client can be held up at national borders, creating a bigger delay than ever expected in the supply chain that has been put in place. Many companies are familiar with the cry 'Our products have arrived in the country but they are being held at the docks'. Common export and import documents required in international shipping are given in Table 17.9.[12] Then Table 17.10 gives a listing of the most common terms related to international transportation.

Trading partners

The international supply chain is made simpler when countries that are physically close create trading partnerships which liberalize trade barriers and permit faster movement of goods across their frontiers. It also makes goods cheaper by eliminating all tariffs and quotas. The leading trading groups include the following.

European Union

As of 1997 there were the 15 countries of the European Union (EU): Austria, Belgium, Denmark, Finland, France, Germany, Greece, Ireland, Italy, Luxembourg, Netherlands, Portugal, Spain, Sweden and the UK, although other countries in the former Eastern Europe have also made application for membership. Within the European Union, the lead time for the movement of goods is considerably shortened, as much of the paperwork and customs inspections have been eliminated. The introduction of a common currency in January 1999 should further facilitate the movement of goods.

North American Free Trade Association

The North American Free Trade Association, or NAFTA, is the trade association between the USA, Canada and Mexico.

Association of South East Asian Nations

The Association of South East Asian Nations (ASEAN) includes the trading partners of Burma, Laos, Brunei, Indonesia, Malaysia, the Philippines, Singapore, Thailand and Vietnam, which have a combined population of 500 million people.

Southern African Development Community

The Southern African Development Community, SADC, includes the trading countries of Angola, Botswana, Democratic Republic of the Congo, Lesotho, Mauritius, Mozambique, Namibia, Seychelles, South Africa, Swaziland, Tanzania, Zambia and Zimbabwe.

ORGANIZATION OF THE SUPPLY CHAIN FUNCTION

The structural organization to manage the logistics function depends on the company. Some manufacturing firms might be organized according to the organization chart given in Figure 17.26. Here the vice president, or manager, is responsible for all the functions related to the manufacturing operation itself including production and design, plus functions that are somewhat peripheral to manufacturing, such as shipping, purchasing, subcontractor liaison and inventory control of both raw materials and finished goods.

A defined logistics function

To manage all the logistics functions better, a possibility is to split the manufacturing responsibility into two functions, production and logistics with a manager for each as illustrated in Figure 17.27. The production manager is now concerned with all of the production aspects proper. The logistics manager is involved with those functions that encircle the manufacturing. In addition, the order compilation (assembling all customer orders) has been removed from the finance function and put under the control of the logistics manager. This new organization now has an individual whose primary concern is managing all the flow of materials from the beginning of the logistics chain to customer delivery. The production manager is involved with all the activities of transformation and capacity planning. Since the logistics manager and the production manager both report to the vice president of manufacturing, this should make for a smooth-flowing organization. If a more stronger logistics control was needed, an alternative organization could be to create a vice president of logistics reporting directly to the president.

Brewery

The organization of a European brewery, identifying the logistics function, is illustrated in Figure 17.28.

Table 17.9 Common export and import documents

Export documents	Description
Ocean bill of lading	This is a receipt for the cargo and a contract between a shipper and the ocean carrier. It may also be used as an instrument of ownership, which can be bought, sold or traded while the goods are in transit.
Dock receipt	This is used to transfer accountability between domestic and international carriers at the ocean terminal. It is the document prepared by the shipper or forwarder, which the ocean carrier signs and returns to the delivering inland carrier, acknowledging receipt of the cargo.
Delivery instructions	These provide specific information to the inland carrier concerning the arrangement made by the forwarder to deliver the merchandise to a particular pier or steamship line.
Export Declaration	Required to control exports, acts as a source document for export statistics and includes complete particulars of the shipment.
Letter of credit	This is a financial document issued by a bank at the request of the consignee, guaranteeing payment to the shipper of the cargo.
Consular invoice	This is used to control and identify goods shipped to a country. It must usually be prepared on special forms and may require legalization by the country's Consul.
Commercial Invoice	This is a bill for the goods from the seller to the buyer. It is often used by governments to determine the true value of goods for the assessment of customs duties and is used to prepare consular documents.
Certificate of origin	This is a document to assure the buying country precisely in which country the goods were produced. The certification of the origin of the merchandise is usually performed by a recognized Chamber of Commerce.
Insurance Certificate	This assures the consignee that insurance is provided to cover loss or damage to the cargo while in transit.
Transmittal letter	This is a list of the particulars of the shipment and a record of the documents being transmitted, together with instructions for disposition of documents. Any special instructions are also included.

Import documents	Description
Arrival Notice	This is sent by the carrier and informs the customer of the estimated arrival date of the vessel and gives information regarding the nature of the goods.
Customs Entries	A form required by countries of goods entering into that country. It provides information about the goods, their origin and estimated customs duties.
Carriers certificate and release order	A document to advise customs of the details of the shipment, its ownership, port of loading, etc. This document is certification of the owner or consignee of the cargo.
Delivery order	This is issued by the consignee, or his customs broker, to the ocean carrier as authority to release the cargo to the inland carrier. It includes all data necessary to ascertain that the cargo can be released.
Freight release	This is evidence that the freight charges for the cargo have been paid.
Customs invoice	A document usually prepared by the exporter or forwarder and used by customs to determine the value of the shipment.

Table 17.10 Terms in international transport

Ex Works	Here the seller's only responsibility is to make the goods available at his premises. It is the buyer who bears the full cost and risk involved in moving the goods from the seller's location to their final destination.
Ex Ship	In this case the seller makes the goods available to the buyer at the destination named in the sales contract. It is the seller who bears the full cost and risk of getting the goods to that point.
Ex Quay	Here the seller makes the goods available to the buyer on the quay at the destination named in the sales contract. Again, it is the seller who bears the full cost and risk of getting the goods to that point.
FOB	This is an acronym for 'free on board' meaning that goods are placed on board a ship by the seller at a port of shipment named in the sales contract. The risk of loss or damage to the goods is transferred from the seller to the buyer when the goods pass the ship's rails.
FOR/FOT	These are 'free on rail', and 'free on truck', with the same obligations as FOB.
Free Carrier	This term meets the requirements of multimodal transport such as containers, or 'roll-on–roll-off' traffic by trailers and lorries. It is based on the same main principle as FOB and the seller's obligations are fulfilled when the goods are delivered to the carrier at a named point.
FOB Airport	This is similar to the ordinary FOB term, but applies to goods sent by air.

FAS	This term means 'free alongside ship'. Under this arrangement the seller's obligations are fulfilled when the goods have been placed alongside the ship in lighters (barges used for loading or unloading). In this case the buyer bears all costs and risks of loss or damage after this activity has been fulfilled. Unlike FOB, FAS means that it is the buyer's responsibility to clear the goods for export.
C & F	This term means 'cost and freight' and it is the seller who must pay the costs and freight necessary to bring the goods to the named destination. However, the risk is transferred from the seller to the buyer when the goods pass the ship's rail in the port of shipment.
Delivered at Frontier	This means that the seller's obligations are fulfilled when the goods have arrived at the frontier, but before the customs borders of the country named in the sales contract.
CIF	This is 'cost, insurance and freight'. It is C&F, but with the addition that the seller has to buy marine insurance against the risk of loss or damage to the goods during transport.
OCP	This means that freight and transport are paid to a named destination by the seller. It is equivalent to C&F but is appropriate for modes of transport other than ships.
CIP	This term is OCP, but with the addition that the seller also buys transport insurance. Again, it is equivalent to CIF, but is appropriate for modes of transport other than ships.
Delivered duty paid	This term, followed by words naming the buyer's premises, is the maximum obligation a seller can accept. The seller takes all risks and expenses in delivering the goods.

Specific activities of the logistics manager

Some of the specific activities of the logistics manager and what that person would do in collaboration with other departments in the organization are given below.

Physical distribution

- Selection of the transportation means such as road or rail. In many cases it would involve selecting the subcontractor who will handle the transportation.

- Scheduling the transportation both incoming and outgoing.
- Organization and planning activities of the distribution centres.

In collaboration with Production

- Establishing the production levels meet sales requirements.
- Optimization of the material flow within the work centre.

Figure 17.26   Organization chart – no logistics function.

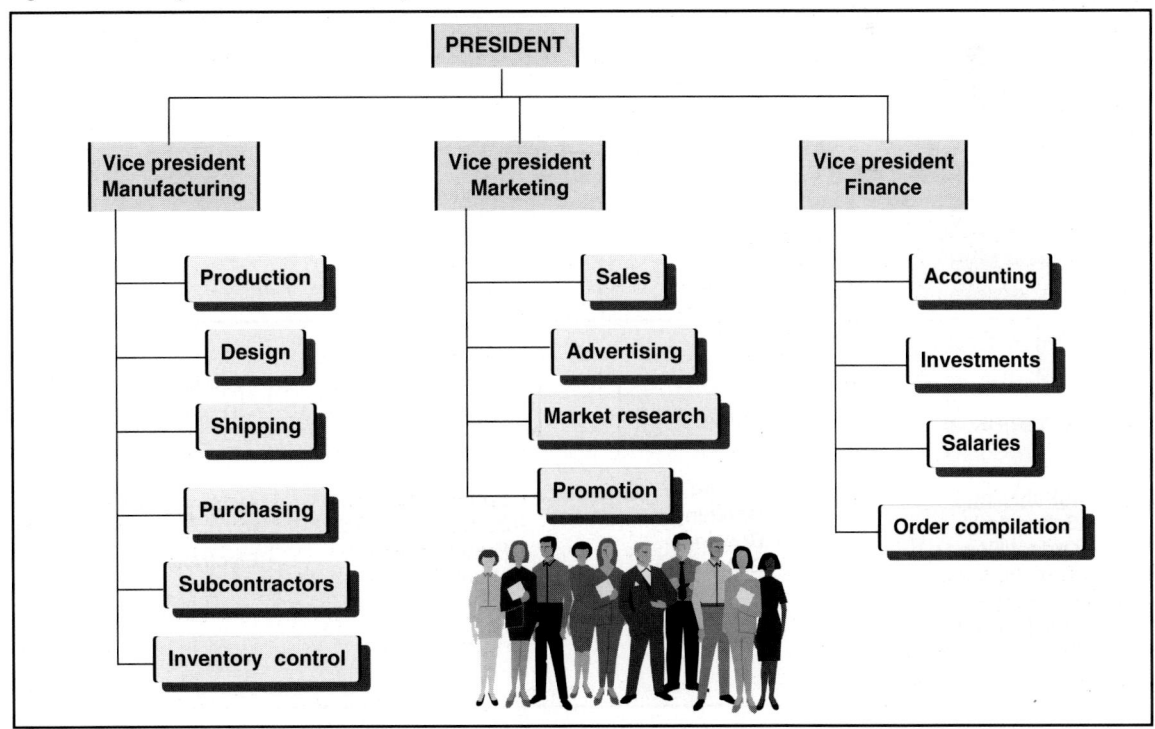

Figure 17.27 Organization chart – with logistics function.

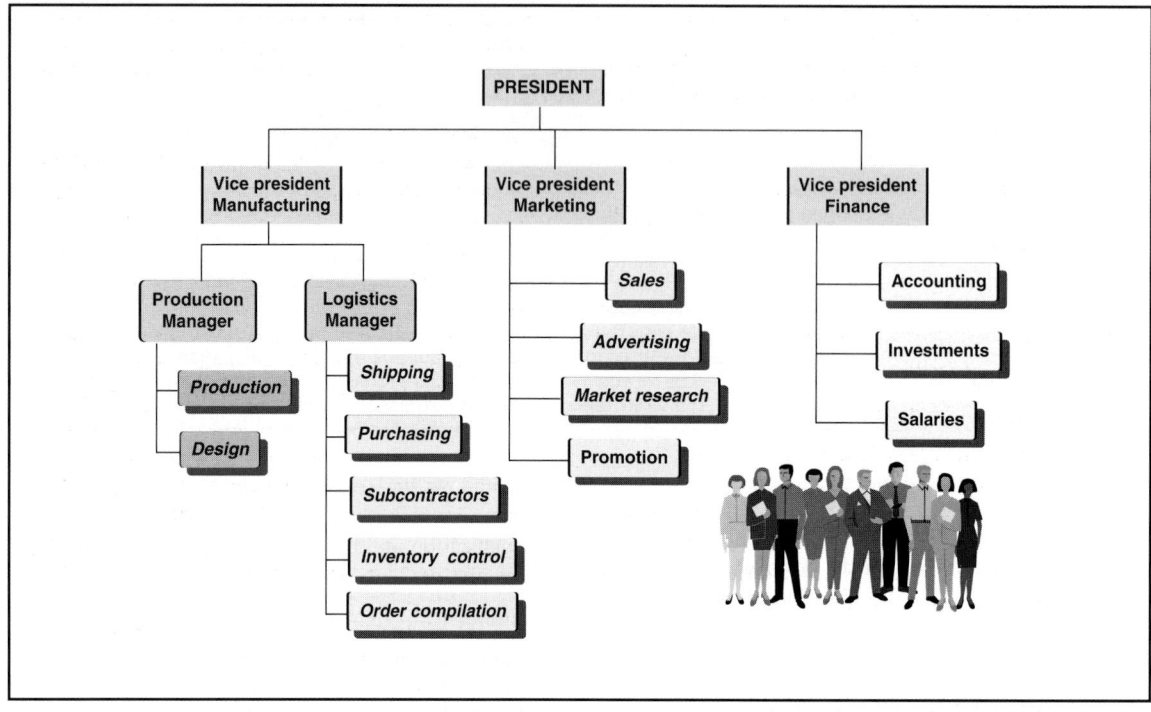

Figure 17.28 Logistics function in a brewery.

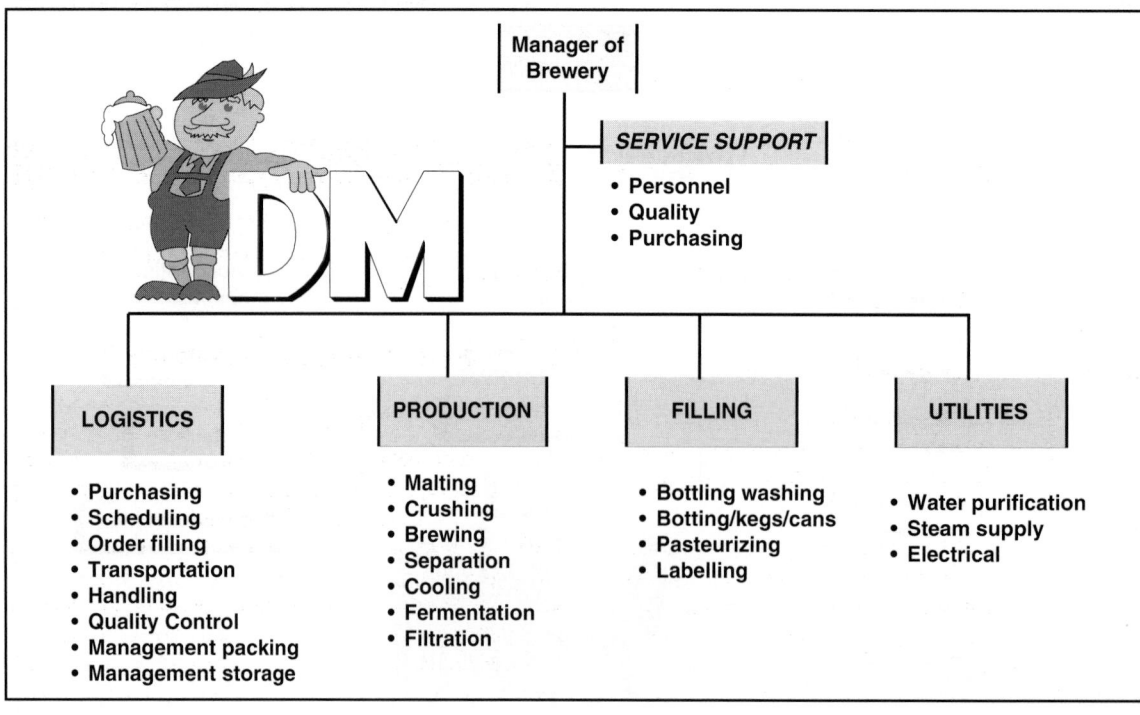

■ Planning and organizing the storage area layouts and the types of handling material employed.

In collaboration with Production and Purchasing

■ Selection of suppliers for the various purchased raw materials and components.

■ Establishing quantity requirements for raw material, price levels and specifications.

■ Selection of subcontractors who perform specific sections of the work.

In collaboration with Marketing

■ Organizing the after-sales service activity, including resolving problems with products supplied.

In collaboration with Marketing and Production

■ Verifying that the sales forecast corresponds to the real needs of the client.

■ Developing delivery schedules that correspond to clients' due dates.

■ Developing packaging that corresponds to clients' needs, has the physical strength for transportation demands, but at an appropriate cost.

Challenges for the logistics manager

It can be seen that the job of a logistics manager is very broad and crosses many functional lines, with challenges to establish the best equilibrium between the following:

■ the sales forecast;

■ the delivery schedules for purchased parts, materials and finished goods;

■ the production schedules and operating plans;

■ the inventory levels of raw materials, in-process materials and finished goods;

■ the flexibility of the production centre.

That is to say, find the best compromise between cost and service, at all times satisfying the client.

Definition of the logistics manager

The supply chain takes its origin from logistics management, which has its roots in wartime. The following gives a 'real' definition of the logistics manager, or the logician.[13]

Logicians are bitter people. They are very much in demand during wartime, but are quickly forgotten in peacetime. They are faced with the difficult task of serving people who are pursuing their dreams. They are present in wartime, because war requires reality. They disappear in peacetime because peace permits all sorts of frivolity. These people who pursue dreams and who have need of logicians in wartime, but ignore them in peacetime, are the army generals. The generals belong to the titled class. They shine with pride and exude power. Like the Olympic gods, they feed on ambrosia and drink nectar. In peacetime they behave magnificently. On a map, they can invade an empire and, with a simple majestic gesture, are able to trace the access routes, scale the gorges and crush all obstacles with their hand.

In times of war, they move more cautiously. Each general has in fact a logician who follows him like his shadow. He knows that at any time the logician can lean over and whisper to him 'No, that's not possible'. The generals are afraid of the logicians in wartime and they try to forget them in peacetime. Generals are accompanied by operational staff officers (tactical and strategic). The logicians scorn the tacticians and the strategists. The strategists and the tacticians ignore the logicians just up to the moment when they themselves become generals, which is often the case.

It sometimes happens that a logician is promoted to a general. In this case he must identify with the hated class of generals. He is followed by a cortege of strategists and tacticians, whom he detests. And, on his back is a logician, whom he fears. That is why the logicians who make it to generals get stomach ulcers and are not able to drink the nectar!

REDUCING SUPPLY-CHAIN COSTS

As for any activity, a key criterion is to keep costs low, and supply-chain management is no exception. The following are some considerations.

Computerized network integration

Accurate scheduling and planning is one of the key elements in managing the supply chain in order to ensure the smooth flow of materials from purchasing, through manufacturing, to the client and at the same time keep costs low. This is one of the functions of integrated MRP-II type systems, discussed in Chapter 13, *Materials Requirements Planning*, organizing all the various planning phases of the purchasing, production and delivery cycle. Companies like SAP of Germany, Baan of the Netherlands, and Oracle, USA, in collaboration with major consulting firms, are booming with their computerized Enterprise Resource Planning tools, which manage the whole supply-chain function from production through distribution. However, although they are effective, the purchase cost and installation of these products does not come cheap and can run into thousands of dollars. For example, Chevron Oil of the US decided to use SAP's software back in 1992 with the objective of reducing the cost of the purchasing activity in the supply chain. Internal estimates had indicated that the SAP system could help Chevron reduce costs by 25 per cent. Five years later, by 1997, although the company had succeeded in cutting purchasing-related expenses by 15 per cent, it had spent $160 million to get SAP operational. In addition, purchase transactions were executed electronically more quickly than the old method, which involved a lot of paper transactions. This considerably helped in improving management and the response time in the supply chain.[14]

Packaging

Packaging is not part of the product, is usually trashed and thus adds little product value in the eyes of the customer. However, packaging is a necessity to protect the product from damage. Chapter 5, *An Environmental Balance*, discussed packaging from an environmental angle. The other angle is the cost of packaging, not just its direct cost, but that part of the shipping costs which can be attributed to the size and weight of the packaging being moved.

A way of keeping packaging-related costs reasonable is to standardize, or modularize, the packaging so that individual packs fit onto a standard pallet. Figure 17.29 illustrates this in the case of canned goods or beverages. Here, individual packs of standard sizes will fit onto a basic module. The basic module can be arranged several ways on the pallets without wasting any space. Computer Aided Packing Simulations are available which optimize the packing of components into standard containers.

To keep costs even lower, it is best to put the pallets into containers and not to unload the container until it has reached its final destination. Containerization is such that, if necessary, the packed goods can be loaded into a truck, off-loaded and then loaded onto a train, and then loaded directly onto a cargo ship without unpacking the unit. Minimizing product handling from supplier to customer reduces the quantity of packaging needed. (See also, Chapter 16, *Purchasing and Subcontracting*, section *Completely Knocked Down*).

Subcontracting or outsourcing

Many companies are finding that in the distribution function of the supply chain, in addition to standard practices such as negotiating long-term transportation contracts, increasing useful capacity of trucks or subcontracting use of trucks on a return journey, the complete distribution function can be subcontracted, as the article in Box 17.3 illustrates.[15] This article highlights activities in Europe and the USA.

Figure 17.29 Modular system for packaging.

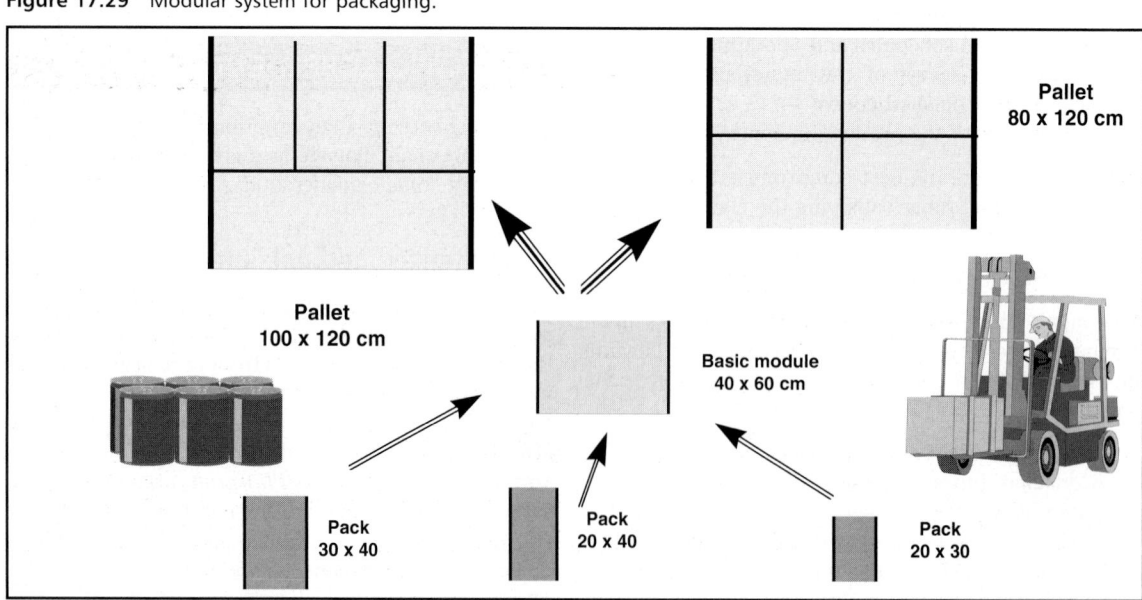

Box 17.3 Driving force. In today's economy, there is big money to be made in logistics. Trucking firms lead way in creating an industry that's bringing in billions. Rotterdam acts as magnet. By Jon Bigness and Martin du Bois, Staff Reporters

It is as dry as toast, but chew on this: Contract logistics has become a $20 billion-a-year business in Europe. And in the U.S., it's expected to more than triple over the next five years to $50 billion in annual revenue. That is a lot of bread for an industry that is about nothing more than moving things around.

But wait. It's important: Virtually the entire industrialized world depends on the arcane and complex science of logistics to get billions of parts and supplies into manufacturing plants on time and to distribute finished products efficiently to customers. Until recently, most manufacturers handled both incoming and outgoing logistics themselves – in the case of giants like General Motors Corp., assigning whole departments to the process.

Now, thanks to deregulation of the U.S. trucking industry, efforts to capitalize on Europe's single-market plan and just some basic philosophical changes in the way businesses are run, more and more manufacturers are outsourcing various portions of their logistics activities.

Moving Ahead

Contract logistics in Europe is growing 15% to 20% a year, analysts say, creating a boom for such shipping and storage companies as Royal Nedlloyd Group NV and Pakhoed Holding NV of the Netherlands, Swiss-based Kuehn & Nagel AG, and Bilspedition AB of Sweden, Scandinavia's biggest air-freight and transport firm.

"Every single company I know that's active in the third-party logistics services is swamped," says Hans Van der Hoop at Logistics International, a Rotterdam-based consulting firm.

"The starting point in Europe is further ahead than in the U.S. [and] there's a lot more growth potential," says Stephen Byrne, a logistics consultant and director of M-Star Systems Ltd., a U.K. designer of logistics software. Logistics is becoming vital for manufacturers not only to reduce costs, Mr. Byrne says, but to keep up with increasingly short product-life cycles, as in the computer industry. "Obsolescence is a huge problem," he says. "My view is that if you can't move it, don't make it."

Quick Response

Of the 23 biggest U.S. logistics companies, 16 were created in the past eight years, according to a recent survey by Robert Lieb, a professor at Northeastern University in Boston, and Hugh Randall, group vice president of Mercer Management Consulting Inc. in Lexington, Massachusetts. Leading the charge to provide these services in the U.S. are the biggest trucking companies, including Ryder System Inc., Roadway Services Inc. and Schneider National Co. The entire manufacturing supply chain – from raw materials to finished goods – increasingly is being analyzed, designed, managed and operated by these trucking companies, which run just-in-time and quick-response deliveries for many Fortune 500 manufacturers.

The difference between a typical shipper/trucker relationship and a shipper/logistician one is that a shipper hires a trucker to deliver its products on a certain day at a certain time. A company hires a logistics outfit to manage a range of shipments and deliveries over a long term, typically three years.

Europe's logistics boom comes as multinationals set up centralized distribution and warehousing facilities for the entire Continent. Half of the 800 largest U.S. and Japanese companies in recent years have established so-called European distribution centers, according to a study by Buck Consultants International in Nijmegen, the Netherlands. Big European companies, which have tended to remain more centered on their national home markets, are now following suit.

Single-Minded

Europe's logistics boom started in the late 1980s, driven by the 1992 single-market program. Also in the 1980s, the British food and retail industries started outsourcing their logistics activities to break the logjam of labor unions, a practice progressively spilling over onto the Continent. During the 1990s, a pan-European wave of corporate restructurings and cost-cutting, as well as the EU's efforts to abolish national restrictions on intra-European transport, added to the momentum.

Europe is actually a step ahead of the U.S., Mr. Van der Hoop says, because U.S. trucking business has been hidebound for so long by restrictions on interstate transport. Cultural differences also play a role: Companies active in Europe need to provide a far greater variety of products to suit national preferences: computers sold in Germany, France or the U.K. all require different keyboard layouts; electrical plugs and sockets come in all shapes and sizes; packaging varies from country to country. That makes it all the more rewarding to cut costs by centralizing logistics.

The real pioneer has been the Netherlands, home to Rotterdam – the world's largest harbor – and to a thriving transport and warehousing industry. "The Dutch are at it first," says Robert Delaney, a logistics expert at CASS Information Systems in St. Louis, Missouri.

The Netherlands is by far the most active European market for logistics services, with an EU market share of nearly 50%, according to the Buck Consultants study. That's because so many multinationals are setting up distribution centers close to Rotterdam. The rest of the market is dominated by Belgium and Germany; Britain and France play minor roles.

Most companies in Europe outsource the management of their European distribution centers to specialized logistics firms. But some have kept the operations in-house: U.S. machinery maker Caterpillar Inc., for example, has built up its own logistics center in Grimbergen, Belgium, into a thriving business selling pan-European logistics services to other multinationals. National postal offices such as the Dutch PTT are also joining the fray.

"The whole thing is in very rapid transformation," says Graham Sharman, a McKinsey director and logistics consultant based in Amsterdam. "The variety of companies entering the logistics business [in Europe] is greater than in the U.S."

Last month, Roadway, one of the largest U.S. trucking companies, spun off its unionized trucking business to focus on its thriving young logistics division and other nonunion activities. Bob Lake, president of Roadway Logistics Systems, says the parent company, based in Hudson, Ohio, isn't abandoning its core transportation business entirely. "But it does mean, on the other side of the coin, that we are going to lengthen our stride in logistics and make it a very key part of the mix," he says.

Printing Kits

Two years ago, Hewlett-Packard Co., the high-tech maker of computer printers, turned over its in-bound raw-materials warehousing in Vancouver, Washington, to Roadway Logistics. The warehouse operates 24 hours a day, seven days a week. Nearly 140 Roadway employees took over for some 250 Hewlett-Packard employees, who were transferred to other H-P activities.

Roadway coordinates the delivery of parts to the warehouse and manages storage. When an order comes from H-P's nearby printer-manufacturing plant, Roadway fills a container, loads it onto a truck and delivers it just in time for assembly. After the containers are emptied by Hewlett-Packard employees, Roadway picks them up, takes them back to the warehouse and prepares for the next trip.

Hewlett-Packard says the arrangement has cut its warehouse-operating costs about 10%, while freeing its own employees to work on the printer business. The savings reflect Roadway's expertise, developed over years in the trucking business, in moving goods from point A to point B, on time and in the correct order.

The outsourcing of logistics has enormous growth potential. U.S. manufacturers today hire third-party companies for only about 12% of their logistics. Mr. Gecowets, the trade-group director, believes that with increased competition in a global economy, companies will find it more efficient to outsource as much as 25% to 30%.

U.S. rethinking on how to organize manufacturing companies started in the auto industry in the early 1980s. As Detroit began to figure out why Japanese auto makers were so much more efficient, the U.S. car companies learned how to save big bucks by shaving factory inventories of parts to the bare minimum necessary to keep a steady flow of production. Now, various versions of Japanese-style just-in-time inventory management practices are in use across U.S. industry, from Microsoft Corp. to Stroh Brewery Co.

Cutting Inventory

Understandably, the new emphasis on lean inventories makes logistics that much more important. If a plant should miss a prompt delivery of brake shoes or computer chips, production could grind to a halt, costing hundreds of thousands of dollars in lost output. This has led to the development of complex computer-tracking technology, and as the demands have grown more sophisticated, specialists have come into greater demand.

The new approach essentially replaces costly inventory with valuable information. And the electronics industry has figured out the implications. A decade or so ago, there were no more than 50-odd computer programs available for logistics management. Today, according to a survey by Rick Haverly, a partner with Andersen Consulting in New York, there are more than 1,300 software packages offered by 900 vendors. There are lots of specialized programs now, including an application that diagrams the optimum pallet-stacking pattern by product. It used to be done by hand.

Union Objections

Labor unions, however, are fighting the outsourcing moves. "It can be a thorny labor issue because the flip side of subcontracting is jobs," says Harley Shaiken, a labor professor at the University of California at Berkeley. Transportation outsourcing is clearly an effective method of cutting costs and improving service, Prof. Shaiken says, but it can also be used to break unions and lower wages. "When that truck pulls out of the lot," Mr. Shaiken says, "the person who drove it sees his job going with it."

When Chrysler Corp. considered outsourcing the transportation operations of its Kokomo, Indiana, transmission plant five years ago, the United Auto Workers union refused to step aside, according to John Guinan, assistant director of the UAW's Chrysler department. The Kokomo site, still operated by UAW workers, supplies all of Chrysler's U.S. assembly plants.

Because the logistics industry is growing so fast, a lot of transportation and warehousing companies are suddenly adding "logistics" to their names. But industry leaders believe that of the nearly 100 trucking companies that identify themselves as logistics providers, fewer than 10 will survive well into the next century.

"There will be a shakeout," predicts Bill Zollars, senior vice president of Ryder. "Customers will begin to figure out who can do what for them."

Wall Street Journal Europe, 12 September 1995
Reprinted by permission of *Wall Street Journal Europe*,
© 1995 Dow Jones & Company, Inc.
All Rights Reserved Worldwide.

Europe

- Contract logistics has become a $20 billion a year business and is growing 15 to 20 per cent a year.
- Half of the 800 largest US and Japanese companies have recently established European distribution centres.
- The Netherlands, with Rotterdam as the world's largest harbour, has developed a thriving transport and warehouse business.
- Most companies in Europe outsource, or subcontract, the management of their European distribution centres to specialized logistics firms.

United States

- Contracting out the logistics function is expected to more than triple over the next five years to $50 billion in annual revenue.
- In 1993, Hewlett-Packard's printer operation turned its in-bound raw materials warehousing in Vancouver, Washington, over to Roadway Logistics. Hewlett Packard claims that this has cut warehouse-operating costs by about 10 per cent, while freeing its own employees to work in manufacturing.
- Labour unions are not happy with outsourcing because this means loss of jobs to their members. An illustration was when Chrysler considered out-

sourcing the transportation operations of its Kokomo, Indiana, transmission plant five years ago. The United Auto Workers union refused to step aside. The Kokomo site is still operated by UAW workers.

SUMMARY OF KEY ELEMENTS

- A supply chain is the integrated network for the physical flow of goods from suppliers, through transformation, to distribution of finished products. In the reverse direction is the information flow.
- A pure service function's supply chain principally involves information flow.
- The supply chain may be in two parts: Materials Management, or the flow of materials from suppliers through to the finished product, and Physical Distribution Management, or the distribution of the finished product to the client.
- Lead times in the supply chain include delivery times of raw materials, operating times, distribution times of finished goods and waiting or non-value idle time.
- A supply chain can be modelled into a series of value-added cells with an input and output. An objective is to have cells which maximize the value-added content.
- Inventory is held in the supply chain because of uncertainty related to suppliers, manufacturing operations and the clients' real needs.
- A pipeline map is a series of horizontal lines (pipeline length) representing processing steps and vertical bars (pipeline height) representing waiting periods. Pipeline volume is the sum of the two and is an indicator of the firm's flexibility.
- A variety funnel shows the reduced flexibility as one moves through the pipeline.
- DRP is the process in the supply chain to ensure that the specified finished goods arrive as planned. A pull-system DRP is when the client triggers the orders. A push system is when the supplier triggers the movement of goods.
- Electronic data interchange (EDI) permits rapid flow of information through a network.
- The Internet's World Wide Web can reduce the supply-chain lead time by permitting direct purchasing, delivery and invoicing of goods.
- The retail fresh-food industry has a supply chain network, which in many cases permits the delivery of fresh foods in a cycle time of less than 24 hours.
- Factors to consider in selecting a distribution centre include location relative to clients and suppliers, capacity, layout, handling equipment and ease of access.
- Management of a distribution centre can be improved by using crossdocking, computer control and benchmarking with similar facilities.
- Criteria for selecting a mode of transport include network availability, distance, speed, volume and weight restrictions, security, regulations and overall costs.
- International considerations in the supply chain include the host country's policies on tariffs, subsidies, product standards, patents and copyrights and investment.
- Shipping regulations and document needs are part of supply-chain management.
- Having in place a defined logistics function can improve a firm's performance.
- Modularized packing and using standard pallets can reduce supply-chain costs.
- European and US firms are subcontracting the distribution activity to reduce costs.

REVIEW AND DISCUSSION QUESTIONS

1 **Pipeline map**. Develop a pipeline map for the supply chain for:
   (a) the growing, cutting, and delivery of lumber to a pulp mill;
   (b) the sale of sugar from the refining to its consumption in a household;
   (c) the production of cotton tee-shirts from raw materials to final sale;
   (d) the publishing of a book from delivery of final manuscript to when the product appears on the bookshelves.
   Indicate on the map which are the process steps and which would be waiting times. Although you may not be able to put in quantitative numbers, indicate on the map your estimation of relative values.

2 **Transportation in Europe**. In Europe, the road networks are heavily congested, particularly around major cities. What do you believe might be some of the solutions to easing the distribution problems? Look at some

of the advantages both from an economic and an environmental point-of-view.

3 **Site selection and the supply chain**. Discuss the relationship between site selection (Chapter 3, *Site Selection*), consumer needs and the supply chain. What developments do you see in emerging markets such as China and what will be the impact on regions like the USA and Europe?

4 **Technology and the supply chain**. Can you identify other technological developments, or the improvement of existing technologies, which might make the supply chain more efficient? What will be its impact?

5 **Comparison of the supply chain**. Compare the differences between the supply-chain network within the USA, Europe and Japan. Identify the reasons.

6 **International supply chain**. A firm has a manufacturing facility in Essen, Germany, which in part uses imported materials from Singapore. Some of the finished products are then exported to Nigeria. In this international supply chain, identify and discuss some of the considerations that a logistics manager overseeing the whole operation must take into account.

EXERCISE PROBLEM: BEER DISTRIBUTION

Situation

A brewing company has four breweries located in Marseille, France, Newcastle, UK, Tarragona, Spain, and Cologne, Germany. It supplies seven distribution centres in Porto, Portugal, Madrid, Spain, Birmingham, England, Bonn, Germany, Paris, France, Lille, France, Brussels, Belgium, and Milan, Italy.

Table 17.11 The weekly supply of canned beer, in units, available from the four breweries, and the units demanded by the eight distribution centres

Brewery	Weekly supply (units)	Distribution centre (units)	Weekly demand (units)
Marseille	3 250	Porto	1 750
Newcastle	5 380	Madrid	2 350
Tarragona	7 750	Birmingham	2 480
Cologne	5 845	Bonn	2 200
Total	**22 225**	Paris	3 785
		Lille	1 980
		Brussels	3 150
		Milan	3 250
		Total	**20 945**

One product that is transported either by truck or by train is canned beer. Before being shipped, the beer is stacked on pallets 100 × 150 cm. A full pallet is considered a unit for shipping purposes.

Table 17.11 gives the weekly supply of canned beer, in units, available from the four breweries, and the units demanded by the eight distribution centres. Transportation costs in dollars per unit are given in Table 17.12.

Required

1 Develop the optimum transportation network.
2 What are the total weekly transportation costs?
3 If the distribution centres are billed for their actual transportation costs, what will be their individual costs?
4 If this situation was, on average, the regular supply and delivery pattern, what changes would you propose?

Table 17.12 Transportation costs ($/unit)

	Porto	Madrid	Birmingham	Bonn	Paris	Lille	Brussels	Milan
Marseille	4.2	3.5	5.2	4.2	1.2	1.4	2.2	2.5
Newcastle	7.5	6.0	2.5	5.0	4.0	3.0	3.5	7.4
Tarragona	1.2	1.5	5.6	4.8	4.0	4.7	4.8	5.2
Cologne	6.2	6.1	2.7	1.7	3.1	3.2	3.0	4.7

EXERCISE PROBLEM: CHIANTI WINE (PART II)

Situation

This is the same as presented in the worked example, *Chianti Wine* (Part I). All quantitative data supplied remains the same.

Required

1 Develop a 'push' distribution requirements plan for the network. Assume that the winery has a master production schedule which bot-

tles 160 cases of wine every two weeks, starting the production operation in the second week. Assume that all inventory on hand, or material received, is available for distribution in the same period. Proportion shipping requirements in the supply chain according to the retail demand, as illustrated below:

- The total demand from Zurich by the three retail outlets is 29 (8 + 9 + 12). The total demand from Torino by the three retail outlets is 55 (15 + 18 + 22). Thus the total demand from the two distribution centres is thus 84 (29 + 55).

- The proportion of cases from the winery going to Zurich is 29/84 = 0.3452. The proportion of cases from the winery going to Torino is 55/84 = 0.6548.
- Since in Week 1 the winery has 80 units on hand, the number of cases going to Zurich is 28, (80 × 0.3452) and the number of cases of wine going to Torino is 52 (80 × 0.6548).
- The quantity sent to each retail outlet from the distribution centre is on a fair share basis in proportion to the amount demanded each week. For example, the proportion of cases going to

Baden is 8/29 = 0.2759. Thus, the quantity from Zurich to Baden is 65 × 0.2759 = 18 cases. Distributions to the other retail outlets are made according to fair-share proportions.

2 What is the criticism of the push system developed in this case?
3 Calculate the average inventory for each week at each retail site.
4 How can the problems that occur with the push system be avoided, without modifying the master production schedule defined in Question 2?

EXERCISE PROBLEM: CUPBOARD

Situation

A furniture manufacturer in Copenhagen makes a wide range of Scandinavian-type modular furniture, which it sells throughout Europe. One if its popular products is a cupboard, the design of which is such that one model type can be assembled in three different ways. For one of its supply networks, the company has distribution centres near Paris, France, and Frankfurt, Germany. The distribution centre in Paris supplies large retail outlets in Nantes, Marseille and Geneva, whilst the distribution centre in Frankfurt supplies retail outlets in Dresden, Hamburg and Essen. Based on past data, the forecast demand for each of the six retail outlets, for the next nine weeks is given in Table 17.13. Whenever an order is required, each retail outlet makes fixed order quantities from the corresponding distribution centre. These amounts, and the current inventory levels at the start of Week 1, are given in Table 17.14.

Table 17.13 The forecast demand for the cupboard for each of the six retail outlets, for the next nine weeks

Week	1	2	3	4	5	6	7	8	9
Nantes	10	6	12	14	16	10	20	22	25
Marseille	14	18	17	25	30	19	15	25	18
Geneva	10	6	14	25	32	17	18	18	22
Dresden	8	14	15	22	23	22	25	14	25
Hamburg	10	12	14	25	23	32	18	17	18
Essen	16	9	28	18	28	24	12	15	14

Table 17.14 Inventory on hand and retail order quantities for the cupboard

Site	Inventory on hand	Order Quantity
Nantes	12	25
Marseilles	14	30
Geneva	19	25
Dresden	18	30
Hamburg	21	35
Essen	32	25

The distribution centre makes orders fixed quantities from the producer. These amounts, and the current inventory levels at the start of Week 1 are given in Table 17.15. Finally, the producer at Copenhagen assembles the cupboards in fixed lot sizes of 150 units. Inventory on hand at the start of Week 1 is 80. Delivery time from the producer to the distribution centre, and from the distribution centre to the retail outlet is one week. This takes into account the actual transportation time and the time for unloading and putting the inventory in storage. Similarly, the production lead time at Copenhagen is one week.

Table 17.15 Distribution-centre order quantities and current inventory levels

Site	Inventory on hand	Order Quantity
Paris	80	65
Frankfurt	110	70

Required

1 Develop a 'pull' distribution requirements plan for the next eight weeks using the weekly demand from each retail outlet as the independent demand that pulls the product through the distribution network.

EXERCISE PROBLEM: HEATING OIL

Situation

A subsidiary of Elf distributes heating oil in the Rhône-Alps region. Heating oil supplies are located at Grenoble, St Etienne, and Annecy. The oil is distributed to centres in Mégève, Vienne, Valence and Mâcon. The supply and demand capacities in litres of oil are given in Table 17.16. The distances between each supply and distribution centre in kilometres are given in Table 17.17. Transportation costs are considered proportional to the distance travelled.

Table 17.16

Factory	Daily supply (litres)	Distribution Centre	Daily demand (litres)
Grenoble	5 700	Megève	4 000
St Etienne	3 700	Vienne	2 500
Annecy	2 750	Valence	4 000
Total	**12 150**	Mâcon	4 000
		Total	**14 500**

Table 17.17 Distances between each supply and distribution centre in kilometres

	Mégève	Vienne	Valence	Mâcon
Grenoble	120	100	95	160
St Etienne	270	55	95	130
Annecy	60	120	155	135

Required

1 Develop the optimum transportation network

CASE STUDY: MACHINE TOOLS (PART II)

Situation

The manufacturing centres, the distribution centres, the network and the unit shipping costs remain as in the worked example, *Machine Tools* (Part I).

Required

1 Develop the optimum transportation network given the following information. Here the total quantity supplied from the production centres is greater than the quantity demanded, as given in Table 17.18.

Table 17.18 Machine tools – Production rate and demand (1)

Factory	Production rate (units/day)	Distribution centre	Daily demand (units/day)
Liverpool	300	Lyon	180
Toulon	275	London	150
Hamburg	325	Frankfurt	185
Total	**900**	Barcelona	235
		Total	**750**

2 Develop the optimum transportation network given the following information. In this case the total quantity demanded by the distribution centres is greater than the supply, as given in Table 17.19.

Table 17.19 Machine Tools – Production rate and demand (2)

Factory	Production rate (units/day)	Distribution centre	Daily demand (units/day)
Liverpool	150	Lyon	180
Toulon	275	London	300
Hamburg	325	Frankfurt	185
Total	**750**	Barcelona	235
		Total	**900**

EXERCISE PROBLEM: REFRIGERATORS

Situation

The Brandit company, which manufactures household appliances, has three factories in Germany located in Frankfurt, Bonn and Munich. The company delivers refrigerators on a weekly basis to four distributors in Lyon, Brussels, Vienna and Leiden, Holland.

The average weekly supply of a particular standard model and the weekly demand from each of the four distributors is as shown in Table 17.20. Transportation costs in German Marks per unit are as shown in Table 17.21.

Required

1 Develop the optimum transportation network.
2 What is the total weekly transportation cost?

3 If the distribution centres are billed for their actual transportation costs, what will be their individual costs?

Table 17.20 The average weekly supply of a particular standard model of refrigerator and the weekly demand from each of the four distributors

Factory	Weekly supply (units)	Distribution centre (units)	Weekly demand (units)
Frankfurt	180	Lyon	144
Bonn	360	Brussels	162
Munich	270	Vienna	216
Total	**810**	Leiden	288
		Total	**810**

Table 17.21 Transportation costs in German Marks per unit

	Lyon	Brussels	Vienna	Leiden
Frankfurt	24	42	42	6
Bonn	72	18	48	48
Munich	48	60	96	30

CASE STUDY: THE INTERNATIONAL AUTOMOBILE

The automobile

The automobile is now as essential to many people as their clothes. Estimates say that, on average, Americans are prepared to walk just 200 metres before using the car. After a house, the automobile is the second largest purchase. People show off in cars. Some live in cars. Others work in cars. Couples make love in cars. In short, the automobile is the indicator of the world's economic strength. The industry has a turnover of more than $1 trillion and employs some 10 million people.[16]

The market

The markets of North America, Japan and Europe account for about 90 per cent of the automobiles sold. By 2000 there will probably be one car for every person aged 20–64 in the USA. The market is saturated, and in some regions there is gridlock. In Southern California, the largest market for automobiles, the average road speed is forecast to be down to 30 km/h by 2010. On the Nuremberg–Berlin motorway on a holiday weekend in Spring 1992 there was a 70 km traffic jam, simply as a result of the volume of traffic. Cars were stuck for up to 18 hours. And, try to go some place fast on the M25 motorway around London on a Friday night, or on the coast roads of Southern France in July and August.[17]

The ability to sell fewer cars, but profitably, will be what counts in the future. After 2000, the main automobile growth will be in Asia, Eastern Europe and Latin America. Further down the road, China, India and Africa will provide millions of new drivers. Most of these developing countries, however, will want to produce their own cars, rather than import them from the major producers. And another threat, as is happening with South Korea and Malaysia, once these countries have learnt how to make cars (with the help of an existing producer), they will then export them to the West.

The producers

The principal top independent worldwide automobile producers number 16 and in 1991 they sold some 40.2 million vehicles.[18] These constructors are given below, and Figure 17.30 gives a breakdown of their status.

Chrysler, USA*
Fiat, Italy
Ford, USA
General Motors, USA
Honda, Japan
Mazda, Japan
Mercedes-Benz, Germany*
Mitsubishi, Japan

Nissan, Japan
Peugeot-Citroên, France
Renault, France
Toyota, Japan
Volkswagen, Germany
Volvo, Sweden
Hyundai, Korea
Suzuki, Japan

* Now merged

Figure 17.30 Automobile market share by the top 12 producers.

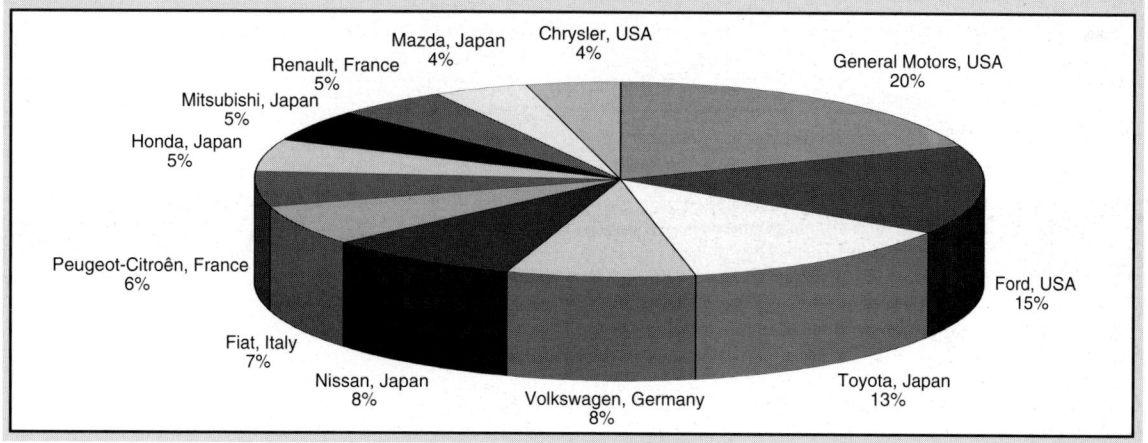

Survival

Not all car makers will survive, even the next decade, at least not in their present forms. To date, Britain's Jaguar has gone to Ford, and Rover to BMW and so now Britain no longer has a major domestic automobile producer. Sweden's Saab and Germany's Opel are controlled by General Motors. Spain's SEAT is a Volkswagen subsidiary. In 1995/1996 Renault and Volvo discussed a marriage that never made it to the altar. On 31 December 1999 the law limiting the number of Japanese cars imported into the European Union will expire. After that, the European market will be a free-for-all.

In 1991, the combined losses of GM, Ford and Chrysler were $7.3 billion. In the early 1990s Japan faced its worst slump in car sales for 50 years. Toyota's worldwide pretax profits in the year ending 30 June 1992 fell by 40 per cent compared to the previous year. Nissan made a loss in the first half of 1992 and for the first time withheld its dividend payment. For the first time in ten years, Renault announced a loss, for 1996 amounting to FF 3 billion ($0.5 billion). Although the other French company, Group PSA announced a profit, it has in two years seen its results divided by three.[19]

In 1996, the European automobile capacity stood at 18 million vehicles, whereas the demand was 12.8 million. Citing the excess capacity, and expecting its 1996 losses, Renault announced plans to close its Vilvoorde, Belgium plant in early 1997.[20] In the USA between 1987 and 1990 there were the closures by US automobile constructors that are shown in Table 17.22.[21] Although General Motors did open the technologically advanced Saturn Facility in Spring Hill Tennessee in 1990, which has an annual capacity of 250 000 vehicles.

Table 17.22   Closures by US automobile constructors, 1987–1990

Location	Vehicle capacity/year	Year
General Motors		
Detroit, Michigan	212 000	1987
Norwood, Ohio	250 000	1987
Leeds, Missouri	250 000	1988
Pontiac, Michigan	100 000	1988
Framingham, Massachusetts	200 000	1989
Lakewood, Georgia	200 000	1990
Pontiac, Michigan	54 000	1990
Chrysler		
Kenosha, Wisconsin	300 000	1988
Detroit, Michigan	230 000	1990
St. Louis, Missouri	210 000	1990

The life of the automobile

One thing that is common to the automobile whether it is a Cadillac from General Motors, a Clio from Renault, or a Rabbit/Golf from Volkswagen, it is international.[22]

Raw materials/components

The primary raw materials that go into the building of a car are sheet steel, various plastics, glass and rubber. These go into making the chassis and component parts. The automobile contains literally thousands of different reference items. And, up to 70 per cent of the value of a complete car is provided by outside suppliers. Some of the major ones are Robert Bosch, Germany, Valéo, France, TRW and Delco, USA, GKN and Unipart, Britain, and Yachiyo Kogyo, Japan.

The origins of some component parts are as shown in Table 17.23.[23] In addition, the relationship of component suppliers to automobile constructor is not the same in different countires, as illustrated in a 1990 survey (Table 17.24).[24]

Table 17.23   The origins of car components

Country	Component
Denmark	Cooling and air-conditioning belts
The Netherlands	Tyres, paint, control systems
Switzerland	Carpeting, speedometer
Norway	Straps for exhaust system, tyres
Germany	Pistons, cylinder bolts, steering column
Austria	Tyres, radiator and heating lines
Japan	Starter, alternator, bearings
USA	Catalytic converter, wheel bolts, windows
Belgium	Inner tubes, seat cushions, brakes and linings
Sweden	Tubular columns, cylinder bolts, stamped sections
Italy	Engine block, carburettor, lights, de-icing system
Spain	Radiator and heater leads, air filters, batteries, rear mirrors
France	Master cylinder, brakes, gearbox casing, waterproof joints
Canada	Windows, radio
Great Britain	Oil pumps, heating system, direction indicators, petrol tank, steering wheel

Table 17.24   Relationships between component suppliers and automobile constructors .

	Japan	USA	Europe
Number of suppliers per assembly factory	170	509	442
Inventory, days (sample of 8 components)	0.2	2.9	2.0
Components delivered just-in-time, %	45.0	14.8	7.9
Components from sole sources, %	12.1	69.3	32.9

Assembly

Figure 17.31 gives the various steps in the construction of the automobile in the assembly line process.[25] The internationalization of this aspect is illustrated in Table 17.25, which gives the percentage of the vehicles constructed according to the assembly site.[26] However, in a survey in 1989, as shown in Table 17.26, the way the three major countries assemble cars is not the same.[27]

Figure 17.31 How the car is assembled.

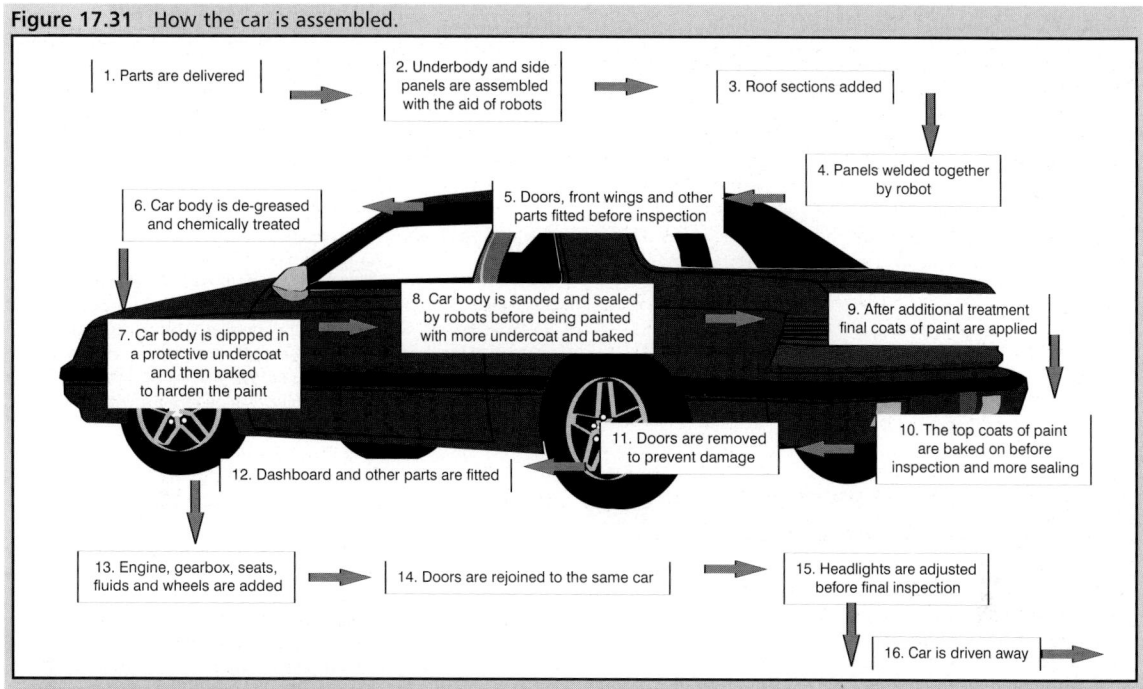

Table 17.25 Percentage of vehicles assembled in different countries

Manufacturer	Country of origin	Bordering countries	Elsewhere
Ford	53	13	34
General Motors	65	10	25
Volkswagen Group	56	25	19
Fiat (not including Iveco)	79	11	10
Renault (not including RVI)	61	34	5
Group PSA	77	20	3
Honda	72	3	25
Nissan	75	4	21
Mazda (including Kia)	65	20	15
Toyota	89	2	9
Mitsubishi	80	13	7

Table 17.26 The way three major countries assemble cars

Criteria (average values)	Japan	USA	Europe
Hours per car	16.8	25.1	36.2
Defects per 100 cars	60	82	97
Factory space (sq. ft/car/year)	5.7	7.8	7.8

Repair area as percentage of assembly area	4.1	12.9	14.4
Workforce in teams (%)	69.3	17.3	0.6
Number of job classifications	12	67	15
Training hours	380	46	173
Automation (percentage of process)			
Welding	86	76	77
Painting	55	34	38
Assembly	2	1	3

Supplying the client

The finished automobile, if necessary, is exported to the country where it is to be sold. Selling is though dealerships, which for the most are exclusive. That is to say, each dealer sells only vehicles made by one producer. The number of car dealers in the USA is now about 23 000, a reduction of 50 per cent since the 1940s. In France there are about 25 000 dealers, but they sell only about one-sixth of the vehicles sold in the US.

Renault

As an illustration, Renault is one of the automobile constructors in the list of 16. Its corporate headquarters are in Paris and the principal manufacturing sites in France are Batilly, Douai, Creil, Dieppe, Flins, Maubeuge and Sandouveille. Other automobile facilities are at Grand-Couronne, Cléon, Dreux, Le Mans and Orléons. Internationally, Renault has the facilities shown in Table 17.27 either partly or wholly owned. About 85 per cent of the sale of Renault automobiles are in Europe.

Table 17.27   Renault's international facilities

Europe	Vilvoorde, Belgium (closure announced)
	Palencia and Valladolid, Spain
	Cacia and Setubal, Portugal
	Novo Mesyo, Slovenia
South America	Venezuela, Columbia, Chile, Uruguay, Argentina
Africa	Morocco
Middle East	Turkey, Iran
Asia	Taiwan, Thailand, Malaysia, Indonesia

Summary

From raw materials and component-part purchases, through production, distribution and sales, together with the appropriate alliances, the automobile industry represents an enormous supply chain. The supply chain is not only physical flow, coupled to quality, cost and delivery times, but also information flow in the reverse sense. For the automobile constructor, managing the supply chain is a survival strategy. This will be tough for producers who are used to home markets that have nearly always expanded. The solution according to many is lean manufacturing and lean selling.

Required

Make an exhaustive analysis of what is involved in the supply chain of an automobile producer. You might consider Renault, but in reality many of the considerations apply to all firms. Consider network integration. What changes do you believe will have to occur? Where might Business Process Engineering play a role? Use whatever tools you feel would be appropriate to illustrate the supply chain (pipeline map, flow sheet, etc.).

NOTES AND REFERENCES

1. Davis, T. (1993) 'Effective supply chain management', *Sloan Management Review*, Summer: 335–46.
2. *L'Usine Nouvelle* (1994) 24 February.
3. Palenet Corporation, Japan (subsidiary of Mitsubishi), 1993. Report of Christine Daval, ESC Lyon.
4. Scott, C. and Westbrook, R. (1991) 'New strategic tools for supply chain management: Supply chain effectiveness can be enhanced by the strategic tools described in the article – the pipeline map, and the supplier relationship grid', *International Journal of Physical Distribution and Logistics Management* 21(1): 23–33.
5. 'Invoice? What's an invoice?', *Business Week* (1996) 10 June: 52.
6. Study at E. M. Lyon (1996).
7. Lavin, D. (1994) 'The mighty Antonov is only way to fly your locomotive: Soviet military relic carries anything; Despite quirks, behemoth does the job', *Wall Street Journal Europe* 30–31 December.
8. 'Europe in figures' (1995) *Eurostat*, 4th edn, Luxembourg: Statistical Office of the European Communities.
9. Abbati, C. degli (1986) *Transport and European Integration*, European Perspectives Series, Brussels, Appendix C.
10. Taylor B. W. III (1996) '*Introduction to Management Science*', Englewood Cliffs, NJ: Prentice Hall, Chapter 7.
11. Gattorna J. L. and Walters, D. W. (1996) 'International Supply Chain Management: Issues and Implications', *Managing the Supply Chain, A Strategic Perspective*, Basingstoke: Macmillan Business: 239–48.
12. The Port Authority of New York and New Jersey, Port Service Improvement Committee, One World Trade Center, New York, NY 10048.
13. *By an anonymous office of the Pentagon.*
14. 'The best software business Bill Gates doesn't own' (1997) *Fortune* 29 December: 68–72.
15. Bigness, J. and du Bois, M. (1995) 'Driving force: In today's economy there is big money to be made in logistics. Trucking firms lead way in creating an industry that's bringing in billions. Rotterdam acts as magnet', *Wall Street Journal Europe* 12 September.
16. 'Car crash ahead' (1997) *The Economist* 10 May: 11–12.
17. 'Survey: The car industry: in trouble again' (1992) *The Economist* 17 October: 5–28.
18. 'L'album Renault: Un voyage dans l'entreprise' (1992) *Régie Nationale des Usines Renault SA*: 25. [Translation: Renault's photograph album: A journey through the firm.]
19. 'Renault et PSA: trop petits, trop français, trop européens' (1997) *Le Monde* 21 February. [Translation: Renault and Group PSA: too small, too French, too European.]
20. 'Renault to axe Belgian plant, take $421.1 million charge' (1997) *Wall Street Journal Europe* 28 February–1 March.
21. Womack, J. P., Jones, D. T. and Roos, D. (1992) Le systeme qui *va Changer le Monde*, Paris: Dunod. Translation of *The Machine that Changed the World* (1991) New York: Harper Perennial.
22. What is called the Rabbit in the USA is called the Golf in Europe.
23. 'Countries participating in the construction of the Ford Escort' (1990) *Economie Mondial*, Paris: Mémo Larousse: 600.
24. Womack, J. P., Jones, D. T and Roos, D. (1992) 'Word Assembly Plant Survey, IMVP, 1990', *Le Systeme qui va Changer le Monde*, Paris: Dunod: 179.
25. Based on GM's Opel plant in Germany – *The Economist* (1992) 17 October: 12.
26. Estimation established by the French Automobile constructors, in *Répertoire Mondial*, Paris (1989) December (From Womack. J. P., Jones, D. T. and Roos, D. *Le Systeme qui va changer le Monde* (1992) Paris: Dunod: 238.
27. Powers, J. D. California, USA – *The Economist* (1992) 17 October: 10.

FURTHER READING

Abbati, C. degli (1986) *Transport and European Integration* European Perspectives Series, Brussels.
Allnoch, A. (1997) 'Efficient supply chain practices mean big savings to leading manufacturers', *IIE Solutions* 29(7): 8–9.
Anscombe, J. (1994) 'The fourth wave of logistics improvement: Maximizing value in the supply-chain', *Logistics Focus*, Yearbook Supplement: 36–40.
Arntzen, B. C., Brown, G. G., Harrison, T. P. and Trafton, L. (1995) 'Global supply chain management at Digital Equipment', *Interfaces* 25(1): 69–93.
Blanchard, B. S. (1992) *Logistics Engineering and Management*, Englewood Cliffs, NJ: Prentice Hall.

Byrne, P. M. and Young, S. V. (1995) 'UK companies look at supply chain issues', *Transportation and Distribution* 36(2): 50–56.

Carter, J. R. and Ferrin, B. G. (1995) 'The impact of transportation costs on supply chain management', *Journal of Business Logistics* 16(1): 189–212.

Cooke, J. A. (1992) 'Supply chain management 90s style', *Traffic Management* 31(5): 57–59.

Cooper J., Browne M. and Peters M. (1994) *European Logistics*, Oxford: Blackwell Business.

Cowdrick, R. M. (1995) 'Supply chain planning (SCP): Concepts and case studies', *Computers and Industrial Engineering* 29(1–4): 245–48.

Coyle J. J., Bardi E. J., Langley, J. C. Jr (1992) *The Management of Business Logistics*, St Paul, MN: West Publishing Company.

Ellram, L. M. (1991) 'Supply chain management: The industrial organisation perspective', *International Journal of Physical Distribution and Logistics Management* 21(1): 13–22.

Falconer, D. (1994) 'The Offsite law: Process engineers pay little attention to off-sites and logistics. David Falconer explains why this could be a financial mistake', *The Chemical Engineer*, 26 May: 40.

Fernie, J. (1995) 'International comparisons of supply chain management in grocery retailing', *Service Industries Journal* 15(4): 134–47.

Fisher, M. (1997) 'What is the right supply chain for your product?', *Harvard Business Review* 75(2): 105–16.

Fitzgerald, K. R. (1996) 'The supply chain: A competitive edge', *Purchasing* 120(1): 44C9–C13.

Gattorna, J. L. and Walters, D. W. (1996) *Managing the Supply Chain, A Strategic Perspective*, Basingstoke: Macmillan Business.

Gentry, J. J. (1996) 'The role of carriers in buyer-supplier strategic partnerships: A supply chain management approach', *Journal of Business Logistics* 17(2): 35–55.

Greenblatt, S. (1993) 'Continuous improvement in supply chain management', *Chief Executive*, Iss. 86, June: 40–43.

Greene, A. H. (1991) 'Supply chain of customer satisfaction', *Production and Inventory Management Review & APICS News* 11(4): 24–25.

Gupta, S. (1997) 'Supply chain management in complex manufacturing', *IIE Solutions* 29(3): 18–23.

Harland, C. M. (1996) 'Supply chain management: Relationships, chains, and networks', *British Journal of Management* 7(Special Issue): 563–80.

Hicks, D. A. (1997) 'The manager's guide to supply chain and logistics problem-solving tools and techniques', *IIE Solutions* 29(10): 24–29.

Horsley, R. C. (1993) 'Integrated Transport', *Logistics Information Management* 6(1): 42–45.

Lee, H. L. and Billington, C. (1992) 'Managing supply chain inventory: Pitfalls and opportunities', *Sloan Management Review* 33(3): 65–73.

Lee, H. L. and Billington, C. (1995) 'The evolution of supply-chain-management models and practice at Hewlett-Packard', *Interfaces* 25(5): 42–63.

Levy, P., Bessant, J., Sang, B. and Lamming, R. (1995) 'Developing integration through total quality supply chain management', *Integrated Management Systems* 6(3): 4–12.

Morash, E. A., Clinton, S. R. (1997) 'The role of transportation capabilities in international supply chain management', *Transportation Journal* 36(3): 5–17.

Muller, E. J. (1993) 'Key links in the supply chain', *Distribution* 92(10): 52–56.

Piszczalski, M. (1997) 'Ball and chain? Or simultaneous supply chain', *Automotive Manufacturing and Production* 109(9): 24–26.

Rheem, H. (1997) 'Logistics: A trend continues', *Harvard Business Review* 75(1): 8–9.

Stevens, G. C. (1990) 'Successful supply chain management', *Management Decision* 28(8): 25–30.

Stuart, F. I. (1997) 'Supply-chain strategy: Organizational influence through supplier alliances', *British Journal of Management* 8(3): 223–36.

Taylor, D. H., Probert, S. (1993) 'European logistics systems employed by UK manufacturing companies', *International Journal of Physical Distribution and Logistics Management* 23(2): 37–47.

Turner, J. R. (1993) 'Integrated supply chain management: What's wrong with this picture' *Industrial Engineering* 25(12): 52–55.

Vaughan, J. (1995) 'Supply chain focus enlivens manufacturing processes' *Software Magazine* 15(3): 96–99.

Wilding, R. D., Yazdani, B. (1997) 'Concurrent engineering in the supply chain' *Logistics Focus* 5(2): 16–22.

Wilson, M. (1994) 'Simulating the supply chain', *Logistics Focus* 2(4): 5–8.

'The Global Trade Game' (1995–96) *The Lamp* (Exxon Corp.) 77(4): 1–4.

18 | **Project management**

Objectives and overview

The objective of this chapter is to present the function and the activities of project management and to show how it is related to the operations and supply-chain management environment. The chapter begins with defining a project, detailing key elements and giving the comparison with operations and the supply chain. The chapter then presents the concept of work packages in a project and the various phases involved from proposal stage through to project completion and hand-over to the client. There is a section on project organization, highlighting the members of a project team, and a section presenting the activity of scheduling and controlling in project management together with analytical tools that might be used. The remainder of the chapter is devoted to the use of network diagrams in project management, including an explanation of the nomenclature and the methods of critical path (CPM) and the Program Evaluation and Review Technique (PERT). The chapter concludes by presenting crashing, or accelerating, a project completion time and how this is evaluated in a network diagram.

DEFINING A PROJECT

A project is an item of work that is unique and which has a start date and a finish date. Project management then involves the planning, scheduling, budgeting and control of this work using an integrated team of workers and specialists. A project can be of any size, as in the following examples.

Complex and unknown projects

Complex and unknown projects are those construction projects that are very large in terms of financial investment, maybe running into billions of dollars, and are complicated because they involve many untested design elements. The time horizon for their completion may be many years. Examples include:

■ The tunnel under the Channel between France and England – part of a physical supply chain.
■ The Aswan Dam in Egypt to provide hydroelectric power to the country and to alleviate flooding.
■ Development of the oil fields in Alaska's North Slope to provide energy sources for the USA.
■ The Three Gorges dam project on the Yangtse River in China. This mega-dollar hydroelectric project, currently under way, will create a reservoir some 400 miles long, submerge 150 000 acres of land, 1500 factories, 160 towns and 16 archaeological sites and require the resettlement of 1.3 million peo-

ple. It is designed to generate over 18 000 megawatts of power, help flood management and improve navigation on the Yangtze River.[1]

Large projects with standard elements

Large projects, with a time frame of perhaps 18 months to five years and costing in the region of thousands of dollars have many standard elements, because in part they duplicate construction work that has been performed before. Examples include:

■ an oil refinery, say for Exxon in France;
■ an industrial automobile complex, say for BMW in the USA;
■ a housing estate for 30 homes;
■ the construction of the section of a motorway – another part of the physical supply chain.

Intermediate projects

Intermediate projects, perhaps of an internal nature, lasting only a matter of months and costing hundreds to a few thousand dollars might include:

■ installing a new offset print machine;
■ installing an Enterprise Resource Planning System (see Chapter 13, *Material Requirements Planning*);
■ implementing a cellular layout in a factory (see Chapter 10, *Design of the Facility Layout*);

- landscaping around an office building.

Small projects

Small projects would be those activities lasting a few weeks, or even a few days, and which are of relatively low cost, for example:

- installing cabling in an office for Internet connections;
- painting an existing home;
- a small consulting or marketing study;
- a SMED application at a work post (see Chapter 15, *Lean production and just-in-time*).

Elements of a project

In all projects, whether internal or external, large or small, there are common elements, which are listed in Table 18.1.

Table 18.1	Elements common to all projects
Objective	There are a series of activities, which serve a well-defined objective.
Plan	There is a defined work plan with corresponding dates for all the milestones in the project.
Schedule	A project has a start date (it is 'kicked off') and a stipulated finish date. To a client these dates are critical, since from the start date to the finish date costs are incurred. And, for certain projects, after the finish date, revenue streams from the project should begin. Thus, a late project can delay the generation of revenues.
Team	A project is made up of a cohesive team, led by the project manager, all with the same objective. The team for the particular project is disbanded once the work is completed.
Budget	All projects have a financial budget attributed to the project and one of the responsibilities of the project manager is to complete the project within budget.

Contracts in a project

For external projects involving several parties, most projects are backed up by some form of a written contract. This might be a fixed-price or cost-plus contract containing as a minimum a penalty clause and a holdback provision. Consider for example a project carried out by a Contractor A for a Client B.

A *fixed-price or lump-sum contract*

In a fixed-price, or lump-sum, contract, Contractor A contracts to do the work for a fixed sum of money for Client B. If this is the case, the work is often of relatively short duration, is well defined and there is low risk. Small engineering design or consulting work is often performed at a fixed price, where the fixed price would cover all costs plus an allowance for profit. With a fixed-price contract, the budget level is critical to the Contractor A of the project, because if the budget is exceeded this will eat into his profit margin. When projects are of a longer duration, with uncertainties, firms are often not willing to offer a fixed-price contract because of the risk.

A cost-plus contract

A cost-plus contract may take various forms, but it is basically when Contractor A contracts to do the work for Client B at Contractor A's cost plus a specified percentage amount above cost to cover profit. This would be for large projects and when the time period is long, such that material and labour costs may be changing, giving the possibility of greater risk. For a cost plus contract, being over budget is perhaps more financially onerous to the client. However, being over budget can impair client–supplier relationships, perhaps obliging the supplier to take part of the financial loss.

Penalty clauses

The purpose of the penalty clause in the contract is to put pressure on the Contractor A so that the work is finished according to schedule. The penalty clause stipulates that if Contractor A is unable to meet the contractual finish date, then Contractor A is obliged to pay a financial penalty to Client B. The objective of this is to offset the loss of revenues that might accrue to Client B. For example, suppose a firm contracts to build an office block for which tenants have already agreed to lease the facility. If the building is late in its completion, then the owner would lose rental fees. A penalty clause in the contract against the constructor would help offset the loss of rental fees should the building be completed after the agreed date.

Holdback provision

The holdback provision is a clause to provide a guarantee that the project is completed according to the specified quality levels and performed according to expectations, as expressed in the contract. The holdback provision is usually a financial amount equal to a percentage of the project cost, or a fixed sum of money. As an illustration, a holdback provision might be 15 per cent of the project cost, which is held back by Client B until he has checked and is satisfied that the completed project meets expectations. Normally, the Client B has a time limit of perhaps 90 days, within which he must reply in writing to the Contractor A to 'sign off' completely on the project, that is to say, that he is completely satisfied. In this case, he is obligated to pay the holdback amount to Contractor A. If not, then Client B indicates in writing the areas of non-conformity that have to be resolved by the Contractor A. When all the conditions are satisfied, the holdback amount is eventually paid to Contractor A.

Turnkey projects

A turnkey project is one that starts from zero to proceed to a finished 'product'. The concept of turnkey is that when the project is finished *one turns a key to set the facility in operation*. The General Motors Saturn plant in the USA was a turnkey project as it was built on a previously virgin site. Another name for turnkey is grass roots, meaning that the plant is built on the *roots of the grass in the field*. As opposed to the expansion, or the extension, of an existing facility.

Projects, operations and the supply chain

The difference between a project and operations is that a project starts and finishes, whereas operations are on-going or continuous. Project management is treated here in a text on operations management with an emphasis on the supply chain, because of the following connections.

Projects are the start of operations

A project is often the start of operations. The project to build the General Motors Saturn plant in the US was the starting point for the operation to build a new models of automobiles. The building of a dam is the start of an operation to supply electricity to a surrounding community. The building of a new hospital is to improve the operations of medical services to a defined region.

Projects have similar functions to operations

Within a project, once it gets underway, there are operations, or many of the activities and functions that are similar, if not identical, to those performed in operations management. There are scheduling activities, management of inventory during the various phases of the projects, human resource management, productivity considerations, quality control, just-in-time planning, purchasing, etc.

A project team composed of operators

In the composition of a project management team there are often operations-related personnel, who have familiarity with the type of project in question, for example engineers, purchasing personnel, planners and schedulers.

Project team members become operators

When a project is terminated, persons who have been involved in a project often become part of the operating team because of their familiarity with the programme from its embryonic stage.

Supply-chain element

A completed project might be any of the physical facilities in a supply chain. For example, consider the supply chain for computers. A project at the start of the supply chain may be the plant for making computer chips, which are considered as the raw material. The project might be the transformation facility where the computers are assembled. The project might be the distribution centre for storing and the delivery area for supplying the computers to the retail outlet. Finally, the project might be the retail store that sells the computers.

PHASES OF A PROJECT

Work packages

Some projects, very often because of their magnitude, are released in phases, or work packages. Projects for the European Commission, or government agencies, are very often awarded in phases. The following are some of the reasons.

Project modification

A phased project gives the client the opportunity to make modifications (even cancel) should market conditions change. In the late 1970s when oil prices started to rise (of the order of $30 per barrel), many projects were awarded in the USA and Canada to produce oil from tar sands and gas from coal. However, when the crisis ended, oil prices dropped and most of these projects were cancelled. Some were only in the engineering stage, but some were in construction. In June 1997, in France, the newly arrived Socialist government cancelled the construction of the Rhine–Rhône canal, which was a project approved by the previous right-wing government.

Level the work load

If one contractor is given one phase of the project and another phase is given to a different contractor, this evens out the work load among companies (a consideration in government contracts).

Ethics

Splitting the work of a large project between several parties helps to keep all the work 'above board'. That is, unethical practices, particularly in purchasing (see Chapter 16, *Purchasing and Subcontracting*) should be eliminated or at least minimized.

Splitting a project into phases adds to the cost since it involves coordination between different organizations and also increases the time for overall completion.

Proposal stage

The proposal stage, or pre-project, is where a proposal is made to the client describing how the supplier firm (engineering and construction company for example) proposes to perform the project. Key elements in the proposal would include:

- cost or budget estimate;
- the schedule or the estimate of when the project will be completed;
- details (resumés) of key persons who will be working on the project;
- draft contract for the project; this would include things such as penalty clauses if the project is not completed according to schedule and budget.

Design and conception

Once the project is awarded, the first phase is the design and the conception of the project. This would involve preliminary designs and estimates, as well as development of the overall project schedule.

Detailed design

This second phase of the project might be, for example in the case of a plant construction project, the detailed design including flow diagrams, piping and instrument diagrams, site planning, detailed estimates, manpower requirements.

Construction

This is the final phase of the project, when all the design work is translated into building the facility. It is at this point that all purchased equipment arrives, the site is prepared and there is a heavy concentration of field craftsmen (electricians, mechanical personnel, riggers, etc.).

Start-up, or hand-over, phase

This is the time when the project is completed and the project is handed over to the client. The client would verify that design, operation, looks, etc. are according to specification.

PROJECT ORGANIZATION

A project team is made up of appropriate personnel in the supplier firm who have experience on that type of project work, say refinery, chemicals, food processing, nuclear power, etc. On projects where the client firm and the supplier are from different organizations, such as, for example, an engineering and construction firm building a brewery for Heineken in Holland, then the client (Heineken) might want to approve the key personnel proposed to work on his project.

Consider, for example, a major construction project such as a dam, building, chemical plant or automobile assembly facility; then key members of the team would include the following, as illustrated in Figure 18.1.

Project manager

The project manager is the key individual in the project. This person is the direct contact with the client, the interface between the client and the top manager of his organization, and responsible for managing the budget and controlling the schedule. Often this lead position, with many cross-functional contacts, gives the project manager high visibility within the organization and an attractive salary.

Engineers

Engineers usually form the nucleus of the project organization. It is these persons who perform the preliminary and detailed design, and might work with field construction personnel.

Scheduler

The scheduler is the person who follows the progress of the work from day to day. This person communicates with the project manager when the schedule falls behind the plan.

Purchasing

Purchasing personnel are those handling all the purchasing of raw materials, equipment and, if necessary,

Figure 18.1 Example of project organization.

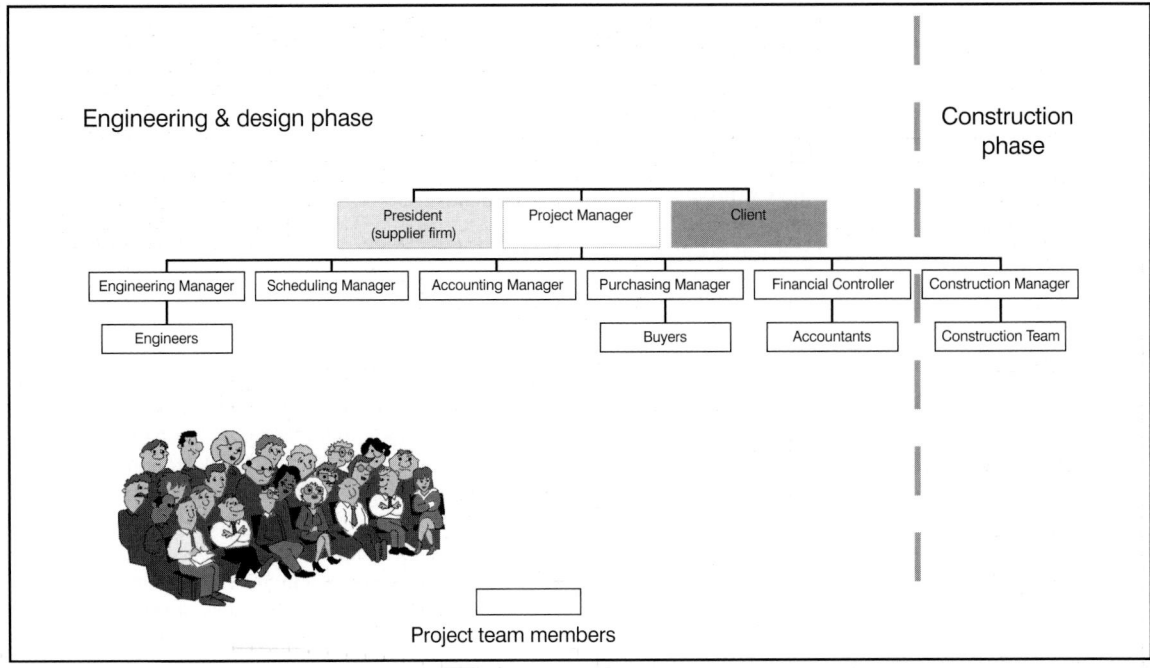

Project team members

subcontractor services. They are the main contact with the suppliers and are responsible for ensuring that material and equipment arrive according to the plan. (See also Chapter 16, *Purchasing and Subcontracting.*)

Controller

The controller is the person responsible for the financial management of the project. This will include paying bills for supplied material, contacting clients for invoice payments and managing day-to-day disbursement of cash.

Construction manager

The construction manager is responsible for the project once it reaches the activity in the field. Depending on the project, this might be in such harsh climates as Alaska, the Middle East or South America. Construction managers are chosen for their international experience as well as their ability to manage, and handle people. The construction manager may be responsible for managing over 10 000 field craftsmen on a single project.

SCHEDULING AND CONTROLLING

Once a project is defined, the principal task of the project team is to complete the project, within schedule,

within budget and according to design specifications. To monitor these activities, the project team reports progress on time, costs and quality to the internal project manager, and also to the client. The following are some tools that might be used.

Gantt charts

Horizontal bar charts are an application of Gantt charts (see also Chapter 14, *Operations Scheduling*). As an illustration, Figure 18.2 gives a Gantt chart for a project that lasts some three years.

Legend

The Gantt charts shows the time frame, and how each bar represents a milestone. There is a legend which is explained in Table 18.2.

Table 18.2 Explanation of Gantt chart legend

Key event	Start or end of phase
Purchase order	When a purchase order is made
Material delivery	When material must be in field or construction site
Construction issue	Construction activity of a phase
Engineering	Time frame for engineering/design work
Construction	Time frame for construction work
Block model	Model ready for design

Figure 18.2   Gantt schedule for high-density polyethylene plant.

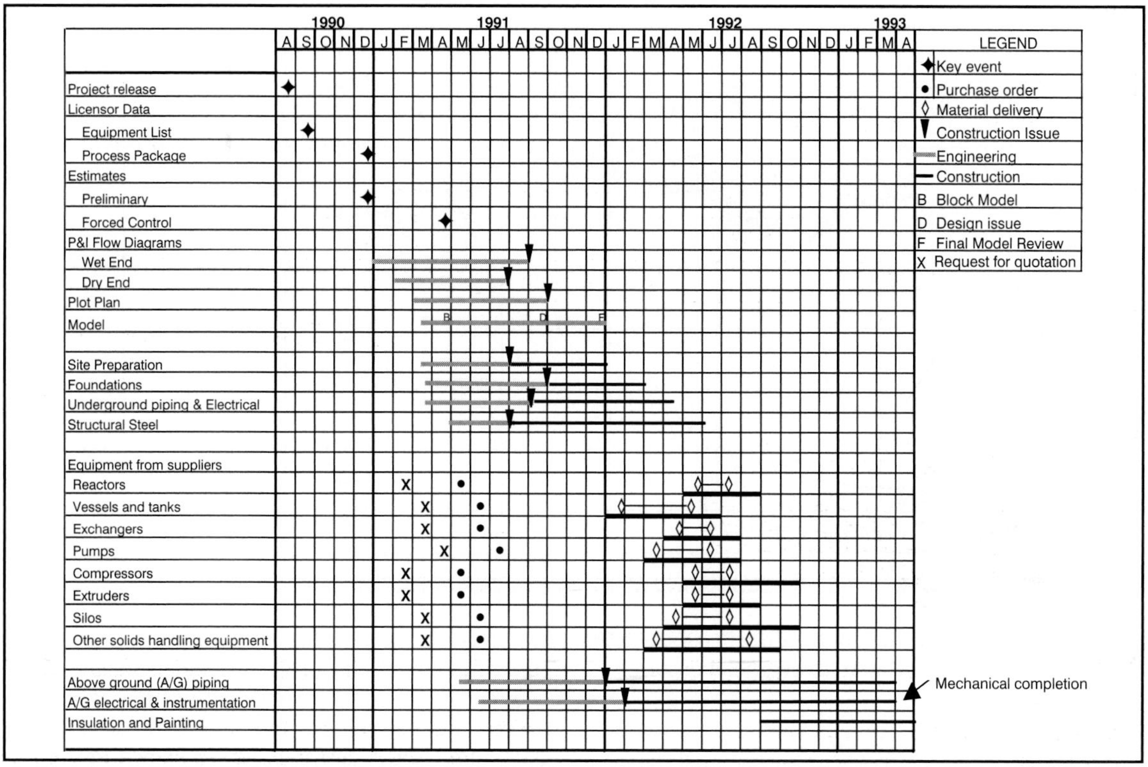

Gantt schedule showing activities from 1990 to 1993 for a high-density polyethylene plant, with rows including: Project release, Licensor Data, Equipment List, Process Package, Estimates, Preliminary, Forced Control, P&I Flow Diagrams, Wet End, Dry End, Plot Plan, Model, Site Preparation, Foundations, Underground piping & Electrical, Structural Steel, Equipment from suppliers (Reactors, Vessels and tanks, Exchangers, Pumps, Compressors, Extruders, Silos, Other solids handling equipment), Above ground (A/G) piping, A/G electrical & instrumentation, Insulation and Painting.

LEGEND:
- ◆ Key event
- ● Purchase order
- ◊ Material delivery
- ▼ Construction Issue
- Engineering
- Construction
- B Block Model
- D Design issue
- F Final Model Review
- X Request for quotation
- ◢ Mechanical completion

Advantages of a Gantt chart

The advantages of a Gantt chart for a project are that they are easy to prepare and of low cost, easy to understand and easy to modify.

Disadvantages of a Gantt chart

On complex projects Gantt charts can become unwieldy and the charts may not indicate the relationship between the project activities.

Project cost curves

Project cost curves are used for monitoring the expenditures of a project. The following are three forms that might be used.

Monthly budget curve

The monthly budget curve plots the planned expenditures for a project, as illustrated in Figure 18.3, which gives the budgeted monthly costs associated with the turnkey high-density polyethylene project. This curve illustrates that at the early engineering phase of the project, costs rise relatively slowly. The principal costs here are the salaries of the design engineers. As the project moves into the construction phase, cost starts to rise more rapidly as earth-moving work is started, heavy equipment is purchased and there are the salaries of the numerous construction workers and craft people in the field. At some point the monthly expenditures peak and then start to fall as the project approaches completion. Towards the end of the project, costs are more associated with personnel such as painters and start up crews.

Cumulative project cost curve

A project manager's responsibility is to see that expenditures are in control and, for this purpose, a cumulative project cost curve might be used, as illustrated in Figure 18.4, which shows the budgeted cumulative cost curve and also the actual costs incurred. Plotting the actual expenditures against budget is a clear way to see if the project is running according to schedule. Shown here, after the 20th week it is clear that the work is running above budget.

Project cost distribution

This curve, as illustrated in Figure 18.5 gives a profile of the cumulative three major costs in a four-year project, showing how the labour, material and overhead costs build up. The usefulness of this type of curve is

Figure 18.3 Monthly project expenditures.

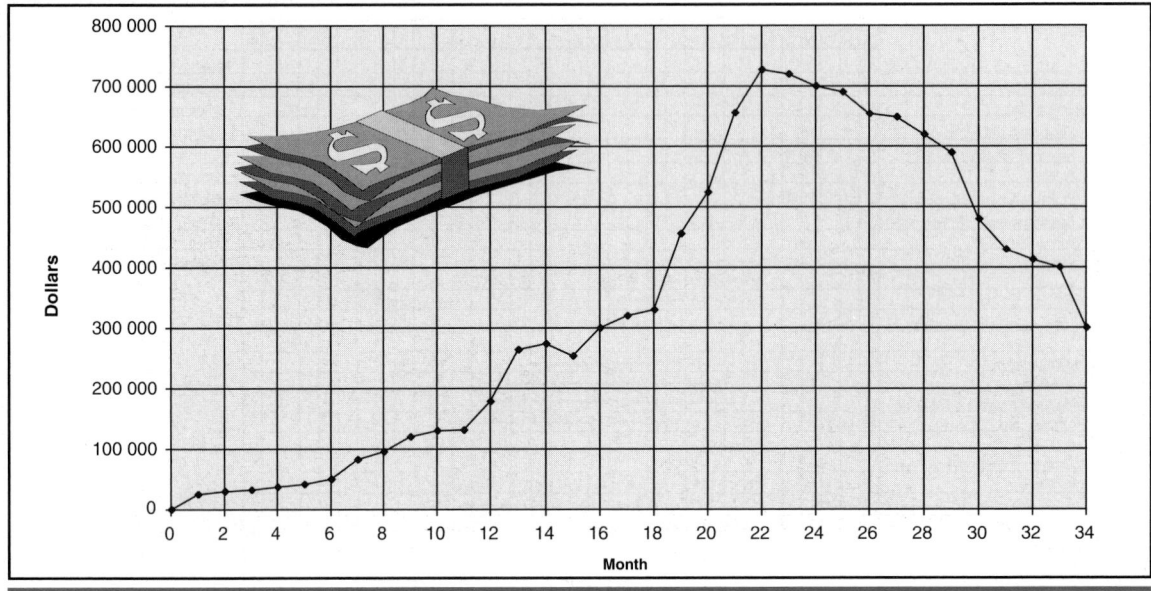

to see the relative magnitude of the direct costs, equipment and labour, and the indirect overhead costs.

Percent completion curve

Another monitoring tool for the Project Manager is a project completion curve, as shown in Figure 18.6. This curve gives the project completion in terms of hours spent on the project, calculated by the relationship (Number of people × hours per month). This representation of the project is independent of the costs since it is only based on the time expended, there is no equipment and people have different salary rates. There are two curves shown in the figure, one for the budgeted time and the other the actual percent completion through the 12th month. Here the curve illustrates that the project is ahead in terms of hourly expenditures.

Figure 18.4 Cumulative project expenditure.

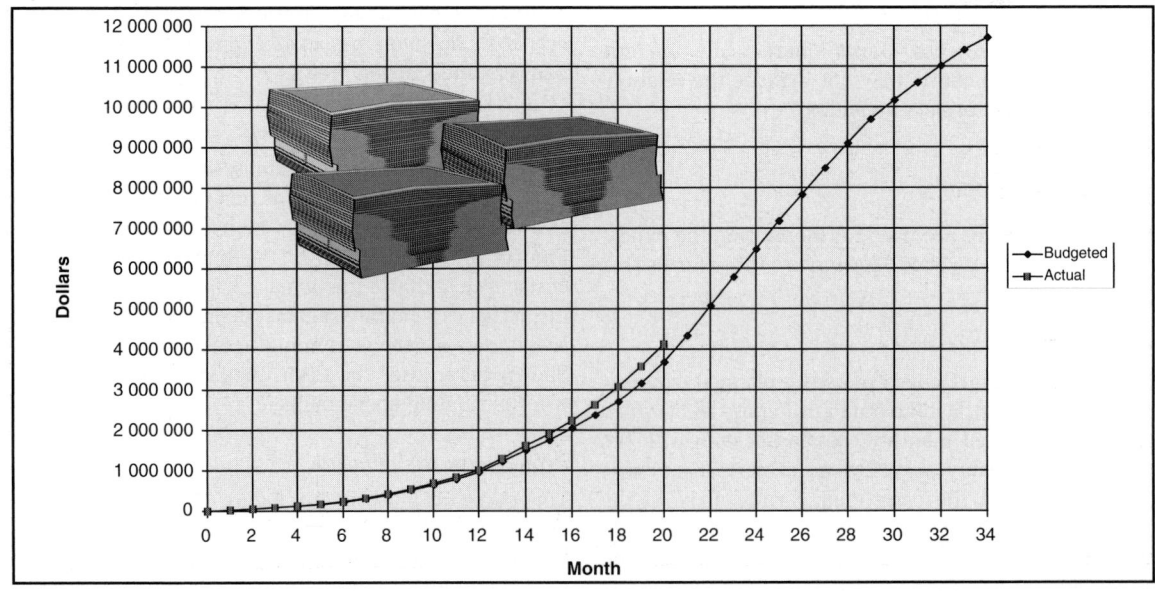

Figure 18.5   Cost breakdown for a project.

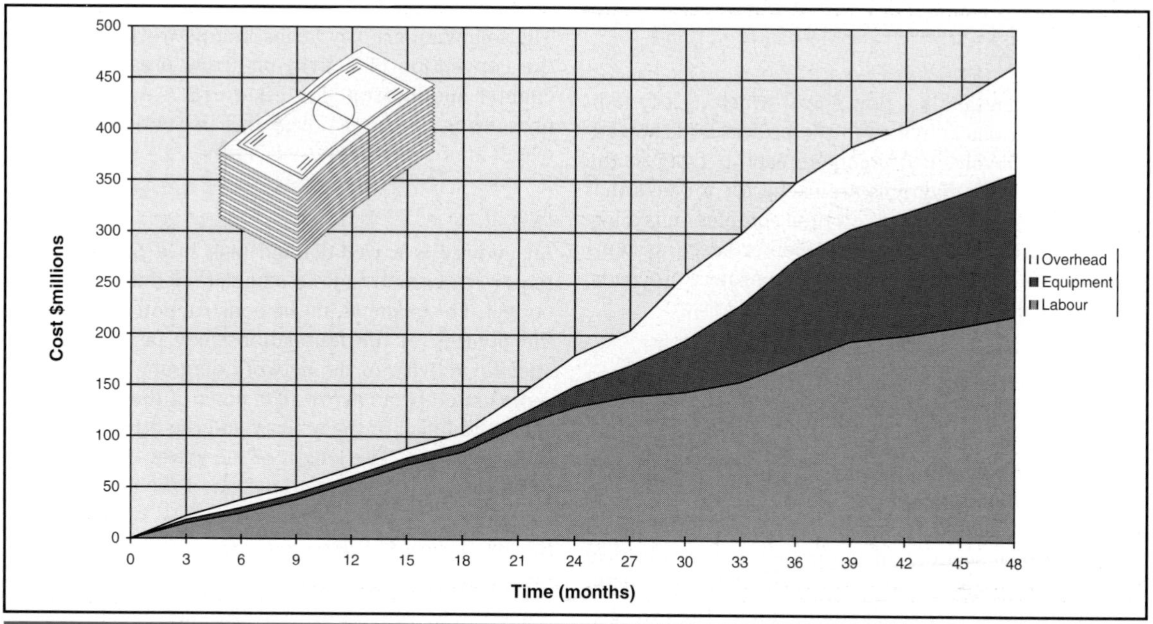

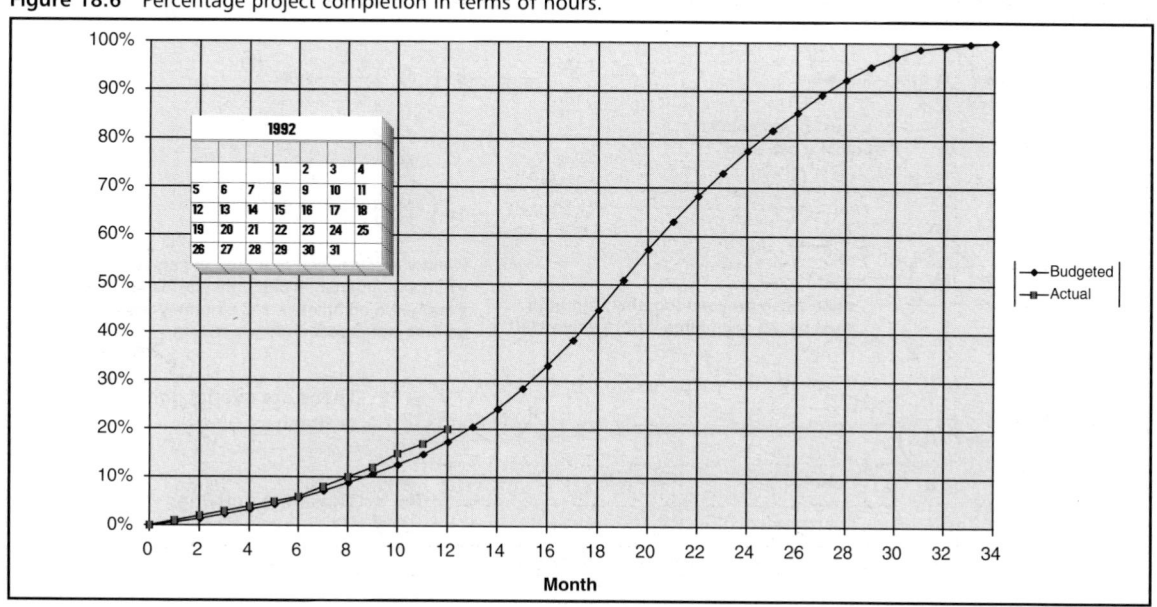

Dynamic monitoring tools

All the monitoring tools, such as Gantt charts, cost curves and per cent completion curves, are dynamic in that they are modified according to changes in the project as work progresses. There may be modifications due to unforeseen circumstances, such as delays, bad weather, industrial disputes, etc. I was involved on a project when one of the barges delivering equipment for an ammonia plant sank! One of the reasons for the delay in the building of the Channel tunnel was that the soil turned out to be much rockier than expected and this increased drilling, and thus overall construction, time.

Figure 18.6   Percentage project completion in terms of hours.

NETWORK DIAGRAMS

Description

A network diagram is a flow sheet, which clearly indicates the various activities in the project and the estimated time involved to complete each activity in the project. Network diagrams are useful for projects that have many activities where on time completion is a key criterion. They are dynamic computer-based systems that can be continually updated as a project proceeds. They provide information such as:

- the date when the project should be finished;
- when each individual part, or activity, of the project is scheduled to start and finish;
- which steps of the project are critical and must be completed on time in order that the overall project is not behind schedule;
- where it might be possible to shift resources from non-critical sections of the project to more critical parts, or those that must be finished on time, without affecting the overall completion of the project;
- from among the many sections of the project where management should concentrate most of its effort.

Terms in network diagrams

The following are key terms in a network diagram for the convention of activity-on-arrow presented in this chapter and illustrated in Figure 18.7. Another way of presenting network diagrams is activity-on-node, which is not used here.

Activity

An activity is a well-defined task in a project, which requires a certain time to complete and has a financial budget. For example, in the construction of a building, the pouring of the foundations may be considered a specific activity. In the network diagram, an activity is represented by an arrow. The point of the arrow represents the finish of the activity and the other end represents the start. The length of the arrow does not have to be related to the time duration of the activity.

Beginning and ending activities in a project

In constructing the network diagrams in the project immediately preceding activities are identified. The starting activities in the project would be those that have no preceding activities. The ending activities would be those which do not precede any other activities.

Figure 18.7 Terms in a network diagram.

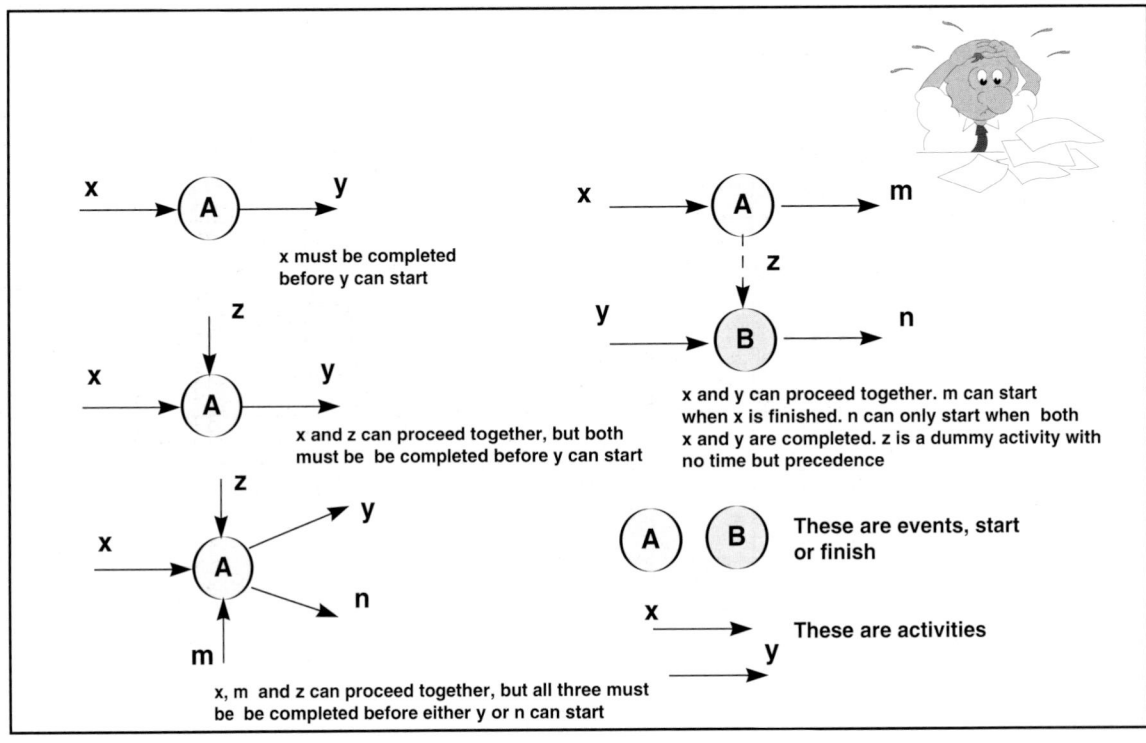

Event

An event is represented by a circle, or node, and occurs at the start or finish of an activity. The event has no time. An activity cannot start from a node until all the activities leading to that node have been completed.

Dummy activity

A dummy activity is a fictitious activity, which is included in a network diagram to indicate a precedence relationship. There is no time involved.

Path

A path is the route taken, passing though several activities to arrive at a specific activity or the end of the project.

Critical path

The critical path is the longest path in the network diagram.

Independence

It is assumed that path duration times are independent of each other. This implies that activity times are independent of each other and each activity is only one path.

Completion

A project is not finished until all paths have been completed. This means not just the critical path, but all the other paths as well, some of which might be delayed.

Network diagram for a house construction

Figure 18.8 illustrates the various activities in the design and construction of a house. Each activity is shown on the arrow, and the beginning and ending of activities are numbered from 1 to 32.

Critical Path Method

The Critical Path Method (CPM) method is a network diagram approach developed in 1957 by J. E. Kelly of Remington Rand and M. R. Walker of Du Pont to help schedule maintenance projects in chemical plants. It is useful for projects that have many activities and where on time completion is imperative. CPM methods are dynamic systems that are continually updated as the project proceeds. The method uses single time estimates, which are considered to be certain, or *deterministic*.[2]

Figure 18.8 Network diagram for house construction (Europe).

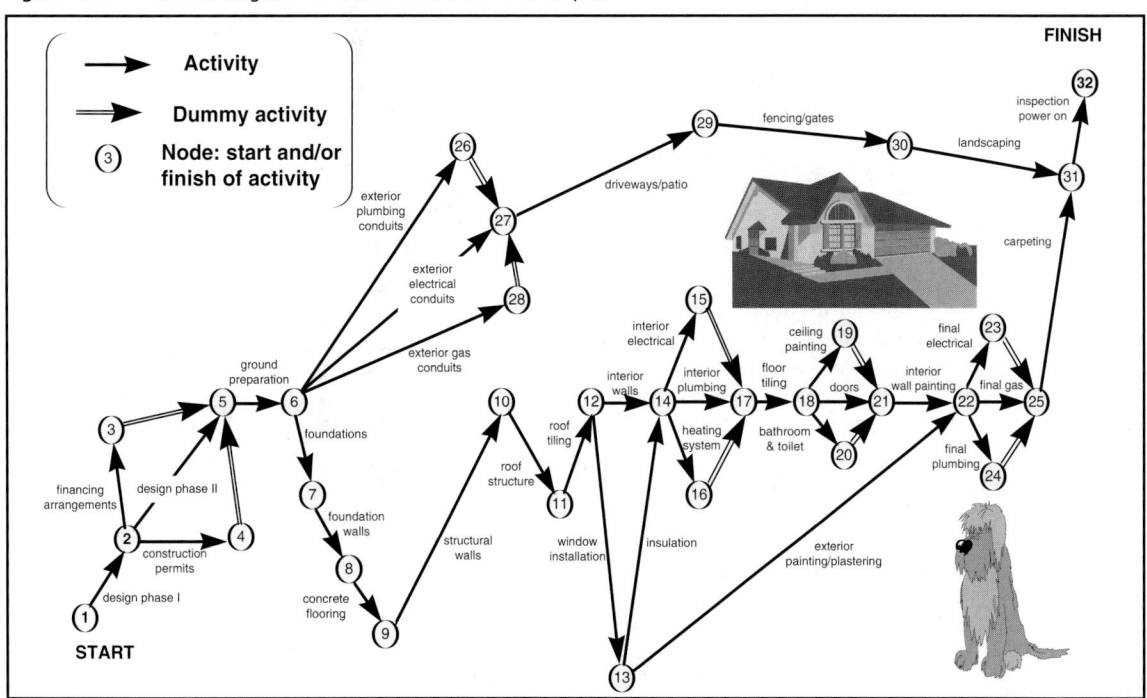

Procedure in the CPM method

The following gives the steps involved in using the CPM method:

1 Draw the network diagram indicating the events on a node, and the activities by an arrow. This gives a global overview of the complete project. By convention, the project starts on the left and finishes on the right.
2 Show on the arrows the time duration (T) of each activity.
3 Starting from the left, calculate the earliest finish time (EF) for each activity. This is given by the earliest possible start time (ES) plus the duration of the activity.
4 When all the calculations are made, the last time will give the finish time for the complete project.
5 Starting from the right-hand side with the overall project duration, determine the latest finish for each activity (LF).
6 Determine the latest start (LS) by deducting the activity duration from the latest finish.
7 For each activity, determine the difference between the latest finish and the earliest finish. This will give the slack time for each activity. Alternatively, the slack can be calculated as the difference between the latest start and the earliest start.
8 Where an activity has a slack time of zero, then this is an activity on the critical path.
9 The critical path for the project is the one where all the activities have a slack time of zero.

The worked example, *Enviroteck* Part I, illustrates the principle of the critical path method.

Program Evaluation and Review Technique

The Program Evaluation and Review Technique (PERT) was developed in 1958 jointly by Lockheed Aircraft, the US Navy Special projects office and the consulting firm of Booz, Allen and Hamilton and specifically directed at planning and controlling the Polaris missile programme. This was a project involving 250 prime or major contractors and over 900 sub-contractors.[3]

PERT is similar to the CPM method regarding functions, network diagrams, internal calculations and resulting project management reports. An exception is that it considers the uncertainty of the duration of activities by incorporating probability values. As such, time estimates, developed by persons familiar with the project concepts, have three values as shown in Table 18.3.

Table 18.3 Values of time estimates in PERT

Time	Explanation
b	Pessimistic time, or worst conditions if bad luck is encountered
m	Most likely time, or the consensus best estimate
a	Optimistic time, or when things go better than expected

Beta probability distribution

A beta probability distribution, illustrated in Figure 18.9, is commonly used in PERT. This distribution has the properties of being entirely contained within a finite interval and the mean and variance of the distribution can be approximated by the pessimistic most likely and optimistic time estimates. It has no predetermined shape, such as the bell shape of the normal curve, and will take on that shape or be skewed, according to the estimates (see also Chapter 20, *Statistical concepts*).

Then mean time t for an activity is given by:

$$t = \frac{a + 4m + b}{6},$$

the variance is given by the relationship:

$$\sigma^2 = \left[\frac{(b-a)}{6}\right]^2 = \frac{(b-a)^2}{36}.$$

The standard deviation for the activity is the square root of the variance:

$$\sigma = \sqrt{\sigma^2} = \left[\frac{(b-a)}{6}\right].$$

The magnitude of the variance reflects the degree of uncertainty associated with the time of an activity. An activity with a variance of 20 would have more uncertainty with respect to its actual duration than one with a variation of 5. The standard deviation of each activity's time is estimated as one sixth of the difference between the pessimistic and optimistic times. This is analogous to all of the area under a normal distribution that lies within plus or minus 3 standard deviations of the mean, or a range of six standard deviations (see again Chapter 20, *Statistical concepts*).

The standard deviation, or variance, can be computed for each path by summing the individual variances, or standard deviations, for each activity path. This enables project managers or schedulers to make probabilistic estimates of the project completion times, for example:

■ The probability a project will be completed with 15 months of start is 92 per cent.
■ The probability that project will take longer than 18 months is 3 per cent.

Figure 18.9 Beta distribution for a PERT diagram.

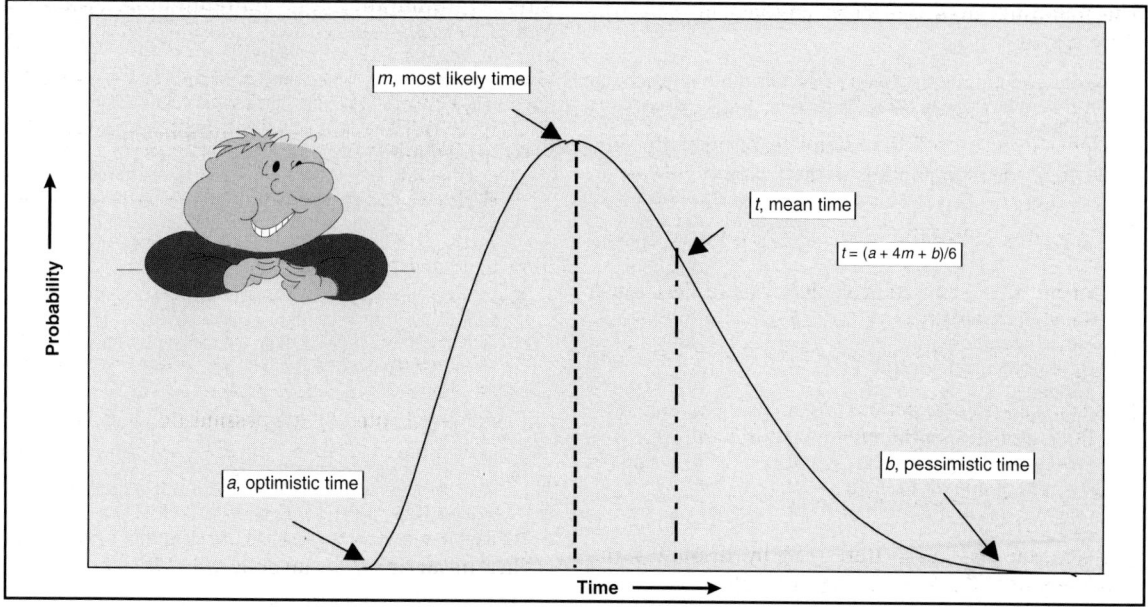

These statements are based on the assumption that the path duration is a random variable that is normally distributed around the expected path time. This is true for large samples and is approximately true for smaller samples.

The worked example, *Biltmore*, illustrates the use of the PERT method. (Since this example uses the principle of probabilities, Chapter 20, *Statistical concepts* may be helpful.)

Advantages of network diagrams

Using network diagrams has the following advantages:

- They force a project manager to organize and quantify available information, and to recognize where and what additional information is needed.
- They provide a graphical display of the project and activities.
- They identify activities that should be closely watched because of the potential for delaying the project.
- They identify activities that have slack time and so can be delayed without affecting project completion time. This raises the possibility of reallocating resources.

Limitations of network diagrams

There are limitations, and caution should be exercised when using network diagrams:

- They are time consuming, and therefore costly. However, this is usually outweighed by their advantages.
- Established precedence relationships may not be correct and this could upset the schedule.
- The time estimates are sometimes difficult to calculate. Similar past projects are useful in this respect.
- The probabilistic capabilities of PERT are open to criticism, because it is difficult enough to make one good time estimate for each activity, as in CPM. Making three accurate time estimates, each with a different meaning, is hard. As such, PERT is more costly than CPM in terms of both dollars and the management effort.

Computerized systems

Today, the network diagram systems are computerized and there are many packages for CPM and PERT methods on the market from such firms as Microsoft, Primavera and IBM.

WORKED EXAMPLE: ENVIROTECK PART I

Situation

The Enviroteck Co. wishes to construct a pilot plant north of Sitges, Spain for the treatment of domestic waste. The activities for this project are as shown in Table 18.4.

Table 18.4 Activities in the Enviroteck project

Activity		Duration (weeks)	Activity immediately preceding
A	Equipment delivery	6	None
B	Site preparation	10	None
C	Development of control systems	14	A
D	Equipment assembly	8	A
E	Underground connections	6	B
F	Process connections	18	B
G	Training of operating team	10	C
H	Delivery and preparation of raw materials	12	F
I	Installation and equipment checkout	6	D, E

Required

1 Identify the critical path. What is the minimum time to complete this project?
2 How can several activities be managed if personnel is limited?

Solution

1 Identify the critical path. What is the minimum time to complete this project?
- Table 18.5 gives the complete calculations.
- Paying attention to the precedence relationship, draw a network diagram. This is given in Figure 18.10. On the diagram are given the times for each activity.

Earliest times

- The earliest start time and the earliest finish time are determined for each activity. It is assumed that the earliest start time for the beginning of the project is 0. The times are shown in Figure 18.11.

- For example, the earliest start time for A is 0, and thus the earliest finish for A is $0 + 6 = 6$ weeks.
- For activity C, the earliest start time is equal to the earliest finish time for A, or 6 weeks. Thus the earliest finish time for activity C is $6 + 14 = 20$ weeks.
- In the case where there is more than one activity arriving at a node, then the activity leaving that node cannot start until all the entering activities have been completed. This is the case at node 4. Activity I cannot start until both activities D and E have been completed. D finishes after 14 weeks and E finishes after 16 weeks. Thus I cannot start until 16 weeks have elapsed.
- In proceeding with the calculation through the whole network, the earliest finish time for the complete project is 40 weeks, as determined by activity H. However, the earliest finish time for activity G is 30 weeks, and 22 weeks for activity I.

Latest times

- Since the project cannot finish until activity H has been completed, then the latest finish date for both activities I and G can also be 40 weeks as there is no urgency to have them finished before H.
- Starting with 40 weeks, determine the latest start for each activity. This is given by the latest finish less the duration.
- For activity G, the latest start is $40 - 10 = 30$ weeks (compared to 20 for the earliest start).
- For activity I, the latest start is $40 - 6 = 34$ weeks (compared to 16 for the earliest start).
- For activity H, the latest start is $40 - 12 = 28$ weeks or the same as the earliest start.
- The latest finish for both activities D and E is 34 weeks, or the same as the latest start for I.
- Determine the slack time for each activity. This is either the difference between the earliest start and the latest start, or the difference between the earliest finish and the latest finish.
- Those activities that have a zero slack time are on the critical path, in this case activities B, F and H.
- The critical path for the project is thus Site Preparation (B), Process Connections (F), and Delivery and preparation of raw materials (H). All this is illustrated in Figure 18.11.

2 How can several activities be managed if personnel is limited?
The project manager can evaluate those non-critical activities where there is slack time (Equipment delivery, Development of control systems, Equipment assembly, Underground connections, Training of operating team and Installation and equipment checkout) to see if resources from these, such as personnel and money, can be utilized on the critical path activities.

Table 18.5 Enviroteck – initial network data

	Activity	Duration (weeks)	Activity immediately preceding	Earliest start date	Earliest finish date	Latest start date	Latest finish date	Slack time (weeks)
A	Equipment delivery	6	None	0	6	10	16	10
B	Site preparation	10	None	0	10	0	10	0
C	Development of control systems	14	A	6	20	16	30	10
D	Equipment assembly	8	A	6	14	26	34	20
E	Underground connections	6	B	10	16	28	34	18
F	Process connections	18	B	10	28	10	28	0
G	Training of operating team	10	C	20	30	30	40	10
H	Delivery and preparation of raw materials	12	F	28	40	28	40	0
I	Installation and equipment checkout	6	D, E	16	22	34	40	18

Figure 18.10 Enviroteck – network diagram with activity times.

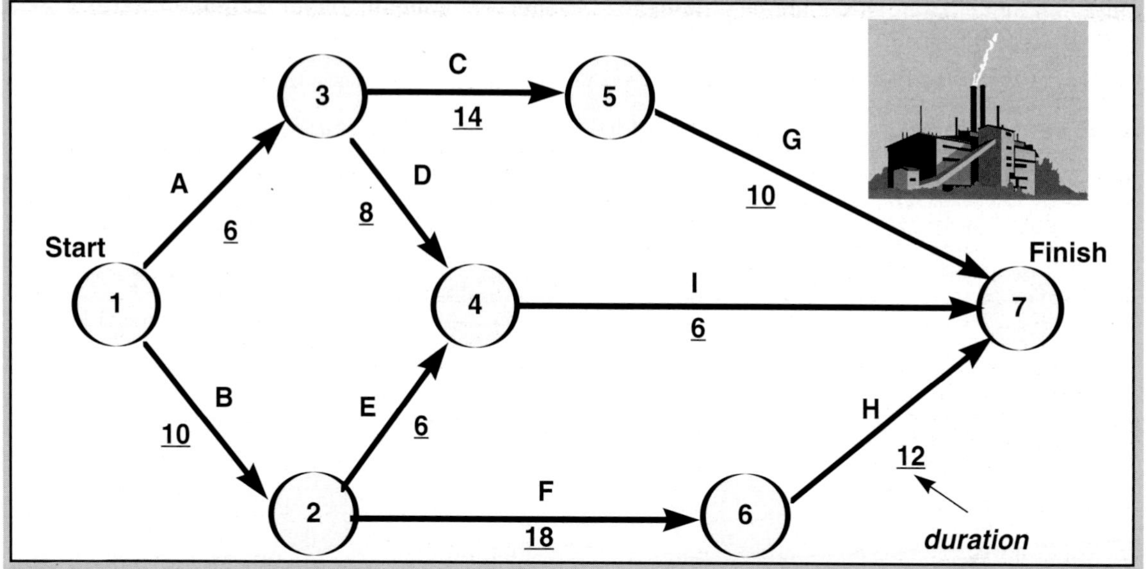

Figure 18.11 Enviroteck– Part I: network with activities, duration, start time and finish time.

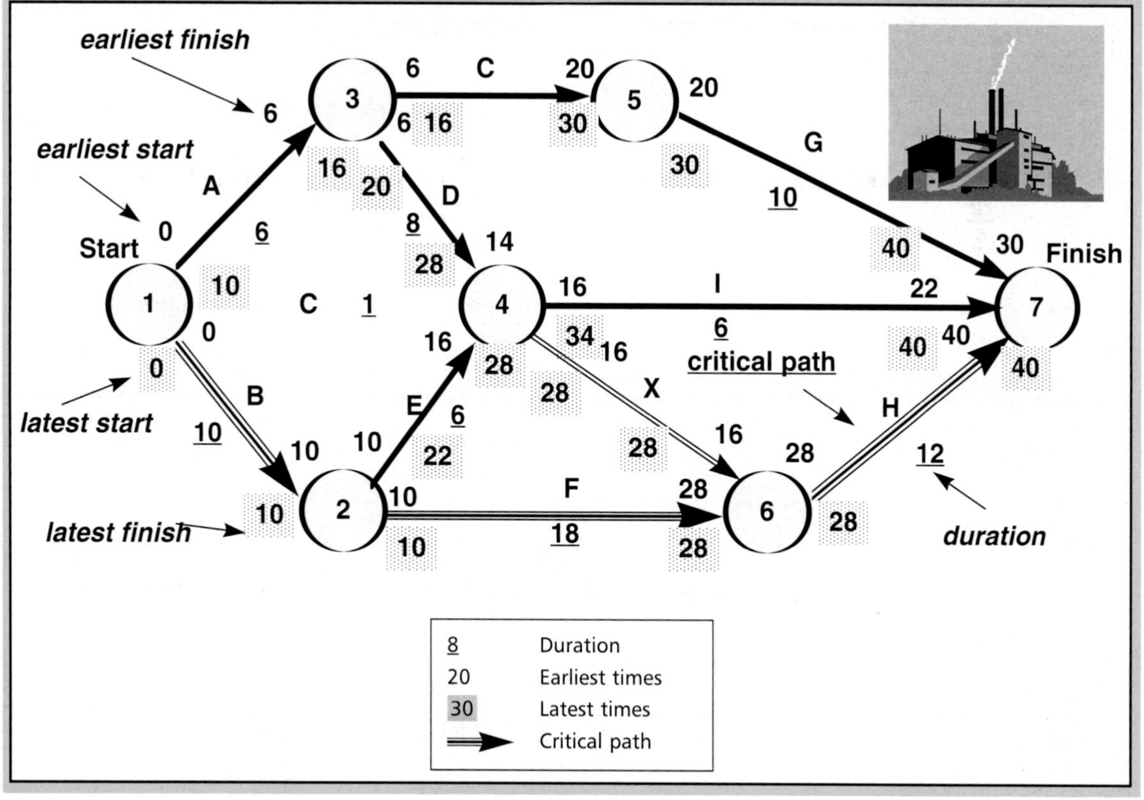

8	Duration
20	Earliest times
30	Latest times
⟹	Critical path

WORKED EXAMPLE: BILTMORE (PART I)

Situation

The Biltmore Co. wants to build a deluxe hotel in Igls, Austria, ready for the ski season. The project manager, together with the project team, has identified the principal activities for the construction, together with time estimates, in weeks, based on pessimistic, optimistic and mean times. These are given in Table 18.6. The pessimistic times are principally due to bad weather which might be encountered. Further, Biltmore is going to use a subcontractor for the construction of the parking and there will be a severe penalty if construction is not completed on the date promised. This is why the optimistic, realistic and pessimistic estimates for this activity are the same.

Required

1 Analyse the project and determine the critical path, the critical time for each activity and the total time for completing the project.
2 What is the probability that the project will take more than 57 weeks to complete?

Solution

1 Analyse the project and determine the critical path, the critical time for each activity and the total time for completing the project.
- The network diagram is given in Figure 18.12.
- The mean time for each activity is calculated from the optimistic, pessimistic and realistic times, using the relationship:

$$t = \frac{a + 4m + b}{6}.$$

These values are given in Table 18.7.

- Using the mean times, the earliest start date, earliest finish date, latest start date and latest finish date are calculated in the same manner as for Enviroteck. The data is shown in Table 18.8.
- The slack time is determined from the difference between the latest and earliest start dates, or the latest and earliest finish dates. This information is given in Table 18.8.
- There is no slack time on the path B-E-F and this is then the critical path.
- Figure 18.13 gives the completed network information. A period of 54.33 weeks is the project completion date based on the information given.

2 What is the probability that the project will take more than 57 weeks to complete?
- The completion time was calculated based on the mean times for each activity. For each of these activities, a pessimistic time was given and it is this data that leads to a probability situation.
- The variance for each activity is given in Table 18.7. It is calculated from the relationship:

$$\sigma^2 = \left[\frac{(b-a)}{6} \right]^2 = \frac{(b-a)^2}{36}.$$

- The sum of the variances for each of the three paths from start to finish of the project is obtained by summing the individual variances for each activity. This is given in Table 18.9.
- The standard deviation of each of the three summed variances is determined by taking the square root. This is also given in Table 18.9.
- The z value, or the number of standard deviations from the mean, is calculated from the relationship:

$$z = \frac{x - \mu}{\sigma} \text{ (see Chapter 20, \textit{Statistical Concepts}).}$$

Table 18.6 Biltmore – activities and time estimates

	Activity	Immediate predecessor	Optimistic time (a)	Realistic time (m)	Pessimistic time (b)
A	Access road	None	15	20	25
B	Foundations	None	8	10	12
C	Landscaping/Pool	A	25	30	40
D	Parking structure	B	15	15	15
E	Hotel structure	B	22	25	27
F	Interior/Exterior – hotel	E	15	20	22
G	Interior/Exterior – parking	D	20	20	22

Table 18.7 Biltmore, activity time data

		Immediate predecessor	Optimistic time (a)	Realistic time (m)	Pessimistic time (b)	Mean time (t)	Variance	Standard deviation
A	Access road	None	15	20	25	20.00	2.78	1.67
B	Foundations	None	8	10	12	10.00	0.44	0.67
C	Landscaping/Pool	A	25	30	40	30.83	6.25	2.50
D	Parking structure	B	15	15	15	15.00	0.00	0.00
E	Hotel structure	B	22	25	27	24.83	0.69	0.83
F	Interior/Exterior – hotel	E	15	20	22	19.50	1.36	1.17
G	Interior/Exterior – parking	D	20	20	22	20.33	0.11	0.33

Figure 18.12 Biltmore – network diagram with activity times.

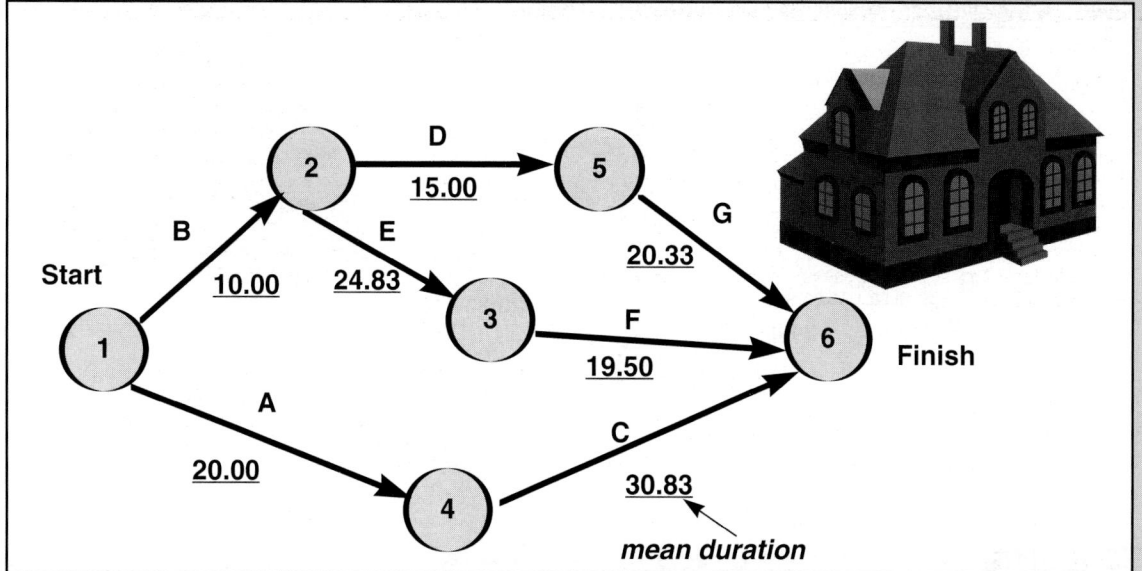

Here, the value of x is 57 weeks, μ is the mean time obtained by summing the mean time for each activity on the path, and s is the calculated standard deviation. The values are given in Table 18.9.

■ The probability of being finished within 57 weeks is determined for each path using the Normal function in Excel. For path B-D-G there is no uncertainty, but for A-C there is a probability of 97.99 per cent of being finished, and for path B-E-F a probability of 95.42 per cent.

■ Since both probabilities need to be considered, then the joint probability of being completed within 57 weeks is the product of the two probabilities, or 93.50 per cent.

■ Thus the probability of the project running over the 57 weeks is 100 per cent less 93.50 or 6.50 per cent. All this is shown in Table 18.9.

Table 18.8 Biltmore, start and finish dates

		Duration (weeks)	Immediate predecessor	Earliest start date	Earliest finish date	Latest start date	Latest finish date	Slack time (months)
A	Access road	20.00	None	0.00	20.00	3.50	23.50	3.50
B	Foundations	10.00	None	0.00	10.00	0.00	10.00	**0.00**
C	Landscaping/Pool	30.83	A	20.00	50.83	23.50	54.33	3.50
D	Parking structure	15.00	B	10.00	25.00	19.00	34.00	9.00
E	Hotel structure	24.83	B	10.00	34.83	10.00	34.83	**0.00**
F	Interior/Exterior – hotel	19.50	E	34.83	54.33	34.83	54.33	**0.00**
G	Interior/Exterior – parking	20.33	D	25.00	45.33	34.00	54.33	9.00

Table 18.9 Biltmore, probabilities

		Weeks	Variance	σ	z	P (finish)	P (not)
Project completion time		54.33					
Required completion data		57.00					
Path	B-D-G, mean time	45.33	0.56	0.7454	15.6525	100.00%	0.00%
Path	A-C, mean time	50.83	9.03	3.0046	2.0524	97.99%	2.01%
Path	B-E-F, mean time	54.33	2.50	1.5811	1.6865	95.42%	4.58%
Probability of finish						**93.50%**	**6.50%**

Figure 18.13 Biltmore – network diagram with critical path.

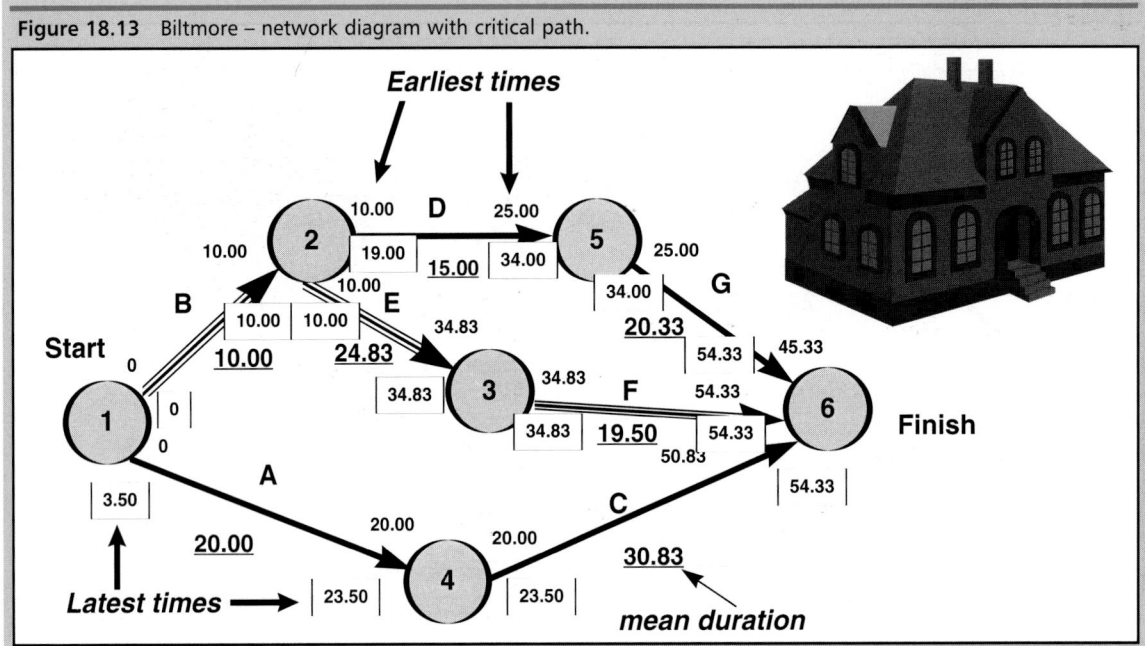

ACCELERATING (CRASHING) A PROJECT

Principle

Project managers may have the option, or may be required, to accelerate, or crash, a project, which means reducing the duration for an additional cost. Project managers would particularly consider this option if the project was in danger of running over schedule, especially if there was a penalty clause in the contract. Options available to accelerate a project include:

- spending more money;
- using personnel on overtime, including weekends and nights;
- subcontracting out some portions of the project;
- expediting materials if this is a reason for the delay;
- hiring more people.

The principle of crashing is illustrated in Figure 18.14. In this illustration a particular project has a normal duration of ten weeks for a total cost of £300 000. The project can be reduced to a duration of three weeks and the cost would be now £1 000 000. Thus, for a reduction in time of seven weeks the cost has increased by £700 000. The illustration here shows a linear reduction, which may not necessarily be the case.

Network diagrams and crashing

In a project that has several activities that can be crashed or accelerated, the following are the general rules to adopt:

1. Crash only critical activities in the network.
2. Do not crash non-critical activities as this will not reduce the project's overall duration.
3. Start by crashing activities with the lowest crashing cost per unit of time and continue until the desired project duration is achieved.
4. When parallel critical paths exist, each of the parallel paths must be reduced since compressing only one of the paths will not reduce the overall project duration.

To crash a project successfully, one examines the network, not its activities, and compares normal costs with crash costs for each activity. The objective is to find those activities on the critical path where time can be cut substantially with minimum expenditure. The objective is the greatest time reduction for the least increase in project cost.

The worked example, *Gibson*, illustrates the principle of crashing a project.

Figure 18.14 Principle of accelerating, or crashing, a project.

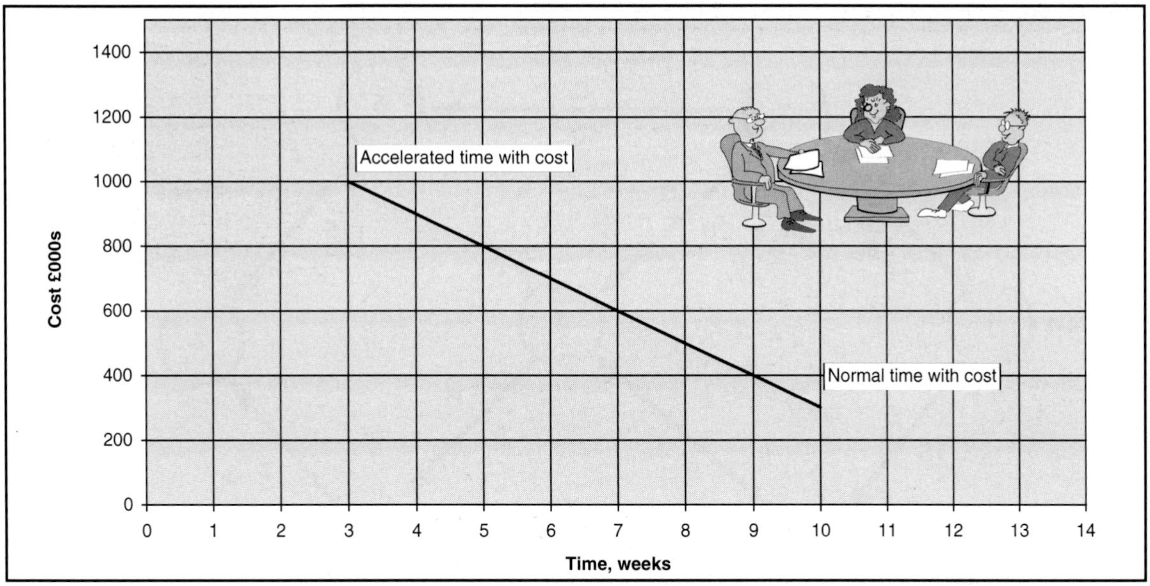

Situation

The activities, duration, schedule and cost data for the construction of a section of an oil rig are given in Table 18.10

Required

1 Develop the network for this project.
2 Determine the following:
  (a) the earliest possible start dates;
  (b) the latest start dates;
  (c) the earliest finish dates;
  (d) the latest finish dates.
3 What is the critical path and the project duration?
4 What is the maximum feasible time by which the project can be reduced and what would be the additional cost to arrive at this time?

Solution

1 Develop the network for this project
  ■ This is given in Figure 18.15, taking into account the precedence relationship.
2 Determine the following:
  (a) the earliest possible start dates;
  (b) the latest start dates;
  (c) the earliest finish dates;
  (d) the latest finish dates.
  ■ These are given in the Table 18.11 using the same criteria as for the worked example, Enviroteck.
  ■ Figure 18.16 shows the activity times, latest and earliest start times and the latest and earliest finish times.
3 What is the critical path and the project duration?
  ■ The critical path is where there is no slack time. This is the path B-F-H-I (shown in bold type in Table 18.11).

Table 18.10 The activities, duration, schedule and cost data for the construction of a section of an oil rig

Activity	Activity immediately preceding	Normal duration (weeks)	Accelerated duration (weeks)	Activity immediately preceding	Normal cost (£000)	Accelerated cost (£000)
A	None	10	9	None	1100	1500
B	None	15	13	None	2000	2500
C	A	10	6	A	900	2000
D	A	20	18	A	2500	3000
E	C	15	10	C	2000	3500
F	B	17	15	B	2000	3000
G	B	12	10	B	1500	2500
H	D, F	9	8	D, F	1200	1800
I	G, H	7	6	G, H	1000	1500

Figure 18.15   Gibson – network with activities and duration.

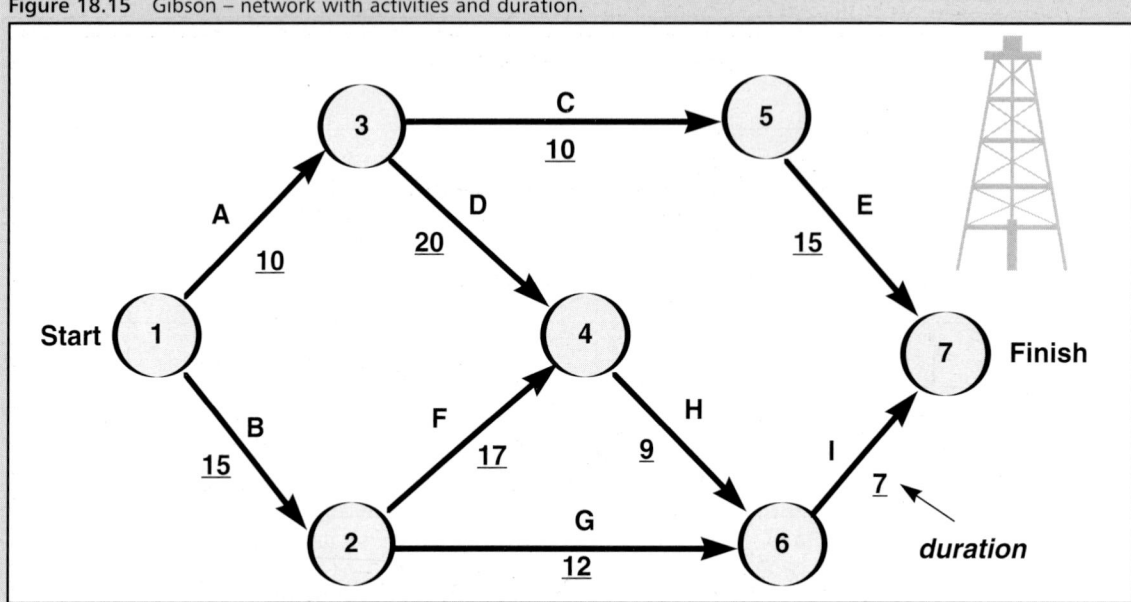

Table 18.11   Gibson – initial network data (critical path when slack time = 0)

	Normal duration (weeks)	Accelerated duration (weeks)	Activity immediately preceding	Normal cost (£000)	Accelerated cost (£000)	Cost to reduce (£000/week)	Earliest start date	Earliest finish date	Latest start date	Latest finish date	Slack time (weeks)
A	10	9	None	1100	1500	400	0	10	2	12	2
B	15	13	None	2000	2500	250	0	15	0	15	0
C	10	6	A	900	2000	275	10	20	23	33	13
D	20	18	A	2500	3000	250	10	30	12	32	2
E	15	10	C	2000	3500	300	20	35	33	48	13
F	17	15	B	2000	3000	500	15	32	15	32	0
G	12	10	B	1500	2500	500	15	27	29	41	14
H	9	8	D, F	1200	1800	600	32	41	32	41	0
I	7	6	G, H	1000	1500	500	41	48	41	48	0

Table 18.12   Gibson Network data with project acceleration – 1. Reducing activity B from 15 to 13 weeks

	Revised duration (weeks)	Accelerated duration (weeks)	Activity immediately preceding	Normal cost (£000)	Accelerated cost (£000)	Cost to reduce (£000/week)	Earliest start date	Earliest finish date	Latest start date	Latest finish date	Slack time (months)
A	10	9	None	1100	1500	400	0	10	0	10	0
B	13	13	None	2000	2500	250	0	13	0	13	0
C	10	6	A	900	2000	275	10	20	21	31	11
D	20	18	A	2500	3000	250	10	30	10	30	0
E	15	10	C	2000	3500	300	20	35	31	46	11
F	17	15	B	2000	3000	500	13	30	13	30	0
G	12	10	B	1500	2500	500	13	25	27	39	14
H	9	8	D, F	1200	1800	600	30	39	30	39	0
I	7	6	G, H	1000	1500	500	39	46	39	46	0

Additional cost (£000s)   500

Figure 18.16 Gibson – network with activities, duration, start time and finish time.

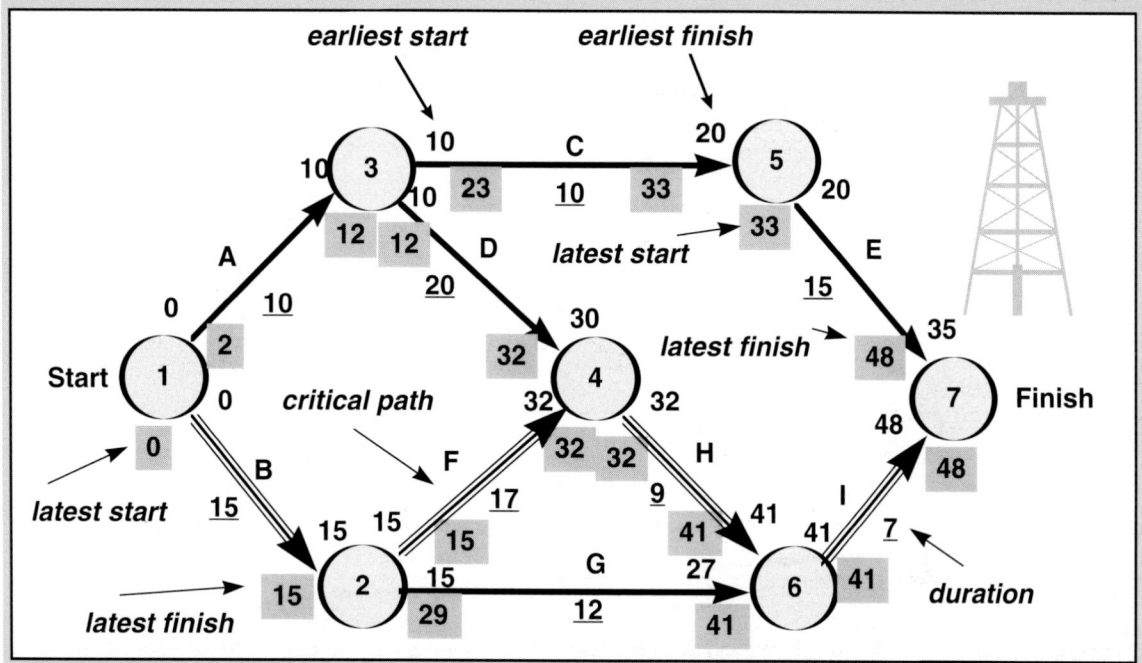

4 What is the maximum feasible time that the project can be reduced and what would be the additional cost to arrive at this time?
- Convert the accelerated costs into a common base or accelerated cost to reduce per week. This is given in Table 18.11.
- Start by crashing on the critical path and selecting that activity which is the least costly to reduce. In this case reduce B from 15 to 13 weeks for an additional cost of £500 000 (Table 18.12).
- Reducing the time of B now also puts A on the critical path. So there are two critical paths for the project, B-F-H-I and A-D-H-I.
- Reduce activity I from 7 to 6 weeks, for a total cost of £500 000 (Table 18.13).

- Reduce activity F from 17 to 15 weeks, for a total cost of £1 000 000. Project critical path is now A-D-H-I Table 18.14).
- Reduce activity H from 9 to 8 weeks, for a total cost of £600 000. Project critical path is still A-D-H-I (Table 18.15).
- Reduce activity D from 20 to 18 weeks, for a total cost of £500 000. Project critical paths are now A-D-H-I and B-F-H-I (Table 18.16). This is the furthest one can go. This is illustrated on Figure 18.17.
- Thus the overall project schedule has been reduced by six weeks from 48 weeks to 42 weeks. The additional cost for accelerating the project is £3 100 000.

Table 18.13 Gibson – network data with project acceleration – 2. Reducing activity I from 7 to 6 weeks

	Revised duration (weeks)	Accelerated duration (weeks)	Activity immediately preceding	Normal cost (£000)	Accelerated cost (£000)	Cost to reduce (£000/week)	Earliest start date	Earliest finish date	Latest start date	Latest finish date	Slack time (months)
A	10	9	None	1100	1500	400	0	10	0	10	0
B	13	13	None	2000	2500	250	0	13	0	13	0
C	10	6	A	900	2000	275	10	20	20	30	10
D	20	18	A	2500	3000	250	10	30	10	30	0
E	15	10	C	2000	3500	300	20	35	30	45	10
F	17	15	B	2000	3000	500	13	30	13	30	0
G	12	10	B	1500	2500	500	13	25	27	39	14
H	9	8	D, F	1200	1800	600	30	39	30	39	0
I	6	6	G, H	1000	1500	500	39	45	39	45	0
Additional cost (£000)		500									

Table 18.14 Network data with project acceleration – 3. Reducing activity F from 17 to 15 weeks

	Revised duration (weeks)	Accelerated duration (weeks)	Activity immediately preceding	Normal cost (£000)	Accelerated cost (£000)	Cost to reduce (£000/week)	Earliest start date	Earliest finish date	Latest start date	Latest finish date	Slack time (months)
A	10	9	None	1100	1500	400	0	10	0	10	0
B	13	13	None	2000	2500	250	0	13	2	15	2
C	10	6	A	900	2000	275	10	20	20	30	10
D	20	18	A	2500	3000	250	10	30	10	30	0
E	15	10	C	2000	3500	300	20	35	30	45	10
F	15	15	B	2000	3000	500	13	28	15	30	2
G	12	10	B	1500	2500	500	13	25	27	39	14
H	9	8	D, F	1200	1800	600	30	39	30	39	0
I	6	6	G, H	1000	1500	500	39	45	39	45	0
Additional cost (£000)		1000									

Table 18.15 Gibson – network data with project acceleration – 4. Reducing activity H from 9 to 8 weeks

	Revised duration (weeks)	Accelerated duration (weeks)	Activity immediately preceding	Normal cost (£000)	Accelerated cost (£000)	Cost to reduce (£000/week)	Earliest start date	Earliest finish date	Latest start date	Latest finish date	Slack time (months)
A	10	9	None	1100	1500	400	0	10	0	10	0
B	13	13	None	2000	2500	250	0	13	2	15	2
C	10	6	A	900	2000	275	10	20	19	29	9
D	20	18	A	2500	3000	250	10	30	10	30	0
E	15	10	C	2000	3500	300	20	35	29	44	9
F	15	15	B	2000	3000	500	13	28	15	30	2
G	12	10	B	1500	2500	500	13	25	26	38	13
H	8	8	D, F	1200	1800	600	30	38	30	38	0
I	6	6	G, H	1000	1500	500	38	44	38	44	0
Additional cost (£000)		600									

Table 18.16 Gibson – network data with project acceleration – 5. Reducing activity D from 20 to 18 weeks

	Revised duration (weeks)	Accelerated duration (weeks)	Activity immediately preceding	Normal cost (£000)	Accelerated cost (£000)	Cost to reduce (£000/week)	Earliest start date	Earliest finish date	Latest start date	Latest finish date	Slack time (months)
A	10	9	None	1100	1500	400	0	10	0	10	0
B	13	13	None	2000	2500	250	0	13	0	13	0
C	10	6	A	900	2000	275	10	20	17	27	7
D	18	18	A	2500	3000	250	10	28	10	28	0
E	15	10	C	2000	3500	300	20	35	27	42	7
F	15	15	B	2000	3000	500	13	28	13	28	0
G	12	10	B	1500	2500	500	13	25	24	36	11
H	8	8	D, F	1200	1800	600	28	36	28	36	0
I	6	6	G, H	1000	1500	500	36	42	36	42	0
Additional cost (£000)		500									
Total cost for acceleration (£000)		3100									

Figure 18.17 Gibson – network with activities after reducing schedule.

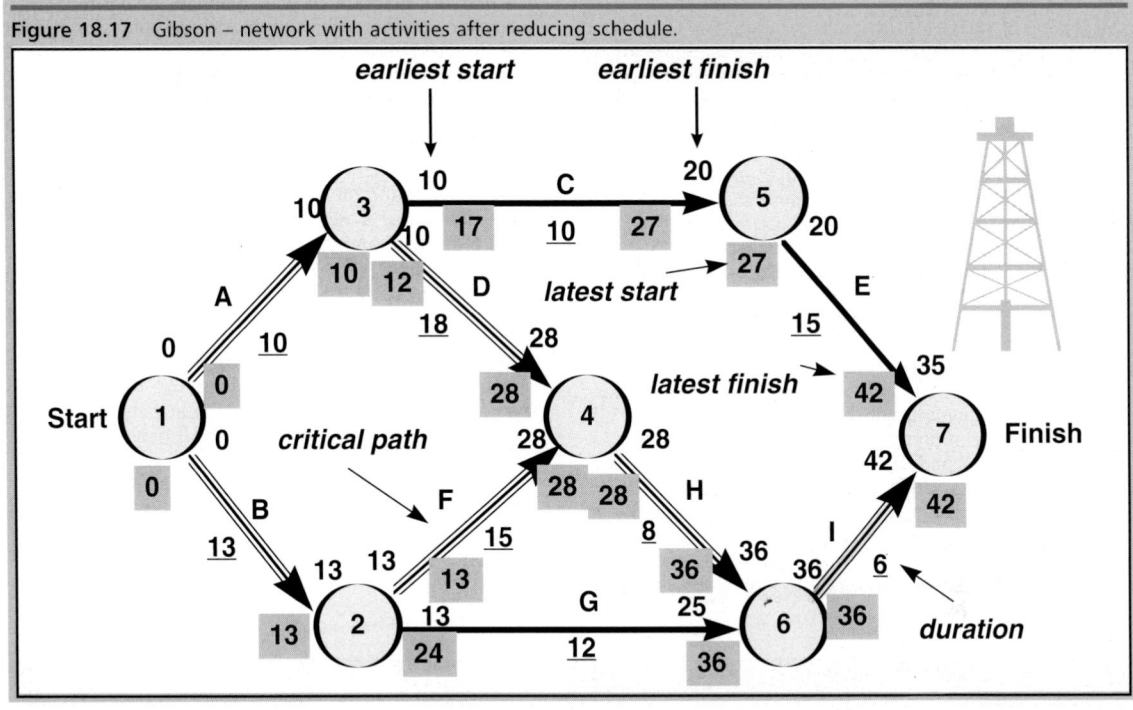

SUMMARY OF KEY ELEMENTS

- A project is a unique item of work. Project management is the planning, scheduling, budgeting and control of this work using an integrated team.
- In a project there is an objective, a plan, start and finish dates and a budget.
- A project performed for a client by a supplier firm might be on the basis of a fixed-price contract, which presents more risk to the supplier firm, or it might be on the basis of a cost-plus contract, which represents more risk to the client.
- A turnkey, or grass roots, project is completely new, built on a virgin site.
- Project and operations are related. A project is often the start of operations. Project activities are similar to operating functions. The project team may be composed of operating personnel. When the project is terminated, some of the project team may be involved in the operations.
- Projects, particularly when government entities are involved, are awarded in phases, or work packages. This permits modifications if market conditions should change, levels the work-load among firms and may avoid unethical situations.
- Project stages go from proposal to design and conception, detailed design, construction and the start-up or hand-over phase.

- A project organization is composed of a project manager, who has overall responsibility, and a team, perhaps of engineers, schedulers, purchasing people, a controller and a construction manager.
- For scheduling and controlling a project, tools that may be used include Gantt charts, monthly and project cost curves and per cent completion curves.
- A network diagram is a flow sheet that clearly indicates the various activities in the project and the estimated time to complete each activity.
- In a network diagram the critical path is the longest path in the network and this is where the project manager should concentrate his attention.
- The critical path method (CPM) in network diagrams uses single time estimates for activities.
- The Program Evaluation and Review Technique (PERT) method in network diagrams uses pessimistic, most likely and optimistic time estimates. The estimations are probabilistic, based on a beta probability distribution.
- Crashing a project involves using additional resources, such as overtime, subcontracting, expediting and hiring, to reduce the time duration of a project.

REVIEW AND DISCUSSION QUESTIONS

1 **Project or operations?**. Review all the activities that you are scheduled to do during the next six months. Classify them accordingly as operations or projects. Justify your reasoning. For those that you consider to be projects, develop a Gantt scheduling chart.

2 **Project proposal**. Consider that you are developing a client proposal for the following projects:
   (a) a marketing study concerning the construction of a polyethylene plant in the Middle East;
   (b) the construction of a new motorway linking two major cities;
   (c) the design and construction of a nuclear repository in Greenland for nuclear waste from nuclear warheads originating from the USA and the former USSR (a consideration by the government in Greenland).
   Indicate the major sections and the type of information that you would include in the proposal. What would be some of the important elements in the contract? What financial terms might you propose?

3 **Network diagrams**. A network diagram is a series of nodes (events) connected by arrows (activities). Develop a network diagram of your planned, or desired, strategy for your life. This should include your strategy for both your personal and professional endeavours. What are some of the risks and uncertainties involved?

4 **Project manager**. Discuss what you believe should be some of the important criteria for the selection of a project manager for the following types of projects:
   (a) the construction of an automobile facility in China;
   (b) a marketing study for the development and introduction of a new pharmaceutical product for the European market;
   (c) a European-government sponsored project for environmental improvement in the European Union.
   Consider some of the elements that would be included in the project.

5 **Technology and project management**. Discuss where you think technology is able to improve the function of project management. Consider the activity from a global perspective, including all of the functions which are managed by the project manager.

6 **Project acceleration or crashing**. This chapter deals with ways in which a project's duration can be reduced (accelerated or crashed). Discuss the impact of the various possibilities on a project and their implications for the project supply chain.

EXERCISE PROBLEM: BILTMORE (PART II)

Situation

In the worked example, *Biltmore*, the owners of the hotel have put a constraint on the project saying that the hotel structure, Activity E, has to be completed before the landscaping and the covered swimming pool, Activity C, can be started.

Required

1 Make the necessary additions/modifications to the network diagram to take into account the new requirements.
2 Illustrate the earliest and latest times on the network diagram.
3 What is the critical path for the project?
4 What is the probability that the complete project will not be finished before 57 weeks? What is the risk that it will run over schedule?

EXERCISE PROBLEM: ENVIROTECK (PART II)

Situation

In the *Enviroteck* worked example, just before starting the project, the project manager learns that the delivery time for equipment delivery has increased from 6 to 17 weeks. This gives the activities and times for the project now as shown in Table 18.17.

Table 18.17 Enviroteck – revised activities and times for the project

	Activity	Duration (weeks)	Activity immediately preceding
A	Equipment delivery	17	None
B	Site preparation	10	None
C	Development of control systems	14	A
D	Equipment assembly	8	A
E	Underground connections	6	B
F	Process connections	18	B
G	Training of operating team	10	C
H	Delivery and preparation of raw materials	12	F
I	Installation and equipment checkout	6	D, E

Required

1 What changes would now occur in the project?
2 If a requirement is that all the underground connections are finished before beginning the delivery and preparation of the raw material, how would the project schedule change. The equipment delivery time remains at six weeks rather than the 17 weeks.

EXERCISE PROBLEM: EUSTON

Situation

The schedule and cost data for the construction of a commercial shopping centre are given in Table 18.18. This information gives the 15 activities, the activities which immediately precede and the normal duration for each activity in months. The cost data includes the direct cost to reduce the duration of the activity by one, two or three months. In addition, the indirect costs for this construction work are estimated at FF 4 000 000 per month.

Required

1 Develop the network scheme for this project.
2 What is the critical path?
3 The client would like to cut six months off the completion time for the project. What would be the additional direct costs required to achieve this?
4 What is the optimal time for reducing this project if all the given costs are taken into consideration? Justify your answer with a graph showing the movement of costs.

Table 18.18   Euston – the schedule and cost data for the construction of a commercial shopping centre

Activity	Immediate predecessor	Normal duration (months)	Crash cost for first month (FF 000)	Crash cost for second month (FF 000)	Crash cost for third month (FF 000)
A	None	5	1800	2200	None
B	None	4	1200	2400	2600
C	None	3	1000	1500	2500
D	A	8	2400	2500	2500
E	B	12	None	None	None
F	C	12	800	1300	None
G	D	7	3000	3000	3500
H	E	5	4000	4000	4000
I	B	6	300	1000	1200
J	F	9	500	1200	None
K	G	4	1500	2000	None
L	I	9	200	700	1000
M	J	8	1400	1500	None
N	K, H	11	3000	3300	3600
P	L, M	1	2600	None	None

EXERCISE PROBLEM: HARBOUR

Situation

A coastal town on the Mediterranean has signed a contract to build a new yacht harbour. The project team who have been assigned have developed a schedule based on a PERT approach. This information is given in Table 18.19.

Table 18.19   PERT data for the new yacht harbour

	Immediate predecessor	Optimistic time (weeks)	Realistic time (weeks)	Pessimistic time (weeks)
A	None	17	20	25
B	None	43	55	64
C	None	62	68	75
D	A	17	15	27
E	D	22	25	35
F	E, B	18	20	28
G	D	22	20	31
H	G	19	22	26
J	G	14	17	21
K	G	20	37	62
L	C, F, H	12	14	25
M	J	18	25	41

Required

1 Develop the network scheme for this project.
2 What is the critical path?
3 Since there is a heavy penalty clause on this project, the project manager wants to know what the probability of completion on schedule will be. Develop a curve showing the probability of completing the project in two years (104 weeks) to two years 4 months (120 weeks) in intervals of one week.
4 Would you be prepared to sign a contract saying the project can be completed in two years? If not, what completion date would you be confident to give to the client?

EXERCISE PROBLEM: LAYOUT

Situation

A company is considering changing the layout of its manufacturing facility in order that it can better incorporate lean production and just-in-time into its operation. Table 18.20 shows the activities and the times in weeks in order that this reorganization can be made.

Table 18.20 Activties and time for layout reorganization

Activity	Immediate predecessor	Normal duration (weeks)
A	None	6
B	A	4
C	None	5
D	C	3
E	B	8
F	B	4
G	B	10
H	D, E	9

Required

1 Develop the network scheme for this project.
2 What is the critical path?
3 What is the total slack time?
4 What would happen if the duration of activity E was reduced by 50 per cent?

CASE STUDY: SANA

Situation

Sana is a subcontractor to the French Government for construction projects related to the Ariane space programme in Guyana. Table 18.21 shows the relevant activities, duration and total cost for the activities for the construction of a section of a launching platform.

Table 18.21 Activities for the construction of a section of a launching platform, with duration and cost

Activity	Duration (months)	Immediate predecessor	Total Cost (FF000)
A	3	None	1200
B	2	None	8000
C	1	A	1600
D	4	A	800
E	5	D	3000
F	2	B, C	4000
G	1	B, C	3000
H	3	E, F	720
I	4	G	9600

Required

As project manager, develop the following for this project:

1 The network diagram for the complete project.

2 The earliest start and finish, and the latest start and finish for each activity.
3 The critical path for the project.
4 The cumulative project completion curve by month, illustrating on the curve each month what activities have been completed. Assume that activities are completed on a linear basis. For example, after one month, one third of activity A would have been completed.
5 Develop the cumulative cost curves for the project based on:
   (a) commencing an activity on the earliest date possible;
   (b) commencing an activity at the latest time possible.
   Use a time period of a month and assume that expenditure per month is linear with the time. For example, for activity A, the duration is three months and the total cost is FF 1 200 000. Thus, the cost per month is FF 400 000.
6 Sana has a FF 100 million line of credit with the BNP to finance this construction activity. The interest rate is nine per cent, compounded daily. Using electronic data interchange, cash is borrowed on the first day of each month, for that month's activity. The total amount of the funds borrowed is repaid to the BNP one year after project completion. Determine the following:
   (a) the total cost of the project (direct cost plus interest costs), if each activity is started on the earliest date possible;
   (b) the total cost of the project (direct cost plus interest costs), if each activity is started on the latest date possible.
   For the purpose of calculations, assume a 30-day month; thus one year is equivalent to 360 days.
7 Discuss your conclusions about this project.

NOTES AND REFERENCES

1. Ex-Im Bank URL: http://www.exim.gov/3gorges.html (5 June 1996).
2. Kelly, J. E. and Walker, M. R. (1959) 'Critical Path Planning and Scheduling', *Proceedings of the Eastern Joint Computer Conference*, Boston: 160–73.
3. *PERT, Program Evaluation Research Task, Phase I Summary Report* (1958) Special Projects Office, Bureau of Ordnance, Department of the Navy, Washington DC, July: 646–69.

FURTHER READING

Babu, A. J. G and Suresh, N. (1996) 'Project management with time, cost, and quality considerations', *European Journal of Operational Research* 88(2): 320–27.

Barkley, B. T. (1993) *Customer-Driven Project Management: A New Paradigm in Managing Total Quality*, New York: McGraw-Hill.

Cammarano, J. (1997) 'Project Management: How to make it happen', *IIE Solutions* 29(12): 30–34.

Chen, Y.-L., Rinks, D. and Tang, K. (1997) 'Critical path in an activity network with time constraints', *European Journal of Operational Research* 100(1): 122–33.

Cox, M. A. A. (1995) 'Simple normal approximation to the completion time distribution for a PERT, network', *International Journal of Project Management* 13(4): 265–70.

Dinsmore, P. C. (1993) *The AMA Handbook of Project Management,* New York: AMACOM.

Harrison, F. L. (1992) *Advanced Project Management: A Structured Approach,* Aldershot: Gower.

Hickman, A. M. (1992) 'Refining the process of project control', *Production and Inventory Management* 12(2): 26, 29.

House, R. (1988) *Human Side of Project Management,* Reading, MA: Addison-Wesley.

Kuklan, H., Erdem, E. and Nasri, F. (1993) 'Project planning and control: An enhanced PERT network', *International Journal of Project Management* 11(2): 87–92.

Lewis, J. P. (1993) 'Project management: Think like your customers', *Transportation and Distribution* 34(7): 26–28.

Lock, D. (1992) *Project Management,* Aldershot: Gower.

Lockyer, K. G. and Gordon, J. (1995) *Project Management and Project Network Techniques,* London: Pitman.

Macleod, K. R. and Peterson, P. F. (1996) 'Estimating the trade-off between resource allocation and probability of on-time completion in project management', *Project Management Journal* 27(1): 26–33.

Magott, J. and Skudlarski, K. (1993) 'Estimating the mean completion time of PERT networks with exponentially distribution duration's of activities', *European Journal of Operational Research* 71(1): 70–79.

Maylor, H. (1996) *Project Management,* London: Pitman.

Penner, D. (1993) *The Project Manager's Survival Guide: The Handbook for Real-World,* Columbus, OH: Battelle.

Pillai, A. S. and Tiwari, A. K. (1995) 'Enhanced PERT for programme analysis, control, and evaluation: PACE', *International Journal of Project Management* 13(1): 39–43.

Reiss, G. (1992) *Project Management Demystified: Today's Tools and Techniques,* London: E & FN Spon.

Rosenau, M. D. Jr. (1991) *Successful Project Management,* New York: Van Nostrand Reinhold.

Shtub, A. (1997) 'Project management: A tool for project management', *International Journal of Project Management* 15(1): 15–19.

Shtub, A., Bard, J. F. and Globerson, S. (1994) *Project Management: Engineering, Technology, and Implementation,* Englewood Clifs, NJ: Prentice Hall.

Soroush, H M. (1994) 'The most critical path in a PERT network: A Heuristic approach', *European Journal of Operational Research* 78(1): 93–105.

Soroush , H. (1993) 'Risk taking in stochastic PERT networks', *European Journal of Operational Research* 67(2): 221–41.

Sung, C. S. and Lim, S. K. (1994) 'Project activity scheduling problem with net present value measure', *International Journal of Production Economics* 37(2,3): 177–87.

Teplitz, C. J., and Amor, J.-P. (1993) 'Improving CPM's accuracy using learning curves', *Project Management Journal* 24(4): 15–19.

Webb, R. P. (1991) *Project Management Basics,* Blue Ridge Summit, PA: TAB Books.

Weiss, J. and Wysock, R. (1992) *Making Project Management Work,* Reading, MA: Addison Wesley.

Zhu, Z. and Heady, R. B. (1994) 'A simplified method of evaluating PERT/CPM network parameters', *IEEE Transactions on Engineering Management* 41(4): 426–30.

19 | Reliability and maintenance

Objectives and overview

The objective of this chapter is to underscore the importance of reliability and maintenance in the supply chain. The chapter opens by giving two real-world examples where poor design and poor maintenance have had costly and, in one case, tragic results. The chapter then goes on to detail the concept of reliability for series and parallel designed, or so-called back-up, systems and then presents terms for measuring reliability. The concept of the Japanese idea of Poka Yoke for minimizing failures is detailed and then Failure Mode, Effect and Criticality Analysis (FMECA) is presented with a real-world illustration related to the pharmaceutical industry. There is a section on maintenance, which discusses the various maintenance procedures including emergency maintenance, preventative maintenance, total productive maintenance and reliability-centred maintenance. The chapter closes by discussing recovering from a failure, including a review of the concept of crisis management.

UNEXPECTED OCCURRENCES

Operations and the supply chain depend on the reliability of people, suppliers, subcontractors, manufacturers and distribution firms. In addition, these separate entities design, produce or use a host of transportation vehicles, sophisticated machines and equipment, the continuous reliable operation of which depends very much on proper maintenance. Failure or unexpected occurrences can have diverse consequences, ranging from customer inconvenience, through lost revenue, delayed production and poor quality to, at the worst, tragedy. Consider the following two incidents, one embarrassing and costly and the other catastrophic and terribly costly.

Poor design: the case of Daimler Benz

In November 1997, the new Mercedes A-class small car, produced by Daimler-Benz, won the satirical 'Golden Steering Wheel' award as 'car' of the year from a German tabloid newspaper. The problem was that the car failed the so-called Elk test, in which a vehicle is subjected to two sharp turns at 65 km an hour, intended to mimic a driver attempting to evade a collision with wildlife that has wandered onto the highway. This incident (in which the car rolled over) was a monu-

mental embarrassment to Daimler-Benz, which had spent DM 2.5 billion to develop the vehicle. After the episode occurred Daimler promised to fit different tyres on the vehicle, blaming the problem on those originally supplied by Goodyear (much to that company's indignation). It also said it would recall cars and fit free some optional drive-control electronics to improve handling. However, as other motoring journals repeated the test and came up with the same results, more orders dried up. On 11 November, after about 2 per cent of the 100 000 orders for the A-class had been cancelled, Daimler admitted that the car was unsafe in extreme conditions. The firm proposed a new chassis design that would lower the body, improve the stability of the axles and require tyres that hold the road better. The cost of the redesign was estimated at DM 300 million ($175 million).[1]

One month later, in December 1998, Daimler-Benz suffered a further embarrassment, when it was forced to suspend the sale to the public of its two-seater Smart car (dubbed the 'Swatchmobile' because Daimler's 19 per cent joint-venture partner is the Swiss-based Société Suisse de Microelectronique et d'Horlogerie SA, which makes the trendy Swatch wristwatches). The reason for the suspension was again that the car flipped over in the Elk test. A subsequent quality audit of the vehicle discovered technical flaws, some related to supplier's parts only three months ahead of the March 1998 introduction date. The Daimler chief executive, Juergen Schrempp, demanded a six-month delay until October 1998 to give engineers time to widen the car's wheel base, shift the vehicle's weight closer to the ground and retool the production line, as well as to upgrade some 5000 parts.[2] The delays with the Smart car were estimated to cost Daimler DM 300 million ($169.1 million).[3]

Poor maintenance: the case of American Airlines

In Chicago, USA, on 25 May 1979 everything happened so quickly. The only remains of American Airlines flight N110AA, a McDonnell Douglas DC-10 on a flight from Chicago to Los Angeles, were the burnt wreckage scattered in a field. Just 31 seconds after take-off from O'Hare airport, the engine broke away from the wing, the aeroplane reared, rolled to one side and the end of its left wing hit the ground. Immediately, the plane was transformed into a fire ball. The 279 passengers and crew were burnt to death, as well as two people on the ground. The subsequent inquiry indicated that there was a mechanical failure caused by the rupture of one of the bolts that secured the engine to the aircraft wing. The maintenance procedures had not verified this anomaly.[4]

On 6 June 1979 the US Federal Aviation Authority (FAA) withdrew the flight-worthy certificate from the 270 DC-10s in service, 58 of which belonged to European airline companies. This grounding resulted in flight cancellations worldwide (including the author's flight to Europe for his wedding!) and millions of dollars in lost revenues. In addition, American Airlines and McDonnell Douglas were subjected to costly lawsuits resulting from the horrible loss of life in the USA's worst commercial airline accident.

The European airlines were angered at the FAA's grounding decision and acted alone. At a meeting on the 12 June in Strasbourg, France, they adopted their own revised aircraft maintenance programme. And, on 18 June, in Zurich, Switzerland, they voted to permit the flying of their DC-10s in spite of the FAA ruling. However, the FAA refused to allow these European planes to fly over US territory and the 138 USA-registered planes remained grounded. It was only after intense pressure from airlines and further research, that the FAA in Oklahoma rescinded the DC-10 grounding on 13 July 1979.[5]

The long-term outcome of this failure and the poor maintenance programme was the complete loss of passenger confidence in the DC-10 jumbo jet (in favour of Boeing's 747). McDonnell Douglas Corp.'s market share of commercial aircraft sales tumbled and it finally stopped production of the DC-10 and essentially pulled out of commercial aircraft manufacture. This episode was the catalyst that resulted in McDonnell Douglas being swallowed by its competitor Boeing in July 1997.[6]

RELIABILITY

Reliability is the confidence one has in a product, process, service, work team or individual to operate under prescribed conditions without failure or stopping, in order to produce the required output. In the supply chain, for example, reliability might be applied to whether the trucks delivering raw materials arrive on time, whether the suppliers produce quality components, whether the operators turn up for work or whether the packing machines operate without breaking down.

Components and reliability in a series system

The more components in a product or process, the more complex is the system and thus the greater is the risk of failure, or unreliability. Consider a product built up in a series arrangement, as illustrated in the upper scheme of Figure 19.1. This is a basic structure which contains n components, where n can take on any integer value. In the series arrangement the relationship between the overall system reliability R_S and the number of interacting parts or components n is a joint probability relationship (see Chapter 20, *Statistical Concepts*), which can be expressed by the relationship.

$$R_S = R_1 \times R_2 \times R_3 \times R_4 \ldots R_n.$$

Here R_1, R_2, etc. are the reliabilities of the individual components. The relationship assumes that each component is independent of the others and that the reliability of one does not depend on the reliability of the others. However, the complete system does depend on all the components functioning; that is, they are interdependent, so that if one fails, then the system fails. For example, in an electric food mixer, there is a switch, a cutting blade and an electric circuit. All are independent units, but if any one fails, the food mixer will not work.

The reliability, or the value of R, is expressed as a percentage, such as 99 per cent, which means that a component will perform as specified 99 per cent of the time or it will fail (100 − 99) or 1 per cent of the time.

Figure 19.1 Reliability: series and parallel systems.

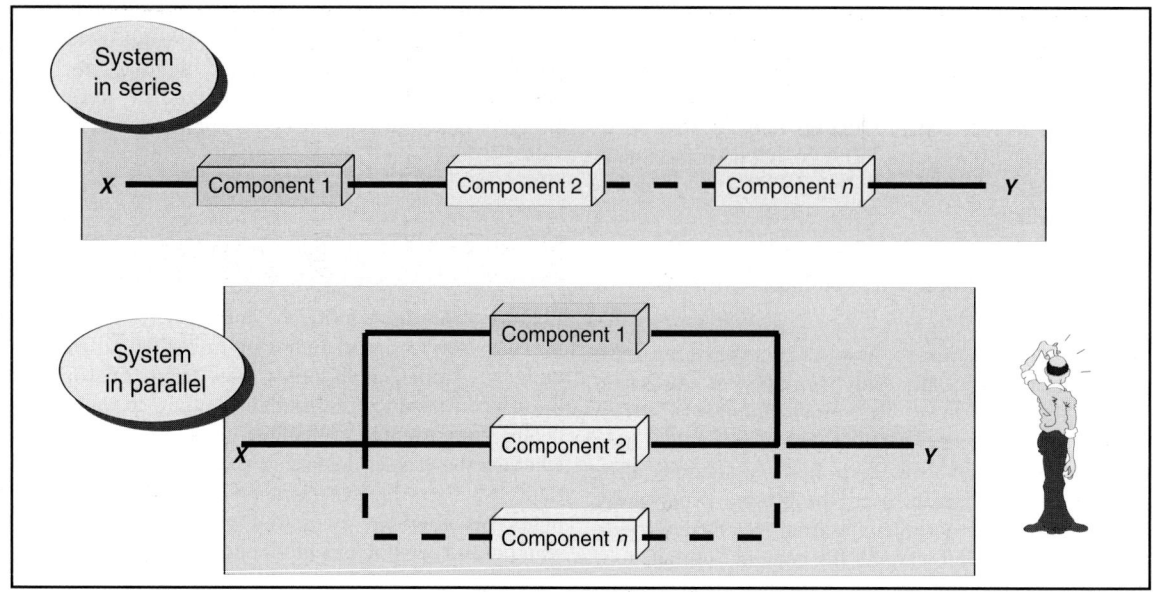

Two components

Consider the system between point X and Y in Figure 19.1 with two components R_1 with a reliability of 99 per cent and R_2 with a reliability of 95 per cent. The system reliability is:

$$R_S = R_1 \times R_2 = 0.99 \times 0.95$$
$$= 0.9405 \text{ or } 94.05 \text{ per cent.}$$

Multiple components

Since R is always less than one (nothing is 100 per cent reliable all of the time), the reliability of the system in a series arrangement decreases with the number of components. This concept is illustrated in Figure 19.2. Here the various curves show the rapid decline in the system reliability as the number of components increase from one to 500 for various average component reliability. For example, as illustrated in Table 19.1, for an average component reliability of 99 per cent, the system reliability drops from 99 to less than 1 per cent as the number of components increases from one to 500. Conversely, this means that the system would be working less than 1 per cent of the time in this worst case.

Equal reliability

In a situation where there are similar components of quantity n, all of which can be considered to have the same reliability, then the system reliability would be given by the relationship

$$R_S = R^n.$$

Back-up or parallel systems

In situations where the failure of a component or system would be problematic, dangerous or catastrophic, then back-up systems would be in place to operate in the eventual failure of the principal system. In this case, the components would be in parallel as illustrated in the lower scheme of Figure 19.1. Hospitals have back-up energy systems in case of failure of the principal power supply. Most banks and other firms have back-up computer systems containing client data should one system fail. Aeroplanes have back-up units in their design such that, in the eventual failure of one component or subsystem, there is recourse to a back-up. For example, a Boeing 747 can fly on one engine, although at a much reduced efficiency. To a certain extent, the human body

Table 19.1 Change in system reliability with an increasing number of components

Number of components	1	5	10	50	100	250	500
System reliability (%)	99.00	95.10	90.44	60.50	36.60	8.11	0.66

Figure 19.2 System reliability according to the number of components.

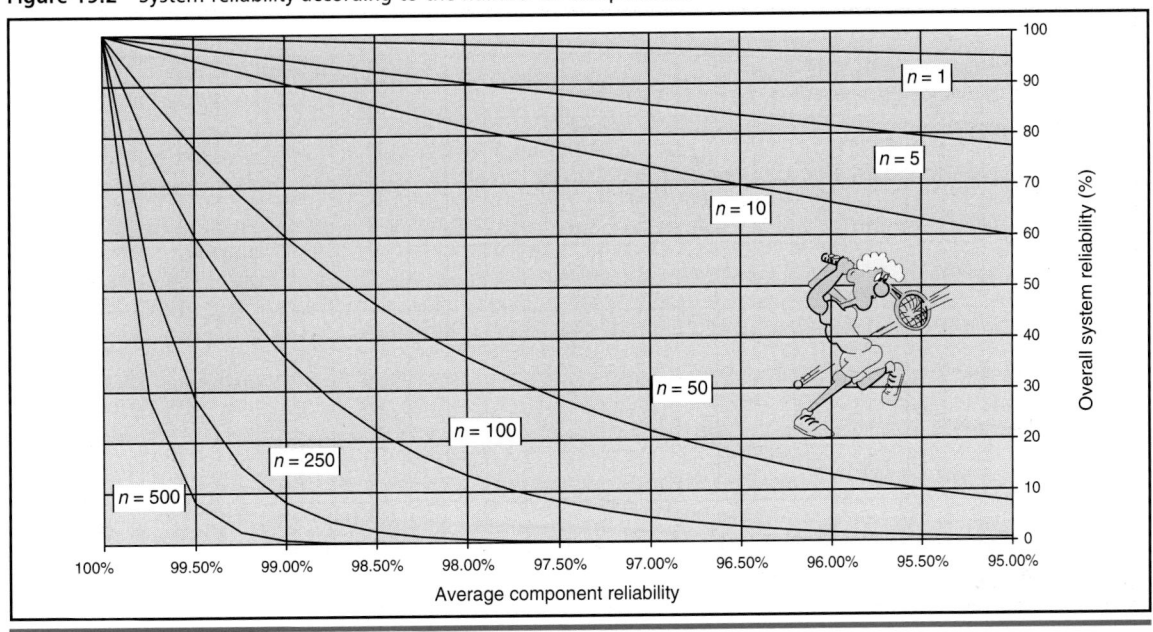

has a back-up system as it can function with only one lung, though again at a reduced efficiency. When back-up systems are in place, this implies redundancy since the back-up units are not normally operational. As a real example consider Box 19.1.[7]

Redundancy improves system reliability

The reliability of the system with backup can be calculated by the relationship:

$$R_S = 1 - (1 - R_1)(1 - R_2)(1 - R_3)(1 - R_4) \ldots (1 - R_n),$$

where R_1, R_2 etc. are the reliabilities of the individual components. The greater the number of backup systems, or the greater the redundancy, then the greater is the reliability of the system.

Two components

As an example, consider from Figure 19.1 a generating system between points X and Y with the principal generator R_1 having a reliability of 99 per cent and R_2 the

back-up generator having a reliability of 95 per cent. The system reliability is:

$$R_S = 1 - (1 - 0.99)(1 - 0.95)$$
$$= 0.9995 \text{ or } 99.95 \text{ per cent.}$$

Thus the system reliability is greater than with a single generator.

Multiple components

The more the number of back-up units, then the greater the reliability as illustrated in Figure 19.3. Here the curves give the reliability with no back-ups to three back-up components. Of course, ideally, one would always want close to 100 per cent reliability; however, with greater reliability, the greater is the cost. For many years, the US Federal Aviation Administration had a requirement that all aeroplanes flying over water for a duration of one hour or longer should have three engines, in case of failure of an engine. Airline manufacturers complained and said

---

Box 19.1 Auckland, New Zealand

Businesses and residents in central Auckland, New Zealand, suffering through the 12th day of a power failure, got more bad news on Wednesday 4 March 98 when they learnt that the blackout would last 10 more weeks. Merchants estimate that they are losing $60 million a week because of the failure of four cables supplying electricity to the centre of New

Zealand's largest city. Two cables repaired by the city's power company, Mercury Energy, failed when tested Wednesday and it was estimated it will take 10 weeks to run a new cable into the central area. Central Auckland has been largely deserted since last month, when cables strained by a heat wave, started to fail. The utility had no backup system.

International Herald Tribune, 5 March 1998

Figure 19.3 System reliability of a parallel back-up system.

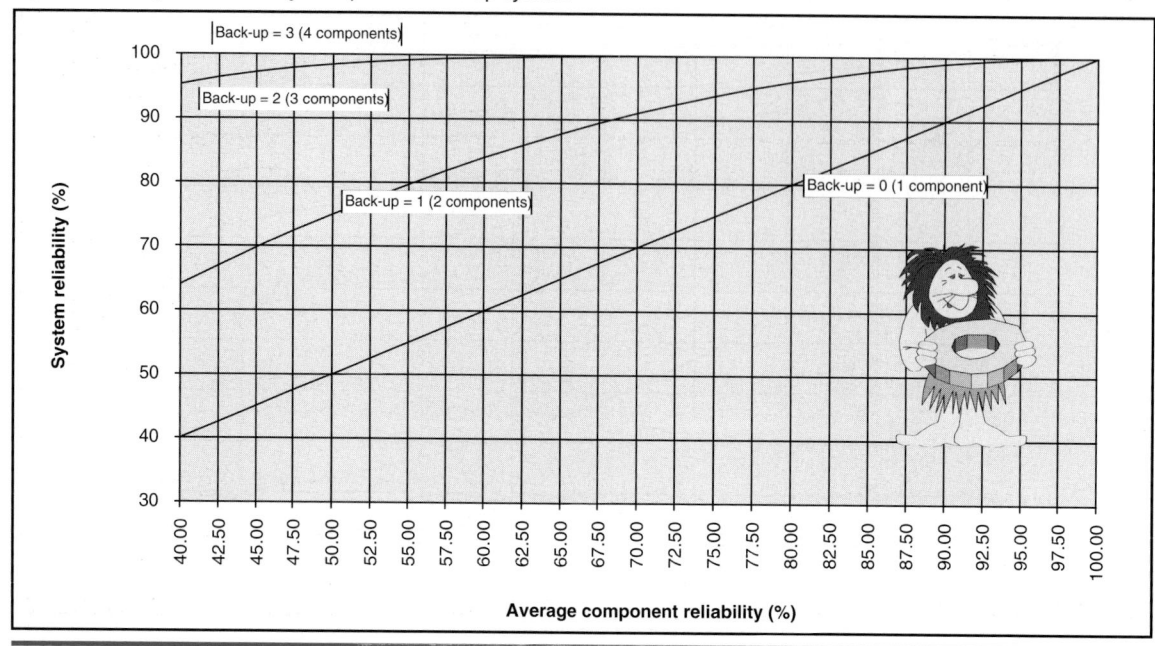

this was an unnecessary expense because of the reliability of the engines. It is only recently that the FAA has permitted commercial airlines with two engines to make transatlantic flights.

Equal reliability

When the back-up components of quantity n have the same reliability, then the system reliability would be given by the relationship:

$$R_S = 1 - (1 - R)^n.$$

Failure rate

The failure rate is a measure of the reliability of products. It might be determined by the number of failures among the total number of products tested and then expressed as a percentage according to the following ratio:

$$\text{Failure rate (\%)} = \frac{\text{Number of products which failed}}{\text{Total number of products tested}}.$$

Alternatively, the failure rate might be expressed as the number of failures during a specified period of time and given by the following ratio:

$$\text{Failure rate } (N):$$
$$= \frac{\text{Number of products which failed}}{\text{Number of unit-hours of operating time}}.$$

Mean time between failures

An often-used measure for reliability is the mean time between failures, MTBF, which is the reciprocal of the Failure rate (T):

$$\text{MTBF} = \frac{1}{\text{Failure Rate } (N)}$$
$$= \frac{\text{Operating time for units}}{\text{Number of products which failed}}.$$

The principle of these measurements of failure rate is illustrated in the worked example, *Toilet Systems.*

Lifetime failure rate

All products and processes fail at some point in their lifetime. The failure-rate profile, illustrated by the bath tub curve in Figure 19.4 (somewhat analogous to the human profile) shows that there are high rates both at the early or infant stage and in old or wear-out failure towards the end of the product's life. There is a relatively low, or what is considered the normal, failure rate in between the two extremes.

Infant mortality

At the early stages of the product life, components may be fragile as they have not been 'run in' or, conversely, operators are not familiar with equipment and,

Figure 19.4 Product lifetime failure rate.

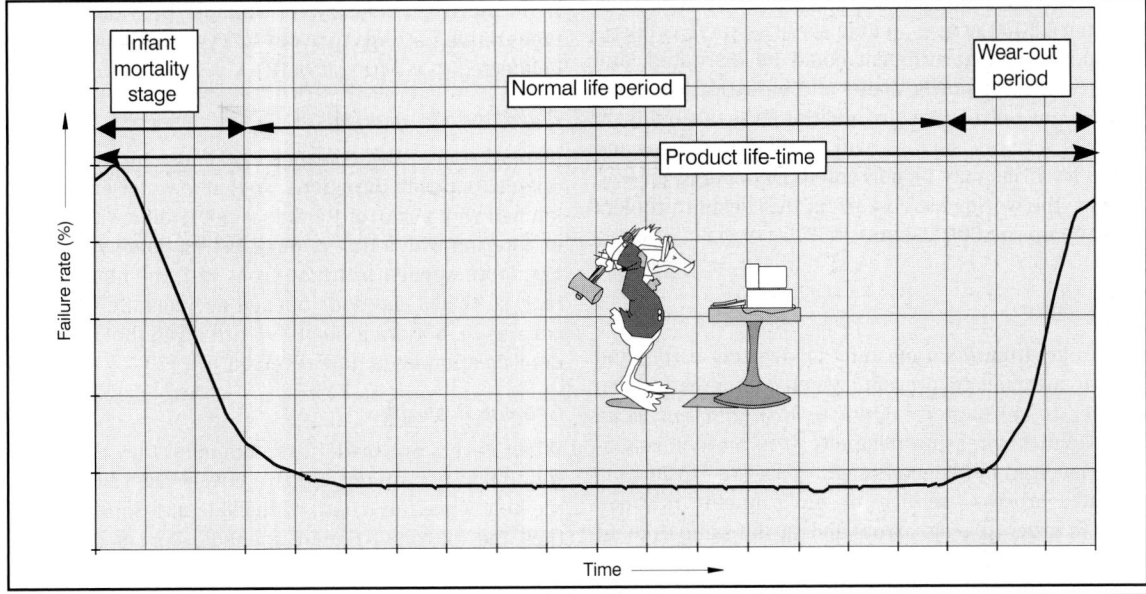

because of bad use, the equipment breaks down. This is often the case with appliances such as washing machines, food mixers or power lawn mowers. Some companies may 'run in' or 'burn in' a product before it is released on the market to ensure that all the teething start-up problems have been overcome. For other products, such as automobiles, the requirement is that an operator does not run it above a certain speed for say the first 3000 km, after which it has to be serviced. To cover the possibility of failure in the early days of a product's life, certain firms provide a 90-day warranty for their products. The term infant mortality is obviously used because young children are fragile at this point in their life.

Normal failure

Once a product has been used for a certain period, it is normally pretty robust and with the correct preventive maintenance will last throughout its expected lifetime. During this period the failure rate is pretty constant and low. Again, the analogy is with the human body, which is pretty robust, though from time to time 'breakdowns' do occur, either through some random occurrence (illness) or improper use (accidents).

Wear-out failure

Towards the end of the life of a product or process, the failure rate starts to increase rapidly again as parts become used or worn and eventually fail. Again, there is the analogy of the human body.

Responsibility and the supply chain

Reliability in the supply chain depends on all team members 'pulling their weight' such that the work in hand is completed according to schedule, budget and at the required quality or specification level. Failure in one phase impacts other elements of the chain. With tangible products, responsibility starts with the design engineers who conceive the product and develop the final design. Purchasing personnel have the responsibility to verify the quality of the purchased materials used in the assembly of the product. Suppliers and subcontractors have the responsibility of delivering parts on time. Operating personnel have the responsibility to verify that products are manufactured according to the established specifications. And, once a product is in service, maintenance personnel have the responsibility to verify that work is properly carried out. (The cases of Daimler-Benz and American Airlines at the beginning of this chapter underscore what could be some of the undesirable outcomes.)

The millennium bug

Probably one of the most expensive, and far reaching, reliability problems to occur is the so called 'millennium bug', which is the responsibility of computer design engineers and programmers, who back in the 1960s, in order to save computer memory, used only two digits, instead of four, to represent a year (69 for 1969 for example). As a result, the digits 00 will be read as the year 1900 and not the approaching year 2000. As a consequence, there is a concern that when 1 January 2000 arrives, public services such as hospitals, police and government could be disrupted, and airports, nuclear power plants and industrial concerns may be uncontrollable. In addition, the accounts in financial services, such as banks, stock exchanges and insurance firms may be corrupted. Depending on who is right, the worldwide cost to fix this design problem could be up to $600 billion.[8]

Poka Yoke

Poka Yoke, from *Poka* meaning inadvertent errors and *Yokeru* meaning to prevent, which has already been referred to in Chapter 4, *Quality Management*, is an approach to increasing reliability. It is an idea originally conceived by Shigeo Shingo of Japan – to make a product, process, service or environment mistake-proof in order to avoid errors and, at the same time, to maintain quality. It is based on the premise that everyone is human and fallible and that on occasions they will do things wrong. The concept is very logical and the following are some examples.

Different diameters

When there are male–female connections on products, make the diameters different if product usage is not the same. For example, the diameter of the petrol filler hole in a vehicle that uses unleaded petrol is smaller than normal so that a leaded petrol filler pistol cannot be inserted.

Guide notches

To avoid an erroneous assembly, install guide notches that match in only one sense on components that are to be joined together. An example is on automobile headlights, so that they cannot be installed upside down.

Alternative fittings

In the electrical industry, for example, provide different types of plug fittings to avoid 120 volt appliances being connected to a 240 volt outlet.

Reverse door openings

In restaurants, the entrance/exit doors in restaurants open in opposite directions, so that a waiter exiting the kitchen with a tray of food does not collide with a waiter entering with a tray of dirty dishes. Some years ago, car doors opened from the front with the hinge at the rear, so that if the door opened accidentally while the car was in motion, it could be torn off in the wind. The door positioning is now reversed.

Geometric shape

When covers are made for containers, they should be round and not square. Square covers can fall through the hole since the length of the side of a square is less then the diagonal. Square manhole covers could fall through the hole into the sewer!

Assembly operations

- In the assembly of products that have different fittings, for example automobile axles, keep components destined for the right-hand side in green containers and those for the left-hand side in red containers.
- To ensure first in, first out usage of components, when there are two delivery conveyers have a system which alternately blocks off one while the other is in use, as illustrated in Figure 19.5.[9] Here, during time n, components are delivered to the right-hand conveyer and are used from the left-hand conveyor. When the left-hand conveyor is empty, at time $(n + 1)$, an arm is swung over so that components can be taken from the right-hand conveyer. This automatically blocks the right-hand side and opens the left-hand side for delivery of components.

WORKED EXAMPLE: TOILET SYSTEMS

Situation

Boeing Aircraft Company is interested in learning something about the reliability of the toilets on its long-haul 747s, noting that there have been passenger complaints. On average, the flight time of these long-haul planes is 11 hours. Boeing tested 12 toilet units for a duration of 50 h each. During the test, one unit failed after 20 h, one after 25 h, and one after 45 h.

Required

Determine the following:

1. the failure as a percentage, FR (%);
2. the number of failures during a period of time, FR(N);
3. the mean time between failures;
4. the estimated toilet failures per 747 trip.

Solution

1. $$\text{Failure Rate (\%)} = \frac{\text{Number of products which failed}}{\text{Total number of products tested}}$$
   $$= 3/12 = 25.00\%$$

2   The number of failures during a period of time, FR(N)
Total unit hours of operating time is $12 \times 50 = 600$.

Non-operating time is the total time the three units were not operating for the full 50 h of the test. For the first unit this is $(50 - 20)$ or 30 h, for the second unit $(50 - 25)$ or 25 h, and for the third unit $(50 - 45)$ or 5 h. Thus total non-operating time is 60 h. Thus, operating time is $600 - 60 = 540$ h.

The failure rate in units per total unit operating time is:

$$\text{Failure rate } (N) = \frac{\text{Number of products which failed}}{\text{Number of unit-hours of operating time}}$$

$$= \frac{3}{540} = 0.005556.$$

3   Mean time between failures is the reciprocal of FR(N) or $1/0.005556$ = 180 h.

4   Average toilet failures per trip is average flight time $\times$ FR(N) = 11 $\times$ 0.005556 = 0.06111.

FAILURE MODE, EFFECT AND CRITICALITY ANALYSIS

A failure mode, effect and criticality analysis, FMECA, is the detailed study of a product design, manufacturing operation or distribution network to determine which features are critical to various modes of failure. The concept was developed in the USA in the 1950s, particularly to increase the reliability for military equipment and in aviation, as well as by NASA (The North American Space Agency) for its space programmes. The FMECA analysis appeared in Europe in the 1970s in the electronics industry and it is now common practice in automobile firms. Using FMECA involves input from other functional areas, including marketing, design, purchasing, production, operations, finance, etc.

Element in the FMECA analysis

The three principal study areas in a detailed FMECA analysis are failure mode, failure effect and failure criticality. These studies may be applied at any stage of conception, design, development, production or final use. However, since the objective of FMECA is to prevent failure, the study is most often applied at the design stage. Perhaps a more rigorous FMECA analysis might have avoided the disastrous explosion and loss of the seven astronauts in the Challenger launch on 28 January 1986.[10]

Figure 19.5   Ensuring components are used on a FIFO basis.

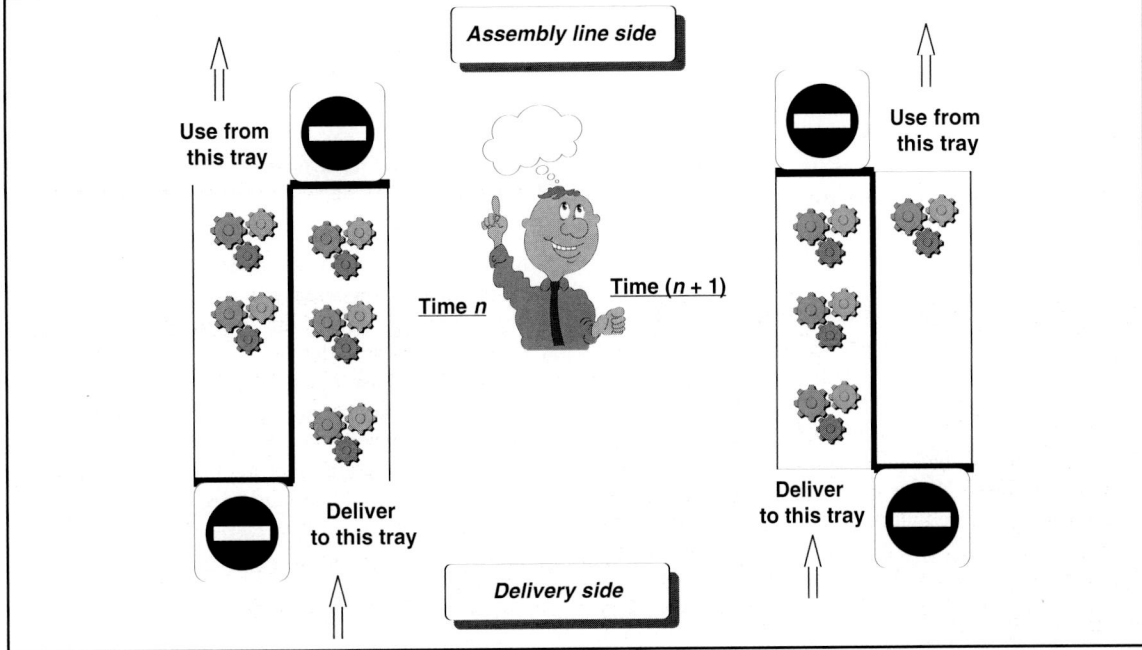

Failure mode analysis

The failure mode is analysing the operation of the product or the process to see what are the most likely modes where failure would occur. This would include describing the conditions, the components involved, the time elements, location, etc.

Failure effect analysis

The failure effect is the study of the potential failures to ascertain the likely impact on the performance of the whole product, the process or service and/or related elements.

Failure criticality analysis

Failure criticality is the examination of the potential failures of the product, process or service to determine how critical the failure would be. The criticality might range from customer irritation, through a lowering of performance, shutdown of an operating plant, a safety problem or an environmental hazard to a catastrophic occurrence.

Procedural steps in the FMECA analysis

The step-by-step procedures in FMECA depend to a certain extent on what service, or product, is being examined, but the following are the key phases:

1 In the product, or the process, identify all the components and assemblies that are part of the operating system.
2 Make an exhaustive listing of all the possible failure modes of each component in the system.
3 Establish the effects that each mode of failure would have on the product, process or service.
4 Make a list of all the possible causes of each failure mode.
5 Assign a numerical value to each occurrence for each of the following criteria:
   ■ *P*, the *probability* of each failure mode occurring;
   ■ *S*, the *seriousness*, or the criticality, of the failure;
   ■ *D*, the *difficulty* of detecting the failure before the product or service is used by the client.
   For example use a scale of 1 to 10, with 1 being low or easy and 10 high. As an illustration, the rating for an automobile hydraulic braking system might be shown in Table 19.2.
6 For each possible failure mode, determine the value of the product $P \times S \times D$, which is considered the criticality index, or the risk priority number, RPN. Using Table 19.2, the maximum value of RPN which would have the highest priority is $10 \times 10 \times 10$ or

Table 19.2 Possible ratings for an automobile hydraulic braking system

Value	1	2	3	4	5	6	7	8	9	10
P		X								
S									X	
D					X					

1000 and the minimum value, with a low priority, is $1 \times 1 \times 1 = 1$. For example, the value of RPN for the automobile brake situation given in Table 19.2 is $2 \times 9 \times 5 = 90$. This index represents the relative priority of each mode in the failure prevention study.
7 Determine the corrective action necessary to avoid the failure in question, and also which department, or function, would be responsible for the corrective action.
8 Rank the RPN for the whole product or process such that the necessary corrective action can be taken in the light of the resources available.

Real-world pharmaceutical application

Table 19.3 gives a selection of some of the elements considered in the preparation of an over-the-counter drug.[11]

It should be noted that in the FMECA analysis, since the value of RPN is the product of three values, the effect of a high value of the seriousness of a failure, *S*, can be reduced by a low value of *D*, the difficulty of detecting the failure. In practice, if the value of *S* is high, then the value of *D* should be low.

MAINTENANCE

Globally, maintenance covers all those operations such as monitoring, inspecting, adjusting, repairing and/or doing whatever is necessary to put or keep a machine, facility, a piece of equipment or transportation vehicle in proper working order. A maintenance programme may consist of just emergency maintenance, simple preventative maintenance or more sophisticated well managed preventive-maintenance-type programmes such as Total Productive Maintenance (TPM) or Reliability Centred Maintenance (RCM).

Emergency maintenance

Emergency maintenance, or run-to-breakdown maintenance, is repairing machines or equipment after a

Table 19.3 FMECA analysis for a pharmaceutical operation for the preparation of a gel for the treatment of insect bites

Component or process	Failure mode	Cause	Failure effect	Detection	P	S	D	RPN
Purified water for dissolving ingredients	Presence of ozone in the mixing vessel	Poor treatment of feed water	Products would be oxidized	Presence of ozone activates alarm	2	6	3	36
Purified water for dissolving ingredients	Microbiological contamination	Water treatment system malfunctioning	Contamination of final product	Quality inspection at treatment facility	1	7	6	42
Active ingredient	Quantity of product insufficient	Loss during transfer in the feed pipe	Concentration too low	Detected by an operator	2	4	6	48
Active ingredient	Not according to specification	Poor mixing of powder upstream	Final production not conforming	Quality control inspection	3	8	2	48
Sodium hydroxide solution	Microbiological contamination	Using dirty utensils	Product toxic	Quality control inspection	2	7	2	28
Sodium hydroxide solution	Concentration too high	Solid ingredients incorrectly weighed	Lot would have to be rejected	Quality control inspection	2	4	1	8
Mixing of all components	Mixture non-homogeneous	Agitation temperature too low	Gelatinization would be impaired	By the temperature controller	3	2	1	6
Mixing of all components	Foam appears on the final solution	Agitation too strong	Gelatinization would be impaired	Visual inspection	4	7	2	56
Gelatinization	Gel non-homogeneous	Machine incorrectly adjusted	Product non-conforming. Lot would be rejected	Final quality control inspection	2	6	3	36
Transfer of gel to filler	Microbiological contamination	Transfer pipes not clean	Lot would be rejected	Inspection prior to filling	3	8	3	72
Filling 30 ml tubes	Tubes incorrectly sealed	Caps of poor quality	Lot to be dumped	Quality control inspection				
Filling 30 ml tubes	Volume too little	Filling machine incorrectly adjusted	Product quantity non-conforming	Quality control inspection	2	6	3	36

failure has occurred. Obviously, this is not an ideal way of keeping equipment operating, but is very often the policy with home users of appliances, such as washing machines, televisions and dishwashers, where the owner waits until the machine breaks down before calling a repairer. Light bulbs are commonly only replaced when they go out. This policy usually creates no safety hazard and is more usually an inconvenience to the user. However, when emergency maintenance occurs in operating equipment, the system capacity is reduced, workers are idle and this causes direct labour costs to rise. Costs increase because of calling in emergency maintenance crews and acquiring the necessary spare parts urgently. Further, client service level drops because units cannot be produced according to the master production schedule, meaning that orders cannot be delivered when promised.

Preventative maintenance

Preventative maintenance is the work activity that has been programmed on a regular basis to inspect a system, to uncover potential problems and to make whatever repairs are necessary to ensure that the system does not fail during normal operation. Studies have indicated that if good maintenance-management practices are applied, and integrated with other operations activities, cost reductions of 35 per cent or more are possible.[12]

Level of preventative maintenance

Maintenance is a cost and to a customer really adds no value to a product. The costs include the salaries of the persons performing the maintenance, inventories kept for the maintenance procedures, such as spares for machines, and the lost time when equipment is down for repairs. The frequency of maintenance must be balanced with the cost if a failure should occur. The breakdown of a piece of equipment upstream of a production line can be costly if it means the shutdown of the whole plant. Besides the cost of lost production, there will be idle employees during the period the maintenance is performed. In some instances, it may be less costly to run a machine until it breaks down and then perform the necessary emergency repairs. The relationship between the maintenance costs and the cost of failures is illustrated in Figure 19.6. This curve illustrates that there is an optimum level when preventative maintenance programmes should be carried out. The exact level depends on the systems in question and the mean time between failures as discussed in the previous section.

An illustration of the costs associated with preventative maintenance programmes is illustrated in the worked example, *Copier Machine*.

Total productive maintenance

Total productive maintenance is a well defined and organized maintenance programme developed in Japan, which places a high value on teamwork, consensus building and continuous improvement, or Kaizen. Reliability and TPM principles call for avoiding crisis, relying on teamwork, maximizing capacity, minimizing costs and continuously improving processes for manufacturing. Specific actions require the following:[13]

- restoring equipment to a like-new condition;
- having operators involved in the maintenance of the equipment;
- improving the maintenance efficiency and effectiveness;
- training the labour force to improve upon their job skills;
- equipment management and maintenance prevention, which is considered inherent in the reliability strategy;
- the effective use of preventive and predictive maintenance technology.

The philosophy in TPM is that if equipment is in good condition and making what it is designed to make, most problems then arise from human error. In which case, firms should aim to employ equipment that is easy to use correctly, but difficult to use incorrectly. Under this approach, TPM thus focuses on improving the reliability of the complete manufacturing system, reducing uncertainty within the supply chain, reducing lead times and increasing customer service level. All this without increasing the level of inventory.[14]

Reliability-centred maintenance

Reliability-centred maintenance (RCM) is a technique that evolved within the civil aviation industry and is based on a 30-year research programme launched in the 1960s. It focuses on establishing what exactly is meant by the right maintenance, rather than just very frequent complete overhaul of equipment. It determines what must be done to ensure that any physical asset continues to fulfil its present operating context, ensuring that equipment and systems work as designed with minimal problems.[15] RCM focuses on function, not equipment, and its ultimate benefit is to drive down

Figure 19.6 Frequency of maintenance and associated costs.

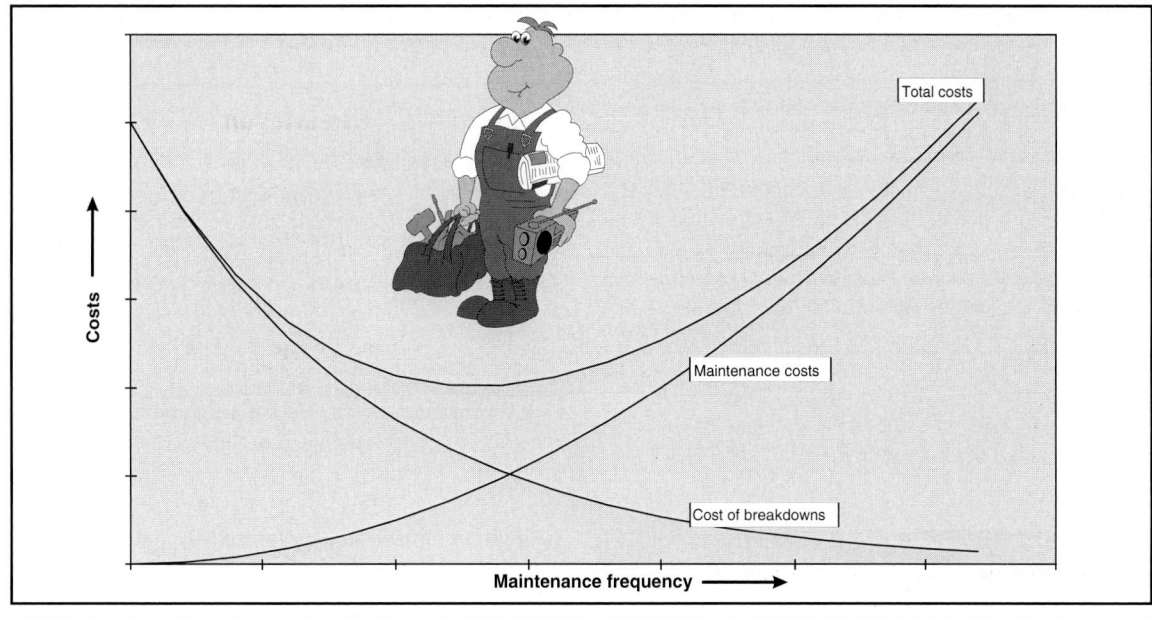

corrective maintenance costs and to reduce costs associated with outages and downtime.[16]

As an illustration, the Madawaska paper mill in Maine, USA implemented RCM and defined its goals for the programme as:

- reducing scheduled maintenance from 2 per cent to 1.5 per cent;
- reducing unscheduled maintenance from 2 per cent to 1.5 per cent;
- achieving a total mill efficiency improvement of 1.5 per cent.

For Madawaska, the change to RCM required maintenance departments to adopt the principles of planning and anticipation in place of policies based on fix-it-and-forget-it. It also obliged maintenance to forge new relationships with engineering and production personnel.[17]

Another illustration of the advantages of RCM is from the Huddersfield, UK, plant of Zeneca, a bio-science company. This firm implemented RCM, at a cost of £11 000 on a 20-year-old ice- manufacturing plant that was critical to the site as this plant supported a range of other facilities. With RCM in place in 1995, the firm was able to reduce downtime by 1500 h, which translated into a savings of £1.5 million.[18]

WORKED EXAMPLE: COPIER MACHINE

Situation

A consulting company in London has a copying machine, which it uses to copy contractual material for its clients. At the present time the firm operates the machine in a run-to-breakdown mode. The company estimates that at present, on average, each time the copier machine breaks down, the cost due to lost time for client work is £500. Based on historical information over the last 2½ years, the number of breakdowns, and the number of months that this level occurred are according to Table 19.4.

Table 19.4 Copier machine breakdowns

Number of breakdowns	0	1	2	3	4	5
Number per month	2	5	4	9	7	3

A service company in the area has proposed a preventative maintenance contract at a cost of £900 per month and with this contract it guarantees that the breakdowns on average will be one every two months.

Required

Determine whether or not the company should change is policy and purchase the preventative maintenance service contract?

Solution

This problem can be resolved using expected values (discussed in more depth in Chapter 22, *Decision Making and Risk Analysis*).

The expected, or average, value of the breakdowns is determined by taking the weighted average of the historical data as shown in Table 19.5:

- The total number of months of the study is 30. The frequency of occurrence for each breakdown is the number per month divided by 30. This frequency is given in Column 3 of Table 19.5.
- Each frequency is multiplied by each of the number of breakdowns. This is given in Column 4 of the table.
- The total of Column 4 is 2.77 and is the average, or expected number, of breakdowns per month.

Table 19.5 Analysis of copier machine breakdowns

Number of breakdowns	Number per month	Frequency (%)	Frequency of breakdowns
0	2	6.67	0.00
1	5	16.67	0.17
2	4	13.33	0.27
3	9	30.00	0.90
4	7	23.33	0.93
5	3	10.00	0.50
Total	30	100.00	2.77

The expected cost of breakdowns per month is then the average multiplied by the monthly cost:

$$2.77 \times 500 = \pounds 1383.33.$$

The monthly cost of the preventive maintenance contract is the cost of the contract itself plus the costs when a breakdown occur in this case. Since one breakdown every two months is equivalent to 0.50/month, then the total cost is:

$$900 + 500 \times 0.25 = \pounds 1150.$$

This amount is less than the run-to-breakdown policy and so the firm would be advised to take out a preventive maintenance contract.

RECOVERY FROM A FAILURE

For all that is said about reliability and maintenance, even with the best programmes in place, in the best of organizations, failures do occur, through poor design, poor operation or poor maintenance. In this event, a firm should have in place programmes or systems in order to recover from the failure, to bring the operation back to its normal operating condition and to minimize the damage.

Just-in-time

The just-in-time philosophy of operations (Chapter 15, *Lean production and just-in-time*) has built in the sense of rapid recovery from failure. In just-in-time, operators are trained to be multiskilled, such that when equipment breaks down, or there is a problem on the production line, operators as a team provide the necessary help to bring the system back to its normal operation in order to minimize downtime. This is a far cry from the time when all operations were strongly unionized and organized by function. As an illustration, the author was a drilling operator in a manufacturing firm in the 1960s. One morning, a screw came loose from the drill machine and the machine shut off. The author could have easily fixed the problem in a few minutes, but was unable to do because of union rules. Instead, he had to fill in a work order for a maintenance man to come and fix the problem. The result was that the assembly operation was down for one hour.[19]

Subcontractor/supplier network

Having in place a reliable subcontractor or supplier network can be extremely helpful in an organization, in that if something goes wrong, such as a machine fails, a truck breaks down or raw materials do not conform, then a firm has outside contacts to call upon in case of emergency situations. Box 19.2 illustrates a situation from Japan, whose strong supplier relationship, or *keiretsu*, made the difference in the recovery from a failure resulting in a disastrous fire.[20]

Box 19.2 To the rescue: Toyota's recovery from factory fire shows firm's clout

No one knows what caused the fire that destroyed Aisin Seiki Co's Factory No 1 in the morning of Saturday 1 February 1997. The fire incinerated the main source of a crucial brake valve that Toyota buys from Aisin and uses in most of its cars. Most Toyota plants kept only a four-hour supply of the $5 valve and without it Toyota had to shut down its 20 auto plants in Japan which build 14 000 cars a day. Some experts thought Toyota couldn't recover for weeks. But just five days after the fire, Toyota's car factories started up again. The secret lay in Toyota's close-knit family of parts suppliers who rushed to the rescue. Within hours they had begun taking blueprints for the valve, improvising tooling systems and setting up make-shift production lines. By the following Thursday, the 36 suppliers, aided by more than 150 other subcontractors, had nearly 50 separate lines producing small batches of the brake valve. In one case, a sewing machine-maker that had never made car parts spent about 500 man-hours refitting a milling machine to make just 40 valves a day.

Wall Street Journal Europe, 12 May 1997

Crisis management

Crisis management is a function in place at major corporations and often governments so that they can respond and recover from a failure, very often on a large scale. Chemical firms have crisis management teams in place to recover from failures resulting from industrial accidents, such as fires or other occurrences which result in plant shutdown or environmental disasters (see Chapter 5, *An Environmental Balance*). Alternatively, governments and some firms may have in place crisis management teams to respond to natural disasters or economic downturn. As an illustration consider Box 19.3.[21]

In crisis management the ultimate objective is to reduce the impact of the failure or a crisis. Activities included in crisis management would involve:

- undertaking a risk evaluation analysis to identify what might be possible occurrences;
- developing appropriate action plans and strategic plans in order to respond to the failure;
- developing failure information systems in order to record and report the occurrences;
- if appropriate, putting in place teams to respond to pressure groups and to respond to the public and to the media.

Like the Heathrow Airport incident, the ultimate effectiveness of crisis management can be measured from the speed with which the organization recovers, the degree to which it recovers, the extent of the operational and organizational improvement added during the recovery and the amount of crisis resistance added since the failure arose.[22]

Box 19.3 London scurries to restore flights

Authorities at Heathrow International Airport London had a crisis on Friday 12 December 97 after a roof fire closed the airport's busiest passenger Terminal 1 for half the day severely restricting operations and forcing flight cancellations for tens of thousands of passengers. Fortunately the fire occurred in the early morning and helped to avoid a replay of the tragic fire that swept through Dusseldorf International Airport in 1996 killing 17 people and causing damage totalling $55 million. Heathrow learnt some lessons from the German fire and credited the rapid control of the blaze to the $1.65 million new investment in fire detection, alarms, and other safety systems.

International Herald Tribune, 13th/14th December 1997

SUMMARY OF KEY ELEMENTS

- Failure of equipment in the supply chain will have diverse consequences, ranging from customer inconvenience, through lost revenue, delayed production and poor quality, to perhaps tragedy.
- Reliability is the confidence one has in a product, process, service, work team or individual to operate under prescribed and expected conditions.
- A product assembled in a series arrangement of components $R_1, R_2, \ldots R_n$ has a system reliability R_S, given by $R_S = R_1 \times R_2 \times R_3 \times R_4 \ldots R_n$.
- If a failure would be problematic, back-up systems operate in the eventual failure of the principal system. Here, components $R_1, R_2, \ldots R_n$ are connected in a parallel, giving a system reliability $R_S = 1 - (1 - R_1)(1 - R_2)(1 - R_3)(1 - R_4) \ldots (1 - R_n)$.
- The failure rate measures the reliability of products. It can be determined by one of the following two ratios:

$$\text{Failure rate (\%)} = \frac{\text{Number of products which failed}}{\text{Total number of products tested}}$$

$$\text{Failure rate } (N) =$$
$$\frac{\text{Number of products which failed}}{\text{Number of unit-hours of operating time.}}$$

- The mean time between failures, MTBF, is the reciprocal of the Failure Rate (T):

$$\text{MTBF} = \frac{1}{\text{Failure Rate } (N)}$$
$$= \frac{\text{Operating time for units}}{\text{Number of products which failed}}.$$

- The failure rate profile can be expressed as a bathtube curve showing high failure rates at the beginning and the end and normal failure between these extremes.
- Poka Yoke is the principle of making products, processes or services fail-safe by incorporating mistake-proof techniques into the design.
- A failure mode, effect and criticality analysis, FMECA, is the detailed study of a system to determine which features are critical to various modes of failure.
- Maintenance is all those operations, such as monitoring, inspecting, adjusting and repairing, to keep machines, equipment or vehicles in proper working order.
- Emergency maintenance, or run-to-breakdown maintenance, is repairing machines or equipment after a failure has occurred.

- Preventative maintenance is programmed on a regular basis to inspect and to make necessary repairs to ensure that the system does not fail during normal operation.
- Total productive maintenance places a high value on teamwork, consensus building and continuous improvement, or *Kaizen*.
- Reliability-centred maintenance determines what must be done to ensure that any physical asset continues to fulfil its present operating context.

- Failures occur and firms must be prepared to respond quickly. Just-in-time has built-in failure recovery, as does a good supplier/subcontractor network
- Crisis management is a function put in place by major corporations and governments to respond to a failure, very often on a large scale.

REVIEW AND DISCUSSION QUESTIONS

1 **Unexpected occurrences**. List unexpected occurrences that have occurred in business in the last five years. Can you describe the reasons for these occurrences and what steps were taken to minimize the subsequent damage.

2 **Back-up or parallel systems**. Other than the examples given in the text, list situations where operations would have in place back-up or parallel systems in case of failure of the main system.

3 **Failure rate**. Would you consider that tangible products produced today have a 'longer life' than similar products produced, say, 15 years ago. Justify your arguments and give illustrations.

4 **Poka yoke**. Other than the illustrations given in the text, give examples of where the concept of Poka yoke is used either in manufacturing or in services.

5 **Human error**. Not infrequently, failure in systems is due to human error. What do think are some of reasons that individuals are the cause of failures? Justify your arguments with examples.

6 **Failure mode, effect, and criticality analysis**. Develop the framework of items of consideration in a FMECA analysis for
   (a) an automobile;
   (b) a house;
   (c) a degree programme (MBA for example).

7 **Run-to-breakdown maintenance**. Give illustrations where the philosophy of run-to-breakdown maintenance is employed. In these instances, what are the advantages and disadvantages of this approach in operations?

EXERCISE PROBLEM: BICYCLE RENTAL

Situation

A company in Switzerland rents out all-terrain bicycles during the summer months for use in the Alps. At one location the firm has just one employee who devotes his time to the rental arrangement. Since he is alone, he has not time to perform preventative maintenance, but only repairs bicycles when a client brings one back after it has broken. If this happens, the firm estimates it loses $30 each time because of customer irritation; also, it is obliged to let the client have more rental time than he or she has actually paid for. Based on data for the last summer period, Table 19.6 shows the breakdown frequency for the bikes.

The firm is thinking of employing another person on a part-time basis, whose sole function will be to perform preventive maintenance on the fleet of bikes. This would cost the firm $280 per month. Even so, with this preventive maintenance there is still expected to be on average one bike broken down per week.

Required

Should the firm hire a second person part-time to perform preventive maintenance or should it stay with its present policy? Justify your response.

Table 19.6 Breakdown frequency for the bicycles

Number of bicycles broken down	1	2	3	4	5	6	7
Number of weeks when this level occurred	2	3	5	4	6	2	2

EXERCISE PROBLEM: BINDINGS FOR SKIS

Situation

A manufacturer of ski equipment wants to learn something about the reliability of its racing ski bindings. It tested 25 units each over a period of harsh treatment for 2000 h each. One unit failed after 200 h, one after 300 h, one after 800 h, one after 1200 h, and one after 1550 h. The firm estimated that these bindings were used on average for 200 hours before being replaced.

Required

Determine the following:

1 The failure as a percentage, FR(%).
2 The number of failures during a period of time FR(N).
3 The mean time between failures.
4 The estimated failures per use of the bindings.

EXERCISE PROBLEM: SMITH

Situation

The Smith Co. makes electronic circuit boards that are used in automatically controlled drilling machines. In one particular circuit board the present design has nine components connected in a series arrangement. The reliability of these nine components is as shown in Table 19.7.

Table 19.7 The reliability of the nine circuit-board components

Component	1	2	3	4	5	6	7	8	9
Reliability	0.99	0.98	0.97	0.96	0.99	0.98	0.99	0.96	0.98

Required

1 What is the reliability of this circuit board with the nine components in a series arrangement?

Figure 19.7 Smith – a possible arrangement of the circuit-board components.

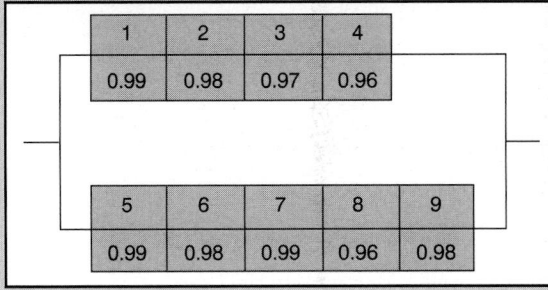

2 How would the reliability change if Smith was able to redesign the system so that the first three components were in series, but these were then connected in parallel to the other five components, which were themselves connected in series according the scheme shown in Figure 19.7.
3 If Smith Co., with a much detailed modification, was able to put components 1 through 3 in series, this combination in parallel with components 4 through 6 themselves in series, and finally this combination in parallel with components 7 though 9, themselves in series as illustrated in Figure 19.8. Then what would be the reliability of the circuit board?

Figure 19.8 Smith – a second possible arrangement of the circuit-board components.

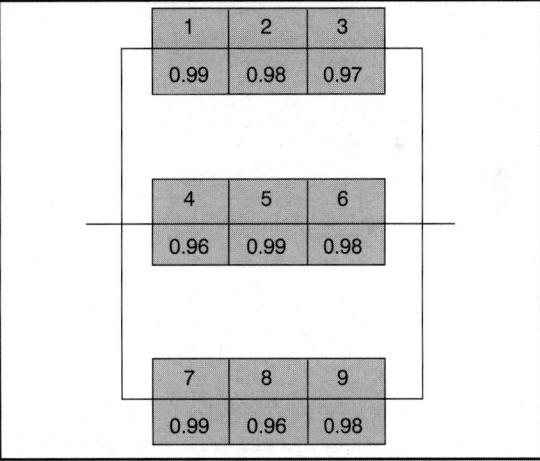

CASE STUDY: A SKI RESORT

Situation

Serre Chevalier, dubbed 'The ski station where all the world descends', is a ski resort in the Southern French Alps, very close to the Italian border. The resort is in fact four separate ski villages, Briançon (named Serre Che 1200), Chantemerle (Serre Che 1350), Villeneuve La Salle (Serre Che 1400) and Monetier les Bains (Serre Che 1500). From the base of these villages one can ski up to an altitude of 2800 m. Table 19.8 lists the ski lifts for the four villages.

At Briancon, the chair lift Serre Blanc is the connection to the neighbouring Chantemerle, and Cucumelle is the connecting chair lift between Villeneuve and Monetier. All of the lift systems are driven by electric motors from the same electric power supply that serves the community of Serre Chevalier. The reliability of all the motors driving the lifts is 95 per cent. Each of the lifts has a back-up motor driven by an oil-driven generator. These back-up systems have a reliability of 90 per cent.

As Serre Chevalier faces south, the snow on the lower slopes thaws easily, exposing rocks and wood stumps. For this reason, and when the snow for the season is poor, at the intermediary level of each of the four villages are snow-making machines that are operated electrically from the community power supply and fed water from the respective villages. There are no back-up systems for these snow making machines. At night-time the slopes are groomed by a fleet of 10 snow cats, which serve the four villages.

Access to the village is from the west over the Col du Lautaret at 2058 m, or, coming east from Turin, over the Col de Montgenèvre. For the convenience of skiers, there is a bus shuttle service between the four villages plus bus services from Lyon, Grenoble and Turin to serve both foreign and French tourists.

Required

1   As the manager responsible for the whole Serre Chevalier ski resort, what would you expect from your maintenance programme, from the points of view of both customer service and safety.
2   Develop a proposed scheme for a FMECA covering the ski lifts.

Table 19.8   Ski lifts for the four Serre Chevalier villages

Briançon	Chantemerle	Villeneuve	Monetier
Prorel (cc)	Aiguilette (cl)	Contillas (tc)	Yret (cl)
Serre Blanc (cl)	Bois des coqs 1 (tb)	Foret 1 (tb)	Corvaria (cl)
Rocher Blanc (cl)	Grand Alps (cl)	Aravet (tc)	Charmettes (tb)
Croix de la Noire (tb)	Combes 2 (tb)	Foret 2 (tb)	Cibouit (cl)
Serre Pelat (tb)	Bletonet 1 (tc)	Tremplin (cl)	Etoile (tb)
Stade de slalom (cl)	Bletonet 2 (cl)	L'Echaillon (tb)	Pre Charbert (tb)
	Prorel 1 (tb)	Cote Chevalier (cl)	Lauzieres (cl)
	Bois des coqs 2 (tb)	Clot Mea (cl)	Chanteloubbe (cl)
	Grand Serre (cl)	Pre du bois (tb)	Cucumelle (cl)
	Grand Alp 1 (cc)	Balme (cl)	
	Bletonet 2 (tc)	Clot Gauthier (cl)	
	Orée du bois (tb)		
	Prorel 2 (tb)		
	Replat (tb)		
	Combes 1 (tb)		
	Grand Alp 2 (cc)		
	Bletonet 1 (cl)		

cc = cable car   cl = chair lift   tb = tow bar   tc = tele cabin (60 people)

NOTES AND REFERENCES

1.   'Car safety: Mercedes bends' (1997) *The Economist* 15 November.
2.   'Daimler hits brakes on second flawed model' (1997) *International Herald Tribune* 19 December.
3.   '"Daimler's Swatchmobile" faces delays' (1997) *Wall Street Journal Europe* 19–20 December.
4.   'Un DC-10 perd un réacteur au décollage' (1992) *Chronique de l'aviation*, Paris: Editions Chronique: 768. [Translation: A DC-10 loses an engine on takeoff.]
5.   'Reprise des vols sur DC-10 autorisée' (1992) *Chronique de l'aviation*, Paris: Editions Chronique: 769. [Translation: Flying for the DC-10s is authorized.]
6.   *Wall Street Journal Europe* (1997) 31 July.

7.   'More dark news for Auckland' (1998) *International Herald Tribune* 5 March: 5.
8.   'The Millennium Bug: Please panic early' (1997) *The Economist* 4 October: 23–27.
9.   Based on an idea by Renault VI, Bridge and Axle Division, Lyon, France (1995).
10.   'Challenger, explose en plein vol' (1990) *Chronique du 20e siècle*, Paris: Larousse. [Translation: Challenger explodes in mid-flight.]
11.   Confidential report.
12.   Sivalingham, Y. (1997) 'Applying best practices to maintenance: A 12-step program for moving down the road to recovery', *Plant Engineering* 51(6): 120, 114.
13.   Moore, R. (1997) 'Combining TPM and reliability-focused maintenance', *Plant Engineering* 51(6): 88–90.

14. McCarthy, D. (1995) 'Total productive maintenance', *Works Management* 48(4): 14–15.
15. Moubray, J. (1995) 'Reliability centred maintenance: Making a positive contribution to asset management strategy', *Works Management* 48(3): 14–15.
16. Smock, R. W. (1993) 'A comprehensive look at reliability-centred maintenance', *Power Engineering* 97(10): 12.
17. Arnold, R. D. and Levasseur, R. (1997) 'Reliability centred maintenance becomes strategic asset at Fraser's Madawaska mill', *Pulp and Paper* 71(2): 55–58.
18. Geraghty, T. (1996) 'Maintenance Matters', *The Chemical Engineer* No. 622: 14–16.
19. Machine operator at the British Oxygen, Edmonton Works, UK, June 1962.
20. 'To the rescue: Toyota's recovery from factory fire shows firm's clout' (1997) *Wall Street Journal Europe* 12 May.
21. 'London scurries to restore flights' (1997) *International Herald Tribune* 13–14 December.
22. Crisis Corp. Ltd. URL: http://www.crisiscorp.com/services.htm – Crisis Management Services.

FURTHER READING

Ackerman, K. and Smit, J. (1997) 'Economic maintenance strategies for the future', *Transmission and Distribution World* 49(2): 40–47.
Ashley, S. (1993) 'Failure analysis beats Murphy's Law', *Mechanical Engineering* 115(9): 70–72.
Bates, A. (1996) 'Effective strategies deliver plant reliability', *Works Management* 49(7): 45–49.
Beckman, L. V. (1992) 'How reliable is your safety system?', *Chemical Engineering* 99(1): 108–14.
Bierbower, W. (1996) 'What every maintenance manager should know', *Metal Center News* 36(1): 52–56.
Bretz, E. A. (1992) 'Planning, design approach help ensure reliability', *Electrical World* 206(5): 58–60.
Chareonsuk, C., Nagarur, N. and Tabucanon, M. T. (1997) 'A multi-criteria approach to the selection of preventive maintenance intervals', *International Journal of Production Economics* 49(1): 55–64.
Chen, F. (1994) 'Benchmarking: Preventive maintenance practices at Japanese transplants', *International Journal of Quality and Reliability Management* 11(8): 19–26.
Davis, R. (1997) 'TPM and RCM: Must it be one or the other?' *Works Management* 50(6): 49–53.
Dixey, M. (1993) 'Putting reliability at the centre of maintenance', *Professional Engineering* 6(6): 23–25.
Eby, M. and Bush, R. (1996) 'Maintenance management techniques for the future', *Transmission and Distribution World* 48(8): 94–103.
Fox, B. H., Snyder, M. G. and Smith, A. M. (1994) 'Reliability-centered maintenance improves operations at TMI nuclear plant', *Power Engineering* 98(13): 75–78.
Hipkin, I. B. and Lockett, A. G. (1995) 'A study of maintenance technology implementation', *Omega* 23(1): 79–88.
Holder, R. (1993) 'Plant maintenance: Just what the plant doctor ordered', *Works Management* 46(6): 37–41.
Hsu, L.-F. (1992) 'Optimal preventive maintenance policies in an M/G/1 queue-like production system', *European Journal of Operational Research* 58(1): 112–22.
Idhammar, C. (1997) 'Responsibility for maintenance costs – partners or customers', *Pulp and Paper* 71(3): 49.

Kelly, A. and Harris, M. J. (1993) 'Uses and limits of total productive maintenance', *Professional Engineering* 6(1): 9–11.
Kiesche, E. (1993) 'Maintenance gears up for higher productivity', *Chemical Week* 152(22): 29–30.
Kumar, D. and Pandey, P. C. (1993) 'Maintenance planning for a refining system in the sugar industry', *International Journal of Quality & Reliability Management* 10(1): 61–71.
Lamb, R. G. (1996) 'Determining true cost of maintenance performance can generate new profits', *Pulp and Paper* 70(10): 93–100.
Levitt, J. (1996) *Managing Factory Maintenance*, New York: Industrial Press.
Lin, T. and Titmuss, D. (1995) 'Critical component reliability and preventive maintenance improvement to reduce machine downtime', *Computers and Industrial Engineering* 29(1–4): 21–23.
Mann, L. Jr. (1983) *Maintenance Management*, Lexington, MA: Lexington Books.
Moubray, J. (1992) *Reliability Centered Maintenance*, , New York: Industrial Press.
Murty, A. S. R. and Naikan, V. N. A. (1995) 'Availability and maintenance cost optimisation of a production plant', *International Journal of Quality and Reliability Management* 12(2): 28–35.
Nakajima, S. (1988) *Introduction to TPM: Total Productive Maintenance*, Cambridge, MA: Productivity Press.
Oliver, K. G. (1989) *Industrial Boiler Management, An Operator's Guide*, New York: Industrial Press.
Ozekici, S. (1995) 'Optimal maintenance policies in random environments', *European Journal of Operational Research* 82(2): 283–94.
Pham, H. and Wang, H. (1996) 'Imperfect maintenance', *European Journal of Operational Research* 94(3): 425–38.
Phillips, T. (1997) 'What's your maintenance strategy?', *Plant Engineering and Maintenance* 21(4): 22–26.
Pujadas, W. and Chen, F. F. (1996) 'A reliability centered maintenance strategy for a discrete part manufacturing facility', *Computers and Industrial Engineering* 31(1,2): 241–44.
Raouf, A. (1993) 'On evaluating maintenance performance' *International Journal of Quality & Reliability Management* 10(3): 33–36.
Richards, D. and Rickaby, R. (1996) 'Software improves system maintenance', *Transmission and Distribution World* 48(9): 54–59.
Sarker, B. R. and Yu, J. (1995) 'A balanced maintenance schedule for a failure-prone system', *International Journal of Quality and Reliability Management* 12(9): 183–91.
Sheu, S.-H. and Jhang, J.-P. (1997) 'A generalised group maintenance policy', *European Journal of Operational Research* 96(2): 232–47.
Tseng, S.-T. (1996) 'Optimal preventive maintenance policy for deteriorating production systems', *IIE Transactions* 28(8): 687–94.
Wheaton, R. (1996) 'Reliability-based maintenance requires mill culture change', *Pulp and Paper* 70(7): 53–61.
Wireman, T. (1994) *Computerised Maintenance Management Systems*, New York: Industrial Press.
Wireman, T. (1990) *World Class Maintenance Management*, New York: Industrial Press.

ⅠⅤ Part IV.
Further Analysis

Operations involves both quantitative and qualitative elements. Part III has already developed some analytical approaches and the purpose of this last part of the book is to go deeper and present other techniques. It begins with Chapter 20 which gives an overview of statistical concepts. Chapter 21 goes further into quantitative forecasting expanding upon Chapter 9, *Forecasting Customer Demand*, of Part III. *Decision making and risk analysis*, Chapter 22, details quantitative approaches to minimizing risk and Chapter 23 on statistical quality control is an analytical component of quality management presented in Chapter 4 of Part I. The theory of waiting lines, although a scheduling and capacity problem, is presented separately in Chapter 24 as it is heavily quantitative. Chapter 25 covers the all important financial aspects of operations. Finally Chapter 26 deals with auditing to improve the efficiency of the operating system from both quantitative and qualitative angles.

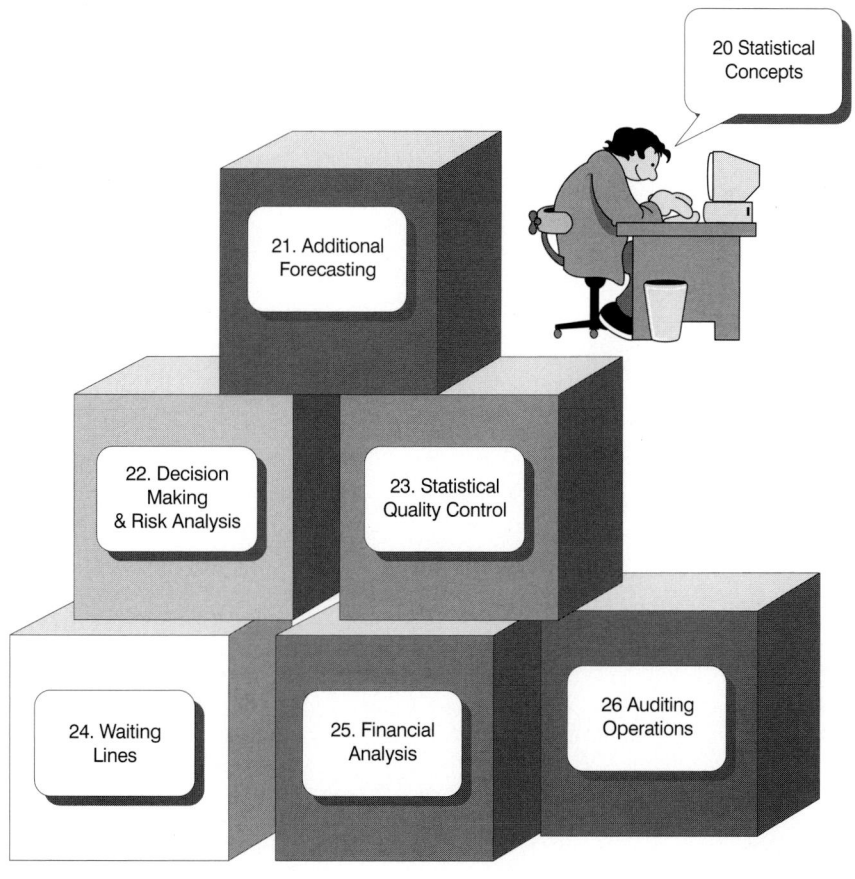

20| Statistical concepts

Objectives and overview

The objective of this chapter is to give a review of basic statistical concepts that are used directly or referred to in this textbook on operations management. The chapter first presents statistical terms most often encountered and then reviews basic probability concepts. The measures of central tendency, such as the mean, median, mode, midrange and geometric mean, are presented, followed by measures of dispersion, including the variance and the commonly used concept of standard deviation. The chapter then has separate sections devoted to probability distributions, including the exponential, normal, binomial, Poisson, student t and beta distributions.

WHY STATISTICS

Areas of use

The operations and supply-chain environment is quantitative. There are costs, profits, sales revenues, units sold, productivity levels, flow rates, capacity factors, inventory quantities, waiting times, delivery periods, etc. Statistical analysis is an important tool, which uses as a base historical or measured data, in order to examine quality conditions or to make estimates or forecasts about actual, or future conditions. Banks and insurance companies use statistics to estimate the evolution of interest rates, or to calculate financial risk. (see Chapter 26, *Decision Making and Risk Analysis*). Manufacturing firms use statistical control on their products (see Chapter 23, *Statistical Quality Control*) and pharmaceutical firms use statistics to test the effectiveness of their products before launching them onto the market. The use of statistics is extensive.[1]

Using statistics never gives a guarantee of a situation, or a future outcome. However, if data measurements are performed correctly and future conditions can be considered to be similar to the past, statistical analysis can be used with a degree of confidence.

General Electric

The importance of statistics is illustrated by the General Electric Co. USA (GE), one of the world's most successful companies, which has a quality programme (borrowed from Motorola, USA), involving training 'Black Belts' for four months in statistical and other quality-enhancing measures. After the training, the 'Black Belts' spend all their time roaming the plants of General Electric and setting up quality-improvement projects. John F Welch, the Chairman of the company, has told young managers that they do not have much future at GE unless they are selected to become Black Belts in statistics and quality control. The company has so far trained 2000 and planned to increase that number to 4000 by the end of 1997, and to 10 000 by the year 2000. In all, it is investing hundreds of millions of dollars in training, in specific projects and in computer systems to analyse and run the statistical-based quality-control programmes.[2]

Microsoft Excel

Almost all of the statistical terms described in this chapter, and used throughout this book, including central tendency, dispersion, random variables, and normal, binomial, Poisson, beta, and t distributions can be generated or calculated by using the built-in statistical functions in Microsoft Excel. This avoids going through the sometimes laborious mathematical calculations.

COMMON TERMS

Data characteristics

Data characteristics are the units of measurement that describe weight, volume, length, production rate, viscosity, etc.

Raw data

Raw data is collected data that has not been organized into any order. Raw data is sometimes referred to as a data set.

Data array

A data array is raw data that has been sorted in either ascending or descending order.

Class

A class is a grouping into which data is arranged. The following age groups would constitute four classes:

- 20 to 30 years;
- 30 to 40 years;
- 40 to 50 years;
- 50 to 60 years.

Discrete data

Discrete data consists of distinct or unconnected information usually obtained from the counting process:

- 9 machines are shutdown;
- 4 units are defective;
- 5 bottles have been sold;
- 7 operators are absent.

It is not possible to have $4\frac{1}{4}$ defector units, $7\frac{1}{2}$ operators absent, $5\frac{1}{2}$ bottles sold or $9\frac{3}{4}$ machines shutdown. Discrete data does not progress from one class or another.

Continuous data

Continuous data is information that progresses from one class to another. The volume of beer in a 33 cl can might be: 32.7954 cl; 32.9271 cl; 33.0094 cl; 33.1000 cl.

A statistic

A statistic describes the characteristic of a sample, taken from a population, such as the weight, volume length, etc.

Descriptive statistics

Descriptive statistics is the analysis of sample data in order to describe the characteristics of that particular sample.

Inferential statistics

Inferential statistics is the analysis of sample data for the purpose of describing the characteristics of the population from which that sample is taken; that is, the population characteristics are inferred from the analysis of the sample. This is the most common practical usage of statistical analysis.

Population

The population is all of the elements being studied, and about which conclusions are being drawn:

- employees with General Motors;
- water in the river Rhône, France;
- the population of China;
- the sheep in Australia.

Parameter

A parameter describes the characteristic of a population, such as the weight, height, or length. A parameter is in contrast to a statistic, which describes a sample.

Sample

A sample is the collection of a portion of population elements:

- A blood sample is used to describe the total blood in the body, and by corollary the health of the individual.
- A sample of ten slabs of chocolate taken from a batch of 50 000 is used to understand the quality of the batch.
- A sample of 15 piston rods taken from the production line in an automobile firm is used to ascertain the quality of the product from the assembly line.

Random sample

A random sample is where each item in the sample has an equal chance of being selected. The selection of one item from the sample has no impact on the chance that any other item is chosen.

Sampling with replacement

Sampling with replacement is taking a sample from a population and, after analysis, returning the sample to the population. One reason for this would be not to change the probability outcome. For example, in a pack of cards, a card is selected:

- The probability of this card being the Ace of Spades is 1/52 or 1.92 per cent.
- Assume this chosen card is not the Ace of Spades and is not replaced.
- Another card is chosen, then the probability of this second card being the Ace of Spades is 1/51 or 1.96 per cent, a slightly higher probability.
- If the first card was replaced, there would be no change in the probability outcome for the second card.

Sampling from an infinite population

Sampling from an infinite population means that, even if the sample is not replaced, then the probability outcome for a subsequent sample would not change markedly. For example, in a population of 10 000 bottled chemical samples, one is believed to be toxic. If one sample is taken, the probability of this sample being toxic is 1/5000 or 0.02 per cent. If the first sample is good and a second is taken, without the first being replaced, the probability of this being toxic is 0.020004 per cent, not very much different from the first sampling.

Frequency distribution

A frequency distribution is a display, in either tabular or graphical form, that illustrates the number of observations (the frequency of occurrence) that fall into each set of mutually exclusive classes. The more frequently data occurs, then the higher is the probability that it will occur again. Frequency distributions are more manageable than raw data and demonstrate trends more easily. The normal, binomial, Poisson and beta distributions are examples of frequency distributions.

Pie chart

A pie chart shows data according to the percentage of certain occurrences. The presentation of work-in-progress times in Chapter 11, *Inventory Management*, (Figure 11.5) is an example of a pie chart.

Histogram

A histogram is a vertical bar chart with the length of the vertical bar proportional to the data value. Histograms are used extensively in Chapter 3, *Site Selection*.

Bar chart

A bar chart is a horizontal histogram. Gannt charts (Chapters 14 and 18, *Operations Scheduling* and *Project Management*) are forms of bar charts.

Polygon

A polygon is a line graph representing a frequency distribution.

PROBABILITY

Probability means the chance that something will happen, or will not happen. It might be expressed in a subjective manner, based on the frequency of past events, or by the application of certain probability rules.

Subjective probabilities

Subjective probabilities are based on the feelings of the person making the judgement. This might be a function of that person's experience in a particular situation:

- A good salesperson may be able to say 'I am 90 per cent certain the customer will buy that product.'
- A competent manager may be able to say, 'I am 95 per cent certain John will finish that project by the end of the week.'

Relative frequency probability

Relative frequency probability assumes that an activity has occurred frequently before, with many recorded observations such that a frequency distribution can be developed. As an illustration, historical data indicates that, in a sample of 3000 bronze castings made, 24 had hairline cracks. Thus, using this data, it can be estimated that in the foundry operation, 0.8 per cent of the castings (24/3000) were of poor quality. Thus, knowing this occurrence from past data, the necessary action can be taken, such as putting into production approximately 101 castings for every 100 demanded.

In relative frequency probabilities, the larger the number of observations, the greater is the reliability of the relative frequency measurement. However, the larger the sample size, the more expensive is the analysis.

Probability rules

In many situations, one is interested in the probability of either of the following:

- when one event, or another, will occur; for example, what is the probability that today's demand for customer orders will exceed the quantity manufactured?
- when two, or more, events occur together; for example, what is the chance that demand for orders will exceed the forecast and that the assembly line breaks down?

Marginal or unconditional probability

In marginal, or unconditional, probability, there is only a single occurrence which assumes that every outcome has an equal possibility. It can be determined by the relationship:

$$\frac{\text{Number of outcomes where the event occurs}}{\text{Total number of possible outcomes}}$$

A simple illustration applies to gambling and the chance of drawing the Ace of Spades from a full pack of cards. This would be:

$$\frac{1}{52} = 1.92 \text{ per cent}$$

If in a sample of 20 chemical vials, one is believed to be off-specification then, the probability of one selected at random being the off-spec sample is 1/20 or 5 per cent.

Joint probabilities of independent events

The probability of two or more independent events A *and* B occurring together, or in succession, is the product of their marginal probabilities:

$$\text{Probability (A and B)} = \text{Probability (A)} \times \text{Probability (B)}.$$

In two packs of cards, the probability of drawing together the Ace of Spades from both packs is:

$$\frac{1}{52} \times \frac{1}{52} = 0.04 \text{ per cent}$$

or *less than* the individual probabilities. If the probability of an operator being absent is 20 per cent and that of a machine breaking down is 30 per cent then the probability of both occurring together is 0.2 × 0.3 = 6.0 per cent. Joint probabilities occur in PERT distributions (Chapter 18, *Project Management*) in determining the probability of a project being finished on time when there is more than one project path to be considered.

Mutually exclusive events

If two events, A and B, are not related to one another (mutually exclusive), then the probability of A or B occurring can be expressed by the addition rule.

$$\text{Probability (A or B)} = \text{Probability(A)} + \text{Probability(B)}.$$

From a pack of cards, the probability of drawing the Ace of Spades or the Queen of Hearts is,

$$P(\text{Ace of Spades or Queen of Hearts}) = \frac{1}{52} + \frac{1}{52}$$
$$= 3.85 \text{ per cent}$$

or *greater than* the individual probabilities. If the probability of an operator being absent is 20 per cent and that of a machine breaking down is 30 per cent, then the probability of either one *or* the other occurring is 0.20 + 0.30 = 50 per cent.

Non-mutually exclusive events

Two events, A and B, are not mutually exclusive when it is possible for both events to occur, for example in the probability of selecting either an ace or a spade from a deck of cards. An ace and spade can occur together since the Ace of Spades could be drawn. Thus, drawing an ace and a spade are not completely mutually exclusive events. In this case, the addition rule is adjusted to avoid double accounting by the probability of drawing the Ace of Spades:

$$\text{Probability (A or B)} = \text{Probability(A)} + \text{Probability(B)} - \text{Probability (AB)},$$

where Probability (AB) is the probability of A and B occurring together. Thus:

$$P(\text{Ace or Spade}) = \frac{4}{52} + \frac{13}{52} - \frac{4}{52} \times \frac{13}{52}$$
$$= \frac{17}{52} - \frac{1}{52} = \frac{16}{52} = 30.77 \text{ per cent.}$$

CENTRAL TENDENCY

Most data is clustered, or grouped, around a central point. This central point is often used to describe the data, or the population, and is used as a reference. The mean (average), median, mid-range, and mode are measures of central tendency.

Mean

The mean (average, arithmetic average or arithmetic mean) is the sum of all values, ΣX divided by the number of elements in the observations, n:

$$X = \frac{\Sigma X}{n}$$

If the recorded temperatures, in °C, at midday at a certain location for one week are;

18   25   22   23   21   20   15

then the arithmetic mean for the week is 22°C (154/7).

The value of the mean is modified by extreme values (very high or very low values relative to others in the data set). However, the value of the mean may not be affected by the number of values.

Median

The median is the middle value of an ordered set of data. The following data set,:

9   13   12   7   6   11   12

must be rearranged in descending, or ascending order. In ascending order this gives:

6   7   9   11   12   12   13

This shows that 11 is the median value. The median can be calculated as shown in the following.

Odd number of values

If n, the number of values, is odd, the median is calculated from, $(n + 1)/2$. If there are seven values, the median is, $(7+1)/2$ or the fourth value.

Even number of values

If n, the number of values, is even, the median is the average of the values $n/2$ and $(n + 2)/2$. If there are six values, the median is the average of values and 6/2 and $(6+2)/2$, or the average of the third and fourth values.

The median value indicates that half of the data lies above the median and half below. For example, in 1990, the median price of a house in California, USA was $200 000. This meant that half of the houses in California were priced above $200 000. The other half were priced below. The median is not affected by extreme values, but it is affected by the number of values.

Mode

The mode is that value that occurs most frequently in data. In the following data:

9   13   17   19   7   3   13   8   22   4   7

the mode is 13 (it occurs twice). The mode is of interest because that value that occurs most frequently is probably a response that deserves further investigation.

The mode is unaffected by extreme values, but may be affected by the number of values if these new values introduce another modal value.

Mode in a qualitative sense

The mode can also be used for qualitative data. In the listing:

yellow   red   green   blue   brown   purple
mauve   blue   violet   grey   green   blue

The modal value is blue (it occurs three times). Thus, if this was a survey of customer preference for a fabric, a manufacturer might carry more inventory of blue stock.

Bimodal

If there are two values in a data set that occur most frequently, then it is bimodal. In:

9   13   17   19   7   3   13   8   22   4   7   9

the values 9 and 13 occur most frequently and so the data set is bimodal. When a data set is bimodal, it indicates that there are two pieces of data that are of particular interest.

Midrange

The midrange is the average of the smallest and largest observation in a data set. In:

9   13   12   7   6   11   12

the midrange is $(6 + 13)/2 = 9.5$.

Like the average, the midrange can be distorted by extreme values and the distortion may be high because the midrange only considers extreme values. In the example above, if the highest value was 26, then the mid-range would be $(6 + 26)/2 = 16.0$. This is the disadvantage with the mid-range as a measure.

Geometric mean

The geometric mean is a special measure of central tendency when data is changing over a period of time. Examples might be the growth of investments, the inflation rate or the growth rate of the gross national product (see Chapter 25, *Financial Analysis*).

Consider the growth of an initial investment of $1000 in a savings account that is on deposit for a period of five years. The interest rate, which is accumulated annually, is variable. Table 20.1 gives the interest and the growth of the investment.

Table 20.1 Interest and growth of an investment of $1000

Year end	Interest rate	Growth factor	Value at year
1	6.0	1.060	$1060.00
2	7.5	1.075	$1139.50
3	8.2	1.082	$1232.94
4	7.9	1.079	$1330.34
5	5.1	1.051	$1398.19

The growth rate, or geometric mean, is given by the relationship:

$$\sqrt[n]{\text{product of growth rates}}$$

In this case the geometric mean is:

$$\sqrt[5]{1.060 \times 1.075 \times 1.082 \times 1.079 \times 1.051}$$
$$= 1.0693$$

or an average growth rate of 6.93 per cent per year. Thus, the value of the $1000 at the end of five years is:

$$\$1000 \times 1.0693^5 = \$1398.19,$$

the same value as calculated in Table 20.1.

If the arithmetic average of the growth rates was used, the mean growth rate would be:

$$\sqrt[5]{1.060 + 1.075 + 1.082 + 1.079 + 1.051}$$
$$= 1.0690$$

or a growth rate of 6.90 per cent per year.

Using this mean interest rate, the value of the initial deposit after five years would be:

$$\$1000 \times 1.0690^5 = \$1396.01.$$

This is less than calculated using the geometric mean. Although the difference is small, in cases where interest rates are widely fluctuating and deposit amounts are large, the difference could be significant.

DISPERSION

Dispersion is a measure of the spread of the data. Data that lies close to the central point has a low dispersion and is more reliable for analysis. On the other hand, data that lies far from the central point or is highly dispersed is less reliable for analysis. Data sets may have the same measure of central tendency (for example the same mean), but have a different dispersion. Some measures of dispersion are the range, variance, standard deviation and fractiles.

Range

The range is the difference between the maximum and minimum values in a data set. In:

$$9 \quad 13 \quad 12 \quad 7 \quad 6 \quad 11 \quad 12$$

The range is $13 - 6 = 7$. Since only extreme values are used to calculate the range, changes in these can distort the value. The conclusion that the larger the range in a data set, then the greater is the dispersion or uncertainty should be treated cautiously because of distortion from extreme values. The range may not be affected by the number of values.

Variance

The variance is the average of the squared difference between each of the observations in a data set and the mean value.

Sample variance

The sample variance is the sum of the squared difference between each observation and the mean, divided by the number of observations minus one:

$$s^2 = \frac{\Sigma \, (x - \bar{x})^2}{(n - 1)},$$

where $\bar{x}$ is the sample mean, s^2 is the sample variance, s is the sample standard deviation, x is a data value and n is the number of values. Using $(n - 1)$ in the denominator removes the bias.

Population variance

The population variance is the sum of the squared difference between each observation and the mean, divided by the number of observations:

$$\sigma^2 = \frac{\Sigma \, (X - \mu_x)^2}{N},$$

where μ_x is the population average, σ^2 is the population variance, σ is the population standard deviation, X is a data value and N is the number of values.

The following apply in either the population or the sample variance:

- Subtracting the mean from each value indicates how far the observation is from the central point (the mean in this case).
- Squaring each difference removes the negative sign.
- Summing, and dividing by N for the population or $(n - 1)$ for the sample gives an average value.

In the data,

9 13 12 7 6 11 12

the sample variance is 7.333 and the population variance is 6.286. Both the sample and population variance are affected by extreme values, but, in contrast to the range, because each value in the data set is taken into consideration, the effect is less marked.

Standard deviation

The standard deviation is the square root of the variance. It is more useful than the variance because as a measure of dispersion it has the same units as the data from which it was calculated. (The units for determining the variance in grams (g), of sample weights, would be g^2. Taking the square root of this gives the units as g.). The standard deviation is the most common measure of dispersion in statistical analysis. Its usefulness is because it takes into account all items in the data set. Like the variance, the sample and population standard deviations are affected by extreme values.

Sample standard deviation

This is given by:

$$s = \sqrt{s^2} = \sqrt{\frac{\Sigma\,(x - \bar{x})^2}{(n - 1)}}.$$

Population standard deviation

This is given by:

$$\sigma_x = \sqrt{\sigma^2} = \sqrt{\frac{\Sigma(X - \mu_x)^2}{N}}.$$

In

9 13 12 7 6 11 12

the sample variance is 2.507 and the population variance 2.708.

Deviations about the mean

The variance and standard deviation measure the average scatter around the mean, showing how larger observations fluctuate above and how smaller observations fluctuate below. Mathematically, the deviation about the mean value must be zero:

$$\Sigma\,(x - \bar{x}) = 0.$$

In,

9 13 12 7 6 11 12

the mean of the data set is 10 and:

$$(9 - 10) + (13 - 10) + (12 - 10) + (7 - 10) +$$
$$(6 - 10) + (11 - 10) + (12 - 10) = 0.$$

Bienayme–Chebyshev Rule

The Bienayme–Chebyshev Rule (after the Russian) relates to the variability of data about the mean point. It states that, regardless of how a set of data is distributed, the percentage of observations that are contained within a distance, k standard deviations, around the mean, must be at least the value calculated by:

$$\left(1 - \frac{1}{k^2}\right) \times 100$$

where k takes on values greater than 1. For example, for $k = 2$ standard deviations the percentage of observations must be greater than:

$$\left(1 - \frac{1}{2^2}\right) \times 100 = 75 \text{ per cent.}$$

In summary, for any type of distribution, Table 20.2 is useful in estimating probabilities.

Table 20.2 Some useful relationships

Number of standard deviations	Percentage of observations between mean and given standard deviation
2	At least 75.00 per cent
3	At least 88.89 per cent
4	At least 93.75 per cent

Fractiles

Fractiles are the division of data into well defined parts, such that a given fraction, or proportion, of the data lies at, or below, a fractile. The most common fractiles are the following.

Quartiles

Quartiles are fractiles that divide data into four equal parts. There are three quartiles.

Deciles

Deciles are fractiles that divide data into ten equal parts. There are nine quartiles.

Percentiles

Percentiles are fractiles that divide data into 100 equal parts. There are 99 percentiles.

50 per cent fractile, or the 50th percentile

The 50 per cent fractile, or the 50th percentile, is also the median, because half the data are less than or equal to this value.

Interfractile range

The interfractile range is a measure of the spread between two fractiles in a data set.

Table 20.3 A data set

0	8	19	27	37	51	58	68	78	89
2	8	19	30	37	52	58	68	80	90
2	9	20	31	38	54	59	69	81	91
2	13	21	33	38	55	59	73	81	93
3	15	22	34	41	56	62	74	84	93
3	16	22	35	41	56	63	75	85	94
5	16	22	35	41	57	66	75	88	94
7	18	22	35	46	57	67	75	88	95
7	19	22	36	49	57	67	76	89	95
8	19	27	36	51	58	68	77	89	98

Interquartile range

The interquartile range, or midspread, is the difference between the third and first quartiles in a data set. In the data set given as Table 20.3:

- The first quartile, Q_1, is 22 and 25 per cent of the data lies at or below 22 and 75 per cent above.
- The second quartile, Q_2, is 51 and 50 per cent of the data lies at or below 51 and 50 per cent above.
- The third quartile, Q_2, is 74 and 75 per cent of the data lies at or below 74 and 25 per cent above.
- The 50th percentile, the median, is 51.
- The interquartile range is:

$$Q_3 - Q_1 = 74 - 22 = 52.$$

The interquartile range considers the spread in the middle 50 per cent of the data.

EXPONENTIAL DISTRIBUTION

The exponential distribution is a mathematical function for which a dependent variable changes (increases or decreases) according to the power, or exponent, of a given independent value. The general form of the exponential equation is:

$$Y = ab^x,$$

where the value of x can be either positive or negative. The exponential distribution is sometimes referred to as the 'function of natural growth' as it is the distribution which explains:

- population expansion;
- the growth of a forest;
- the spread of disease.

Growth

The exponential increase is illustrated in Figure 20.1 for the function:

$$Y = ab^x.$$

In this case $a = 1$ and $b = 3$. This exponential format would illustrate, for example the growth of the sales of automobiles, new technology (see Chapter 1, *Positioning Operations Management*) or population. It implies that there is really no limit.

Decline

This change is illustrated in Figure 20.2 for the function:

$$Y = ab^{-x}.$$

Again $a = 1$ and $b = 3$. This exponential format would illustrate, for example, the learning rate of new ideas (Chapter 8, *Human Resources in the System Design*) or average cost curves (Chapter 11, *Inventory Management*), when there is at first a very rapid decrease but the rate of change slows down, although it never becomes horizontal.

Increase to a maximum

This change is illustrated in Figure 20.3 for the function:

$$Y = 1 - ab^{-x}.$$

Again $a = 1$ and $b = 3$. Here the value of Y reaches a maximum value of unity or 100 per cent. The form of this curve is similar to the ABC inventory analysis (Chapter 11, *Inventory Management*).

Natural logarithm

Other exponential distribution curves may be based on some form using e, the natural logarithm, where $e = 2.718281$. A general form thus would be:

$$Y = e^x \quad \text{or } Y = e^{-x} \quad \text{or } Y = 1 - e^{-x}.$$

NORMAL DISTRIBUTION

Definition

A normal distribution, as illustrated in Figure 20.4 is a continuous probability distribution illustrating the frequency of occurrence of a random variable. It was developed by the German, Karl Friedrich Gauss

Figure 20.1 Exponential curve when x is positive: $Y = ab^x$.

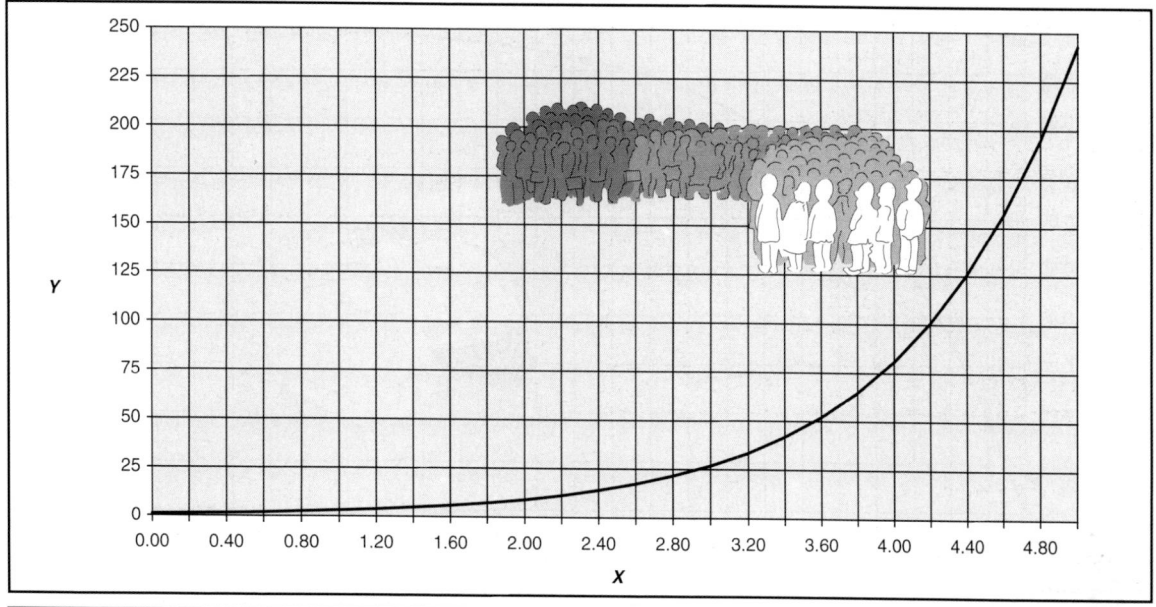

Figure 20.2 Exponential curve when x is negative: $Y = ab^{-x}$.

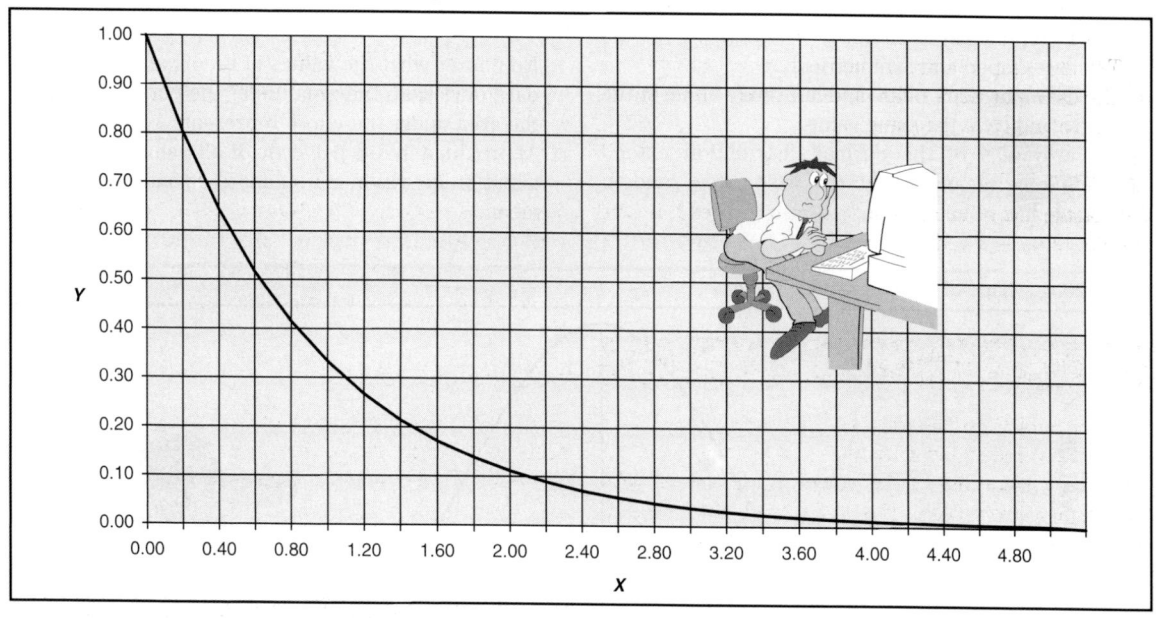

Figure 20.3 Exponential curve when *x* is negative: $Y = 1 - ab^{-x}$.

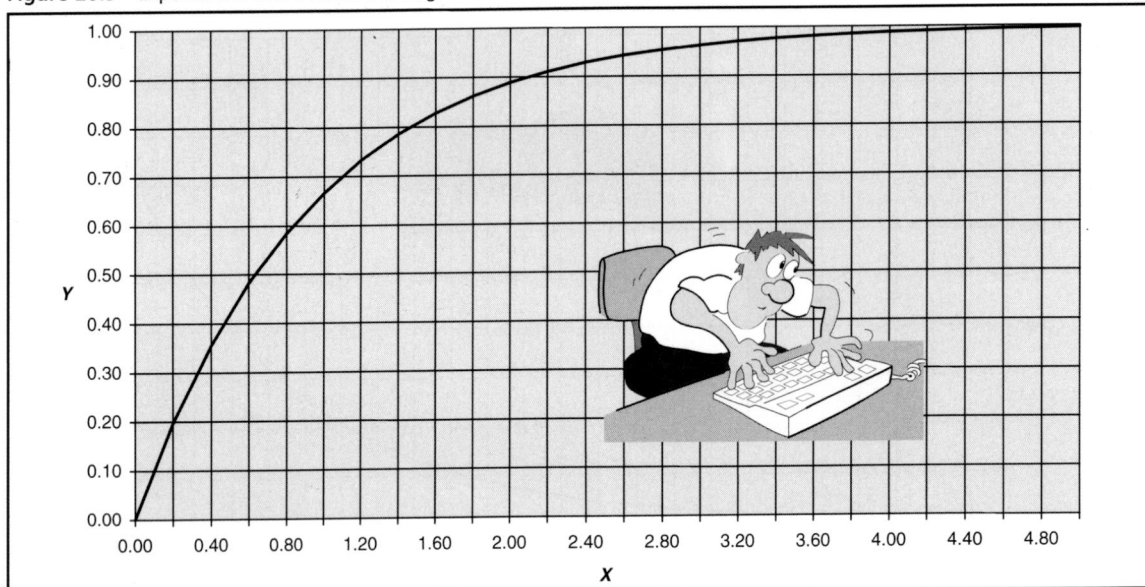

(1777–1855) and thus is also known as the Gaussian distribution. The characteristics are:

- It is a continuous distribution.
- It is bell-shaped and symmetrical.
- The mean, median, mode and midrange all lie at the centre and have the same value.
- The two tails of the normal distribution extend indefinitely, meaning that the associated random variable has infinite range: $(-\infty < x < +\infty)$.

The area under the normal distribution

The following are quantitative measures regarding the area under the normal distribution:

- No matter what the values of the mean, or the standard deviation, the area under the curve is 1.00, or the area under the curve represents 100 per cent.
- Approximately 68 per cent of all values in the distribution lie within ±1 standard deviations from the mean.

Figure 20.4 Shape of the normal distribution.

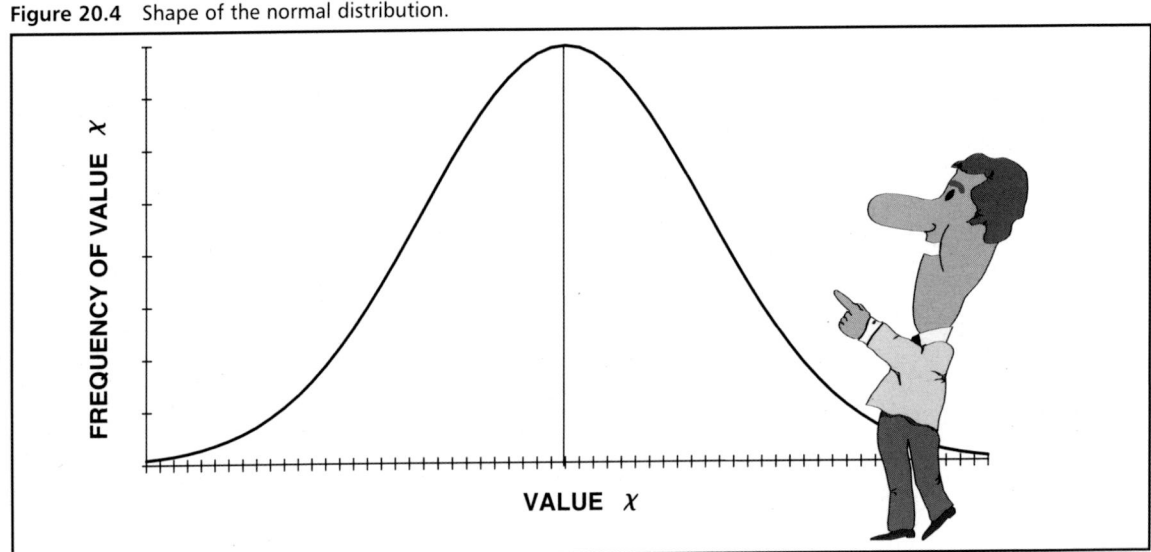

- Approximately 95.5 per cent of all values in the distribution lie with ±2 standard deviations from the mean.
- Approximately 99.7 per cent of all values in the distribution lie within ±3 standard deviations from the mean.
- All intervals containing the same number of standard deviations from the mean will contain the same proportion of the total area under the curve for any normal probability distribution.

Mathematical expression

The mathematical expression for the normal distribution, where $f(X)$ is the probability density function, is:

$$f(X) = \frac{1}{\sqrt{2\pi}.\sigma_x} \exp\{-(1/2)[X - \mu_x)/\sigma_x]^2\}$$

where $\exp(x) = e^x$.

It is from this equation that the normal distribution curve is developed.

Transformation formula

A convenient way to use the normal distribution is to convert measured data into a standard form using the transformation formula:

$$z = \frac{X - \mu_x}{\sigma_x},$$

where X is the value of the random variable, μ_x is the mean of the distribution of the random variables, σ_x is the standard deviation of the distribution and z is the number of standard deviations from X to the mean of this distribution.

Normal distribution and risk

The concept of the normal distribution is illustrated by the following risk assessment in stock trading.[3]

Stock trading

A trader wants to assess the risk of buying 100 shares of a stock currently selling at $100 per share (total price $10 000) and selling them the following day. Historical data on the daily price of the stock, measured over the past 12 months, shows that it follows a normal distribution with an average price of $100 per share. This normal distribution curve, and its associated standard deviation, represents the volatility of the stock. An overnight volatility of 1 per cent means that the price can swing $1 in either direction (1 per cent of $100 is $1).

Two standard deviations means that the swing of the price of the stock will cover 95 per cent (actually 95.5 per cent) of the possible movements, or a swing between $98 and $102. This also means that there is a 5 per cent chance that the price will be more than $102 or less than $98. Since the curve is symmetrical, there is a 2.5 per cent chance that the price will be less than $98 and 2.5 per cent chance that the price will be more than $102. Thus, if the trader buys the share at $100 there is a 2.5 per cent chance (risk) that the price will be less than $98 the following day and, if the trader sells, he will lose money.

The real world

Sample data does not always follow a normal distribution, but the normal distribution can be approximated to give reasonable estimates of probability. Its use is illustrated with the worked example, Drive Shaft.

WORKED EXAMPLE: DRIVE SHAFT

Situation

A company has a factory where it machines drive shafts used in the manufacture of motors. The production manager wants to know what the probability is that a randomly selected shaft will last more than 12 000 h before failure so that he can better define its warranty requirements.

Required

Determine the probability that a shaft will last more than 12 000 h if it is known from historical data that the average life of a drive shaft is 11 000 h, the standard deviation of the life is 500 h, and the life of a drive shaft follows a normal distribution.

Solution

From the transformation formula:

$$z = \frac{x - \mu_x}{\sigma_x}$$

X is 12 000 hours, μ_x is 11 000 hours and σ_x is 500 hours. Therefore

$$z = \frac{12\,000 - 11\,000}{500} = 2.00$$

From the Microsoft Excel function menu, or standard distribution tables, this value of z gives a value of 0.47725. This means that the area of the curve between 11 000 and 12 000 hours is 0.47725. However, the question asks 'more than 12 000 hours', so the area of the curve of interest is that portion to the right of 12 000 hours. Since the area of the curve to the right of the mean is 0.5, then the area of the curve to the right of 12 000 hours is:

$$0.5 - 0.47725 = 0.02275.$$

Thus, the probability of the drive shaft lasting longer than 12 000 hours is about 2.275 or about 2 per cent. This information is illustrated in Figure 20.5.

Figure 20.5   Life of the drive shaft.

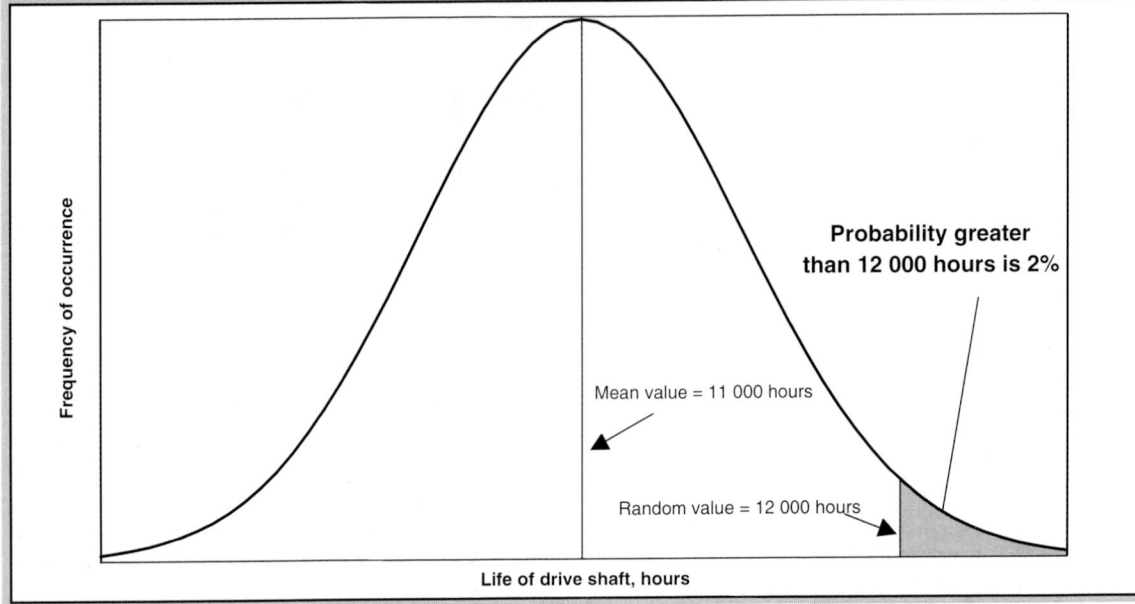

BINOMIAL DISTRIBUTION

Characteristics

A binomial distribution is a discrete probability distribution when there are only two possible outcomes for each trial of an experiment, for example:

■ In tossing a coin, the only two possible outcomes are heads or tails. The probability of obtaining one, two, three, four or five heads in successive throws of a coin would follow a binomial distribution.

■ In the manufacture of a product, quality control might be to test whether an inspected item is good or defective. The probability outcomes for analysing several products would follow a binomial distribution.

■ In a market survey a client might be questioned whether he liked or disliked a product. In surveying several clients, the response under this criterion would be a binomial distribution.

Validity

In order for the binomial distribution to be valid:

1   Each observation is considered as having been selected either from an infinite population, without replacement or from a finite population, with replacement.

2   Each sample, or trial, has two possible outcomes
   ■ success or failure;
   ■ win or lose;
   ■ good or bad;
   ■ present or absent;
   ■ on time or late;
   ■ open or closed.

3   The probability p of obtaining the desired result (success) remains fixed over time. Since the sum of the probabilities is unity (there are only two possible outcomes) the probability of failure q is $(1 - p)$. In the case of tossing a coin, the distribution is symmetrical. Here $p = q = 0.5$.

4   The outcome of any observation is independent of the outcome of any other observation. In tossing a coin for the first time, the outcome of the toss has no bearing on the outcome of the second toss.

Deviations

Meeting the conditions for a binomial distribution is not always evident. Consider the following.

Fixed over time

Rule 3 requires that the probability of success remains fixed over time. In, say, a drilling operation, each time a hole is drilled, there is wear on the machine and the drill. Thus, in time, the hole drilled may not be according to specification.

Observations are independent

Rule 4 requires that the outcome of any observation is independent of the outcome of other observations. In personnel evaluations, a positive evaluation of one person can cause a less positive evaluation of another, and vice-versa. Assume that candidates are being interviewed for a senior job position. Candidate A is rated negatively. The next candidate B is rated more positively because B is compared with A. Interviewers often make a subliminal comparison of competing candidates.

Mathematical expression

The following equation, which is the probability of r successes in n trials, describes the binomial distribution. It was developed from experiments carried out by the Swiss mathematician (of French origin), Jacques Bernoulli (1654–1705):

$$P(X) = \frac{n!}{r!(n-r)!} \, p^r \, q^{(n-r)}$$

- ■ p is the characteristic probability, or probability of success (0.5 for toss of a coin).
- ■ $q = (1-p)$ = probability of failure (equals 0.5 for the coin toss experiment).
- ■ r = number of successes desired.
- ■ n = number of trials undertaken.

If $p = 0.5$, the distribution is symmetrical, regardless of the values of n. When p is not equal to 0.5, the distribution is skewed.

Dissecting the binomial equation

The expression: $p^r q^{(n-r)}$ is the probability of obtaining exactly r successes out of n observations in a particular sequence. The relationship:

$$\frac{n!}{x! \, (n-r)!}$$

indicates how many combinations of the r successes, out of n observations, are possible.

Mean value of the binomial distribution

The mean value, also known as the expected value $E(x)$, is given by the product of the number of trials and the characteristic probability:

$$\text{mean} = \mu_x = E(x) = np.$$

Standard deviation of the binomial distribution

The standard deviation is the square root of the variance. The variance is the product of the number of trials, the characteristic probability of success, and the characteristic probability of failure:

standard deviation,

$$\sigma_x = \sqrt{\text{var}(x)} = \sqrt{np(1-p)} = \sqrt{npq}.$$

Binomial distribution situations

1 In gambling, what is the probability that an ace and a jack will occur once, in 50 rounds of blackjack (vingt-et-un, pontoon, twenty-one)?
2 In quality control, what is the probability that in a sample of 1000 computer cards, none will be defective? Historically, it is known that 0.02 per cent of all cards produced are defective.
3 In finance, what is the probability that the price of Texaco stock will increase next week, if price changes are random?
4 In education, what is the probability that a student will pass a 100-question multiple choice exam, each with five choices, if the student guesses each question? Passing is considered obtaining a score greater than 70 per cent.

Approximating to the normal distribution

The binomial distribution can be approximated to the normal distribution in the following circumstances:

- ■ When the product of sample size and probability of success is greater or equal to five: $n \times p \geq 5$.
- ■ When the product of sample size and probability of failure is greater or equal to five: $n \times q \geq 5$.

In the binomial distribution, the mean $\mu = np$ and the standard deviation $\sigma = \sqrt{npq}$. From the transformation formula $z = (x - \mu)/\sigma$, so that, substituting from the binomial relationships, $z = (x - n\,p)/\sqrt{npq}$.

The worked example, *Hair Dryers*, illustrates the use of the binomial distribution.

WORKED EXAMPLE: HAIR DRIERS

Situation

Historical data indicates that 65 per cent of defective hair driers assembled by an electrical company can be repaired by simply replacing the heating coil. Since the units can either be repaired or they cannot, the probability of success is considered to follow a binomial distribution.

Required

1 Develop a distribution of the probability of repairing a hair drier if there is a quantity of 10 units that are defective.
2 What is the probability that six of the defective units can be repaired?
3 What is the probability that at least six can be repaired?
4 What is the probability that no more than six can be repaired?

Solution

- The characteristic probability is 0.65 or 65 per cent.
- The number of trials is 10.
- The outcome of units that can be repaired ranges from 0 to 10.

1 The probability distribution (using the binomial distribution function in Microsoft Excel) is as shown in Table 20.4. The histogram for this distribution is given in Figure 20.6

Table 20.4 The probability distribution for hair-drier repair

Number that can be repaired	Probability that exactly this number can be repaired (%)	Probability that this number, or fewer, can be repaired (%t)
0	0.00	0.00
1	0.05	0.05
2	0.43	0.48
3	2.12	2.60
4	6.89	9.49
5	15.36	24.85
6	23.77	48.62
7	25.22	73.84
8	17.57	91.40
9	7.25	98.65
10	1.35	100.00

2 The probability that six of the defective units can be repaired is 23.77 per cent.
3 The probability that at least six can be repaired (7 through 10 units) is 51.38 per cent.
4 The probability that no more than six (0 through 6) can be repaired is 48.62 per cent.

Figure 20.6 Repair of hair driers.

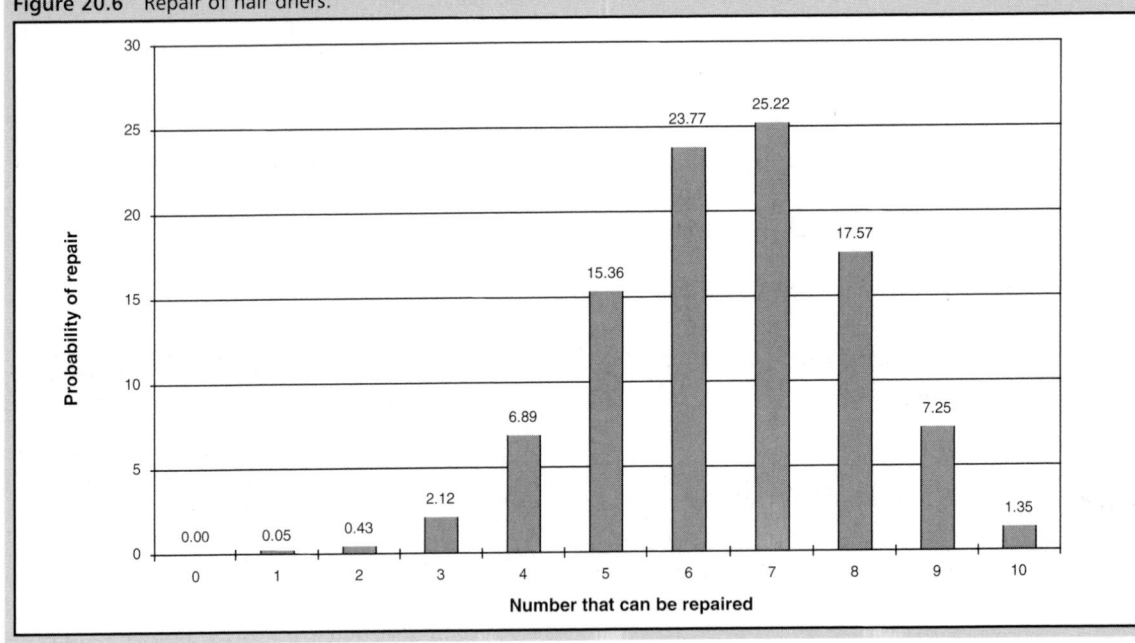

POISSON DISTRIBUTION

Characteristics

The Poisson distribution, named after the Frenchman Denis Poisson (1781-1840), is another discrete probability distribution. It is often used to describe waiting-line situations, such as the number of patients arriving at a doctor's surgery, the arrival of vehicles at a toll booth or the number of customers arriving at a credit card/cash distribution machine (see Chapter 24, *Waiting Lines*).

Requirements

The number of vehicles arriving at a road tunnel at rush hour would be an example of a Poisson distribution. The requirements and conditions would be:

1 The mean number of vehicles arriving per hour can be estimated from past data.
2 If the rush-hour period is divided into single seconds, the following would be approximately true:
   ■ The probability that exactly one vehicle will arrive at the tunnel mouth per second is a very small number and is constant for every one second interval.
   ■ The probability that two or more vehicles will arrive within a one-second interval is so small that it can be considered zero.
   ■ The number of vehicles that arrive in a given one second interval is independent of the time at which that one-second interval occurs during the overall prescribed time period.

■ The number of arrivals in any one-second interval is independent of the number of arrivals in any other one-second interval.

Mathematical expression

The equation describing the Poisson probability of occurrence, $P(x)$, is:

$$P(x) = \frac{\lambda^x e^{-\lambda}}{x!},$$

Where λ (lambda) is the mean number of occurrences, e is the base of the natural logarithm, $e = 2.71828$, and $P(x)$ is the probability of exactly x occurrences.

Poisson distribution as an approximation of the binomial distribution

The Poisson distribution can be a reasonable approximation of the binomial distribution if the sample size n is greater than or equal to 20 and p the characteristic probability, is less than or equal to 0.05.

If this requirement is met, then the mean of the binomial distribution, which is given by the product $n \times p$, can be substituted for the mean of the Poisson distribution λ. The probability function then becomes:

$$P(x) = \frac{(np)^x e^{-(np)}}{x!}.$$

The use of the Poisson distribution is illustrated by the worked example, *Petrol Pump*.

WORKED EXAMPLE: PETROL PUMP

Situation

A petrol service station is interested to learn about the utilization of its single automatic petrol pump, which is operated by the insertion of a credit card. In order to know if he is recouping his investment, the franchise owner of this service station wants some assurance that there is a probability of greater than 50 per cent that ten or more customers in any hour use the automatic pump. Past data indicates that on average eight customers per hour use the automatic pump.

Required

1 Develop a Poisson distribution for the utilization of this petrol pump.
2 Should the franchise owner be satisfied with the utilization, based on the data given?

Solution

1 Using the Poisson distribution, where $\lambda = 8$, the probability of customers using this machine during any hour is given in Table 20.5 and illustrated in Figure 20.7.

Table 20.5 Probability of customers using the automatic pump

Customers using pump	Probability of this number using pump (%)	Cumulative probability of this number, or fewer, using pump (%)
0	0.03	0.03
1	0.27	0.30
2	1.07	1.38
3	2.86	4.24
4	5.73	9.97
5	9.16	19.13
6	12.21	31.34
7	13.96	45.30
8	13.96	59.26
9	12.41	71.66
10	9.93	81.59
11	7.22	88.81
12	4.81	93.62
13	2.96	96.58
14	1.69	98.27
15	0.91	99.18
16	0.45	99.63
17	0.21	99.84
18	0.09	99.93
19	0.04	99.97
20	0.02	99.99
21	0.01	100.00

2   The table and figure indicate that the probability of ten or more people using the pump in any hour is $(100 - 71.66)$ or 38.34 per cent. Thus, utilization is below the requirements of the franchise. Appropriate steps should be taken to increase usage, such as by publicity, price or other incentives.

Figure 20.7 Use of the petrol pump.

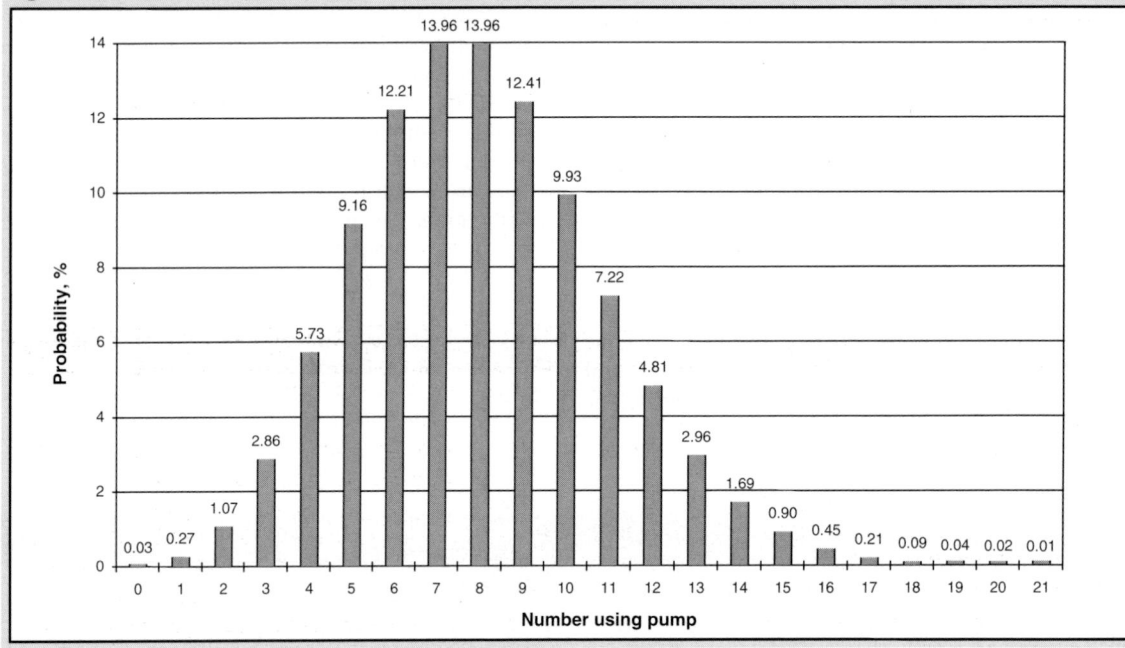

STUDENT t DISTRIBUTION

Characteristics

A t distribution is another continuous probability distribution, similar to the normal distribution in that it is bell-shaped and symmetrical. However, the t distribution is lower at the mean and higher in the tails than the normal distribution. The t distribution was developed by William Gossett of the Guinness Brewery in Dublin, Ireland, in the early 1900s. He referred to it as the student's t distribution because Guinness would not let him use his own name for the discovery.

Degrees of freedom

There is a different t distribution for each possible degree of freedom. Consider the following equation containing five variables:

$$\frac{A + B + C + D + E = 13.}{5}$$

If the four variables A, B, C, and D are given the values 14, 16, 12 and 18, then the fifth variable E is automatically fixed at a value of 5 in order to maintain the validity of the equation. Thus, in general terms for a sample size of n units, the number of degrees of freedom is $(n-1)$.

Using a *t* distribution

A t distribution is used when the sample size n is less than 30 and the population standard deviation is unknown. There is a different t distribution for each sample size. As the sample size increases, the t distribution approaches the normal distribution. When n is greater than 30, the normal distribution can be used. In this case, the sample standard deviation s approaches the population standard deviation σ.

BETA DISTRIBUTION

Definition

A beta distribution is commonly used to describe the inherent variability between various samples, such as the time certain groups take to perform a specific activity, for example, students completing an exam, the time sample groups watch television or the time people sleep. The distribution has the properties of being entirely contained within finite limits and it can be symmetrical or skewed to the right or the left according to the nature of the activity.

Network diagrams

The beta distribution is used in PERT project management network diagrams, where three time estimates are considered and a mean value is calculated. For example, if b is a pessimistic time, a is an optimistic time and m is the most likely time, then the mean time t for an activity is given by:

$$t = \frac{a + 4m + b}{6}$$

The variance is given by the relationship:

$$\sigma^2 = \left[\frac{(b-a)}{6}\right]^2 = \frac{(b-a)^2}{36}.$$

The standard deviation for the activity is the square root of the variance:

$$\sigma = \sqrt{\sigma^2} = \left[\frac{(b-a)}{6}\right].$$

This is used in Chapter 18, *Project Management*.

SUMMARY OF KEY ELEMENTS

- Discrete data is distinct information, usually obtained from counting. This is in contrast to continuous data that progresses from one class to another.
- Inferential statistics is the analysis of sample data for the purpose of describing the characteristics of the population from which that sample is taken.
- A random sample is where each sample item has an equal chance of being selected. The selection of one item from the sample has no impact on the chance that any other item will be chosen.
- A frequency distribution is a display that shows the number of observations that fall into each set of mutually exclusive classes. The more frequently data occurs, then the higher the probability that it will be repeated in the future.
- Probability means the chance that something will or will not happen. Probability may be subjective, based on the frequency of past events, or be estimated by the application of certain probability rules.

- Most data is clustered around a central point. This central point is often used to describe the data, or the population, and is used as a reference. The mean, median, midrange, mode and geometric mean are central tendency measures.
- Dispersion is a measure of the spread of data. Data that lies close to the central point has a low dispersion and is more reliable for analysis, whereas data that lies far from the central point is more dispersed and is less reliable.
- An exponential distribution is where a dependent variable changes according to the power, or exponent, of an independent value. Population expansion, the growth of a forest, or the spread of disease often follow an exponential distribution.
- A normal distribution is symmetrical and bell-shaped. No matter what the value of the mean, or the standard deviation, the area under the curve is 1.00. Approximately 68 per cent of all values lie within ± 1 standard deviations from the mean, 95.5 per cent within ± 2 standard deviations, and

99.7 per cent within ±3 standard deviations from the mean.

■ A binomial distribution is a discrete probability distribution with only two possible outcomes for each trial, such as success or failure, present or absent, win or lose, on time or late, good or bad and open or closed.

■ The Poisson distribution is a discrete distribution used to describe waiting lines, such as the number of patients arriving at a doctor's surgery, the arrival of vehicles at a toll booth or the number of customers arriving at a cash register.

■ A t distribution is another continuous probability distribution, similar to the normal distribution in that it is bell-shaped and symmetrical. There is a different t distribution for each possible number of degrees of freedom.

■ A beta distribution, used in PERT network diagrams, describes inherent variability between various samples, such as the time to perform a specific activity. It has the properties of being entirely contained within finite limits and can be symmetrical or skewed to the right or the left according to the nature of the activity.

REVIEW AND DISCUSSION QUESTIONS

1 **Distributions.** What type of probability distributions might apply to the following situations:
   (a) Delivery vehicles waiting to unload at a hypermarket on a Monday morning?
   (b) A passenger driving to the airport trying to get the 12:00 flight from Los Angeles to London?
   (c) The lengths of 50 000 screws in a lot with a nominal length of 5 cm?
   (d) The test to see if a watch works?
   (e) The estimated chance that a construction project will be completed on time when there are four activity paths leading to the completion?
   (f) Stock-market prices as they are currently quoted on the New York Stock Exchange?
   (g) Stock market prices as they are presented on dividend investment statements?

2 **Probability.** What type of probability might be used in the following situations:
   (a) Whether a client will sign a contract for the purchase of a line of clothing.
   (b) That an aircraft engine may, at the same time, lose an impeller blade and break away from its wing mounting. The two events are unrelated.
   (c) The rolling of two fair dice such that 12 comes up the first time.

   (d) An insurance company's estimation of the life expectancy of men in the United Kingdom
   Justify your reasoning.

3 **Life and death.** Even as the European Union (EU) gets ready to enlarge by taking in new member states, the existing members are slowly shrinking. Eurostat, the EU's statistical branch, predicts that the bloc's share of the global population could drop to just 3 per cent in the year 2050, compared with 7 per cent today and 12 per cent back in the 1950s. As women have fewer children or put off motherhood, fertility rates in the EU are at an all-time low of 1.45 children per woman. Eurostat also says that women are living longer than ever before, with the current life expectancy at 87 years.[4]
   (a) This information is based on what type of probabilities?
   (b) The life expectancy of 87 years is what type of statistical term? How would this statement apply to a sample of 5000 women? What type of distribution might it represent?
   (c) What impact does this information have globally on the operations and supply chain?

4 **Percentiles.** Statistical analysis indicates that US high-school students are in a lower percentile on maths scores than some European and Asian Countries.
   (a) In simple words this means what?
   (b) Upon what type of statistical analysis is this based?
   (c) What might be the impact of this fact on future international business?

EXERCISE PROBLEM: CHILDREN

Situation

Derek and Christine are newly married, they come from big families and they themselves would like to have seven children. Based on their family history, the probability of having a boy is 50 per cent and there is no incidence of twins in the history.

Required

1 Develop a probability distribution histogram for all the possibilities of having a boy.
2 What is the probability they will have all boys?
3 What is the probability they will have all girls?

4 What is the probability they will have four or more boys?
5 What is the probability they will have three or fewer girls?
6 What is the probability of having two or three boys?

Assume that the probability of having a boy is now 52 per cent. (more males die at a younger age).

7 Develop a probability distribution histogram for all the possibilities of having a boy or a girl under this new situation.
8 What is the probability they will have all boys?
9 What is the probability they will have all girls?
10 What is the probability they will have four or more boys?
11 What is the probability they will have two or fewer girls?
12 What is the probability of having two or three boys?

EXERCISE PROBLEM: COLA

Situation

A food manufacturing company has a bottling process for making its own recipe of Cola. The Cola is made in large mixing vessels and then sent to the filling area where one litre polyethylene terephthalate (PET) bottles are filled. The bottling line moves very rapidly and sometimes a bottle, after filling, is ejected from the moving line and splits open on impact. Past data indicates that 0.25 per cent of the bottles are ejected from the line. This type of operating problem follows a Poisson Distribution.

Required

1   For 1500 filled bottles, develop a probability histogram for zero to 20 bottles falling from the line.

2   What is the probability that in 1500 filled bottles none are ejected from the line?
3   What is the probability that in 1500 filled bottles five are ejected from the line?
4   What is the probability that in 1500 filled bottles at least six are ejected from the line?
5   What is the probability that in 1500 filled bottles fewer than four bottles are ejected from the line?

EXERCISE PROBLEM: DELIVERY VEHICLES

Situation

A food distribution company has a fleet of 1500 trucks that it uses for delivering products from its distribution centre to retail outlets. Based on records, the trucks travel on average 120 000 km per year with a standard deviation of 25 000 km. The distance travelled by the trucks approximates a normal distribution.

Required

1   Make an estimation of what proportion of trucks can be expected to travel between 75 000 and 130 000 km per year?

2   What is the probability that a randomly selected truck travels less than 60 000 km per year?
3   What percentage of trucks can be expected to travel more than 145 000 km per year?
4   How many of the trucks in the fleet are estimated to travel between 40 000 and 90 000 km per year?
5   How many miles will be travelled by at least 90 per cent of the trucks?

EXERCISE PROBLEM: DIPLOMA

Situation

E M LYON, a business school in Ecully, France, has a double diploma programme for its student participants. In this programme, participants are able to spend a year studying at universities such as Bocconi, Italy, Lancaster, England, and Texas and Connecticut in the USA.
The competition for this programme is high. Candidates are selected on their language ability, motivation and GMAT score. Past data indicates that 60 per cent of the candidates are accepted for this programme. Acceptance or rejection follows a Bernoulli process.

Required

1   Develop a table showing all the possible exact probabilities of acceptance if 15 candidates apply for this programme.

2   Develop a table showing all the possible cumulative probabilities of acceptance if 15 candidates apply for this programme.
3   Illustrate, on a histogram, all the possible exact probabilities of acceptance if 15 candidates apply for this programme.
4   If 15 candidates apply, what is the probability that exactly five candidates will be accepted?
5   If 15 candidates apply, what is the probability that exactly ten candidates will be accepted?
6   If 15 candidates apply, what is the probability that at least ten candidates will be accepted?
7   If 15 candidates apply, what is the probability that fewer than eight candidates will be accepted?

EXERCISE PROBLEM: SALARIES

Situation

The database shown in Table 20.6 represents the starting annual salary in 1996, converted into pounds sterling, for a sample of graduate engineers in the 15 European countries. The industries surveyed included automobiles, chemicals, refining, food, pharmaceuticals and textiles.

Table 20.6 Database of salaries (converted to £)

17378	15098	14582	18511	16421	14178	21752	15690	15515	14183
12850	20375	16506	16863	18797	16519	15002	16694	19112	14864
16700	17725	15829	17522	18052	13947	18612	17377	16561	16155
16900	13831	16604	15876	19862	16933	18016	17066	15090	16190
15817	12185	17568	16929	15228	15269	14526	14898	17489	14555
17393	16968	16793	15265	15284	15589	12326	13790	20080	16963
16964	16466	15387	15457	18375	13640	13443	16576	18290	17662
13978	13008	12901	14861	17227	17982	11641	14954	14886	13600
18599	15528	17426	15185	15414	13388	14325	16979	14487	17602
13376	14239	14632	18949	16362	17041	14974	17205	16228	14964
16442	12987	10783	13155	15918	17949	13698	14146	17892	16110
12171	18151	16092	17394	16049	15022	15805	18141	12421	12371
14757	17783	13778	19943	15734	16651	18990	19087	17822	18685
17536	13700	17919	14929	12031	14303	14006	17221	17509	15819
13077	14853	16925	14334	15935	12786	13288	14379	16290	12057
17439	15930	15608	15834	18745	21036	14621	14043	12527	16624
16827	12946	17451	16647	15856	16156	13773	15736	17010	16352
20101	13626	14435	18207	14793	14453	17717	17166	16782	17134
12123	17607	16551	14637	14727	17063	14706	15794	15383	15526
17307	15815	15512	14621	15462	17516	18667	13330	18308	12671
15038	15951	17557	16174	20592	14486	17294	13656	15202	15739
13211	15824	16539	16820	17120	12816	12264	15594	15003	17325
14233	13808	16997	17684	16902	13525	17035	18006	18205	15920
19891	14189	14664	18072	16505	14296	16391	18387	19572	18451
14331	13761	14600	15996	15282	15381	12930	17810	12596	20745
17125	12606	17839	12456	17824	18311	18442	14744	14530	19346
14526	16942	17601	19412	16688	18244	15991	17451	16534	17259
12573	13917	19495	17472	11697	15138	18562	13378	16071	15194
13812	14359	18414	13264	14584	15806	14411	14648	14187	14995
15457	17406	18754	15223	17695	19458	16921	12721	14044	14117
17326	17143	13237	17697	18318	17298	18098	16206	15636	15911
14848	16776	14450	15192	16137	11160	14467	17869	18005	19519
11022	17011	18875	13573	17285	14757	15521	15336	16741	17387
18259	14819	14488	15573	19217	13734	19785	14251	15881	19300
13567	16167	13964	15575	15929	15772	13627	13858	20741	13541
16235	14064	14292	16560	18382	17725	16427	15924	16737	13421
16698	13679	16916	19044	17537	14557	13190	15628	18540	14811
16530	12713	15808	15938	17919	14688	18327	15199	18015	17098
14866	14872	15272	15927	15442	11884	15760	15168	13721	14898
19651	12712	14462	16036	14602	17453	16217	11855	15982	16664
19978	16693	19092	17663	17234	18808	17794	18656	16242	14761
15666	17568	17593	16482	15981	17035	20698	14085	17676	15650
12095	18646	16573	16486	15130	15589	13386	19688	15930	18540
16284	13995	16189	11254	16322	13579	15934	16525	14812	16184
14088	13832	15920	13400	16626	16311	17983	14632	15773	13146
15558	15417	15127	15345	11965	15601	16083	15198	16849	14852
15748	16865	15857	17023	14878	19186	17833	15672	17988	16518
13750	16941	20248	16109	15055	18084	15827	14440	13751	14541
18262	15256	16941	17175	19531	12337	16692	13736	10977	13967
16673	16713	15861	14783	15500	15261	16971	16245	17567	14822
19377	16107	15610	16302	11794	14824	16235	19412	15410	17147
11428	14757	14000	17699	15967	13552	17497	12503	15593	17582
14176	13313	18026	15567	17032	16093	14862	18484	16279	17298
17323	14916	16892	18173	16846	20591	14687	18287	13434	18798

12566	15309	11842	16959	17668	13431	17878	15877	14045	14118
15390	16447	13304	15445	16765	17105	15536	18371	16491	20888
16625	18418	16195	14813	19321	14703	13543	13951	18185	15261
14786	15472	16500	17157	15574	17650	12008	13939	19409	16955
13419	17107	16735	15535	16050	14491	13816	14216	15927	16426
16298	12905	18213	16726	15852	17469	15352	17868	17341	18350
17119	13506	17406	15312	15209	17365	16567	15346	16071	17225
17383	15912	14563	17297	15544	19664	13838	17259	15148	17871
11415	16666	16743	15772	16466	14798	14314	17831	13762	17537
18689	16713	15168	14731	16090	17765	18144	16074	13869	15055
14805	14626	18189	16816	14287	13038	16559	14330	17985	17903
15349	16310	14321	17869	17372	17414	14760	11838	16212	16269
13891	14531	13633	15458	14934	14873	17988	16102	15496	17550
19082	15349	15501	17138	15423	14976	13986	17742	15906	16310
15987	15966	16674	13734	16868	13550	15560	15246	19605	14155
13608	15714	16634	14598	14934	17892	15969	16785	13650	18607
14379	15484	16701	18155	18686	17745	17627	11728	14814	14983
16051	20523	15752	13281	16700	14384	16135	13863	16211	15252
13831	14922	15089	16971	16397	13768	13677	14877	15907	14713
15749	19650	13371	20286	18051	16475	10188	17946	14627	18111
15440	15020	12680	18002	14296	14667	13480	12989	13608	16146
16545	13913	15526	15887	16281	16056	13193	18778	14277	11524
18088	13696	18608	12157	12205	18152	14784	16607	15642	18632
12759	16809	18109	15574	13310	15589	15745	14169	13385	15749
15702	16103	17276	17421	13332	12480	16399	11428	16541	16257
13428	14836	16893	15251	15883	15927	17725	14594	16346	14915
14429	18154	15146	15149	16062	15865	16767	17720	14495	14803
14777	12531	14251	17194	15526	17413	17012	16963	16165	16730
16108	16080	20321	13993	16520	18199	18042	12832	14926	18700
14837	16550	16024	15303	17451	17269	16219	14422	15251	14589
13328	13365	13345	15618	17894	14719	16544	14465	13671	16035
18343	15393	13682	17785	19695	14129	17951	16929	13871	15679
19881	16693	18775	15326	12469	16926	15254	15211	17011	14895
16658	13300	14958	15781	11046	16499	17373	17670	15168	16128
15168	15731	15959	15997	12520	15493	16110	13415	14441	14713
16524	15755	16691	16340	17901	18352	14918	15580	16659	12912
18844	17191	17252	15934	15436	18078	21296	16818	19435	12735
17329	15215	18030	18653	19524	17667	14299	16332	17479	19707
21393	21629	17630	17534	15227	15440	17388	14971	13072	13216
12968	15684	13496	13226	14042	14018	14390	18191	17624	16463
18331	13528	13881	14308	17421	14291	18930	15567	18352	14996
18780	16054	14679	13781	14745	15658	17795	16760	15231	14401
17886	17110	17245	14612	18655	15123	13960	15000	17572	14907
14292	16101	17825	12437	18047	17387	19313	15260	12375	14289
19590	15085	15110	14782	17153	16917	17184	13672	16274	16351
15396	11730	15651	14736	12765	14514	17175	16874	17765	15866

Required

1 Illustrate that a normal distribution is a reasonable representation of this salary data. Use a bar width of £1000 starting at £10 000.

2 For this data determine:
   (a) the maximum value;
   (b) the minimum value;
   (c) the mean;
   (d) the median;
   (e) the standard deviation.

3 Based on the assumption that the distribution follows a normal distribution, what proportion of engineers started with a salary of more than £20 000 per year?

4 Based on the assumption that the distribution follows a normal distribution, what proportion of engineers started with a salary of less than £15 000 per year?

5 From the data, how many engineers earned more than £20 000 per year? What is the difference between this and the answer to question 3?

6 From the data, how many engineers earned less than £15 000 per year? What is the difference between this and the answer to question 4?

7 Based on the assumption that the distribution follows a normal distribution, 10 per cent percent of the engineers have an annual starting salary greater than what amount?

8 From the frequency distribution, 10 per cent percent of the engineers have an annual starting salary greater than what amount?

NOTES AND REFERENCES

1. 'Les statisticiens montent en puissance dans les entreprises' (1997) *Le Monde* 22 October. [Translation: Statisticians increase their power in business.]
2. 'Charging ahead: To keep GE's profits rising, Welch pushes quality control plan. "Black Bets" are roaming its plants to weed out foul ups and slash costs. Some gripes ate high levels' (1997) *Wall Street Journal Europe* 14 January.
3. Based on Robert MARK, Chemical Bank (1993) *The Economist* 10 April.
4. EU Notebook (1997) *Wall Street Journal Europe* 26 June.

FURTHER READING

Anderson, D. R., Sweeney, D. J. and Williams, T. A. (1997) *Essentials of Statistics for Business and Economics*, St Paul: West Publishing.

Anderson, D. R., Sweeney, D. J. and Williams, T. A (1996) *Statistics for Business and Economics*, St Paul, MN West Publishing.

Barrow, M. (1996) *Statistics for Economics, Accounting and Business Studies*, London: Longman.

Berenson, M. L., Levine, D. M. and Rindskof, D. (1988) *Applied Statistics: A First Course*, Englewood Cliffs, NJ; London: Prentice Hall.

Black, K. (1997) *Business Statistics: Contemporary decision making* St Paul, MN: West Publishing.

Bowers, D. (1991) *Statistics for Economics and Business* Basingstoke: Macmillan.

Brockett, P. and Levine, A. (1984) *Statistics and Probability and their Applications*, Philadelphia, PA: Saunders College Publishing.

Fergus, D., Jones, C., Lunn, D., Hand, D. and McConway, K. (1995) *Elements of Statistics*, Wokingham; Reading, MA: Addison-Wesley.

Fleming, M. and Nellis J. (1996) *The Essence of Statistics for Business*, New York, London: Prentice Hall.

Harnett, D. L. and Soni, A. K. (1991) *Statistical Methods for Business and Economics*, Reading, MA: Wokingham: Addison Wesley Longman.

Hildebrand, D. and Ott, R. L. (1991) *Statistical Thinking for Managers*, Boston, MA: PWS-Kent.

Ingram, R and Hoyle, K. (1991) *Statistics for Business*, Oxford: Butterworth and Heinemann.

Keller, G. and Warrack, B. (1997) *Statistics for Management and Economics*, Belmont, CA; London: Duxbury.

Kohler, H. (1993) *Statistics for Business and Economics*, Hinsdale, IL: HarperCollins.

Kvanli, A. H., Guynes, C. S. and Pavur, R. J. (1996) *Introduction to Business Statistics: A Computer Integrated Approach*, St Paul, MN: West Publishing.

Larsen, R. Marx, M. and Cooil, B. (1997) *Statistics for Applied Problem Solving and Decision Making*, Pacific Grove, CA; London: Duxbury.

Levin, R., I. and Rubin, D. S. (1994) *Statistics for Management*, London: Prentice Hall International.

Mann, P. S. (1995) *Statistics for Business and Economics*, New York; Chichester: Wiley.

Mendenhall, W., Reinmuth, J., E. and Beaver, R. (1993) *Statistics for Management and Economics*, Belmont, CA: Duxbury.

Minium, E. W. and Clarke, R. B. (1982) *Elements of Statistical Reasoning*, New York; Chichester: Wiley.

Morse, L. (1993) *Statistics for Business and Economics*, New York: HarperCollins.

Neufeld, J. L. (1997) *Learning Business Statistics with Microsoft Excel*, Upper Sadelle River, NJ: Prentice Hall.

Owen, F. and Jones, R. (1994) *Statistics*, London: Pitman.

Sanders, D. H. (1990) *Statistics: A Fresh Approach*, New York; London: McGraw Hill.

Spooner, A. and Lewis, C. (1995) *An Introduction to Statistics for Managers*, Hemel Hempstead; Prentice Hall.

Stockton, J. R. and Clark, C. T. (1980) *Introduction to Business and Economic Statistics*, Cincinatti, OH: South Western.

Summers, G. W., Peters, W. S. and Armstrong, C. P. (1985) *Basic Statistics in Business and Economics*, Belmont, CA: Wadsworth Publishing.

Triola, M. F. (1998) *Elementary Statistics*, Reading, MA; Harlow: Addison-Wesley.

Weiss, N. A. (1996) *Elementary Statistics*, Reading MA; Wokingham: Addison-Wesley.

Weiss, N. A. (1995) *Introductory Statistics*, Reading, MA: Addison-Wesley.

21 | Additional forecasting

Objectives and overview

Chapter 9, *Forecasting Customer Demand*, covers both qualitative and quantitative approaches to estimating, or forecasting the needs of the customer. This is an important function since it triggers all the operating activities in the operations and supply chain. The objective of this chapter is to expand on the quantitative forecasting methods already presented, to give the basis for their development and to describe the reliability and confidence of some of the methods. The first section gives the basis for exponential smoothing and this is followed by more on model accuracy by illustrating the various approaches of error measurement. There is a section detailing simple linear regression, with attention given to accuracy and confidence, and this is followed by a section on multiple regression, particularly as it might apply to a sales situation. Non-linear regression is covered, including exponential and polynomial changes, and finally, the last section describes the use of control charts to monitor forecasts.

MORE ON EXPONENTIAL SMOOTHING

Exponential profile

In Chapter 9, *Forecasting Customer Demand*, exponential smoothing was developed as a quantitative method to estimate future demand. This section elaborates further on the concept, illustrating the impact of the alpha factor on the actual data in the forecast, with as an illustration an alpha factor of 0.4.

The general equation

The general equation for exponential smoothing is

$$F_{n+1} = F_n + \alpha (A_n - F_n).$$

The second period

For the second period, the forecast is given by:

$$F_2 = F_1 + \alpha (A_1 - F_1) = F_1 + \alpha A_1 - \alpha F_1$$
$$= (1 - \alpha) F_1 + \alpha A_1.$$

Thus, for this period, the contribution of A_1 to the forecast is αA_1 and, with an alpha value of 0.4, the forecast data contains 0.4 of actual data from Week 1.

The third period

For the third period, the forecast is given by:

$$F_3 = F_2 + \alpha (A_2 - F_2) = F_2 + \alpha A_2 - \alpha F_2$$
$$= (1 - \alpha) F_2 + \alpha A_2.$$

Substituting the value of F_2 in the equation for F_3 gives:

$$F_3 = (1 - \alpha)[(1 - \alpha)F_1 + \alpha A_1] + \alpha A_2$$
$$= (1 - \alpha)^2 F_1 + \alpha (1 - \alpha)A_1 + \alpha A_2.$$

Thus, here the contribution of A_1 to the forecast is, $\alpha (1 - \alpha) A_1$ and, for an alpha value of 0.4, the forecast data contains 0.24 of the actual data from Week 1 calculated from:

$$\alpha (1 - \alpha) = 0.4 (1 - 0.4) = 0.24.$$

The fourth period

For the fourth period, the forecast is given by:

$$F_4 = F_3 + \alpha (A_3 - F_3) = F_3 + \alpha A_3 - \alpha F_3$$
$$= (1 - \alpha) F_3 + \alpha A_3.$$

Substituting the value of F_3 in the equation for F_4 gives:

$$F_4 = [1 - \alpha] [(1 - \alpha)^2 F_1 + \alpha (1 - \alpha) A_1 + \alpha A_2] + \alpha A_3$$
$$= (1 - \alpha)^3 F_1 + \alpha (1 - \alpha)^2 A_1 + \alpha (1 - \alpha) A_2 + \alpha A_3.$$

Thus, for the fourth period, the contribution of A_1 to the forecast is $\alpha (1 - a)^2 A_1$ and, for an alpha factor of 0.4, the forecast data contains 0.144 of the actual data from Week 1 as calculated from the relationship:

$$\alpha (1 - \alpha)^2 = 0.4 (1 - 0.4) (1 - 0.4) = 0.144.$$

Subsequent periods

The progression is similar for subsequent weeks in the forecast time horizon. For the nth period, the contribution of A_1 to the forecast is, $\alpha (1 - \alpha)^{n-2}$, illustrating that the inclusion of the actual data for the first period, A_1, decreases exponentially with the increase in time.

This exponential decline of the forecast data is illustrated in Figure 21.1, which is supported from the data in Table 21.1. Actual data from Week 2 and Week 3 follow the same exponentially decline as illustrated except that there is a lag of one period in the fraction of data included.[1]

Table 21.1 Forecast data

Week	Fraction of actual data from Week 1 in forecast	Fraction of actual data from Week 2 in forecast	Fraction of actual data from Week 3 in forecast
1			
2	0.4000		
3	0.2400	0.4000	
4	0.1440	0.2400	0.4000
5	0.0864	0.1440	0.2400
6	0.0518	0.0864	0.1440
7	0.0311	0.0518	0.0864
8	0.0187	0.0311	0.0518
9	0.0112	0.0187	0.0311
10	0.0067	0.0112	0.0187
11	0.0040	0.0067	0.0112
12	0.0024	0.0040	0.0067
13	0.0015	0.0024	0.0040
14	0.0009	0.0015	0.0024
15	0.0005	0.0009	0.0015

MORE ON FORECASTING MODEL ACCURACY

Introduction

In Chapter 9, the model accuracy of averaging and exponential smoothing methods was presented using the mean average deviation. This section presents various other methods for testing forecast model accuracy by considering the following situation for a bakery.

Scenario

The Ringe family has a bakery shop for which a forecast model over a two-week period has been developed for determining future sales of croissants. This information is given in Table 21.2. Figure 21.2 gives a graph of this data and, further, Figure 21.3 gives the above actual and forecast data, plus procedures for determining model accuracy, which are explained below.

Table 21.2 Forecast data for future sales of croissants

Day	Forecast sales (000s)	Actual sales (000s)
1	510	480
2	460	520
3	620	690
4	510	410
5	540	480
6	370	350
7	460	390
8	440	410
9	470	590
10	380	425
11	250	300
12	320	350
13	480	440
14	485	465

Forecast error

The period forecast error is the difference between actual and forecast sales, as shown in Column 4 of the table in Figure 21.3. Mathematically the period forecast error is given by the following equation:

$$\text{Forecast error} = (Y - \hat{Y}).$$

The cumulative forecast error is the sum of each period forecast error as shown in Column 5. The forecast error gives the direction of the forecasting model. When the value is positive, then forecast sales are lower than the actual sales. When the forecast error is negative then the forecast is higher than actual sales.

Mean error

The mean error, or bias, is the average of the forecast error for the number of data points considered. The equation is:

$$\text{Mean error} = \frac{\Sigma\,(Y - \hat{Y})}{n}.$$

The calculated data is given in the shaded cell at the bottom of Column 4:

- If the mean value is positive, then overall the forecast is low and the model exhibits a bias by forecasting values lower than actual.
- If the average value is negative, then on average the forecast is high and the model exhibits a bias by forecasting values higher than actual.

If a forecast is required for period 15, and the same forecast model is used, then the mean forecast error should be added (or subtracted) to the forecast made

Figure 21.1 Exponential smoothing: fraction of actual data in forecast.

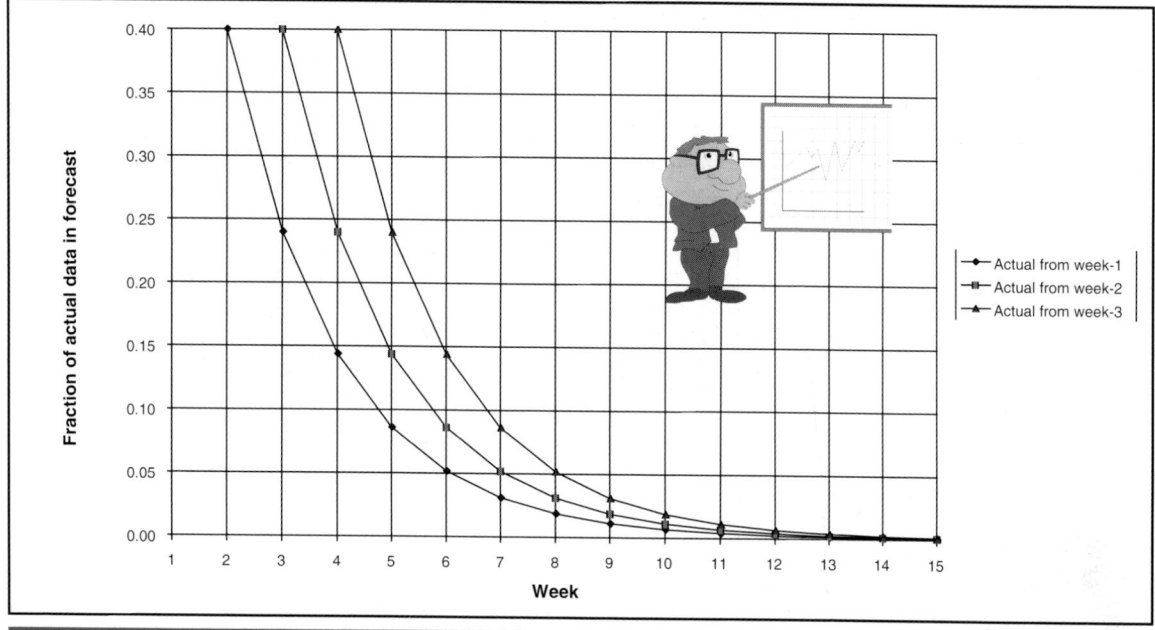

Figure 21.2 Ringe – sale of croissants.

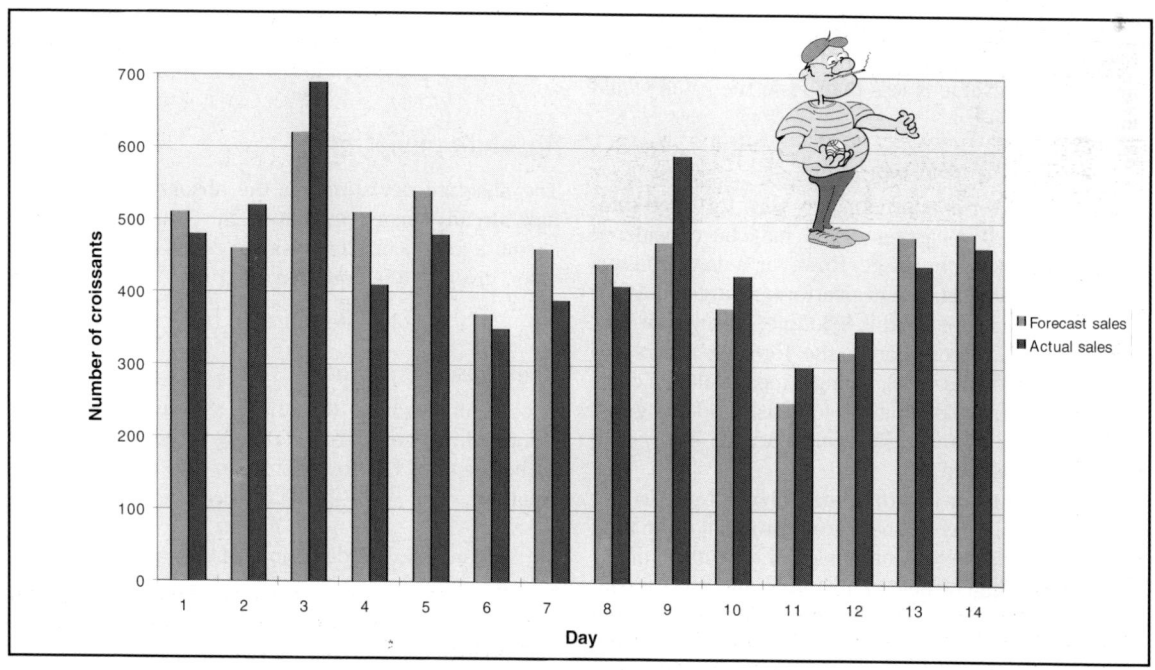

Figure 21.3 Ringe – sale of croissants.

[1]	[2]	[3]	[4]	[5]	[6]	[7]	[8]	[9]	[10]	[11]
Day	Forecast (000s)	Actual (000s)	Forecast Error	Cumulative Forecast Error	Absolute Deviation	Cumulative Absolute Deviation	Mean Absolute Deviation	Tracking Signal (No of MAD)	Squared Error	Mean Percentage Error
[1]	[2]	[3]	[3] - [2]	Cum [4]	Abs [4]	Cum [6]	[7]/[1]	[5]/[8]	[4]²	[4]/[3]
1	510	480	-30	-30	30	30	30,00	-1.00	900	-6.25%
2	460	520	60	30	60	90	45,00	0.67	3 600	11.54%
3	620	690	70	100	70	160	53,33	1.88	4 900	10.14%
4	510	410	-100	0	100	260	65,00	0.00	10 000	-24.39%
5	540	480	-60	-60	60	320	64,00	-0.94	3 600	-12.50%
6	370	350	-20	-80	20	340	56.67	-1.41	400	-5.71%
7	460	390	-70	-150	70	410	58.57	-2.56	4 900	-17.95%
8	440	410	-30	-180	30	440	55.00	-3.27	900	-7.32%
9	470	590	120	-60	120	560	62.22	-0.96	14 400	20.34%
10	380	425	45	-15	45	605	60.50	-0.25	2 025	10.59%
11	250	300	50	35	50	655	59.55	0.59	2 500	16.67%
12	320	350	30	65	30	685	57.08	1.14	900	8.57%
13	480	440	-40	25	40	725	55.77	0.45	1 600	-9.09%
14	485	465	-20	5	20	745	53.21	0.09	400	-4.30%
Total	6 295	6 300	5,00		745				-5.58	51 025	-9.66%
Mean	449.64	450.00	0.36		53.21				-0.40	3 645	-0.69%
sq root										60.37	

for period 15, because on average it means that the forecast is off by this amount. In the example given here the mean value is less than 1, so the value would not change.

The mean error is zero

If the mean error is approximately zero for large samples, then the forecasting model may be considered accurate over the long range. However, a danger in this analysis is that mistakes in overforecasting are offset by underforecasting. In this example, if only the first four periods are considered, the forecast errors are –30, +60, +70, and –100, giving a mean value of zero. It might be concluded that the forecast model is good. In fact, individual forecasts exhibit a wide divergence from the actual data.

If the mean error is zero, then individual under- and overforecasting may not be a great problem if the time periods are relatively short and if the product under consideration can be held in inventory and used in subsequent periods, for example, standard products like compact discs, dry food or clothing. The principal operating problem in this case is that there will be stocking costs, or at the worst, stockouts. However, if the inventory items are perishable food items, such as in this case for croissants, then high forecasts period by period will result in overstocking and thus waste and a higher than desirable cost.

Absolute deviation

The absolute deviation, or the absolute error, which has already been presented in Chapter 9, is the absolute value, or the positive value, of the forecast error, given by the equation:

$$\text{Absolute deviation} = |(Y - \hat{Y})|.$$

Mean absolute deviation

The mean absolute deviation, a common measurement used to compare averaging forecasting models, is the mean of the forecast error and is given by the equation:

$$\text{Mean absolute deviation (MAD)} = \frac{(Y - \hat{Y})}{n}.$$

In the table in Figure 21.3, Column 7 gives the cumulative absolute deviation and Column 8 the mean absolute deviation on a period-by-period basis, with the cumulative data divided by the number of periods under consideration. In this example, the mean absolute deviation for the 14 days is 53.21.

Mean squared error

The mean squared error is given by the general equation:

$$\text{Mean squared error} = \frac{\Sigma\,(Y - \hat{Y})^2}{n}.$$

The forecast error for each period, as given in Column 4, is squared, and this removes the negative sign, as shown in Column 10. The mean of this is the mean squared error.

Standard error

The standard error is the square root of the mean squared error, as given by the equation, and for this example, as shown in the last cell of Column 10, this is 60.37:

$$\text{Standard error} = \sqrt{\frac{\Sigma\,(Y - \hat{Y})^2}{n}}.$$

The standard error is referred to as the consistency of the forecast. It is analogous to the population standard deviation already presented in Chapter 20, *Statistical Concepts*:

Population Standard Deviation, σ_x

$$\sigma_x = \sqrt{\sigma_x^2}$$

$$= \sqrt{\frac{\Sigma\,(X - \mu_x)^2}{N}}.$$

Note, that in a rigorous statistical analysis in samples from a population, the standard error, or called the standard error of the estimate, as discussed in the next section), is given by

$$\text{Standard error} = \sqrt{\frac{\Sigma(Y-\hat{Y})^2}{n-2}}$$

This compares to the sample standard deviation, or

$$s = \sqrt{\frac{\Sigma(x-\bar{x})^2}{(n-1)}}$$

However, when the value of n is large, the difference between using n, or $n-2$ in the standard error equation is small.

Comparing mean average deviation and standard error

If the errors that occur in a forecast can be considered as normally distributed, then the relation between the mean absolute deviation and the standard deviation is:

One standard error (one standard deviation)

$$= \sqrt{\frac{\pi}{2}} \times \text{MAD}.$$

One standard error is equal to approximately 1.2533 of the mean absolute deviation or, conversely, 1 MAD = 0.80 standard deviations.

In the example given here:

■ mean absolute deviation = 53.21;
■ standard error = 60.37.

If the mathematical relationship between mean absolute deviation and standard error is used, the standard error would be 1.25 × 60.37 = 66.69, a difference of about 9 per cent from the calculated value.

Percentage error

The percentage error is the forecast error divided by the actual sales for the corresponding period:

$$\text{Percentage error} = \frac{(Y - \hat{Y})}{Y} \times 100.$$

This data is given for each period in Column 11 of the table in Figure 21.3 and the mean percentage error is calculated for the 14 pieces of data.

Which error method?

Table 21.3 summarizes the errors from this illustration for the four approaches. The standard error, compared to the other methods, puts a greater emphasis on large individual errors since it squares the individual errors. Thus, if one is more concerned about minimizing large errors, the standard error might be used. If all errors have equivalent importance, then the other methods are appropriate.

Table 21.3 The errors in the Ringe example

Method	Value for the example Ringe
Bias	0.36
Standard error (SE)	60.37
Mean absolute deviation (MAD)	53.21
Mean percentage error (MPE)	−0.69

Very often, as already presented in Chapter 9, the mean average deviation is used to test the forecast models, for example in the Averaging Methods. In regression analysis, a form of the standard error is used and this is discussed in the next section.

MORE ON SIMPLE LINEAR REGRESSION

In Chapter 9, *Forecasting Customer Demand*, linear regression was developed for a time-series analysis, including when a seasonal variation exists, and for causal forecasting. The results were developed using the Microsoft Excel regression functions. This section gives the basis for regression calculations and illustrates additional information that can be obtained from the results. It uses as the basis the example of operator absenteeism already presented in Chapter 9.

Least-squares method

In linear regression, the objective is to develop a linear relationship of the general form:

$$\hat{Y} = a + bX,$$

where a is a constant and the intercept on the y axis, b is a constant and the slope of the line, X is the independent variable and $\hat{Y}$ is the predicted value of the dependent variable.

The method of least squares determines the best straight line by minimizing the error between the points estimated from the calculated line and the actual observed points used to draw the line. From the least-squares method the values of a and b are given by:

$$a = \frac{\Sigma X^2 \Sigma Y - \Sigma X \Sigma XY}{n\Sigma X^2 - (\Sigma X)^2}$$

$$b = \frac{n\Sigma XY - \Sigma X \Sigma Y}{n\Sigma X^2 - (\Sigma X)^2}.$$

Alternatively, a and b can be calculated from the relationships below using the linear equation of the line:

$$a = \overline{Y} - b\overline{X}$$

$$b = \frac{\Sigma XY - n\overline{X}\,\overline{Y}}{\Sigma X^2 - n(\overline{X})^2},$$

where $\overline{X}$ is the mean of the X values, and $\overline{Y}$ is the mean of the Y values.

Operator absenteeism

Table 21.4 gives the original data for the operator absenteeism situation and the calculation of some of the various terms given in the above equations.

From this data, the following are the values for the terms in the equations:

$$\Sigma X = 171.00 \qquad \Sigma Y = 383.00$$
$$\Sigma X^2 = 2571.00 \qquad \Sigma Y^2 = 15\,535.00$$
$$\Sigma XY = 6094.00 \qquad n = 12.$$

When these are substituted in the equations, then:

$$b = \frac{\Sigma XY - n\overline{X}\,\overline{Y}}{\Sigma X^2 - n\overline{X}^2} = 4.7393$$

$$a = \overline{Y} - b\overline{X} = -35.6182.$$

Standard error of the estimate

The standard error of the estimate measures the amount of variability, or scatter, around a regression line. The regression equation is established such that the vertical distance between the observed values Y and the predicted values $\hat{Y}$ balance out when all the values above and below the line are considered:

$$\Sigma (Y - \hat{Y}) = 0.$$

The standard error of the estimate, for n data points, is given by:

$$S_{Y/X} = \sqrt{\frac{\Sigma (Y - \hat{Y})^2}{n - 2}},$$

which can be rewritten by using the identity:

$$\Sigma (Y - \hat{Y})^2 = \Sigma Y^2 - a\,(\Sigma Y) - b\,(\Sigma XY),$$

giving:

$$S_{Y/X} = \sqrt{\frac{\Sigma (Y - \hat{Y})^2}{n - 2}} = \sqrt{\frac{\Sigma Y^2 - a(\Sigma Y) - b(\Sigma XY)}{n - 2}}.$$

In the linear regression equation for employees and absenteeism the following values were calculated:

$$\Sigma Y^2 = 15\,535 \qquad \Sigma Y = 383 \qquad \Sigma XY = 6094$$
$$a = -35.6183 \qquad b = 4.7393 \qquad n = 12.$$

Substituting these values into the standard error of the estimate equation gives a value:

$$S_{Y/X} = 5.4361.$$

The standard error of the estimate, written as $S_{Y/X}$ or s_e has the same units as the dependent variable Y and in

Table 21.4 Data on operator absenteeism and some calculated variables

X	15	13	12	11	13	9	12	16	14	20	21	15
Y	45	35	19	17	23	9	13	41	25	59	62	35
X²	225	169	144	121	169	81	144	256	196	400	441	225
Y²	2025	1225	361	289	529	81	169	1681	625	3481	3844	1225
X × Y	675	455	228	187	299	81	156	656	350	1180	1302	525

this case is the number of defects per week. The standard error of the estimate is analogous to the standard deviation in that the standard deviation measures variability around the mean (for example), whereas the standard error of estimate measures variability around the regression line. One difference is that in the standard deviation for a sample $(n - 1)$ is used in the denominator whereas here $(n - 2)$ is used. Two degrees of freedom are lost because two statistics, a and b, are used in the standard-error equation in order to compute the standard error. Like the standard deviation, the closer the value is to zero, the better the linear regression model fits the observed data.

Certainty and confidence limits

Assume that the question is asked, 'What is the 90 per cent confidence limit for a predicted number of defective parts?' The confidence interval is given by the relationship:

$$\hat{Y} \pm zs_e \text{ or } \hat{Y} + ts_e \text{ for small sample sizes.}$$

For the operator absenteeism relationship:

■ The sample size n is 12. Since it is less than 30, t rather than z tables are used.
■ The number of degrees of freedom is 10.
■ $t = 1.8125$.
■ Standard error = 5.4364.
■ $t \times$ standard error = $5.4364 \times 1.8125 = 9.8534$.
■ Upper limit = $49.6892 + 9.8534 = 59.54245$ (say 60).
■ Lower limit = $49.6892 - 9.8534 = 39.8356$ (say 40).

Thus, the response to the question would be that the estimate of defective parts is 50 and there is a 90 per cent confidence that the number of defective parts will be between 60 and 40.

Coefficient of determination

In regression analysis the coefficient of determination r^2 measures the variation in the dependent variable Y that is explained by the fitted simple regression equation. r^2 is calculated from the ratio of the explained variation to the total variation:

$$r^2 = \frac{\text{Explained variation}}{\text{Total variation}}$$

$$= \frac{\text{Sum of squares due to regression}}{\text{Total sum of squares}}$$

$$= \frac{\text{SSR}}{\text{SST}} = \frac{\Sigma \ (\hat{Y} - \bar{Y})^2}{\Sigma \ (Y - \bar{Y})^2},$$

where:

$$\text{Total variation} = \text{Explained variation} + \text{Unexplained variation}.$$

Then the coefficient of determination can also be written:

$$r^2 = \frac{\text{Total variation} - \text{Unexplained variation}}{\text{Total variation}}$$

$$= 1 - \frac{\text{Unexplained variation}}{\text{Total variation}}.$$

or:

$$r^2 = 1 - \frac{\text{Error sum of squares}}{\text{Total variation}}$$

$$= 1 - \frac{\text{SSE}}{\text{SST}} = \frac{1 - \Sigma \ (Y - \hat{Y})^2}{\Sigma \ (Y - \bar{Y})^2}.$$

Using the summation rules, the coefficient of determination can be rewritten as:

$$r^2 = \frac{a \ (\Sigma \dot{Y}) + b \ (\Sigma XY) - \dfrac{(\Sigma Y)^2}{n}}{\Sigma Y^2 - \dfrac{(\Sigma Y)^2}{n}}.$$

The coefficient of determination is always positive. The closer the value of r^2 is to unity, the more the value of Y is explained by the regression model containing the independent variable X. Figure 21.4 illustrates the terms total variation, unexplained variation and explained variation for the employee-absenteeism situation. In the calculation of the total variation for describing product defects in terms of employee absenteeism, the following values were obtained:

■ Explained variation (sum of squares due to regression), SSR = 3015.40.
■ Total variation (error sum of squares), SST = 3310.92.

Substituting these values in the expression for the coefficient of determination gives:

$$r^2 = \frac{3015.40}{3310.92} = 91.07.$$

This can be interpreted by saying that 91.07 per cent of the product defects are explained by the simple linear regression equation based on absenteeism. Thus one can say that there is a strong linear relationship between product defects and absenteeism.

Coefficient of correlation

In regression analysis the coefficient of correlation r explains the relative importance of the association

Figure 21.4 Measure of variation in a regression line.

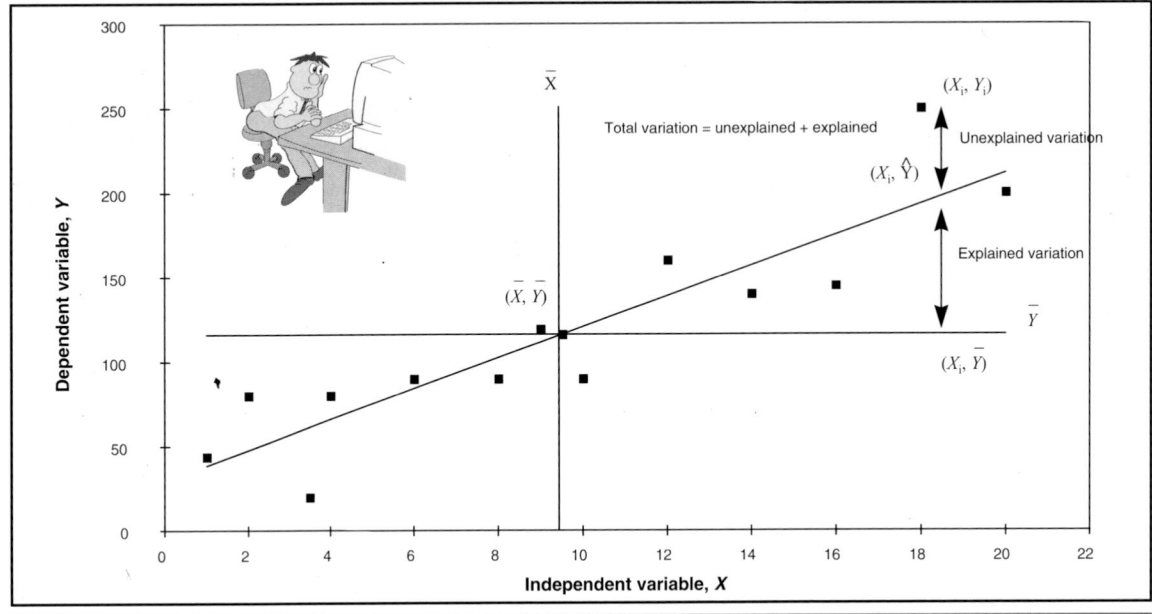

between the independent variable X and the dependent variable Y. The coefficient of correlation can take a value between $+1$ and -1. A value of -1 indicates a perfect negative relationship (Y decreases as X increases). A value of $+1$ indicates a perfect positive relationship (Y increases as X increases). Zero would mean that there is no relationship between X and Y. Thus, when r has a low value, regression analysis as a tool for forecasting is not appropriate.

Microsoft Excel and the regression functions

Figure 21.5 illustrates the regression line and the statistical variables, as obtained from Microsoft Excel. In using the regression function from Excel, a two by five matrix (2 columns, 5 rows) is provided, which gives the various statistical functions in the format shown in Table 21.5.

MULTIPLE REGRESSION

In multiple regression analysis for forecasting there is more than one independent variable in the forecasting model, or regression equation. For example, it may be determined that the sales of a particular product are a function of variables such as the advertising expenditure, the number of sales persons, the number of sales contacts, the number of sales offices, etc.

Two independent variables

If it is believed that sales are a function of advertising expenditures and the size of the sales force, then perhaps a multiple regression equation model could be developed to describe the movement of sales. The regression equation would take the form:

$$\hat{Y} = a + b_1 X_1 + b_2 X_2 ,$$

Table 21.5 Format of functions provided by Excel

b	Slope due to variable X	a	Intercept on Y-axis
se_b	Standard error for slope, b	se_a	Standard error for intercept a
r^2	Coefficient of determination	s_e	Standard error of estimate
F	F-ratio for analysis of variance	df	Degrees of freedom ($n-2$)
SS_{reg}	Sum of squares due to regression (explained variation)	SS_{resid}	Sum of squares of residual (unexplained variation)

Figure 21.5 Operator absenteeism and defective components: summary.

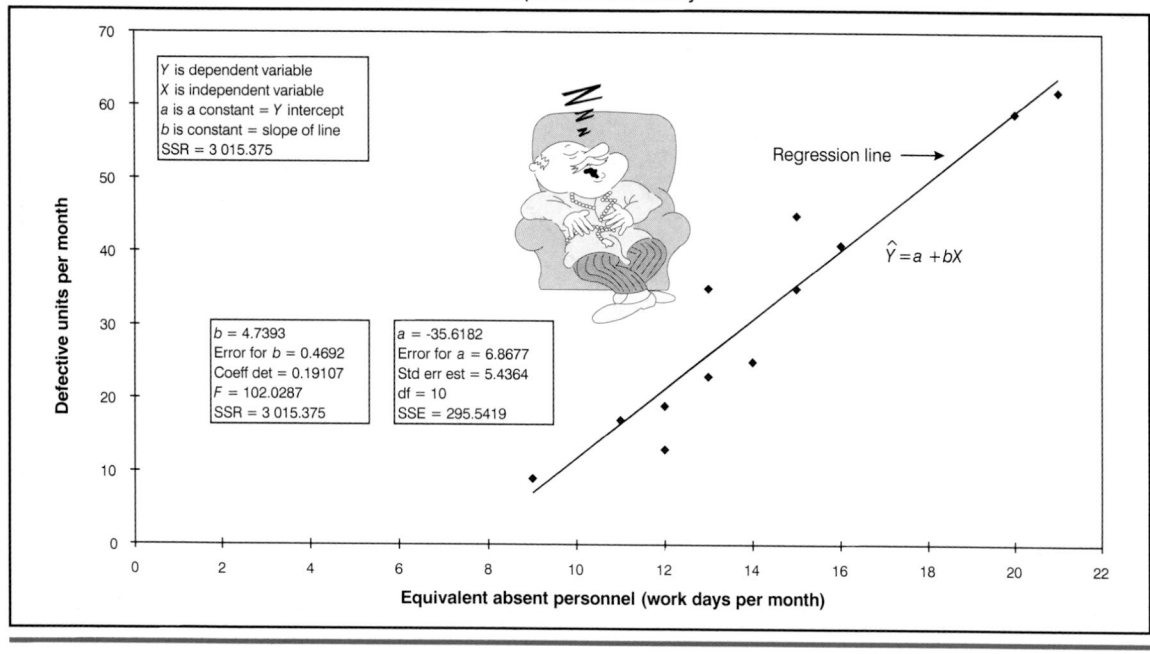

Where a is a constant and the intercept on the Y axis, X_1 and X_2 are the independent variables (number of sales persons and advertising budget, for example), b_1 and b_2 are constants and the slopes of the line corresponding to X_1 and X_2 and $\hat{Y}$ is the forecast value given by the best straight line for the actual data.

With two independent variables the data can be represented graphically on a three-dimensional axis, as illustrated in Figure 21.6.

To calculate the best straight line, the least-squares method can again be used. This locates the plane that minimizes the sum of the squares of the errors or the distance from the actual data points near the plane to the corresponding points on the plane. With the actual data, the following three equations can be used to calculate the values of the constants:

$$\Sigma Y = na + b_1 \Sigma X_1 + b_2 \Sigma X_2$$
$$\Sigma X_1 Y = a\Sigma X_1 + b_1 \Sigma X_1^2 + b_2 \Sigma X_1 X_2$$
$$\Sigma X_2 Y = a\Sigma X_2 + b_1 \Sigma X_1 X_2 + b_2 \Sigma X_2^2.$$

In the first equation, n is the number of data points. These three equations can be solved to determine the values of the intercept a on the y axis and the values of the slopes b_1 and b_2 relative to the x_1 and x_2 axes. The use of multiple regression using two variables is illustrated by the first part of the worked example, *Catalogue Sales*.

Multiple independent variables

The regression model may contain multiple independent variables. In this case, the regression equation would be represented by the form:

$$\hat{Y} = a + b_1 X_1 + b_2 X_2 \ldots b_k X_k,$$

where k would take the value of the number of independent variables being considered. The greater the number of independent variables, the more complex is the model and the more uncertain are the predicted values.

As for simple linear regression, multiple regression functions can be solved using a computer program such as the 'Linear Regression' in Microsoft Excel. In Excel, when the Y data and the X matrix are entered into the regression function, the various statistical data are computed according to Table 21.6.

The use of multiple regression using three variables is illustrated by the second part of the worked example, *Catalogue Sales*.

Standard error of estimate

The standard error of the estimate s_e (also known as the root-mean square error or mse) measures the degree of dispersion around the multiple-regression plane. The value is given by:

Figure 21.6 Multiple regression plane.

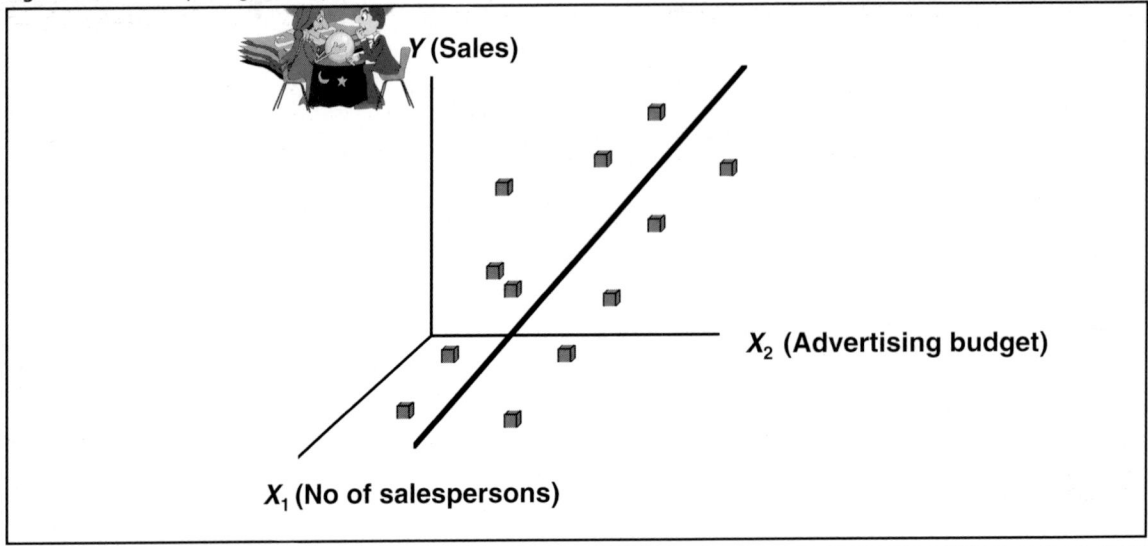

$$s_e = \sqrt{\frac{\Sigma (Y - \hat{Y})^2}{n - k - 1}},$$

Where Y is an actual value of the dependent variable; $\hat{Y}$ is the estimated value of dependent variable predicted from the regression equation, n is the number of data points in the sample and k is the number of independent variables.

The denominator $(n - k - 1)$ is the number of degrees of freedom. For example, in a situation where there are ten data points for simple linear regression:

$n = 10$; $k = 1$; degrees of freedom is $10 - 1 - 1 = 8$.

Where there are three independent variables, then:

$n = 10$; $k = 3$; degrees of freedom is $10 - 3 - 1 = 6$.

Again, the smaller the value of the standard error of the estimate, the better is the fit of the regression equation.

Confidence intervals

The confidence intervals of the predicted value are:

$$\hat{Y} \pm t \times s_e.$$

Coefficient of multiple determination

The coefficient of multiple determination r^2 measures the strength of the relationship among the independent variables, which represents the proportion of the total variation of Y that is 'explained' by the regression plane.

Table 21.6 Table for computing statistical data for multiple regression functions

bk Slope due to variable X_k	b_{k-1} Slope due to variable X_{k-1}	b_2 Slope due to variable X_2	b_1 Slope due to variable X_1	a intercept on Y axis
se_k Standard error for slope b_k	se_{k-1} Standard error for slope b_{k-1}	se_2 Standard error for slope b_2	se_1 Standard error for slope b_1	se_a Standard error for intercept a
r^2 Coefficient of determination	s_e Standard error of estimate			
F-ratio	df Degrees of freedom			
^{ss}reg Sum of squares due to regression (explained variation)	^{ss}resid Sum of squares of residual (unexplained variation)			

WORKED EXAMPLE: CATALOGUE SALES

Situation

The Chelsea company is a distributor of a vast range of consumer products, ranging from televisions and audio visual equipment to kitchen utensils. The company publishes a catalogue of its products, which is a key to its sales. Customer contact is either direct or by telephone. The Chelsea company wants to see if there is any relationship between sales revenues, advertising budget, sales staff and client contact made either direct or by telephone. The historical data in Table 21.7 was available on a monthly basis.

Table 21.7   Historical data for catalogue sales

Sales (US $)	Advertising budget (US $)	Sales persons	Number of sales contacts
72 120	7 200	42	27 500
47 000	4 712	21	18 412
57 000	5 512	28	22 478
51 000	4 985	22	20 554
31 540	3 000	22	15 487
58 750	6 245	32	18 724
61 580	6 352	35	22 845
59 450	5 847	35	23 448
57 450	4 897	28	22 045
26 500	3 000	16	9 998

Required

Develop forecast models for two and three independent variables.

Two independent variables

1   Develop a two-independent-variable multiple regression model for the sales volume as a function of the advertising budget and the number of sales persons.
2   Does the relationship appear strong? Quantify.
3   Assume for a particular month that it is proposed to allocate a budget of US $4000 and to use 30 sales persons. Then, what would be an estimate of the sales for that month?
4   What are the 90 per cent confidence intervals?

Three independent variables

5   Develop a three-independent-variable multiple regression model for the sales volume as a function of the advertising budget, the number of sales persons and the number of sales contacts made.
6   Does the relationship appear strong? Quantify.
7   Assume for a particular month that it is proposed to allocate a budget of US $4000 to use 30 sales persons, with a target to make 21 000 sales contacts. Then, what would be an estimate of the sales for that month?
8   What are the 90 per cent confidence intervals?

Solution

The solution for this problem is given as tables in Figure 21.7. The upper table gives the regression constants for two variables and the lower table the regression constants for three variables. The format of the table is according to the Microsoft Excel regression function.

Two independent variables

1   The regression equation is:

$$\hat{Y} = 1198.09 + 8.76 \times \text{Ad. budget} + 204.02 \times \text{No. sales persons.}$$

2   A test for the strength of the relationship is the coefficient of multiple regression. In this case for two independent variables, the coefficient of multiple determination is 0.9413. This means that 94.13 per cent of sales are explained by the advertising budget and the number of sales persons.

3   Inserting the corresponding values in the regression equation gives an estimate of sales of $42 339.

4   Here for two independent variables for a 90 per cent confidence level:
   ■   Sample size is 10.
   ■   Standard error is 3825.67.
   ■   Upper limit is 49 587.
   ■   Number of degrees of freedom is 7.
   ■ t is 1.8946.
   ■   Lower limit is 35 091.

This can be translated as saying that the estimated sales with an advertising budget of $4000 and 30 sales persons is 42 339 and one is 90 per cent certain that sales will lie between $49 587 and $35 091.

Three independent variables

5   The regression equation is:

$$\hat{Y} = -3909.69 + 6.53 \times \text{Ad. budget} - 99.88 \times \text{No. sales persons} + 1.25 \times \text{No. sales contact.}$$

6   A test for the strength of the relationship is the coefficient of multiple regression. In this case, for three independent variables, the coefficient of multiple determination is 0.9824. This means that 98.24 per cent of sales are explained by the advertising budget, the number of sales persons and the number of sales contacts.

7   Inserting the corresponding values in the regression equation gives an estimate of sales of $45 442.

8   Here for three independent variables for a 90 per cent confidence:
   ■   Sample size is 10.
   ■   Standard error is 2264.48.
   ■   Upper limit is 49 843.
   ■   Number of degrees of freedom is 6.
   ■ t is 1.9432.
   ■   Lower limit is 41 042.

This can be translated as saying that the estimated sales with an advertising budget of $4000, 30 sales persons and 21 000 sales contacts is $45 442 and one is 90 per cent certain that sales will lie between $49 843 and $41 042.

Figure 21.7 Multiple regression – catalogue sales (Microsoft Excel format).

Two independent variables

Sales	Advertising Budget (X1)	Sales Persons (X2)		Sales persons	Advertising Budget	Y intercept A
72,120	7,200	42		204.02206	8.7551481	1198.0886
47,000	4,712	21		369.053843	2.14710352	4966.22781
57,000	5,512	28		0.9413447	3825.6676	#N/A
51,000	4,985	22		56.1706958	7	#N/A
31,540	3,000	22		1644198562	102450128	#N/A
58,750	6,245	32		#N/A	#N/A	#N/A
61,580	6,352	35		#N/A	#N/A	#N/A
59,450	5,847	35		#N/A	#N/A	#N/A
57,450	4,897	28		#N/A	#N/A	#N/A
26,500	3,000	16		#N/A	#N/A	#N/A

			t	t*std err	Upper	Lower
42.339	4.000	30	1.8946	7.248.11	49.587	35.091

Three independent variables

Sales	Advertising Budget (X1)	Sales Persons (X2)	Sales Contacts (X3)	Sales contacts	Sales persons	Advertising Budget	Y intercept A
72,120	7,200	42	27,500	1.2494287	-99.87572	6.52760037	-3909.68902
47,000	4,712	21	18,412	0.33417288	233.0806	1.40362324	3241.52987
57,000	5,512	28	22,478	0.98238505	2264.47648	#N/A	#N/A
51,000	4,985	22	20,554	111.539945	6	#N/A	#N/A
31,540	3,000	22	15,487	1715881568	30767122.3	#N/A	#N/A
58,750	6,245	32	18,724	#N/A	#N/A	#N/A	#N/A
61,580	6,352	35	22,845	#N/A	#N/A	#N/A	#N/A
59,450	5,847	35	23,448	#N/A	#N/A	#N/A	#N/A
57,450	4,897	28	22,045	#N/A	#N/A	#N/A	#N/A
26,500	3,000	16	9,998	#N/A	#N/A	#N/A	#N/A

				t	t*std err	Upper	Lower
45.442	4.000	30	21.000	1.9432	4.400.33	49.843	41.042

Case 1   Y = 1198,089+8,76*(Ad budget)+204,02*(sales persons)

Case 2   Y = -3909,69+6,53*(Ad budget)-99,88*(sales persons)+1,25*(sales contacts)

NON-LINEAR REGRESSION

Linear and multiple forecasting regression models assume that the forecast changes linearly, or at a constant amount according to the slope, with the change in the dependent variable. There are many situations when this is not the case, and the increase is a non-linear, or curvilinear function of the independent variable, for example:

- the rapid increase in demand for electronic calculators in the 1980s after they were first introduced by Texas Instruments;
- the rapid increase in demand for personal computers in the late 1980s and early 1990s;
- the sharp decline in the demand for 33 rpm records in the early 1990s after the introduction of the compact disc.

The curvilinear function can be a complex relationship between the dependent and the independent variables. Some basic forms include an exponential function and a polynomial, where the independent variable takes on integer values or non-integer values.

Exponential change

An exponential change moves according the general function, $Y = ab^x$ (see section Learning curves in Chapter 8, *Human Resources in the system design*). The following provides an illustration.

Sales increasing

A curvilinear function may be exponential, of a similar form to a learning curve (see section Learning Curves in Chapter 8 *Human Resources in the system design*). Figure 21.8 shows an exponential relationship for an increase in sales of over a twelve-month period. This is a progression that might explain the sale of computers or electronic calculators mentioned above.

Sales decreasing

Alternatively, Figure 21.9 illustrates a declining trend, such as might have been experienced in the sale of 33 rpm records, hand lawnmowers, manual-shift automobiles in the USA and other types of products that have been replaced by products using different technologies.

If analysis of data indicates that the trend is exponential, then forecast models can be developed on this

Table 21.8 Data for increasing and decreasing sales

(Sales)	Increasing sales		Decreasing sales	
	Sales ($000)	Log$_{10}$ (Sales)	Sales ($000)	Log$_{10}$
January	50.00	1.70	582.08	2.76
February	62.50	1.80	465.66	2.67
March	78.13	1.89	372.53	2.57
April	97.66	1.99	298.02	2.47
May	122.07	2.09	238.42	2.38
June	152.59	2.18	190.73	2.28
July	190.73	2.28	152.59	2.18
August	238.42	2.38	122.07	2.09
September	298.02	2.47	97.66	1.99
October	372.53	2.57	78.13	1.89
November	465.66	2.67	62.50	1.80
December	582.08	2.76	50.00	1.70

Polynomial

A polynomial function with integer values of X takes on the general form:

$$Y = a + bX + cX^2,$$

where a, b and c are constants and X is the dependent variable, the time in a time series analysis or another variable in the case of causal analysis.

Curvilinear with a non-integer value of X

In this case, the general form of the forecasting equation is

$$Y = aX^b.$$

Again, the values of a and b are constants, but in this relationship, X is a non-integer value.

basis. A logarithmic function applied to exponential functions gives a straight line, as illustrated on the two curves. The data for these two curves is given in Table 21.8.

For example in the case where sales are increasing, then the logarithmic value for sales in February is given by $\log_{10}(62.50) = 1.80$. Thus, if actual sales are monitored, and the model indicates that the trend is exponential, then a logarithmic function can be developed. This function extrapolated can then be used to estimate future sales.

Comparison of forecast models

The following compares forecast models that might be obtained from exponential changes, polynomial changes and curvilinear changes, with non-integer values of x. These results are then compared with the linear regression approach using the coefficient of determination as the basis for comparison.

Table 21.9 gives the collected data on the relationship between house prices and house-plot surface area in a certain community.

Figure 21.8 Curvilinear increase of sales.

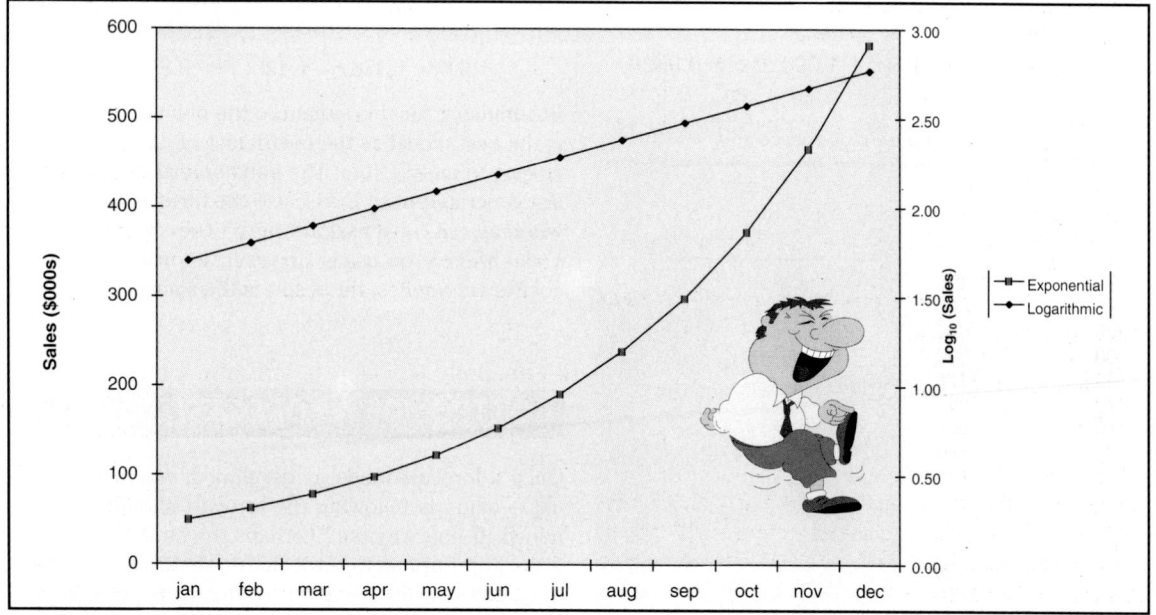

Figure 21.9 Curvilinear decrease in sales.

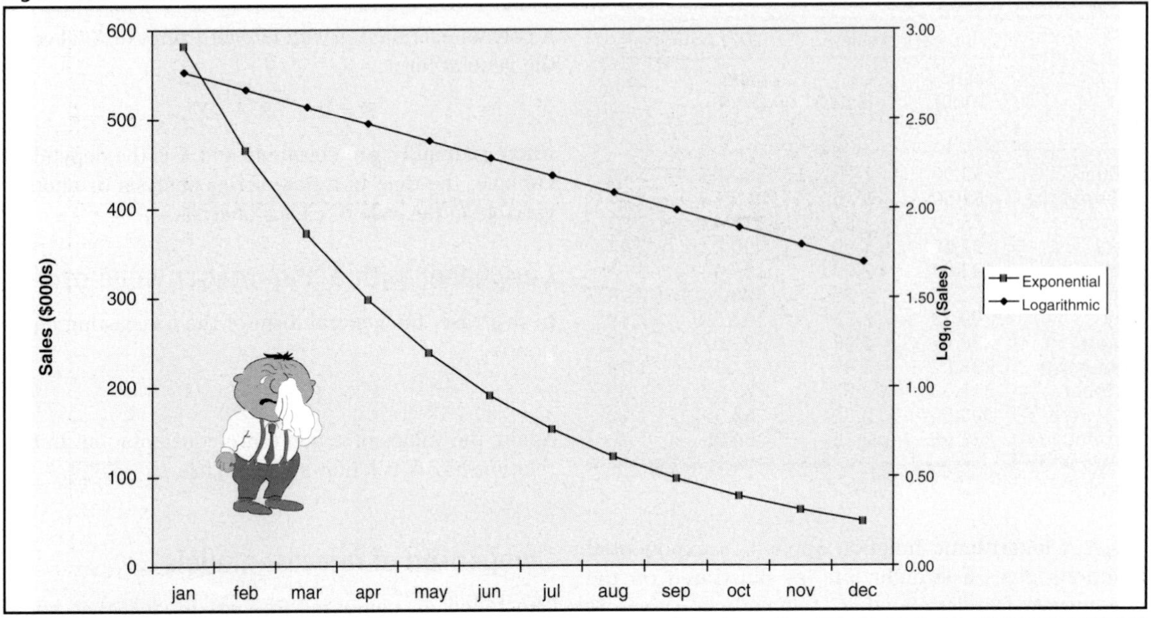

Exponential

The exponential form is given in Figure 21.10. The model describing this movement and the corresponding coefficient of determination are:

$$Y = 125.32e^{0.009x}; \qquad r^2 = 0.9202.$$

Polynomial

The polynomial form is given in Figure 21.11. The model describing this movement and the corresponding coefficient of determination are:

$$Y = 0.0005x^2 - 1.2499x + 1.094.2; \quad r^2 = 0.9628.$$

Table 21.9 Price and house-plot surface area

Surface area (sq. feet)	Price ($000)
900	250
1550	400
1600	590
2200	900
3200	2100
1820	750
1710	684
1000	680
950	175
3100	2800
2300	1100
4000	5200
3750	3550
3500	3750

Curvilinear with a non-integer value of X

The form with a non-integer value of X is given in Figure 21.12. The model describing this movement and the corresponding coefficient of determination are:

$$Y = 0.0005X^{1.9099}; \quad r^2 = 0.8899.$$

Linear regression

As a comparison, the linear regression form is given in Figure 21.13. The model describing this movement and the corresponding coefficient of determination are:

$$Y = 1.376x - 1.466; \quad r^2 = 0.8715.$$

In summary, for this situation, the polynomial function is the best model as the coefficient of determination is closest to unity. (Note: The polynominal graphs, which are generated from Excel, use the form $Y = aX^2 + bX + c$ whereas in discussion here the general form $Y = a + bX + cX^2$ is used. However, knowing where the coefficient applies, the result is the same.)

CONTROL OF A FORECAST

Once a forecast model is developed, whether the actual demand is following the forecast should be determined. If not, why not? Perhaps the model being used is not appropriate. Control charts, similar to those used in quality control, using a tracking signal, can be used to monitor the forecast.

Figure 21.10 House prices – exponential curve.

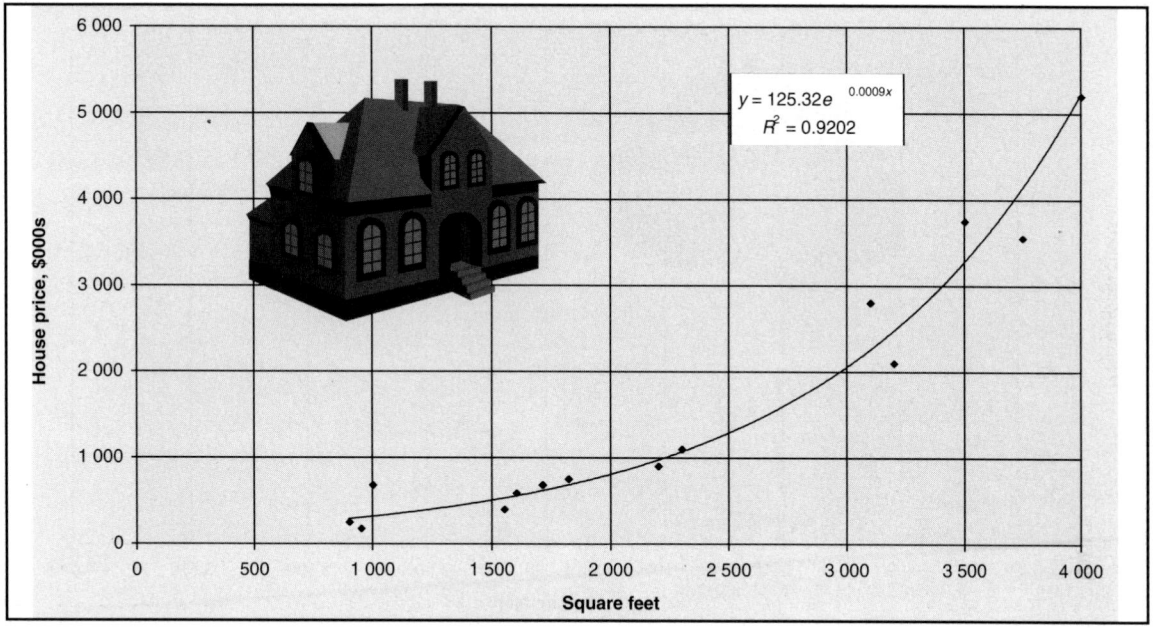

$$y = 125.32e^{0.0009x}$$
$$R^2 = 0.9202$$

Figure 21.11 House prices – polynomial.

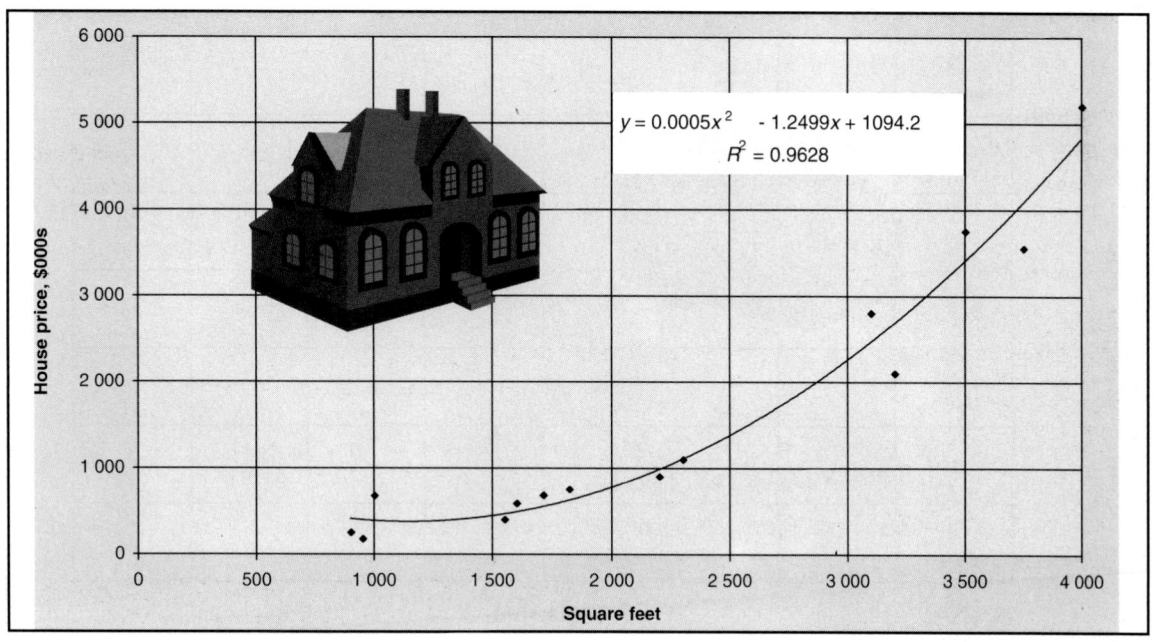

$$y = 0.0005x^2 - 1.2499x + 1094.2$$
$$R^2 = 0.9628$$

Figure 21.12   House prices – non-integer.

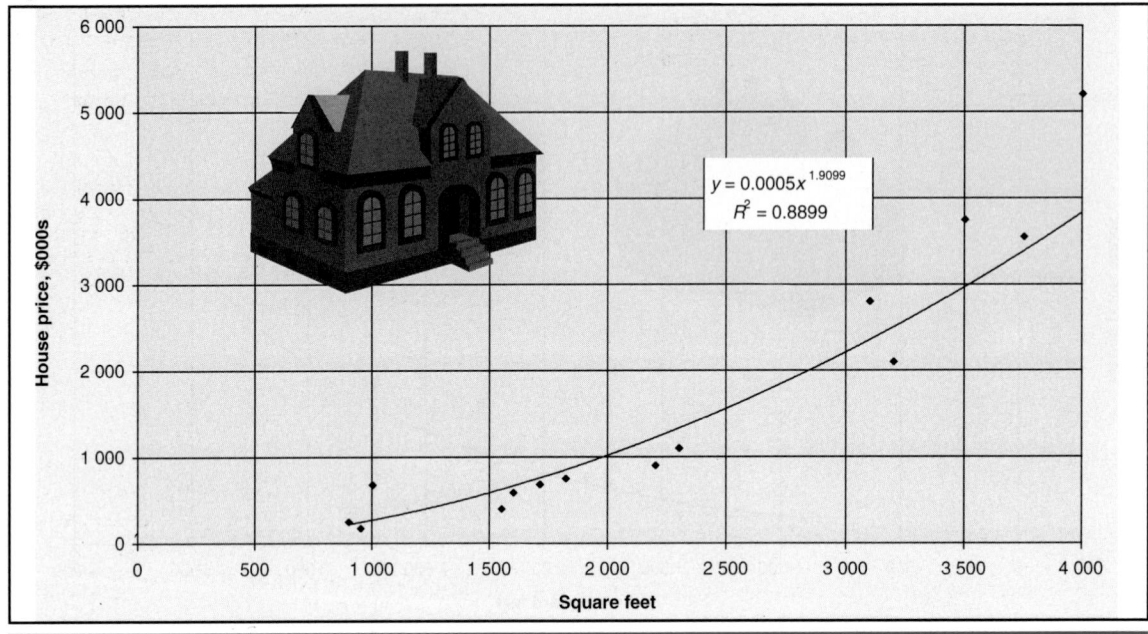

$y = 0.0005x^{1.9099}$
$R^2 = 0.8899$

Figure 21.13   House prices – regression.

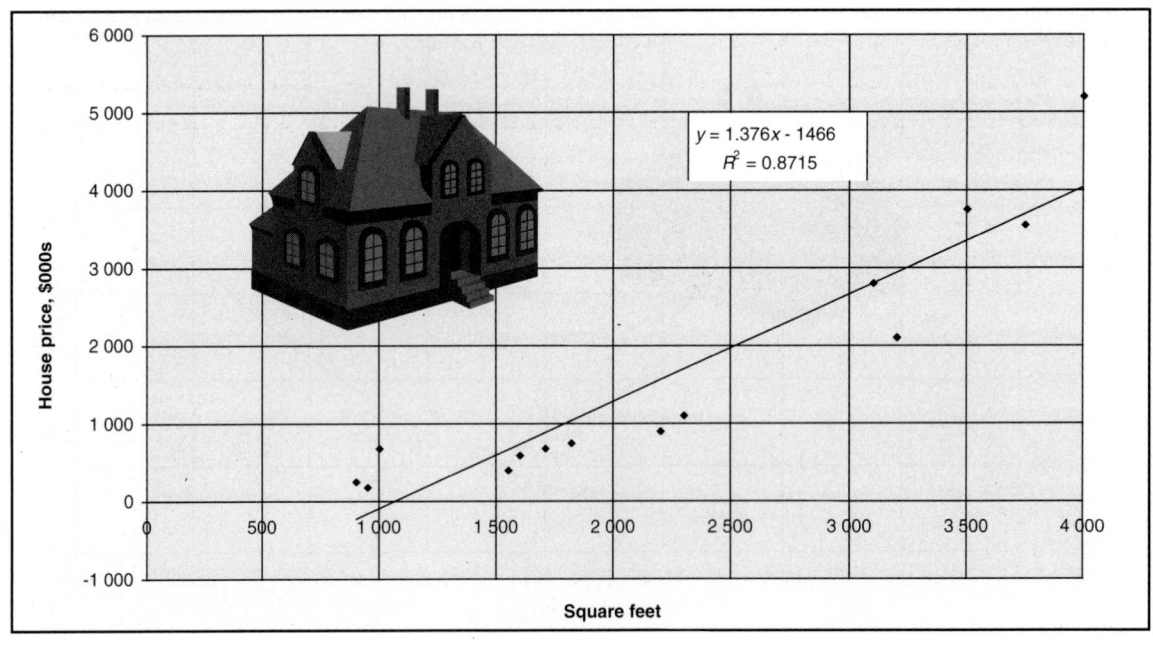

$y = 1.376x - 1466$
$R^2 = 0.8715$

Tracking signal

The tracking signal indicates how well the forecast is predicting the actual data. The tracking signal at time period T is given by:

$$\frac{\text{Cumulative forecast error (period } T)}{\text{Mean average deviation (period } T)}$$

$$= \frac{\Sigma\,(Y - \hat{Y})}{\Sigma\,|(Y - \hat{Y})|/n}.$$

In the Ringe example:

- The cumulative forecast error is given in Column 5 of the table in Figure 21.3.
- The mean absolute deviation day by day is given in Column 8.
- The tracking signal is Column 9 (Column 5/Column 8).

The tracking signal may be positive or negative and it indicates how many mean average deviations the cumulative forecast error deviates from the actual value at any particular time period. If the tracking signal hovers around zero, then it means that the actual values are corresponding well to the forecast. If the tracking signal errs on the positive side, then it means the forecast is predicting low (it is pessimistic). If the tracking signal errs on the negative side, then it means the forecast is predicting high (it is optimistic). It is to be accepted that a forecast is just that, a forecast, and that there will be differences between the actual and estimated values. The question is how much deviation can be accepted before it is concluded that the forecast model is not valid. It is for this reason that control charts are useful.

Control charts

A control chart, and these will be discussed further in Chapter 23, *Statistical Quality Control*, contains:

1 a centre line, CL which is the zero value of the difference;
2 an upper control limit, UCL;
3 a lower control limit, LCL.

Figure 21.14 illustrates the movement of the tracking signal with control limits set at plus and minus two mean average deviations. This control chart illustrates that after the fourth day the tracking signal starts decreasing (forecasts are continually higher than actual sales) and that in period 7 and 8, the lower control limit is exceeded.

Control limits

Control limits should be established such that:

- They are not too wide, such that large errors between the forecast and actual data are continually overlooked.

Figure 21.14 Ringe – tracking signal.

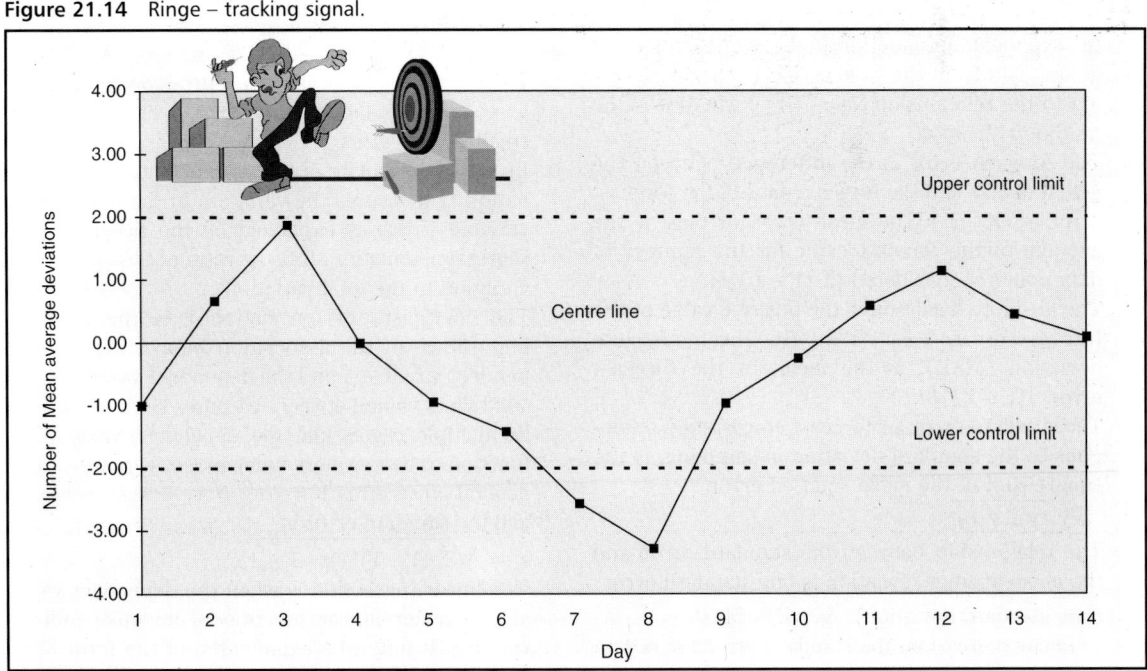

■ They are not too narrow, such that limits are exceeded at a small difference between the forecast and actual data, which results in continuing doubt over the validity of the forecast model being used. It has to be accepted that there will always be differences.

Table 21.10 gives the relationship between the value of the mean average deviation (MAD) the standard error and the percentage of data falling within the corresponding range. For example, if control limits are set at ±2 MADs, then about 89 per cent of the data will be contained within the control limits, assuming that the data can be considered to follow a normal distribution. Alternatively, with control limits of ±2.5 MADs (about ±2 standard deviations), then about 95 per cent of the data will be contained within the limits, assuming a normal distribution.

Choosing the right model

There are no real hard and fast rules for choosing the right forecasting model. It starts with the trial-and-error process of selecting a model and testing it against actual data. Models can be complex. In the 1980s, in a marketing function, the author worked on a team to develop a forecast model for world crude-oil prices. This was needed in order to estimate financial returns

Table 21.10 The relationship between the value of the mean average deviation, (MAD), the standard error, and the percentage of data falling within the corresponding range

MAD	Standard deviation	Percentage of data	Standard deviation	MAD	Percentage of data
±1	±0.7979	57.2	±1	±1.2533	68.26
±2	±1.5958	89.4	±2	±2.5066	95.44
±3	±2.3937	98.2	±3	±3.7599	99.72

from future oil drilling, exploration, refinery and chemical plant operations. The model developed was curvilinear and incorporated variables in the US economy including GNP changes, interest rates, energy consumption patterns, chemical production, demographic changes, US taxation, capital expenditure, seasonal effects and political risk.

Care should be taken in using polynominal type forecasting models as the predicted value of Y changes rapidly with values of X. This would not make sense in sales forecasting because there are always limits. In the house example, using the polynominal function, a surface area of 10 000 square feet forecasts a sales price of $63.59 million! ($0.0005 \times 10\,000 \times 10\,000 - 1.2499 \times 10\,000 + 1094.2$.)

SUMMARY OF KEY ELEMENTS

■ In exponential smoothing, the contribution of actual data from the first period declines according to the relationship $\alpha(1 - \alpha)^{n-2}$, where n is the period in question.

■ The forecast error is the difference between the actual data Y and the forecast data $\hat{Y}$, the forecast error $= (Y - \hat{Y})$. The mean error, or bias, is the average of the forecast error for the number of data points n considered $[\Sigma (Y - \hat{Y})]/n$.

■ The absolute deviation is the positive value of the forecast error, $|(Y - \hat{Y})|$. The mean absolute deviation (MAD), is the mean of the forecast error, $|(Y - \hat{Y})|/n$.

■ The standard error, or forecast consistency, analogous to the standard deviation in sampling, is the square root of the mean squared error,
$$\sqrt{\Sigma (Y - \hat{Y})^2/n}.$$

■ The relationship between the standard error and the mean average deviation is one standard error (one standard deviation), $\sqrt{\pi/2} \times$ MAD.

■ In linear regression, the standard error for n data points is

$$s_e = \sqrt{\Sigma (Y - \hat{Y})^2/(n - 2)}.$$

■ The confidence interval of a regression forecast is given by the relationship, $Y \pm zs_e$, or $\hat{Y} \pm ts_e$ for small sample sizes.

■ In regression analysis, the coefficient of determination r^2 measures the variation in the dependent variable Y that is explained by the fitted simple regression equation. It is the ratio of the explained variation to the total variation.

■ The coefficient of correlation r is the relative importance of the association between the independent variable X and the dependent variable Y. It can take a value between +1 and –1.

■ In multiple regression, the dependent value is a function of two or more independent variables. The general equation is $\hat{Y} = a + b_1X_1 + b_2X_2 \ldots b_kX_k$ and the standard error is

$$s_e = \sqrt{\Sigma (Y - \hat{Y})^2/(n - k - 1)}.$$

■ Non-linear regression is when the dependent variable is a curvilinear function of an independent variable. It might be exponential of the form $Y = ae^{bx}$, polynomial of the form $Y = a + bX + cX^2$ or, when x has a non-integer value, of the general form $Y = ax^b$ or multiples of all these possibilities.

■ A control chart, plotting the ratio of the cumulative forecast error to the mean absolute deviation can be used to monitor the accuracy of the forecast.

REVIEW AND DISCUSSION QUESTIONS

1 **Multiple regression**. What are the criticisms of using multiple regression in forecasting. In what areas do you think multiple regression is the most appropriate?
2 **Forecast errors**. Regardless of the type of forecast one is making, what are some of the factors that lead to errors in the analysis?
3 **Erroneous forecasts**. Can you cite some real examples, either in business or other areas, where forecasts have turned out to be wrong?

4 **Non-linear regression**. Give some other illustrations when the sales activity or some other progression of events has followed, or will probably follow, a curvilinear change either in a negative or in a positive sense.
5 **Controlling a forecast**. Discuss the advantages and drawbacks of using a tracking signal in the control of a forecast. Illustrate your arguments by presenting some practical situations.

EXERCISE PROBLEM: CONSULTING

Situation

A consulting company that has a major activity related to the installation and integration of systems software for enterprise resource planning wishes to see if there is any correlation between the profits generated in this sector and various variables related to its practice. For this particular sector of the work, these are the average number of consultants on projects, their average experience and the percentage of time that the consultant spends away from his or her office; this means that the consultant is either travelling or working at the client's facility.

The historical data in Table 21.11 is available on a quarterly basis.

Table 21.11 Consulting – historical data

Profits $US	Years of experience	Number of consultants	Time away from office (%)
4 501 000	15	27	55
3 241 000	6	45	27
8 745 100	18	112	75
6 984 210	23	80	62
3 421 800	8	35	55
5 845 600	10	98	57
6 854 200	8	80	75
3 589 500	5	30	49
9 542 300	21	120	82
5 689 250	10	54	62

Required

Two independent variables

1 Develop a two-independent-variable multiple regression model for profits as a function of the years of experience and the number of consultants on the projects.
2 Does the relationship appear strong? Quantify.
3 What would be an estimate of profits for a particular quarter, if the average experience of consultants on projects was 15 years and the average number 50?
4 What are the 90 per cent confidence intervals?

Three independent variables

5 Develop a three-independent-variable multiple regression model for profits as a function of the years of experience, the number of consultants on the projects and the time spent away from the office.
6 Does the relationship appear strong? Quantify.
7 What would be an estimate of profits for a particular quarter, if the average experience of consultants on projects was 15 years, the average number 50 and the percentage of time away from the office 60 per cent?
8 What are the 90 per cent confidence intervals?

EXERCISE PROBLEM: TUBE PASSENGERS

Situation

The number of travellers on tubes and buses in London, England, during the summer months (June, July and August) is believed to be heavily tied to the number of tourists visiting the city. Over the last 12 years the data in Table 21.12 has been collected:

Table 21.12   Data on tourists and bus/tube ridership

Year	Number of tourists (millions)	Passengers (millions)
1986	5.30	1.90
1987	6.20	2.10
1988	7.30	2.50
1989	8.20	2.70
1990	9.00	2.90
1991	8.70	2.70
1992	10.10	3.10
1993	11.10	3.20
1994	10.00	3.00
1995	13.20	4.10
1996	11.30	3.50
1997	10.70	3.20

Required

1   Show that a linear regression line is a reasonable model for this data. What quantitatively justifies your argument?
2   What is the expected passengers if ten million tourists visit the city in a year?
3   What are the 90 per cent confidence limits for this value?
4   What if no tourists visit the city? Why is the interpretation of this question difficult from the data given?

NOTES AND REFERENCES

1.   Gardner, E. S. (1985) 'Exponential Smoothing: The State of the Art', *Journal of Forecasting* 4: 1–28.

FURTHER READING

Alstrom, P. and Madsen, P. (1994) 'Evaluation of forecast models used for inventory control during a product's life cycle', *International Journal of Production Economics* 35(1–3): 191–200.

Batchelor, R. and Dua, P. (1995) 'Forecaster diversity and the benefits of combining forecasts', *Management Science* 41(1): 68–75.

Chase, C. W. Jr (1995) 'Measuring forecast accuracy', *Journal of Business Forecasting Methods and Systems* 14(3): 2.

Cipra, T. (1992) 'Robust exponential smoothing', *Journal of Forecasting* 11(1): 57–69.

Forst, F. G. (1992) 'Forecasting restaurant sales using multiple regression and Box–Jenkins analysis', *Journal of Applied Business Research* 8(2): 15–19.

Jonsson, B. (1994) 'Prediction with a linear regression model and errors in a regressor', *International Journal of Forecasting* 10(4): 549–55.

Gaynor, P. and Kirkpatrick, R. (1994) *An Introduction to Time Series Modelling and Forecasting for Business and Economics*, New York; London: McGraw-Hill.

Macdonald, D. G., Power, M. and Fuller, J. D. (1994) 'A new discovery process approach to forecasting hydrocarbon discoveries', *Resources and Energy Economics* 16(2): 147–66.

Magiera, F. T. (1995) 'Decomposition of earnings forecast errors', Journal of Business Forecasting Methods 14(3): 11–13.

Matthews, B. P. and Diamantopoulos, A. (1994) 'Towards a taxonomy of forecast error measures: A factor-comparative investigation of forecast error dimensions', *Journal of Forecasting* 13(4): 409–17.

Mentzer, J. T. and Gomes, R. (1994) 'Further extensions of adaptive extended exponential smoothing and comparison with the M-Competition', *Journal of the Academy of Marketing Science* 22(4): 372–82.

Miller, T. and Liberatore, M. (1993) 'Seasonal exponential smoothing with damped trends: An application for production planning', *International Journal of Forecasting* 9(4): 509–15.

Montgomery, D. C. and Friedman, D. J. (1993) 'Prediction using regression models with multicollinear predictor variables', *IIE Transactions* 25(3): 73–85.

Narula, S. C. and Korhonen, P. J. (1994) 'Multivariate multiple linear regression based on the minimum sum of absolute errors criterion', *European Journal of Operational Research* 73(1): 70–71.

Newsome, B. A. and Zietz, J. (1992) 'Adjusting comparable sales using multiple regression analysis: The need for segmentation', *Appraisal Journal* 60(1): 129–35.

Ohtani, K. (1994) 'The density functions of R squared and the adjusted R squared, and their risk performance under asymmetric loss in misspecified linear regression models', *Economic Modelling* 11(4): 463–71.

Ou, C. S. (1996/1997) 'A misconception about exponential smoothing', *Journal of Business Forecasting Methods and Systems* 15(4): 15–16.

Pantazopoulos, S. N. and Pappis, C. P. (1996) 'A new adaptive method for extrapolative forecasting algorithms', *European Journal of Operational Research* 94(1): 106–11.

Patel, M. H. (1995) 'A linear program to detect extrapolation in predicting new responses of a multiple linear regression model', *Computers and Industrial Engineering* 28(4): 787–91.

Pecar, B. (1994) *Business Forecasting for Management*, London; New York: McGraw-Hill.

Rosas, A. L. and Guerrero, V. M. (1994) 'Restricted forecasts using exponential smoothing', *International Journal of Forecasting* 10(4): 515–27.

Steigerwald, D. G. (1992) 'Adaptive estimation in time series regression models', *Journal of Econometrics* 54(1–3): 251–75.

Toothaker, L. E. (1994) 'Multiple regression: Testing and interpreting interactions', *Journal of the Operational Research Society* 45(1): 119–20.

Willemain, T. R., Smart, C. N., Shockor, J. H. and Desautels, P. A. (1994) 'Forecasting intermittent demand in manufacturing: A comparative evaluation of Croston's method', *International Journal of Forecasting* 10(4): 529–38.

22| Decision-making and risk analysis

Objectives and overview

The objective of this chapter is to present the many quantitative methods for decision making and risk analysis that have application in the operations and supply-chain environment. The chapter opens by reviewing decision making and associated risks, the concept of trade-off and prioritizing when there are several alternatives in the decision process. The chapter then presents the magnitudes of decision making from intuition to using a task-force approach and it then gives a step-wise approach to making decisions. There is a section which elaborates the environment for decision making, including decision making under certainty, decision making under risk and decision making under uncertainty. Then the chapter develops decision theory for each of these possible environments, including the concepts of maximin, maximax, equally likely and minimax regret for decision making under uncertainty and the use of decision trees for decision making under risk when probabilities can be assigned. The concept of expected value of perfect information is presented and also sensitivity and a 'what if?' analysis. Other methods described include payoff tables, marginal analysis, utility in decision making, cost–benefit analysis and finally linear programming. All the methods are fully explained by giving detailed worked examples.

THE ELEMENT OF RISK

Making decisions is part of life. Business is no exception:

- What products to make?
- Which markets to pursue?
- When to invest in new technology?
- Who to hire?
- How much raw material to purchase?
- When to start a production run?
- When to purchase new equipment?
- Should we merge with another company?

Whenever a decision is made, there is always an element of risk. Plans may not proceed as desired, markets may alter, technology may change, or the cost of materials may increase unexpectedly. The more systematic the analysis of all the variables involved in a decision, the less likely is the downside risk. A decision is usually made from a combination of quantitative analyses, such as cost, price information, statistics, historical data and market factors, plus subjective reasoning based on the experience of persons involved in the decision-making process.

Wrong decisions

A wrong decision can be costly. Some classic examples follow.[1]

Ford Motor Company and the Edsel

In 1957 Ford, USA, launched a new medium-priced automobile, the Edsel. This decision was taken after 10 years in research and development. Some $50 million was spent in establishing new independent dealers, advertising and promotion in the year it was launched. Ford's market analysis indicated that this project was almost risk free. In fact, the Edsel was a financial disaster. In three years, only 109 466 Edsels were sold, which was far below forecast. In 1959, the production was halted after an estimated loss of $100 million on the original investment and another $100 million in operating losses. Some of the reasons for this poor decision were:

- Competition, particularly General Motors, was very strong.
- A recession in 1958 affected sales.
- The power and performance of the Edsel were the subject of extreme criticism by the National Safety

Council and the Automobile Manufacturing Association.

- Demand for smaller cars was taking hold, and the size and style of the Edsel did not have the expected consumer demand.
- Ford tried to 'push' as many Edsels as possible onto the market immediately after its introduction and, as a result, quality suffered.
- The network of controllers, dealers, marketing managers and industrial relations persons created within Ford to launch the Edsel was complicated and inefficient.

Dupont and Corfam

In 1964 Dupont, USA, introduced a synthetic leather, Corfam, as a substitute material for shoe manufacture. Corfam was promoted as a light material, which breathed and flexed easily, kept its shape, was water resistant, stood up well to abrasion and did not have to be polished. Dupont took some 13 years to develop the product and spent $2 million in advertising in the first year of introduction. After seven years of losses ranging from $80 to $100 million, and even after the introduction of a new version of Corfam in 1970, Dupont abandoned the product in 1971. Some of the reasons for this poor decision were:

- The leather industry attacked Corfam as a poor substitute for leather.
- Quality-control problems occurred in production, causing costs to rise. Higher costs put Corfam in the $15 to $20 shoe-price range, which comprised only 10 per cent of the shoe market. A lower price might have enabled Corfam to capture a larger market share.
- In 1969, less expensive vinyl and fabric materials entered the market. The leather industry began to promote soft leather. Imports infiltrated the USA market, and Corfam's sales declined by 25 per cent.

Coca-Cola and New Coke

Coca-Cola, USA, decided in 1984 that it must act boldly to reverse its 20-year market share decline against Pepsi. Coca-Cola decided that the correct strategy was to replace the 98-year old coke with a better tasting cola, and label it 'New Coke'. With much fanfare, New Coke was launched onto the market in April 1985. It was a flop. One reason for the poor decision was that in launching the new product, the company decided not to present the option of keeping 'Old Coke' on the market (79 days after the launch of New Coke, the old-formula coke was brought back).[2]

System

A business can be considered to be a system comprising principally three subsystems, Marketing, Operations and Finance (see Chapter 1, *Positioning Operations Management*). Decisions made at the level of one subsystem will impact the other subsystems. A decision that seems logical for one subsystem may not appear so for the other:

- Marketing wishes to introduce another product line. There is a risk that this would saturate the capacity of the production (operations) department and a risk that it would also strain the financial situation of the company.

In arriving at the final decision, the system has to be considered in its entirety, not only at the subsystem level.

Trade-offs

In decision making, trade-offs occur. A trade-off is making a choice between one decision and another. With both there is a risk and both have advantages and disadvantages:

- The Finance department wants Production to keep inventories at the lowest possible level, to reduce the financial investment. Production wants to keep levels reasonably high because of the uncertainty of supplier deliveries and fluctuations in final product demand. There is trade-off on what levels of inventories should be held.
- In Quality Control there is a trade-off between the extent of product inspections (an internal cost) and the number of defects that slip through the production process (an external cost). There is a trade-off on the level of inspection.

Priority recognition

Managers at all levels are confronted with numerous decisions. One task is to sort the decisions in order that priority is given to the most important:

- Should the problem of quality control in the plant in Europe be dealt with now or should the new client in Japan be contacted?
- Should the purchase decision of raw materials be made now, in order to get a preferential price, or should the sales negotiations be finalized first?
- Should we start hiring now to meet the expected market demand or should we wait and see if the market expands as forecast?

MAGNITUDE OF THE DECISION MAKING PROCESS

The depth of analysis for making decisions depends on its complexity, the costs involved and the time horizon:

- A decision on purchasing a new quantity of raw material may be relatively short term and simple to make. (The raw material should be consumed within a few days under just-in-time operation.)
- Deciding on the purchase of a new printing press make take three months to finalize with a long-term impact on the outcome (five to ten years' use of the equipment).
- The decision for a German company to build a new production centre in the USA has very long-term consequences.

The following illustrates concepts in the magnitude of decision making, which are also summarized in Figure 22.1.

Intuition

The sales vice president of a fashion company in Paris receives a telephone call from a prospective client in the USA. She decides to leave that night for New York to meet the customer, even though it means cancelling other critical appointments. She goes because, intuition tells her, she knows this particular customer, that he is likely to place a substantial order.

Quick and dirty

The vice president is on the plane back from New York. The customer has given her a large order for ladies' apparel at a price lower than usual. The vice president is not immediately clear on the profit margin. The customer wants an answer as soon as she arrives back in Paris. She does some 'quick and dirty' calculations on the flight back.

Figure 22.1 The magnitude (and cost) of making a decision.

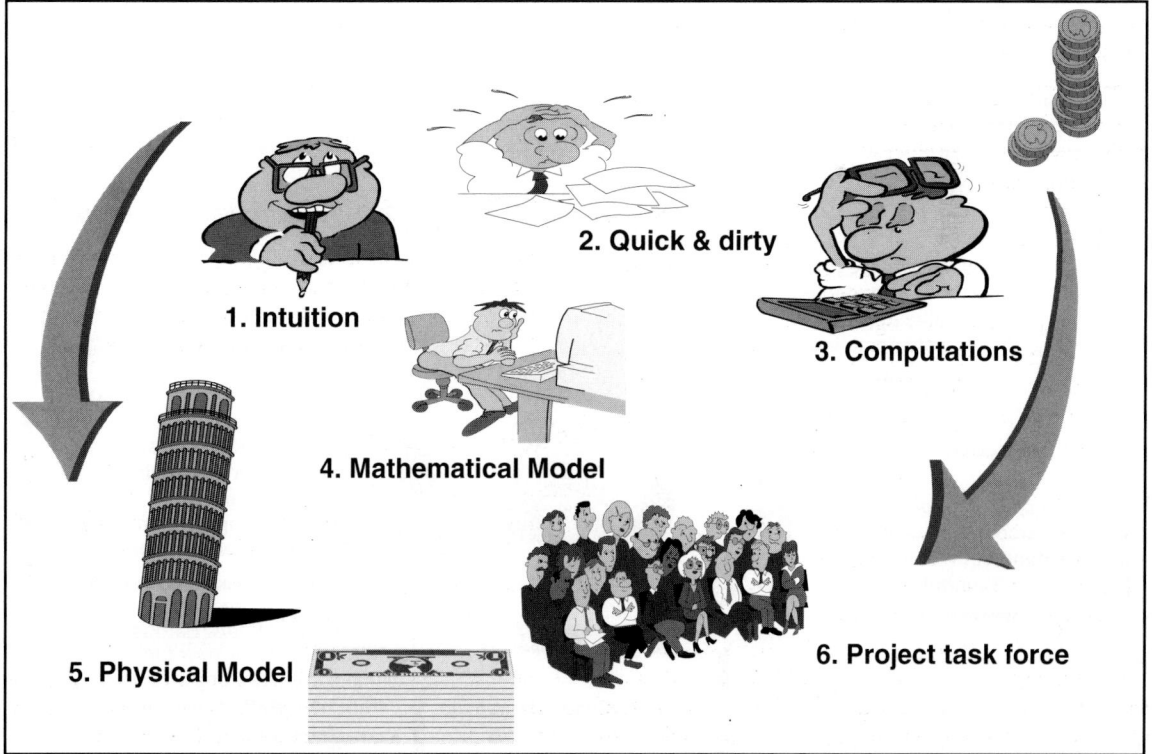

1. Intuition
2. Quick & dirty
3. Computations
4. Mathematical Model
5. Physical Model
6. Project task force

Computations

The sale is a bit more complicated, as it potentially involves future sales on other clothing items. The vice president spends a day at the office doing some additional computations and talking with design and production people.

Model building

A model represents a simplified version of the real thing and is used as a tool to aid in decision making (see Chapter 9, *Forecasting customer demand*):

■ An oil company is deciding on whether to drill for oil in the Ukraine. Before a final decision is made, financial models are developed looking at costs, expected revenues and the probability of locating oil.

■ A food company is considering acquiring a small chocolate manufacturer. Before a decision on the acquisition is made, financial models are developed to analyse the expected revenues from the acquisitions and the impact of the additional debt on net returns.

■ A construction company develops a proposal for constructing a new hotel in Las Vegas, USA. Three physical scale models are constructed as an aid to the client to make a decision on the final design.

■ A boat builder is developing a new sail boat as an entrant for the America's Cup. A model is built to decide on the final aerodynamic design.

Task Force

A company is deciding whether to build a large petrochemical facility in Kuwait. A team, comprising a project manager, a market analyst, an estimator, a scheduler and two engineers, is sent over to Kuwait to analyse the proposition. This task force then returns to the home office with a recommendation based on their work in Kuwait City. (The author was part of such a task force.)

THE DECISION PROCESS

The process of decision making depends on the magnitude of the decision being made and the extent of risk, should the wrong decision be made. Steps in the decision process might include the following and are summarized in Figure 22.2.

Figure 22.2 The decision-making process.

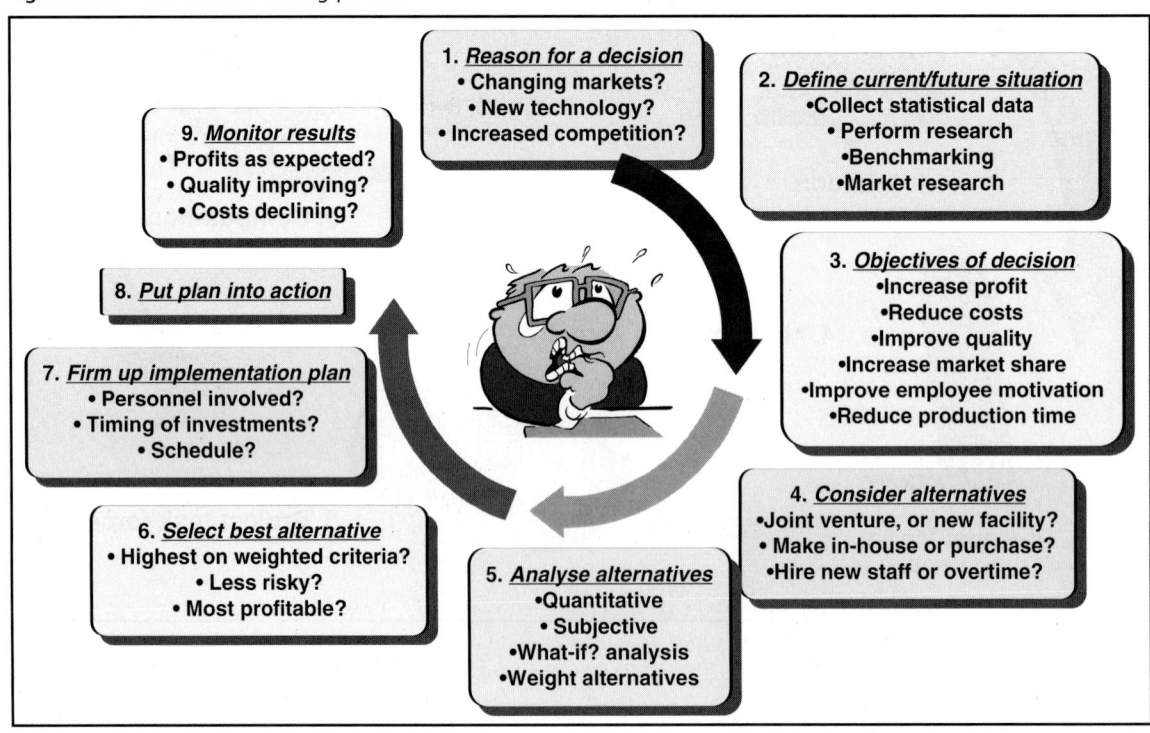

What is the reason for requiring a decision?

Perhaps markets have changed, the competition has increased or new technology has been developed. This would apply to computer hardware companies such as IBM, Dell, Hewlett Packard, Compaq and Bull:

- The markets have increased as personal computers become more accepted for both business and personal use.
- The competition is extremely strong among computer manufacturers.
- Technology is constantly changing with new software offered by Microsoft and more powerful computer chips (for example, the Pentium).

In a production operation, perhaps a reason for the decision is that there are continuing complaints from customers regarding product quality.

Define the current and future situation

This would involve analysing the situation by gathering cost, price and market data, doing research, interviewing personnel and bench-marking or analysing the competition. (See also Chapters 4 and 26, *Quality Management* and *Auditing Operations*).

If there is a problem (for example, poor quality of end products), the decision should not be to remove the symptoms leaving the basic problem unresolved. (The non-conforming products are repaired rather than the cause of the poor quality investigated.)

Define objectives

The criteria by which the proposed solutions will be judged should be clearly defined. These might include:

- costs;
- profits;
- return on investment;
- increased productivity;
- risk to the organization;
- company image;
- impact of demand;
- quality level.

Develop alternatives

Is there more than one solution that would be acceptable or one that is less costly? For example, there is a rush order for a supply of office furniture to a customer. If the order is not ready on time for the customer, the order will be lost and quite possibly repeat business from this customer. Possible alternative ways of tackling the problem are:

- putting the factory on overtime;
- hiring additional workers;
- renting additional factory space;
- subcontracting the work – but perhaps sacrificing quality;
- purchasing semi-finished units from elsewhere and finishing them in your factory;
- promising the customer the furniture, but putting a penalty clause in the contract so that, if deliveries are not on time, you pay a penalty.

Analyse alternatives

Quantitative methods, as well as subjective analyses, may be used to look at the other options in the decision process. Probability analysis is a useful tool, as is using some other forms of weighting on all the possible criteria.

Select the best alternative

The best alternative may be the one that scores best on a weighting criteria; it may be the less risky alternative; or it might be the alternative that is the most profitable.

Firm up a plan for implementation

During the decision-making process, consideration has to be given to implementing the final decision (the planning steps can impact the decisions). This firm-up step is finalizing the implementation plan:

- personnel involved;
- timing of investments (see Chapter 18, *Project Management* and particularly the case study, *Sana*);
- schedule.

Monitor results

Once the decision has been made and implemented, results should be monitored to be sure that they are according to expectations. If not, why not (perhaps another decision):

- Are profits as expected?
- Is quality improving?
- Are costs declining?
- Is productivity improving?
- Has delivery time been reduced?

THE ENVIRONMENT FOR DECISION MAKING

Decision making under certainty

Decision making under certainty implies that all relevant parameters in the decision, such as cost, capacity, market demand, price and style, have values that are known in advance and will not change during the life of the decision made:

- A production decision is required concerning 500 engine parts. If the units are made in house, the production costs per unit are $20. Thus, for certainty the total cost will be $10 000. If the parts are purchased outside, the price paid (cost) per unit is $19.50 or a total cost of $9750.
- An investment decision is required. US government certificate of deposits are currently giving an annual yield of 7.5 per cent. Thus, $200 000 invested for one year will give a return of $15 000.
- A marketing decision is required concerning 750 office desks that a manufacturer has in stock that cost FF 4800 per unit to produce. One client wishes to purchase all these office desks and has agreed to pay FF 5500 per unit. Thus, the profit to be realized is FF 700 per unit or a total of FF 525 000. Another client wishes to purchase 700 of these desks at a price of FF 5585 per unit. This would yield a profit of FF 549 500.

All the parameters are known and the decision most likely to be taken is the one that maximizes outcome.

Decision making under risk

In decision making under risk there is no certainty of the final outcome, but a probability of success can be estimated, implying that certain parameters have probabilistic outcomes:

- Selling price per unit of an item is $40. Based on previous experience, there is a 75 per cent probability of selling all the 500 units made. What is the expected revenue?
- A contractor is 70 per cent certain that it will receive a building contract that has a value of DM 23 million.
- A software dealer is 90 per cent certain that this year's profits will exceed the forecast.
- A production manager is 10 per cent sure that a machine can exceed capacity.

Here the probabilities would be taken into account in order to try and maximize the benefits of the expected outcomes.

Decision making under uncertainty

In this situation it is extremely difficult, or impossible, to assess the likelihood of various possible future events. Assigning probabilities would be wild:

- Selling price is $40 per unit. Sales demand is unknown and thus revenue is uncertain.
- In 10 years what will be profits realized in the former East German market?
- If a new chemical is found to replace chlorofluro-carbons in refrigeration systems, will the new product eventually prove hazardous to the environment?
- If new investments are made in new nuclear technology, will this industry be profitable in the next 30 years?
- Will the income from the investment in stock A be more than income from Stock B in 15 years?
- Will Hong Kong, under Chinese rule, maintain the same spectacular growth?

Decisions made under uncertainty are often long term and complex, involve many players and sometimes involve governments and politics, which makes them very uncertain!

DECISION THEORY

Some of the decisions characterized previously lend themselves to an approach called decision theory. Decision theory is an aid to managers to decide on the most attractive alternative. The elements of decision theory are discussed below and then illustrated afterwards by a worked example, *Polyethylene Facility*, concerning a company's decision to add new plant capacity.

Characteristics

In decision theory, the following characteristics exist:

- There are several possible future external conditions that will influence the final decision. Usually, these future conditions are beyond the manager's control.
- There is one or more alternatives from which to choose.
- For each alternative there is a financial payoff under each future condition.

Stages

The stages in using decision theory are described in the following.

Identify future conditions

The future conditions are those that are likely to impact the final outcome, for example:

- Product demand is expected to be high, low or flat.
- A competitor will introduce a new product or there is not expected to be any new competition.
- Interest rates are expected to increase, decrease or remain about the same.

These future conditions are known as states of nature. They are external events, over which one usually has little control.

List of alternatives

Develop a list of possible alternatives in the decision-making process. There will always be alternatives, even if the only one is not doing anything.

Payoff

Most business decisions are based on financial returns. Therefore, estimate the payoff associated with each alternative for every possible future condition.

Probability

Estimate the likelihood, probability, chance of each of the possible future conditions.

Alternatives

Evaluate alternatives according to some decision criteria, such as maximum profits, minimum cost, maximum market share, a certain growth rate, etc.

Decision making under certainty

In decision making under certainty it is known for certain which of the possible future conditions will actually happen. In this case, the decision is relatively straightforward in that the choice is the alternative with the highest payoff under that state of nature.

Decision making under uncertainty

In decision making under uncertainty there is no clear information on the likelihood of the states of nature. There are no probability values (see Chapter 20, *Statistical Concepts*). The following are some criteria for making a decision.

Maximin

In the maximin approach, first the worst, or minimum, possible payoff for each alternative is identified. This might be the lowest profit, highest cost or lowest market share. The decision is made to choose the alternative that has the best or the maximum of all of the worst payoffs. This is a pessimistic approach and, although the actual outcome may not be as bad as selected, the maximin criterion establishes a guaranteed minimum level if the given base information is correct.

Maximax

In the maximax approach, first the best or maximum possible payoff for each alternative is identified. This might be the highest profit, lowest cost or highest market share. The decision is made to choose the alternative that has the highest or maximum of all of the best payoffs. This is an optimistic approach as the decision maker has targeted what appears to be the best payoff.

Equally likely

In the equally likely approach, first the average payoff is determined for each alternative. The decision is made to choose the alternative with the highest average payoff. This approach treats the states of nature as equally likely and would be an approach for someone who is middle-of-the-road in nature.

Minimax regret

The minimax regret is the 'regret' or disappointment resulting from making a decision that is wrong, or not the best. The degree of regret is the difference between the choice that is made and what turns out to be the best choice.

In decision making under uncertainty, there are criteria but no firm basis for preferring one decision over another. Each decision is a function of the 'feeling' of the decision maker. Setting up the matrix does not create certainty where none exists, nor does it attempt to include an element of risk. What it does is to organize the various outcomes so that decision makers can organize their thoughts, crystallizes prejudice about caution and highlights information that is needed to improve upon the decision.

Decision making under risk

In the case of risk there are probabilities of occurrence because the states are mutually exclusive (see Chapter 20, *Statistical Concepts*). For example, interest rates will either increase, decrease or remain the same. They cannot do all three! If all possible probability outcomes are considered, then they must add up to unity. In decision making under risk, the concept of expected value (EV) is used, which is the result obtained by weighting the outcomes according to the probability data provided. The decision that has the highest expected value (for profit) or lowest (for cost) would then be the preferred decision.

In this approach, the expected value is only a quantitative theoretical value used for making the decision. The calculated value cannot be the actual payoff because of the mutual exclusivity of the states of nature. Only one of the states of nature can occur.

Decision trees

A decision tree is a schematic representation of the alternatives involved in decision making and is particularly useful in a situation of decision under risk. A decision tree has nodes, branches, and payoffs as illustrated in Figure 22.3. The conventions are described in the following.

Square nodes

There are square nodes (1, 4 and 5 in Figure 22.3), which denote decision points. This is where the decision maker has control. The manager makes the decision.

Circular nodes

There are circular nodes (2 and 3 in Figure 22.3), which denote external chance events. The decision maker has little, if any, control.

Branches

Branches (the straight lines in the figure) indicate the direction in which the decision is being made. The length of the branches themselves has no bearing on the decision process.

Payoffs

All the possible financial outcomes, or payoffs, in the decision-making process are listed on the right of the tree for each alternative and probability of occurrence. From the decision tree, branches are cut (de-branched) by drawing a double line across the branch if an alternative is less attractive than another:

- Consider the decision point No. 4. If Payoff 3, for choice C, is greater than Payoff 4 for choice D, then the branch for choice D is de-branched.
- Consider the decision point No. 5. If Payoff 6, for choice F, is greater than Payoff 5 for choice E, then the branch for choice E is de-branched.

The expected values (EV) for each node are then calculated:

$$\text{EV(node 2)} = \text{Payoff 1} \times p_1 + \text{Payoff 2} \times p_2 + \text{Payoff 3} \times p_3$$
$$\text{EV(node 3)} = \text{Payoff 6} \times p_1 + \text{Payoff 7} \times p_2 + \text{Payoff 8} \times p_3.$$

Figure 22.3 Decision tree layout.

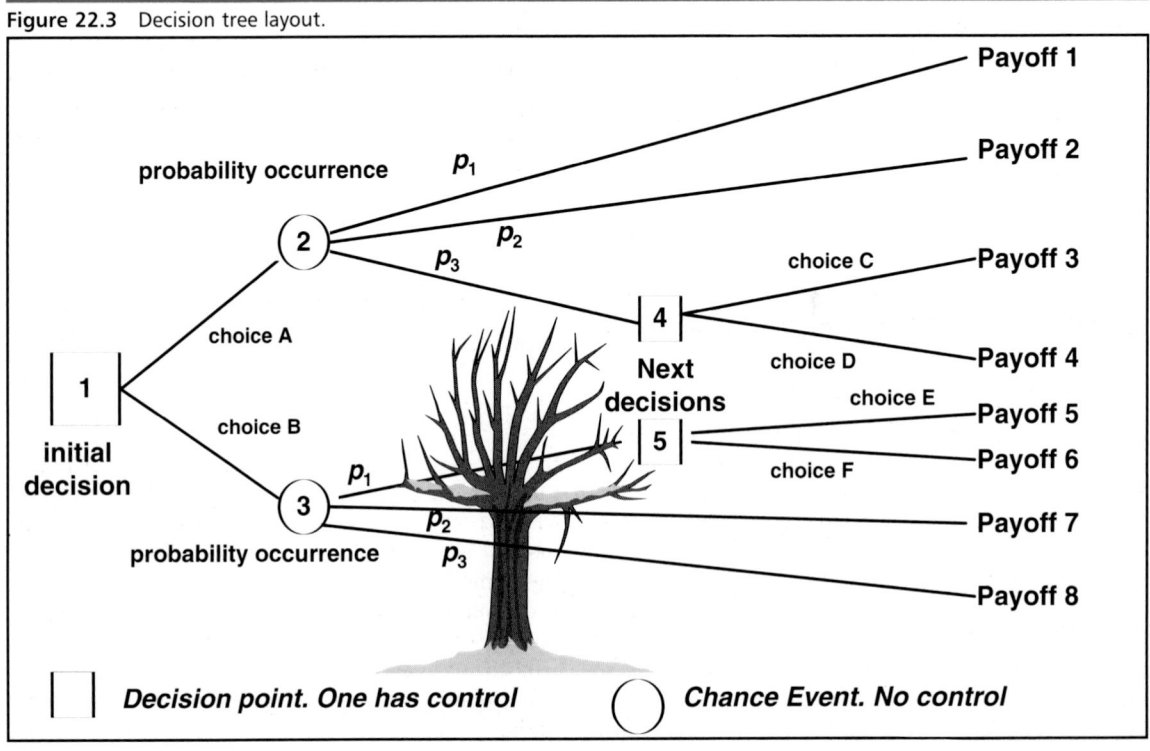

Assume that the expected value at Node 2 is greater than the expected value at Node 3, then the branch for choice B is de-branched. The preferred decision route is then choice A. The decision made is then described as follows for choice A:

- If the probability turns out to be p_1, then the result would be Payoff 1.
- If the probability turns out to be p_2, then the result would be Payoff 2.
- If the probability turns out to be p_3, then decide on alternative choice C. This would give Payoff 3. (Pay off 4 has already been de-branched.)

Expected value of perfect information

The expected value of perfect information (EVPI) is the difference between the expected payoff under certainty and the expected payoff under conditions of risk. The purpose of determining this value is that, in decision making, it would not make sense to pay more than the expected value of perfect information to be more certain of an alternative.

The EVPI is determined by the expected payoff 'value' under certainty (EVUC) less the expected payoff 'value' under conditions of risk (EVUR).

What-if? and sensitivity analysis

In making a decision, the final outcome can be sensitive to the assumed future external events. This always leads to the question, 'What if this happens? Or, what if that occurs? The following provides an illustrative example.

Construction of cruise ships

The demand for holiday cruises increased at an annual average rate of 9 per cent between 1980 and 1993.

Based on this rapid growth, major cruise line companies such as Carnival, Royal Caribbean Cruises and Princess Cruises (owned by Peninsular & Oriental Steam Navigation Co. – P&O) are adding new cruise ships to their fleet, as indicated in Table 22.1. Some of these ships include casinos, an 18-hole miniature golf course and a wedding chapel. They cost up to $400 million.[3]

Table 22.1 Passenger growth on cruise lines

Cruise line	1 April 1995 passenger capacity	Net estimate 1988 (includes retirements)	Growth (%)
Carnival	23 995	40 041	67
Royal Caribbean Cruises	13 216	24 724	87
Princess Cruises	10 070	16 570	65
Kloster Cruise	9 539	9 735	2
Cunard Line	6 896	5 319	–23
Celebrity Cruises	4 760	10 150	113

In 1994 passenger growth dropped to 2.2 per cent. Thus, there is a big risk in constructing new ships. Demand is very sensitive to passenger growth and the question being asked in the industry is, 'What if the passenger growth fails to materialize?' All this extra capacity will be underutilized at an enormous cost.[4]

Under decision making with conditions of risk, the choice of the decision is a function of, or sensitive to, the probability values. Probabilities are difficult to quantify exactly and thus there is a risk in making a decision based on precise probabilities. A sensitivity analysis will show how the final decision might change with various probabilities.

WORKED EXAMPLE: POLYETHYLENE PROJECT

Situation

An international chemical company is considering increasing its worldwide polyethylene capacity. The following are the possible alternatives being considered:

- build a new grassroots facility;
- expand an existing plant;
- establish a joint venture with another overseas company.

After some extensive studies, and initial designs, the estimated net present value of the payoff (net return) for the three alternatives at three different levels of future polyethylene demand are as given in Table 22.2.

Table 22.2 Future demand for polyethylene ($ million)

Alternative	Low	Stable	High
Grass roots	–50	30	100
Expansion	–25	50	75
Joint venture	10	30	45

Required

1 What would be the preferred decision if management was:
 (a) pessimistic?
 (b) optimistic?
 (c) middle-of-the-road?
 (d) used to analysing the degree of regret or disappointment?

2　After a further market study was performed, the company developed some probability estimates for the market outcome, which are given in Table 22.3. Using this information what would be the preferred decision?

Table 22.3　Polyethylene markets – Probability estimates for market outcome

Future market	Probability (%)
Low	20
Stable	35
High	45

3　Develop a decision tree to illustrate the situation and the solution, under a condition of risk. How would the decision be interpreted?

4　What is the expected value of perfect information (EVPI)? How is this interpreted?

5　Management believes that, although the probability of a stable market at 35 per cent is a reasonable estimate, there is uncertainty in the probabilities for the low and high market demand. Some persons involved in the analysis believe that the value of 20 per cent for a low market demand is too high. Others believe it is too low. Illustrate, on a graph, the sensitivity of the decision process for all possible ranges of a low demand. (Since the stable market probability is considered fixed at 35 per cent, the possible range of the low probability is 0 to 65 per cent. Correspondingly, the range of high demand will then be from 65 per cent to 0 per cent, since the total probabilities must add up to unity.)

6　After further discussion, management came up with the following modified situation:
■ If the grass-roots alternative was selected, and the market demand was high, the company had an option to expand the capacity. In this case, the estimated payoff would be $125 million instead of $100 million.
■ If the joint-venture alternative was selected, and the market demand was high, the company had an option to increase its percentage share in the joint venture. In this case, the estimated payoff would be $65 million instead of $45 million.

Use decision trees to illustrate the preferred decision for management.

7　What is the expected value of perfect information for this modified situation?

Solution

1　In this first situation, no estimates of probability are given and so this is decision making under uncertainty:
(a) Pessimistic is a maximin approach. Here, the decision would be to select the joint-venture alternative since $10 million is the 'best' of the worst alternatives.
(b) Optimistic is a maximax approach. Here the decision would be to select the grass-roots facility since $100 million is the maximum possible outcome.
(c) Middle-of-the-road is an equally likely approach. Here, expansion would be the preferred alternative as the average value of the outcome is the highest at $33.33 million.

$$\text{Average of grass-roots option} = \frac{-50 + 30 + 100}{3} = \$26.67 \text{ million.}$$

$$\text{Average of expansion option} = \frac{-25 + 50 + 75}{3} = \$33.33 \text{ million.}$$

$$\text{Average of joint-venture option} = \frac{10 + 30 + 45}{3} = \$28.33 \text{ million.}$$

In practice if all the payoff values are realistic numbers, the $33.33 is not a realizable value since the future market can only be either low, stable or high, but not all three. The equally likely calculated value is just a quantitative indicator used as a form of hedging to 'optimize' the best decision.
(d) From the payoff tables, the 'best' outcome is determined:
■ The difference between the best outcome and the selected option according to the environment is calculated. This is the regret in financial terms of not deciding on the choice.
■ The maximum regret for each decision is determined.
■ The minimum of the maximum is determined, which is the least painful regret.

The details of the decisions to make are given in Table 22.4 and 22.5.

Table 22.4　Polyethylene project – decision making under uncertainty (the best results according to the environment are given in bold)

	Payoff values ($ millions), according to market		
	Low	Stable	High
Grass roots	−50	30	100
Expansion	−25	50	75
Joint venture	10	30	45
Maximin	**Minimum**		
Grass roots	−50		
Expansion	−25		
Joint venture	10		
Maximum	10　Select joint venture		
Maximax	**Maximum**		
Grass roots	100		
Expansion	75		
Joint venture	45		
Maximum	100　Select grass roots		
Average	**Average**		
Grass roots	26.67		
Expansion	33.33		
Joint venture	28.33		
Maximum	33.33　Select expansion		
	Payoff values ($millions), according to market		
Minimax regret	Low	Stable	High
Grass roots	−50	30	**100**
Expansion	−25	**50**	75
Joint venture	**10**	30	45

Table 22.5 Polyethylene project – regret matrix. The table gives the maximum 'regret' disappointment in not selecting the best decision; the min then would give the least painful regret.

	Difference between 'best' and selected option		
	Low	Stable	High
Grass roots	60	20	0
Expansion	35	0	25
Joint venture	0	20	55
	Maximum regret		
Grass roots	60		
Expansion	**35**		
Joint venture	55		
Min of max	35	Expansion	

2 Since there is now an estimate of the probability of the outcomes, this represents decision making under risk. To decide on the preferred alternative, the expected value of the outcome is determined by weighting using the probability values.

Expected values

Grass roots $= -50 \times 0.20 + 30 \times 0.35 + 100 \times 0.45$
$= \$45.50$ million.

Expansion $= -25 \times 0.20 + 50 \times 0.35 + 75 \times 0.45$
$= \$46.25$ million.

Joint venture $= 10 \times 0.20 + 30 \times 0.35 + 45 \times 0.45$
$= \$32.75$ million.

The expansion project has the highest expected value and, thus, this represents the best alternative. The expected value is not a realizable value (only one of the future market conditions is possible). The expected value is a quantitative indicator used as a type of hedging to minimize risk by taking into account all the possibilities.

3 Figure 22.4 gives the decision tree for this situation. The square node No. 1 is the starting point for the decision process. The circular nodes, Nos 2, 3 and 4, represent the states in the environment. The payoff for each possible alternative is indicated on the right of the diagram. Figure 22.5 is the analysis for this situation. The expected value calculations (already developed in Question 2) are presented above each of the circular nodes. The branches for the grass-roots and joint-venture options are crossed with a double line (de-branched), illustrating that these are not the preferred decision since their expected values are lower, \$45.50 and \$32.75 million respectively, compared to the expansion option (the preferred decision) with an expected value of \$46.25 million. The interpretation of the decision to expand an existing facility is that the company will realize:

- a net payoff of \$75 million if the market change is high;
- a net pay off of \$50 million if the market remains stable;
- a loss of \$25 million if the market demand is low.

4 The expected value of perfect information is the difference between the expected value under certainty and the expected value under risk.

Figure 22.4 Polyethylene project – initial situation.

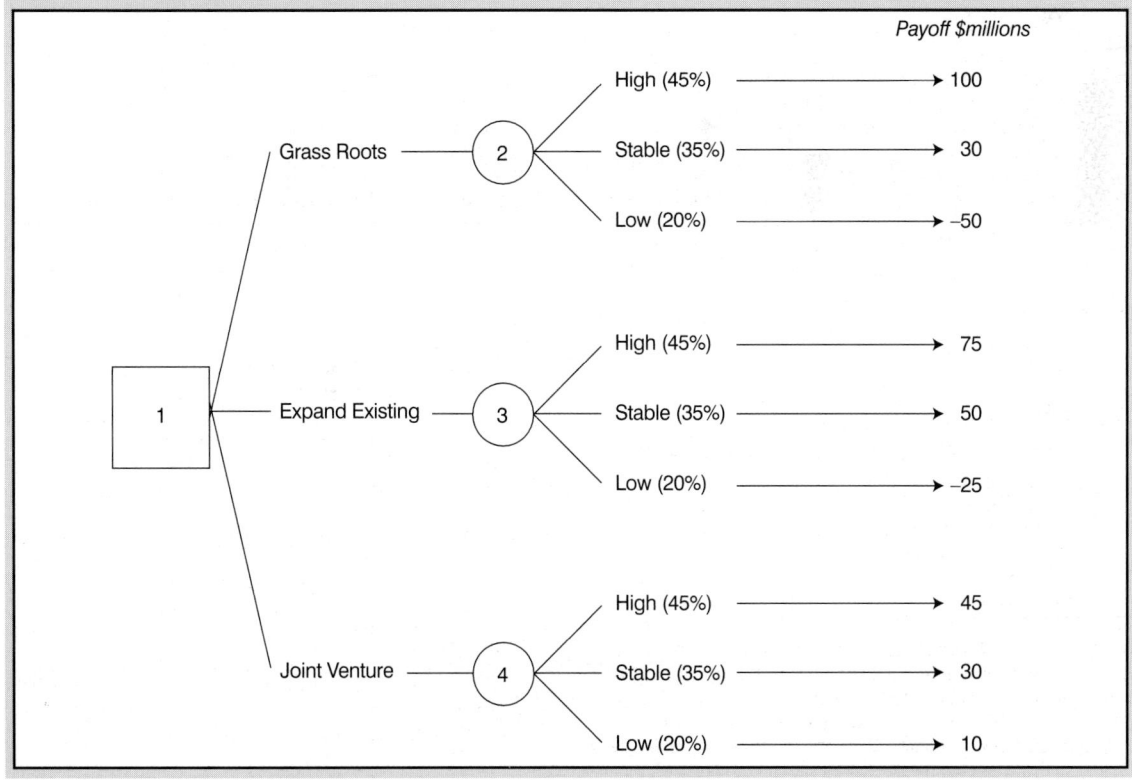

Figure 22.5 Polyethylene project – solution to initial situation.

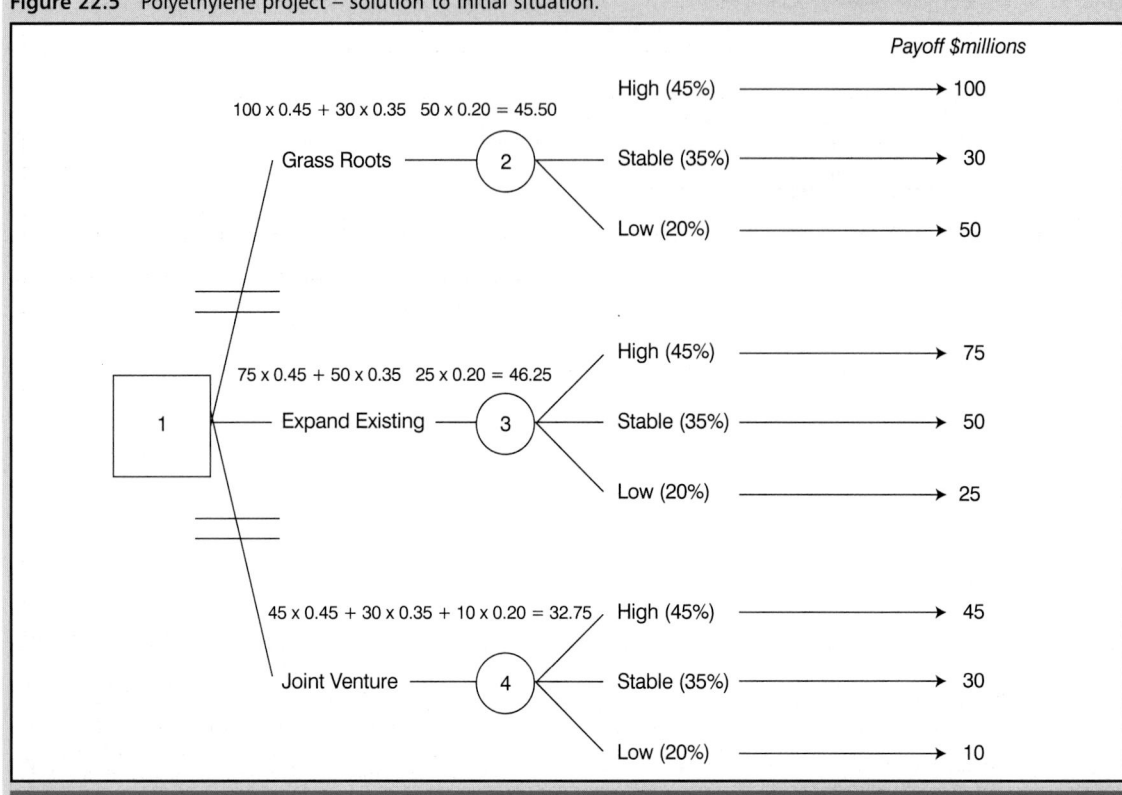

Payoff $millions

Grass Roots — (2)
100 x 0.45 + 30 x 0.35 50 x 0.20 = 45.50
- High (45%) ⟶ 100
- Stable (35%) ⟶ 30
- Low (20%) ⟶ 50

Expand Existing — (3)
75 x 0.45 + 50 x 0.35 25 x 0.20 = 46.25
- High (45%) ⟶ 75
- Stable (35%) ⟶ 50
- Low (20%) ⟶ 25

Joint Venture — (4)
45 x 0.45 + 30 x 0.35 + 10 x 0.20 = 32.75
- High (45%) ⟶ 45
- Stable (35%) ⟶ 30
- Low (20%) ⟶ 10

Expected value under certainty

- If it was known in advance that the market for polyethylene would be high, the decision would be to build a grass-roots facility, giving a net payoff of $100 million.
- If it was known in advance that the market for polyethylene would be stable, the decision would be to expand an existing facility, giving a net payoff of $50 million.
- If it was known in advance that the market for polyethylene would be low, the decision would be to go into a joint venture, giving a net payoff of $10 million.

The expected value under certainty is thus the weighted probability of the best payoff for each alternative:

$$10 \times 0.20 + 50 \times 0.35 + 100 \times 0.45 = \$64.50 \text{ million.}$$

Expected value under risk

This is the best outcome considering probabilities for each alternative. The value was calculated in the answer to Question 2 and is $46.25 million for the expansion option. Thus:

$$\text{EVPI} = 64.50 - 46.25 = \$18.25 \text{ million.}$$

This means that $18.25 million is the maximum amount one should be willing to spend to obtain perfect information. It would not make sense to spend more than $18.25 million to develop a more detailed market survey, or to sign contracts with prospective clients to guarantee future sales of polyethylene. More than $18.25 million would mean that it is better to take the risk and choose the project with the highest expected value (the expansion project in this case)

In this situation, obtaining perfect information for a future market is impossible. However, the example illustrates that there is a limit to how much one should be willing to spend to minimize risk. Expected value of perfect information is a value to be taken into consideration when contracts are being considered for 'guaranteeing' a certain sales level.

The probability data for the future market demand is given as precise figures. Probabilities in reality may be different to that which is assumed and, as such, a decision is sensitive to the external environment.

Figure 22.6 shows the change in expected values as the probability of a low market increases from 0 to 65 per cent (this means that, correspondingly, the probability of a high market decreases from 65 to 0 per cent) on the assumption that the probability of a stable market remains fixed at 35 per cent. The graph illustrates that:

- At a probability of low demand between 0 and 18.50 per cent the decision to build a grass roots facility would be the preferred decision.
- At a probability of low demand between 18.50 and 40.77 per cent the decision to expand an existing facility would be the preferred decision.
- At a probability of low demand between 40.77 and 65.00 per cent the decision to establish a joint venture would be the preferred decision.

The values 18.50 and 40.77 per cent are the break-even probabilities between the grass roots and expansion options and between the expansion and joint-venture options respectively. The break-even values are determined as follows:

$$\text{EV (Grass roots)} = p_L \times GR_L + p_S \times GR_S + p_H \times GR_H$$

Figure 22.6 Polyethylene facility: sensitivity..

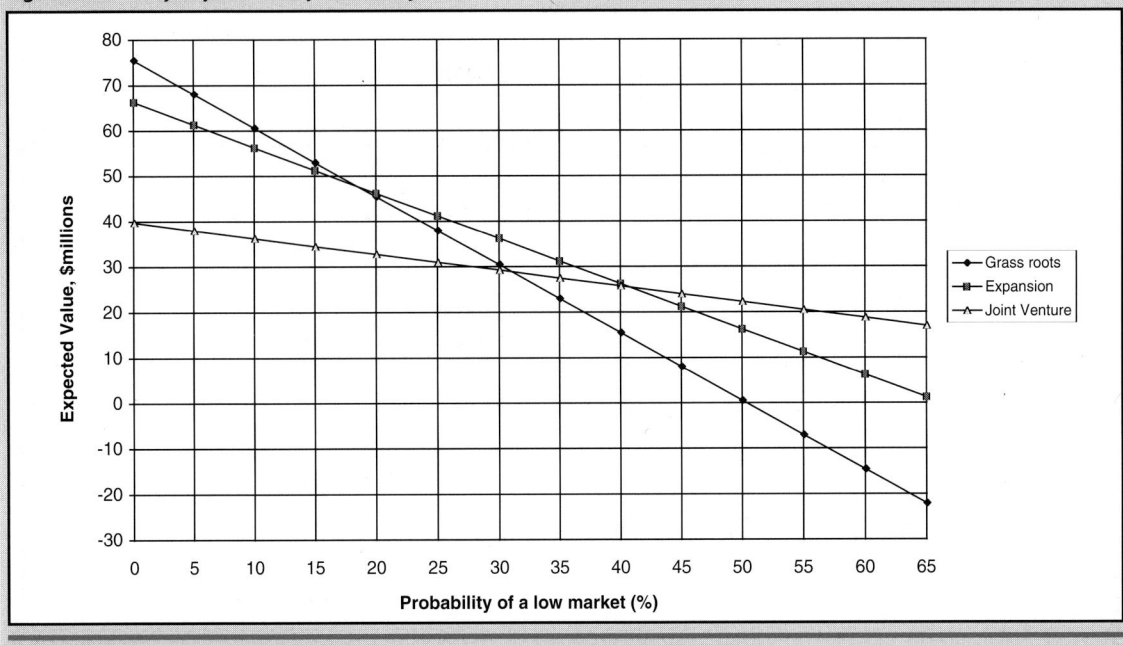

$$EV \text{ (Expansion)} = p_L \times EX_L + p_S \times EX_S + p_H \times EX_H$$
$$EX \text{ (Joint venture)} = pL \times JV_L + p_S \times JVs + p_H \times JV_H,$$

where GR, EX and JV refer to the payoff values for the grass roots, expansion and joint venture options respectively and p_L, p_S and p_H are the probability values for low, stable and high market demand.

The break-even point between the grass-roots decision and expansion is given when their expected values are equal:

$$p_L \times GR_L + p_S \times GR_S + p_H \times GR_H$$
$$= p_L \times EX_L + p_S \times EX_S + p_H \times EX_H,$$

Since

$$p_H = 1 - p_L - p_S,$$

then

$$p_L \times GR_L + p_S \times GR_S + (1 - p_L - p_S) \times GR_H$$
$$= p_L \times EX_L + p_S \times EX_S + (1 - p_L - p_S) \times EX_H,$$

or

$$= p_S \times EX_S - p_S \times GR_S - GR_H + p_S \times GR_H + EX_H - p_S \times EX_H,$$

giving

$$p_L = \frac{p_S (EX_S - GR_S + GR_H - EX_H) - GR_H + EX_H}{(GR_L - GR_H - EX_L + EX_H)}.$$

In a similar fashion, the probability at break-even between the expansion and joint venture options is given by the following relationship:

$$P_L = \frac{P_S (JV_S - EX_S + EX_H - JV_H) - EX_H + JV_H}{(EX_L - EX_H - JV_L + JV_H)}.$$

The computations for the data are given in Table 22.6.

The information illustrates the sensitivity of the decision to the probability. If the probability of low demand drops from 20 per cent and high demand increases from 45 per cent (the given values) to say 18 and 47 per cent respectively (a small variation), then the best decision would be to build a grass-roots facility.

6 Figure 22.7 gives the decision tree for this problem. The new square nodes, Nos 5 and 6, are the additional decisions to be made if either the grass-roots option is selected, and the market demand is high, or the joint-venture option is selected, and the demand is high.

Figure 22.8 gives the analysis and path for the preferred decision. The grass-roots option is now the preferred decision, with an expected value of $56.75 million. This is arrived at as follows:

■ De-branch the path, maintain capacity for the alternative at node 5 for the grass-roots option, since 'maintain capacity' has a lower payoff than 'expand'.
■ De-branch the path 'maintain share' for the alternative at node 6 for the joint-venture option since 'maintain capacity' has a lower payoff than 'increase share'.
■ Calculate the expected value at each of the three circular nodes, 2, 3 and 4 using the payoff value of $125 million for the payoff if there is high demand for the grass-roots option and $65 million for the payoff if there is high demand after the joint venture option has been selected.

7 The EVPI is the difference between the expected value under certainty and the expected value under risk.

Expected value under certainty

■ If it was known in advance that the market for polyethylene would be high, the decision would be to build a grass roots facility and then expand it, giving a payoff of $125 million.
■ If it was known in advance that the market for polyethylene would be stable, the decision would be to expand an existing facility, giving a net payoff of $50 million.

Table 22.6 Polyethylene facility: sensitivity

| | Payoff values ($millions), according to market | | |
	Low	Stable	High
Grass roots	–50	30	100
Expansion	–25	50	75
Joint venture	10	30	45

| Probability (%) | | | Alternative | | | |
Low	Stable	High	Grass roots	Expansion	Joint venture	Max value
0	35	65	**75.50**	66.25	39.75	75.50
5	35	60	**68.00**	61.25	38.00	68.00
10	35	55	**60.50**	56.25	36.25	60.50
15	35	50	**53.00**	51.25	34.50	53.00
20	35	45	45.50	**46.25**	32.75	46.25
25	35	40	38.00	**41.25**	31.00	41.25
30	35	35	30.50	**36.25**	29.25	36.25
35	35	30	23.00	**31.25**	27.50	31.25
40	35	25	15.50	**26.25**	25.75	26.25
45	35	20	8.00	21.25	**24.00**	24.00
50	35	15	0.50	16.25	**22.25**	22.25
55	35	10	–7.00	11.25	**20.50**	20.50
60	35	5	–14.50	6.25	**18.75**	18.75
65	35	0	–22.00	1.25	**17.00**	17.00

| Breakeven Point | Probability | | | |
	Low	Stable	High	Expected value ($million)
Grass roots/Expansion	18.50	35.00	46.50	47.75
Expansion/Joint Venture	40.77	35.00	24.23	25.48

■ If it was known in advance that the market for polyethylene would be low, the decision would be to go into a joint venture, giving a net payoff of $10 million.

The expected value under certainty is thus the weighted probability of best payoff for each alternative:

$$10 \times 0.20 + 50 \times 0.35 + 125 \times 0.45 = \$75.75 \text{ million.}$$

Expected value under risk

This is the best outcome, considering the probabilities for each alternative. The value was calculated in the answer to Question 6 and is $56.75 million for the grass roots option. Thus:

$$\text{EVPI} = 75.75 - 56.75 = \$19.00 \text{ million.}$$

Figure 22.7 Polyethylene project – modified situation.

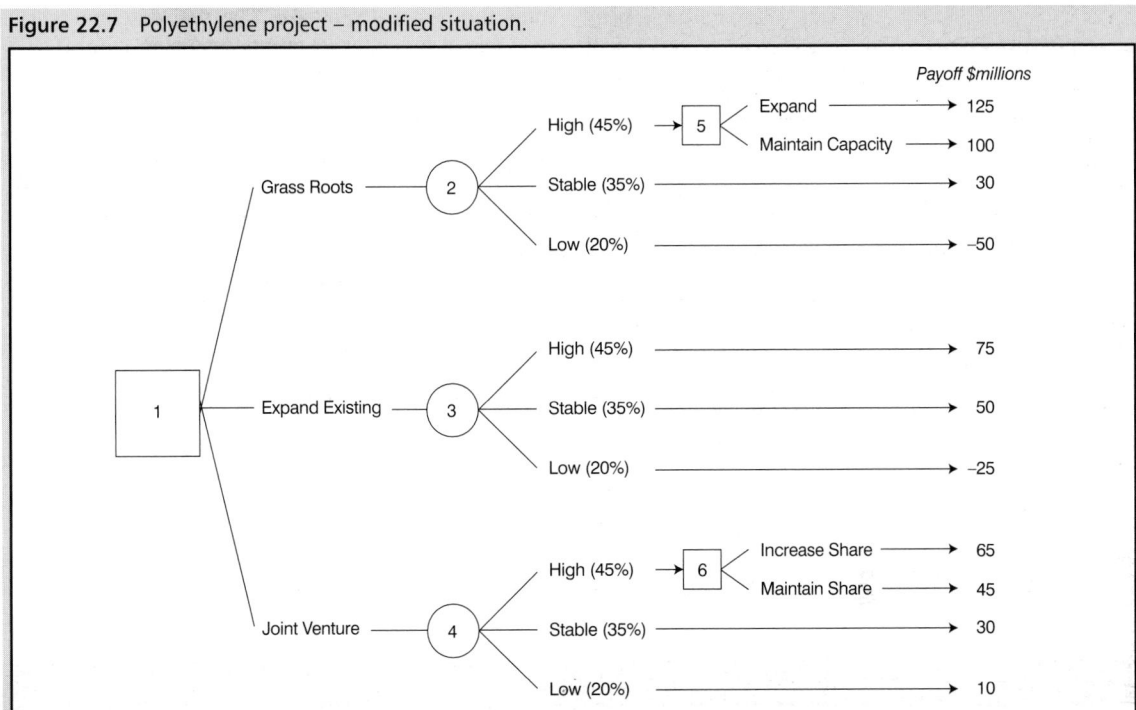

Figure 22.8 Polyethylene project – solution to modified situation.

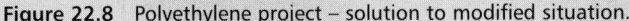
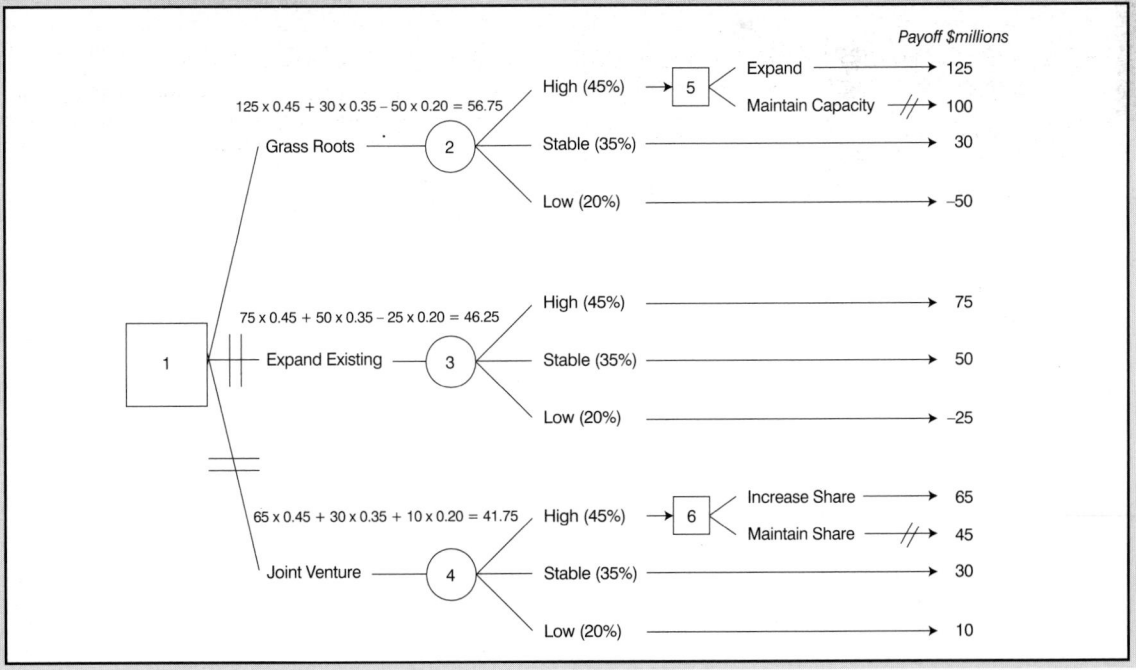

PAYOFF TABLES

Payoff tables are another way of using expected values to analyse the various alternatives available in decision making. There use was considered in Chapter 11, *Inventory Management*, for long and short costs.

Method

A matrix is prepared showing all the possible outcomes for the various options available, according to the likely external events. To determine the expected values, these outcomes are then weighted according to the given probabilities. The alternative that has the highest value is chosen.

Analysis

Again, since only one state of nature is possible, the expected value is only a quantitative measure to deter-

mine the best path to take. The real outcome will be only one of the external events (states of nature) since they are mutually exclusive.

When a situation is a recurring event, such as an inventory stocking, using payoff tables may not give the optimum result each time. What payoff tables do is to optimize the best alternative in the long run on the assumption that the probability data remains constant. Again, there is the question of sensitivity in that the chosen decision is based on the probability estimates. If these change, then the decision alternative may be modified.

The use of payoff tables is illustrated by the following worked example, *Sierra Produce*.

WORKED EXAMPLE: SIERRA PRODUCE

Situation

Jack Komiko owns Sierra Produce, a retail outlet for all types of vegetables and fruit for the San Gabriel Valley residents in north-east Los Angeles. One of Sierra Produce's most exotic products is mangos imported from the Far East at a purchase price of $56.00 per case. Jack normally stocks 11, 12, 13 or 14 cases of mangos each week. For each case that he sells, he realizes a profit of $35.00. However, since Jack always wants to sell fruit of top quality, and as the mangos soon get soft, Jack must dump the unsold fruit at the end of the week. Based on past experience, Jack knows that there is a probability of 35 per cent of selling 11 cases, 35 per cent also of selling 12 cases, 20 per cent of selling 13 cases and only 10 per cent probability of selling 14 cases.

Required

1 What is the recommended stocking level, if there is no value for the dumped fruit?
2 What is the recommended stocking level, if Jack could sell the soft mangos at the end of the week, at a profit of $10.00 per case, to a small company that makes fruit juices?

Solution

The selling price is $91/case (56 + 35). Figure 22.9 gives the solution for making this decision. The results are arrived at as follows:

1 No value for dumped fruit:
   ■ If 11 cases are stocked and 11 cases are demanded, then all the inventory is sold and the profit would be $385 (11 × 35). This is the value in the top left cell of the shaded area of the profit table shown in Figure 22.9.

■ If 12 cases are stocked and 11 cases are demanded, then only 11 cases are sold and one is trashed. The profit would be $329 (11 × 35 − 1 × 56). This is the value in the first cell, second row of the shaded area of the profit table.
■ If 13 cases are stocked and 14 cases are demanded, then all the 13 cases are sold. The profit would be $455 (13 × 35). This is the value in the fourth cell, third row of the shaded area of the profit table. In this case, no consideration is given to opportunity costs (lost sales)
■ If 14 cases are stocked and 12 cases are demanded, then only 12 cases are sold and two are trashed. The profit would be $308 (12 × 35 − 2 × 56). This is the value in the second cell, fourth row of the shaded area of the profit table.
The other profit figures are calculated in a similar manner. The expected value is greater ($388.15) if 12 cases are stocked. In this case the outcome for Jack would be:
■ a profit of $329/case if 11 cases are demanded;
■ a profit of $420/case if 12 cases are demanded;
■ a profit of $420/case if 13 cases are demanded;
■ a profit of $420/case if 14 cases are demanded.
2 Sells mangos for fruit juice:
   ■ If 11 cases are stocked and 11 cases are demanded, then all the inventory is sold and the profit would be $385 (11 × 35). This is the value in the top left cell of the shaded area of the profit table in Figure 22.9.
   ■ If 12 cases are stocked and 11 cases are demanded, then 11 cases are sold for their full profit and one is sold for juice manufacture. The profit would be $395 (11 × 35 + 1 × 10). This is the value in the first cell, second row of the shaded area of the profit table.
   ■ If 13 cases are stocked and 14 cases are demanded, then all the 13 cases are sold. The profit would be $455 (13 × 35). This is the value in the fourth cell, third row of the shaded area of the profit table. In this case, no consideration is given to opportunity costs (lost sales)

Figure 22.9 Sierra produce.

Selling price, $/case	91
Purchase cost, $/case	56
Profit, $/case	35
Profit on soft mangos, $/case	10

Case 1: End of week mangos dumped

PROFIT TABLE

		Cases demanded				
		11	12	13	14	Exp Val
Stocking	11	385.00	385.00	385.00	385.00	385.00
level in	12	329.00	420.00	420.00	420.00	388.15
number	13	273.00	364.00	455.00	455.00	359.45
of cases	14	217.00	308.00	399.00	490.00	312.55

Probability		0.35	0.35	0.20	0.10	1.00

Case 2: End of week mangos sold for fruit juice

PROFIT TABLE

		Cases demanded				
		11	12	13	14	Exp Val
Stocking	11	385.00	385.00	385.00	385.00	385.00
level in	12	395.00	420.00	420.00	420.00	411.25
number	13	405.00	430.00	455.00	455.00	428.75
of cases	14	415.00	440.00	465.00	490.00	441.25

Probability		0.35	0.35	0.20	0.10	1.00

■ If 14 cases are stocked and 12 cases are demanded, then 12 cases are sold for their full profit and two are sold for juice manufacture. The profit would be $440 (12 × 35 + 2 × 10). This is the value in the second cell, fourth row of the shaded area of the profit table.

The other profit figures are calculated in a similar manner. The expected value is greater ($441.25) if 14 cases are stocked. In this case the outcome for Jack would be:

■ a profit of $415/case if 11 cases are demanded;
■ a profit of $440/case if 12 cases are demanded;
■ a profit of $465/case if 13 cases are demanded;
■ a profit of $490/case if 14 cases are demanded.

MARGINAL ANALYSIS

Decision making using marginal analysis is an evaluation involving probabilities, and expected values, that considers the additional benefit of taking some particular action, compared to the outcome if that action is not taken.

Probability relationship

Consider the situation of a company that makes standardized products for sale:

■ MP is the marginal profit obtained from making an additional item of inventory which is subsequently sold.
■ ML is marginal loss from making an additional item of inventory which remains unsold in inventory.
■ p is the probability of selling this additional unit.
■ Thus, $(1 - p)$ is the probability of not selling this additional unit. This is a binomial situation.

■ Expected marginal profit is the probability that unit will be sold multiplied by the marginal profit, or $p \times MP$.
■ Expected marginal loss is the probability of not selling that unit multiplied by the marginal loss, or $(1 - p) \times MP$.

If a marginal analysis approach was used in decision making, an additional unit would only be made if the subsequent marginal profit was greater than, or equal to, the marginal loss:

$$p \times MP \geqslant (1 - p) \times ML.$$

If this is reorganized to make p the subject of the equation:

$$p \times MP \geqslant (1 - p) \times ML$$
$$p \times MP \geqslant ML - p \times ML$$
$$p \times (MP + ML) \geqslant ML$$

$$p \geqslant \frac{ML}{(MP + ML)}.$$

- The value of p given by the above expression is now the minimum required probability of selling at least one additional unit of stock that would justify the making of that additional unit.
- It would only make sense to make additional units as long as the probability of selling at least one additional unit is greater than p.

The use of marginal analysis is illustrated in the worked example, *Adhesive Product*.

Normal probability distributions and marginal analysis

If the assumption can be made that the distribution of the sale or stocking of a product follows a normal distribution, then marginal analysis can be used in conjunction with the normal distribution.

A normal distribution is given in Figure 22.10. Shown on this distribution is:

- the mean value μ and a standard deviation σ;
- the value of x at the extreme left of the curve, $(\mu - 3\sigma)$;
- the value of x at the extreme right of the curve, $(\mu + 3\sigma)$.

If the normal distribution is applied, the probability of occurrence is as follows:

- The probability of selling $(\mu - 3\sigma)$ units or more is 100 per cent.
- The probability of selling μ units or more is 50 per cent.

Figure 22.10   Normal distribution.

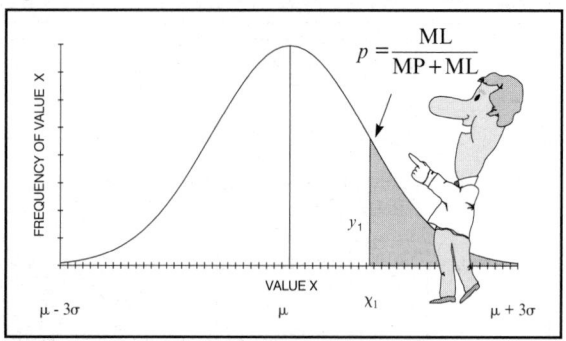

$$p = \frac{ML}{MP + ML}$$

- The probability of selling $(\mu + 3\sigma)$ units or more is zero.

Thus, the more one moves from left to right on the curve, the probability of selling a certain quantity of units declines. Putting it another way, the area to the right of any particular point is the probability of selling that quantity of units, or more.

On the curve is a vertical line y_1 at a value of $X = x_1$. The probability of selling this quantity, or more, is given by the area of the curve to the right of the line y_1. As one moves more to the right, the probability diminishes. In marginal analysis this probability value is given by:

$$p \geq \frac{ML}{(MP + ML)}.$$

This idea is illustrated in the worked example, *Ardeche*.

WORKED EXAMPLE: ADHESIVE PRODUCT

Situation

Jameyson Brothers is a small company specializing in carpet laying. Jameyson purchases the organic-based adhesive it uses for carpet laying in drums from a large chemical company. This adhesive dries very quickly, allowing a newly carpeted room to be used within two hours. However, the adhesive product has the disadvantage that, if the drums, even if unopened, are not used within a week, the adhesive is unusable because it hardens in the drums. In this case, it is sold back to the supplier who recycles the material. On the basis of past data, Jameyson developed Table 22.7, which shows drums of adhesive demanded and the probability of these levels being demanded.

Table 22.7   Probability of demand for drums of adhesive

Drums of adhesive demanded	Probability of this level being demanded	Drums of adhesive demanded	Probability of this level being demanded
0	0.02	6	0.16
1	0.06	7	0.13
2	0.08	8	0.10
3	0.10	9	0.07
4	0.12	10	0.02
5	0.14		

Also, in costing the carpet laying operation Jameyson calculated that the marginal profit on stocking an additional drum of adhesive was $1.70 and the marginal loss was $2.90.

Required

1   What is the optimum stocking level for Jameyson? At this level what is the expected marginal profit and expected marginal loss.

Solution

The tables in Figure 22.11 give the solution for this problem.

Column 3 gives the probability values when the probability is equal to, or greater than, the amount at a particular demand level, for example:

- At a demand of zero units, the probability is 0.02. Any demand greater than, or equal to, zero must have a probability of all that is left, or 1 or 100 per cent.
- At a demand of one unit, the probability is 0.06. Any demand greater than, or equal to, one unit must have a probability of $(1 - 0.02)$ or 0.98.

- At a demand of two units, the probability is 0.08. Any demand greater than, or equal to, two units must have a probability of $(1 - 0.02 - 0.06)$ or 0.92.
- At a demand of three units, the probability is 0.10. Any demand greater than, or equal to, three units must have a probability of $(1 - 0.02 - 0.06 - 0.08)$ or 0.84.

The minimum probability to optimize the stocking level is given by:

$$p \geqslant \frac{ML}{(MP + ML)},$$

Where p is the probability, ML is the marginal loss and MP is the marginal profit:

$$p \geqslant \frac{2.9}{(1.7 + 2.9)}$$

Figure 22.11   Solution for adhesive products.

1	2	3		
Demand units	Prob of demand	Prob this or greater	Exp MP	Exp ML
0	0.02	1.00	1.7000	0.0000
1	0.06	0.98	1.6660	0.0580
2	0.08	0.92	1.5640	0.2320
3	0.10	0.84	1.4280	0.4640
4	0.12	0.74	1.2580	0.7540
5	0.14	0.62	1.0540	1.1020
6	0.16	0.48	0.8160	1.5080
7	0.13	0.32	0.5440	1.9720
8	0.10	0.19	0.3230	2.3490
9	0.07	0.09	0.1530	2.6390
10	0.02	0.02	0.0340	2.8420
Total	1.00		0.0000	2.9000

	4	5
Marginal profit, $/drum		1.7
Marginal loss, $/drum		2.9
$p > $ or $=$ to		0.63
Optimum stocking level in drums		4
If 4 drums are stocked		
Expected marginal profit		1.258
Expected marginal loss		0.754
If 5 drums are stocked		
Expected marginal profit		1.054
Expected marginal loss		1.102

Figure 22.12   Adhesive products: expected marginal loss and expected marginal profit.

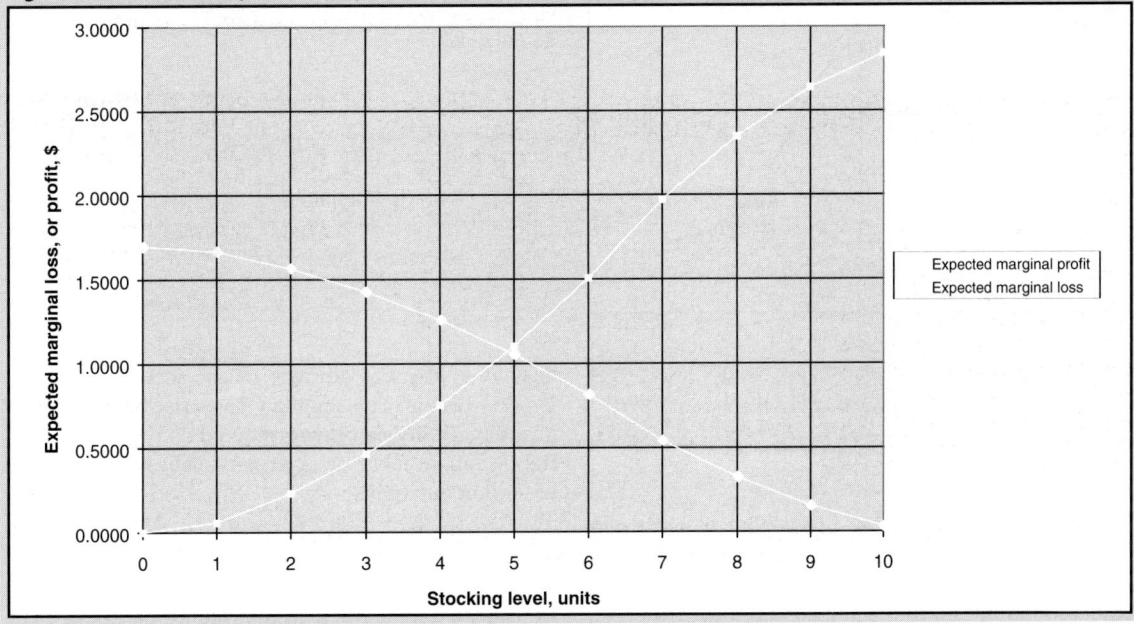

or p must be greater than or equal to 0.6304. In which case, this would mean stocking four drums of adhesive where the probability of using four or more drums is 0.74.

The calculation is shown for the marginal loss and marginal profit if four or five drums are stocked.

If four drums are stocked

- Marginal profit = $1.7 \times 0.74 = \$1.258$.
- Marginal loss = $2.9 \times (1 - 0.74) = \$0.754$.

The marginal profit is greater than the marginal loss.

If five drums are stocked

- Marginal profit = $1.7 \times 0.62 = \$1.054$.
- Marginal loss = $2.9 \times (1 - 0.62) = \$1.102$.

The marginal profit is less than the marginal loss. Figure 22.12 shows the results graphically.

WORKED EXAMPLE: ARDÈCHE

Situation

The Servillon family in Ardèche, France, make cheese from the milk they obtain from their cows. The cheese-making process is simple. To the milk is added rennet, which makes the milk curdle. Additives are added for flavour and then the product is air dried and cut into portions. The cheese is sold at the local market.

From past data the average daily sale of cheese is 25 kg with a standard deviation of 6.50 kg. The cheese is sold at FF 5.35/kg and costs FF 2.35/kg to make. The customers who buy the cheese want it fresh so that any taken to the market and not purchased is sold to the local farmer for pig feed for FF 0.95/kg.

Required

What is the optimum cheese production level to the nearest kilogram for the Servillons?

Figure 22.13 The probability curve for cheese making in the Ardèche.

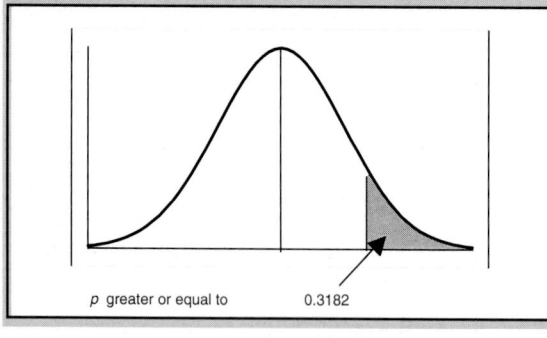

p greater or equal to   0.3182

Solution

The solution is given in Table 22.8 and Figure 22.13. The optimum level is 28 kg.

Table 22.8 Cheese making in the Ardèche; $p = ML/(MP + ML)$

Per kilogram	
Sales price, FF	5.35
Cost, FF	2.35
Pigfood price, FF	0.95
ML = Cost − salvage	1.40
MP = Price − cost	3.00
p (greater than)	0.3182
Area is to right of mean	
z	0.4728
Mean	25.00
σ	6.50
std $\times z$	3.07
kg to make	28.07
Round down	28

Check		
	Production, kg	Profit
	28.00	84.00
	28.07	84.21
	29.00	82.91

WHEN EXPECTED VALUES ARE NOT THE DECISION-MAKING CRITERIA

Utility

To use expected values, the probability of each outcome is multiplied by the payoff (net return) of that outcome. The alternative that produces the highest expected value is the selected option. However, because of fear, gut feeling or risk-averse personalities, decisions are not always made according to the expected value. This anomaly gives rise to the concept of utility. Utility can be considered as the satisfaction, the disappointment or even nervousness as the result of certain outcomes.

Gambling

Consider a gambler at a casino (Monte Carlo). In a certain blackjack game, the probability of winning is 70 per cent. Alternatively, the probability of losing is 30 per cent (100 – 70), as illustrated in Table 22.9 for expected gains for gambling when placing bets of FF 5, 50, 500, 5000, 50 000 and 100 000.

In all cases, the 'expected gain' is greater than the 'expected loss', or the level of bet. Thus, if expected value was the decision criterion used, the gambler would always play. However, in reality, this is not the case:

■ Placing a bet of FF 5 causes little concern, even if one loses. The payoff, if the gambler wins, is FF 500 with an expected outcome of FF 350 (500 × 70%).
■ In the next situation, one might be a more cautious of putting down FF 50, even though the potential winnings are FF 5000, with an expected gain of FF 3500.

As the value of the bet placed becomes higher, a gambler (usually!) becomes more and more cautious about placing a bet and may refuse to place bets at the FF 50 000 and FF 100 000 levels, even though the expected gain is greater than the expected loss or the value of the bet. In this case, the prospect (utility) of losing FF 50 000 or FF 100 000 outweighs the prospect of winning.

The utility concept is illustrated in Figure 22.14. Utility is given an arbitrary index number ranging from 0 to 200 (satisfaction) and 0 to –500 (disappointment or fear). The satisfaction (utility) of winning up to FF 100 000 increases with the amount of gain. However, the fear (utility) of losing decreases (increases negatively) at a much sharper rate. There are different utility curves for different individuals, as some people fear loss more greatly than others.

Managers with different personalities

Figure 12.15 illustrates the concept of utility and risk. Here, utility has been given an index of 0 to 10 (positive utility, or satisfaction) and 0 to –10 (negative utility, or disappointment).

Risk taker

The lowest curve is for the risk taker. For this person, taking a great risk is a big challenge. He gets a 'high'. Thus, his satisfaction of reaping great rewards (an acquisition, a new product, a stock investment) increases sharply. Thus, with high profits, the slope of his utility curve is high (the portion of the curve to the right of the y axis). In contrast, his disappointment, or loss, is relatively less intense as illustrated by the smaller slope to the left of the y axis.

Risk averse

The upper curve is for the risk averse. Here the situation is reversed. The thought of a loss sharply decreases his utility (left of the y axis). The idea of a gain, although it increases his utility, is much less marked.

Middle of the road

The centre curve is for the middle-of-the-road manager, where utility (satisfaction or disappointment) is of equal value, whether the outcome is a gain or a loss.

Insurance

The insurance industry makes its fortune on risk.

Industrial insurance

A company operates a small manufacturing operation producing steel and aluminium aircraft components. The facility is constructed of brick. The company is valued at £2 million. The probability of the company being destroyed by fire is 0.001 per cent based on historical data of industrial accidents in England. The insurance premium is £2500 per year:

■ Expected loss is £2 000 000 × 0.00001 = £20.

On the basis of the expected-value criterion, the expected loss of £20 is less than the insurance premium of £2500 and so one would not take out insurance. However, most, if not all, manufacturing concerns have

Table 22.9	Chances of winning at blackjack				
Level of bet (FF)	Potential winnings (payoff) (FF)	Probability of winning (%)	Probability of losing (%)	Expected gain (FF)	Expected 'loss' (FF)
5	500	70	30	350	150
50	5 000	70	30	3 500	1 500
500	50 000	70	30	35 000	15 000
5 000	500 000	70	30	350 000	150 000
50 000	5 000 000	70	30	3 500 000	1 500 000
100 000	10 000 000	70	30	7 000 000	3 000 000
1 000 000	100 000 000	70	30	70 000 000	30 000 000

Figure 22.14 Utility of profit and loss.

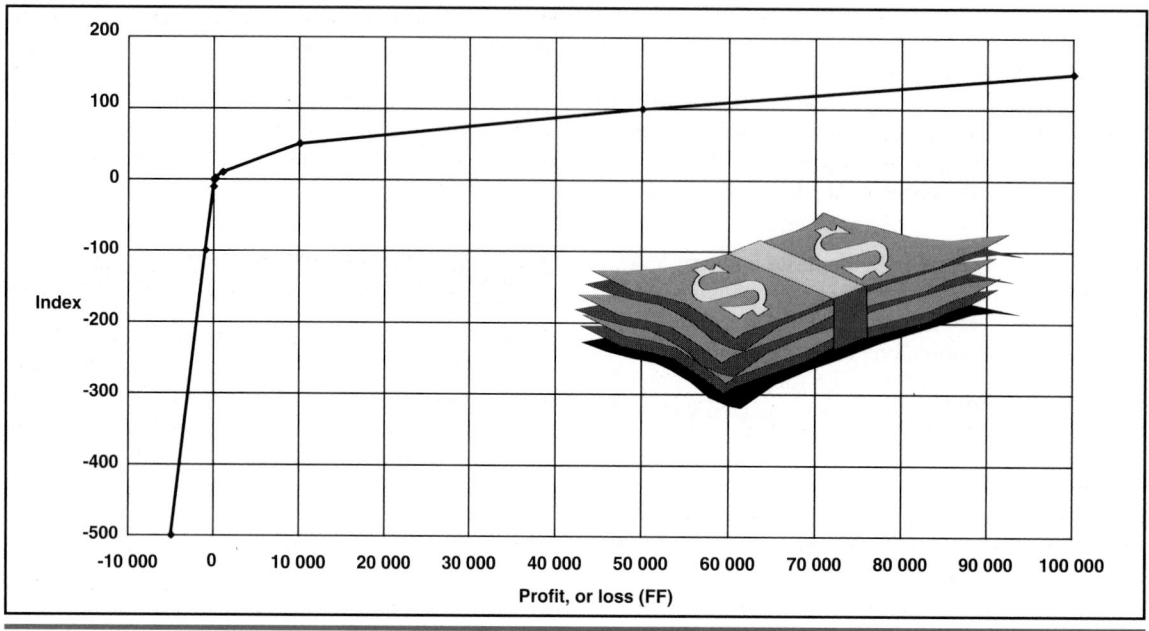

Figure 22.15 Utility curves for managers with different personalities.

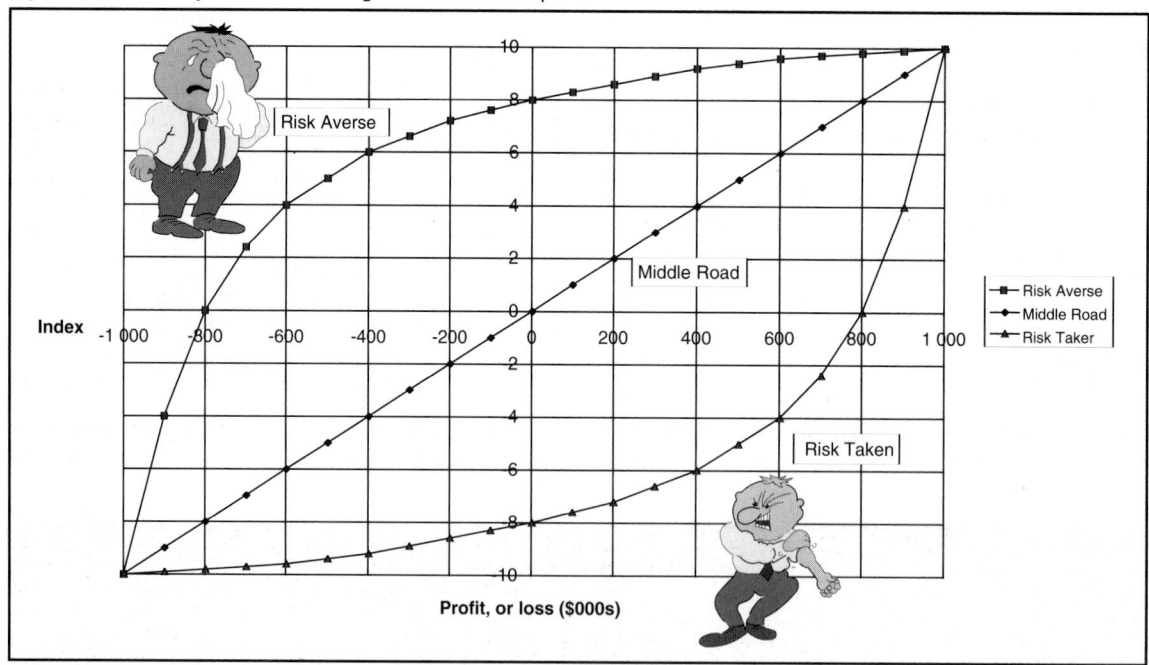

insurance. The thought (utility) of losing £2 million in assets far outweighs the cost of the premium.

Transportation insurance

A US manufacturer of compressors sends a new installation to Germany for use in a pharmaceutical operation. The value of the equipment is $4 million. The probability of the equipment being damaged, or lost, is 1 in 10 000, or 0.01 per cent.

- Expected loss is $4 × 0.0001 = $400.
- Insuring the equipment costs $2000.

Since $2000 is greater than the $400, using the expected-value criterion, one would not insure the merchandise. However, losing $4 million would be very heavy for the company and it takes out insurance.

Earthquake insurance

Some homes in Southern California (Beverly Hills, Brentwood, San Marino) have market values in excess of $1 million. The possibility of a home being completely destroyed by an earthquake is small (though not remote according to geologists' reports on the San Andreas fault). Many people have earthquake insurance, which can cost upwards of $1000 per year. This is greater than the expected loss. The thought (utility) of losing one's home greatly outweighs the insurance cost.

Flight insurance

Insurance companies – Travellers is one in the USA – have 'do it yourself' insurance booths at major airports. Here, for example, for $10 one is able to take out a life insurance of, say, $100 000 in the event the aeroplane crashes:

- The probability of the plane crashing is 1 in 500 000 or 0.0002 per cent.
- Expected loss, if an accident, is 100 000 × 0.000002 = $0.20.

This expected loss is less than the insurance premium and, under the expected value criterion, one would not take out life insurance. However, many travellers do since, if there is an accident, the loss of the family breadwinner would be disastrous.

Overall, life insurance is a bad investment (the probability of dying prematurely is low) but with the concept of utility many people have life insurance – with good returns to the insurance companies!!

COST–BENEFIT ANALYSIS

Cost–benefit analysis is an analytical tool to decide whether expenditures for a certain project are greater or less than the 'financial' benefits that would be obtained if the project was executed. If the costs are less, then the decision should be made to go ahead with the project. And the reverse, if the costs are greater.

Governments

A cost–benefit analysis is a decision tool often used in government agencies. In the USA it was popular under the administrations of Presidents Kennedy and Johnson in the 1960s. It is often used related to environmental situations as the following illustrates.

Phelps Dodge

Phelps Dodge Corporation operated a copper smelter in Douglas, Arizona, USA, for nearly 80 years. For nearly a decade, in the 1970s and early 1980s, the facility failed to meet US Environmental Clean Air laws. After a cost–benefit analysis, the company decided to close permanently the facility in 1987. It was felt that the benefits to the operation by the installation of new pollution control equipment to reduce sulphur dioxide emissions were far outweighed by the millions of dollars required to do the work. The plant closure put 347 persons out of work and removed $10 million from the local economy.[5]

The worked example, *Grivel Foundry*, illustrates the use of cost–benefit analysis.

WORKED EXAMPLE: GRIVEL FOUNDRY

Situation

The Grivel foundry, established in 1937, just north of Rennes in France, is a combination foundry and machinery operation turning out flanges, elbow joints and cooling-block parts for the refinery, chemical and food industries. The basic operation is that pieces are forged in alloyed materials of zinc, copper and nickel before passing to machining where the units are cleaned, drilled, polished and semi-assembled. They are then dispatched to the final customer. There are 55 people employed in the foundry and 73 people in machinery. Machining adds about 80 per cent of the net income to the company and 20 per cent comes from the foundry operation.

As a result of a directive from the European community, Grivel has to clean up considerably the pollution emanating from the foundry operation. This work centre uses oil-fired units that are old and inefficient. To bring the foundry to within conformity, and particularly to reduce the sulphur dioxide and nitrogen oxide emissions, will involve the installation of some rather expensive equipment.

Management at Grivel was wondering whether installing the equipment was really worth the additional cost. They were of the opinion to close the foundry and concentrate on the machining part of the business. Rough-forged components would be purchased from subcontractors and the machinery work would continue as before. This decision would involve laying off the 55 foundry workers. The disadvantages of this approach was that they would lose some flexibility in planning as they would be entirely dependent on the subcontractors. In addition, they would have to rely on the subcontractors for quality control of the forged pieces.

Before management made a final decision, they performed internally an analysis on the cost and benefits involved in installing the new equipment. This data on an annual basis over five years is given in Table 22.10.

Table 22.10 Costs and benefits associated with installing new equipment (FF)

Annual costs	
Capital cost (depreciated over five years)	11 000 000
Annual operating cost	500 000
Increased energy costs	100 000
Lost revenue (a shutdown is necessary to install the equipment)	50 000
Annual benefits	
Employee relations	6 000 000
Company image (increased sales)	750 000
Gain to local community	1 250 000
Specification control	1 250 000
Flexibility	1 750 000

The explanation of the benefits is given in the following.

Employee relations

Avoiding laying off the foundry workers would maintain morale and thus productivity in machining. In addition, it would avoid the possibility of a strike on the part of the machining personnel.

Company image (increased sales)

If the company maintained the foundry operation, it would give a good image to clients, who would feel that Grivel were able to give them a complete service.

Gain to community

It was felt unlikely that the 55 foundry workers would be able to find other employment in the community. Thus, if employed by Grivel, they would add purchasing power and tax revenue.

Specification control

Keeping the foundry would mean that Grivel would have better control of the specification and of the quality of the units produced.

Flexibility

Planning would be much easier if Grivel continued with the foundry operation.

Required

1   Develop a cost–benefit analysis for Grivel. Based on the results of this what decision should Grivel take?
2   One member of the Grivel management, who was somewhat out of touch with the human relations at the foundry, felt that the FF 6 000 000 per year allocated for employee relations was far too high. He believed that, since there was little other work in the community, there might be a loss of productivity, but the threat of industrial action was slight. On this basis, the 'benefit' of employee relations could be reduced to FF 400 000 a year, instead of the original FF 6 000 000. How would this change the cost–benefit analysis and the subsequent decision of the Grivel Co.?
3   On further discussing the project with union leaders, Grivel learnt that, if the foundry operation was closed, there would be a strong risk of prolonged industrial action. If this was the case, it was felt that a more realistic 'benefit' to Grivel concerning employee relations would be FF 20 000 000 a year, rather than FF 6 000 000. How would this change the cost–benefit analysis and the subsequent decision of the Grivel Co.?
4   Develop a curve showing the sensitivity of the cost–benefit ratio to the 'benefit' value of employee relations. In addition to the three figures given, use FF 5, 7, 8 and 10 million. What are your observations?

Table 22.11 Grivel foundry – Cost/benefit analysis of installing new equipment (For 7 differetn 'benefits')

Cost of new equipment (FF)	1	2	3	4	5	6	7
Capital cost of equipment	11 000 000	11 000 000	11 000 000	11 000 000	11 000 000	11 000 000	11 000 000
Operating Cost	500 000	500 000	500 000	500 000	500 000	500 000	500 000
Increased energy cost	100 000	100 000	100 000	100 000	100 000	100 000	100 000
Lost output	50 000	50 000	50 000	50 000	50 000	50 000	50 000
Total	11 650 000	11 650 000	11 650 000	11 650 000	11 650 000	11 650 000	11 650 000

Benefit of new equipment (FF)	1	2	3	4	5	6	7
Employee relations	400 000	5 000 000	6 000 000	7 000 000	8 000 000	10 000 000	20 000 000
Company image (increased sales)	750 000	750 000	750 000	750 000	750 000	750 000	750 000
Gain to community	1 250 000	1 250 000	1 250 000	1 250 000	1 250 000	1 250 000	1 250 000
Specification control	1 250 000	1 250 000	1 250 000	1 250 000	1 250 000	1 250 000	1 250 000
Flexibility	1 750 000	1 750 000	1 750 000	1 750 000	1 750 000	1 750 000	1 750 000
Total	5 400 000	10 000 000	11 000 000	12 000 000	13 000 000	15 000 000	25 000 000
Cost/benefit	2.16	1.17	1.06	0.97	0.90	0.78	0.47

Solution

Table 22.11 and Figure 22.16 give all the cost–benefit analysis for all the 7 different 'benefits' for employee relations:

1 The cost–benefit ratio is 1.06 (Column 3 of Table 27.11). Thus, since the costs seem to be just higher than the benefits, management should close the foundry.
2 The cost/benefit ratio is 2.16 (Column 1). Thus, since the costs are more than double the benefits, there would seem to be a strong argument for closing the foundry operation.
3 The cost/benefit ratio is 0.47 (Column 7). Thus, since the benefits are more than double the costs, there would seem to be a strong

argument for keeping the foundry operation and installing the new equipment.
4 The curve illustrates that the decision swings from closing the foundry (a low benefit from employee relations) to keeping the foundry (a high benefit from employee relations).

Cost–benefit analysis is useful in this type of decision making, but the 'benefit' values are hard to quantify. Management must be attentive to this fact. All else being equal, the preferred decision in this situation is to install the new equipment and keep the foundry operating. A motivated work force is critical, as is flexibility and quality control. Further, an improved marketing effort may be able to increase the contribution of the foundry operation.

Figure 22.16 Grivel Foundry: cost/benefit analysis for installing new equipment.

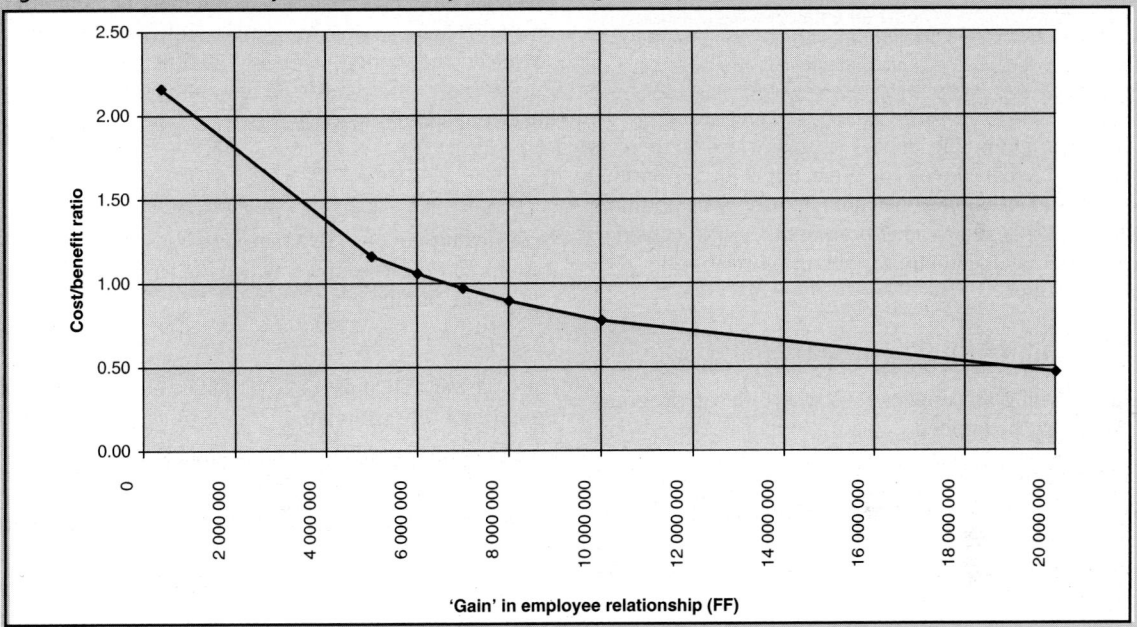

LINEAR PROGRAMMING

Linear programming is a powerful quantitative tool for decision making, which can be used to optimize decisions both at the operating and strategic levels. It determines the values of variables that would achieve a particular objective such as to:

- maximize revenues;
- maximize profits;
- minimize costs;
- maximize market share.

Restrictions

In the decision-making process, there are restrictions on arriving at desired objectives, which might be resource-related or legal requirements.

Resource availability

There may be restrictions on availability of resources, such as those shown in Table 22.12.

Table 22.12 Resources

Raw materials	Crude oil for refining, steel for producing pipe, wheat for food processing
Time	For completing a project according to schedule, for meeting a client's purchase order or meeting a flight schedule
Floor space	Surface area for new machines, additional offices or storage space
Labour	Construction labour for a building, operating labour for production or labour in a service environment
Money	For capital appropriation, equipment purchases or employee salaries
Land	For the construction of a new facility or for expansion of an existing plant

Legal codes and specifications

Legal codes and specifications are enormous. Table 22.13 gives some illustrations.

Table 22.13 Examples of legal requirements

Minimum composition specifications	Composition of fertilizers (percentage of nitrogen, phosphate and potassium) or the minimum vitamin requirements in food
Design specifications	These may have to comply with earthquake codes or fire or safety measures
Working week	This would cover the maximum hours an employee could work, including overtime (see Chapter 3, *Site Selection*)

Linear programming solves situations when there is quantitative data involved. What might be an optimal solution quantitatively may not necessarily be optimum when other qualitative factors are taken into consideration such as capability of labour, motivation level or productivity.

Application of linear programming

The following are applications where linear programming might be applied.

Product mix

This would be to select the required mix of product components, or services, that results in maximizing profits or minimizing costs, but at the same time satisfying required specifications:

- petrol in order to satisfy 'knock' requirements;
- concrete composition to satisfy strength requirements;
- food-compositions in order to satisfy regulations, such as ingredients in chocolate;
- animal-feed composition in order to satisfy minimum protein requirements;
- products to manufacture to satisfy client demand;
- placement of investments to maximize return according to guidelines (proportion in stocks, certificates of deposits and government bonds, for example).

Transportation

This would be to design a distribution network for delivery of products that would minimize total transportation costs.

Production plan

This would be to select the amount of products, or services, to be produced on both straight-time and overtime labour during each month of the year to minimize costs of labour and carrying inventory.

Assignment

This would be to assign products, or jobs, to individuals or departments so that the total costs are minimized during the planning period.

Objectives in linear programming

In linear programming, there must be a well-defined single objective in the decision to be made, such as, revenues must be maximized, costs must be minimized or the value of some objective must be defined in advance; the budget equals £10 000, for example. Furthermore, there must be alternative ways of arriving at the stated objective.

Constraints

In achieving the objective there are constraints, or limitations, on the resources available. These constraints might take on one of three forms.

Less than

Here the variable must be less than or equal to ($\leqslant$) the upper limit. For example:

- less than or equal to 100 machine hours;
- less than or equal to $900 worth of raw materials;
- less than or equal to 40 hours of labour hours per week.

Greater than

The variable must be greater than or equal to ($\geqslant$) the lower limit. For example:

- greater than or equal to 11 per cent alcohol content (wine for example);
- greater than or equal to 25 per cent of the RDA (recommended daily allowance) of protein;
- greater than or equal to $50 earnings per share next quarter.

Equal to

The variable must be equal (=) to a required amount:

- equal to 400 kg in total weight;
- equal to 900 machine hours;
- equal to a surface area of 1000 m^2.

Formulating the linear function

In formulating the decision to be optimized, the objective and the variables with their constraints must be expressed as linear mathematical functions. The objective will be to maximize, minimize or equal some given objective. In addition, the constraints, 'greater than or equal to', 'less than or equal to', or 'equal to', need to be represented as linear functions in terms of the variable values. The function is linear which means the following:

- No variable can have an exponent more than unity. X and Y are possible but not X^2, Y^3 or X^4 etc.
- There is no combination of variables. For example, if X and Y denote two of the variables, then $X \times Y$ is not permitted.

Negative values in the solution are not permitted. Additionally, in certain situations, only integer values are acceptable, such as the number of people, number of trucks or number of machines.

Tools for solving linear-programming problems

The Simplex method is a common tool for solving linear programs. An alternative to Simplex is Kamarkar's algorithm, which was developed by Narendra Karmarker in 1984.[6] Compared to Simplex, this algorithm usually takes significantly less computer time to solve complex linear-programming situations. In transportation and assignment linear programming,

methods include the North West Corner Rule, Vogels Approximation Method and the MODI method.[7]

Linear-programming problems are solved by computer and linear-programming packages can be purchased and used without the user understanding the tedious arithmetical gymnastics involved in solving linear-programming problems. Microsoft Excel is a well-known spreadsheet computer program that incorporates a linear-programming tool called Solver, which is used in this text. Linear-programming examples using the Microsoft Solver Macro have already been presented for job assignment situations in Chapter 14, *Operations Scheduling*, and a transportation problem in Chapter 17, *Managing the Supply Chain*.

Two variables

If there are only two variables in an operating situation, a linear program situation can be presented and/or solved graphically. The ability to present the information on a graph is useful in that it gives a clear illustration of the interconnection between the constraints and the objectives. This idea is illustrated with the two worked examples, *Braun Engineering* and *Vogler Confectionery*. In practice, however, business is usually more complex and involves more than two variables.

WORKED EXAMPLE: BRAUN ENGINEERING

Situation

The Braun engineering services company in Alhambra, California, USA, uses Senior and Junior Engineers on its design projects. Senior Engineers are more experienced, but command higher salaries than Junior Engineers. However, Senior Engineers require less supervision and less computer assistance than Junior Engineers.

Senior Engineers cost Braun $16.00 per hour compared to $7.50 per hour for Junior Engineers. Each hour of senior engineering time requires 5 min of supervision by the Project Manager and 15 min of computer time. Every hour of junior engineers requires 30 min of supervision from the Project Manager and 25 min of computer time. It is the Junior Engineers who do the bulk of the computer work.

The Braun company has just been awarded a design project and needs to decide on the mix of Senior and Junior Engineers to execute the project. In bidding for the project, it budgeted a maximum total labour cost for Senior and Junior Engineers of $75 000. There is available for the project a maximum of 1000 hours of supervision by the Project Manager and 2500 hours of computer time. The project will be billed at an hourly rate, such that the time of Senior Engineers will yield a profit of $2.50 per hour, whereas Junior Engineer's time will yield a profit of $3.75 per hour.

Required

1 What is the maximum profit attainable for this project within the constraints given and what is the corresponding mix of Senior and Junior Engineers?

2 Illustrate the optimum solution on a graph.

Solution

1 Profit and engineering mix – let:

P = profit;
X_s = Number of Senior Engineer hours;
X_j = Number of Junior Engineer hours;

Then, the objective function P, which is the function to maximize, is given by:

$$P = 2.50X_s + 3.75X_j.$$

Constraints are:

$16.00X_s + 7.50X_j \leq 75\ 000$ (Cost of Senior and Junior Engineers);
$5/60X_s + 30/60X_j \leq 1000$ (Hours of supervision);
$15/60X_s + 25/60X_j \leq 2500$ (Computer time).

Figure 22.17 gives the arrangement to solve using Microsoft Solver:

- Cell B-3 is the maximum cost possible.
- Cell B-4 is the maximum supervision hours possible.
- Cell B-5 is the maximum computer hours possible.
- Cell B-6 contains the formula for calculating the profit objective, (C-6)*(C-8) + (D-6)*(D-8). This is the cell to maximize in Solver.

Figure 22.17 Braun Engineering: layout of problem.

	A	B	C	D	E
1		Maximum	Senior	Junior	Actual
2			Engineers	Engineers	
3	Cost	75 000.00	16.00	7.50	0.00
4	Supervision	1 000.00	0.0833	0.5000	0.00
5	Computer time	2 500.00	0.2500	0.4167	0.00
6	Profit		2.50	3.75	
7					
8	Hours required		0.00	0.00	
9					

Figure 22.18 Braun Engineering: solution of Microsoft Solver.

	A	B	C	D	E
1		Maximum	Senior	Junior	Actual
2			Engineers	Engineers	
3	Cost	75 000.00	16.00	7.50	75 000.00
4	Supervision	1 000.00	0.0833	0.5000	1 000.00
5	Computer time	2 500.00	0.2500	0.4167	1 567.80
6	Profit	15 127.12	2.50	3.75	
7					
8	Hours required		4 067.80	1 322.03	
9					

- Cell C-3 is the $/h cost for senior engineers.
- Cell C-4 is the hours of supervision time each hour for senior engineers.
- Cell C-5 is the hours of computer time each hour for senior engineers.
- Cell C-6 is the $/h profit for senior engineers.
- Cell C-8 contains the senior engineering hours to maximize profit. This is a variable value in Solver and is initially zero at the start of the solution.
- Cell D-3 is the $/h cost for junior engineers.
- Cell D-4 is the hours of supervision time each hour for junior engineers.
- Cell D-5 is the hours of computer time each hour for junior engineers.
- Cell D-6 is the $/h profit for junior engineers.
- Cell D-8 contains the junior engineering hours to maximize profit. This is a variable value in Solver and is initially zero at the start of the solution.
- Cell E-3 contains the formula for calculating the cost, (C-3)*(C-8) + (D-3)*(D-8). This is the first 'less than or equal to' constraint with the maximum constraint value given in cell B-3.
- Cell E-4 contains the formula for calculating the supervision hours, (C-4)*(C-8) + (D-4)*(D-8). This is the second 'less than or equal to' constraint with the maximum constraint value given in cell B-4.

- Cell E-5 contains the formula for calculating the computer hours, (C-5)*(C-8) + (D-5)*(D-8). This is the third 'less than or equal to' constraint with the maximum constraint value given in cell B-5.

Figure 22.18 gives the solution for this linear programming problem:
- Profit is $15 127.12.
- Senior Engineer Hours are 4067.80.
- Junior Engineer Hours are 1322.03.

Graphical presentation – Figure 22.19 gives the graphical presentation of this problem. The three straight lines are arrived at as follows:

Cost

The constraint function is converted to an equation:

$16.00X_s + 7.50X_j = 75\ 000$ (Cost of Senior and Junior Engineers).

When:

$$X_s = 0, \text{ then } X_j = 75\ 000/7.50 = 10\ 000;$$
$$X_j = 0, \text{ then } X_s = 75\ 000/16.00 = 4687.50.$$

This give two points to construct the cost curve.

Supervision

The constraint function is converted to an equation:

Figure 22.19 Braun Engineering: linear programming.

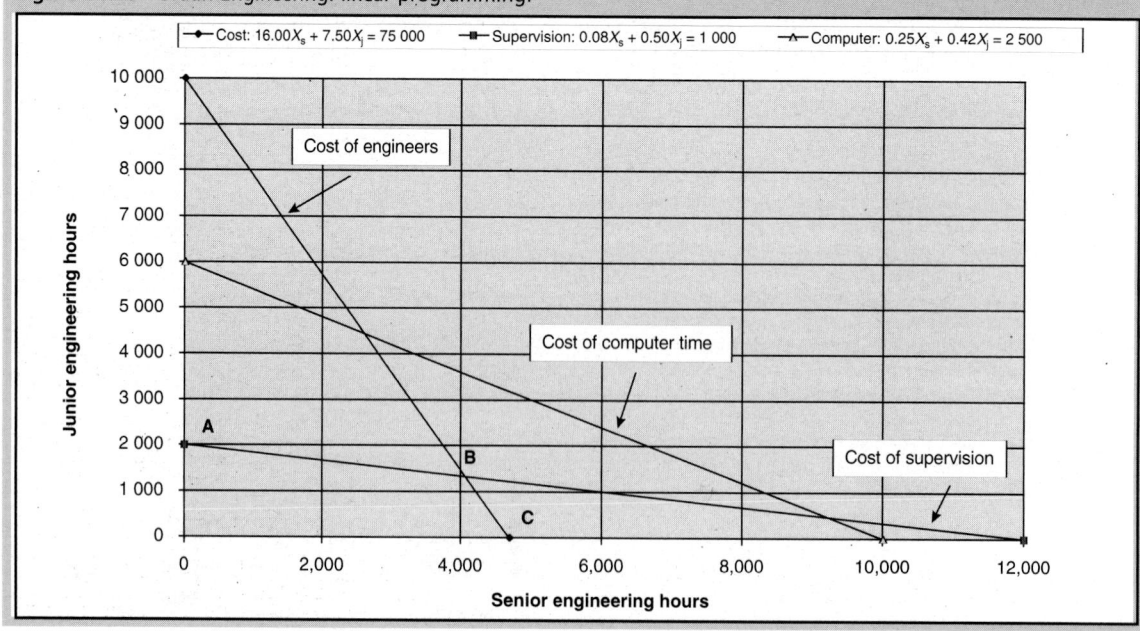

$5/60X_s + 30/60X_j = 1000$ (Hours of supervision).

This can be simplified to:

$0.08X_s + 0.50X_j = 1000$ (Hours of supervision).

When:

$X_s = 0$, then $X_j = 1000/0.50 = 2000$;
$X_j = 0$, then $X_s = 1000/0.08 = 12\ 000$.

This give two points to construct the supervision curve.

Computer time:

The constraint function is converted to an equation:

$15/60X_s + 25/60X_j = 2500$ (Computer time).

This can be simplified to:

$0.25X_s + 0.42X_j = 2500$ (Computer time).

When:

$X_s = 0$, then $X_j = 2500/0.42 = 5999.52$;
$Xj = 0$, then $X_s = 2500/0.25 = 10\ 000$.

This give two points to construct the computer curve.

To satisfy the constraints of this situation all three must be satisfied. In this case, the solution must lie in the quadrangle ABCO in Figure 22.19, since this is a 'less than or equal to' situation. Any values outside ABCO will not satisfy all of the constraints.

The optimum solution is the intersection of the supervision and cost curves, point B, which corresponds to the results given by Solver. At this point, the cost of the project is at the limit of the constraint ($75 000, the value in cell E-3). The supervision also is at the limit of the constraint (1000 hours, the value in cell E-4). However, the computer time is not at the maximum (1567.80 hours as opposed to a maximum possible of 2500 hours, cell E-5). This is also illustrated by the fact that the point B does not lie on the curve for computer time.

WORKED EXAMPLE: VOGLER CONFECTIONERY

Situation

The Vogler Confectionery Co. in St. Etienne, France, is a small manufacturing company that produces many types of confectionery products. Two of its main products are plain and milk chocolate bars sold in 100 g tablets. In setting up the production run for the month the company needed to decide on the quantity of plain and milk chocolate to produce to minimize manufacturing costs. Manufacturing costs per ton are FF 800 for plain chocolate, and FF 700 for milk chocolate. The difference is principally due to the use of superior quality cocoa beans for the plain chocolate.

There were several constraints for the production operation. Marketing stipulated that for their needs they would require at least 8 tons (80 000 tablets) of plain chocolate and at least 14 tons (140 000 tablets) of milk chocolate for the coming month. The Finance department set the objective that the profit made on this month's production should exceed FF 60 000. The profit per ton of chocolate was FF 2500 for plain and FF 1200 for milk chocolate. Finally, for scheduling purposes, production wanted to be sure that at least 2400 h of total labour time was used in this section of the work centre. Historical data indicated that labour time was 50 h/ton for plain chocolate and 75 h/ton for milk chocolate. The difference was principally due to the additional mixing and controlling needed for the milk chocolate.

Required

1 What is the minimum production cost for Vogler and what are the corresponding production levels for plain and milk chocolate?
2 Illustrate the optimum solution on a graph.

Solution

1 Production cost, and tonnage – let:

$C = $ cost;
$X_b = $ tons of plain chocolate;
$X_m = $ tons of milk chocolate.

Then the objective function C, which is the function to minimize, is given by:

$$C = 800X_b + 700X_m.$$

Constraints are:

$2500X_b + 1200X_m \geqslant 60\ 000$ (Profit, FF);
$X_b \geqslant 8$ (Market demand for plain chocolate);
$X_m \geqslant 14$ (Market demand for milk chocolate);
$50X_b + 75X_m \geqslant 2400$ (Production time, h).

Figure 22.20 gives the arrangement to solve using Microsoft Solver:

■ Cell B-3 is the minimum profit required.
■ Cell B-5 is the minimum production time needed.
■ Cell B-6 contains the formula for calculating the cost objective, (C-6)*(C-8) + (D-6)*(D-8). This is the cell to minimize in Solver.
■ Cell C-3 is the profit/ton in FF for plain chocolate.
■ Cell C-4 is market demand for plain chocolate. This is one of the minimum constraints in the problem.
■ Cell C-5 is the labour hours/ton for plain chocolate.
■ Cell C-6 is the cost/ton in FF for plain chocolate.
■ Cell C-8 is the tons of plain chocolate to produce to optimize the problem. This is a variable in Solver.
■ Cell D-3 is the profit/ton in FF for milk chocolate.
■ Cell D-4 is market demand for milk chocolate. This is one of the minimum constraints in the problem.
■ Cell D-5 is the labour hours/ton for milk chocolate.
■ Cell D-6 is the cost/ton in FF for milk chocolate.
■ Cell D-8 is the tons of milk chocolate to produce to optimize the problem. This is a variable in Solver.

Figure 22.20   Vogler Confectionery: layout of problem.

	A	B	C	D	E
1		Minimum	Plain	Milk	Actual
2		Needs	Chocolate	Chocolate	
3	Profit	60 000	2 500	1 200	
4	Market	0	8	14	
5	Production	2 400	50	75	
6	Cost		800	700	
7					
8	Production, tons		0.00	0.00	
9					

- Cell E-3 contains the formula for calculating the actual profit, (C-3)*(C-8) + (D-3)*(D-8). This is one of the constraints in the problem with the minimum constraint value given in cell B-3.
- Cell E-5 contains the formula for calculating the production time, (C-5)*(C-8) + (D-5)*(D-8). This is another constraint with the minimum constraint value given in cell B-5.

Figure 22.21 gives the solution using Microsoft Solver:

- Cost is FF 29 733.33.
- 8.00 tons of plain chocolate should be produced.
- 33.33 tons of milk chocolate should be produced.

2 Graphical presentation – Figure 22.22 gives the graphical presentation of this problem. The four straight lines are arrived at as follows.

Profit

The constraint function is converted to an equation:

$$2500X_b + 1200X_m = 60\,000 \text{ (Profit, FF).}$$

When:

$$X_b = 0, \text{ then } X_m = 60\,000/1200 = 50.00;$$
$$X_m = 0, \text{ then } X_b = 60\,000/1600 = 24.00.$$

This gives two points to construct the cost curve.

Market demand for plain chocolate

The constraint function is converted to an equation:

$$X_b = 8 \text{ (Market demand for plain chocolate).}$$

No matter what, the market demand for plain chocolate is a vertical line, parallel to the y axis.

Market demand for milk chocolate

The constraint function is converted to an equation:

$$X_b = 14 \text{ (Market demand for milk chocolate).}$$

No matter what, the market demand for milk chocolate is a horizontal line, parallel to the x axis.

Production time

The constraint function is converted to an equation:

$$50X_b + 75X_m = 2400 \text{ (Production time, h).}$$

When:

$$X_b = 0, \text{ then } X_m = 2400/75 = 32.00;$$
$$X_m = 0, \text{ then } X_s = 2400/50 = 48.00.$$

This gives two points to construct the production-time curve.

To satisfy the constraints of this situation all four must be satisfied. In this case, the solution must lie to the right of and above the area denoted by ABCDE, since since is a 'greater than or equal to' situation.

The optimum solution is the intersection of the market demand for plain chocolate, and the profit curve, point B, which corresponds to the results given by Solver. At this point the production cost is at the limit of the constraint (FF 60 000, the value in cell E-3). The production of plain chocolate (8 tons) is also at the limit of the minimum market demand (Cell C-4). However, the tonnage of milk chocolate (33.33 tons) is above the minimum amount of 14 tons (Cell D-4) and the labour time (2900 hours, Cell E-5) is above the minimum requirement of 2400 hours (Cell B-5). This is also demonstrated by the fact that both these curves lie below point B.

Figure 22.21   Vogler Confectionery: solution using Microsoft Solver.

	A	B	C	D	E
1		Minimum	Plain	Milk	Actual
2		Needs	Chocolate	Chocolate	
3	Profit	60 000	2 500	1 200	6 0000
4	Market		8	14	
5	Production	2.400	50.00	75.00	2900
6	Cost	29 733.33	800	700	
7					
8	Production, tons		8.00	33.33	
9					

Figure 22.22   Vogler Confectionery: linear programming.

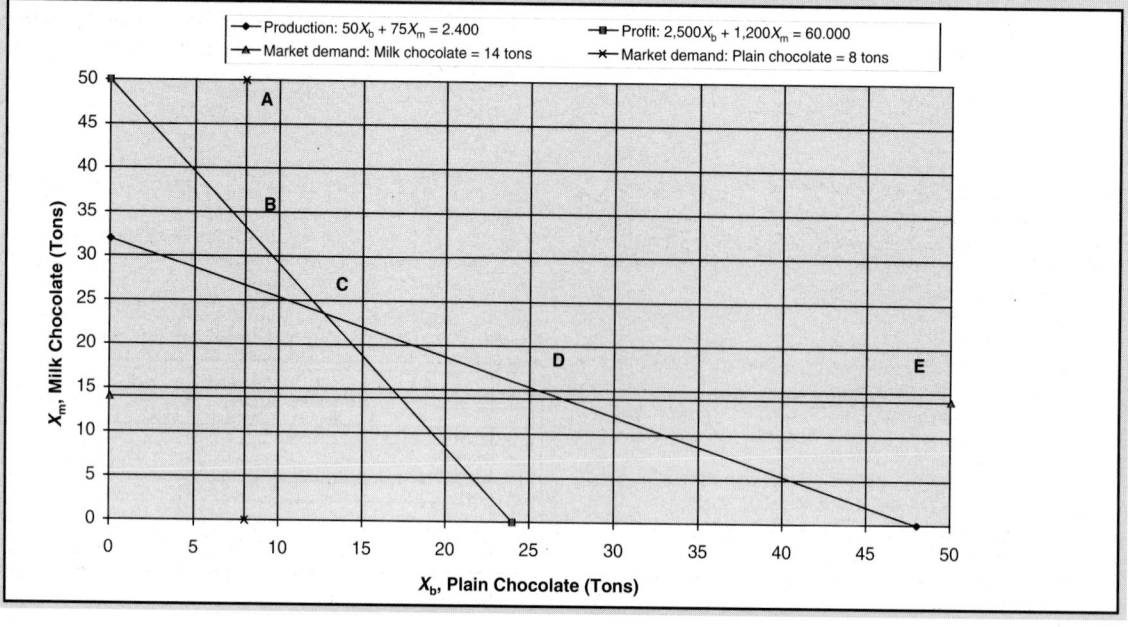

SUMMARY OF KEY ELEMENTS

- Any aspect of business (or life) involves making a decision, which, as a corollary, invokes risk. The more systematic one is in analysing the variables involved in the decision, the less likely is the downside risk.

- A trade-off is making a choice between one outcome and another, where both have advantages and disadvantages.

- When there are several decisions to make, it is helpful to prioritize them.

- The magnitude of decision making can range from intuition, through quick and dirty, computations and model building, to implementing a task force.

- The decision process involves understanding the reasons for a decision, analysing the situation, defining objectives, developing and analysing alternatives, selecting the best alternative, executing plans and afterwards monitoring the results.

- The environments for decision making include decision making under certainty, decision making under risk and decision making under uncertainty.

- In decision theory there are environmental changes, over which a manager has no control. However, there is more than one alternative and each offers some financial payoff.

- In decision making under certainty the future outcomes are known with certainty.

- In decision making under uncertainly, there is no clear information on the external environment, so it is difficult to establish probabilities. Criteria for decisions include maximin, maximax, equally likely and minimax regret.

- In decision making under risk, probabilities can be assigned to outcomes. Then expected values can be determined which can be used as criteria for a decision.

- A decision tree shows the alternative decisions using square nodes for the decision point, circular nodes for external events where probabilities can be assigned, branches for the direction of the decision and payoffs for the possible outcomes.

- Many decisions are dependent on the external environment. A 'what if?' analysis looks at the sensitivity of the decision with assumed changes in the environment.

- A payoff table is a matrix showing all the possible outcomes for various options available according to the likely external events. These outcomes are then weighted according to the given probabilities to determine expected values.

- Marginal analysis uses probabilities and expected values to consider the benefit of some action, as opposed to the outcome if that action is not taken. The minimum probability is the ratio of marginal loss to the sum of marginal loss and marginal profit.

- Utility is the satisfaction or disappointment derived from certain outcomes. People have different utility levels and this can impact the apparent logic of a decision.

- A cost–benefit analysis is a tool to decide whether the expenditures for a certain project are greater than the perceived financial benefits if the project were executed.

- Linear programming is a method to optimize a decision in situations such as maximizing revenues or profits or minimizing costs. The method creates a linear function taking into account constraints involved in the decision situation.

REVIEW AND DISCUSSION QUESTIONS

1 **Personal decision making**. What are some of the biggest decisions you have made in your life? What was the element of risk? Did you make an in-depth analysis before you took the decision? Did the result turn out as planned?

2 **Cost–benefit analysis**. What are some of the elements you would consider in a cost–benefit analysis for the following situations:
(a) Tree cutting in the Brazilian Rain Forest?
(b) A recycling programme for plastic bottles?
(c) Building a new town hall in your community?
(d) Closing hospitals in Britain?
Indicate those elements which you believe are difficult to quantify. What are some of the elements which should be taken into account, but which probably do not enter into the decision process?

3 **Magnitude of decision making**. Considering the magnitude of decision making, under which category would you put the following decisions:
(a) Purchasing a new suit?
(b) Building an express train link between Berlin and Paris?
(c) Deciding whether to take early retirement?
(d) Deciding whether to give your child a university education at a private institution in the United States?

4 **Decision trees**. Develop a decision tree showing the various paths in your professional career up to retirement. Indicate on the tree the decisions over which you believe you have control and the states of nature over which you have little control. Attempt to put in probabilities on the decision tree. How sensitive is your plan to the environment?

5 **Utility**. In the concept of utility, would you consider yourself a risk taker, risk averse or middle-of-the-road? Give examples to justify your classification. If you are not satisfied with your analysis, what might you be able to do to change?

6 **Linear programming**. Give at least five additional examples where linear programming might be used effectively. Indicate the objectives, variables and constraints for each situation.

EXERCISE PROBLEM: BED AND BREAKFAST

Situation

Sally Stock is considering opening a bed and breakfast (B&B) operation in Sydney, Australia. This will be Sally's sole source of revenue. She is thinking of building either a small B&B with 12 rooms, a large B&B with 50 rooms or she may abandon the idea altogether. She is considering leasing, for five years, one of two facilities in the Sydney area for her project.

A friend, Bill, will perform a market survey. Sally has estimated that if she establishes a large B&B and the market is favourable, she can earn $A60 000 over a five-year period, but will lose $A40 000 if the market is unfavourable. The small B&B will return a $A30 000 profit with a favourable market and a $A10 000 loss if the market is unfavourable.

At the present time, Sally believes there is a 50/50 chance that there will be a favourable market. Bill will charge Sally $A5000 for the market survey. Bill has estimated that there is a 60 per cent probability that the market survey will be favourable. What is more, he believes that there will be a 90 per cent probability that the market will be favourable, given a favourable outcome of the market survey. However, Bill has warned Sally that there is a probability of only a 12 per cent favourable market, if the results of the market survey are not favourable.

Required

Develop a decision tree indicating what would be the best approach for Sally.

EXERCISE PROBLEM: BOVINE

Situation

Britain has been preoccupied with the possibility of an outbreak of Creutzfeldt–Jakob disease caused by exposure to beef with BSE. A major decision by the government was the extent of destruction of cattle in order to minimize contamination. Reaction in other European countries was total destruction of the herds of cattle. For Britain this would have been an horrendous cost and financial ruin for many farmers.

Assume that the ability of BSE to infect humans can be categorized at the levels of zero, low, medium and high. Furthermore, the government's policy to the crisis could be to do nothing, mild intervention, which would mean selective killing of cattle, or strong intervention, which means complete destruction of all the cows.

The basis for a cost matrix is considered by saying that the 'cost' if nothing is done by the government, under the four possible assumptions would be as in Table 22.14. The cost of action by the government, under the zero assumption of infection is considered to be as shown in Table 22.15. Furthermore, the assumption is that selective culling reduces the rate of infection by 45 per cent and the total destruction reduces it by 85 per cent.[8]

Table 22.14 Cost matrix for government doing nothing about BSE (arbitrary units)

	Assumptions about infection			
	Zero	Low	Medium	High
Do nothing	0	3000	6000	10 000

Table 22.15 Cost of action on BSE under zero assumption of infection (arbitrary units)

	Zero infection
Do nothing	0
Mild intervention	1500
Strong intervention	4500

Required

1 Develop the complete cost matrix for this situation.
2 Under the maximax criteria, which would be the proposed action?
3 Under the maximin criteria which would be the proposed action?
4 Develop a regret matrix. Using this evaluation, what would be the proposed action?

EXERCISE PROBLEM: CONSTRUK

Situation

Construk Inc. in Southern California performs engineering, design and construction work for international and domestic clients. Next year it has a potential project from a French/Chinese consortium to perform design work on the reactor system of a nuclear power plant. The work is very specialized and Construk will need to hire engineers trained in this area. The extent of the design work has not been completely defined, but is expected to be between 19 600 hours and 27 440 hours. This is indicated in Table 22.16, with the estimated probabilities for the work being released.

Table 22.16 Extent and probability of design work for Construk

Customer job hours	19 600	21 560	23 520	25 480	27 440
Probability of this level (%)	20.00	45.00	30.00	4.00	1.00

Engineers are paid an average of $35/h on the basis of 2080 hours per year. However, included in these 2080 hours are three weeks' paid vacation. (The working week is 40 h). If engineers are hired and the work level does not materialize, they will be retained by the company and assigned to developing equipment specifications (indirect work). This indirect work is not billed to the client. That is, these engineers will be paid their hourly salary and this represents a cost to Construk. It is budgeted that the work will be finished within the year.

The customer is billed at a rate of $42/h, but only for the time that the engineers work on the project.

Required

1 Using the concept of expected values, without any financial considerations, estimate how many engineers should be hired?
2 Using an expected profit table (taking into account the financial information), how many engineers should be hired to maximize the expected profit? What is this expected profit?
3 What is the expected value of perfect information (EVPI)?
4 How might the concept of EVPI be interpreted in this particular situation?

EXERCISE PROBLEM: CRUISE

Situation

A boat construction company on the East Coast of the USA is considering adding to its fleet of cruise ships for the Caribbean region. It is considering four options:

- build a large luxury boat;
- build a medium boat;
- build a smaller boat;
- build in a joint venture with a French company.

The estimated net present value (NPV) of the returns, according to the market demand as defined by the company, for cruise vacations is as given in Table 22.17.

Table 22.17 The estimated net present value (NPV) of the returns ($) for cruise vacations

| | Market change | | |
	Increase	Stable	Decline
Large boat	2 750 000	750 000	−1 500 000
Medium boat	1 500 000	500 000	−100 000
Small boat	1 000 000	400 000	−10 000
Joint Venture	550 000	150 000	0

Required

1 If a manager was pessimistic in his approach, which decision would be taken?
2 If a manager was optimistic in his approach, which decision would be taken?
3 Using the concept of regret, which decision would be taken?
4 If there was a 50 per cent chance of an increase in the market, and a 50 per cent chance of a declining market, which decision would be made based on the concept of expected values? (In this risk situation a stable market is not an option.)
5 In the case of the 50/50 probability from Question 4, what would need to be the NPV for the large boat in order that the expected value of returns for the large boat and medium boat gives a break-even situation?

EXERCISE PROBLEM: DRILLING EQUIPMENT

Situation

The Santa Rosa Drilling Co. in Texas, USA, is planning to purchase additional drilling equipment to aid in the exploration of new offshore oil fields.

The company is considering three types of new equipment, Snowcat, Wildcat and Madcat. The possible annual outcome from the purchase of this equipment is shown in Table 22.18.

Table 22.18 The possible annual outcome ($) from the purchase of new drilling equipment

Equipment	Favourable market	Unfavourable market
Snowcat	3 000 000	−2 000 000
Wildcat	2 500 000	−1,000 000
Madcat	750 000	−180 000

Required

1 What type of decision is the Santa Rosa company facing?
2 What decision criteria should be used?
3 Which alternative is best?

EXERCISE PROBLEM: HANSON

Situation

John Hanson is the Operations Manager of a manufacturing facility that makes automobile engine parts. The facility uses flexible manufacturing and John is able to change from one product range to another relatively easily. The capacity of John's facility is now saturated and he has to make a decision on adding new machines to handle the combined drilling, milling and welding operations. This automated equipment is expensive.

John knows that he wants to purchase equipment manufactured by Brown-Boveri and he has narrowed his requirements down to one or two machines. If just one machine is purchased now, and demand for engine parts turns out to be more than expected, a second machine can be purchased at a later date. However, in this case, purchasing a second machine later would cost more than if both machines were purchased together because of higher unit transportation and installation costs.

Based on knowledge of the business, John estimates that the probability of low demand is about 40 per cent, and high demand 60 per cent.

If John purchases two machines at the same time, and demand for engine parts is high, then the net present value (NPV) of profits associated with the machines would be $520 000. If demand turns out to be low, then the NPV of profits will be only $300 000 as one machine would be running below capacity.

If John purchases only one machine now, and demand is low, then the NPV of profits is estimated at $360 000. However, if the demand turns out to be high, then John has three options:

1 Do nothing. This means losing potential business and the NPV of profits would stay at $360 000.
2 Subcontract the additional business, which would yield a NPV of profits to John of $440 000.
3 Purchase another machine, which would result in a NPV of $400 000.

Required

1 Draw a decision tree showing the various options available to John Hanson.
2 On the decision tree, show the value of all the expected outcomes.
3 Based on the data given above, what decision should John make concerning the purchase of machines?
4 If the estimated NPV of profits for the subcontracting option was $480 000 instead of $440 000, what impact would this have on John's decision?

EXERCISE PROBLEM: IPRAS

Situation

Tugrul Osmal is the Chief Engineer at the Ipras Oil Refinery in Izmit, Turkey. He is considering adding a new Unit A to the present catalytic cracking unit to upgrade petrol production. It is not certain that this Unit A will work, because the crude used at Ipras is high in sulphur and excessive sulphur levels in the Unit A would poison the catalyst. However, if the Unit A works, Ipras could realize a return of $350 000 per year. If the unit does not work, the company stands to lose $150 000 per year. At the present time, Tugrul estimates that there is a 40 per cent chance that the Unit A will work.

An alternative option for Tugrul is to build a pilot plant first to test a smaller version of the Unit A. Based on the results of that, Tugrul could then decide whether to build a commercial version of Unit A. Constructing and operating the pilot plant would cost an annualized $45 000. There is a 50 per cent chance that the pilot plant would work. If the pilot plant works, there is then a 90 per cent probability that the commercial Unit A,

if subsequently built, would perform correctly. If the pilot unit does not work, there is only a 20 per cent chance that the commercial plant, if constructed, would work.

Required

1 Develop a decision tree based on the above information.
2 Show quantitatively on the decision tree, and explain, the best strategy for Tugrul.
3 Tugrul, after discussing the project with a US engineer, decides that the probability of the commercial facility working with no pilot plant could be increased to 55 per cent from the original 40 per cent. In this case, would this cause a change in the decision for Tugrul? Justify your response.
4 What can you say about the sensitivity of this decision situation?

EXERCISE PROBLEM: NAVAJO TRIBE

Situation

The Navajo Co. is considering building a facility near Page, Arizona, to produce Indian jewellery, pottery and sculptures typical of the Navajo tribe. The decisions being considered, with an estimate of the possible outcomes, are given in Table 22.19.

Table 22.19   The options for Navajo Co., together with estimated outcomes ($)

Decision	Favourable market (40%)	Unfavourable market (60%)
Build large plant	400 000	−300 000
Build small plant	80 000	−100 000
Don't build	0	0

Required

1 Construct a decision tree.
2 Determine the best strategy using expected monetary value (EMV).
3 What is the expected value of perfect information?

EXERCISE PROBLEM: PILLER

Situation

Ron Piller is a baker in Normandy. One of his specialities is a black forest chocolate cake, which he sells in his bakery shop for FF 105. The cost of making the cake, including his time and the ingredients, is FF 54. Ron bakes his cakes in the morning before 7:00 and hopes to sell them that same day before he closes the store at 19:00. Any of these black forest cakes remaining at the end of the day are sold to the local retirement home for FF 20. There is never any problem in selling his cakes to the retirement home.

Based on past data, the probability of selling the chocolate cakes fresh (that is the same day they are baked) is given in Table 22.20.

Table 22.20   Piller – the probability of selling the chocolate cakes fresh

Cakes demanded	Probability of this demand
20	0.02
21	0.05
22	0.07
23	0.09
24	0.12
25	0.14
26	0.18
27	0.20
28	0.10
29	0.02
30	0.01

Required

1 Using marginal analysis, determine the minimum required probability in order to justify Ron making an additional cake.
2 At the probability level in question 1, what would be the number of cakes to make?
3 Verify your answer with a table showing expected marginal loss and expected marginal profit for each level of the number of cakes demanded.
4 Convert the table in Question 3 into a histogram.

EXERCISE PROBLEM: TENNIS

Situation

A community is facing pressure from its residents to construct several tennis courts in its town. A cost–benefit approach to the project yields the information in Table 22.21.

Table 22.21   Costs and benefits (£) of constructing tennis courts

Cost	
Administration	15 000
Salaries of employees (3)	40 000
Maintenance	12 500
Energy	7 500
Benefits	
Social (enjoyment of playing)	8 000
Community image	6 000
Social (occupies youth)	15 000
Income to restaurant/shops	20 000

Required

1 Based on a cost–benefit analysis, using the information provided, would the tennis facility be constructed?
2 How could the costs be adjusted to make the project more feasible?
3 What major cost is missing from the data?

NOTES AND REFERENCES

1. Hisrich, R. D. and Peters, M. P. (1984) *Marketing Decisions for New and Mature Products*, Columbus, OH: C. E. Merrill: 16–17.
2. 'So you fail: Now bounce back' (1995) *Fortune* 1 May: 45.
3. *Business Week* (1995) 1 May.
4. 'The Love boats are brawling: They're launching lush new ships – and small lines may sink' (1995) *Business Week* 8 May: 64.
5. Shields, T. (1987) 'Smelter's billows depart Arizona sky', *USA Today* 15 January: 3A.
6. Ferris, M. C. and Philport, A. B. (1988) 'On the performance of Karmarkar's Algorithm', *Journal of the Operational Research Society* 39: 257–70.
7. Taylor, B. W. III (1996) *Introduction to Management Science*, Englewood Cliffs, NJ; London: Prentice Hall.
8. Based on 'Apocalypse maybe: Sometimes governments must respond to unknown probabilities of extremely unpleasant outcomes. Can economic theory help?' (1996) *The Economist* 30 March: 84.

FURTHER READING

Al-Harbi, K. A.-S., Selim, S. Z. and Al-Sinan, M. (1996) 'A multiobjective linear program for scheduling repetitive projects', *Cost Engineering* 38(12): 41–45.

Al-Shammari, M. and Dawood, I. (1997) 'Linear programming applied to a production blending problem: A spreadsheet modelling approach', *Production and Inventory Management Journal* 38(1): 1–7.

Anderson, D. R., Sweeney, D. J. and Williams, T. A. (1997) *Introduction to Management Science: Quantitative Approaches to Decision Making*, St. Paul, MN: West Publishing.

Anderson, D. R., Sweeney, D. J. and Williams, T. A. (1995) *Quantitative Methods for Business*, St Paul, MN: West Publishing.

Ansell, J. and Wharton, F. (1992) *Risk: Analysis, Assessment and Management*, Chichester; New York: Wiley.

Ball, R. (1991) *Quantitative Approaches to Management*, Oxford: Butterworth-Heinemann.

Balson, W. E., Welsh J. L. and Wilson, D. S. (1992) 'Using decision analysis and risk analysis to manage utility environmental risk', *Interfaces* 22(6): 126–39.

Berger, D. (1995) 'A measure of success: The cost-benefit analysis equation', *Plant Engineering and Maintenance* 18(2): 10.

Bernstein, P. L. (1996) *Against the Gods: The Remarkable Story of Risk*, New York; Chichester: Wiley.

Bonini, C. P., Hausman, W. H. and Bierman, H. (1981) *Quantitative Analysis for Business Decisions*, Homewood, IL: Irwin.

Carter, M. and Williamson, D. (1996) *Quantitative Modelling for Business and Management*, London: Pitman.

Curwin, J. and Slater, R. (1991) *Quantitative Methods for Business Decisions*, London, New York: Chapman & Hall.

Dillinger, A. M., Stein, W. E. and Mizzi, P. J. (1992) 'Risk averse decisions in business planning', *Decision Sciences* 23(4): 1003–08.

Earl, M. J. (1996) 'The risks of outsourcing IT', *Sloan Management Review* 37(3): 26–32.

Erikson, W. and Hall, O. P. (1986) *Computer Models for Management Science*, Reading, MA: Addison-Wesley.

Fiora, G. and Specht, P. G. (1992) 'Cost-Benefit analysis and risk: In the hands of the Supreme Court', *Professional Safety* 37(4): 24–28.

Gilliland, S. W., Schmitt, N. and Wood, L. (1993) 'Cost-benefit determinants of decision process and accuracy', *Organisational Behaviour & Human Decision Processes* 56(2): 308–30.

Hackett, G. and Caunt, D. (1994) *Quantitative Methods*, Oxford; Cambridge, MA: Blackwell.

Haraden, J. (1992) 'Cost-benefit analyses for the development of magma power', *Energy Economics* 14(4): 255–64.

Jablonowski, M. (1992) 'Expert systems for risk management', *Risk Management* 39(9): 56–60.

Jansen, B., Jong, J. J. de, Roos, C. and Terlaky, T. (1997) 'Sensitivity analysis in linear programming', *European Journal of Operational Research* 101(1): 15–28.

Jennings, D. and Wattam, S. (1994) *Decision Making*, Pitman.

Knowles, T. W. (1989) *Management Science: Building and using models*, Homewood, IL: Irwin.

Krum, F. V. and Rolle, C. F. (1992) 'Management and application of decision and risk analysis in Du Pont', *Interfaces* 22(6): 84–93.

Kuula, M. (1993) 'A risk management model for FMS selection decisions: A multiple-criteria decision-making approach', *Computers in Industry* 23(1): 99–108.

Lee, S. M. (1983) *Introduction to Management Science*, Fort Worth, TX: Dryden Press.

Lindley, D. V. (1985) *Making Decisions*, London; New York: Wiley.

McKim, R. A. (1992) 'Risk Management: Back to Basics', *Cost Engineering* 34(12): 7–12.

Moses, L. N. and Savage, I. (1997) 'A cost–benefit analysis of US motor carrier safety programmes', *Journal of Transport Economics and Policy* 31(1): 51 – 67.

Nadiminti, R., Mukhopadhyay, T. and Kriebel, C. H. (1996) 'Risk aversion and the value of information', *Decision Support Systems* 16(3): 241–54.

Nainar, S.M. K. and Shehata, M. (1993) 'Decision making under uncertainty: Some experimental evidence from auditing', *Managerial Finance* 19(5): 28–42.

Ossenbruggen, P. J. (1994) *Fundamental Principles of Systems Analysis and Decision Making*, New York: Wiley.

Rivett, P. (1994) *The Craft of Decision Modelling*, New York; Chichester: Wiley.

Sarin, R. K. and Weber, M. (1993) 'Risk-value models', *European Journal of Operational Research* 70(2): 135–49.

Shenkar, O., Hattem, E. and Globerson, S. (1992) 'Cost-Benefit analysis of quality circles: A case study', *Human Systems Management* 11(1): 35–40.

Shogan, A. W. (1988) *Management Science*, Englewood Cliffs, NJ: Prentice Hall.

Silver, E. and Peterson R. (1985) *Decision Systems for Inventory Management and Production Planning*, New York: Wiley.

Stevenson, W. J. (1989) *Introduction to Management Science*, Homewood, IL: Irwin.

Target, D. (1996) *Analytical Decision Making*, London: Pitman.

Turban, E. and Meredith, J. R. (1994) *Fundamentals of Management Science*, Homewood, IL: Irwin.

Waters, D. (1998) *A Practical Introduction to Management Science*, Harlow: Addison Wesley Longman.

Waters, D. (1997) *Quantitative Methods for Business*, Harlow: Addison Wesley Longman.

Wemple, W. B. (1992) 'Risk management and quality: An integrated approach', *Bankers Magazine* 175(6): 57–61.

Winston, W. L. (1994) *Operations Research: Applications and algorithms*, Belmont, CA: Duxbury Press.

Winston, W., Albright, S. C. and Broadie, M. (1997) *Practical Management Science*, Belmont, CA: Duzbury Press/Wadsworth.

Wisniewski, M. (1997) *Quantitative Methods for Decision Makers*, London: Pitman.

23 Statistical quality control

Objectives and overview

The objective of this chapter is to underscore the importance, use and application of statistical quality control and it draws very heavily on Chapter 20 *Statistical Concepts*. This chapter begins by describing what is meant by statistical quality control and the meaning of lots, and explains the difference between attributes and variables. The chapter then presents the activity of sampling, describing the central limit theory and the single, double and sequential methods of sampling. There is a section on acceptance plans, which discusses the criteria for acceptance sampling, operating-characteristic curves, the notion of producer and consumer risk and average outgoing quality levels. Statistical process control is then presented with its application to both manufacturing and services. The use of the *p*-chart and the *c*-chart for controlling attributes, and the *x*-bar chart, combined with the range chart for controlling variables, are then presented in detail and worked examples given.

DEFINING STATISTICAL QUALITY CONTROL

Manufacturing

In manufacturing, statistical quality control covers the sampling and analysis of purchased raw materials or components, manufactured products and other units used in any part of the supply-chain operation to determine if these are in accordance with certain specifications. If they are not, corrective action is taken.

Services

In services, statistical quality control is sampling and analysing, often for customer satisfaction, activities such as:

- on-flight arrival and departure times in the airline industry;
- room service, restaurant facilities and cleanliness in the hotel business;
- delivery conditions for merchandise in distribution and transportation;
- quality of products in retail outlets.

Again, if certain standards are not met, appropriate corrective action would be taken.

Origin

The technique of statistical quality control has its roots in the research work of Walter A. Shewart, Harold F. Dodge, and H. G. Romig in the 1920s and 1930s. These persons, who worked at the Bell Telephone Laboratories, USA (since September 1996, as a result of the AT&T de-merger, part of Lucent Technologies) developed analytical methods using random samples, statistical control charts and statistical acceptance of products based on sampling from lots.

Lots or series

In production, units are often made in discrete groups called lots, or series. These groups of units will have been produced under the same operating conditions such as:

- on the same machine;
- with the same operator
- using raw material from the same batch;
- in the same time period;
- during the same shift;
- under the same process conditions.

The particular quantity of units in a manufactured lot might be:

- an amount, simply based on economics;
- the amount ordered by a client;
- a batch (made in fixed quantities such as pharmaceutical products, chemicals, wines, etc.) rather than a continuous process; the size here is limited by the volume of the production vessel;
- that quantity of units which is the most practical to produce at any one time, given the equipment, raw materials and operating team available.

Production by lots occurs in many manufacturing concerns, such as the food, automobile, textile, paper, printing and chemical industries.

Quality characteristics of units

In production, the ultimate goal is to make specification-quality units. The test of quality might be that the product works or does not work. This is considered an *attribute*.[1] Alternatively, the test might be that the unit is within a given *variable* range to meet certain specifications, such as colour, weight, length, diameter, viscosity, volume or hardness.

Attributes

Attributes are characteristics, which can be either only one of two outcomes, or a binomial classification. In general terms, examples of binomial outcomes are:

- yes or no;
- open or closed;
- pass or fail;
- go or no-go;
- defective or non-defective;
- good or bad;
- on time or late;
- sharp or dull (blades).

In production, for attribute classification, basically a product works or it does not:

- A battery generates a current when it is connected to a circuit or it does not.
- A wrist watch tells the correct time or it does not.
- A bulb illuminates or it does not.

Similarly, in services:

- The train arrives on time or it is late.
- The bank statement is correct or it is wrong.
- The quantity of goods delivered was according to the order or it was not.

Attribute data are count data. For example, ten of the samples inspected were found to be defective. For attribute data, a discrete probability distribution, such as the binomial, or Poisson, serves as the basis for statistical inference (see Chapter 20, *Statistical Concepts*).

Variables

Variables are characteristics that can be measured on a continuous scale, where there is a range of acceptance. For example, the diameter of a motor shaft can be measured by a dial micrometer. If the diameter is between the minimum and maximum allowable diameters, the shaft passes the inspection. For most work, the narrower the specification range, the better is the quality of the units produced (see Chapter 4, *Quality Management*, particularly the section on Taguchi methods). Normal distributions often serve as the basis for statistical inference (see Chapter 20, *Statistical Methods*).

The goal of statistical quality control

The ultimate objective of statistical quality control is not to find out if units are good or bad, but to avoid the production of poor quality items in the first place. It is always more economic to produce products that conform, rather than having to repair products later that do not conform. In addition to measurable costs, there is the intangible customer damage.

SAMPLING

Lots of materials, assemblies and finished products are sampled at random to see if these pieces conform to appropriate specifications. If they do, under statistical inference, it is assumed that the entire lot from which these samples are taken meets the desired quality control standards. If they do not, it is assumed that the entire lot is defective. This is where probabilities are involved. If a sample of, say, 25 units has more than 3 per cent defective units, one might say that the probability is that the entire lot has more than 3 per cent defective units. However, this may not be the case as the 25 units in the sample may not have been representative of the lot.

Random sample

A random sample is one where each unit in the lot has an equal chance of being selected. It is because of this randomness that the sample is considered representative of the lot. In random sampling, either attributes or variables can be measured and compared to standards.

Central limit theory

The foundation of sampling is based on the central limit theory. This states that in sampling, as the size of the sample increases, there comes a point when the sampling distribution of the mean can be approximated by the normal distribution, even though the distribution of the population is not necessarily normal.

Sampling distribution of the mean

The sampling distribution of the mean is a probability distribution of all the possible means of samples taken from a population. Assume that an analysis of the water quality of the River Saône, France is being made to determine the level of phosphates. Ten one-litre samples are taken each day, over a period of 120 days, and the phosphate level in parts per million is measured. Thus, each day, ten phosphate measurements are obtained and, from these, a mean value is calculated. Repeating this exercise for each day of the 120-day period gives 120 average, or mean, values. Plotting this data as a frequency distribution (Chapter 20, *Statistical Concepts*) gives a sampling distribution of the mean.

Sample size

- For most population distributions, regardless of shape, the sampling distribution of the means will be approximately normally distributed if samples of at least 30 units each are withdrawn from the population.
- If the population distribution is symmetric, the sampling distribution of the means will be approximately normal if samples of at least 15 units are withdrawn from the population.
- If the population is normally distributed, the sampling distribution of the means will be normally distributed, regardless of sample size withdrawn.

Mean of the sample means and the population mean

The mean of a sample is $\bar{x}$ (x-bar). The mean of all the samples withdrawn from the population is $\bar{\bar{x}}$ (x-double bar). From the central limit theory, the mean of the sample means can be considered equal to the population mean, μ_x:

$$\bar{\bar{x}} = \mu_x.$$

Standard error of the sample

By the central limit theory, the standard deviation of the sampling distribution, $\sigma_{\bar{x}}$, also known as the standard error of the sample means, is related to the population standard deviation σ_x and the sample size n by the following relationship:

$$\sigma_{\bar{x}} = \frac{\sigma_x}{\sqrt{n}}.$$

This indicates that, as the size of the sample increases, the standard error decreases, or the sample means lie closer to the population mean.

The practicality of the central limit theory is that by taking samples, either sampling from non-normal populations or sampling from normal populations, inferences can be made about the population parameters without having any information about the shape of the population distribution other than the information obtained from the sample, as illustrated in Figure 23.1.

Sampling techniques

Three techniques for sampling to see whether a lot conform are:

- single sampling;
- double sampling;
- sequential sampling.

Single sampling

In single sampling (Figure 23.2) there is one upper limit of c defective units in the sample. A random sample is withdrawn from the lot and tested for conformity. If the number of defective units c' in the sample does not exceed c, the lot is considered good and accepted. If the number of defective units c' exceeds c, the lot is considered bad and rejected

Double sampling

In double sampling (Figure 23.3) there are two limits of non-conformity, a lower limit c_1 and an upper limit c_2. In this plan, a random sample is taken from the lot and tested:

- If the number of defective units c' is less than or equal to c_1, then the lot is accepted.
- If the number of defective units c' in the sample is greater than c_2 the lot is rejected.
- If the number of defective units c' lies between c_1 and c_2, then a second random sample c' is taken from the lot and tested. If the sum of the defective units from both samples ($c' + c''$) is greater than c_2, the lot is rejected. If the sum of the defective units is less than c_2, the lot is accepted.

Double sampling is more rigorous than a single sampling plan and, as such, is more time consuming and costly.

Sequential sampling

In sequential sampling, lots are rejected (Figure 23.4) or accepted (Figure 23.5) according to a pre-established

Figure 23.1 Comparison of population distribution and sampling distribution.

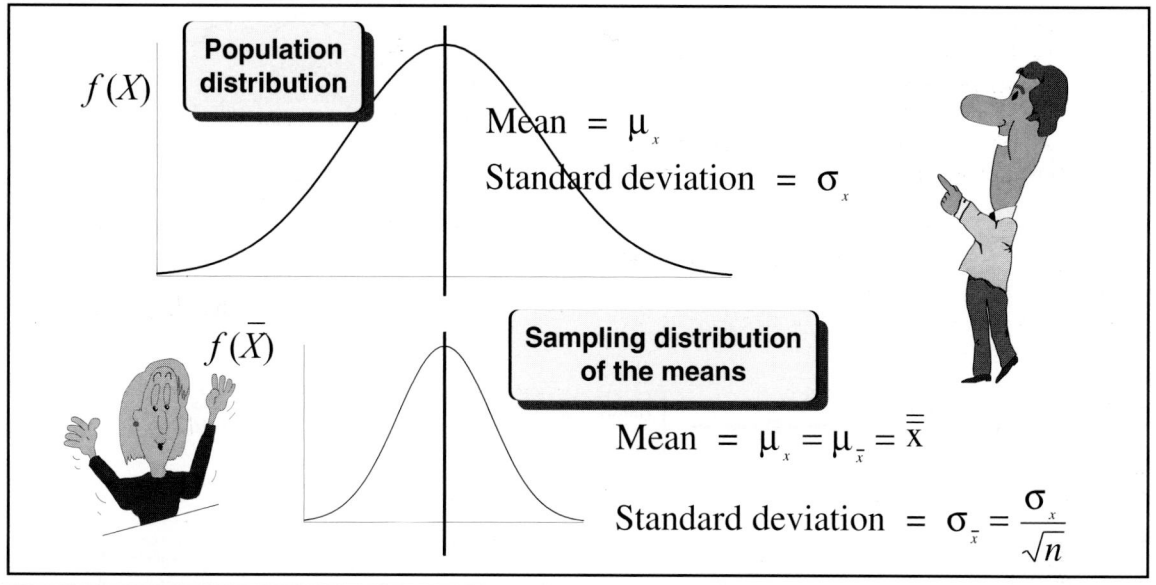

Figure 23.2 Single sampling plan.

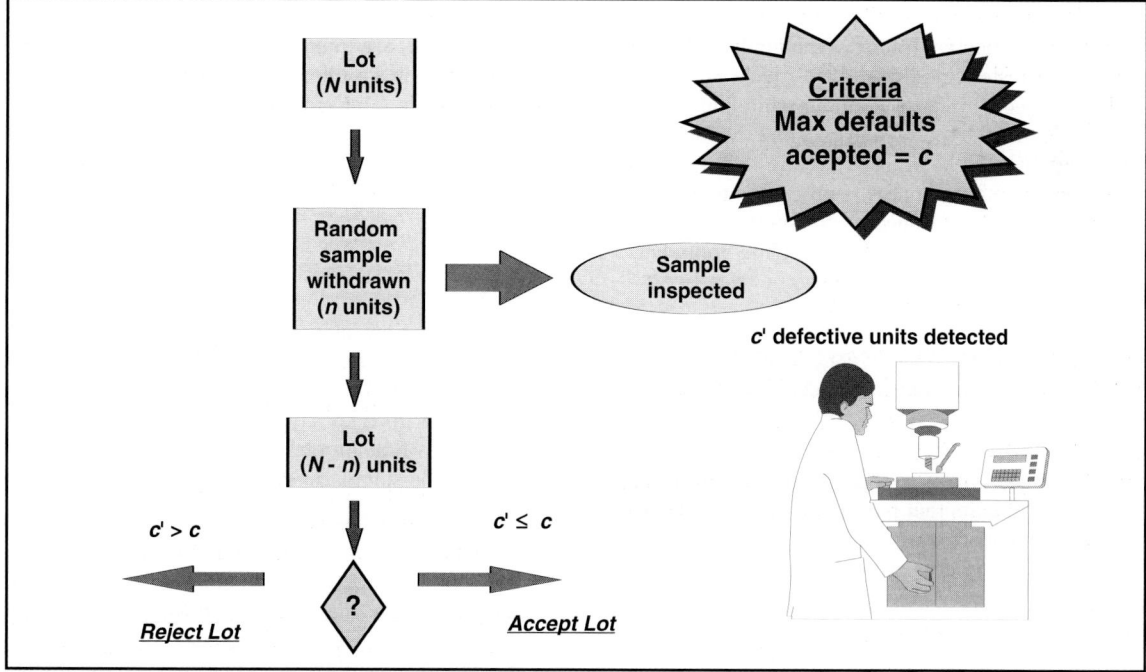

Figure 23.3 Double sampling plan.

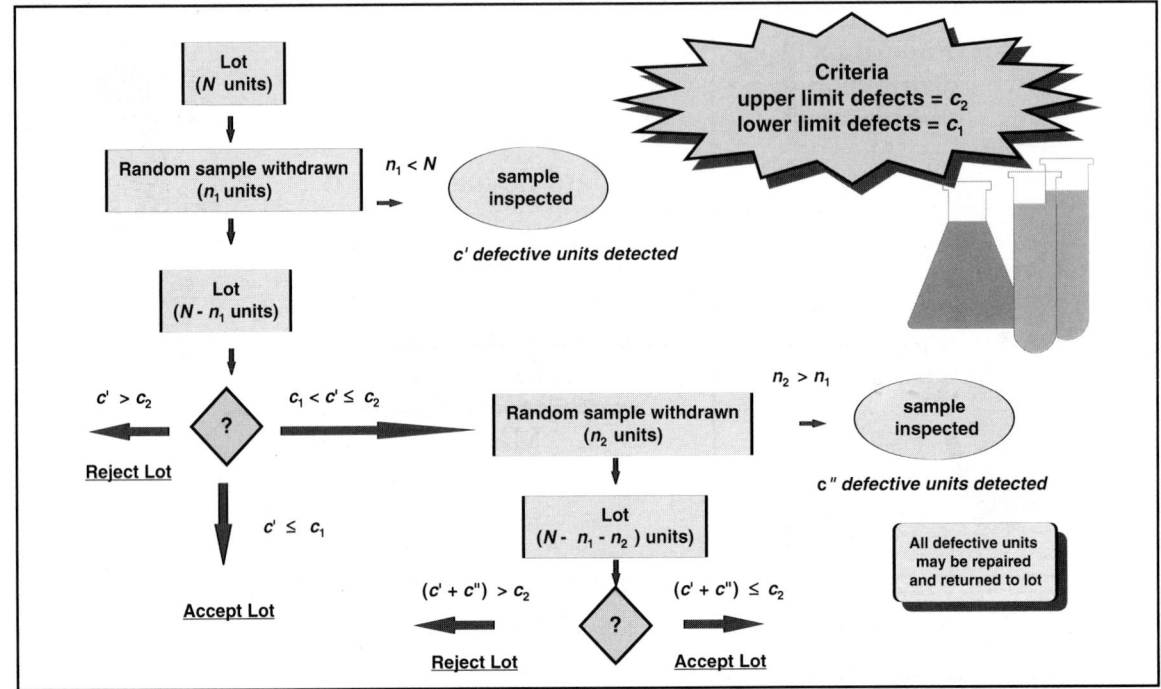

sampling programme. Units are randomly selected from the lot and tested one by one. After each unit has been tested, a reject, accept or continue sampling decision is made according to the sample plan and the total number of units that have been tested. If the number is in the continuous sampling zone, the process continues until a decision has been reached as to whether to accept or reject the lot. In the sequential sampling approach, it is conceivable that an entire lot could be tested.

ACCEPTANCE PLANS

Acceptance sampling

Acceptance sampling applies to whether to accept or reject a lot of units that has already been made. This is as opposed to inspecting items that are part of an ongoing production process, which is statistical process control (SPC). Consider a company that purchases from an external supplier a lot of 1000 electrical switches that are to be installed in refrigerator units.

Switches, Case 1

To be certain of that all of the switches work, the purchaser tests all of them. Of the 1000 units tested, 80, or 8.0 per cent, are found to be defective. These 80 are sent back to the supplier, who promptly replaces them with good units. This can be summarized as follows:

- The purchaser has spent his time, and money, in verifying the quality of the supplier's units.
- The supplier has avoided any expense for quality control. The purchaser has done it all for him!

Switches, Case 2

The purchaser now takes a random sample of 50 switches from the lot and tests them. Of the 50, four, or 8.0 per cent, are found to be defective. Based on this sampling, the purchaser does not consider the lot acceptable, and he sends the whole lot of 1000 units back to the supplier. This can be summarized as follows:

- The purchaser has only expended about 5 per cent of his time and cost compared to Case 1 (50/1000).
- The supplier, probably irritated, now has the burden put on him and he is obligated to spend time and money on rechecking the quality of his switches (assuming he wants to keep business with his client).

Case 2 illustrates the idea of acceptance sampling, which is to decide whether to accept lots of units (parts, raw materials or finished products) that have

Figure 23.4   Sequential sampling plan – 1.

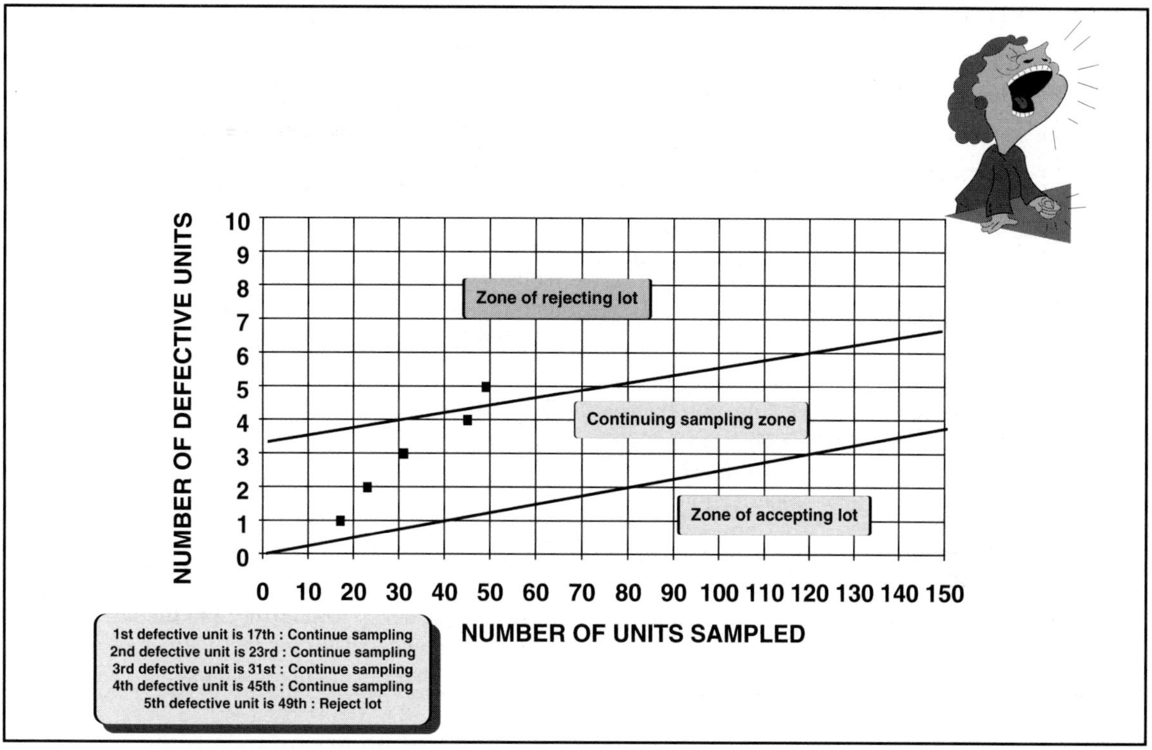

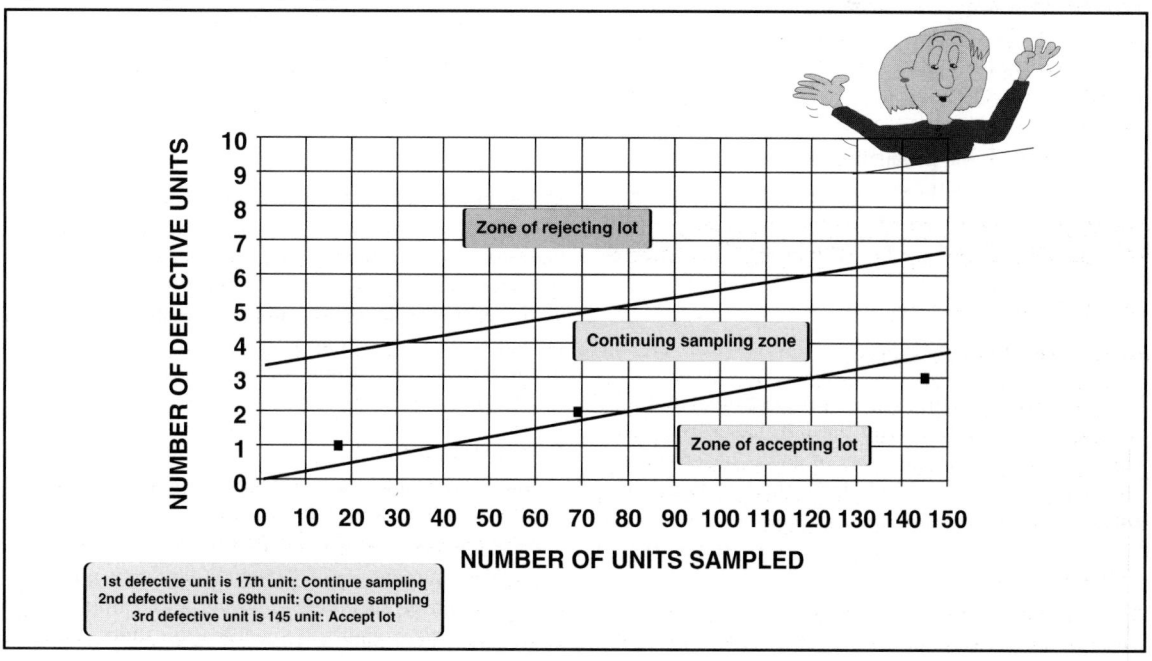

Figure 23.5   Sequential sampling plan – 2.

already been delivered to the client or are at the supplier's facility being prepared for delivery.

Rejected lots

Acceptance sampling is to decide if a lot satisfies predetermined standards. The lot is either rejected or accepted. If a lot is rejected:

- The entire lot may be inspected and faulty items repaired (when the supplier/consumer are the same firm).
- If the lot was purchased, it may be returned to the supplier.
- If it is not possible to repair the lot, it may be sold as a downgraded item of inferior quality, such as textiles that are not exactly the right colour, paper that does not have the exact surface finish or ceramic products that have some imperfection.

Criteria for acceptance sampling

Acceptance-sampling procedures are usually employed when:

- A large number of items have been supplied, produced, or prepared ready for shipment.
- Unit cost is relatively low and the cost consequence of passing a defective unit is not excessively high.
- Destructive testing is required.

High-value goods

Units which have a high added value, such as engines, refrigerators or computers, exhibit attribute characteristics (they work or they do not). However, in light of their high value, they are usually 100 per cent inspected before they leave the production or assembly operation. A faulty unit such as these could have severe costly consequences downstream and could impair customer relations. Hewlett Packard, for example, in France checks each computer unit before it leaves the factory.

Acceptance plan

An acceptance plan is the programme, mutually agreed to by a supplier and the purchaser, regarding whether to accept an entire lot of goods based on simply testing a random sample from the lot. As an illustration, if an acceptance plan permits a maximum of 5 per cent defective items and the sample tested shows 7 per cent of the items are defective, then under the acceptance plan the entire lot would be rejected and returned to the supplier. The goal in the development of the acceptance plan is to have one

that passes good lots and fails bad lots. Acceptance-sampling programmes can be applied to both attributes and variable criteria.

Attributes

With attributes, the interest is: 'What is the maximum percentage of defectives that can be found in a sample and the lot still be accepted by the client?'

Variables

With variables, the interest is: 'What is the largest and smallest sample mean and sample range that can be detected and the lot still be accepted by the client?'

Operating-characteristic curves

An operating-characteristic curve (OC) is a graphical relation illustrating how well an acceptance plan discriminates between *good* and *bad* lots. The discriminating ability depends on the shape of the curve, which is a function of:

- the sample size n withdrawn from the lot;
- the acceptance level c or the number of allowable defective units found in the sample.

Outcomes of an acceptance plan

In sampling with an acceptance plan, there are four possible outcomes:

- Desirable:
  1 A *good* lot can be accepted.
  2 A *bad* lot can be rejected.
- Undesirable:
  3 A *good* lot can be rejected.
  4 A *bad* lot can be accepted.

In the acceptance plan, it is hoped that only the first and second outcomes occur. However, there may be occasions when the third or fourth occurs. With a lot, or series, it is never known with certainty the quality of all the products. Drawing a random sample from the lot does not tell with certainty the quality of the products in the lot. The only thing that is known with certainty is the quality of the products in the sample.

Rejected good lot

Assume that there is a lot of 20 000 units of stainless-steel rods. In these 20 000 units, 15, or 0.075 per cent, have diameters that are outside the required specifications. This percentage of defects is low and, normally, the lot would be accepted. However, in a sample of 20 rods, there were eight off-specification units. That is, eight of the total of 15 defective units appeared in this sample. This number of 8 is 40 per cent and, based on the sample, the lot would be rejected. In fact, it is a *good* lot.

Accepted bad lot

Assume in another situation that there are 20 000 rods where actually there are 1000 defective units. This represents 5 per cent and is probably sufficiently high to reject all of the lot. If a sample of 20 rods is taken, there could be no off-specification units. The *bad* lot would then be accepted.

From information about the small proportion of the products in the sample, the quality of all the products in the lot must be inferred and this is the nature of, and the risk in, acceptance plans. For attribute sampling, where lots are considered either good or bad, the operating characteristic curve is developed from the binomial distribution, or under certain conditions the Poisson distribution. These both describe discrete distributions.

Perfect discriminating operating curve

Figure 23.6 illustrates an ideal discriminating operating curve with an acceptance level of 2 per cent. Here all lots with 2 per cent, or less, defective units would be accepted. All those lots with greater than 2 per cent defective units would be rejected. This curve is only theoretical, since to obtain perfect discrimination would require inspection of all the units in the lot and, for products of relative low unit value, this would be uneconomic.

Practical operating characteristic curves

Practical operating characteristic curves are illustrated by the worked example, *Switches*.

Inspection and quality

Ideally, the client would like to receive from the producer a lot with zero per cent defectives, one of the goals in just-in-time management. However, this might involve 100 per cent inspection of the lot, which would be costly (the cost being passed on to the consumer in the unit price). If the client accepts that, because of the type of operation being used by the producer, there may be some defective units in the lot, then there are two levels accepted by both parties:

- acceptable quality level;
- lot tolerance per cent defective.

Acceptable quality level

The acceptable quality level (AQL) is the level of quality of a product, often expressed as a percentage, that is considered acceptable for the production. Broadly, it

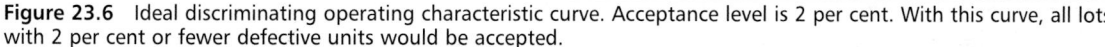

Figure 23.6 Ideal discriminating operating characteristic curve. Acceptance level is 2 per cent. With this curve, all lots with 2 per cent or fewer defective units would be accepted.

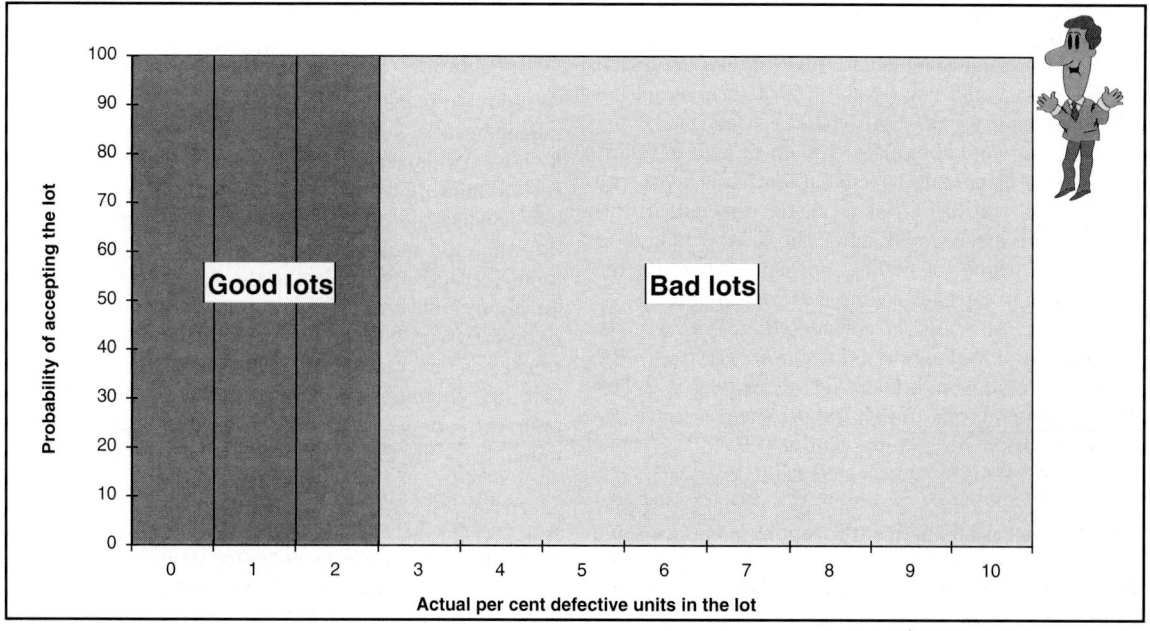

defines the maximum defective level, which is still considered a 'good lot'. For example, in the production of computer chips an AQL might be one defective unit in 10 000, or 0.01 per cent. For the manufacture of light switches, the AQL may be, say, 2 per cent or 40 units in a lot of 2000. The AQL is a standard established by the product manufacturer, or by the purchaser of the product. The lower the value of the AQL the more rigorous is the production process, and the higher is the cost of quality, a cost that is passed onto the purchaser.

Lot tolerance per cent defective

Lot tolerance per cent defective (LTPD), is the level of quality considered unacceptable, or bad. Lots at this level, or higher, need to be rejected by the acceptance plan. Broadly speaking, the LPTD is the lower level of defects which still constitutes a 'bad lot'. In the production of computer chips a LTPD might be ten defective units in 10 000, or 0.1 per cent. In the case of the light switches the LTPD might be 5 per cent, or 100 units in a lot of 2000.

Producer and consumer risk

In the agreed sampling plan, even though the AQL and the LTPD have been defined, there is a risk for both parties concerned.

Producer's risk

The producer or supplier of the units wants to avoid having a good lot rejected by the acceptance plan. The producers risk (α) involves the taking of a random sample that results in a higher portion of defects in the sample than is actually present in the lot. For example, a good lot of 10 000 units with only ten defectives, or 0.1 per cent, could conceivably result in a sample of 100 containing all the ten defective units or 10 per cent. This lot would be rejected, even though in reality it has only 0.1 per cent defective units. Thus, a lot with a given AQL still has a risk of being rejected. In this case, the producer would suffer the loss of having to inspect the whole lot at his expense, discarding the whole batch or perhaps selling it at a discount.

The producer's risk is considered a Type I error (rejecting a null hypothesis when it is true). The acceptance plan would reject the lot, when it is in fact good. A sampling plan might be designed to have the producers risk α set at 5 per cent or 0.05.

Consumer's risk

The consumer wants to avoid accepting a bad lot since if the lot is accepted he would be responsible for rectifying faulty units. The consumer's risk (β) involves the taking of a random sample that results in a much lower portion of defects in the sample than is actually present in the lot. For example, a lot of 10 000 units with 2000 defectives could produce a sample of size 100 with no defective units. The lot would be accepted. Thus, a lot with a given LTPD still has a risk of being accepted

The consumer's risk is a Type II error (accepting a null hypothesis, when it is false). A sampling plan might be designed to have the consumer's risk β set at 10 per cent or 0.10.

Sample size of 100

Figure 23.7 shows an operating characteristic curve with:

- the producer's risk at 5 per cent;
- the consumer's risk at 10 per cent;
- an acceptable quality level (AQL) of 2 per cent;
- lot tolerance per cent defective (LTPD) of 8 per cent.

Here there is a 5 per cent risk of rejecting a good lot (95 per cent probability of accepting the good lot) and a 10 per cent risk of accepting a bad lot (90 per cent chance of rejecting a bad lot). The development of this curve is given in Table 23.1.

Sample size of 200

If the sample size was increased to 200 and a value of $c = 8$, then the risk levels are decreased for the same values of AQL and LTPD. (Figure 23.8 shows the operating curve with:

- the producer's risk at 2.2 per cent.
- the consumer's risk at 2.7 per cent.
- an acceptable quality level (AQL) of 2 per cent.
- lot tolerance per cent defective (LTPD) of 8 per cent.

Average outgoing quality

Acceptance plans in statistical quality control provide managers with some assurance that the average quality level, or per cent defective items, will not exceed a certain limit. In a sampling procedure, if a lot is rejected because the AQL does not meet the criteria, then the whole lot might be inspected and all the defective items replaced. By replacing the defective items in the lot, then the average outgoing quality (AOQ) in terms of defective units is improved. In a sampling plan that replaces all encountered defective items, and if the per cent defective items for the lot is known at the beginning, the average outgoing quality (AOQ) can be determined from the following relationship:

$$\text{AOQ} = \frac{P_t P_a (N - n)}{N},$$

where P_t is the per cent defective items in the incoming lot; P_a is the probability of accepting the lot, N is the lot size and n is the sample size used in the inspection plan.

Figure 23.7 Operating characteristic curve showing level of risk (sample size = 100, c = 4).

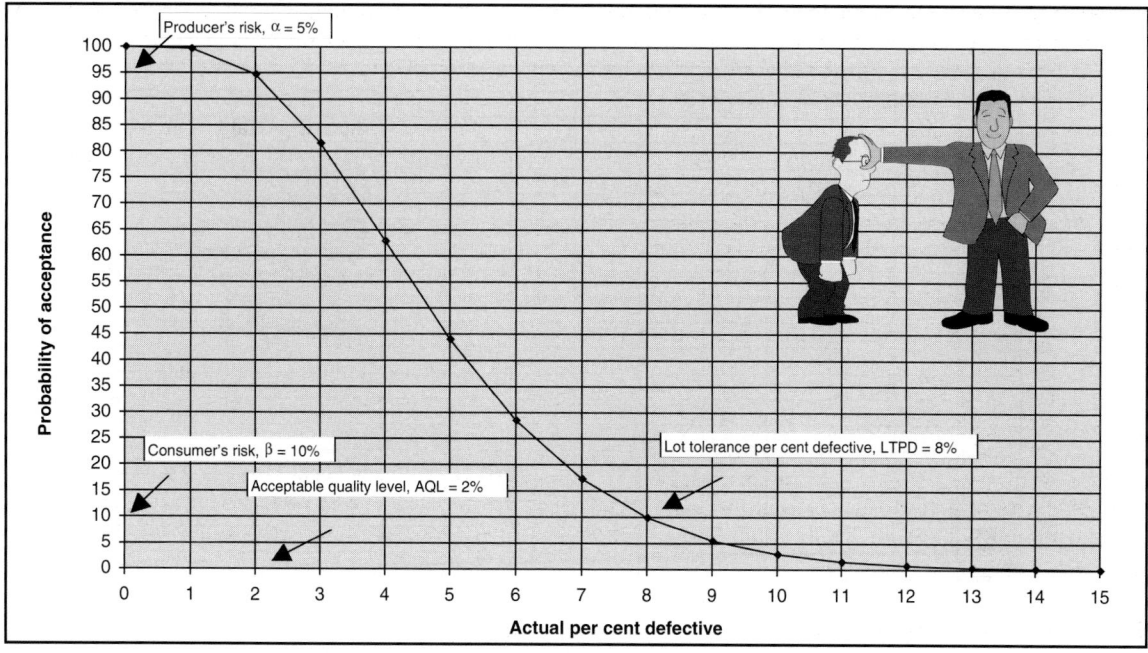

Table 23.1 Operating characteristic curve showing risk levels: $P(x) = \dfrac{(np)^x\,e^{-(np)}}{x!}$

Per cent defective units	λ ($n \times p/100$) Sample size				Probability of acceptance Sample size			
	25	50	100	200	25	50	100	200
					Value of c			
					1	2	4	8
0	0.00	0.00	0.00	0.00	100.00	100.00	100.00	100.00
1	0.25	0.50	1.00	2.00	97.35	98.56	99.63	99.98
2	0.50	1.00	2.00	4.00	90.98	91.97	94.73	97.86
3	0.75	1.50	3.00	6.00	82.66	80.88	81.53	84.72
4	1.00	2.00	4.00	8.00	73.58	67.67	62.88	59.25
5	1.25	2.50	5.00	10.00	64.46	54.38	44.05	33.28
6	1.50	3.00	6.00	12.00	55.78	42.32	28.51	15.50
7	1.75	3.50	7.00	14.00	47.79	32.08	17.30	6.21
8	2.00	4.00	8.00	16.00	40.60	23.81	9.96	2.20
9	2.25	4.50	9.00	18.00	34.25	17.36	5.50	0.71
10	2.50	5.00	10.00	20.00	28.73	12.47	2.93	0.21
11	2.75	5.50	11.00	22.00	23.97	8.84	1.51	0.06
12	3.00	6.00	12.00	24.00	19.91	6.20	0.76	0.02
13	3.25	6.50	13.00	26.00	16.48	4.30	0.37	0.00
14	3.50	7.00	14.00	28.00	13.59	2.96	0.18	0.00
15	3.75	7.50	15.00	30.00	11.17	2.03	0.09	0.00
16	4.00	8.00	16.00	32.00	9.16	1.38	0.04	0.00
17	4.25	8.50	17.00	34.00	7.49	0.93	0.02	0.00
18	4.50	9.00	18.00	36.00	6.11	0.62	0.01	0.00
19	4.75	9.50	19.00	38.00	4.97	0.42	0.00	0.00
20	5.00	10.00	20.00	40.00	4.04	0.28	0.00	0.00

Figure 23.8 Operating characteristic curve showing level of risk (sample size = 200, c = 8).

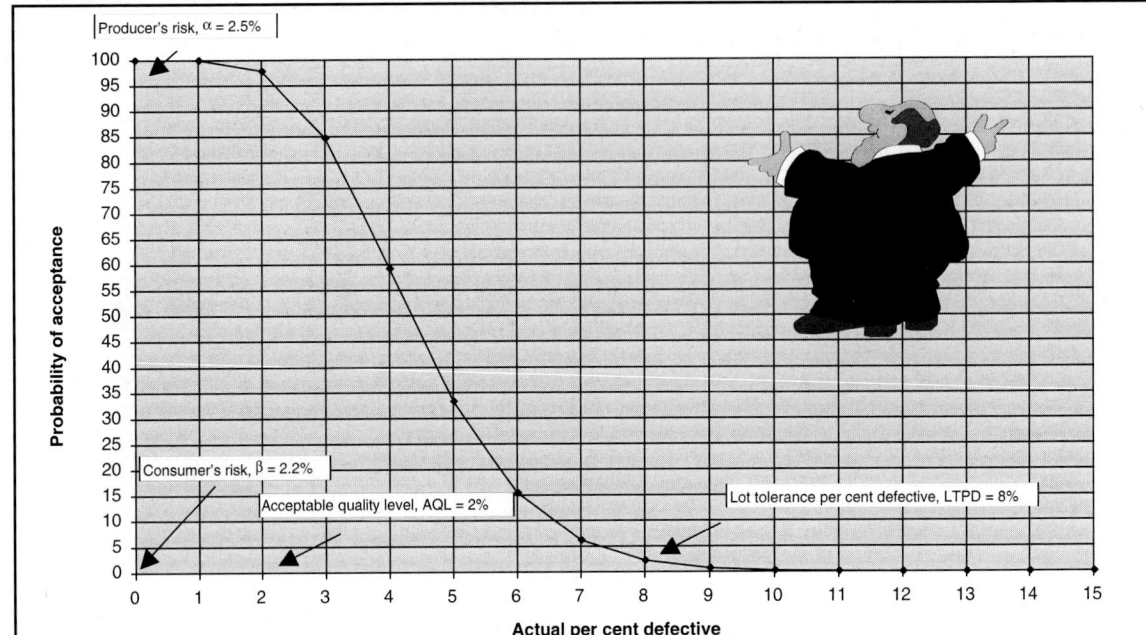

Development of AOQ curves

Normally in the AOQ relationship, the values of P_t and P_a are not known. However, for a particular sampling plan, an AOQ curve can be developed by assuming different values of P_t and calculating the value of P_a from the Poisson relationship. Figure 23.9 gives four AOQ curves for different acceptance plans. These curves were developed as follows:

- Lot size N is assumed as 2000 units.
- Sample size n is 50 random units.
- Values of defective units in the lot, p (equal to P_t), were considered from 0 to 20.
- Four acceptance plans are considered for values of c (defective units in the sample) of 0, 1, 2 and 3.
- The value of λ (lambda) is calculated from the relationship, $n \times p$ (divided by 100 since the p is a percentage).
- The probability of acceptance P_a is calculated from the Poisson relationship for each value of p for the value of $c = 0$:

$$P_a(c) = \frac{(np)^x e^{-(np)}}{c!}.$$

- The value of P_a is calculated, at each level of p, for values of $c = 0$, 1, 2 and 3.
- The average outgoing quality is then calculated from the relationship:

$$\text{AOQ} = \frac{P_t P_a (N - n)}{N}.$$

- As the actual per cent defectives in a production lot increases – moves along the horizontal axis from left to right – the effect initially is for lots to be passed, even though the number of defective units has increased. Consequently, the number of defective units passed along to the customer increases.
- If the trend continues, however, the acceptance plan begins to reject lots. When lots are rejected, the lots are usually 100 per cent inspected. The defective units are replaced with non-defective ones. Thus, the net effect of rejecting lots is to improve the average quality of the outgoing lots, because the rejected lots that are ultimately shipped contain all non-defective units.
- As the actual per cent defectives increases, the average outgoing quality improves because more and more lots are rejected. They are 100 per cent inspected and the defective units replaced. The extreme condition is when all lots are rejected and thus the per cent defectives going to customers approaches zero.

The maximum value of the AOQ curve (average outgoing quality limit, AOQL) gives the highest average per cent defective, or the lowest average quality for a par-

Figure 23.9   Average outgoing quality curve (lot size is 2000, $n = 50$).

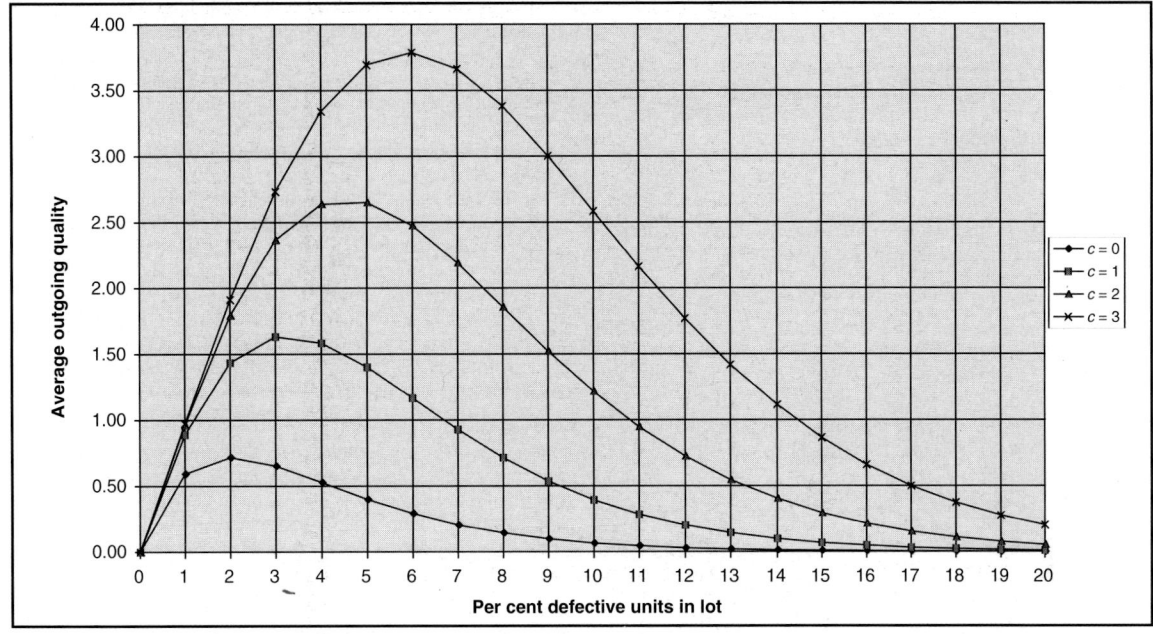

ticular sampling plan. For example, consider the sampling plan when $c = 3$ defective units in a sample of 50.

■ The highest average per cent defective (AOQL) is about 3.8 per cent for an incoming quality in the lot of 6 per cent.

■ This means that units are about 96.2 per cent good when the incoming quality in the lot is equal to 6 per cent.

WORKED EXAMPLE: SWITCHES

Situation

A small electrical manufacturing company in Dresden, Germany, makes a variety of electrical switches in lot sizes of 2000 units used in domestic power circuits, in batteries and for automobile use. The company wants to develop a statistical quality control programme for testing the attribute function of its products. The first step was to develop operating characteristic curves for its sampling programme to see what the effect of sampling limits and sample sizes would have on the probability of accepting good lots, and rejecting bad lots.

Required

1 Develop operating characteristic curves for a fixed sample size of 50 units, for 0, 1, 2 and 3 defective units in the sample.
2 Using the operating characteristic curves developed in an answer to question 1, what is the probability of accepting the lot when the actual per cent defective units in the lot is 2, 4, 6 and 8 per cent?. What are the conclusions from this information?
3 Develop operating characteristic curves for sample sizes of 25, 50, 75 and 100 units, for a level when the per cent defects in the sample is always at 4 per cent.

4 If the acceptance plan is to reject all lots where the actual per cent defective units in the lot is 2 per cent, using the operating characteristic curves developed in the answer to question 3, what is the probability of accepting the lot when the actual per cent defective units in the lot is 1, 2, 3, 4, 6 and 8 per cent? What are the conclusions from this information?

Solution

1 The operating characteristic curve is developed from the modified Poisson distribution:

$$P(x) = \frac{(np)^x e^{-(np)}}{x!}$$

where $P(x)$ is the probability of accepting the lot, n is the sample size (number of units in the sample), p is the actual per cent defective units in the lot, x is the number of defective units permitted in the sample and np is the mean value of defective units in the sample.

Here $n = 50$ and p is given selected values of 0 though 15 per cent in increments of 1 per cent. Four separate curves are developed for values of $x \, (= c) = 0, 1, 2$ and 3. The data are shown in Table 23.2 and Figure 23.10.

Table 23.2 Switches – Fixed sample size (= 50) changing values of c

$$P(x) = \frac{(np)^x e^{-(np)}}{x!}$$

Per cent defective units	λ (np/100)	Operating characteristic curve Probability of acceptance Value of c (= x)			
		0	1	2	3
0	0.00	100.00	100.00	100.00	100.00
1	0.50	60.65	90.98	98.56	99.82
2	1.00	36.79	73.58	91.97	98.10
3	1.50	22.31	55.78	80.88	93.44
4	2.00	13.53	40.60	67.67	85.71
5	2.50	8.21	28.73	54.38	75.76
6	3.00	4.98	19.91	42.32	64.72
7	3.50	3.02	13.59	32.08	53.66
8	4.00	1.83	9.16	23.81	43.35
9	4.50	1.11	6.11	17.36	34.23
10	5.00	0.67	4.04	12.47	26.50
11	5.50	0.41	2.66	8.84	20.17
12	6.00	0.25	1.74	6.20	15.12
13	6.50	0.15	1.13	4.30	11.18
14	7.00	0.09	0.73	2.96	8.18
15	7.50	0.06	0.47	2.03	5.91
16	8.00	0.03	0.30	1.38	4.24
17	8.50	0.02	0.19	0.93	3.01
18	9.00	0.01	0.12	0.62	2.12
19	9.50	0.01	0.08	0.42	1.49
20	10.00	0.00	0.05	0.28	1.03

2 The probability of accepting the lot for the given values of the actual per cent defective units in the lot is as given in Table 23.3. The operating characteristic curve with the tighter limits (low value of c) is less likely to accept the lot (more likely to reject the lot) at whatever the actual percent defect units in the lot. At the lower end, for small value of the actual percent defective units in the lot it is less likely to accept the lot (even though it is a good lot). Thus, except for low values of c in the sample, the best discriminating curve is the one that has smaller values of c in the sample.

3 In order to keep the value at 4 per cent defective units in the sample, Table 23.4 shows the number of defective units at each sample size. The modified Poisson distribution is used in the same way to develop the operating characteristic curves. The data for these operating characteristic curves are shown in Table 23.5 and Figure 23.11.

4 The probability of accepting the lot at the given actual percent defective units in the lot are as given in Table 23.6. When the actual per cent in the lot is 1 or 2 per cent, there is a higher probability of accepting the lot (a good lot) than with the large sample size.

When the actual percentage of defective units in the lot is 3 per cent or more (a bad lot) the operating characteristic curve at the larger sample size is less likely to accept the lot (more likely to reject the lot). Thus, for a given percentage of defectives, the larger the sample size, the more discriminating is the operating characteristic curve.

Thus, in summary, the better discriminating operating characteristic curve is either:

■ having a very low tolerance of defect units in the sample (low value of c);
■ for given fraction defective units in the sample, having a larger sample size.

In either case, the cost will be higher. The first indicates that the process producing the lots must be very reliable (avoid producing defective units). In the second case, the cost of sampling is higher.

Figure 23.10 Switches: operating characteristic curve (sample size n = 50)

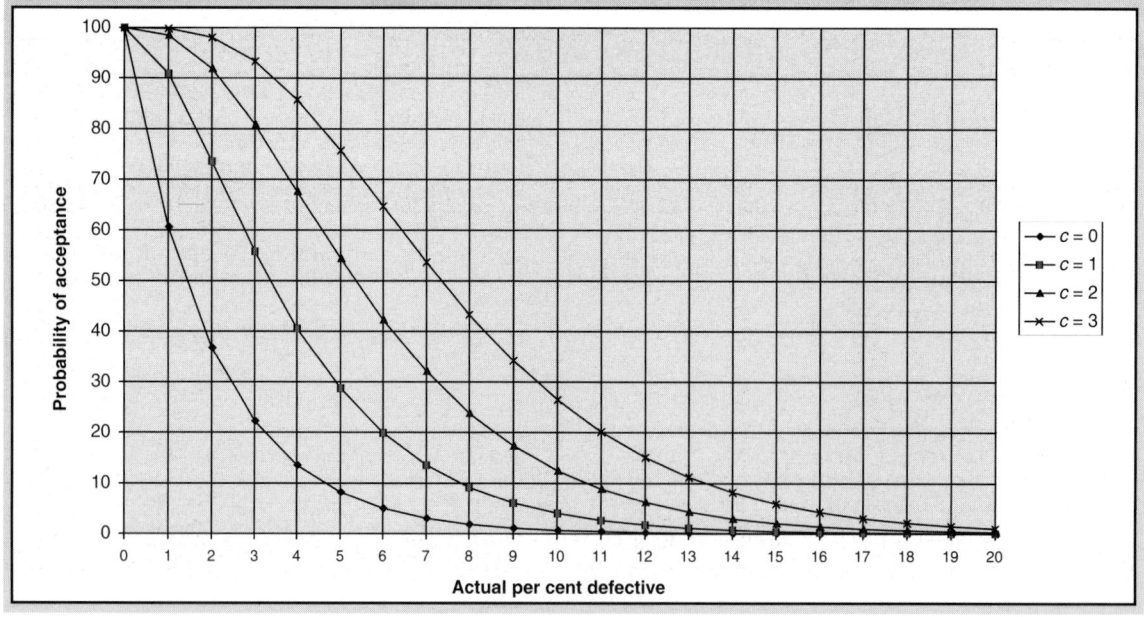

Table 23.3   The probability of accepting the lot for the given values of the actual per cent defective units in the lot

Actual per cent defective units in lot	Probability (%) of accepting lot Curve: c = 0	Probability (%) of accepting lot Curve: c = 1	Probability (%) of accepting lot Curve: c = 2	Probability (%) of accepting lot Curve: c = 3
1	60.65	90.98	98.56	99.82
2	36.79	73.58	91.97	98.10
4	13.53	40.60	67.67	85.71
6	4.98	19.91	42.32	64.72
8	1.83	9.16	23.81	43.35

Table 23.4   The number of defective switches at each sample size

Sample size	Number of defective units
25	1
50	2
75	3
100	4

Table 23.5   Switches – fixed per cent defective (4 per cent); changing sample size

$$(P(x) = \frac{(np)^x e^{-(np)}}{x!}$$

Per cent defective units	λ (np/100) Sample size = n				Operating characteristic curve Probability of acceptance Sample size			
	25	50	100	200	25	50	100	200
					Value of c (= x in Poisson)			
					1	2	4	8
0	0.00	0.00	0.00	0.00	100.00	100.00	100.00	100.00
1	0.25	0.50	1.00	2.00	97.35	98.56	99.63	99.98
2	0.50	1.00	2.00	4.00	90.98	91.97	94.73	97.86
3	0.75	1.50	3.00	6.00	82.66	80.88	81.53	84.72
4	1.00	2.00	4.00	8.00	73.58	67.67	62.88	59.25
5	1.25	2.50	5.00	10.00	64.46	54.38	44.05	33.28
6	1.50	3.00	6.00	12.00	55.78	42.32	28.51	15.50
7	1.75	3.50	7.00	14.00	47.79	32.08	17.30	6.21
8	2.00	4.00	8.00	16.00	40.60	23.81	9.96	2.20
9	2.25	4.50	9.00	18.00	34.25	17.36	5.50	0.71
10	2.50	5.00	10.00	20.00	28.73	12.47	2.93	0.21
11	2.75	5.50	11.00	22.00	23.97	8.84	1.51	0.06
12	3.00	6.00	12.00	24.00	19.91	6.20	0.76	0.02
13	3.25	6.50	13.00	26.00	16.48	4.30	0.37	0.00
14	3.50	7.00	14.00	28.00	13.59	2.96	0.18	0.00
15	3.75	7.50	15.00	30.00	11.17	2.03	0.09	0.00
16	4.00	8.00	16.00	32.00	9.16	1.38	0.04	0.00
17	4.25	8.50	17.00	34.00	7.49	0.93	0.02	0.00
18	4.50	9.00	18.00	36.00	6.11	0.62	0.01	0.00
19	4.75	9.50	19.00	38.00	4.97	0.42	0.00	0.00
20	5.00	10.00	20.00	40.00	4.04	0.28	0.00	0.00

Figure 23.11 Switches: operating characteristic curve (defect amount = 4 per cent).

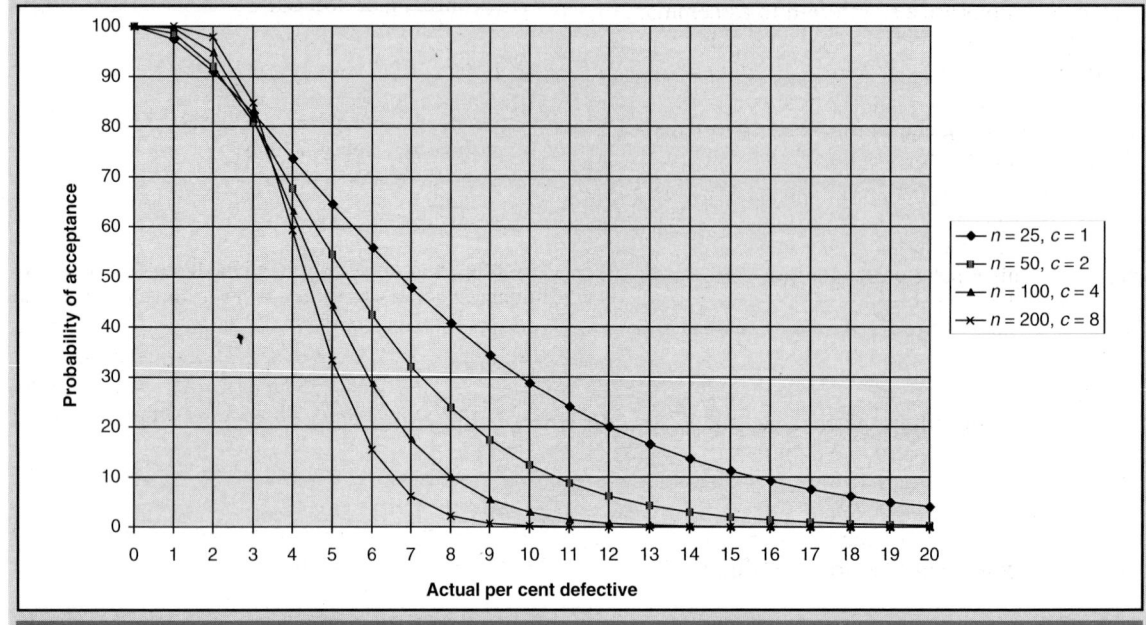

Table 23.6 Probability of accepting the lot at the given actual per cent defective units in the lot

Actual per cent defective units in lot	Probability (%) of accepting lot $n = 25: c = 1$	Probability (%) of accepting lot $n = 50: c = 2$	Probability (%) of accepting lot $n = 75: c = 3$	Probability (%) of accepting lot $n = 100: c = 4$
1	97.35	98.56	99.27	99.63
2	90.98	91.97	93.44	94.73
3	82.66	80.88	80.94	81.53
4	73.58	67.67	64.72	62.88
6	55.78	42.32	34.23	28.51
8	40.60	23.81	15.12	9.96

STATISTICAL PROCESS CONTROL

Statistical process control (SPC) is the periodic sampling and analysis of units, items or activity, to determine if the system is performing as expected, according to some pre-determined target or within design limits. The primary purpose of SPC is to analyse the process to verify that it is operating correctly. It is not to analyse the produced units to see if they conform to specifications. This is the objective of acceptance sampling.

Manufacturing

Statistical process control in manufacturing is the periodic sampling of production units from the operating line to determine if a process, such as drilling, soldering, bottle filling, assembly, etc., is performing according to the required conditions. If the units are acceptable, no action is taken. If the output is not acceptable, the process is stopped and corrective action is taken.

Services

Statistical process control in services is the periodic sampling of activities, such as the arrival time of aeroplanes, the quality of a professor's teaching, the accuracy of bank statements, etc., to determine if the activity is according to some acceptable level. If not, corrective action is taken.

Variations in a process

The objective of statistical process control is to determine if there is variation in a process. There are two types of variations, random and assignable.

Random variations

Random variations are also referred to as common, or inherent, variations. For example, in a drilling operation of 5 cm diameter holes it is very unlikely to always have exactly holes of 5 cm diameter owing to the nature of the drilling equipment being used (there will be slight sideways movements of the drill) and the material into which the holes are being drilled (it may not always be structurally the same). As such, some holes will be slightly larger, and some will be slightly smaller and this results because of random variations. To accommodate these variations, a specification for the holes is established, 5 ± 0.01 cm for example.

Assignable variations

In the drilling operation, after time, the drill will become dull and the clamps holding the material may loosen. In this event, the holes being drilled will become larger than the specification. These are assignable, or systematic variations, because one is able to identify why changes are occurring.

In quality control, the emphasis is always on continuous improvement. However, for a given process, little can be done for random variations unless the production operation is changed. The purpose of statistical process control is to detect the assignable variations. When such variations occur, the process is considered out of control.

In services such as measuring on-time arrivals, quality of teaching, statement errors, ideally there should be no variation. However, since services are performed by people, who sometimes have their 'off-days', a small amount of variation may be tolerated.

Control charts

A control chart is the evaluation tool in statistical process control. The elements of control are the same, whether the objective is to control quality, costs, absenteeism, accidents, temperature, time, etc. A control chart includes:

- a lower control limit (LCL);
- a centre line (CL): this is the target point;
- an upper control limit (UCL).

The steps in quality control using charts are as described in the following.

Define

The specification that is to be measured needs to be established. This might be:

- Manufacturing:
  - weight (chocolate bars, bread);

- colour (paper, textile, linoleum);
- hardness (gear wheels);
- viscosity (oil, ointments).
- Services:
  - arrival time (plane, train, bus);
  - errors (printing, statements, records);
  - evaluation level (teaching);
  - absenteeism (personnel).

Control limits

The upper and the lower control limits must be set (though, in some situations, a lower limit may have no importance). It is outside these limits that a process is considered 'out of control', or the performance is not acceptable. When established, the control limits become the benchmark with which to compare future samples.

Measure

Analysis needs to be made to measure the variable and compare it to the standard.

Action

If a variable falls within the control limits, take no action. If not, investigate the cause and take appropriate measures. This might include:

- Manufacturing
  - replacement of worn tools;
  - adjustment of machines;
  - retraining of operating staff.
- Services
  - modify the schedule (transportation);
  - replace the professor (teaching);
  - motivation programmes (personnel).

Control charts for attributes

Two charts that might be used for control of attributes are:

- the *p*-chart, which indicates the percentage, or fraction, of defective units in a sample;
- the *c*-chart, which indicates the number of defective units in a sample.

p-chart

Since a p-chart is a measure of discrete data, a binomial distribution is the correct probability function. However, for large sample sizes, the normal distribution can be approximated for the binomial distribution. The limits in the *p*-chart are:

centre line (CL) = p;
upper control limit (UCL) = $p + z\sigma_p$;
lower control limit (LCL) = $p - z\sigma_p$;

where p is the targeted fraction, or percentage, of defective units in the sample and represents the centre line of the control chart. If there is no target level, then the value of p is given by $p = \bar{p}$, where $\bar{p}$ is the average fraction of defectives in many samples, z is the number of standard deviations and σ_p is the standard deviation of the sampling distribution, which can be estimated from the relationship:

$$\sigma_p = \sqrt{\frac{\bar{p}\,(1 - \bar{p})}{n}}\,.$$

Thus, in a situation where the centre line is p, the control limits would be given by:

$$\sigma_p = \bar{p} \pm z \sqrt{\frac{\bar{p}\,(1 - \bar{p})}{n}}\,.$$

Very often, control charts with a value of $z = 3$ are used. From the normal distribution relationship this would cover 99.7 per cent (or essentially all) of the data. This would mean that the limits are quite loose. If the limits were set for $z = 2$ (95.5 per cent of the data), then the control would be more rigid and if for $z = 1$ (68 per cent of the data) even more rigid (Taguchi's idea of quality; see Chapter 4, *Quality Management*). The development of p-charts, and the effect of tighter limits, is illustrated with the worked example, *Printed Circuits*.

c-charts

A c-chart might be used where counting the number of errors makes more sense than a percentage, or fraction, value. For example:

- the number of imperfections on a one square metre sample of fabric;
- the number of blemishes on given surface area of a bobbin of paper;
- the number of imperfections on a piece of wooden furniture;
- the number of typing errors in one page of type-set material.

The Poisson distribution, which has a variance equal to its mean, is the basis developing for c-charts. In this case c is the mean number of defects per unit:

$$\bar{c} = \frac{\Sigma c}{n}\,.$$

The limits in the c-chart are:

centre line (CL) = $\bar{c}$;

upper control limit (UCL) = $\bar{c} + z \sqrt{\bar{c}}$

lower control limit (LCL) = $\bar{c} - z \sqrt{\bar{c}}$,

where $\sqrt{\bar{c}}$ is the standard deviation.

The use of c-charts is illustrated with the worked example, *Paper making*.

Control charts for variables

Variables are those characteristics that can take on a range of values such as kilograms, decibels, metres, litres, km/h, gallons, etc. In quality control for variables, samples are withdrawn from populations of products and are described by the sample mean $\bar{x}$ and the sample range R; an $\bar{x}$ (x-bar) chart and R chart need to be used together to monitor quality of products.

A range chart is necessary

Consider the following example. A chocolate manufacturer purchases sacks of sugar by the lorry load from a local supplier. The weight of each sack should be 25 kg. From a supplied lot, a sample of 10 sacks is removed and weighed. These weights are: 21; 24; 23; 29; 25; 27; 28; 25; 22 and 26kgs respectively.

The average weight of these ten samples, x, is 25 kg, or according to specifications. However, the range is 8 kg, which is exceedingly large, so there is obviously a problem. Having dual monitoring controls both the average values and variation of values from their means. It cannot be concluded that a process is in control by just monitoring sample means; the variation (range) within a sample must also be monitored.

Sample mean control chart

- The centre line is $\bar{\bar{x}}$ or the average of all the sample averages.
- The upper and lower control limits are:

$$\text{UCL} = \bar{\bar{x}} + z\sigma_{\bar{x}}$$
$$\text{LCL} = \bar{\bar{x}} - z\sigma_{\bar{x}}.$$

In situations where the standard deviation is unknown, or difficult to determine, it can be replaced with the average range of values, $\bar{R}$. (The range is a measure of deviation – see Chapter 20, *Statistical Concepts*) Then the control limits become:

$$\text{UCL} = \bar{\bar{x}} + A\bar{R}$$
$$\text{LCL} = \bar{\bar{x}} - A\bar{R},$$

where A is a factor given in a table of control chart factors for variables (Table 23.7). The values are a function of sample size.[2]

Sample range control chart

Centre line = $\bar{R}$
Lower control limit = $B\bar{R}$
Upper control limit = $C\bar{R}$

Where B, and C are also factors given in the table of control chart factors for variables (Table 23.7). Sample ranges R are compared with the R chart that monitors the variation of range among the items within samples.

Table 23.7 Control chart factors for variables; for sample sizes greater than 25 the given expressions are linear approximations for constructing control charts

Sample size, n	Control limit factors		
	Sample means	Sample ranges	
	A	B	C
2	1.880	0.000	3.269
3	1.023	0.000	2.574
4	0.729	0.000	2.282
5	0.577	0.000	2.114
6	0.483	0.000	2.004
7	0.419	0.076	1.924
8	0.373	0.136	1.864
9	0.337	0.184	1.816
10	0.308	0.223	1.777
11	0.285	0.256	1.744
12	0.266	0.283	1.717
13	0.249	0.308	1.692
14	0.235	0.328	1.672
15	0.223	0.347	1.653
16	0.212	0.363	1.637
17	0.203	0.378	1.622
18	0.194	0.391	1.609
19	0.187	0.403	1.597
20	0.180	0.414	1.586
21	0.173	0.425	1.575
22	0.167	0.434	1.566
23	0.162	0.443	1.557
24	0.157	0.452	1.548
25	0.153	0.460	1.540
> 25	$0.751/\sqrt{n}$	$0.45 + 0.001n$	$1.55 - 0.001n$

The control limits are based on the sampling distribution. Each sample mean, or sample range, is plotted on the appropriate control chart and provides the information on whether the process mean has shifted. This type of control chart is illustrated with the worked example, *Filling Machine*.

Setting control limits

A process that is considered in control when 3σ limits are used ($z = 3$) may not be in control if tighter limits are used, ($z = 2$) or ($z = 1$) for example. This is illustrated in Figure 23.12, which shows that the process is in control with the broader limits, but more and more samples lie outside the limits in going from $z = 3$ to $z = 1$.

Precautions with control limits

The following should be noted with regard to control limits:

■ Even if all observations are within limits, it does not guarantee that assignable variations are not present, that is, that there is a problem with the process.

■ Even if all observations appear outside one of the control limits, this does not guarantee that assignable variations are present.

■ If 2σ limits are used, 95.5 per cent of sample means should be within limits and 4.5 per cent outside limits when only random variations are present.

■ If 1σ limits are used, 68 per cent of sample means should be within limits, and 32 per cent outside limits when only random variations are present.

■ Using 3σ limits will reduce the risk of concluding that process is out of control when in fact only random variations account for points outside the control limits. However, wider limits make it more difficult to detect non random variations when they are present.

Possibilities in the outcome of control charts

In summary, there are three commonly used quality control charts, the p-chart, the c-chart and the x-bar chart (with the R-chart) – Figure 23.13. The following summarizes the possible outcomes of sampling results from any of these types of charts.

Sample means lie close to the centre line

In Figure 23.14, the sample means lie close to (hug) the centre line, which indicates that the process is well in control. This is the expectation in the Taguchi Methods of quality control (see Chapter 4, *Quality Management*). Under this situation, one should tighten up the control limits (bring them closer to the centre line).

Sample means within limits, but wide variation

In Figure 23.15, the sample means are within limits, but there is wide fluctuation, which means that, although this indicates that the process is in control, the variation is too much and the process is sloppy. An analysis should be made to find out why this is happening.

Sample means within limits, but there is an alarming trend

In Figure 23.16, the sample means are within limits, but there is an alarming trend, which means that, although the samples are at present within the limits, there is an upward trend and it seems that the process will soon be out of control. The process should be stopped and investigated.

Sample out of control

In Figure 23.17, the sample means are beyond upper limit, which shows that, from the beginning, the process is out of control. The system should be shut down and investigated.

Figure 23.12 Control chart.

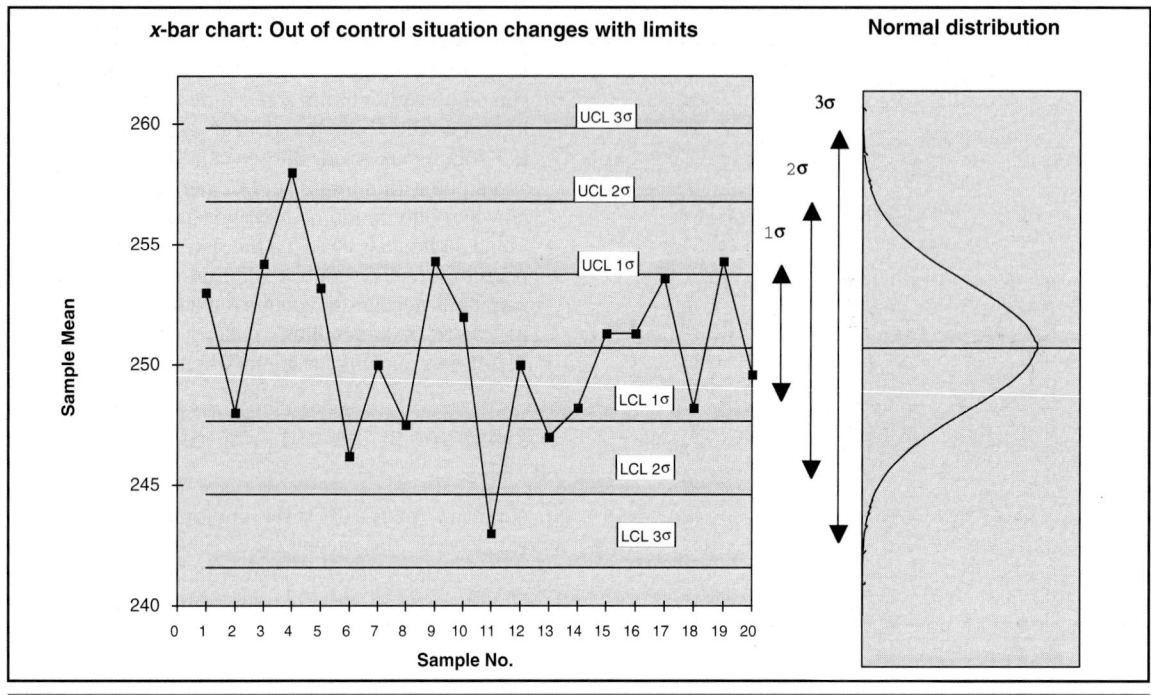

Change in the process

In Figure 23.18, the sample means are within limits, but there has been an abrupt change in the process operation. At first, sample data is between the centre line and the upper control limit. Then suddenly the performance of the process has improved and data points begin to hug the lower limit. This situation is worthy of investigation.

Figure 23.13 Quality control charts.

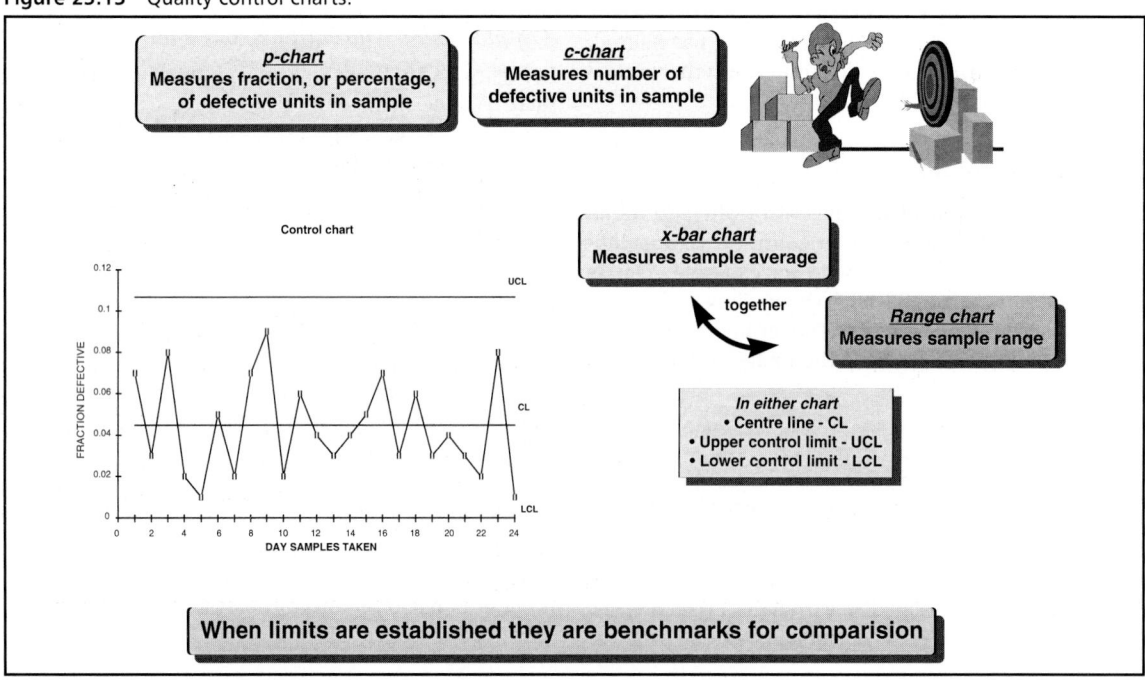

Figure 23.14   Sample means lie close to (hug) the centre line.

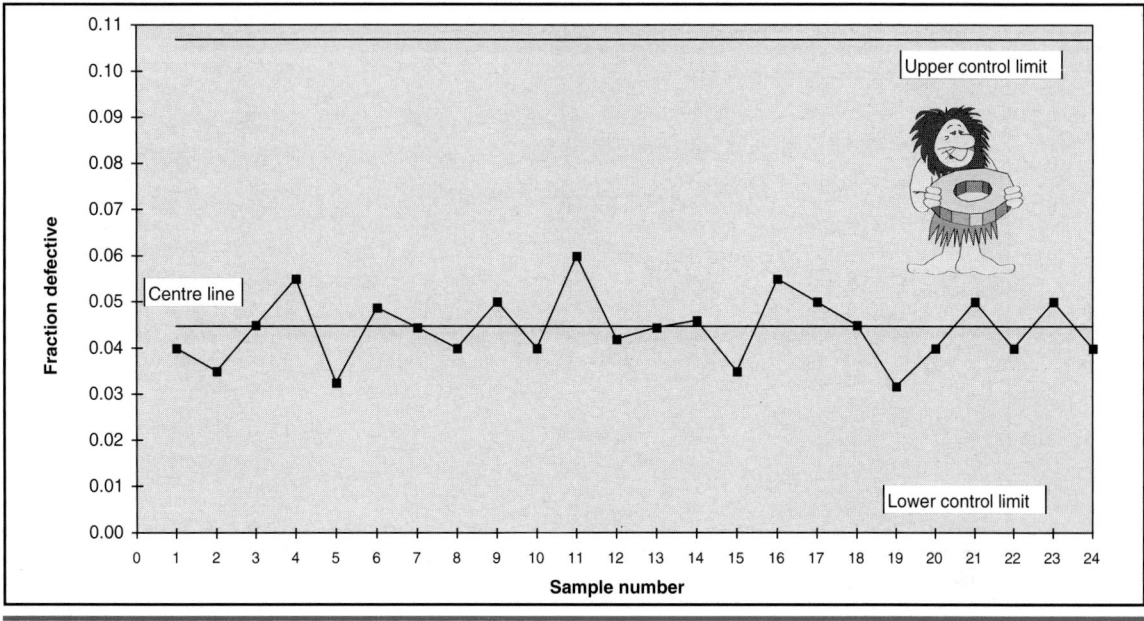

Figure 23.15   Sample means within limits, but wide fluctuation.

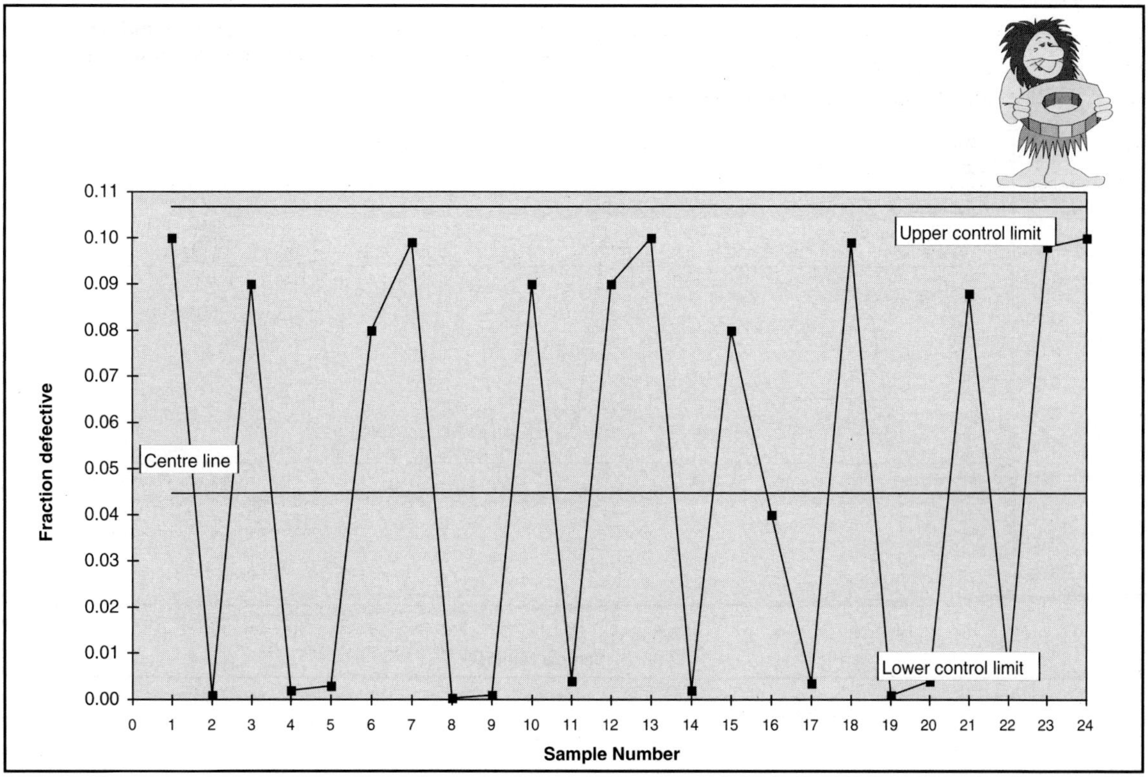

Figure 23.16 Sample means within limits, but there is an alarming trend.

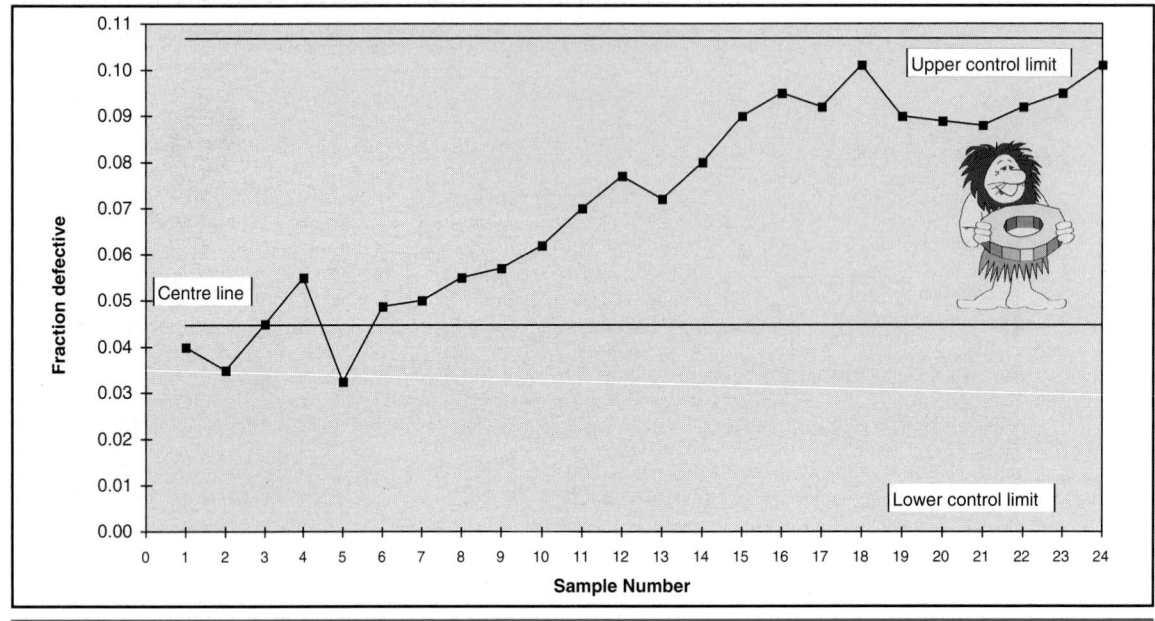

Figure 23.17 Sample means beyond upper limit, out of control.

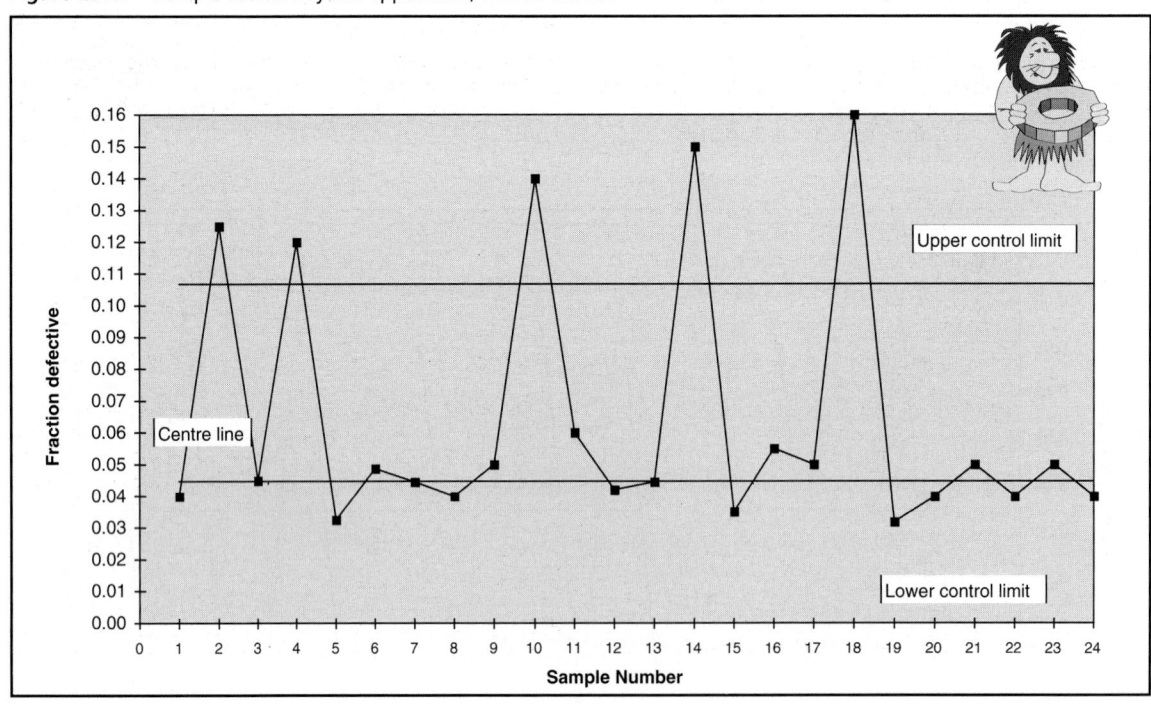

Figure 23.18   Sample means within limits, but there has been an abrupt change in the process.

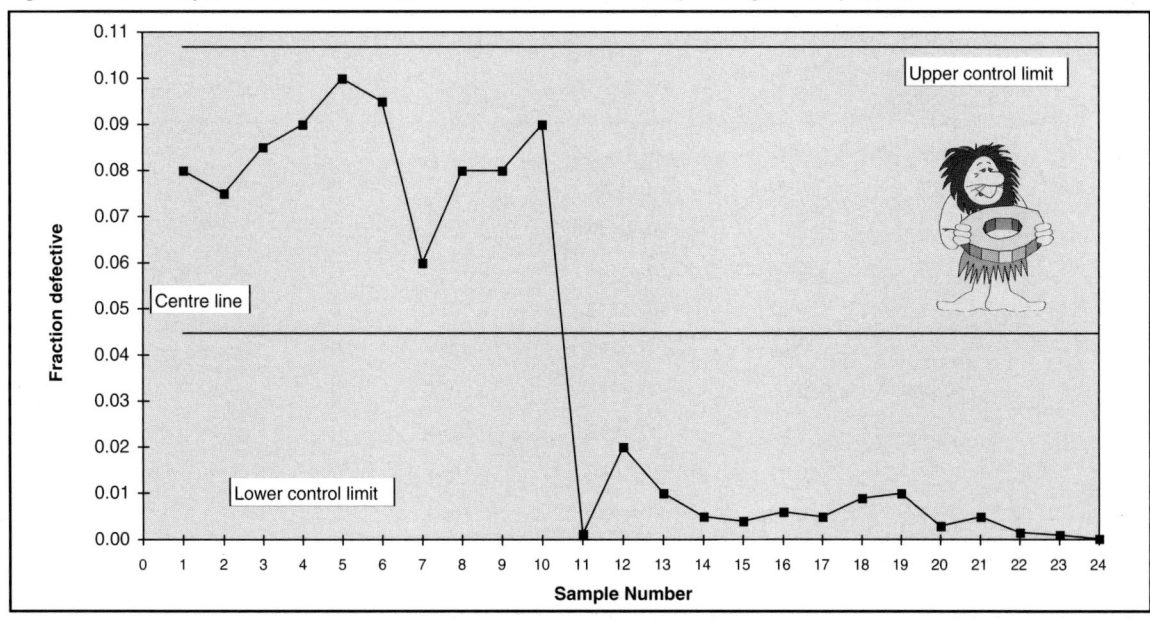

WORKED EXAMPLE: PRINTED CIRCUITS

Situation

A company makes small inexpensive printed electrical circuits and most of the soldered connections are performed by hand. The company wants to develop a process control chart to see if the operation is in control. Samples of size 100 are withdrawn over a 24-hour period and inspected. These results are shown in Table 23.8.

Table 23.8   Printed circuits – results of inspection

Sample No.	Number of defective circuits	Sample No.	Number of defective circuits
1	7	13	3
2	3	14	4
3	8	15	5
4	2	16	7
5	1	17	3
6	5	18	6
7	2	19	3
8	7	20	4
9	9	21	3
10	2	22	2
11	6	23	8
12	4	24	1

Required

1   Develop a 3-standard-deviation p-chart, the required control chart.
2   Would one conclude that the process in control?
3   What comments do you have regarding random sampling for printed circuits?

Solution

1   Table 23.9 gives the calculation for developing the p-chart with 3σ limits and Figure 23.19 shows the 24 sample data. The lower control limit is at zero because in practice the calculation indicates a negative value of p, which is impossible.

2   Since all the samples fall within the limits, the process is considered in control.

3   One word of caution that should be noted is that, even though the process is in control according to the company's requirements, having even one faulty printed circuit for use in downstream use can have serious consequences to the company (faulty products, poor customer relationship, expensive rework operations).

Table 23.9 Circuits – calculation for developing the p-chart

Sample No.	Number of defective circuits	Fraction of defective circuits	CL	UCL	LCL
0					
1	7	0.07	0.0438	0.1051	0
2	3	0.03	0.0438	0.1051	0
3	8	0.08	0.0438	0.1051	0
4	2	0.02	0.0438	0.1051	0
5	1	0.01	0.0438	0.1051	0
6	5	0.05	0.0438	0.1051	0
7	2	0.02	0.0438	0.1051	0
8	7	0.07	0.0438	0.1051	0
9	9	0.09	0.0438	0.1051	0
10	2	0.02	0.0438	0.1051	0
11	6	0.06	0.0438	0.1051	0
12	4	0.04	0.0438	0.1051	0
13	3	0.03	0.0438	0.1051	0
14	4	0.04	0.0438	0.1051	0
15	5	0.05	0.0438	0.1051	0
16	7	0.07	0.0438	0.1051	0
17	3	0.03	0.0438	0.1051	0
18	6	0.06	0.0438	0.1051	0
19	3	0.03	0.0438	0.1051	0
20	4	0.04	0.0438	0.1051	0
21	3	0.03	0.0438	0.1051	0
22	2	0.02	0.0438	0.1051	0
23	8	0.08	0.0438	0.1051	0
24	1	0.01	0.0438	0.1051	0
Mean defectives	4.3750	0.0438			
Sample size, n	100				
Fraction good		0.9563			
standard deviation $\sigma = (pq/n)^{0.5}$		0.0205			
3σ		0.0614			

Figure 23.19 Printed circuits: *p*-control chart.

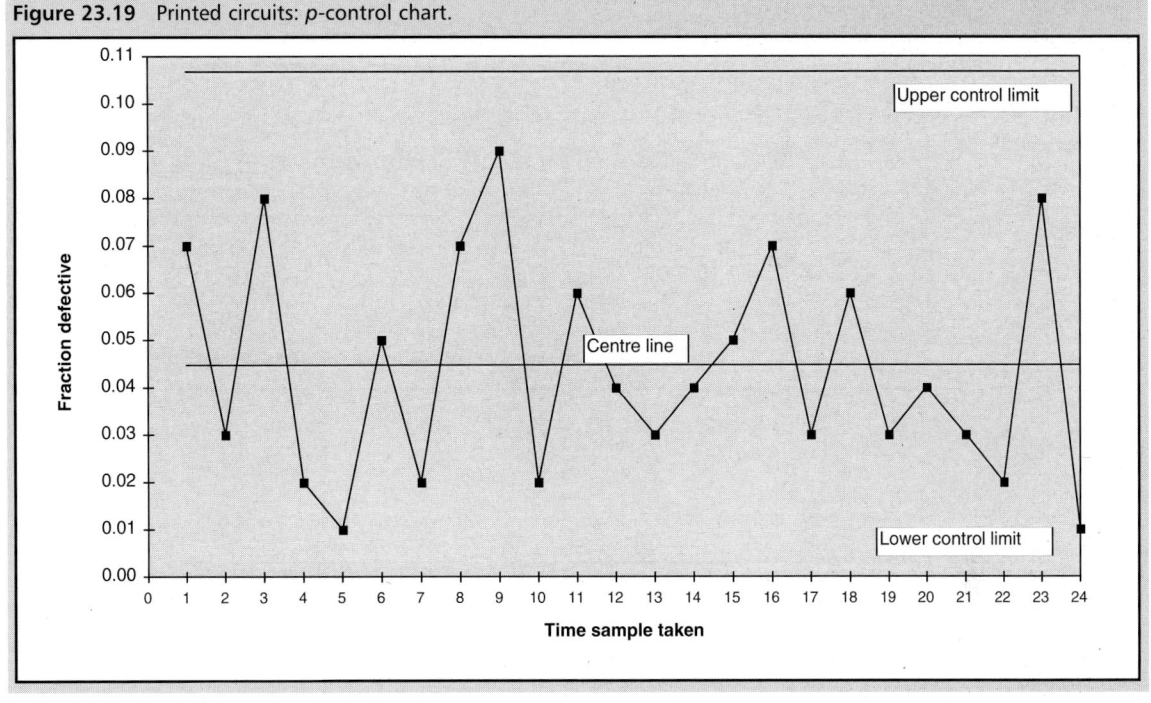

WORKED EXAMPLE: PAPER MAKING

Situation

A company proposes to modify its paper-making process using pulp from a foreign supplier, rather than its normal domestic suppliers. It wants to be sure that it can use this raw material in its paper-making operation and obtain the same quality paper as it does with domestic pulp. Prior to running the foreign pulp, it takes paper from its normal suppliers for one week and analyses the blemishes on the paper. On a total of 32 m² of paper tested during one week it found 350 blemishes. The company then ran the paper-making machines with the foreign pulp and in five bobbins of paper tested it obtained the average blemishes per square metre on the paper as shown in Table 23.10.

Table 23.10 Average blemishes per square metre on the paper made from the foreign pulp

Sample No.	Average blemishes per square metre
1	30
2	19
3	6
4	25
5	3

Required

1. Establish a *c*-control chart for 3σ control limits using the domestic paper test.

2. Show the information from the foreign paper on the control chart. What are your comments about the foreign paper? Do you have any suggestions?

Solution

1. Table 23.11 gives the calculation for the control limits for the test data. Figure 23.20 shows the five sample data on the control chart.

Table 23.11 The calculation for the control limits for the paper-making test data

Square metres tested	32
Total blemishes	350
Average faults/m²	10.9375
Standard deviation	3.31
z value	3
Limits, + and −	9.92
UCL	20.86
CL	10.94
LCL	1.02

2. The quality of paper seems erratic. Two averages are outside the limits, one is pretty close to the upper limit, and two are below the centre line. The company should analyse the quality of the raw material and perhaps re-evaluate the operating procedures, such as drying time, tension etc. for paper making using this new raw material.

Figure 23.20 Papermaking: c-control chart.

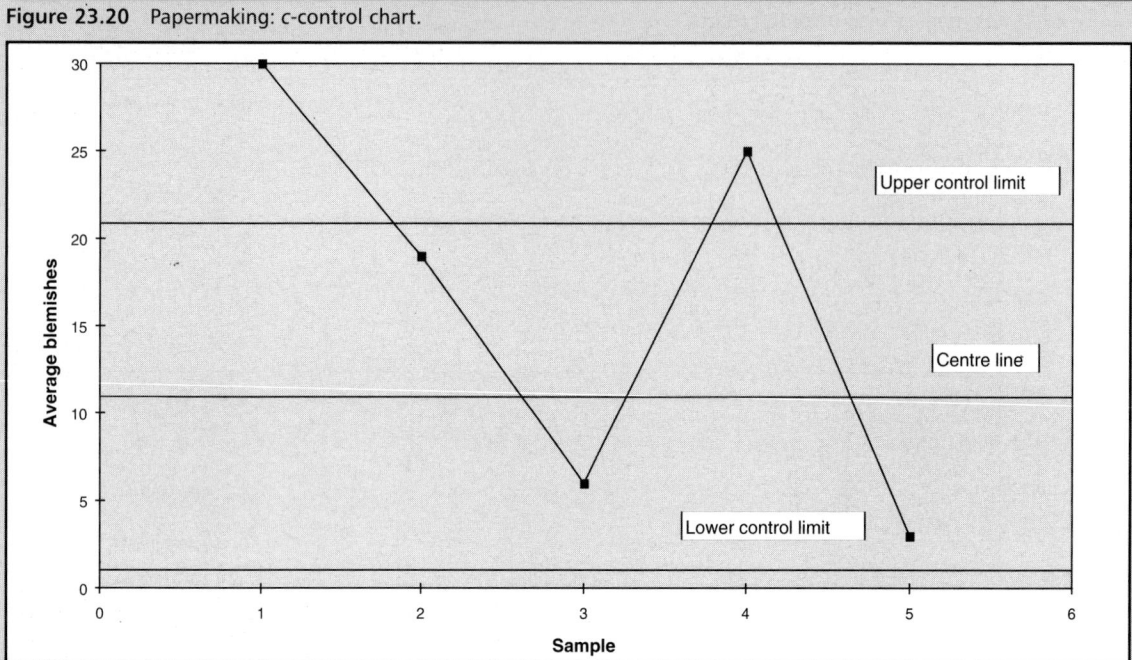

WORKED EXAMPLE: FILLING MACHINE

Situation

A confectionery company in St. Etienne, France, has an automatic filling machine which allows 250 grams of sweets to be put into plastic bags before they are sealed. The company is concerned about the reliability of this machine and decides to carry out a statistical process control study. First, the filling line is shut down and adjusted according to specifications. The line is then put into operation and 20 random samples each of 25 units, are taken during eight hours of operation. For each of the samples taken, the average weight is determined, and the maximum and minimum weight is also recorded. This information is given in Table 13.12.

Table 23.12 Average, maximum and minimum weights (g) of confectionery samples

Sample No.	Average weight	Maximum weight	Minimum weight
1	253.00	262.00	232.00
2	248.00	261.00	232.00
3	254.20	269.00	242.00
4	256.00	265.00	248.00
5	253.20	262.40	247.00
6	246.20	261.40	235.00
7	250.00	254.00	230.00
8	247.50	265.00	229.00
9	254.30	275.00	242.00
10	252.00	258.00	241.00
11	246.10	278.00	237.00
12	250.00	265.00	235.00
13	247.00	265.20	241.00
14	248.20	263.20	242.10
15	251.30	270.20	247.20
16	251.30	265.20	248.10
17	253.60	257.20	248.80
18	252.70	259.20	248.20
19	254.30	259.00	247.90
20	255.20	260.10	251.00

Required

1 Develop the two appropriate control charts to analyse this filling operation.

2 What are the conclusions from these control charts?

Solution

1 The average values for the weights and the range are calculated as shown in Table 23.13. The coefficients A, B and C according to the sample size are taken from Table 23.7 and the two charts are constructed as given in Figures 23.21 and 23.22.

2 Both charts illustrate that there is a problem with the filling machine. In the x-bar chart the early results are erratic, some falling within the range, and samples 4 and 6 falling outside. As the sampling proceeds, the average weights are erring on the high side and the 20th sample indicates that the average weight is outside the limit. Although this would not be of concern to the consumer, it is costing more than is necessary to the producer.

The machine should be shutdown and checked for operation.

Table 23.13 Filling machine operation

Sample No.	Average weight	Maximum weight	Minimum weight	Sample range	x-bar chart			Range chart		
					CL	LCL	UCL	CL	LCL	UCL
1	253.00	262.00	232.00	30.00	251.21	247.76	254.65	22.54	10.37	34.71
2	248.00	261.00	232.00	29.00	251.21	247.76	254.65	22.54	10.37	34.71
3	254.20	269.00	242.00	27.00	251.21	247.76	254.65	22.54	10.37	34.71
4	256.00	265.00	248.00	17.00	251.21	247.76	254.65	22.54	10.37	34.71
5	253.20	262.40	247.00	15.40	251.21	247.76	254.65	22.54	10.37	34.71
6	246.20	261.40	235.00	26.40	251.21	247.76	254.65	22.54	10.37	34.71
7	250.00	254.00	230.00	24.00	251.21	247.76	254.65	22.54	10.37	34.71
8	247.50	265.00	229.00	36.00	251.21	247.76	254.65	22.54	10.37	34.71
9	254.30	275.00	242.00	33.00	251.21	247.76	254.65	22.54	10.37	34.71
10	252.00	258.00	241.00	17.00	251.21	247.76	254.65	22.54	10.37	34.71
11	246.10	278.00	237.00	41.00	251.21	247.76	254.65	22.54	10.37	34.71
12	250.00	265.00	235.00	30.00	251.21	247.76	254.65	22.54	10.37	34.71
13	247.00	265.20	241.00	24.20	251.21	247.76	254.65	22.54	10.37	34.71
14	248.20	263.20	242.10	21.10	251.21	247.76	254.65	22.54	10.37	34.71
15	251.30	270.20	247.20	23.00	251.21	247.76	254.65	22.54	10.37	34.71
16	251.30	265.20	248.10	17.10	251.21	247.76	254.65	22.54	10.37	34.71
17	253.60	257.20	248.80	8.40	251.21	247.76	254.65	22.54	10.37	34.71
18	252.70	259.20	248.20	11.00	251.21	247.76	254.65	22.54	10.37	34.71
19	254.30	259.00	247.90	11.10	251.21	247.76	254.65	22.54	10.37	34.71
20	255.20	260.10	251.00	9.10	251.21	247.76	254.65	22.54	10.37	34.71
Mean	251.205			22.54						
Count	20									

Sample size, n	25
Average of sample mean	251.21
Average of sample range	22.54
For sample size of 25	
A	0.153
B	0.46
C	1.54
x-bar chart	
CL	251.21
LCL	247.76
UCL	254.65
Range chart	
CL	22.54
LCL	10.37
UCL	34.71

Figure 23.21 Filling machine: *x*-bar chart.

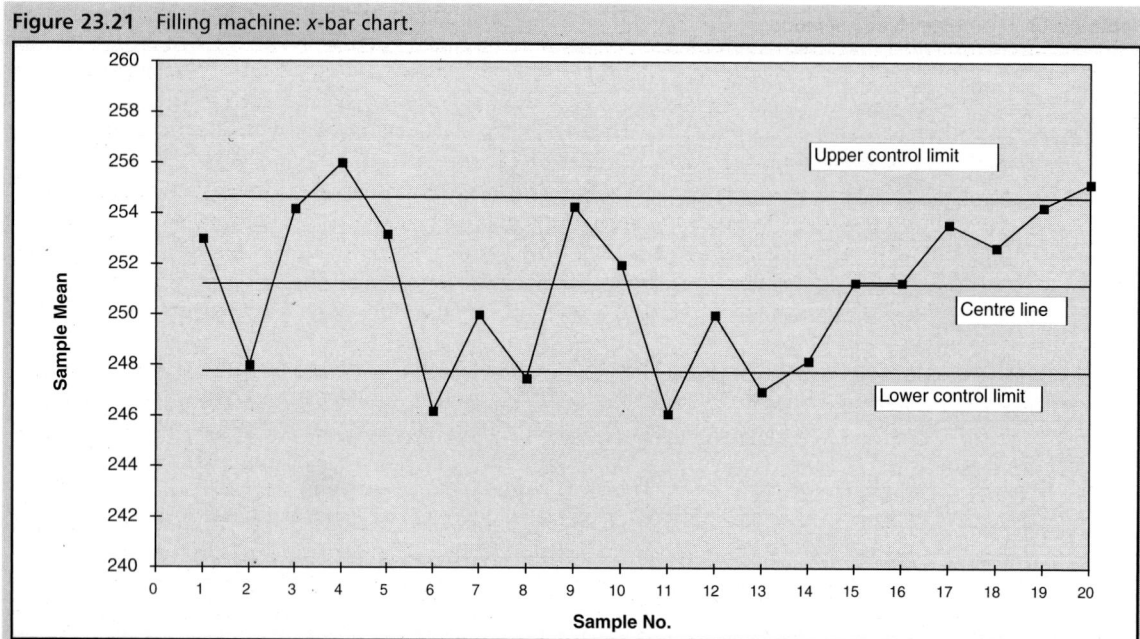

Figure 23.22 Filling machine: range chart.

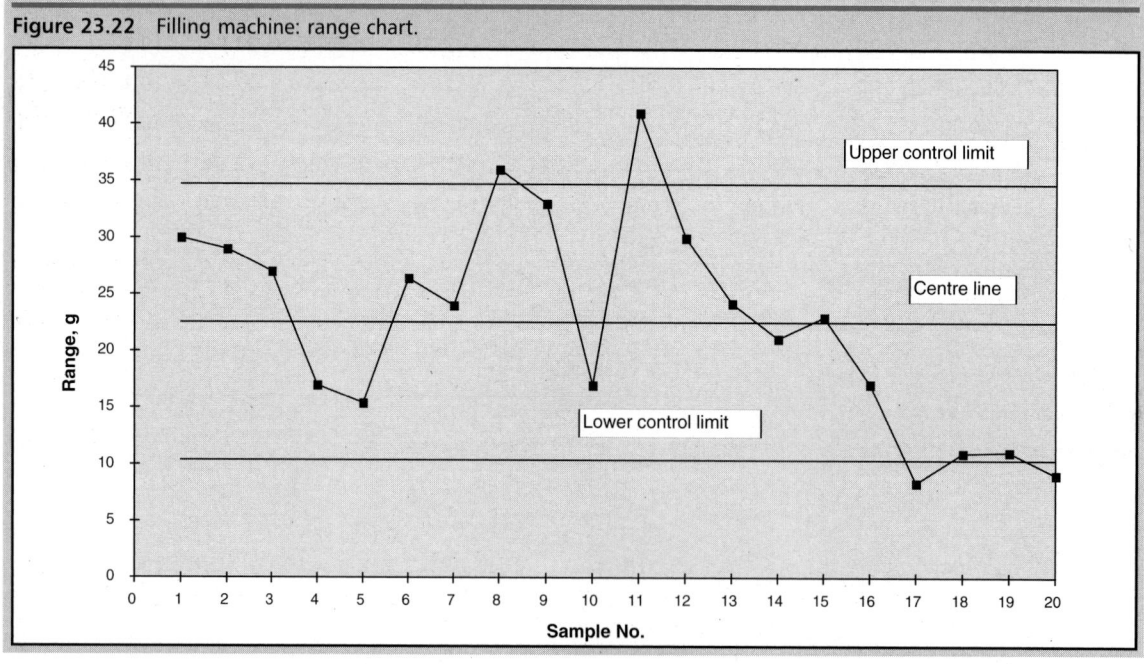

SUMMARY OF KEY ELEMENTS

- In manufacturing, statistical quality control is the sampling and analysis of units to determine if these are in accordance with specifications. In services, statistical quality control is often carried out to determine customer satisfaction.

- The ultimate objective of statistical quality control is not to find out if situations or units are bad, but to avoid poor quality in the first place. It is more economic to operate in a quality mode than to have to repair damage later.

- There are statistical quality control measures for attributes, whether a product works or not, or for variables, to see whether a product is within a specified range.

- Three quality control methods are single, double and sequential sampling.

- An acceptance plan is mutually agreed to by a supplier and a purchaser, regarding whether to accept a lot of goods based on sampling and testing from the lot.

- An operating characteristic curve shows how well an acceptance plan discriminates between good and bad lots. Discriminating ability depends on the shape of the curve, which is a function of sample size and the number of defective sample units.

- With an acceptance plan four things can happen. A good lot can be accepted, a good lot can be rejected, a bad lot can be rejected or a bad lot can be accepted. Sampling from the lot gives no guarantee of the quality of the lot, only of the sample.

- The acceptable quality level (AQL) is the level of product quality considered acceptable and is a standard established by the manufacturer or the purchaser. The lower the value, the more rigorous is the process, and thus the higher is the cost of quality.

- Lot tolerance per cent defective (LTPD) is the level of quality considered unacceptable or bad. Lots at this level, or higher, need to be rejected by the acceptance plan.

- The producer of units wants to avoid having a good lot rejected by the acceptance plan. The producer's risk (α) involves the taking of a random sample that results in a higher portion of defects in the sample than is actually present in the lot.

- The consumer wants to avoid having a bad lot accepted by the acceptance plan. The consumer's risk (β) involves the taking of a random sample that results in a much lower portion of defects in the sample than is actually present in the lot.

- Statistical process control (SPC) is the periodic sampling and analysis of units or activity to determine if the system is performing according to some specified target. It tests for assignable, but not random, variations in the system.

- A control chart is the evaluation tool in statistical process control. It has a centre line, an upper control limit and a lower control limit.

- Control charts for attributes are p-charts, which show the percentage of defective units in a sample, and c-charts for the number of defective units in a sample.

- There are two control charts for variables, an x-bar chart for sample means x and a sample range chart R.

- In SPC, if all observations are within limits, it does not guarantee that a process is in control; nor, if observations are outside limits, does it guarantee that a process is out of control.

REVIEW AND DISCUSSION QUESTIONS

1 **Acceptance sampling and SPC**. Acceptance sampling and statistical process control are different concepts. However, if improvements were made through statistical process control, what might be the impact on the acceptance plan?

2 **Attributes and variables**. Which of the following would fall into the category of attributes and which into the category of variables:
   (a) The quality of a German shepherd (Alsatian) in a dog show?
   (b) The volume of wine in a ¾ litre bottle of Bordeaux wine?
   (c) A soft-boiled egg, which is ordered in a restaurant for breakfast?
   (d) Exam results, such as in A level Physics or on the French Baccalaureate?
   (e) An incandescent light bulb?
   (f) A neon light bulb?
   (g) The weight of a pound of beef?
   (h) Making a plane connection at London's Heathrow after taking a flight from Paris to London?
   Are your responses completely black and white?

3 **Lots and series**. The following products are usually made in lots:
   (a) flu vaccine;
   (b) chocolate;
   (c) cotton fabric for shirts;
   (d) paper for printing;
   (e) screws.
   Discuss some of the factors that dictate manufacture of these by products as lots, rather than as individual units.

4 **Control limits**. Which of the following products would have tight control limits, and which would be somewhat looser:
   (a) penicillin;
   (b) gasket seals on a rocket booster for space flight;
   (c) five-inch nails;
   (d) the surface finish on an automobile;
   (e) the grading of an essay in an English Literature exam;
   (f) the thickness of icing on a wedding cake.
   Discuss, in general terms, the criteria that establish control limits.

5. **Standards or control charts**. What do you think would be some of the variables measured, and compared to standards or to control charts, for the following:
   (a) a brewery;
   (b) an airline company such as British Airways, Air France or Lufthansa;
   (c) an automobile company;
   (d) a blood test;
   (e) pharmaceutical ointment;
   (f) distribution of a consignment of goods from one location to another.

EXERCISE PROBLEM: CANDY CO.

Situation

The Candy Co., outside Berlin, Germany, manufactures a large variety of sweets. One of its principal products is Gumbo Bears (jelly sweets in the shape of the German Bear.) After production, the Gumbo Bears are cooled and packed in 250, 500 and 1000 gram plastic bags. The Gumbo Bears are fed automatically into the bags, which are then sealed by a hot press. Lately, the manager of production has noticed that there have been problems with the hot-press sealer and he wonders if this has something to do with the filling operation. This has particularly occurred with the 500 gram bags.

The company decided to investigate the operation of the automatic filling machine and asked Michael Grand to undertake the analysis. The filling machine was first shut down and checked to see if was operating properly. This was just a very quick check and no extensive adjustments were made. Next Michael randomly sampled the bags of Gumbo bears and weighed the contents. Sample sizes were 20 bags each, and in total 200 samples were taken. The average of the 200 sample means was 250.50 grams. The average of the sample range was 24.20 grams. Michael used this information to construct control charts for sample means, and sample ranges.

The following week Michael, together with his assistant, Anne Box, carried out a detailed analysis of the filling machine. Each hour, they took random samples of the 500 gram bags of Gumbo Bears. Michael took samples for the first 8 hours, and Anne took samples for the next 8. Thus in total they took 16 samples. As before, there were 20 bags in each sample. The mean weight of the sample was determined, and also the heaviest, and the lightest bag in each sample was recorded. This data is given in Table 23.14.

Table 23.14 The sample weights of the bags of Gumbo bears

Sample No.	Sample Average	Maximum Weight	Minimum Weight
1	504.00	508.00	499.20
2	502.00	510.00	485.50
3	501.00	512.60	496.50
4	501.30	514.90	498.60
5	499.20	520.20	487.20
6	501.00	504.90	489.50
7	502.10	508.60	489.60
8	499.20	512.50	475.60
9	498.20	509.60	499.20
10	499.80	507.60	499.60
11	500.90	503.20	498.40
12	501.30	514.60	486.50
13	501.90	521.00	498.60
14	501.70	521.20	485.60
15	502.10	521.90	475.60
16	503.20	512.80	498.20

Required

1 Develop a control chart for the sample mean and the sample range.
2 Plot the data for the 20 samples on the corresponding control charts.
3 What are your conclusions about the automatic filling machine?

EXERCISE PROBLEM: CARPET MAKING

Situation

A carpet maker in India wishes to install a quality control programme for the production of its carpets. It takes at random 250 carpets of similar size and counts the total number of faults on this sample. The number was 970.

Then at random for one week, Monday to Friday, the producer takes one carpet each from its two work centres and counts the number of blemishes on the carpet. This information is given in Table 23.15. The number in parenthesis after each day indicates the work centre.

Table 23.15 The number of faults in the carpet samples

Day	Number of faults
Monday (1)	2

Monday (2)	12
Tuesday (1)	3
Tuesday (2)	13
Wednesday (1)	3
Wednesday (2)	10
Thursday (1)	2
Thursday (2)	8
Friday (1)	2
Friday (2)	11

Required

1 Establish a c-control chart for 3σ control limits.
2 Present the test data on the control chart. What conclusions might you draw?

EXERCISE PROBLEM: INTERNET

Situation

A consulting firm in France is looking into modifying its information systems network because of problems with the present arrangement. Before any action is taken, a control was made over a three-week period, Monday to Friday, for the time taken to access the first search screen of Internet. During one-hour periods throughout the day consultants were asked to record the response time for connecting to Internet. For each hour period, data for 12 consultants picked at random was tabulated. This information is given in seconds, in the Table 23.16 for the mean of the 12 response times, plus the range.

Required

1 Construct the appropriate control charts to see if the response time of the process is 'in control' according to the information provided.
2 What conclusions might you draw from your control charts?
3 What was your reason for selecting the control chart you used for your interpretations?

Table 23.16   Data for Internet access times

Time	Week 1 Mean	Range	Week 2 Mean	Range	Week 3 Mean	Range
08h–09h	8.25	5.20	2.25	14.50	5.20	23.60
09h–10h	10.65	12.20	5.86	26.20	4.60	45.20
10h–11h	9.45	22.90	13.25	15.20	3.50	12.60
11h–12h	9.86	18.00	10.56	32.00	3.60	23.60
12h–13h	12.24	14.60	13.46	14.60	4.50	25.40
13h–14h	20.25	23.70	20.45	41.20	13.60	25.60
14h–15h	32.40	21.00	30.25	12.60	9.50	12.60
15h–16h	40.20	25.00	35.21	23.50	12.60	18.60
16h–17h	45.70	26.30	40.56	18.50	13.50	21.60
17h–18h	55.23	30.20	47.50	19.60	20.60	23.60
18h–19h	56.20	23.60	48.60	21.30	25.60	5.60

EXERCISE PROBLEM: METERS

Situation

The Gerber company, in the Paris region of France, manufactures various types of flow meters for use in the gas and petroleum industry. The critical part of these meters is a rotating cylinder positioned inside a gas-tight casing. The cylinders are cut from aluminium tubing on a large automatic saw. It is critical that the length of these cylinders lies within the given specification or else the meters do not function correctly.

Gerber operates on a 40-hour week, Monday to Friday. In the cutting operation the automatic machine is regulated twice each day, once in the morning at 08:00 and once in the afternoon at 13:00. The production manager has been unhappy with the quality of the meters being made and has authorized a quality control analysis to take place. This analysis was carried out over a one-month period when cylinder reference No 45983-M was being produced. This cylinder had a specified length of 3.8 cm.

Samples of 15 units were taken twice a day at 09:30 and 15:30 and the sample average and sample range were determined. This data is given in Table 23.17.

Required

1 Construct the x-bar control chart with the centre lines and the upper and lower limits.
2 Construct the range chart indicating the centre lines and the upper and lower limits.
3 Do either of the charts indicate any cause for concern? If so what do you suggest might be happening?

Table 23.17   Data for cylinder-length samples (reference no. 45983-M)

Day	Time	Week 1 x-bar (cm)	Range (cm)	Week 2 x-bar (cm)	Range (cm)	Week 3 x-bar (cm)	Range (cm)	Week 4 x-bar (cm)	Range (cm)
Monday	09:30	3.8900	0.0855	3.7800	0.1140	3.8640	0.0950	3.8960	0.0950
Monday	15:30	3.8420	0.0950	3.7900	0.1045	3.8043	0.1045	3.8640	0.1000
Tuesday	09:30	3.8095	0.0950	3.8380	0.0855	3.8245	0.0950	3.8040	0.0895
Tuesday	15:30	3.8080	0.1045	3.8157	0.0950	3.8190	0.0855	3.8190	0.0855
Wednesday	09:30	3.8285	0.0855	3.8138	0.1045	3.8123	0.0950	3.8320	0.0950
Wednesday	15:30	3.8095	0.1045	3.8185	0.0855	3.8190	0.1045	3.8190	0.1045
Thursday	09:30	3.8285	0.1045	3.8157	0.0960	3.8200	0.0855	3.8268	0.0855
Thursday	15:30	3.8190	0.0950	3.8275	0.0860	3.8100	0.0855	3.8170	0.0855
Friday	09:30	3.8200	0.1045	3.8340	0.0950	3.8280	0.0755	3.8050	0.0878
Friday	15:30	3.8700	0.0950	3.8700	0.0880	3.7810	0.0855	3.7700	0.0855

EXERCISE PROBLEM: SANTA CLAUS

Situation

The Cusin company in Chambery is a family-owned toy business. One of its products for Christmas is a Santa which walks, rings a bell and sings 'Merry Christmas'. Cusin manufactures the Santa itself and imports the electrical/mechanical movement from the Chang company in Seoul in South Korea.

A shipment of 4000 movements has just been received in the Cusin warehouse. Chang and Cusin have jointly agreed to an acceptance plan where the producer's risk is 5 per cent, the consumer's risk is 10 per cent, the acceptable quality level (AQL) of 1 per cent and the Lot Tolerance Per cent Defective (LTPD) is 6 per cent.

Required

1   Develop an operating characteristic curve for a sample size of 100 and for 3 or less defective units (value of c) in the sample, using a value of p from 0 to 15 per cent in 1 per cent intervals. Would this satisfy the acceptance plan of Chang and Cusin?

2   Redo the operating characteristic curve for a sample size of 200 and a value of c of 6 or less. What are your observations?

3   Develop an average outgoing quality level (AOQ) curve for the sampling situation given in Question 1.

4   If the actual percentage of defectives from an incoming lot is 3 per cent, then, given the AOQ curve developed in the answer to Question 3, what is the average outgoing quality (AOQ) in per cent defectives for the Santa movement?

EXERCISE PROBLEM: WATCH MANUFACTURE

Situation

The Picasso company, outside Barcelona, Spain, assembles inexpensive watches for sale in the European market. Most of its watches are aimed at the market for children or young adolescents. The company imports the printed circuit from Singapore and then assembles the watches with the frames made in its own factory. The watches are sold through distributors situated throughout Europe.

Assembly is quite straightforward. It involves laying the printed circuit into the watch frame then making six solder connections. The battery is then inserted and the back is snapped onto the frame. The company works seven days a week. The weekend employees are a mixture of temporary and permanent staff.

Of late, Picasso has been receiving complaints from its distributors about defective watches being sold. As a result, Picasso has decided to investigate its assembly operation.

Picasso is carrying out sampling over a continuous 28-day period, starting on a Monday. Each day, for the 28 days, it takes a random sample of 150 finished watches from that day's assembled lot and tests them, simply to see if they work. The criterion is that the watches operate or they do not. The data for this sampling is given in Table 23.18

Table 23.18   Results of tests on Picasso watches

Day	Quantity of defective watches	Day	Quantity of defective watches
1	3	15	1
2	2	16	4
3	5	17	3
4	4	18	2

5	1	19	9
6	12	20	13
7	16	21	19
8	3	22	5
9	0	23	3
10	2	24	1
11	0	25	0
12	7	26	5
13	11	27	13
14	14	28	18

Required

1 Construct a p-chart for this operation, using a z value of 3 (99.7 per cent confidence limit).
2 What are your observations from this p-chart?
3 Construct a new p-chart, just using the Monday through Friday data (thus 20 pieces of data).
4 What are your observations from new this p-chart?

NOTES AND REFERENCES

1. Baillargeon, G. (1990) *'Plans d'Echantillonnage en Contrôle de la Qualité: Contrôle par Attributs'*; Editions SMG, (Eclipse-marketing)
2. Bell Telephone Laboratories (1931) *Economics Control of Manufactured Products*, Litton Educational Publishing, Van Nostrand Reinhold Co.

FURTHER READING

Benneyan, J. C. and Chute, A. D. (1993) 'SPC, process improvement, and the Deming PDCA circle in freight administration', *Production and Inventory Management Journal* 34(1): 35–40.

Buch, K. and Wetzel, D. (1993) 'The evolution of SPC in manufacturing', *Journal for Quality and Participation* 16(6): 34–37.

Duncan, A. (1986) *Quality Control and Industrial Statistics*, Homewood, IL: Irwin.

Esposito, P. (1993) 'Applying statistical process control to safety', *Professional Safety* 38(12): 18–23.

Freeman, J. D. (1993) 'Metrology and statistical quality control', *Quality* 32(4): 18–22.

Gaafar, L. K. and Keats, J. B. (1992) 'Statistical process control: A guide for implementation', *International Journal of Quality and Reliability Management* 9(4): 9–20.

Harris, C. R. and Yit, W. (1994) 'Successfully implementing statistical process control in integrated steel companies', *Interfaces* 24(5): 49–58.

Hill, S. (1994) 'Real-time SPC has sparked a real debate', *Manufacturing Systems* 12(6): 14–18.

Hryniewicz, O. (1997) 'Statistical process control with the help of international statistical standards', *Human Systems Management* 16(3): 201–06.

Keats, J. B., Miskulin, J. D. and Runger, G. C. (1995) 'Statistical process control scheme design', *Journal of Quality Technology* 27(3): 214–25.

Kumar, S. (1997) 'Using SPC in the semiconductor industry', *Industrial Management* 39(1): 5–8.

Kumar, S. and Gupta, Y. P (1993) 'Statistical process control at Motorola's Austin assembly plant', *Interfaces* 23(2): 84–92.

Litsikas, M. (1996) 'SPC cuts inspection time by 95 per cent', *Quality* 35(12): 58–60.

Litsikas, M. (1997) 'SPC time cut by 80 per cent', *Quality* 36(4): 110–11.

Maki, R. G. and Milota, M. R. (1993) 'Statistical quality control applied to lumber drying', *Quality Progress* 26(12): 75–79.

Marquardt, D. W. (1993) 'Estimating the standard deviation', for statistical process control', *International Journal of Quality and Reliability Management* 10(8): 57–64.

Maul, G. P., Richardson, R. and Jones, R. (1996) 'Statistical process control applied to gas metal arc welding', *Computers and Industrial Engineering* 31(1,2): 253–56.

McWilliams, T. P. (1994) 'Economic, statistical, and economic-statistical x-chart designs', *Journal of Quality Technology* 26(3): 227–38.

Montgomery, D. C. (1990) *Introduction to Statistical Quality Control*, Wiley: 740.

Montgomery, D. C. (1992) 'The use of statistical process control and design of experiments' in product and process improvement', *IIE Transactions* 24(5): 4–17.

Morrison, S. J. (1992) 'What's wrong with sampling inspection?', *Professional Engineering* 5(6): 16–17.

Noaker, P. M. (1995) 'Sizing up SPC software', *Manufacturing Engineering* 114(4): 32–36.

Norton, L. (1997) 'What do you see in the mirror when SPC fails?', *Manufacturing Engineering* 118(4): 16.

Oakland, J. S. and Followell, R. F. (1996) *Statistical Process Control*, Oxford: Butterworth-Heinemann.

Pitt, H. (1994) *SPC for the Rest of Us: A personal path to statistical process control*, Reading, MA: Addison-Wesley.

Porteus, E. L. and Angelus, A. (1997) 'Opportunities for improved statistical process control', *Management Science* 43(9): 1214–228.

Quesenberry, C. P. (1993) 'The effect of sample size on estimated limits for sample mean and x control charts', *Journal of Quality Technology* 25(4): 237–47.

Rauwendaal, C. (1995) 'Statistical process control in extrusion', *Plastics World* 53(3): 59–64.

Roberts, H. V. (1998) *Total Quality Management and Statistics*, Oxford: Blackwell.

Roes, K. C. B., Does, R. J. M. M. and Schurink, Y. (1993) 'Shewhart-type control charts for individual observations', *Journal of Quality Technology* 25(3): 188–98.

Runger, G. C. and Montgomery, D. C. (1993) 'Adaptive sampling enhancements for Shewhart control charts', *IIE Transactions* 25(3): 41–51.

Saniga, E. M. (1993) 'Decision support and statistical quality control', *International Journal of Quality and Reliability Management* 10(2): 9–17.

Shamma, S. E. and Shamma, A. K. (1992) 'Development and evaluation of control charts using double exponentially weighted moving averages', *International Journal of Quality and Reliability Management* 9(6): 18–25.

Stapenhurst, T. (1995) 'SPC and Business Improvements', *Journal of the Operational Research Society* 46(8): 1036–37.

Stuart, M., Mullins, E. and Drew, E. (1996) 'Statistical quality control and improvement', *European Journal of Operational Research* 88(2): 203–14.

24 Waiting lines

Objectives and overview

The objective of this chapter is to present the characteristics and theory of waiting lines, or queuing. Although waiting lines are both a scheduling and capacity problem, the topic is presented here in a separate chapter as the subject has a rather special approach. The chapter opens by discussing the relationship between load and capacity and then illustrating some practical illustrations, causes and characteristics of waiting lines. There is a section which describes the various terms encountered in waiting-line theory, including the probability distributions that are applied, the nature of arrival patterns and service rates and a description of the channel and service phases. Modelling of single-channel single-phase queuing systems is presented and this is followed by a detailed explanation of how a Monte Carlo Simulation can be used to manage waiting lines better.

LOAD AND CAPACITY

Waiting lines, or queues, occurring sporadically or continuously in any part of the supply chain, illustrate a bottleneck situation. They are evident in service situations when people are standing in a line and in manufacturing when there is upstream inventory of component parts waiting to be worked upon. Waiting lines are both a load-scheduling and a capacity-planning problem; a scheduling concern because better planning of people, machines or work posts may reduce the bottlenecks and a capacity problem because better design of the operating system may also reduce or eliminate the waiting lines. (Regarding bottlenecks, see also the section Optimized production technology in Chapter 14, *Operations Scheduling*.)

Balancing the system

The balance of a waiting line can be represented by a seesaw arrangement, where the load is on the left-hand side of the seesaw and the capacity of the system is on the right-hand side.

Load greater than capacity

When the load is greater than the capacity, the seesaw is unbalanced and tips to the left (Figure 24.1). People, inventory units or transportation equipment are waiting. There is a bottleneck and clients are waiting.

Capacity greater than load

When the capacity is greater than the load then the seesaw is unbalanced and tipped to the right (Figure 24.2).

There is no bottleneck, but the capacity resources are underutilized, meaning an unnecessary cost. There are more machines, transportation equipment, cashiers in the system than is needed at that point of time.

Load and capacity balanced

When the load and capacity are balanced, the seesaw is horizontal (Figure 24.3). The system is optimized and there are essentially no waiting lines. In a manufacturing organization this would approach a just-in-time operation (see Chapter 15, *Lean Manufacturing and Just-in-Time*).

WAITING LINES IN PRACTICE

Daily occurrences of waiting line

When there are waiting lines, there is inefficiency. Waiting is a non-value added activity. Some illustrations follow.

Retail stores

A checkout counter at a supermarket or hypermarket, for example, customers are waiting to pay for purchases. The waiting line is often greater during lunchtime and early evening, but sometimes non-existent in the morning or late evening.

Government owned or managed

■ There will be a queue waiting to pass through customs or passport control at major international airports, such as London's Heathrow, Los Angeles

Figure 24.1 Seesaw illustration of load and capacity: load greater than capacity.

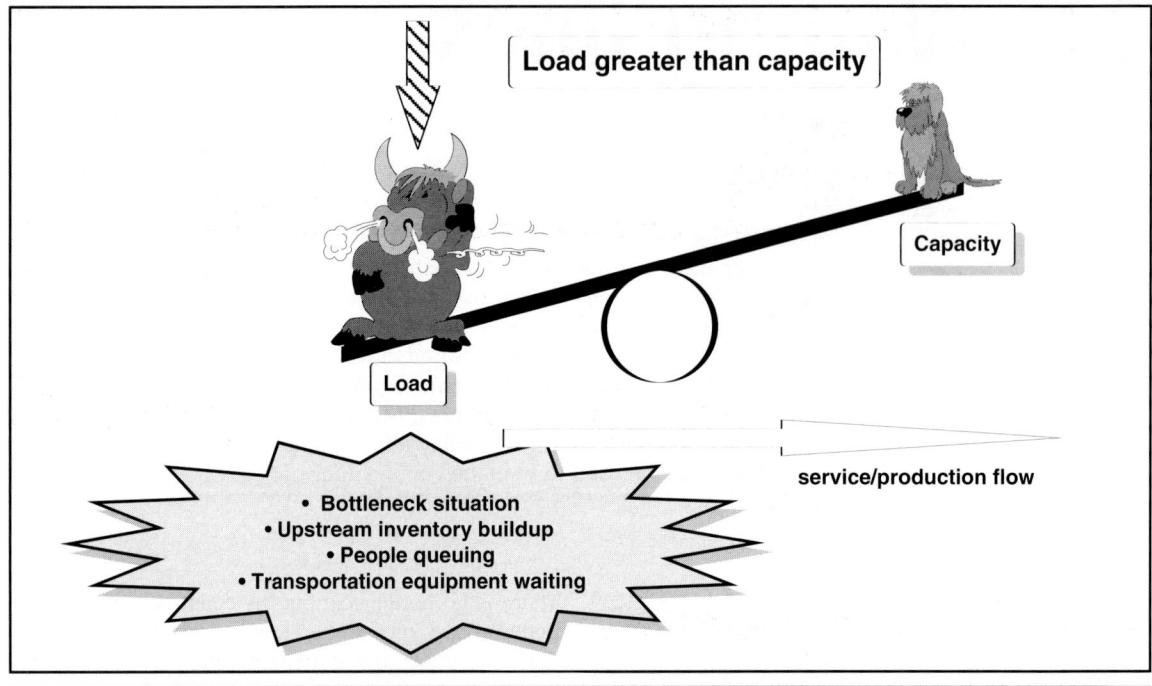

Figure 24.2 Seesaw illustration of load and capacity: capacity greater than load.

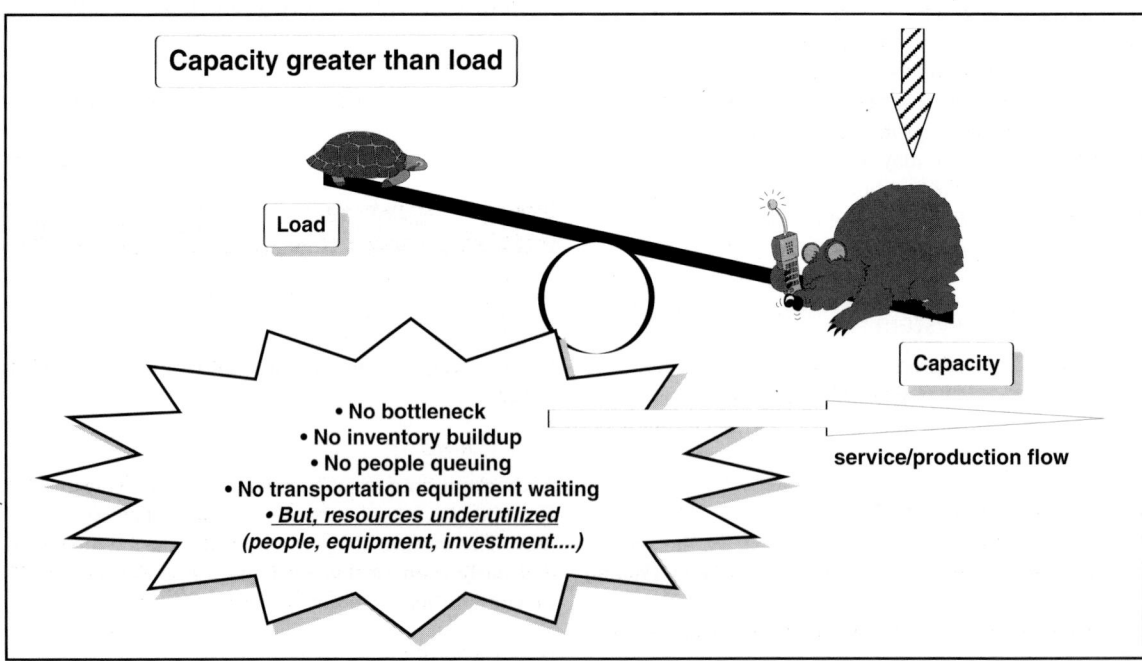

Figure 24.3 Seesaw illustration of load and capacity: load equals capacity.

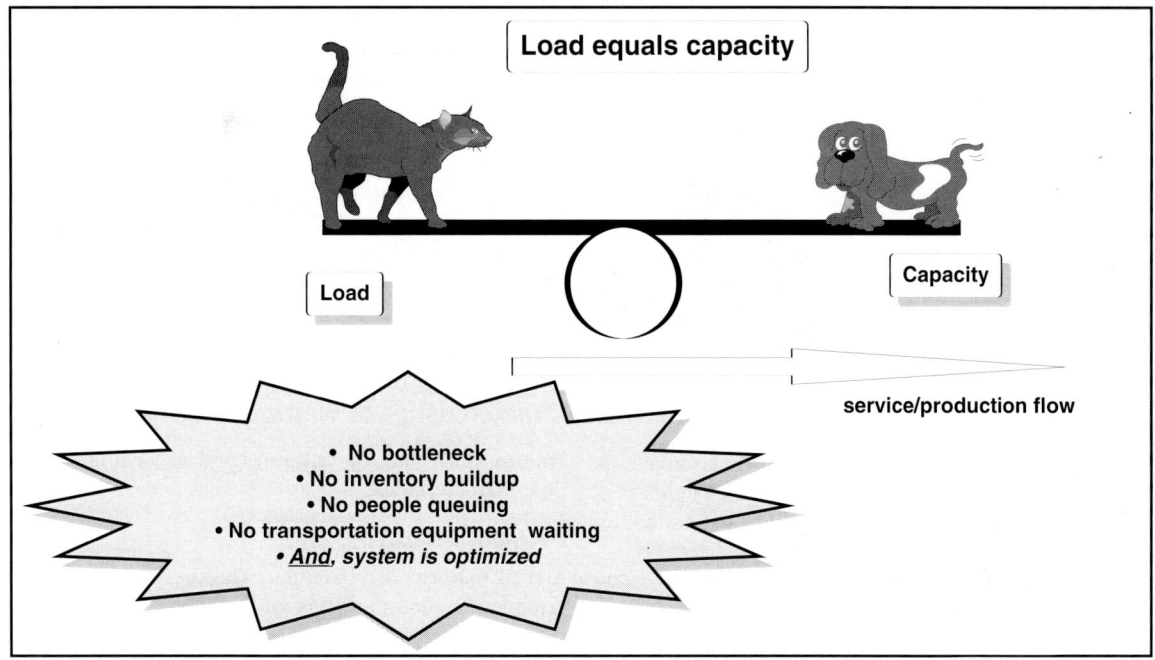

International or Kennedy, New York. If three 747s arrive within several minutes of each other, then the waiting line can be very long.

- Customers queue at a post office.
- People wait at a passport office to obtain a passport or a visa. (On one occasion, the author arrived at the Los Angeles Passport office at 02:00 and left at 15:00!)

Transportation networks

- Automobiles wait to pass through a tunnel (for example, the Fourvière tunnel into Lyon, France).
- Automobiles wait to pass through automobile toll booths.
- Automobiles wait to board a cross-channel ferry.
- Aeroplanes wait for take-off clearance.
- People wait for a bus

Service centres

- Patients wait at a medical centre (doctor, dentist, hospital etc.)
- Cars wait to be serviced at an automobile repair centre.
- Customers queue to use an automatic teller machine.

Sports and entertainment

- Skiers wait for a chair lift.

- People queue for an attraction at a theme park (Disneyland, Paris).
- People wait for the cinema.

Manufacturing

- Forged pieces wait to be drilled, cut and polished in a job shop.
- Finished automobiles wait to be shipped to dealers.

Communication

- You wait for your telephone call to be answered.

Causes of waiting lines

Some of the reasons for waiting lines are discussed in the following.

Poor scheduling

Poor scheduling can include, for example, a doctor scheduling more patients than can be treated in a certain time period. If this is a regular occurrence, it means that the doctor is not able to, or does not want to, balance the load with his service capacity.

Badly designed systems

There may be a badly designed system, such there are frequently numerous customers who arrive at random and there are only one or a few service personnel to attend to them. The system is under capacity relative to the load.

The system has reached saturation

The system used to be able to handle the load, but the capacity is now saturated:

- the London and Paris underground systems;
- road networks (M25 in England, the Santa Monica Freeway in Los Angeles, the Fourvière tunnel in Lyon, France);
- a machine shop's orders, which have increased although the machines available to perform the work remain the same.

Irregular patterns

People, parts, machinery or automobiles can arrive at a service centre in an irregular pattern. The capacity of the service centre cannot immediately be expanded, or contracted, to meet client needs exactly.

Unknown service time

The time it takes to service a customer is not known with certainty. In a supermarket, some people may have a lot of products to buy, while others may have very few. Some pay with a cheque, some with cash and some with a credit card. The times for these types of transactions are different.

Benefit of waiting lines to the operator

Sometimes the waiting line may 'add value' to the operator.

Additional time to buy

A limited queue in a supermarket gives customers time to buy display items, such as sweets, magazines and batteries at the checkout counter.

Quality perception

A line in a restaurant gives the impression to prospective clients that the food must be good. Thus, the total number of customers serviced is greater and hence the revenues are also greater.

Dissuasive element

A long line in an immigration office may 'dissuade' those seeking residency papers.

Customers' behaviour in waiting lines

Not all customers who see a queue accept that they should wait in line. They may balk or renege.

Balk

Balking is when customers refuse to join the queue because they do not like to wait under any circumstances, or the particular queue is too long.

Renege

Reneging is when a customer enters a waiting line but becomes impatient and leaves. Thus, for a part of the time they form part of the waiting line, but never receive service. Reneging customers can be detrimental to the operator, because if one customer leaves the line it can have a snowball effect and other customers decide to leave too.

Characteristics of waiting lines

Waiting lines may be differentiated according to certain characteristics.

Irregular arrival

Arrival patterns are irregular. The average number of arrivals per time period is known, but it is not known how many will arrive in a specific time period. The average daily customers in a post office can be reasonably estimated from past data, but it is not known if they arrive in the morning, afternoon or early evening.

Variable service requirements

Service varies between arrivals. One may know the average time necessary to service an arrival (from past data), but one does not know in advance how long it will take to service each arrival. A client at a supermarket may have five articles, 25 or a whole basket load. A medical patient may just want a repeat prescription or may require an X-ray of a broken arm.

Fixed service rate

Service is a fixed rate whose time is known before hand. This is the case with automatically controlled facilities such as:

- an automatic car wash;
- a park attraction at a theme park (The Matterhorn Ride at Disneyland);
- drilling a standard part on a numerically controlled drilling machine;
- a coffee machine;
- an automatic washing machine.

Unlimited waiting line

The waiting line until the facility closes is unlimited, or infinite. This is the case with automobiles at a toll booth, skiers waiting for a chair lift and often customers at a hypermarket.

Waiting line is limited

The waiting line for a specific service is limited to a maximum finite value because the capacity of the system is fixed. This is the case for:

- a transportation system, such as a cross-channel car ferry or aeroplane;
- a cinema;
- a hotel;
- a restaurant.

TERMS IN MODELLING A WAITING LINE

To aid in managing waiting lines, systems can be modelled (see also Chapter 9, *Forecasting Customer Demand*, Modelling). The following are terms associated with modelling of waiting lines.

Probability distributions

The Poisson distribution, perhaps modified by the binomial distribution, and the normal distribution are the probabilities used in queuing or waiting-line situations (see Chapter 20, *Statistical Concepts*).

Queue

A queue, as mentioned, is another name for a waiting line. Organized queues are usually very evident in Anglo-Saxon countries (particularly Britain!), but much less so in countries of Latin origin!

Queue discipline

A queue discipline is the scheduling rule that determines the order in which arrivals are served through the service system (see also Chapter 14, *Operations Scheduling*); for example:

- first come, first served (this is perhaps the most common queue discipline);
- shortest processing time;
- longest processing time;
- critical ratio (time to completion/processing time);
- most valuable customer.

Arrival

An arrival is when one unit (person, automobile, work piece) arrives in the system and requires service. Each of the units may continue to be called an arrival while in the service system.

Arrival rate

The arrival rate λ is the frequency at which the units arrive, or the average units per period. The units may be persons per hour, components per minute, automobiles per day. For analytical purposes, the arrival rate is usually considered to follow a Gaussian (normal) or a Poisson distribution (see Chapter 20, *Statistical Concepts*).

Service rate

The service rate μ is the rate that arrivals are serviced or helped, expressed in arrivals per unit of time; for example, arrivals per minute, per hour etc. Service rate is considered as one of the following:

- constant;
- normally distributed;
- Poisson distributed;
- exponentially distributed.

Service time

The service time t_h is the time it takes to service (help) an arrival. This is expressed in time per arrival. It does not include waiting time. The average service time is given by:

$$\bar{t}_h = \frac{1}{\mu}.$$

Channels

The channels N are the number of waiting lines in a service system.

Single channel

A single-channel system has only one line, for example:

- a single ticket-sales booth at the theatre;
- a medical centre where there is only one doctor;
- one cash register servicing a food line;
- one automatic cash dispensing machine.

Multichannel

A multichannel system would have two or more waiting lines, for example:

- a supermarket checkout counter;
- a toll booth on a motorway;
- a ticket booth at a major railway station (Waterloo, London; Gare de Lyon, Paris).

Service phases

The service phases are the number of steps involved in servicing arrivals.

Single channel, single phase

A single-channel, single-phase (Figure 24.4) might be the case with a queue in a small grocery store, where there is only one cashier for all the customers.

Single channel, multiple phase

A single-channel, multiple-phase system (Figure 24.5) might be the case with a medical health service where there is one nurse and one doctor. The patients first give all medical information to the nurse and then pass to the second phase to see the doctor.

Multiple channel, single phase

A multiple-channel, single-phase system (Figure 24.6) might be the case with a queue in a country passport office, where there are several assistants to serve the line of customers.

Multiple channel, multiple phase

A multiple-channel, multiple-phase system (Figure 24.7) might be the case with a queue at an airport terminal, where passengers pass first through immigration control, where there are several officers, and then through customs inspection, where there are several inspectors.

SINGLE-CHANNEL, SINGLE-PHASE QUEUING MODELS

Single-channel, single-phase models can be analysed by relatively simple mathematical formulas.[1]

Conditions

In single-channel, single-phase queuing models arrivals form a single line and wait to be serviced at a single station. These models apply under the following conditions:

- Arrivals are served on a first-come-first-served basis.
- Every arrival waits to be served, regardless of the length of the queue.
- Arrivals are independent of previous arrivals.
- Arrivals come from a population that is considered infinite.
- The average arrival rate does not change over time.
- Arrivals are described by a Poisson probability distribution.
- Service times may vary from one arrival to the next and are independent of each arrival. However, the average service time is known.
- Service times vary according to an exponential or Poisson distribution.
- The service rate is faster than the arrival rate.

Utilization of service system.

Utilization (P_n) is the probability that the service system is occupied by an arrival, or λ/μ. Thus, if the mean number of arrivals is eight per hour and the service rate on average is ten per hour, then the utilization is 8/10 or 80 per cent.

By corollary, the probability that the system is idle, or there are no units in the system, is $1 - (\lambda/\mu)$. With the data given, the probability that the system is idle is $100 - 80 = 20$ per cent. The probability of more than k units in the system is $(\lambda/\mu)^{k+1}$.

Variable service rate

Here the service rate is variable, because it depends to a certain extent on the ability of the person performing the service and on the requirements of the arrival. The service rate may follow a Poisson or exponential distribution.

Waiting time

The waiting time t_w is the amount of time an arrival spends in queue. The average waiting time is $\bar{t}_w$, which is given by:

$$\bar{t}_w = \frac{\lambda}{\mu\,(\mu - \lambda)}.$$

Figure 24.4 Queuing: single-channel, single-phase system.

Figure 24.5 Queuing: single-channel, multiple-phase system.

Figure 24.6 Queuing: multiple-channel, single-phase system.

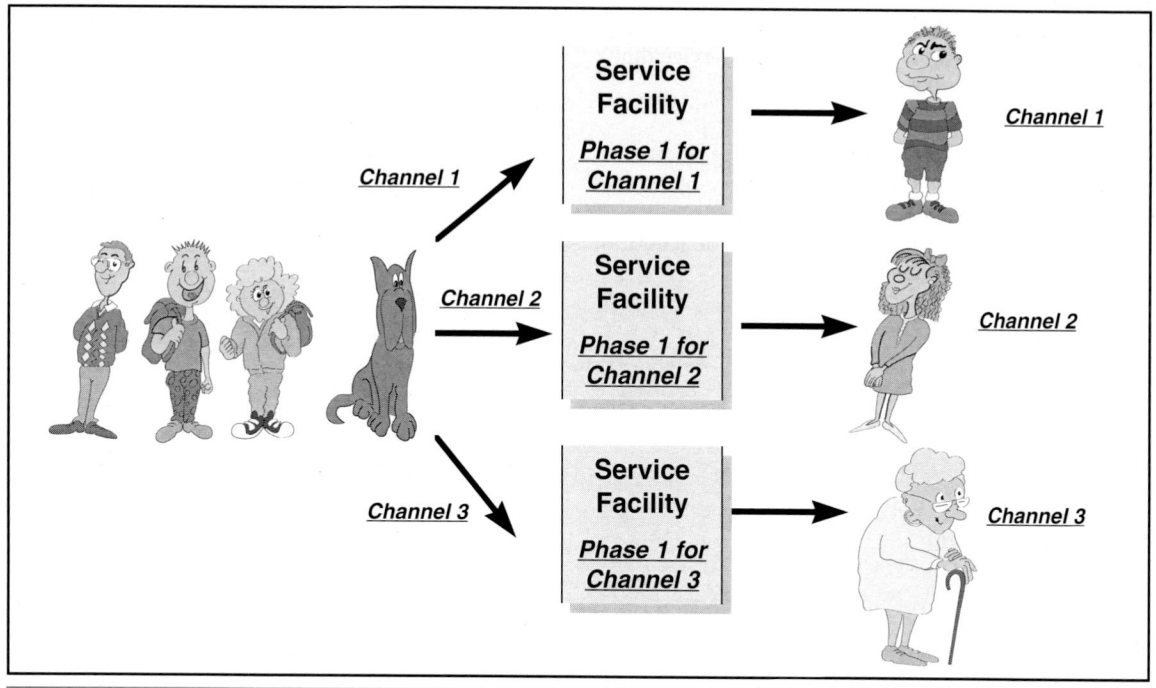

Figure 24.7 Queuing: multiple-channel, multiple-phase system.

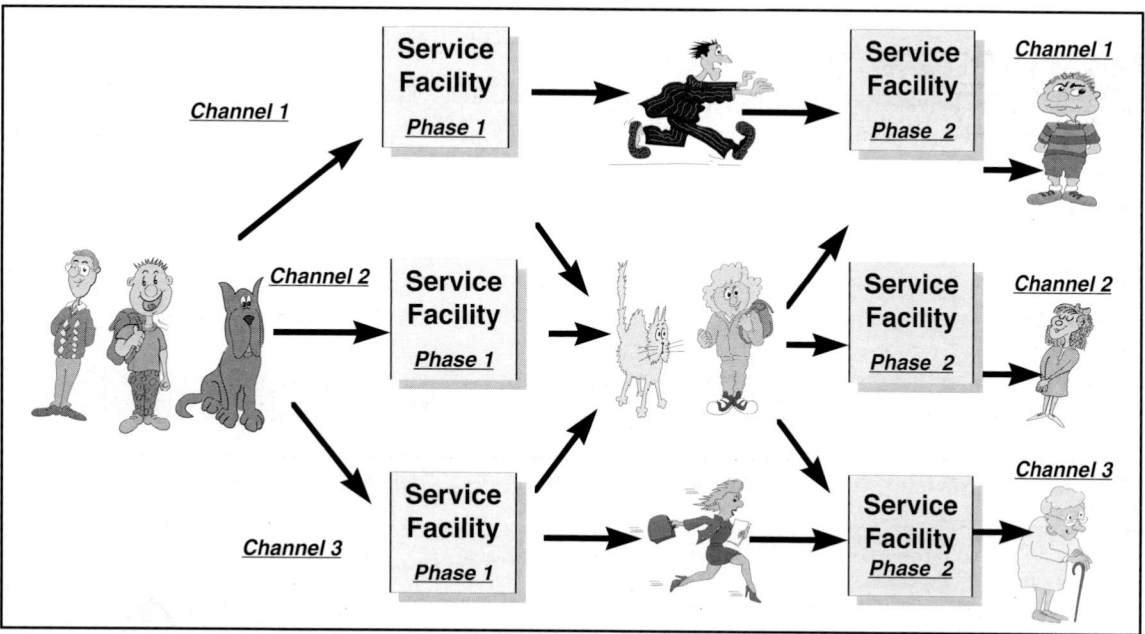

Time in the system

The time in the system $(t_w + t_h)$ is the total time that arrivals spend in system (waiting time + service time). The average time in the system is given by:

$$\bar{t}_w + \bar{t}_h = \bar{t}_s = \frac{\lambda}{\mu\,(\mu - \lambda)} + \frac{1}{\mu} = \frac{1}{(\mu - \lambda)}.$$

Number waiting

The average number of arrivals waiting (the length of the queue) is given by the relationship:

$$\bar{n}_w = \frac{\lambda^2}{\mu\,(\mu - \lambda)}.$$

Number being serviced

The average number of arrivals being serviced is given by the relationship:

$$\bar{n}_h = \frac{\lambda}{\mu}.$$

Number in system

The average number of arrivals in the system (waiting + being serviced) is given by:

$$\bar{n}_s = \bar{n}_w + \bar{n}_h = \frac{\lambda^2}{\mu\,(\mu - \lambda)} + \frac{\lambda}{\mu} = \frac{\lambda}{(\mu - \lambda)}.$$

This model is illustrated by the worked example, *Town Hall*.

Constant service rate

In this model the service rate is fixed as the station is automated (coffee, washing or automatic carwash machines).

Waiting time

The waiting time t_w is the amount of time an arrival spends in queue. The average waiting time $\bar{t}_w$, is given by:

$$\bar{t}_w = \frac{\lambda}{2\mu\,(\mu - \lambda)}.$$

Time in the system

The time in the system $(t_w + t_h)$ is the total time that arrivals spend in system (waiting time + service time). The average time in the system is given by:

$$\bar{t}_w + \bar{t}_h = \bar{t}_s = \frac{\lambda}{2\mu\,(\mu - \lambda)} + \frac{1}{\mu} = \frac{2\mu - \lambda}{2\mu\,(\mu - \lambda)}.$$

Number waiting

The average number of arrivals waiting is given by the relationship:

$$\bar{n}_w = \frac{\lambda^2}{2\mu\,(\mu - \lambda)}.$$

Number being serviced

The average number of arrivals being serviced is given by the relationship:

$$\bar{n}_h = \frac{\lambda}{\mu}.$$

Number in system

The average number of arrivals in the system (waiting + service) is given by:

$$\bar{n}_s = \bar{n}_w + \bar{n}_h = \frac{\lambda^2}{2\mu\,(\mu - \lambda)} + \frac{\lambda}{\mu}$$
$$= \frac{\lambda(2\mu - \lambda)}{2\mu(\mu - \lambda)}.$$

This model is illustrated by the worked example, *Coffee*.

WORKED EXAMPLE: TOWN HALL

Situation

A Town Hall has a department for issuing official documents, such as residency papers, marriage licences, fishing permits, etc. At any given time there is one employee who is handling the customers. On average, the Town Hall employee takes 12 minutes to service a client and, on average, one client arrives every 20 minutes. The arrival and service rates follow the assumptions for a single channel, single phase queuing model.

Required

1 The average time a customer spends in the system (waiting and being helped).

2 The average time waiting in line.
3 Average utilization of the system.
4 Develop a probability histogram of there being more than k units in the system with a value of k from 0 to 10.
5 What is the probability that there will be more than four people in the system?

Solution

The calculation steps are given in the Table 24.1 below. The average service rate of 12 min per unit is converted to five units per hour and the arrival rate of every 20 min to 3 per hour.

Table 24.1 Town Hall

Criterion	Formula	Value
Average service rate, min/unit		12
Average arrival rate, min/unit		20
Average service rate, units/h	μ	5
Average arrival rate, units/h	λ	3
Average units in system	$\lambda/(\mu - \lambda)$	1.50
Average time in system	$1/(\mu - \lambda)$	0.50
Average units waiting	$\lambda2/[\mu(\mu - \lambda)]$	0.90
Average time waiting, hours	$\lambda/[\mu(\mu - \lambda)]$	0.30
Utilization	λ/μ	0.60
Idle percentage	$1 - (\lambda/\mu)$	0.40
More than k in system	$(\lambda/\mu)^{k+1}$	
Value of k	0	60.00%
	1	36.00%
	2	21.60%
	3	12.96%
	4	7.78%
	5	4.67%
	6	2.80%
	7	1.68%
	8	1.01%
	9	0.60%
	10	0.36%

1   The average time a customer spends in the system (waiting and being helped) is $0.5 \times 60 = 30$ min.
2   The average time waiting in line is $0.3 \times 60 = 18$ min.
3   The average utilization of the system is 60 per cent.
4   Develop a probability histogram of there being more than k units in the system, with a value of k from 0 to 10.
    The answer to this question is given in the graph, Figure 24.8. Data from the graph is based on the probability values in the table.
5   What is the probability that there will be more than four people in the system? About 8 per cent.

Figure 24.8 Waiting at the Town Hall.

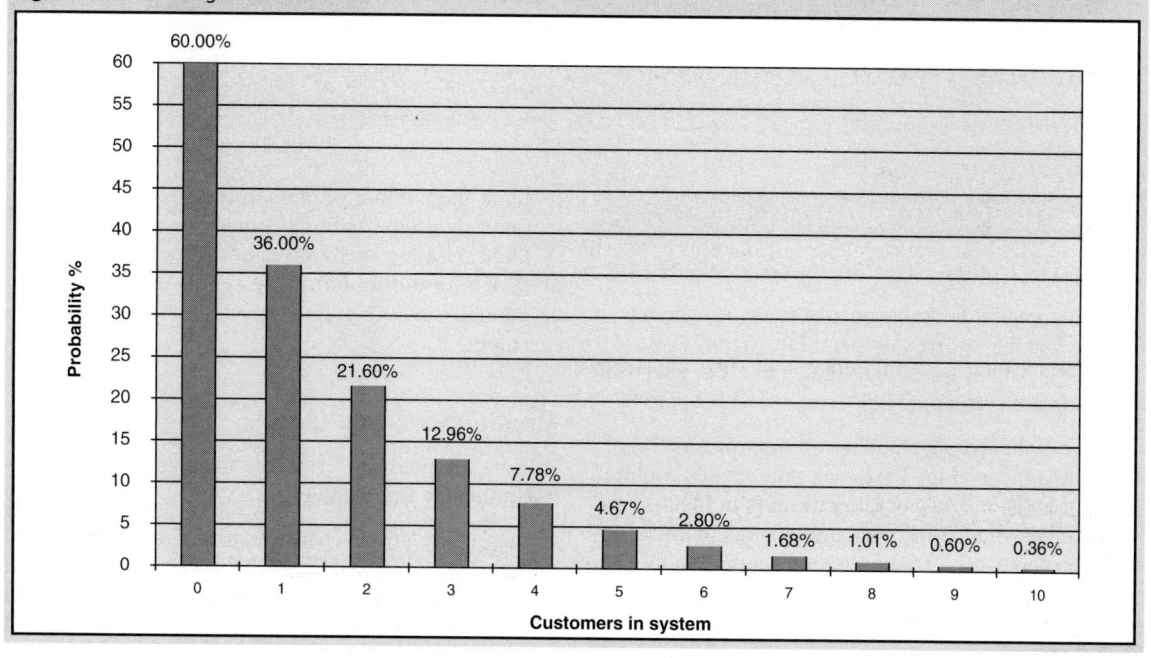

WORKED EXAMPLE: COFFEE

Situation

A company restaurant has an area where it serves coffee to employees. The present arrangement is one lady who makes and pours the coffee. The average arrival rate at the coffee area is ten people per hour and the average service rate is 14 per hour. This activity is assumed to following the single-phase, single-channel model with variable service rate. The cost for a client in the system is estimated at $20 000 per year for every hour in the system.

Management is considering replacing the server by an automatic coffee machine, which has a fixed rate for making and distributing the coffee. In this case, the model would now be a single-phase, single-channel model with a fixed service rate.

Required

How much would the company save on waiting time in the system if the automatic coffee machine was installed? Assume that the average arrival and service rates remain unchanged.

Solution

The solution is given in Tables 24.2 and 24.3. Table 24.2 is the calculation for the variable situation, and Table 24.3 that for the coffee machine. The savings would be an estimated $1786.

Tables 24.2 Coffee – variable

Criterion	Formula	Value
Average service rate, units/h	μ	14
Average arrival rate, units/h	λ	10
Average units in system	$\lambda/(\mu - \lambda)$	2.50
Average time in system	$1/(\mu - \lambda)$	0.25
Average units waiting	$\lambda^2/[\mu(\mu - \lambda)]$	1.79
Average time waiting, h	$\lambda/[\mu(\mu - \lambda)]$	0.18
Each hour unit in system costs £/yr	20 000.00	
Total cost of being in system, £		5 000.00

Table 24.3 Coffee – fixed

Criterion	Formula	Value
Average service rate, units/h	μ	14
Average arrival rate, units/h	λ	10
Average units in system	$[\lambda(2\mu - \lambda)]/[2\mu(\mu - \lambda)]$	1.61
Average time in system, h	$(2\mu - \lambda)/[2\mu(\mu - \lambda)]$	0.1607
Average units waiting	$\lambda^2/[2\mu(\mu - \lambda)]$	0.89
Average time waiting, h	$\lambda/[2\mu(\mu - \lambda)]$	0.0893
Each hour unit in system costs, £/yr	20 000.00	
Total cost of being in system, £		3 214.29
Difference in cost		1 785.71

MANAGING THE WAITING LINE

Needs to analyse in waiting-line situations

A service system is designed to service, on average, a certain number of arrivals per time period (hour for example). Some questions that may be asked in analysing the system are:

- What is the average number of units waiting?
- What is the average time each unit spends waiting?
- What is the average number of units in the system?
- What is average time each unit spends in system?
- What percentage of time is the system empty (not used)?
- What is the probability that n units will be in the system?

Good management policy

Management should attempt to have the following attitude towards waiting lines:

- Limit the number of units waiting.
- Limit the number of units in the system.
- Limit the time each unit waits.
- Limit the time each unit is in the system.
- Maximize utilization of the service system, that is, minimize the percentage of time the system is empty.

Managed waiting lines

Policies adopted by firms to 'manage' waiting lines might include the following:

- In grocery stores, when waiting lines occur, managers, shelf stackers and even warehouse people can help at the checkout stands. Some supermarkets have a policy that no more than, say, five people will be waiting in line before another checkout is opened.
- Part-time workers can be used for weekend and evening operations.
- There can be an express checkout in a supermarket for, say, less than five articles.
- There can be a special checkout for those who use the store's own credit card.

- Appointment schedules can be arranged for, say, a hairdresser, doctor or dentist.
- Use take-a-number at the customer service desk. This will reduce waiting lines if customers holding a number can do other things, such as shop elsewhere in the store, if they are able to estimate when their number will be called.
- Entertain those waiting in line, or inform them of the waiting time. This is done for customers waiting in line in Disney attractions at Disneyland, Paris.

WAITING LINE SIMULATION

Defining simulation

Simulation, like modelling, is trying to create the real environment using smaller systems, very often computer driven. Airline pilots use flight simulators in training to aid them in flying the real aeroplane. Wind-tunnel simulators are used to mimic the atmospheric conditions to which aircraft might be exposed. Whirlpool Co. simulates conditions for testing its washing machines for quality control purposes. In waiting lines, simulation usually means using computer-based systems to create the real environment, so that scheduling and capacity can be better optimized in situations where mathematical models, such as those presented earlier, are not appropriate for the waiting-line situation.

Elements in the waiting line

In a waiting line situation, there are both variables and parameters.

Variables

The variables in the waiting line are those that vary randomly in the system, such as the customer arrival rate, the service rate, the time of arrival, etc.

Parameters

The parameters in the waiting line are those elements that are constant and established by economics,

management policy or technology, such as the number of channels, the number of phases or the service time in automated systems.

Monte Carlo process

Some operating systems may be difficult to solve analytically because variables are random and are better represented by probability distributions. The Monte Carlo process is a technique using random numbers to simulate arrival patterns and service rates in an operation based on probability distributions.[2] When a system has been satisfactorily simulated, variables can be managed by adjusting the parameters of the system.[3] The Monte Carlo concept originates from the gambling casino in Monaco, where clients attempt to select the correct sample from a population, for example, three oranges in a one-armed bandit spun at random, the correct numbers from the throw of two dice or numbers from a roulette wheel. The use of the Monte Carlo process using random numbers is detailed in the worked example, *Motorway* (part I).

Computer packages

There are many commercial computer packages used as management tools for simulating waiting-line situations. These are particularly useful when the system is complex, such as the multiple-channel, single-phase system or the multiple-channel, multiple-phase system handling a large number of clients. As an illustration, Carrefour, a hypermarket in Ecully, France, has 69 checkouts which handle on average 50 000 customers during a six-day week. Their computer simulator gives information on the store arrivals, service rates and the loading on each cashier, which provide the criterion for opening or closing a checkout. Carrefour's checkouts are of three types, Normal (any customer), Fast (those with five articles or less) and Membership card (those that possess the Carrefour credit card). The basis for the computer simulator is very similar to that described in the worked example, *Motorway* (part I).

WORKED EXAMPLE: MOTORWAY PART I

Situation

A company owns a petrol station on a major motorway in Europe. In addition to selling petrol and diesel fuel, the store also sells products that customers may purchase for a driving trip, including sweets, food, maps, small gift items and the like. At the present time there is one person at the cash register who handles payment for petrol purchases and other items that are bought. Most of the transactions are either by credit card or cash, though occasionally cheques are used. The owner of the retail outlet wants to understand more about the loading on the cashier, that is, is she occupied most of the time with customers, probably resulting in customer waiting, or are there long periods of idle time for the cashier?

Required

Use the Monte Carlo random number approach to simulate the waiting-line situation for this motorway outlet for 50 customers. What are your conclusions? The following information is provided.

Arrival time

Based on historical data, Figure 24.9 gives the probability distribution of the arrivals at the cashiers. This graph can be interpreted as saying, for example, that for 22 per cent of the time customers arrive at one-minute intervals, for 30 per cent of the time they arrive at two-minute intervals, etc. For the purpose of this simulation, discrete time data has been assumed although, in reality, customers will arrive at fractions of minutes.

Service time

Based on historical data, Figure 24.10 gives the probability distribution of the service times with the cashier. This graph can be interpreted as saying, for example, that for 1 per cent of the customers the service time is 0.50 min, for 6 per cent the service time is one minute, etc. Again, for the purpose of this simulation, discrete time data has been assumed, although in reality customers will be serviced in fractions of minutes.

Random numbers

Figure 24.11 gives a print-out of 500 random numbers ranging from 0 to 99 generated from Microsoft Excel.

Solution

The first step in generating the simulation is to establish the range of random numbers that correspond to the probability distributions for the arrival patterns and the service rates.

Arrival intervals

Table 24.4 gives the probability distribution for the arrival intervals, as presented in the histogram (Figure 24.9). The range of possible random numbers is from 0 to 99, or a total of 100. Thus, if the arrival interval of 1.00 minute is considered, with a probability of 22 per cent, then the random number range is from 0 to 21 (a total of 22 possible numbers or 22 per cent of the possible 100). For the arrival interval of 2.00 minutes, the probability is 30 per cent and so the random numbers of between 22 and 51 have been assigned (a total of 30 or 30 per cent from the possible 100). This is repeated for the complete distribution

Table 24.4 The probability distribution for arrival intervals at the motorway cashier

Arrival intervals (min)	Probability (%)	Cumulative probability (%)	Lower limit of random number	Upper limit of random number
1	22	22	0	21
2	30	52	22	51
3	18	70	52	69
4	13	83	70	82
5	8	91	83	90
6	5	96	91	95
7	3	99	96	98
8	1	100	99	99

Service rates

Table 24.5 gives the probability distribution for the service rates, as presented in the histogram (Figure 24.10). Again, the range of possible random numbers is from 0 to 99, or a total of 100. Thus, if the service time of 0.50 minutes is considered, with a probability of 1 per cent, then the

Figure 24.9 Motorway – arrival patterns.

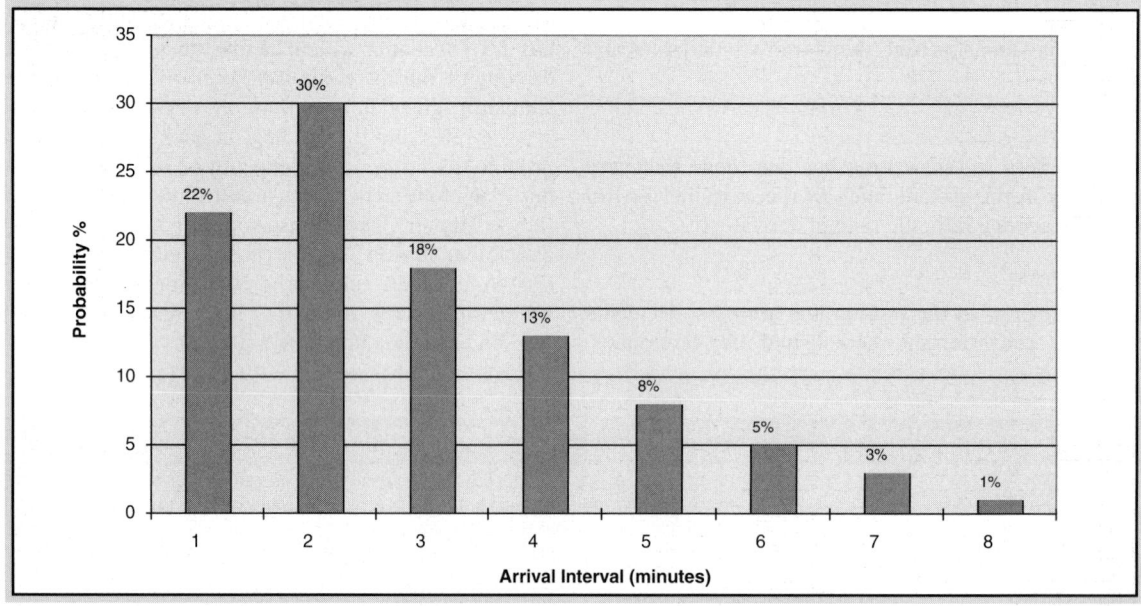

Figure 24.10 Motorway – service time patterns.

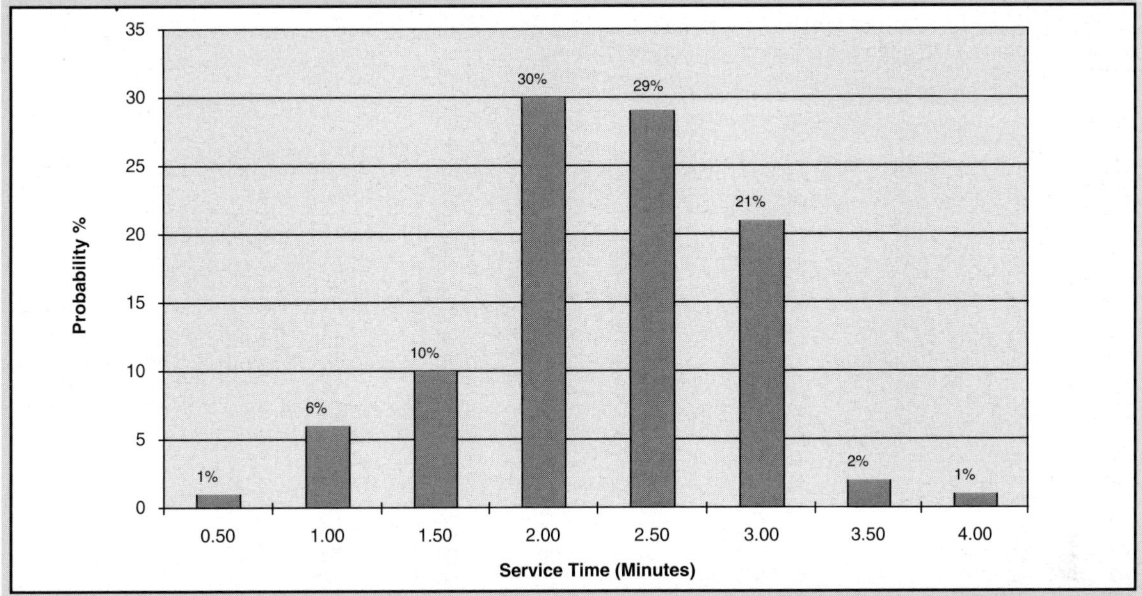

Figure 24.11 Motorway – table of random numbers.

	A	B	C	D	E	F	G	H	I	J
1	76	39	63	41	88	35	98	45	64	11
2	5	98	42	22	57	60	90	14	4	6
3	91	58	55	8	71	2	37	68	98	88
4	20	58	59	30	81	2	50	18	8	32
5	7	50	52	50	12	48	83	27	83	71
6	85	65	60	76	48	79	88	73	29	80
7	67	31	29	82	59	40	36	10	78	29
8	5	51	84	77	65	66	9	59	88	71
9	59	90	40	20	69	33	57	30	77	94
10	41	62	30	19	65	93	26	53	1	61
11	80	80	53	5	57	68	75	51	42	48
12	15	48	59	21	9	99	48	31	61	21
13	87	37	82	83	3	59	71	64	83	36
14	94	91	67	18	52	85	82	74	60	87
15	42	70	37	13	60	38	6	80	94	18
16	6	64	42	86	83	23	46	51	10	64
17	3	92	94	86	23	15	95	8	98	92
18	47	29	23	96	13	80	54	79	77	61
19	23	23	32	6	30	45	65	87	9	9
20	36	38	44	75	24	22	33	42	85	85
21	48	80	55	61	52	19	24	71	33	13
22	5	65	8	0	32	5	92	2	83	45
23	44	19	89	71	60	9	99	63	1	69
24	56	19	94	8	24	56	9	68	74	55
25	79	94	71	63	66	43	67	50	83	36
26	60	77	43	79	42	26	63	31	91	36
27	3	27	42	89	51	59	87	1	4	7
28	88	32	4	65	29	79	34	27	93	7
29	47	83	35	1	68	90	21	76	35	87
30	61	37	20	99	71	63	86	50	61	21
31	6	37	64	95	44	90	45	74	70	19
32	40	64	12	8	21	50	67	21	79	47
33	83	84	25	93	41	70	33	39	83	40
34	38	50	99	13	61	50	73	36	95	23
35	97	99	5	27	29	70	52	95	38	33
36	52	84	13	85	61	29	25	73	6	6
37	46	34	56	32	95	76	89	92	42	88
38	4	7	17	4	12	98	24	49	48	3
39	31	16	32	54	86	76	82	38	39	18
40	25	84	15	86	93	66	89	4	14	58
41	96	6	48	76	13	28	50	61	7	4
42	7	65	80	17	23	11	7	54	30	54
43	80	8	10	48	89	59	22	71	89	71
44	32	8	74	88	18	19	30	1	64	33
45	82	75	30	41	80	80	49	14	60	38
46	46	20	35	31	86	19	14	13	59	4
47	67	79	50	92	73	26	0	77	18	48
48	48	32	99	54	5	93	33	67	67	29
49	69	52	5	61	31	7	16	56	80	54
50	54	41	7	85	7	64	84	87	68	96

random number range is just the number 0 (a total of 1 possible numbers or 1 per cent of the possible 100). For the service time of 1.0 minute, the probability is 6 per cent and so the random numbers of between 1 and 6 have been assigned (a total of 6 or 6 per cent of the possible 100). Again, this is repeated for the complete distribution.

Table 24.5 The probability distribution for service times at the motorway cashier

Service times (min)	Probability (%)	Cumulative probability (%)	Lower limit of random number	Upper limit of random number
0.5	1	1	0	0
1.0	6	7	1	6
1.5	10	17	7	16
2.0	30	47	17	46
2.5	29	76	47	75
3.0	21	97	76	96
3.5	2	99	97	98
4.0	1	100	99	99

Simulation

The completed simulation is shown in Table 24.6. The explanation of each column is as follows.

Table 24.6 Motorway: Monte Carlo simulation

Client number (min)	Random number (1) (min)	Arrival interval	Time entering (min)	Random number (2) (min)	Service time (min)	Waiting time (min)	Time leaving (people)	Time in system	Queue length	System status
1			0	39	2.00	0.00	2.00	2.00	0	
2	5	1	1	98	3.50	1.00	5.50	4.50	1	occupied
3	91	6	7	58	2.50	0.00	9.50	2.50	0	empty
4	20	1	8	58	2.50	1.50	12.00	4.00	1	occupied
5	7	1	9	50	2.50	3.00	14.50	5.50	2	occupied
6	85	5	14	65	2.50	0.50	17.00	3.00	1	occupied
7	67	3	17	31	2.00	0.00	19.00	2.00	0	occupied
8	5	1	18	51	2.50	1.00	21.50	3.50	1	occupied
9	59	3	21	90	3.00	0.50	24.50	3.50	1	occupied
10	41	2	23	62	2.50	1.50	27.00	4.00	1	occupied
11	80	4	27	80	3.00	0.00	30.00	3.00	0	occupied
12	15	1	28	48	2.50	2.00	32.50	4.50	1	occupied
13	87	5	33	37	2.00	0.00	35.00	2.00	0	empty
14	94	6	39	91	3.00	0.00	42.00	3.00	0	empty
15	42	2	41	70	2.50	1.00	44.50	3.50	1	occupied
16	6	1	42	64	2.50	2.50	47.00	5.00	1	occupied
17	3	1	43	92	3.00	4.00	50.00	7.00	2	occupied
18	47	2	45	29	2.00	5.00	52.00	7.00	2	occupied
19	23	2	47	23	2.00	5.00	54.00	7.00	2	occupied
20	36	2	49	38	2.00	5.00	56.00	7.00	3	occupied
21	48	2	51	80	3.00	5.00	59.00	8.00	3	occupied
22	5	1	52	65	2.50	7.00	61.50	9.50	3	occupied
23	44	2	54	19	2.00	7.50	63.50	9.50	3	occupied
24	56	3	57	19	2.00	6.50	65.50	8.50	3	occupied
25	79	4	61	94	3.00	4.50	68.50	7.50	3	occupied
26	60	3	64	77	3.00	4.50	71.50	7.50	2	occupied
27	3	1	65	27	2.00	6.50	73.50	8.50	3	occupied
28	88	5	70	32	2.00	3.50	75.50	5.50	2	occupied
29	47	2	72	83	3.00	3.50	78.50	6.50	2	occupied
30	61	3	75	37	2.00	3.50	80.50	5.50	2	occupied
31	6	1	76	37	2.00	4.50	82.50	6.50	2	occupied
32	40	2	78	64	2.50	4.50	85.00	7.00	3	occupied
33	83	5	83	84	3.00	2.00	88.00	5.00	1	occupied
34	38	2	85	50	2.50	3.00	90.50	5.50	1	occupied
35	97	7	92	99	4.00	0.00	96.00	4.00	0	empty
36	52	3	95	84	3.00	1.00	99.00	4.00	1	occupied
37	46	2	97	34	2.00	2.00	101.00	4.00	1	occupied
38	4	1	98	7	1.50	3.00	102.50	4.50	2	occupied
39	31	2	100	16	1.50	2.50	104.00	4.00	2	occupied
40	25	2	102	84	3.00	2.00	107.00	5.00	2	occupied
41	96	7	109	6	1.00	0.00	110.00	1.00	0	empty
42	7	1	110	65	2.50	0.00	112.50	2.50	0	occupied
43	80	4	114	8	1.50	0.00	115.50	1.50	0	empty
44	32	2	116	8	1.50	0.00	117.50	1.50	0	empty
45	82	4	120	75	2.50	0.00	122.50	2.50	0	empty
46	46	2	122	20	2.00	0.50	124.50	2.50	1	occupied
47	67	3	125	79	3.00	0.00	128.00	3.00	0	empty
48	48	2	127	32	2.00	1.00	130.00	3.00	1	occupied
49	69	3	130	52	2.50	0.00	132.50	2.50	0	occupied
50	54	3	133	41	2.00	0.00	135.00	2.00	0	empty
Average		2.71			2.40	2.23		4.63	1.26	

- *Client number*. This is the sequential number of customers who arrive from 1 to 50.
- *Random number (1)*. This is the random number that is used to determine the arrival time for each of the customers. In this illustration the random numbers from Column A of the random number table have been used, starting from Cell A-1. Any column could have been used.
- *Arrival interval*. This is the arrival interval in minutes, corresponding to the random number for that client, and taken from the arrival table interval above, for example:
  - For Client No. 2, the random number is 5 and this corresponds to an arrival interval of 1 minute.
  - For Client No. 3, the random number is 91 and this corresponds to an arrival interval of 6 minutes.

  For the first client, random numbers are not used. It is assumed that the client arrives as soon as the simulation starts.
- *Time entering*. This is the time at which a client enters the system, where the client either waits in the line to be served or is directly served by the cashier. Numerically, the time entering is the sum of all the arrival times, for example:
  - Arrival time of the sixth customer is the sum of the arrival intervals of customers 1 through 6 or $(0 + 1 + 6 + 1 + 1 + 5) = 14$.
- *Random number (2)*. This is the random number that is used to determine the service time for each of the customers. In this illustration, the random numbers from Column B of the random number table have been used, starting from Cell B-1. Any column could have been used.
- *Service time*. This is the service time, in minutes, for the client. The value corresponds to the random number for that client, taken from the service-time table above, for example:
  - For Client No. 1, the random number is 39 and this corresponds to a service time of 2 minutes.
  - For Client No. 2, the random number is 98 and this corresponds to a service time of 4 minutes.
- *Waiting time*. This is the waiting time, in minutes, for which the client stands in the queue waiting to be assisted by the cashier. It is calculated by the relationship:

$$WT_n = WT_{n-1} + ST_{n-1} - AI_n,$$

where WT are waiting times and ST is the service time, AI is the arrival interval and n is the client in question. If the value of the WT_n is negative, then there is no waiting time and the client is served immediately, for example:
- For Client No. 7, $WT_7 = WT_6 + ST_6 - AI_7 = 0.50 + 2.50 - 3.00 = -0.50$ and so there is no waiting time.
- For Client No. 8, $WT_8 = WT_7 + ST_7 - AI_8 = 0.00 + 2.00 - 1.00 = 1.00$ and so the client stands in line for one minute.

The waiting time for each client is given by the histogram in Figure 24.12.

- *Time leaving*. This is the time that the client leaves the system, or the service area. It is the sum of the time entering plus waiting and service times.
- *Time in system*. The time in the system is the sum of the waiting time and the service time.
- *Queue length*. The queue length is given in terms of the number of people waiting. It is a function of the service time necessary to serve the people, for example:
  - Client No. 14 arrives; there is no waiting time and so the queue length is zero.
  - Client No. 15 arrives; there is a waiting time of 1.00 minute and so the queue length is one unit.
  - Client No. 16 arrives; there is a waiting time given by $WT_{16} = WT_{15} + ST_{15} - AI_{16} = 1.00 + 2.50 - 1.00 = 2.50$ minutes while Client No. 15 is being served. Thus the queue length is one unit.
  - Client No. 17 arrives; there is a waiting time given by $WT_{17} = WT_{16} + ST_{16} - AI_{17} = 2.50 + 2.50 - 1.00 = 4.00$ minutes. In this case, Client No. 16 still has not been serviced, since Client No. 16 still has a wait time given by WT_{16} (when client 17 arrives) $= WT_{16} - AI_{17} = 2.50 - 1.0 = 1.50$ minutes. Thus the queue length is two units (Client Nos 16 and 17).

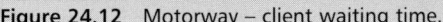

Figure 24.12 Motorway – client waiting time.

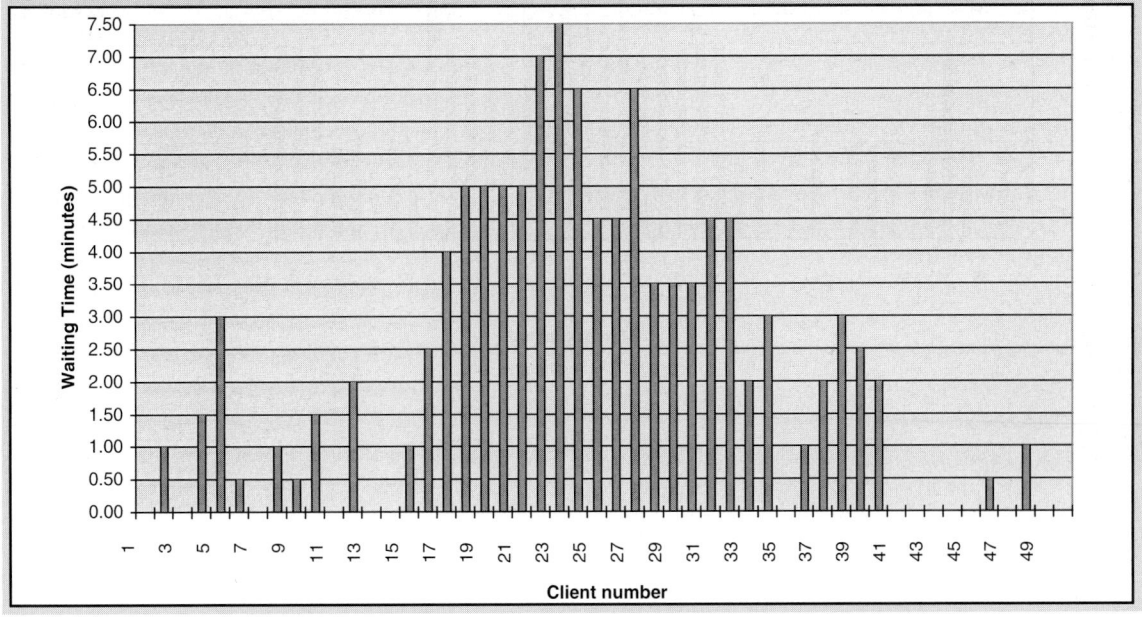

- Client No. 20 arrives; there is a waiting time given by $WT_{20} = WT_{19} + ST_{19} - AI_{20} = 5.00 + 2.00 - 2.00 = 5.00$ minutes. In this case, neither Client No. 19 nor Client No. 18 has been serviced. The queue length for each client is given by the histogram in Figure 24.13.

■ *System status.* This column indicates whether the cashier is busy or not. If there is waiting time, then the cashier is occupied. The cashier may be occupied even though the waiting time is zero, because it means that as the last customer has finished being serviced, then the next one arrives immediately.

Characteristics of the operation

The last line of the simulation table (Table 24.6) gives the characteristics of the waiting line situation. In summary these are as follows:

■ Average arrival interval (min) = 2.71
■ Average service time (min) = 2.40
■ Average waiting time (min) = 2.23
■ Average time in system (min) = 4.63
■ Average queue length (units) = 1.26

From this data, the system is not overloaded from a customer perspective, in that neither the average waiting time nor the average queue length is excessive. However, the cashier is occupied for most of the time. This means that there is little time for other activities, such as answering the telephone, shelf stacking or, say, doing something special for a customer, such as wrapping a gift.

Expected values

For this simulation, which is a sample for 50 clients of the activities of a larger population, the average service time is 2.40 minutes. From the basic data, the average service time (expected value) calculated from the sum of the service time and the probability, or $\Sigma ST_n \times P_n$, is 2.28. The difference is that the value of 2.40 is based on the simulation, which is a sample, whereas 2.28 is for the whole population. The larger the sample size, the closer the value will be to the expected value.

Similarly, from the simulation, the average arrival interval is 2.71 minutes. Using expected values from the relationship $\Sigma AI_n \times P_n$, the arrival interval is 2.87. Again the difference is explained by one being a sample, the other a population.

In this simulation the data will vary according to the random numbers obtained. This can be demonstrated using Excel, where the random numbers are continuously changing. This is the very nature of probabilities. Another consideration is that the simulation was started with no-one in the system so that in reality the simulation has to function for a while before the real conditions are obtained. Alternatively, it could have been generated by assuming that there already was a load on the system.

Figure 24.13 Motorway – queue length.

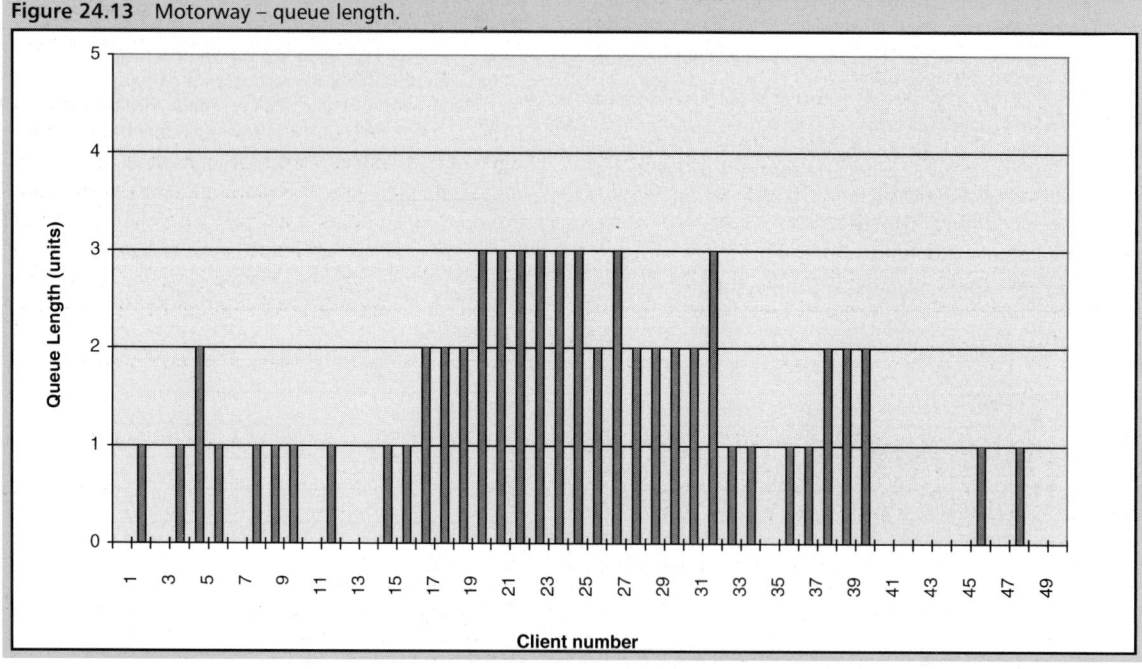

SUMMARY OF KEY ELEMENTS

- Waiting lines are both a load scheduling and a capacity planning problem. They are a scheduling concern because better planning of people, machines or work posts may reduce the bottlenecks and a capacity problem because better design of the operating system may reduce or eliminate the waiting lines.

- When the upstream load is greater than the system capacity, there is a bottleneck and the system is unbalanced. Conversely, when the capacity is greater than the load, there is no bottleneck but the system capacity is overdesigned. The ideal system is when the capacity matches the demand on the system.

- Bottlenecks are evident in service systems when people are waiting to be served and in manufacturing when upstream inventory accumulates.

- Excess capacity is evident when machines are not running or operating personnel are idle.

- Some benefits of a waiting line to a system operator are that it may give customers 'more time to make impulse purchases', it may give a quality perception in the case of restaurant or it might 'dissuade' people seeking a government service.

- Not all customers accept standing in a waiting line. They may balk and refuse to join the waiting line under any circumstances, or they may renege and leave the waiting line after a certain time.

- The characteristics of waiting lines include irregular arrival patterns of customers, variable service rates, fixed service rates and limited or unlimited waiting lines.

- Probability distributions that are used in waiting line theory include Poisson, normal and binomial distributions.

- The most common form of queue discipline in waiting lines is first come, first served, although other disciplines might be shortest processing time, longest processing time, the critical ratio (time to completion divided by processing time) and the most valuable customer.

- A channel is the number of waiting lines in the service system. There may be a single channel with just one waiting line or multiple channels with two or more waiting lines.

- The service phases are the number of steps involved in assisting arrivals. The phase might be single channel and single phases, single channel and multiple phase, multiple channel and single phase or multiple channel and multiple phase.

- Waiting lines might be better 'managed' by using other employees when the system becomes heavily overloaded, using 'take a number' systems, having express counters or using appointment schedules when appropriate.

- Computer simulations can be used to understand waiting lines better and thus improve their management. A Monte Carlo simulation is one such approach, which uses random numbers to simulate the system variables, such as the arrival interval of customers or the service rate. Knowing the movement of these variables makes it easier to control the parameters such as the number of checkouts to install.

REVIEW AND DISCUSSION QUESTIONS

1 **Airports**. Many airports are notorious for waiting lines, either for the passengers or the aeroplanes (which include the passengers).
   (a) What are the reasons for waiting lines at airports?
   (b) How can waiting lines be better managed?
   (c) What is the impact of some of the proposed solutions to reduce the waiting lines at airports?

2 **Queuing experience**. In the past month you have probably experienced a waiting-line situation. If this is the case:
   (a) Describe the circumstances of the waiting line.
   (b) What has been the 'lost time' to you?
   (c) Can you put a financial value on this lost time?

   (d) How do you think the waiting line could have been better managed?

3 **Variables in waiting lines**. How would the following impact waiting lines in department stores:
   (a) Promotions?
   (b) Vacation periods?
   (c) The four seasons?

4 **Technology and waiting lines**. How has technology improved the management of waiting lines on:
   (a) Transportation systems?
   (b) Retail stores?
   (c) University registration for the next trimester course?
   (d) Financial services?

5 **Fixed capacity systems**. Identify some fixed capacity systems. Indicate the parameters that mean that they are 'fixed'. How does management try to manage the waiting lines in these fixed-capacity systems?

EXERCISE PROBLEM: CAMPING

Situation

A small camp site in Ardèche, France, has one automatic washing machine for the clients of the camp site. It takes 50 minutes to do a complete wash. The average arrival time for campers to use the machine is one per hour. The proprietor of the camp site is considering installing a second, identical washing machine in the washing area.

Required

1 Develop the waiting line characteristics for one machine, showing the queuing time, waiting time in the system, average people queuing and average persons in the system.

2 Develop a probability histogram of the utilization of the single washing machine.
3 How would the profile of waiting times change with the addition of a second machine?
4 Show a new probability of utilization of two machines, alongside that for one machine.

EXERCISE PROBLEM: GRAVEL

Situation

A company is building an underground parking structure in the centre of London. Part of the construction work involves dumping gravel at the concrete preparation area at the site. When the lorry arrives, it has to wait in line while the first lorry is dumping its load. The dumping process involves the lorry driver raising the back of the lorry to dump the gravel with the aid of construction workers who rake the gravel from the lorry. On average, the time to unload the lorry is 7.5 minutes/unit and a lorry arrives every 12 minutes. Lorry drivers are paid on average £9 an hour. The arrival and service rate of the lorry follows the assumption of single channel, single phase queuing model.

Required

1 The average time a truck spends in the system (waiting and unloading).
2 The average time waiting in line.
3 Average utilization of the system.
4 What is the average hourly cost for trucks waiting and unloading, based on the drivers' wages?
5 Develop a probability histogram of there being more than k trucks in the system with a value of k from 0 to 10.
6 What is the probability that there will be more than three trucks in the system?

EXERCISE PROBLEM: MOTORWAY (PART II)

Situation

The basic data for this problem is identical to that given in the worked example, *Motorway (part I)*. Redo the simulation on the following basis, assuming that as soon as the simulation starts, the first customer arrives. The random-number table used is given as Figure 24.14.

Required

1 In the random-number table use Column C for the arrival patterns and Column D for the service time (instead of Columns A and B) and recreate the simulation. What are your conclusions? Why is there a difference?
2 In the random-number tables use the Column E for the arrival patterns and Column F for the service time (instead of Columns A and B) and recreate the simulation. What are your conclusions? Why is there a difference?
3 In the random number tables use the Column G for the arrival patterns and Column H for the service time (instead of Columns A and B) and recreate the simulation. What are your conclusions? Why is there a difference?
4 In the random number tables use the Column I for the arrival patterns and Column J for the service time (instead of Columns A and B) and recreate the simulation. What are your conclusions? Why is there a difference?
5 In the random number tables use the Column B for the arrival patterns and Column A for the service time (instead of Columns A and B) and recreate the simulation. What are your conclusions? Why is there a difference?

Figure 24.14   Motorway – second table of random numbers.

	A	B	C	D	E	F	G	H	I	J
1	76	39	63	41	88	35	98	45	64	11
2	5	98	42	22	57	60	90	14	4	6
3	91	58	55	8	71	2	37	68	98	88
4	20	58	59	30	81	2	50	18	8	32
5	7	50	52	50	12	48	83	27	83	71
6	85	65	60	76	48	79	88	73	29	80
7	67	31	29	82	59	40	36	10	78	29
8	5	51	84	77	65	66	9	59	88	71
9	59	90	40	20	69	33	57	30	77	94
10	41	62	30	19	65	93	26	53	1	61
11	80	80	53	5	57	68	75	51	42	48
12	15	48	59	21	9	99	48	31	61	21
13	87	37	82	83	3	59	71	64	83	36
14	94	91	67	18	52	85	82	74	60	87
15	42	70	37	13	60	38	6	80	94	18
16	6	64	42	86	83	23	46	51	10	64
17	3	92	94	86	23	15	95	8	98	92
18	47	29	23	96	13	80	54	79	77	61
19	23	23	32	6	30	45	65	87	9	9
20	36	38	44	75	24	22	33	42	85	85
21	48	80	55	61	52	19	24	71	33	13
22	5	65	8	0	32	5	92	2	83	45
23	44	19	89	71	60	9	99	63	1	69
24	56	19	94	8	24	56	9	68	74	55
25	79	94	71	63	66	43	67	50	83	36
26	60	77	43	79	42	26	63	31	91	36
27	3	27	42	89	51	59	87	1	4	7
28	88	32	4	65	29	79	34	27	93	7
29	47	83	35	1	68	90	21	76	35	87
30	61	37	20	99	71	63	86	50	61	21
31	6	37	64	95	44	90	45	74	70	19
32	40	64	12	8	21	50	67	21	79	47
33	83	84	25	93	41	70	33	39	83	40
34	38	50	99	13	61	50	73	36	95	23
35	97	99	5	27	29	70	52	95	38	33
36	52	84	13	85	61	29	25	73	6	6
37	46	34	56	32	95	76	89	92	42	88
38	4	7	17	4	12	98	24	49	48	3
39	31	16	32	54	86	76	82	38	39	18
40	25	84	15	86	93	66	89	4	14	58
41	96	6	48	76	13	28	50	61	7	4
42	7	65	80	17	23	11	7	54	30	54
43	80	8	10	48	89	59	22	71	89	71
44	32	8	74	88	18	19	30	1	64	33
45	82	75	30	41	80	80	49	14	60	38
46	46	20	35	31	86	19	14	13	59	4
47	67	79	50	92	73	26	0	77	18	48
48	48	32	99	54	5	93	33	67	67	29
49	69	52	5	61	31	7	16	56	80	54
50	54	41	7	85	7	64	84	87	68	96

NOTES AND REFERENCES

1. Griffin, W. (1978) *Queuing: Basic Theories and Applications*, Columbus, OH: Grid Publishing.
2. Lee, S. M. (1983) *Introduction to Management Science*, Fort Worth: TX: Dryden Press.
3. Cooper, B. (1980) *Introduction to Queuing Theory*, New York: Elsevier North Holland.

FURTHER READING

Ackere, V. A. and Ninios, P. (1993) 'Simulation and queuing theory applied to a single-server queue with advertising and balking', *Journal of the Operational Research Society* 44(4): 407–14.

Allen, G., Gunn, E. and Rutherford, P. (1993) 'Improving throughput of a coal transport system with the aid of three simple models', *Interfaces* 23(4): 88–103.

Amiri, A. (1998) 'The design of service systems with queuing time cost, workload capacities and backup service', *European Journal of Operational Research* 104(1): 201–17.

Atkinson, B. (1995) 'Queuing theory in manufacturing systems analysis and design', *Journal of the Operational Research Society* 46(1): 137–38.

Banks, J. and Dai, J. G. (1997) 'Simulation studies of multiclass queuing networks', *IIE Transactions* 29(3): 213–19.

Barlach, Z. and Morrison, K. R. (1992) 'Waiting time calculations for *K* machines with two service facilities', *Computers and Industrial Engineering* 23(1–4): 85–88.

Chao, X. (1995) 'Networks of queues with customers, signals, and arbitrary service time distributions', *Operations Research* 43(3): 537–44.

Chebat, J.-C. and Filiatrault, P. (1993) 'The impact of waiting in line on consumers', *International Journal of Bank Marketing* 11(2): 35–40.

Daniel, J. I. (1995) 'Congestion pricing and capacity of large hub airports: A bottleneck model with stochastic queues', *Econometrica* 63(2): 327–70.

Deng, C. C. (1992) 'A modelling study of a taxi service operation', *International Journal of Operations and Production Management* 12(11): 65–78.

Duff, J. R. (1992) 'Shortening the manufacturing queue', *Professional Engineering* 5(5): 20–21.

Goddard, W. E. (1994) 'Don't get buried by WIP queues!', *Modern Materials Handling* 49(9): 41.

Griffiths, J. D. (1995) 'Queuing at the Suez Canal', *Journal of the Operational Research Society* 46(11): 1299–309.

Jackman, J. and Johnson, E. (1993) 'The role of queuing network models in performance evaluation of manufacturing systems', *Journal of the Operational Research Society* 44(8): 797–807.

Jewkes, E. (1994) 'A queuing analysis of priority-based scheduling rules for a single-stage manufacturing system with repair', *IEE Transactions* 26(4): 80–86.

Khan, M. R. and Callahan, B. B. (1993) 'Planning laboratory staffing with a queuing model', *European Journal of Operational Research* 67(25): 321–31.

Lamrecht, M. R., Chen, S. and Vandaele, N. J. (1996) 'A lot sizing model with queuing delays: The issue of safety time', *European Journal of Operational Research* 89(2): 269–76.

Lin, C., Madu, C. N., Chien, T. W. and Kuei, C.-H. (1994) 'Queuing models for optimising system availability of a flexible manufacturing system', *Journal of the Operational Research Society* 45(10): 1141–155.

Lynes, K. and Milenburg, J. (1994) 'The application of an open queuing network to the inventory and cost in the batch production system of a microelectronics manufacturer', *International Journal of Production Economics* 37(2): 189–203.

Mascolo, M. D. (1996) 'Analysis of a synchronisation station for the performance evaluation of a kanban system with a general arrival process of demands', *European Journal of Operational Research* 89(1): 147–63.

Papadopoulos, H. T and Heavey, C. (1996) 'Queuing theory in manufacturing systems analysis and design: A classification of models for production and transfer lines', *European Journal of Operational Research* 92,Iss.(1): 1–27.

Proctor, R. A. (1994) 'Queues and the power of simulation: Helping with business decisions and problems', *Management Decision* 32(1): 50–55.

Rao, S. S. (1992) 'The relationship of work-in-process inventories, manufacturing lead times, and waiting line analysis', *International Journal of Production Economics* 26(1–3): 221–27.

Ross, K. W., Tsang, D. H. K. and Wang, J. (1994) 'Monte Carlo summation and integration applied to multiclass queuing networks', *Journal of the Association for Computing Machinery* 41(6): 1110–35.

Shi, L. (1995) 'Approximate analysis for queuing networks with finite capacity and customer loss', *European Journal of Operational Research* 85(1): 178–91.

Springer, M. C. and Makens, P. K. (1992) 'Queuing models for performance analysis: Selection of single station models', *European Journal of Operational Research* 58(1): 123–45.

Stein, W. E. and Cote, M. J. (1994) 'Scheduling arrivals to a queue', *Computers and Operations Research* 21(6): 607–14.

Tang, L. C. and Chew, E.-P. (1997) 'Order picking systems: Batching and storage assignment strategies', *Computers and Industrial Engineering* 33(3): 817–20.

Tetxlaff, U. A. W. (1996) 'A queuing network model for flexible manufacturing systems with tool management', *IIE Transactions* 28(4): 309–17.

Van Dijk, N. M. (1997) 'Why queuing never vanishes', *European Journal of Operational Research* 99(2): 463–76.

Wang, P. P. (1996) 'Queuing models with delayed state-dependent service times' *Journal of the Operational Research Society* 47(1): 122–35.

Wang, P. P. (1997) 'Optimally scheduling N customer arrival times for a single-server system', *Computers and Operations Research* 24(8): 703–16.

Wang, P. P. and Wilson, G. R. (1994) 'Approximations for the mean and variance of the throughput of flexible manufacturing cells', *International Journal of Production Economics* 37(2,3): 275–84.

Zipkin, P. (1995) 'Processing networks with planned inventories: Tandem queues with feedback', *European Journal of Operational Research* 80(2): 344–49.

25 Financial analysis

Objectives and overview

All activities should consider the financial aspects. The objective of this chapter is to highlight the importance of costs and pricing in operations management and associated supply chains. The chapter opens by illustrating the various approaches to product pricing, including market price, published prices, cost plus margin price and a price based on target cost. The chapter then reviews variable, or direct, costs and then reviews the difference between the FIFO, LIFO and weighted-unit-averaging methods of valuing inventory. Fixed costs are reviewed, together with the way they are handled for depreciation purposes and their analyses by using the payback and net present value methods. Activity-based costing is discussed and compared to traditional cost accounting and a review of the importance of non-value added activity and cost allocation is given. Short-run production costs are then presented in detail with the importance of marginal costs to the operations manager emphasized. The final section of the chapter covers long-run production costs, the advantage of the economies of scale to some firms and the disadvantages to others.

PRODUCT PRICING

Product price and the operations manager

A firm is in business to make money and it generates this income from the sale of goods or services, that is, the end products of the integrated supply chain. Very simply, net income is the difference between sales revenues and costs, the sales revenue being the product of units sold and product price. Although the operations manager may not be directly involved in product pricing, an awareness of a company's pricing strategy facilitates effective cost management of the operations function. As illustrated for Hershey Foods in Chapter 2 *Strategy of organizations*, cost reductions, for given sales revenues, can have significant impact on net income. While some firms consider that the Client is King, others say that Cost is King!!

For a given price, lower product costs translate into a higher profit margin. Thus, in establishing a product price, a prime objective is to maximize the total profit margin. However, the price should not be too high so that market share is low, nor should the price be too low so that costs are barely recuperated. The following are some approaches to product pricing.

Market price

The market price, or the price the market will bear, is the amount customers are willing to pay for the product. For products that are a monopoly in the market, the price may have little relationship to cost, as is illustrated below for Johnnie Walker Scotch whisky.[1]

Johnnie Walker Scotch whisky

Johnnie Walker Scotch whisky, brewed in the United Kingdom, sells for $30 in New York City, USA, which is a high market price relative to production and distribution costs. Here for the $30 retail price, $15 is the mark-up, with half for the retail liquor merchant and half for the producer (Guinness in this case); see Figure 25.1. (A fifth is a unit of measure equal to one-fifth of a US gallon.)

For new products introduced into the market, prices may be very high at first in order to recoup earlier development costs (See Chapter 6, *Design of the Product*). As more competitors enter the market, companies are forced to lower prices in order to keep customers. However, this may not have an equivalent impact on margins, as a result of the learning curve with increase in production volume (see Chapter 8, *Human Resources in the System Design*):

■ When Texas Instruments introduced their calculators in the early 1970s, prices were very high at the beginning (over $250) but dropped to below $100 in a period of only a few months.
■ In the late 1980s the price of personal computers was very high but dropped dramatically in the 1990s.
■ Air fares in real terms have fallen since the 1980s (part of this has been the result of deregulation in the USA and now in Europe).

Figure 25.1 Breakdown of the price of a fifth of Johnnie Walker Scotch whisky, which costs $30 in New York City.

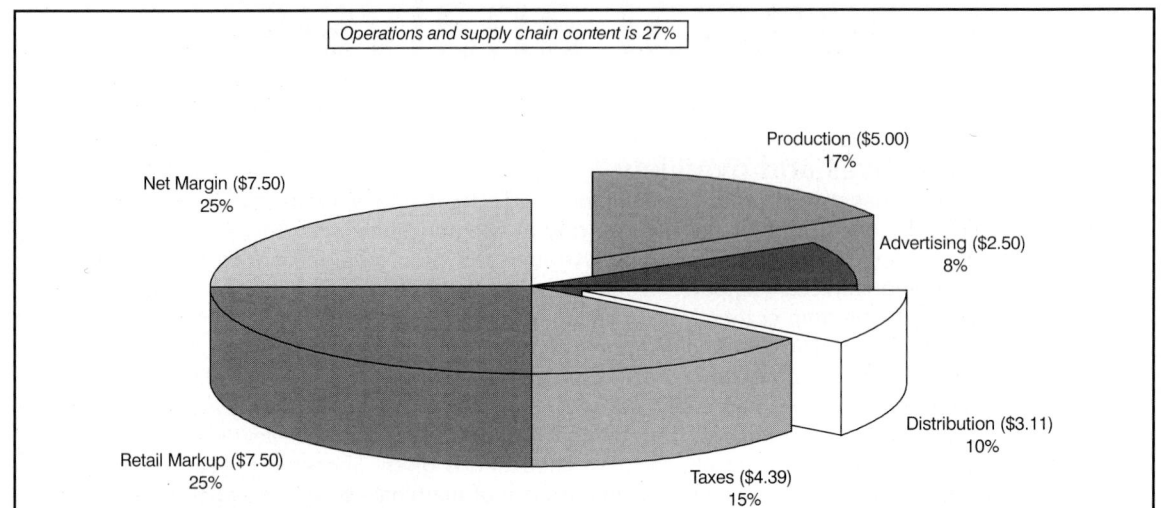

When there are many competitors offering similar products, and the product is fairly standard, the price level, or range, is usually already established and will lie between quite close limits as for example:

- services: restaurants with similar menus;
- consumer products: blue jeans;
- industrial products: stainless-steel tubing.

Catalogue price

A catalogue price is similar to the market price in that it is a price already published in a catalogue. A company bringing out a similar product that cannot be differentiated from competitive products, would probably follow the catalogue price. For example, in the case of industrial goods:

- screws, bolts, nails, etc.;
- PVC pellets for making plastic;
- corrugated cardboard.

Price equal to cost plus margin

Here a company would add up all the costs going into the product and then add a profit margin (say 15 per cent) to give the market price. This approach is illustrated in Figure 25.2.[2]

Price based on target cost

The target cost is a market-driven cost in competitive industries, determined from the sales price necessary to capture a predetermined market share:

Target cost = Sales price (for expected market share) – profit.

Thus, from this relationship, assuming that the profit level is pre-established, if the target cost is lower than the standard, or budgeted, costs, cost reductions have to be implemented. This means that all groups involved in commercializing the product, through design, engineering, suppliers, manufacturing and operations, have to implement continuous cost-reduction programmes. Here again a learning curve approach may be appropriate as increased volumes of products result in lower unit costs; see Figure 25.3.[3] An illustration is as follows.

Heinz pet foods

With a process dubbed price-based costing, Heinz figured the price that shoppers were willing to pay for a can of 9-Lives cat food, or of Star-Kist tuna, and then worked backward, cutting expenses to arrive at that price and preserve the company's margins. Starting in the late 1980s, $50 million in annual costs were slashed from the pet-food business and prices were cut. Volume grew and within five years the Heinz pet food business doubled its sales and profit margins and quadrupled its profits.[4]

Exchange rates

Companies that export may find that, because of changes in exchange rates, the sales price of their products rises on foreign markets, making them less attractive to consumers. This has been the case for Japanese and German products when the Yen and the Mark have strengthened in relation to the US dollar. To

Figure 25.2 Product price based on cost plus margin.

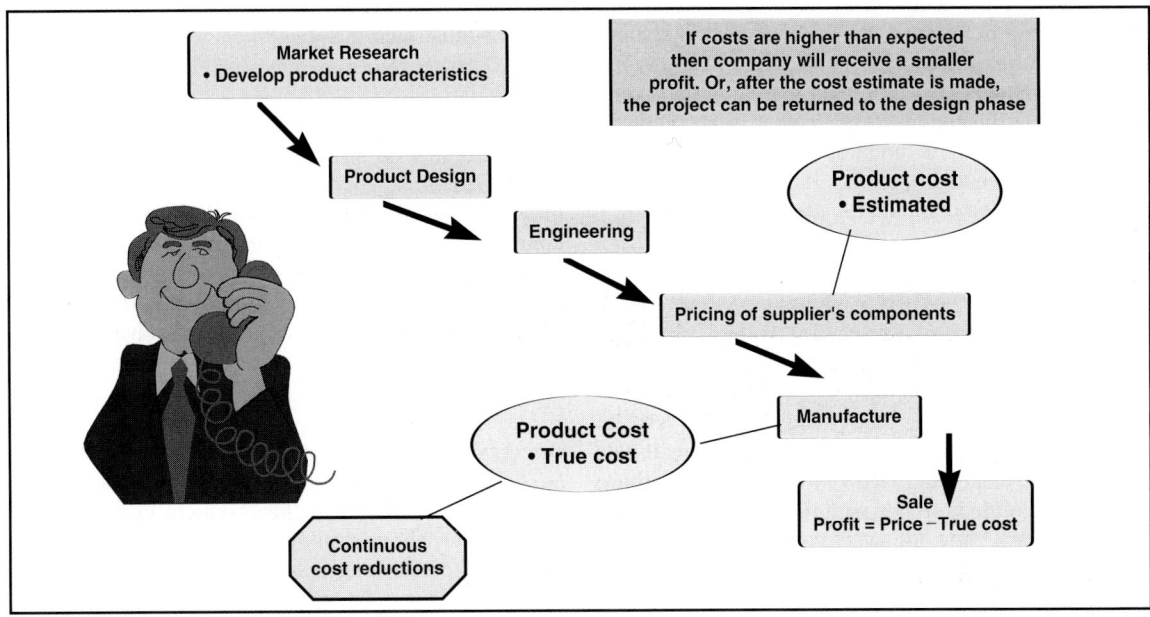

Figure 25.3 Product price based on target cost.

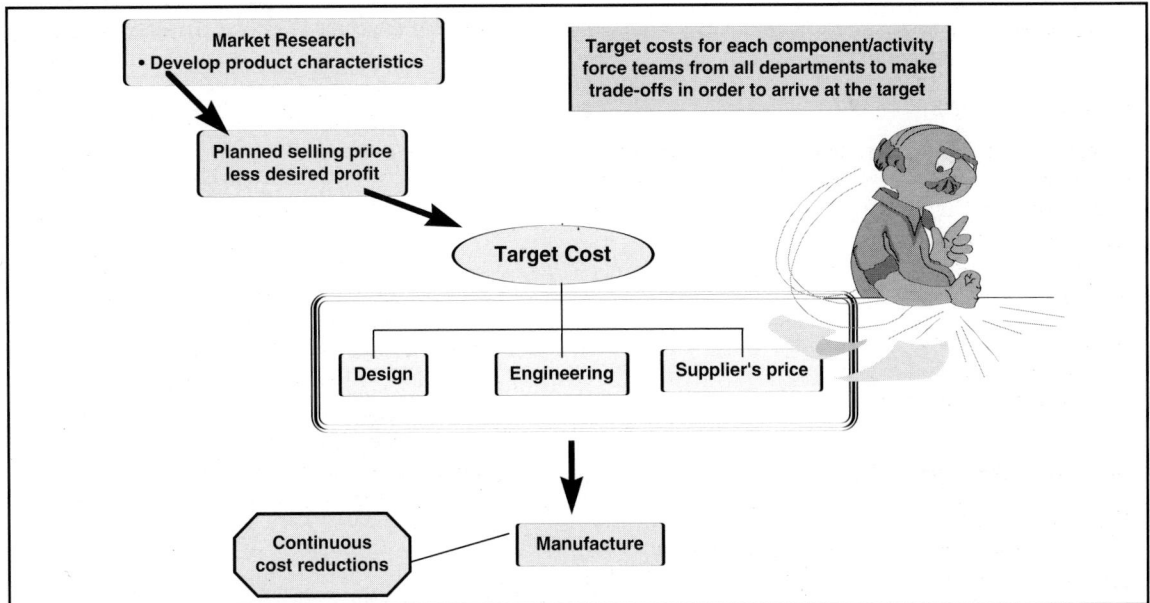

counteract this, companies are pushed to drop their prices and, if the same profit level is desired, this means a drop in target cost. For example, to achieve this, Japanese automobile companies like Toyota, Nissan and Honda are cutting out extras on their vehicles, such as heated mirrors, leather seats and all-round disc brakes. In addition, their manufacturing processes are changing so that hidden parts, such as the fuel tanks and drive shafts, are left unpainted.[5]

VARIABLE COSTS

Definition

Variable costs are those that change with the level of products produced and include direct labour, materials used in the product and factory overhead. Since these costs are identified directly with the products, or services produced, they are also considered the direct costs. In slow periods, variable costs can be reduced by cutting back purchases and making employees redun-

dant. The development of the unit cost of a product, and how it is presented on a company's financial statement, is illustrated in Table 25.1.

Raw material cost

Raw material cost, shown in the Table by the line item *Raw materials*, covers the purchase price paid to external suppliers for things like raw materials, components, subassemblies and packaging. For components made in one work centre of the same company and then used by another work centre, the 'price' or material cost would be an established transfer cost.

Direct labour cost

Direct labour cost, shown in the Table by the line item *Direct labour*, is that which can be directly accounted for in the production of the products in question. It would cover labour employed for things like operating machines, performing assembly operations and packaging. The direct labour cost is not only the wages

Table 25.1 Cost of goods sold ($), year ending 31 December 1995

	$	$	$
Work in process, 1 January 1995			5 176 000
Raw materials			
Inventory, 1 January 1995		2 943 500	
Purchases	4 712 500		
Less: purchase returns, and allowances	214 100		
Net purchases		4 498 400	
Total cost of materials available		7 441 900	
Less: inventory, 31 December 1995		3 532 200	
Cost of materials put into production		3 909 700	
Direct labour		2 079 000	
Factory overhead			
Indirect labour	184 800		
Repairs	72 150		
Energy (heating, light, power)	5 780		
Water	1 500		
Depreciation – machinery and equipment	24 150		
Factory supplies (oil, cleaning fluids, gloves)	1 800		
Patents expense	2 750		
Insurance	5 780		
Total factory overhead		298 710	
Total manufacturing costs			6 287 410
Work in process during 1995			11 463 410
Less: work-in-process inventory, 31 December 1995			7 246 400
Costs of goods sold			4 217 010
Units sold in 1995	27 400		
Unit cost price of manufactured goods in 1995			153.91

paid, but also the burden. The burden is made up of the the mandatory social charges, such as medical insurance, retirement, unemployment, holiday pay, etc.

The importance of labour costs in product cost

The element of labour costs in production is one reason why companies are transferring their manufacturing operations from countries of high labour cost, such as Germany, Switzerland and France, to regions of low labour cost, such as Mexico, China and Brazil. (see Chapter 3, *Site Selection*). As an illustration, Table 25.2 gives the estimated cost of a silk shirt, in $US, manufactured in Lyon, France and Shanghai, China.[6]

Table 25.2 The estimated cost of a silk shirt, in $US, manufactured in Lyon, France and Shanghai, China

Item	Shanghai	Lyon
Raw materials	5	7
Labour	1	18
Margin	5	6
Transportation to Europe	1	0
Total product cost	12	31
Labour as percentage of product cost	8	58

Factory overhead

In traditional accounting, factory overhead includes all those costs that can be allocated to a particular manufacturing process used in making the product. It might include energy costs, lubricating fluids, maintenance costs and a portion of machinery depreciation used in the manufacture. This is shown in the line item, 'Factory overhead'.

Value of inventory

In Table 25.1 there are line items for inventory (see Chapter 11, *Inventory Management*). The price paid for inventory items changes with time. As an example, in paper manufacture, the raw pulp, purchased in one period may increase in price when the identical raw

material is purchased six months later. Physically, the component is the same and the price makes no difference in the operation of the manufactured end product. However, the question arises as to what is the value of inventory to be used to calculate the final cost of goods sold. Methods used include the following.

First in, first out

In first in, first out (FIFO) the first items of inventory obtained are charged against sales. Since the first items will probably have cost less than later items, the cost of goods sold will be the lowest possible. The effect on the income statement will be to indicate a higher gross profit. The value of inventory remaining will be accounted at a relatively high value.

Last in first out

In last in, first out (LIFO) the last items of inventory obtained are charged against sales. Since the last items will probably have cost more than earlier items, the cost of goods sold will be the highest possible. The effect on the income statement will be to indicate a lower gross profit. The value of inventory remaining will be accounted at a relatively low value.

Weighted unit average cost

In weighted unit average cost (WUAC) the average value of the inventory items obtained is charged against sales. This will balance out the value of the cost of goods sold and the value of inventory remaining.

In the USA, the LIFO or FIFO methods of accounting are permitted for reporting financial results. The FIFO method would be very optimistic in determining profits and report high in-process inventory values, which could impact insurance or taxation levels. With LIFO, profit figures are conservative with a low value of inventory remaining. In France, the weighted average unit cost is the accepted accounting method for inventory valuation. These three methods of valuing inventory are illustrated by the worked example, *Rosehead*.

WORKED EXAMPLE: ROSEHEAD CO.

Situation

The Rosehead Co. in England makes specialized electric pumps, for which it buys the electrical winding units from outside. At the end of September 1995 it has 1000 inventory items of these electrical windings. The quantity, date acquired and the unit cost paid for these units is as shown in Table 25.3.

Table 25.3 Rosehead – quantity, date acquired and the unit cost paid for units held at the end of September 1995

Quantity	Date acquired	Unit cost
400	1 January 1995	£4.00
300	1 April 1995	£6.00
300	1 July 1995	£8.00

During the period 1 January 1993 through 30 September 1993 the company uses 300 of the electrical windings to make pump units. Each pump unit is sold for £10.00.

Required

1 Determine the gross margin for Rosehead, and the value of the inventory remaining using:
   (a) first in, first out inventory valuation;
   (b) last in, first out inventory valuation;
   (c) weighted unit average method of inventory evaluation.

Solution

1 Table 25.4 gives the solutions for the inventory value methods, while Table 25.5 summarizes the results.

Table 25.5 Gross margin and inventory values for different inventory value methods

Method	Gross margin (£)	Value of inventory remaining (£)
FIFO	1800	4600
LIFO	600	3400
WUAC	1260	4060

Table 25.4 Rosehead – solutions for inventory value methods (all financial figures in £s)

	Quantity	Date acquired	Unit cost	Value
	400	1 January 95	4.00	1600
	300	1 April 95	6.00	1800
	300	1 July 95	8.00	2400
Total	1000			5800
Weighted unit average cost			5.80	
Quantity of end products sold (units)	300			
Price per unit (£)	10.00			
Revenues generated (£)	3000.00			
Inventory units remaining	700			
FIFO				
Cost per unit of inventory	4.00			
Revenues		3000.00		
Cost of inventory units		1200.00		
Gross Margin		1800.00		
Value of inventory remaining	4600			
LIFO				
Cost per unit of inventory	8.00			
Revenues		3000.00		
Cost of inventory		2400.00		
Gross Margin		600.00		
Value of inventory remaining	3400			
WUAC				
Cost per unit of inventory	5.80			
Revenues		3000.00		
Cost of inventory		1740.00		
Gross Margin		1260.00		
Value of inventory remaining	4060			

FIXED COSTS

Definition

Fixed costs are derived from the capital assets used for running a business and normally have a useful life of over one year. (Chapter 11, *Inventory Management*, differentiates capital assets from inventory). Capital assets include machinery, computers, transportation equipment, buildings, office furniture, etc. In operations planning, the need to acquire capital assets, and the timing, are important as these are charged as a cost to the operation in the form of depreciation.

The need for additional capital assets may arise as a result of expansion due to increased sales or new markets. Alternatively, existing capital equipment may need to be replaced because it is worn or obsolete, or because technological sophistication necessitates replacement. Normally, the purchase of capital assets is made by top management, but those in operations are very often required to justify their acquisition. Capital assets are being used proportionately more and more, relative to labour, in flexible manufacturing systems. Land is a capital asset, but its financial treatment is different from equipment as it does not 'wear out'.

Depreciation

Depreciation is the accounting method by which a capital asset is charged to the business. Though payment for the capital asset is normally made at the time the asset is acquired (though this depends on terms with the supplier), depreciation is a periodic non-cash charge. It indirectly impacts the cash flow or profits through its effect on income tax, as illustrated in Table 25.6. Since tax rates, and depreciation methods vary from country to country, the magnitude of the tax advantage will not be the same in every country.

Table 25.6 The effect of depreciation on tax

Financial entry	No depreciation allowance	Depreciation allowance
Income, before depreciation and taxes	500 000	500 000
Less depreciation	0	35 000
Taxable income	500 000	465 000
Taxes payable @ 45 per cent	225 000	209 250
Income after taxes	275 000	255 750
Tax advantage with depreciation	0	19 250

Calculation of depreciation

The way depreciation is calculated, and applied for the cost of a capital asset, affects the annual cash flow. Three accounting methods are the straight-line method, the sum-of-years digits method and the declining-balance method.

Straight-line method

The straight-line method divides into equal portions the cost of the fixed asset C over the period of its estimated life, n years. If there is a salvage value S then the amount of depreciation applied each year is:

$$\text{Depreciation amount} = \frac{C - S}{n}.$$

Assume that an asset is purchased for $510 000. The life of the asset is seven years and the salvage value is $20 000. The depreciation is then given by:

$$\text{Depreciation amount} = \frac{510\,000 - 20\,000}{7}$$

$$= \frac{490\,000}{7}$$

$$= \$70\,000 \text{ per year.}$$

Thus, amounts charged to depreciation each year are as given in Table 25.7.

Table 25.7 Amounts charged to depreciation under the straight-line method

Year	Depreciation amount ($)
1	70 000
2	70 000
3	70 000
4	70 000
5	70 000
6	70 000
7	70 000
Total	490 000

Sum-of-the years digits method

Here, the sum of the years' digits are totalled to give the denominator to proportion the depreciation amount. For an asset with a seven-year life, the sum of the years' digits is:

$$7 + 6 + 5 + 4 + 3 + 2 + 1 = 28.$$

The numerator is the year in question. For example, for the asset with a cost price of $510 000 and a salvage value of $20 000, the depreciation amounts are:

$$\text{Depreciation, year 1} = \frac{7}{28} \times (510\,000 - 20\,000)$$

$$= \$122\,250$$

$$\text{Depreciation, year 2} = \frac{6}{28} \times (510\,000 - 20\,000)$$

$$= \$105\,000$$

$$\text{Depreciation, year 3} = \frac{5}{28} \times (510\,000 - 20\,000)$$

$$= \$87\,500$$

$$\text{Depreciation, year 4} = \frac{4}{28} \times (510\,000 - 20\,000)$$

$$= \$70\,000$$

$$\text{Depreciation, year 5} = \frac{3}{28} \times (510\,000 - 20\,000)$$

$$= \$52\,500$$

$$\text{Depreciation, year 6} = \frac{2}{28} \times (510\,000 - 20\,000)$$

$$= \$35\,000$$

$$\text{Depreciation, year 7} = \frac{1}{28} \times (510\,000 - 20\,000)$$

$$= \$17\,500.$$

Total depreciation is $490 000. With this method, higher amounts are charged in the earlier years and less in the later periods.

Declining-balance method

This method applies a constant depreciation rate to a gradually reducing balance. It applies a higher depreciation rate in early years and lower rates in later years. A commonly used rate is twice the straight-line rate, or double declining balance. The rate is applied to cost and not the cost less salvage.

As an illustration, in the straight line method the rate used is 1/7, while in the double declining balance the rate is 2/7. Depreciation is:

$$\text{Year } 1 = \frac{2}{7} \times (510\ 000) = \$145\ 714:$$

Remaining is $(510\ 000 - 145\ 714) = 364\ 286$

$$\text{Year } 2 = \frac{2}{7} \times (364\ 286) = \$104\ 082:$$

Remaining is $(364\ 286 - 104\ 082) = 260\ 204$

$$\text{Year } 3 = \frac{2}{7} \times (260\ 204) = \$74\ 344:$$

Remaining is $(260\ 204 - 74\ 344) = 185\ 860$

$$\text{Year } 4 = \frac{2}{7} \times (185\ 860) = \$53\ 103:$$

Remaining is $(185\ 860 - 53\ 103) = 132\ 757$

$$\text{Year } 5 = \frac{2}{7} \times (132\ 757) = \$37\ 931:$$

Remaining is $(132\ 757 - 37\ 931) = 94\ 826$

$$\text{Year } 6 = \frac{2}{7} \times (94\ 827) = \$27\ 093:$$

Remaining is $(94\ 826 - 27\ 093) = 67\ 733$

$$\text{Year } 7 = \frac{2}{7} \times (67\ 733) = \$19\ 352:$$

Remaining is $(67\ 733 - 19\ 352) = 48\ 381$

The total depreciation is $461 619.

Depreciation tables

For income tax purposes, taxing authorities in some countries publish depreciation tables according to the type of capital. As an illustration, two depreciation tax tables used for the United States are given in Appendix III.

FINANCIAL TREATMENT OF FIXED ASSETS

Payback method

The payback method gives an indication of how long it takes to recover the initial investment for the purchase of an asset with operating cost savings, or other financial expenses taken into account. The payback period is dependent on the depreciation method employed and it should be considered on an after-tax basis to give meaningful results; otherwise, the time period determined may be quite wrong. The method does not consider the time value of money, but its calculation is straightforward and the results are easy to understand. The payback method of financial analysis is illustrated in the first part of the worked example, *OTL Co.*

Net present value

Net present value (NPV) analysis considers the time value of money and discounts the value of all after-tax cash flows back to the present time. Investments in the asset are outflows, or a negative value. Savings, as a result of improved operations, are positive flows. A positive net present value indicates that the value of the investment has been recuperated during the life of the investment considered.

The basis of the net present value calculation is that an amount of money invested today, say in a certificate of deposit, will be worth more in the future because of the interest on the investment. Assume the following:

- P is the initial investment;
- i is the interest rate;
- n is the period of investment;
- F is the future value of the initial investment after n years.

Future values

For annual compounding:

$$F = P\,(1 + i)^n;$$

for daily compounding:

$$F = P\left(1 + \frac{i}{365}\right)^{n \times 365}.$$

Some financial institutions may use 360 instead of 365 days.

Assume that £2500 is invested for a period of six years at a rate of 5 per cent. The value of the investment at the end of the period, for annual compounding, is:

$$F = 2500\,(1 + 0.05)^6 = 2500 \times 1.3401$$
$$= £3350.24,$$

while, for daily compounding, the value is:

$$F = 2500\left(1 + \frac{0.05}{365}\right)^{6 \times 3} = 2500 \times 1.3498$$
$$= £3374.58.$$

Present values

By corollary in the NPV concept, the present value of a future sum of money is less in absolute terms because future values implies accrued interest. To obtain the present value, all accrued interest has to be removed. Thus, reversing the relationships above gives, for annual compounding:

$$P = \frac{F}{(1 + i)^n} \; ;$$

for daily compounding:

$$P = \frac{F}{\left(1 + \dfrac{i}{365}\right)^{n \times 365}} .$$

Thus, the present value of £3350.24 to be received five years from now would be £2500 at an interest rate of 5 per cent compounded annually. The present value of £2500 to be received five years from now at a rate of 5 per cent is:

$$P = \frac{F}{(1 + i)^n} = \frac{2500}{(1 + 0.05)^6} = \frac{2500}{1.3401}$$
$$= £1\,865.54.$$

The net present value method of financial analysis is illustrated in the second part of the worked example, *OTL Co.*

Internal rate of return

The internal rate of return method computes the discount rate that equates the present value of all net cash inflows (positive values) with the cost of the capital asset (negative values). The calculation approach is similar to that of the net present value method, except that in the NPV approach the discount, or interest rate, is specified.

WORKED EXAMPLE: OTL CO.

Situation

The OTL Co. in northern England is a small printing company that prints brochures, catalogues and posters for a wide variety of customers. It is planning to purchase a new offset press at a cost of £375 000 to replace an existing printing press. The economic life of the new machine is considered to be ten years, after which the salvage value is expected to be £35 000. The old machine currently has a salvage value of £12 500. For purposes of financial analysis, the discount rate is considered fixed at nine per cent, the tax rate is 40 per cent and straight line depreciation is considered. Operating cost savings with the new machine are estimated as shown in Table 25.8

Table 25.8 OTL – Operating cost savings with the new press

Year	Operating cost saving (£)	Year	Operating cost saving (£)
1	41 000	6	82 000
2	51 250	7	82 000
3	61 500	8	82 000
4	82 000	9	82 000
5	82 000	10	82 000

Required

1. Determine the payback period in years if income taxes are taken into consideration.
2. Determine the payback period without tax considerations.
3. Illustrate graphically the cumulative cash flow movements for both payback methods.
4. What is the net present value of the investment? Based on the NPV, does the investment seem sound?

Solution

Tables 25.9 to 25.14 give the calculation methods.

Table 25.9 OTL Co. – supplied data

Purchase price of asset (£)	375 000
Economic life of asset (years)	10
Tax rate	40.00%
Cost saving (£)	
Year 1	41 000
Year 2	51 250
Year 3	61 500
Year 4	82 000
Year 5	82 000
Year 6	82 000
Year 7	82 000
Year 8	82 000
Year 9	82 000
Year 10	82 000
Total	727 750
Salvage value new equipment (£)	35 000
Salvage value old equipment (£)	12 500
Asset cost less salvage	327 500
Discount rate	9.00%

Table 25.10 OTL – Tax savings (£) with depreciation

Year	Annual depreciation	Accumulated depreciation	Annual tax savings
1	34 000	34 000	13 600
2	34 000	68 000	13 600
3	34 000	102 000	13 600
4	34 000	136 000	13 600
5	34 000	170 000	13 600
6	34 000	204 000	13 600
7	34 000	238 000	13 600
8	34 000	272 000	13 600
9	34 000	306 000	13 600
10	34 000	340 000	13 600
Total	340 000		136 000

1   Table 25.11 gives the calculation with tax considerations. The payback is between six and seven years. By linear interpolation, as shown on Table 25.14, the exact period is 6.1 years or six years and five weeks.

$$6 + \frac{6\,050}{56\,750 + 6\,050} = 6.10.$$

2   Table 25.12 gives the calculation without tax considerations. The payback is between three and four years and by linear interpolation, as shown on Table 25.14, the exact period is 3.62 years or about three years and 32 weeks:

$$3 + \frac{71\,750}{71\,750 + 44\,250} = 3.62.$$

3   The graph is given in Figure 25.4.

4   The net present value flows are shown in Table 25.13. Yes, the NPV is positive when all the cash flows are considered, so on this basis it would seem a sound investment.

Table 25.11 OTL – Cash flows (£) with tax taken into account

Payback period (years)	After-tax operating cost savings (1 − rate) × savings	After-tax savings from depreciation	After-tax savings total	After-tax savings and outgoings	Cumulative cash flows
0				−327 500	−327 500
1	24 600	13 600	38 200	38 200	−289 300
2	30 750	13 600	44 350	44 350	−244 950
3	36 900	13 600	50 500	50 500	−194 450
4	49 200	13 600	62 800	62 800	−131 650
5	49 200	13 600	62 800	62 800	−68 850
6	49 200	13 600	62 800	62 800	−6 050
7	49 200	13 600	62 800	62 800	56 750
8	49 200	13 600	62 800	62 800	119 550
9	49 200	13 600	62 800	62 800	182 350
10	49 200	13 600	62 800	62 800	245 150
Payback period (years)	6.10				

Table 25.12 OTL – Cash flows (£) without taxes taken into account

Payback period (years)	Cost savings	Annual depreciation	Savings + depreciation	Outgoings and savings	Cumulative outgoings and savings
0				−327 500	−327 500
1	41 000	34 000	75 000	75 000	−252 500
2	51 250	34 000	85 250	85 250	−167 250
3	61 500	34 000	95 500	95 500	−71 750
4	82 000	34 000	116 000	116 000	44 250
5	82 000	34 000	116 000	116 000	160 250
6	82 000	34 000	116 000	116 000	276 250
7	82 000	34 000	116 000	116 000	392 250
8	82 000	34 000	116 000	116 000	508 250
9	82 000	34 000	116 000	116 000	624 250
10	82 000	34 000	116 000	116 000	740 250
		340 000			
Payback period (years)	3.62				

Table 25.13   OTL – net present value (£)

			After tax cash flows			
Year	Purchase	Salvage	Operating savings	Savings from depreciation	Total flows	Present value
0	–375 000	12 500			–362 500	–362 500
1			24 600	13 600	38 200	35 046
2			30 750	13 600	44 350	37 329
3			36 900	13 600	50 500	38 995
4			49 200	13 600	62 800	44 489
5			49 200	13 600	62 800	40 816
6			49 200	13 600	62 800	37 446
7			49 200	13 600	62 800	34 354
8			49 200	13 600	62 800	31 517
9			49 200	13 600	62 800	28 915
10		35 000	49 200	13 600	97 800	41 312
Net present value						7 718

Table 25.14   OTL – exact payback period

Year	With tax	Without tax
0	–327 500	–327 500
1	–289 300	–252 500
2	–244 950	–167 250
3	–194 450	–71 750
4	–131 650	44 250
5	–68 850	160 250
6	–6 050	276 250
7	56 750	392 250
8	119 550	508 250
9	182 350	624 250
10	245 150	740 250
Payback period (years)	6.10	3.62

Figure 25.4   OTL: payback period.

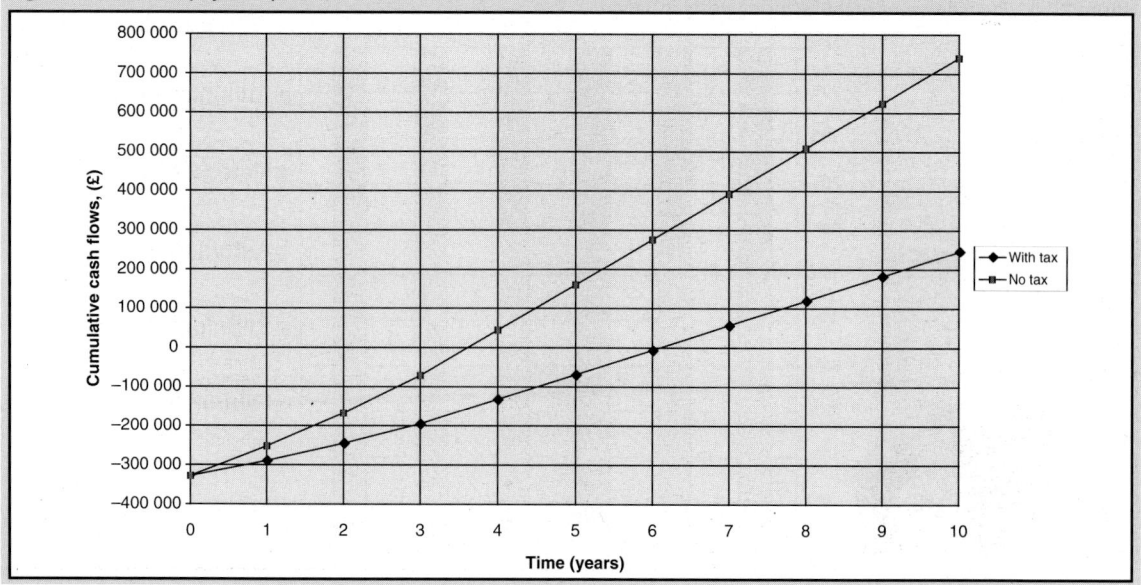

ACTIVITY-BASED COSTING

Traditional cost accounting

Traditional cost accounting involves assigning to the product the direct labour and materials and then attributing a proportion of factory overhead to this figure. This gives a cost price from the production centre, as already illustrated in Table 25.1. To this is then added a proportionate amount to include sales and administrative costs to arrive at a global product cost price. If a company produces a limited range of products, and the proportions of labour and materials used in the operation are high, then this method of cost accounting may be appropriate.

Operating changes

Today, many companies produce a wide range of products. In addition, they are increasingly using computers, robots, CAD/CAM equipment, etc., displacing the labour input and reorganizing the work centre using just-in-time and related methods. As such, there is a justification for modifying how costs are allocated.

Figure 25.5, which is based on a study by the Tokyo Metropolitan University of Japan, illustrates how manufacturing costs have changed over almost the last 50 years.[7] Of significance is the reduction in proportion of labour and materials and the increase in the proportion of subcontracting and automation. Thus, proportioning overhead in the traditional cost-

accounting way may give a false interpretation of product cost. Possible pitfalls are illustrated in the worked example, *Lorain Co.*

The principle of activity-based costing

The principle of activity-based costing is to analyse in depth actual product costs by specifically identifying all those activities associated with a product at each step in the flow of that product through the manufacturing or service-centre supply chain. In manufacturing, these items include not only the production, or transformation, step, but the technology used and non-value activities that take time, such as rework, bottlenecks, material delays, inventory in storage, etc. These costs are then assigned to the product concerned. This keeps the allocated overhead proportion to a minimum. Using activity-based costing highlights all the activities in the operating process, including inefficiencies. Conventional accounting does not take this into consideration.

The histograms (Figure 25.7) in the Example, *Lorain Co.*, illustrate the difference in costing presentations. The last histogram (Added value) illustrates the activity-based approach. The cost of the raw materials and components is the same as with direct costing, but in the activity-based costing there is the 'value' added, which includes all the activities associated with the product. Some activities may add value to enhance the product, while other activities may be non-value-added activities.

Figure 25.5 Breakdown of manufacturing costs in Japan.

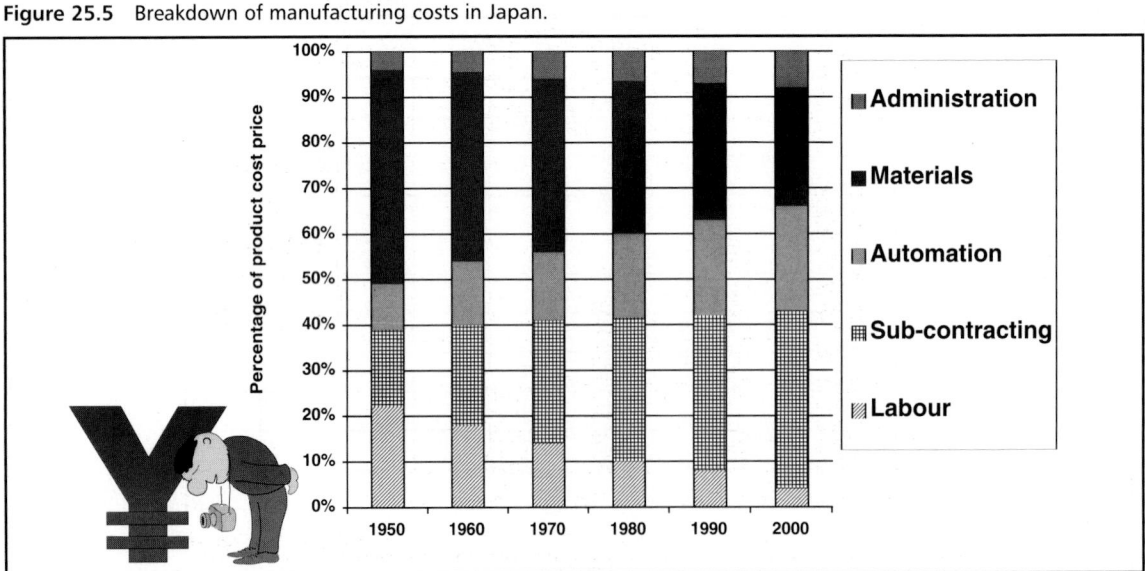

Non-value-added activities

A non-value-added activity is one that involves the expenditure of time, money and other resources, although, to the client, there is no apparent improvement in quality, performance, function or perceived value for the product. Activity-based costing identifies these non-value-added activities to provide a basis for their reduction and/or elimination.

Time

In Chapter 11, *Inventory Management*, the activities (times) associated globally with the transformation of a product were:

Activity time = Processing + (Waiting + Transfer + Queuing + Set-up).

Combining the non-value activities gives:

Activity time = Processing + Non-value-added time.

The efficiency of the operation can be represented by:

Operating efficiency =

$$\frac{\text{Processing time}}{\text{(Processing time + Non-value-added time)}}.$$

The non-value-added time might be reduced by:

- improving equipment effectiveness;
- SMED analysis to reduce set-up times;
- just-in-time Kanban systems;
- minimizing idle time as a result of worker pause and lunch breaks by staggering these times;
- improving layout to have a more streamlined flow;
- simplifying product design to reduce operating time;
- working closely with suppliers to reduce delays.

Reducing the non-value-added time by improving the balance of the operation by continuous flow increases the efficiency and reduces the wasted time. Schematically, the concept is illustrated in Figure 25.6. The difference in product costs between traditional accounting and activity-based costing in considering waiting time is illustrated in the worked example, *Balekjian Co.*

Henry Ford

Henry Ford (1921) said that 'Time waste differs from material waste in that with time there can be no salvage. The easiest of all wastes, and the hardest to correct, is the waste of time, because wasted time does not litter the floor like wasted material.'

Inventory holding costs

Holding inventory, whether it be raw materials, in-process or finished goods, is a non-value-added cost. Financing this inventory must be made though internal cash, or external debt and equity. Costs associated with

Figure 25.6   Reducing non-value-added activities.

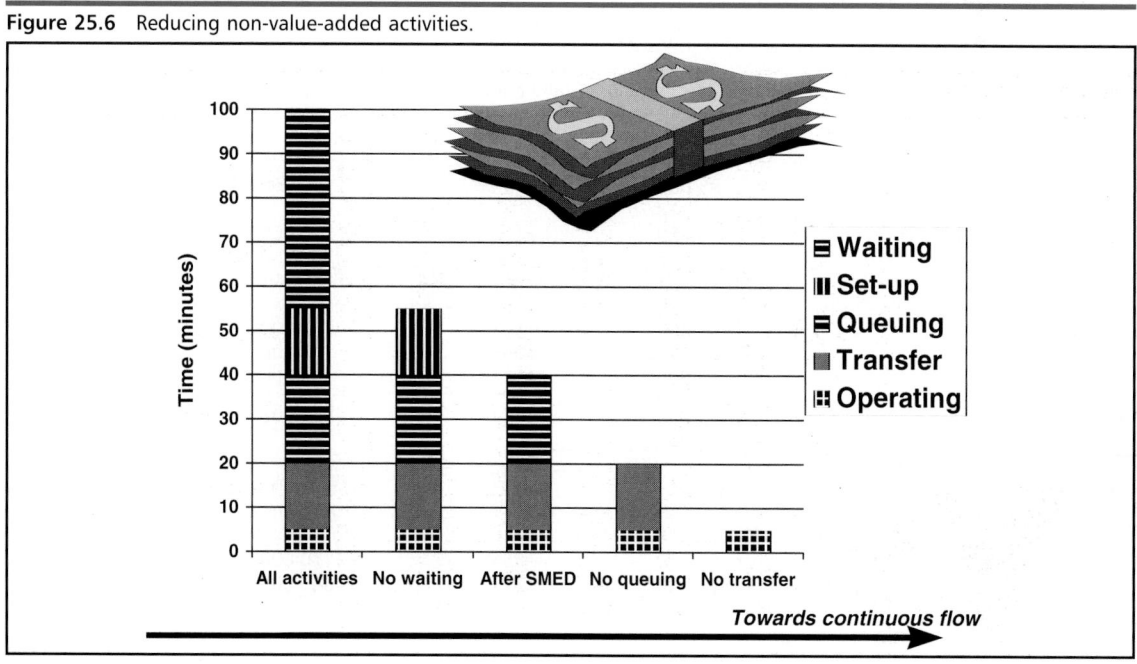

holding assets are often buried in overhead and ignored in real product costing.

Depreciation charges

In the traditional accounting for depreciation the assumption is that technology becomes obsolete over time and that the costs are recovered over a fixed period. The depreciation of the equipment is part of the overhead charge, but it can distort product costs if the technology is lumped into overhead when it is not evenly used for all products. This concept is illustrated by the worked example, *Techno Co.*

WORKED EXAMPLE: LORAIN CO.

Situation

Lorain Co. is a small business in England that assembles electronic components. It has two principal products, references DW-1705 and CW-1905. In 1995 the production quantity of these two products was 85 000 units each. The unit cost of raw materials and components was £13.75 for DW-1705 and £14.25 for CW-1905. Other costs associated with the two products in 1995 are as shown in Table 25.15.

Table 25.15 Lorain – Costs (£), other than raw materials and components

Other costs	Purchasing	Manufacturing	Sales and administration
Salaries	45 000	550 000	650 000
Expenses	25 000	105 000	150 000
Depreciation	45 000	750 000	55 000

The production time (elapsed time) per unit was 6.50 h for DW-1705 and 1.50 h for CW-1905. A major reason for the difference in time was that DW-1705 was produced on an old, poorly organized assembly line with machines that required long set-up times, while, CW-1905 was produced in a newer part of the factory, where machines were more recent and a just-in-time Kanban organization was in effect.

The sales prices were £36.00 per unit for DW-1705 and £21.00 for CW-1905.

Required

1 Determine a contribution margin for each product by allocating:
  - purchasing costs according to the value of raw material;
  - manufacturing costs according to the manufacturing time;
  - sales and administrative costs according to total costs less administration costs.
  What conclusions might be drawn from these results?
2 Develop an income statement for the organization based on the two products. What is the annual profit?
3 What would be the profit for the organization:
  (a) If only product DW-1705 was produced?
  (b) If only product CW-1905 was produced?
  Assume that all the other costs remain unchanged and that the total time used for manufacturing is the same as that used in Question 1.
4 What is the added value for the two products?

Solution

The financial analysis is given in Tables 25.16 to 25.20 and the final results presented in Figure 25.7:

Table 25.16 Lorain – product cost calculations: question 1 (all financial data in £)

Product	DW-1705	CW-1905	Total	
Annual production units	85 000	85 000	170 000	
Unit cost of raw materials	13.75	14.25		
Total cost of raw materials	1 168 750	1 211 250	2 380 000	
Other costs	Purchasing	Manufacturing	Sales & Admin	Total
Salaries	45 000	550 000	650 000	1 245 000
Expenses	25 000	105 000	150 000	280 000
Depreciation	45 000	750 000	55 000	850 000
Total	115 000	1 405 000	855 000	2 375 000
Manufacturing time Product	DW-1705	CW-1905	Total	
Time per unit (h)	6.50	1.50		
Annual production	85 000	85 000	170 000	
Total time (h)	552 500	127 500	680 000	

Allocating purchasing costs

Total material purchased	2 380 000
Purchasing costs	115 000 ›
Total	2 495 000
Total/material cost (Allocation factor)	. 1.05

Allocating manufacturing costs

Manufacturing costs	1 405 000
Manufacturing time	680 000
Costs/h (Allocation factor)	2.07

Allocating sales & administration

Total costs (materials, salaries, other)	4 755 000
Administration	855 000
Total costs – sales/administration	3 900 000
Total costs/(Total costs – Sales/ Administration) (Allocation factor)	1.22

Contribution margin per unit for each product

Product	DW-1705	CW-1905	DW/CW
Raw materials	13.75	14.25	0.96
Factor for allocating purchasing costs	1.05	1.05	1.00
Allocating purchasing charges	14.41	14.94	0.96
Manufacturing time/unit (h)	6.50	1.50	4.33
Factor for allocating manufacturing costs	2.07	2.07	1.00
Allocated manufacturing costs	13.43	3.10	4.33
Cost price at factory	27.84	18.04	1.54
Factor for allocating general overhead	1.22	1.22	1.00
Total cost price	33.95	21.99	1.54
Sales price	36.00	21.00	1.71
Margin	2.05	−0.99	−2.07
Margin/sales price (%)	5.70%	−4.73%	
Annual production (units)	85 000	85 000	
Unit margin	2.05	−0.99	
Margin/sales price (%)	5.70	−4.73	
Total margin	174 342	−84 342	
Margin company (profit)			90 000

Table 25.17 Lorain – Product cost calculations: Question 2 (all financial data in £)

Income statement	DW-1705	CW-1905	Total
Revenues	3 060 000	1 785 000	4 845 000
Raw materials	1 168 750	1 211 250	2 380 000
Salaries			1 245 000
Expenses			280 000
Depreciation			850 000
Total costs			4 755 000
Profit			90 000
Profit/Revenues (%)			1.86

Table 25.18 Lorain – product cost calculations: Question 3 (all financial data in £)

	Only DW-1705	Only CW-1905	DW/CW
Time per year	680 000	680 000	1.00
Time/unit	6.50	1.50	4.33
Units per year	104 615	453 333	0.23
Income statement			
Revenues	3 766 154	9 520 000	0.40
Raw materials	1 438 462	6 460 000	0.22
Salaries	1 245 000	1 245 000	1.00
Expenses	280 000	280 000	1.00
Depreciation	850 000	850 000	1.00
Total costs	3 813 462	8 835 000	0.43
Profit	−47 308	685 000	−0.07
Profit/sales (%)	−1.26	7.20	

Table 25.19 Lorain – product cost calculations: Question 4 (all financial data in £)

Per unit	DW-1705	CW-1905
Sales price	36.00	21.00
Raw materials	13.75	14.25
Added value (Sales – raw materials)	22.25	6.75
Manufacturing time/unit (h)	6.50	1.50
Added value/h	3.42	4.50

Note: Reducing manufacturing time (just-in-time for example) increases rate of added value

Total	DW-1705	CW-1905	Total
Annual production (units)	85 000	85 000	
Manufacturing time/unit (h)	6.50	1.50	
Total activity time (h)	552 500.00	127 500.00	680 000.00
Added value/h	3.42	4.50	
Total added value	1 891 250.00	573 750.00	2 465 000.00
Other costs (less raw materials)			2 375 000.00
Added value – other costs			90 000.00

	Only DW-1705	Only CW-1905
Time per year	680 000.00	680 000.00
Time/unit	6.50	1.50
Units per year	104 615.38	453 333.33
Added value/hour	3.42	4.50
Total added value	2 327 692.31	3 060 000.00
Other costs (less raw materials)	2 375 000.00	2 375 000.00
Added value – other costs	–47 307.69	685 000.00

Table 25.20 Lorain – ways of presenting financial data (see also Figure 25.7)

Revenues	4 845 000	4 845 000	4 845 000
	Profit	Margin	Added value
Cost of raw materials	2 380 000	2 380 000	2 380 000
Direct labour costs	550 000	550 000	
Purchasing costs	115 000		
Variable O/H	855 000	855 000	
Sales and Administration	855 000		
Profit	90 000		
Margin		1 060 000	
Added value			2 465 000
Total	4 845 000	4 845 000	4 845 000

1 The margin for the two products is as shown in Table 25.21. Thus, based on this, a conclusion might be drawn either to increase the sales price of CW-1905 or to cease its production.

Table 25.21 Lorain – margin for the two products

Product	DW-1705	CW-1905
Annual production, units	85 000	85 000
Unit margin	2.05	–0.99
Margin/sales price (%)	5.70%	–4.73%
Total margin	174 342	–84 342

2 The profit is £90 000 and the profit as a percentage of sales is 1.86 per cent.

3 Producing the products separately has the results shown in Table 25.22. Thus conclusion might be to produce CW-1905 only.

Table 25.22 Lorain – Results for producing DW-1705 and CW-1905 separately

Product	DW-1705	CW-1905
Profit (£)	–47 308	685 000
Profit/sales (%)	–1.26	7.20

4 Even though the added value per unit is less for CW-1905 when the manufacturing time is taken into account, the added value per unit is more. Thus, product CW-1905 contributes more to the other operating costs of the firm.

Figure 25.7 Lorain – ways of presenting data.

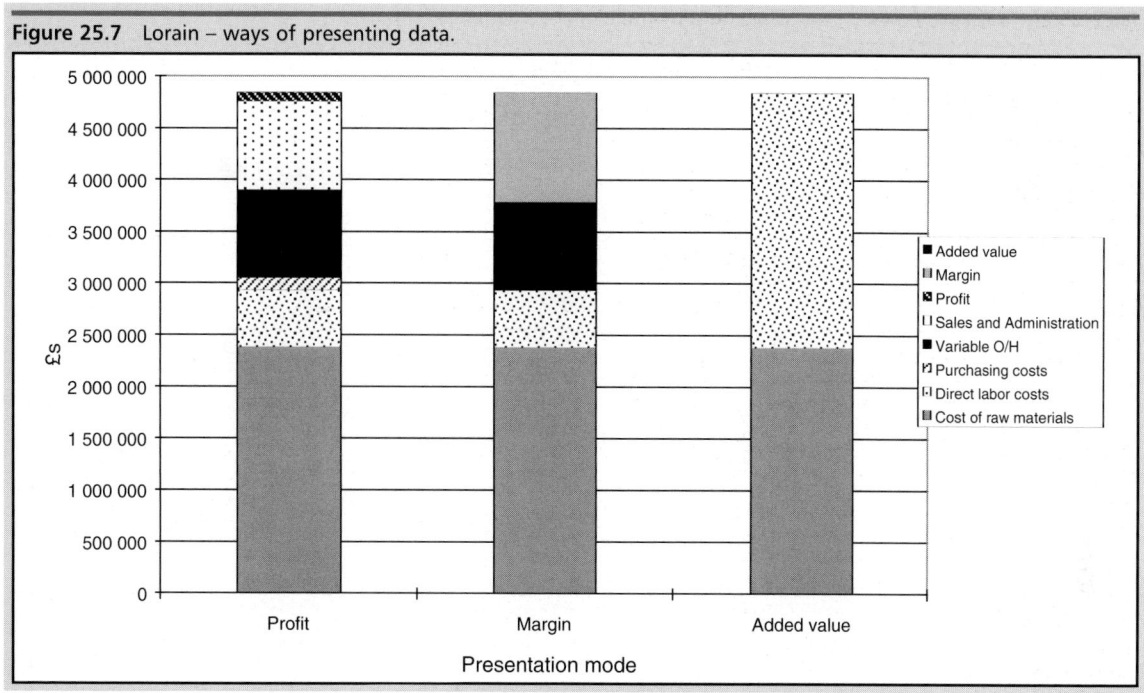

WORKED EXAMPLE: BALEKJIAN CO.

Situation

The Balekjian Co. is a small manufacturing company in the San Gabriel Valley, Southern California, USA, which makes a variety of small control units used on petrochemical and chemical facilities. In one particular month, 240 each of two models, A and B, were assembled. The cost data for these two products is given in Table 25.23.

Table 25.23 Balekjian – Cost data for products A and B

	Product A	Product B	Total
Units produced per month	240	240	480
Labour cost ($/h)	15.00	15.00	
Labour hours/unit	0.50	2.50	
Labour cost ($/unit)	7.50	37.50	
Material cost ($/unit)	17.50	17.50	
Monthly factory overhead			500
Sales and Administrative ($/month)			5 000
Total direct labour (h/month)	120	600	720

Required

1. Based on the data, determine cost prices for Product A and Product B by allocating the factory overhead and sales and administrative costs according to direct-labour hours used.

2. The layout of the assembly of Product A is very linear, equipment set-up times are low and in-process inventory is a minimum. For the month, the total inactive time for the 240 units was estimated at 5h. On the other hand, assembly of product B was more batch-based and, with the equipment used, there were significant set-up times. For the month, the total delay for Product B was estimated at 90 h. Using the activity-based costing approach, by allocating the overhead costs according to the total activity time, develop product costs for A and B.

Solution

Tables 25.24 and 25.25 give the cost prices for these two methods.

1. The product costs are $28.82 for A and $74.10 for B.
2. The product costs are $45.27 for A and $57.64 for B. This means an increase of 57 per cent for Product A, and a reduction of 22 per cent for Product B over the costs calculated with the traditional cost-accounting method.

Table 25.24 Balekjian Product cost calculations by traditional accounting

	Product A	Product B	Total			
Units produced per month	240	240	480			
Labour cost ($/h)	15.00	15.00				
Labour (h/unit)	0.50	2.50				
Labour cost ($/unit)	7.50	37.50				
Material cost ($/unit)	17.50	17.50				
Monthly factory overhead			500			
Sales and administrative ($/month)			5 000			
Total direct labour (h/month)	120	600	720			

					Percentages	
Total costs				A	B	Total
Labour	1 800.00	9 000.00	10 800.00	26.02	50.61	43.72
Material	4 200.00	4 200.00	8 400.00	60.72	23.62	34.01
Variable overhead	83.33	416.67	500.00	1.20	2.34	2.02
Total direct costs	6 083.33	13 616.67	19 700.00	87.95	76.57	79.76
Sales and administrative	833.33	4 166.67	5 000.00	12.05	23.43	20.24
Total cost	6 916.67	17 783.33	24 700.00	100.00	100.00	100.00
Cost per unit	28.82	74.10				

Note: Both Variable overhead and Sales and administrative were allocated on the basis of direct-labour hours

Table 25.25 Balekjian – Product cost calculations by activity-based costing

	Product A	Product B	Total			
Units produced per month	240	240	480			
Labour cost ($/h)	15.00	15.00				
Labour (h/unit)	0.50	2.50				
Labour cost ($/unit)	7.50	37.50				
Material cost ($/unit)	17.50	17.50				
Monthly, factory overhead			500			
Sales and administrative/month			5 000			
Total direct labour (h/month)	120	600	720			
Other activity time for 240 units, hrs	90	5	95			
Total activity time	210	605	815			

					Percentages	
Total costs				A	B	Total
Labour	1 800.00	9 000.00	10 800.00	16.57	65.06	43.72
Material	4 200.00	4 200.00	8 400.00	38.65	30.36	34.01
Variable O/H	128.83	371.17	500.00	1.19	2.68	2.02
Total direct costs	6 128.83	13 571.17	19 700.00	56.41	98.10	79.76
Sales & Administrative (b)	4 736.84	263.16	5 000.00	43.59	1.90	20.24
Total Cost	10 865.68	13 834.32	24 700.00	100.00	100.00	100.00
Cost price/unit	45.27	57.64				

Note 1: Both Variable overhead and Sales and administrative were allocated on the basis of total activity time
Note 2: Increase in cost of Product A is 57.09 per cent and decrease in cost of Product B is 22.21 per cent

WORKED EXAMPLE: TECHNO CO.

Situation

The Techno Co. is a manufacturer of electrical appliances. It has two assembly lines, I and II, which can both be used for assembly of similar products. Line II is a much newer, and more automated, line using computers and automated equipment, while Line I, which has been in operation since the company started, is much more labour intensive.

The cost data for the two production lines is given in Table 25.26.

Table 25.26 Techno – the cost data for the two production lines

	Line I	Line II	Total
Units produced per month	700	1000	1700
Labour cost ($/h)	15.00	15.00	
Labour hours/unit	3.25	0.25	
Labour cost ($/unit)	48.75	3.75	
Material cost ($/unit)	17.50	17.50	
Monthly factory overhead			8750
Total direct labour (h/month)	2275	250	2525

Table 25.27 Techno – Product pricing by traditional accounting

	Line I	Line II	Total
Units producer per month	700	1000	1700
Labor cost ($/h)	15.00	15.00	
Labor hours/unit	3.25	0.25	
Labor cost ($/unit)	48.75	3.75	
Material cost ($/unit)	17.50	17.50	
Monthly factory overhead			8750
Total direct labour (h/month)	2275	250	2525

				Line I	Line II	Total
Total costs						
Labour	34 125.00	3 750.00	37 875.00	62.89	16.96	49.59
Material	12 250.00	17 500.00	29 750.00	22.58	79.13	38.95
Monthly factory overhead	7 883.66	866.34	8 750.00	14.53	3.92	11.46
Total costs	54 258.66	22 116.34	76 375.00	100.00	100.00	100.00
Cost per unit	77.51	22.12				

Note: Monthly factory overhead allocated by direct labour hours

Required

1 Based on the data, determine a unit product cost for Line I and Line II by allocating the factory overhead according to direct labour hours used.
2 If the depreciated charge for Line II was $8,750 per month, what would be the new product cost, with only the remaining factory overhead allocated according to direct labour hours.

Solution

Tables 25.27 and 25.28 give the cost prices for these two methods.

1 The product costs are $77.51 for Line I and $22.12 for Line II.
2 The product costs are $66.80 for Line I and $29.62 for Line II. This means a decrease of about 14 per cent for Line I and an increase of 34 per cent for products from Line II.

Table 25.28   Techno – Product pricing by activity-based costing

	Line I	Line II	Total
Units producer per month	700	1000	1700
Labour cost ($/h)	15.00	15.00	
Labour hours/unit	3.25	0.25	
Labour cost ($/unit)	48.75	3.75	
Material cost ($/unit)	17.5	17.5	
General factory overhead			425
Technology component			8325
Monthly factory overhead			8750
Total direct labour (h/month)	2275	250	2525

				Percentages		
Total costs				Line I	Line II	Total
Labour	34 125.00	3 750.00	37 875.00	72.98	12.66	49.59
Material	12 250.00	17 500.00	29 750.00	26.20	59.09	38.95
General factory overhead	382.92	42.08	425.00	0.82	0.14	0.56
Technology component		8 325.00	8 325.00	0.00	28.11	10.90
Total factory overhead	382.92	8 367.08	8 750.00	0.82	28.25	11.46
Total costs	46 757.92	29 617.08	76 375.00	100.00	100.00	100.00
Cost per unit	66.80	29.62				

Note 1: Factory overhead allocated by direct labour hours
Note 2: Decrease in unit cost in Line I is 13.82 per cent and increase in unit cost in Line II is 33.91 per cent

SHORT-RUN PRODUCTION COSTS

Chapter 12, *Operations and Capacity Planning*, presented short-term capacity planning, where, in the short run, to increase capacity or output, variable resources such as labour and materials can be increased. (By definition, in the short run, a plant size cannot be changed and fixed costs, such as depreciation of the building and machines employed, are independent of the output.) However, increasing labour in the short run has limitations, as illustrated in the following with reference to the short-term production of men's suits.

Diminishing marginal returns

In the short run, to increase output, labour can be increased to work on the machines in the fixed physical plant. If necessary, a second and even a third shift can be added. At first, hiring more people will increase output. However, as the facility and machines become saturated, there comes a point when increasing labour no longer results in a corresponding output. The building space is insufficient and there are not enough machines, so that some employees are idle. As hiring

continues, a situation is reached when the total output actually decreases because additional workers have no machines on which to work, and the presence of these new hires hinders other operators. This situation is quantified in Table 25.29 for the production of men's suits, where the number of employees increases from 0 to 20 and the corresponding output in suits is given.

Table 25.29   Production of men's suits

Workers	Production units/week	Average units per employee	Marginal units per employee
0	0	0	0
1	6	6.00	6
2	13	6.50	7
3	22	7.33	9
4	34	8.50	12
5	50	10.00	16
6	68	11.33	18
7	81	11.57	13
8	92	11.50	11
9	102	11.33	10
10	110	11.00	8
11	116	10.55	6
12	120	10.00	4

13	123	9.46	3
14	126	9.00	3
15	126	8.40	0
16	122	7.63	−4
17	112	6.59	−10
18	100	5.56	−12
19	88	4.63	−12
20	75	3.75	−13

Total output

Figure 25.8 shows the weekly production output in terms of the number of employees. The output increases at an increasing rate up to seven suits, then increases at a declining rate to 15 suits. At this point the output drops as more operators are added to the work centre.

Average and marginal production

The average production is given by:

$$\frac{\text{Total output}}{\text{Number of employees}}.$$

The marginal production is the extra output obtained by adding an extra employee and calculated by:

Unit output with ($n + 1$) employees
– Unit output with n employees.

Both the average and marginal production are illustrated in Figure 25.9. This shows that the average pro-duction per employee increases to a maximum at seven suits, after which it declines. The marginal production is a maximum at six suits and declines to zero at 15 suits, from which point it becomes negative.

Total costs

The costs for an operation are the sum of the fixed and variable costs:

Total costs = Fixed costs + Variable costs.

In the short run fixed costs are considered independent of output. The variable costs are given by the sum of the labour costs plus the material costs, or variable cost is equal to:

(Labour rate, £/h) × (hours/week) × (Number of employees) + (material cost/unit) × (number of units).

The calculation for this information is in Table 25.30. Figure 25.10 illustrates the data.

Average and marginal costs

The average and marginal costs for suit production are also determined in Table 25.30 for positive values of marginal costs:

Average fixed costs (£/unit)

$$= \frac{\text{Total fixed costs (£)}}{\text{Total output (units)}}$$

Figure 25.8 Total production of men's suits.

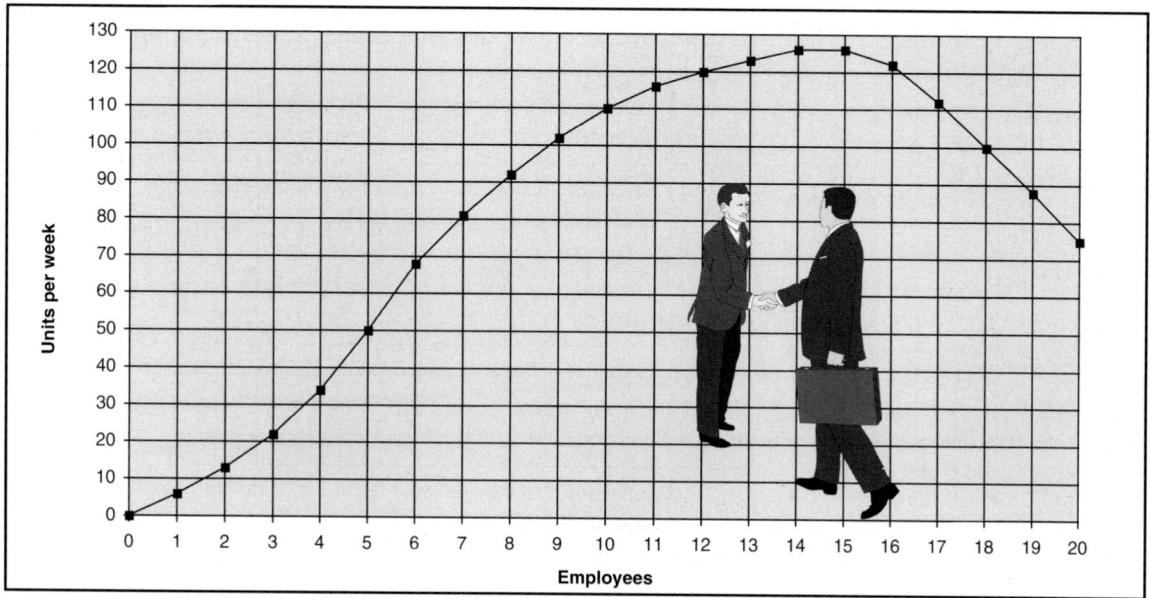

Table 25.30 Costs for suit manufacture.

Wages (£/h)	12
Material costs (£/unit)	35
Hours/week	40

Workers	Production units/week	Variable costs (£)	Fixed costs/week (£)	Total costs/week (£/week)	Average variable costs (£/unit/week)	Average fixed costs (£/unit/week)	Average total costs (£/unit/week)	Marginal costs (£/unit/week)
0	0	0	1 500	1 500	–	–	–	
1	6	690	1 500	2 190	115.00	250.00	365.00	115.00
2	13	1 415	1 500	2 915	108.85	115.38	224.23	103.57
3	22	2 210	1 500	3 710	100.45	68.18	168.64	88.33
4	34	3 110	1 500	4 610	91.47	44.12	135.59	75.00
5	50	4 150	1 500	5 650	83.00	30.00	113.00	65.00
6	68	5 260	1 500	6 760	77.35	22.06	99.41	61.67
7	81	6 195	1 500	7 695	76.48	18.52	95.00	71.92
8	92	7 060	1 500	8 560	76.74	16.30	93.04	78.64
9	102	7 890	1 500	9 390	77.35	14.71	92.06	83.00
10	110	8 650 ·	1 500	10 150	78.64	13.64	92.27	95.00
11	116	9 340	1 500	10 840	80.52	12.93	93.45	115.00
12	120	9 960	1 500	11 460	83.00	12.50	95.50	155.00
13	123	10 545	1 500	12 045	85.73	12.20	97.93	195.00

Average variable costs (£/unit)

$$= \frac{\text{Total variable costs (£)}}{\text{Total output (units)}}$$

Average total costs (£/unit)

$$= \frac{\text{Total variable + fixed) costs (£)}}{\text{Total output (units)}}$$

Marginal cost (£/unit)

$$= \frac{\text{Change in total cost}}{\text{Change in units produced}}.$$

These costs are illustrated in Figure 25.11.

Figure 25.9 Production of men's suits: average and marginal output.

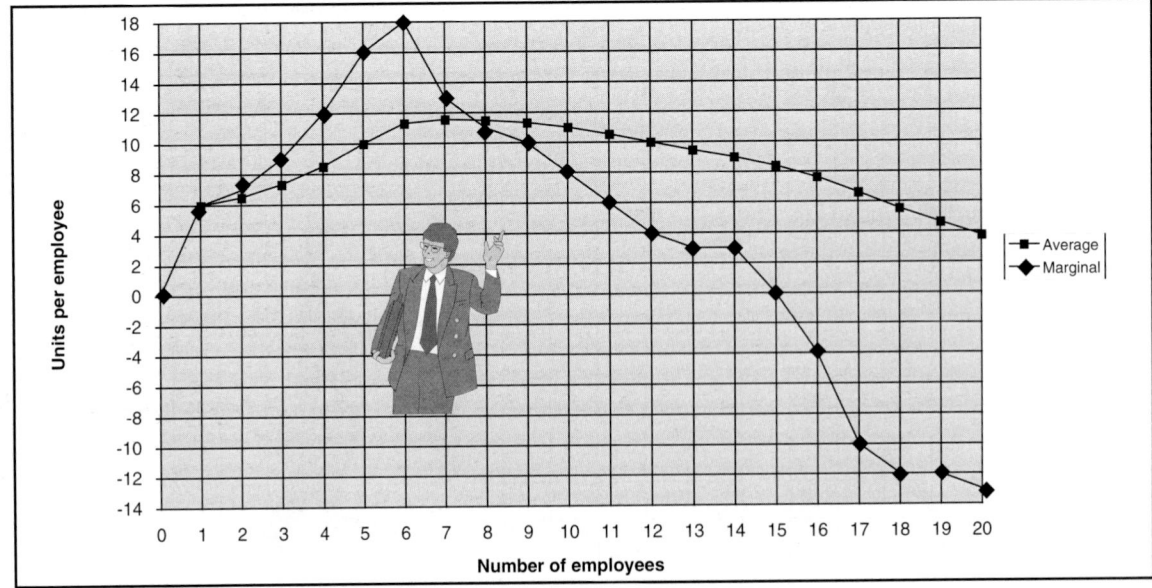

Figure 25.10   Production curve costs for suit manufacture.

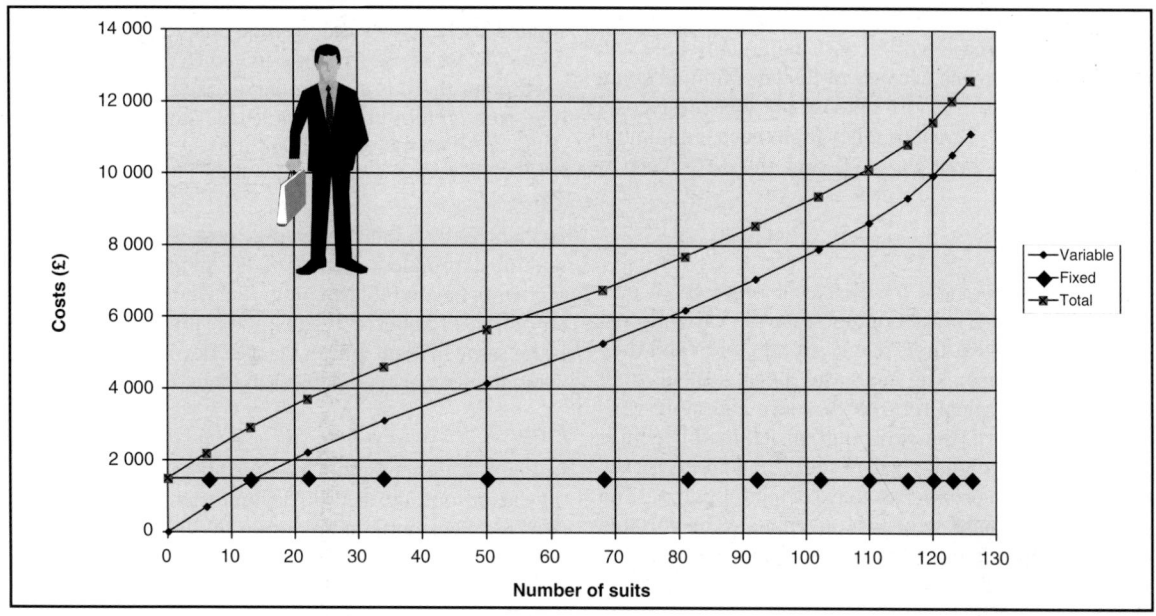

Figure 25.11   Average and marginal cost of suits.

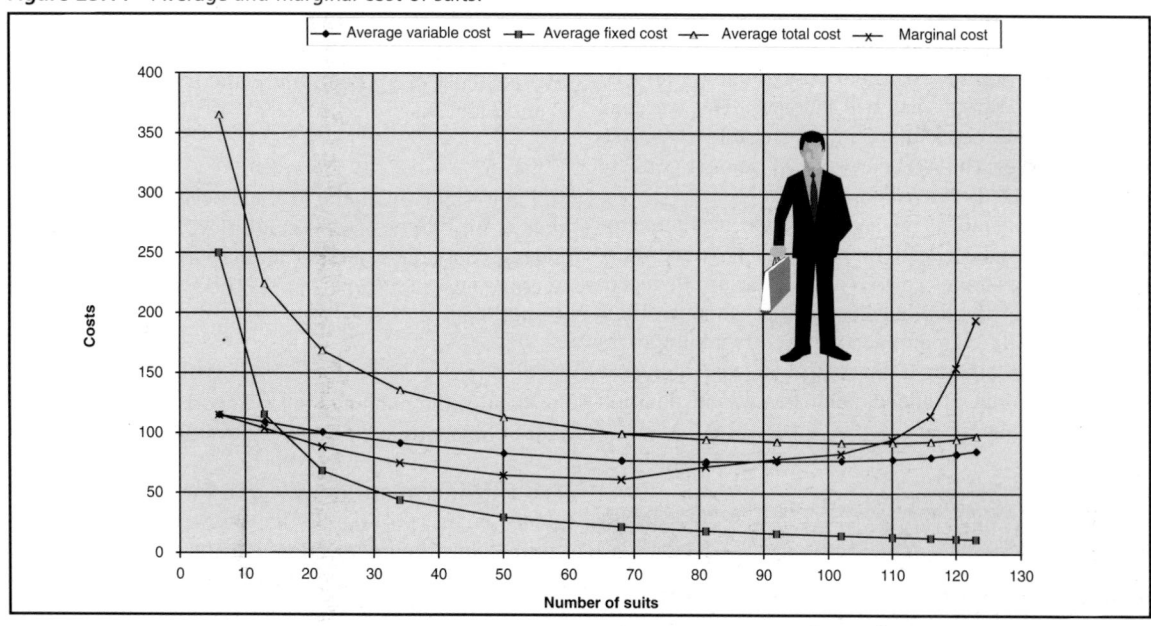

Average costs

The average variable cost (AVC) and the average total cost (ATC) decrease at first to a minimum value and then start to increase because of the law of diminishing marginal returns. As more persons are hired, the costs per unit initially decreases. They then reach a minimum point, at which both the AVC and the ATC start to increase.

Marginal costs

The marginal cost (MC) is that cost required to produce an additional unit of output. Like the variable cost curve, it declines at first, reaches a minimum and then starts to increase. The increase reflects the law of diminishing marginal returns. As more and more variable input is used, the extra output obtained becomes smaller as it eventually takes more and more of the variable input to produce each extra unit of output. The marginal cost only depends on changes in variable costs and not on fixed costs. The fixed cost is independent of output.

The marginal cost curve intersects the ATC curve and the AVC curve at their respective minimum points since the marginal cost is the last number added to both the ATC and the AVC when these values are calculated. When the marginal cost is below the AVC and the ATC, these values will continue to decline. Conversely when the marginal cost is above the ATC and the AVC, these costs will increase. The marginal cost curve intercepts the average variable cost first, since it is below the ATC curve by an amount equal to the average fixed cost (AFC).

The marginal cost is not a value that is accounted for in the firm. Total costs are presented on financial statements and average costs can be easily deduced. However, it is the marginal cost that an operations manager should take into account before adding extra input such as labour. If the marginal cost increases when extra input is added, then the wrong decision would have been made.

LONG-RUN PRODUCTION COSTS

In the long run, management can expand (or contract) the capacity of the physical plant and the corresponding number of machines to accommodate the demand requirements. In the long run, all costs can be considered variable. However, at any specific time period, an operation would be confined to a plant of a certain physical size or capacity and the short-term criteria for costs would apply.

Long-run cost curves

Figure 25.12 shows the average cost curves for manufacturing suits in five possible different plants. For each plant there is a minimum average cost corresponding to a certain production level. The details of these costs are then given in Table 25.31.

Plant 1

In Plant 1 the minimum average cost is about £109 per unit at a production level of 80 suits. As the output increases beyond this amount, the average cost rises. At an output of about 125 suits, the average cost per unit is the same in Plant 1 as in Plant 2. Beyond 125 units the average cost per unit is lower in Plant 2 than in Plant 1.

Plant 2

In Plant 2, the minimum average cost is about £91 per unit at an output of 220. Beyond this point, the average cost rises until, at an output of 255 suits, the average cost of £138 per unit is again a trade-off between Plant 2 and Plant 3. Beyond 255, the lowest average cost lies in the production at Plant 3.

Plant 3

In Plant 3, the minimum average cost is about £81 per unit at an output of 470 suits. Beyond this point, the average cost rises until, at an output of 490 suits, the average cost of £90 per unit is the same in both Plant 3 and Plant 4.

Plant 4

In Plant 4, the minimum average cost is about £73 per unit at an output of 620 suits. Beyond this point the average cost rises until, at an output of 710 suits, the average cost of £95 per unit is the same in both Plant 4 and Plant 5.

Plant 5

In Plant 5, the minimum average cost is about £90 per unit or higher than the minimum average cost in Plant 4.

The long-run average cost curve for all five possible plants is the portion of the short-run average cost curve below the intersection. Portions above the intersection are not included in the long-run cost curve because they do not represent the minimum possible cost when all inputs are variable.

Flexibility

In the long run, the optimum long-run cost is the minimum cost when all the inputs (labour, material and

Table 25.31 Long-run production costs for mens' suits.

Output units per week	Plant 1 Total costs (£/week)	Plant 1 Average total costs (£/unit/week)	Plant 2 Output units per week	Plant 2 Total costs (£/week)	Plant 2 Average total costs £/unit/week	Plant 3 Output units per week	Plant 3 Total costs (£/week)	Plant 3 Average total costs (£/unit/week)	Plant 4 Output units per week	Plant 4 Total costs (£/week)	Plant 4 Average total costs (£/unit/week)	Plant 5 Output units per week	Plant 5 Total costs (£/week)	Plant 5 Average total costs (£/unit/week)
0	1 500	0	90	14 000	155.56	210	38 000	180.95	350	42 000	120.00	620	65 000	104.84
10	2 190	219.00	100	15 000	150.00	220	34 000	154.55	380	43 000	113.16	650	66 000	101.54
20	2 915	145.75	120	16 800	140.00	230	34 000	147.83	410	44 000	107.32	680	67 000	98.53
30	3 710	123.67	130	17 300	133.08	240	34 500	143.75	440	44 500	101.14	710	67 500	95.07
40	4 610	115.25	140	18 200	130.00	250	35 000	140.00	470	44 550	94.79	740	68 000	91.89
50	5 650	113.00	150	19 000	126.67	260	35 200	135.38	500	44 555	89.11	770	69 000	89.61
60	6 700	111.67	160	19 000	118.75	270	35 400	131.11	530	44 559	84.07	800	72 000	90.00
70	7 695	109.93	170	19 200	112.94	280	35 300	126.07	560	44 560	79.57	830	82 000	98.80
80	8 700	108.75	180	19 100	106.11	290	35 350	121.90	590	44 570	75.54	860	95 000	110.47
90	9 900	110.00	190	19 105	100.55	300	35 360	117.87	620	45 000	72.58	890	107 000	120.22
100	11 100	111.00	200	19 110	95.55	310	35 365	114.08	650	53 000	81.54	920	129 000	140.22
120	16 800	140.00	210	19 115	91.02	320	35 366	110.52	680	57 000	83.82	950	185 000	194.74
130	21 000	161.54	220	20 000	90.91	330	35 367	107.17	710	69 000	97.18	1000	230 000	230.00
140	25 000	178.57	230	22 000	95.65	340	35 368	104.02	740	79 000	106.76			
			240	27 000	112.50	350	35 369	101.05	770	92 000	119.48			
			250	33 000	132.00	380	35 911	94.50	800	107 000	133.75			
			260	39 000	150.00	410	35 912	87.59	830	132 000	159.04			
			270	53 000	196.30	440	35 913	81.62						
						470	38 000	80.85						
						500	47 000	94.00						
						530	59 000	111.32						
						560	74 000	132.14						
						590	88 000	149.15						
						620	120 000	193.55						
						650	160 000	246.15						

Figure 25.12 Suit production: long-run costs.

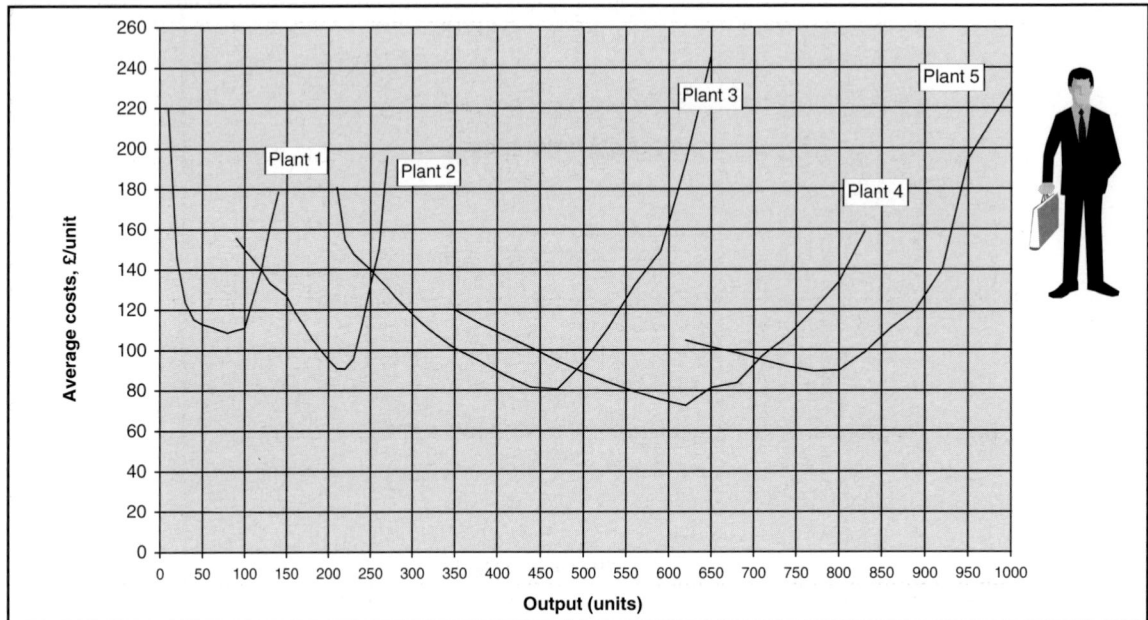

physical plant capacity) are variable. The difference between long-run and short-run operation is flexibility, because in the long run management has the option of modifying not only the people and materials, but also the size and the number of physical plants. There is the phenomenon of economies of scale.

A smooth long-run cost curve exists when there is the flexibility to vary plant size, so that the output corresponding to the minimum possible average unit cost for each plant is just one unit greater than output from the previous plant. This would occur when one is able to add, say, an additional square metre to the plant surface area and/or a fraction of a machine hour, whenever necessary. This is different from the example with the five specific plants, where there is only a step-wise, rather than a smooth, transition. A smooth long-run cost curve is illustrated in Figure 25.13, when there is continuously variable plant size and the long-run cost curve is made up of the minimum of many average cost curves. Moving to the right on the curve corresponds to a slightly larger plant. In the graph, for an output of about 7000 units, the plant size would be the one that has a minimum average cost of £20 750 per 7000 units.

Economies of scale and their benefit

As a firm's operation becomes bigger, it can benefit from the economies of scale because of increased productivity of inputs and the specialization of labour.

Specialization of labour

In the suit production, some workers can be specialized in the dyeing, some in cutting, some in sewing, etc., rather than having all operators doing a portion of each. Thus with this specialization, ten workers may have more than twice the output of five.

Automation

As a firm gets bigger, machinery can be employed, rather than labour. As the suit production increases, automatic machines can be employed for sewing, rather than using hand sewing.

Bulk purchases

With increase in size, the firm can purchase the raw materials, fibre and cloth, in bulk and thus get attractive price breaks, which will reduce the product cost.

When economies of scale exist, the larger firms become more competitive as they can produce at lower average costs. This explains the large size of oil-refining operations, power-generation facilities and the large farms in the USA.

Economies of scale and their disadvantages

With economies of scale, the larger firms become more competitive and thus the small operator gets pushed out of the market place. This explains the following.

Figure 25.13   Smooth long-run average cost curve.

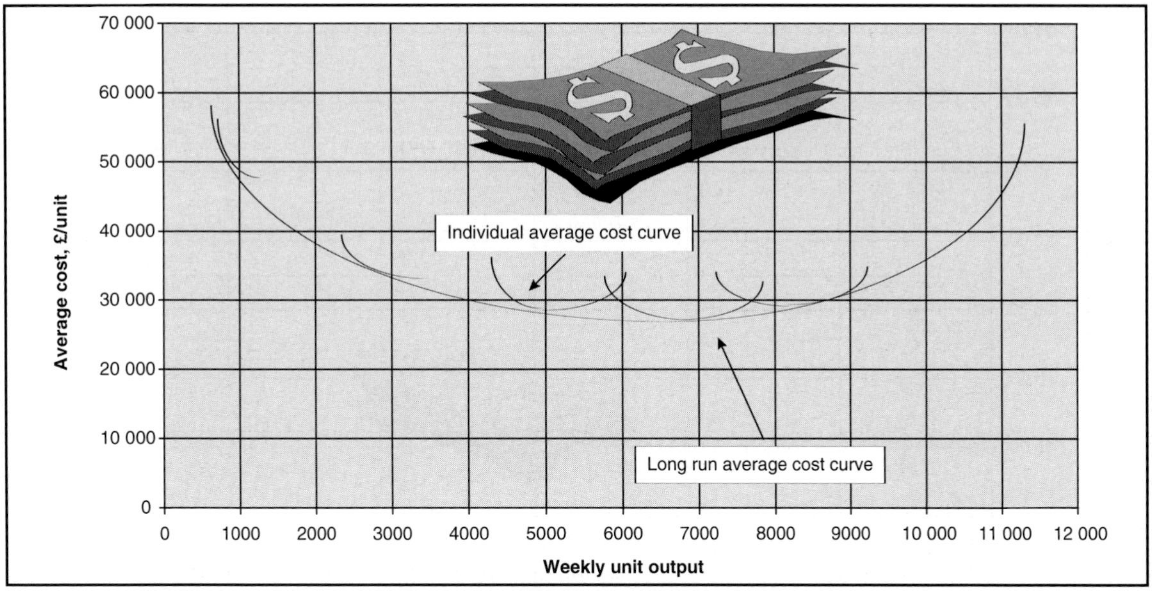

Village grocery store

The small grocery store cannot compete with the large surface area of hypermarkets. This is one reason why, in France, there is now a law forbidding the construction of any more hypermarkets.

Boutiques and small retail stores

Similarly, boutiques and retail stores can be forced out of business by the large shopping malls. This explains the demise of down-town areas, particularly in the United States.

Custom tailors

Customized tailors, such as on Saville Row in London, cannot compete on price with the mass produced clothing industry. Production technology used in the mass clothing industry can provide good quality products at much lower prices.

Farming

Small farmers cannot compete with the larger mechanized operations. This is one reason for their demand for government subsidies.

The economies of scale also explain the demise of exclusive car makers such as Ferrari, Lotus, Maserati, Jaguar, Bentley and Rolls-Royce who have all been purchased by larger, foreign companies. The small market share of these former independent firms made their production activity uneconomic.

Diseconomies of scale

As a firm increases in size, it may encounter diseconomies of scale, which means that the average cost is increasing with output. This may arise because there are too many people and management becomes difficult, workers are lost in the size and become lazy or just avoid doing their work. Diseconomies of scale depend on the industry and in fact may never occur for some firms. Diseconomies of scale are part of the reason why some job-shop operations, such as car repair, dry cleaning and bakeries (in France), remain relatively small.

Constant economy of scale

It may be that the long-run average cost curve is horizontal, or near horizontal (Figure 25.14), so that the minimum on the average cost curve is the same for the small firm as for the large firm. In this case, the large firm would have no significant economic advantage over the small firm, because the average cost remains essentially constant regardless of the output.

Capital outlays and capacity

The article in Box 25.1 illustrates situations regarding long-run production costs, capital expenditure and capacity.[8]

Figure 25.14 Constant economy of scale.

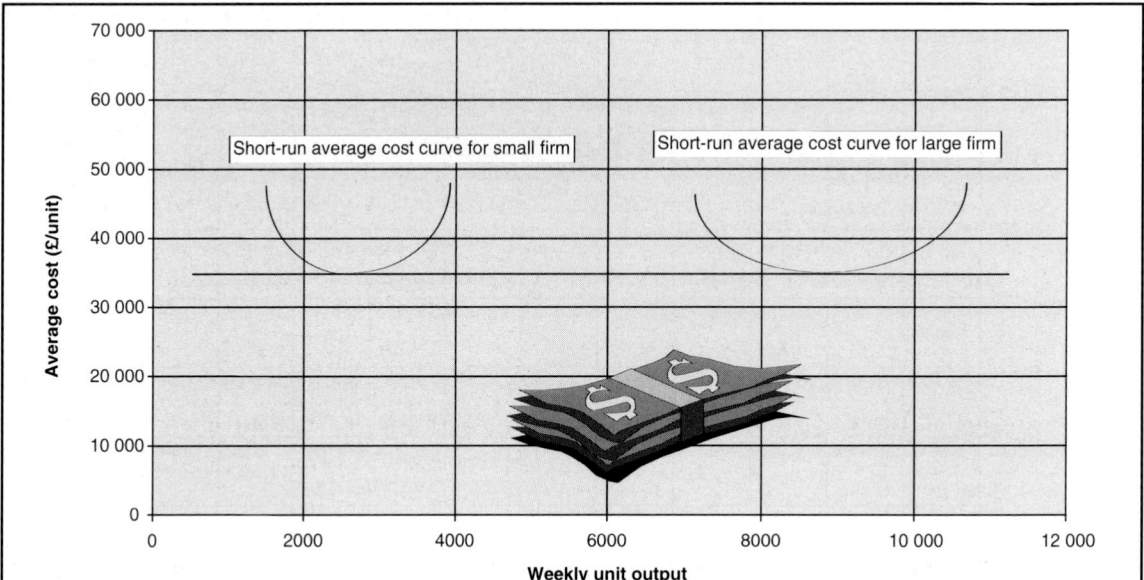

Box 25.1 Lower capital outlays at U.S. factories may boost companies' capacity for trouble. By Fred R. Bleakley, Staff Reporter

Monsanto Corp. scrambled last year to expand its production of nylon fiber when orders poured in faster than expected. It made the St. Louis chemical and agricultural company wish it had planned to boost its plant capacity sooner.

More and more companies may be in the same boat this year if the U.S. economy grows anywhere near as fast as it did in 1996. During the past year, the pace of factory construction and expansion has slowed sharply from the rapid rate of the previous two years. Among the 500 largest manufacturing companies in the U.S., capital outlays for new and expanded plants both at home and abroad plunged by almost 50% in 1996, to about $50 million from nearly $100 million the year before, according to Cimtek Thomas Inc., a Johnson City, Tennessee, firm that tabulates plant-spending announcements. That represents a four-year low in new plant and equipment spending, says Cimtek.

Some Economists Surprised

Such a falloff in outlays won't be a problem as long as the U.S. economy starts to slow, and some recent data indicate it has. But the strength and durability of the current business expansion has surprised many economists and corporate executives, so there's no guarantee that any slowdown will be long or very deep.

As a result, some manufacturers could be caught short even if the economy grows only between 2.5% and 3% this year instead of at last year's fourth-quarter rise of 3.4% from the same period of 1995.

Bottlenecks in production could develop, leading to higher prices and/or a loss of market share to foreign competitors, say some economists. And even if companies try to catch up now with new expansion plans, it would take about 10 to 12 months before any new plant could be up and running.

"If the business expansion continues at a fairly fast clip companies will not have the supply of new production coming on stream that they need," says Joseph Carson, chief fixed-income economist for Deutsche Morgan Grenfell Inc.

He said he expects tighter supplies, followed by higher prices, to show up first in the intermediate stage of the production pipeline – in industries such as paper, industrial chemicals, and rubber and plastics.

Those industries already are running at higher-than-average capacity, and the Cimtek Thomas data show that they are among those that have cut back on expansion plans.

Of course, companies have increasingly found ways to add capacity by modernizing equipment, improving inventory controls and production processes without having to build new plants.

Compaq Computer Corp. has followed that rule in going from a $3 billion-in-sales company a few years ago to $18 billion last year, says Gregory Petsch, the company's senior vice president. In that time, Compaq has increased manufacturing capacity 50% without adding new production space. One way: halving the space for raw materials in existing plants by using hub warehouses, among other things. Compaq also outsources about 15% of its production to other manufacturers around the world.

But Deutsche Morgan Grenfell's Mr. Carson believes many companies "are running close to the end of squeezing every last ounce of capacity out of existing structures." Tighter utilization rates, he expects, will lead to intermediate producer price gains of 3% to 4% this year, after showing a slight decline in 1996.

Price Increases Seen

There is some support for his view in the year-end 1996 survey of members of the U.S. National Purchasing Managers Association. Although overall inflation is seen remaining quiescent, the survey shows that many of the industries running at the highest capacity-utilization rates – including textiles, petroleum, printing and publishing and primary metals – also expect to have the chance to pass along the largest price increases this year.

"We are beginning to move into capacity-utilization rates where price increases are far more likely this year," says Gail Fosler, an economist at the Conference Board, a New York-based business research group. Historically, utilization rates of about 82% begin to give companies more power over setting higher prices because customers are eager to have their orders filled in an expanding economy, she notes. The manufacturing industry's capacity-utilization rate rose to 83.5% in December from 83.1% at the end of the summer.

Still, companies often don't have the luxury as they did in the past of adding new plant space on top of pushing through higher prices. Monsanto wasn't able to raise prices for nylon fiber (used in carpeting) last year just because it was running full out. When that occurred, some of its customers merely switched to a different kind of nylon fiber made by a competitor.

"There were times in the past year when we could have sold more production than we had in place," says Monsanto's chief economist, Nicholas Filipello. The company now has all the production it needs, "but we would have liked to have the capacity in place sooner than we did."

Maria Fiorini Ramirez, who heads her own economic-consulting firm in New York, says price increases may not happen as quickly as they did in the past. "A shortage of capacity in the U.S. now may simply mean more imports," she explains: "In a global economy, there is always someone in the world able to produce at a cheaper rate."

Michael Bradley, Cimtek Thomas's president, agrees, saying that the firm's data indicate U.S. companies could be facing a loss of market share to foreign companies that didn't back off heavy plant-spending plans last year. "The bottom line is that in many industry groups, huge international capacity coming on stream in 1997 may inhibit price pressures in the U.S. and take business away from U.S. firms," says Mr. Bradley.

Wall Street Journal Europe, 11 February 1997
Reprinted by permission of *Wall Street Journal Europe*,
© 1997 Dow Jones & Company, Inc.
All Rights Reserved Worldwide.

SUMMARY OF KEY ELEMENTS

■ Although an operations manager may not be involved in product pricing, an awareness of a firm's pricing strategy greatly facilitates the effective cost management of operations.

■ The market price, or the price market will bear, is the amount customers are willing to pay for the product. For products that are a monopoly in the market, the price may have little relationship to cost.

■ A catalogue price is similar to the market price in that it is a price already published. A company bringing out a similar product that cannot be differentiated from competitive products will probably follow the catalogue price

■ A product price equal to cost plus margin is where a firm adds up all the costs going into the product and then adds a profit margin to give the market price.

■ The target cost is a market-driven cost in competitive industries determined from the sales price necessary to capture a predetermined market share. Target cost is given by the sales price less profit.

■ Variable, or direct, costs are those that change with the level of products produced. They include direct labour, materials used in the product and factory overhead.

■ FIFO inventory management puts a low value on product cost, but a high value on remaining inventory. LIFO puts a high value on product cost, but a low value on remaining inventory. The weighted unit average cost balances out the cost of goods and the value of inventory.

■ Fixed costs are the capital assets for running a business, such as buildings, machines and equipment, and normally have a life of over one year. Depreciation is a way of accounting for fixed assets.

■ Three methods for calculating depreciation are the straight-line method, the sum-of-years digits method and the declining-balance method.

■ Analysing the effectiveness of fixed assets can be made by using the payback, net present value or internal rate of return methods.

■ Activity-based costing is to analyse in depth actual product costs by identifying all those activities associated with the product at each step in the supply chain. In particular, this includes non-value-added time.

■ When capital equipment is used in an operation at the expense of labour, the way this fixed cost is allocated can impact the value put on the product cost.

■ In the short run, the capacity of an operation can be increased by increasing labour. However, there comes a point at which the marginal cost declines. The marginal cost is not an accounted cost but it is a value that the operations manager should take into account in short-term capacity planning.

- In the long run, plant capacity can be increased so that all resources, labour, material and physical plant, are variable. Then there is an economy of scale, in which firms benefit by labour specialization, automation and bulk purchases. This often disadvantages small firms, which cannot take advantage of the economies of scale.

REVIEW AND DISCUSSION QUESTIONS

1 **Product pricing**. What do you think are the main elements in price structure which differentiate the prices of the following products? Indicate which is normally the less expensive to purchase:
   (a) Baby nappies carrying the label Proctor and Gamble and nappies carrying a private label (Tesco, Carrefour, Safeways, etc.).
   (b) An 18 ct gold chain necklace and an identical 14 ct gold chain.
   (c) A silk shirt made in France and a similar silk shirt made in China.
   (d) A compact disc purchased in Germany and the same compact disc purchased in the United States.
   (e) A 1996 Bordeaux wine and a similar wine bottled in 1985.
2 **Retail stores**. In the United States, small boutiques and small grocery stores have almost disappeared in the large urban areas. In Britain, France and other European countries the same is happening, such that governments are enacting laws to 'prevent the decimation of the small communities'. Discuss, in terms of product prices and fixed and variable costs, why the small store is having difficulty surviving.
3 **Service industries**. What are the principal variable costs in the following types of service industries:
   (a) Financial services?
   (b) A medical centre?
   (c) An educational establishment?
   (d) The film industry?
   (e) A department store?
   Why is it difficult to control these costs? What are some of the trends in these industries to reduce these variable costs?
4 **International operations**. Discuss what might be some of the major differences in a cost analysis for a television manufacturer in the Netherlands and a television manufacturer in China? Consider both the variable and fixed costs plus overhead allowances.
5 **Marginal costs**. How would you use the concept of marginal costs to describe the following activities:
   (a) Increasing the level of finished goods inventory?
   (b) Increasing the class size for a university course in Operations Management?
   (c) Increasing the number of skiers permitted to use a certain ski area?
   (d) Increasing the number of grape harvesters in a given vineyard?
   What action is often taken in these situations as a result of marginal impacts?
6 **Economies of scale**. Give some real examples, and justify, where the economy of scale has had the following effects:
   (a) benefited industry and, as a corollary, the consumer and society;
   (b) benefited industry, but to the detriment of some consumers and society.

EXERCISE PROBLEM: ALUMNI

Situation

A small team of ex-students decide to launch a new monthly magazine of 50 glossy colour pages advertising good rates for ski and surfing holidays for alumni of their university. After some discussion, they decide to call their magazine *Second Ecstasy*. Their intent is that the magazine will only be available by subscription at a price of £1.50 a copy. Their analysis yields the following financial information:

- personnel, salaries and secretaries will cost £24 000 per annum.
- Other fixed charges including advertising, telephone, office rental type and photosetting will cost £16 000 per annum.

In addition, the total cost of printing, paper and delivery of each monthly copy will vary with production run, as shown in Table 25.32.

Table 25.32 *Second Ecstasy* – costs for printing, paper and delivery

Number of copies	Variable costs (£)
0	0
10 000	7 575
15 000	10 780
20 000	13 630
25 000	16 170
30 000	18 440
35 000	20 490
40 000	22 350
45 000	24 060
50 000	25 670

Required

1 Present the information graphically for total variable costs, total fixed costs, total costs, revenues and profits according to production levels.
2 From the graph at what level of sales will the students break even?

3 Present the same information on a unit basis, that is, the average variable cost, average fixed cost and the average total cost according to production level. What is the break-even level?
4 What is the difference between the two ways of presenting the cost and profit information?

EXERCISE PROBLEM: GAREN CO.

Situation

Garen Co., in Manchester, England makes metal cabinets for control systems, which are sold to industrial users. The cabinets are standard products and they are published in Garen Co's. catalogue. The average operating data for two of Garen's main products are given in Table 25.33. Garen Co. adds 15 per cent to the product cost to establish the price for its products. The catalogue price for Product STA-3 is £36 per unit, and that for product DIS-8 is £53 per unit.

Table 25.33 Garen – operating data.

	Product STA-3	Product DIS-8
Production costs		
Units produced per month	720	800
Labour cost (£/h)	9.50	9.50
Labour hours/unit	0.75	2.75
Material cost (£/unit)	17.50	17.50

Other costs

Monthly factory overhead (£)	1 500
Sales and administrative (£/month)	5 000

Required

1 If Garen allocates both the overhead quantities according to direct labour hours, how would its product prices compare to competitors' catalogue prices.
2 Assume that, in addition to direct labour hours, there are other activity times associated with the products, including machine time, waiting and storage time of 250 h for product STA-3 and 50h for product DIS-8.

If the overhead was now allocated according to total hours for the product (labour hours + other activity hours), how would this change the proposed product prices for the two products? Would they be competitive in the catalogue of similar articles?

EXERCISE PROBLEM: LAMPS

Situation

The Rey company in England assembles table lamps from components purchased from outside. The inventory records file for all the components that go into making a lamp purchased in the last three quarters is as shown in Table 25.34.

Table 25.34 The inventory records file for all the components that go into making a lamp

	Quantity	Date purchased	Unit cost (£)
First period	3500	1 January 1996	5.50
Second period	3200	1 April 1996	6.75
Third period	2800	1 July 1996	7.75

On 1 August 1996, Rey assembles 8000 lamps using the inventory according to the above records file. No other units were manufactured from this inventory before 1 August. One item of inventory as listed goes into assembling the lamp. Labour costs for the assembly are £3.00 per unit, and the fixed costs, charged against the assembly of the 8000 units, are £18 000.

Required

1 Using the FIFO method of accounting, determine the following:
(a) the gross margin;
(b) percentage mark-up on unit cost;
(c) value of inventory remaining.
2 Using the LIFO method of accounting, determine the following:
(a) the gross margin;
(b) percentage mark-up on unit cost;
(c) value of inventory remaining.
3 Using the LIFO method of accounting, determine the following:
(a) the gross margin;
(b) percentage mark-up on unit cost;
(c) value of inventory remaining.
4 In economic terms, how would you describe the first nine months of 1996 from these purchase price changes? Was this in fact the case? Why does this sort of economic environment make financial planning difficult?

EXERCISE PROBLEM: MANNING

Situation

Frank Manning lives in the Wasdale area of the Lake District, England and is a carpenter who makes hand-made good-quality wooden benches from oak. There are no nails and screws in the assembly, which comprises all dovetail joints secured by a horse-resin waterproof glue. Frank's principal costs are the raw materials, which include the oak slats that he purchases from a supplier in Gosforth, the glue, varnish stain and his tools, for which he needs to replace the cutting blades from time to time. When Frank's production increases beyond a certain level, he uses the services of Willie Greenup, who lives just up the road. Willie is not too efficient, but he helps Frank out with some of the wood-cutting work and, as such, Frank is able to keep up with the scheduled delivery dates. The costs for making the benches according to the number made is given in Table 25.35.

Table 25.35 Frank Manning's costs (£) for making the benches according to the number made

Quantity	Cost	Quantity	Cost	Quantity	Cost
1	464.48	11	1 624.96	21	2 961.92
2	660.08	12	1 700.08	22	3 223.52
3	829.84	13	1 780.00	23	3 520.64
4	976.72	14	1 867.84	24	3 856.40
5	1 103.92	15	1 966.64	25	4 233.76
6	1 214.48	16	2 079.52	26	4 655.84
7	1 311.52	17	2 209.52	27	5 125.84
8	1 397.92	18	2 359.68	28	5 646.64
9	1 476.96	19	2 533.04	29	6 229.25
10	1 551.60	20	2 732.80	30	6 898.23

Required

1 Show graphically the marginal costs and the average cost for Frank according to the number of benches made. Explain the profile of these curves.
2 If Frank sells the chairs for £200 each, show the movement of the total profit and the marginal profit. How does the total profit change when the marginal profit remains positive and when the marginal profit changes to a marginal loss?
3 Determine graphically the quantity Frank must sell to maximize the total profit at a unit price of £200. What is the total profit?
4 Explain why the total maximum profit does not correspond with the number of units sold for which the average cost is a minimum?
5 Below what price does Frank have no interest in producing? Why?
6 If Frank sold the benches at £160, what level of production would maximize Frank's profit?
7 If the Frank sold the benches at £240, what level of production would maximize Frank's profit?

EXERCISE PROBLEM: MOTORS

Situation

After a technical study, a company that manufactures small motor units established that the variation CT of the total daily costs, according to the function of the units produced, could be represented by the following function:

$$CT = 10Q^3 - 200Q^2 + 5000Q + 5000.$$

Required

1 What type of cost does the last term represent? What is represented by the sum of the three first terms?
2 From the above equation giving the total cost, develop a function for the average cost.
3 From Table 25.36 for the average cost, show on a graph the evolution as a function of the motors produced.
4 Market conditions due to competition impose a unit sales price of FF 5000. Above what production level will the firm start to make a profit? Does the shape of the average cost curve show that there is always a profit made above the break-even point?
5 At what number of units sold will the profit be a maximum at a unit sales price of FF 5000?
6 Calculate the total profit that corresponds to a maximum unit profit.
7 Calculate the marginal cost for the twelfth unit, and also for the thirteenth unit. Compare these values to the average cost. What are your observations?
8 What are the shapes of the average cost curve when the marginal cost is less and when it is greater? How does the level relative to the marginal cost compared to the average cost? Explain the evolution of the latter.
9 Calculate the total profit for the company if it can sell 13 units at FF 5000 per unit? Compare this profit with that obtained for a sale of 12 units. Why does a maximum unit profit not necessarily correspond to a total maximum profit? Can the firm continue to increase its total profit by producing and selling 14 units instead of just 13?

Table 25.36 The average cost (FF) of motors

Units	Average cost	Units	Average cost
1	9810	11	4465
2	7140	12	4457
3	6157	13	4475
4	5610	14	4517
5	5250	15	4583
6	4993	16	4673
7	4804	17	4784
8	4665	18	4918
9	4566	19	5073
10	4500	20	5250

EXERCISE PROBLEM: PUMPS

Situation

A company makes industrial pumps for the pharmaceutical, food and chemical industries, principally out of stainless steel. There is both a labour and a machining operation for the pumps. Machining is carried out on automatic numerically controlled units. Table 25.37 gives the processing and financial data for two major models, DIW-17 and GDW-14. There are 125 units of each model produced per month.

Table 25.37 Pumps – processing and financial data for two major models, DIW-17 and GDW-14

	DIW-17	GDW-14
Labour rate (£/h)	15.00	15.00
Labour hours/unit	3.75	17.25
Average material cost (£/unit)	4.25	6.75
Quantity of material (kg)	5.50	3.50
Machine cost (£/h)	25.00	25.00
Machine time (h/unit)	12.25	3.75
Sales and Administration for the firm	£12 250	

Required

1 The firm wishes to establish a product cost based on allocating sales and administrative costs according to labour time and then adding 20 per cent for profit. On this basis, what would be the quoted sales price of the pumps?

2 If the firm allocated sales and administrative costs according to machine time and then added the 20 per cent for profit, would this change the quoted price of the units?

3 Which do you believe is the better method? Or do you believe the firm should take another approach?

EXERCISE PROBLEM: STAMPING

Situation

A company that makes aluminium parts for the automobile and aircraft industries is considering replacing one of the stamping presses it has in its work centre. The new stamping press is faster and almost completely automated, so that, if it were purchased, there would be a big saving in labour costs. Prior to the commitment of purchase the company has established the financial information shown in Table 25.38.

Table 25.38 Financial information relating to the stamping press

Purchase price of asset (£)	1 572 500
Economic life of asset (years)	10
Tax rate (%)	38.00
Cost saving (£)	
Year 1	175 800
Year 2	219 750
Year 3	263 700
Year 4	351 600
Year 5	351 600
Year 6	351 600
Year 7	351 600
Year 8	351 600
Year 9	351 600
Year 10	351 600
Total	3 120 450
Salvage value, new equipment (£)	550 000
Salvage value, old equipment (£)	148 000
Asset cost less salvage	874 500
Discount rate (%)	12.00

Required

1 Based on this information, determine the payback period in years if income taxes are taken into consideration?

2 What would be the apparent payback period if income taxes were not taken into consideration?

3 Illustrate graphically the cumulative cash-flow movements for the two payback considerations.

4 What is the net present value of the investment? Based on the NPV does the investment seem sound?

NOTES AND REFERENCES

1. 'Why whisky costs so much' (1996) *Fortune* 25 November: 18.
2. Based on *Fortune* (1991) 12 August.
3. Based on 'Japan's smart secret weapon: It's a unique cost-management system, and it helps Japanese companies to cut costs, undersell Western competitors, and beat them with new products' (1991) *Fortune* 12 August.
4. *Wall Street Journal Europe* (1997) 11 March.
5. 'Lean enough? Japan's car makers are cutting costs by simplifying their cars rather than slimming their work-forces. This could prove a costly mistake' (1996) *The Economist* 10 February: 61–62.
6. ICBT Company, Rhône-Alps, France.
7. 'Costing the factory of the factory of the future: Factories run by numbers. Numbers to calculate profit and losses to analyse the costs of new products; and to chart corporate strategy. But a lot of managers are relying on the wrong numbers' (1990) *The Economist* 3 March.
8. Bleakley, F. R. 'Lower capital outlays at US factories may boost companies' capacity for trouble' (1997) *Wall Street Journal Europe* 11 February.

FURTHER READING

Alnestig, P. and Segerstedt, A. (1996) 'Product costing in ten Swedish manufacturing companies', *International Journal of Production Economics* 46–47: 441–57.

Bailes, J. C. and Kleinsorge, I. K. (1992) 'Cutting waste with JIT', *Management Accounting* 73(11): 28–32.

Benjamin, C. O., Siriwardane, H. P and Laney, R. (1994) 'Activity-based costing in small manufacturing companies: The theory/practice gap', *Engineering Management Journal* 6(4): 7–12.

Berliner, C. and Brimson, J. A. (Eds) (1988) *Cost Management for Today's Advanced Manufacturing: The CAM-I Conceptual Design*: Boston, MA: Harvard Business School Press.

Block, S. and Hirt, G. (1997) *Foundations of Financial Management*, Chicago; London: Irwin.

Brookes, R. (1995) 'Strategic implications for fresh produce suppliers', *Journal of Business Research* 32(2): 149–61.

Byrns, R. T. and Stone, G. W. (1989) *Economics*, Glenview, IL: Scott, Foresman and Co.

Dhavale, D. G. (1992) 'Activity-based costing in cellular manu-facturing systems', *Industrial Engineering* 24(2): 44–46.

Flesher, D. L. (1992) 'Activity base costing for manufacturers', *National Public Accountant* 28(10): 36–39.

Gagne, M. L. and Discenza, R. (1992) 'Accurate product costing in a JIT environment', *International Journal of Purchasing and Materials Management* 28(4): 28–31.

Gooley, T. B. (1995) 'Finding the hidden cost of logistics', *Traffic Management* 34(3): 47–53.

Griggs, G. (1994) 'Activity-based costing for marketing and manufacturing', *Journal of the Academy of Marketing Science* 22(3): 298–99.

Gruber, R. (1994) 'Why you should consider activity-based costing', *Small Business Forum* 12(1): 20–36.

Harrington, L. H. (1996) 'Logistics assets: Should you own or manage?' *Transportation and Distribution* 37(3): 51–54.

Harrington, L. H. (1995) 'It's time to rethink your logistics cost-ing, Part 2', *Transportation and Distribution* 36(7): 27–30.

Hegde, G. G. and Nagarajan, N. J. (1992) 'Incentives for over-head cost reduction: Set-up time and lot size considera-tions', *International Journal of Production Economics* 28(3): 255–63.

Hicks, D. T. (1992) 'A modest proposal for pricing decisions', *Management Accounting* 74(5): 50–53.

Hobdy, T., Thomson, J. and Sharman, P. (1994) 'Activity-based management at AT&T', *Management Accounting* 75(10): 35–39.

Kaplan, R. S. (1990) *Measures for Manufacturing Excellence*, Boston, MA: Harvard Business School Press.

Kaplan , R. S., Weiss, D. and Desheh, E. (1997) 'Transfer pric-ing with ABC', *Management Accounting* 78(11): 20–28.

Kloock, J. and Schiller, U. (1997) 'Marginal costing: Cost/budg-eting and cost variance analysis', *Management Accounting Research* 8(3): 299–323.

Koons, F. J. (1992) 'Introducing activity-based costing into manufacturing', *American Association of Cost Engineers Transactions* 2: T41–44.

Koons , F. J. (1994) 'Applying ABC to target costs', *American Association of Cost Engineers Transactions*, pp. CSC111–14.

Krupnicki, M. and Tyson, T. (1997) 'Using ABC to determine the cost of servicing customers', *Management Accounting* 79(6): 40–46.

Lere, J. C. (1995) 'Simulations testing the performance of three product pricing rules when applied using data on past oper-ations', *Managerial and Decision Economics* 16(1): 15–32.

Lere , J. C and Saraph, J. V. (1995) 'Activity-based costing for purchasing managers' cost and pricing determinations', *International Journal of Purchasing and Materials* 31(4): 25–31.

Malik, S. A. and Sullivan, W. G. (1995) 'Impact of ABC informa-tion on product mix and costing decisions', *IEEE Transactions on Engineering Management* 42(2): 171–76.

Merz, C. M. and Hardy, A. (1993) 'ABC puts accountants on design team at HP', *Management Accounting* 75(3): 22–27.

Miller, J. (1996) *Implementing Activity-Based Costing in Daily Operations*, Chichester; New York: Wiley.

Nash, K. S. (1995) 'Oracle plugs new product, priding, and packaging', *Computerworld* 29(12): 75.

Pirrong, G. D. (1993) 'As easy as ABC: Using activity based costing in service industries', *National Public Accountant* 38(2): 22–26.

Pirttila, T. and Hautaniemi, P. (1995) 'Activity-based costing and distribution logistics management', *International Journal of Production Economics* 41(1–3): 327–33.

Pohlen, T. L. and La Londe, B. J. (1994) 'Implementing activi-ty-based costing (ABC) in logistics', *Journal of Business Logistics* 15(2): 1–23.

Rodgers, J. L., Comstock, S. M. and Pritz, K. (1993) 'Customize your costing system', *Management Accounting* 74(11): 31–32.

Shapiro, J. F. (1992) 'Integrated Logistics Management: Total cost analysis and optimisation modelling', *Logistics Management* 22(3): 33–36.

Shim, E. and Sudit, E. F. (1995) 'How manufacturers price products', *Management Accounting* 76(8): 37–39.

Tatikonda, L. U. and Tatikonda, M. V. (1994) 'Tools for cost-effective product design and development', *Production and Inventory Management Journal* 35(2): 22–28.

Tippett, D. D. (1993) 'Activity-based costing: A manufacturing management decision-making aid', *Engineering Management Journal* 5(2): 37–42.

Waeytens, D. and Bruggeman, W. (1994) 'Barriers to successful implementation of ABC for continuous improvement: A case study', *International Journal of Production Economics* 36(1): 39–52.

Westervelt, R. (1995) 'New entry complicates propylene oxide pricing', *Chemical Week* 156(10): 9.

Woodside, A. G. (1995) 'Pricing an industrial technological innovation: A case study', *Industrial Marketing Manager* 24(3): 145–50.

Zhuang, L. and Burns, G. (1992) 'Activity-based costing in non-standard route manufacturing', *International Journal of Operations and Production* 12(3): 38–60.

'Pushing the pace: The latest big thing at many US firms is speed, speed, speed. They change manufacturing, order taking, office jobs, to cut costs, lift quality. Gillette retrains its workers' (1994) *Wall Street Journal Europe* 27 December.

26 Auditing operations

Objectives and overview

In business one needs to be efficient, perform quality work and operate at low cost. The purpose of this chapter is to highlight areas to be considered in an operational audit, which is a starting point for efficiency improvements and cost reductions. Some aspects of audits may have already been touched upon in previous chapters, the purpose here is to bring them together under one heading. The chapter begins by defining the audit and then stressing the importance of customer satisfaction and various elements in a customer analysis in order to improve the *customer satisfaction index*. There is a section on the working environment and elements to consider in order to maintain, or improve, productivity. The chapter then discusses key functional areas to consider and presents indicators related to customer satisfaction, inventory, purchasing, quality and production that are useful in measuring the effectiveness of functional activities. There is a section on the supply chain, giving suggested financial measurements and analytical tools specifically directed at this area. The chapter then presents various analytical tools, including Ishikawa Diagrams and a Pareto analysis, with examples, in both service and manufacturing industries. The chapter concludes by discussing benchmarking, giving guidelines for this audit approach.

AN AUDIT

An operational audit, or diagnostic, is a detailed analysis of the firm, the operation or the supply chain to obtain an in-depth understanding of current performance. An audit is conducted because there is a perception that improvements can be made and the audit gives a baseline from which to start making these changes.

Auditor

Who performs the audit depends on the resources available to the firm. A competent external auditing firm, or consultants, can often provide an unbiased opinion of a firm's business. They are able to 'see the wood from the trees'. However, external auditors can be very expensive and often take time to understand the firm in question. An internal audit, by current staff members, is less costly and has the advantage that those involved know the firm. However, it can be biased in that individuals cannot recognize their own difficulties. To avoid this, an internal audit is best carried out with the aid of at least one outside competent consultant. The duration of an audit again depends on the size of the company, and on what is being targeted. It may be a few days or up to several months.

Starting point

Performing an audit, or diagnostic, of an operation takes time (and is thus expensive). One approach for starting is to take a global look at the supply chain from purchasing, through transformation to delivery, particularly noting the level of customer satisfaction (discussed in the next section). Then, once a global viewpoint has been established, break the whole operation into manageable 'blocks' and conduct a detailed audit sequentially on each.

Audit check sheets

Contained in Appendix IV are five useful audit check-sheets for carrying out an audit.

CUSTOMER SATISFACTION

A key starting area in an audit should be at the customer level. The client is king. Firms are in business to make a profit and this implies satisfying the customer with desired products, expected quality and promised delivery. It is the customer who is pulling the products through the supply chain, or is demanding the services of the firm. Customer satisfaction is at the level of the finished product. Satisfied customers, for either industrial products or consumer products, increases market share and thus increases activity at the operational level.

J. D. Power

In the USA, J. D. Power and Co., California regularly carries out customer satisfaction surveys on automobiles sold in the USA, using a customer satisfaction index. One such analysis is illustrated in Figure 26.1.[1] The object of this survey was to position US automobiles with respect to imports. As the article in Box 26.1 indicates, a good satisfaction index from this consulting company can turn a car into an enormous hit. A low index can kill it.[2]

Europe

European auto makers treat Dave Power III (the head of J.D. Power) like a leper. For almost ten years they have done the maximum to prevent him from getting a toehold in Europe, including denying him access to information on their cars and customers. However, their efforts have been in vain. Starting in the UK in 1993 the firm, jointly with the British Broadcasting Corporation, began taking note of drivers' opinions of their cars. In their 1997 survey of 87 models, European models were the worst, while Japanese and other Asian-designed models occupied 24 of the top 40 spots. Sales of Japanese cars, some of which are made in England, are climbing, while those of Ford, Vauxhall (a unit of General Motors) and Rover (BMW Germany) are slowing.[3]

Customer analysis

The following are considerations at the customer level presented in question form. The response is binomial, 'yes' or 'no'. If the answer is no, then there is obvious room for improvement.[4]

Customer levels

Do you have as many customers as you would like?

- The bottom line, or profit, can never be too healthy.
- A growth-oriented company can never have too many customers.
- Customers are the engine that generates revenues.

Customer loyalty

Are the customers as loyal as you would like?

- It is one thing to gain customers. It is another thing to keep them!

Figure 26.1   Top automobiles in the USA, 1989, according to J. D. Power.

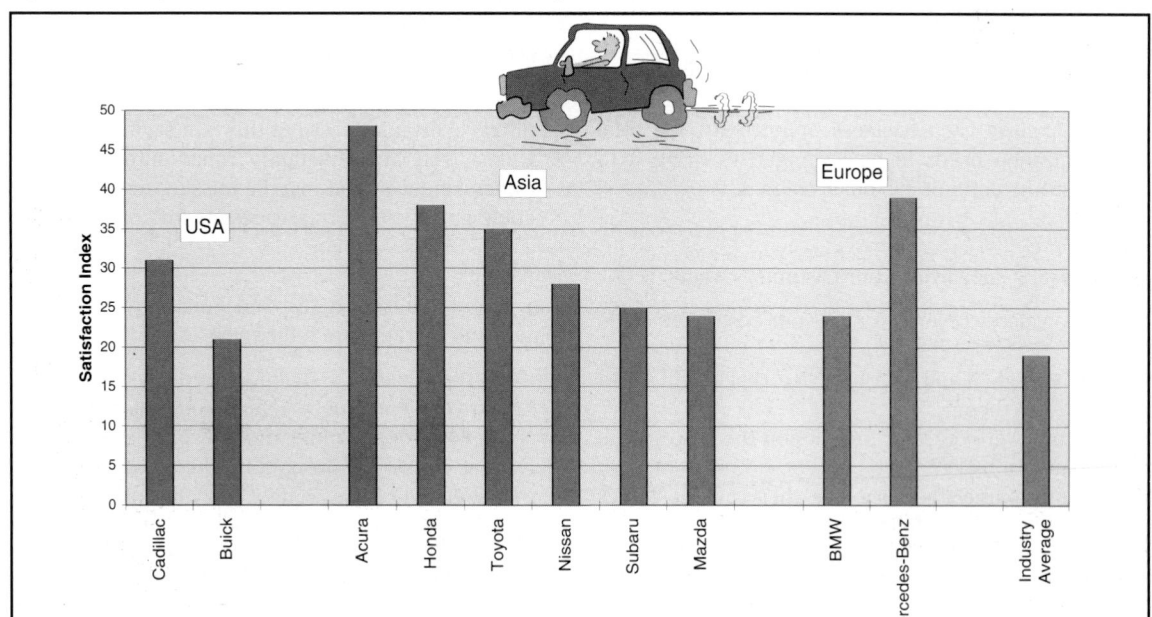

Box 26.1 The power of Power, Agoura Hills, California.

IN THIS rural suburb of Los Angeles, a 59-year-old from New England has become the car industry's most revered, and feared, oracle. A good word from Dave Power can turn a car into an enormous hit; a bad word can wreck it. Mr Power's company, J.D. Power and Associates, is the most influential market-research company in the car business.

A former financial analyst with Ford, Mr Power set up shop in 1968. But he climbed to his current pre-eminence only after spotting that the competitive battleground in the car market was shifting from styling and speed to quality. In 1981 he launched the first of a series of closely watched consumer surveys.

The best known of the Power surveys is the Customer Satisfaction Index, which asks 30,000 drivers to rate the quality of their vehicles and the standard of service provided by dealers a year after their purchase. Other surveys in the Power stable measure the opinions of owners three months (the Initial Quality Survey) and five years (the Vehicle Dependability Index) after purchase.

Mr Power says that if the 1980s were the decade of quality, then the 1990s will be the decade in which car makers pay more attention to distribution. By that Mr Power means everything from advertising to warranty repairs, which can together account for about 35% of the price of an average car in America. In Europe and Japan such costs are an even greater proportion of the final price.

Top ten

Trouble-free models, 1990

1	Toyota Cressida
2	Mercedes-Benz E-Series
3	Toyota Camry
4	Lexus (Toyota) LS400
5	Mercedes-Benz S-Class
6	Buick LeSabre
7	Nissan Maxima
8	Infiniti (Nissan) Q45
9	Toyota Corolla
10	Mazda Miata/MX-5

Source: J.D. Power and Associates

So what does the expert reckon is the best car to buy? Mr Power gives his stock reply: "You should be dealing with a retailer you feel comfortable with." Some help. Mr Power himself drives an 1987 Oldsmobile. That never did very well in any of his surveys.

The Economist 27 April 1991
© *The Economist* 1991

■ The strength of a firm depends very much upon the ability to sustain a strong relationship with customers.

Business volume

Do you generate as much business from each customer as you would like?

■ Critical to business growth is continually increasing sales.
■ To maximize each business opportunity, the total organization needs to be leveraged to bring it to bear at the point of customer contact.

Comprehension

Do you really know what your customers want?

■ Are you alert to every product your customers could use?
■ Do you understand every service that might be of interest to them?
■ Are you aware of every transaction the customer is prepared to make?
■ Do you appreciate every sale that your customer would allow you to follow through?
■ Are you completely tuned into your market?

Team work

Does your entire organization know what your customers want?

■ Customer orientation has limited value unless it is embedded in the very heart of the enterprise. This means at all levels and at every place that directly or indirectly involves the customer.

Communication

Is your information network focused on helping you hear what customers and markets are trying to tell you?

■ The next best thing to reading your customers' minds is listening to what they are saying.
■ Unless you are constantly tuned into your customers' signals, you may be missing messages that could guide you to greater results for your business.

Lead time

Can your organization respond quickly to what customers and markets are telling you?

■ If the flow lines of your information system are not within your customers' reach, you may not always sense when opportunity knocks.
■ Even if customers are getting the message, it may not be enough if you cannot reply rapidly to market signals with information, products and services. In this case, important revenues will be lost.

Proactive response

Does the information network enable a proactive delivery of information to customers?

- Some business plans underestimate the power of information to build customer relationships.
- There is tremendous advantage in using information technology to transform customer information into customers who are generating revenue for your business.

Accessibility

Are the full capabilities of the organization accessible to customers at all locations?

- An office, a branch, a retail site, a representative – these are to a customer your company, a part of the subsystem that is your system or the whole organization.
- It is strategically important to leverage your entire organization by extending its capabilities to each and every point of customer contact.

Service

Does your information network reflect the bottom line importance of customer service?

- Business is built on customers.
- Without customers, there is no business. There is no bottom line.
- Government is also built on customers. The public.
- Whether one is in business, commerce or the business of government, no objective of an information network is more fundamental than enhanced customer service.

The customer is not always the final purchaser of the product. The customer is any group, organization or person downstream of the operation – the next work post, the adjacent work centre, the parent company or the final consumer.

THE SUPPLY CHAIN

An integrated supply chain includes the purchasing of raw materials, manufacturing/assembly and distribution (see Chapter 17, *Managing the Supply Chain*). A global audit of the integrated supply chain might be carried out by analysing the various costs relative to revenues.

Financial measurements

Table 26.1 gives some simplified financial measurements for auditing a supply chain for several products for a certain period. The centre column includes the revenues and costs in pounds sterling. The right-hand column gives the ratio of the absolute financial figures

as a percentage of revenues. This is not a statement that would be found in an accounting document since it includes items that are not easy to measure, such as storage costs and stockouts. However, as was discussed in Chapter 11, *Inventory Management*, these occurrences are important since they represent a measure of the client service level and should be measured in an operational audit.

Tables 26.2 and 26.3 review these indicators, what they measure, comments, their impact on the operation and some considerations for improvement.

WORKING ENVIRONMENT

A good diagnostic also includes analysing the work environment. A poor work environment can be the reason for poor quality, high cost and low morale. Some considerations are given below and these underscore the human relations discussion in Chapter 8, *Human Resources in the System Design*.

Management

Good management is the driving force for a successful operation in order that it can respond to market needs.

Absenteeism

If the absentee level is high in a company, there is a problem. Personnel are unhappy with the management organization and the decision-making process.

Turnover

In a vibrant economy, a low staff turnover (1–2 per cent) is an indicator of motivated employees.

Training

Personnel cannot improve, or be motivated, if management does not make available appropriate training.

Changes

Are changes accepted as a way of improvement? If so, this means that management encourages new ideas, input and recommendations from employees.

Communication with peers

Is the environment created by management such that there is free and easy communication between operators and peer level employees. Do people 'trust' one another and work as a team?

Management communication

Is there free and easy communication between operators and management? Does management have an

Table 26.1   Simplified financial measurements for auditing a supply chain

	£	Percentage of revenues
Distribution Centre		
Total sales revenue	39 648 615	—
Special delivery costs for customer	80 900	0.20
Stockout costs of finished products	1 431 960	3.61
Distance travelled by trucks (km)	198 685	0.50
Total hours (weekly charge)	446 235	1.13
Storage costs of finished goods	436 357	1.10
Total distribution costs	2 594 137	6.54
Margin from delivery	37 054 478	93.46
Production centre		
Storage costs	3 799 118	9.58
Labour costs	8 540 277	21.54
Hiring and termination costs	372 600	0.94
Transfer of personnel costs	0	0
Raw materials purchased	20 448 520	51.57
Total production costs	33 160 515	83.64
Bottom line		
Profit	3 893 963	9.82

Table 26.2   Analytical indicators, as a percentage of revenues, for a distribution centre

Indicator	Measures	Comments	Impact	Considerations
Special deliveries	For unplanned or urgent deliveries to satisfy client demand	Poor planning of deliveries to distribution centre Underestimated forecast Not confident of client's needs Client has last minute changes	High cost (additional planning, special truck, driver at last minute	Work closer with client Integrated MRP/DRP system Modify forecasting methods
Stockout	Inability to satisfy client demand at the right time	Production plan not matching forecast Unforeseen occurrence in production Last-minute client needs	Loss of revenues Loss of clients	Work closer with client Integrated MRP/DRP Modify forecasting methods Higher level of safety stock
Distance travelled by trucks	Charge for distance travelled between work centre and distribution outlet	Normal charge, but may be high as a result of poor route planning	Costs higher than normal eat into margin	Improve route planning (computer tools) Ensure that trucks are full
Weekly charge for truck	Fixed charge for truck based on a normal week Additional costs for overtime Includes loading and unloading time	Normal charge Underutilization of truck because of poor planning engenders unnecessary cost	Costs higher than normal eat into margin	Improve planning Subcontract transportation
Storage costs	Costs associated with holding inventory at distribution centre	Poor planning tied in with customer requirements	Ties up capital More capacity than really needed	Just-in-time management might help
Margin from delivery	Contribution to final profit (revenues less total business logistics costs)	Stockout cost not an accountable cost		

Table 26.3   Analytical indicators, as a percentage of revenues, for a production centre

Indicator	Measures	Comments	Impact	Considerations
Storage costs	Costs for holding raw materials, in-process and finished goods inventories	Some inventory usually necessary for unplanned occurrences Raw materials may be higher because of discounts	Ties up capital Increases storage area Increased management	Just-in-time planning reduces this cost. Reduce product references
Labour costs	Normal labour time and overtime to perform the work	Regular hours a normal cost, but attention should be made to keeping idle time to a minimum Overtime, in the short term, is usually cheapest way to handle excess load	High labour translates into high production costs	Move to low labour areas Automate labour-intensive operations Keep idle time to a minimum Reduce set-up time (SMED)
Hiring/termination	Costs associated with increasing or reducing employment levels Includes interviewing and training for new hires Social and outplacement costs in the case of termination	Hiring policies should be well planned to ensure that growth is sustained Termination demotivates remaining employees May include in the learning curve concept the fact that new hires are not immediately 100 per cent operational	Under normally accounting, not a direct charge to the operation, but an overhead charge Activity-based costing treats this as a direct cost	Improve forecasting, planning to minimize labour fluctuations Use temporary/part time labour
Transfer of personnel	Charges for transferring employees between work centres Includes training, (learning-curve principle)	Employees motivated if they change worktype from time to time Cost is kept to a minimum if employees are multi-skilled	May not always translate into costs as transferred employees may be highly motivated	Optimize to maintain employee moral but keep costs to a minimum
Raw materials	Price paid for raw materials, whether payment is paid on reception, orother terms (2/10 net 30)	Raw material should be received only when needed Timing of payment depends on terms and conditions	Ties up capital More capacity than really needed	Use just-in-time purchasing
Stockout costs	Costs for not having materials to meet production requirements	Results from poor planning Assembly line shut down means labour idle Not a normal accountable cost	Inactive production line is costly Snowballs into stockouts of finished products	Optimize MRP system Reliable suppliers for lead times Include a safety stock
Production costs	Variable costs. Distribution margin less production costs gives operating profit	In accounting includes labour, raw materials and variable overhead	Low production costs (controllable cost) a key to maintaining profit margins	

'open door' policy so that employees are free at any moment to discuss problems.

Objectives

Has management defined a common objective in the organization? A common objective improves motivation and encourages team work.

Customers

Has management ensured that everyone's attention is focused on satisfying customers? All employees must have the customer in mind, whether the customer is the final client or the downstream workstation.

Promotion

Does management make its best efforts to see that career movement and promotion is from within? When there are new opportunities in the firm, effort should be made

to promote from the existing work pool. If this is not possible, the reasons why should be clearly explained.

Performance measurements

Is performance judged by objectives? Setting objectives, and measuring against this baseline, is an equitable way of managing and is what everyone understands.

Decision-making

Is decision-making by consensus? If a large number of people are involved in the decision process, it is easier to put that decision into effect (see the section 'Attitude toward employers', in Chapter 8, *Human resources in the system design*).

Personnel involvement

Management leads, and the employees follow that lead. The measure of management's success can to a certain extent be measured by how easy it is for other employees to become involved.

Motivation

Are personnel motivated at all levels in their work? Everyone in the organization must be motivated, from those who take care of cleaning and warehouse managers, up to the supervisory and middle-management level. All employees must be made to feel they are part of a team.

Quality

Are personnel encouraged to do the job right the first time? Quality the first time minimizes waste, and hence cost. Quality training programmes need to be available.

Stopping the facility

In any production, can operators stop the facility if there is a problem? Giving operators this responsibility lets them know they are part of the 'big picture'. This is enriching and motivating.

Multiskilling

Are personnel encouraged to be multiskilled? To be multiskilled involves taking advantage of additional training, and there has to be a motivation to take this training, for example, the prospects of a more interesting job, greater security of employment, international assignments, a higher salary, etc.

Documentation

With the different technologies employed, activities in different languages and conformity to certain standards, either client specifications or norms such as ISO-9000 (see the Chapter 4, *Quality Management*) or ISO-14000 (see Chapter 5, *An Environmental Balance*), documentation is always needed.

Availability

Is the documentation easily available? Instruction manuals should always be near the workstation. (This is also a requirement of the ISO-9000 quality certification.)

Ease of use

Easy language should be used so that operators can easily follow instructions. If necessary, documetation should be available in all languages of the employees.

Detail

The documentation should be sufficiently detailed. Missing information can cause problems.

Up to date

Documentation should be up to date and correspond to the system or equipment in use. Out of date documentation wastes time and may be a safety problem.

Physical environment

Is the work facility organized, clean, pleasing and efficient? Does it have a low noise level? Is it safe? The Japanese are very rigorous in this respect (see the section on the five S rules in Chapter 15, *Lean Production and Just-in-Time*).

KEY FUNCTIONAL AREAS

Areas to consider in an audit, and what data to collect, depend very much on the firm and the type of operation. A service organization would be different from a manufacturing or distribution firm where material goods are being handled. However, key general areas to consider that apply to many organizations are discussed in the following.

Forecasting

- What are the forecasting procedures for determining client needs?
- What forecasting tools are used?
- How accurate are forecasts compared to actual requirements?
- How good are the forecasts for managing the production operation?
- If client demand changes, has the production operation the flexibility to respond?

Chapters 9 and 21, *Forecasting Customer Demand* and *Additional Forecasting*, give more detail.

Purchasing

- In what quantities are raw materials and component parts delivered?
- How many suppliers are there?
- What are the lead or delivery times for raw materials, component parts and packaging (boxes, cartons, bottle tops, labels, etc.)?
- Is the quality of goods received according to specification?
- How quickly do the raw material goods turn over?
- What is the order processing cost per cycle?

See also Chapter 16, *Purchasing and Subcontracting*.

Inventory management

- What is the inventory policy for raw materials, packaging, in-process inventory and finished goods?
- How many product references are there?
- What is the average value of inventory during a cycle?
- What is the inventory carrying cost?
- What is the inventory turnover?
- What is the record accuracy?
- What is the ratio of inventory to sales?
- What is the value of working inventory?
- What is the value of safety stock?
- What is the value of waste?
- What is the value of work-in-process inventory at each value-added step?
- What is the value of raw materials?
- When is the supplier paid for raw materials?
- What is the value of finished goods inventory?
- Are finished goods made to order or made to stock? Producing to order simplifies the production forecast.
- Is there a certain shelf life for the products (perishable or obsolete)?
- What is the quality of finished goods as measured by customer complaints?
- What is the basis for keeping stock. Is it:
  - Uncertainty of customers?
  - Long supplier delivery times?
  - Lack of confidence in suppliers?
  - Lack of sufficient production capacity?
  - Insufficient transportation needs?
  - Poor scheduling?

See Chapter 11, *Inventory Management*, for more detail.

Production operation

- Are production quantities made as an economic batch, or just-in-time?
- Does an integrated planning system exist?
- Are there frequent changes to satisfy important clients?
- What is the average run length of operations?
- How quickly can the firm respond to customer demands?
- Is the facility layout optimum for the production operation?

- Are employees motivated?
- What is the level of manual labour compared to automation?

See Chapters 10, *Design of the facility layout*, 12 *Operations and capacity planning* and 13, *Material requirements planning*, for more information.

INDICATORS

The following are some indicators that can be used to determine how well operations, and functions within those operations, are being managed. These indicators rely on accurate records being kept of past operating performance. Also, to be meaningful, they should be calculated periodically for a set time period, say one year, to see if improvements are being made. An analysis every month, or every quarter, might be an appropriate time scale, although again this depends on the type of business.

Customer service level

Customer service level is a measure of customer satisfaction regarding delivery of specific identified goods or services. Some measurements would include the following.

Service according to availability of orders of finished product

This is the product availability as a percentage of the orders demanded by the customer. It is given by:

$$100 - \frac{\text{number of incomplete orders} \times 100}{\text{Total orders demanded}}$$

For example, a food company may have given a producing firm 25 orders for different products. How many of these orders can be filled out of existing inventory, or produced in time to meet the required delivery date? How many of the orders have to be put on backorder? If two out of the 25 were incomplete, the customer service level would be 92 per cent:

$$100 - \frac{2 \times 100}{25} = 92 \text{ per cent}$$

Service according to availability of units of finished product

This indicator is similar to the previous one, except that it measures the service level as a percentage of the number of units supplied:

$$100 - \frac{\text{Stockouts in units for period} \times 100}{\text{Total units demanded}}$$

If a client puts in an order for 250 units, maybe with many different references, and out of these only 240 can be supplied (stockout of 10), then the customer service level would be 96 per cent:

$$100 - \frac{10 \times 100}{250} = 96 \text{ per cent}$$

Delivery

Delivery service level to the client can be measured by:

Delivery service level (%) =

$$\frac{100 - \text{Number of late (or early shipments)}}{\text{Total number of shipments ordered}}.$$

A client makes an order for 20 shipments of items, which are promised on a certain date, or on certain dates. One is not delivered on time and thus the service level is 95 per cent:

$$100 - \frac{1 \times 100}{20} = 95 \text{ per cent}$$

Order cycle time

The order cycle time, or the production lead time, is the elapsed time from the customer placing the order to when the customer receives the order. It is an indicator of the flexibility of an organization. One of the challenges to industry is to reduce lead times. One of the strategies of the Hewlett-Packard company is to cut production lead times by 50 per cent. This may be less than a day (local suppliers) or several weeks.

Product availability combined with order cycle time

This quantitative measure might be, for example, that 95 per cent of orders can be delivered within one week.

System flexibility

This is the ability of a firm, in time units (hours, days, weeks) to respond to special and/or unexpected needs of a customer by expediting the required order.

The information system

A firm's information system must be able to respond in a timely and accurate manner to a customer's request for information about a product or a service. For example, can the customer make contact directly though electronic mail?

System malfunction

This is concerned with the efficiency, procedures and time required to recover from a system malfunction, such as a billing error, a wrong shipment, a shipping damage claim, etc.

After-sales service

This is the efficiency (time) in providing product support, such as technical help, after delivery of the product or service.

Minimum order size

This is the minimum order size a firm is willing to supply to a client. Are you prepared to provide service to your small clients, who may only ask for one item?

Emergency orders

Are you willing, and able, to supply units outside normal working hours, such as at night, at weekends and during vacation periods?

Delivery frequency

Are you able to deliver frequently in small lot sizes, so that the client can operate in a just-in-time mode?

Delivery reliability

When a delivery date is fixed, are you able to keep to this date and time?

Inventory management

Inventory management is a key indicator of how efficiently a manufacturer or a distribution company is operating. Holding inventory is costly. It can become obsolete, spoil (perishable products), be damaged or be stolen.

Average inventory level during a cycle

During the inventory cycle (the period between one order and the next) the average inventory is:

$$\frac{\text{(Beginning value of inventory} + \text{Ending value of inventory}}{2}.$$

The average inventory for each reference item should be measured and not the total inventory.

Order processing cost per cycle

This ordering cost is given by:

$$\frac{\text{(Total demand in units)} \times \text{(Cost of each order)}}{\text{Units per order}}.$$

and can be applied if orders are purchased from outside. If orders are placed inside, they involve set-up and other preparation costs.

Inventory carrying cost

This covers the total cost of financing, warehousing, insurance, theft, waste, obsolescence, etc.

Inventory turnover

This is defined as:

$$\frac{\text{Cost of goods sold}}{\text{Value of inventory}}$$

Thus, the greater the inventory turnover, the more efficient is the operation and the lower is the inventory holding cost. Box 26.2 gives an illustration.[5]

Inventory-to-sales ratio

This ratio:

$$\frac{\text{Value of inventory}}{\text{Sales volume}}$$

gives the value of the finished goods inventory (for example) relative to the sales for a given time period. The lower the value, the more efficient is the firm in turning over the inventory. This is a similar measure to inventory turnover, but in the reverse sense.

Record accuracy

Mistakes can be made in the recording of inventory. Records may indicate that there is more inventory in stock than is in fact the case. Thus, when the time comes to use this 'inventory' for a production operation, it is not available. Alternatively, when the time comes to supply the customer with the finished goods, the products are not there. Record accuracy can be measured by:

$$\frac{\text{Number of inaccurate records during a cycle count}}{\text{Number of items counted during cycle}}$$

Box 26.2 Electronics industry

Pittiglio Rabin Todd & McGrath indicated that in their study of US electronics companies the inventory turnover had improved some 15 per cent per year in the period 1981 to 1990 (Figure 26.2). They stress the importance of improving inventory turnover to free up assets that can be used in other ways to improve operating performance, such as investment in new products, stock buyback, or upgrading capacity. This figure gives the reduction in inventory investment of their study for the average electronics company as a function of the cumulative incremental investment. For example, if the inventory turnover increases one turn, from say two to three, then the reduction in inventory investment would go from $130 million to $220 million or a difference of $90 million. For two turns the difference would be $150 million ($280 million less $130 million).

From *Insight* (1991) Fourth quarter

Figure 26.2 Inventory turnover in the US electronics industry.

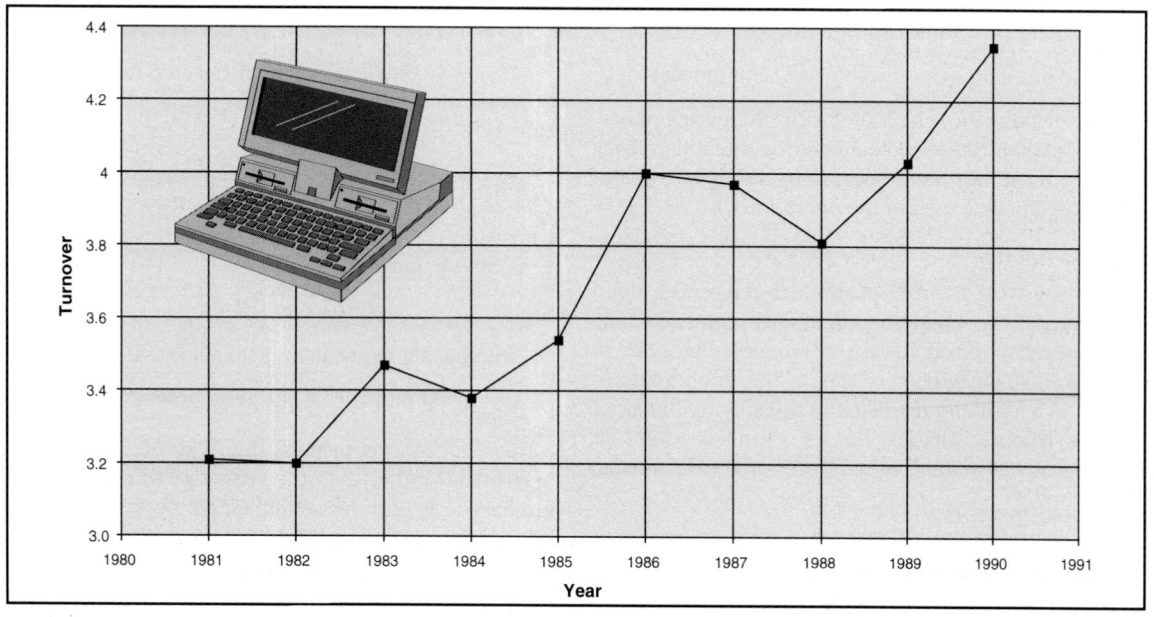

Record accuracy is improved by using bar coding on items, at purchase, in process or at finished-goods stage.

The average value of working inventory

This is the amount of money invested in the inventory that goes up to make the working material of the organization. To keep this value to a minimum, quantity discounts are an advantage. However, if this means buying in large quantities, it may not effectively reduce the value of the working inventory. The value is calculated by

$$\frac{(\text{Number of items ordered}) \times (\text{Value})}{2}.$$

The value of safety stock

This is:

Total inventory value – Value of working inventory.

Obviously the closer this value is to zero, the better. Safety stock is dead stock and only adds to the cost of doing business. Safety stock can be reduced by minimizing the uncertainty of the operation, for example, choosing suppliers who are reliable on delivery dates and material quality, fine tuning the production operation so that unplanned shutdowns are minimized or trying to anticipate customer needs better.

Inventory as a percentage of assets

This is given by:

$$\frac{\text{Value of inventory}}{\text{Value of total assets (inventory + equipment)}}.$$

The lower this ratio, again the better the performance. (Benchmarking these indicators with dissimilar firms may not be appropriate, because of different types of capital equipment used in the operations.)

Product references

This is the total number of product references managed during the operation. Customer demands may result in many different item references, but even so some products may be very similar (fasteners that are similar in length and diameter, plastics components of varying colours, chassis frames of many different sizes). A higher number of different references means:

- greater inventory;
- increased ordering costs;
- larger stocking costs;
- more management attention;

- the greater the possibility of errors.

Henry Ford (Chapter 1, *Positioning Operations Management*) had this in mind in the production of the Model T automobile. His operating approach was that, 'A customer can have what car he likes as long as it is black!' Thus, with this very standard product, the number of product references of automobile components was kept very low. An audit should ask the question, 'Can the number of references be reduced without jeopardizing customer satisfaction?'

Waste

Material lost is throwing money out of the window. Waste can be accounted for as follows and every effort needs to keep this value as low as possible:

$$\frac{\text{Cost of material lost in period}}{\text{Average value of material in period}}.$$

Product quality

Some indicators for the quality of products received, or delivered are:

- in terms of lots:

$$100 - \frac{\text{Number of lots rejected}}{\text{Total number of lots received}};$$

- in terms of components rejected:

$$100 - \frac{\text{Number of parts rejected}}{\text{Total number of parts received}};$$

- in financial terms:

$$100 - \frac{\text{Financial value of rejected items}}{\text{Total financial value of shipments}};$$

Purchasing costs

A measure of the efficiency of the purchasing department can be measured by:

$$\text{Costs per order} =$$

$$\frac{\text{Purchasing department asministrative costs}}{\text{Total number of purchase orders}}.$$

This indicator considers the cost of running the department, rather than the costs tied to the products purchased. It can be manipulated by issuing more orders for smaller quantities, whereas real purchasing efficiency may be in the opposite direction (issuing fewer orders for larger quantities).

Production

Some indicators of product efficiency are as follows.

Set-up time of a machine

In a given period, say one week:

$$\text{Set-up time (\%)} = \frac{\text{Total set-up times}}{\text{Operating + Set-up time}}.$$

Time loss due to machine breakdowns

In a given period, say one week:

$$\text{Downtime (\%)} = \frac{\text{Total time machines are down}}{\text{Total time (running + shutdown)}}.$$

Time loss due to rework of components

In a given period, say one week:

$$\text{Lost time (\%)} = \frac{\text{Time spent on rework}}{\text{Total time spent on producing units}}.$$

Production costs

Production costs, or the total unit cost for producing an order (by product), eat into the profit margin. If production costs can be reduced, then for the same sales price, margins can be increased. Alternatively, lower production costs may allow a reduced sales price, which could increase market share. (see the Hershey Co. example in Chapter 2, *Strategy of organizations.*)

Use of data processing

Verbal orders, paper commands or checkboards can be misread or misinterpreted. Using data processing can increase speed and reduce errors, thus allowing a better response to customer needs. The indicator is:

$$\frac{\text{Orders sent by EDI in a certain period}}{\text{Total orders dispatched in the same period.}}$$

Support services

The support personnel compromise all support services, such as maintenance, subcontractors, inspectors, part-time labour, administration, etc. Those services that are not adding value to the production operation should be kept to a bare minimum. Operators should be their own inspectors and, where possible, perform maintenance. Record keepers can be reduced by using data processing. The indicator is:

$$\frac{\text{Number of support personnel in the operating unit}}{\text{Total personnel in the same operating unit.}}$$

ANALYTICAL TOOLS

Analytical tools are the instruments available to carry out the audit. They may be quantitative or qualitative in nature. Some have already been treated in previous chapters, but for completeness they are referred to again in this section.

Pipeline map

A pipeline map is an analysis carried out in order to understand the activities in the physical supply chain and would include raw materials, components, packaging, reception, transformation and transportation. A pipeline map is broken down into 'length' and 'volume' to represent the leanness and flexibility of the system. (see Chapter 17, *Managing the Supply Chain*).

Process flow chart

A process flow chart shows the flow of materials between successive units in order to locate the value-added and non-value-added activities (see Chapter 7, *Process Design and the Operations Network*).

Ishikawa diagrams

An Ishikawa diagram, named after its inventor and also known as a fishbone diagram because of its shape, can be used to examine an operation in detail. It is a very useful brainstorming tool for looking first at all eventualities.

Manufacturing operation

Figure 26.3 is a fishbone analysis that might be used to analyse why an excessive number of defective products are being produced. In this example there are six major potential problem areas, together with identifiable situations within each area:

- the physical work environment;
- labour employed;
- machines employed;
- management;
- methods;
- materials.

Other areas that might be considered include financial – insufficient capital, inadequate cash flow, late payment by customers, high costs and the like.

Figure 26.3 Ishikawa diagram for a manufacturing operation.

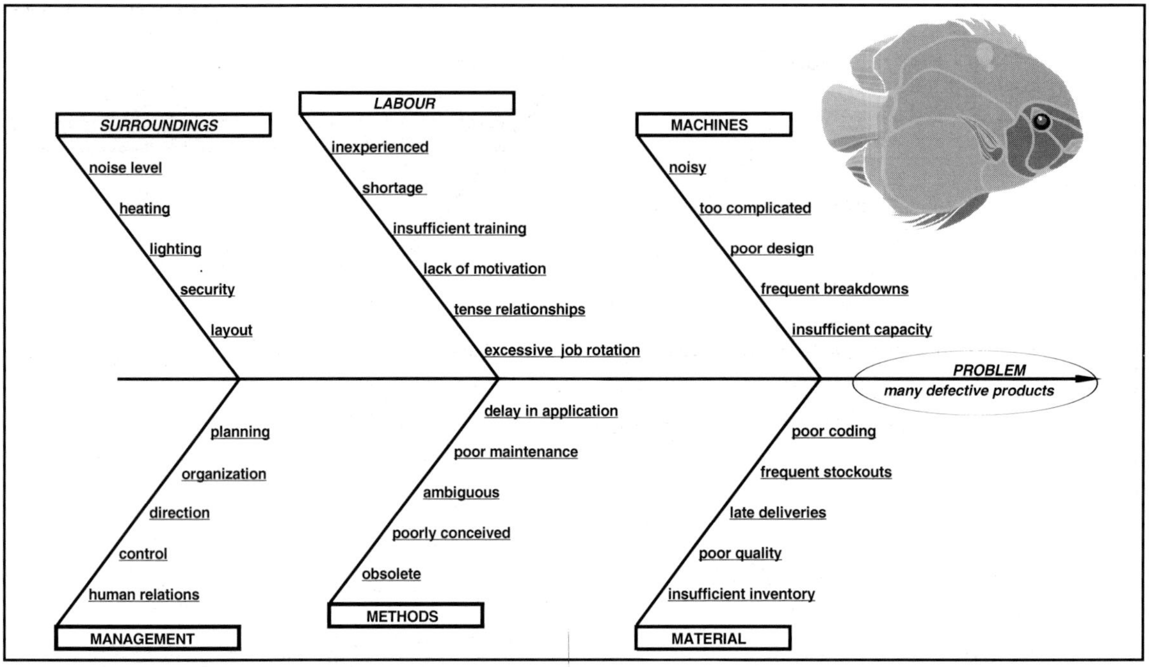

Service operation

Figure 26.4 gives some of the considerations in analysis of a service operation such as a restaurant. In this example, there are six major potential problem areas, together with identifiable situations within each area:

- delay;
- food;
- environment;
- employees;
- beverages available;
- services offered.

An Ishikawa diagram can be developed for just about every operation. As an analytical tool, it is best used by starting from the right-hand side (the head of the fish bone), which is the principal indicator for the operation and then working backwards identifying specific elements.

Frequency checksheet

A frequency checksheet can be used to indicate how often any problem may be occurring with a particular product. For example, Table 26.4 gives a checksheet for problems occurring in a food production unit. This can be further developed into a Pareto analysis.

Table 26.4 A checksheet for problems occurring in a food production unit

Production line	Problems occurring in one week
Slab chocolate	12
Boiled sweets	15
Soft sweets	8
Mustard	4
Spices	3
Mixed chocolates	8
Total	50

Pareto analysis

A Pareto analysis, after Vilfredo Pareto a 19th century Italian economist, is a graphical representation showing the frequency of the causes of a problem (see Chapter 20, *Statistical Concepts*). The following are three examples, which give a histogram for the exact frequency of occurrence and a line diagram giving the cumulative amounts.

Manufacturing

A Pareto analysis for lost time on a machine is shown in Figure 26.5. Non-quality material is the major problem, which may be directly related to suppliers.

Figure 26.4 Ishikawa diagram for a restaurant.

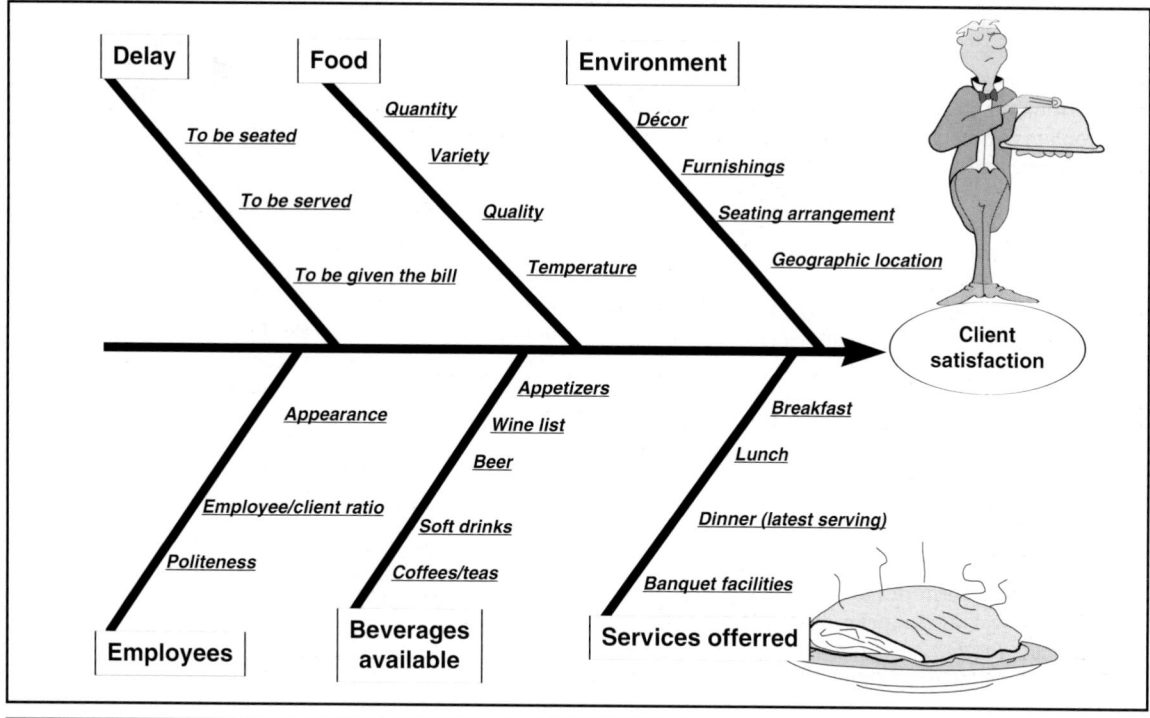

Figure 26.5 Pareto analysis: lost time on a machine.

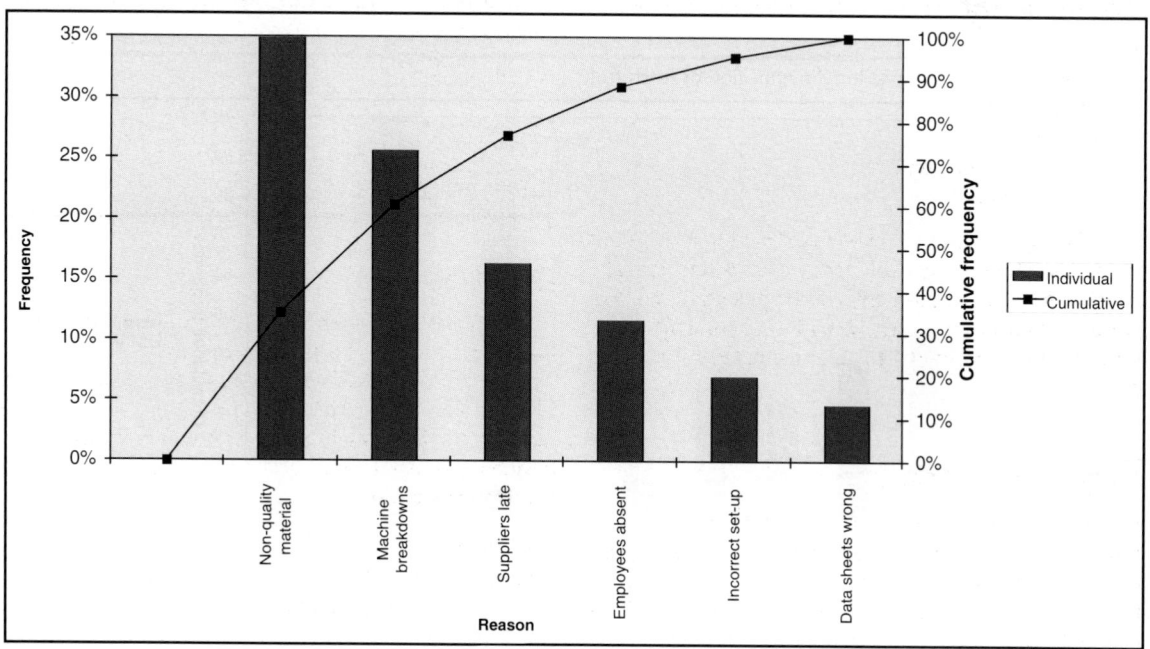

Distribution

A Pareto analysis for lorry distribution of fresh fruit is given in Figure 26.6. Fruit squashed is the problem that occurs most frequently (about 40 per cent of the time). However, bacteria on fruit may be a more critical problem (occurring about 3 per cent of the time) in the case of the delivery of fresh fruit.

Services

A Pareto analysis for the most valuable benefits of airport executive lounges is given in Figure 26.7.[6] Peaceful surroundings are the most important, though communication and eating facilities are close behind.

The principle of these Pareto analyses is to concentrate first on solving the most critical, often the most frequently occurring, activity before devoting resources to the less frequently occurring areas.

ABC analysis

This is a special form of Pareto analysis to determine the financial value of stocks relative to the quantity (Chapter 11, *Inventory Management*) or the number of suppliers relative the value of purchases (Chapter 16, *Purchasing and Subcontracting*).

Improvement monitoring charts

In setting up a programme to improve an operation, it is necessary to monitor if progress is being made.

This has to be illustrated by comparing earlier results with current results. For example, assume that the interest was to reduce the number of defective products being made in an assembly operation. The percentage of defectives would be the indicator. Sampling would be carried out at specified periods and results compared. If at the start of the quality programme the percentage of defects was 8 per cent, three months later, 6.5 per cent, and then three months after that, 4.7 per cent, then an apparent conclusion is that the quality plan is working. Figure 26.8 illustrates a general situation in which the progress is being made over time as the value of the indicator decreases. An indicator can be anything, such as employee absenteeism, product composition, delivery times, inventory levels, etc.

Statistical quality control charts

Statistical control charts (Chapter 23, *Statistical Quality Control*) are analytical tools for determining whether a production operation or service system is operating according to certain specifications. Three charts that are commonly employed include:

- the p-chart for measuring proportions, or the fraction of defective units;
- the c-chart for measuring the absolute number of defective units;
- the x-bar chart, together with a range chart, for measuring the output of variables in an operation.

Figure 26.6 Pareto analysis: lorry distribution of fresh fruit.

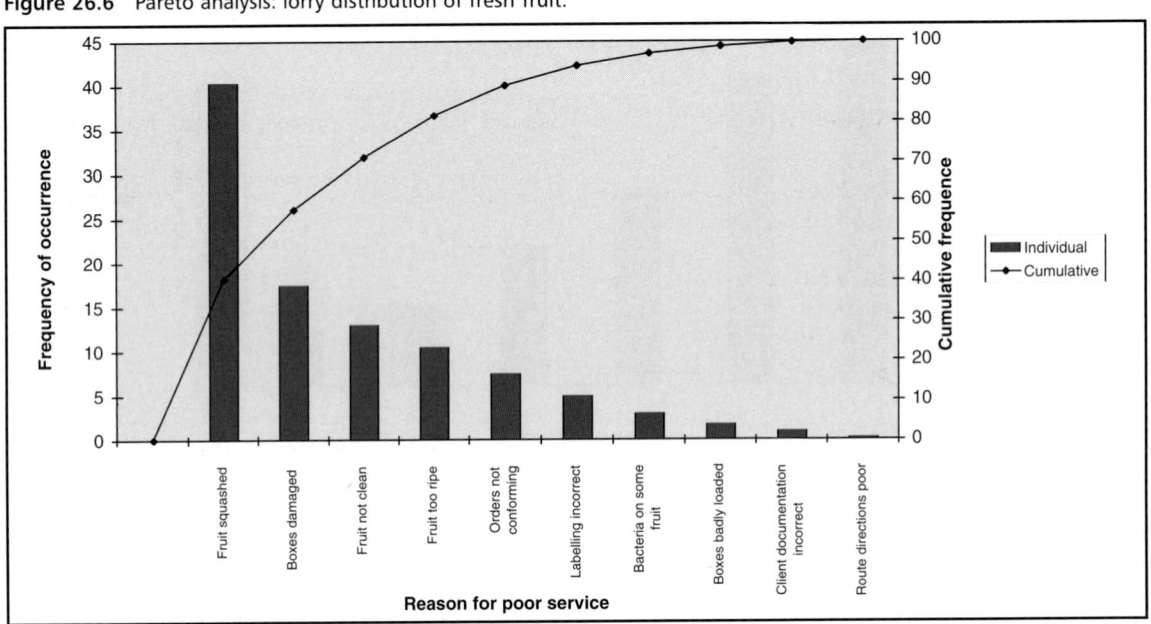

Figure 26.7   Pareto analysis: most valuable benefits of airport executive lounges.

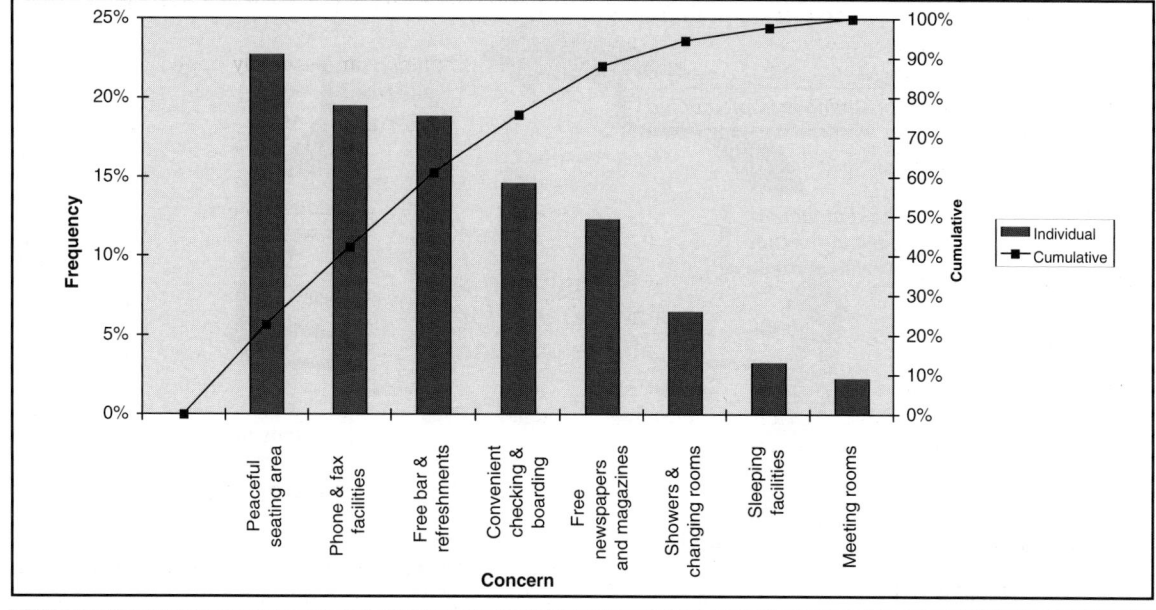

Scatter diagrams

A scatter diagram is a presentation of the dependent operating variable in terms of an independent variable. The purpose of the scatter diagram is to see if there is a correlation between the two variables. If so, can a quantitative model be developed which will forecast, or estimate, certain outcomes? Chapter 9, *Forecasting Customer Demand*, gives a scatter diagram for operator absenteeism (independent variable) against faulty units (dependent variable) and then develops an appropriate regression model.

Quality function deployment

Quality function deployment (QFD) is an analysis method that focuses and coordinates capabilities within an organization in order to design, manufacture and market goods that are desired by the customers. Products should be designed to reflect customers' preferences and priorities. As a result, marketing people, design engineers, operating personnel and suppliers must work very closely together in order to produce a product that will meet the customer's requirements (see Chapter 6, *Design of the Product*).

Quality circles

A quality circle, originated by the Japanese, is a small group of employees (the average number is nine), who volunteer to meet regularly to analyse work-related projects with the objective of advancing the company, improving working conditions and spurring mutual self-development, by using quality-control concepts.[7] Participation is voluntary and there are no direct cash incentives. The principal reasons are personal satisfaction and achievement and recognition given at regional and national quality-control meetings. The process is illustrated in Figure 26.9.

Failure mode, effect and criticality analysis (FMECA)

A failure mode, effect and criticality analysis is the detailed study of a product design, manufacturing

Figure 26.8   Operational improvements are shown by measuring changes.

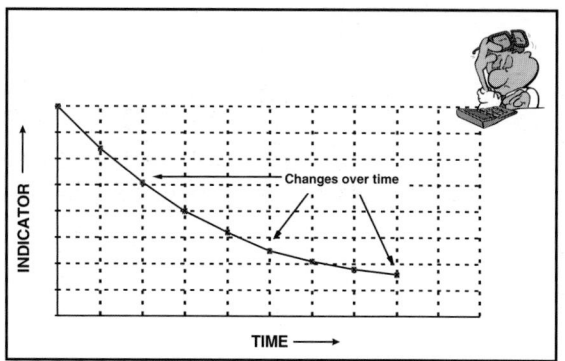

Figure 26.9 Quality circles.

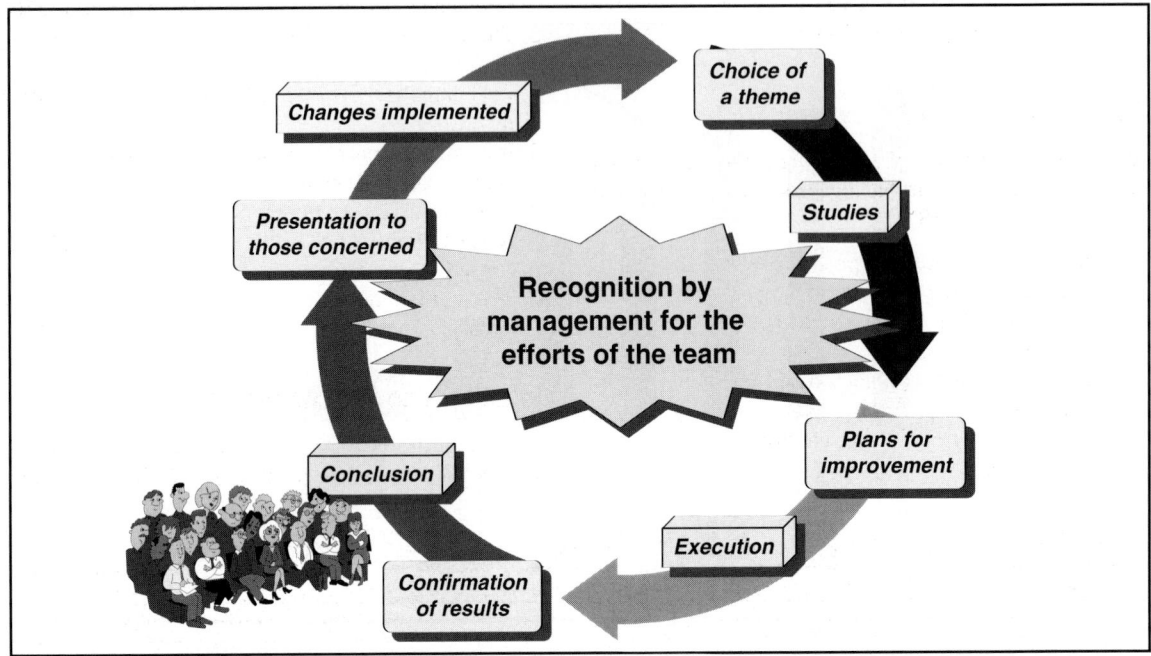

operation or distribution network to determine which features are critical to various modes of failure. The method has been covered in detail in Chapter 19, *Reliability and Maintenance*.

Overall equipment effectiveness

Chapter 15, *Lean Manufacturing and Just-in-Time*, illustrates this approach, where analysing the activities of a machine might include:

- operator breaks;
- machine breakdowns;
- unplanned interruptions;
- machine set-up;
- speed less than design;
- waste products.

BENCHMARKING

Benchmarking is an analytical tool, but is somewhat special in that it involves comparison of firms rather than a stand-alone internal analysis. Benchmarking is the continuous process of measuring a firm's products, services and operating practices against competitors, or those recognized as leaders. Benchmarking may not only include direct competitors but even how a company compares to other firms the products of which are

not the same. For example, a food company might compare its indicators with those of a computer firm or a furniture manufacture. US companies used benchmarking to analysis the production methods of Japanese automobile producers, which then ultimately led them to implement just-in-time production and other forms of lean manufacturing in many types of industries (see Chapter 15, *Lean Production and Just-in-Time*).

Operating level

Specific areas to benchmark at the operating level might include the following:

- customer service levels;
- inventory management;
- inventory control (extent of automation);
- purchasing;
- billing and collection;
- production operations;
- purchasing practices;
- quality process;
- warehousing and distribution;
- transportation.

European firms

As an illustration of benchmarking Table 26.5 compares major European manufacturing and service firms with their competition on the bases of revenue growth, profitability, stock price increase, international business and perceived company image.[8]

Petroleum industry

The following are ten of the conclusions of a benchmark study on the purchasing practices of the petroleum industry in 1988.[9]

1 The amount of money spent with vendors accounted for 9 per cent of sales revenues.
2 It cost less than $0.01 to purchase $1 worth of goods or services.
3 Purchasing staff represented 0.6 per cent of total employees.
4 There was one purchasing employee per $104 million of sales.
5 There was $8.5 million in purchases made by the purchasing department per employee in purchasing.
6 There were 102 active suppliers per purchasing employee.
7 Each supplier received $96 000 in company orders in 1988.
8 Inventory of purchased items accounted for 1 per cent of sales revenues.
9 Inactive inventory, or that which had not moved in at least three years, was 21 per cent of total purchased inventory.
10 The number of suppliers decreased by 7 per cent from 1987 to 1988.

Guidelines to benchmarking

Companies approach benchmarking in different ways. IBM has a four phase step approach, AT&T has a nine-

Table 26.5   Benchmarking comparision of some leading European companies

Company	Country	Activity	Revenue growth	Profitability	Stock price increase	International	Company image	Score
Elf	France	Oil and					X	1
Shell	UK/Netherlands	chemicals	X	X	X	X		4
Rhone-Poulenc*	France	Chemicals and				X		1
Hoechst*	Germany	pharmaceuticals	X	X	X		X	4
Groupe PSA	France	Automobiles	X					1
Volkswagen	Germany			X	X	X	X	4
L'Oréal	France	Cosmetics and	X	X	X		X	4
Benckiser	Germany	beauty products				X		1
Aérospatiale	France	Aeroplanes	X			X		2
British Aerospace	Britain	and components		X	X		X	3
Schneider	France	Heavy equipment				X		1
ABB	Sweden/Switzerland		X	X	X		X	4
Usinor-Sacilor	France	Steel and	X			X	X	3
British Steel	Britain	steel products		X	X			2
Lafarge	France	Cement	X	X			X	3
Holderbank	Switzerland				X	X		2
Bull	France	Computers		X		X	X	3
Olivetti	Italy		X		X			2
Alcatel	France	Electronics and					X	1
Siemens	Germany	telecommunications	X	X	X	X		4
LVMH	France	Drinks	X	X	X	X	X	5
Vendome	Switzerland							0
Danône	France	Food	X					1
Nestlé	Switzerland			X	X	X	X	4
Carrefour	France	Retail distribution	X	X	X	X	X	5
Metro	Germany							0
Accor	France	Hotels				X		1
Granada	Britain		X	X	X		X	4
UAP	France	Insurance	X					1
Allianz	Germany			X	X	X	X	4

* now in merger talks

step approach and Xerox a ten-step method. In all these however are the general guidelines.[10]

Do not go on a fishing expedition

When preparing a benchmark study, pick a specific area in the organization that needs improving. This may be quality, customer satisfaction, accounts payable or delivery time, for example. Then do your homework, including thoroughly reviewing your own process and procedures before picking a company that excels in the particular area chosen.

Use company people

The people who are going to implement changes need to see and understand for themselves, so it is they who should make the site visits and have discussions with the people concerned. It is difficult to implement changes if senior management or outside consultants do the benchmarking and return to tell the process operators what to do. Furthermore, keep site visits short and working teams small.

Exchange information

You should be ready to exchange information and provide answers in turn to any questions that you might ask another company.

Legal concerns

Avoid legal problems, which might arise as a result of discussions that might imply price fixing, market allocation or other illegal activities. This could lead to problems. Do not expect to learn much about new products. Most benchmarking missions focus on existing products, business practices, human resources and customer satisfaction.

Confidentiality

Respect the confidentiality of data obtained. Companies that agree to share information with you may strongly object if that information leaks out to a competitor.

SUMMARY OF KEY ELEMENTS

- An operational audit, or diagnostic, is an analysis intended to provide an in-depth understanding of performance of the firm. It is performed because there is a perception that improvements can be made and the audit gives a baseline from which to start making these changes.
- A starting area in an audit should be at the customer level. The client is king. Firms are in business to make a profit and this implies satisfying the customer with desired products, expected quality and promised delivery.
- In the integrated supply chain, financial performance measures of a distribution centre include special delivery costs, stockout costs, distance travelled by trucks, total operating hours (weekly charge), storage costs of finished goods, total distribution costs and the operating margin. In the production centre they include costs associated with storage, direct labour, hiring and termination, personnel transfer and raw materials purchased.
- A work environment should be established such that absenteeism and staff turnover are low, training is provided, communication is transparent, company objectives are identified, promotion is from within, there are appropriate performance measurements and the work environment is agreeable. These are all management's responsibility.

- Service indicators include service according to availability of orders or units, delivery, order cycle time, product availability combined with order cycle time, system flexibility, use of information systems, speed to recover from a system malfunction, after sales service, minimum order size, emergency orders, delivery frequency and delivery reliability.
- Inventory management indicators include average inventory level during a cycle, order processing cost per cycle, carrying cost, inventory turnover, ratio of inventory to sales, record accuracy, average value of working inventory, value of safety stock, inventory as a percentage of assets, inventory references and inventory waste.
- The product quality of tangible goods may be measured in terms of lots, components rejected or in financial terms.
- Non-value-added activity, such as production set-up time, time loss due to breakdowns, time loss due to rework and level of support services, should be minimized.
- Analytical tools include pipeline maps, process flow charts, Ishikawa diagrams, frequency checksheets coupled to a Pareto analysis, ABC inventory analysis, improvement monitoring charts, statistical quality control charts, scatter diagrams, quality function deployment, quality circles, failure

mode effect and criticality analysis, and an overall equipment effectiveness analysis.

■ Benchmarking involves comparison with the products, services and operating practices of other firms, both competitors and other firms recognized as leaders. Guidelines for benchmarking include being objective, using company personnel, exchanging information, being aware of legal concerns and respecting confidentiality.

REVIEW AND DISCUSSION QUESTIONS

1 **Customer satisfaction**. Consider the last purchase, or purchases, you made. Were you satisfied with the service and the product you bought? If yes, indicate why you come to this conclusion. If the answer is no, discuss how the supplying organization could improve its customer service.

2 **Working environment**. You work or study (or have worked or studied) in some organization. Evaluate the working environment. Are (were) the considerations satisfactory? Consider ease of communication (with the professor!), training, possibilities, physical conditions, motivation, etc. If there is or was dissatisfaction, what improvements would you propose?

3 **Ishikawa diagram**. In the following situations the system is not operating or performing as expected by the customer or user:
(a) a university or business school;
(b) a supermarket, hypermarket or grocery store;
(c) a road system around where you live and work (or study);
(d) your residence (house, apartment or hall of residence);
(e) a ski resort;
(f) a Club Mediterranean resort;
(g) a manufacturer of running shoes;
(h) a rail transportation network;
(i) a hospital.
The 'effect' is that the product, process or service is of poor quality or below expected standards. Develop a detailed Ishikawa diagram, after brainstorming, showing what you believe might be possible causes grouped in the fishbone branches according to generic causes.

4 **Benchmarking**. Perform a benchmarking analysis, using literature or the Internet, of the following:
(a) your university, with others;
(b) the life style in your country of residence or birth, compared with the countries where you live, are familiar with and the USA; thus, there are several 'benchmarks',

Figure 26.10   Operational audit of a firm.

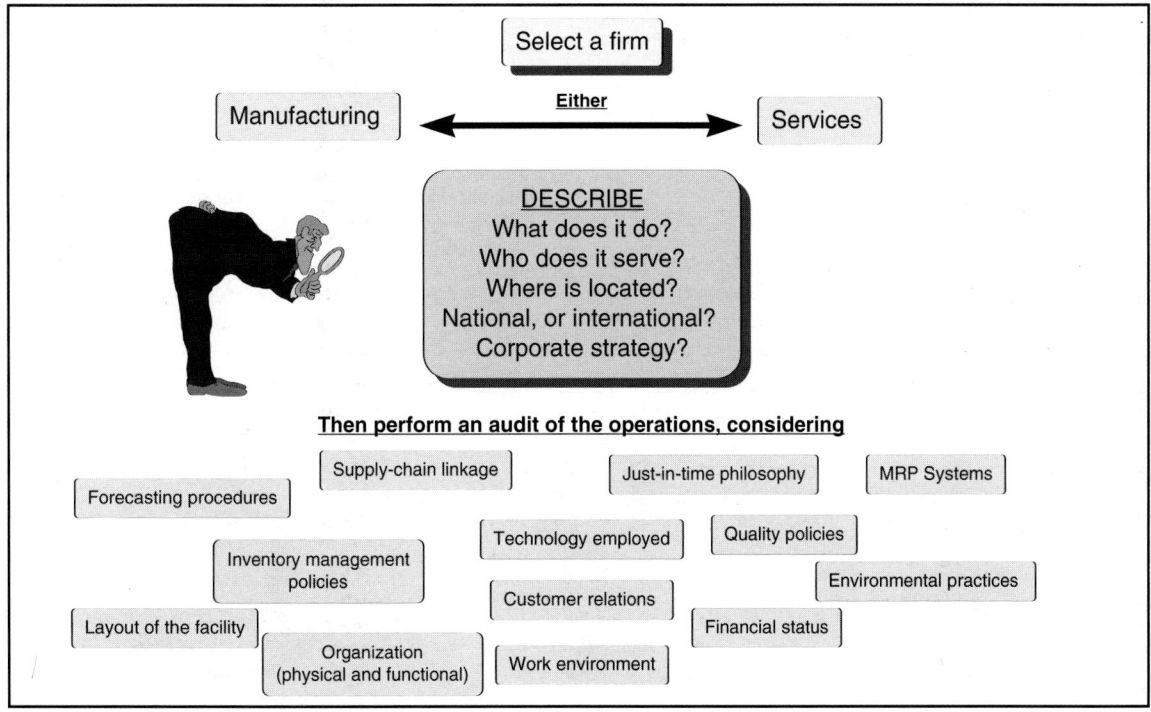

(c) an automobile company in your country, with others not in your country;

(d) environmental standards where you live, compared with other countries on the same continent and the USA;

(e) the transportation network where you live, compared with other countries on the same continent and the USA;

(f) the government system where you live, compared with other countries.

5 **Audit of an operation**. Using Figure 26.10 and the elements discussed in the text, develop an operational audit of a firm in either manufacturing or services.

CASE STUDY: BERGER CO.

Situation

The Berger Co. near Birmingham, England is a subsidiary of a major US conglomerate and makes electrically operated metering instruments used for flow measurement for gas, oil and water. The clients for Berger are utility companies, the oil industry and chemical firms such as Esso, EDF of France, Texaco, Total and British Petroleum.

Product

The metering instruments are similar in their basic design in that they have a casing made of stainless steel, cast iron, ordinary carbon steel or aluminium. The choice of material depends on the service in which the instrument is to be used. For all corrosive conditions, stainless steel is employed. The dimensions of the meters depend on the volume of fluid flow and the operating pressure. For most of the meters the casings are purchased from outside subcontractors.

The operating and strategic part of the instrument is a rotating-piston arrangement, which is manufactured by Berger. The piston arrangement is made of stainless steel, aluminium, or, in a few cases, carbon steel. The meters are controlled by electronic motors. All of these are purchased from subcontractors.

There are three principal models manufactured by the company. These are shown in Figure 26.11. The product structure of these three meters, given in Figure 26.12, illustrates how the meters are assembled from the various machined or purchased parts.

Work centre

Figure 26.13 shows the work-centre arrangement. The following is a description.

Receiving and shipping

This is where the raw materials (sheet steel, aluminium rods, rubber for gaskets, wiring, paint, etc.) and assemblies made by subcontractors (cas-

ings and electric motors) are received. It is also the area where the final product is packaged and shipped to the customer.

Storage raw materials

This is the storage area for all received materials, except motors and casings.

Rough machining

This is the first machinery operation for the preparation of the meters. The various operations in sequence are:

1 **Cutting**. Here the aluminium and steel is cut to shape and length. There are two cutting work posts.

2 **Drilling**. Here holes of varying dimensions are cut into the metal pieces according to specifications. There is one drilling work post.

3 **Drilling and boring**. This is a specialized step for certain models in which the drill holes are much smaller. The boring operation puts a high tolerance on the units. There is one combined drilling–boring operation.

4 **Turning**. This is where appropriate meter components are reduced to the correct diameter on a lathe. There is one lathe.

5 **Burring**. Here all the rough edges are removed from the cut pieces.

6 **Reaming**. This is another operation for giving fine tolerances on the meters. Not all models pass through this step. There is one reaming work post.

Precision machining

This work area is where the working parts of the meters are closely matched, aligned and adjusted before final assembly.

7 **Alignment**. There are four work posts.

8 **Balancing**. Here the meters are balanced so that they will respond correctly to whatever media they will be measuring. There are two balancing work posts.

9 **Adjusting**. Final adjustments are made at this work post. There is one work post here, and all of the meters pass through this work area.

Figure 26.11   Berger Co. meters.

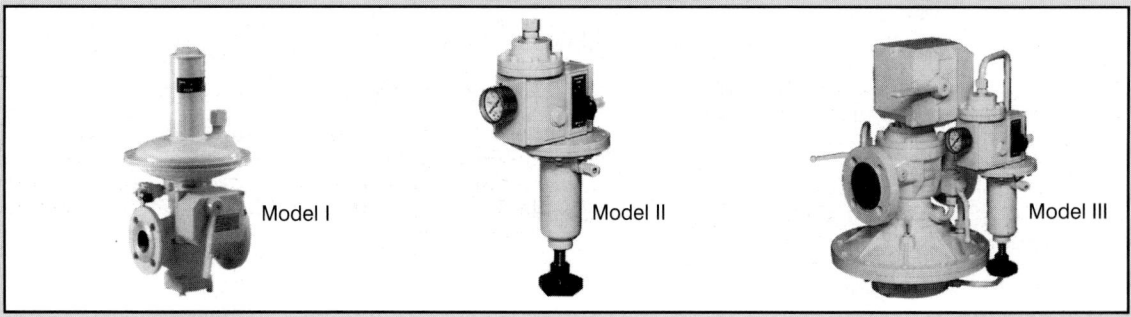

Model I   Model II   Model III

Figure 26.12   Berger Co. – product structure.

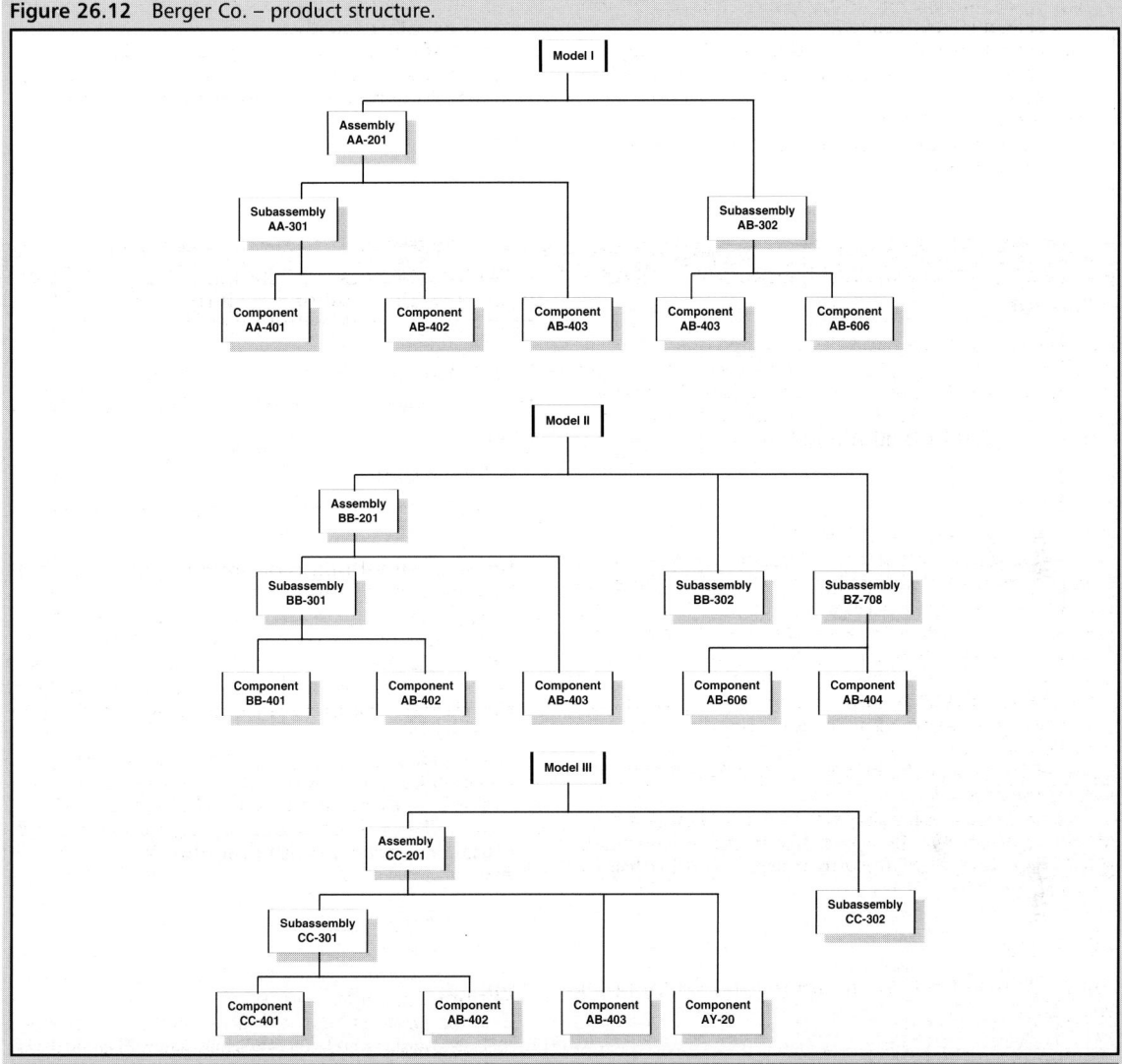

Assembly

This is where the final product is assembled. The assembly involves installing the piston unit in the casing, bolting and sealing with gaskets and then attaching the electric motor. Assembly is a sequential operation going from Post 1 to Post 5.

Testing

From assembly the end products go to testing to confirm that they operate according to specification. From here they go to the receiving and shipping zone.

Storage tables

Each of the storage tables shown in the layout can hold up to 35 semi-finished units.

Personnel

Information concerning the personnel working in rough machining, precision machining, and assembly is given in Table 26.6

The production manager has the responsibility for all the activities shown on the Berger plan layout.

Quality control

The quality of the instruments is important. A poorly operating instrument in use in the field is a serious problem and could result in accidents, particularly in the case of dangerous fluids. For this reason, in addition to the final testing of the instrument, quality control inspectors are employed as shown in Table 26.7.

Figure 26.13 Berger Co. – layout.

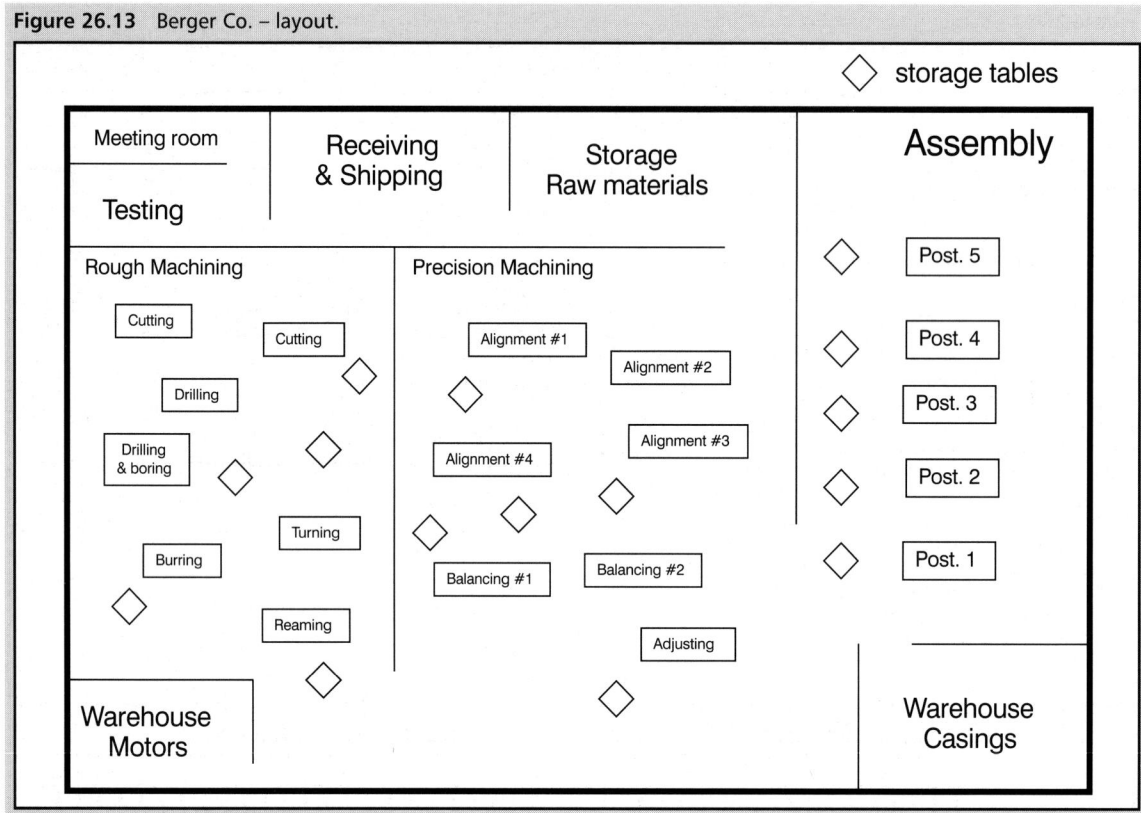

Table 26.6 Berger – personnel information

	Name	Year of birth	Start date		Name	Year of birth	Start date
1	Framer	1942	1958	19	Arce	1945	1966
2	Berge	1937	1952	20	Boldon	1939	1957
3	Jones	1936	1953	21	Barish	1961	1980
4	Seidel	1952	1972	22	Cusin	1964	1983
5	Forgeon	1948	1966	23	Cornford	1975	1992
6	Caumont	1961	1976	24	Nicholson	1947	1978
7	Wilson	1935	1960	25	Schmitz	1942	1982
8	Stanford	1947	1972	26	Brown	1941	1960
9	Zukowski	1951	1968	27	Jacobs	1958	1990
10	Manfred	1938	1968	28	Harold	1959	1988
11	Duong	1965	1987	29	Alision	1955	1976
12	Faseil	1958	1977	30	Wheeler	1952	1982
13	Revault	1942	1967	31	Atmal	1950	1975
14	Abdulla	1959	1989	32	Olson	1940	1980
15	Hannan	1948	1973	33	Heath	1957	1978
16	Ringe	1961	1993	34	Cerder	1959	1978
17	Joffrey	1971	1989		Production Manager	1942	1961
18	Fagiano	1958	1974				

Table 26.7 Berger – quality control

Work area	Time spent on quality control (job hours/week)
Receiving and shipping	32
Rough machining	16
Precision machining	24
Assembly	48
Testing	On-going operation

Planning

The planning of the production operation is under the responsibility of the Production Manager. He develops a bar (Gantt) chart each Monday morning for the coming week's operation. Copies of this planning chart are given to each of the superintendents in Rough Machining, Precision Machining and Assembly. Any modifications to the plan, which may occur midweek, are discussed at a meeting at the end of Wednesday.

A typical bar chart for Berger for the third week of October 1995 is given in Figure 26.14. This indicates the status at the end of Wednesday. The letters A, B, C, D, etc. represent job orders for specific customers. A job order is a particular quantity of units for a customer.

The time is the end of December 1995 and the anticipated demands, including actual orders and forecasts for 1996, have been prepared by the Sales Department as shown in Table 26.8.

Table 26.8 Berger – anticipated demand

Month	Model I	Model II	Model III	Total
January	380	785	560	1 725
February	325	645	450	1 420
March	310	870	158	1 338
April	380	821	489	1 690
May	420	745	753	1 918
June	280	610	489	1 379
July	290	845	167	1 302
August	410	879	962	2 251
September	385	960	523	1 868
October	345	450	895	1 690
November	386	562	991	1 939
December	325	876	451	1 652
Total	4 236	9 048	6 888	20 172
Average/month	353	754	574	1 681

The production manager has developed a proposed aggregate plan based on this expected demand for 1996. This is given in Tables 26.9 and 26.10.

Figure 26.14 Berger Co. – Gantt chart.

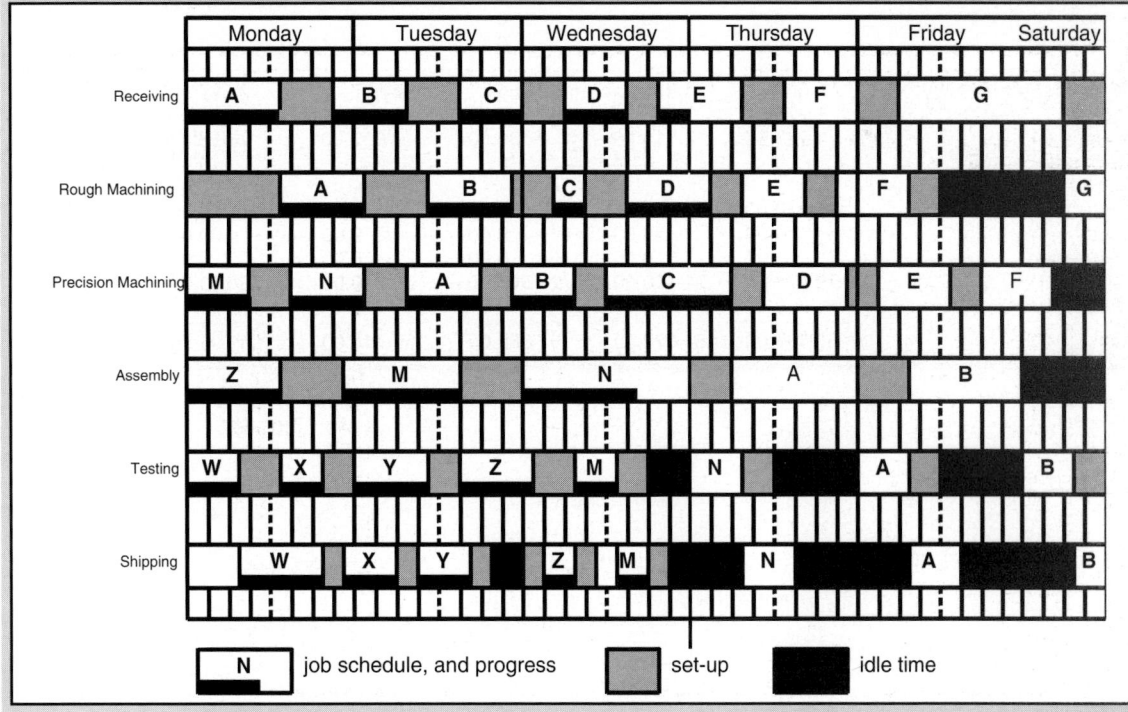

Table 26.9 Berger – aggregate plan: given date

Ending December inventory (units)	2000
Stockout costs (£/unit)	35.00
Holding cost (£/unit/week)	2.50
Hiring cost/employee (£)	350.00
Termination cost/employee	275.00
Labour cost (£/h)	8.00
Overtime cost (£/h)	12.00
Subcontracting cost (£/unit)	35.00
Labour hours/unit	3.20
Production December	1800
Working week (h)	40
Maximum overtime/week (h)	10
Weeks/month	4
Units/month/person (normal hours)	50.00
Units/month/person (overtime hours)	12.50

Financial performance

The financial performance of Berger, for the last two years, is given in Table 26.11. The complete data for 1995 is estimated.

Table 26.10 Aggregate plan: monthly breakdown (buffer with inventory).

Month	December	January	February	March	April	May	June
Demand		1 725	1 420	1 338	1 690	1 918	1 379
Labour							
Production (units)		1 681	1 681	1 681	1 681	1 681	1 681
Labour hours		5 379.20	5 379.20	5 379.20	5 379.20	5 379.20	5 379.20
Staff		33.62	33.62	33.62	33.62	33.62	33.62
Staff (rounded)	34	34	34	34	34	34	34
Actual production		1 700	1 700	1 700	1 700	1 700	1 700
Hiring		0	0	0	0	0	0
Termination		0	0	0	0	0	0
Inventory							
Beginning		2 000	1 975	2 255	2 617	2 627	2 409
Ending		1 975	2 255	2 617	2 627	2 409	2 730
Average		1 987.50	2 115.00	2 436.00	2 622.00	2 518.00	2 569.50
Stockouts		0	0	0	0	0	0
Costs							
Production		43 520.00	43 520.00	43 520.00	43 520.00	43 520.00	43 520.00
Hiring		0.00	0.00	0.00	0.00	0.00	0.00
Termination		0.00	0.00	0.00	0.00	0.00	0.00
Carrying		19 875.00	21 150.00	24 360.00	26 220.00	25 180.00	25 695.00
Stockouts		0	0	0	0	0	0
Total		63 395.00	64 670.00	67 880.00	69 740.00	68 700.00	69 215.00

continues

Table 26.10 *Continued*.

Month	July	August	September	October	November	December	Total
Demand	1 302	2 251	1 868	1 690	1 939	1 652	20 172
Labour							
Production (units)	1 681	1 681	1 681	1 681	1 681	1 681	20 172
Labour hours	5 379.20	5 379.20	5 379.20	5 379.20	5 379.20	5 379.20	64 550
Staff	33.62	33.62	33.62	33.62	33.62	33.62	
Staff (rounded)	34	34	34	34	34	34	
Actual production	1 700	1 700	1 700	1 700	1 700	1 700	20 400
Hiring	0	0	0	0	0	0	0
Termination	0	0	0	0	0	0	0
Inventory							
Beginning	2 730	3 128	2 577	2 409	2 419	2 180	
Ending	3 128	2 577	2 409	2 419	2 180	2 228	
Average	2 929.00	2 852.50	2 493.00	2 414.00	2 299.50	2 204.00	
Stockouts	0	0	0	0	0	0	0
Costs							
Production	43 520.00	43 520.00	43 520.00	43 520.00	43 520.00	43 520.00	522 240.00
Hiring	0.00	0.00	0.00	0.00	0.00	0.00	0.00
Termination	0.00	0.00	0.00	0.00	0.00	0.00	0.00
Carrying	29 290.00	28 525.00	24 930.00	24 140.00	22 995.00	22 040.00	294 400.00
Stockouts	0	0	0	0	0	0	0.00
Total	72 810.00	72 045.00	68 450.00	67 660.00	66 515.00	65 560.00	816 640.00

Table 26.11 Berger Co. – Financial statements

Income and Expenditure statement (£000)

	1995	1994
Net sales	8350	6852
Cost of goods sold		
Direct labour	1008	715
Materials	3124	2540
Manufacturing overhead	1212	1105
Total cost of goods	5344	4360
Gross profit	3006	2492
G & A	442	359
Marketing	1090	989
R & D	1208	902
Total	2740	2250
Profit before taxes	266	242
Tax provision	95	108
Net profit	171	134

Balance Sheet (£000)

	1995	1994
Assets		
Current Assets		
Cash	18	121
Accounts receivable	1470	1274
Inventory	3025	2012
Other	42	54
Total current assets	4555	3461
Net fixed assets	521	520
Total assets	5076	3981
Liabilities		
Current liabilities		
Notes payable	1800	845
Accounts payable	934	672
Accruals	356	570
Total current liabilities	3090	2087
Long-term debt	600	542
Capital stock & surplus	602	654
Earned surplus	784	698
	1386	1352
Total liabilities	5076	3981

Required

Based on the information given, make an audit (diagnostic) of the Berger Co.

1   What improvements would you suggest?

2   What are some of the areas to which attention should be given?
3   If appropriate, add any other ideas, even though they may not be directly referred to in the case given above.

CASE STUDY: THE HECK TRAVEL AGENCY

Situation

Margrit Heck was Austrian, from Innsbruck. As a young girl, she spent most of her weekends skiiing in the mountains close to her home. She lost her parents during the early part of the second World War and, in 1944, when she was only 15, she fled to England with a friend. Life was pretty tough. Not having too much of an education, Margrit flitted from job to job, searching for something more satisfying than an employer could give. In December 1954 she learnt that an uncle of hers had died and she was the sole legatee of a small sum of money. She returned to her native country for the first time since the war and settled the arrangements concerning her inheritance. She spent the remaining part of December and all of the following January in Austria taking the opportunity to do some skiing, something that she hadn't done for many years. While there, she met several British people, mostly middle class, who were skiing. She spent a lot of time with the British people, discussing their vacation ideas, why they came to Austria and what they enjoyed about their trip. These discussions germinated an idea. Why not organize package ski holidays from England available not only to the well off?

Early start

When she returned from her stay in Austria, Margrit set to work on her idea. First she made arrangements to have her inheritance transferred to Barclays Bank in Piccadilly Circus, London. This took some time as exchange controls were in force and Margrit still retained her Austrian nationality. Margrit was enthused about her venture and set her mind to having it up and running by the ski season 1955/56. When her inheritance came through, she quit her job and started to organize.

Margrit first did a rather 'back of the envelope' market survey to decide who would be her most likely customers. In the 1950s ski vacations were principally taken by single people and those who had a reasonable disposable income. She felt that London would be her best target area, particularly the west side (Earl's Court, Kensington, South Kensington and Chelsea) as here there was a reasonably large concentration of young doctors, engineers, accountants, lawyers and financial types who worked in the City. With this decided, and using part of her inheritance as collateral, she rented a small, rather dingy office on the Cromwell Road in South Kensington, London.

Since money was tight, Margrit started off by doing everything herself. She decided that she should start by concentrating on providing packages to four well known ski resort areas in Austria: Igls, near Innsbruck; Soëlden/Hochsoëlden, Lech/Zur and Kizbühel. Using telephone directories she had picked up in Austria, she either wrote or sent telegrams to hotels in the selected ski areas outlining her idea and indicating that in June/July 1955 she would be in Austria and would like to establish some tentative contracts. Regarding transportation, it was least expensive, and most reliable, to use flights from Gatwick, south of London, to Munich, Germany. From Munich, buses would then take the skiers to their respective resorts. With this in mind, Margrit made contact with British European Airways (now British Airways), Caledonian Airways and other charter companies to organize the transportation.

In the summer Margrit went out to Austria. She took the ferry from Dover to Ostend and then the train through Belgium to Innsbruck. From here she took local transport to the four ski areas she had selected and established some rather loose contracts with hotels in these resorts. Most hotels wanted skiers to come on 'full pension', taking breakfast, lunch and dinner. In this way, hotels could more easily schedule their restaurant services, and the profit margin to them was more attractive. Along with this was added a lift pass for six days. At each resort she made arrangements to have a hostess meet the skiers, direct them to their hotels and be available to answer any concerns. In addition, she visited local ski shops to work out deals for ski rental.

Returning from Austria at the end of July, Margrit began pricing the ski packages. The direct costs for skiing included:

- air transportation from Gatwick to Munich;
- bus transfer to and from the designated ski resort;
- fee to the resort hostess;
- hotel accommodation at 'full pension';
- the cost of a lift ticket;
- a cocktail on arrival.

To this Margrit added her estimated total indirect costs (office rental, communications, advertising and the services of an assistant, whom she felt would be necessary). She added 10 per cent of this to each one-week package deal. Finally, she added 20 per cent to cover profit. With this information, she put together a publicity brochure. For the first year this was quite simple. It explained the package, the price and the conditions. In addition, she contacted the *Evening Standard* (a London evening newspaper) and arranged to have an announcement appear every Friday night from September through to the end of January.

Thus, by the end of September, Margrit was ready to launch her first ski package holidays under the name of 'Heck's Travel Agency'. At first, business was a little slow, then through word of mouth it picked up pretty well in November when the snow in Austria was proving to be plentiful. In the first year, Margrit made a slight loss. She wasn't too disappointed and felt that she had at least started to carve out a niche for her business.

Growth

Each ski season Margrit's business improved a little, though not without problems. Selling, organizing and communicating with the resorts presented headaches. Margrit had difficulty planning the number of clients each ski season. This made booking the seats on the charter plane difficult, and the charter company with whom she was working was not that flexible. Another difficulty was in Munich. Often the buses in Munich were not full, and so she was obliged to share space with other holiday organisers. This meant that the bus would have to stop at several hotels between Munich and the resort areas. In addition, although Margrit had a representative in Austria to act as a hostess to meet her clients, the hostess was often also working with other holiday groups.

Expansion of the ski territory

In the 1960s and the early 1970s Margrit's business became well established. However, there were ups and downs. The clientele started to change somewhat. Originally, the skiers were single people, with money and free time. As the standard of living improved in England, families began to book ski holidays. Their requirements were quite different from the 'single' free-wheeling crowd. With the increase in business, Margrit hired three additional assistants for the office. She rented additional space on the floor above in Cromwell Road, where she established her personal office. Competition was becoming more pronounced now. To combat this, she began to improve her advertising, expanded into more resorts in Austria and started to use charter flights to Innsbruck and Salzburg, in addition to Munich.

In the late 1970s and early 1980s, as the income of British people was increasing, vacation time increasing to four weeks per year on average, the demand was not only for ski packages to Austria, but also to France and Switzerland. Margrit was quite unfamiliar with these areas, but with the aid of additional staff, some part-time, she began to target areas around Chamonix/Mégève in France and Zermatt/Saas-Fee in Switzerland. Her package trips in these areas were moderately successful.

Summer vacations

The revenue flows for Margrit were very cyclical. They started growing in November, peaked in January, and then declined to a trickle in early April. To give a more balanced aggregate plan, Margrit decided to launch into summer package vacations. British people were always seeking the sun in the summer, to escape the sometimes dreary British weather. Her company was well known in Britain now, with offices in London, Manchester, Newcastle and Bristol, and clients were often asking, 'Do you have summer package deals?'

Margrit targeted Spain (the coastal area around Barcelona, Tarragona and Valencia), Italy (the regions of La Spezia and Viareggio) and Yugoslavia (Split and Dubrovnik). She had a lot of difficulty making a success of these vacation packages. Business was very competitive and clients were always looking for the cheapest deals. As a result, she had difficulty breaking even on her summer activity.

Change of ownership

In 1990, Margrit was approached by a large competitor in Britain with an offer to buy her travel business. Margrit, now 61, was fairly tired, having spent many years dealing with customer problems. In addition, business with her company was flat and almost in decline as a result of several quality problems. She had amassed a reasonable sum of money for herself and decided to accept the purchase offer. In the summer of that year, the Heck travel agency was under new onership.

Required

You have been on vacation and possibly on a ski vacation. Thus, as a client, you are aware of the demands that will be interpreted as the quality of the product and will have a bearing on the operation of a travel business.

1 As a consultant to the new owner of the Heck Travel Agency, make an audit of the situation, including developing an Ishikawa Fishbone to diagnose the business with the objective of identifying actual or *potential* quality problems. The ideas you develop may have been enumerated in the case given above or they may be others associated with the travel industry.

2 In order of importance, list those areas of analysis for a Pareto-type analysis.

NOTES AND REFERENCES

1. J.D. Power and Associates, Agoura Hills, California.
2. *The Economist* (1991) 27 April: 78
3. 'J.D. Power looks critically at European cars. U.S. Survey firm makes further inroads on continent' (1997) *Wall Street Journal Europe* 25 June.
4. Adapted from advertising announcements of Unisys in *International Management* (May 1994).
5. *Insight* (1991) 4th Quarter.
6. *Wall Street Journal Europe* (1996) 11/12 October.
7. Oakland, J. (1989, 1992) *Total Quality Management*, Oxford: Heinemann: 252.
8. *Le Nouvel Economiste* (France). (1996) 7 June: 44.
9. Center for Advanced Puchasing Studies, PO Box 22160, Tempe, AZ 85285-2160.
10. 'How to steal the best ideas around. Benchmarking is a perfectly legal way of copying the smartest business practices. Ford Motor, Xerox, AT&T, Motorola, Du Pont, and others are using it to bound ahead' (1992) *Fortune* 19 October: 86-89.

FURTHER READING

Anderson, R. (1996) 'Internal audit taps new sources', *Journal of Business Strategy* 17(2): 22–24.
Bernthal, P. R. (1996) 'Comparing performance management practices in the United States and Pacific Rim', *Advances in International Comparative Management*, 11: 1–29.
Butler, R. H. (1995) 'Key indicators can help improve the performance of your business', *Industrial Management*, 37(3): 2–3.
Butler , R. H. (1996) 'Key indicators can help improve the performance of your business', *Supervision* 57(3): 3–5.
Cerullo, M. V. and Cerullo, M. J. (1993) 'Operational audits of computer information systems: A general framework', *Internal Auditing* 8(3): 44–52.
Collins, M. J. (1995) 'Benchmarking with simulation: How it can help your production operations', *Production* 107(7): 50–51.
Collins , R., Cordon, C. and Julien, D. (1996) 'Lessons from the, "Made in Switzerland" study: What makes a world-class manufacturer?', *European Management Journal* 14(6): 576–589.
Coonen, R. (1995) 'Benchmarking: A continuous improvement process', *Safety and Health Practitioner* 13(10): 18–21.
Copacino, W. C. (1994) 'The ultimate supply-chain vision', *Traffic Management* 33(5): 29–30.
Drach, B. (1994) 'Use manufacturing standards to drive continuous cost improvement', *Production and Inventory Management Journal* 35(1): 20–25.
Hill, S. (1994) 'Want better customer service? Think logistically', *Manufacturing Systems* , 12(3): 11.
Hitchcock, N. A. (1993) 'Benchmarking bolsters quality at Texas Instruments', *Modern Materials Handling* 48(3): 46–48.
Johnson, W. (1995) 'Benchmarking procurement: More to performance than price', *Purchasing and Supply Management* March: 8–9.
Kaplan, R. S. (1990) *Measures for Manufacturing Excellence*, Boston, MA: Harvard Business School Press.

Korpela, J. and Tuominen, M. (1996) 'Benchmarking logistics performance with an application of the analytic hierarchy process', *IEEE Transactions on Engineering Management*, 43(3): 323–333.

Oliver, N., Delbridge, R. and Lowe, J. (1996) 'Lean production practices: International comparisons in the auto components industry', *British Journal of Management* 7(Special Issue), March: S29–44.

Patrick, M. S. (1992) 'Benchmarking: Targeting best practices', *Healthcare Forum* 35(4): 71–72.

Petrick, J., Scherer, R., Westfall, F. and Wilson, J. C. (1994) 'Benchmarking and improving core competencies', *Journal for Quality and Participation* 17(4): 82–85.

Posson, M. C. and Barney, C. A. (1993) 'Environmental auditing and continuous improvement at Lockheed', *Total Quality Environmental Management* 2(3): 267–272.

Pullat, B. M. (1994) 'Process Improvements through benchmarking', *TQM Magazine* 6(2): 37–40.

Roper, W. L. (1994) 'Improving customer service can be as simple as ABC', *Industrial Engineering* 26(8): 39–41.

Rowat, C. (1994) 'Benchmarking warehouse operations', *Logistics Focus* 2(1): 8–9.

Santhouse, D. (1994) 'Benchmarking distribution/logistics: Against industry best practices', *Logistics Focus* 2(1): 2–4.

Schefczyk, M. (1993) 'Industrial benchmarking: A case study of performance analysis techniques', *International Journal of Production Economics* 32(1): 1–11.

Seaman, J. K. (1995) 'Dollarizing audits', *Internal Auditor* 52(5): 42–44.

Sill, B. (1994) 'Operations engineering: Improving multiunit operations', *Cornell Hotel and Restaurant Administration Quarterly* 35(3): 64–71.

Smith, P. (1996) 'World-class new product development: Benchmarking best practices of agile manufacturers', *Journal of Product Innovation Management* 13(6): 567–568.

Stewart, G. (1995) 'Supply chain performance benchmarking study reveals keys to supply chain excellence', *Logistics Information Management* 8(2): 38–44.

Voss, C. A., Chiesa, V and Coughlan, P. (1994) 'Developing and testing benchmarking and self-assessment frameworks in manufacturing', *International Journal of Operations and Production Management* 14(3): 83–100.

Yasin, M. M. and Zimmerer, T. W. (1995) 'The role of benchmarking in achieving continuous service quality', *International Journal of Contemporary Hospitality Management* 7(4): 27–32.

Zairi, M. (1996) *Benchmarking for Best Practice: Continuous Learning through Sustainable Innovation*, Oxford: Butterworth-Heinemann.

V Part V. Appendices

I   Appendix

Major *selected* international manufacturing firms in 1998, according to category, are given in Table AI.1.[1,2] Similarly *selected* major international service companies firms in 1998, according to category, are given in Table AI.2.[2,3]

Table AI.1   International manufacturing companies according to industry

Industry	Companies
Aerospace	Aérospatiale, France; Boeing, USA; Bombardier, Canada; British Aerospace, UK
Apparel	Benetton, Italy; Berkshire Hathaway, USA; Fruit of the Loom, USA; Levi Strauss, USA
Beverages	Coca-Cola, USA; Cadbury-Schweppes, UK; Asahi Breweries, Japan; Seagrams, Canada; Heineken, Netherlands
Building materials and glass	Saint-Gobain, France; Asahi Glass, Japan; Pilkington, Britain; Corning, USA; Italcementi, Italy
Chemicals	Du Pont, USA; Hoechst, Germany; ICI, UK; Rhône-Poulenc, France; Montedison, Italy; Norsk-Hydro, Norway
Computers and office equipment	IBM, USA; Toshiba, Japan; Olivetti, Italy; Bull, France; Compaq, USA;
Electronics and Electrical equipment	ABB ASEA Brown Boveri, Switzerland; Electrolux, Sweden; Ericsson, Sweden; GEC, UK Hitachi, Japan; General Electric, USA; Samsung, South Korea; Siemens, Germany; Philips, Netherlands; Alcatel Alsthom, France
Food	Nestlé, Switzerland; Danône, France; General Mills, USA; Tate & Lyle, Britain; Südzuker, Germany; Unilever, UK/Netherlands
Forest and paper	Fletcher Challenge, New Zealand; Nippon Paper, Japan; Saint Louis, France; Stora, Sweden; Weyerhaeuser, USA; UPM-Kymmene, Sweden
Industrial and farm equipment	Mannesmann, Germany; Caterpillar, USA; Kawasaki Heavy Industries, Japan; BTR, UK; Sulzer, Switzerland; IRI, Italy; Deere, USA; Thyssen, Germany
Jewellery and silverware	Citizen Watch, Japan; Seiko, Japan;
Metal products	Pechiney, France; Alcan, Canada; Gillette, USA; Johnson Mathey, UK;
Metals	Sandvik, Sweden; Sumitomo Electric Inds, Japan Nippon Steel, Japan; Usinor-Sacilor, France; British Steel, UK; Reynolds Metals, USA; Metallgesellschaft, Germany; Alcoa, USA; Kobe Steel, Japan; Krupp, Germany
Mining	Ruhrkohle, Germany; RTZ, UK; De Beers, South Africa; CRA, Australia; Oil & Natural Gas Corp., India
Motor vehicles and parts	General Motors, USA; Toyota, Japan; Daimler-Chrysler, Germany; Fiat, Italy; Renault, France; Groupe PSA, France; Ford Motor, USA; PSA (Citrôen and Peugeot), France; Nissan motor, Japan
Petroleum refining	Exxon, USA; Shell, UK/Netherlands; Elf Aquitaine, France; Eni, Italy; Pemex, Mexico; BP-Amoco, UK; PDVSA, Venezuela; Petronas, Malaysia; SK, South Korea; Statoil, Norway
Pharmaceuticals	Novartis, Switzerland; Johnson & Johnson, USA; Glaxo–Wellcome, Britain; Sankyo, Japan; Pharmacia, Sweden; Bristol–Myers Squib, USA; Merek, USA; Roche Holding, Switzerland; SmithKline Beecham, UK
Publishing and printing	Bertelsman, Germany; Lagardère Groupe, France; News Corp., Australia; Reed Elsevier, UK/Netherlands; Readers Digest, USA; Dai Nippon Printing, USA
Rubber and plastic products	Bridgestone, Japan; Goodyear, USA; Michelin, France; Pirelli, Italy; Continental, Germany
Scientific and photographic	Kodak, USA; Xerox, USA; Fuji Film, Japan; Carl-Zeiss, Germany; Siebe, Britain; Minnesota Mining and Mfg, USA
Soaps and cosmetics	Proctor & Gamble, USA; Henkel, Germany; Kao, Japan; L'Oréal, France; Reckitt & Colman, Britain; DMC, France; Colgate–Palmolive, USA
Textiles	Toray Industries, Japan; Hyosung, South Korea; Haci Ömer Sabanci, Turkey; Coats Viyella, Britain; DMC, France
Tobacco	RJR Nabisco, USA; Japan Tobacco, Japan; Rothmans, UK/Netherlands; Seito, France; BAT Industries; Philip Morris, USA
Toys	Nintendo, Japan; Yamaha, Japan
Transportation equipment	Hyundai Heavy Industry, South Korea; Kvaerner, Norway; Schlindler Holding, Switzerland

Table AI.2 International service companies according to industry

Airlines	AMR (American Airlines), USA; Japan Airlines, Japan; Lufthansa Group, Germany; British Airways, UK; Air France Group, France; Delta Airlines, USA
Banks (Commercial and savings)	Deutsche Bank, Germany; Citicorp, USA; Industrial Bank of Japan; Crédit Agricole, France; ABN Amro Holding, Netherlands; Crédit Suisse, Switzerland
Computer services and software	Baan, Netherlands; Electronic Data Systems, USA; Microsoft, USA; Oracle, USA; SAP, Germany
Diversified financials	ING Group, Netherlands; ITT, USA; Cie De Suez, France; Federal National Mortgage, USA; American Express, USA
Engineering and construction	Kajima, Japan; Lyonnaise des Eaux, France; Bouygues, France; Fluor, USA; Bechtel, USA; Vivendi, France
Entertainment	CBS, USA; TIme Warner, USA; Viacom, USA
Food and drug stores	Daiei, Japan, Kroger, USA; J Sainsbury, Britain; Promodès, France; Koninklijke Ahold, Netherlands; Auchan, France; Carrefour, France; Casino, France; George Weston, Canada; ITO–Yokado, Japan; Koninklijke Ahold, Netherlands; Kroger, USA; Metro, Germany; Promodès, France; Safeway, USA; Tesco, UK
General merchandise	Daiei, Japan; Karstadt, Germany; K-Mart, USA; Marks & Spencer, UK; Pinault-Printemps, France
Healthcare	Columbia/HCA Healthcare, USA; Pacificare, USA; United Healthcare, USA
Hotels	Marriot International, USA; Ladbroke Group, Britain; Accor, France; Bass, UK
Information service	Dun & Bradstreet, USA
Insurance	Aetna Life, USA; Nippon Life, Japan; CNP Assurances, France; Sun Life Assurance, Canada; Prudential, UK
Mail, package and freight delivery	U.S. Postal Service, USA; United Parcel Service, USA; Japan Postal Service; Deutsche Post, Germany; Royal Mail, UK
Insurance (mutual)	Nippon Life, Japan; State Farm Group, USA; Swiss Life, Switzerland; Standard Life Assurance, UK; Principal Mutual Life, USA; Cathay Life, Taiwan; Nippon Life, Japan
Rail transportation	East Japan Railway, Japan; Deutsche Bahn, Germany; SNCF, France; CSX, USA; Kinki Nippon Railway, Japan
Savings institutions	Great Western Financial, USA; Raiffeisenbanken, Switzerland; La Caixa, Spain; BHW Holding, Germany; Abbey National, UK
Tele-communications	AT&T, USA; Nippon Tel. & Tel., Japan; Deutsche Telekom, Germany; Öesterreichische Post, Austria; France Télécom, France; BCE, Canada
Trading	Misui, Japan; Veba Group, Germany; Ssangyon, South Korea; Sinochem, China; SHV Holdings, Netherlands, Antilles
Utilities: Electric and gas	Tokyo Electric Power, Japan; Electricité de France, France; Enel, Italy; British Gas, UK; Korea Electric Power, South Korea; PGKE, USA
Waste management	WMX Technologies, USA

REFERENCES

1. 'World's largest industrial corporations' (1994) *Fortune International* 130(2), 25 July.
2. 'The Fortune Global Five Hundred', *Fortune*, 3 August 1998, pages F-1 to F-42.
3. 'World's largest service corporations' (1994) *Fortune International* 130(4), 22 August.

II Appendix

Table AII.1 gives prominent discoveries and inventions since the eighteenth century.

Table AII.1 Discoveries and Inventions

Eighteenth century – from the start of the industrial revolution

1733	Flying shuttle loom for weaving invented in Britain by John Kay
1747	Rubber tree discovered in Guyana by François Fresneau, France
1751	Nickel discovered by Cronstedt, Sweden
1754	Aluminium discovered in Germany by Andreas Sigismund Marggraf
1759	First factory for printed linen, Jouy-en-Josas, France by Christophe Philippe Oberkampf
1764	First mechanical weaving machine 'spinning jenny' by James Hargreaves, Britain
1765	Steam engine of Newcomen perfected by the Scottish James Watt
1774	Magnesium and chlorine discovered by C W Scheele, Germany
1783	First manned flight (in a balloon) in France By François Pilâtre de Rozier and François d'Arlandes
1785	Mechanical weaving machine perfected by Edmund Cartwright, Britain
1789	Uranium and zirconium discovered by Martin Heinrich Klaproth, Germany
1790	Preserving jars for food perfected in France by Nicolas Appert
1793	Cotton gin to quickly comb the seed from cotton invented in Britain by Eli Whitney
1794	First graphite pencil developed by Nicolas Jacques Conté, in France

Nineteenth century

1804	First steam locomotive put into service in Britain by Richard Trevithick
1807	First steam boat *Clermont* on the Hudson River between New York and Albany, USA (Robert Fulton)
1813	First steam locomotive to utilize traction by friction the *Puffing Billy* by William Hedley, Britain
1814	The steam locomotive the *Rocket* developed by George Stephenson in Britain
1816	Principle of photography invented in France by Nicéphore Niepce
1819	First Atlantic crossing by a steam boat, the *Savannah*
1824	Composition of Portland cement established by Joseph Aspdin in Britain
1826	Benzene discovered by Michael Faraday in Britain
1828	First train put into service in France between Saint-Etienne and Andrézieux, France
1830	First patent for the sewing machine deposited by the Frenchman Barthélemy Thimonnier

1836	Discovery of acetylene by Edward Davy in Britain
1837	First demonstration of the commercial version of the telegraph by Samuel Morse in the USA
1839	Vulcanization of rubber discovered by Charles Goodyear in the USA
1840	First electric transformer constructed Antoine Masson and Louis Brégue in France
1841	Invention of the rheostat by Johann Christian Poggendorff in Germany
1843	First steel boat driven by propeller, the *Great Britain,* launched by Isambard Kingdom Brunel, Britain
1844	First intercity telephone call (between Washington and Baltimore, USA) using Samuel Morse's system
1845	Rotating printing press developed by Richard Marsh Hoe, USA
1845	Inflatable rubber tyre developed Robert William Thompson, Britain
1847	Invention of photography on a glass plate by Abel Niepce de Saint-Victor, France
1851	Sewing machine perfected by Isaac Merrit Singer, USA
1851	First undersea cable (between Dover, UK and Calais, France)
1852	First steam-driven warship built, the *Napoléon,* by Henri Dupuy de Lôme, France
1853	Discovery of aspirin by Charles Gerhardt, France
1854	First tar road surfacing by Henri Sainte-Claire-Deville, France
1855	Discovery of isopropyl alcohol by the French chemist, Pierre Berthelot
1856	The Bessemer process for making steel developed by Henry Bessemer in Britain
1857	First elevator (lift) installed in New York, USA by Elisha Graves Otis
1859	First oil drilling and production operation, Titusville, Pennsylvania, USA (Edwin Laurentine Drake)
1860	Manufacture of linoleum perfected by J Walton, Britain
1861	Development of the process for producing sodium carbonate by Ernest Solvay, Belgium
1861	First large hydraulic press constructed by John Haswell, Austria
1862	Patent deposited for the four-cycle internal combustion engine by Alphonse Beau de Rochas, France
1865	Commercialization of the first rotating printing press (front and back) by William A Bullock, USA
1865	First patent of a railway sleeping carriage in USA by George Mortimer Pullman and Ben Field
1866	Invention of dynamite by Alfred Nobel, Sweden
1866	Introduction of automatic train signals (automatic blocks) by Thomas Hall, USA
1867	Principal of antiseptic to aid surgical procedures discovered by Joseph Lister, Britain
1867	First typewriter built by Christopher Latham Sholes, USA

1869	First skin graft by Jacques Louis Reverdin, Switzerland
1869	Margarine discovered by Hippolyte Mèges-Mouriès, France
1869	Invention of the vacuum cleaner by I G McGaffe, USA
1869	Invention of the ball-bearing by J Suriray, France
1871	Invention of the pneumatic hammer by Simon Ingersoll, USA
1871	Invention of the photographic gelatine emulsion bromine/silver by Richard Leach Maddox, Britain
1872	First use of compressed air brakes on trains by George Westinghouse, USA
1872	Patent for the petrol engine by George B Brayton, USA
1872	Laying of the first transatlantic cable between Europe and South America
1873	First transmission of electric energy at Vienna, Austria, by Hippolyte Fontaine
1873	Perfection and assembly line production of the typewriter by Philio Remington, USA
1875	Long-distance transport of refrigerated meat (Buenos Aires/Le Havre) by Ferdinand Carré, France
1875	Remington launched the production of the typewriter from the invention of L Sholes
1876	Invention of the telephone by Alexander Graham Bell, USA
1876	Four-stroke internal combustion engines, Nokolaus Otto/Gottlieb Daimler/Wilhelm Maybach, Germany
1877	Invention of the record player by Thomas Alva Edison, USA
1878	Construction of the two-stroke petrol engine by Carl Benz, Germany
1878	First photographic plates of silver bromide emulsion by George Eastman, USA
1878	Invention of the incandescent light bulb by Thomas A Edison, USA
1878	Invention of the centrifuge by Gustaf De Laval, Sweden
1879	First vaccination experiments on animals by Louis Pasteur, France
1879	First electric locomotive built by Werner von Siemens, Germany
1880	First electrical distribution system on a transatlantic boat (*Columbia*), Thomas A Edison, USA
1882	Construction of the first industrial alternator, Sebastiano Ziani de Ferranti, Britain (origin Italian)
1882	Invention of the electric fan by Schuyler Skoats Wheeler, USA
1883	First internal combustion engine automobile driven by Edouard Delamare-Deboutteville, France
1884	Discovery of the bacterial nitrification of soil by Jean-Jacques Schloesing, France
1884	Invention of the transformer by Lucien Gaulard, France
1884	Invention of the steam turbine by Charles Parsons, Britain
1884	Invention of the first artificial textile fibre by Hilaire Bernigaud, France
1884	Invention of the first fountain pen by Edson Waterman, USA
1884	Invention of the first photographic film by George Eastman, USA
1885	Invention of the first adding machine by William Steward Burroughs, USA
1886	First automobile driven by a four-stroke petrol engine (three wheels), Carl Benz, Germany
1886	First offshore drilling in California, USA
1887	Carburettor and two-stroke petrol engine invented, Gottlieb Daimler & Wilhelm Maybach, Germany
1888	First special steels developed, Robert Abbot Hadfield, Britain
1888	Pneumatic tyre developed by John Boyd Dunlop, Scotland
1890	First underground railway (tube/metro) line in London, England
1891	First petrol-driven automobile by René Panhard and Emile Levassor, France
1891	Invention of the replaceable inflatable tyre for the bicycle by Edouard Michelin, France
1892	First patent for the internal combustion engine, Rudolf Diesel, Germany
1892	Refinement of the electric oven, Henri Moissan, France
1893	Invention of the thermos flask for liquefied gases, James Dewar, Scotland
1893	Invention of the radio antenna, Aleksandr Stepanovitch Popov, Russia
1894	Invention of the replaceable inflatable tyre for the automobile, Edouard Michelin, France
1895	Discovery of the X-ray by Wilhelm Conrad Röntgen, Germany
1895	Invention of cinematography by Louis and Auguste Lumière (brothers), France
1895	First use of the electric train in Baltimore, USA
1896	Discovery of naturally occurring uranium, Henri Becquerel, France
1896	Wireless telegraphy patented by Gugliemo Marconi, Italy
1896	First electrical record player, or pick-up, Frantz Dussaud, Switzerland
1896	The telephone dialler is invented; operators are no longer needed to connect all calls
1897	Demonstration that yeast from beer is the fermentation agent for alcohol, Edouard Buchner, Germany
1897	Invention of the cathode ray oscilloscope, Karl Ferdinand Braun, Germany
1898	Hydrogen gas liquefied by James Dewar, Scotland
1898	Radium and polonium discovered Pierre and Marie Curie, France
1899	First Morse code sent over a long distance (40 km) by Gugliemo Marconi, Italy
1899	First bus built by Gottlieb Daimler in Germany
1899	First electrified rail line in Europe (Switzerland) by Burgdorf-Thourne

Twentieth century

1901	Battery with electrodes of iron and nickel invented by the German, Junger
1902	Synthesis of methane realized by Paul Sabatier in France
1902	Invention of electric lighting using a magneto by Robert Bosch in Germany
1903	First powered aeroplane flight *Kitty Hawk* by Orville and Wilbur Wright, in North Carolina, USA

1904	Invention of the electric vacuum tube by John Ambrose Fleming in England
1904	Invention of colour photography by Auguste and Louis Lumière, France
1905	First industrial production of offset printing in the USA by Ira W Rubel
1906	Ammonia synthesized in Germany by Fritz Haber
1909	First flight across the English Channel by the Frenchman Louis Blériot
1913	First flight across the Mediterranean by the Frenchman Roland Garros
1913	Invention of the cathode ray tube for the production of X-rays, Hans Geiger, Germany
1913	Invention of the first gas-field electric bulb by the American Irving Langmuir
1913	Opening of the first assembly-line car production operation by Henry Ford, USA
1915	First aeroplane constructed entirely of metal by Hugo Junkers, Germany
1916	Stainless steel invented by Henry Brearly in England
1918	First hybrids of corn developed by the American Donald Jones
1920	Opening of the first radio station in Pittsburgh, Pennsylvania, USA
1920	Invention of steel–nickel alloy for manufacture of clock springs, Charles Guillaume, Switzerland
1920	Commercialization of isopropyl alcohol by Exxon, giving birth to the petrochemical industry
1923	Invention of the bulldozer in the USA
1925	First automobile made with a single body of metal, André Citroën, France
1925	First short-wave intercontinental radio-telephone contact between Sydney and London, Gugliemo Marconi.
1926	First demonstration of colour television by the Englishman John Logie Baird
1926	Invention of pre-stressed concrete by Eugène Freyssinetn, France
1927	First talking movie by Warner and Fox, USA
1927	Non-stop transatlantic air crossing by Charles Lindbergh, USA
1928	Penicillin discovered by Alexander Fleming, Britain
1928	Invention of the electric razor by the American Schick
1930	Invention of the particle accelerator by Robert Jemison Van de Graff, USA
1931	Invention of the synthetic rubber, neoprene by Wallace Hume Carothers, USA
1932	Discovery of Heavy Water and deuterium by Harold Urey, USA
1932	Installation of the talking clock at the Paris observatory, Ernest Esclangon
1933	Development of the insecticide DDT by Herman Müller, Switzerland
1934	Development of nuclear fission by the Italian Enrico Fermi
1934	Invention of the iconoscope for television by Vladimir Zworykin, USA (originally Russian)
1935	Invention of radar by Robert Alexander Watson-Watt, Britain
1935	Invention of the fountain pen with a refillable reservoir
1938	Uranium fission discovered by the Germans Otto Hahn and Friedrich Strassmann

1939	First flight in Germany a turbine driven aeroplane (Heinkel He-78)
1939	First helicopter with a propeller anti-couple by Igor Sikorsky, USA
1939	Ball-point invented by the Hungarian L Biro and put into production by the firm Reynolds, USA
1941	Plutonium discovered by the Americans Ewin Mattison McMillan and Glenn Seaborg
1941	Discovery of silicones by Frederic Stanley Kipping
1941	First flight of a turbine-driven aeroplane perfected by Frank Whittle, Britain
1942	First atomic pile built at the University of Chicago, USA, by the Italian Enrico Fermi
1943	Commercialization of the first polyacrylic fibres
1944	Production of the electro-mechanical calculator by Howard Aiken and IBM, USA
1945	First atomic bomb explosion in New Mexico, USA
1945	Atomic bombs dropped on Hiroshima and Nagasaki, Japan
1946	Computer ENIAC 'Electronic Numerical Integrator & Calculator', USA, John Ecket/John Mauchy
1948	Transistor invented by John Barden, Walter Brattain and William Shockley, the Bell Laboratories, USA
1948	Development of the instantaneous photographic camera by Edward Herbert Land, USA
1950	First numerical-controlled machine tool (milling machine), USA
1951	Colour movies (Eastman Colour) launched by Eastman Kodak
1951	First electronic calculator, UNIVAC, for management applications, Remington Rand, USA
1952	First commercial computers (IBM 701)
1952	First television link between Britain and France
1953	Cinemascope developed by 20th Century Fox
1954	First nuclear-powered submarine Nautilus launched in USA
1955	Polymerization of ethylene (polyethylene) achieved in Germany by Karl Ziegler
1955	Technique for making artificial diamonds discovered by Percy William Bridgman, USA
1955	First automobiles with hydraulic suspension (DS 19 Citroën)
1955	Two locomotives in France reach the speed of 331 km/h
1955	First flight of the French Caravelle jet with rear engines
1955	First nuclear power plant put into service (Calder Hall), UK
1956	Fortran becomes the first computer programming language, John Backus, IBM
1956	Laying of first undersea telephone cable between the USA and Britain
1956	General Electric (USA) begins producing industrial diamonds
1956	Lever Brothers launches Wisk, America's first liquid laundry detergent
1957	First satellite put into orbit by the Russians (Sputnik 1)
1957	Ford introduces the Edsel (loses more than $250 million in two years)
1958	First automobile with an automatic gearbox, DAF, Netherlands
1958	Launching of the first nuclear-powered ice-breaker

1958	Pan American Airways (USA) inaugurates New York to Paris commercial jet service
1958	Integrated circuit developed by Kilbey at Texas Instruments and Noyce at Fairchild, USA
1958	Bank of America issues BankAmericard (later called Visa)
1959	Hovercraft put into service, C Cockerell, Britain
1959	Haloid Xerox introduces plain paper copier, USA
1960	The Food and Drug Administration (FDA), USA approves Searles Enovid as the first oral contraceptive
1960	Construction of the first laser by Theodore Harold Maiman, USA
1962	Telstar 1, a communications satellite, is launched into orbit, USA
1962	First transatlantic TV satellite emission (Andover, USA, and Plemeur-Bodou, France)
1962	First industrial robot commercialized in USA
1962	Philips, the Netherlands, introduces the compact cassette
1963	Pepsi Cola introduced, USA
1964	Blue Ribbon Sports (Nike) introduces its first running shoes, USA
1964	First typewriter with a memory, IBM, USA
1964	Ford introduces the Mustang, USA
1966	Carbon fibres developed in Britain by W Watt, L N Phillips and W Johnson
1967	Amana introduces countertop microwave oven, USA
1967	First flexible factories, Sundstrand Aviation, Rockford, USA and IBM, Deptford, Britain
1968	First supersonic transport plane, Tupolev Tu-144, USSR
1968	Cameron printing press for large volumes in the USA
1968	Burroughs, USA, produces first computers (B2500 and B3500) using integrated circuits
1969	Integrated circuit (CDD Charge Coupled Device) of silicon, Boyle and Smith at Bell Labs, USA
1969	Citroën, France, commercializes fuel injection systems
1969	Moon landing (Neil Armstrong and Edwin Aldrin), USA
1969	US Department of Defense creates ARPAnet, forerunner of the Internet
1970	Pan Am inaugurates wide-body jet service with flights between New York and London
1971	Intel, USA, commercializes first microprocessor (2300 transistors on 7 mm^2 of silicon)
1971	Intel, USA, produces micro-processor
1972	Fibre-optics developed by Corning Glassworks, USA
1972	Pong, the first home video game is introduced
1972	First colour home VCR is produced by Philips, the Netherlands
1972	First pocket calculators, Texas Instruments, USA
1972	EMI of the UK introduces the CT scanner
1972	Colour TVs outnumber black and white sets
1972	Kevlar, artificial fibre commercialized by Dupont, USA
1973	Sharp, Japan, introduces calculators with LCDs (liquid crystal displays)
1973	10 000 components are placed on a 1cm^2 chip
1973	Invention of the scanner for medical work by Godfrey Newbold Hounsfield, Britain
1974	The first international fax standard transmits one page in six minutes
1974	Intel's second-generation microprocessor makes personal computers possible, USA
1974	First programmable calculators, Hewlett-Packard, USA
1975	Development of Computer Aided Design (CAD)
1976	Supercomputer Cray 1 capable of performing 250 million operations, USA
1977	Apple II by Apple, USA, first PC able to generate colour graphics; has a keyboard and power supply
1977	CompuServe, a computer information service, goes on-line, USA
1978	Genentech, USA, clones first recombinant DNA product, human insulin
1979	First laser printers, IBM, USA
1979	Compact disc developed by Philips, the Netherlands
1979	IBM PC launched, USA
1980	First experiments at video conferencing
1980	First phone cards introduced
1981	Development of interferon, Charles Weissmann, Switzerland
1981	IBM adopts Microsoft's industry standard disc operating system (DOS)
1981	Xerox PARC, USA, introduces graphical user interface
1981	First systems of computer aided design and computer aided manufacturing (CAD/CAM), USA
1982	First compact discs introduced
1983	First cellular telephone system introduced in the USA by Motorola
1983	Sega, Japan, introduces a three-dimensional video game
1983	MCI orders first big fibre-optic system from Corning and Siecor, USA
1983	Chrysler, USA, introduces the minivan
1984	Philips (the Netherlands), and Sony (Japan) develop the compact disc read-only memory (CD-ROM)
1984	Commercialization by Seiko, Japan, of the first colour portable TV with a flat screen
1984	Apple, USA, introduces the Macintosh, a powerful and user-friendly desktop computer
1985	A single optical fibre transmits the equivalent of 300 000 simultaneous phone calls
1986	First laser robots used in a mechanical production centre
1987	First virtual-reality products sold commercially
1988	Hewlett-Packard, USA, develops the DeskJet printer in just 22 months
1989	Lotus, USA, introduces Notes groupware
1990	Internet World Wide Web developed by Tim Berners-Lee at European Particle Physics Lab, Grenoble, France
1990	Saturn, GM's first new car division since 1919, rolls out first car
1991	Compact disks outsell cassettes
1993	Intel's Pentium microprocessor enables personal computers to run thousands of programs
1993	Mosaic, a free software program, can be used to surf the World Wide Web
1994	Netscape creates its Navigator software for browsing the World Wide Web

1994	Digital Satellite System provides up to 175 TV channels using an 18-inch satellite dish
1995	US Federal Communications Commission (FCC) begins auctioning broadband spectrum licenses for personal communications services
1995	Microsoft introduces Windows 95, an upgrade of its operating system

SOURCES

Chronique du 20e siècle (1990) Paris: Larousse.
Fortune.
History of the World (1951) Odhams Press Ltd.

Pears Cyclopaedia 1993–94 (1993) London: Pelham Books.
International Herald Tribune.
Petit Larousse illustré (1986) Paris: Libraire Larousse.
Petit Robert, 2, Universel des Noms Propres (1989) Paris: Dictionnaires Le Robert.
Sunday Times Makers of the 20th Century (1991) London: Times Newspapers Ltd.
The Economist.
Wall Street Journal.

III Appendix

Table AIII.1 gives an illustration of depreciation tables for the United States. It gives the recovery period in years for common assets and is taken from the Federal Income Tax Tables.

In the Modified Accelerated Cost Recovery System the percentages applied each year to the asset depend on whether a half-year or quarter-year convention is used. As an illustration of the half-year convention, the applied percentages are given in Table AIII.2.

Table AIII.1 US depreciation tables for assets placed in service after 1986

Assets used in all business activities	Modified accelerated cost recovery system (MACRS)	Alternative depreciation system (ADS)
Office furniture and equipment	7	10
Computers and peripheral equipment	5	5
Typewriters, calculators, copiers	5	6
Aeroplanes (non-commercial) and helicopters	5	6
Automobiles	5	5
Light general-purpose trucks (less than 13,000 lb)	5	5
Heavy general-purpose trucks (13,000lb or more)	5	6
Tractor units (for over-the-road use)	3	4
Trailers	5	6
Vessels, barges, tugs and similar water transportation equipment	10	18
Assets used in agricultural activities		
Agricultural machinery and equipment	7	10
Breeding or dairy cattle	5	7
Breeding or work horses, 12 years or less	7	10
Racehorses, more than two years old	3	12
Breeding hogs	3	3
Breeding sheep and goats	5	5
Farm buildings, other than single purpose	20	25
Trees and vines, fruit or nut bearing	10	20
Drainage tile, culverts	15	20
Assets used in mineral extraction		
Mining assets to mine sand, gravel, clay, etc.	7	10
Assets used in drilling oil and gas wells	5	6
Assets used in exploration and production of oil and gas	7	14
Assets used in manufacturing activities		
Manufacture, packaging and finishing of apparel and textiles	6	9
Assets used in manufacture of wood products and furniture	7	10
Assets for distributive trades and services		
Wholesale and retail trade, personal and professional services	5	9
Marketing petroleum and petroleum products	5	9
High-technology medical equipment	5	5
Real property		
Land improvements (sidewalks, roads, bridges, fences, towers)	15	20
Residential property	27.5	40
Non-residential real property (in service before 13 May 1993)	31.5	40
Non-residential real property (in service after 13 May 1993)	39	40

Other

Assets used in construction	5	6
Assets used in recreation activities	7	10
Timber-cutting equipment	5	6

Table AIII.2   MACRS (US) half-year convention, applied percentages

Recovery year	Three-year	Five-year	Seven-year	Ten-year	Fifteen-year	Twenty-year
1	33.33	20.00	14.29	10.00	5.00	3.750
2	44.45	32.00	24.49	18.00	9.50	7.219
3	14.81	19.20	17.49	14.40	8.55	6.677
4	7.41	11.52	12.49	11.52	7.70	6.177
5		11.52	8.93	9.22	6.93	5.713
6		5.76	8.92	7.37	6.23	5.285
7			8.93	6.55	5.90	4.888
8			4.46	6.55	5.90	4.522
9				6.56	5.91	4.462
10				6.55	5.90	4.461
11				3.28	5.91	4.462
12					5.90	4.461
13					5.91	4.462
14					5.90	4.461
15					5.91	4.462
16					2.95	4.461
17						4.462
18						4.461
19						4.462
20						4.461
21						2.231
Total	100.00	100.00	100.00	100.00	100.00	100.00

IV Appendix

AUDIT CHECK SHEETS

The six tables given here (Tables AIV.1 to AIV.5) are audit checksheets that summarize areas in Chapter 26, *Auditing Operations*, and can be used to evaluate how well an operation is performing. These checksheets are of a general nature and may need to be adjusted for the specifics of a firm.

Table AIV.1 Are you customized?

Criteria	1	2	3	4	5
Do you have all the customers you would like?					
Are the customers as loyal as you would like?					
Do you generate as much business from each customer as you would like?					
Do you really know what your customers want?					
Does your entire organization know what your customers want?					
Is your information network focused on helping you hear what customers and markets are trying to tell you?					
Can your organization respond quickly to what customers and markets are telling you?					
Does your information network enable the proactive delivery of information to your customers?					
Are the full capabilities of your organization accessible to your customers at all your field locations?					
Does your information network reflect the bottom-line importance of customer service?					

Key: 1. Never; 2. Rarely; 3. Sometimes; 4. Most of the time; 5. All the time
Note 1: This checksheet may be simplified by having a binomial, yes/no response.
Note 2: It is useful if the analysis is performed periodically, say once a quarter or once every six months, to see if improvements are being achieved.

Table AIV.2 Working characteristics of an organization

Criteria	1	2	3	4	5
Are changes accepted as a way of improvement?					
Are operators encouraged to be multiskilled?					
Are operators motivated at all levels in their work?					
Are personnel motivated to do quality work?					
Can operators stop a facility if there is a problem?					
Is attention focused on satisfying customers?					
Is career movement and promotion from within?					
Is decision making by consensus?					
Is operational documentation easily available?					
Is operational documentation easy to use?					
Is operational documentation sufficiently detailed?					
Is operational documentation up to date?					

Criteria	1	2	3	4	5
Is performance judged by objectives?					
Is the plant always well organized?					
Is the plant always clean?					
Is the absenteeism low?					
Is the facility neat and organized?					
Is the noise level low?					
Is there adequate training for personnel?					
Do peer members communicate easily?					
Does management have an open-door policy?					
Is there a common objective in the organization?					

Key: 1. Never; 2. Rarely; 3. Sometimes; 4. Most of the time; 5. All the time
Note 1: This checksheet may be simplified by having a binomial, yes/no response.
Note 2: It is useful if the analysis is performed periodically, say once a quarter or once every six months, to see if improvements are being achieved.

Table AIV.3   Inventory management

Indicator	Calculation	Today	In three months	In six months	In nine months	In one year
Average inventory level during a cycle	$$\frac{(\text{Beginning} + \text{ending value of inventory})}{2}$$					
Order processing cost per cycle	$$\frac{(\text{Total demand in units}) \times (\text{Cost of each order})}{\text{Units per order}}$$					
Inventory carrying cost	Cost of financing, warehousing, insurance, waste, etc.					
Inventory turnover	$$\frac{\text{Cost of goods sold}}{\text{Value of inventory}}$$					
Record accuracy	$$\frac{\text{Number of inaccurate records during a cycle}}{\text{Number of items counted during a cycle}}$$					
Inventory-to-sales ratio	$$\frac{\text{Inventory}}{\text{Sales}}$$					
Average value of working inventory	$$\frac{(\text{Number of items ordered}) \times (\text{value})}{2}$$					
Value of safety stock	Total inventory value − Value of working inventory					
Customer service level according to availability of units (%)	$$100 - \frac{\text{Number of incomplete orders} \times 100}{\text{Total orders demanded}}$$					
Customer service level according to availability of units (%)	$$100 - \frac{\text{Stockouts in units for period} \times 100}{\text{Total units demanded}}$$					
Inventory as a percentage of assets	$$\frac{\text{Value of inventory}}{\text{Value of total assets (inventory} + \text{equipment})}$$					
Number of references for raw materials, in-process and finished goods	Number of product references managed					

Table AIV.4 Operational Measurements

Indicator	Calculation	Today	In 3 months	in 6 months	in 9 months	In 1 year
Production lead times (days	Elapsed time between receiving the customer's order and delivery					
Production Costs	Total unit cost for producing order (by product)					
Use of data Processing	$\dfrac{\text{orders made by data processing}}{\text{Total orders made}}$					
Waste	$\dfrac{\text{cost of material lost in period}}{\text{average value of material in period}}$					
Level of Support services	Maintenance, sub-contractors, part-time labour, etc.					
Product quality (lots)	$100 - \dfrac{\text{Number of lots rejected}}{\text{Total number of lots received}}$					
Product quality (components)	$100 - \dfrac{\text{Number of parts rejected}}{\text{Total number of parts received}}$					
Product quality (financial)	$100 - \dfrac{\text{Financial value of rejected items}}{\text{Total financial value of shipments}}$					
Purchasing operating costs	$\text{Costs per order} - \dfrac{\text{Purchasing department administration costs}}{\text{Total number of purchase orders}}$					
Set-up time of a machine	$\text{Set-up time (\%)} - \dfrac{\text{Total set-up times}}{\text{Operating + set-up times}}$					
Time loss due to machine break-downs	$\text{Downtime (\%)} - \dfrac{\text{Total time machines are down}}{\text{Total time (running + down)}}$					
Time loss due to rework of components	$\text{Lost time (\%)} - \dfrac{\text{Time spent on rework}}{\text{Total time spent on producing units}}$					

Table AIV.5 Delivery service attributes

Delivery service criteria	1	2	3	4	5
Delivery completeness					
Delivery reliability					
Delivery frequency					
Order status information					
Order lead time					
Minimum order quantity					
Delivery hours					
Delivery precision					
Ability to make emergency orders					

Key: 1. Never achieved; 2. Rarely achieved; 3. Achieved sometimes; 4. Achieved most of the time; 5. Achieved all of the time
Note 1: This checksheet may be simplified by having a binomial, yes/no response.
Note 2: It is useful if the analysis is performed periodically, say once a quarter or once every six months, to see if improvements are being achieved.

Table AIV.6 Quality of restaurant service (better understanding your tastes to better serve you)

Criteria	1	2	3	4	5
Friendliness of the personnel?					
Speed of the service?					
Quality of the food?					
Quantity of food served?					
Presentation of the food?					
General cleanliness of the restaurant?					
Relationship quality/price?					
Are you staying at the hotel?	Yes*	No*			
Are you here for the first time?	Yes*	No*			
Do you come to the region for:	Tourism*	Business*			

*Delete as appropriate
Key: 1. Very poor; 2. Poor; 3. Good; 4. Very good; 5. Excellent
Note: It is useful if the analysis is performed periodically, say once a quarter or once every six months, to see if improvements are being achieved.

Glossary

Note: Words in *italic* are cross-references and defined in the glossary.

A

A classification, part of the *VAT classification*, means that from a multitude of raw materials, parts and components (the base of the A) is made a single product, or a few products, (the apex of the A), such as a cruise ship or a jumbo jet.

ABC inventory management is a way of classifying *inventory* components. It is based on a *Pareto* analysis in which units are grouped according to annual cost. Inventory having a high total annual cost is considered in the A classification, inventory with the lowest cost in the C classification and inventory with intermediate costs in the B classification.

Acceptable quality level (AQL) is the level of product quality, often expressed as a percentage, considered acceptable. It is a standard established either by the manufacturer or by the purchaser of the product. The lower the value of the AQL, the more rigorous is the production process, and the higher is the *cost of quality*.

Acceptance plans are the agreed programmes between suppliers and purchasers for *random sampling* and testing, of a quantity of goods to decide whether to accept the entire *lot* based on the quality of a tested sample.

Acid rain is principally derived from fossil fuels, particularly oil and coal, which produce sulphur dioxide and sulphur trioxide when burnt. These gases, dissolved in atmospheric moisture, constitute acid rain, which is a constituent of air pollution.

Activity in a project is an identifiable and well-defined task. For construction, activities might include laying of foundations, frame construction and electrical connections.

Activity-based costing is analysing the cost of an operation at each processing step. In addition to measuring direct costs like materials and labour, it covers rework, bottlenecks, delays and other time-related activities. In this way, activity-based costing highlights areas of inefficiency in an operation.

Activity chart is a tool used to analyse the activity of an operator and machine, or a combination of a crew of operators with a park of machines, with the objective of improving the utilization of man/machine.

Activity on arrow in a *PERT* or *CPM* chart is the convention for designating an activity where the arrowhead shows the direction of flow. The length of the arrow does not have to be proportional to the time of the activity.

Activity scheduling chart is an alternative name for a *Gantt* or *bar chart*.

Activity time estimate is the estimated time to complete a project *activity* in a *PERT* or *CPM* network diagram.

Adaptive smoothing is a type of *exponential smoothing* forecast where the smoothing constant is automatically adjusted to keep forecasting errors to a minimum.

AFL-CIO is the biggest US labour movement formed by the merger of the American Federation of Labour and the Congress of Industrial Organisations in 1955.

Agency shop is a labour–management agreement where workers who refuse to join the union represented in the firm are expected to pay the union for the benefits derived through collective bargaining. In this condition of employment, non-union workers cannot be criticized for 'getting a free ride', even though they are not union members.

Aggregate demand is the total client demand for a product or service, as opposed to the demand for the individual products.

Aggregate inventory is the total inventory maintained by a firm, rather than specific quantities of the different materials and products contained in a storage area.

Aggregate planning is the development of a production plan to efficiently use available resources, such as labour, machines and subcontractors, in order to satisfy expected demand.

Air freight is merchandise that is transported by air. It is the most expensive way to expedite goods and is usually reserved for perishable or urgently required items.

Air pollution is caused by chemicals or solid particles in the air principally from industry and transportation. In humans this can lead to respiratory or other health problems. It is also destructive to plant and animal life and causes corrosion on buildings and equipment.

Alpha risk, in statistics – also known as a *Type I error* – is the risk of rejecting a null hypothesis when it is in fact true.

American Production and Inventory Control Society (APICS) is a US-based professional organization associated with operations management activities.

Analogue computer carries out calculations by taking measurements of *continuous variables*, such as temperature, pressure or flow rates, which are then translated into understandable mechanical or electrical values. Analogue devices are often used in *process industries*.

Analysis of variance (ANOVA) is a technique useful in *statistical quality control* enabling the testing of the significance of the difference between two or more sample means.

Annual operating plan, developed from the firm's *strategic plan*, details the actions to be taken, the budget to be allocated, and a forecast of expected results.

Annual report is a document that, by law, is published every year by corporations or organizations whose shares are publicly traded. The report includes financial data for the corporation and also information covering the company's activities, personnel, achievements, environmental record and perhaps future strategies.

Annuity is a series of payments, or receipts, of equal amounts which usually occur at the end of a period. A life insurance policy, when matured or activated, can pay an annuity to the beneficiary of a fixed sum of money each month or each year

Appointment book is a planning document often used in the service industry, for example in medical centres as a master schedule for patient appointments. It is analogous to the *master production schedule* in manufacturing.

Apprentice system is where inexperienced workers are assigned to master craftsmen, or experienced workers, who supervise and monitor the apprentice's activity for a certain period. During this time it is expected that the apprentice will become knowledgeable about his trade and at the end of his 'time' will be able to obtain the appropriate apprentice certification.

Approved list is a list of those suppliers that have been pre-selected by a purchasing authority. Preselection may have been based on such factors as price, reliability, service or quality. When a supplier is selected from an approved list, there is an assurance that the supplier meets the purchasing organization's requirements.

Approved supplier is one providing raw materials, or parts, who is given preferential treatment in purchasing activities, because the supplier scores high on price, quality, reliability, delivery, service and stability of its business.

Arbitration is negotiation and conflict resolution where an impartial third party is involved in hearing and settling the dispute. This arbitrator decides which evidence can be heard and how the dispute should be resolved. Binding arbitration is often used in labour disputes where both parties agree to abide by the decision of the arbitrator.

Area of feasibility in two dimensional linear programming is the region bounded by the graphs, and the axes containing feasible solutions to the linear programming model.

Arrivals are the number of units or people arriving at a service area and forming a *waiting line* or *queue*. A knowledge of the pattern of arrivals, size, service time and the like is necessary in order to design the service centre handling the arrivals.

Artificial intelligence is an aspect of information technology and broadly, is the use of computers to mimic or copy aspects of human intelligence such as learning languages, making decisions, and performing physical actions.

Assembly chart, also known as a *Gozinto Chart* after the Italian mathematician Zepartzat Gozinto, uses information from an *assembly drawing* to indicate how parts fit together, the order of assembly and perhaps the material flow pattern.

Assembly drawing is an exploded view of a product, showing component parts and where they are interconnected. It is used to facilitate the final assembly of the product.

Assembly line is a plant layout where a product is progressively assembled at successive work posts; Transfer from one work post to another may be on a belt, on roller conveyers or with overhead cranes. An assembly line is designed using *assembly line balancing*.

Assembly line balancing is the assignment of tasks or activities on an *assembly line* operation so that each workstation is balanced with its immediate upstream, and downstream posts. The objective is to optimize the assembly operation, avoiding bottlenecks and excessive accumulation of inventory and minimizing employee idle time.

Assembly operation is that part of the manufacturing process where subassemblies, or the end products, are put together.

Assembly-time chart is a planning document indicating when to order, or manufacture, component parts in order to meet scheduled completion dates for finished products. The assembly-time chart is derived from the *material requirements plan*.

Assignable variations in an operation are those that can usually be identified or assigned to a specific cause. They may be due to worn tools, badly adjusted equipment, defective materials or human error.

Assignment method is a linear programming method that assigns jobs or functions to resources such as machine operation, territories to specific representatives or tasks to various employees. The objective is to match the task with the resource to optimize performance according to criteria such as cost, profit, efficiency and rate.

Associative forecasts are estimates of future demands that rely on identification of related variables for prediction. Sales of a particular computer may be directly related to its price, to the price of a competing model or to the capacity of the model. The essence of associative forecasting is to develop an equation, or model, to predict future demands.

Attribute inspection involves controlling according to the desired *attribute*, rather than to the degree of failure. The inspection of a light bulb would be attribute inspection as it either works or does not work.

Attributes are used in the classification of products where there are only binomial or two possible states, such as it works or it does not work, good or bad, pass or fail, fits or does not fit. Either a watch works or it does not and a student passes an exam or fails it.

Authorized requisition is a purchase agreement where certain persons, or situations, allow its execution. The requisition may be authorized because the activity is below a certain budget or a certain quota, or because the purchasing manager may automatically have signature authorization.

Autocratic leader is a manager who make most of the decisions himself, rather than depending on a consensus opinion.

Automated guided vehicles (AGVs) are computer-controlled chariots, often used in manufacturing to move parts and equipment between workstations or storage areas.

Automated storage and retrieval systems are computer-controlled systems in warehouses, where inventory is automatically added or withdrawn and forklifts, bins, conveyers and inventory records are managed by a central control system.

Automated teller machine (ATM) is a computer-controlled cash distributor.

Automated warehouse is a storage facility managed and operated principally using computers, automatic equipment, robots and conveyers, rather than a lot of manual labour.

Automatic vending is the sale of products using automatically controlled machines, rather than sales people, for items like food, beverages, newspapers and stamps.

Automation is the manufacture of products, or the distribution of services, using computer-operated equipment rather than human labour. In the long term, automated production produces more uniform products and unit costs are generally lower.

Autonomous production or assembly is when all work on a certain product is performed at a single workstation, rather than being processed at successive work stations. Artisans may be autonomous in producing wood furniture, for example.

Average forecasting models average or smooth past data in order to develop a forecast. The models may be *simple moving averaging* or *weighted moving averaging*.

Average inventory is the mean quantity maintained during a certain period and can be calculated by the simple arithmetic mean of the beginning and ending inventories.

Average outgoing quality (AOQ) is the percentage of defective items in an average lot size of products that have been inspected through acceptance sampling.

B

Baan is a Netherlands based company, founded in 1978, specializing in the development of computer-based *material resource planning* or *enterprise resource planning* tools.

Backlog is made up of customer orders not yet shipped and may be expressed in terms of units, or in financial terms. Backlog is usually encountered for custom, or produce-to-order, goods

Backorder is when an out-of-stock item has been reordered from the supplier but has not been delivered.

Back-up systems are in place when the failure of the principal system would be of concern. The back-up, or *parallel system*, cuts in if the principal system fails. Hospitals have back-up electrical generators and aeroplanes have back-up control systems.

Backward integration is when a company purchases, or merges with, another company, which is a supplier of its raw materials. This is a strategy that helps to ensure a continued supply of those raw materials, for example a paper company purchasing forestry land.

Backward scheduling determines when to start production or to place purchase orders to meet client needs. Scheduling begins with the product due date and then subtracts the various lead times from this to determine when production or purchasing should begin.

Baldrige, Malcolm was the US Secretary of Commerce under President Reagan, from 1981 until his death in a rodeo accident in 1987. That year the US Congress created an internationally recognized award entitled 'The Malcolm Baldrige Quality Award'.

Balk occurs in systems where *waiting lines* occur, such as at a bank till or grocery checkout. Arriving customers decide to wait, to wait a while and then leave or to leave immediately, or balk at waiting in line.

Bar chart, also called a *Gannt chart*, indicates scheduling activities. Horizontal bars show the various activities, the start and finish times, with the length of the bar proportional to the time taken for execution of a particular activity.

Barcode scanner is used for reading the barcode stamped or printed on an article. The scanner is often integrated with a computer program to record inventory movements.

Barcoding uniquely identifies a product by a series of wide and narrow strips, or bars, stamped or printed onto the product label. The barcode incorporates symbols, letters and numbers to identify a product, which can thus be identified by a *barcode scanner*. Barcoding is common in retail stores, where the code incorporates the product price.

Bargaining is negotiating a work contract, such as for salaries or other conditions. If unions are involved, collective bargaining replaces individual bargaining and the union is the bargaining agent between company management and its members. In some cases (*agency shops*), the union may also be the agent for some or all of the non-union employees.

Base stock system is where inventory is replenished at a scheduled shipment date with the quantity equal to the actual usage for the previous period.

Batch processing is the manufacture or processing of products or units in bulk, or in large lots. The preparation of a batch of die in the textile industry, printing a certain quantity of a book or the seating of passengers in a Boeing 747 would be batch processing.

BATNEEC principle or the *Best Available Technology Not Entailing Excessive Cost*, is the principle that if the costs of technology are reasonable and also would make a product more environmentally acceptable, then this should be the chosen production technology.

Bayesian decision theory is the concept of revising one's decision as more information related to that decision becomes available, because, with more information, the probability of making the correct decision becomes more likely.

Behavioural approaches to management emphasize the understanding of people in increasing performance and productivity. The belief is that if managers understand their people, and adapt their organizations to them, company success usually follows.

Bell curve for projects is the profile of financial expenditures over time. At the design stage, costs rise slowly, being related just to personnel charges. When major equipment is purchased, earth work and construction-start costs rise rapidly. Towards completion, costs decline, again being associated with personnel such as operators, painters and start-up crews.

Benchmarking is rating a firm's products, processes and policies, in comparison with other companies in the same, or another, business. The objective is to see how the company is performing, particularly relating to quality, service and unit cost.

Bernoulli equation is the expression to describe a *binomial distribution*. It was developed on the basis of experiments carried out by the seventeenth century Swiss mathematician, Jacob Bernoulli. Tossing a coin a fixed number of times is a Bernoulli process.

Beta distribution, which has the properties of being entirely contained within a finite interval, is a probability distribution commonly used in *PERT* network diagrams. The. mean and variance of the distribution can be determined, by the estimated *optimistic, pessimistic* and *most likely times*.

Bhopal is the site in India that suffered a catastrophic accident in 1984 as the result of the release of toxic methyl isocyanate gas in a pesticide facility owned by Union Carbide.

Bienayme-Chebyshev rule concerns the variability of data about the mean point. The rule says that, regardless of how a set of data is distributed, the percentage of observations contained within a distance of two standard deviations around the mean is at least 75.00 per cent. For 3 standard deviations,the percentage is at least 88.89 per cent and, for four standard deviations at least 93.75 per cent.

Bill of labour is the labour requirements for producing an end-item tangible product or service and specifies the labour specialization required, the quantity and the hourly rate.

Bill of material is a listing of the parts, subassemblies, assemblies and raw materials that go into making a finished product.

Bill of sale is a legal document, signed by the seller, giving evidence of the transfer of the title or ownership of a product, real estate or other asset.

Bimodal is when there are two values in a data set that occur most frequently.

Binary code, the arithmetic of computers, is based on two digits, zero and one. A digit, either the 0 or the 1 in the binary code, is called the *bit*, or binary digit. When a binary digit is moved one space to the left and a zero is placed after it, the resulting number is twice the original number.

Binary digit is another term for a *bit*.

Binomial distribution is the probability distribution of discrete probabilities when there are only two possible outcomes for each trial of an experiment, such as yes or no, good or bad, open or closed.

Biodegradable materials are materials that will break down under natural conditions to become harmless substances. Vegetable matter and, to some extent, paper are biodegradable.

Biodiversity refers to the earth's multitude of plant and animal species. Human activity, population growth and economic progress contribute to the reduction of biodiversity.

Biotechnology is producing products through recombinant genetics, or gene splicing.

Bit, or *binary digit* is either the 0 or the 1 in the *binary code*.

Blacklist in labour circles is a secret list of union organizers and members that is compiled by employers' associations and circulated among the members for the purpose of denying employment to the listed persons. It is regarded as an unfair labour practice under a ruling of the US National Labour Relations Board.

Blanket orders are used when a company has a continuous, but perhaps varying, need for relatively low-cost items. This purchase order usually covers a given time, and deliveries are arranged by sending a simple release notice to the supplier. Price, and other specifications, have previously been established in the principal blanket-order contract.

Blister pack is transparent plastic packaging that is made up of a matrix of air pockets, which give added protection by preventing a transported product being directly in contact with the outside packing container. Blister packaging is not biodegradable.

Block models are a scale representation of a construction project, such as a chemical plant. These plastic blocks, built during the projects design stage, aid *facility layout*.

Blue-collar workers are those, in a manufacturing environment, who work in the factory.

Board of directors is that group of people ultimately responsible for directing the affairs of a corporation; directors are typically elected for a three-year period.

Bonus payments are a form of incentive pay given by firms to employees in addition to normal wages. These bonuses are frequently paid on a yearly basis and may be related to length of service and company profitability.

Bottleneck is when some equipment, facility or other resource reduces the normal operating rate of a process because it does not have the capacity to meet the upstream load.

Bottom-round management is a consensus approach to management, often employed in Japanese firms where all parties are involved in the decision making. It is also known as consensus management, committee management or bottom-up management.

Brainstorming is a process where a small group of people in a company, often from different departments, meet and, without any inhibitions or pre-conceived notions, put forward their ideas related to company issues such as new products.

Breakeven is the point at which there is a balance between costs and revenues, or the point at which two or more operating centres exhibit equal costs.

Breaking the china is an expression used to describe what occurs when a firm applies business process re-engineering, starting all over again and being brave enough to ignore, or even destroy, the process design activities that went on before.

Buffer stock is inventory kept to smooth out an irregular operation, or to avoid stockouts with clients. If there is uncertainty in the delivery of raw materials, a buffer stock may be held to avoid a possible shutdown of a production operation.

Building codes are rules, usually legally enforceable, on the conditions for construction of buildings, bridges and the like. Codes differ from region to region and may be based on safety regulations or aesthetic considerations.

Bulk products are those quoted, sold or transported in significantly large quantities, such as coal, wood and plastic fibre.

Business cycle is the period of prosperity, or depression, for business activity. During periods of prosperity, the volumes of production, employment, company profits and prices rise, while the reverse applies during a depression. When the downward part of the business cycle is short, the period is referred to as a recession, rather than a depression.

Business ethics concern the standards of conduct for doing business. The standards of conduct vary between companies, countries and people, which often creates difficulties for firms involved in international business.

Business game is a simulation of an actual business activity, maybe computerized, and often used as an aid to teaching in universities and business schools.

Business process re-engineering is the means by which an organization may achieve radical change in performance, as measured by cost, cycle time, service and quality, by applying tools and techniques that focus on the business as a set of related customer-oriented core business processes, rather than a set of organizational functions.

Buyers' expectations is a qualitative approach to sales forecasting by soliciting opinions from prospective buyers. It is most commonly used for *industrial goods*.

Buying is the purchasing of goods and services from external sources. Often buyers are specialized according to a commodity, such as copper, steel, valves, ladies clothing, floor coverings or other unique items. This specialization allows buyers to become experts at purchasing their particularly commodity.

C

C-chart is a control tool in *statistical process control* to monitor the number of defects found on a surface area or a unit, such as on woven fabric, paper, the surface of an item of furniture or the errors on a page of newsprint.

Cabotage is a European Union system which decides the conditions under which domestic road transport in one Member State may be undertaken by a haulier registered in another Member State.

Capacity is the ability of an operating system to handle a certain load.

Capacity-constrained resource is one in which utilization is very close to capacity such that bottlenecks could occur if workcentre scheduling is not properly managed.

Capacity control is the management of a work centre such that equipment, people and materials are being fully utilized, but not overloaded.

Capacity cushion is the amount of capacity of a resource in excess of its planned charge. If a work centre has a monthly production capacity of 12 000 units, and the planned charge is 10,000 units, then the capacity cushion is (12 000 – 10 000)/10 000 or 20 per cent.

Capacity planning is the management of resources, such as labour, equipment and material, typically over a medium-term planning horizon such as a few weeks to perhaps 18 months.

Capacity requirements planning is the management of resources such as labour, equipment and material that tests the *master production schedule* to see if sufficient capacity is available for the operation.

Capacity utilization rate is the extent to which an organization uses its available capacity and is given by the ratio of capacity used to design capacity.

Capital assets include equipment, buildings, fixtures, patents and land.

Capital investment is the amount of funds used to purchase *capital assets*.

Carbon dioxide is an odourless, colourless gas formed under normal conditions by the burning of hydrocarbon fuels and considered a contributor to the *greenhouse effect*.

Carload lot, in train shipments, is that quantity of material that completely fills a railroad car. In this way unit shipping costs are less than if the wagon was only partly full.

Carousel is an inventory storage or retrieval system that rotates in a horizontal plane. In manufacturing, carousels are used to move inventory from storage to the working area and in airport terminals to move passenger luggage from the aeroplane to the client.

Carrying costs are those costs associated with holding of inventory, including borrowing costs for purchasing the stock, warehouse rent or depreciation, operating cost of the warehouse, inventory insurance, warehouse taxes, taxes on the inventory, losses due to theft, damage or obsolescence, and labour costs concerned with storing and handling.

Cash budget is a series of monthly or quarterly schedules showing cash receipts, cash payments and the borrowing requirements for meeting financial obligations. The cash budget is developed from the *pro forma financial* statement and other supporting data.

Cash discounts allow a reduction in price of goods if payment is made within a specified period. A 2/10, net 30 cash discount means that the price is 2 per cent less if payment is made within ten days after billing; otherwise, the full amount must be paid within 30 days.

Causal forecasting incorporates into the forecast model factors that could influence the forecast. For kitchen appliances, the forecast could be a function of housing construction; for car sales a function of interest rates; or for housing a function of immigration.

Cause and effect chart is another name for a *fishbone chart* or *Ishikawa diagram*.

Cellular layout is the arrangement of a work centre such that many different operations can be performed on one product.

Cellular manufacturing is production using a *cellular layout*.

Central limit theorem in statistical sampling says that, as the sample size increases, there is a point when the sampling distribution of the mean can be approximated by the normal distribution, even though the distribution of the population is not necessarily normal.

Central tendency implies that most *data sets* cluster around a central point. The mean, median, mode and midrange are measures of central tendency.

Centralized purchasing is the buying of goods and services from a common location rather than each individual user making his or her own purchases.

Centre of gravity method for site selection determines the central location at which total transportation costs to and from that site to other locations are minimized.

Centred moving average in forecasting is the average of data around a middle point.

Changeover time is the requirement to switch from one operation to another.

Chi-square test in statistics indicates whether the difference between several sample analyses is just due to chance or if there is a justifiable reason for the difference.

Chlorinated fluorocarbons (CFC), sometimes referred to as *freons*, are chemical compounds containing chlorine, fluorine and carbon. The chlorine in these is the constituent that damages the ozone in the upper atmosphere.

Clayton Act is a 1914 US law related to *purchasing*, extending the earlier *Sherman Act* covering price discrimination, tying clauses requiring the purchase of another item with the purchase of the desired item and exclusive dealings.

Client is not just the end user, but also the immediate downstream work post.

Client is king is the philosophy that the client, or customer, must receive the best service and is always right. The idea is that in business the object is to serve the customer and, if this is not done, there will be a problem. This concept is very dominant in the USA.

Client-server systems are where one computer (server) acts as a central repository for files and programs that can be shared by a number of personal computers (clients) connected by a network. This system replaces the mainframe-centric arrangement.

Closed loop material requirements planning manages material movement, *production planning, master production scheduling* and *capacity requirements planning*. An execution function covers *shop floor* control, scheduling, dispatching and delay reports. Being closed loop provides feedback and control between the execution and planning.

Closed system is where machines, organizations, or programmes are not constrained or do not interact with the external environment. In the short run, a manufacturing assembly operation could be considered as a closed system.

Cluster sampling is the division of the population into clusters and sampling one or more clusters. If London is targeted for analysis, it could be divided into clusters using a city map and then an appropriate number of clusters selected for study.

Coefficient of correlation r in *regression analysis* explains the relative importance of the association between the independent variable, x, and the dependent variable, y. It can take a value between $+1$ and -1, where -1 indicates a perfect negative relationship and $+1$ a perfect positive relationship. Zero would mean that there is no relationship between x and y.

Coefficient of determination r^2 measures the variation in the *dependent variable* y that is explained by the fitted simple *regression equation*. It is the square of the *coefficient of correlation* and thus always has a positive value.

Coefficient of variation is the relative analysis of the standard deviation of a distribution σ and its mean μ, given by the ratio σ/μ.

Coincident indicators or simultaneous indicators, are ones in harmony with the associated economic activity, such as GNP, unemployment rate, retail store sales, or index of industrial production

Completely knocked down (CKD) is a term used for companies that export their products in a disassembled, or kit form. In this way, products can be purchased at a lower price, shipping costs are less as the product can be packaged more precisely, and customs duties are lower because there is often a lower tariff for components than for finished goods.

Compound sum is the future value of a single amount of money, or an annuity, when compounded at a given interest rate for a specified time period.

Computer aided design (CAD) is the use of computer software to aid engineers to design products or process schemes using graphic and three-dimensional displays.

Computer aided manufacturing (CAM) is the technology where in manufacturing CAD provides tooling departments with data and generates codes for numerically controlled machines. The two concepts are thus integrated, resulting in CAD/CAM systems.

Computer integrated manufacturing (CIM) is a flexible system connecting engineering, production and inventory control, where computers generate electronic codes to control numerically controlled machines and material handling equipment.

Concurrent engineering is the practice where design engineers work closely, or in parallel, with production people to ensure that a product can be easily and cost-effectively manufactured, avoiding costly design changes and waste at a later stage.

Consumer price index is a measure of the inflation rate, or an indicator of the level of consumer prices. It estimates how much it would cost an urban middle class family to buy a market basket of goods in comparison with the purchase of the same goods a year earlier.

Consumer surveys are analyses of consumers' wants and tastes, often used by marketing departments to determine future product needs.

Consumers risk (β) is taking a random sample that shows a lower proportion of defects in the sample than actually present in the lot. A lot of 10 000 units with 2000 defectives could produce a sample with no defects, in which case the lot would be accepted.

Contact distance analysis is a *facility layout* method when there is contact with various functional departments. This approach involves adopting a department layout where the product of the total number of physical contacts and the distance travelled is a minimum. The logic is similar to that of *load–distance analysis*, except that material flow is not involved.

Contingency table is a cross-classification of data in statistical analysis to determine if data exhibits a pattern and, if so, to determine the reasons.

Continuous flow manufacturing is the term used to describe *just-in-time* production.

Continuous improvement is always looking for ways to improve a process or product, but not necessarily making radical changes. The principle is that, if the basic idea is sound, then building upon it will improve quality. The Japanese refer to this as *Kaizen*.

Continuous process is an operation having a very long and continuous cycle, where output volumes are high but the product variety is usually low. Oil refining is a continuous process operating continuously, perhaps for 350 days per year. The product range is limited to propane or butane gas, petrol, kerosene, diesel and heavy oils.

Contribution margin is the contribution to fixed costs from each unit of sales and is given by the difference between the sales price per unit and the cost per unit.

Control limits, in statistical quality control are the upper and lower limit of variables such as temperature and length, outside which a process is considered to be malfunctioning.

Corporate towns are those that grew up, or were established, by a corporation who located in that area, such as Bourneville, UK, established by Cadbury's, the chocolate company.

Cost of non-quality is associated with items produced below specification and discovered internally or externally, such as those concerned in a product recall.

Cost of quality is the cost of attaining a certain quality level. It might include employee training programmes, systems development for quality improvement, pilot plants, costs related to quality assurance and costs connected with detection and/or evaluation.

Cost–benefit analysis is a decision method showing whether expenditures for a project are greater or less than the '*financial*' benefits ultimately realized. If the costs are less, then the decision would be to proceed and, if costs are greater, the reverse.

Counting rules are the mathematical relationships that describe the number of possible outcomes, or results, of various types of experiments or trials.

Crisis management is a function that is often put in place by major corporations and governments, to respond to and to recover from a failure or accident, usually on a large scale.

Critical path is the longest path in a project *network diagram*.

Critical Path Method (CPM) is a *network diagram* analysis technique, originally developed to schedule maintenance projects in chemical plants. The method is useful for projects that have many activities and where on time completion is imperative.

Critical ratio, of the time to due date to the remaining process time, is an *order sequencing* rule, where the next job processed among those waiting is that with the lowest critical ratio.

Crosby, Philip B, of the USA is a quality management expert recognized for his 1979 book, *Quality is Free*, where he contended that any level of defects is too high and that companies should have programmes that will lead them towards the goal of zero defects.

Cross-classification table is an alternative name for a *contingency table*.

Crossdocking is the practice, when goods arrive at a warehouse, in which they simply 'cross the dock' to be shipped out, rather than being unloaded, logged in, broken down into smaller units, and reloaded onto a truck. This minimizes labour costs of handling.

Cumulative frequency distribution is a tabular or graphical display of data, showing how many observations lie above or below certain values.

Customer service level related to inventory is a measure of the probability that a client can be supplied goods immediately from stock.

Cutting fluid is a liquid used to cool and lubricate a work piece and tool in a machining operation. These fluids, which are difficult to purify, are potential pollutants.

Cycle time is the elapsed period between two successive operations, or when products come off a production line.

D

Data array is the arrangement of *raw data* in either ascending or descending order.

Data base is a set of records, perhaps computerized, containing specific information on such things such as clients, subcontractors, employees, inventory, etc.

Data set is a collection of data, not necessarily in order.

Decentralized purchasing is where individual sites of the same firm make their own purchase decisions and transactions.

Deciles are special forms of *fractiles*, which divide data into ten equal parts.

Decision environment is the conditions under which decisions are made.

Decision making under certainty is knowing for certain which of the possible future conditions will actually happen. In this case, decision-making is straightforward in choosing the alternative with the highest payoff under that state of nature.

Decision making under risk implies probabilities of occurrence exist, such as 60 per cent that the market conditions will be favourable and thus 40 per cent that they will not.

Decision making under uncertainty is when there is no clear information on the likelihood of the states of nature which may occur or when one is not able to assess probabilities for each possible outcome.

Decision tree is a pictorial representation of the possible outcomes and alternatives in decision making. The tree has nodes and branches, where a square node denotes a decision point and a circular node denotes an external chance event. The branches indicate the direction of the next decision point, state-of-nature or outcome.

Deforestation is the massive destruction of forests for economic development. Trees are an inventory of oxygen and absorb the *greenhouse gas*, carbon dioxide. Furthermore, destroying trees reduces the ability of the soil to absorb rain, causing flooding and erosion.

Degrees of freedom are the choices available for making a decision. In a two-variable linear equation there is only one degree of freedom because, if one variable is given, the other is automatically fixed.

Delay is the time lag between starting and finishing an operation. In inventory management it is the elapsed time, or *lead time*, between making and receiving an order.

Delphi method, for long-range forecasting, was developed by the Rand Corporation, of Santa Monica, California, USA. It originally was used to assess the potential impact of a nuclear bomb attack on the USA, but since has had other uses in forecasting. The method involves three key groups, decision makers, staff people and the respondents.

Demand during lead time is the quantity of a product demanded during *lead time*. This amount demanded is critical because it is when inventory levels are low that an unexpected surge in demand might result in stockouts.

Deming, W. Edwards, who died in 1994, was a quality guru known for his 14 criteria for quality improvement. By training he was a statistician, a professor at New York University, as well a consultant. He worked with Japanese industries so successfully that the Japanese established the annual Deming prize for innovation in quality management.

Dependent inventory is material for which the quantity demanded is a function of a finished product, for example the number of wheels demanded for an automobile is five.

Descriptive statistics is the collection and analysis of a *data set* in order to describe that set of data and not the *population* from which the data was drawn.

Design review is a formal, documented, comprehensive and systematic examination of a design to evaluate the design requirements, to determine its capability to meet these requirements and to identify problems and thence to propose appropriate solutions.

Discrete data is normally obtained from the counting process and does not progress from one class to the next without a break.

Discrete distribution is a probability distribution of *discrete data*, such as the *binomial* or *Poisson* distribution.

Dispersion is a measure of the spread of data, such as given by the *range* or *standard deviation*.

Distribution requirements planning (DRP) is the planning step in the supply chain to move finished goods from the production or storage source to the client. The DRP is very often a computerized module in an overall *enterprise resource planning* system.

Double sampling plan is where two samples may be taken from a lot and there are upper and lower defective limits. If in the first sample the number of defective units is below the lower limit, the lot is accepted, and it is rejected if the number is above the upper limit. If the result is between the two limits a second sample is withdrawn and tested and the results from the two samples combined.

Drucker, Peter, is a specialist in human relations and has writtten extensively on employee motivation and the role of management in organizations. He was responsible for establishing the idea of *management by objectives*.

Dummy activity is a fictitious activity included in a *network diagram* to indicates a precedence relationship, although for this activity no time span is involved.

E

Earliest due date in order-sequencing is when the next job to be processed among those waiting is that which has the next earliest date at which the job is promised to a client.

Earliest finish in network diagrams for *project management* is the earliest date that an activity can be completed.

Earliest start in network diagrams for *project management* is the earliest date that an activity can begin.

Eco-labeling is affixing a label to a product, or its packaging, to indicate that the product is environmentally acceptable. For the producer this helps to enhance the sale of its product and to a consumer it gives some assurance that the product is less environmentally damaging

Economic order quantity (EOQ), in inventory management, is the amount of material to order which has the least overall cost with inventory carrying costs, inventory ordering costs and stockout costs taken into account.

Economies of scale are the concept that, as a production facility increases in size, the average production costs per unit fall because each new unit absorbs part of the fixed cost of the plant, implying that larger firms would be more efficient than smaller ones.

Effective capacity is another expression for *capacity utilization rate*.

Efficiency in operations is another way of expressing *productivity*.

Elastic product is one for which the quantity demanded changes markedly with price, for example expensive goods like perfume, high priced wines, or expensive cars.

Elasticity of demand refers to the change in the quantity of a product demanded relative to its price. Products may be classified as *elastic* or *inelastic*.

Electronic data interchange (EDI) is communication using computer networks employing fibre-optic cables, or other relay sources.

Emergency maintenance involves repairs when a facility unexpectedly breaks down.

Emission is the discharge of materials that may pose an environmental hazard.

Employee benefits include health insurance, retirement, vacation and the like, which have to be added to employee wages to determine the total labour costs.

Empowerment is an extension of *job enrichment*, giving complete employee trust and responsibilities not originally associated with the job.

End item is the finished unit in an operating function.

Enterprise resource planning is the extension of MRP-II systems to the management of the complete business function.

Entitlement is a legal obligation for governments to pay certain benefits to employees such as health care, retirement or unemployment benefit. They are a reason why balancing the budget is difficult, since entitlements have to be paid regardless of tax revenues collected and demographically the proportion of retirees to active employees is increasing.

Environmental auditing is a management tool comprising a systematic, documented, periodic and objective evaluation of how well environmental organization, management and equipment are performing with the aim of helping to safeguard the environment.

Environmental balance implies balancing economic or production output with safeguarding the environment by minimizing pollution.

Environmental Protection Agency (EPA) is the USA government environmental watchdog.

Environmentally friendly product is one that is designed, produced or used in such a manner that it minimizes the adverse impact on the environment.

Equally likely is a decision-making process under uncertainty where the arithmetic average of all the possible outcomes is considered.

Ergonomics is balancing the work of the employee with the machine or the task at hand in order to minimize human effort and to make the work as comfortable as possible.

Ethics in buying refers to situations where buyers may feel obligated to sales persons who have given them gifts and thus they may not act in the best interest of their own organizations.

Expected demand during lead time (EDDLT) is the mean value of inventory consumed during the time between a new order being placed and its delivery.

Expected value is the weighted average of all possible outcomes.

Event is an activity. The tossing of a coin is an event.

Expected value of perfect information (EVPI) is the difference between the *expected value under certainty* and the *expected value under risk*.

Expected value under certainty is the weighted average of the probability of best payoff for each alternative.

Expected value under risk is the weighted average using the probabilities of all the possible outcomes.

Expediting is the delivery of a product in an urgent situation.

Experience curve is another name for the *learning curve*.

Expert systems are knowledge-based systems that emulate expert thinking, or human logic, to solve complex problems in a particular domain, such as the design of a process network.

Explained variation is the variation in the regression equation relating y to x.

Exponential smoothing in forecasting uses a single smoothing factor alpha, to forecast the next period's activity, where the alpha value takes on a value between 0 and 1.

External faults in quality control are those that occur when a product has left the production site and is in the hands of the consumer.

F

Facility layout is the arrangement of machines, workstations, storage areas, etc. to enable an operation to function efficiently, safely and in a cost-effective manner.

Facility location is the siting of a manufacturing facility, retail store, warehouse, office or other facility to optimize the supply chain of that organization.

Failure is when a product or service ceases to function according to requirements.

Failure mode effect and criticality analysis (FMECA), developed originally for military equipment, is the detailed study of a product design, manufacturing operation or distribution network to determine which features are critical to various modes of failure.

Feasibility studies are detailed analyses of a product design, process or other system to see if it is reasonable in terms of design, operating capability, acceptability and cost.

Feasible region in linear programming is the area in which all the constraints and objectives are met.

Feigenbaum, Armond V, a proponent of quality management, who, in 1983, published a book, *Total Quality Control*, in which he emphasized that the responsibility for quality has to rest with the persons who perform the associated work, or *quality at the source*.

Finite population is a collection of data that has a stated or limited size.

First in, first out (FIFO) in inventory accounting is where the first items acquired are charged against sales. As these probably will have cost less than the last items, the income statement will indicate a higher gross profit. However, this method causes the value of the inventory remaining to be higher.

First come, first served is an *order-sequencing* rule in which the next job to be processed among the jobs waiting is the one that arrived first.

Fish bone chart, another name for an *Ishikawa diagram*, or *cause and effect* chart, is referred to in this way as it resembles the skeleton of a fish.

Fixed capacity refers to systems that have little flexibility to increase capacity. Cinemas, restaurants and aeroplanes have fixed capacity, limited by seat availability.

Fixed costs are derived from *capital assets*, usually in the form of depreciation. These costs are charged to operations and are thus independent of the level of production.

Fixed order interval in inventory planning means that new orders of inventory are made at regular intervals, such as every two days, every week, etc.

Fixed order period model for inventory is based on ordering at *fixed order intervals*. The quantity ordered is determined from the amount remaining so that, with a new order, the inventory in storage is brought up to some pre-established level. The quantity ordered each time is usually not the same since consumption in each order period varies.

Fixed order quantity model for inventory is based on the criterion that the same quantity is ordered each time material is requisitioned. Orders would be placed when the inventory in storage falls to a certain pre-established minimum level.

Fixed position layout is an arrangement of a work centre where the product being produced, because of its weight, size or character, such as a bridge or cargo vessel, does not move. The workers, machines and tool areas rotate around the stationary product.

Flexitime is when employees have variable hours regarding starting and finishing, though normally they have to be present during a certain core period of the day.

Flexible manufacturing systems are clusters of computer controlled machines that produce a variety of products. The computers give instructions, robots handle materials and machine settings are automatically changed to produce the different products.

Focused factory is one that is dedicated to one, or a few types of, product.

Ford, Henry, developed one of the first major assembly-line operations in the USA in 1913 for the manufacture of the Ford Model T automobile.

Forecast error is the difference between actual data and that estimated from the forecast.

Forecast horizon is the time span of the forecast, in which the longer the span, the more unreliable will be the estimates.

Forecasting is estimating future outcomes using statistical data or a qualitative approach.

Fractile is a division of data into well defined parts such that a given fraction, or proportion, of the data lies at, or below, a fractile. The *median* is the 50 per cent fractile, or the 50th *percentile*, because half the data are less than or equal to this value.

Fraction defective in a lot is that proportion of products that do not conform.

Free on board price (FOB) is the price of a manufactured product on a delivered basis, including all transport, insurance and handling.

Frequency distribution is a table or graph in which data are arranged into unique class groupings, which are more manageable than *raw data* and demonstrate trends more easily.

Frequency polygon is a line graph of a *frequency distribution.*

Functional layout is the organization of a work centre according to speciality, such as a manufacturing firm organized according to cutting, grinding, drilling and assembly.

Fuzzy logic deals with the use of approximate values, influences or ambiguous data in making decisions. Chefs with years of experience know when to add ingredients in order to make meals taste good, though their logic for the modifications is ill defined.

G

Gantt chart, after *Henry L Gantt* is a horizontal bar chart, used in operations or project scheduling. It shows activities that need to be completed and their start and finish times.

Gantt, Henry, an American engineer (1861–1919) who was interested in both the human and scientific approaches to management. His perception of managers was that they were slave drivers forcing workers to do jobs in which they had little interest, under poor conditions. On the scientific side, he was responsible for developing the *Gantt chart* for scheduling.

Gaussian distribution, after Karl Gauss, is an alternative for the *normal distribution.*

Geometric mean, a measure of *central tendency*, used for data that changes over time such as the growth of investments, the inflation rate or the GNP. Over a period of n years, the geometric mean is given by the relationship, $\sqrt[n]{\text{product of growth rates}}$.

Gilbreth, Frank and Lilian, were the USA husband and wife team who analysed operations management as a science in the period 1900–1910. Their primary research tool was motion studies in order to reduce a job to its most basic movements and was used to establish performance standards and to eliminate unnecessary physical movements.

Gozinto chart is another name for an *assembly chart.*

Grade is an indicator of category, or rank, applied to products, processes or services that are intended for the same functional use, but for an otherwise different set of needs. Hotels and restaurants have grades, as do clothing and work tools like sandpaper.

Grass roots is a term used in *project management* for a project that is built from scratch on virgin land or 'grass roots'.

Graveyard shift is one which starts around midnight and finishes around 08:00.

Green product is one that is considered environmentally friendly, or at least one less damaging to the environment than perhaps another product that has similar uses.

Greenhouse effect is the accumulation of gases, principally carbon dioxide, in the upper atmosphere, preventing heat from escaping and thus causing the earth's temperature to increase

Gross National Product (GNP) is the total value of goods and services, usually during a one year. It is used as an economic indicator and a measure of the well-being of a country.

Group technology identifies components by a code that specifies the type of processing, such as milling, and the parameters of processing, such as shape. Machines then process families of parts as a group, minimizing set-ups, materials handling and routing.

Growth stage refers to the period when a new product has been introduced on the market and is growing in acceptance by consumers and expanding in market share.

H

Halons are gaseous chlorine and bromine compounds, which, when emitted alone, or combined with other chemicals, attack and destroy the upper atmosphere ozone layer.

Hard copy is a printed version on paper of computer-based information.

Hardware is the physical equipment used in information technology, such as the computers, printers, terminals, scanners, etc.

Hawthorne Studies, by Elton Mayo and others, between 1927–1932 at the US Western Electric plant, studied human relations in the work environment. They looked at the effect of lighting on productivity and the human side. They concluded that the role of individuals is more important in productivity than physical elements such as lighting.

Herzberg, Frederick, on human motivation at work in the 1960s, concluded that there were two variables that influenced people. One was hygiene, or maintenance factors that impacted job dissatisfaction and related to the work environment. The other was motivating factors, which affected job satisfaction and were connected to the work itself.

Heuristic methods, from the Greek 'heuristic – I have found', are those which provide a solution to a problem, but may not be optimum and are difficult to justify, but nevertheless work.

Hierarchy of needs includes those five human desires developed by *Abraham Maslow* and from first to last include physiological, security, social, esteem, and self-actualization.

Histogram is a graph of a *data set*, made up of rectangles, where each is proportional in width to the range of values in a class and proportional in height to the number or fraction of items falling in that class. A histogram may represent a *frequency distribution*.

Holdback provision is a proportion, or an amount, of money not paid to a supplier of services until there is assurance that the work performs according to specification.

Horizontal integration is fusion of firms that have similar products and compete in the same markets. Integration may give the combined organization bigger market clout.

Hoshin is the Japanese idea of searching for simple practical solutions for improving an operation by working at the shop-floor level with operators familiar with the work.

Hoteling is an open plan office at its very extreme, where private offices are eliminated to provide temporary space for employees such as consultants, only when they are in town. This saves money on rent and gets employees out spending more time with customers.

House of quality is another name for *quality function deployment*.

Human resource management is the management of all personnel in an organization, including work assignments, salaries, promotion, training, etc.

Hydrocarbons contain the atoms of carbon and hydrogen and are a natural product of plant life. They are also a constituent of petrol and thus one of the components in automobile exhaust *emissions*. By the action of sunlight, hydrocarbons react with other substances causing smog, an environmental concern in large cities.

Hypermarkets are those retail stores that have a very large surface area and sell just about everything including food, clothing, appliances, books, garden tools, plants, furniture, etc.

Hypothesis testing is when decisions are made about population characteristics based only on information from a sample. One hypothesis is called the null hypothesis, compared to which there will always be an alternative hypothesis.

I

IBM-compatible is a personal computer (PC) that can be used interchangeably with an IBM PC and run operating systems MS-DOS and Windows and related programs.

Income statement indicates the profitability (or loss) of an organization over a period of time. All costs and expenses are subtracted from sales to arrive at the net income.

Independent inventory is an item, the quantity of which is not a function of other units; this is most often a finished product. A bicycle would be independent inventory and the wheels *dependent* inventory. Spares also constitute *independent inventory*.

Independent variable in forecasting is one that has no direct relationship to the one being estimated and graphically is always plotted on the *x axis*.

Industrial goods are those manufactured by one firm destined for another firm, such as engine parts. They are sometimes referred to as intermediary goods.

Industrial park is a zone established, usually outside a town, purely for industrial firms.

Industrial revolution (1733–1878) is considered to have heralded in the beginning of technological inventions and industrial growth. It started with the invention of the flying shuttle for weaving textiles by John Kay of Britain in 1733.

Inelastic product is one for which quantity sold does not vary much with price. Usually these are basic products such as milk, cheese and margarine.

Infant mortality is the early stages of product life where components are fragile because they have not been 'run-in', or operators are not familiar with equipment and it breaks down as a result on inappropriate use. The term relates to the vulnerability of infants at this point in their lives.

Inferential statistics is the estimation of the *population* characteristics based on sampling. Population characteristics, such as weight, are inferred from the sample.

Infinite population is one whose size is so large that for analytical purposes taking a sample from the population does not change the characteristics of that population.

Information systems are made up of the network and architecture for communicating and include data bases and computer links with purchasing, manufacturing, distribution and clients.

Infrastructure for a project is all the support facilities enabling a project to operate. The infrastructure for an airport would include parking, restaurants, access roads, etc.

Inspection in *quality control* covers measuring, examining, testing or gauging the characteristics of a product, process or service, and comparing these with specifications.

Institute of Industrial Engineers is a US-based professional group.

Interfractile range measures the spread between two fractiles in a *data set*.

Internal faults are those occurring before the product or service has left the facility.

International Standards Organization (ISO) is a Swiss-based non-governmental group founded in 1947, with the goal of decreasing trade barriers by promoting worldwide product standardization. The *ISO-9000* series for quality and *ISO-14000* for the environment are two commonly applied standards.

Internet is a sophisticated form of *electronic data interchange*, where one is able to communicate via a worldwide network on literally thousands of topics.

Interquartile range is a measure of dispersion and the difference between the third *quartile* and the first *quartile* in a data set. The *midspread* is another name.

Inventory is material consumed during the normal course of business, including raw materials, *work in process*, finished goods, packing, spares, supplies and small tools.

Inventory carrying costs is an alternative term for *carrying costs*.

Inventory management involves keeping inventory costs to a minimum, but at the same time providing the most economic service level to clients and to the production centre.

Inventory models are mathematical expressions describing the movement of inventory.

Inventory ordering costs are those costs associated with obtaining the inventory, such as salaries of purchasing staff, communication costs, receiving, handling and inspection costs. For inventory produced by the same company the costs include preparation of production orders, preparation of materials and tools and set-up of machines.

Inventory records file is a *database* of information about the status of inventory.

Inventory stockout costs occur when there is not sufficient inventory to satisfy demand and include loss of revenues, loss of clients and expediting to make up for the stockout.

Inventory turnover is a measure of how a firm uses its inventory. The greater the inventory turnover, the more efficient is the operation, and the lower is the inventory holding cost. It is calculated as the ratio of the cost of goods sold to the value of inventory.

Irregular components in a time-series analysis refer to changes that are the result of infrequent activities, such as machine failure, truck strike and absence in the work force.

Ishikawa diagram, after its inventor, is a tool to determine the causes of quality-related problems. It is also known as a *cause and effect diagram* or a *fishbone analysis*.

ISO-9000 series, including 9001, 9002 and 9003, is the international quality standard.

ISO-14000 is the international standard covering environmental concerns.

J

Jidoka is the Japanese word that means stop everything if something has gone wrong.

Job enlargement avoids an employee being trapped in a *job specialization* by improving the variety within the sphere of a person's ability and interest. A cutting operation could be enlarged by adding shaping and forming, that is horizontal expansion of the job.

Job enrichment is expanding a job vertically, such as by adding design and planning elements. A purchasing secretary whose basic job is the correspondence of the department, could have the job enriched by being given responsibility for planning work assignments, by being an intermediary in customer contacts and maybe by helping in proposal evaluation.

Job lot is a batch of parts or units that have been produced together.

Job rotation is moving from one activity to another to add interest and avoid boredom.

Job shop is a *functional organization* where departments are organized around special equipment or operations, such as cutting, drilling, milling or heat treatment, in manufacturing. Products flow through departments in batches often corresponding to individual orders, either as stock for inventory or for specific customer orders.

Job specialization relates to the knowledge and training in just one particular job activity, such as mining or typing.

Johnson's rule is a method for scheduling jobs through two, or in special circumstances three, work centres, giving an order sequence that minimizes the total processing time.

Joint probability is when two or more independent events occur together, or in succession, and is calculated by the product of the individual marginal probabilities.

Joint venture is when two or more firms work together on a project to minimize the individual risk, to pool financial or other resources, or perhaps for governmental reasons.

Juran, Joseph M, was another pioneer in the 1970s and 1980s in helping the Japanese to improve product quality. Like *Deming*, he believed in top-management commitment and involvement in quality and also in team work to continually strive to raise standards.

Jury of executive opinion is consolidating the opinions of top management or executives in order to develop a forecast of future activity for the firm.

Just-in-time (JIT) is a management practice where the exact quantities of a product are produced, purchased or delivered only when needed. Delays and inventory levels are kept to an absolute minimum, the philosophy being that unnecessary inventories, or delays, are an inefficient use of resources. Practising JIT enforces adherence to quality.

K

Kaizen is the Japanese word meaning *continuous improvement*.

Kanban, from the Japanese meaning card or ticket, refers to the technique of managing the flow of materials, principally in manufacturing. Kanbans are used to communicate the need for parts from one work centre to another, replacing written work orders. The card 'pulls' the needed parts from the upstream supply post to the downstream client post.

Kanban square is an area marked out on the floor, or bench, that represents the storage area for a specific referenced component part. A supplying workstation has authority to furnish more parts only if there is space available in this Kanban square.

Karmarkar's algorithm is a mathematical expression in linear programming.

Keiretsu is the Japanese word for the integrated network of distributors and clients.

KISS principle meaning, *K*eep *I*t *S*imple *S*tupid, implies that the less sophisticated a product or service is, the less likely there will be quality problems.

Kurtosis is the characteristic of the peak of a frequency distribution curve. Distributions may have the same mean, but different standard distributions, which changes the sharpness of the peak. Three classifications are *leptokurtic*, *platykurtic* and *mesokurtic*.

L

Labour is the human resources of a firm and includes current employees, new hires, workers on recall, part-time employees and overtime.

Labour costs are those associated with employing human resources, including basic salary or wages plus social and other charges paid to the employee, or paid by the employer for the employee. Social charges include medical insurance, social security, paid vacations, retirement benefits, unemployment benefits and paid education.

Labour organizations are unions that represent the workers in a firm.

Labour standard is the basic hours needed to carry out a task and this standard is often used to plan and price a job.

Labour turnover is a measure of the change of employment in a firm. A repeated high level is probability associated with motivational factors.

Lagging indicators in the economy are those that reach a high, or low, after the economic activity has occurred, such as labour cost per unit of production, commercial and industrial loans and book value of inventories.

Laser scanner is the instrument used to read *barcode* charts.

Last in, first out (LIFO) is an inventory policy where the last items of inventory acquired are charged against sales. As these normally cost more than earlier items, the cost of goods sold will be high, indicating a lower profit on the *income statement*. The value of inventory remaining will be accounted at a relatively low value.

Layout refers to *facility layout*.

Lead time is an alternative for *delay*.

Leading indicators are those that reach a high, or a low, before a related economic activity and are thus useful in forecasting. Construction contracts, equipment orders, new business incorporation, capital appropriation and manufacturing orders are examples.

Lean production means having the most efficient operation possible, avoiding waste and giving employees maximum responsibility.

Learning curve, or *experience curve*, shows labour hours against the quantity of products produced. It decreases exponentially, meaning that starting with a new operation, as the number of units produced increases and operators become familiar with the task, the number of hours required per unit decreases.

Least changeover cost is an *order sequencing rule* where the next job processed among those waiting is the one that involves the least machine set-up cost. Some jobs are better suited to this sequencing operation because of the similarities of machine settings.

Least slack rule is an *order sequencing rule* where the next job processed among those waiting is the one where the difference between due date and operating time is the least.

Least-squares method is used for determining the best straight line from a set of data. The method minimizes the error between the estimated points on the calculated line and the actual observed points used to draw the line.

Leptokurtic is a measure of kurtosis in a frequency distribution curve, meaning that the peak is sharp, so that data dispersion is small and the standard deviation is low; lepto (Greek) = slender.

Level of analysis refers to the depth of decision making and might range from intuitive analysis, through quick-and-dirty, computations and model building, to project teams.

Level production is the production of goods or services at a relatively constant output from period to period, thus simplifying planning and perhaps minimizing costs.

Life cycle analysis is the evaluation of the life of a product from conception, through design, production, distribution and use, to disposal at the end of its useful life. The objective is to manage so that environmental damage from the product is a minimum.

Line balancing is a *facility layout* procedure that determines which tasks each employee will perform and how they are grouped at workstations to optimize the system.

Line function is one that has direct responsibility over operations.

Linear programming is a mathematical technique for optimization.

Linear regression is the development of a straight line relationship between a dependent variable, for which future values need to be forecast, and another independent variable.

Load–distance analysis is a *facility layout* procedure to identify the layout with the least product or material travel per time period.

Long cost is the cost of stocking one inventory unit that is not demanded, meaning that the unit is in inventory but there is no client need. This cost is associated with carrying costs, handling and other expenses involved in carrying a unit from one period to another.

Longest processing time is an *order sequencing rule* according to which the next job processed among those waiting is the one that has the greatest processing time.

Lot sizing is determining the optimum quantity of units to make or purchase.

Lot tolerance percentage defective (LTPD) in *statistical quality control* is the level of quality considered unacceptable, or bad, such that a lot should be rejected.

Lot-for-lot is producing or purchasing exactly that quantity of material that is required by the client or the downstream work post.

Love canal is an abandoned canal along the Niagara River, in New York State, USA where between 1942 and 1953 Hooker Chemical and Plastics dumped tons of toxic chemicals. This material contaminated a housing zone constructed later, resulting in a major environmental disaster costing the US government millions of dollars.

Low-level coding in a bill of materials is coding an item at the lowest level at which it appears.

M

Macroeconomic factors include GNP, interest rates and inflation rates, all of which can impact the forecast of future sales and business activity.

Make-or-buy is the decision whether to buy a component or to make the part. Sometimes firms can make parts for lower cost, at better quality, faster delivery, than purchasing them. Generally, for small or specialized orders, it is more cost-effective to purchase. A *break-even analysis* is useful to decide whether to make or buy a product.

Management by objectives, the concept of *Peter Druker*, is where employees mutually agree to goals that they attempt to achieve in a reasonable time. Performance reviews are conducted periodically to see how near the individuals are to achieving these objectives and rewards are given on the basis of how close they are to reaching their objectives.

Manufacturing resource planning (MRP-II) is the expansion of *materials requirement planning* to include other functions such as marketing, finance, engineering, distribution and human resource planning. Commercially MRP-II is now referred to as *enterprise resource planning*.

Marginal cost is the cost to produce an additional product.

Maslow, Abraham, of the USA is best known for his 1943 publication, *A Theory of Human Motivation*, in which he theorized that people have five basic requirements, which he put into a pyramid as a *hierarchy of needs*.

Mass production is the production in high volume of standard-type products in an *assembly line* operation.

Master production schedule is a planning tool in operations, with a time horizon in weeks or months, showing what *end items* are required and the timing necessary to satisfy client demands.

Material requirements planning (MRP) is a computer-based tool for materials management in manufacturing. It is used when there is *dependent demand*.

Materials management refers to the purchasing of raw materials and components, through transformation to the storage of the finished product.

Maximax is an optimistic approach to *decision making under uncertainty* when management selects the maximum of the best of the possible outcomes.

Maximin is a pessimistic approach to *decision making under uncertainty* when management selects the maximum of the worst of the possible outcomes.

McGregor, Douglas, in studying human relations, identified people as Theory X type, who usually had negative assumptions about other people, and Theory Y, who had positive ideas. In the management environment the implications were that Theory X managers were bad and Theory Y managers were good and made the best managers.

Mean absolute deviation is a measure of the forecast error given as the average of the absolute deviation between the actual and forecast values for all the data points.

Mean squared error for forecasting is the average of the sum of the squared difference between the actual and the forecast values.

Mean time between failure in product *reliability* is the average time between when a product fails.

Minimax regret is a method for *decision making under uncertainty* when management selects the minimum of the worst regret, or disappointment, of an outcome.

Mission statement globally defines the business and objectives of an organization and is the start point of the strategic plan.

Modelling is the development of a mathematical or physical representation of the real thing and is used as a tool in planning, management and decision making.

Monte Carlo simulation in *queuing* systems uses random numbers as an approach to modelling the waiting times and queue length.

Most likely time in a *PERT* network is the time that would most frequently occur if the activity were repeated many times.

Motion study is analysing the time to perform a specified activity and is often the basis for developing *labour standards*.

Moving average forecasting is developing a forecast model based on the average of past data, say three periods, and then dropping the oldest data point as one moves on in time.

Multiskilled, or polyvalent, means having the expertise to perform several tasks.

Multiple regression is when there is more than one independent variable to estimate a value for the dependent variable. Sales may be dependent on the sales budget, the number of sales persons and the number of sales contacts, three independent variables.

N

Naive approach to forecasting assumes that the forecast activity for the next period is equal to the actual immediate past period's result.

Net present value is the value of a future stream of incomes recalculated to the present, taking into account the time value of money.

Net requirements in an inventory situation are the gross requirements required by the customer less the amount of inventory in stock.

Network diagrams in *project management* are flow schemes that show the various activities and their beginning and start points.

Neural networks are computer-based programs patterned on the human brain's mesh like network of interconnecting cells, programmed to recognize patterns for problem solving.

Nitrogen is a gas which makes up 78 per cent of air. When it is heated, such as in the engine of an automobile, it reacts with oxygen to give nitrogen oxide and nitrogen dioxide. These gases, known as NO_x react with moisture in the atmosphere to give nitric acid or acid rain.

Noise pollution is the nuisance or pollution caused by excess noise. Sound levels are measured in decibels and the addition of 10 decibels doubles the sound level, with 85 decibels considered the maximum level safe for the human ear. Continuous exposure to noise leads to health problems and in a work environment lowers *productivity*.

Normal distribution, or *Gaussian distribution*, is a graph of the frequency of occurrence of a random variable. The distribution is continuous, bell-shaped and symmetrical and the two tails extend indefinitely. The mean, median, mode and midrange are equal and lie at the centre of the distribution.

Not-for-profit organizations are those that do not declare a profit and often have a preferential tax status.

Numerically controlled machines have control systems that read instructions and translate these into machine operations. Machines are preprogrammed with computer commands to perform a repeat cycle of operations, which replaces manual machine settings.

O

Objective function in linear programming defines the goal of the decision process, such as maximizing profits or minimizing costs.

Office layout is the efficient arrangement of workers, equipment and offices.

Ogive is a *cumulative frequency distribution* useful in decision making, showing how many observations, or the percentage of the data, lie above or below certain values.

Open system is an organization, programme, department or machine that under normal operation has continuous interaction with the external environment, for example marketing.

Operating budget is that money allocated in advance, or forecast, for a business operation, such as for sales activity, a projected building or research and development.

Operating characteristic curve in *quality control* is a graph illustrating how well an *acceptance plan* discriminates between good and bad lots. The discriminating ability depends on the shape of the curve, which is a function of the sample size withdrawn from the lot, and the acceptance level, or the number of allowable defective units in the sample.

Operations management is the effective planning, organizing and control of all resources and activities necessary to provide the market with tangible goods and services. It applies to manufacturing, service industries and *not-for-profit organizations.*

Optimized production technology (OPT) is a planning and scheduling tool for coordinating engineering, manufacturing and marketing for a job shop, or repetitive manufacturing. It is based on nine rules, which revolve around the concept of *bottlenecks.*

Optimistic time in a *PERT* network is the shortest possible time within which an *activity* could be completed if everything went right.

Oracle is a California based company developing *enterprise resource planning* tools.

Order point is the time when a new order is placed for additional inventory.

Order sequencing is the timing within which a group of orders, such as assembling machine parts, packing of items or machining operations, is processed at a work centre.

Ordering costs are those costs associated with purchasing or making new inventory.

Outsourcing, or *subcontracting*, is contracting work to another firm.

Overall equipment effectiveness is the real output of a machine, given by the theoretical output less downtime due to operator pauses, machine breakdowns, unplanned interruptions, machine set-up, low performance and nonconforming material.

Ozone, a gas comprising three atoms of oxygen per molecule, is formed from the action of sunlight on vehicle emissions. At ground level it causes respiratory problems.

Ozone layer in the upper atmosphere is a barrier to the sun's ultraviolet rays. Ozone is destroyed by chlorine compounds like *chloroflurocarbons*, allowing higher concentrations of ultraviolet rays to penetrate to the earth's surface. This leads to higher incidence of skin cancer, glaucoma and other health and environmental problems.

P

P-chart in *statistical process control* indicates the proportion or percentage of defective products in an operation.

Parallel system is an alternative term for a *back-up system.*

Parameter is a measure that describes the characteristics of a population.

Pareto Analysis, after the Italian Vilfredo Pareto, is a tool based on a frequency distribution for quality control and is also used in *ABC analysis* for inventory management.

Part period balancing is a lot sizing method that balances set-up costs with holding costs. It is dynamic as it reflects requirements for future demand requirements.

Payback period is the time taken to recover an original investment made in a capital project, machine, equipment or other *capital asset.*

Percentiles are special forms of *fractiles* and divide data into 100 equal parts.

Periodic order quantity is a *lot sizing* method where a quantity of parts is produced at regular periods. This simplifies planning as set-up needs are known in advance.

Pessimistic time in a *PERT* network is the longest possible time the activity would require to be completed assuming everything went wrong.

Physical distribution management concerns the delivery, storage and other activities of delivering finished goods to clients.

Pictogram is a picture, or sketch, representing quantitative data.

Pie chart is a circle representing data, divided into segments, portions of a pie, where segments are proportional to the data represented. The circle is 100 per cent of the data.

Piece work is where employees are paid on the basis of the volume of work they produce.

Piggybacking is a transportation mode where container trucks can be directly loaded onto the wagons of trains, avoiding unloading and repackaging.

Pipeline is another term used for the *supply chain.*

Pipeline map is a linear flow scheme of the *supply chain*, highlighting each operation by processing time and the holding time that material stays in the supply chain.

Piping and instrument diagram (P&I) is the engineering drawing of a facility showing pipelines, instruments, valves and other key control equipment.

Planned ordered deliveries are the materials scheduled to be delivered at a given date.

Planned ordered receipts is that material scheduled to be received at a given date.

Planned ordered release is that material to be released to meet a planned delivery date.

Planning horizon is the time period for an organizations various planning programmes.

Platykurtic describes the peak of a frequency distribution that is relatively flat. This distribution has a large dispersion and a high standard deviation; platy (Greek)= broad or flat.

Point estimate is a single figure, or statistic, to estimate the true population parameter.

Poisson distribution, after the Frenchman Simeon Denis Poisson, is a *discrete* probability distribution often used to describe *waiting line* situations.

Poka Yoke, is a fail safe approach incorporating devices to make products, processes or services mistake proof in order to avoid errors and at the same time maintain quality.

Polynomial regression is the relationship between the dependent value y and the independent value x when there are values of x in the equation other than unity for example x^2.

Polygon is a line graph representing a *data set*.

Population is a collection of all the elements being studied.

Power, J D, is a California-based firm which regularly carries out quality-based surveys on automobiles using a customer satisfaction index.

Preventative maintenance is the work activity that has been programmed on a regular basis to inspect a system, uncover potential problems and make whatever repairs are necessary to ensure that the system does not fail during normal operation.

Pro forma financial statements are those which are an estimate of future performance.

Probabilistic time estimates are those used in *PERT* network diagrams to estimate the duration of the various activities.

Process control charts in *quality control* indicate the performance of an operation.

Process flow chart shows the flow of materials between successive operating units; its usefulness is to locate the value-added and non-value added activities.

Process flow diagram shows sequentially all the activities in a production operation.

Process-focused factories are facilities equipped to produce non-standard products in relatively small batches. They are sometimes referred to as *job shops*.

Process liability is the risk a producer or others take regarding the responsibility for the personal injury, or harm resulting from the use of a process that they have supplied.

Produce to order is supplying goods or services, often non-standard items, only when requested by the customer.

Produce to stock is making products, often of standard design, that go into inventory.

Producer risk involves the taking of a random sample that results in a higher portion of defects in the sample than is actually present in the lot.

Product-focused factories are facilities arranged to produce many products of a relative standard design using a *product layout*. Usually the *assembly line* is the layout arrangement of a product-focused factory where the finished items go into inventory.

Product layout describes the arrangement for a *product-focused factory*.

Product liability is the risk a producer or others take regarding the responsibility for the personal injury, or harm resulting from the use of a product that they have supplied.

Product life cycle is the duration of the life of products ranging from, development, birth or introduction, through growth, maturity and decline, to death.

Product structure shows the make-up of a product from its various components.

Product-analysis matrix is a tool using weighting to evaluate the viability of new products.

Production permit, or deviation permit, is written authorization, prior to production to depart from specified requirements, a specified quantity or a specified time.

Productivity measures *efficiency* and can be calculated by the ratio of outputs to inputs.

Program evaluation and review technique (PERT) is technique in *project management* using network diagrams to determine the critical path. It relies on three time estimates for the activity duration and is thus a probabilistic method.

Project acceleration is employing resources necessary to reduce the time of a project.

Pull system is one where a product moves through the *supply chain* as a result of customer demand 'pulling' the item.

Purchasing is the selection, and ultimate acquisition, of raw materials, components or equipment for a manufacturing or service organization.

Purchasing managers index measures the level of purchasing activity. It is related to economic activity as a high index signals an increase, and vice versa.

Push system is where the producer 'pushes' his products through the *supply chain* relying on marketing to sell them to the client.

Q

Qualitative data is categorical or subjective information.

Qualitative forecasting is based on subjective opinions.

Quality assurance includes those planned and systematic actions necessary to provide confidence that a product, process or service will satisfy given quality requirements.

Quality at the source implies that all those persons responsible for an activity are also responsible for its quality, thus avoiding non-value quality inspection.

Quality audit is a systematic, and independent, examination to determine whether quality activities and results comply with planned arrangements and also whether these arrangements are effectively implemented and are suitable to achieve objectives.

Quality circle is a small group of employees who voluntarily meet regularly to analyse work-related projects with the objective of improving company operations. There are no direct cash incentives and the principal reason for participation is personal satisfaction.

Quality control includes the operational techniques and activities that are used to satisfy quality requirements, such as inspection, measuring and testing.

Quality function deployment (QFD) is a method to ensure that a new product or service satisfies clients. Its goal is to develop an appropriate design and then translate this into targets throughout product development and production. QFD is also known as the *house of quality* because of its shape, or the *voice of the customer*, because of its purpose.

Quality is the totality of features and characteristics of a product, process or service that bear on its ability to satisfy stated or implied needs.

Quality loop is a conceptual model of interacting activities that influence the quality of a product, process or service in the various stages, ranging from identification of needs to the assessment of whether these needs have been satisfied.

Quality loss function, an element of *Taguchi's* robust design, is a relationship that identifies costs L associated with poor quality. It shows how costs increase as the product deviates from specifications and is given by $L = D^2 \times C$ where D is deviation from the target specification and C is the cost of avoiding the deviation.

Quality management, the responsibility of top executives, is that aspect of the overall management function that determines and implements the quality policy.

Quality plan is a document setting out the specific quality practices, resources and activities relevant to a particular product, process, service, contract or project.

Quality robust refers to products designed to function under adverse conditions.

Quality spiral is an alternative name for a *quality loop*.

Quality surveillance is the continuing evaluation of the status of procedures, methods, conditions, products, processes and services and the analysis of records in relation to stated references to ensure that quality requirements are being met. It is often performed independently by customers or third parties to ensure that contractual requirements are met.

Quality system is the organizational structure, responsibilities, procedures, activities, capabilities and resources, aimed at ensuring that products, processes or services will satisfy stated or implied needs.

Quality system review is a formal management evaluation of the status and adequacy of the *quality system* in relation to *quality policy* and new objectives, arising from changing circumstances.

Quantitative data is numerical information that can be rigorously analysed.

Quantitative forecasting is forecasting using *quantitative or statistical data.*

Quantity discount is a reduction offered per unit in buying bulk purchases.

Quartile deviation is one half of the *interquartile range.*

Quartiles are special forms of *fractiles* that divide data into four equal parts.

Queuing is an alternative term for *waiting lines.*

R

Random sample is where each item has the same chance of being selected.

Random variations are those for which there are no assignable causes.

Range chart is an analytical tool in *statistical process control* for monitoring the sample range of continuous variables. Range charts are used in conjunction with *x-bar charts.*

Range is a measure of the dispersion of data.

Raw data is information before it is arranged or analysed by statistical or other methods.

Re-engineering is used as an alternative to *business process re-engineering.*

Relative frequency distribution is the display of a data set that shows the fraction, or percentage, of the total data set that falls into each of a set of mutually exclusive classes.

Reliability is the ability of an item to perform a required function, under stated conditions, for a specified period of time.

Reliability-centred maintenance focuses on function and equipment by establishing what is meant by the right maintenance, rather than just very frequent overhauls. It determines what must be done to ensure that physical assets continue to fulfil their operating context and that systems work as designed with minimal problems.

Renege relates to *waiting lines* when a customer enters the queue but becomes impatient and leaves. Thus for a part of the time the customer forms part of the queue, but never receives service.

Reorder point is the level of inventory in storage at which another order is placed.

Repatriation of earnings refers to the transfer of income from a foreign operation back to the home office.

Request for proposal (RFP) is the formal demand from a user to suppliers of services or goods to present a technical and financial proposal of their proposed offer.

Reverse osmosis is a filtering process in which very small molecules are removed.

Robot is an automatic, computer driven, flexible machine that can hold, turn, lift and perform other activities according to electronic impulses.

Run length is an alternative term for *lot size.*

Run-out method of scheduling is a procedure based on when stock of a product would be depleted. For production in fixed lot sizes, this is the ratio of current inventory to demand. Alternatively inventory can be aggregated to determine at what point in time inventory will be depleted, or will 'run out'.

S

Safety stock is inventory for unplanned purposes, such as transport strikes, delivery delays due to bad weather, unreliable suppliers or unexpected increase in demand. Safety stock reduces the probability of stockouts, but increases *inventory carrying costs.*

Sales force composite is a judgemental forecast where opinions are solicited from line sales at the regional level and then these sales forecasts are compiled at headquarters.

Salvage value is the value of equipment at the end of its life when it is sold for scrap.

Sample is a collection of some, but not all, of the elements of a population being studied.

Sampling distribution of the mean is a probability distribution of all the possible means of samples taken from a population.

Sampling with replacement is taking an item from a population for analysis, and then putting this sample back into the population. For a *finite population* the probability of a sample being selected is then always the same.

Sampling without replacement is taking an item from a population for analysis, and not putting this sample back into the population. For an *infinite population* the probability would not change, but it would for a *finite population*.

Sandoz, now Novartis, has a chemical plant in Basel, Switzerland, which as a result of a fire in 1986 caused an environmental disaster. Water used for the fire's containment flowed into the Rhine, carrying with it tons of toxic chemicals that killed fish and contaminating drinking water in Switzerland, France, Germany and the Netherlands.

Scatter diagram is a graph showing the x and y measurements of various observations.

Scheduled receipt is that planned quantity of inventory due to arrive at a given date.

Scheduling is the preparation of a timetable, and sequencing order, for activities that have to occur to achieve a set of objectives.

Scientific management was an approach put forward by theorists in the period from about 1875 to 1925, whose objectives were to treat the activity of workers in a logical, scientific way by using time, motion and methods study. The ultimate goal of this analytical approach was to increase worker output, efficiency and productivity and to reduce production costs.

Seasonal index is a factor in a time series showing the magnitude of seasonal effects.

Segmentation is the separation of consumer and industrial markets into identifiable groupings for the ultimate purpose of increasing a company's marketing success.

Seiketsu is a Japanese word meaning to standardize. Applied to operations, it means that with standardization jobs and activities are performed in a consistent manner.

Seiro is a Japanese word meaning to remove. In operations, it means remove from the work area unneeded tools, materials, equipment, or documents. The idea being that 'if it's not needed, don't have it cluttering the area because it gets in the way and slows down activity.'

Seiso is a Japanese word meaning to keep clean, which in a manufacturing environment, keeping the working area clean, is appropriate from a health and safety point of view.

Seiton is a Japanese word meaning to organize. In operations, it means organizing materials, tools, pencils, papers, computer diskettes and documents. Classification of these work items will help to reduce the time spent in searching for these when they are needed.

Sensitivity analysis is determining how a given solution reacts to changes in values. In decision making, the best result might be chosen but it can be sensitive to small changes.

Sequencing rules are rules that govern the order for scheduling work.

Sequential sampling in *statistical quality control* is where lots are rejected or accepted according to a pre-established programme. Units are randomly selected from the lot and tested, after which a reject, accept or continue sampling decision is made according to the sample plan and the region in which the total number of units that have been tested fall.

Service industries are those industries that do not transform materials in the classic sense and the term applies to such industries as transportation, financial services, retailing and leisure.

Service level is that proportion of customer orders that can be completed from existing inventory. A 95 per cent service level means that 95 per cent of customers can be supplied out of existing inventory, while 5 per cent cannot, or the probability of a stockout is 5 per cent.

Set-up time is the *delay* involved in regulating a machine such that it can work on a component part. Set-up times maybe reduced by *SMED* or automating procedures.

Sherman Act, a 1890 USA law, prohibits price fixing among competitors, group boycotts, allocation of customers or markets and agreements between a manufacturer and customers that they will not buy a competitor's products.

Shitsuke is a Japanese word meaning to respect the rules. In business it underscores that firms and society function through teamwork and cooperation, or respecting rules.

Shop floor refers to the area where the manufacturing and assembly activities occur.

Short cost in inventory management is the cost of not stocking a unit demanded, meaning that there is a customer need but the unit is not in inventory. This cost is associated with stockouts and includes lost revenue and charges for special handling and expediting to satisfy the customer.

Short-run production costs relate to labour, materials and variable overhead, which can change in the short run. Not included is physical capacity, which is fixed in the short run.

Shortest processing time is an *order-sequencing* rule according to which the next job to be processed among the jobs waiting is the one that involves the shortest operating time.

Simplex method is a tool for linear programming.

Simulation is duplicating activity that occurs in the real world, often using computers.

Single channel, multiple phase in queuing is where there is one line but several phases such as in a medical centre where a patient first sees a nurse and then the doctor, and finally pays.

Single channel, single phase in queuing is where there is one line and one service area, such as a grocery store with only one cashier.

Single minute exchange of die (SMED) from Toyota is a procedure to try and reduce machine set-up times to less than 10 minutes (a single number of minutes).

Single sampling in *statistical quality control* has one upper limit of permitted defective units. A random sample is withdrawn from the lot and tested. If the number of defective units in the sample does not exceed the limit, the lot is accepted, if it does exceed the limit, the lot is rejected.

Site selection is the decision involving establishing the location for an operating facility.

Smith, Adam, 1723–1790, an early theorist of scientific management, suggested in his book *The Wealth of Nations* that labour specialization could reduce labour costs.

Smoothing constant is the alpha factor in forecasting using exponential smoothing.

Solid waste pollution is dumping untreated commercial, consumer or industrial waste on land. Besides being an eye-sore, toxic products from waste can percolate into water sources.

Specification is the document that describes in detail the requirements that a product, process or service has to meet.

Staff functions are those that have no direct responsibility in production output, such as a *quality control* inspector.

Standard deviation is a measure of the dispersion of a data set, applied to either a population or a sample and given by the square root of the variance.

Standard error of estimate measures variability or scatter around a regression line.

Standard error of the mean measures the variability of the means of each sample.

Standard time is the practical time needed to perform work and on which labour costs are often based.

State of nature is the condition in the external environment governing decision making.

Statistic is a measure that describes a characteristic of a sample, such as weight.

Statistical process control is the procedure to verify that a process operates correctly.

Statistical quality control covers all the quantitative analytical procedures used to verify that a process, product or service is according to specification.

Stem-and-leaf display is a method of data presentation highlighting which data occurs most frequently. The stem shows the principal value of the *data set* and the leaf intermediate values. It is useful when dealing with a large quantity of *raw data.*

Stockout costs are those associated with being unable to satisfy demand. They include lost sales, lost customers or activities needed to eventually satisfy the customer.

Straight-line depreciation is the allocation of depreciated costs linearly over the life of the *capital asset.*

Strategic plan is the detail of how an organization proposes to arrive at its desired objectives. The plan is often long term, though firms may have short-term strategies, and gives the time frame, the *mission statement,* or *charter* for *non-profit organizations.*

Stratified sampling is a survey approach in which the population is divided into homogeneous groups or strata, such as according to age.

Student's *t* distribution is an alternative for *t distribution.*

Suboptimality is the condition that exists when optimization of a component or subsystem gives less than optimal performance of the larger system and vice-versa.

Subcontracting is giving work to another firm enforced by a legal contract.

Subcontractor networks cover the contacts, services, relationships and availability of third parties available to perform work. The network, called *keiretsu* in Japan, can

be critical to the flexibility and the performance of the firm.

Sum-of-years digits is a depreciation method in which the sum of the years' digits is calculated to give the denominator for proportioning the depreciation amount.

Supply chain is a network, which for tangible goods covers purchasing of raw materials, manufacturing, assembly and distribution of finished goods to the client.

Sustainable development is the management of economic growth avoiding irreparable damage to the environment. By balancing economic demands with ecological concerns, the needs of people are satisfied without jeopardizing the prospects of future generations.

SWOT analysis is a management planning tool for analysing a company's future strategy and an acronym for the firm's internal, *S*trength and *W*eaknesses and the external *O*pportunities and *T*hreats. A SWOT analysis assumes that, if managers carefully review such elements, then an appropriate long-term programme for success will emerge.

Synchronized production is producing a product at the same rate as demanded.

System is a group of interdependent components, variables, activities or departments.

Systematic layout planning rates the relative importance of the closeness of departments, considering factors, such as the type of customers, the ease of supervision, common personnel and common equipment, and then selecting a layout according to the importance of the closeness.

Systematic sampling is where elements are selected and analysed from a population at a uniform interval of time, order or space. Analysing the surface condition of a motorway, by sampling every half mile, would be systematic sampling.

T

T classification, part of the *VAT classification*, is where products are similar in their functionality, but used in different services or applications. Components may be common in each product but, towards the end of assembly, combining certain subassemblies produces different products such as flow control valves for water, gas and other fluids.

_t_ distribution is a continuous probability distribution, like the *normal distribution* in that it is bell-shaped and symmetrical, except that it is lower at the mean and higher in the tails. A *t* distribution is used when the sample size *n* is small and the population standard deviation is unknown. There is a *t* distribution for every sample size.

Taguchi methods are aimed at quality improvement based on making designs robust by building in tolerances for manufacturing variables known to be unavoidable. Taguchi's philosophy is that missing the quality target in a consistent manner can be better than hitting it a few times with the rest being scattered all over the board.

Takt time, meaning in rhythm with the conductor, is synonymous in operations for being in rhythm with the client demands; Takt (German) = time in music.

Taylor, Frederick Winslow, of the USA (1856–1915) is considered the father of scientific management. He rigorously examined the field of operations as a science, proposing to increase worker efficiency by job design. His logic was that there was one best way to work and it was this way that should be developed and put into action.

Taylorism is the scientific approach to management based on *Taylor's* theories. For many it is synonymous with rigidity, inflexibility and demotivation.

Theory X is a concept proposed by *Douglas McGregor*, in which Theory X type of people have negative opinions about others and make bad managers.

Theory Y is a concept proposed by *Douglas McGregor*, in which Theory Y type of people have positive opinions about others and make good managers.

Time fences in the *master production schedule* refer to the frozen, fixed, full and open time periods, providing a scale of rigidity for planning purposes.

Time series are historical data, such as sales revenues, GNP or cash flow, that have been compiled over a regular period of time and may be used to forecast future values.

Time value of money refers to the fact that value declines over time. £100 today will not have the same value five years from now.

Tolerance limits refer to the upper and lower values, say in length, within which a unit or work piece is considered acceptable.

Total productive maintenance is a well defined and organized programme that places a high value on teamwork, consensus building and continuous improvement, or *Kaizen*.

Total Quality Management (TQM) is where attention to quality pervades the whole operation, not just one particular sector, with the driver being top management.

Total sum of squares in a regression equation, also called the *total variation*, measures the variation of the observed Y values around the mean value of Y.

Traceability is the ability to trace the history, application or location of an item or activity, or similar items or activities, by means of recorded identification.

Tracking signal in forecasting indicates how well the forecast is predicting actual data.

Trade-off in decision is making a choice between two or more possibilities when there are advantages and disadvantages attached to all of them.

Trading pollution rights is a market-based approach for firms, involving buying or selling the right to pollute with the objective of reducing the overall pollution levels.

Transportation method is a linear programming technique to determine the lowest-cost plan for the distribution of goods from multiple origins to multiple destinations.

Two-dimensional template is a technique for *facility layout*, where cut-outs, on the same scale as the floor plan, are made of the equipment to be located. These cut-outs are moved around by trial and error until the desired floor plan is achieved.

Two-bin system is a *fixed order* inventory management approach in which inventory is held in two bins. The first, the principal storage container, has a large capacity. The capacity of the second is based on *demand during lead time*. When the first bin is empty, a new order is placed; meanwhile withdrawal is from the second bin.

Type I error α in *statistical control* is accepting a null hypothesis when it should be rejected. If a Type I error involves the time and cost of remaking a batch of vaccine that really was acceptable, while a *Type II error* means taking a chance that users of the vaccine could be sick, then management would prefer to make a Type I error.

Type II error β in *statistical control* is accepting a null hypothesis when in fact it should be rejected.

U

UK Best Factory Awards is a quality awards programme operated by Cranfield Business School and the publication, *Management Today*, which annually identifies those plant sites in the UK considered 'the best' according to industry sector.

Unbalanced transportation problem in linear programming is when the total supply of a product is greater than total demand, or total product demand is greater than total supply.

Uncertainty in decision making implies that probabilities cannot be assigned to outcomes.

Utilization rate is the time that a production unit must be on line to produce the required output. It is given by the ratio of the total operating time to the total time available.

Utility in *decision making* refers to the pleasure, or displeasure, as the result of a certain outcomes. Managers are not the same and may make different decisions in the same situation; this, in part, is related to their utility.

V

V classification, part of the *VAT classification*, is where from one raw material, or a few (the base of the V), a variety of different end products can be produced. From petroleum a vast range of chemicals can be made.

Vacation days are the number of holiday days per year allotted to an employee and paid by the employer. The greater the number of days given, the higher are the labour costs which in part explains the differences in labour costs between Europe and the USA.

Valdez principal, after the Exxon Valdez oil spill, calls on companies to make organizational changes and appoint an environmentalist to the corporate board, and also to conduct an annual public audit of the company's environmental progress.

Value added tax (VAT) is a surcharge added to the sales price, or the cost of goods or services, in theory based on the 'value added' to that product.

Value analysis or *value engineering*, very often a practice in purchasing, is the evaluation of the expected performance of a product relative to its price.

Value engineering is similar to *value analysis*.

Variable costs are those which change with output, such as labour, materials and variable overhead.

Variety funnel illustrates the reduction of flexibility with raw materials and components as the operation moves through the supply chain.

VAT classification is grouping items according to the type of end product and, to a certain extent, by the manufacturing process employed.

Vendor analysis is the comparison of vendors, or suppliers, based on criteria such as price or global cost, delivery time, quality, availability of spares and after-sales service.

Venn diagram is a rectangular scheme used to illustrate visually the probability outcomes of events that are mutually or not mutually exclusive.

Vertical integration is the combination, under single ownership, of two or more stages of production and/or distribution in the supply chain of entities normally separate. An oil refiner that owns the crude oil, refinery, oil tankers and retail outlets is an example.

Virtual systems are those which perform a function but do not physically exist or only exist at the instant they are needed.

Voice of the customer is another name for *quality function deployment*.

W

Waiting Line or *queue* is people or units in a system waiting to be serviced.

Water pollution describes the discharge of toxic products directly into rivers, lakes and the sea or dumping on land because toxic chemicals can percolate into water sources.

Web page is a block of information that can be called up on the world wide web. It is a way of organizing data on the Web and such pages are prepared by individuals, manufacturers, universities, publishers, hospitals, restaurants, etc. as a means of advertising their activity.

Weighted moving average forecasting is applying a weighting factor to each period, rather than using the straight average as in *simple moving average forecasting*.

Weighted unit average cost for inventory accounting is when the average value of inventory items is charged against sales. This gives a 'fair' value of the cost of goods sold and the value of inventory remaining.

What-if analysis in decision making looks at alternative outcomes by posing the questions, 'What if this happens? What if this decision is made?'

White-collar worker is a term referring to managers or supervisors.

Work in process is that raw-material inventory to which some processing has been applied although it is still not a finished product.

Work order is the instruction for producing a given quantity of items usually according to a required schedule.

Working week is the number of hours per week that an employee works usually according to law. A longer working week usually results in lower unit product costs.

World wide web (the Web, or WWW) is a set of standards on the Internet for storing, retrieving, formatting, and displaying information using a client/server architecture. Using the Web one can be connected to information at another site perhaps many kilometres away.

X

x **axis** is the horizontal axis, or abscissa, of a graph and in forecasting is used for the independent variable.

x **bar chart** is a graph used in *statistical process control* to monitor the average value of continuous variables such as hardness, height, temperature and weight. *Range charts* are used in conjunction with x-bar charts in order to give correct monitoring.

Y

y **axis** is the vertical axis, or ordinate, of a graph, which in forecasting is used for the dependent variable.

Yield rate in a production process is the percentage of starting material that actually ends up in the product with scrap taken into account scrap. It is calculated as $100 -$ scrap percentage.

Z

z **value** in a *normal distribution* is the number of standard deviations a random variable, x, lies from the mean, μ. It is calculated as $(x - \mu)/\sigma$, where σ is the standard deviation.

Zero inventory is the ultimate objective of an operation that uses the *just-in-time* approach. Zero breakdowns, zero defects, zero delays and zero paper are other related goals. Together they are known as the five zeros targeting ultimate efficiency. By corollary, zero accidents is a sixth.

Index